ENCYCLOPEDIA
OF EMERGING
INDUSTRIES

FOURTH EDITION

HIGHLIGHTS

The fourth edition of the *Encyclopedia of Emerging Industries* details the inception, emergence, and current status of 115 flourishing U.S. industries and industry segments.

EEI's focused essays unearth for users a wealth of relevant, current, factual data previously accessible only through a diverse variety of sources. This volume provides broad-based, highly-readable, industry information under such headings as Industry Snapshot, Organization and Structure, Background and Development, Industry Leaders, Current Conditions, America and the World, Pioneers, and Research and Technology.

WHAT'S NEW FOR THIS EDITION

The essays in this edition have been completely revised, with updated statistics and the most current information on industry trends and developments. In addition, we have added essays on some of the most interesting and influential new business fields. Among these are

- Application Service Providers

- Concierge Services, Corporate and Personal

- Entrepreneurial Training and Advisory Services

- Fuel Cells

- Logistics Outsourcing Services

- Pharmacogenomics

- Tissue Engineering.

INCLUDES GRAPHS, PHOTOS, AND SIDEBARS

Enhancing the text are dozens of visual elements. Graphs, charts, and tables may detail sales figures, market share, forecasts, and user trends. Photographs of people, places, products, and procedures lend context to the data featured within the essays. Sidebars provide a unique addition to the information found in *EEI,* focusing on anecdotal statistics, unique incidents, trends, and key individuals.

ADDITIONAL FEATURES

- Contents are arranged alphabetically

- General Index lists company names, people, legislation, court cases, significant terms, and provides broad subject access via cross-references

- Industry Index offers access to essays via Standard Industrial Classification (SIC) codes

- Two Conversion Tables function as keys to SIC codes and to North American Industry Classification System (NAICS) codes

- Further Reading sections suggest avenues for continued study

A valuable addition to the Gale Group's business resource collection, *EEI* pinpoints emerging industries while they are still well in the spotlight.

ENCYCLOPEDIA OF EMERGING INDUSTRIES

FOURTH EDITION

JANE A. MALONIS, EDITOR

GALE GROUP

Detroit
New York
San Francisco
London
Boston
Woodbridge, CT

ENCYCLOPEDIA OF EMERGING INDUSTRIES, 4TH EDITION

Jane A. Malonis, *Senior Editor*

Erin Braun, *Managing Editor*
Rebecca Marlow-Ferguson, *Contributing Editor*

Synapse, the Knowledge Link Corporation, *Indexer*

Mary Beth Trimper, *Production Director*
Evi Seoud, *Assistant Production Manager*

Cynthia Baldwin, *Product Design Manager*
Pamela A. E. Galbreath, *Senior Art Director*

Barbara J. Yarrow, *Graphic Services Manager*
Randy Bassett, *Image Database Supervisor*
Robyn Young and Pamela A. Reed, *Image Coordinators*

Maria Franklin, *Permissions Manager*

Andrew Malonis, *Technical Training Specialist*

ISBN 0-7876-4676-8
ISSN 1096-2433

TABLE OF CONTENTS

INTRODUCTION

Welcome to the fourth edition of the *Encyclopedia of Emerging Industries (EEI)*. In this volume readers will find essays covering specific businesses as well as broad business sectors that have, for the most part, shown evidence of significant growth in the recent past or potential for exemplary growth in the near future. In some cases, these areas of commerce fall within older, well-established industries—prominent examples include semiconductors, beverages, and tourism. More commonly, the essays focus on offshoots of relatively new industries, such as developments in electronic commerce, Web development, minimally invasive medical technologies, and genetic engineering. Students, entrepreneurs, investors, and job seekers alike will find information on technical subjects as arcane as optical sensing or encryption systems, and on topics as commonplace as juice bars and gambling casinos.

CONTENT AND ARRANGEMENT

Arranged alphabetically within the book, essay titles are cross-referenced in the General Index. Within essays, readers may encounter statements referring them to related areas of potential interest, such as: "Also see the essay in this book on Fertility Medicine."

Supplementing the text are photographs, charts, graphs, and sidebars. In each essay, readers may expect to find some or all of the following aspects discussed:

- **Industry Snapshot.** Provides a brief overview of the topic and identifies key issues.

- **Organization and Structure.** Discusses the configuration and functional aspects of the business, including sub-industry divisions.

- **Background and Development.** Relates the genesis and history of the industry to date, including major technological advances, scandals, pioneering companies, major products, important legislation, and other shaping factors.

- **Pioneers.** Discusses individuals who have made significant contributions to the development of the industry.

- **Current Conditions.** Provides information on the status of the industry in the late 1990s well into 2000, with an eye toward challenges on the horizon.

- **Industry Leaders.** Profiles major companies, and may include discussion of financial performance.

- **Work Force.** May contain information on the size, diversity, and characteristics of the industry's labor force, as well as discussion of skills needed by employees.

- **America and the World.** Contains information on the global marketplace in relation to the topic discussed.

- **Research and Technology.** Furnishes information on cutting edge developments, areas of research, and their potential to impact the industry.

- **Further Reading.** Provides users with specific source citations. These sources, many of which have been used to compile the actual essays, are publicly accessible materials such as articles from professional and academic periodicals and journals; books; corporate annual reports; documents from government sources, as well as material supplied by industry associations. Included are references to numerous reputable Internet sites; whenever available, the URLs for these sources are included.

INDEXES AND CONVERSION TABLES

The General Index contains alphabetic references to items mentioned within the essays such as significant terms, companies, trade and professional associations, government agencies, names of individuals, significant court cases, and key legislation.

The Industry Index contains a listing of many 1987 Standard Industrial Classification (SIC) references, with page numbers as they pertain to the book's subject coverage.

Two industry classification tables allow cross-referencing of SIC categories used in the Industry Index with the 1997 North American Industry Classification System (NAICS) codes.

TOPIC SELECTION AND INCLUSION CRITERIA

In determining topic selection, the editors found it best to rely upon several means, a portion of which were decidedly subjective. (Users will note that we have chosen to employ the term "emerging industries" rather loosely, often referring not only to entire *industries,* but to specific industrial and business *sectors,* discrete types of business *enterprises,* and sometimes simply to describe a particular *range of products or services.*) In considering inclusion, the questions we repeatedly asked ourselves revolved around these central points:

- Is the industry experiencing a period of significant growth, either financial or otherwise?

- Has the business been the recent focus of much public attention and, if so, why?

- Is the product or service being newly marketed in a particularly innovative way?

- Is the business involved in the use or production of cutting edge technologies?

Ideas for topics were culled, in part, from a wide assortment of variously ranked lists detailing the recent accomplishments of promising or well-established companies. Assorted content experts, along with our team of advisors, also provided myriad suggestions and assisted in refining the coverage within *EEI*. Finally, we relied to a certain degree on hunch, experience, and intuition, predicting to the best of our ability which emerging business areas our users would want and need to know more about.

The *EEI* series will be published annually. Chapters in future volumes will be comprised of fresh updates to selected existing topics, and will explore new industries that have entered the spotlight. Enhancements in essay comprehensiveness will be a focus.

ACKNOWLEDGMENTS AND ADVISORS

The editor would like to sincerely thank the members of the *EEI* advisory board for their invaluable assistance with this edition:

- **Galen Avery,** Librarian, Spengler Nathanson PLL, Toledo, Ohio.

- **Susan G. Neuman, Ph.D.** Librarian, Katz Graduate School of Business Library, University of Pittsburgh, Pittsburgh, Pennsylvania.

- **Judith M. Nixon,** Management and Economics Librarian, Purdue University, West Lafayette, Indiana.

Special thanks also to Andrew Malonis of the Gale Group, for his technical assistance in preparing the manuscript for typesetting.

COMMENTS AND SUGGESTIONS

Comments and suggestions, including ideas for future essays, are most welcome. Readers are invited to send their thoughts to:

Editor/Encyclopedia of Emerging Industries
Gale Group, Inc.
27500 Drake Rd.
Farmington Hills, MI 48331-3535

Toll-free phone: 1-800-347-GALE
Toll-free fax: 1-800-339-3374
Editor E-mail: jane.malonis@galegroup.com

ADULT AND RETIREMENT COMMUNITIES

Adult and retirement communities were among the housing industry's prize sectors in the 1990s, and demographics promised a healthy market well into the 21st century; the elderly portion of the U.S. population was not expected to peak for another two decades. And while supply outpaced demand in the late 1990s, leading to some minor market jolts in 1998 and 1999, there were few fears of anything short of explosive growth in the 2000s. The seniors housing industry at the end of the 20th century included over 50,000 properties containing about 3.5 million units.

The increasingly competitive market forced the industry to diversify rapidly, and thus facilities and services became increasingly tailored to specific categories of seniors. The independent-living sector, the least tapped segment in the 1990s boom, witnessed some of the largest growth by early 2000. But affordability remained the most prominent differentiating feature as of 2000, according to *National Real Estate Investor.*

Furthermore, retirement communities were looking younger all the time. As wealthy baby boomers decided to retire early, seniors housing was increasingly filled by those who did not even merit the title "senior." This dynamic, expected to continue for the foreseeable future, also recast the nature of retirement communities, and many began offering services to appeal to those who remained relatively youthful.

By the 21st century, America's elderly population was rapidly expanding—with women aged 80 and older as one of the fastest-growing segments of the U.S. population. The trend is expected to continue as approximately 77 million baby boomers enter their retirement years, beginning in 2010. The Administration on Aging estimates that by the year 2030, the United States will have more than 85 million people over the age of 60. Further, the U.S. Census Bureau's projections reflect an increasingly aged population as well. In 2000 there will be approximately 72,000 people 100 years of age or older. By 2050, they are projected to number more than 84,000 and the over-65 population is expected to exceed 78 million, up from over 34 million in 2000.

ORGANIZATION AND STRUCTURE

The adult and retirement communities industry consists of a variety of facility options catering to the needs of residents aged 55 or older. These communities offer residences and, at times, special care for their occupants. According to the National Investment Center in Annapolis, Maryland, which monitors growth in the seniors housing industry, the four categories of senior living include senior apartments, active adult communities, and owner-occupied housing; continuing-care retirement communities (CCRCs), congregate-care facilities, independent-living units in CCRCs, and board and care living facilities; assisted living in congregate and CCRCs and board and care facilities; and nursing homes and skilled nursing units in congregate, CCRCs, and hospitals. CCRCs often evolve around a certain theme; for instance, a resort community may offer recreational activities while a health-care community may offer nursing care.

Since 1992 the American Seniors Housing Association (ASHA) has followed and reported on the adult

Social hour at an upscale retirement community. (*Stock Market*)

housing industry. The association was started by the National Housing Council and, along with Coopers & Lybrand, L.L.P, publishes annually the leading 25 managers and owners of seniors housing in the United States. ASHA also serves as a membership organization for companies involved in seniors housing. In 2000 the association had more than 300 firms as members. Another major resource and forecaster in the seniors housing industry is the National Investment Center (NIC), which held its first conference in 1991. NIC's research publications, available for sale through their Web site, include *Lender and Investor Survey Results: Preferences and Trends in Financing Long Term Care and Senior Living Projects* and *National Survey of Assisted Living Residents: Who Is the Customer?*

The industry seemed headed toward some type of government involvement. In the mid-1990s, the majority of senior housing was private pay, but some states had begun to allow Medicaid waivers for assisted living residences. Government involvement was expected to come mainly by way of regulations imposed as a condition of state and federal reimbursements. While many industry players, such as market leader Colson & Colson/Holiday Retirement Corp., decried government intervention as a stifling intrusion, others, especially those in the nursing home sector,

found themselves pushing for greater government involvement in the late 1990s. The federal role in the nursing home industry was diminished in some ways, particularly in federal budgetary cuts on subacute nursing home care, which would probably increase the pace at which nursing home operators scrambled to attract private investment.

Like the housing industry as a whole, the retirement communities and seniors housing industries were exceptionally cyclical. The industry's nearest relatives were the hotel and multifamily sectors. In general, however, both occupancy rates and rents were slightly higher in the seniors housing industry than for either multifamily housing or lodging, thus yielding greater revenues.

BACKGROUND AND DEVELOPMENT

Adult and retirement communities first began as simple housing options for people entering their retirement years. The basic focus of these communities was to lure those seniors who were able to remain independent and who were willing to give up their homes in favor of living in a residential area with other people their age. Unfortunately, until the 1980s the industry was not able to attract the number of seniors it had anticipated. Leaders in the seniors housing market discovered that seniors were not interested in giving up their homes unless new adult communities could provide value-added services as they grew older. Once builders and managers realized what it took to attract seniors, the industry, especially assisted living facilities, took off, increasing by 24 percent during the 1980s.

The dramatic growth in the retirement sector through the 1980s, however, resulted in a glut by the end of the decade, leading to massive financial restructuring. Analysts attributed the overbuilding to unchecked exuberance among investors and builders and inadequate research into target markets and prospective rental rates. The industry took note, and worked extensively to remedy such shortcomings.

In that spirit, the National Investment Center (NIC) was formed in 1991 to act as an information conduit between the investment community and the industry's owners and managers. The NIC mobilized quickly to provide comprehensive research and information to investors and lenders to help them understand the specific nature of the seniors housing market, and particularly to spell out the tremendous growth opportunities it offered. Thus, the NIC took it upon itself to attract capital flows into the industry.

NIC conducts research independently and also jointly with other major senior resource organizations, including ASHA and the American Health Care Association. NIC hosts an annual conference that provides industry information. Among the members of the research projects committee are leaders in the field of real estate investment in housing for seniors.

These and similar efforts paid off handsomely, and the industry dusted itself off and charged into the 1990s full force. The market exploded throughout the decade, particularly beginning in the mid-1990s as major investors dived in to make a killing.

PIONEERS IN THE FIELD

A true pioneer of American retirement living is Del Webb. In the late 1950s Webb started to develop the idea. He would end up, a few years later, successful in finding retirees who were healthy enough to live independently in their own homes and luring them to the desert outside of Phoenix. In 1960 his Sun City, Arizona, development opened; Webb created the model for America's retirement communities. By the end of the 1970s that idea had been successfully realized on 8,900 acres when the first development came to fruition. Retirees fleeing the cold of the East Coast and Great Lakes flocked to the age-segregated, planned community. Until that time, many northern retirees went only to Florida. The Del Webb Corp. led the way to the future of comfortable living for people on fixed incomes—many of whom suffered through the Great Depression, fought in World War II, and worked hard in factories to save for a time of leisure as they aged. By the late 1970s, Sun City's 46,000 residents made it the nation's largest retirement community. Other Sun City retirement communities grew up elsewhere, including Tucson, Arizona; Hilton Head, South Carolina; and Roseville, California.

By 2000, the corporation was at work in more than 10 Sun Cities, pushing into new geographical regions and expanding the range of services. In the late 1990s, Sun City was moved north, to the cold, bleak farmland of northern Illinois about 50 miles northwest of Chicago. Sun Cities are built around an 18-hole golf course and include an indoor recreation lodge, artificial lakes, and tennis courts. At least one of the resident spouses must be 55 or older. In the northern communities natives were tied to the land—and their grandchildren. The idea of living closer to the family they loved and the countryside that was familiar, not far from the city that might nurture them for many

years, was seen as the crucial element in the expected success of Sun City in the Frost Belt. Meanwhile, the newest Sun Cities were equipped with spa facilities to supplement golf and other physical activities, providing a place to relax and stay fit with a wide range of holistic health treatments and facilities.

Moreover, the company seemed to be just getting going at the turn of the century. In January 2000 Del Webb launched its very first branding campaign, a $7 million effort that included 60- and 30-second television spots.

CURRENT CONDITIONS

While the tremendous industry growth through the 1990s attracted the attention of large institutional investors and lenders, the investment climate for the seniors housing industry remained tumultuous, leading to several large sell-offs in the late 1990s. Still, overall confidence in the industry remained exceptionally high, as returns remained healthy compared with other real estate-based investments.

As ever in the housing business, there were fears just below the surface of a possible glut in some geographic locations, particularly in the Northwest, though for the most part, building and investment patterns, as well as demand for seniors housing, revealed little panic. The industry first started to register concern in late 1998 following the massive financial turmoil in foreign markets, after which investors started to flee the building industries, and thus many retire-

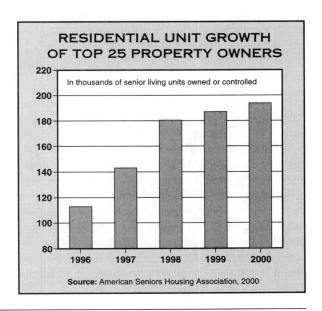

RESIDENTIAL UNIT GROWTH OF TOP 25 PROPERTY OWNERS

In thousands of senior living units owned or controlled

Source: American Seniors Housing Association, 2000

ment-based companies saw their capital pulled out from under them. The market jolts of 1998 and 1999, however, may have even served as a preemptive strike against possible overbuilding, according to many analysts. Though the industry remained in sound overall financial shape in 2000, the number of new units was still expected to decline from about 65,000 in 1999 to 40,000.

Some industry sectors learned the hard way that the sheer number of seniors was not enough to maintain a healthy market. Alterations to the Medicare payment systems cut into nursing home revenues, and thus investor confidence, in the late 1990s, and the sector was rife with executives calling for greater help from the government to provide more solid footing. Two leading nursing home operations, Assisted Living Concepts Inc. and Sunrise Assisted Living, Inc., achieved disappointing earnings, and some industry players feared an avalanche of bad news.

The NIC released a new brand of study for the industry in 1999 that compared the seniors market to that of the multifamily housing and hotel lodging sectors. The study, entitled *Size, Scope and Performance of the Seniors Housing & Care Industry: A Comparative Study with the Multifamily and Lodging Sectors,* revealed the industry's quickly realized maturity.

For instance, the seniors housing industry emerged as such a powerful force by the late 1990s that it exceeded even the revenues of the apartment and hotel industries in 1997. The industry's total valuation crept into the territory of the other two as well. Seniors housing and care was valued at $206 billion in 1998, compared with $293 billion for the lodging sector and $546 billion for multifamily housing. The industry had also stabilized somewhat; by the end of the 1990s the same firms topped the industry for several years at a time. In ASHA's ranking of the top 25 owners and managers in 2000, 92 percent of the firms had been so ranked before.

As Americans grow older and health care prolongs the lives of people suffering from chronic diseases, assisted living and continuing care facilities have had to expand their services to provide for residents who require additional care. According to some estimates, up to 30 percent of assisted living residents suffer from various degrees of Alzheimer's disease or other forms of dementia, and such communities are filled with growing numbers of frail residents who require the special assistance that trained specialists provide. As a result, costs are expected to rise as these operations attempt to retain staff qualified to handle increasingly acute cases of such conditions.

In addition to self-contained retirement communities, or assisted living centers, the housing market began designing homes for the retirement leisure. The increasingly youthful character of the retirement communities market, as 50-something empty nesters left the responsibilities of household maintenance behind them for the comforts of adult communities, forced an industry-wide shift in design and services. For starters, independent-living facilities were among the fastest-growing segments of the industry. Moreover, retirement communities were built adjacent to golf courses and other amenities that promoted an active lifestyle. As baby boomers move into retirement age in droves, industry analysts expected the 50-something market to fuel the industry's most dramatic growth and drive the next industry-wide building boom in the 2000s. Fortunately, the younger residents were near the age of those designing and building the communities. Such relationships often saved the expense of research because the developers understood the people who had always been their customers. In a market ever-evolving due to the vastly diverse population of aging adults, sometimes the best investment was directed by the intimate knowledge of developers at the local level.

As the "graying of America" increases, the seniors housing industry is expected to continue to grow and thrive. More than 6,000 Americans were turning 65 each day by the end of the 1990s. That figure didn't include the crop of baby boomers who would start retiring in the 2000s. According to a report by Timothy Boyce, a member of the Real Property Division's I-2 Committee of the American Bar Association, by the year 2003, 21 percent of the U.S. population will be over 65 years old, compared with only 11 percent in 1997.

According to the State of Seniors Housing 1999 survey conducted by ASHA, NIC, and PricewaterhouseCoopers, occupancy rates remained exceptionally strong, at 92 percent for the entire industry. The highest occupancy rates (95 percent) were found in congregate residences, followed by assisted living facilities (93.7 percent), and CCRCs (92.7 percent). These sectors likewise registered the highest turnover rates. Assisted living facilities accounted for 70 percent of all seniors housing projects in the late 1990s, and by 2000 the vacancy rate for such operations stood at 8 percent, with an average rent of $1,839, according to a report by the Seattle-based real estate company Marcus & Millichap.

In addition, retirement communities operating with a focus on health care continued to alter their perspective at the end of the 1990s. Typical of some of these changes was The Washington House (TWH) in Alexandria, Virginia, which operates as a nonprofit corporation. TWH offers an array of options for living within the community. A companion program called "Community Washington House" was created to assist older adults in their own homes, and to assist their caregivers. This program was a modification of what was predicted as a possible wave of the future: long-term care without walls. Membership, according to TWH president and CEO, Judith Braun, R.N., Ph.D., offers senior citizens the option of staying in their own homes longer. Community Washington House was unique as late as 1999 because it did not include an insurance component for payment of services, as did other similar programs. As past president and as a fellow of the National Gerontological Nursing Association, Braun witnessed the changing landscape of retirement living beginning in the late 1970s.

Programs such as this one reflected the knowledge and commitment to ongoing care. Comprehensive membership in Community Washington House includes use of the fitness center, which is also offered for memberships separately; monthly wellness seminars; utilization of a personal liaison to coordinate home chores through the use of local service providers; and the benefit of social activities at the retirement community. Washington House gives seniors exercising this option the additional reassurance of priority placement on a waiting list.

Decision making as people age and require additional care is a burden that many similar communities alleviated. Such arrangements encompassed three levels of care on the site, thus providing the security from upheavals at the times when illnesses made such moves unduly traumatic. The options of either living independently at home or retiring to a nursing home when a person could no longer deal with increasing frailty due to illness and age had been nudged aside by the end of the 20th century. Braun noted that CCRCs and nursing home facilities of the late 1990s looked very much like hospitals of the early 1980s. Length of stay was measured in weeks, rather than years. Many industry observers were looking to CCRCs, such as Washington House, as the "potential sleeper" that was likely to surge within the early years of the 21st century.

A major development in the future of retirement living occurred on 2 March 1999. Residents of the Leisure World retirement community in Laguna Hills, California, voted to incorporate as a city. With an average age of 77, the 18,000 residents proved that aging Americans exercised political clout, in addition to their increasing economic influence. Other unincorporated communities, including the Sun City developments, continue to enjoy their status.

The business side of seniors housing had grown large and specialized enough to even work its way into the academy at the end of the 20th century. At the NIC Annual Conference in 1999, it was announced that NIC Seniors Housing & Care Program had partnered with Johns Hopkins University to begin offering a graduate program dedicated to the field through the university's Real Estate Institute. A number of companies both inside and outside the industry, including Marriott Senior Living Services, GMAC Commercial Mortgage, and Senior Campus Living, kicked in funding for the program. The courses, beginning in fall 2000, were open to the school's M.B.A. students as a specialty field, which covers the issues of marketing, development, financing, quality of care, and other areas.

INDUSTRY LEADERS

In 2000, ASHA released a list of the top-25 seniors housing owners. Leading the list were Colson & Colson/Holiday Retirement Corp. based in Salem, Oregon; Alterra (formerly known as Alternative Living Services) of Brookfield, Wisconsin; Nationwide Health Properties of Newport Beach, California; and Atria, Inc. of New York City.

Colson & Colson/Holiday Retirement Corp., a private company, was the leading owner and manager on the top-25 list. With sales of $674.7 million in 1998, the most recent figure available, and 6,500 employees, Colson & Colson, majority-owned by the Colson family, enjoyed seven consecutive years at the reigning position. One hundred percent of their sales come from private pay, a fact that William Colson, the firm's president, considered to be a source of pride; he insisted that they do not want to work with the government in any capacity. In 2000, the company maintained nearly 27,450 units on 229 properties in the United States, with an additional 2,270 units on 23 properties abroad. The firm was also the market leader in Europe (where it was one of the few U.S. seniors housing companies to enjoy any significant presence) and placed third in Canada. Colson had not moved aggressively into building assisted living residencies, instead preferring to acquire those that had undergone bankruptcy.

Alterra Healthcare Corp. focused solely on private-pay clients, a strategy that greatly helped the company as Medicare pay structures reduced the total amount of revenue flowing toward its competitors.

Its ownership portfolio boasted 21,119 units on 453 properties, the bulk of which were aimed at residents with few special nursing needs. Founded as Assisted Living Services (ALS) in 1981, the company was a long-time industry leader by the late 1990s. After going public in 1996, Alterra made a series of acquisitions to emerge as the nation's largest assisted living firm. In 1999 ALS partnered with HCR Manor Care to purchase and codevelop a series of assisted living centers, with an emphasis on residents suffering from Alzheimer's disease. The company achieved sales of $376.2 million in 1999, up from $244.4 million the year before.

Nationwide Health Properties was a leading real estate investment trust (REIT) in the industry, with sales of $163.6 million in 1999, up from $144.9 million in 1998. The company maintained an ownership portfolio of 11,529 units in 128 properties. Alterra was responsible for about 12 percent of Nationwide's revenues. The REIT was involved in purchasing, mortgaging, and building retirement communities, nursing homes, and assisted living centers in addition to various health-care facilities.

Atria, Inc. of New York City boasted a portfolio of 9,704 units on 100 properties. 1,750 employees. The product of a merger between Atria Communities, Kapson Senior Quarters, and The Arbor Company, Atria's aims its facilities at seniors in need of daily assistance but who don't require skilled nursing care.

Health Care REIT, Inc. of Toledo, Ohio was another mainstay on ASHA's Top-25 list. The company maintained a staff of 23 at the end of 1999, when it recorded revenues of $129.4 million, an increase of 32 percent from 1998. The firm was one of a handful of real estate investment trusts topping the list of seniors housing owners in 1999. About half of the company's investments were in assisted living facilities, and another third were based in nursing homes. The remainder was divided between retirement communities catering to more active residents and specialty care hospitals. Health Care REIT maintained a portfolio of 8,066 units in 128 properties.

Other key players in the list of the top-25 owners, as designated by ASHA, included Senior Lifestyle Corporation, a public company founded in 1985 and headquartered Chicago, Illinois. In 2000 they operated over 60 assisted living communities and approximately 9,650 units, and employed over 3,000 people. Sunrise Assisted Living, Inc. of Fairfax, Virginia

pushed its way to seventh on ASHA's list, maintaining 7,966 units on 120 properties; Crestline Capital Corp. of Bethesda, Maryland operated 7,497 units on 31 properties; and Health Care Property Investors, Inc. of Newport Beach, California maintained 7,297 units on 92 properties.

FURTHER READING

American Seniors Housing Association. "Top 25 Owners and Managers," 2000. Available from http://www.asha.nmhc.org/toppers/default.html.

Beirne, Mike. "Del Webb Antes $7M for Sun City." *Brandweek,* 17 January 2000.

Catinella, Rita F. "America Is Growing Older, and New Technologies Will Allow the Aging to Live Where They Want—at Home." *Architectural Record,* July 1999.

Gamzon, Mel. "Back to Basics." *National Real Estate Investor,* 31 March 2000.

Johnson, Ben. "NIC Study Makes Strong Case for Seniors Investing." *National Real Estate Investor,* 31 October 1999.

Mines, Cynthia. "Assisted Living Growth Slows Down (For Now). . . ." *Midwest Real Estate News,* March 2000.

Pappas, Lorna. "Seniors Investment Potential Wide Open." *National Real Estate Investor,* July 1999.

Peck, Richard L. "What Is Assisted Living?" *Nursing Homes Long Term Care Management,* March 2000.

Resor, Joseph T., III. "Troubled Times Don't Necessarily Mean Gloom and Doom." *Nursing Homes Long Term Care Management,* March 2000.

Saphir, Ann. "Code Red Finds Code Blue: At Meeting, Nursing Home Operators Tell Their Sad Story and Future Hopes to Investors." *Modern Healthcare,* 11 October 1999.

Schless, David S. "1999: Nation's Top Seniors Housing Companies Hold Firm." *National Real Estate Investor,* October 1999.

Shapiro, Joseph P. "No Sunset for Sun City." *U.S. News & World Report,* 28 June 1999.

Terry, Don. "In This Brand-New City, No Shortage of Elders." *New York Times,* 4 March 1999.

Ursery, Stephen. "NIC and Johns Hopkins University Team up to Start Unique Graduate Program." *National Real Estate Investor,* November 1999.

———. "Seniors Housing Beat." *National Real Estate Investor,* February 2000.

AIDS Testing, Treatment, and Services

Since it was first uncovered as a distinct new syndrome in 1981, acquired immune deficiency syndrome (AIDS) has emerged as one of the most pressing concerns and most significant health phenomena of the modern era. While public attitudes towards AIDS, along with effective treatments for its patients, have evolved considerably since the condition was first diagnosed, the disease remains mired in a range of social, political, economic, ethical, religious, and cultural debates and concerns. Hampered for years by political complacency and social bigotry, AIDS testing, treatment, and services have blossomed into enormous industries scrambling to deal with the disease on a variety of levels, including research into a vaccine; development of drugs to combat symptoms; information resources for researchers, patients, and the public; support centers for patients and their families; and others.

AIDS is the name given to a range of diseases and complications that compromise the body's immune system and thereby increase the body's vulnerability to other infections. As of 2000, AIDS, generally thought to be the result of the human immunodeficiency virus, or HIV, was always fatal, though thanks to rapidly developing drug treatments, patients were increasingly able to live healthy lives for well over a decade after contracting HIV. There are four primary ways in which a person can become infected with HIV: through unprotected sexual contact with an infected partner; by sharing intravenous needles with an infected person; prenatally from an infected mother; or by receiving infected blood through a transfusion. Especially in the United States and other industrialized nations, this last avenue for infection was becoming quite rare.

On a global scale, the AIDS crisis has reached pandemic levels. Approximately 5.4 million new infections were reported in 1999, occurring at a rate of nearly 15,000 per day. About 95 percent of these took place in the world's developing countries. That year, 2.8 million individuals lost their lives to AIDS-related illnesses, the highest total in the disease's history, despite improved antiretroviral therapy. Dr. Anthony Fauci at the National Institute of Allergy and Infectious Diseases ranked AIDS as one of the most devastating microbial scourges in the history of humankind. In total, by June 2000 about 18.8 million people had died from AIDS since the epidemic's beginning, while 34.3 million people were living with the HIV virus.

In the United States, the trends were slightly less horrific, but still alarming. While by the end of the 1990s effective treatments were largely credited with bringing the number of AIDS-related deaths down by 60 percent, from 50,000 at their peak in 1995 to 20,000, the number of new infections held steady at about 40,000 cases per year, half of which were in individuals less than 25 years of age.

AIDS is a vast subject, and discussing it in dollar terms is somewhat problematic. Figures that might assist in the understanding of AIDS as a public health problem and as an industry are usually outdated by the time they become available to the general public. The U.S. Public Health Service estimated that total cost for treating an HIV-positive patient throughout his or her lifetime averaged $119,000. Those figures have continued to rise. Multiplying that number by the Centers for Disease Control and Prevention's (CDC) numbers of identified AIDS cases, the estimated cost of treating all HIV-infected individuals during their lifetimes rises to in excess of $84 billion.

One way to define the scope and impact of the domestic AIDS-related industry is to look at infection and mortality rates. As of 1 January 2000, the CDC, based in Atlanta, Georgia, indicated a total of 733,374 AIDS cases have been reported in the United States since these statistics have been kept. Of that number, 609,326 were males and 124,045 were females. In that same period, 29,629 people between the ages of 13 and 24 were diagnosed with the AIDS virus, as were 8,718 below the age of 13. AIDS deaths totaled 430,411 by January 2000. The causes of AIDS transmission, in the 84 percent of cases where a cause had been clearly identified, were broken down as follows: 47 percent were men who had sex with men, 25 percent originated with injected drug users, and 10 percent of the cases were the result of heterosexual contact (chiefly by sexual contact with an injecting drug user).

Several elements of AIDS-related industries are more visible than others. Possibly the most visible of these are pharmaceutical companies. Research and development is the hub of the AIDS industry and accounts for the most spending, in part because this area carries with it the promise of finding a cure for AIDS.

A second major arm of the AIDS-related industries is not a business, but government agencies. In the United States, much of the focus of AIDS policy, as well as the source of research funding, has rested with two agencies: the National Institutes of Health (NIH) and the CDC. These agencies are part of the U.S. Department of Health and Human Services, which contributes to the underwriting of research at drug companies and at educational institutions throughout the country. NIH is the principal biomedical research arm of the federal government. The CDC, part of the U.S. Public Health Service's efforts to control infectious diseases, works with state health officials and is a repository of statistical information about AIDS and other diseases. This country's general AIDS policy is formulated through the Presidential Commission on AIDS, established under the administration of President Ronald Reagan in 1987. This commission has been a source of controversy since its inception. High-profile members, such as basketball great Magic Johnson, have resigned from the commission, complaining the body was not serious about addressing all AIDS-related issues, including directing enough funding to research and development. During the early years of

the disease's appearance on the national scene, both the Reagan and the Bush administrations were roundly criticized for what critics saw as a half-hearted commitment to finding a cure for AIDS.

The third major segment of the AIDS-related industries involves the private and quasi private, locally funded, service-oriented, and/or foundation-based enterprises classified as AIDS service organizations, or ASOs. Some of the largest ASOs generate and distribute millions of dollars for research and education and prevention efforts. Smaller ASOs may be involved in work at the community level, such as distributing condoms or helping individuals find medical testing or housing. While dwarfed by government agencies and the large pharmaceutical companies, ASOs generate funds used in research, provide direct services, and are beneficiaries of funding from government sources. Related businesses, such as condom manufacturers, medical supply companies, health-food stores, and home health-care aides, are also affected by AIDS, but do not generally break down the impact the disease has on their financial operations.

The CDC issues a handbook each year listing national organizations providing HIV and AIDS services. Virtually all of these are either governmental or nonprofit. Some are funded by significant private donors such as the Rockefeller Archive Center. Others are funded by religious organizations, such as the Presbyterian AIDS Network. Many are community-based, such as the Gay Men's Health Crisis Center in New York, the San Francisco AIDS Foundation—two of the largest—and the Madison, Wisconsin-AIDS Network. Although it is entirely inaccurate to characterize AIDS as only a homosexual disease, many ASOs are based in communities where substantial gay populations are located. The National Prevention Information Network (formerly the National AIDS Clearinghouse) reported there were more than 19,000 ASOs, many of which cropped up in the years 1982-86, when the general public's awareness of AIDS also increased. Such organizations, however, were subject to criticism as well. Some critics suggested that the proliferation of AIDS-related organizations had a tendency to divert money from services and research into salaries and organization-based expenses.

Federal funds directed toward AIDS research, treatment, prevention, and education (other major elements of the AIDS industry) are the result of passage by the U.S. Congress of the Ryan White Act of 1990. Named for a teenager from Indiana who died as a result of receiving an HIV-contaminated blood transfusion, the act authorized $4.5 billion in federal spending for five years (from 1991 through 1996). Though the funding was authorized, the appropriation did not begin until 1994. The vast majority of the funding was directed toward research and development and treatment, although a portion was also directed toward education programs in schools and prisons and toward minorities. In December 1998 President Bill Clinton announced the release of an additional $479 million in new Ryan White funding money. This time, most of the money went to primary health-care and supportive services for people living with HIV/AIDS. Since that time, AIDS organizations have continued their private fund-raising and continued to pressure the federal government to budget additional money to eradicate AIDS. In November 1999, however, the Ryan White Foundation was forced to close its doors due to lack of funding. Meanwhile, the Ryan White Act was set to expire in September 2000, leading to waves of outcry from interest groups and spurring movement in Congress to initiate legislation to extend the act and provide new money to the foundation. In October 2000, Congress easily passed legislation reauthorizing the Act for five years, during which Congress will appropriate $1 billion annually for prevention and treatment programs.

The president's Millennium Vaccine Initiative was launched in March 2000 to devote research and money to bringing vaccines for infectious diseases, including AIDS, to the developing nations of the world. As part of a government/industry alliance, the initiative brings Merck and Co. and Glaxo SmithKline into partnership with the federal government to develop vaccines for strains of AIDS found worldwide.

Insurance companies also comprise a major part of AIDS-related industry. While initial reports of HIV and AIDS generated considerable confusion and concern over possible impacts on the insurance industry, those impacts have not materialized. It was presumed that insurers would take a financial hit as the number of HIV-infected individuals and persons with AIDS grew. *Life Association News,* however, reported that AIDS has not had a significant negative impact on the insurance business. The debate is less over how much of the cost of HIV/AIDS treatments is covered (although that is a concern given the high cost of medications and care) than over what some have called the "buying off" of persons with AIDS. This area, where insurance companies have found themselves in an unwanted spotlight, involves something called viaticals. The word is from the Latin *viaticum,* which refers either to the rites administered to dying persons in the Roman Catholic Church, or to the provisions for a journey. It has come to mean a new growth segment of the AIDS-related insurance industry.

A small number of companies—usually not an individual's life insurer—have entered into Living Benefits arrangements with AIDS patients. These individuals tend to be unable to find employment and may have to rely on assistance programs such as Social Security disability payments or public relief payments. The viatical companies agree to "buy" the life insurance policy of an AIDS sufferer for between 50 and 80 percent of its face value. The policyholder gets access to needed money; the viatical company collects on the life insurance policy when the individual with AIDS dies. This approach has both supporters and detractors. Although someone with AIDS may not be able to work (either because of health considerations or because of de facto job discrimination), living expenses continue. Added to daily living costs are increasing costs for medicines and health-related services. Additionally, the ability to pay off student loans, make automobile payments, or be responsible for any kind of debt, means the cost of having AIDS quickly mounts. The viatical approach has been viewed as a way for needed funding to get into the hands of those suffering from AIDS at a time when they really need the money—while they are still alive. The viatical insurance industry was generating an estimated $300 million in annual receipts in the mid-1990s. By 2000, however, the industry had decidedly slacked off, not only because of the increased life span of AIDS patients due to medical advances, but also because of negative media attention directed at the industry.

Yet another element in the AIDS-related industry is equipment, ranging from extremely expensive machines used in the treatment of blood and blood-related products to disposable plastic gloves and condoms. Prior to the 1980s, condoms were rarely seen in public and were not widely marketed. With the onset of AIDS and public education campaigns, including announcements by Surgeon General C. Everett Koop, suggesting condom use was one way to minimize exposure to HIV, condoms became a product for mass marketing. With considerable fanfare (and inevitable controversy), condoms were advertised on television, with their regular use endorsed by sex therapist Dr. Ruth Westheimer. After basketball star Magic Johnson's November 1991 announcement that he was HIV-positive, stock in condom companies soared. Today, condoms are widely publicized and are easily available in a variety of locations.

There have been other, sometimes questionable, products and services resulting from AIDS. Author Elinor Burkett, who coined the phrase "AIDS Industrial Complex" in her book *The Gravest Show on Earth,* listed a wide array of activities ranging from well-meaning failures to tasteless exploitation to outright scams. Some health-food stores claimed certain vitamins could cure AIDS, and a Texas company peddled what it also claimed was an AIDS cure. There was an advertisement in a national magazine for Lasting Impression cards (sold for $19.95) for terminally ill patients to send to loved ones, and a $15 red rhinestone version of the AIDS ribbon often seen at entertainment events.

Virtually all branches of the AIDS-related industries have come under criticism at one time or another for their failure to eradicate AIDS. Stories about advances seem to be balanced by stories of failures and rising death rates; therefore, it is unclear whether anything short of total eradication of HIV and AIDS would satisfy critics. Given the nature of the disease, that was still projected to be at least several years off in 2000.

BACKGROUND AND DEVELOPMENT

The study of the origin of AIDS has been rather contentious in recent years. While scientists have generally come to accept the theory that the disease has its origins in Africa, the precise timing and method of transmission to humans is still up in the air. While a subsequent examination of medical records suggests that people may have died of AIDS-like diseases throughout history, awareness of AIDS as an identifiable condition was first observed in the late 1970s. At that time, there were large population shifts in coun-

tries such as Zaire, with thousands of rural dwellers moving to the cities, resulting in increased overcrowding and increased prostitution, which led to the spread of the disease. There had been plagues earlier in history, such as the Black Death that ravaged Europe in the Middle Ages and the worldwide influenza epidemic of 1918 to 1920, which killed more people than had died in World War I. But the causes of those plagues had long before been identified. That is not yet the case with AIDS.

Initially, it was believed this disease was spread only by inoculation, that the virus must somehow be injected into an individual's bloodstream. That thinking made intravenous drug users, who often shared needles, prime candidates for the syndrome. But in 1981, physicians in New York and San Francisco began noticing a high death rate among gay males from such opportunistic diseases as Kaposi's sarcoma, a form of cancer thought to be isolated in Africa. Medical personnel also noticed that individuals who had exceptionally low T-cell counts were virtually unable to fight off even simple infections. Initially, causes of death among this group of people were attributed to the infections. After these findings were revealed, other physicians reported that they had run into similar cases over the previous few years, but these cases went unexplained.

AIDS was formally identified as a syndrome (or series of diseases, opportunistic infections, and conditions) in 1981. It was believed AIDS originated in Africa as a result of human-animal sexual activity and/or bites from infected animals, then spread to

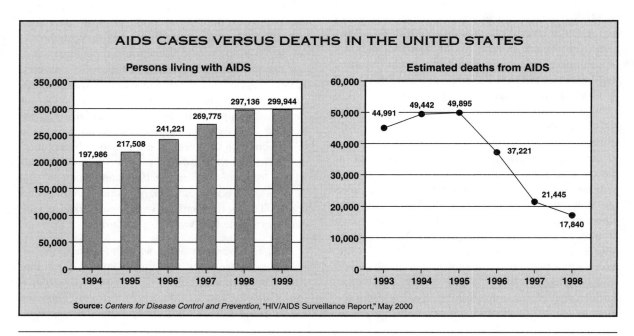

AIDS CASES VERSUS DEATHS IN THE UNITED STATES

Persons living with AIDS

197,986 (1994), 217,508 (1995), 241,221 (1996), 269,775 (1997), 297,136 (1998), 299,944 (1999)

Estimated deaths from AIDS

44,991 (1993), 49,442 (1994), 49,895 (1995), 37,221 (1996), 21,445 (1997), 17,840 (1998)

Source: *Centers for Disease Control and Prevention, "HIV/AIDS Surveillance Report," May 2000*

Western countries primarily through homosexual activity. By the late 1990s, the debate heated up considerably. British journalist Edward Hopper revealed his findings suggesting that AIDS was born of early polio-vaccine experiments in Africa in the 1950s that utilized infected chimpanzee cells, based on admittedly circumstantial evidence of the coincidence of the earliest AIDS cases and vaccine testing. The vaccine researchers vigorously deny using chimpanzee cells at all. Shortly thereafter, Los Alamos National Laboratory scientist Bette Korber reported that, in light of her recent findings, Hopper's theory was highly unlikely, given that Korber traced the virus back to sometime between 1915 and 1941. The theory most widely accepted by scientists holds that the virus was transmitted via the hunting and butchering of chimpanzees infected with simian immunodeficiency virus (SIV, closely clinked genetically with HIV), although direct connections between SIVs and the dominant strains of HIV are still lacking.

In 1983 scientists identified HIV as the probable cause of AIDS, setting the stage for most subsequent research. Initially thought to be a gay male's or drug user's disease, AIDS deaths began to multiply among persons young and old who received blood transfusions from HIV-positive individuals, as well as those who engaged only in heterosexual practices. By the late 1980s, AIDS was everyone's concern.

AIDS quickly became a sensitive political and social issue. President Ronald Reagan's administration was viewed as largely unresponsive to AIDS, prompting considerable protest and rhetoric. While President George Bush gave more attention to the problem, AIDS surfaced as a campaign issue in 1992 when Bush was challenged for the presidency by Arkansas Governor Bill Clinton. During Clinton's two terms as president, he greatly expanded government's role in research, treatment, education, and prevention—with a substantial amount of money and effort still devoted to educating people about how AIDS is contracted and what should be done to minimize exposure to the disease. During this same period, the American Red Cross took extraordinary precautions to prevent the spread of AIDS through the blood supply.

In the mid-1990s there was an increase in AIDS-related lawsuits. One of the more significant lawsuits pitted Jackson National Life against Mrs. Frank Deramus, whose husband had died of AIDS. Mrs. Deramus sued the insurance company for not informing her husband that he had AIDS. A court ruled that insurers had no responsibility to notify those they insured of medical information to which the companies had access. Another significant set of cases involved a Japanese government AIDS researcher, Takeshi Abe, who in 1983 received donations from five different blood product manufacturers that were accused of having sold HIV-tainted products. Similar cases involving HIV-tainted blood also surfaced (and have been settled) in Canada and France.

CURRENT CONDITIONS

One of the most difficult and persistent problems in developing drugs to combat AIDS is that the HIV virus is notorious for its mutation ingenuity. That is, the virus has a way of "changing" when it reproduces in an individual's blood cells. Consequently, an individual's ability to fight off a wide range of infections is substantially compromised, and it means a drug or combination of drugs may work for one person but not for another. That has kept a number of pharmaceutical companies continuing research to find either a cure or a way to substantially prolong the lives of AIDS-infected persons.

Still, a variety of drugs and treatments have proven successful in treating those infected from birth. Some of the oldest HIV-infected individuals in this category living in the late 1990s were 17 years old, significantly older than doctors had predicted was possible. In 1999 researchers welcomed the positive result of a multiyear study showing that shorter-term medication for HIV-infected babies born to infected women was nonetheless effective. While results were hopeful for developing countries, the study was not without controversy. One concern was the trial testing, which gave real medicine to only half the study's infected mothers, thus building into the study model a mortality statistic that was considered by many as unethical. Simply put, the study might have saved many more otherwise doomed infants, but those that have survived now may be orphaned because of untreated mothers. The alternative, argued scientists from the United Nations AIDS program, was to let the babies die.

AZT, also known as azido-deoxythymidine, as zidovudine (ZDV), or by its trademarked name Ritrovir, was the first and probably the best known of the battery of drugs used to keep AIDS at bay. Most doctors start antiviral therapy (when a person has some symptoms of HIV) with this drug. As the first HIV drug to receive U.S. Food and Drug Administration (FDA) approval, it has been widely studied. Since there is no generic version of this drug, and since only one company manufactures it, Glaxo SmithKline has been in the forefront of AIDS-related industries.

While AZT is still considered the first-line treatment of HIV, it brings with it a wide array of negative side effects, and the drug may produce a harsh interaction with other drugs used as part of the drug "cocktail" approach now used to stave off HIV and to treat AIDS. In 1999, it was shown that AZT and 3TC, another drug, together could substantially reduce risk to newborns, even when given during a smaller window period during the mother's pregnancy and postpartum days. New treatments involving antiviral protease inhibitor drugs have had mixed reviews, although the majority have been positive. More alarming than mixed treatment prognoses are the financial aspects of AIDS. Many patients cannot get the costly medicines needed to keep their conditions under control because of restrictions imposed on them by their health maintenance organizations and state programs set up to assist low-income persons. The kinds of drug combinations recommended by doctors treating AIDS patients generally cost about $12,000 per year—a cost likely to stay at its prohibitive height for as long as the individual is being treated for AIDS.

New fusion inhibitors, meanwhile, were rapidly speeding through the pipeline. In 1997 antiviral protease inhibitors were among the most promising of the new drugs in the developing HIV/AIDS arsenal. These drugs interrupt the way HIV uses a healthy cell to make more viruses. In April 1999 the FDA approved Agenerase, generically known as amprenavir, the first new protease inhibitor approved since 1997.

The drug cocktail appears to be capable of eliminating nearly all detectable levels of HIV in the body tissues where the virus is known to reside, although traces still appear under intense magnification. Previous studies have shown that these drugs can reduce the level of HIV in the bloodstream. But the virus is known to hide in the tonsils, lymph nodes, spinal fluid, and semen. Canadian scientists have found that drug cocktails have been most effective with individuals who have not been ill with HIV for a long time. Unfortunately, while these protease inhibitors were highly effective in prolonging patients' lives when mixed in drug cocktails, the patients' HIV levels return to their high levels when the treatment is discontinued. Thus, the treatment curtails but does not destroy the virus.

One set of cocktail drugs is produced by Glaxo SmithKline and Abbott Laboratories and utilizes the drugs AZT, 3TC, and Norvir. A separate study found that the combination of AZT, 3TC, and Viramune (manufactured by Boehringer Ingelheim) had a similar effect. This approach, known as HIV therapeutics, was welcomed at the twelfth International Conference on AIDS held 28 June through 3 July 1998 in Geneva, Switzerland, and has generated optimism within the research community.

While drug cocktails in combination with other anti-HIV treatments is becoming the standard of care, it has not yet been determined which of the anti-HIV drug combinations are the most effective and consistent. What is clear is that the stronger the anti-HIV effects of a drug combination, the less likely it is that HIV will become resistant to the effects of the drugs. This will keep the world's drug manufacturers involved in research for the near future.

Since the introduction of the protease inhibitors around 1995, HIV/AIDS patients no longer have to endure long and painful stays in hospitals, and are generally much more able to lead healthy lives. Still, however, such patients must be meticulous in their daily medication, keeping to strict time and dosage regiments and continuously monitoring side effects.

According to many critics, one unfortunate side effect of improved drugs and treatments allowing for longer, healthier lives for those living with HIV and AIDS is that public visibility has diminished, and with it the sense of the disease's urgency. For instance, some surveys reported a decline in philanthropic donations to HIV/AIDS groups of 22 percent between 1997 and 2000, and "risky" behavior was generally viewed as on the upswing as the disease came to be conceptualized increasingly as a chronic condition, in the manner of diabetes, rather than as a fatal infection. Meanwhile, the disease is still spreading at a rate of 40,000 each year in the United States.

Researchers made tremendous progress toward the development of a vaccine in the late 1990s, building on improved genetic and viral understandings to produce treatments and vaccine tests ranging from methods to teach the immune system to attack the virus to isolating the vulnerable components of the virus itself.

Most vaccination programs have focused on mimicking an infection in order to stimulate the immune system in one of two ways. First, the body's immune system can be taught to recognize an HIV invasion by injecting a protein that surrounds the HIV virus into the bloodstream, thereby causing the system to shoot antibodies at the intruder in attempts to neutralize it. While such experiments traditionally found that the stimulated antibodies were still far too weak to properly combat the virus, improved technologies have continued to maintain this technique as a viable option for vaccine development. The other route is to mimic an actual infection in order to prompt the

An AIDS-prevention discussion and condom distribution program assists high-risk women. *(Stock Market)*

body's T cells into action. In this case, a few HIV genes are injected, causing cells to create HIV proteins, thereby telling the body's T cells to carry out a seek-and-destroy mission. Recent years have witnessed the proliferation of such experiments whereby genetically engineered HIV proteins are injected on the backs of previously successful vaccine "carriers," such as those for smallpox.

These methods, however, fail to focus the immune system's full attention on its target, because the system will instinctively respond to the proteins from the carrier as well. For this reason, scientists have begun to utilize genetic-engineering technology to introduce vaccines carrying DNA that interacts with cells to produce HIV proteins. In the meantime, genetic manipulation has been successful in making the HIV genes more similar to human genes, thereby producing greater levels of HIV proteins and, as a result, greater T-cell response.

Another area of concern for scientists developing a vaccine is the level of specialization such a solution would have to incorporate. The most common strain of HIV in Kenya, for instance, was about 90 percent identical with the dominant North American strain, but scientists were unclear on whether this difference would require alternate vaccinations. Nonetheless, re-

searchers and companies, such as Merck & Co., Inc., were committed to the development of vaccines of all known strains.

The most advanced vaccination program in 2000 was that developed by Dr. Donald P. Francis at Vax-Gen, Inc of Brisbane, California. After beginning human test trials in 1998, Francis oversaw the initial advanced-stage trial of a potential HIV vaccine, called AIDSVAX, in late 1999, with results expected by fall 2001. The vaccine was administered to over 8,000 patients in the United States and Thailand, endorsed by the Joint United Nations Programme on HIV/AIDS. While there were skeptics aplenty, most viewed the Phase III trial as a crucial test to determine whether a viable vaccine was in sight. This was, in fact, the first AIDS vaccine to move into Phase III trials, at which the vaccine's effectiveness in preventing infectious disease is determined.

INDUSTRY LEADERS

While a number of companies are involved in the development and testing of the wide array of expensive drugs used to treat persons with HIV and AIDS, the first name that comes to the minds of medical practitioners and their patients is Glaxo SmithKline. Formed by the merger, between SmithKline Beecham and AZT developer Glaxo Wellcome, the company was the world's largest pharmaceutical maker. The firm is also the manufacturer of the new protease inhibitor Agenerase, approved by the FDA in April 1999 for treatment of HIV infections. Abbott Laboratories joined Glaxo in bringing commercial treatments to the market; Abbott's Kaletra protease inhibitor was approved by the FDA in 2000. The three leading producers of protease inhibitors, a major pharmaceutical component of AIDS treatment, are Merck & Co., Abbott Laboratories, and Hoffmann-La Roche, Inc. Serono Laboratories, Inc. has produced a drug called serostim, which is designed to address AIDS-wasting syndrome. Several pharmaceutical companies were engaged in trying to develop a vaccine for AIDS. The largest among these included Merck, Wyeth-Ayerst Laboratories, and Rhone-Poulenc's Pasteur Merieux Connaught unit.

WORK FORCE

The frontline workers in the AIDS battle are clinical physicians, related clinic- and hospital-based professionals, and home health-care workers. Also part of the army of AIDS industry workers are the research scientists, pharmacists, related direct-care providers, and the educators, outreach workers, and fund-raisers who help keep the issue of AIDS in the public consciousness.

Biomedical researchers are the behind-the-scenes workers who rarely come into direct contact with AIDS patients. Many of them work for the National Institutes of Health, the Food and Drug Administration, and the Centers for Disease Control and Prevention. A substantial number of university-based researchers and individuals working for private pharmaceutical manufacturers also contribute to the $12 billion research industry.

A number of other occupations are also a part of AIDS-related industries. Particularly significant are manufacturing jobs. These include those involved in the production of treatment equipment and items for prevention, such as condoms and latex gloves. Except for doctors and other health-care workers treating AIDS patients, very few persons in the AIDS industry run any risk of infection through their jobs.

Initially, there was dramatic fear that HIV and AIDS could be spread through casual contact with an infected individual; a number of medical workers be-

came infected as a result of being stabbed by instruments that had touched virus-infected blood. While there are still some personnel who refuse to provide treatment to or come in contact with an HIV-positive/AIDS-infected individual—something the American Medical Association has condemned as a violation of its code of ethics—precautions in all areas of medical practice have improved to the point where the risk of accidental infection is almost nil.

AMERICA AND THE WORLD

AIDS knows no political, social, or racial boundaries; it is a global phenomenon. While the relatively rich United States has undertaken efforts on all fronts to deal with all aspects of HIV and AIDS, other countries are only beginning to come to grips with the disease and the magnitude of its destruction.

In June 2000 the Joint United Nations Programme on HIV/AIDS (UNAIDS) updated its basic statistics, evincing a pandemic rather than epidemic crisis. More than 18.8 million people had died worldwide since the epidemic began—15 million of them were adults; 3.8 million were children under the age of 15. In 1999 alone, a total of 5.4 million new cases were reported, including 620,000 children. Of adults, just over half of all new cases were women.

Internationally, UNAIDS reports what they call an alarming increase in HIV and AIDS worldwide among persons aged 13 to 24. Rates in foreign countries are also rising dramatically. A study by Louis Harris & Associates indicated that 25 percent of HIV/AIDS patients in the United States do not follow treatment guidelines developed by the U.S. Department of Health and Human Services, even when they have AIDS-related symptoms.

Figures from UNAIDS concluded that more than half of all new HIV infections acquired after infancy occur among young people between the ages of 10 and 24. Of the estimated 34.3 million people worldwide living with HIV, about half were under 25 years of age; by the year 2020, there will be more than 40 million orphans under the age of 15 in the 23 countries most affected by HIV, one-third of them under the age of 5. These children will have lost their parents to AIDS.

More than 1.7 million young people aged 13 to 24 are infected with HIV every year in Africa. South of the Sahara Desert, about 24.5 million Africans are living with HIV, and countries of that region account for the 21 highest HIV prevalence rates in the world. An alarming 71 percent of the world's HIV/AIDS sufferers live in sub-Saharan Africa. Indicative of the urgency with which African countries are racing to find a remedy, the South African AIDS Vaccine Initiative announced its intention to generate a locally produced vaccine by 2005, when nearly one-quarter of the South African population was expected to be infected, and five years before the target date set by U.S. President Clinton.

In South and East Asia, the numbers are rising as well, with over 6 million living with HIV, especially concentrated in areas with high poverty rates. India has nearly 4 million people living with HIV, and more than 700,000 young people in Asia and the Pacific contract HIV each year. The totality of these staggering figures shows that more than 95 percent of all HIV-infected people now live in the developing world, with a correlative 95 percent of all AIDS-related deaths.

At one time, it was believed infection rates in Eastern European and Central Asian countries were relatively small. That has changed. By the end of 1999, more than 420,000 people in the region were living with HIV, representing a sharp increase from just a few years before. In fact, Uganda and Thailand were the only developing countries studied by Dr. David Heymann with the World Health Organization that have declining HIV rates.

While many developing countries have embarked on strong prevention programs, their HIV and AIDS rates have not dropped, and these countries have neither the infrastructure nor the funding capabilities to make strong inroads without outside financial assistance.

Some developed nations have registered negative trends as well. Disturbingly, the United Kingdom, unlike other European Union nations, has witnessed an increase in mother-baby HIV transmissions in recent years. About 50 children are born HIV-positive in Britain each year, accounting for about 2 percent of the nation's 34,000 sufferers. Moreover, the number of adults in the U.K. living with HIV rose 29 percent between 1995 and 1998. A significant portion of this rising figure, however, was attributed to improved drug treatments allowing for longer lives of those suffering with the disease, according to the U.K. Public Health Laboratory Service's HIV division. Indeed, AIDS-related deaths fell from 1,236 in England and Wales in 1996 to 395 in 1998, though that figure rebounded to 450 in 1999.

France, whose researchers narrowly edged out Robert Gallo of the National Cancer Institute in Bethesda, Maryland, for credit in isolating HIV as the cause of AIDS in 1983, has had its own problems with public perceptions. Researchers in the United States and abroad have suggested that France's hierarchical research system has stunted the ability of researchers to effectively continue AIDS-related research. And France's problems worsened in 1999. Former French Prime Minister Laurent Fabius and two administration members were on trial for manslaughter for failing to act on available tests to detect HIV-infected blood back in the mid-1980s. The result, said prosecutors, was the AIDS infection of more than 4,000 people from tainted blood transfusions, 40 percent of whom have since died. (The defendants were acquitted in March 1999.)

On a global scale, the efforts to combat AIDS assumes social and political, in addition to scientific and medical, dimensions. Couched within broader fears of proprietary Western pharmaceutical companies pushing products for profit and market dominance, some leaders, such as South Africa's Thabo Mbeki, called into question the remedies to the escalating epidemic being propagated, such as AZT and drug cocktails. Mbeki called for more research into the basis of AIDS science and the reasons for the disease's prevalence in sub-Saharan Africa, even seeking input from San Francisco biochemist David Rasnick, who forwarded the controversial and much-derided theory that the disease does not stem from a virus and that popular Western drug cocktails are toxic. Such scientists held that diseases associated with damaged immune systems could very easily be brought on by the high rates of poverty and malnutrition, which compromise the body's defense mechanisms, found in such regions. While these factors are taken seriously, researchers gathered at the XIII International AIDS Conference in South Africa in July 2000 roundly criticized Mbeki's extreme interpretation and what they felt were irresponsible policies. Although President Mbeki has stepped up his government's commitment to the prevention and treatment of AIDS, he has been less enthusiastic about devoting government resources to the purchase of anti-HIV drugs.

The intersection of AIDS, politics, and economics found U.S. Vice President Al Gore in hot water with AIDS activists in 1999 and 2000. Gore, who headed a bilateral commission on U.S.-South Africa relations, was accused of protecting the profits of major drug companies at the expense of AIDS sufferers in sub-Saharan Africa because of Washington's official policy of protecting restrictive intellectual property rights, thus prohibiting the manufacture of generic pharmaceuticals at a price more readily affordable to Africa's impoverished populations. Meanwhile, since the successful treatments enjoyed by those in the

United States are generally far too expensive for those in the developing world, a vaccine was widely seen as the only possible remedy for the vast majority of the world's sufferers. At the International AIDS Conference in 2000, HIV-infected South African high-court Justice Edwin Cameron noted that he was able to address the crowd only because he could afford the enormous costs of maintaining his health, an inequity he called "shocking and monstrous." These comments brought long-standing activist criticisms to a high level of prominence, and helped push several major drug companies into a commitment to cut the inequities in treatment availability.

The United States, which itself has been the target of substantial worldwide criticism for its AIDS policies, has begun to question the effectiveness of UNAIDS. A General Accounting Office (GAO) analysis of UNAIDS concluded that this United Nations agency has had little success in its two years of operation. According to the GAO report, the United Nations has not increased AIDS spending, despite its goal of expanding the fight against the disease, particularly in the developing world. The report also said United Nations' efforts to coordinate its AIDS and health activities in various countries have gotten off to a slow start. The report did, however, praise UNAIDS for research it has sponsored to identify which programs work to curb the spread of AIDS.

RESEARCH AND TECHNOLOGY

Researchers and activists awaited a slate of new possibilities in understanding the precise causes of AIDS and the body's reaction to the HIV virus afforded by the mapping of the complete human genome, the first draft of which was completed in 2000. After deciphering the 3 billion bits of genetic information, scientists will begin to research the meanings and functions of the body's genes and use that knowledge to develop drugs aimed at combating ailments at their sources.

In connection, another viable research area is centered in the biochip industry. Also known as DNA arrays, biochips are microscopic devices studded with a kind of molecular "tweezer" that grips human DNA, the genetic code carried in all cells of a person's body. These chips allow medical researchers to study thousands of genes at once. By mapping genes, scientists may learn how cells mutate and may eventually be able to stop HIV before it takes over a human organism. Gene mapping may also open the door to immune reconstitution following successful suppression of

HIV replication. Pathogenic events surrounding primary HIV infection are being actively studied by several groups throughout the world.

Help for AIDS patients moved online, as well, in the late 1990s. To help patients taking the cocktail therapy, Minnesota-based Chronimed Inc. developed an online information system to gather and process key data and indicators from patients in order to alert the patients' clinicians, pharmacists, and case managers of crucial changes in condition, reactions to certain drugs, and so on. Using encryption technology, the service can also track a patient's history to enable more informed decision making.

What may be the most welcome news to drug companies and AIDS researchers is a finding by Dr. Beryl Koblin and colleagues of the New York Blood Center that a large percentage of individuals—77 percent—who are considered at high risk of HIV infection say they are willing to participate in HIV vaccine trials. The study included responses from homosexual men, intravenous drug users, and women at risk of HIV infection from heterosexual sex. An HIV vaccine, as well as a "day-after" pill or medicine, remains the goal of researchers grappling with this frustrating disease.

FURTHER READING

Altman, Lawrence K. "A Big Maybe about AIDS." *New York Times,* 5 December 1999.

Bisseker, Claire. "The Race to Beat the Virus before It Beats Us." *Financial Mail* (South Africa), 26 November 1999.

Burkett, Elinor. *The Gravest Show on Earth: America in the Age of AIDS.* Boston: Houghton Mifflin, 1995.

Carey, John, and Amy Barrett. "An AIDS Vaccine Is No Longer a Dream." *Business Week,* 6 September 1999.

Carey, John, Amy Barrett, and Heidi Dawley. "'We Have to Find a Solution.'" *Business Week,* 6 September 1999.

CDC National Prevention Information Network. April 2000. Available from http://www.cdcnpin.org/.

Centers for Disease Control and Prevention. "Basic Statistics," September 2000. Available from http://www.cdc.gov.

———. "HIV/AIDS Surveillance Report: U.S. HIV and AIDS Cases Reported Through December 1999, Year-End Edition," 31 May 2000. Available from http://www.cdc.gov/hiv/stats/hasrlink.htm.

———. "Recent HIV/AIDS Treatment Advances and the Implications for Prevention," April 2000. Available from http://www.cdc.gov/nchstp/hiv_aids/pubs/facts/treatmnt.htm.

———. "Testing a Vaccine Designed to Help Curb the Devastating Toll of HIV in the Developing World," April 2000. Available from http://www.cdc.gov/nchstp/hiv_aids/pubs/facts/vaccinefact.htm.

Chenault, Kathy, John Carey, and Paul Magnusson. "Will the AIDS Plague Change U.S. Trade Policy?" *Business Week,* 13 September 1999.

Cohen, Jon. "AIDS Virus Traced to Chimp Subspecies." *Science,* 5 February 1999.

———. "Cheap Treatment Cuts HIV Transmission." *Science,* 12 February 1999.

———. "Companies, Donors Pledge to Close Gap in AIDS Treatment." *Science,* 21 July 2000.

———. "Searching for the Epidemic's Origins." *Science,* 23 June 2000.

———. "South African Leader Declines to Join the Chorus on HIV and AIDS." *Science,* 14 July 2000.

DeNoon, Daniel J., and Salynn Boyles. "AIDS Pandemic Seen Worsening Next Century." *AIDS Weekly Plus,* 11 October 1999.

Gillespie, Greg. "HIV/AIDS Data on the Internet." *Health Data Management,* August 1999.

Gordimer, Nadine. "Africa's Plague, and Everyone's." *New York Times,* 11 April 2000.

"HIV Cases at Highest for Decade." *Pulse,* 4 December 1999.

"House Clears AIDS-HIV Bill." *The Washington Post,* 6 October 2000.

Jemison-Smith, Pearl. "Legacy of Ryan White Lives on via AIDS Assistance Legislation." *Los Angeles Times,* 9 April 2000.

Joint United Nations Programme on HIV/AIDS. "Report on the Global HIV/AIDS Epidemic," June 2000. Available from http://www.unaids.org/epidemic_update/report/index.html.

Key, Sandra W., Daniel J. DeNoon, and Salynn Boyles. "AIDS Is World's Fourth-Largest Killer." *World Disease Weekly Plus,* 24 May 1999.

Licking, Ellen, and John Carey. "Turning Data into Drugs—Fast." *Business Week,* 6 March 2000.

Masland, Tom, and Patricia King. "Flirting with Strange Ideas." *Newsweek,* 17 April 2000.

Shapiro, Joseph P. "Feeling the Pinch." *U.S. News & World Report,* 1 November 1999.

Veash, Nicole. "Living in the Shadow of AIDS." *Observer,* 15 August 1999.

Weissman, Robert. "Are U.S. Anti-AIDS Drug Makers Being Unfair to Africa?" *Insight on the News,* 13 September 1999.

Wright, L. N., P. F. Smith, et al. "Decrease in AIDS-Related Mortality in a State Correctional System-New York, 1995-1998." *JAMA,* 10 February 1999.

ALTERNATIVE ADULT EDUCATION

Participation in adult education grew steadily from 1970 to 2000, increasing to 90 million adults (46 percent of the population) in 1999. American adults desperately need further education; according to the U.S. Department of Commerce, by 2005, 60 percent of all U.S. jobs will require skills currently held by only 20 percent of the population. About 40 million adults possess poor or no reading skills. Though the number of college students in the United States was expected to reach 3.2 million by 2004, only one in five post-secondary education students is 18 to 22 years old, attends school full-time, and lives on campus. About 44 percent of students are working adults over age 24. The tight U.S. labor market also heightened the importance of corporate investment in education as a means of retaining skilled workers. Finally, the overall aging of the population, with people living longer and healthier lives, meant many more retirees would seek education as a path to personal enrichment.

Adults were most likely to participate in work-related courses and personal development courses. Participation rates overall are associated with prior educational attainment. About two in 10 adults without a high school diploma participated in any educational activities, compared to more than six in 10 with a B.A. or higher. The apparent direct relationship between participation in adult education and educational attainment, on closer examination, however, may result from participation of more highly educated adults in work-related educational activities.

The popularity and proliferation of Internet-based, online (or "distance") learning represented the dominant trend in alternative adult education by the end of the 1990s; the global market was poised to leap from \$4 to \$15 billion between 1998 and 2002, and was projected to reach \$50 billion by 2005. International Data Corp. indicated that 710,000 students were enrolled in e-courses in 1998 and predicted an increase to 2.2 million by 2002. The medium seemed especially well suited to business education and on-going professional training. Even prestigious institutions of higher education, such as the University of Chicago and Columbia University, scrambled to ally with start-up online providers. More than one observer predicted e-learning would spell the demise of face-to-face, classroom-based instruction altogether, at least in some fields. As the cost of attending traditional educational institutions continued to escalate, many employers found that continuing, online education for their employees made simple mathematical sense. And the flexibility of Internet courses, which can often be accessed at all hours, meshed with the time constraints of many already overscheduled working adults.

Corporate universities, such as General Electric Co.'s in Crotonville, New York, and McDonald's Hamburger University, also sprang up, growing from 400 in 1990 to about 2,000 by the decade's end, while enrollments increased about 30 percent each year.

The trend has not gone unopposed, particularly among some members of the higher-education community itself. Critics warn that e-learning will transform post-secondary institutions into "McUniversities" and that Web courses showcasing star professors will result in the "Hollywoodization" of academia.

ORGANIZATION AND STRUCTURE

From 1987 to 2000, over 100 traditional, four-year colleges in the United States closed; during the same period, the number of for-profit colleges or universities increased from 400 to 1,600. Many analysts say that in the future, higher education will move away from traditional liberal studies—which they charge are aimed at elites—and toward more practical education that stresses skills immediately applicable in the job market. The new trends target middle-class, working adults over 24, who make up an increasingly large percentage of the $200 billion per year higher education market.

Adult education is defined in a variety of ways. The National Center on Education Statistics adopts a broad definition, and includes voluntary and required educational activities that involve the presence of an instructor. These encompass courses teaching English as a second language; adult basic education, General Educational Development preparation classes, and adult high school; and credential programs leading to a college or university degree or a postsecondary vocational or technical diploma.

VOCATIONAL EDUCATION

The 1990 Perkins Act defines vocational education as "organized educational programs offering a sequence of courses which are directly related to the preparation of individuals in paid or unpaid employment in current or emerging occupations requiring other than a baccalaureate or advanced degree." Postsecondary occupational curricula typically offer programs in the following categories: agriculture; business and office; marketing and distribution; health; home economics; technical education, including protective services and computers and data processing; engineering, science, and communication technologies; and trade and industry. Vocational education is also provided at the secondary level.

The National Assessment of Vocational Education found that 5.8 million students were enrolled in post-secondary vocational education in 1990, making up about 35 percent of all undergraduate post-secondary enrollment. Vocational enrollment represented an even larger share of the non-baccalaureate undergraduate population, approximately 50 percent of which reported majoring in a vocational program area.

PRIVATE, FOR-PROFIT INSTITUTIONS

Proprietary, for-profit colleges set up campuses in locations such as shopping malls, near where working adults live, and schedule classes for evenings and weekends. Many focus offerings in business and technical fields and stress job placement. Examples include DeVry Technical Institute, the University of Phoenix, and ITT Educational Services, Inc. They pose a challenge to traditional colleges and universities, particularly the United States' 1,250 community and technical colleges. Private, for-profit institutions enroll 8 percent of all post-secondary students, but 16 percent of all black students, 14 percent of Hispanic students, and 4 percent of Native American students, according to the U.S. Department of Education. Proprietary schools target under-served students, such as working parents, returning students, and employees who need ongoing training.

DISTANCE INSTRUCTION

By the late 1990s, two forms of distance instruction existed: traditional correspondence-based instruction, which is oriented for independent study, and telecommunications-based instruction, which offers the teaching and learning experience simultaneously. Some scholars distinguish between distance learning and distance education, instead of using the term "instruction." Distance learning is exemplified by programs designed to encourage self-directed learning, such as do-it-yourself books, while distance education requires formal evaluation and two-way communication with an institution, as well as independent study.

Distance instruction is delivered through media such as audiotape, videotape, radio and television broadcasting, and satellite transmission. Microcomputers, the Internet, and the World Wide Web are shaping the current generation of distance learning. The next generation may be built on virtual reality, artificial intelligence, and knowledge systems. Although broadcast television was often used for distance instruction in the mid- to late 1990s, it may be used more rarely in the future, as media such as print, audiocassette, and telephone access prove to be more convenient.

Two primary forms of communication are used to deliver distance instruction—asynchronous and synchronous. The main distinction between the two is whether teachers and learners are participating at the same time. Asynchronous methods use recorded instructional materials that allow participants to be separated in time and distance. Thus, telecommunications systems such as television, or electronically stored media such as video, audio, and computer software, are among the technologies employed. Synchronous programs use technologies offering live, interactive instruction. Instructional Television Fixed Service and point-to-point microwave are among the most common live interactive systems linking classrooms within the regional area surrounding an institution; the students are able to see and hear one another, as well as the instructor. Other examples of synchronous communications include audio conferencing and real-time computer communications.

The organization and administration of distance instruction in the late 1990s varied according to the type of institution offering the instruction. Some universities offer distance-learning programs exclusively, while others provide distance instruction as one of a number of programs. Entire degree programs, at both the undergraduate and graduate levels, can be obtained via Web-based courses over the Internet.

Accreditation of distance-instruction establishments vary by state and region. Institutions that also maintain a traditional campus often have the distance-instruction component accredited as part of the main institution. One accrediting body specific to the industry is the Distance Education and Training Council (DETC)—formerly the National Home Study Council—founded in 1926 in Washington, D.C. The DETC is an association of distance learning and correspondence schools recognized by the U.S. Department of Education and the Commission on Recognition of Post-Secondary Accreditation.

PROPRIETARY COLLEGES

Proprietary, for-profit colleges and universities emerged after World War II. While nonprofit universities reinvest surplus revenue in further educational efforts, proprietary institutions return it to shareholders. In 1972, amendments to the Higher Education Act allowed for-profit college students access to federal student loans to pay for their education; their default rate, however, is higher than that of other students.

Perhaps the most well known such provider is the University of Phoenix, founded in 1976 by a former political science professor from San Jose State University and accredited since 1978. The university admits only employed students over 23 years old. Offering classes in 15 states, plus Puerto Rico and British Columbia, it enrolled over 66,000 students in 2000, making it the largest private university in the United States. The university leases its classroom space; most faculty are part-timers with M.A.s. The University of Phoenix also offers courses in a distance-learning format.

BACKGROUND AND DEVELOPMENT

For well over a century, a debate was fought in the United States over how to prepare students to become adult workers. Until the country's economy was transformed from an agricultural to a manufacturing base, children received a common core curriculum of academic subjects, and most left school before the end of the eighth grade. In 1900, 6.5 percent of students were graduated from high school, as compared to about 72 percent in the mid-1990s.

As the manufacturing-centered economy took hold, changes in vocational education were required. Some policy makers proposed setting up separate vocational education programs to prepare young people for work. Others, especially John Dewey (1859-1952), urged the integration of academic and vocational instruction so that all students could learn the same academic material, but in the context of occupations and adult experiences. The federal government, however, created distinct programs of vocational instruction when it passed the Smith-Hughes Act of 1917. Eventually, most schools divided students into "academic" and "vocational" tracks, and in the 1920s, many schools added a general track to give students a sampling of both. Although commissions and studies throughout the 20th century have endorsed this approach to vocational education, many schools and school districts still designated vocational education as a separate track designed primarily to prepare students for work.

As high school graduates were increasingly seen as under-qualified to perform the technical jobs for which vocational education supposedly had trained them, adult vocational training took on added importance. In addition, improvements were sought in secondary school vocational training, notably in the Carl Perkins Vocational and Applied Technology Education Act of 1990, which promoted the integration of academic and vocational learning. The Perkins Act requires each state to use academic achievement as a measure of success, and it encourages linkages between secondary and post-secondary course work through tech-prep education. Another statute designed to improve vocational education was the School-to-Work Opportunities Act of 1994, which sought to raise educational standards and prepare students for post-secondary education.

In the early 1990s, the most popular post-secondary vocational program of study was business, with about 17 percent of all non-baccalaureate students declaring a major in that area. This was followed in popularity by health, with 11 percent, and trade and industry, with 8 percent. The combined technical fields—computers and data processing, engineering and science technologies, protective services, and communications technologies—accounted for 12 percent of all non-baccalaureate majors.

Pioneer WILLIAM RAINEY HARPER (1856-1906) EDUCATING AMERICA

William Rainey Harper (1856-1906) was one of America's great education pioneers. Harper was born in New Concord, Ohio, to Ellen Rainey and Samuel Harper, a grocer. He entered Muskingum College preparatory department when he was eight years old, and at 10 became a freshman at the "college on the hill." At 16 he attended Yale University, and within three years had earned a doctorate. His first teaching job was at Denison University. A year later he took a teaching position at the Baptist Theological Seminary in Chicago.

In 1891, John D. Rockefeller called on 35-year-old Harper to help organize and run a new private, nondenominational, coeducational university—a "Harvard of the Midwest." On October 1, 1892 classes began at the University of Chicago. So great was the university's promise that eight college and university presidents resigned their posts in order to teach there. Harper was the university's first president, and he envisioned a modern research university, combining an English-style under-

graduate college and a German-style graduate research institute.

Harper encouraged administrators to seek new disciplines and ambitious faculty. The University of Chicago quickly became a national leader in higher education and research, despite the fact that Harper was outspoken and scorned tradition. For example, seizing an opportunity generated by academic unrest at another institution, he visited Clark University and recruited two-thirds of the faculty and half of the graduate students, generating a solid core upon which to build his vision.

Harper was an innovative force in education throughout his career. Some of his greatest accomplishments included establishing the first Department of Sociology in the world and the first university extension program in the United States. He also founded a "core curriculum," which became the model for colleges throughout the United States for more than 60 years. Finally, Harper advocated the admittance of women and minorities to all academic programs.

At the post-secondary level in the 1990s, community and technical colleges served a broad range of students, including those still in high school, recent high school graduates, college graduates returning for specific technical skills, adult workers returning for retraining, welfare recipients, and adults with limited basic skills. Community colleges and private proprietary schools redesigned curricula to deal with a changing student body and the added burdens on adult education.

Public two- to three-year institutions, including community colleges, enrolled 60 percent of all non-baccalaureate post-secondary students reporting a vocational major. The second-largest providers were private proprietary institutions, which educated about 22 percent of non-baccalaureate vocational students.

THE GROWTH OF DISTANCE INSTRUCTION

As early as 1728, advertisements appeared in the Boston *Gazette* soliciting students for shorthand lessons by mail. In 1840, Isaac Pitman (1813-1897) offered shorthand courses by mail in Bath, England. The 1880s saw the founding of private British correspondence colleges. Schools such as Skerry's College and University Correspondence College, established by the University of London, prepared students for post-secondary examinations. Correspondence schools also found fertile soil on the European continent. In Berlin, Germany, a modern-language correspondence

school was established by Charles Toussaint and Gustav Langenscheidt in 1856; this school still published instructional materials in the late 1990s.

American academic distance learning began in 1874 at Illinois' Wesley University, which offered both undergraduate and graduate degrees by correspondence. In 1883 the Correspondence University was established in Ithaca, New York. Study outside the traditional classroom was furthered by Anna Eliot York, who founded the Society to Encourage Study at Home in 1873. Home reading circles for adults were created by John Vincent, who became a founder of the Chautauqua movement. The aim of this popular education society was to extend educational access to all Americans, and the movement has been called "the first significant distance-education effort in America." Chautauqua continued to play a role in distance instruction when William Rainey Harper, called by many the father of American correspondence study, established a correspondence program for his students. Chautauqua later became an accredited university in New York State, and Harper became the first president of the University of Chicago and founder of the first university-level correspondence study division in the United States.

The growth of distance-instruction centers spawned growth in other media. The first federally licensed radio station devoted to educational broadcasting, WHA, evolved from an amateur wireless station started by University of Wisconsin professors in 1919. The birth of educational television broadcasts occurred at the University of Iowa between 1932 and 1937.

A remarkable example of the potential for adult distance instruction can be seen in the Open University of the United Kingdom, established in 1971. In its first 10 years, the school enrolled 60,000 to 70,000 students per year. By the mid-1980s, more than 70,000 students had earned a bachelor's degree from the university. American attempts to emulate the Open University met with limited success. In 1974 the University of Mid-America was founded, aiming to create distance education in seven Midwestern states. The university, despite large enrollments over the years, closed its doors in 1982.

Of concern is the potential spread of "bogus" degrees from "diploma mills," especially on the Internet. Since accreditation is largely nonregulated, online colleges and universities can offer degrees costing thousands of dollars and offering little, if any, substantive education. Many people assume that the U.S. government regulates the industry and they are misled by advertisements boasting of full accreditation from an important-sounding accrediting entity. But as of the late 1990s, the only nationally recognized accrediting agency that evaluates distance-education programs is the Accrediting Commission of the Distance Education and Training Council.

The Higher Education Act of 1998 created a special liaison in the U.S. Department of Education to represent proprietary schools and it included them in the category of "institutions of higher education" that could benefit from Title IV federal financial-aid funds. Prior to the Act, proprietary schools were defined separately from other institutions of higher education, and were thus excluded from bills that affected post-secondary education overall. The 1998 Act also allowed for-profits to appeal default sanctions that might imperil their access to financial aid for high student-loan default rates.

CURRENT CONDITIONS

In 1991 an estimated 58 million adults in the United States participated in adult education, including part-time credential programs; by 1999, this number rose to an estimated 90 million. Participation in adult education was approximately four times the enrollment in higher education overall in 1991, and six times the higher education enrollment in 1999. The 1999 National Household Education Survey, the most

recent available, revealed that adult education is prevalent and increasing in American society, with a 46 percent participation rate reported for 1999. Enrollment in higher education overall remained relatively constant at 7.6 to 7.9 percent of the adult population throughout the 1990s. Adults were most likely to participate in work-related courses and personal development courses (23 percent for each). About 9 percent of adults participated in credential programs, about 2 percent in ABE/GED classes, about 2 percent in apprenticeship programs, and about 1 percent in English as a second language classes.

Much of the industry is still unregulated. The question of whether existing standards for accrediting traditional post-secondary schools apply equally to online learning has yet to be ironed out. Another question is who owns the intellectual property rights for online courses—whether the professors who develop such courses or the universities that employ them should earn royalties for subsequent use. In 1999, Professor Arthur R. Miller of Harvard Law School made news when he supplied video-taped lectures for a course at Concord University School of Law, an entirely online institution that is not accredited by the American Bar Association. Harvard officials claimed that Miller violated university regulations by supplying course material to another law school without permission; Miller, however, contended that his rights over the material were similar to those he would have when publishing an academic book. The entire question of Web-based courses designed by "star" faculty members led Professor Arthur Levine of Columbia University's Teachers College to forecast the "Hollywoodization of academia" with "academic free agents," popular professors who peddle their intellectual wares to the highest bidders.

The overall education sector was worth about $780 billion by 2000, of which for-profit companies accounted for only 10 percent. Market capitalization of education stocks amounted to less than 1 percent of U.S. capital markets in 1999. Venture capital poured into the sector at the end of the 1990s, with about $4 billion estimated to be available in 2000, according to Eduventures.com, Inc. However, education stocks generally disappointed through 2000.

CORPORATE TRAINING
Within the industry, ongoing corporate training—a $63-billion segment—did particularly well. An April 1999 study by Merrill Lynch stated that annual corporate training expenditures totaled at least $60 billion, not counting government-training subsidies of $38 billion. Outsourcing comprised nearly one-third

of all outlays and was growing at three times the rate of overall expenditures. By 2000, there were also more than 2,000 corporate universities in the United States, 10 times the number in 1970. International Data Corp. estimated that the 2000 corporate-training, e-learning market of $1 billion would increase to $11.4 billion by 2003. Typically e-training costs about one-half of what traditional classroom instruction costs; e-training should account for about 51 percent of all corporate training by 2003. Providing such training increasingly became a key element in employee retention. While some employers, such as Aetna Life Insurance, have used distance learning in their corporate training programs for over 15 years, many other employers are quickly embracing the medium. In 2000 even the U.S. Army offered extensive access to online college courses to its enlisted personnel while on active duty, in an attempt to retain qualified recruits in the extremely tight labor market of the late 1990s and early 2000s.

VOCATIONAL EDUCATION

The 1990s saw a continued increase in vocational school enrollment by adult learners. As almost 6 million students sought to improve career-related skills, vocational education in the United States was on track to surpass traditional academic post-secondary education in enrollment, especially among students in non-baccalaureate programs.

DISTANCE INSTRUCTION

According to the Department of Education, distance-learning programs doubled between 1997 and 2000. By 2000, approximately 75 percent of U.S. colleges and universities offered courses over the Internet; 34 percent also supplied accredited, online degree programs. Costs were usually equal to those for traditional courses. With interest in easily accessible course work growing, some analysts predicted online courses could surpass traditional classrooms as the primary vehicle for higher education.

About 700,000 learners logged onto distance courses in 1999; Eduventures.com estimated that number would triple by 2002. According to the National Center for Education Statistics, over one-tenth of the 2 million students enrolled in graduate courses were taking distance-education classes.

One dilemma facing the large numbers of traditional colleges and universities seeking to enter the online education market is the strain of managing a business enterprise necessary to a successful distance-education program. Another difficulty is the great cost associated with the technology necessary to establish effective distance instruction. For students, access to education for those who do not attend classes on campus could be a question of their access to technology. Some critics wonder whether this could lead to a divide between the "technology rich" and the "technology poor."

Many traditional colleges and universities entered the distance-learning realm by 2000, often in the midst of considerable controversy and resistance from their own faculties. Temple University launched a for-profit corporation to market its online offerings under the name Virtual Temple, aimed specifically at continuing education and international students. The new corporation contracts with individual faculty and programs to sell their materials to the corporation. Despite the fact that Temple already hosted 85 online courses, and that other institutions such as New York University and Columbia had similar programs, some Temple professors felt that authorizing a for-profit corporation jeopardized the university's fundamental mission and would take jobs away from doctorate-holders in favor of business executives and poorly paid part-time adjunct instructors.

The move to online instruction raises many problems, among them the issue of intellectual property rights. Though professors usually own their syllabuses and class materials, and universities generally have no claim on royalties to books written by faculty members, the rules don't easily apply to online courses whose implementation requires input from programmers and other designers. Most colleges and universities making the leap to cyberspace were only beginning to hammer out the policies that would govern their online offerings.

In 1999 a report by the American Association of University Professors criticized the practice of allowing universities to retain the sole copyright on professors' work as "deeply inconsistent with fundamental principles of academic freedom." Adverse faculty reaction to the broader phenomenon of the move away from classroom-based education to the Internet, a decision often made by university trustee boards without much initial faculty input, included fear of the loss of face-to-face relationships that characterize the best in traditional education. They raise questions about integrity and student cheating, and concerns that for students to succeed online, they must be self-motivated and highly disciplined.

Business programs, health care, and education curricula seem to translate well to the online environment, while law schools have had more difficulty.

Many business schools have entered e-learning with courses geared specifically to middle- and upper-level managers who want to pursue degrees for career advancement, but who can't sacrifice the time away from the job to do so. The flexibility and cost savings have attracted many corporate employers, who no longer have to send employees away from work for professional training. Furthermore, advances in technology have greatly enhanced the level of vitality and interactivity possible in virtual classrooms. Columbia University's Business School contracted with UNext.com, a fledgling venture financed by former junk-bond guru Michael Milken, to market its online courses to corporate employees. Stanford University, the University of Chicago, and the London School of Economics have also signed on with UNext.com. The courses are provided through Cardean University, an institution created by UNext to award degrees and credits.

Capella University, an accredited, for-profit, entirely online university, received a $35 million investment from Forstmann Little & Co., a New York investment firm. Capella offers undergraduate and graduate degrees in five subject areas. Capella also announced it would collaborate with SmartForce PLC to provide online computer training to employees of 2,500 companies.

Not all distance instruction may be offered for a profit, however. In 2000, D.C. billionaire Michael Saylor, who made his fortune in high tech, announced he would donate $100 million to create an online university that he prophesied would offer "Ivy-caliber" courses free of charge to anyone in the world who logged on. Saylor felt certain that the instructors of his free e-university, all stars from academe, would gladly contribute their expertise unpaid to help generate a "genius knowledge bank."

INDUSTRY LEADERS

Alternative education industry leaders are as diverse as the field itself. The market included providers of vocational, career, and leisure/enrichment education for adults, traditional universities offering courses and degrees online, and institutions existing solely online. Distance instruction caused some overlap. For example, providers of vocational education often provide course work online or in some other distance environment, and traditional universities offering online courses may also teach career courses.

An industry leader in vocational education was DeVry, Inc., of Oakbrook Terrace, Illinois. One of the largest publicly owned international education companies in North America, DeVry has offered technology-based career training to high school graduates for more than 65 years. Its Institutes are located on 30 campuses in the United States and Canada, with more than 38,000 students. DeVry's 1999 fiscal year sales were $419.4 million, an increase of 19.2 percent from 1998. DeVry's Keller Graduate School of Management is one of the nation' largest part-time graduate schools for working adults, and operates 30 sites in major metropolitan areas with attendance by about 6,000 students.

Another leader in alternative education was Sylvan Learning Systems, Inc., of Baltimore, Maryland. Sylvan's 1999 global revenues were $338.5 million. The company provides supplemental and remedial educational services. Sylvan sold its Prometric division, which delivered computer-based testing for academic admissions and professional certification and which provided 60 percent of its revenues, to concentrate on its teaching operations. Part of the sale proceeds went to set up an Internet incubator in collaboration with Apollo Management and Rare Medium Group.

The Caliber Learning Network, a joint initiative of Sylvan and MCI Communications Corp., provides educational and training programs through video-conferencing and the Internet. It went public in 1998 and posted revenues of $26 million in 1999. Caliber supplies classrooms for corporate education. Faculty-student interaction is facilitated by in-room cameras and by computers. Caliber estimated that the cost of e-learning saves two-thirds to four-fifths the cost of traditional classes, because it eliminates travel and facility expenses. The company provides graduate-level learning and professional training through a network of more than 40 campuses. Caliber offers classes to working adults through partnerships with universities (including the Wharton School of the University of Pennsylvania) and corporations (such as Compaq and Nabisco).

The Apollo Group of Phoenix, Arizona, operates five for-profit subsidiaries that provide ongoing education for working adults, among them the University of Phoenix. In 1999 Apollo posted an income of $59 million, an increase of 27.4 percent, on revenues of $499 million. Apollo took the Internet division of the University of Phoenix public as a tracking stock. Another operator of for-profit adult-education institutions was Argosy Education Group, Inc. of Chicago. Offering degrees programs in psychology, business, and information technology, Argosy operated 17 campuses in nine states and Ontario and posted a 1999 net income of $4.6 million, an annual increase of 206.7 percent, on sales of $37 million.

ICS Learning Systems, a subsidiary of National Education Corp. and of Harcourt General, Inc., was the first distance-education provider to offer nationwide job placement opportunities to students. The company targets both the degree and professional education markets, offering allied health, accounting, and law courses. In 1999, the ICS student body contained over 350,000 men and women studying in 150 countries; 2,000 American corporations use ICS training systems with their employees.

Among distance-learning providers, the $100 million start-up UNext.com—founded in 1998—partnered with some of the most prestigious names in traditional higher education, such as the University of Chicago, Columbia University, and the London School of Economics. Faculty from participating schools create the content of its online courses; UNext then designs compatible learning exercises for each class. Classes are taught by UNext-supplied faculty. UNext.com is 20 percent owned by Knowledge Universe, itself owned by investor Michael Milken and Oracle's CEO Lawrence Ellison.

ITT Educational Services, Inc., based in Indianapolis, was the largest U.S. provider of adult technical education. Its 26,000 students were enrolled in courses at 68 sites in 28 states; two-thirds pursued course work in electronic engineering technology. ITT reported sales of $316.4 million and net income of $23.6 million in 1999.

An expanding field is computer education for senior citizens. San Francisco-based SeniorNet is a nonprofit corporation offering classes from basic computer literacy skills to opening e-mail sites and surfing the Internet. In 1995 William Ashkin, then a 94-year-old retired dentist, created Century Club, a Web page and computer forum for adults over the age of 90. Over the Internet, seniors play bridge or exchange recipes with others from places such as Norway and London, and stimulate interest in other seniors to take basic courses in computer technology.

ucation and making education accessible to all. The conference held several key seminars directed toward accessibility technology, women, global minorities, and the physically and developmentally challenged.

One topic that challenged the conference attendees concerned the state-of-the-art transmission of educational knowledge and information, not only from one global community to another, but from one culture or subculture to another. New technology has employed the introduction of international symbols through media tools such as videotapes and interactive compact discs. These new devices could cut through the barrier of language, as well as distance. The challenge of electronic transmission of educational materials to diverse adult cultures and peoples remains a global priority into the 21st century.

The Global Alliance for Transnational Education was formed in 1995 and remains a respected entity for certifying international institutions, both online and off. England's Labour Party gained wide support in its preelection speeches addressing the "lifelong learning" needs of adults. In 1998 Britain's Department for Education proposed the University for Industry, a vocational and technical initiative comparable to the successful Open University, and complete with governmental financial assistance in the form of "individual learning accounts." These proposals addressed the fact that while the majority of existing educational subsidies and post-school education budget funds go to universities, only one-fourth of the nation's 5 million over-16 learners attended universities.

Sylvan Learning Systems announced in January 1999 plans to implement a network of about a dozen for-profit, private universities overseas, opening about one per year. The director of the U.S. Information Agency was to head the endeavor. Putting its plan into action, the company acquired 54 percent of the Universidad Europea de Madrid, a private, for-profit university in Spain.

AMERICA AND THE WORLD

In 1997 the United Nations Educational, Scientific, and Cultural Organization held its fifth International Conference of Adult Education in Hamburg, Germany, with over 1,500 attendees from around the world. The conference published a broad policy statement, the *Declaration of Adult Learning,* and more detailed proposals in its *Agenda for the Future.* The overall theme was to promote democratic understanding through ed-

FURTHER READING

Blumenstyk, Goldie. "Market Intensifies in Distance Learning." *Chronicle of Higher Education,* 4 April 1999.

———. "Sylvan Learning Systems Moves into the Higher-Education Market." *Chronicle of Higher Education,* 12 March 1999.

Carnevale, Dan, and Jeffrey Young. "Who Owns Online Courses? Colleges and Profits Start to Sort It Out." *Chronicle of Higher Education,* 17 December 1999.

Carr, Sarah. "Amid High Expectations, UNext.com Tests Its First Online Courses." *Chronicle of Higher Education,* 27 April 2000.

Dervarics, Charles. "On the Hill, For-Profits Reap Some Rewards, Wait for Others." *Community College Week,* 24 January 2000.

Distance Learning Resource Network. "What Is Distance Learning?" Available from http://www.wested.org/tie/dlrn/distance.html.

Evelyn, Jamilah. "A Coming of Age: Proprietary Colleges." *Community College Week,* 24 January 2000.

Gertzen, Jason. "Booming Firms Deliver Bytes of Knowledge." *Milwaukee Journal Sentinel,* 13 August 2000.

Hall, Brandon. "Corporate Distance Learning: The Future Is Now." *Inc.,* May 1999.

Hayward, Ed. "Mass. Gives OK for State's First For-Profit University." *Boston Herald,* 12 March 2000.

"Intelligence on E-Learning." *Inc.,* July 2000.

Jones, Del. "Will Business Schools Go Out of Business? E-Learning, Corporate Academies Change the Rules." *USA Today,* 23 May 2000.

Kirschner, Ann. "Making Education an Online Brand." *New York Times,* 23 April 2000.

Kleiner, Carolyn. "The Best Graduate Schools: More People Are Getting Degrees without Stepping onto a University Campus." *U.S. News & World Report,* 10 April 2000.

Kwang, Kim, and Sean Creighton. "Participation in Adult Education in the United States: 1998-99." *Education Statistics Quarterly,* Winter 1999. Available from http://nces.ed.gov/pubs2000/qrtlyspring/6life/q6-1.html.

Mangan, Katherine. "A Struggling Law School Turns Its Management over to a Chain of Proprietary Schools." *Chronicle of Higher Education,* 24 September 1999.

———. "Top Business Schools Seek to Ride a Bull Market in Online M.B.A.'s." *Chronicle of Higher Education,* 15 January 1999.

Marcus, David L. "A Scholastic Goldmine." *U.S. News & World Report,* 24 January 2000.

McMurtrie, Beth, and Katherine Mangan. "Education Department and Career Schools Clash over Accrediting of Distance Learning." *Chronicle of Higher Education,* 17 December 1999.

Meister, Jeanne. "Savvy E-Learners Drive Revolution in Education: The Case for Corporate Universities." *Financial Times* (London), 3 April 2000.

Melcher, Richard. "Education Industry Outlook." *Business Week,* 11 January 1999.

Michaels, James W., and Dirk Smillie. "Webucation." *Forbes,* 15 May 2000.

Murphy, Lee. "Stock Market Turn a Lesson for Argosy." *Crain's Chicago Business,* 14 February 2000.

Myers, Michele Tolela. "CyberU: What's Missing." *Washington Post,* 21 March 2000.

National Center for Education Statistics. "International Comparisons of Adult Literacy." 1999. Available from http://nces.ed.gov/pubs99/condition99/Indicator-8.html.

Rosenbaum, James. "Give and Take." *Chronicle of Higher Education,* 17 December 1999.

Symonds, William. "Industry Outlook 2000: Education." *Business Week,* 10 January 2000.

Thor, Linda. "Understanding the Appeal of For-Profit Colleges." *Community College Week,* 24 January 2000.

Wieffering, Eric. "Deals Give Online University Big Boost." *Minneapolis Star Tribune,* 18 May 2000.

Winston, Gordon. "For-Profit Higher Education: Godzilla or Chicken Little?" *Change,* January/February 1999.

Woody, Todd. "Ivy Online: Elite Universities and Professional Schools Are Scrambling to 'Leverage Their Brands' and Make Extra Money through Online Education." *Industry Standard,* 22 October 1999.

Wyatt, Edward. "Investors See Room for Profit in the Demand for Education." *New York Times,* 4 November 1999.

ALTERNATIVE MEDICINE

Alternative medicine is for the most part a Western term. Worldwide, the use of such methods as acupuncture, aromatherapy, herbal remedies, homeopathy, and hypotherapy has been part of the medical mainstream for centuries. For this reason, the undeniable growth of the alternative medicine industry during the 1990s represents a dramatic shift not only in the traditional Western medical industry, but in Western thought itself. Historically, alternative therapies such as those mentioned above were used by only a small portion of the population in the United States, and were considered by many Western doctors to be opposed to traditional Western medical practice. By 2000, however, more than 60 percent of U.S. doctors reported that they not only approved of, but have referred their patients to practitioners of alternative medicines. This increased acceptance in the medical community has combined with a new wealth of information and alternatives, made available by increased access to the Internet. The result was a growing trend away from traditional Western medicine as a sole solution.

Another important development in the growth of alternative medicine was the introduction of the Access to Medical Treatment Act. The bill, proposed in the late 1990s, would allow consumers to choose any medical treatment that was not proven to be dangerous, had fully disclosed side effects, and fell within the scope of a provider's expertise. It would also allow for a new definition of health-care providers as "any properly licensed medical doctor, osteopath, chiropractor or naturopath."

Unable to overlook these trends, 29 major insurance providers offered at least partial coverage by 2000 for many therapies that had historically been considered experimental or alternative. With such strong trends emerging, the alternative medicine industry is poised for record growth in the 21st century.

ORGANIZATION AND STRUCTURE

While the term "alternative medicine" encompasses a wide range of loosely related therapies and practices, the common denominator of all alternative medicines is their holistic focus—the treatment of an illness by considering the role played by both the body and the mind. Demand for alternative medicines in the United States ballooned in the 1990s; by the year 2000, nearly 50 percent of Americans had used, or were continuing to use, alternative medicine, and the industry was generating annual revenues in excess of $20 billion, according to *American Medical News*. The leading fields of alternative medicine include mind/body medicine, chiropractic therapy, massage therapy, homeopathy, and acupuncture.

MIND/BODY MEDICINE

Mind/body medicine is the most popular form of alternative medicine, according to the *New England Journal of Medicine*. While traditional Western medicine focuses solely on reactions in the body, mind/body medicine explores the role the mind plays in healing, as well as the role the body plays in healing the mind. Although mind/body medicine is not a treatment in the traditional sense of the word, it is a method of influencing and controlling the reactions and responses of the body. The ultimate goal of all forms of mind/body medicine is to achieve relaxation or the reduction of stress, which is considered the catalyst for many kinds of illness. Consequently, mind/body medicine is largely a complementary form of treatment, not a primary form. Standard medical testing procedures demonstrate the power of the mind to overcome poor health. Patients who have been given placebos, such as sugar pills, often report feeling relief from their symptoms.

Mind/body techniques include meditation; progressive relaxation, which is similar to meditation; autogenic training, which is the use of autosuggestive phrases such as "I'm calm"; hypnosis; and biofeedback or amplification of body signals so that patients can hear or see signs of stress and learn how to control stress. All of these techniques seek to counteract the body's reaction to stressful situations. When experiencing stress, the body releases various chemicals that affect the body by causing the heart rate to speed up, blood pressure to rise, and the muscles to become tense. Frequent and long-term stress impairs the immune system and can cause insomnia, high blood pressure, and depression, among other things. Although biofeedback therapy requires special training and a state license, other forms of mind/body medicine do not; however, practitioners of these other therapies often hold licenses in other fields.

CHIROPRACTIC THERAPY

Chiropractic therapy, the second-most popular form of alternative medicine, assumes that an inherent healing mechanism strives to return the body to a state of balance and, therefore, health. Chiropractic theory holds that the nervous system is responsible for maintaining the body's balance. Subluxations (bones out of alignment within joints) and fixations (motion anomalies) obstruct the flow of nervous impulses and, consequently, the body's natural healing system. By manipulating the bones and their respective joints and muscles—especially the spine—chiropractic therapy seeks to undo motion anomalies. Chiropractic therapy is employed to relieve or alleviate a wide range of illnesses, including: arthritis, asthma, back pain, carpal tunnel syndrome, headaches, premenstrual syndrome, and tendinitis.

While still considered an alternative form of medicine, chiropractic therapy is widely accepted. Chiropractic services are covered by Medicare and Medicaid in many states, as well as by most of the large private insurers. In addition, the practice is licensed in all 50 states and taught at special chiropractic colleges. Chiropractic licenses are governed by the Council of Chiropractic Education and the Federation of Chiropractic Licensing Boards. Moreover, chiropractors

make up the second-largest group of primary care providers, behind physicians, with more than 45,000 practitioners, and they receive about 66 percent of all visits for back pain. By the year 2000, 32 percent of the U.S. population had used chiropractic therapy at least once, and 10 percent underwent chiropractic therapy on a continuing, regular basis

Daniel David Palmer, originally a magnetic healer, founded the practice of chiropractic therapy in 1895. Palmer manipulated a man's ill-aligned vertebra and cured his deafness. He considered this proof that misaligned spines could cause poor health and that manipulation of the spine could restore health by correcting the flow of nervous impulses. In 1897 Palmer established the first chiropractic school, which his son managed.

However, one of the school's instructors, John Howard, disputed Palmer's contention that subluxations caused disease. Consequently, he left Palmer's school and founded his own—the National College of Chiropractic. Howard's school relied on some of Palmer's basic teachings but tempered them with standard scientific and medical thought and evidence. Hence, the split created two camps of modern practitioners: the straights, who follow Palmer, and the mixers, who follow Howard. Straights focus solely on the manipulation of the spine, whereas the mixers integrate other techniques such as massage and nutritional therapy.

MASSAGE THERAPY

Massage therapy ranks as the third-most frequently used form of alternative medicine. In the year 2000, there were more than 47,000 practicing massage therapists, and the American Massage Therapy Association was one of the fastest-growing associations of health-care professionals. Numerous schools or forms of massage therapy exist, including shiatsu (acupressure), deep tissue massage, neuromuscular massage, Swedish massage, and Esalen massage.

The myriad forms of massage therapy are based on a series of common tenets: circulation of blood, release of tension, release of toxins, and reduction of stress. Massage therapy holds that proper blood circulation is essential for health. Tension can impede circulation, thus interfering with the flow of nutrients and the removal of waste and toxins and possibly causing psychological and immune-system problems. Hence, by releasing tension in muscles and other soft tissues, massage therapists strive to improve the circulation of blood, which will bring about the removal of toxins and the reduction of stress, which some believe cause over 80 percent of all illnesses.

An herbalist preparing an herbal remedy. (Custom Medical Stock Photo, Inc.)

Considered by many to be one of the oldest health-care techniques, mention of massage use can be found in Chinese records dating back about 3,000 years, but its use probably predates these documents by many years. Physicians and health-care practitioners from many cultures and from many eras have practiced massage therapy. In Germany, Japan, and China, for example, massage therapy has continued to be used as it has for centuries, and massage therapists work alongside doctors.

The medical use of massage began to decline in the United States in the early part of the 20th century as surgical and pharmaceutical approaches to medicine began to blossom. Physicians began to view massage as too time-consuming so they delegated it to aides—who evolved into modern-day physical therapists. Massage therapy began to turn professional in 1943 when the graduates of massage schools decided to found the American Massage Therapy Association.

HOMEOPATHY

Homeopathy represents another one of the largest sectors of the industry. The word homeopathy comes from the Greek *homios,* meaning "like," and *pathos,* meaning "suffering." Thus, the term implies its conceptual underpinnings, to treat "like with like." Contrary to traditional Western (allopathic) medicine,

which hastens to suppress, alleviate, or obliterate symptoms, homeopathy works with a patient's symptoms, not against them. Homeopaths view a sick person's symptoms, such as a dry cough or runny nose, as the body's attempt to heal itself. The remedies, therefore, often attempt to stimulate the exacerbation of existing symptoms, thus triggering the sick body's natural healing response to cure the patient.

Because homeopathic remedies are based on such inexpensive natural substances as plants, herbs, or minerals, homeopathy is often conflated with other forms of alternative medicine such as aromatherapy, acupuncture, massage, herbal medicine, and chiropractic care. In its purest form, homeopathy is not really aligned with these other forms, many of which are allopathic in approach and methodology. Nonetheless, the association has hardly hurt the industry, as a "back to basics, back to nature" mentality swept across America and the world. Continually barraged with news of oil spills, toxic exposures, hormonal additives in food sources, chemical and often-carcinogenic sprays and herbicides on fresh produce, and untoward side effects of conventional pharmaceutical and prescriptive medications, the public's resurgent interest and search for homeopathic and other natural alternative medicines was all too apparent and predictable. This conveniently combined with a renewed interest in preventive, rather than palliative, medicine, as people learned how to prolong their health and life expectancies through natural diet, exercise, and therapy. Health-food stores became one of the hottest industries in the 1990s—with shelves loaded with herbal teas, megavitamins, natural mood enhancers, stimulants, depressants, aphrodisiacs, and purportedly natural cures for everyday ailments. Caught up in the momentum of all this, "homeopathy" became a household term. According to the American Homeopathic Pharmaceutical Association, sales of homeopathic remedies climbed by as much as 25 percent annually from 1988 to 1998. With the proliferation of online advertising and storefronts, sales rose nearly 30 percent between 1998 and 1999, and more than 37 percent between 1999 and 2000.

Homeopathic methods have remained popular for more than two centuries, despite criticism from some doctors that these methods rely more on anecdotal than empirical knowledge. Since the 1970s, many people suffering from common chronic ailments found relief through homeopathy, leading some doctors, researchers, lawmakers, and insurance carriers to become more open to sanctioning homeopathy. Led by consumer demand, homeopathy and homeopathic medicine are poised for even greater public acceptance and new growth. In 1997 the American Homeopathic Pharmaceutical Association estimated sales at about $230 million per year; by the year 2000, this number had nearly doubled. So, incidentally, did the average cost of homeopathic remedies: in 1997 the average homeopathic remedy cost $3-$7 per bottle; by 2000, this had risen to an average price per bottle of $10 to $15.

A survey of homeopathic practitioners found homeopathy most effective in treating common ailments such as colds and flu, chronic headaches, arthritis, allergies, asthma, premenstrual syndrome, and menopause. Homeopathic treatments have also been used for depression and anxiety, as well as common childhood conditions such as earaches, colic, and teething. Patients can get these remedies from mainstream pharmacies, natural pharmacies, and health-food stores, or from catalogs featuring alternative health-care products. Several catalogs and pharmacies sell home treatment kits that contain 20 or more vials of common homeopathic remedies. Included in these kits are reference materials that can be used to explain which remedy to use to treat specific ailments. Homeopathic remedies typically come in liquid, tablet, or granule form.

To practice homeopathy in the United States, one must be a licensed health-care provider. All states have laws that allow medical doctors (MDs) and osteo-

pathic doctors (DOs) to diagnose and treat illnesses. A few states—including Alaska, Arizona, Connecticut, Hawaii, Montana, New Hampshire, Oregon, Utah, and Washington—license naturopathic doctors (NDs) to do the same. An MD or DO can be certified as competent to practice homeopathy through the American Board of Homeotherapeutics, which grants a DHt certification. NDs go through the Homeopathic Academy of Naturopathic Physicians, which grants a DHANP certification. All health-care providers can be certified through the Council for Homeopathic Certification. The Council on Homeopathic Education monitors these educational programs. Moreover, the U.S. Food and Drug Administration regulates all homeopathic remedies, but because homeopathic products contain little or no active ingredients, many are exempt from the same regulations as other drugs.

More On INDUSTRY ASSOCIATIONS

Those looking for homeopathic physicians can consult the *Directory of Homeopathic Practitioners,* published by the National Center for Homeopathy (NCH) in Alexandria, Virginia. The NCH serves as both a lobbying and educational organization for homeopathy in the United States. The NCH also encourages home study groups for people who wish to self-treat common ailments after learning about homeopathy. The NCH recognizes 165 self-help homeopathic study groups in North America, and reports that these groups grow at the rate of three per month. Because most homeopathic remedies are nontoxic and sold without a prescription, educated patients can treat themselves relatively safely.

Other related entities include the American Homeopathic Pharmaceutical Association/Homeopathic Pharmacopoeia of the United States, headquartered in Valley Forge, Pennsylvania, and the American Institute of Homeopathy. The NCH also provides information regarding the location of facilities offering education in the field.

ACUPUNCTURE

Acupuncture, like other forms of traditional Chinese medicine, dates back roughly 4,500 years. While its practice in the West has been slow to catch on, it has received steady interest. A 1971 *New York Times* story acted as the catalyst that led to growth of acupuncture in the United States. Acupuncture is based on the concept of *Chi,* which is the life force that circulates through the body within 14 channels called "meridians." When *chi* flows freely, people experience good health. When *chi* is blocked or flows slowly, however, people experience poor health.

Consequently, the goal of acupuncture is to stimulate proper flow of *chi*. To do so, acupuncturists insert very thin sterilized needles to penetrate the area just under the surface of the skin, where the *chi* passageways, or acupoints, are said to be. Acupuncturists insert the needles less than an inch into the skin in some cases and three to four inches in others. They also rotate the needles and the entire procedure causes little pain. Acupuncture, in Western parlance, builds host resistance, which is the body's natural defenses and its ability to fight illness.

Acupuncture's primary application in the United States has been the alleviation of pain caused by a plethora of illnesses including arthritis, back pain, headache, gout, stress pain, and toothache. Nevertheless, acupuncturists are beginning to use this technique to relieve symptoms of other kinds of illnesses, such as those of addiction and stroke. Of the 12,000 acupuncturists in the United States, about 3,000 are licensed medical doctors. Many doctors of traditional Western medicine, however, still find it hard to accept the theory of invisible flowing energy, and contend that acupuncture produces nothing more than a placebo effect. Despite the criticism, scientific research indicates that acupuncture helps to improve health and relieve pain by stimulating the body's production of natural pain killers (endorphins and enkephalins) and a natural anti-inflammatory substance (cortisol).

CURRENT CONDITIONS

Because alternative medicine is such a broad term, and encompasses so many specialized fields that are often hard to track, exact figures regarding the value of the industry are hard to come by. In 1997, sales from all forms of alternative medicine in the United States were estimated at between $21 and $34 billion, up from about $14 billion in the early 1990s. Alternative therapies accounted for about $19.6 billion, herbal medicine for about $5 billion, and therapy classes and materials for about $4.7 of the industry's overall sales, according to the *Journal of the American Medical Association (JAMA)*. By 2000, overall sales were estimated at approximately $45 billion. The largest growth segment was in herbal remedies, which jumped from $5 billion to nearly $9 billion in annual sales between 1997 and 2000. *JAMA* also reported that the largest growth in the industry came from "herbal medicine, massage, megavitamins,

self-help groups, folk remedies, energy healing, and homeopathy." Demand for alternative medicine grew rapidly throughout the 1990s, with more than 42 percent of the population using these treatments and therapies by the year 2000, up from only 33 percent a decade earlier.

INDUSTRY LEADERS

Complete Wellness Centers, Inc. and American HealthChoice, Inc. ranked among the leading providers of alternative medicine therapies, offering these therapies along with conventional health-care services. Founded in 1994, Complete Wellness Centers established and runs over 140 diversified medical centers throughout the country. Complete Wellness Centers offer acupuncture, chiropractic, and massage therapy. In addition to providing services by physicians and alternative medicine practitioners, the company has programs to help patients quit smoking and lose weight. In 1999 the company reported revenues of $12.9 million and had approximately 110 employees at 11 different facilities.

American HealthChoice, Inc. owns and manages 15 medical centers, including primary care, urgent care, physical therapy, and chiropractic clinics in Georgia, Louisiana, and Texas. While the company had owned some unprofitable medical centers, it sold them and sought to acquire new, more promising operations. However, such efforts haven't panned out; the company was operating under Chapter 11 bankruptcy protection in late 2000 and was actively seeking acquisition. American HealthChoice posted sales of $4.8 million in 1999 and employed 65 workers.

In the homeopathy sector, two of the highest-grossing remedy makers include the Boiron Group and Dolisos Homeopathic Pharmacology Laboratories. Boiron, based in France, reported worldwide annual sales of $225 million and net profits of $14.9 million in 1999. The company's work force totaled more than 2,200 employees. The company has 29 units for production, distribution, and information in France, and 18 establishments worldwide. The Boiron Group produces 100 million single and multidose tubes of homeopathic medicine each year, covering a range of 200 homeopathic remedies. The company was formed in 1932 by three French homeopathic pharmacists.

While Boiron enjoyed success in its early years, it did not achieve significant growth until 1965 when the French Pharmacopoeia included homeopathy, thus including the medicines they produced in the health-care system coverage. Boiron grew steadily from 1968 on and expanded worldwide through the 1990s with establishments in Italy, India, the United States, Canada, Poland, and Bulgaria. The company was privately held until June 1987 when the Boiron family first listed it on the French stock exchange. In 1988 Boiron merged with Laboratoires Homeopathiques de France. In 1990 they bought another competitor, Herbaxt. Since the mid-1990s, the company has maintained the Institute Boiron, an independent homeopathic laboratory staffed with more than 100 clinical physicians working on research and development. Their research has developed products for veterinary and medical prescriptions, as well as products and guidelines for pharmacies and home medication.

The other prominent industry leader in the homeopathic sector, Dolisos, also of France, reported annual sales of more than $120 million and employed approximately 200 people in the late 1990s. Dolisos claimed to be the world's biggest investor in homeopathic research, while Boiron claimed the most sales. In 1996 the world's leading seed-producing company, Groupe Limagrain, acquired Dolisos, allowing their new subsidiary to keep its own name. Dolisos was founded in 1937 by Dr. Jean Tetau, a French pharmacist. In 1978 Dr. Tetau directed the firm to be the first homeopathic laboratory with independent research facilities. Next, the company established links between their industry and university researchers. The company specializes in homeopathic medicines available primarily through prescriptions. Anticipating future interest, the company began selling and researching homeopathic veterinary drugs during the mid-1990s. Their plant produces active ingredients for pharmacists to blend, or finished products ready for the patient.

RESEARCH AND TECHNOLOGY

In 1995 the Office of Alternative Medicine (OAM) appointed a new director, Wayne Jonas, a retired military physician who had run the Medical Research Fellowship program at Walter Reed Army Institute of Research in Washington, D.C. Of interest to proponents of alternative medicine was that Dr. Jonas himself had been trained in bioenergetics, homeopathy, acupuncture, and spiritual healing, and he had used such treatments in his family medical practice. When Jonas addressed the first International Congress on Alternative and Complementary Therapy, he cautioned against self-conclusions about the efficacy of alternative medicine without the support of corroborative data. Shortly thereafter, in October 1995, OAM announced the funding of eight additional centers for alternative medicine research. Of these, at least two were cited for specific research in homeopathy—The University of California-Davis and Harvard Medical School's Beth Israel Deaconess Medical Center in Boston, Massachusetts. As of late 2000, study reports and findings were not yet available.

In a comprehensive study reported in the 20 September 1997 edition of the respected medical journal, *Lancet,* scientists concluded that they could neither endorse nor dispel the critical and stigmatic hypothesis that the clinical effects of various forms of alternative medicine were the result of a "placebo effect." Nor could they conclude one way or the other, having found insufficient evidence, that these remedies were effective for any single clinical condition. They enthusiastically supported, however, the need for additional "rigorous and systematic" research in this area. At a minimum, advised George Washington University School of Medicine's Megan A. Johnson (not a member of the above study) in her 1998 *JAMA* published essay, homeopathy could complement modern medicine as "another tool in the bag."

FURTHER READING

Alternative Advisor. Alexandria, VA: Time-Life Books, 1997.

Avalon, Bruce B. "Homeopathy for Homesteaders." *Mother Earth News,* April/May 1998.

"Boericke & Tafel, Inc." 1997. Available from http://www.hpr.room.net/hprcat1.html.

"CAM Facts." *National Center for Homeopathy.* 2000. Available from http://www.healthy.net/nch/cam.htm.

Collinge, William. *The American Holistic Health Association Complete Guide to Alternative Medicine.* New York: Warner Books, 1996.

Comarow, Avery. "Going Outside the Medical Mainstream." *U.S. News & World Report,* 23 November 1998.

"Dolisos Answers Your Homeopathy Questions." 1997. Available from http://www.lyghtforce.com/Dolisos/QuesAnsw.htm.

Eder, Rob. "Is the Bloom Off the Rose?" *Drug Store News,* 14 August 2000.

———. "New Products Battle Heart Disease the Natural Way." *Drug Store News,* 11 September 2000.

Eisenberg, David M., et al. "Trends in Alternative Medicine Use in the United States, 1990-1997." *Journal of the American Medical Association,* 11 November 1998.

"Herbal Medicine: Safe and Sound?" *Chemist & Druggist,* 22 July 2000.

"The History of Dolisos." 1997. Available from http://www.lyghtforce.com/Dolisos/Dolisos.htm.

"Homeopathy Sales Defy Critics." *CQ Researcher,* 14 February 1997.

Jarvis, William. "Health Fraud Leader Speaks out on Homeopathy." *FDA Consumer,* 6 April 1997.

Johnson, Megan A. "Homeopathy: Another Tool in the Bag." *Journal of the American Medical Association,* 4 March 1998.

Linde, Karl, et al. "Are the Clinical Effects of Homeopathy Placebo Effects? A Meta-Analysis of Placebo-Controlled Trials." *Lancet,* 20 September 1997.

Stapleton, Stephanie. "Alternative Medicine: Time to Talk." *American Medical News,* 14 December 1998.

Stehlin, Isadora. "Homeopathy: Real Medicine or Empty Promises?" *FDA Consumer,* December 1996. Available from http://www.fda.gov.

Wheeler, David L. "From Homeopathy to Herbal Therapy: Researchers Focus on Alternative Medicine." *Chronicles of Higher Education,* 27 March 1998.

ALTERNATIVE VEHICLE FUELS

A number of factors powered the alternative-fuels industry at the dawn of the 21st century. In addition to concerns over the pending depletion of the world's petroleum reserves, alternative fuels—including liquefied petroleum gas, methanol, ethanol, compressed natural gas (CNG), hydrogen, biomass, and mixtures of these with regular gasoline—were gaining increasing favor due to test results demonstrating their significantly more benign effects on the ozone layer and their reduction of pollutant emissions. The quest for viable alternative fuel technologies on a consumer level generally centered on day-to-day issues such as fuel economy and convenience, although evolving world attitudes toward concerns about the environment and sustainable supplies played an increasingly influential role, as did contemporary medical research linking illnesses and cancers to petroleum by-products or burn-off.

The impact of a mass alternative-fuel-based economic conversion was a sticky issue, both domestically and globally. The tenuous balance of geopolitical power and international governmental alliances is intricately tied to control over energy supplies, which has served as the backdrop to wars and less dramatic international tensions. On the domestic front, some of the nation's largest enterprises staked their fortunes on traditional energy sources slated for replacement by alternative fuels. Power companies, electricians, coal companies, and oil firms are just a handful of the players throughout the economy that will need to scramble for a meaningful place in a dramatically changed market.

In the industrial realm, automotive companies have been among the most farsighted in this regard; all the world's leading auto makers have invested heavily in alternative-fuel research and development, particularly in fuel cells, which convert methanol, CNG, or hydrogen to electricity capable of powering a car or truck, emitting only clean—even drinkable—water as a by-product. (See the essay in this book entitled Fuel Cells.) Hydrogen energy alone was expected to reach into the trillion-dollar stratosphere as an industry by 2010, expanding at about 30 percent annually. Still, the penetration of all alternative-fuel vehicles (AFVs) was slight; of the 212 million motor vehicles gracing U.S. roads in 1999, only 1 million, or .4 percent, were AFVs.

While the depletion of world oil reserves remains a central long-term impetus for the conversion to alternative fuels, petroleum will face no major challenges as the energy of choice for several decades. The Environmental Information Agency credits newly discovered reserves and streamlined technologies in drilling, refining, and engines with portending the satisfaction of increasing demand for oil through 2020, and most analysts expect world oil reserves to last for nearly a century. The extensive resources, however, in terms of private investment and public policy, required to maintain the stability of the U.S. oil supply create an enormous incentive for the introduction of viable alternative-fuel technologies on a mass level. Skyrocketing prices at gas pumps in summer 2000 energized new debate over the reliance on fossil fuels, and contentious policy debates loomed. One of the biggest challenges facing the industry was to incorporate such fuels into vehicles and power systems on a mass scale without sacrificing everyday conveniences and comforts, all while keeping costs down. The question of how best to accomplish this task amidst the range of hurdles—logistic, economic, and environmental—is not so easily answered, and remains the most nebulous aspect of the alternative-fuels industry.

ORGANIZATION AND STRUCTURE

Because of the interrelationship and interdependency between transportation fuels and the national economy, as well as national security, both gasoline and alternative-fuel industries are heavily structured, controlled, and regulated by federal and state interests. Control spills over into the user market in that private industry must not only produce alternative-fuel vehicles, which can compete with the price and efficiency of traditional gasoline-fueled vehicles, but must also meet strict emissions and other environmental regulation standards.

The Energy Information Administration reports that the primary determinant of the choice and scale of alternative-fuel production is governmental policy, noting that use of such technology takes off only following public policy initiatives, whereas incentive seems to be in short supply absent government spurs. Not surprisingly, then, federal funding remains a cornerstone of alternative-fuels development programs. The Clinton administration requested $439 million in the fiscal year 2001 budget for the development of bioenergy, including ethanol fuels and energy derived from agricultural and other waste products.

INDUSTRY REGULATION

To ease the pain of regulation as well as stimulate interest, numerous laws and tax incentives are directed toward both producers *and* users of domestically produced alternative fuels, giving them a chance to compete with the oil industry and its monopolized hold on the global market. Some of the more important federal legislation supporting biofuels include: the Energy Security Act (1978); the Energy Tax Act (1978); the Gasohol Competition Act (1980); the Crude Oil Windfall Profit Tax Act (1980); the Energy Security Act (1980); the Surface Transportation Assistance Act (1982); the Tax Reform Act (1984); the Alternative Motor Fuels Act (1988); the Omnibus Budget Reconciliation Act (1990); the Clean Air Act Amendments (1990); the Energy Policy Act (1992); the Building Efficient Surface Transportation and Equity Act (1998); and the Energy Conservation Reauthorization Act (1998). These acts are administered and overseen by the U.S. Department of Energy (DOE).

The manner in which these laws affect and interface with private industry can be summed up by the Alternative Motor Fuels Act of 1988. Its stated objective is to encourage the widespread development and use of methanol, ethanol, and natural gas as transportation fuels. Section 400AA requires the U.S. government to acquire the maximum number of alternative-fueled vehicles in its fleets as is practical. Importantly, the vehicles are to be supplied by original equipment manufacturers (OEMs), thus stimulating private industry. The act also mandates that the DOE must assist state and local governments in developing public transportation buses capable of operating with alternative fuels.

Concurrently, acts such as the Clean Air Act and its amendments continue to focus on reducing the amount of pollutants emitted from motor vehicles. The U.S. Environmental Protection Agency (EPA) also remains greatly involved in the monitoring of environmental effects caused by vehicular traffic and fuel by-products. In the late 1990s, for example, the EPA ruled that particulates, microscopic specks of carbon emitted from diesel engines that can lodge in lungs and cause a host of medical complications (including death), constituted air-quality health hazards.

To monitor progress under the Energy Policy Act of 1992 (EPAct), which extends the Alternative Motor Fuels Act by requiring the incorporation of AFVs into the fleets of federal and state governments, the DOE reports to Congress annually on the progress of the act's focus, which is to encourage use of alternative fuels. Field researchers, OEM markets, and fuel suppliers complete lengthy annual surveys that primarily address the number and type of alternative-fuel vehicles available; the number, type, and geographic distribution of these vehicles in use; the amount and distribution of each type of alternative fuel consumed; and information about the refueling/recharging facilities. As the data builds from year to year, the DOE paces its monetary funding and program initiatives accordingly.

Moreover, the United States was increasingly participating in international environmental agreements, such as the Kyoto Accords and the deal with China in 1999 that, among other things, provided for U.S. investment in an onshore natural-gas pipeline in China. In February 2000 the U.S. government signed a Memorandum of Understanding (MOU) with the United Nations implementing a number of environmental provisions, including a "Drive Green" initiative designed to promote alternative fuels. As the world's largest single energy consumer at about 2 percent of total consumption, the U.S. government has its own considerations, such as reducing its energy budget, very much in mind. The Drive Green program will funnel matching funds up to $4 million through the DOE to federal agencies engaged in converting fleets to AFVs.

BACKGROUND AND DEVELOPMENT

It would be remiss not to begin the industry's history by emphasizing the enormous economic influence that gasoline had over both Western and Eastern countries. In the United States for example, a single dollar increase in the price per barrel of crude oil could lead to a $1 billion change in oil imports. In fact, gasoline supply disruptions between 1974 and 1984, such as those surrounding the 1973 Arab Oil Embargo and the 1979 Iranian Oil Embargo, cost Americans $1.5 *trillion*. In the late 1990s, petroleum imports accounted for nearly half of the U.S. trade deficit, and were expected to rise to 60 to 70 percent within the next 10-20 years, even though Congress voted in 1990 that a dependence on foreign oil of more than 50 percent would constitute a "peril point" for the United States.

The additional cost in terms of military security and protection of foreign oil interests cost the United States an estimated $365 billion between 1980 and 1990. The Persian Gulf War alone cost $61 billion. Factoring in these energy security costs results in the astounding reality that the true financial cost of oil consumption in the late 1990s was approximately $5 per gallon.

These factors helped stimulate efforts toward near-total replacement of gasoline fuels with renewable alternative fuels. Henry Ford himself, back in 1908, well expected his Model T automobile to be fueled by ethanol, the most viable alternative fuel at that time. In fact, an ethanol-gasoline mix (25 percent ethanol) was rather successfully marketed by the Standard Oil Co. in the 1920s. When high corn prices, doubled with storage and transportation costs, made ethanol less feasible, federal and state initiatives were undertaken to keep interest alive. Ford again reentered the picture and joined others to establish a fermentation plant in the Corn Belt, capable of producing 38,000 liters per day. But the efforts could not effectively overcome the low petroleum prices, and ethanol production plants closed down in the 1940s.

Interestingly, at about the same time Ford was developing prototype vehicles, Rudolf Diesel was perfecting his diesel engines to run on peanut oil, with the intention that eventually they would be able to operate on several types of vegetable oils. It is unfortunate that both Ford's and Diesel's hopes were relegated to the back burners of a hot petroleum market with which these resourceful fuels could not then compete. It was not until the critical gasoline market in the 1970s that momentum was reestablished. Ethanol-gasoline blends were again reintroduced to the U.S. market in 1979. These blends, however, were marketed not as gasoline replacement fuels but as "octane enhancers" or "gasoline extenders." This may have diminished any sense of urgency in the public's mind to accelerate conversion of a transportation economy so comfortable with inexpensive gasoline. Along the same lines, the federal government created the Strategic Petroleum Reserve (SPR) to stockpile nearly 6 million barrels of oil (about 75 days' worth of fuel at 1998 consumption rates) in an underground facility in Louisiana. Since 1993, no oil has been added to the reserves and the facility's $200 million annual operating cost ultimately prompted Congress to mandate selling the reserve oil at half price.

But complacency again reverted to a proactive attitude during the 1990s as Americans became more

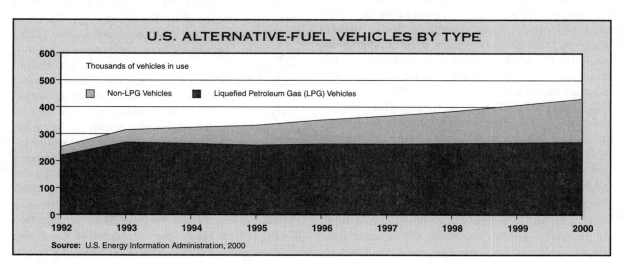

U.S. ALTERNATIVE-FUEL VEHICLES BY TYPE

Thousands of vehicles in use

◻ Non-LPG Vehicles   ◼ Liquefied Petroleum Gas (LPG) Vehicles

Source: U.S. Energy Information Administration, 2000

sensitive about environmental issues and economic dependency. The Clean Air Act Amendments of 1990 required that special fuels be sold and used in areas of the country with harmful levels of carbon monoxide. This resulted in the development and promotion of a cleaner-burning and lighter gasoline product known as "reformulated gasoline"; California had its own formula. Again, ethanol blends and other alternative-fuel choices caught the public's attention. Concurrently, the federal government continued to infuse money into numerous projects for biofuel development, also giving private industry a stake in the results. By the end of the 1990s, the alternative-fuel industry had been resurrected.

CURRENT CONDITIONS

A standard for AFV technology was a long way off in 2000. A host of AFV types existed, each with their own particular benefits and drawbacks. Dedicated alternative-fuel vehicles, for instance, utilize only one alternative fuel, the most common being liquefied petroleum gas (LPG). Bi-fuel vehicles house separate tanks for regular gasoline and one type of alternative fuel. Flexible fuel models utilize a gas-alcohol mixture, such as the popular E85 which blends a maximum of 85 percent ethanol and 15 percent gasoline, in one tank.

The Energy Information Administration (EIA) estimated that over 430,000 AFVs cruised U.S. highways in 2000. LPG vehicles accounted for almost half that total, with their compressed natural gas (CNG) cousins totaling 101,000. While electric fuel-cell vehicles were widely expected to emerge as the AFV of choice sometime over the next decade, such vehicles took a backseat to natural-gas and alcohol-based AFVs through the 1990s. Vehicles powered by the M85 ethanol-gasoline mixture numbered about 30,000, while the M85 methanol version declined slightly to under 19,000. Many such automobiles met the criteria for Low Emissions Vehicles, designed specifically to target the emissions standards established by the U.S. Environmental Protection Agency, which call for undercutting U.S. governmental standards by 70 percent in the field of smog-forming hydrocarbons and by 50 percent in the realm of nitrogen oxides. The EIA predicted continued steady growth of AFVs at about 6.2 percent, consistent with trends dating back to 1992.

Natural gas seemed poised to remain the AFV industry's lifeline in the first decade of the 21st century. As the market awaits more sophisticated and affordable fuel-cell vehicles, natural-gas and alcohol fueling systems will represent the most efficient mass solution to the demand for more efficient and clean-burning vehicles. For all hydrocarbon emissions, CNG vehicles save up to 48 percent and LPG cars cut emissions up to 31 percent.

Cost remains a primary impediment to mass consumption of AFVs. Vehicles powered by natural gas, for instance, cost about $3,000 to $5,000 more than standard gasoline vehicles, according to the U.S. General Accounting Office (GAO). And while alternative-fuel technology was still more or less in the gestation process in 2000 in terms of achieving mass viability of AFVs, competition was already intense. Most auto manufacturers, as well as the research firms they have forged contracts with, were becoming notoriously tight-lipped about their development programs for fear of tipping off competitors or breaching restrictive confidentiality agreements.

GOVERNMENTAL EFFORTS

The Clinton administration's Partnership for a New Generation of Vehicles (PNGV), established in 1993, created an industry-government consortium with the ultimate goal of phasing out gasoline engines over the next 20-30 years. The federal government pledged an annual investment of $500 million (half of which included direct federal funds) to help the industry. The University of Illinois received such a prize in 2000 to build a "biorefinery" devoted to the production and commercialization of Pure Energy Corp.'s P-Series ethanol-based fuel. The refinery was scheduled to begin production of no-sulfur P-Series fuel, a blend of ethanol, natural-gas liquids and biomass, at a price comparable to gasoline by 2002. Meanwhile, the consortium's automakers introduced their concept vehicles to the press and Vice President Gore in March 2000.

Long a leader in the development and employment of environmentally friendly energy, California launched an ambitious zero emission vehicle (ZEV) program to aggressively boost fuel economy and mitigate periodic price fluctuations like the one that so angered consumers in summer 2000. A study by the California Air Resources Board (CARB) conservatively concluded that ZEVs consumed about 25 percent less energy than conventional vehicles. In the late 1990s, moreover, CARB reported that the gasoline refining, marketing, and distribution system resulted in hazardous water contamination, particularly by the oxygenate methyl tertiary butyl ether (MTBE), which is produced from methanol and added to gasoline to enhance octane levels. In July 2000, Senator Bob Smith (R-New Hampshire), chairman of the Senate Environment and Public Works Committee (EPW), introduced "The Federal Reformulated Fuels Act", which was designed to eliminate MTBE from U.S. gasoline within four years, or allow the EPA to cap MTBE at 1 percent volume if it determines that a total ban isn't necessary to protect air, water, and health.

Arizona was another aggressive promoter of alternative fuels, offering attractive incentives to individuals and businesses to convert to AFVs utilizing various fuels, including dollar-for-dollar tax credits to consumers reaching up to $5,000 or 30 percent of the total vehicle cost. In early 2000, Pennsylvania, a state with a history of smog problems, allocated $1.2 million to organizations around the state for use and development of cleaner fuels to reduce tailpipe emissions and hazardous ground level ozone.

Other governments moved into direct production of alternative fuels. San Diego, for instance, constructed a gas liquefaction plant to provide energy to its packer trucks. One-third of the city's packer-truck fleets will incorporate dual-fuel systems utilizing liquid natural gas and diesel gasoline; eventually, the entire fleet will be converted.

CORPORATE EFFORTS

U.S. auto manufacturers took the new technology seriously enough as a fixture in their operations that they began to bypass the traditional outsourcing methods for gas power conversions in favor of investment in plants specifically devoted to alternative-fuel vehicles. Ford Motor Co. also broke new ground by initiating a new brand specifically devoted to ecologically friendly vehicles when it established its Th!nk Group. Ford, which manufactures about 90 percent of the AFVs sold in North America, saw its sales growth in this sector reach 24 percent in 1999. The company committed over $1 billion in research by 2005 to develop its alternative-fuel capacity. In 2000 the firm tested a new hydrogen-based internal combustion engine, a spin-off of its development of fuel-cell vehicles. Its major competitors, such as Daimler-Chrysler, General Motors, and Honda, have responded in kind with development programs of their own.

Other transportation-based companies likewise hoped to capitalize on growing demand for what they saw as a niche product. Budget Rent-a-Car introduced the Ford Taurus 2000 flexible-fuel vehicle (FFV) into its fleet. The Taurus 2000 was designed to run on unleaded gasoline or a mix of ethanol and gasoline, while sensors configure the engine to the specific fuel composition. Budget also offers natural-gas and electric vehicles in select U.S. markets, and was an early renter of LPG vehicles in the United Kingdom.

HURDLES

Hampering the proliferation of automobiles powered by LPG and CNG was the finding by researchers from BP Amoco and Ford that the retrofitting of traditional fueling systems for use of LPG and CNG can in fact lead to more rather than less net emissions. Similarly, skeptics of alcohol-based fuels such as ethanol have called for studies of the entire production process. That is, while studies have found significant emission reduction in ethanol fuels, critics have claimed that the entire process from development to delivery to emission actually results in a net increase in greenhouse gasses. Two California agencies—the California Air Resources Board and the California Energy Commission embarked on just such a study in 2000.

Despite the tremendous headway, moreover, alternative fuels continue to fall short of goals. The GAO determined that the nation would fail to meet the goals of 10 percent alternative-for-gasoline substitution by 2000 as well as the 30 percent substitution by 2010. Though consumer interest is in place and auto makers have shown a heightened willingness to embrace the new technology, the relative cost advantages of gasoline (even at the soaring prices of 2000) and the plentiful availability of gasoline for the foreseeable future have placed overall priorities for the conversion on the back burner.

The infrastructure to support alternative fuels also failed to materialize. The GAO reported that fewer than 7,000 commercial alternative-fuel stations were in place in 1999, making customers reluctant to shift consumption patterns. The GAO went on to state that 10 times that number would need to exist in order to meet the 2030 substitution goal.

Moreover, while environmentalists wholeheartedly supported and had long spearheaded the push toward more efficient energy, some claimed that the efforts made by auto manufacturers to shift the nation's automobile population to alternative fuels, and to paint themselves "green," was overstated. They noted that the federal tax credits auto makers receive for producing such vehicles allow for greater leverage to produce lucrative but inefficient gas guzzlers such as sport-utility vehicles (SUVs) at a continued pace, at a ratio of two SUVs to one AFV, according to Sierra Club lobbyist Dan Becker. Such incentives, activists claimed, negate the purpose of introducing AFVs by relieving automakers of the necessity to improve the efficiencies of their traditional models. Ford Motor Co. acknowledged that the tax credits have helped the auto giant meet the soaring demand for its high-consumption SUVs while still meeting its fleet emissions requirements.

AMERICA AND THE WORLD

The tightly regulated European market offers expansive opportunities for alternative-fuel vehicles. With high congestion and a long-standing commitment to greater fuel efficiency, Europe has attracted the world's major automakers as a prime target for introducing AFV automobiles to a mass audience. By 2000, however, some proponents of alternative fuels were taking shots at major European countries such as Germany and the United Kingdom for failing to match rising consumer support for more efficient fuels with an infrastructure to support it. The United Kingdom, for instance, maintained fewer than 20 commercial stations offering CNG or LPG.

Around the world, several countries increased efforts to develop alternative-fuel technologies, not only for their own economic safety, but also to be first at the finish line and cash in on America's needs. In 1999 Alternate Power Products Asia Limited announced its version of an electric vehicle, and selected Agar, Uttar Pradesh, India, as its demonstration project site. Canada introduced its Bombadier electric vehicle in 1999, which it called an NEV, for "neighborhood electric vehicle." And China focused on the development of hydrogen as a viable transportation fuel source.

In the Americas, Brazil's vibrant alternative-fuels industry was badly derailed in the late 1990s. One of the only countries to have adopted the technology on a mass scale, particularly focused on alcohol-based fuels, the debt crisis and strikingly low sugar prices squeezing farm owners made it increasingly difficult for them to economically meet the appropriate yield of sugarcane necessary to distill ethanol. Nonetheless, the Brazilian government, determined to shore up the country's alternative-fuel commitment, has maintained its policy of strongly promoting alcohol-based fuels by offering tax credits to taxi drivers who utilize alcohol fuels, increasing the already-high alcohol content in bi-fuel mixtures, and drastically boosting the percentage of government fleets devoted to alcohol. While a declining currency and other economic woes have unleashed waves of anger against government policy, analysts note that the Brazilian alcohol program has emerged as an important component of the Brazilian economy—employing 1.1 million workers, propping up the real in currency markets, and alleviating environmental degradation.

RESEARCH AND TECHNOLOGY

The real potential for alternative fuels remains that they are not only renewable resources, but by 2000, were increasingly made of environmental waste, or "biomass." This subcategory of alternative fuels, known as "biofuels," converts agricultural and forestry residue, and even municipal solid and industrial waste, into bioethanol, biodiesel, biomethanol, and pyrolysis oil fuels. Biofuels are, by composition, alcohols, ethers, esters, and other chemicals made from cellulosic biomass.

But the conversion from biomass to biofuel is not without complication. Biomass energy at the plant cellular level is comprised of complex lignocellulosic compositions that include hemicellulose, cellulose, lignin, and extractives; cellulose also has hydrogen bonds that form crystalline structures. These long chains of sugarlike molecules have resistant linkages that inhibit the release of potential energy. In the latter 1990s, the Office of Fuel Development initiated the Bioethanol Project, which was devoted to the commercial production of waste-based bioethanol.

In concert with private companies, the Bioethanol Project focuses on developing four process technologies. The first, concentrated acid cellulose conversion, uses recombinant microorganisms to separate sugars and acids. Basically a hydrolysis process, the technology is being used by Arkenol and the Masada Resource Group in specially located plants in California and New York, respectively. Arkenol, which already holds several patents on acid-based ethanol development, is working with the Department of Energy (DOE) to establish a commercial facility for the conversion of rice straw to ethanol. Masada, on the other hand, plans to establish a facility to process the lignocellulosic portion of municipal solid waste into ethanol, using concentrated sulfuric acids.

Breakthroughs in the use of biomass for fuel have been at the forefront of industry development. In 2000 scientists at the University of California at Berkeley, sponsored by the DOE, discovered a process by which green algae, known affectionately as "pond scum," ceases oxygen production in favor of hydrogen. Algae-generated hydrogen was known to scientists for years, but dislodging the element under controlled circumstances proved troublesome.

The Berkeley team found that the answer lay not in the molecular structure of hydrogen, but in its diet. By effectively starving the algae of the sulfur it requires to produce protein, the scientists halted its oxygen production, thereby forcing the algae to switch its emissions to hydrogen to survive. As a bonus, they found that hydrogen was emitted in much greater quantities when sulfur was cut off than researchers had believed possible. The team added that the metabolic switch does not kill the algae, which can be reused over and over. After a few days of sulfur starvation, all the plant's production capacity is exhausted, at which point sulfur is reintroduced to its diet allowing it to regenerate its necessary carbohydrates for protein production.

Though the integration of the process into a large industrial framework remains to be configured, requiring alternative land-use strategies, its potential benefits include vastly more efficient, cost-effective, and ecologically sound energy production than oil drilling and coal mining. A researcher on the project, Michael Seibert of the DOE's National Renewable Energy Laboratory in Golden, Colorado, surmised that algae-production lands covering the size of New Mexico would sufficiently supply all the energy needs in the United States.

The expanding market for alternative fuels has inevitably led to a market for alternative-fuel components. Among the most potentially useful of these are hydrogen sensors. In the form of tiny chips, hydrogen sensors monitor the amount of hydrogen circulating through a fuel system, sending signals to the engine to adjust its operations accordingly. Most analysts expect that hydrogen sensors will be a standard component on any hydrogen-fueled vehicle, especially on fuel-cell cars. Thus, as the alternative-fuel market grows, so goes the sensor market. Ion Optics, for example, received a Department of Transportation grant in January 2000 to develop for use in emissions testing its portable sensor, the MicroSpe, designed to resist the highly volatile temperature fluctuations and vibrations found in most marine fueling systems.

Other technologies deal with pollutant emissions after the fact. A process called "Gas-to-Liquids," patented by Colorado-based Rentech, Inc., was developed to capture solid, liquid, and gas carbon dioxide industrial emissions for conversion into hydrocarbons. The process was slated for use in the manufacturing facilities of Oroboros AB, a Swedish steel firm. Whereas industrial greenhouse gases are typically flared into the atmosphere at standard facilities, the Gas-to-Liquid process will capture hydrogen and carbon monoxide and convert the materials into safe, usable energy, reducing by an estimated 200 tons the plant's carbon dioxide emissions.

Ethanol remains the most widely marketed biofuel. Made from brewed starch crops such as corn or, in the case of bioethanol, from cellulosic biomass, it was marketed in the late 1990s as an octane-booster and a cleaner emissions fuel additive. In 1999 more than 1.4 billion gallons were sold as gasoline-blend additives. It could be used in its pure form or, more often, blended as E10 (10 percent ethanol) on up to E85 blends. Ethanol derived from biomass generates emissions reductions of up to 90 percent, and can be used in traditional vehicle infrastructures, thus making it a popular new alternative for auto manufacturers who would prefer that the overhaul of their production processes be kept to a minimum. But ethanol tax incentives will end in 2007; therefore, the Ethanol Project has developed a research plan with a stated goal of reducing the cost of bioethanol technology by a minimum of 40 cents per gallon by 2010. The ethanol industry alone created more than 200,000 jobs, and by the year 2002 will have added $51 billion to the U.S. economy.

Biodiesel fuel is made from soybean, rapeseed, vegetable, or animal oils. Combined with alcohol, it is then chemically altered to form fatty esters in a process referred to as "transesterification." It is typically marketed as a fuel additive in a 20 percent blend. Biodiesel was approved as an alternative fuel by the DOE in 1998 under amendments to the Energy Policy Act of 1992 (EPAct), which allow regulated fleets to use up to 450 gallons of biodiesel per vehicle per year to qualify for EPAct credit. Increasingly, it is replacing traditional fuel in work environments that require exposures to diesel exhaust, such as near airports or locomotive systems. As of 2000, however, biodiesel suffered from production costs, which the DOE pinned at about three times those of traditional diesel.

The DOE also gave the thumbs up in late 1998 to Pure Energy's P-Series fuel, developed by researchers at Princeton University, that derives ether from wood and paper waste. The P-Series production process erodes cellulose-based waste—including office paper, food wrappers, sawdust, and hard wood—into organic acid. P-Series fuels use ether in about one-quarter of the mixture, with the balance supplied by liquid natural gas, butane, and ethanol. Princeton physicist Stephen Paul, who designed the pilot program, estimated that one ton of office wastepaper could generate ether for 100 gallons of P-Series fuel. The catalytic conversion process does result in the production of significant residue, though Paul noted that what was generated could be sold as industrial solvent or organic acid. The DOE estimated that P-Series could substitute for up to 100 billion gallons of gasoline by 2005.

One of the original criticisms of alternative fuels was their ostensibly lower "energy density," technical jargon for the formularized relationship between weight or mass of the energy source and the energy it would produce. Historically, gallon for gallon, alternative fuels offered smaller driving ranges, less acceleration capability, and more vulnerability at high speeds or in heavy traffic situations than their gasoline counterpart. But interestingly, most of the energy in gasoline and diesel fuel was burned off as combustible heat and friction, not as locomotive power. Notwithstanding, it was true that gasoline engines were distinguishable for rapid acceleration capability, a desirable quality in a nation with as many freeway systems as the United States.

Conversely, alternative fuels such as ethanol and methanol burned cleaner than gasoline, an important consideration in urban areas plagued with smog. Beginning in the latter 1990s, federal Clean Air laws began to require automobile manufacturers to increase the number of vehicles offered that met the newly mandated Ultra Low Emissions Vehicles standards. Ultimately, vehicles will be required to meet Zero Emissions Vehicle standards, and clearly, alternative-fuel vehicles held the competitive edge in this arena. In fact, combustible natural gas was so clean burning that the only by-products were carbon dioxide and water vapor. Still, gasolines have been purified and made to burn cleaner over the years and, in 1998, the most desirable choice following gasoline was diesel, not alternative fuel.

FURTHER READING

Acohido, Byron. "Firm Tests Auto Fuel Derived from Waste." *Waste News,* 30 August 1999.

"Alternative Fuels Data Center." Washington: Office of Transportation Technologies, 2000. Available from http://www.afdc.doe.gov.

Barham, John. "Sour Taste for Brazil's Sugar Growers." *Financial Times* (London), 20 July 1999.

Burt, Tim. "Environmental Issues Move to Centre Stage." *Financial Times* (London), 3 December 1999.

———. "Filling Stations for Cleaner Fuels 'Held Back by Planners.'" *Financial Times* (London), 28 September 1999.

———. "Push for Alternative Fuels Moves up a Gear." *Financial Times,* (London) 3 December 1999.

Chang, Thi. "U.S. Consumption of Alternative Fuels Growing." *Oil & Gas Journal,* 12 July 1999.

Cole, Carol. "Energy Diversity Goals in ZEV Program Target Oil Use." *Octane Week,* 2 October 2000.

———. "United Nations, U.S. Sign Environmental Cooperation Agreement." *Oxy-Fuel News,* 7 February 2000.

Dye, Lee. "You'll Never Look at Algae the Same Way Again—Or So Some Researchers Hope." *Los Angeles Times,* 28 February 2000.

Joyce, Mary. "U.S. Alternative Transportation Fuels Industry." *Oil & Gas Journal,* 10 July 2000.

Keplinger, Carolyn. "California Studies Complete Emissions Benefits of Alt Fuels." *Oxy-Fuel News,* 28 February 2000.

———. "GAO: U.S. Not Going to Achieve EPAct's Alternative Fuel Goals." *Oxy-Fuel News,* 28 February 2000.

Office of Transportation Technologies. "National Biofuels Program." Washington: U.S. Department of Energy, 2000. Available from http://www.ott.doe.gov/biofuels.

"Policy Seen Affecting Choice of Alternative Motor Fuels." *Federal Technology Report,* 7 October 1999.

Thompson, Jake. "Omaha, Neb., Driver Complains about Ethanol-Based Fuel." *Omaha World-Herald,* 12 October 1999.

Whalen, Peg, Kenneth Kelly, Richard L. Bechtold, and David E. Rodgers. "DOE Documents Alternative Fuel Success in Niche Markets." *Oil & Gas Journal,* 12 July 1999.

Wiles, Russ. "Natural-Gas Vehicles Appear to Catch On in Arizona." *Arizona Republic,* 31 August 1999.

Anti-Aging Products and Services

With a baby boomer turning 50 every seven seconds in the United States, by the dawn of the 21st century the market for anti-aging products was booming too. Extended longevity and a decade of unprecedented prosperity have given aging U.S. consumers the desire and the means to purchase cosmetics, nutritional supplements, and surgical procedures that promise to mask, stave off, or even reverse the effects of growing older. Three-quarters of boomers believe that it's important to look younger than one's calendar age. Retail sales of anti-aging products, which tripled between 1994 and 1998, were predicted to reach $4.3 billion by 2000, according to Kalorama Information, a market research firm. Cosmetic surgery, a market worth over $1 billion, grew by 44 percent in 1999 alone. But shaving off the years didn't come cheaply: some procedures, such as hormone injections, could run from $12,000 to $15,000 a year.

Anti-aging products encompass items meant to be taken internally, such as "nutraceutical" vitamin and mineral dietary supplements, and items applied externally, such as skin-care and cosmetic preparations. Many of the latter have moved beyond traditional cosmetics into the realm of "cosmeceuticals." Cosmeceuticals don't simply camouflage the signs of aging; instead, they contain ingredients intended to reduce or delay those signs. Such ingredients include vitamins, antioxidants, hormones, amino acids, and botanicals. In general, anti-aging products have become more scientific and technical in their makeup.

Drugstores continued to dominate the channels for sales of cosmeceuticals and other anti-aging products, with a 29 percent share of sales. They were followed by department stores, with 26 percent; and mass merchandisers, such as Wal-Mart and Kmart, with 24 percent. Although grocery stores did not perform competitively in this sector, consumer-direct sales through such venues as Internet sites claimed an increasing presence in the anti-aging sales landscape.

ORGANIZATION AND STRUCTURE

Large pharmaceutical companies and cosmetics manufacturers produce most cosmeceuticals. Many of the largest cosmetics companies are part of multinational personal hygiene and home care product manufacturers. Both the large cosmetics companies and the pharmaceutical manufacturers have access to internal research and development resources, giving them an inestimable advantage in the ever-evolving anti-aging products market.

Hormonal compounds used for medicinal purposes are manufactured primarily by pharmaceutical companies, and are subject to U.S. Food and Drug Administration (FDA) scrutiny and approval. Hormonal preparations used in dietary supplements, such as dehydroepiandrosterone (DHEA), are not subject to governmental regulation at present, and, as such, are manufactured by a wide range of companies.

Amino acids and enzymes, including alpha- and beta-hydroxy acids, are essential components of many cosmeceuticals and dietary supplements. Like cosmeceuticals, these substances are produced primarily by large pharmaceutical and cosmetics manufacturers, although some independent chemical laboratories and a few small firms are also engaged in their production.

Herbal anti-aging preparations and dietary supplements are manufactured primarily by small companies. As is the case with hormones used in dietary supplements, herbal supplements are not subject to governmental regulation, which enables companies to develop new products with far less expenditure on research and development. (Also see the essay in this book entitled Dietary Supplements.)

Within the anti-aging products industries, a strict dichotomy exists between those sections of the market that come under federal regulatory scrutiny and those that do not. Under the provisions of the Food, Drug, and Cosmetic Act of 1938, the FDA must approve pharmaceutical preparations only. The distinction between cosmetics and pharmaceuticals was quite clear at the time of the act's passage, but modern cosmeceuticals have made changes in the act a possibility. Many countries, including Japan, have amended similar regulatory rules to classify cosmetics that alter physiology as pharmaceuticals subject to regulation. While companies in the anti-aging products industries dread increased regulation, the trend in the United States has not been in this direction. In fact, the Dietary Supplement Health and Education Act of 1994 exempted "natural substances"—including human hormones, herbal compounds, amino acids, and enzymes—from regulation so long as these substances were included in dietary supplements rather than medicines. Increasing reports of dangerous side effects and drug interactions suffered by people taking herbal and hormonal dietary supplements, however, may trigger increased regulatory scrutiny of these products.

BACKGROUND AND DEVELOPMENT

Medical science has been aware of the therapeutic uses of hormones since the 1930s, but they were not widely used in over-the-counter preparations until the Dietary Supplement Health and Education Act of 1994. While the efficacy of medical hormonal therapies such as estrogen replacement has been demonstrated irrefutably, the effectiveness and safety of hormonal dietary supplements remains questionable. Small manufacturers produce most of these substances. In fact, many local health-food stores are able to manufacture their own DHEA, a human hormone synthesized by the adrenal glands. DHEA was one of the first hormones recognized to play a role in the aging process, as its level drops markedly as individuals age. DHEA replacement, however, has not been demonstrated to slow or reverse the aging process, and has caused troubling side effects in those who ingest more

than 50 milligrams per day. Other popular, and controversial, hormone-replacement therapies include human growth hormone injections, which are said to boost stamina, sex drive, and muscle mass; testosterone for men; and melatonin. The National Institute on Aging has criticized the use of hormone therapy to combat aging until further studies have been undertaken.

During the mid-1970s, the popular solution of alpha-hydroxy acid was first used in cosmetic preparations, but it did not attract widespread consumer attention until the 1992 release of Avon's Anew line of skin-care products. The Anew product line achieved sales of over $190 million in 1997, and its phenomenal success led other major cosmetics manufacturers to launch competing compounds. These new products enabled the skin-care products industry to grow 12 percent overall in 1993 and 14 percent overall in 1994, reaching a total market size of $5.1 billion in the United States alone by the end of that year. Industry growth has slowed since the initial onslaught of alpha-hydroxy products, but new innovations have enabled individual companies to post fabulous growth rates in the mid- to late 1990s.

Antioxidants and vitamins, including beta carotene and vitamins A, C, E, and K, have long been observed to protect cells from certain forms of damage caused by environmental factors. As customers became increasingly concerned about the potential effects of environmental degradation on their health, and in particular, the effects of increased ultraviolet radiation on their skin, demand for skin-treatment products that incorporated antioxidant vitamins soared. Antioxidants are useful in treating far more aging problems than previously thought—research conducted in 1998 found that antioxidants showed great promise for preventing chronic aging diseases such as Alzheimer's, cataracts, heart disease, and cancer.

Hair restoration services traditionally did not involve medication, but rather physical replacement of hair. The introduction of Rogaine with minoxidil by the Upjohn Co. in 1988 revolutionized this portion of the anti-aging industry, enabling individuals suffering hair loss to enjoy some renewed growth through application of the product. Rogaine's limited efficacy allowed hair weave and other services to survive, but the product continued to post steady success into the late 1990s.

The problem of impotence received its first medicated treatment when Pfizer Inc. introduced its new impotence drug, Viagra, in the United States in 1998 and received instant phenomenal success, garnering worldwide sales of $193 million. One in three U.S. doctors has written a prescription for Viagra, and it

A wide variety of anti-aging books and products are available to consumers. *(FieldMark Publications/Robert J. Huffman)*

has recently been approved in 77 countries around the world. Research has shown that while Viagra doesn't increase libido or boost sexual desire, it does enhance normal physiological response.

Passage of the Dietary Supplement Health and Education Act of 1994 provided great impetus to the herbal remedy and dietary supplement industries. Herbs have been used to treat a variety of maladies from prehistoric times. While the therapeutic properties of some herbs, including gingko biloba and aloe vera, were proven, many others were subject to question. Of particular concern were the effects of ingesting high concentrations of the active ingredients present in herbs, as these ingredients often interact harmfully with medications. Such concerns notwithstanding, small manufacturers readily filled the huge public demand for herbal anti-aging remedies, dietary supplements, and skin-care products, with global demand for herbal preparations reaching $12 billion by the mid-1990s.

CURRENT CONDITIONS

The U.S. Census Bureau predicted that by 2030 the number of Americans over the age of 65 will reach more than 70 million, one-fifth of the entire popula-

tion. There will be 9 million people over 85 and, by 2050, 40 percent of Americans will be 50 or older. As long as economic prosperity continues, these individuals will be well disposed to devote part of their discretionary income to purchase products that promise to make them look and feel younger than their age. The Freedonia Group reported that expenditures on cosmeceuticals alone increased 7 percent each year since 1998. But not only aging baby boomers fueled that growth. Increasingly younger consumers, especially affluent women between 20 and 30 years old, are investing in preparations that will act as preventive "medicine" in the battle against aging.

Alpha- and beta-hydroxy acids, Retin-A, and the antioxidant vitamins A, C, and E dominated the mass skin-care market in the late 1990s. Products also featured natural ingredients in anti-aging preparations, especially grapeseed extract, olive leaf, and green sea moss. Datamonitor reported that consumers wanted quicker results from products and that the overall trend moved toward combination products that could deliver more than one result, such as anti-aging moisturizers that also contained sunscreens. Poly-hydroxides were introduced as milder versions of alpha- and beta-hydroxies; similarly, new polymer and protein-based delivery systems made vitamin-enhanced formulations much less irritating to skin. In general, sales of premium products outpaced mass-market items in the late 1990s.

Although demand for cosmetics containing alpha-hydroxy acids slowed by the mid-1990s, the skin-care industry as a whole continued to boom, reaching $25 billion in U.S. sales by 1998. The cosmeceutical portion of the skin-care industry was dominated by cosmetic firms Estée Lauder, Procter & Gamble, Cosmair, Maybelline, and Avon Products, Inc., each of which has incorporated anti-aging substances in product lines to some degree. Notable product roll-outs in 1999-2000 included Nivea's Visage CoQ10, a competitor to hydroxy acids and retinol products; its manufacturer claimed it actually replenished the level of the coenzyme Q10—found in young skin—rather than merely affecting the surface layer of the epidermis.

Although the only anti-aging, skin-care products with established scientific backing are the prescription retinoic acids (such as Retin-A and Renova), which have received FDA testing, and the alpha-hydroxy acids, numerous manufacturers touted new, "breakthrough" ingredients in their product roll-outs. For example, copper peptide emerged as a new formulation in skin-care products. ProCyte Corp. debuted its Neova line of skin products, and touted the role of its peptide copper complexes in tissue repair. The Neova line included eye gel, skin lotions, and creams. The Japanese company Kosei promoted the marine carotenoid astaxanthin, an antioxide, in its skin-care line, noting that the ingredient could reverse photo-damage to the skin.

Botanicals were another prominent new ingredient category. ICN Pharmaceuticals, Inc. launched its highly successful Kinerase skin products that contained the plant growth factor N6-furfuryladenine, which it claimed resisted the results of photo-aging. In its first four months on the market, the product line generated sales of about $6 million. Soliance was investigating wheat soramides and Mu Laboratoires, pine bark and black currants. Even the sap of the *Acer saccharum* tree, used to make maple syrup, found its way into a Canadian skin-care line. Chemist Ben Kamins included the sap in B. Kamins' Menopause Cream and Revitalizing Booster Concentrate for sunburn, reasoning that if the sap helped maple trees survive harsh northern winters, it might also improve the condition of aging boomers' skin.

Other producers, such as Christian Dior, RoC, and Plenitude, all launched preparations containing nonprescription doses of the proven antiwrinkle ingredient, retinol. Another development was the introduction of home-use versions of products usually applied only in dermatologists' offices, such as Fairchild's YouthfulYou facial peel.

Special, multipurpose anti-aging centers also sprang up to deliver clinical services alongside cosmetic ones. For example, John Sperling, the founder of the for-profit University of Phoenix, unveiled the Phoenix Kronos Clinic, the first in a planned string of nine such centers to be opened in retiree-dense Arizona and California. Clinic patients can submit themselves to a comprehensive series of tests intended to generate their complete aging profile, including their hormone levels, risk of various cancers, and cardiac health. The clinic then can tailor and provide a full battery of remedies, ranging from cosmeceutical preparations and nutrition to more advanced medical procedures, to help them stave the effects of time.

Nutrition science has played an increasing role in the attempts to slow the aging process from the inside out. Reliv International, Inc., a nutritional-supplements manufacturer, released in 2000 a dietary supplement it claimed replenished key anti-aging hormones. The product, ReversAge, was designed to "promote longevity, enhance wellness, and reduce the effects of aging at the cellular level." The mix included 7 KETO, symbiotropin, antioxidants such as coenzyme Q10, and herbs such as gingko biloba and maca. Also in 2000, Royal BodyCare of Irving, Texas announced the introduction of a new mineral antioxidant, which it sold under the name Microhydrin, and which it claimed improved cell hydration and reduced lactic-acid accumulation during exercise. Fairchild brought out a YouthfulYou supplement line to complement its cosmeceuticals of the same name, including Lover's Delight-V, for sexual enhancement, and an anti-aging dietary supplement that contains L-lysine, glucosamine, and chondroitin. Liddell Laboratories' Age Defying line was the first anti-aging supplement to be delivered in oral spray form. Liddell announced that the product, which was hormone-free, "supports the body's release of human growth hormone." Other ingredients included ginseng, amino acids, and pituitary extract.

At the low-tech end of the nutritional spectrum, the humble blueberry was also trumpeted for its anti-aging virtues. A study by Dr. James Joseph of the Human Nutrition Center on Aging at Tufts University linked blueberries and their active ingredient anthocyanine to a reversal of age-related dysfunctions, such as balance and memory loss, in lab mice. Blueberries were ranked first in antioxidant activity among 40 fruits and vegetables.

Vitamins were also meant to be applied to the exterior of bodies to prevent aging. By 2000, the vitamin of choice was C. Added to skin products at doses

About ANTI-AGING TREATMENTS: VANITY MEDICINE OR CURE FOR AGING?

By 2000, Dr. Ronald Klatz, founder of the American Academy of Anti-Aging Medicine (A4M), declared that aging was a "disease" that could be combated and cured in the foreseeable future. Created in 1993, A4M was the only professional organization of practitioners devoted to the emerging discipline of anti-aging, or "regenerative," medicine—a specialty that has been labeled "vanity medicine" by some critics. Numbering only 12 members at its inception, by century's end A4M boasted 8,500 card-carrying individuals in 55 countries, whose professional specializations ranged from cosmetic surgery and endocrinology to nutrition science. A4M promotes an aggressive anti-aging research and treatment agenda encompassing diverse remedies, and its founder believes that a healthy life span of up to 120 years lies just on the medical horizon for many people.

The organization's outspoken agenda has not been immune to criticism. Nonmembers from the medical community have questioned the qualifications of some of A4M's members; even Klatz acknowledged that many were not board-certified specialists. The National Institute on Aging also took a critical stance on some of A4M's assertions.

The current race to provide anti-aging treatments may also lead to insufficient training in some practitioners. For example, in December 1999 the Florida *Fort Lauderdale Sun Sentinel* conducted a study of anti-aging treatments, which it dubbed "vanity medicine," and the medical profession in its community. It found that spe-

cializations such as liposuction, hair transplants, cosmetic surgery, and hormone therapies accounted for one of every 17 physicians in the area. The study further speculated that this high consumer demand for services provided by this lucrative sector was luring under-prepared practitioners as health maintenance organizations drained the profits from more mainstream practices.

Nonetheless, recent breakthroughs linked to animal cloning may indeed portend sweeping changes for the future of anti-aging medicine. In April 2000, researchers at Advanced Cell Technology (ACT) in Worcester, Massachusetts, cloned six calves whose cells appeared to be about 50 percent younger than those of calves born at the same time. Previously cloned animal replicas—such as the famous, first successful mammal clone, the Scottish sheep Dolly—possess cells the same age as those of their donor originals, raising questions about whether such animals would age and die prematurely. When Dolly was cloned in 1996, for example, her cells were as "old" as those of the six-year-old ewe from which she was cloned. The telltale markers of cell age are telomeres, rodlike caps on the ends of cells that shorten as the cells age. In contrast to Dolly, the ACT calves, which had been cloned from cells of a 45-day-old fetus, boasted telomeres that were actually 50 percent longer than those of the parent cells. This implied that cloning may be able to "reset" the "telomere clock" of mature cells, leading to promising treatments for diseases linked to cellular degeneration.

---

of more than 20 percent, however, it tended to create irritation. Murad Inc. introduced its 30 percent Vitamin C Home Facial, which it claimed delivered antioxidant benefits directly into the skin without irritation. Vitamins A, C, and E were particularly prominent in skin-care products.

Many manufacturers combined both high-tech and natural ingredients in new anti-aging lines. For example, Procter & Gamble's Olay premiered its global launch of the Total Effects subline in January 2000. The products' ingredient list includes niacin, B3, E, and provitamin B5. Rochas introduced Futuressence Nourishing, Anti-Wrinkle, and Moisturizing Firming Stimulating Treatments, which contains glucan, antioxidant vitamins, liposomes, amino acids, and oils of rose, camomile, and marjoram.

Since nearly 90 percent of skin aging results from photo-damage, increased consumer concern over the effects of ultraviolet radiation on the skin led to a booming market for sunscreens and related products from the mid-1990s. In spring 2000 the first internal

sunscreen appeared. Developed by Protective Factors, Inc. of Boston, the patent-pending sun protectant—an oral supplement, Sunray Defense—contained antioxidants such as Lutein, which help cells to absorb ultraviolet (UV) rays and block the formation of UV-induced free radicals.

Hormone replacement therapy, delivered both orally and through injections, also emerged as a means—though a controversial one—to combat aging. Going beyond the familiar estrogen-replacement therapies available for menopausal and postmenopausal women, the field encompassed genetically engineered human growth hormone (HGH). Though it is promoted as an injectable, anti-aging treatment that retards loss of muscle and bone density, it may represent a cancer risk, according to Dr. Samuel Epstein, chairman of the Cancer Prevention Coalition. Among the risks associated with HGH were colon, prostate, and breast cancers. Although approved by the FDA in 1994 for limited medical disorders, such as dwarfism, HGH has not been endorsed by the FDA for anti-aging therapies.

Pharmacia & Upjohn, Inc.'s domination of the hair restoration medication market was challenged in 1998 with the introduction of Propecia, an orally administered hair restoring pharmaceutical by Merck & Co., Inc. Though sales of Rogaine slumped in 1997 and 1998, increased advertising and the introduction of Rogaine for Women helped mitigate the slump. Hair treatment and hair care overall were expected to see continued growth, reaching $910 million by 2003, according to the Freedonia Group.

Researchers also uncovered more anti-aging powers of simple aspirin. In addition to its well-publicized work in fighting the risk of heart attack, it also helps promote blood flow in diabetics, reduces the likelihood of bowel cancer, and may stave off Alzheimer's disease.

INDUSTRY LEADERS

Large cosmetics companies, some of which were owned by multinational pharmaceutical manufacturers, dominated the cosmeceuticals industry. Avon Products, Inc., originator of Anew, the first cosmetic product to include alpha-hydroxy acids, remains a major player in the industry with sales of $5.3 billion for the 1999 fiscal year. Avon's competitive position was enhanced when it added retinol, a vitamin A-based compound said to help protect skin from ultraviolet radiation, to its original Anew formula. In 1998 Avon introduced Avon Basics worldwide; this line of vitamin-enriched skin care broadened its sunscreen formula to encompass all skin types. In 1999, it introduced coenzyme-containing Anew Clearly C10% to the Anew product family.

L'Oréal SA, of Clichy, France, was the world's leading cosmetics' manufacturer. Its product lines included Maybelline, Biotherm, and Lancôme≥; 1999 sales topped $10.8 billion, of which its cosmeceuticals accounted for about 5 percent. Corporate subsidiaries operate in medical and pharmaceutical research and development, and support L'Oréal's creation of new cosmeceutical products.

Estée Lauder Companies Inc. accounts for nearly half of the sales of prestige women's cosmetics in the United States and showed a net sales of $1.4 billion in 1999. Its Diminish Retinol eye cream was among the biggest sellers in anti-aging skin care; the skin-care category accounted for about 35 percent of overall product sales. Estée Lauder's brand lines include Clinique, Aveda, and Origins. Revlon,

Inc. has also entered the anti-aging cosmetics market with its Almay and Color Stay product lines.

Large, diversified consumer-goods manufacturers also play a key role in the anti-aging products industry. Procter & Gamble (P&G), whose brand names include Cover Girl, Olay, Max Factor, and Noxema, is one such corporation. P&G's rival, the consumer-products behemoth Unilever, included among its truckload of brands the Chesebrough Pond's line of cosmetics and toiletries. Health-care product manufacturer Johnson & Johnson (J&J), of New Brunswick, New Jersey, was the world's third-largest pharmaceutical maker, with sales of more than $27.5 billion in 1999. It participates in the cosmeceuticals industry through its Neutrogena product line, which it purchased in 1994. Neutrogena's Healthy Skin line enjoyed a 46 percent sales increase in 1999. In addition to cosmeceuticals, J&J developed Retin-A and the antiwrinkle treatment Renova, which won FDA approval in 1996.

Small, independent laboratories and other corporations continue to produce the majority of the nonpharmaceutical hormones and hormone-based dietary supplements and cosmeceuticals.

Two companies dominate the hair replacement portion of the anti-aging products industry: Pharmacia and Upjohn, manufacturer of Rogaine, and Merck & Co., Inc., manufacturer of Propecia. Since these were the only proven hair restoration medications on the market, the companies faced no competition apart from each other in the late 1990s. Pharmacia and Upjohn has dominated the hair restoration market since the introduction of Rogaine—and its active ingredient, minoxidil—in 1988.

As is the case with hormonal anti-aging products, herbal-based anti-aging compounds are primarily produced by small, independent concerns. Natrol, Inc., a California-based producer of melatonin, and Sunsource International, a Hawaii-based producer of melatonex—melatonin to which vitamin B6 has been added—are typical of these concerns. An exception to this rule is Yamanouchi Pharmaceutical Co., a Tokyo-based corporation that produces herbal remedies and supplements in the United States under the Shaklee Corp. name. Nature Made is another important player in this sector of the anti-aging products.

AMERICA AND THE WORLD

Demand for anti-aging products is centered in the West and the economically developed areas of Asia, particularly Japan, which represents the second-highest cosmetic and the highest skin-care sales in the world. Euromonitor released a study in April 2000 that revealed 1999 skin-care product sales experienced double-digit growth in the United States, Japan, France, Spain, Germany, and the United Kingdom. Among emerging markets, Chile represented the highest per capita expenditure on skin care in Latin America and Poland led the countries of Eastern Europe.

Manufacturing of anti-aging products is also concentrated in Europe and the United States. Multinational giants Unilever, P&G, and their subsidiaries play a prominent role in the industry globally. Production of herbal and hormonal cosmetics and dietary supplements is fragmented among small manufacturers, although Europe accounted for approximately one-half of worldwide demand for herbal remedies in the late 1990s. Despite the predominance of the West in the anti-aging products industry, production and exportation of nonpharmaceutical quality hormones, most notably DHEA, by the People's Republic of China led the value of these substances to fall dramatically in 1996.

RESEARCH AND TECHNOLOGY

Research and development has driven the growth of the anti-aging products industry throughout the 1990s. As advances in medical understanding of the aging process reveal the therapeutic properties of new substances, cosmetics and pharmaceutical firms adapt these substances for use in their products. The industry also expends a great deal of effort identifying the exact effects of anti-aging compounds. This is particularly true of the anti-aging hormones and herbs.

In cosmeceutical research, Fairchild announced a partnership with Proxis Pharmaceuticals, Inc. to invest $950,000 in the development of two over-the-counter anti-aging, carbohydrate therapeutic remedies to attack deep skin wrinkles, a feat no over-the-counter product has yet been proven to accomplish. The topical remedy could supply a replacement for depleted natural collagen, and substitute for the painful injection therapy of bovine-derived collagen currently in use.

The mode of application for anti-aging products also formed the target of new technology. IntegreMed LLC announced its Sonophoresis technology at the American Academy of Dermatology's 2000 annual meeting. The patented, ultrasound-based technique uses low-intensity ultrasound to increase the permeability of the skin's outer layer, which the manufac-

turer claimed increases the skin's receptivity to skin-care products.

A new surgical technique also appeared under development. Nanotechnology, being pioneered by Zyvex, the first company dedicated to this technology, will provide doctors with surgical tools to repair age-related molecular and cellular damage, by supplying highly controlled nutritional and metabolic support to tissues that have ceased functioning on their own.

The biotech sector approached the U.S. government to supply more funding for, and less regulation of, anti-aging research. In 2000, about 25 U.S. biotech firms focused on cutting-edge, anti-aging research, such as genetics, stem cell biology, and tissue engineering, according to the nonprofit Alliance for Aging Research. This field of regenerative medicine seeks to retard aging through the prevention and treatment of age-related diseases, such as cancer, heart disease, and Alzheimer's. If and when the field succeeds, it might obliterate the need for many more superficial anti-aging treatments. As of 2000, however, no readily available cosmeceuticals or procedures had emerged to rival the age-slowing effects of adequate rest, balanced diet, mental stimulation, and plenty of exercise.

FURTHER READING

"American Academy of Dermatology Adding Vitamins to the Mix: Skin Care Products That Can Benefit the Skin." *PR Newswire,* 10 March 2000.

"Anti-Aging Substance Developed by Cosmetics Maker." *Japan Chemical Week,* 23 September 1999.

"Anti-Aging Therapies." *Mayo Clinic Health Letter,* May 1999.

"Baby Boomers Cry Out For Specialized Items." *MMR,* 4 September 2000.

Baird, Pat. "Offerings Vary in the Fountain of Youth." *Times-Picayune,* 18 July 1999.

Boyd, Brian. "The Underdog Wonderdrug." *Irish Times,* 31 May 1999.

Bucalo, Anthony. "State of the Industry." *Global Cosmetic Industry,* June 1999.

Carey, Benedict. "Can Doctors Really Turn Back Time?" *Los Angeles Times,* 8 May 2000.

Cookson, Clive. "Hopes Rise for Anti-Ageing Drug." *Financial Times* (London), 18 November 1999.

"Cosmeceutical Market to Continue Growth." *Cosmetic Insider's Report,* 6 September 1999.

"Cosmeceuticals Market Expected to Surpass $4 Billion in 2003." *Chemical Market Reporter,* 11 October 1999.

"Feeding the Face." *Functional Foods,* December 1999.

"Formulating the Future." *Soap, Perfumery & Cosmetics,* May 1999.

Gizowska, Eva. "Paintwork." *Independent* (London), 9 April 2000.

Grossman, Andrea M. "Anti-Aging Products Top Skin Care Sales." *Drug Store News,* 22 May 2000.

———. "Competition Heats Up in Anti-Aging Segment." *Drug Store News,* 19 July 1999.

———. "War against Wrinkles Sparks Anti-Aging Growth." *Drug Store News,* 15 November 1999.

Holmes, Anna. "Flapjacks and Flapjills." *New York Times,* 30 January 2000.

"Ingredients." *Soap, Perfumery & Cosmetics,* May 1999.

Jennings, Lisa. "Finding Youth in a Lotion: Few Products Are Backed by Scientific Data." *Chicago Sun-Times,* 3 September 1999.

Lasalandra, Michael. "Bio 2000: Biotech Asks for Hike in Anti-Age $$." *Boston Herald,* 28 March 2000.

"Murad Changes the Face of Vitamin C Skincare Products." *Business Wire,* 15 May 2000.

"The Next Secret Ingredient?" *Natural Health,* March 2000.

"ProCyte in License Agreement with Neutrogena: Deal Introduces ProCyte's Copper Peptide Technology to the Worldwide Consumer Market." *PR Newswire,* 19 April 2000.

"Reliv International Launches New Anti-Aging Product." *PR Newswire,* 22 May 2000.

"Risks Increase as Vanity Medicine Grows." *American Health Line,* 13 December 1999.

Saltus, Richard. "Cell Discovery Might Be Step to Anti-Aging Process." *Montreal Gazette,* 28 April 2000.

Schnirring, Lisa. "Healthy Aging or Anti-Aging?" *Physician and Sportsmedicine,* June 2000.

Shaw, David. "Medical Miracles or Misguided Media?" *Los Angeles Times,* 13 February 2000.

Siegel-Maier, Karyn. "Peel away Wrinkles—Without Plastic Surgery." *Better Nutrition,* March 2000.

"Something New under the Sun: Internal Sunscreen Guards against UV Rays." *PR Newswire,* 4 April 2000.

Stuttaford, Thomas. "You Can't Beat a Good Surgeon." *Times* (London), 27 November 1999.

Tenerelli, Mary Jane. "The State of the Skincare Industry Revealed." *Global Cosmetic Industry,* June 1999.

Vogel, Gretchen. "Cell Biology: In Contrast to Dolly, Cloning Resets Telomere Clock in Cattle." *Science,* 28 April 2000.

"Wild Blueberries, Nature's Healthy Food." *Canada NewsWire,* 16 May 2000.

Williams, Jack. "New Products Join Age-Old Battle to Remain Young." *San Diego Union-Tribune,* 8 May 2000.

Zuidhoff, Heiko. "Hydroxy Acids in Action." *SPC Asia,* November 1999.

ANTIBACTERIAL PRODUCTS

Antibacterial products have enjoyed rising popularity as consumers aspire to eradicate germs from their surroundings. Between 1992 and 2000, upwards of 700 new antimicrobial products were introduced in the United States. According to one estimate, the consumer market for disinfectants and antimicrobials was rising 6.1 percent a year in the early 2000s, compared to 3 to 4 percent growth in more established soap and detergent lines.

Today the mix of products with antibacterial properties extends well beyond household cleaners and hand sanitizers to a surprising array of merchandise, including everything from pillows and diapers to toothbrushes and touch-screen displays. While manufacturers of these products sometimes shy away from making overly specific claims for fear of regulatory headaches, the marketing behind antibacterial products assures users that their homes and businesses will be cleaner, safer places thanks to embedded germ-killing agents.

Some medical and health experts caution, however, that the flood of antibacterial products could be encouraging development of more resistant strains of harmful bacteria. This assertion hasn't been rigorously tested, and has been challenged by some researchers. Still, a 1998 poll conducted by CBS News indicated that at least 52 percent of U.S. consumers would always choose antimicrobial or antibacterial products whenever possible.

ORGANIZATION AND STRUCTURE

The U.S. Food and Drug Administration (FDA) oversees the production of pharmaceuticals, or any products that include regulated, approved medicinal or health benefits. With such a product as soap, for instance, the FDA has very clear guidelines. According to the FDA Office of Cosmetics Safety, there are two categories of soap: "true" soaps, made up solely of fats and an alkali, and synthetic "detergent products." "True" soaps are regulated by the Consumer Product Safety Commission, not the FDA, so they do not require labeling. Most synthetic soaps come under the regulation of the FDA, as do any "true"soaps that make a so-called cosmetic claim, such as having moisturizing or deodorizing properties. Words such as "antibacterial" push a product into the drug category, which is subject to additional requirements.

Products with disinfectant qualities that are used on inanimate surfaces (in other words, not on or in the human body) fall under the purview of the U.S. Environmental Protection Agency (EPA). That agency's involvement stems from the federal government's classification of disinfectants as pesticides, which are also under the EPA's jurisdiction. Disinfectants are thus registered through the Antimicrobials Division of the EPA's Office of Pesticide Programs. The agency has been criticized for taking too long to review products and costing manufacturers too much; on the other hand, the EPA was also criticized for allowing disinfectants with questionable merits on the market. In the late 1990s the EPA took steps to improve its record on both counts, and therefore some of its policies (or at least their enforcement) were in flux.

Antibacterials classified as homeopathic, or alternative medicine, are not regulated by the FDA. In essence, they are unregulated and could make any claim, valid or questionable, regarding their effectiveness in fighting bacteria. In the area of plastics that use antibacterial protections, all industry standards pertaining to their occupational safety, along with consumer protection guidelines, direct production.

BACKGROUND AND DEVELOPMENT

The market for antibacterial products owes its success to the origins of bacterial study and Sir Alexander Fleming, a Scottish researcher who joined the research department of St. Mary's Hospital in London in 1906. Fleming's experiences during World War I as a soldier in France presented him with the terrible reality of infectious wounds.

World War I brought horrors that other wars had not due to modern artillery, machine guns, and bombs. Physical disfigurements, infections, and wounds that resulted from the new technology inspired many medical breakthroughs. In addition to Fleming's commitment to finding medicines that would attack infections, much of modern-day plastic surgery underwent its earliest experiments during this time. According to Ted Gottfried, for *Scotsmart Books* in an online biography, "Fleming discovered in 1928 that an unwashed and bacterially infected flask appeared to be disinfected by mould which had grown from airborne spores. Penicillin's use in combating bacterium had been discovered." After World War II, thanks to Fleming's discovery, penicillin began to be used to treat people in the fight against infections.

The onset of the use of antibiotics, such as penicillin and its derivative administered orally or intravenously, remained the focus of medical research and pharmaceutical companies. Products that employed antibacterial safeguards in surgical products such as heart catheter tubes were crucial in hospitals and other medical care settings to offset the chance of spreading disease. In alternative medical arenas, various herbal compounds and natural plants were the basis for homeopathic remedies and beauty products. As far back as ancient times, natural poultices, creams, and herbal drinks were taken for the cure of infections. Although the industry had supplied antibacterial items to hospitals and medical supply companies, not until Safeguard, a soap from the Procter & Gamble Co., was introduced in the early 1970s did most Americans see the term "antibacterial" appearing on any product, even though products such as Lysol disinfectants and Listerine mouthwash had been available for decades. Safeguard soap was introduced into hospitals first, and was then advertised to the American consumer. Procter & Gamble kept it on the market due to its well-received response for the product in terms of sales.

Despite warnings of the possible harmful aspects of nontraditional practices, the alternative medicine industry managed to grow into an $18 billion market by 1996, as reported by the *Nutrition Business Journal* and as referenced in a series of investigative articles in the *Los Angeles Times*. They reported that even insurance companies began to look at various alternative treatments as viable and offered some reimbursement for certain procedures. The market for homeopathic remedies in California alone enjoyed an income of $3.65 billion, up 100 percent in the period between 1994 and 1998. Every one of hundreds of natural-health companies offered some line of antibacterial products, both for personal and household use. The products include soaps, lotions, herbs, teas, vitamins, and household cleaning products, all thought to improve physical health and immunity. The natural-products industry vigorously pursued the consumer market that continually sought out products to destroy the harmful effects of bacteria.

CURRENT CONDITIONS

The U.S. market for all forms of disinfectants and antimicrobial compounds reached $455 million in 1998, the most recent year for which statistics were available, according to published figures from the Freedonia Group. This included disinfectants used in commercial and industrial applications, as well as those marketed to consumers. The overall market was expected to grow at a compound average of 3.6 percent a year through 2003, but the consumer segment was forecast to outpace it at 6.1 percent a year. By 2003, Freedonia projected the total market to be worth $620 million, including $110 million worth of consumer products. Market growth of antibacterials in more conventional soap and detergent products was expected to significantly outperform growth in plastics and other products with embedded antibacterial agents.

NEW PRODUCTS KEEP COMING

Manufacturers continue to unveil a spate of new products with antibacterial and disinfectant properties. Procter & Gamble (P&G) had at least three recent entrants to the field: Mr. Clean antibacterial towelettes for cleaning kitchens and baths, Tide with Bleach for sanitizing laundry, and Fit Fruit and Vegetable Wash for ensuring fresh produce is germ-free. Other soap and detergent makers such as Clorox Co. and Colgate-Palmolive have kept pace with P&G in the antibacterial cleaning product arena.

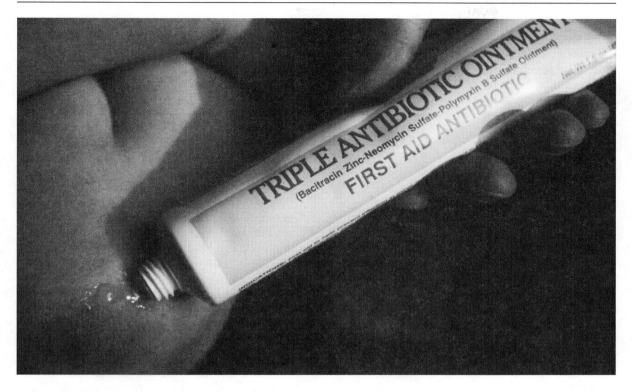

Antibacterial ointment being applied to the skin. (FieldMark Publications/Robert J. Huffman)

Among other debuts, computer peripheral maker MicroTouch Systems Inc. released CleanScreen, an antibacterial touch-screen display. It's intended for computer systems in businesses and commercial environments where many people are touching the same interactive screen. Similar devices have been used in restaurants in Japan, and in addition to food-service applications, the potential market includes medical settings and public information kiosks.

WEAK SPOTS

Not all antibacterial products have experienced unqualified success. Antibacterial toothbrushes, for instance, have proven a problematic category. Johnson & Johnson ran into a roadblock with its antibacterial Reach toothbrush in 1998 when the EPA fined the company for misleading consumers about its health benefits. In a retreat, the company could claim only that the antibacterial in the plastic handle could protect the user's hands from transmitting bacteria. Separately, HealthShield Technologies in 1999 was trying to revive the antibacterial toothbrush, as well as introduce other kinds of germ-fighting brushes, using special bristles and filaments made by DuPont Filaments.

Another antibacterial category with a troubled history is diapers. Drypers Corp., the first company to

market such a product, announced in 1999 it was ceasing production of its Drypers Supreme with Germ Guard because of disappointing sales. A company representative acknowledged that the product had a small but loyal following.

SCIENTISTS DECRY ANTIBACTERIAL TREND

Widespread use of antibacterial products has drawn pointed criticism from certain scientists and medical experts. An October 1998 article in the *Tufts University Health & Nutrition Letter* entitled "Antibacterial Overkill" laid out some of their objections. According to a growing number of medical researchers, said the article, "Using a special antibacterial cleanser when ordinary soap will do the job just as well (and it will) is a form of overkill that can backfire. It can lead to the development of bacteria that will be able to withstand the action of antibacterial agents should they ever really be needed."

"It's the same with antibacterial compounds used in common household cleaners," the article continued. "The more they're used, the more the bacteria that they are supposed to destroy—*E. coli, Salmonella,* and other germs that make their way into food—will undergo mutations that only serve to strengthen them by allowing them to 'resist' the antibacterial attacks. The upshot: the germs will thrive on kitchen counters, floors, sinks, dishes, and hands, and more people could potentially be sickened by bacteria contaminated food." The piece argued, moreover, that antibacterial compounds wouldn't work at times when they're needed most, such as when a patient's immune system is weakened.

The root of the problem, a number of researchers have concluded, is with triclosan, the major ingredient in antibacterial cleansing agents, soaps, and lotions. Stuart B. Levy, M.D., director of the Center for Adaptation Genetics and Drug Resistance at the Tufts University School of Medicine, probed to find the way triclosan actually works. It was first thought that triclosan worked simply by "punching holes" in bacterial membranes, but when Levy published his results in *Nature,* he reported that his research group determined that the agent destroys *E. coli* by simply killing a single gene. If that gene underwent a mutation, the *E. coli* bacteria would be able to fight off the force of the triclosan and continue to live and grow. More importantly, a gene similar to the mutated one in the Tufts experiment was found in a strain of bacteria that caused tuberculosis.

Levy, a microbiologist whose work on triclosan has been widely cited, admitted that such a condition had not yet been observed outside of a laboratory environment. Still, he and others have warned that before all of the evidence was examined over a long period, caution should be used. Antibacterial products are sometimes necessary, but not always. He also noted that while bleach and chlorine-containing products are not labeled as antibacterial products, they were still effective in wiping out entire bacteria colonies.

ANTIBACTERIAL PLASTICS UNDER SCRUTINY

In the late 1990s, the Environmental Protection Agency (EPA) publicly reprimanded the toy maker Hasbro and a number of their manufacturers for leading the consumer to believe that a germicide embedded into their plastic products would fight the spread of disease-producing germs. In an article for *Health* in the spring of 1998, Deborah Franklin quoted Brenda Mosley, a microbiologist at the EPA, as saying, "If that evidence exists, we haven't seen it." One plastic distributor, Neste Polyester, entered into a licensing agreement with Microban Products Co. to put antibacterial, antimold, and antimildew protection into polyester gelcoat applications used for surfacing reinforced plastics products in everything from bathroom fixtures to boats. The Microban antibacterial protection was listed on the *Plastic Distributor & Fabrica-*

tor Magazine Web site as "a proprietary technology that inhibits the growth of a broad range of bacteria, mold, mildew, and fungus in polymeric products. . . . Unlike surface coating, the antibacterial protection is incorporated directly into the polymer's molecular structure."

SOME EVIDENCE SUPPORTS ANTIBACTERIAL USE

According to Franklin, there were some benefits to antibacterial products and cleansers. Franklin reported that "In a hospital nursery several years ago, for example, *Staphylococcus aureus* sickened 22 newborns over the course of seven weeks, despite control measures. The problem was squelched only after the staff started using antibacterial hand soap—of the same strength as versions found in the supermarket—to wash their hands and bathe their babies." Marsha Koopman, a nurse epidemiologist at the University of California at Davis Medical Center, explained in a university health publication that washing hands remained the best protection against bacteria, at least in the average situation. "It's not just the soap that accomplished this, it's also the friction caused by rubbing your hands together and rinsing them with water," Koopman said.

INDUSTRY LEADERS

The Procter & Gamble Co. (P&G), one of the world's largest consumer products firms, has courted the antibacterial market aggressively as it tries to break out of the revenue doldrums of its maturing cleaning and paper products businesses. The company has rolled out an extensive line of new products and brand extensions with antimicrobial claims, including dish detergent, hand soap, hand sanitizer, face soap, laundry detergent, cleaning towelettes, and produce wash.

Once part of P&G, The Clorox Co. manufactures Clorox bleach, Pine-Sol, and Soft Scrub cleaners, among many others. The company's traditional bleach products all have antibacterial properties, and Clorox has used these to its advantage in marketing. It competes head-on with P&G in several antibacterial product categories.

GoJo Industries was one of the industry's category-defining companies in the late 1990s with its introduction of Purell waterless hand sanitizer. The product, which contains alcohol in a moisturizing gel, appeals to people at work, in transit, or in other places where they might not have access to wash their hands by conventional means. GoJo is still the leader in the consumer hand-sanitizer segment.

AMERICA AND THE WORLD

While the market for antibacterial products is ripe in a germ-conscious culture such as America, other countries do not necessarily share in the zeal. As reported by Lynn Payer in *Medicine and Culture,* the French medical establishment has suggested that germs are healthy for people. Some diseases, they argue, such as hepatitis A, when contracted in childhood through a natural sort of vaccination, are much milder and protect from further dangers in adulthood. American doctors tend to disagree with this medical philosophy, although they do acknowledge that antibacterial artillery might not be as beneficial and that some exposure to bacteria and germs provide a defense rather than an attack.

Drugstores in the United States, often selling many of these antibacterial products, continue to thrive. The boom that started at the very end of the 20th century for antibacterial products shows no immediate signs of subsiding. It is an area, however, that calls for close attention. With continuing research on any possible negative effects of such products by medical researchers, scientists, and the FDA, a turn in another direction might possibly affect production and sales.

FURTHER READING

"Antibacterial Overkill." *Tufts University Health & Nutrition Letter,* October 1998.

"Antibacterial Protection for Gelcoats." *Plastics Distributor & Fabricator Magazine,* 29 April 1999. Available from http://pdfm@plasticsmag.com.

Colwell, Shelley M. "Disinfectants: Lethal Weapons." *Soap-Cosmetics-Chemical Specialties,* May 1997.

Couzin, Jennifer. "Battling Bugs in the Home." *U.S. News & World Report,* 10 May 1999.

Fayerman, Pamela. "Skin Glue Replaces Stitches for Injured Kids." *Vancouver Sun,* 21 May 1997.

Franklin, Deborah. "Gel Crazy." *Health,* May/June 1998.

Gottfried, Ted. "Famous Scots: Sir Alexander Fleming." 2 May 1999. Available from http://scotsmart.com.

Harvilicz, Helena. "Procter & Gamble Introduces Home Wash for Fresh Produce." *Chemical Market Reporter,* 24 January 2000.

Liddle, Alan. "'Touching Technology' Touted as Microbe Murderer." *Nation's Restaurant News,* 24 January 2000.

Monmaney, Terence, and Shari Roan. "Alternative Medicine: The 18 Billion Dollar Experiment." *Los Angeles Times,* 30 August 1998.

Neff, Jack. "Drypers Calls It Quits on Germ-Fighting Line." *Advertising Age,* 29 November 1999.

Schmidt, Bill, and Claudia Hume. "Surfactants Suppliers Turn Up the Heat." *Chemical Week,* 26 January 2000.

"A Silver Bullet for Bacteria." *Business Week,* 5 July 1999.

"Too Clean?" *The Boston Globe,* 24 July 2000.

U.S. Food and Drug Administration. "Guideline No. 18 Human Health Safety Criteria." Washington, 26 April 1999. Available from http://www.fda.gov.

———. "Office of Cosmetics Fact Sheet." Washington, 3 February 1995. Available from http://www.fda.gov/CFSAN.

Wilson, Sue. "Maybe We're Disinfecting Ourselves Too Much." *Fortune,* 11 October 1999.

APPLICATION SERVICE PROVIDERS

Application service providers (ASPs) are reviving some old practices in the computer business. And they're doing it with a vengeance. Building on the long-established paradigms of high-end software rental and computer time-sharing—updated with Web savvy—ASPs are challenging the supremacy of user-licensed and user-maintained software in the corporate information technology (IT) market.

The ASP model represents a shift both in pricing and, many proponents hope, in the total cost of owning (or using) software. Traditional software licensing involves buying application licenses based on the number of simultaneous users, sometimes called seats, of the program. Copies of the application are then installed and maintained on each machine that will need to run the program.

CONVENTIONAL LICENSES SEEN AS TOO COSTLY, INEFFICIENT

This poses several disadvantages for the software buyer. For one, an occasional user must pay the same price as a frequent user. When it's a very expensive piece of software in question, the economic disparity in cost-per-use under conventional licensing could be enormous. An even more nagging problem for software licensees, however, is the cost of installing and maintaining it over time. In a large organization, the cumulative cost of maintaining packaged software—mostly in terms of staff hours—can easily exceed the cost of the software itself. For problem-prone applications and ones with frequent upgrades, ownership costs are only compounded.

ASPs OFFER ATTRACTIVE ALTERNATIVES

Exploiting the Web's nearly universal connectivity, ASPs are positioning themselves as a remedy for the ills of software ownership. ASPs host software applications remotely and allow companies (and individuals) to tap into them through a secure Internet site. All software maintenance is done by the ASP; the customer simply needs a computer equipped with a compatible Web browser. Although they operate under a variety of pricing structures, usually their services are subscription-based, meaning that customers pay a periodic (often monthly) flat rental fee based on how much they use the application. Use can be measured in terms of users, bandwidth consumed (the amount of data traveling to and fro), or other metrics.

IMPACT COULD BE MASSIVE

All of this adds up to a potentially massive recasting of the software and IT services businesses. A number of prominent market research organizations, including International Data Corp. (IDC), have predicted that ASPs will disrupt the conventional software industry and perhaps even shift the balance of power from software code writers such as Microsoft to the large service providers who deploy and manage their programs. In addition, as some ASPs develop their own custom software, they will provide new competition for existing software firms.

Estimates of the market for online application hosting still vary widely. IDC's has been conservative, calling for a $7.8 billion global market by 2004, up from $2 billion in 2000. At the other extreme, the Gartner Group predicted a whopping $24 billion market by 2004 from $3.6 billion in 2000. The Yankee Group forecast a $17 billion market by 2003. Still another forecast by Forrester Research envisaged a $6 billion world market as of 2001. Part of the disparity lies in how each one defines the industry; the different analysts also disagree on historical revenues. A few things seem certain, though: ASPs will be one of the biggest and fastest-growing new segments in IT services, and will wield mounting influence over hardware makers and other established players in the broader IT sector.

ORGANIZATION AND STRUCTURE

DEFINING ASPs

The fact market analysts can't agree on a consistent definition of the industry points to the broader debate in the business over what exactly constitutes an ASP. The ASP Industry Consortium, the leading trade group for the fledgling industry, defines an ASP broadly as any firm that hosts and manages applications over a wide area network (such as the Internet) for multiple clients.

Most businesspeople seem to understand the concept in more specific terms, according to a survey by the Information Technology Association of America (ITAA), an influential trade organization. The ITAA's study found that two-thirds of respondents defined ASPs as companies that provide "specific business applications on a subscription basis via the Internet or other networked arrangement." The key difference here is the assumption that software is leased on a subscription basis, such as through a flat monthly payment, whereas the ASP Industry Consortium doesn't consider pricing structure a defining feature. It's also interesting to note that survey respondents' most common definition assumes ASPs are geared toward businesses, not consumers.

In the same survey, two other competing definitions were espoused by a noteworthy minority of survey respondents. The first, supported by 15.2 percent of respondents, held that ASPs are for-profit entities that offer aggregated IT resources over a network to remotely connected customers. This notion encompasses a wider array of services such as hardware management and even programming services that some view as part of a complete ASP package. The third most common definition of an ASP, chosen by 12.9 percent of respondents, was simply a company that offers "outsourcing/hosting of hardware and/or software," again a broader definition that doesn't specify pricing method or even mode of delivery.

If potential customers can't agree on what an ASP is, neither can the ASPs themselves. A study by Cahners In-Stat Group in 2000 found that most ASPs had remarkably broad ambitions about whom they wanted to reach and what they wanted to offer. Most, it seems, wished to be a nonstop source for all applications and IT infrastructure services. Industry observers, however, question whether such an unfocused approach is sustainable.

TECHNICAL PORTRAIT

In simplest terms, an ASP consists of a Web site that provides some user-oriented application or function. Familiar consumer applications on the Web include free Web-based e-mail services such as Hotmail and Yahoo! Mail and personal calendar/scheduling applications by the same vendors.

Application hosting for businesses follows a similar approach on a much grander scale—and is usually more lucrative for the ASP. At a minimum, the ASP provides packaged or custom applications through a secured portal. The software in question might be a familiar desktop productivity suite such as the Microsoft Office or StarOffice. Or more often, it may be a high-end program tailored to some business process or functional department: order processing, sales force management, accounting and finance, human resources, manufacturing systems, supply-chain management.

Indeed, some of more popular packages served up by such leaders as USinternetworking, Inc. are the so-called enterprise resource planning (ERP) suites by software developers such as PeopleSoft and Lawson. These multiapplication suites, often industry-specific, are designed to provide broad, efficient, and powerful functionalities that all organizations of a certain type might need (say, banks or telecommunications companies), but without the costs of developing a set of completely custom applications. ERP software grew intensely popular with large corporations in the latter part of the 1990s, but also became notorious for being difficult and expensive to implement internally. The ERP deployment process was often slow and disruptive and prone to setbacks due to the complexity of the systems and the ambitious goals set out for them. With the rise of ASPs, ERP has become a leading candidate for outsourcing because, in theory, corporations can leave the implementation and maintenance to the ASP and simply enjoy the benefits of the software.

In addition to merely providing a networked conduit to popular applications, ASPs handle scores of back-end system management tasks. These range from routine data backups and software upgrades to software customization and hardware maintenance. Often, an ASP commits to a minimum level of service as measured in application availability ("up time") or some other performance gauge. If the ASP fails to deliver as promised, the customer is usually entitled to some type of discount or credit. This guarantee is formalized in a contract frequently called a service-level agreement, a document that both ASPs and customers alike must scrutinize to ensure they're not leaving themselves open to tremendous liabilities or insufficient remedies should problems arise.

While access via public Web space is most commonly associated with ASPs, many also furnish their services over private networks using high-speed leased lines or fiber-optic cable. Having a private connection is especially important when the customer has large amounts of mission-critical data flowing into and out of the remote application. The application interface may still be viewed through a Web browser, but the communications channel isn't the Web.

MARKET STRUCTURE

All ASPs aren't for all companies. While some have cast their nets widely during the industry's formative stages, fundamentally there are separate markets for different kinds of applications and a single ASP is unlikely to serve all markets equally well.

For instance, there are applications geared toward big businesses and others aimed at small businesses. Large companies typically require much more elaborate functions and the ability to effectively manage tremendous amounts of data—and have deep pockets to pay for it all. Many large corporations could afford to go it alone if they had to, but choose ASPs for the sake of long-term efficiency and cost savings. Small businesses, by contrast, tend to have simpler needs and more limited means. They possibly don't possess or can't afford the expertise needed to effectively manage a slew of different applications, and would be satisfied to get reliable access to a few good programs without many bells and whistles.

Thus not all ASPs offer the same applications or levels of service. They likewise differ in the kinds of bundled services they offer, such as connectivity, maintenance, consulting, customized programming, Web site hosting, and the like. ASPs that concentrate on applications hosting are often termed "pure-play" ASPs because subscription applications are their primary line of business.

A similar breed of outsourcing services is known as application maintenance outsourcing providers or application hosts. These firms differ from the common definition of an ASP in that the customer still purchases an ordinary software license from a software vendor, only the application host takes responsibility for running the software and providing remote access. In essence, the application maintenance provider acts as a manager of the client's own software, which is typically run on the provider's hardware.

Still, market segmentation by ASPs remains somewhat blurred as providers get a feel for what market needs are out there and how they can profitably meet those needs. Clearly, there are already some ASPs directed solely at small businesses only or larger organizations, and the process of specialization is likely to accelerate once the most capable ASPs begin building a meaningful presence in the market.

BACKGROUND AND DEVELOPMENT

As they're understood today, ASPs are of very recent vintage, dating only to 1998 or so. Many of the underlying principles and practices, however, are firmly rooted in high-end computer sales and service conventions set forth as early as the 1950s and 1960s.

Before 1969, when a bit of trust-busting by the U.S. Justice Department forced IBM Corp. to uncouple its software and hardware distribution, software acquisition was generally tied to the purchase or rental of hardware. Since computers in those days were phenomenally expensive by today's standards, combined software and hardware rental was a regular occurrence in the business world. And because computers were such large investments and so few people were familiar with them, high-end systems tended to come with a great deal of support and ongoing service that later began to be scaled back and billed separately.

System manufacturers and software writers such as IBM weren't the only ones involved in high-end computer support. A cadre of service providers, including Electronic Data Systems Corp. (EDS) and Remington Rand (maker of the pathbreaking UNIVAC computers and forebear to present-day Unisys Corp.), became involved in outsourced data processing and computer facilities management.

TIME-SHARING SERVICES THRIVE

Remote data-center and application hosting flourished in the 1970s as a bevy of service providers made inroads into the market by offering so-called computer time-sharing services. Under these arrangements, customers accessed databases and software applications maintained by the time-sharing company through a network connection (often a dial-up connection). The end user typically did so via a "dumb terminal," one that had no processing or storage capacity of its own. This meant that users often could only view information on their screen, but not print it or store it locally. What's more, the software interfaces were universally text-based and nongraphical.

"Time-sharing" was then a general computing term for multiuser systems, and in this case carried the special significance that different customers were sharing access to the same computer—often being billed for the amount of time they used it. Soon, the phrase also carried the negative connotation that users had to wait their turn at using the remote system, as they didn't always possess 24-hour access to the remote computers.

While such limitations are apparent in hindsight, they didn't stop time-sharing from becoming a fast-growing, multibillion-dollar enterprise during the 1970s and early 1980s. Some of the era's big names included Tymshare, EDS, General Electric Information Services, Comshare, and Automatic Data Processing. They didn't all fare so well by the mid-1980s, but their vision was strikingly similar to that of present-day ASPs—an economical, scalable alternative to owning software and hardware.

PC REVOLUTION, SOFTWARE LICENSING OVERSHADOW TIME-SHARING

As companies began adopting personal computers (PCs) wholesale in the 1980s, interest in time-sharing waned. Personal computers were seen as relatively inexpensive and surprisingly powerful tools that some believed would curtail the need for high-end multiuser systems in general. Although that prediction didn't pan out, companies focused on developing in-house IT infrastructure using PCs. Many chafed at the lack of control in time-sharing arrangements and yearned for the independence and ease of use PCs seemed to promise. Coupled with time-sharing firms' poor marketing and seemingly stagnant offerings, time-sharing was relegated to an increasingly obscure and ridiculed niche by the late 1980s.

With PCs, the software paradigm was almost entirely license-driven from the get-go. This occurred in part because PCs relied more heavily on packaged software and third-party software than had larger systems. Moreover, a different breed of software developers—Microsoft, for one—began catering to the PC market and their dominant mode of distribution was licensing.

Since PCs were considered relatively small-ticket items (at least on an individual basis) and were always located on premises, companies focused on acquiring legions of PCs for their employees and, as a consequence, outfitting each machine with the requisite operating systems, spreadsheets, word processors, and so on. The licenses, and later, support needs, began racking up. As well, PC networks quickly came into vogue, creating demand for client/server and networking software, which was also primarily licensed and run on internal servers.

INTERNET AND THIN-CLIENT COMPUTING OPEN NEW POSSIBILITIES

Commercialization of the Internet in the mid- and late 1990s provided an opportunity to revisit outsourcing software and hardware. The Internet provided nearly universal connectivity across far-flung locations. Moreover, its primary mode of access—Web browsers—enabled the same content and functions on a Web site to be shared on disparate computers without installing or maintaining any software locally aside from the browser. Growing antipathy toward aggressive software publishers, especially Microsoft, which by the late 1990s had become the world's biggest software company, also fueled interest in alternatives to software licensing.

At the same time, larger companies lamented the expense and complexity of maintaining the sprawling PC networks they had assembled. Upgrading software was commonly a major ordeal, and troubleshooting PC and network problems consumed corporate IT staff hours. Some dissatisfaction with distributed computing was channeled toward so-called network computers (NCs) and NetPCs, bare-bones network-centric workstations that run centralized applications off a network server. NCs and similar devices were part of a broader thin-client movement, where full-featured PCs running their own space-hungry applications are known as "fat clients." (Web browsers are considered thin clients in the software realm.)

The ultimate extension of thin-client computing, in fact, was the adoption of updated versions of the once-derided dumb terminal. Late-1990s terminal systems, such as Windows-based terminals, were a far cry from the brooding monochrome text screens of yesteryear, however. They supported graphical interfaces, Web browsing, local printing, point-and-click operations, and in large part provided the look and feel of a PC—and at a fraction of the cost.

While thin-client hardware was making its revival, a complementary and much bigger movement began to unfold on the software side. As Web programming grew more robust and stable, various parties began developing software applications that could be accessed through browsers. Corporate intranets put common internal information and functions—employee information, message boards, operating data—within reach of any Web browser. Extranets did the same for sharing information and data with suppliers and customers.

ASPs Emerge

With electronic commerce (e-commerce) on a steep rise, it was just a short leap to online application hosting and subscription services being conducted over the Web. The first companies dedicated to serving up applications over the Web (and browser-friendly private networks) sprang up in 1998 with the formation of leading pure-play ASPs such as USinternetworking, Inc. and Corio, Inc. These companies marketed themselves as solutions to the hassles of licensing software and maintaining it on unwieldy and resource-sapping internal PC networks. Although sales were not immediately off the board—USinternetworking generated less than $5 million in revenue in 1998—nascent ASPs met with strong interest and even stronger growth prospects in future years. Venture capitalists poured millions into ASP start-ups, and a few of the larger ones began going public in 1999.

The year 1999 proved a watershed for the industry, with a huge influx of new investors, competitors, and customers. In addition to service providers focused solely on application hosting, a large number of IT service and consulting firms and Internet access companies began touting themselves as ASPs. Software publishers such as Oracle Corp. and Sun Microsystems, Inc. also became outspoken proponents of Web-enabled software rental. The industry received extensive coverage in the business and technology press, and by the end of the year even Microsoft, which had publicly criticized the ASP model, began to warm up to the idea of letting its titles be rented online.

CURRENT CONDITIONS

While ASPs made immeasurable gains in public awareness during 1999, the market for online application hosting remained subdued in dollar terms, as many services were just coming online that year. Worldwide ASP revenues in 2000 approached $2 billion, according to research by International Data Corp., but were expected to grow at a furious 90 percent rate per year well into the early 2000s. Other organizations estimated that the market will be worth significantly more than that.

Market research suggests, not surprisingly, that the ASP concept is most appealing to users who need enterprise-level software and e-commerce capabilities. A survey by the Information Technology Association of America (ITAA) found that just over half of business respondents who weren't currently using an ASP said their companies were interested in obtaining e-commerce applications through an ASP. Slightly fewer respondents would seek a customer relationship management application—a trendy new class of software aimed at improving customer handling and focus at medium and large companies—from an ASP. Other popular types of software sought from ASPs, based on the ITAA survey, included applications for accounting and financial, human resources, and e-mail.

Other research suggested that online collaboration tools—such as those for e-mail, document sharing, and online meetings—are the online applications actually being adopted most rapidly. This is likely the case because such programs are easier to implement and tend to be cheaper—even free—compared to high-end applications.

Meanwhile, debates over ASP pricing continue. While most of the mainstream vendors (and customers) are committed to flat monthly subscription fees, some providers caution that flat-rate pricing may not be cost-effective for ASPs in the long run. They would rather see customers billed on a per-use basis, which some argue is also a fairer deal for light users.

As customers test-drove the new technology and began to demand more immediate return on their ASP investments than have so far been realized, ominous rumblings threatened the industry. Analysts anticipated that most of today's ASPs wouldn't survive long enough to enjoy the windfall expected in the early 2000s. The Gartner Group predicted that fully 60 percent of existing ASPs would collapse by the end of 2001. This pending shakeout would result from consolidation, scarcity of venture capital, bankruptcy, and market competition.

INDUSTRY LEADERS

A market report in 2000 by Internet Research Group (IRG) ranked USinternetworking, Inc. (USi) the largest U.S. ASP based on market share. According to IRG, USi held a dominant 36 percent of the nascent market by value of active contracts. In 1999 the publicly traded company posted about $35.5 million in revenue, with slightly more than half coming from its managed application subscriptions. The rest came from general IT services. Software available from USi included packages from Ariba, BroadVision, Lawson, Microsoft, Oracle, PeopleSoft, and Siebel. With applications ranging from human resources and finance to professional services management, USi's target market is mid-market companies with revenues of $50 million to $1 billion.

Breakaway Solutions, Inc. was ranked by IRG as the second-leading ASP in the United States. Claiming 16 percent of the market, Breakaway was founded in the early 1990s as a systems integrator and IT consulting firm. As a result, it has considerable experience developing custom solutions for businesses, and its services tend to be wider yet more customer-specific than those of dedicated application hosts. A publicly held company, Breakaway concentrates on e-commerce and enterprise applications and services. It took in $25.4 million in 1999.

At 9 percent of active ASP contracts, Corio, Inc. was tied for third with Oracle Corp. in IRG's market-share study. Corio hosts enterprise software packages such as those of SAP and PeopleSoft, as well as packages for internal process automation and business analysis. As a pure-play application service, Corio enjoys better name recognition than many of its competitors. The company, which has filed for an initial

SOFTWARE APPLICATIONS DRAWING THE MOST INTEREST FROM POTENTIAL ASP CUSTOMERS

Application	Percent
E-commerce	51.2
Customer relationship management	49.3
Accounting/financial	42.3
Human resources	33.8
E-mail	32.7
Office productivity	29.9
Enterprise resource planning	27.4

Source: Figures based on a survey of businesses by the Information Technology Association of America, 2000.

public offering of its stock, recorded just $5.8 million in sales during 1999, including only three-quarters of a million dollars in actual application hosting revenues.

Another notable competitor is FutureLink Corp. Established through a series of mergers and acquisitions beginning in 1998, the company has its roots as a systems integrator for implementing Citrix terminal and thin-client hosting systems for companies both large and small. In 1999 FutureLink began refashioning itself as an ASP, finding that setting up internal terminal systems for delivering packaged software was closely related to delivering such applications independently over the Web. It snatched up an executive from USinternetworking and acquired several other companies that were well positioned to enter the ASP market. The company's first hosted applications included such popular desktop suites as Microsoft Office and Corel WordPerfect, as well as low-end functional suites for accounting, customer relationship management, and manufacturing management. FutureLink markets its ASP solutions primarily to small businesses with fewer than 200 employees. In 1999 it posted $13.6 million in sales, but only a small portion came from application hosting.

FURTHER READING

Cherry Tree & Co. *Application Service Providers: Spotlight Report.* Edina, MN: Cherry Tree & Co., 1999.

Cope, James. "Definition for ASPs Emerging." *Computerworld,* 24 April 2000.

Gerwig, Kate. "Pending Payout." *tele.com,* 2 October 2000.

Information Technology Association of America. *The ITAA ASP Customer Demand Survey.* Arlington, VA: Information Technology Association of America, 2000.

Kara, Dan. "Software as Service." *Software Magazine,* December 1999.

Ladley, Eric. "What Will ASPs Grow up to Be?" *ISP Business News,* 29 May 2000.

Legg Mason Wood Walker, Inc. "Application Hosting Market." *Equity Research: Industry Update,* 30 December 1999.

Maselli, Jennifer. "ASPs Gain Ground." *InformationWeek,* 9 October 2000.

Menezes, Joaquim. "ASPs Disrupting IT World: Study." *Computing Canada,* 3 December 1999.

Soat, John. "IT Confidential." *InformationWeek,* 25 September 2000.

"Technique: ASPs Struggle to Make a Profit." *Computing,* 12 October 2000.

BIOMETRICS

Imagine a world in which you didn't have to remember multiple computer passwords and IDs, didn't have to carry car keys, credit cards, and automated teller machine (ATM) cards, and didn't have to worry about the security of electronic commerce (e-commerce) transactions. Such a streamlined world is closer than you think, according to spokespeople in the emerging biometrics industry. Biometrics measures physical characteristics unique to each human being—such as fingerprints, retinal and iris patterns, facial structure, even vocal inflections and the rhythms of an individual's signature and typing strokes. These measurements are then stored in a computer database and used in security applications to recognize or verify that person's identity.

Once relegated to the realm of comic books, science-fiction films, and Orwellian predictions of oppressive governmental surveillance of civilian populations, biometrics systems have been used for some time by sectors such as law enforcement, defense installations, and nuclear facilities because of the extremely high level of security they demand. But the rapid proliferation of electronic record keeping, ATM banking, e-commerce, and widespread air travel has created new demands for increased security in many venues of ordinary life. Producers of biometric devices are rushing to meet those needs, and also to provide identification systems that monitor those entering college dormitories, seeking driver's licenses, claiming welfare payments, or trying to immigrate.

But such convenience and security come attached with serious ethical and legal questions concerning individual privacy. Fears of an all-out governmental scheme to map citizens' identities down to the last gene strand may be overblown, but they do point out the need for policy guidelines and regulations about exactly what information can be measured and stored about whom and by whom. The extent to which both government and business may peer into the identities of ordinary individuals is a question that industry and government have finally started to fully address.

Decreasing costs and increasing technical sophistication of products mean that biometrics is gradually penetrating many kinds of transactions, especially to prevent credit-card fraud and to simplify authorized access to computer information networks. In 1999, however, governmental applications remained the predominate market for biometrics. The International Biometrics Industry Association (IBIA) estimated that sales of biometric hardware would jump from $100 million in 2000 to $600 million in 2006. The New York-based consulting firm International Biometric Group was more optimistic, predicting sales of $600 million as early as 2003.

ORGANIZATION AND STRUCTURE

VERIFICATION AND IDENTIFICATION

Biometric devices record and store a template of unique biological or behavioral features. That template is later matched against features obtained from an individual for purposes of verification or identification. In the former case, a person uses two forms of input (for example, a personal identification number, or PIN, and a biometric), and a computer verifies whether the data match. In the latter, a person provides a biometric (such as a picture taken at a border crossing), and a computer uses that data to identify the person.

Most biometrics systems can only verify. Identification systems have to be more powerful because they don't involve cues from PINs or access cards. The computer has to search its entire database and compare biometric data for all its enrolled users—a time-consuming enterprise—until a match is made or the data is rejected as unidentified.

Biometric systems often include safeguards to ensure that a live person is the source of the data. A fingerprint system, for example, may require the detection of body heat before it will validate a fingerprint. Similarly, a voice-recognition system may look for air pressure to prevent the use of a tape recording.

TYPES OF BIOMETRICS

Fingerprints. With as many as 60 variations to analyze and compare, fingerprints are the most widely used biometric in forensic and government databases. The trend is toward compiling databases into national, statewide, and regional networks. Technology is becoming available to allow sharing of fingerprint data from dissimilar systems. The Federal Bureau of Investigation (FBI) maintains the integrated Automated Fingerprint Identification System; with 630 million images, it's the world's largest fingerprint database. Biometric devices may measure prints, dimensions, patterns, or topography of fingers, thumbs, or palms. At one time fingers were inked and pressed on paper to create a print, but by the late 1990s fingerprint scanners, such as those used by the California Department of Motor Vehicles, required no ink. With a mere touch of a glass plate or silicon chip, details of one's print are recorded and stored in an electronic database. Scanners can be integrated into keyboards, notebooks, and mice, such as American Biometric's BioMouse.

Fingerprinting is gaining popularity. Many banks use thumbprints to identify customers. Toronto-based Mytec Technologies Inc. developed a fingerprint scanner used by the Royal Canadian Mounted Police to identify individuals and by the Louvre museum in Paris to control access to secured areas. Fingerprint readers at an Amsterdam airport let frequent flyers avoid long lines at passport control. In addition, many state governments in the United States use fingerprint data to verify eligibility for welfare. The city of Oceanside, California, purchased 2,400 finger scanners and BioLogon software from Identix, Inc. to evade the costs and hassles of having to change forgotten municipal-employee passwords; the city often received as many as 75 password-change requests per day before the switch to biometrics. The analyst firms the Gartner Group and Forrester reported that password management can cost an organization an average of $200 per year per user.

Hand geometry. To measure hand geometry, two infrared photos of a person's hand—one shot from above, one from the side—record more than 90 measurements such as length, width, thickness, surface area, finger shape, and joint positions. First developed for nuclear power plants, hand scanners were used in prisons, universities, airports, and hospitals in the late 1990s. Many manufacturing and construction sites rely on hand scanners to provide a biometric "time card" to verify attendance. (Nicks and dirt do not significantly alter readings.)

National research labs were among the first users of Recognition Systems Inc.'s ID3D HandKey Biometric System. Industry has followed suit, however. For example, HandKey identifies workers at L.L. Bean, parents at a day-care center run by Lotus Development Corp., and people trying to get free food at the University of Georgia's cafeteria. In addition, HandKey controlled the access of more than 65,000 athletes, trainers, and support staff to the Olympic Village in Atlanta, Georgia. A similar technology measuring finger geometry grants access to season pass holders at some Walt Disney facilities. Hand scanners also monitor employee attendance and punctuality. Recognition System's Handpunch 4000 also permits employees who "punch" in to retrieve messages and to review their work schedules.

Facial recognition. Individual face patterns are unique, even between identical twins. While some systems evaluate shadow patterns on a face illuminated in a specific way, others use an infrared camera to record multiple heat patterns (thermal images) at points around the cheekbones and eyes. Face recognition is growing in popularity because the hardware is inexpensive: manufacturers are already building camera lenses into computer monitors to accommodate videoconferencing. TrueFace, a system from Miros, Inc. of Wellesley, Massachusetts, compares images obtained from a security camera with stored images of preauthorized individuals. Facial scanners are sometimes considered less intrusive than retinal scanners and less demeaning than fingerprinting.

In another venture, the company has teamed with Computer Associates International to store images in a database, Jasmine. The partnership enables users to search a large database for a live-image match. Applications include identification of missing children and terrorists, as well as registering employees' time and attendance. A Miros system also secures the Pentagon's computer network. A neighborhood in East

London, U.K., coupled FaceIt software with 144 surveillance cameras positioned throughout town to monitor the likenesses of known criminals contained in their visual database. Casinos also stand to benefit from remote facial scanners to compare the facial scans of suspicious individuals against those of known grifters stored in the database.

Eye scans. Retina scanners flash an infrared light into the eye and examine the distinct pattern of blood vessels behind the retina. Retinal-scanning data occupies less memory space in a computer than does fingerprinting data, so it could be useful in decreasing the time necessary to search the large databases used for identification. Retina scanning, however, is perceived as intrusive by some. When military pilots were first subjected to retinal scans, they refused them, thinking the scans might impair their visual acuity (despite the fact that no evidence indicated this would happen). Both the iris and retina contain more identification points than a fingerprint. At distances up to 12 inches, for instance, iris scans can measure 400 unique characteristics, such as freckles, contraction furrows, rings, and darkened areas, which remain stable from infancy. Even identical twins do not have the same features. Iris scans convert the distinct details of the colored part of the eye into a biological "bar code" that acts as a unique identifier. Positive identification can be made through glasses, contact lenses, and most sunglasses.

Iris scanning debuted at the 1998 Winter Olympics in Nagano, Japan, when security officials required biathletes to undergo scans to check out their rifles. The iris also can be scanned without the knowledge of the subject, which could be useful in applications such as airport security and terrorist detection. Sensar, Inc. licensed the camera technology from Sarnoff Corp. in Princeton, New Jersey, which originally designed it for taking ground surveillance photos from high-flying military helicopters. According to Sensar, the matching probability of their iris scanning process is greater than that of DNA technology. In fact, they continue, iris identification is the only form of personal electronic identification that has never granted a false acceptance.

Spring Technologies will support iris recognition programs at the Summer Olympics in Sydney, Australia; the Charlotte/Douglas International Airport, in North Carolina; and airlines in Europe, the United States, and Latin America. Other iris scan tests planned for 2000 included consumer authorization for individuals who initiated e-commerce purchases with debit cards.

Bank United of Houston was the first U.S. institution to test iris recognition. It installed iris-scanning ATMs in supermarket branches in Dallas, Fort Worth, and Houston. Consumer response was favorable, with 98 percent of the 130 users surveyed reporting a positive first experience.

Voice verification. Voices may sound similar, but no two are alike. The unique topography of a person's mouth, teeth, and vocal cords produces inimitable pitch, tone, cadence, and dynamics. Character, expression, and regional dialects also influence voice patterns. Voice systems are an obvious choice for phone-based applications; they are also suitable for use with personal computers (PCs). SAFlink Corp. offered voice-activated software, SafetyLatch, that scrambled files on command.

Signature dynamics. The speed and style with which a person signs his or her name is a unique behavioral biometric. Signature dynamics measure the pressure, angle of attack, and stroke characteristics with which a person writes. They have been used to verify identity for banking transactions, insurance forms, and electronic filing of tax returns. Chase Manhattan was the first bank to test this technology.

Keystroke dynamics. Individuals are unique in how they work a keyboard, and these differences can be exploited as a means of identification. WonderNet of Bnei Brak, Israel, developed PenFlow software, to be used with an electronic pen, that even compensated for variations in an individual's signature due to haste, mood, and available space for writing. The software tracks pen movements on a grid, rather than capturing a visual image of the signature. Those measurements are then encrypted into a signature "formula" that even reflects the distance of the nib above the writing surface between strokes.

Net Nanny of Bellevue, Washington, planned to introduce Biopassword LogOn for Windows NT, which uses algorithms to measure the keystrokes of its user. The method, intended to prevent employees from sharing passwords, would be the only U.S. commercial technology on the market.

Future identifiers may include measurements of lip and ear shape, knuckle creases, wrist veins, and even vibrations from major body organs. IBM's Blue Eyes was researching "attentive user interfaces," such as gaze tracking. This technology involves a computer camera, mounted to a display, that follows the user's iris movements and calls up information from sites when the eye focuses on the monitory, without the need to click a hyperlink.

APPLICATIONS

Biometric devices were first developed to keep unauthorized persons out of military installations and nuclear power plants. The FBI's Automated Fingerprint Identification System (AFIS) came next, drawing upon technologies developed by defense industries. In 1968 a Wall Street brokerage became the first financial institution to apply biometrics when it used fingerprints to open vaults that stored stock certificates. Biometrics currently plays a role in security and identification across industry lines.

Finance. Banks testing or using finger-based biometrics include Bank of America, Citicorp, Mellon Bank, Bankers Trust, and Chevy Chase Savings and Loan Association. Perdue Employees' Federal Credit Union in West Lafayette, Indiana, was the first U.S. bank to implement finger imaging to identify customers.

InnoVentry Corp.—a partnership of San Francisco's Wells Fargo and Cash America International of Texas—rolled out a new line of ATMs at Texas Kroger grocery stores. Dubbed rapid pay machines (RPMs), they scan users' faces to verify identity, thus eliminating the need for bank cards or PINs. About 300,000 users signed up for check-cashing privileges by submitting to a facial scan and by inputting personal information on a keypad at the kiosk. On subsequent visits, a new scan is compared to the stored image, customers enter their Social Security or driver's license number, and a credit authorization is done on the spot. The RPMs utilize Visionics' FaceIt and Miros' TrueFace biometric identification technology. InnoVentry planned to establish 5,000 RPMs in 30 cities across the United States by 2001. The technology was originally developed to restrict access at the Pentagon. Fees varied according to the type of financial transaction conducted. RPMs were also being used to reach out to the "unbanked"—roughly 40 million Americans who lack bank accounts or who rely on check-cashing businesses to cash their checks.

Biometrics and smart cards becoming more commonplace in PCs. Compaq, Hewlett-Packard, and IBM all offer such built-in security systems in their models; Microsoft Windows 2000 includes a smart-card version. Even palm-sized computers complete with smart-card slots, bar-code readers, and fingerprint reading terminals are on the market or under development by Compaq, NEC Technologies, and DataStrip.

Retail. Biometrics may even eliminate the need for cashiers and baggers at grocery stores. Utah-based International Automated Systems Inc. (IAS) announced a $35 million agreement with Pittsburgh-based Schematics Inc. to operate 10 U-Check cashierless supermarkets in the eastern United States. The stores are fully automated and rely on IAS's proprietary fingerprint identification technology. Consumers' fingerprint data and their debit or credit-card information are stored on a proprietary magnetic-stripe card. Upon verification of their fingerprint image when swiped through a payment terminal, the system assigns an ID number to the transaction information kept in a central database. Company officials claimed the system would eliminate cashier-induced losses, such as fraud, chargebacks, and duplicate postings.

E-commerce. E-commerce may provide the most amenable entry for wide biometrics penetration of American markets, in the form of swipeable smart cards encoded with digital signature technology to be used with card readers and the appropriate software when making online purchases. Though often preloaded with a monetary value, virtually any type of biometrics data can be stored on the card, allowing security systems to verify without storing the information in large databases. In addition to e-commerce, smart cards are useful in PC security and regulating medical prescriptions. Widely accepted throughout the rest of the world, they have received a lackluster welcome in the United States. The European Smart Card Industry Association reported that the United States accounted for only a fraction of the 1.4 billion smart card shipments in 1999. However, the U.S. market is ready to take off; according to a report by Frost & Sullivan, smart card shipments in the United States will leap from 14.4 million units in 1999 to 114.7 million units in 2006. Encryption and digital signature authorization safeguard the sensitive information embedded in the cards.

Cash Technologies Inc. of Los Angeles announced it would collaborate with MP3.com, Inc., a provider of digital music over the Internet, and Princeton, New Jersey-based Sensar, which makes iris recognition biometrics identification products. They will test online debit cards to purchase music through MP3.com's Web site, enabling online debit cards to buy products over the Internet using Cash Technology's EMMA transaction processing system, which chooses a network to route a transaction and uses a Sensar iris camera to identify a card user.

Other Applications. One of the most innovative applications of biometrics technology emerged in the wake of the tragic U.S. school shootings in the late 1990s. Responding to public calls for improved gun safety features, gun-maker Smith & Wesson announced in early 2000 its prototype "smart gun"—at least two years away from commercial development—that used a biometric verification system developed by Mytec to prevent anyone but an authorized user from firing the weapon. The prototype was equipped with a cartridge attachment that can be removed only when the user slides his or her fingerprint across a tiny, battery-powered optical scanner. The ammunition clip can then be inserted into the handgun and the gun can be fired.

Airports. Airport entryways in San Francisco, New York, and Toronto are equipped with HandKey hand-geometry readers for access control. Authorized personnel swipe access cards, then place their hands into entryway readers to gain access. In 1997 Malaysia's Langkawi Airport installed the first face-recognition technology to increase airport security. The system, by Visionics Corp. and TL Technology, matches a passenger's face with an image encoded in the boarding pass during check-in. Unisys developed iris-pattern scanners to permit frequent flyers to by-pass long airport lines. The International Civil Aviation Organization was assessing various biometric technologies that might be used to establish international airport standards.

Correctional institutions. Inmates in some prisons speak a password into a phone to verify their presence. Since the early 1990s, a federal Georgia prison used a hand-geometry biometric system to monitor staff and inmate movements. The first six months' use of fingerprint readers in the Pima County, Arizona, jail, exposed 300 inmates who had given false identities.

In Great Britain a partnership between the Advanced Fingerprint Recognition system (AFR), the world's largest of its kind, and several technology providers has brought live-scan fingerprinting at low cost to its prisoner handling centers. Processing nearly 83,000 sets of fingerprints exposed 3,800 prisoners as having given false identities. Upon release, former inmates can use a biometric system to report to their parole officers without actually meeting in person. At a prearranged time, the parolee goes to a kiosk similar to an ATM, enters an identification number, and is verified by a hand-geometry reader. The parolee receives messages from the parole officer on a display terminal. The kiosk system has a better attendance rate than personal meetings. If a parolee fails to appear for a check-in, an intense follow-up is initiated.

Colleges and universities. With hand templates encoded in photo identification cards, colleges and universities can better manage physical access for large student populations. At the University of Georgia, hand-geometry readers allow access to the student cafeteria. Since 1992, hand readers have controlled se-curity turnstiles at New York University dormitories. At the University of Montreal, students use a hand scanner to enter an athletic complex. Similar arrangements are in use at health clubs and day-care centers.

Government. The U.S. Government Services Administration (GSA) conducted a multiapplication smart-card pilot with 400 employees to determine the feasibility of rolling out smart cards to all federal government employees. The agency wanted to adopt a card to provide access to buildings and computers, and to contain biometric information to verify the card user's identity. Projects were scheduled to continue through 2001, after which other government groups could submit orders for specific smart-card needs, such as credit and debit applications. The government also considered adopting public key infrastructure technology to boost security capabilities. The U.S. Navy budgeted $20 million in 2000 and $27 million in 2001 for similar programs. It expected to save almost $1 million over five years by using smart cards. If government agencies adopted smart cards, it could generate up to $100 million in initial sales and more than $30 million per year to maintain the programs.

Pharmacies. Online pharmacy drugemporium .com, which offers online prescriptions and advice from pharmacists, became a test site in 1999 for BioNetrix Sciences Corp. of Vienna, Virginia. It tested BioNetrix's Authentication Suite, which features an open platform to manage such disparate authentication venues as passwords, tokens, fingerprints, and retinal scans. Since drugemporium.com operates in 26 states, it must meet diverse regulations governing authentication for doctors and pharmacists.

CURRENT CONDITIONS

Growth in the biometrics industry has been gradual. Market growth has been limited by high prices, performance problems, and poor user acceptance, though security applications provided a major market with steady growth. Many consumers associate fingerprint scanning with criminal law enforcement. Also, the scanning, comparison, and storage of unique biological traits makes some feel their privacy is being violated. Health care organizations adopted biometric security faster than any other industry. The International Biometric Group found that fingerscanning was the leading biometrics application, with a market share of 34 percent. Hand geometry followed at 26 percent, face-recognition systems captured 15 percent, retina-scanning and voice-verification equipment each received 11 percent.

Industry claims of accuracy may be overstated, since the controlled conditions under which most accuracy estimates were tested failed to accurately mimic the less optimal conditions of the real world. Biometrics have a harder time dealing with problems such as calloused fingertips, some sunglasses, or a head cold that might alter voice patterns. A recent study by International Biometric Group, backed by Visa, Chase Manhattan, and Citibank, analyzed eight finger-scanning and two face-scanning systems to see whether the accuracy claims made based on laboratory tests held up under real-world usage. The study concluded that results often varied significantly when the systems operated under unpredictable real-world variables; for example, bright lights directly above some finger scanners completely obliterated the finger images.

Several stumbling blocks obstructed rapid adoption of biometric technologies. More than 330 products, according to the 1999 biometrics survey conducted by the International Computer Security Association, were marketed by a diverse pool of vendors, generating concerns over standards, integration with existing systems and long-term support. The market, however, gave hints of consolidation as device vendors teamed up with software makers.

Several standards proposals were underway. Human Authentication Application Programming Interface (HA-API) provided an interface with various biometric technologies, but only under the Win32 platform. In March 2000, a consortium of vendors announced the adoption of the BioAPI standard, which provided an operating-system-independent standard and made the API biometric-independent. Microsoft, a member of the BioAPI Consortium, soon afterwards announced it would, with I/O Software, apply I/O's Biometric Application Programming Interface (BAPI) standard to biometrics operations within Windows. This development created more animosity within the industry, and it was unclear whether these two standards would be capable on interfacing, leading to fears that Microsoft's proprietary standards would hamper the industry-wide adoption of biometrics.

Prices of biometric devices are dropping. From 1990 to 1997, the cost of biometric devices dropped 70 percent, according to CardTech/SecurTech Inc., sponsors of an industry trade show. Identix's DirectFingerprint Reader 300 is based on a new chip from Motorola and combines a transparent folded optical reader that sits on top of the silicon chip. The scanner, bundled with Identix's proprietary Bio-Logon 2.0 software, can be purchased in bulk for about $20 per workstation, a five-fold decrease from the previous year's price. Costs are about one-third of what they were at the beginning of the 1990s. And research suggests that deliveries of biometric products increase as price declines; deliveries were expected to grow from 1,675 units in 1991 to 412,335 in 2001.

THE EFFECTS OF REGULATION
Laws dealing with welfare reform, immigration control, and identification of commercial drivers have played important roles in supporting the biometrics industry.

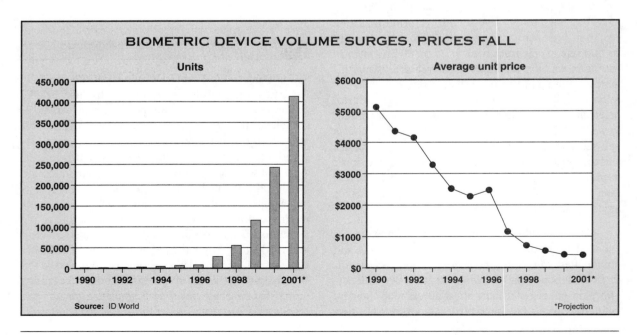

BIOMETRIC DEVICE VOLUME SURGES, PRICES FALL

Units

Average unit price

Source: ID World

*Projection

Welfare. In 1998 more than 20 states verified welfare eligibility with fingerprints. The state of Connecticut saved more than $9 million by using fingerprints to reduce welfare fraud.

Immigration. In the late 1990s, an open-skies agreement between the United States and Canada called for the increased use of biometrics. INSPASS, a large air-travel biometric application, helps speed frequent travelers through immigration lines. It is part of the Immigration and Naturalization Service's future automated screening for travelers (FAST) program. Travelers' passports, nationalities, and security details are verified, and a system encodes their hand-geometry templates into INSPASS cards, which are later used to verify authorization for entry into the host country. The system has processed more than 25,000 entries at major airports in New York, New Jersey, and Toronto. Immigration officials worldwide are now considering encoding biometrics into passports.

The Immigration and Naturalization Service (INS) awarded Digital Biometrics Inc. a contract for 276 TENPRINTER live-scan fingerprint systems valued at in excess of $8.8 million. The INS's IDENT border control program scans left and right index fingerprints and photographs of recidivist individuals and stores them in a database. Fingerprint and facial recognition readings taken of persons suspected of criminal activity are compared with the stored images. The system is designed to easily identify individuals accused of repeatedly crossing the border into the United States in violation of immigration laws.

Similar biometric surveillance methods were being adopted by foreign governments. In 2000, Israel's Ministry of Defense announced that it would employ a smart card and biometrics system to identify workers entering or leaving the country. About 200,000 cards would be distributed for use at 70 crossing areas. The contactless cards store the user's face and hand geometries in the microprocessor chip. Workers entering or leaving the country waive the card; their hands and faces are scanned for verification. The system is faster than magnetic stripe cards and boasts added security features. On Track Innovations provided the smart-card technology, Visionics Corp., of Jersey City, New Jersey, the facial recognition system, and Recognition System Inc., of Campbell, California, the hand-geometry readers. Pakistan was developing a comprehensive database that would link birth certificate, driver's license, and other civil registration information for its citizens. The British Ministry of Defense has the Communication Electronic Security Group to overview biometric considerations and Japan's Ministry of International

Trade and Industry sponsored a year-long study of biometrics.

GOVERNMENTAL REGULATION AND PRIVACY CONCERNS

Americans are renowned for their intense focus on protection of personal privacy, a trait less marked in some other parts of the globe. This national characteristic has hampered the biometrics industry's efforts to expand its presence in U.S. markets. The pressure to view increased biometric identification as an unwelcome intrusion even led the 15-nation European Union to take the lead in calling for international privacy standards with its Data Protection Directive. The U.S. government also appointed its first privacy advocate to coordinate development of federal policies aimed at e-commerce, databases, and information technology. Peter Swire, a professor of privacy law at Ohio State University, was named to the post and will be instrumental in drafting an Electronic Bill of Rights. Swire, the Chief Counselor for Privacy for the Office of Management and Budget (OMB), will serve under the OMB's Office of Information and Regulatory Affairs.

Biometrics industry advocates counter that biometric verification, since it circumvents such easily tampered-with items as passwords and physical credit cards or keys, works as a "privacy protection tool," rather than a privacy menace. But the industry will have to make some decisive statements to allay the fears of those who believe that increasing digitalization of personal data will lead to lost control over financial and medical records, and thus perhaps cost them jobs, credit, or health insurance. In response, the industry formed the International Biometrics Industry Association in 1998, to draft statements on ethics, security, and privacy that would help win skeptical members of the consuming public to its side. In May 1999 the group announced a four-pronged statement on privacy principles that it vowed would govern future industry developments.

Individual states also pursued regulatory action. In 1999 at least 12 different bills covering biometric privacy were under consideration in California alone, including one introduced by State Assemblywoman Liz Figueroa (D-Fremont) that would fine those who deliberately shared medical biometric data for commercial use $10,000 per violation. Several independent watchdog groups monitor industry conditions.

The Clinton administration earmarked $91 million in the fiscal 2001 budget to increased surveillance of computing-systems security. In addition, in June

2000, interest in biometric computer security was propelled by the signing by President Clinton of the Electronic Signatures in Global and National Commerce Act.

The industry itself began promoting self-regulation, to stave off more burdensome governmental legislation. In 1999 the BioAPI Consortium and the Human Authentication Application Programming Interface Working Group merged to supervise all biometric applications and programming interface efforts under one organization.

FURTHER READING

"ADC on the Shop Floor." *ADC News & Solutions,* 29 February 2000.

Beiser, Vince. "Casinos Fight Back with Tech." *Wired News,* 4 May 1999.

Bell, Bonnie. "Uncle Sam Wants YOU@el3to Use Smart Cards." *Card Technology,* November 1999.

"Biometric Keys to Networks, PCs Finally Come Alive." *Security,* 1 September 2000.

"Biometrics-Based Supermarket System Expanding." *Card Fax,* 4 April 2000.

"Biometrics, Smart Cards on the Rise." *Information Security,* June 2000.

Bowman, Eric. "Government ID: A Public Sector Biometric Test Ground." *ID World,* January 2000.

Burnell, John. "Hacking out a Niche." *Automatic I.D. News,* December 1999.

"Cash Technologies Biometric Debit Plans." *Card Fax,* 19 November 1999.

Curtin, Leah L., and Roy L. Simpson. "Biometrics, Technology and Nostradamus." *Health Management Technology,* February 2000.

Dussault, Raymond. "Support Tech: Cause and Effect." *Government Technology,* April 2000. Available from http://www.govtech.net/publications/crimetech/Apr00/CTEFingerprints.shtm.

Evangelista, Benny. "Your Body Is Your Password; Biometrics Lets Machines Recognize Specific Humans by Their Physical Traits." *San Francisco Chronicle,* 21 February 2000.

"An Evolving Biometrics Market." *ID World,* November 1999.

Gignac, Tamara. "Biometrics Waits for Thumbs-up from Customers." *Computer Dealer News,* 11 February 2000.

Gips, Michael. "The Name's the Game." *Security Management,* September 1999.

Guyette, James E. "Group Announces Privacy Principles for Biometrics Use." *Automatic I.D. News,* May 1999.

———. "ID Enigma: Are Biometrics a Threat to Privacy or the Key to Protecting It?" *Automatic I.D. News,* May 1999.

Hallenborg, John C. "The Identification Standards Movement." *ID World,* November 1999.

Hancock, Bill. "Fingerprint Biometrics Devices Just Not Catching on in the Real World." *Computers & Security,* 1 July 1999.

Harrison, Ann. "Online Pharmacy Tests Biometrics." *Computerworld,* 8 November 1999.

Hildreth, Elizabeth. "Sci-Fi Biometrics Turn up in the Here and Now." *Card Technology,* November 1999.

Hopkins, Richard. "An Introduction to Biometrics and Large Scale Civilian Identification." *International Review of Law, Computers & Technology,* December 1999.

Komando, Kim, Tobey Grumet, and Steve Ditlea. "Technology. The Komando Report: Computers." *Popular Mechanics,* July 1999.

Kriz, Heidi. "Boosting Biometric Privacy." *Wired News,* 30 March 1999.

Lee, Thomas. "They Aim to Join 'Smart-Gun' Market." *Seattle Times,* 28 January 2000.

Marks, Paul. "It's Gotta Be You." *New Scientist,* 26 February 2000.

McCullagh, Decian. "DNA Databases Go Too Far." *Wired News,* 26 April 1999.

McGarr, Michael S. "Tuning in Biometrics to Reduce E-commerce Risk." *Electronic Commerce World,* February 2000.

"The Measure of Man." *The Economist,* 9 September 2000.

Miles, Stuart. "If Your Face Fits You're In." *Times* (London), 18 October 1999.

Mitchell, Richard. "A United States Chip Card Initiative." *ID World,* November 1999.

Moody, Scott. "Biometrics Must Get Back to Basics." *Electronic Engineering Times,* 24 May 1999.

Moss, Brenda. "Biometrics, Software Propel Time & Attendance." *Security: For Buyers of Products, Systems & Services,* March 2000.

Nanavati, Samir. "The Marketing and Reality of Biometrics Don't Go Hand in Hand." *Automatic I.D. News,* May 1999.

Neeley, DeQuendre. "An Eye for Security." *Security Management,* March 2000.

Nicholson, Leslie. "Card Technology Could Speed up Air Travel." *Philadelphia Inquirer,* 1 March 2000.

O'Shea, Timothy M., and Mike Lee. "Biometric Authentication Management—Biometric Authentication Systems

Are Being Integrated into Desktop Systems." *Network Computing*, 27 December 1999.

Pankanti, Sharath, and Ruud M. Bolle. "Biometrics: The Future of Identification." *Computer*, February 2000.

Redman, Russell. "Wells Fargo in Venture to Roll out Biometrics-Based, Check-Cashing Kiosks." *Bank Systems & Technology*, November 1999.

Rosen, Jody Beth. "Making Passwords Passe." *Home Office Computing*, March, 2000.

Salamone, Salvatore. "Vendors Simplify Authentication Using Tokens and Biometrics." *Internetweek*, 7 June 1999.

Soto, Monica. "Keystrokes Tell Net Nanny Who's Typing." *Seattle Times*, 22 March 2000.

Stock, Helen. "Firm Uses Biometrics to Serve the Unbanked." *American Banker*, 1 October 1999.

Suydam, Margot. "Taking (Health) Care." *Information Security*, March 2000.

Taneja, Sunil. "Keep an Eye on Biometrics." *Chain Store Age*, July 1999.

Thieme, Michael. "Mapping Form to Function." *Information Security*, March 2000.

———. "Privacy Boon or Bane?" *Information Security*, March 2000.

Trembly, Ara C. "Who Goes There? Biometrics Knows." *National Underwriter/Property & Casualty Risk & Benefits*, 10 January 2000.

Wayman, James L. "Federal Biometric Technology Legislation." *Computer*, February 2000.

Webb, Julia. "Embedded Solutions Key in Secure Biometrics." *Electronic Engineering Times*, 2 August 1999.

Whitford, Marty. "DNA Shows the Way: Door-Lock Manufacturers Weigh Pros, Cons of Biometrics-Based Security Solutions." *Hotel & Motel Management*, 3 May 1999.

Young, Eric. "Smart ATMs Can Identify Your Face." *Minneapolis Star Tribune*, 24 October 1999.

CALL CENTERS

The experience is familiar to most: you call a company to inquire about your latest bill, and you are routed through a series of push-button options before you speak with a customer-service representative with the inside scoop on your account. This represents call centers in action. For more and more companies, call centers were positioned as the hub of all customer-service operations, and the list of services provided via call centers was expanding rapidly by 2000. Used by banks, health-care operations, telemarketers, retailers, catalog companies, industrial firms, and a host of other industries, call centers were, by the end of the 20th century, the most popular medium of contact between companies and customers. Roughly 5 percent of the GDP's transactions in the United States are routed through call centers.

ORGANIZATION AND STRUCTURE

Call centers typically are highly automated telephone systems that customers call with a service or billing question, purchase request, or some other inquiry, depending on the nature of the company. Conversely, many firms also use their call centers to place calls to customers, including those with regular accounts and those targeted as potential new business. In a way, call centers are indicative of the never-ending race to squeeze costs and boost the volume of business. More broadly, however, call centers served as a central buffer between the company and the public, filtering questions and requests so as to free up other workers to concentrate on their particular areas.

Most indicators for measuring call-center performance included the amount of time the average call took up, the number of calls each agent handled, and so on. In this way, the emphasis tended to rely far more on quantity than on quality. The logic goes that by squeezing the average time per call and expanding the number of calls per agent, the company will reap higher benefits from its call center. Many analysts were seriously challenging that logic, however, noting that it betrays an outlook on call centers from a cost-centered, rather than revenue-centered, perspective. Instead, such critics contended that the call center could be more fruitfully utilized as a creative new business strategy that aimed to generate increased revenue through enhanced quality and expansion of available services, not to mention promoting new sales.

Indeed, a growing number of companies were beginning to catch on to that possibility. About one-third of call centers surveyed by Ernst & Young in 1999 planned to devote more resources to gearing their call centers toward customer access and sales opportunities rather than simply handling customer-service inquiries.

BACKGROUND AND DEVELOPMENT

The call center as a major component of the U.S. business environment had its genesis in the mid- and late 1980s during the massive downsizing and corporate restructuring trends. In part, call centers offered firms undergoing such transformation a cost-effective way to process a greater number of customer services and requests, since a large number of employees could be accommodated in a small office space, thus cutting down on overhead. As call centers moved ever closer to the mainstream, customers came to expect the quick access and convenience they offered, though call centers certainly generated their share of complaints related to the long periods customers spent on hold, a reputation that centers were far from shaking off by 2000.

CURRENT CONDITIONS

By the late 1990s the call-center market was growing about 40 percent each year, though within that surging growth, assessments were mixed. Ernst & Young LLP conducted a survey in 1999 comparing call centers by industries, and found, unsurprisingly, that banking companies and health-care operations housed the most sophisticated and successful call centers. The varying nature of industries, however, ensured that call centers were more easily integrated into some industries than into others. For example, the study found that utilities were among the least successful industries in the application of call centers. In large part, this was due to the large amount of information, such as service schedules and payment histories, that must be verified and processed before utilities customers could be provided with information.

The American Bankers Association conducted a study in 2000 of call centers in the banking industry, which found that nearly a quarter of all U.S. banks considered their call centers to be top of the line. A mere 14 percent of those banks surveyed, however, considered the call center as a source of profit in itself, and, perhaps as a result, a majority of banks failed to allocate the resources necessary to adequately train call-center managers or keep tabs on customer satisfaction with call centers.

Banking call centers were relied upon to handle a range of products and services, including general account information and maintenance, mortgages, credit cards, and home equity lines of credit. One of the banking industry's most pressing problems with call centers is that they are famously troublesome to integrate into the strict data-handling environments that banks rely on. Moreover, call centers were generally viewed by banks as extra to or outside of their normal operations, and as a result few were reaping the types of benefits proponents claimed are waiting to be realized.

The managed health-care industry was another hotbed for call centers. One of the central features of demand management among health maintenance organizations (HMOs) was the nurse call center, versions of which were used by more than half of all HMOs to reduce costs and boost efficiency. Nurse call centers provide customers with 24-hour access to health professionals. Many industry analysts, however, felt that nurse call centers, too, fell short of their potential, even though customers reported satisfaction rates exceeding 90 percent, and despite the fact that HMOs typically figured that call centers drastically reduced both emergency-room and physician visits. Critics held that HMOs had done too little to promote nurse call centers to make them a regular recipient of patient requests. Most patients still immediately call a hospital or physician directly, and were not used to calling up a nurse call center to receive answers to their medical questions. In addition to the time this takes up for the physicians, it amounts to a waste of the HMOs' call-center investments, all of which eats into the providers' profits. Moreover, nurse call centers are far more heavily focused on dispensing advice about minor illnesses and symptoms than about more serious medical problems. Still, the HMO industry remained confident in the utility of call centers, noting that some 30-40 percent of all physician visits were in fact unnecessary, and positioning call centers as a potential remedy for that problem.

Some of the disappointment in call centers, however, seemingly had as much to do with the method of valuation as the quality of the service itself. For instance, the majority of banks quantified the value of their call centers on a cost-per-minute basis, whereby the cost of the service was measured against the total duration of the average call. Such measurements, however, failed to take into account the added revenue afforded by increased customer satisfaction. And, proponents noted, once corporations begin to more aggressively conceptualize call centers as an untapped revenue source rather than as a necessary service feature, the typical valuation methods currently employed will become but a pale reflection of the centers' actual worth.

WORK FORCE

An estimated 5 million workers are directly employed as call center agents. The American Bankers Association survey of banks with call centers revealed that call-center managers listed employee hiring, retention, and training as their three most pressing concerns. In part, this was attributed to the demographic from which most call-center employees were drawn. The bulk of the industry's employees were between the ages of 25 and 34, and thus less settled on their careers. Call center agents generally earn between $8 and $15 an hour. As call centers increasingly moved to the front lines of companies' relations with customers, however, demand increased for high-caliber, professional call-center personnel.

A survey conducted by Fantus Consulting, a division of Deloitte & Touche LLP, revealed that in 1997 a total of 61,000 new call-center jobs opened up in North America, concentrated mostly in markets that already had a significant call-center presence over the previous decade, such as Florida, Missouri, Virginia, and Texas.

AMERICA AND THE WORLD

Many U.S. firms looked to European markets to establish their call-center operations. Frost & Sullivan predicts that the number of European call centers with at least 11 agents will soar from 12,750 in 1999 to nearly 28,300 in 2006, and that the portion of those centers that are Web-enabled will skyrocket from 1 percent to 80 percent. Largely due to favorable tax conditions, Holland contained the highest concentration of call centers in Europe. Major U.S. firms such as Adobe, Apple, Cisco Systems, Hewlett-Packard, IBM, Microsoft, and many others have established major call centers in Holland. Other factors contributing to Holland's strong presence in the international call-center market were its advanced telecommunications infrastructure and a relatively strong labor pool for such operations. The United Kingdom was also experiencing rapid growth in its call-center market. One study estimated that by 2002 nearly 2 percent of the United Kingdom's entire work force would be employed in call centers.

RESEARCH AND TECHNOLOGY

Due to the relative difficulty of developing call centers and integrating them with a company's existing operations, a bevy of software packages have hit the market tailored to the implementation of call centers. Indicative of the expected growing popularity of call centers, the London research firm Ovum Inc. expected the world market for call-center software to leap from $580 million in 1998 to $3.1 billion by 2003.

Meanwhile, moves to integrate the Internet with the call center were in full swing. Though only a novelty just a few short years ago, Web-enabled call centers were increasingly popular, particularly in the financial services industries. As more and more banking and other financial transactions were performed over the Web, such firms sought ways to integrate their call centers with the burgeoning online financial market, creating an all-in-one Internet stop to handle all of a client's needs. Though e-mail was the most common form of integration, a number of firms offered manual hot links, which linked Web sites to call centers via telephone connections through the user's computer. Multimedia personal computers allowed users to speak with customer representatives and interact with them as in a phone conversation, but with the added option of exchanging information right over the Web.

Obviously, though, this type of service required an enormous amount of bandwidth, and was thus out of reach to most people in 2000. Less sophisticated Web-enabled call centers featured text-chat capabilities, in which customers interact with agents via live e-mail. Canada's ING Group banking corporation used the call center/Internet combination to eliminate banking branches altogether, thereby saving money in overhead. All their transactions were conducted via telephone, Internet, or mail through the ING Direct Investment Savings Account.

New customer-relationship management (CRM) software was rolled out in the late 1990s for implementation in call-center systems. Lucent Technologies Inc. introduced the CRM Central 2000 to automate the exchange of customer information between a system's computers. Nuance Communications, meanwhile, launched its Customer Support Suite and Order Management Suite, which utilized CRM techniques in a voice recognition program.

Lucent Technologies also was a leader in the development of computer telephony integration (CTI), which integrated a company's phone system into its customer database. Thus, if a customer places a call into the call center, the CTI device instructs the system to bring up that customer's records so that the representative is ready with that customer's information when the call is received.

Related technologies include auto dialers and predictive dialers. Auto dialers simply relieve the representative of having to actually dial the phone, saving valuable seconds that add up to hours after a few hundred calls. Predictive dialers anticipate the representative's next call; thus, when the agent hangs up with one customer, the predictive dialer automatically moves to the next person on the list, and the call can be waiting for the representative as soon as the first call is completed.

FURTHER READING

Ash, Nigel. "Dutch Bank on Brains." *Corporate Location,* January/February 1999.

"Bank Call Centers Need Strong Infrastructure." *Communications News,* March 2000.

"Bank-ING on the Internet." *Fairfield County Business Journal,* 18 October 1999.

Bielski, Lauren. "Get These Four Right—and Run a Better Call Center." *ABA Banking Journal,* September 1999.

"Call Centers Flock to Common Ground." *Facilities Design & Management,* December 1998.

Emrich. "Technology Will Keep Telemarketers on Phone." *Grand Rapids Business Journal,* 29 November 1999.

Jarvis, Steve. "Call Centers Raise Bar on Hiring Criteria." *Marketing Newsl,* 11 September 2000.

Lynch, Wendy D., and James H. Otis. "Stop! In the Name of the Bottom Line." *Managed Healthcare,* March 2000.

Power, Carol. "Banks Top Retailers in 6 of 7 Call Center Categories." *American Banker,* 24 August 1999.

Sinderman, Martin. "Call Centers Offer Multiple Uses and Multiple Problems." *National Real Estate Investor,* 15 September 1998.

Sweat, Jeff, and Brian Riggs. "Call Centers Gain Integrated CRM." *Internetweek,* 6 September 2000.

Tehrani, Nadji. "Here We Go Again. . .Wall Street Is Focused on CRM and Call Centers." *C@ll Center Solutions,* March 2000.

"Utility Call Centers Lag behind Other Industries." *Electric Light & Power,* August 1999.

"Virtual Call Centers Predicted to Become the Norm Within Three Years." *Network News,* 13 September 2000.

Walmsley, Mike. "All Together Now." *Telephony,* 18 September 1999.

Weitzman, Jennifer. "Study: Cost Focus Makes Call Centers Underachievers." *American Banker,* 26 January 2000.

Wineberg, Jonathan. "Well Connected." *Credit Union Management,* April 1999.

CHARTER SCHOOLS

While charter schools enjoyed robust growth in enrollments throughout the late 1990s, the future of the industry was up in the air. The topic generates heated arguments from proponents and critics alike, from the grassroots level to the halls of Congress. In the short term, their growth was all but certain, as more states adopt legislation to grant charters to organizations wishing to establish an educational alternative. But charter schools' ability to deliver superior educational results and to spur competitive innovation among mainstream public schools remains undetermined. Assessments of the industry to date have been highly mixed.

Though publicly funded, charter schools are free from many of the restrictions that govern other public schools. In exchange for such autonomy, a charter school agrees to abide by the terms regulating its operations as set forth in a contract (or "charter") between the school and the authority that sponsors it (either the local school board, the state, or a public university). If the charter school fails in its obligations, its charter may be revoked and the school closed down. Charter schools must be tuition-free and nonsectarian and observe open admissions policies. Most charter schools are run by parent or educational groups, but several for-profit companies have become involved in this arena as "education-management organizations," hoping to mimic the success of health maintenance organizations in the health-care industry.

Advocates promote charter schools as a welcome remedy to what they see as the excessive bureaucracy and stifling regulatory atmosphere in the failing public school system that hinders educational creativity.

A more competitive, market-oriented climate would, according to proponents, foster innovation and efficiency in moribund public schools. Detractors counter that the independence of charter schools paves the way for plummeting accountability, financial mismanagement, and diminishing educational standards, jeopardizing children's right to a decent education.

Despite the controversy, charter schools were in a state of ongoing expansion at the turn of the 21st century, and were assured increased federal support for years to come. In August 1999, President Bill Clinton announced that more than $95 million in federal grants would be disbursed to charter schools through the U.S. Department of Education. Clinton also requested $250 million from Congress to be included in the fiscal year 2001 federal budget to support continued expansion of charter schools and school choice nationwide.

ORGANIZATION AND STRUCTURE

As of October 2000, 36 states, the District of Columbia, and Puerto Rico had passed legislation allowing charter schools. In the 2000-2001 school year, there were over 2,000 charter schools (including multiple branches located on the same campus) operating in 31 states and Washington, D.C., and enrolling about 519,000 students, according to the Center for Education Reform. From 1998-1999 to 2000-2001 alone, the number of students attending charter schools rose by more than 150,000. The 1999-2000 academic year saw the greatest growth in charter start-ups since their inception, with 421 schools opening in that year alone. Another 400 or so sprang up the following year. Charter-school enrollments, however, still accounted for only 1 percent of all public school students. By 1999-2000, only 59 charter schools had been closed.

Each state determines its own set of regulations stipulating how a charter school may be organized, receive funding, and assess its students' performance. Charter schools may be newly created institutions, or existing public or private schools that have converted to charter status. In addition, some states allow charters to hire only state-accredited teachers, while other states are more lax about qualifications. Some proposed schools must win support in their local communities, while others are not so required; and some states allow only public schools or public school per-

sonnel to set up such schools. Others place a cap on the maximum number of charter schools in the state. All of these differences make it hard to determine an overall financial analysis for this field.

Perhaps one of the most important, yet least clear, aspects of charter schools is how they receive their funding. Some districts give charter schools 100 percent of the per-pupil funding that the other public schools receive, while others allot only a portion of that amount. In addition, charters may or may not be permitted or eligible for monies for special-education students or other entitlement programs. Minnesota totally funds its charter schools, while Louisiana state-approved charter schools do not receive any district funding.

Most charter schools are relatively small, with a median enrollment of 137 students, compared to 475 for public schools overall. Thus, start-up capital was one of the greatest problems facing such schools. In general, this difficulty has abated somewhat. According to the U.S. Department of Education's Fourth-Year Report on the State of Charter Schools, 39 percent of charter schools reported lack of start-up funds as the greatest obstacle they had to contend with in 1998-1999, down 20 percent from the previous year. This is due largely to increased federal allocations for charter schools and to increased venture capital available to fund for-profit companies entering the charter-management arena.

BACKGROUND AND DEVELOPMENT

In 1988, politicians, as well as some private citizens, started calling for more "choice" in public education in the form of vouchers, waivers, and alternative schools. In 1991 Minnesota passed legislation allowing the formation of charter schools; numerous other states soon followed. According to the North Central Regional Educational Laboratory, over 50 percent have been set up in Arizona, California, Michigan, and the District of Columbia, all places with "strong" charter laws.

Support for charter schools has come from diverse sources. Reasons for supporting charters range from a desire for public school options to a belief that such competition will strengthen all public schools. Proponents also hope that since they are free of bureaucratic strictures, these schools will initiate reforms not possible at other public schools and that education will improve because these schools are held accountable for student performance. Indeed, the Fourth-Year Report on Charter Schools stated that two-thirds of all

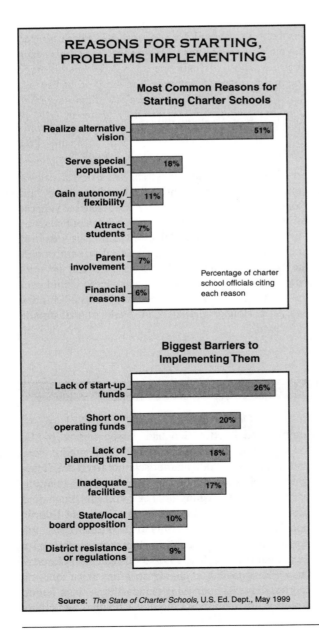

REASONS FOR STARTING, PROBLEMS IMPLEMENTING

Most Common Reasons for Starting Charter Schools

Realize alternative vision — 51%
Serve special population — 18%
Gain autonomy/ flexibility — 11%
Attract students — 7%
Parent involvement — 7%
Financial reasons — 6%

Percentage of charter school officials citing each reason

Biggest Barriers to Implementing Them

Lack of start-up funds — 26%
Short on operating funds — 20%
Lack of planning time — 18%
Inadequate facilities — 17%
State/local board opposition — 10%
District resistance or regulations — 9%

Source: *The State of Charter Schools*, U.S. Ed. Dept., May 1999

charters are started to "realize an alternative vision of schooling."

Critics are just as vocal and diverse. They argue that charter schools will destroy standard public education, are too limited in scope, and do not serve children with special needs. In addition, critics believe that charter schools are not adequately accountable for financial viability and students' academic improvement, since they do not face the same scrutiny as public schools.

By 1992 private education-management companies were eyeing the charter-school field. That year, the Baltimore Board of Education signed an agreement with Education Alternatives, Inc. (EAI) to run nine of the district's schools for a five-year period; in just three short years, however, the board ended its relationship with EAI, citing continued antagonism between EAI and the Baltimore teachers union and EAI's failure to disclose financial information to the Baltimore city council. Student scores had also not shown the improvement originally anticipated; in fact, EAI admitted to having inflated student test scores. In 1995 EAI also contracted to run all of the 52 schools in the Hartford, Connecticut school district, but the deal was canceled a few months later.

Even the Edison Project, started in 1991 by Chris Whittle of Whittle Communications, found that it would have to rein in its originally ambitious plans. Whittle initially proclaimed he would set up 1,000 schools within a few years of launching his operation; by the 2000-2001 academic year, the Edison Project, now known as Edison Schools, Inc., was operating only about 80 public charter schools nationwide.

CURRENT CONDITIONS

Despite the torrent of opinions both pro and con charter schools, perhaps the most crucial sector for determining the future of the charter-school movement—the general public—seems the least well-informed about the charter-school debate. A June 1999 poll of 1,200 individuals conducted by the nonpartisan Public Agenda and funded by the Charles A. Dana Foundation determined that 81 percent of those surveyed—including 52 percent of parents of school-aged children who lived in districts containing operational charter schools—knew "little or nothing" about them, even though a majority of the public (62 percent) believed that the public schools in general needed major reforms. Once the fundamental concepts behind charter schools had been explained to them,

however, 54 percent said that they would consider sending their children to charters.

Many charter schools are small and focus on a specific student population or curriculum. The "typical" charter is also mission-driven. Beyond that, drawing generalizations about charters becomes difficult. Successful charters enjoy a high degree of parental and community involvement in their ongoing operations. According to the U.S. Department of Education, three-fifths of charters schools in 1998-99 enrolled a higher percentage of nonwhite students than the regular public schools, but fewer special-needs students than public schools overall (8 percent versus 11 percent). Charters also possessed a slightly lower student-to-teacher ratio than other public schools—16 to 1 versus 17.2 to 1. Finally, charters included a larger grade span than public schools, though most charters educate primary and secondary, rather than high school, students. Seventy-two percent of all charters that opened in 1998-99 were newly created schools, rather than conversions of existing institutions.

Many charter schools have found a niche serving at-risk students, those students who often fall through the cracks in a traditional school setting. Charter schools can be more responsive to these students because the schools have greater flexibility and can accommodate individual student needs. According to the U.S. Department of Education, one-fourth of all new charters are created to target a distinct student population. Conversion schools often find that receiving a state charter provides additional financial resources. Notably, however, education-management organizations (EMOs) frequently steer away from special-needs students, since they cost more to educate than other students. A study released in fall 1999 by Michigan State University, for example, found that most Michigan charters run by EMOs geared their services to primary students and offered relatively few services addressed to special-needs students.

Charter schools have received some strong criticism from teachers' and other educational organizations. The American Federation of Teachers (AFT) concluded in a 1996 study that the majority of charters failed to target low achievers or at-risk students, preferring to draw less difficult-to-manage populations. Its study also asserted that many of the instructional programs employed by charters were "hardly 'innovative' by any common understanding of the word" and that the methods for success broadcast by many charter schools—such as back-to-basics curricula, longer school days, increased parental involvement, and character education—were also in use in mainstream public schools.

In sum, the AFT cautioned that all sweeping assessments of charter-school effectiveness were premature and most preliminary findings highly mixed, because charters haven't been operating long enough to generate meaningful assessment data. It stressed the need for greater accountability across the board, from financial management to gauging student scholastic achievement, so that future progress could properly be measured. The AFT noted that, of the 25 charter schools it surveyed for its report, only 17 required students to take state tests, only six mandated that all teachers be certified, and six charter-friendly states did not require charter schools to meet state educational standards. Charters' overall impact on the nation's educational system, it remarked dryly, was "as a whole limited thus far." These sentiments were echoed by the National Education Association in a 1998 report on charter-school accountability, which revealed that most state laws still did not require the reporting of charter-school baseline data and that fewer than half of existing accountability plans could be implemented without additional revisions.

Still, the pressure brought down on mainstream public schools by charter-school competition seems to have spurred some change. For example, the Toledo school district declined an offer from Edison to run a local charter, opting instead to set up the Grove Patterson Academy charter school under its own auspices, with help from the Toledo Federation of Teachers. The kindergarten through fourth grade, 220-student school provides early instruction in foreign languages, home computers for the students, and boasts a waiting list of about 400. Research conducted by Berkeley education graduate student Eric Rofes on the impact of competition from charters in 25 school districts in eight states and Washington, D.C., discovered that the presence of charters had led half these districts to institute moderate to substantial changes in attempts to retain student enrollments and hence, educational funds. Rofes's conclusions were reinforced by findings of similar studies undertaken by researchers at Western Michigan University, James Madison University, and for the Pioneer Institute. The latter study of 10 Massachusetts districts revealed that it took the loss of 2 to 3 percent of the student population to galvanize traditional public schools to imitate charter schools' educational strategies to staunch the outflow of students.

SCHOOL CLOSING

Sometimes institutions that provide much-needed services for at-risk children can find themselves at risk. In January 1999 the Chicago Preparatory Charter High School was shut down after being in operation for two and a half years. The school served teenagers with alcohol or drug abuse problems and had been founded through the Mayor's Office on Substance Abuse Policy. The school did not keep attendance records or transcripts and, as a consequence, the 45 students who were enrolled at the time of the closing were not awarded academic credit. The school's failure raised the issue of the need to monitor charter schools. Following the Chicago Prep woes, the Illinois State Board of Education asked for legislation that would require charter schools to report information, such as test scores and graduation rates, the same as all other public schools. In Washington, D.C., charter schools are already required to submit such data. In addition, volunteer monitors make regular visits to the schools. The purpose of these visits is to allow the monitors to examine files and financial statements. These actions are part of the D.C. Public Charter School Board's accountability plan for charter schools. In 2000 the board was responsible for twelve of the area's 27 charter schools.

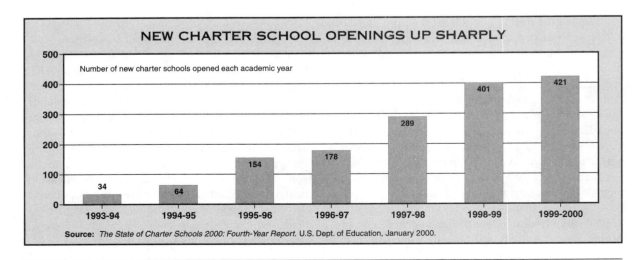

NEW CHARTER SCHOOL OPENINGS UP SHARPLY

Number of new charter schools opened each academic year

1993-94	34
1994-95	64
1995-96	154
1996-97	178
1997-98	289
1998-99	401
1999-2000	421

Source: *The State of Charter Schools 2000: Fourth-Year Report.* U.S. Dept. of Education, January 2000.

Even as charter schools make inroads in addressing special-needs children, it is unclear if they will prosper in more affluent areas where good public school systems are already in place. While charter schools in the city of Chicago have waiting lists, the outlying suburban areas have been less enthusiastic to the charter concept. One proposed charter school in the northwest suburbs of Chicago has had an uphill battle since organizers announced their intentions to create the Jefferson Charter School. Despite opposition from the local Elk Grove Township Elementary District 59, Jefferson School finally received its charter from the state of Illinois after three years of legal wrangling. When Jefferson School finally opened enrollment for the 1999-2000 school year, however, the response was lukewarm. During the two-day advance registrations in January 1999, 50 students signed up, far short of the 96 needed to satisfy state requirements, and much less than the 220 that Jefferson School officials had hoped for.

In 1998, according to the Reason Public Policy Institute and John M. McLaughlin, head of the Education Industry Group (EIG), charter schools had become the fastest-growing portion of the approximately $310 billion spent annually on public kindergarten through 12th-grade education. EIG reported that only about 10 percent of these charter schools are managed by larger private companies intent on making a profit from running them.

FUNDING SOURCES

Funding is crucial for a charter school. The U.S. Department of Education acknowledged that one of the most difficult tasks facing proponents of charter schools was raising the needed capital. Some schools became extremely innovative with ways to cut initial start-up costs by holding classes in churches, local YMCA facilities, and other spaces, including—in the case of Cesar Chavez Public Charter School in Washington, D.C.—in a few rented rooms in a shopping-mall basement. In addition to federal support, several states, including Louisiana, Minnesota, Pennsylvania, and Ohio, have all allocated either low- or no-interest loans for charters. To minimize operating expenses, charters often contract with outside vendors to supply food and transportation services or forgo them altogether. According to the U.S. Department of Education's Fourth-Year Report on the State of Charter Schools, only half of charters offer athletic programs; electives and extracurricular activities are also frequently omitted to save money.

Several major foundations assisted charter schools in the 1990s. Donald and Doris Fisher, founders of Gap, Inc., pledged $25 million to help San Francisco schools bring in The Edison Project, while A. Alfred Taubman, chairman of Sotheby's, put up $680 million to launch his own for-profit charter-school management company, the Leona Group. Moreover, the Walton family members offered $350,000 of their Wal-Mart fortune to promote charter schools. Manufacturer J. C. Huizenga bankrolled the National Heritage Academies, a for-profit education management firm that runs Michigan charters that stress moral values along with academics in their curricula.

Companies were also looking at other ways to fund and support these schools. For example, Charter School USA's CEO John Hage has launched what he termed the "second generation" of charter schools, and depends on his clients to pay for school buildings. Thus, Ryder System Inc. financed the construction of a charter school across from its headquarters in Florida; in exchange, children of Ryder employees will be given first chance at the spaces in the new school. Such an arrangement, however, would not work in the many states that, unlike Florida, prohibit preferential access to charter enrollments.

More obstacles than just a shortage of funds plague charter start-ups. Little advance lead-time to get up and running, uneven cash flow even when funds are available, and frequent opposition from local school boards and teachers unions hamper efforts to implement often-experimental curricula and upgrade substandard facilities. Furthermore, the absence of comprehensive accountability guidelines in many state charter laws injects uncertainty for charter-school personnel into the process of determining exactly what information and how much of it should be tracked and disclosed.

Wall Street analysts argue that the for-profit management of this field holds as much promise of financial growth as that of the health-care industry. To date, however, none of these for-profits has made an impressive financial showing. Among publicly held EMOs, only Nobel Learning Communities, Inc., is profitable, and it is lightly traded.

INDUSTRY LEADERS

New York-based Edison Schools, Inc., formerly The Edison Project, was founded in 1991. The most widely known for-profit company involved in charter-school management, Edison derives much of its recognition from its founder, Chris Whittle, of Whittle

More On **SOME CHARTERS DON'T MAKE THE GRADE**

Despite their growing popularity, charter schools have not enjoyed a track record of resounding successes. Early forays into charter-school management by for-profit firms such as Education Alternatives, Inc. (EAI) and Edison Schools occasionally resulted in the cancellation or revocation of even district-wide charter agreements. And regardless of who is administering such schools, the very newness of the charter-school concept almost guarantees that there will be some notable failures. Unfortunately, the costs of such failures can be exceedingly high, not only to investors in the charter-school concept, but also to the children whose education is at stake.

Charter schools' independence from school-board regulations, teachers unions, and state curriculum guidelines can lead to a lack of scrutiny into their day-to-day operations. Some of the abuses that have come to light have been egregious. For example, in July 1999, the Emma L. Harrison Elementary School in Waco, Texas, became the first Texas charter school to have its contract revoked, after investigations by the Texas Education Agency (TEA) uncovered gross fiscal mismanagement that included unpaid teachers' salaries, missing financial ledgers, bounced payroll checks, and incomplete tax forms; it turned out that despite receiving public monies, Harrison was operating with a budget deficit of $400,000. Further probes into the background of the school's CEO, a former postmaster, revealed a personal history of unpaid rent and property taxes, and filing for Chapter 7 bankruptcy protection. Denied an appeal, the former CEO subsequently filed suit against the TEA in federal court seeking reinstatement of the charter and $250 million in damages. At the same time, another Texas charter—the Ramses School—had been charged with inflating attendance records to draw extra state funds, which follow pupils to the school. Three other Texas charters were under investigation for financial mismanagement and four charter schools operated by Life's Beautiful Education Centers returned their charters when questions arose concerning their money management.

In November 1999 the Massachusetts Office of the Inspector General issued a review of the state's 24 commonwealth charter schools, which found that many had taken out loans to pay for facilities. The report concluded that if any of the charters closed and defaulted, the cost would be passed on to the taxpayers. Furthermore, four of the charters had contracted with education-management organizations (EMOs) that lacked requirements for measuring students' academic achievement. Some management contracts also based the contractors' compensation on a percentage of school expenses or surplus revenues, and a few did not accurately reflect the actual compensation arrangements between the schools and vendors. Independent auditors reported that 17 of the schools possessed deficient internal fiscal-oversight systems and more than half lacked written purchasing policies. The report concluded that although Massachusetts maintained a strong charter-school oversight system, its requirements have not been met. The report appeared at a time when the state was debating whether to raise the cap on the number of charters that could open.

Charters can stumble in other areas as well. In 1997 the U.S. Department of Education's office of civil rights ruled that the Renaissance charter school in Boston, run by Edison Schools, had discriminated against a disabled kindergartner by placing him in class with an inadequately trained teacher; the child was suspended almost 20 times. Charter-school curricula also can blur the separation of church and state that public schools must observe. As of 1999, the Michigan branch of the American Civil Liberties Union and several parents had a suit pending in a U.S. district court against the Michigan-based National Heritage Academies, charging it with promoting religion along with education, including prayer sessions for parents. And National Heritage's Rochester Leadership Academy in New York state intended to teach creationism alongside evolution and other scientific theories to its 436 elementary school students. When seeking to expand into New York, National Heritage presented its curriculum to state educational authorities, but omitted any mention of creationism.

Communications. A former owner of *Esquire* magazine, Whittle created Channel One in 1989, an electronic news system that beams educational programming, along with commercials, into classrooms. Edison raked in $132.8 million in sales in 1999, an increase of 91.3 percent from the previous year. The company has continued to experience net losses, however, which amounted to $49.4 million for 1999. Even though Edison did not take off as quickly as Whittle had hoped, the company has continued to expand, growing from four schools in 1995 to 80 schools in 2000-2001. Edison has invested heavily in these schools, which supply computers to their students for home use and telephones and televisions in the classrooms. In November 1998, Edison initiated a stock-option plan for its staff in Miami, Dade County, Florida, a move backed by the Miami teachers union. The company went public in November 1999; its initial public offering generated $122 million, though shares sold for a very lackluster $18.06, barely above the offering price of $18. John M. McLaughlin, editor of the *Education Industry Report*, proclaimed the offering a "momentous event" that provided the education-management industry with a prominent, publicly traded company. A *Business Week* commentary, however, graded the IPO a "D-."

TesseracT Group, formerly EAI, moved its headquarters from Minneapolis, Minnesota, to Scottsdale, Arizona, in May 1999. The company reported sales of $37.3 million in 1999, which represented sales growth of 143.8 percent in one year, and employed 980 workers. In 1998 the company acquired Sunrise Educational Services, which operated 16 charter schools in Arizona. The financial fortunes of TesseracT declined since the early 1990s; shares traded for less than $1 at the end of the decade, down from a high of $49 in 1993. In January 2000 the Nasdaq threatened to delist the company's shares. In February 2000, TesseracT's interim CEO Martha Taylor Thomas and chief financial officer Richard Yonker both resigned, citing differences of opinions with the board of directors over the future direction of the company. Ongoing disputes with its D.C. charter school, the Southeast Academy of Scholastic Excellence, further troubled its standing.

Alternative Public Schools also changed its name, becoming Beacon Education Management, LLC in 1997. Beacon is headquartered in Westborough, Massachusetts. According to the Center for Education Research, Analysis, and Innovation, in 1999-2000 Beacon managed nine charter schools in Illinois, Massachusetts, Michigan, and Missouri. Its affiliate JCR & Associates administered an additional 14 charters in Michigan.

Among publicly traded EMOs, Nobel Learning Communities, Inc., of Media, Pennsylvania, was among the very few turning a profit in 2000, derived from sales of $127.4 million, an increase of 16 percent over 1999. The company, which employed 3,800 workers, administered schools in 13 states.

Other emerging EMOs are the Leona Group and National Heritage Academies, both based in Michigan, and Advantage Schools of Boston.

FURTHER READING

American Federation of Teachers. *Charter School Laws: Do They Measure Up?* August 1996. Available from http://www.aft.org/research/reports/charter/csweb/sum.htm.

Brady, Diane. "Chris Whittle's New IPO Deserves a D-." *Business Week,* 6 September 1999.

Budge, David. "Private Troubles Nag Model Academies." *The Times Educational Supplement,* 16 June 2000.

Center for Education Reform. "Answers to Frequently Asked Questions about Charter Schools." Center for Education Reform, 2000. Available from http://edreform.com/school_reform_faq/charter_schools.htm.

Center for Education Research, Analysis, and Innovation. *Profiles of For-Profit Education Management Companies, 1999-2000.* Compiled by Alex Molnar, Jennifer Morales, and Alison Vander Wyst. Milwaukee: University of Wisconsin—Milwaukee, March 2000. Available from http://www.uwm.edu/Dept/CERAI/edpolicyproject/cerai-00-02.htm.

"Clinton Announces $95 Million in Support for Charter Schools." U.S. Government Press Release, 28 August 1999. Available from http://www.ed.gov/PressReleases/08-1999/support.html.

"Clinton Urges $250 Million to Lift Ailing Public Schools." *New York Times,* 27 February 2000.

Dunham, Richard. "A Rush to the Head of the Class: Presidential Rivals Strain for an Edge on Education." *Business Week,* 20 September 1999.

Ferrechio, Susan. "Charters in Our Midst: An Overview." North Central Regional Educational Laboratories, January 1998. Available from http://www.ncrel.org/sdrs/pbriefs/97/97-1over.htm.

———. "Verdict Not In on Charter Schools' Performance; Oversight Panels Reserve Judgment." *Washington Times,* 23 March 1999.

Good, Thomas, and Jennifer Braden. "The Charter School Zeitgeist." *Education Week,* 15 March 2000. Available from http://www.edweek.org/ew/ew_printstory.cfm?slug=27good.h19.

Lewin, Tamar. "Edison Group Say Students Gain." *New York Times,* 7 April 1999.

Lord, Mary. "Unhappy? Do It Yourself." *U.S. News & World Report,* 9 October 2000.

Massachusetts Office of the Inspector General. *A Management Review of Commonwealth Charter Schools.* November 1999. Executive summary available from http://www.magnet.state.ma.us/ig/publ/chscx.htm.

Mollison, Andrew. "Boom in Charter Schools Continues Despite Mixed Results." *The Atlanta Journal and Constitution,* 24 September 2000.

National Education Association. *Charter Schools: A Look at Accountability.* April 1998. Available from http://www.nea.org/issues/charter/accnt98.html.

———. "NEA Calls for Stronger Charter School Laws to Spur Innovation." News Release, 14 April 1999. Available from http://www.nea.org/nr/nr990414.html.

———. *NEA in Brief: Charter Schools.* November 1999. Available from http://www.nea.org/issues/charter/resources.html.

Naylor, Janet. "State Lures For-Profit Schools: Two More Open in Metro Detroit." *Detroit News,* 19 August 1999.

North Central Regional Educational Laboratory. "Charter Schools: Developing Policy and Practice." Region VI Charter Schools Conference. Minneapolis, Minnesota, 24-25 September 1998.

Osborne, David. "Healthy Competition: The Benefits of Charter Schools." *New Republic,* 4 October 1999.

Poole, Claire. "An F for Effort." *Texas Monthly,* December 1999.

Public Agenda Online. *On Thin Ice: How Advocates and Opponents Could Misread the Public's Views on Vouchers and Charter Schools.* Funded by the Charles A. Dana Foundation. November 1999. Available from http://publicagenda .org/specials/vouchers/voucherintro.htm.

Schnaiberg, Lynn. "Report Urges More Oversight of Massachusetts Charter Schools." *Education Week,* 12 January 2000. Available from http://www.edweek.org/ew/ewstory .cfm?slug=17charter.h19.

Strauss, Valerie. "Charter Schools Proliferating, Study Finds." *Washington Post,* 15 February 2000.

Symonds, William. "For-Profit Schools." *Business Week,* 7 February 2000.

Toch, Thomas. "Sugar Daddies for Charters." *U.S. News & World Report,* 27 April 1998.

U.S. Charter Schools. *Reports & Research on Charter Schools,* February 2000. Available from http://www.uscharterschools.org/uscs_1/visit?x-a=v&x-id=3442.

U.S. Department of Education. *The State of Charter Schools 2000: Fourth-Year Report,* January 2000. Available from http://www.ed.gov/pubs/charter4thyear/es.html.

Walsh, Mark. "Edison Faces Tough Task Trying to Educate Wall St." *Crain's New York Business,* 15 November 1999.

Wildavsky, Ben. "More Growth in Charter Schools." *U.S. News & World Report,* 11 September 2000.

————. "Why Charter Schools Make Inkster Nervous." *U.S. News & World Report,* 28 June 1999.

Wyatt, Edward. "Charter School to Raise Topic of Creationism." *New York Times,* 18 February 2000.

CHILDREN'S EDUCATIONAL FRANCHISES

INDUSTRY SNAPSHOT

Beyond the basics of reading, writing, and arithmetic, children's education was increasingly viewed as big business. Although by 2000 for-profit educational franchises accounted for less than 10 percent of the $380 billion spent in the United States on K-12 (kindergarten through twelfth grade) education, proponents claimed that the "education industry" was poised for explosive growth. Behind that growth are U.S. demographics—enrollments that were expanding and expected to outstrip even the numbers of the baby boomers in their school days. The market grew by 6 percent in 2000, and optimists foresaw revenues increasing at 15 to 20 percent in the early 21st century. Merrill Lynch & Co., Inc., in a 1999 industry overview entitled "The Book of Knowledge," estimated that the overall for-profit education industry would generate revenues of $100 billion by 2001. Eduventures Inc., a Boston-based market research firm, issued a brighter projection of $123 billion in revenues for 2000.

For-profit charter schools were among the most visible—and controversial—components of the children's educational franchise industry. Likened to health maintenance organizations, these so-called EMOs, or education-management organizations, were promoted as a panacea for the ills of an ineffective and inefficient national public school system. Education is the last large segment of the economy controlled by the government, and penetration by the private sector accelerated at the century's end as companies went after the largely untapped market of 53 million students enrolled in K-12. And a mini-baby boom was anticipated to swell the K-12 population by an additional 2 million from 2000 to 2005.

Other industry providers specialized in delivering computers, tutoring, Web-based curricula, textbooks, and other instructional aids to both school districts and individual parents. At-risk youth, often expelled from public schools for drug and weapons violations, formed a challenging and emerging target population for specialized educational franchises.

ORGANIZATION AND STRUCTURE

According to Eduventure's overview, "The Education Industry: Markets and Opportunities," the industry can be divided into three segments: schools, educational products, and educational services.

The most prominent component of the schools sector was for-profit charter schools—schools that, though publicly funded and tuition-free, can be managed by organizations that seek to generate a profit from their operation. Charter schools operate according to a charter drawn up between the school and its sponsoring organization, usually a local school board or the state. In exchange for freedom from the restrictions that govern other public schools, the charter school must live up to the terms of its charter or its administering organization may lose the contract. For-profits receive the same per pupil allotment as public schools in a district; after operating costs are deducted from that amount, the company keeps the remainder. Though for-profit charters have been enthusiastically backed by Wall Street investors and many parent groups and school boards, no for-profit operator has yet turned a profit and the very arrangement has drawn heavy criticism, especially from teachers' organizations that argue that profit is inimical to the very idea of an equal opportunity, public education for all American schoolchildren.

Some noneducational corporations also sponsor elementary and secondary public schools. For example, the American Bankers Insurance Group (ABIG) operates a "learning center" for kindergarten through second grade in Miami, Florida. Although the building belongs to ABIG and only children of its employees attend the center, the Dade County public school district provides the books, teachers, furniture, and other supplies. Florida law permits property tax exemptions for corporate-owned buildings that house such educational endeavors; Honeywell ran a similar operation in Clearwater. And the Walt Disney Co.'s Celebration School, in Celebration, Florida, operates in tandem with the Osceola County school district.

The products sector encompasses producers of educational supplies and equipment for classroom and home use, such as instructional-materials developers Harcourt General Inc. and Scholastic Corp., and electronic-media firm the Learning Co. ZapMe! installs free computer labs in schools. By 2000, the company had installed labs in 1,200 schools. EduClick.com, another electronic-commerce start-up, sells education-specific books, software, audiotapes, and videotapes online directly to educational purchasers, who can use school purchase orders for payment, rather than personal credit cards. Family Education Network develops educational Web sites, including one that permits parents to connect with their children's schools. About 9,000 schools had signed on, and Family Education Network reported 2.5 million visitors to its sites in November 1999 alone. Bigchalk.com, of Wayne, Pennsylvania, developed Web tools for educators of K-12 students. A joint venture of Bell & Howell Co. (a half-owner) and Infonautics, Inc., Bigchalk.com grants access to its Electronic Library of over 2,600 publications.

The services sector contained not only more-traditional tutoring endeavors, but also specialized providers who serve at-risk students. For example, Community Education Partners operated two campuses for approximately 2,000 students who required extra surveillance in the Houston school district; one opened in 1997 and one in 1998. Security and supervision are much greater than at ordinary district schools and much of the learning that occurs is self-paced, often taking place on computers. Furthermore, teachers are more likely to have backgrounds in corrections work, counseling, or communications than in education. Although all possess at least bachelor's degrees, only about 15 percent are certified instructors.

PIONEERS IN THE FIELD

One of the leaders in the move to privatize elementary and secondary education is Christopher Whittle, the media entrepreneur who developed Channel One, a commercial educational news program intended for broadcast within school classrooms. By the early 1990s, Whittle was airing the idea of creating a company that would operate public schools and turn a profit, in somewhat the same manner as health maintenance organizations operate health-care facilities. Although Whittle's initial projection of building 1,000 such schools within the first few years of operation turned out to be premature, his new venture, Edison Schools, Inc. (initially The Edison Project) became the largest manager of for-profit public schools by 2000; it went public in November 1999, raising $109 million in the process. In 2000, Edison signed its first contract with a state government when it agreed to run three low-performing schools in the Baltimore school district. (Also see the essay in this book entitled Charter Schools.)

CURRENT CONDITIONS

The privatization of K-12 education was spurred in the late 1990s by a huge infusion of private venture capital, which quadrupled to $3.3 billion in 1999 and was projected to rise to $4 billion in 2000, according to Eduventure. Parental clamor for more school choice and changing American demographics were also behind industry development.

Nonetheless, the sector's stock performance was shaky, despite the runaway success of the U.S. economy overall. Eduventure tracked an index of 30 major education stocks and reported they were down by 25 percent by December 1999. In November 1999, Edison Schools, the largest of the for-profit K-12 school operators, went public, though the stock market's response was lukewarm. Despite the less than spectacular performance of its stocks, Wall Street warmly backed the education industry. In particular, the role of the Internet and other technology applications in education has generated a new focus among investors on the education sector. Sylvan Learning Systems, for instance, sold off its testing business in 2000 to generate funds for a new Internet-related strategy, a move of which many investors took notice.

The Center for Education Research, Analysis, and Innovation reported that by 2000 there were 20 companies running at least 230 U.S. public schools for profit in 21 states, educating about 100,000 students.

Charter schools emerged from the school choice movement, which was concerned with combating the problems of overcrowding and substandard achievement that characterized many of the U.S. public K-12 school facilities. For-profit charters multiplied from fewer than 100 nationwide in 1994—the first year they went into operation—to approximately 2,300 in 2000. By the turn of the century, however, none had yet turned a profit. And besides opposition from many teachers' groups, charter schools have had to contend with many of the same negative factors that hinder the performance of regular public schools, such as a shortage of qualified teachers and tight funds for building maintenance and classroom supplies.

The K-12 sector may be the slowest-growing segment of the education industry. The second annual industry survey released by Knowledge Quest Ventures LLC, a New York consulting firm, revealed that precollegiate education ranked lowest in the sights of venture capitalists. Top areas for investing were corporate training and the Internet-based education business.

At-risk students and those who have been expelled from public schools constituted a population that children's educational franchises increasingly sought to address. Many alternative for-profit schools designed to serve this population were filled to capacity and expanding to meet increasing demand as public schools failed to adequately grapple with students who had been removed from the public system for drug use or carrying weapons. Schools for troubled youth often set up in such states as Utah and Montana, whose relaxed regulatory climate and remote locations are well adapted for the purpose. No single type of institution predominates in this young industry sector, and the total number of such schools in operation is unknown. Facilities range from small, independent home-schooling ventures to large corporations that provide psychiatric and therapeutic services in addition to academic instruction and room and board. Complete costs can range up to $40,000 per year per pupil.

Growth in the sector, estimated at about 25 percent per year, was prompted in large part by federal legislation in 1996 that mandated a no-tolerance policy for students found carrying drugs or weapons in public schools. Districts that don't expel such students risk losing their federal funding.

One alternative education franchise devoted to this student population is Richard Milburn High School Inc., which CEO Robert Crosby characterized as the "Edison of the at-risk school world." The company has contracted with districts to run for-profit schools for at-risk students for about a quarter century; annual earnings were projected to total $30 million in the early 2000s. The Milburn schools employ certified teachers and adopt curricula similar to those used in the surrounding district's other public schools.

Such schools, however, have come under scrutiny for focusing too heavily on drug rehabilitation and job training, and not enough on academics. A common pedagogical practice is to stress individual, often computer-based learning, at the expense of class lectures and collaborative projects. Many schools individualize lesson plans because students enter the schools on a rolling basis, rather than all together at the beginning of the semester.

INDUSTRY LEADERS

Edison Schools, Inc., founded by Chris Whittle, was the nation's largest operator of for-profit public charter schools at the start of the 21st century. By 2000, Edison managed 80 charter and contract schools in 16 states. Edison schools feature a longer-than-usual school day and year; in addition, Edison provides each student in grades three or higher with a computer to take home and use free of charge. In fall 1999, the company went public. Though it sold at barely more than its initial offering, by 2000 the company announced it was experiencing a positive cash flow. Sales revenues were $132.8 million in 1999, which represented a net loss of $49.4 million, but a one-year sales increase of 91.3 percent. Edison's high-profile leadership included chairman Benno Schmidt, former president of Yale University; chief education officer John Chubb, of the Brookings Institute; and charter-division head, the Rev. Floyd Flake, a former congressman and senior pastor of the Allen African Methodist Episcopal Church in Jamaica, Queens.

Sylvan Learning Systems, Inc. of Baltimore, Maryland, runs the nation's largest network of contract tutoring centers. With 1999 sales of $338.5 million, Sylvan operated 800 tutoring centers in North American and an additional 900 in Europe and employed 7,437 workers. Having shed its testing subsidiary Prometric, Sylvan embarked on an ambitious plan to overhaul and expand its technology-based education operations. The company also entered into a new venture, called MindSurf, with a number of companies devoted to installing mobile computer infrastructures in elementary and high schools.

Nobel Learning Communities, which was founded in 1984 to run a string of child-care centers, later expanded to operate elementary and high schools.

In 1999, it ran a system of 145 schools in 13 states, including child-care centers, corporate-sponsored schools, facilities for learning-challenged students, and charter schools. In early 2000 it announced a five-year contract to manage the Philadelphia Academy Charter. Fiscal year 2000 saw sales of $127.4 million, a 16 percent increase over 1999; its $2.5 million net income represented an annual increase of 56.3 percent. Nobel employed about 3,800 workers.

TesseracT Group, Inc., of Scottsdale, Arizona, operated both charter and private schools. Among its ventures is its Sunrise Educational Services unit, which managed 20 preschools, mostly in Arizona. The company's 1999 sales totaled $37.3 million, for sales grow of 143.8 percent. This represented, however, a net operating loss of $10.7 million for 1999.

KinderCare Learning Centers, Inc. led the United States in providing child care and educational services for preschool-age children. The Portland firm in 1999 operated 1,170 centers in 39 states in the United States and another two in Great Britain, which enrolled a total of 123,000 children paying a weekly tuition of $115. KinderCare brought in revenues of $696.8 million in 2000, up from $633 million the year before, and generated net income of $20 million.

WORK FORCE

Many of the driving personalities behind the new for-profit education ventures are the so-called education entrepreneurs—business professionals who are seeking to transform and privatize public education. They are spurred by the belief that free market forces will boost the efficiency of school performance, increase the range of educational options available to parents and students, and improve the quality of instruction through competition. In the process, they feel that public schooling can be made to turn a profit and that underperforming schools will be weeded out.

Many workers in the new for-profit educational franchises are former elementary and secondary teachers who are unsatisfied with making relatively low wages after years of teaching service or frustrated by the layers of bureaucracy that come with public school systems. They have decided to jump on the entrepreneurial bandwagon and move into the sector of the educational industry that seems most likely to bring financial rewards for risk-taking, innovation, and a more "businesslike" approach to teaching youngsters.

One example is Paul Wetzel, a former middle school teacher in Greenville, South Carolina, who started Wetzel Educational Services, a private tutoring firm that employs about 30 full- and part-time workers to provide test preparation and individual and group tutoring for both elementary and secondary students. Chris Yelich, executive director of the Association of Educators in Private Practice, which represents such education entrepreneurs, is himself a former high school science teacher.

At the other end of the spectrum are businesspeople, some of whom have prior experience working for investment banking or venture capital firms. Among such businesspeople is J. C. Huizenga, cousin of H. Wayne Huizenga (the chairman of AutoNation and owner of the Miami Dolphins football team). J. C. Huizenga created National Heritage Academies as a for-profit educational franchise whose curriculum stresses discipline and morals and character development along with academics. Based in Grand Rapids, Michigan, National Heritage Academies expanded from one fledgling charter school of about 200 students to 22 charters and 7,900 students in Michigan and North Carolina by 2000.

Many schools have similarly sought out high-level industry executives to serve as school administrators. The Michigan-based Leona Group recruited former General Motors marketing manager Rod Atkins to serve as principal of its Voyageur Academy elementary school in Detroit, despite his lack of experience in the educational field. Moves such as these highlight for-profits' desire to operate less like a traditional educational institution and more like a modern business.

Ironically, for-profit educational franchises often pay less than their public school counterparts and thus tend to hire inexperienced teachers. Some critics charge that stock options and merit pay can't compensate for the lower salaries that are often coupled with longer days and school years than in the public school system. When Edison's Boston Renaissance school, which enrolls primarily low-income, minority kindergarten through eighth grade students, raised salaries and shortened the academic calendar, teacher turnover decreased and student performance improved.

AMERICA AND THE WORLD

The concept of for-profit education was being exported by the United States to many overseas destinations. Tony Blair's New Labour government in Great Britain, for instance, warmly welcomed the notion in 1999. Some state schools, such as King's

Manor in Surrey, and some faltering local education authorities, such as those in Hackney and Islington, had been turned over to for-profits for administering. Canada similarly was considering the concept.

FURTHER READING

Applied Research Center. "The Education Industry Fact Sheet." Available from http://www.igc.org/trac/feature/education/industry/fact.html.

"Argosy Education Group Reports First Quarter Revenues and Earnings." *Business Wire,* 10 January 2000.

Asimov, Nanette. "Most Edison Teachers Ready to Quit in Fall; SF School Is Privately Run." *San Francisco Chronicle,* 10 May 2000.

Blumenstyk, Goldie. "Sylvan Learning Systems Moves into the Higher-Education Market." *Chronicle of Higher Education,* 12 March 2000.

Carter, Samuel Casey. "A Question of Capacity." *Policy Review,* January/February 1999.

Doclar, Mary. "Texas School Shows Perks, Problems with For-Profit Education." *Fort Worth Star-Telegram,* 2 March 2000.

Hill, David. "Would You Buy an Education from This Man?" *Teacher Magazine,* February 1999.

"KinderCare Announces Second Quarter of Fiscal Year 2000 Results." *PR Newswire,* 10 January 2000.

Marcus, David L. "A Scholastic Gold Mine." *U.S. News & World Report,* 24 January 2000.

Mathews, Jay. "New School of Thought: Making Education Pay." *Washington Post,* 19 April 2000.

"New Schools Venture Fund Participates in Conference to Investigate New Public Education Models." *Business Wire,* 11 January 2000.

"Nobel Learning Communities, Inc. Announces a 153 Percent Increase in Its First Half Earnings." *PR Newswire,* 25 January 2000.

Portner, Jessica. "For-Profit Alternative Schools Are Hot Commodities." *Education Week,* 8 July 1998.

"The Privatization of Public Schools." *American School & University,* February 2000.

Schnaiberg, Lynn. "Entrepreneurs Hoping to Do Good, Make Money." *Education Week,* 1 December 1999.

Singhnania, Lisa. "Charter Schools Push Reading, Writing, Arithmetic—And Profits." *Associated Press,* 17 May 2000.

Snyder, Susan. "Philadelphia May Hire Private Firm to Teach Difficult Students." *Philadelphia Inquirer,* 19 January 2000.

Stone, Amey. "It's Time for a Refresher Course in Education Stocks." *Business Week,* 7 February 2000.

Symonds, William. "For-Profit Schools." *Business Week,* 7 February 2000.

———. "Industry Outlook 2000: Education." *Business Week,* 10 January 2000.

"$250 M Private Equity Group Founded to Invest in Education and Training." *Lifelong Learning Market Report,* 15 December 1999.

Walsh, Mark. "Though Investors See Opportunity in Education, K-12 Ranks Low." *Education Week,* 29 September 1999.

———. "Two Reports Offer Bright Outlook for Education Industry." *Education Week,* 19 May 1999.

Woodall, Martha. "Media, PA-Based Education Company Sees 64 Percent Earnings Increase." *Philadelphia Inquirer,* 26 January 2000.

Wyatt, David. "Investors See Room for Profit in the Demand for Education." *New York Times,* 4 November 1999.

COMPUTER ANIMATION ENTERTAINMENT

By 2000, movie and television audiences could watch celestial collisions pulverize Earth, realistic dinosaurs hunting terrified scientists around an island, and insects and toys living out their own dramatic fantasies in feature-length films. Moreover, all of this looked perfectly normal. Elaborate computer-generated special effects have become the motion-picture industry's standard. Developments in computer animation reached a fever pitch by the turn of the 21st century, and studios raced to employ the latest developments in order to showcase the most dazzling, amusing, and terrifying effects Hollywood had to offer. Moreover, in their zeal to wow audiences, directors and studios took turns beating each other over the head with their checkbooks. Films such as *Twister, The Matrix, Titanic,* and a host of others all carried computer animation budgets that alone would have made studios of yesteryear blanch. And costs show no immediate signs of slowing down. In 1991, James Cameron's *Terminator 2: Judgment Day* made many movie executives shudder with its budget exceeding $100 million. In 1996, two films surpassed that mark. By 2000, however, such figures were par for the blockbuster course.

Animation, the art of producing the illusion of movement from a sequence of two-dimensional drawings or three-dimensional objects, has long been a staple of the entertainment industry. Animation can take on many shapes, ranging from primitive drawings in television cartoons such as the *Flintstones,* to complex, dinosaur-sized creatures in *Jurassic Park.* The 1990s saw an animation renaissance and, during this period, the animation studios and production companies that were able to find the right combination of creative talent and technical wizardry found a burgeoning marketplace for their products. Computer animation's entertainment uses were spread far and wide. From the dreamlike landscapes of *What Dreams May Come* to the intricately detailed talking mouse of *Stuart Little* to the resurrection of U.S. presidents to interact with characters in *Forrest Gump,* computer animation was transforming the face of cinematic reality.

ORGANIZATION AND STRUCTURE

Animation has always been a labor-intensive process and, as a consequence, most animation projects are collaborative efforts integrating the talent of animators, technical directors, producers, artists, and engineers. Even though computer animation is technology driven, the workflow for an animated feature movie is still essentially the same as it was in the earliest days of animation. While the computer has replaced some hand drawings, it has not entirely eliminated pen-and-ink sketches. An animation project begins with the creation of a storyboard, a series of sketches outlining the important points of the story and some of the dialogue. When animation was strictly done by hand, the workload would then be distributed between senior artists, who sketched the frames where the most action was occurring and junior artists, who filled in the in-between frames. When computers are used, artists use the storyboard sketches to create clay figures that are made into digitalized three-dimensional (3-D) characters, which are then manipulated by animation artists who also create the background fill. Altogether, an animated feature is the collective work of many people, including animators, lighting experts, story writers, and sound technicians.

BACKGROUND AND DEVELOPMENT

From the very beginning, studios employed animation artists—people who could painstakingly draw quirky animated characters by hand; before the arrival of computers, in fact, all animation was created in this way. Production teams simulated motion by drawing a series of successive, incrementally altered frames. In order to trick the eye into seeing motion, each second of animated sequence for film requires 24 frames. In the earliest cartoons, each one of the frames was hand drawn, thereby creating a tremendous workload just to complete a short cartoon. For instance, the 1910 cartoon *Gertie the Trained Dinosaur,* which was primitive compared to later animation, required 10,000 separate drawings. In 1915 Earl Hurd streamlined the process by developing a time-saving method known as cel animation whereby each individual character is drawn on a separate piece of transparent paper, while the background is drawn on a piece of opaque paper. When the animation is shot, the transparent paper is overlaid on the opaque. With this method, the background was drawn once, and only the parts that needed to be changed had to be redrawn instead of the entire frame. The animation industry flourished from the 1930s to the 1950s, largely through the efforts of pioneer Walt Disney, who produced such full-length animated movies as *Dumbo, Bambi,* and *Snow White and the Seven Dwarfs.*

For many decades, hand-drawn animation was the industry standard. Filmmaker John Whitney began to change that in the late 1950s and early 1960s; Whitney pioneered motion graphics using equipment that he purchased at a government war-surplus auction. These precise instruments allowed Whitney to develop motion control of the camera, zoom, and artwork. Later these techniques would be used to create the stargate slit-scan sequence in Stanley Kubrick's *2001: A Space Odyssey* (1968). In 1986 Whitney received an Academy of Motion Pictures Arts and Sciences "Medal of Commendation for Cinematic Pioneering" in recognition of his contribution.

The 1960s saw another development that led to the eventual rise of computer animation. In 1963 Ken Knowlton, who worked at Bell Laboratories, created a programming language that could generate computer-produced movies. It was not until 1982, though,

with the release of Disney's *Tron,* that computer-generated imaging (CGI) would be explored as a serious moviemaking technique. The widespread arrival of computers in the 1980s marshaled in teams of new workers (namely scientists, engineers, and programmers) capable of developing complex animation software. Computers thus revolutionized the animation process, supplementing traditional animation methods with hardware and software capable of creating realistic on-screen characters.

Advancements in the computer animation field swept the entertainment industry in the 1990s. Before 1995, conventional wisdom held that CGI was too inexact a science to replace hand-drawn animation, which many felt was the only way to capture small, quirky facial and body movements. In 1995, however, Pixar Animation Studios and its partner, The Walt Disney Co., showed that computer animation wasn't just an ancillary technique with the release of *Toy Story,* the first fully computer animated feature-length movie. The success of *Toy Story,* which grossed $350 million in worldwide box-office sales, proved that computer animation was a viable moviemaking art form—one that requires constant research and development. Pixar had already greatly advanced its computer animation techniques by the time it began work on its next project, *A Bug's Life,* which was released in 1998. The movie's director, John Lasseter, noted that *A Bug's Life* utilized 12 times the computing power employed in *Toy Story.*

PIONEERS IN THE FIELD

There is perhaps no name more well known in the field of animation than that of Walt Disney, the cartoon artist who founded the mega-entertainment empire that bears his name. Disney, who was born in Chicago in 1901, left school at 16 and later studied briefly at art schools in Chicago and Kansas City, Missouri. Disney's 1928 cartoon *Steamboat Willie* was a first on two accounts. It was the first cartoon that was synchronized with sound, and it also introduced Mickey Mouse, his enduringly popular cartoon character. Disney would go on to many other firsts in the field of animation. In 1932 he used full color in a cartoon for the first time in the film *Flowers and Trees.* He also created the first full-length animated feature with his 1937 *Snow White and the Seven Dwarfs,* which was produced with 400,000 sketches. Disney's production company ushered in the golden age of animation with film classics such as *Pinocchio* (1940), *Fantasia* (1940), and *Bambi* (1942). At that time, all

---

Trends   BUT WHAT'S HIS
                TAX POLICY?

In the age of the television-ready president, some have surmised that even Abraham Lincoln couldn't get elected. John F. Kennedy's charming smile in the first televised presidential debate in 1960 may have won that election from Richard Nixon's scowl. Undoubtedly, campaign advisers have learned their lesson: image matters.

In that spirit, those who criticize the often-cartoonish nature of presidential politics in the United States received some more ammunition early in the 2000 campaign when the "Doonesbury" comic strip's Uncle Duke announced his candidacy for the Free World's highest office.

Duke was not the first cartoon to throw his hat into the presidential ring, of course. A number of drawings have run for the office of chief executive since Mutt and Jeff's bid on the ill-fated Bughouse ticket of 1908. Duke, however, was the first in that valiant line to exist in real time, able to interact with and berate audiences on the spot.

The Duke 2000 Campaign team received its soft money and management from a partnership between Universal Press Syndicate, Excite, and the San Francisco animation company Protozoa.

Addressing his constituency live from the U.S. Comedy Arts Festival in Aspen, Colorado, a fully animated Duke gave a short stump speech, outlining a political philosophy that "Doonesbury" creator Garry Trudeau described as hovering somewhere between compassionate fascism and coerced libertarianism, before fielding questions from and delivering blunt insults to a live audience.

Utilizing a technique called motion capture, the voice of Duke, Fred Newman, hidden backstage at the theater, wore a sensor-riddled suit that sent signals to hardware and software to mimic Newman's movements, creating a fully responsive, and abusive, Uncle Duke on the theater's screen. Though cynical observers may fail to discern the novelty of such a concept as it applies to presidential candidates, the feat is a timely display of the latest computer animation technology. The motion capture system, also called digital puppetry, further enables the quick and relatively simple transfer into a Web-based format, another crucial element of postmodern campaigning.

The Duke 2000 Campaign shortly afterwards swung by *Larry King Live.*

---

animation work was done by hand with Disney overseeing the productions. Before he died in 1966, Disney had expanded his enterprise to include the Disneyland Theme Park in Anaheim, California; numerous syndicated comic strips featuring his cartoon characters; and television programs such as *The Mickey Mouse Club* and *Walt Disney's Wonderful World of Color,* while Disney himself received 32 Academy Awards.

CURRENT CONDITIONS

By 2000, CGI was not only a proven quantity, but a powerful market force, and as such, a host of new productions were rushed through the pipeline to cash in on the newest, most awe-inspiring computer animation. The animation industry even won Academy prestige in 2000, when it was announced that animated features would have their own Oscar category, perhaps beginning in 2002, marking the first new Oscar category since 1981.

Animators continued to push the limits of CGI's capabilities at the turn of the 21st century. The release of *Toy Story 2* in 1999 showcased the collaborative efforts of over 250 artists, animators, and technicians using 1,200 individual models, 18 virtual sets, and about 10,000 painted images used to define skin characteristics. The film's digital innovation was such that, because shading and rendering technology had improved facial mobility and realism to such a great extent, most of the cast had to be completely redesigned. *Toy Story 2*'s release capped the most highly animated year in film history, which included *The Prince of Egypt* and *Tarzan,* among others. The following year, a record five animated features hit the nation's screens during the summer blockbuster season, no less than a dozen animated features were expected by year's end. In addition to feature-length cartoons, nearly all the major blockbusters were augmented with, or even written around, computer-animated special effects. Before Jar Jar Binks was a ubiquitous mass-merchandising item, he was the computer-generated amphibian comic relief in the highly successful *Star Wars Episode One: The Phantom Menace,* which also featured enormous battle scenes between computer animated creatures.

Actors, meanwhile, welcomed the new technology with a degree of caution. While the technology remained crude as of 2000, a burgeoning CGI devel-

---

The film "Antz" made full use of computer animation techniques. (FieldMark Publications/Robert J. Huffman)

opment was the creation of digital actors and actresses from the ground up, thereby bypassing the need for high-paid talent. Although the ability to create intimate levels of realism was not yet ready to push such virtual actors onto the big screen, developers were working toward the day when screen stars could be created to feature all the ideal visual characteristics as well as the ability to perform superhuman feats. In the meantime, computer animation will certainly continue to help stretch the abilities of the traditional flesh-and-blood talent.

Computer animation also offered a glimmer of hope for the democratization of film production. As CGI fuels further sophistication of interactive video games, high-tech moviemaking capabilities creep ever closer to the hands of the average amateur tech wizard. In March 2000 Sony unveiled its PlayStation 2, armed with powerful new graphic capabilities. By that time, as well, an animation technique known as Machinima, which draws from the rendering techniques employed in 3-D video games, provided amateur filmmakers with the ability to create nearly Hollywood-quality short animated films. A number of feature films were already released and screened at technology showcases.

INDUSTRY LEADERS

Many of the leading animation firms bring together powerhouse names from the entertainment and computer fields. The cofounders of Microsoft Corp. and Apple Computers, Inc. have both paired up with influential filmmakers to produce animated movies. The results of these ventures have generally been financial successes and, as a consequence, new animation studios and production companies have started to form around the world.

DREAMWORKS SKG

DreamWorks SKG, based in Universal City, California, coproduced the highly successful 1998 animated feature *Antz*. DreamWorks produces films, television shows, software, and records. It represents the collaborative effort of three founding partners—movie producer Steven Spielberg, former Disney executive Jeffrey Katzenberg, and music industry mogul David Geffen, who each received a 22 percent share of the company for individual investments of $33 million. The main shareholder, at 24 percent, is Paul Allen, the cofounder of computer software giant Microsoft. In 2000, DreamWorks' major animation film project was *Chicken Run,* featuring the voice of Mel Gibson, while another major hit, *Gladiator,* utilized extensive computer animation to recreate the Roman Colosseum as a backdrop to bloody fight sequences. The company employed 1,600 workers in 2000.

INDUSTRIAL LIGHT & MAGIC

Filmmaker George Lucas's Industrial Light & Magic (ILM), part of Lucas Digital, is an outgrowth of the special-effects team that worked on the box-office smash *Star Wars,* and was the world's largest digital production facility. The San Rafael, California-based company has been supplying special effects in Hollywood since the mid-1970s. ILM was responsible for creating dinosaurs in Steven Spielberg's *The Lost World,* rampaging fire in *Backdraft,* and water for *The Abyss.* Overall, ILM provided the special effects for eight of the 15 highest-grossing box-office hits of all time, raking in 14 Academy Awards for best visuals.

PACIFIC DATA IMAGES

Located in Palo Alto, California, Pacific Data Images (PDI) produces high-end animation and visual effects for feature films and projects in the commercial and entertainment industries. PDI, along with partner DreamWorks SKG, produced the 1998 full-length animation feature *Antz*. It took a team of 27 PDI animators 18 months to create the film. PDI developed software that controls precise movements of body parts and facial features, such as the eyes or mouth, allowing for the creation of complex facial expressions without having to memorize facial musculature. Two new animated features, *Shrek* and *Tusker* were to be released 2001. PDI also created animation for Pepsi and Gatorade commercials, among others. The private company employed 300 workers in 2000.

PIXAR ANIMATION STUDIOS

Steve Jobs, cofounder of Apple Computers, put up $50 million of his own money to purchase Richmond, California-based Pixar Animation Studios from George Lucas. Under Jobs's leadership, Pixar went on to create *Toy Story,* the first fully computer animated movie, in partnership with The Walt Disney Co. *Toy Story,* created by a team of 60 Pixar animators, was the highest-grossing film released in 1995. Pixar has developed proprietary software in the areas of modeling, animating, lighting, production management, and image rendering. Pixar's RenderMan software was used to create dinosaurs in *Jurassic Park.* Its Marionette and Ringmaster software programs complement RenderMan to control the entire range of animated production. Pixar licenses its software to other production companies. In 1997 Pixar and Disney announced a five-movie deal. As part of the agreement, Disney handles marketing and distribution of the movie while Pixar maintains creative control. The first fruit of the arrangement was *A Bug's Life,* released in 1998. Much of Pixar's success is credited to John Lasseter, who worked for Disney and at George Lucas's special-effects company and now oversees creative development at Pixar. *Toy Story 2,* released in late 1999, cheated the dreaded sequel curse, garnering tremendous acclaim and financial rewards. Pixar's revenues in 1999 reached $121 million, up from only $14.3 million the year before. In 2001, Pixar will complete the next installment in its Disney coproductions, *Monsters, Inc.* The firm employed 430 people in 2000, a sizable expansion over the company's six employees in 1986.

WALT DISNEY CO.

The Walt Disney Co., headquartered in Burbank, California, was an early pioneer in full-length animated feature movies and continued its dominance in the 1990s. Disney produced two of the top-grossing animated features of all time—*The Lion King,* which had grossed nearly $400 million by 2000; and *Aladdin,* which recorded domestic box-office sales of $250 million. In 1991 Disney entered into a three-movie deal with Pixar Animation Studios, which resulted in the 1995 animated feature *Toy Story,* a film that earned

$1 billion in box office, video, and licensing sales. The companies renegotiated and signed a five-picture agreement in 1997, allowing Disney to purchase 5 percent of Pixar. Subsequent successes include *A Bug's Life* and *Toy Story 2.* Disney is the second-largest media company in the world and operates theme parks, television and film studios, publishing companies, a cruise line, and professional sports teams. Disney's total operation had sales of $23.4 billion and maintained a payroll of about 117,000 employees in 1999.

WORK FORCE

The computer animation industry is characterized by a well-educated work force, populated with people who combine computer expertise and creative ability. While there is some on-the-job training, to learn an individual company's proprietary software programs for instance, production studios generally don't train employees in technical areas such as creating special effects or programming languages. These skills, in addition to basic animation drawing, are learned in specialized computer animation programs offered in colleges, universities, and art schools. A typical computer animation program includes the following classes: life drawing, character animation, color and design, character design, animation layout, storytelling, 3-D character computers, and background painting. Most animators enter the job market with degrees in computer animation, and because of the high level of technical sophistication required, many workers with advanced degrees come from disciplines such as mathematics or computer programming. Quite often, these programs work closely with companies in the industry and tailor their curriculum to meet the marketplace's needs. For instance, in addition to funding an animation program at the California Institute of the Arts (CalArts), Disney Studios hires graduates of the program. Alumni of the CalArts program include filmmaker Tim Burton and Pixar's John Lasseter.

AMERICA AND THE WORLD

While U.S. companies, such as Pixar and Disney, dominate the computer animation field, it is a truly global industry. Canadian companies, for instance, are leading-edge innovators in animation technology. In the late 1990s Toronto-based Nelvana Ltd. and Vancouver-based Mainframe Entertainment Inc. both created 3-D computer-generated television shows for children. Nelvana created, along with partner French

MediaLab, "Donkey King Country," a 3-D cartoon series. Nelvana also partnered with another French company, Sparx, to create a series of half-hour 3-D television shows called *Rolie Polie Olie*. It took a team of 20 employees one year to complete the show's 13 episodes. Mainframe contracted with Hasbro Properties Group to create a series of half-hour Action Man cartoons created exclusively with CGI technology. Meanwhile, Pixar formed an alliance with the Canadian firm Maya Unlimited to provide geometric modeling for future Pixar film projects.

Hollywood has often sent animation work overseas, especially to companies in the Far East. In Korea though, one firm has made its own bid into the market. Graphic Animatio Visual and Multimedia, owned by Shon Dong-soo, is the only Korean company to produce CD-ROMs, computer games, television shows, music videos, Internet sites, stop-motion clay animation, and video magazines. Shon, the first person in his country to use computer animation, began experimenting with the process in 1993 after a tour of NHK studios in Japan. By 1999 Shon had created an award-winning educational CD-ROM featuring Ricky and Ralph, a small boy and his fuzzy yellow friend. Shon's long-term goals include producing a full-length animated movie.

International partnerships also hoped to improve on the prehistoric realism of one of the most utilized purposes of CGI—dinosaur creation. In early 2000 the BBC in the United Kingdom hooked up with the Discovery Channel to re-create the Jurassic lizards in "Walking with Dinosaurs," a miniseries that recaptured dinosaurs as they lived in their natural habitat. Touching up the California redwood forest, Chilean volcanoes, and the Arizona desert with animation effects, the digital dinosaurs were layered over authentic photographic backgrounds. The animation team at London-based Frame-Store created scale dinosaurs, scanned them into computers, and refitted the creatures' actions to suit the scenery. The computerized material was then shot again with the cameras to create lifelike scenes of dinosaurs in their own habitat. After its British debut on the BBC, the ambitious miniseries, which cost $9.8 million, made its rounds into over 30 international markets, attracting record ratings in several of them.

RESEARCH AND TECHNOLOGY

Creating animated characters out of thin air is a long, laborious process. While computers play a large role in animation, hand drawings are still the first step.

Artists' sketches develop the story line and characters. As an example, it took 27,000 such sketches to define the plot and personalities of the characters in *A Bug's Life*. The design department then used these sketches to model clay figures of the insects. These clay figures gave the animators an idea of how the characters moved. From there, the clay figures were transformed onto a computer screen as 3-D wire-frame models. Technical directors put opaque-surfaced polygons over the wire-frame models. The purpose of the opaque surfaces was to show the animators how light would reflect off the figures. Afterwards, animators brought the 3-D images to life, while technical artists filled in the background and applied the final touches to the characters. When animators want to create animated human figures, they use a motion capture booth, which records a person's movements and translates them into 3-D images. Rainbow Studios has an 800-square-foot motion capture booth that it uses in the development of animated video games for Microsoft.

The computer can transform or alter an on-screen image. For instance, morphing, a popular special-effect technique that blends one image into another and was first used in the movie *Willow* in 1988, is created by technicians providing the computer with the first frame in the transformation sequence and the last frame. The computer then automatically generates the fill-in frames segueing from one image to the other. While computers can add images to the screen, they also can erase what is there. This technique was used to digitally remove the cable that helped Julia Roberts to fly as Tinkerbell in *Hook* (1991).

One of the difficulties for animators, even with high-level computers, was the need to get the complete drawings exactly correct, or else spend valuable time re-creating the animation sequence from scratch. In 1999, New York-based Improv introduced its Siggraph technology, which animators can use to store animation sequences for use in overlaying various scenes and activities. In this way, if a certain portion of an animation sequence is not to a director's liking, the particular components can simply be overlaid with a new component pulled from a stored sequence library, saving the time, effort, and money of re-creating the entire sequence. After building up a library over time, animators could conceivably create entirely new scenes using a simple cut-and-paste approach.

FURTHER READING

Alexander, Kieth L. "Studios in Animated War for Viewer Hearts, Wallets." *USA Today,* 30 June 2000.

"Animated Films Get Own Oscar." *The Atlanta Journal and Constitution,* 29 September 2000.

Graser, Marc, and Jon Herskovitz. "Sony Plays Through: PlayStation 2 to Go Out to Stores in March." *Daily Variety,* 14 September 1999.

Gritten, David. "Back to the Age of 'Dinosaurs': Computer-Generated Images Have Made Series a Hit Wherever It's Been Shown." *Los Angeles Times,* 15 April 2000.

Kahney, Leander. "Making Animation Child's Play." *Wired,* 11 March 2000. Available from http://www.wired.com/news/culture/0,1284,34871,00.html.

Kempley, Rita. "Turning Points of a Century: Movies; Digital Darwinism: Tech It to the Limit; The Special Effects Revolution Is Giving Reality a Bad Name." *Washington Post,* 26 December 1999.

Mallory, Michael. "How Much Further Can Computer Animation Go? Disney and Pixar Stretch the Limits in *Toy Story 2.*" *Los Angeles Times,* 18 November 1999.

Matthews, Jack. "Moviegoers, Stay 'Tuned': This Year's Screen Gems Promise to Be Highly Animated." *New York Daily News,* 9 January 2000.

O'Marcaigh, Fiachra. "Toys Will Be Toys, Once Again." *Irish Times,* 7 February 2000.

"Platform Development: Improv Brings Life to Computer Animation." *Multimedia Week,* 9 August 1999.

Solomon, Charles. "Uncle Duke's Multimedia Run for the White House: An Animated Version of the 'Doonesbury' Character Will Declare His Intentions—And Field Questions." *Los Angeles Times,* 11 February 2000.

Computer Network Support Services

Complicated technology, rising costs, and a dearth of information technology (IT) workers have made network support services a fast-moving business. According to one estimate, in 1999 network support services, broadly defined, were worth more than $100 billion. Growing 17 percent a year, moreover, industry revenues were forecast to pass the $200 billion milestone by 2003.

Although many customers have approached IT outsourcing with trepidation, fearing poor service and lack of accountability, service-level agreements (SLAs)—detailed contracts specifying a minimum quality of service and monetary penalties for the service vendor if the standard isn't met—have done much to allay concerns. Businesses that use outside network support are also increasingly selective about which tasks they farm out, so they are less likely to find themselves in an unsatisfactory blanket arrangement. Cost savings remain a key motivator for companies that hire network support services.

With service options proliferating and quality improving, some analysts envisage IT services growing ever more pervasive in network computing—to a point where a company doesn't need its own network, but relies entirely upon services. High-speed fiber-optic networks, the ubiquity of the Internet, and new networking paradigms such as virtual private networks have all helped make this possible on a limited scale, and point to a future where network services figure prominently.

ORGANIZATION AND STRUCTURE

In a typical network support agreement, the service provider may assume daily responsibility of a local area network or wide area network and guarantee a specified response time to all problems and difficulties. Additional services may include 24-hour, 7-day-a-week support; planning for optimal capacity; and preventive maintenance activities such as scheduled upgrades. Help desk services include handling trouble calls, resolving problems, and staging or coordinating inventories. Often the network support services provider becomes the liaison contact with other computer vendors involved with the contracting company including software, hardware, and telecommunications providers. Profit comes only with experienced personnel and volume—additional customers are incremental costs to a support operation.

Companies supplying computer network support services range in size from large vendors, such as AT&T Solutions Group and Compaq Computer Corp., down to much smaller resellers. Resellers, often called value-added resellers (VARs), may partner with larger corporations; that is, the VAR enters into a reseller agreement with the large corporation, and the giant wholesales its hardware and/or software to the reseller. VARs such as CompuCom Systems and Entex Information Services, Inc. customize products channeled from the vendor, bundle them with network and other services, and add value in other ways. VARs serve as the distribution channel for vendors and are often the primary source of computer equipment and services for small and medium-sized companies.

Due to growing client demand for support services and escalating hardware and software complexity, the interaction between large vendors and VARs is not always clearly defined. There is money to be made in services, and it seems everybody wants to take advantage of the opportunity. In response to the demand, and in an effort to boost revenues, vendors such as Hewlett-Packard Co. and IBM Corp. run integration, consulting, and service units or divisions that often compete with their channel partners for customers.

To gain an edge on the competition, a VAR can concentrate on available niche opportunities that are more appropriate for their smaller, more tightly focused organizations, or the reseller can work in a joint-venture or subcontract mode with a large services provider. A third option, which allows the reseller firm to be acquired by the giant, nets a nice profit for the business owner at the cost of the VAR's independent existence.

Because of the shortage of qualified IT personnel, the large corporations often cooperate with smaller firms in an attempt to provide enough quality consultants to implement the services that have been marketed. For example, during the 1990s Hewlett-Packard partnered with other large consulting firms, other information technology firms that maintained high staffing levels, and VARs who had specialized expertise not available internally at Hewlett-Packard. Intrachannel competition and cooperation work most smoothly for both parties when the large vendor operates under a set of consistent guidelines so that the VARs know when and where they will need to compete.

Telephone companies and their subsidiaries, such as Bell Atlantic Network Integration, perform network support and systems integration without a direct stake as reseller or vendor channel. Telecommunications companies such as MCI WorldCom and AT&T have become active in providing network support services and systems integration.

Finally, consulting firms such as Andersen Consulting and staffing service firms such as Adecco and Modis Professional Services provide network support services from a large pool of technical personnel.

BACKGROUND AND DEVELOPMENT

In the 1980s and early 1990s, network was a simple noun referring to "a group of computers and associated devices that are connected by communications facilities." It was easy to define and easy to visualize. A network's activities, which consisted mostly of making shared files and printers available to network members, were coordinated by a network operating system installed on a server. The network's activities were fairly limited and routine; a few information technology professionals could tame, control, and manage it.

By the mid-1990s, hardware and software advances had gradually expanded the basic network, as local area networks (LANs) supported more and more

users and demand for wide area networks (WANs), metropolitan area networks (MANs), and other configurations surged. Networks were the infrastructure for the fast-growing client/server paradigm. Added to the mix was a range of Internet technologies, which gobbled up resources on both the public network and the private networks that interfaced with it. The Internet's popularity brought an onslaught of new traffic to private networks in the form of e-mail, Web browsing, and related applications.

Stretched to the limit, companies turned to vendors or third-party companies for help installing, configuring, managing, maintaining, and troubleshooting their increasingly complex networks. By 1996, according to a *PC Week* feature, all Fortune 1000 companies had implemented outsourcing contracts with third-party companies for network support services. Computer network support services was becoming a rapidly growing, highly profitable industry niche.

A larger shift by corporations toward outsourcing nonessential functions also gave the industry a boost. According to a 1997 survey, almost 73 percent of IT managers reported outsourcing some of their technical needs. The top function outsourced was network maintenance (46.6 percent), followed by software development (42.5 percent), mainframe/legacy migrations (37 percent), software maintenance (32.9 percent), and Web site hosting (24.7 percent). According to another study, 27 percent of surveyed companies were considering outsourcing remote network management services as well.

The foremost problem with external service and support, according to a 1996 survey, was cost. Outsourcing expenses depended on the services required and the system's complexity. One company, NetSolve, offered a service called ProWatch Exchange for $5,500 per month for a 30-site network. Other companies offered more configurable pricing arrangements. AT&T Managed Network Solutions charged a base rate of $225 per site per month for a managed router contract, but it added $50 for each additional LAN or WAN connection. Additional problems identified in the same survey were poor responsiveness and lack of multivendor expertise.

CURRENT CONDITIONS

Demand for network support services remains very robust and is expected to continue rising. Among the forces fueling the market has been the spate of companies wishing to build or enhance their e-com-

---

Trends   **SIMPLER NETWORK DEVICES HAVEN'T SAPPED DEMAND FOR SUPPORT SERVICES**

Introduced in the mid-1990s, the network computer (NC) has so far been a negligible, if unpredictable, factor in the market for network support services. Touted as a solution to the complexities of the personal computer (PC), NCs don't contain all the software, hardware, and features that a PC does, thereby reducing costs and alleviating some support problems. Instead, NCs retrieve applications and files from a central computer as needed, so they require only a simple operating system and no local storage. Conceivably, this could reduce network administration markedly if NCs were widely deployed. They have not yet been widely deployed, however, and there have been few indications they will be. While one survey found 69 percent of Fortune 1000 chief information officers anticipated purchasing an NC by 2001, actual sales of the machines have been slack.

In a separate trend, though, sales of other thin-client devices known as Windows-based terminals (WBTs) soared in the late 1990s. The terminals, which are more bare-bones than NCs and are based on different technology, mirror mainframe-style centralized processing and storage, but to the end-user function much like any PC. They reportedly use less network bandwidth and work with a wide range of servers. As with NCs, WBTs could drastically simplify networking if they came into mass use.

---

merce capabilities. In doing so, they need anything from consulting and design services to integration services to hosting and management services. The proliferation of wireless network availability and related integration adds a boost to outsourcing demand. Other trends driving demand include the wider availability and flexibility of remote administration services, where the service provider performs diagnostics and system management tasks off-site using a network connection and special software, and brisk demand for network security services.

The fast-growing market for network support services has enticed a number of large players to bolster their presence through acquisitions and joint ventures. Market analysts at International Data Corp. suggested that as the computer hardware business grows less profitable, top hardware companies will gravitate toward services to sustain their business. Providing one example, Cisco Systems, the network hardware colossus, weighed in with heavy investments in the IT consulting wings of Cap Gemini and KPMG. The deals gave Cisco a hand in the service business and potentially opened new distribution channels for its hardware. Similarly, Lucent Technologies made a pair of acquisitions that added substantial heft to its already large network services concern (see below).

INDUSTRY LEADERS

AT&T SOLUTIONS GROUP

AT&T Solutions Group is one of the world's largest network support services, offering network design and analysis, installation, management, and train-

ing services. The AT&T unit drew favorable publicity in 1999 when it took over IBM's Global Network operations in a complex $5 billion transaction that brought 3,000 IBM employees to AT&T and sent 2,000 AT&T data-center workers over to IBM. AT&T renamed the service AT&T Global Network Services. Excluding that acquisition, AT&T Solutions' 1999 revenues totaled $1.6 billion, up 48 percent from the previous year. AT&T Corp. as a whole took in over $62 billion in 1999.

LUCENT TECHNOLOGIES INC.

Best known as a hardware vendor, Lucent Technologies Inc. is also a prominent provider of network support services. In 1997 the company formed Lucent NetCare Services, which offered clients consulting, management, and maintenance services for enterprise voice, data, and video networks. By 1999 Lucent had expanded its NetCare support capabilities to customers in 93 countries. The same year it acquired International Network Services and Ascend Communications, which added 2,200 employees to NetCare and bolstered its strength in network technologies such as asynchronous transfer mode (ATM) and Internet protocol (IP). At the end of 1999, NetCare had some 5,500 employees and approximately $760 million in annual revenue; NetCare accounted for just 2 percent of Lucent's $38 billion in company-wide sales.

IBM GLOBAL SERVICES

The world's largest IT services vendor, IBM's Global Services division posted 1999 revenues of $32.2 billion, up 11 percent from 1998. This increase came in the wake of the company's sale of the IBM

Global Network to AT&T. Network support, however, makes up only a small portion of IBM's service portfolio, which includes a full array of consulting, programming, maintenance, and integration services. IBM services chief Douglas T. Elix expressed his wish in 2000 to turn Global Services into IBM's biggest division by doubling sales within four years, a feat that Elix predicts will come largely from the integration of clients' systems into an e-business network.

HEWLETT-PACKARD CO.

Hewlett-Packard's $6.2 billion service business (as of fiscal 1999) supplies almost 15 percent of the integrated computer and peripheral device manufacturer's revenue. The company's highly regarded service organization, one of the world's largest, is part of its Enterprise Computing unit. In September 2000, Hewlett-Packard announced its plans to increase efforts to link service to hardware sales through the acquisition of the consulting branch of PricewaterhouseCoopers for $18 billion.

COMPAQ COMPUTER CORP.

Compaq emerged as a major network support services player after its purchase of Digital Equipment Corp. (DEC) in 1998. Nearly all of Compaq's service business originated from that acquisition, as DEC was a large and renowned service provider in its own right. In 1999 Compaq integrated its service arm into its Enterprise Solutions and Services (ESS) group, a unit that sells hardware, software, and services to large corporate clients. In 1999 ESS revenues reached $20 billion. Service revenues, which included network support and other services, contributed $6.6 billion, up sharply from $3.7 billion in 1998 due in part to the acquisition's timing.

WORK FORCE

At the end of the 20th century, the United States was experiencing a dramatic shortage of IT workers. The Information Technology Association of America estimated that there were 346,000 unfilled IT positions at U.S. firms in 1999. Demand for IT workers showed no sign of flagging either. The U.S. Bureau of Labor Statistics (BLS) predicted in 1998 that computer scientists, computer engineers, and systems analysts would be the three fastest-growing occupations through 2006. The forces cited by BLS as driving the demand for systems analysts included the expansion of client/server environments and increasing demand for networking to share information.

Computer network support services rely on highly trained and technologically proficient employees to garner contracts and produce profits. The BLS projected that the number of jobs nationwide for database administrators, computer support specialists, and other computer professions would more than double from 212,000 in 1996 to 461,000 by 2006.

According to a 1999 national salary survey by J & D Resources, Inc., typical salaries for network administrators ranged from $40,000 to $58,000, while network analysts, managers, and LAN/WAN specialists averaged between $50,000 and $75,000. For help-desk support technicians, average salaries ranged from $35,000 to $42,500. At the higher end, network architects typically earned $60,000 to $80,000, and systems architects pulled in $70,000 to $95,000.

AMERICA AND THE WORLD

GLOBAL MARKET OPPORTUNITIES

Western Europe was expected to offer sizable opportunities for support service vendors. The WAN-services market, for example, was projected to grow from $980 million in 1999 to more than $4 billion in 2001. Indeed, network management outsourcing services in general were forecast to top $9.5 billion in 2002, quadrupling from $2.3 billion in 1997.

In the late 1990s Australia was an estimated $2.4 billion computer services market, and it was expected to grow as systems became more complex and technical requirements for staff expertise became more rigorous. Services in demand included systems management, consulting, and education, which included training and help-desk services.

Latin America also presented a growing market opportunity for computer services with its information services market estimated at $6.3 billion. Of that market opportunity, Brazil had the largest share ($3.3 billion). With markets emerging for online databases and electronic data interchange, network support services were expected to make up a significant percentage of the overall market for services as the 21st century began.

FURTHER READING

Aragon, Lawrence. "In Pursuit of Service." *VARBusiness*, 6 July 1998. Available from http://www.techweb.com/se/directlink.cgi?VAR19980706S0020.

Bliss, Jeff. "Deathwatch for Desktops?" *Computer Reseller News*, 10 March 1997.

Booker, Ellis, and Chuck Moozakis. "Cisco, Lucent Buy into Consulting Biz." *Internet Week,* 16 August 1999.

Briere, Daniel. "Network Integrators Can Be Lifesavers." *Network World,* 24 February 1997.

"A Call to Action: ITAA's Efforts to Address the Information Technology Skills Gap." 9 May 1999. Available from http://www.itaa.org/workforce/resources.

Connor, Deni. "HP Makes SAN Strides." *Network World Fusion,* 4 May 1999. Available from http://www.nwfusion.com/news/1999.

Dash, Julekha. "Care and Feeding for Desktops." *Software Management,* December 1996.

"Discussion Papers on Services, Information Technology and Electronic Commerce." *Free Trade Area of the Americas,* August 1997. Available from http://www.alcs-ftaa.oas.org/EnglishVersion/Services/its.htm.

Dix, John. "NW 200: Bigger and Better." *Network World,* 20 April 1998. Available from http://www.nwfusion.com/news/nw200.

Duffy, Jim. "Cisco, Cap Gemini Create Consulting Company." *Network World Fusion,* 9 March 2000. Available from http://www.nwfusion.com.

Dzubeck, Frank. "Managed Services Spell an End to Private Networking Era." *Network World,* 22 February 1999.

Gallant, John. "Handing Off Your Net Management Burden." *Network World,* 7 April 1997.

Greene, Tim. "Paying the Price for Good Network Service and Support." *Network World,* 25 March 1996.

Horwitt, Elisabeth. "Go Boldly: Leading-Edge Corporate Users Recommend an Aggressive Approach toward Adopting New Technologies." *Network World,* 3 May 1999. Available from http://www.nwfusion.com/news/1999.

Jacobs, April. "Start-ups Lead the Way." *Network World,* 3 May 1999. Available from http://www.nwfusion.com/ news/1999.

Levine, Ron. "What's Your Level?" *Communications News,* March 1999.

Lieberman, Lenny. "Going Global." *Internet Week,* 29 June 1998. Available from http://www.techweb.com/se/directlink.cgi?INW19980629S0065.

Lindstrom, Annie. "Outsourcing: A Bridge over Trouble IS Waters." *America's Network,* 1 October 1998.

Madden, John. "IT Services Expected to Soar as E-Commerce Takes Hold." *PC Week,* 24 May 1999.

Marion, Larry. "At Your Service; Expanding Services Industry." *PC Week,* 15 January 1996.

Merrill, Kevin. "Entex Beefs Up Network Integration Business." *Computer Reseller News,* 24 June 1996.

"Network Support Contract Spending Projected at $6 Billion by 2001." *EDP Weekly,* 26 March 1997.

Nicolle, Lindsay. "Freedom or Folly?" *Computer Weekly,* 24 June 1999.

Radcliffe, Deborah. "Hot on the Asset Trail." *Software Magazine,* December 1996.

Roberts, John. "Network Spending Will Continue to Surge." *Computer Reseller News,* 22 December 1997.

Rocks, David. "IBM's Hottest Product Isn't a Product." *Business Week,* 2 October 2000.

Rohde, David. "Managed Net Costs Add Up." *Network World,* 21 April 1997.

Russo, Anthony. "Outsourcing Managed Network Services." *Telecommunications,* February 2000.

Thyfault, Mary E. "AT&T's Network Menu." *Informationweek,* 17 February 1997.

U.S. Bureau of Labor Statistics. "Computer Scientists, Computer Engineers, and Systems Analysts." *1998-99 Occupational Outlook Handbook,* 9 May 1999. Available from http://www.bls.gov/oco.

Weil, Nancy. "Wireless LANs Take Flight." *PC World Online,* 20 April 1999. Available from http://www.pcworld.com/shared/printable_articles.

Weinberg, Neil. "Networks of the Future." *CNN Interactive,* 5 May 1999. Available from http://www.cnn.com/TECH/computing/9905/netpredict.ent.idg.

Weston, Rusty. "Why Fight IT?" *PC Week,* 22 July 1996.

Wolfenberger, Mark. "Close-Up: Computer Services." *Upside,* March 1997.

"World of Service, Support Opportunity." *Computer Reseller News,* 23 December 1996.

Wreden, Nick. "Plug Into Wireless Management." *Informationweek,* 8 May 2000.

Wright, John W. *The American Almanac of Jobs and Salaries.* New York: Avon Books, 1996.

Zarley, Craig. "The New Face of Client/Server: Channel Conflict Looms, but So Does Opportunity." *Computer Reseller News,* 1 January 1996.

COMPUTER SECURITY

With millions of consumers and businesses connected to the Internet and billions of dollars in transactions bouncing around cyberspace, computer crime is a mounting concern to many. Although the frequency and cost of computer crime are hard to pinpoint—most crimes go unnoticed and many that are noticed aren't reported—the Federal Bureau of Investigation (FBI) estimated the annual cost in the United States is about $10 billion.

Most applications and systems software—Web browsers, e-mail programs, operating systems, databases, and the like—have historically provided only rudimentary security at best, and are often easily vulnerable to devastating attack or misappropriation. While security in ordinary desktop applications is improving, to help users withstand such intrusions computer security companies market a diverse range of products and services to combat fraud, sabotage, and other unauthorized uses of computer resources:

- security consulting services
- virus detection software
- firewall hardware and software
- encryption software
- intrusion detection and analysis software
- specialty devices for user authentication (biometrics, voice recognition)

The market for all of these has been burgeoning. Sales of Internet-related security software alone were expected to rise more than 17 percent a year between 1998 and 2003, according to forecasts by International Data Corp. Corporate spending on such software in 2000 was estimated at $6.6 billion, and spending on network security services was expected to surpass $900 million.

ORGANIZATION AND STRUCTURE

The field of computer security is diverse and one in which opportunities are abundant for those with a wide range of skills. It has three main levels—physical, software, and administrative controls. Each level is addressed by a different specialist using different skills.

Physical security addresses problems such as fire, theft, sabotage, and malicious pranks. Systems analysts and security officers can address these types of problems.

Software security involves factors such as accidental disclosures caused by partially debugged or poorly designed programs, and active or passive infiltration of computer systems. Active infiltration includes such activities as using legitimate access to a system to obtain unauthorized information, obtaining identification to gain access through improper means, or getting into systems via unauthorized physical access. Passive infiltration includes activities such as wiretapping on data communications lines or databases and using concealed transmitters to send or retrieve data in central processing units, databases, or data communications lines. People involved in software security include analysts, network administrators, programmers, auditors, and security officers.

Administrative controls involve issues such as controls on personnel for fraud protection, controls on

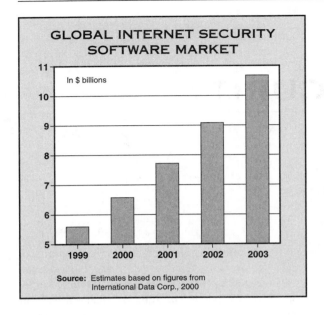

GLOBAL INTERNET SECURITY SOFTWARE MARKET

In $ billions

Source: Estimates based on figures from International Data Corp., 2000

sensitive programs, security of remote terminal access, software security, and file reconstruction capability. Auditors, programmers, systems analysts, security officers, and network administrators are involved in addressing the development and implementation of administrative controls.

While different specialists often address all of these security issues, the need for multilevel controls is increasing as the number of computers grow—one more indication that additional computer security is a continuing demand. The industry will no doubt grow to accommodate the problem.

BACKGROUND AND DEVELOPMENT

Computers for commercial use date back to the 1940s. Since that time, computers have evolved from gigantic board-wired, cathode-ray tube, card-deck-operated machines that literally filled climate-controlled glass houses into desktop machines that are many more times powerful than their larger predecessors.

By the 1990s people in every walk of life were using computers to perform a variety of tasks ranging from mixing recipe ingredients to desktop publishing. In many cases, they were tied into networks such as wide area networks, local area networks, and the Internet. The increasing reliance on networks has created a greater demand for security since networks allow for more opportunities to compromise files and databases.

Businesses in particular have been using more powerful computers for every function possible. Naturally, the almost infinite growth in data processing has led to computer-related problems such as crime, terrorism, and harassment from hackers who break into computer systems; and crackers who deliberately damage others' computers. The need for protection against hackers and crackers has prompted corporations and individuals to seek the help of security specialists.

The development of computer security procedures paralleled developments in the data processing industry. Each succeeding generation of computers has been accompanied by concomitant developments in security measures. Originally, computer security involved controlling access to computer rooms. It was concentrated in the industrial arena, since computers were rarely found outside industry. Computer security specialists were generally senior-level members of a company's data processing staff.

In the early days, computers were generally stand-alone units. Gradually, manufacturers added components such as modems that allowed computers in remote locations to communicate with one another. In the 1980s and 1990s businesses rapidly deployed legions of personal computers (PCs) and Unix-based workstations, often networking them so information and resources could be shared.

HACKERS, CRACKERS, AND THIEVES

Along with its many benefits, the rise of networking brought with it a multitude of security risks, as each computer on a network is a potential entry point for outside hackers and internal miscreants. In most cases the technology to exchange data between computers greatly outpaced the technology to keep them secure, and aside from a few rudimentary measures, security was often an afterthought.

Computer security accounted for about 2 percent of companies' information technology expenditures in 1998, according to International Data Corp. (IDC). Some hackers breached computers just for the fun of it, while others hoped to gain wealth, information, cause harm, or wreak havoc.

In 1998 IDC said that roughly 70 percent of Fortune 1000 companies had hired an ethical hacker to try and break into their own computer system. Such penetration testing to check firewalls will become a necessary part of every security consulting package in the future, according to the market-research firm.

he increase in computer crime in turn gave rise to a new breed of law enforcement officials who were experts in computer use. The need for specialists who could help law enforcement officials and others involved in the criminal justice system, such as lawyers and judges, familiarize themselves with security procedures concerning computers also grew. These technical advisers and consultants have been responsible for much of the research and new product development in the industry today.

The Adaptive Network Security Alliance, a coalition of 40 hardware and software vendors, tries to promote and enforce industry-wide standards to ensure all security products work well together. With the integration of automated tools, network administrators can plug a breach in a firewall in nanoseconds.

COMPUTER SECURITY AND THE LAW

One of the unique aspects of the computer security industry is its connection to the criminal justice system. Many of the activities computer security deals with are illegal. Thus, these activities fall under the broad heading of computer crime.

There are three primary areas of computer crime: data security and integrity, national security threats, and protection of software copyright. Currently, there is a technological gap between the criminal justice system and the enforcement of laws designed to prosecute computer criminals. This lag opens the door for more computer security experts among attorneys, law enforcement agencies, the military, and government organizations.

In August 1998 the nation's top antiterrorism chief discussed the threat of computer warfare that could cripple the United States. Potential targets include banks, airports, stock markets, telephones, and power suppliers. Richard Clark, the first national coordinator for security, infrastructure protection, and counter terrorism, proposed backup plans and vigilance to foil a coordinated multipronged attack from a foreign military, terrorist, or intelligence group.

CURRENT CONDITIONS

Needless to say, computer security has been a growth industry. As companies and individuals flock to the Internet, the public network is a growing source of intrusion. Accordingly, the market for Internet security software is growing swiftly. Worldwide, according to estimates by International Data Corp. (IDC), the corporate market for Internet security software totaled $6.6 billion in 2000, and was expected to top $10 billion by 2003. Firewalls, software that at-

tempts to create a barrier against outside access, were forecast to be the fastest-growing mode of Internet security, reaching $1.5 billion in global sales by 2003. Meanwhile, authentication and administration programs were expected to remain the top-selling software category, rising to $3.7 billion in 2003.

In the smaller field of network security services even faster growth was expected. Based on IDC figures, the world market for these services, which include security management and disaster recovery, was expanding at a compound rate of 34 percent a year between 1998 and 2003. The market approached $924 million in 2000 and was projected to hit $2.2 billion by 2003.

The U.S. government continues to fund research on information security. In 2000 the federal government budgeted $1.75 billion for this cause, and the Clinton administration boosted that to $2 billion for 2001. On the legislative front, a variety of bills were under consideration during the 1999 and 2000 sessions, including the controversial Cyberspace Electronic Security Act backed by the Clinton Justice Department. The bill, a counterpoint to the administration's easing of encryption software exports in 1999, would give law enforcement new powers to access encrypted information and conduct electronic searches. By fall 2000, the bill's fate was uncertain.

RECENT INCIDENTS

In April 1999 the FBI initiated the largest Internet manhunt ever to catch the world's fastest-spreading computer virus to date. The virus, known as Melissa, replicated itself through e- mail. All totaled, the FBI estimated that the virus infected more than 100,000 computer systems in commercial, government, and military installations, forcing some administrators to shut down their e-mail systems for a week. Investigators tracked down the originator with the help of a controversial serial identification number—called a Global Unique Identifier or GUID. In the end, authorities charged a 30-year-old computer programmer with creating Melissa. The following summer, a similar virus was spread to computers around the world, via an attachment with the disarming name "I Love You." Beginning in Asia, the virus spread by infecting the entire email systems of its recipients, who then inadvertently sent it on to others.

A much different kind of attack was mounted in February 2000, when several popular Web sites were disrupted with so-called denial-of-service attacks. The sites, including such mainstays as Amazon.com, eBay, and Yahoo!, were effectively taken offline when the host computers were inundated with bogus traffic generated by a handful of computers. As a result, legitimate users weren't able to access the sites. These sorts of attacks had erupted before periodically, but never on the same scale or with the same coordination. The episode highlighted the vulnerability of even the biggest sites.

EXTENT OF RISKS DETAILED

A prominent annual survey found that 62 percent of respondents from government and private industry in 1999 reported computer security breaches within the previous year. The study, conducted by the Computer Security Institute (CSI) and the FBI, pegged total losses due to security breaches at more than $123 million for the 163 organizations that disclosed losses. Heisted proprietary information and financial fraud were the most expensive breaches.

Consistent with previous research, the survey found that disgruntled workers represented the most likely source of attacks on business computer systems. Independent hackers placed second, while domestic industry competitors ranked the third most likely source. Fourth and fifth place went to foreign competitors and foreign governments, respectively. The Internet was blamed as the most frequent point of attack, reflecting a steady increase of incidents involving the Internet, but illicit access through internal systems and remote dial-up were also common.

The 1999 CSI/FBI survey further found that 55 percent of attacks on computer networks came from inside the organization. Another survey by NetVersant discovered that 83 percent of employees admitted to little or no compliance with their company's network security policies.

Meanwhile, the federal government itself was found to be seriously lagging behind in the effort to create secure computer environments. A study by the Subcommittee on Government Management, Information and Technology of the federal government's 26,000 separate computer systems found them to be in need of serious security overhaul. Issuing letter grades, the committee awarded no As, while about half the agencies received Ds and Fs. The General Accounting Office concluded that the government was riddled with serious and widespread security weaknesses.

PASSWORDS ON THE LOOSE

One of the most common ways of getting into a company's computer system involves little technical skill at all—computer criminals let themselves in thanks to shoddy password control. To the extent that passwords are a frontline defense against breaches, this is more a policy issue than a technical one. Sometimes termed social engineering, tactful hackers frequently persuade employees who have access to passwords to divulge them, often through some distracting pretense. In other cases employees leave their passwords written down in obvious places, which allows unauthorized users easy access. By one estimate, up to a third of all breaches involve password carelessness. The conventional logic in the computer security field is that companies need to articulate and enforce strict password-protection policies. Biometric authentication, one-time passwords, and multicriteria authentication are other ways to lessen the risk.

PIRACY AT THE WORKPLACE

Unlicensed software duplication, or piracy, has become a problem for some government agencies. For example, the city of Philadelphia paid a $120,000 fine in July 1997 because employees in two agencies installed pirated software.

Software piracy is not always intentional, however. In some cases, the laws are vague and potential pirates don't understand relevant copyright laws. The Federal Copyright Act of 1976, for example, allows users to copy their purchased software once, making a single copy for backup. Another subtle distinction: users don't purchase software, but licenses to use the software. To make matters more complicated, some software vendors explicitly allow a licensee to install their programs on multiple computers, such as a desktop computer and a notebook, provided that only one copy is in use at a time. Once a single licensed copy is on multiple computers, it's a slippery slope to violating the license, even for users who don't intend to.

LOSSES DUE TO COMPUTER CRIME

There are other significant and growing risks associated with the increase in computer usage. A 1985 survey of 1,000 organizations assessed verifiable computer crime-related losses as somewhere between $145 and $750 million. More recent figures from the FBI suggest that in the late 1990s the cost of computer crime ran $10 billion or more a year. When the value of stolen proprietary information is considered, a breach that manufacturers are particularly susceptible to, one study places losses at close to $50 billion. True figures are difficult to determine, though, because computer crime victims are not always willing to divulge actual loss figures in order to protect themselves and to prevent other violators from compromising their systems.

ENCRYPTION DILEMMA

Companies often use data-scrambling technology to protect their proprietary data and that of their clients. But the U.S. government insists that special access keys be built into encrypted messages, allowing law enforcement personnel to read them when they need to in order to solve crimes or prevent terrorist activity. The federal government also restricts U.S. firms from exporting top-quality encryption products, citing a concern that spies or terrorists may use the stolen software to evade government wiretaps. The Clinton administration, however, eased the export ban substantially in 1999 after years of political wrangling. The industry had long complained that the ban lost them billions of dollars in international sales that went to their foreign-based competitors.

Free speech and privacy advocates are pushing for stronger encryption to maintain the confidentiality of corporate records and the privacy of personal data. The existence of built-in loopholes undermines general public confidence in the security of their data. Resolving this issue, strong encryption for privacy versus built-in government access for law enforcement and national security, will be an important step in the development of secure communications over a global network.

INDUSTRY LEADERS

With revenues of $112 million in 1999, AXENT Technologies is a top supplier of risk-assessment and intrusion detection products. The company's sales rose 11 percent that year. By one estimate, AXENT controlled in 1999 some 40 percent of the global market for intrusion detection software. The company is also a leading marketer of firewalls under the Raptor Systems name, reflecting its merger with Raptor. In 2000 AXENT agreed to a deal whereby the firm would be acquired by Symantec for $875 million.

Symantec Corporation, based in Cupertino, California, was a giant security software firm, with its Norton Antivirus and other Norton Utilities generating enormous consumer sales. The company was using that leverage to shore up its security products designed for businesses and Internet firms. Founded by artificial-intelligence scientist Gary Hendrix in 1982, the company steadily grew through a series of acquisitions of smaller, niche-market software vendors. In the late 1990s, Symantec picked up IBM's and Intel's antivirus operations, and acquired its rival AXENT Technologies. Symantec recorded sales of $747.5 mil-

MOST COMMON COMPUTER SECURITY TOOLS

Tool	Percentage
Encrypted files	61
Encrypted login	46
Intrusion detection	42
Digital IDs	34
Biometrics	9

Percentage of companies reporting use in 1999

Source: *1999 Computer Crime and Security Survey,* Computer Security Institute

lion in fiscal 2000, nearly 60 percent of which derived from its computer security business.

Another leading security software vendor, Network Associates was created in 1997 through the merger of McAfee, maker of virus detection software, and Network General, which didn't compete in the security market. Early in 1998 Network Associates acquired Trusted Information Systems, a supplier of firewalls and intrusion-detection software. The merged company posted sales of $684 million in 1999. The same year Network Associates spun off its McAfee.com consumer virus-detection software site as a separate publicly traded company.

Check Point Software Technologies is one of the world's top producers of firewall software and other security programs. Its $219 million in 1999 sales represented a one-year increase of 55 percent, driven by new product introductions, partnerships, and strong demand. Among other new products, the company was targeting software at users of household broadband connections, such as digital subscriber line (DSL) and cable Internet services, which are particularly vulnerable to intrusion.

Internet Security Systems, a subsidiary of ISS Group Inc., is a leader in the risk-assessment, intrusion-detection, and adaptive security software segments. In 1999 the parent company's sales more than doubled to $116 million as a result of acquisitions and solid internal growth. The company also launched a security consulting service, although services in 1999 accounted for just over 10 percent of revenues.

WORK FORCE

The computer security industry is a component of the larger computer and data processing industry, and it is only recently that computer security technicians (or their equivalent) have become specialists within the industry. The *Career Security Technicians,* however, published by the U.S. Department of Labor, does acknowledge that security analysts belong to one of the small, rapidly growing specialties within the classification.

As the number of computers in use grows, so will the number of security analysts. Employment in the industry was projected to grow 90 percent between 1990 and 2005, making it the third-fastest growing industry in the economy. One out of every four employees in the industry is a computer programmer or computer systems analyst. Three of every four workers are between the ages of 25 and 44. The average firm in the industry employs only 18 workers.

Computer security specialists are also responsible for detecting illegalities in software copyright and bringing them to the attention of the proper authorities. In some cases, law enforcement agencies offer employment opportunities for security analysts. In other cases, computer security experts act alone to detect illegal or fraudulent activities. The variety of available experiences illustrate the numerous opportunities available to security experts who wish to become consultants in the field.

EMPLOYMENT OPPORTUNITIES

Security staffing levels have increased dramatically, nearly doubling since 1989. Information security staff, including consultants, contractors, and temporary workers, made up about 0.061 percent of total staff head count for North American companies that responded to a survey published in the spring 1998 issue of *Computer Security Journal.*

In firms with national security requirements, such as defense contractors and other government-affiliated organizations, information security staffing levels are higher (.121 percent) than in firms without national security requirements (.052 percent). In other statistics resulting from the survey, the responding companies devote 38.9 percent of their information security budget to in-house security staff and outsource 5.8 percent of their information security activities. Overall, as the demand for computers escalates in the coming years, opportunities will abound for people interested in entering the computer security field.

AMERICA AND THE WORLD

Along with the advantages of the growing industry of computers and networks is the disadvantage of the computer crimes becoming universal. People in the 1990s had access to an international network of computers, which made it more difficult for security experts to detect and prosecute computer criminals. For example, if a New York City Police Department computer security expert detects a computer criminal operating in Thailand or Chad, the security expert is not likely to be able to make an immediate arrest. Even if an arrest were possible, prosecution is often delayed, or even prevented altogether by international extradition treaties and cultural differences in approaches to criminal activity. Examples such as this highlight the complexities involved in detecting and halting computer crime and explain why computer security specialists emerge from such a diverse range of backgrounds.

SECURITY IS A WORLDWIDE CONCERN

The CERT Coordination Center (CERT/CC), based in Pittsburgh at the Carnegie Mellon University Software Engineering Institute, is a U.S. government-funded center used to coordinate communication during major computer security breaches. Established in 1988, CERT/CC strives to minimize the threat of future incidents by operating a 24-hour point of contact that can respond to security emergencies anywhere on the global Internet. The organization also facilitates communication among experts around the world who are working to solve security problems.

CERT/CC-developed incident response procedures have become the model for more than 69 incident response teams worldwide, including the Forum of Incident Response and Security Teams (FIRST). FIRST consists of individual incident response teams that focus on special national, industrial, and/or academic communities. Each FIRST team establishes contacts within its community, making it possible for FIRST members to meet the community's security needs, collaborate on incidents that cross national boundaries, and post transnational alerts and advisories on problems with local and/or global relevance. More than 50 FIRST teams work together in this global effort, including groups from Australia, Germany, the United Kingdom, Israel, and France.

RESEARCH AND TECHNOLOGY

Information security consultants and companies use a number of strategies to counter the threat of computer crime. The most commonly used security technologies are: antivirus software, which detect and nullify the effect of software "viruses" or programs that destroy or garble data when they're run on an unsuspecting victim's computer system; access control procedures, including the use of passwords and other user authentication techniques; physical security such as locked doors, guarded rooms, and other barriers to physical access; firewalls or software programs that restrict incoming and outgoing network traffic; and encryption or coding messages to make data illegible without the decoding key.

NEW SECURITY PRODUCTS

There is a constant need for new security-related computer products. One contemporary way of improving computer security is through keystroke analysis. This system, developed by New Mexico State University professor Juris Reinfelds and two associates, allows computer access only to individuals based on their typing styles. The system is relatively simple. It monitors the pace of users' keystrokes. A timing device or box traps keyboard signals before they reach the computer processor. The box then sends out two signals. One goes to the computer, and the second shows how many milliseconds have elapsed since the last keystroke. If the typing patterns do not match, the computer denies further access. The developers say the system detects impersonators 99 percent of the time. Moreover, it detects unauthorized users even after they enter legitimate passwords.

Another high-end line of products by Miros Inc. uses biometrics technology to fend off intruders. TrueFace Network, which rolled out in 1998, records the faces of authorized personnel to build a database of users. To log on to a personal computer or workstation, a user must face an attached video camera so the computer can compare the facial image to stored images. Recognition gains appropriate access in seconds. As a further fraud deterrent, TrueFace stores all log-on attempts and notifies administrators of unauthorized attempts. Miros also came up with the first facial recognition product used in check-cashing automatic teller machines worldwide.

Also in 1998, Compaq Computer Corp. came out with a low-cost fingerprint identification device that plugs into the home or office computer. To start, authorized users stick a finger inside the device, which takes a picture of the print. Then built-in software turns the print into a point map, which is stored for future reference. To log on, a user holds up the fin-

ger to the camera, and the computer checks the database. A matched print gains access to the hard drive or network.

FIREWALLS

Firewalls are another method of monitoring access to computers. There is some debate as to how effective firewalls can actually be, however. Some experts believe they are easy for hackers and crackers to get around. Even though there is much debate over their effectiveness, this has not prevented firewalls from becoming popular. Different types of firewalls offer different levels of security. The lowest-level firewall uses a technology called *packet filters*. The system examines the address from which data enters a system or the address to which it is going. It decides whether to let the data pass through based on its analysis.

Mid-level firewalls are circuit-level gatekeepers that prevent systems from coming into direct contact with the outside world. More advanced systems go well beyond examining the addresses or prohibiting direct contact. High-level programs look at the content of messages as well as the "to" and "from" addresses. Of course, prices of such packages and ease of installation are based on the level of the firewall, ranging in cost from $3,000 to $100,000. Installation of the more expensive packages can be time consuming and must be performed by security experts.

HARDWARE SECURITY

Researchers are developing security packages for hardware as well as software. Some are applicable to personal computers (PCs) as well as to computers owned by corporations. For example, the CompuTrace security system, developed by Absolute Software, instructs a PC modem to dial the company's toll-free number hotline at least once a week. Via the phone call, the modem reports its location through a caller-ID system, and all calls are logged. If the PC has been reported stolen, its new location is monitored and reported to local police.

One important feature of CompuTrace that lends to its success as a security method is that it acts like a computer virus—one of the computer security breaches that experts are defending against. CompuTrace does not show up in a computer's file directory, and it survives the reformatting of the hard disk on which it resides. If the phone line is inaccessible at the regularly scheduled call-in time, or if the connection is broken, the modem makes its check-in phone call when the line is free or when the connection is restored. CompuTrace also turns off the modem speaker before dialing. Perhaps the greatest draw to CompuTrace is its cost, which is under $100 per year for the software and service.

In 1999 a security breakthrough caused a stir amongst privacy advocates. Reacting to a boycott threat, industry giant Intel Corp. agreed to deactivate the identification system imbedded on Pentium III computer chips. With the system activated, online vendors can trace any transaction to a particular machine. The chips use a 96-digit serial number for the trace, similar to caller-ID devices for phones. Although deactivated for shipment, consumers can activate their system any time after purchase. Critics still worry that Web site proprietors and software vendors might make activation a condition of access to popular sites and programs.

Computer technologies change so rapidly that researchers are not always able to keep up. One source of help to deal with technological changes is the Internet. Computer users and security experts can access programs and Web sites designed to facilitate security. The Security Analysis Tool for Auditing Networks (SATAN) helps systems administrators recognize common network security problems. SATAN reports the problems without actually exploiting them. The Conduit is another computer security Web site that provides helpful information and links regarding network security. The concern about computer security is prompting people in diverse fields to develop new products designed to enhance network, individual PC, and stand-alone integrity. This continued focus guarantees an expansion of computer security efforts to protect owners and users against problems.

FURTHER READING

Alpert, Bill. "As E-Tailing Booms on the 'Net, So Does the Demand for Virtual Security." *Barron's,* 25 January 1999.

Banham, Russ. "Attack of the Cyber Villians." *World Trade,* August 2000.

Computer Security Institute. "1999 CSI/FBI Computer Crime and Security Survey." *Computer Security Issues and Trends,* winter 1999.

"Cyber Crime." *Business Week,* 21 February 2000.

Gips, Michael A. "Is Your Web Site a Hacker's Delight?" *Security Management,* August 1999.

Govea, G. Ernest. "Comparing Information Protection Practices." *Security Management,* September 2000.

Hamilton, David P. "Redesigning the Internet: Can It Be Less Vulnerable." *Wall Street Journal,* 14 February 2000.

Hancock, Bill. "Fortune 1000 Companies' IS Losses in 1998 over $45 Billion." *Computers & Security,* November 1999.

Harbert, Tam. "Supreme." *Electronic Business,* May 1999.

Hare, Chris. *Internet Firewalls and Network Security.* Indianapolis, IN: New Riders Publishers, 1996.

"How We Invaded a Fortune 500 Company." *Fortune,* 3 February 1997.

Information Security: Assessing Risks and Detecting Intrusions. Framingham, MA: Hurwitz Group, 1998.

Koerner, Brendan, and Jeff Glasser. "Who Can Stop Cybervandals?" *U.S. News & World Report,* 28 February 2000.

Lardner, James. "Intel Even Move Inside." *U.S. News & World Report,* 8 February 1999.

Lodin, Steve. "Firing up Data Defenses." *Security Management,* October 1999.

MacLachlan, Malcolm. "Companies Big and Small to Profit from Computer Security." *Business Journal Serving San Jose and Silicon Valley,* 2 March 1997.

Schafer, Sarah. *Digital Security, Inc.* November 1996.

Schwartz, Mathew. "Good Fences, Good Neighbors." *Computerworld,* 2 October 2000.

Simonds, Fred. *Network Security: Data and Voice Communications.* New York: McGraw-Hill, 1996.

Thibodeau, Patrick. "Federal Agencies Get Poor Grades for Security." *Computerworld,* 18 September 2000.

Wallack, Todd. "Computer Security Companies Are Making It Big Business in Massachusetts." *Boston Herald,* 31 August 1998.

Wood, Charles Cresson. *1998 Information Security Staffing Levels and the Standard of Due Care.* San Francisco: Computer Security Institute, 1998.

Young, Jeffrey. "Play to Hack Your Own System." *Forbes,* 4 June 1996.

Concierge Services, Corporate and Personal

INDUSTRY SNAPSHOT

In this workaday world, who has time for such headaches as picking up the laundry from the dry cleaners or returning that overdue library book? If corporate and personal concierge services firms have their way, the answer will be nobody. While the U.S. population had not yet entirely forsaken its routine personal chores to professionals, the concierge industry was exploding by the start of the year 2000.

As employees become increasingly swamped with work and its related stresses, many companies have begun to offer concierge services as part of their benefits packages. In this way, it was hoped that not only would employees be more likely to withstand the high pressure and long hours the jobs entail, but they would be more relaxed and focused on the tasks at hand. Concierges were charged with the performance of an almost limitless array of tasks tailored to individuals' particular needs. Usually, these are centered around basic chores such as grocery shopping, feeding pets, and running routine errands, but the tasks can include more personalized requests, such as researching golf-course locations, locating good insurance deals, and sending flowers to spouses.

Corporate concierge services essentially bring the outsourcing model to their employees' personal lives. The division of labor, so the theory goes, generates increased workplace productivity and boosted employee satisfaction.

ORGANIZATION AND STRUCTURE

The young concierge services industry was quite varied in its organization. Some corporations hired their own concierge staff to function as part of their payroll, while others contracted with local concierge firms to provide services on call. Concierge companies themselves sometimes employed as many as 200 concierges, while others featured only a local mother picking up extra cash by offering to run errands part-time.

For ongoing services, a company will typically pay concierges an annual fee of $1,000 to $5,000, depending on the size of the employer, though the multinational corporations may pay much more for more extensive services. At that point, the concierge's services are available to any employee needing a hand with personal chores. In many local markets, concierges also arrange special discounts with local businesses with the promise of regular patronage from those businesses.

Companies work out a variety of deals with concierge firms, tailoring the range of services and payments to suit their needs. Companies will sit down and decide which services they want to retain and which employee requests they will subsidize. Some companies simply set up an account with a concierge firm and allow employees to use the personal services at their own expense, although these employees typically pay less through the company's discount than they would if they had contracted with the concierge individually. Other firms may pay all or part of an employee's expense, in which case the company will typically put a rein on the type and extent of services an employee may request.

Though concierge services are most heavily utilized among larger corporations, they are quite popular among smaller businesses in several major cities, such as New York, Chicago, Boston, Los Angeles, Washington, D.C., San Francisco, and Atlanta.

BACKGROUND AND DEVELOPMENT

The concierge's connection to the hospitality industry actually dates back to the Middle Ages, when concierges were charged with catering to royal visitors and maintaining the keys of the royal government. The word "concierge" (pronounced cone-see-airge) stems from the French *comte des cierges,* meaning "keeper of the candles." Today's corporate and personal concierge services grew out of the hotel industry, which, especially among luxury operations, have offered such services to guests and regular clients for years.

As the U.S. work environment grew increasingly rushed and stressful for a greater number of employees, enterprising individuals and groups took notice of the fact that, on average, folks spent some 30 percent of their daytime hours taking care of personal and business logistical arrangements, and that spare time was a quickly vanishing commodity. Thus, they took the hotel industry's concept and applied it to a new business strategy. Such services could be expanded and offered directly to individuals or to companies seeking to augment their benefits packages and extract harder, higher-quality work out of their employees. The industry kicked into high gear beginning in the early 1990s, mainly at large companies such as PepsiCo and Andersen Consulting. Notoriously on-the-go consultants were among the earliest recipients of concierge services in the corporate world. By 2000, however, the practice knew few occupational boundaries, though it was still in the gestation period.

CURRENT CONDITIONS

As corporations began moving more and more personal amenities—such as gymnasiums, basketball courts, kitchens, and lounge areas—inside their buildings, they saw another opportunity to place even more personal time on the company clock. At first, the introduction of concierges to the workplace was seen as a way of avoiding the loss of work time to employee errands. Increasingly, however, concierges were seen as the answer to stress and preoccupation for employees while on the job. The perceived "time famine" among American workers, as they began working longer, harder, and faster, virtually created the industry explosion of the late 1990s.

The time famine, in fact, has alarmed many observers who saw in it an odd reversal of expectations as the United States grew increasingly prosperous through the late 20th century. The Families for Work Institute issued the reports of their survey in the late 1990s revealing that the average workweek expanded from 43.6 hours in 1977 to 47.1 hours in 1997, by which time 60 percent of those surveyed said they "never seem to have enough time to get everything done" at work, up from 40 percent in 1977. Many such employees therefore came to view concierge services as a blessing. And in the tight labor market of the late 1990s, workers increasingly began to scout out potential employers with a checklist that included concierge services.

Human resource departments have found concierge services particularly attractive since, after contracting with the concierge, a good chunk of their work is done. Very little ongoing maintenance is necessary once a concierge service has been established. It is usually simply a matter of introducing employees to the new service.

Concierge services still found their greatest employment among the larger, more prestigious corporations. Twenty-six of the companies listed on *Forbes'* list of the 100 Best Companies to Work For offered concierge services at the end of 1999, up from 15 just two years earlier, as did 11 of 1999's Fortune 100 companies.

While those grinding through the daily rat race may find the availability of such services a welcome relief, however, those viewing the trend toward concierge services through a wider critical lens sounded several alarm bells, contending that the practice exhibits a form of surrender of one's personal life to an employer—the logical next step following 24-hour voice mail, e-mail, and laptops for home work. Critics charge that the concierge practice removes individuals from their family and personal lives, and these charges are highlighted by several of the most extreme requests. For instance, the Atlanta concierge service My Gal Friday reported purchasing and wrapping one family's entire list of Christmas presents, and even filed divorce papers for one executive. Panic notwithstanding, the U.S. workplace seemed to be in no mood to slow its pace by 2000, and as such concierge services were expected to find themselves increasingly popular for years to come.

INDUSTRY LEADERS

Most concierge services firms were rather small and served only a local market, though by 2000 a few had graduated to serving regional or even national

About... AUTO CONCIERGES

In a move that ruffled a few auto dealers' feathers, Ford Motor Co. rolled out a new "auto concierge" service in 1998. With pilot projects in Los Angeles (where the company employed 17 concierges) and Chicago (with 10), Ford provided concierges to owners of Fords and other models to see to the vehicles' maintenance, cleaning, and purchasing needs. To generate business, these concierges were charged with trying to contact 20 customers each day. The company planned to introduce similar services in the 25 largest markets. On top of the cost of the car wash, oil change, or other services, customers paid a service fee to the concierge. In addition to car washes and tune-ups, Ford's concierges also help independent vehicle sellers place classified sales advertisements and handle purchasing inquiries.

Local Ford dealers, however, were none too pleased with the concierge service, which they viewed as severing the ties between customers and local dealers. Ford defended itself from these charges by countering that most of the services provided by the concierges were not typically offered at local dealerships.

But perhaps the most controversial aspect of the Ford program is its provision of auto concierge services to owners of cars of any make, a move that infuriated dealers who claimed that the company was driving away business. Again Ford disagreed, claiming that presenting itself as a service-friendly company would generate new business. By reaching out to customers who did not traditionally shop at Ford, and offering friendly, valuable service, the company hoped that more and more drivers would be steered toward Ford.

---

clientele. One such firm was aptly named 2 Places at 1 Time. Based in Atlanta, Georgia, 2 Places at 1 Time boasted such clients as Ernst & Young, Andersen Consulting, and PricewaterhouseCoopers, and recorded revenues of $5 million in 1999, up from $3.1 million in 1998. The company was founded in 1991 as a personal-errand service for individuals. By 2000, 2 Places at 1 Time employed 134 concierges in 41 offices throughout the United States and Canada, most of which worked for corporations on site. Other leading concierge firms included Pampered Professional Ltd., a personal-concierge service based in New York City that focused its business exclusively on individuals, many of them corporate executives; and Capital Concierge, based in New York, which focused on both individual and corporate clients throughout the greater New York area.

WORK FORCE

A typical concierge combines outstanding personal skills with resourcefulness and organization. Working on a company's payroll or as an outside vendor, concierges—or concierge teams, depending on the size of the company—typically organize an entire payroll's personal requests and schedule their fulfillment in accordance with an overall company plan so as to make sure the employees' needs are met in a cost-effective manner. Though the industry remained small at the start of the 21st century, concierges were beginning to gain some strong recognition. *Entrepre-*

neur magazine even listed the concierge profession as one of the hot new careers of 1999.

RESEARCH AND TECHNOLOGY

Since a good deal of one's personal chores are now conducted via cyberspace, that fact has not been lost on the concierge services industry. Cyber-concierges, also known as "compcierges," have cropped up in hotels to help travelers establish Internet connections from their laptops. Compcierges in fact offer a full range of computer support to hotel guests, and were offered as features catering to the business traveler. Other businesses, meanwhile, have placed their entire concierge operations online, inviting individual users to fill out requests on the World Wide Web. By 2000 this industry segment was consolidating in a hurry, providing one-stop shopping sites where consumers could upload a list of requests in one neat package.

FURTHER READING

Allerton, Haidee, and David Malpus. "Trick or Treat?" *Training & Development,* July 1996.

Amundson, Mavis. "From Finding Grave Sites to Gifts, Concierges Do it All." *Puget Sound Business Journal,* 21 January 2000.

"At Your Service." *Boston Business Journal,* 22 October 1999.

Caudron, Shari. "At Your Service." *Industry Week,* 18 January 1999.

Connelly, Mary. "Ford Dealers Lash Concierges." *Automotive News,* 16 August 1999.

Evarts, Eric C. "Masters of Your Tasks." *The Christian Science Monitor,* 24 July 2000.

Freaney, Margie. "In an Era of Workaholics, it's Getting Tougher to Figure Out When to Stop." *Atlanta Business Chronicle,* 30 April 1999.

Garrett, Echo Montgomery. "At Your Service." *Business Week,* 12 June 2000.

Graulich, David. "It's a Helping Hand That Holds You in the Workplace." *Business Press,* 23 June 1995.

Huang, Alarice. "Concierge Services Free Employees from Distractions." *HR Focus,* July 1999.

Marini, Mary. "In the Background." *Business Journal* (Phoenix), 25 February 2000.

McMenamin, Brigid. "Rent-a-Mom." *Forbes,* 21 February 2000.

Nemes, Judith. "When Computer Support Outweighs Theater Tickets." *Crain's Chicago Business,* 7 February 2000.

Taylor, Karla. "May I help You, Pleas?" *HRMagazine,* August 2000.

Useem, Jerry, and Ann Harrington. "Welcome to the New Company Town." *Fortune,* 10 January 2000.

Valigra, Lori. "401k. Vacation. Dog Food? Traditional Benefits Get Makeover to Fit Needs of Today's Worker." *Boston Globe,* 16 April 2000.

Waggoner, Jeff. "Concierge's Clients Keep Calendars Clear." *Capital District Business Review,* 24 May 1999.

CREDIT-CARD ISSUING

Unprecedented prosperity in the 1990s and at the start of the 21st century meant that American consumers were spending like crazy—and with an average of five cards in every cardholder's wallet, spending more with plastic than ever before. Total outstanding consumer credit rose from $119 billion in 1968 to $1.46 trillion in 2000 (in constant 2000 dollars). Qualitative changes abound, as well. Instead of reserving their cards to finance big-ticket items such as home appliances, consumers increasingly viewed credit cards as a convenient cash substitute, and used them more often to pay for groceries and other necessities. Though credit-card balances grew by 23 percent (accounting for inflation) in the 1990s, however, 40-50 percent of cardholders paid off their balances in full each month in 1999, compared with 20 to 30 percent in 1991. And according to Moody's Investors Service, delinquency rates dropped from 5.19 percent in 1999 to 4.83 percent in 2000.

Paradoxically, this consumer responsibility put card issuers in a bind. As more cardholders proved to be good credit risks, income derived from revolving balances—the primary source of revenue for card companies—dwindles. And with consumers in the driver's seat when shopping for cards, card firms were forced to lower interest rates, introduce zero or minimal introductory "teaser" rates, and pump up incentives to lure new customers. To recoup lost revenue, card companies raised penalty fees for over-limit charges and late payments, shortened grace periods, and introduced brand-new service fees, such as currency-conversion fees on purchases made outside of the United States. Some even charged "inactivity" fees to users who failed to exercise their plastic purchasing power at least once every six months. Fee income reached $20 billion in 1999, up from $7.3 billion five years earlier.

Card companies had to scramble in pursuit of new cardholders. While still relying on old recruitment techniques, such as direct mailings and telemarketing, card issuers also turned to ad campaigns aimed at tech-savvy generation X-ers and offered nearly "instant" credit approval via online applications. They stepped up efforts to cross-sell new programs to current cardholders. In addition, they courted untapped pools of potential card issuees, such as the newly affluent and small business owners. They even approached heretofore off-limits demographic pools, such as college students, teens, and those they formerly shunned—individuals with poor credit histories.

Changes in consumer spending habits also spurred new credit-card products and marketing strategies. The growing popularity of online financial transactions and shopping, which offer alternate modes of payment to conventional credit cards, meant that card companies had to adapt quickly to the world of Web commerce. Credit cards must contend with stored-value cards, electronic checks, and direct electronic bill-payment options. Chip-embedded "smart cards," already used in many countries, emerged in the United States as the most promising new card technology, though consumers were only gradually being won over.

Analysts foresee consolidation among top credit-card issuing banks, an increasing focus on overseas markets, and relatively low growth overall due to industry maturation. The Internet will occupy an ever-greater share of issuers' attention as they try to make their presence felt in the new e-commercialism. But the new century might bode a little better for credit cards. Card issuers reported profitability was up slightly in 1999 for the first time since 1994, with after-tax profits on card assets rising to 1.86 percent from 1.5 percent, according to an industry overview by R.K. Hammer Investment Bankers.

ORGANIZATION AND STRUCTURE

CREDIT, CHARGE, AND DEBIT CARDS

Traditional credit cards—magnetic-stripe plastic cards that, when accompanied by the holder's signature, entitle the bearer to draw on a revolving line of credit—still dominated the landscape of noncash transactions in the United States. Cardholders who carry over part of their balances to the next pay period are charged an annual rate of interest that varies according to their income and past credit history. Card firms often also levy an annual fee for use of their cards, plus additional penalties and other fees for charging over the approved card limit, making purchases outside of the United States, or failing to use the card within a specified period.

Some credit cards are affinity cards, which are offered jointly by two organizations; one is a financial institution and the other a nonfinancial group, such as a university or sports team. Cobranded cards are issued by financial institutions and collaborating retailers such as department stores or airlines. The cards bear the names of both organizations. MBNA Corp. dominates the domestic affinity-card market.

Charge cards are similar to credit cards, except outstanding balances must be paid in full by each due date. No interest is charged for their use. American Express and Diners' Club are the most well-known charge-card brands.

Debit cards are bank cards that, like checks, draw funds directly from the holder's bank account. The amount is taken out immediately with online cards, but is delayed by up to 72 hours with offline versions. Both MasterCard and Visa offer debit cards in addition to credit cards.

PRIVATE-LABEL CARDS

Retailers can issue private-label cards, which bear the retailer's logo. They are accepted only by issuer, which partners with financial companies to back the cards. About 10 percent of mass-market retailer Target Corp.'s $8.56 billion sales in 1999 were processed through its private-label card. Also in 1999, the globe's number-one retailer, Wal-Mart, jumped on the private-label bandwagon for the first time in its 37-year history. In February 2000 Staples debuted a no-fee, private-label credit card targeted at small business owners. Ford Motor Co. also developed a private-label card for small businesses; cardholders who service their cars at participating dealers earn discounts toward the purchase or lease of their next Ford.

THE INTERNET AND SMART CARDS

Smart cards (or chip cards) contain computer chips, some of which can hold up to 16K of memory. When read by special terminals, they can access data stored on the chip. They can be used as cash cards, identification cards, or credit cards, and offer potential for enhanced security for online financial transactions. By 2000, most smart cards functioned as memory-only cards, with stored monetary values, and thus served as a replacement for cash at photocopying machines, subways, and public phones. Smart cards have already been implemented in over 90 countries; Germany, for example, has 85 million national insurance smart cards. Smart cards are widely viewed as the next wide-scale development in the card industry. (Also see the essay in this book entitled Smart Cards.)

Though familiar in Europe, smart cards have yet to gain wide acceptance in the United States. American Express got the jump on the domestic smart-card market in 1999 when it premiered its Blue card, promoted as a "one-click, e-shopping tool" that doubles as a conventional credit card. The Blue card is used with a card reader that plugs into the holder's computer. The chip stores a digital-data certificate that enables the customer to shop online. To make purchases, the user inserts the card in the reader and types in a personal identification number, which permits the certificate to be read and unlocks the user's e-wallet. E-wallets function as secured locations for storing information required to complete purchases on the Internet, such as personal data, shipping addresses, and credit-card numbers and expiration dates. When the wallet is unlocked (opened) to make a purchase, it automatically fills out the online order form. The information in e-wallets can be stored on the shopper's desktop or at a remote location controlled by the issuer. Wallets can also remember user names and passwords to frequently visited Web sites.

BACKGROUND AND DEVELOPMENT

In 2000 the modern credit card completed its fifth decade. The concept of credit cards appeared much earlier, in Edward Bellamy's futuristic 1888 novel, *Looking Backward*. Proprietary credit cards, honored only at a single establishment, appeared in the 1920s, when a California gas-station chain issued cards to its regular customers. Departments and hotels followed suit. In 1947 Flatbush National Bank collaborated with nearby retailers in an arrangement that permitted customers to charge their purchases; the result was the first known third-party charge card.

The charge card burst onto the national scene in 1950 with the Diners' Club card, which a number of hotels and restaurants agreed to accept. In 1958 American Express (AmEx) created its own charge card to rival the industry pioneer. Although early versions were made of cardboard, AmEx introduced plastic cards and computerized billing in the 1970s.

Also in 1958, Bank of America premiered Bank Americard (known as Visa since 1976), the first true credit card. With it, customers didn't have to pay off their card balances each month. Instead, they could make a minimum payment and be charged interest on the remaining revolving balance. The initial offer of a $500 line of credit with an 18 percent interest rate drew about 60,000 members. In 1966 Bank of America started licensing the card to other financial institutions. Competition grew with the creation of Master Charge (now MasterCard) in 1977, a new credit card backed by a consortium of Midwestern banks.

Governmental regulation of the industry really began with congressional passage of the Truth in Lending Act (TILA), part of the Consumer Protection Act, in 1968. TILA was intended to protect consumers against abusive lending practices and to mandate comprehensible disclosure of credit terms so that consumers could make more informed credit decisions. The act has been amended numerous times. Other important legislation includes the Equal Credit Opportunity Act; enacted in 1974, it prohibits creditors from discriminating against consumers on the basis of sex or marital status. Two years later its scope was enlarged to bar additional discrimination based on race, color, religion, national origin, age, or receipt of public assistance. In 1989 Senator Charles Schumer won approval for Regulation Z to become part of the Fair Credit and Charge Card Disclosure Act. It required that key credit information, such as annual interest rate, fees, and grace periods, be grouped together on applications and displayed in what became known as the "Schumer box." Some issuers circumvented the regulation by printing the box in small type and placing it in an unobtrusive location on the forms. In May 2000 the Federal Reserve Board proposed an amendment to Regulation Z, stipulating that the Schumer box must appear in "reasonably understandable form" and be "prominently located."

PIONEERS IN THE FIELD

FRANK McNAMARA

The man behind the first widely accepted charge card was Frank McNamara, a World War II veteran, who founded Diners' Club in 1950. McNamara claimed he dreamed up the idea of presenting an authorized cash substitute, the value of which the carrier would pay at a later date, one evening in New York City when he couldn't foot the dinner bill while entertaining a business client. Dubbed the "last supper," the incident was later revealed to be a promotional yarn.

McNamara, however, did persuade a group of New York restaurateurs to take cardboard cards in lieu of hard cash from customers, on the understanding that the cards were backed by a financially reliable third party—Diners' Club. Diners' Club paid the restaurant bills, retained a 7 percent service fee, and then in turn was paid by its cardholders. Within two years, approximately 150,000 diners had become card-carrying members.

In the long run, this scheme didn't benefit McNamara, though. He sold his interest in Diners' Club in 1952 for $500,000, believing that charge cards were merely a passing trend. After having tried his luck with real estate, in 1957 he died penniless of a heart attack at age 40.

CURRENT CONDITIONS

Americans love plastic; in 1999 they charged over $1 trillion on their Visa, MasterCard, American Express, and Discover cards. About 78 million of the 105 million U.S. households used at least one credit card, and 1.306 billion credit, debit, and charge cards were in circulation. Households that didn't pay off their cards in full each month carried an average balance of $7,564, up from $2,985 in 1990. The number of those paying in full, however, rose from 29 percent in 1991 to 44 percent in 1999, according to CardWeb.com.

Consumers drove card issuing in the 1990s and early 2000s. Their relative affluence and prompt balance payoffs enabled them to shop selectively for the

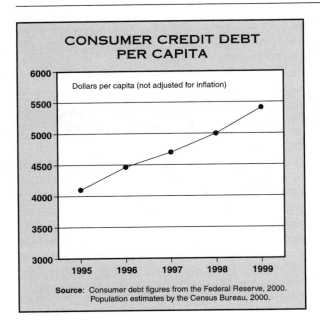

CONSUMER CREDIT DEBT PER CAPITA

Dollars per capita (not adjusted for inflation)

Source: Consumer debt figures from the Federal Reserve, 2000. Population estimates by the Census Bureau, 2000.

best deals. They demonstrated little loyalty, switching cards as soon as prime teaser rates expired or an issuer upped its fees.

ISSUERS PURSUE NEW BUSINESS

Issuers became increasingly aggressive in pursuing new accounts. They continued to employ such standard customer-recruitment techniques as direct mailings and telemarketing, while devising new promotional strategies. These included streamlined, Web-based application procedures, chip-embedded smart cards, and tempting perks such as free computers or trips to the World Series. They also set their sights on undertapped pools of potential cardholders, such as small businesses, college and high school students, and individuals with poor credit histories.

Traditional recruiting techniques fared badly in the highly competitive atmosphere of the 1990s and the start of the next decade. Consumers turned an especially blind eye to direct-mail solicitations. ConsumerAffairs.com noted that fewer than 1 percent of such mailings generated new business in 1999. Switching the venue for pitches from the U.S. mail to the Web didn't help; the response rate for online solicitations hovered around 1 percent as well. Including the messages "invited to apply" or "pre-approved" generated higher response rates, especially from individuals with poorer credit profiles. Still, amidst the generally low response rates and the heightened selectivity of issuers in a period of improving credit quality, card issuers scaled back their solicitations in 2000.

NEW PRODUCTS

Affinity cards remained a popular means of generating accounts. First USA pledged $16 million to the University of Tennessee, payable over seven years, in exchange for exclusive rights to market its Visa affinity cards to the university's students, staff, and alumni. In addition, the university received 5 percent of every transaction charge. Schools are often paid $20-$50 for each account generated. Sometimes issuers earmark contributions for specific endeavors, such as tutoring centers, athletic programs, or campus radio stations—raising concerns that they may exercise at least indirect influence over the functioning or content of such programs. MBNA, the foremost affinity issuer, entered a marketing agreement with Virtual Communities, Inc. of New York to issue affinity cards focused on the ethnic-identity groups featured on each of its ethnic Web sites.

Other tried-and-true draws were rebates or discounts on selected products, or other incentives for card members. Perhaps the most well known of these are frequent-flier miles. Visa scored a success in 1999 with its "Once in a Lifetime NFL Fantasy" incentive. People who made transactions in September and October were entered into a lottery for the chance to participate in a National Football League half-time show. First USA teamed up with computer distributors People PC and Free Mac to attract new customers to its online WingspanBank.com by giving away Mac computers. Even altruistic incentives were tried. AmEx donated 10 cents for every transaction processed on its cards in September and October 1999 to the Breast Cancer Research Foundation.

Some issuers began offering online procedures that featured anonymity and accelerated approval. But according to the *1999 Comprehensive Credit Card Holder* survey by J.D. Power and Associates, online applicants often have poorer credit profiles than those who respond to other solicitations. Nearly 26 percent of consumers who applied online in 1998 failed to pay their bills promptly, versus 13 percent of applicants who chose other application venues. Web applicants also proved less loyal. But they also owed a higher average annual balance, and thus represented a potentially lucrative source of fee income for issuers ready to take on risks. In addition, a 2000 survey conducted by New York-based Cyber Dialogue Inc. further found that online credit applicants maintained a slightly higher net worth than the average Internet user. Online applications were in their infancy at the end of the 1990s; only 4 percent of the 10,420 cardholders surveyed by J.D. Power used the Internet to apply. But Forrester Research predicted that by 2003 one in every six cards would be obtained through on-line applications.

In 1997 NextCard became the first company to approve all its cards online instantly. As the only purely Internet card company, all its account management, from application to bill payment, can be done online through its NextBank.com. As part of its 1999 marketing strategy, NextCard worked with Gator.com to give away adjunct e-wallets for use with their cards. Customers download Gator software and set up a Gator icon on their desktop. The Gator automatically pops up whenever an online merchandise order form appears. Clicking on the Gator fills out the form.

Despite the fanfare that accompanied AmEx Blue, the United States remained a tough chip sell. Nevertheless, MasterCard launched its own chip card in 1999, M/Chip Lite, which cost 60-70 percent less than its M/Chip Select; it was based on the Multos operation system for multiapplication smart cards. Providian offered an online Aria Visa and First USA had cobranded Internet cards with America Online and Yahoo!

NEW TARGETS

Issuers also strove to reach new groups of potential members. For example, small businesses were identified as an underserved and very promising market. Of the 14-20 million small business owners in the United States, only 17.3 percent used business cards for transactions in 1992. But usage tripled by century's end, according to a survey by the National Small Business United and Arthur Andersen's Enterprise Group. Only 100 of the 21,000 financial institutions that issued Visa cards offered debit or credit cards tailored for small businesses in the late 1990s. Visa tried to persuade existing consumer credit members with small businesses to take on business-only cards. AmEx courted small businesses with card-related product and service discounts with retailers such as IBM, Federal Express, Mobil, and Hertz, as well as a Blue Business card. In 1999 LiveCapital.com was the first institution to offer small-business-oriented cards on its online site.

Visa USA president and CEO Carl Pascarelli identified business-to-business (B2B) online transactions as the largest unconquered market on the horizon. Global transactions were expected to increase to $7 trillion by 2004 from $109 billion in 1999, and the United States would account for approximately 60 percent of that activity. The sector could outstrip consumer electronic commerce spending by 10 to 20 times. But Internet application providers such as Ariba and Clarus, and emerging B2B Web sites such as Metal Site, could challenge card issuers. Since they typically trade with a limited number of partners and have less need for general payment forms, private-label payment options could dominate this arena.

Potential customers that issuers used to approach with caution drew increased attention. So-called tweeners—people with emerging credit, such as recent immigrants, and formerly good customers whose credit ratings slipped because of temporary financial difficulties—form the exclusive market for some card companies, such as CompuCredit of Atlanta. Providian Financial concentrates on wooing customers many of its competitors spurn. Using direct mail and the Internet, it targets subprime customers with poor credit records or who tend to maintain credit-card balances. Providian claimed 12.4 million accounts in 2000, signing so many new members that it experienced a 664 percent gain in loans outstanding, the biggest such gain among all top-10 issuers.

But with U.S. affluence at record levels in 2000, perhaps the most prized target market was the wealthy. Visa's Signature, MasterCard's World Card, and American Express's Centurion Card all paved the way for a new round of competition with premium-level fee-based products. Largely targeting the scores of new professionals that emerged in the late 1990s, such programs seek to mitigate the industry's over-reliance on squeezing fees out of the lower end of the consumer market. Typical perks of such cards also reflect their audience: travel benefits and advice, concierge services, shopping privileges, and other special offers. AmEx's Centurion carries a whopping $1,000 annual fee, in return for which customers receive discounts on card expenditures. The popularity of these cards created an industry buzz at the turn of the century. Visa attracted over 1 million customers to its Signature Card in about two years.

INDUSTRY TROUBLES

Visa and MasterCard were enmeshed in several lawsuits in the late 1990s. Wal-Mart led a group of 4 million retailers in a lawsuit against the two companies, attacking their debit-card policy. Debit-card issuers require that merchants accept their debit cards as readily as credit cards, and charge similar fees to process both. But debit cards, unlike credit cards, don't encourage shoppers to spend more than they can immediately afford, so retailers find little reason to pay high fees on the Visa and MasterCard debit cards, especially when regional networks such as STAR, Cir-

Trends

TARGETING TOMORROW'S SPENDERS TODAY

American teenagers present a tantalizing market for issuers—yet one that remained largely beyond their grasp. Like many others, teenagers have reaped the benefits of U.S. prosperity. About 31 million teenagers spent nearly $153 billion in 1999, up 8.5 percent from the previous year, according to Teenage Research Unlimited. Their numbers are expected to reach 35 million by 2010. And they make up the largest demographic segment of Web users, with 88 percent logging on to the Internet. They are too young to qualify for credit cards of their own, however, and only 9 percent possessed parent-sponsored cards by 2000.

Frustrated by the untapped potential teens represent, companies devised numerous schemes to extend credit to them in hopes of hooking them as long-term, card-carrying customers when they come of age. Some firms, such as Illinois-based PocketCard, offer Visa debit cards, which are linked to spending limits prepaid by the teen's parents and which can be used at most retailers. Debit cards are being challenged by online accounts, furnished by such companies as RocketCash and Doughnet.com, which teens can open jointly with their parents. These accounts facilitate online teen shopping, while permitting parents to designate the Internet retailers their children may buy from using the accounts. To circumvent often-unwelcome parental surveillance, San Francisco's Cybermoola.com introduced prepaid cards that can be funded by check or debit card. When users register, they receive an account number and password. Prepaid cards were also available for purchase at retail outlets.

Cobaltcard, a San Francisco start-up, planned to introduce a Visa card especially for 13- to 22-year-olds, which would be connected to deposit accounts into which young people or their parents transfer funds. Unlike most secured cards, for which collateral remains in the account, Cobaltcard cardholders will replace account funds as they make purchases. Young people can apply for themselves, but will not be able to evade restrictions entirely, since the card includes a built-in coding mechanism to block purchases from "inappropriate" e-retailers.

College students formed another youthful target. Professor Robert Manning, a sociologist at Georgetown University, found that about 70 percent of all students at four-year schools possessed at least one card and that card debt among college students nearly tripled since 1990. Students, however, constitute an attractive new customer base because on average they retain their first credit card for about 15 years. And despite their often-low incomes, they can prove good credit risks, because their parents frequently make their payments when they are unable to do so.

Not everyone endorsed targeting those under 21. In 1999 an amendment was introduced to the Bankruptcy Overhaul Bill to bar issuers from authorizing cards for those under 21 without parental permission or clear evidence of financial ability to repay. Senator Ted Kennedy championed the amendment, citing that in the last eight years bankruptcy filings by those under 25 increased by 50 percent and that 9 percent of all college students carried a credit-card debt of $3,000 to $7,000; 5 percent were indebted for more than $7,000. In an unlikely pairing, Senator Orrin Hatch joined his opposition. These arguments, however, failed to sway most lawmakers, who quashed the amendment.

---

rus, or NYCE charge much less. The plaintiffs sought compensatory damages for the difference, which estimates placed at $8.1 to $63 billion. In June 2000 the U.S. Department of Justice took Visa and MasterCard to court for antitrust violations, complaining that the two prohibit their shared network of banks from issuing the cards of competitors such as American Express and Discover. In August, the DOJ issued its proposed final judgment, calling on the companies to require of their respective board members exclusive dedication to their companies, and to repeal their exclusionary practices. A third antitrust lawsuit was filed against Visa and MasterCard in the California State Superior Court of Alameda County. It contested the 1 percent fee that they charge for currency conversion. Consumers incur the fee when they make purchases abroad. The lawsuit alleged that "there is no rational relationship between the additional cost to the defendants of a foreign card charge and the currency conversion fee defendants levy." Furthermore, the suit claimed that over four years, Visa made about $500 million in currency conversion fees, and MasterCard about $200 million. Among other charges were that the fee is not disclosed to consumers, and violates the Truth in Lending Act.

Card-issuing banks also received scrutiny. Payment-posting practices at First USA in particular caused concern. The Office of the Comptroller of the Currency, which regulates national banks, received 2,793 complaints about First USA in the first half of 1999, more than for the next nine largest bank issuers put together. First USA responded that it reviewed all affected accounts and refunded late fees and interest charges as appropriate. It also severed connections with all three of its outside payment-processing centers.

INDUSTRY LEADERS

The industry overview by the Nilson Report, a trade publication covering consumer payment systems, revealed that giant Visa overshadows all its rivals in the industry. In 1999 Visa claimed 48.8 percent of the U.S. general-purpose card market, trailed by MasterCard with 27.7 percent, and American Express with 17 percent; Diners' Club and DiscoverCard accounted for most of the remainder.

Visa International, based in Foster City, California, remained the reigning monarch of the consumer loans industry, with 800 million Visa cards in circulation worldwide. About 21,000 banks own Visa Corp. and each issues and markets its own Visa cards. The VisaNet payment system authorizes and processes transactions for all the owner-banks. Besides plastic credit cards, Visa offers debit cards, value-stored cards, and online payment systems. Visa's 1999 sales were $2.8 trillion for a one-year sales growth of nearly 10 percent. Visa reported $721.1 billion in consumer and business purchases made on its cards for 1999, an 18 percent increase from 1998 and the largest such growth the company has experienced. Its debit-card purchases rose even faster—36 percent in the same period. E-Visa transactions lagged, with only 2 percent of all 1999 Visa transactions made with its online card. But the company predicted that figure would reach 10 percent by 2003.

Number-two MasterCard International, Inc., in Purchase, New York, is owned by more than 22,000 financial institutions. Like VisaNet, MasterCard handles marketing and account approval and processing for all its products, including its MasterCard credit and debit cards and its European Maestro debit cards. MasterCard grew 13 percent in 1999, with U.S. transactions totaling $352.1 billion, roughly equivalent to 49 percent of industry-leader Visa's volume. MasterCard also offered Click Credit, an online only product.

Third-ranked American Express Co. (AmEx) is headquartered in New York City. In the late 1990s it broadened its palette of card offerings (the standard green American Express card and its upscale cousin AmEx gold) with the launch of smart-card AmEx Blue, and superelite AmEx Centurion (AmEx Black card) in the United Kingdom. AmEx posted 1999 sales of $21.3 billion, for a one-year growth of just over 11 percent. Almost 1.6 million cardholders were registered with American Express Online Services, which permits them to review accounts and pay bills online. Worldwide, its total cards in force increased by 9 percent.

DiscoverCard, the credit-card issuer for Morgan Stanley Dean Witter & Co. of New York, claimed about 46 million members and formed the largest independent credit network in the United States. The card is well known for its annual CashBack bonus. MBNA, the leading affinity-card issuer, reported 1999 sales of $6.47 billion, an increase of 24.5 percent for one year. MBNA boasts affinity relationships with over 500 universities and colleges.

Among Internet credit-card issuers, First USA led the field with 1.7 million accounts, followed by NextCard Inc.'s 250,000, and Providian's (Aria) 220,000. NextCard Visa cardholders can access account information via the Web. NextCard's NextBank (formerly Textron National Bank) enables it to take deposits and generate its own credit cards. Customers can also pay bills online, via PayTrust. Its 1999 sales of $26.6 million represented a whopping one-year sales growth of 2,116.7 percent. NextCard also offers a cobranded online card with Amazon.com.

Providian's net income grew by 86 percent in 1999 to $550.3 million. But Providian's practices drew scrutiny in 1999 and shares dropped 20 percent when the Connecticut attorney general and California district attorney launched probes into the company's issuing and billing practices. Charges alleged that Providian unfairly imposed late fees when it failed to record payments promptly as they were received. Several investors brought a class-action suit against in company in late 1999, for which the company paid out hefty settlements in 2000.

New York's Citigroup Inc., created by the merger of Citibank and Travelers Group, recently stole the lead from First USA Bank in U.S. card issuing. Ranked seventh in the Fortune 500, it had operations in over 100 countries and 1999 sales of approximately $82 billion. Its AAdvantage card was the most successful cobranded card in the industry. First USA Bank, a Bank One subsidiary, boasts 56 million cardholders of its own Visa cards, as well as cards for over 1,500 retailers, financial institutions, and universities.

AMERICA AND THE WORLD

American card issuers must envy their Icelandic counterparts. By the end of the 1990s, Iceland had become the world's most "cashless" society—only 14 percent of all financial transactions involved the use of hard currency. By the early 2000s, even parking meters would accept stored-value cards.

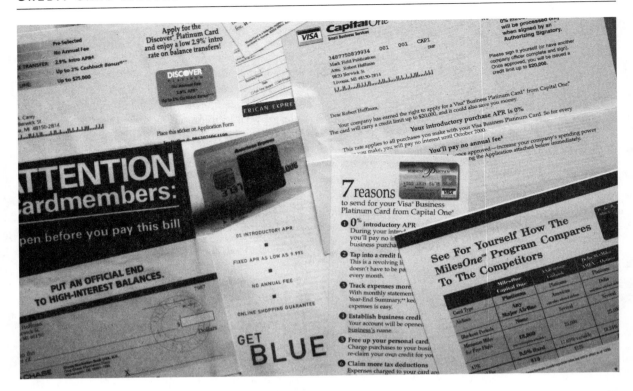

The typical consumer is bombarded by credit-card offers via mail. *(FieldMark Publications/Robert J. Huffman)*

In the rest of the globe, however, the acceptance of plastic has been less all-embracing. Most European cards are debit cards, like Maestro, rather than credit cards. With the proliferation of smart cards, some countries previously not receptive to credit cards seemed poised to avoid their implementation altogether. Instead, they were moving directly to the adoption of smart-card technology. Visa was pursuing collaborations with 22 global vendors to develop off-the-shelf packages for smart-chip card compatibility that included cards, terminals, and software. MasterCard's European affiliate Europay required that all of its 170 million Maestro cards, 2.3 million point-of-sale terminals, and 234,000 automated teller machines be smart-card compliant by 2005. Visa International pushed for an even earlier deadline of 2001 for chip compliance in its European region.

American Express introduced its super-elite Centurion, or AmEx Black card, in the United Kingdom, which was available by invitation only. Intended for the extremely wealthy, it is delivered in a velvet-lined box by private security personnel and comes with such perks as upgrades on the Concorde and private shopping hours at Saks and Neiman Marcus. Visa signed on with the French smart-card firm Gemplus to permit mobile payment services on cell phones, and with the Swedish mobile phone company Ericsson and Finnish Nokia to embed credit-card data directly into the phone. This technology verifies the identity of the phone user.

Brazil has been tagged as a promising chip-card market by both Visa and MasterCard, who predicted the country will go all-chip by 2003. In Asia, where one-sixth of households shop online, MasterCard International expected e-shopping purchases to reach $900 million in 2000, three times the total spent in 1998.

RESEARCH AND TECHNOLOGY

According to MasterCard International, the near future could see a refrigerator capable of monitoring the freshness of its contents and generating lists it could electronically communicate to a "thinking" countertop that keeps a shopping list. The "smart" countertop could trigger a message to the supermarket, so the week's groceries could be waiting at the store. MasterCard would be the payment vehicle for that transaction.

In a less science-fiction-like scenario, in 2000 Wells Fargo & Co. announced it was developing an arrangement with e-Bay, the online auction house, to create an entirely new credit-card niche: consumer-to-consumer credit-card transactions. Through Billpoint, a payment service provider, customers who sell on e-Bay could accept payments directly from their online customers. Such payments would go directly into the sellers' checking accounts. Wells Fargo would furnish the transaction processing services.

FURTHER READING

Bloom, Jennifer Kingson. "Visa Stands by Updated Debit Card, Though Banks' Response Is Cool." *American Banker*, 28 July 1999.

Brown-Humes, Christopher. "Land of Ice and Plastic: The Cashless Society." *Financial Times* (London), 3 May 2000.

Campbell, Tricia. "Card for the Future." *Sales & Marketing Management*, December 1999.

"Cash Remains King." *Economist*, 19 February 2000.

Casison, Jeanie. "Case for Incentives." *Incentive*, October 1999.

Connelly, Mary. "Ford Hopes New Credit Card Will Attract Small Businesses." *Automotive News*, 1 May 2000.

Coolidge, Carrie. "Card Tricks." *Forbes*, 15 November 1999.

"Credit Cards Given to College Students a Marketing Issue." *Marketing News*, 27 September 1999.

Daly, James J. "Many Happy Returns." *Credit Card Management*, May 2000.

"A Diverse Lot of Online Applicants." *Credit Card Management*, June 2000.

Durkin, Thomas A. "Credit Cards: Use and Consumer Attitudes, 1970-2000." *Federal Reserve Bulletin*, September 2000.

"E-cash 2.0." *Economist*, 19 February 2000.

Fickenscher, Lisa. "Credit Card Profitability Growth in '99 First in 5 Years." *American Banker*, 10 January 2000.

———. "Going after Wary Web Shoppers, Citi Offers Card That Isn't a Card." *American Banker*, 28 October 1999.

———. "Some On-Line Card Issuers Offer Fast Approval, Instant Shopping." *American Banker*, 7 March 2000.

———. "Visa, Mastercard Fees Kindle Yet Another Suit." *American Banker*, 10 April 2000.

Fitzgerald, Kate. "The Battle at the High End." *Credit Card Management*, February 2000.

"Five to Watch: Citibank Builds Online Business Model for 2000 Push." *Card Marketing*, January 2000.

Garver, Bob. "Fed Proposes Stronger Card Solicitation Rules." *American Banker*, 19 May 2000.

Janik, Art. "Is the Recent Web Scam Reason to Fear?" *Money*, April 2000.

Kilpatrick, Christine. "New Economy Inspires a Little Old World Caution." *San Francisco Business Times*, 24 March 2000.

Kover, Amy. "Charged! Credit Card Outfits Face Antitrust Suits." *Fortune*, 18 April 2000.

Leuty, Ron. "Credit Card Titans Battle to Rule Net." *San Francisco Business Times*, 25 February 2000.

"The Long Climb Ahead." *Card Technology*, March 2000.

Mackintosh, James. "Barclaycard May Give out Smartcard Readers." *Financial Times* (London), 10 December 1999.

"MBNA Signs Ethnic Web Sites." *Card Fax*, 23 February 2000.

"Nordstrom Enhances Retail Cards." *Card Fax*, 5 April 2000.

Ody, Penelope. "Time to Get Clever in the New Age of E-commerce." *Financial Times* (London), 5 April 2000.

Orr, Bill. "Easy Money." *ABA Banking Journal*, March 2000.

Pal, Uday Lai. "India Plays Catch-up on Smart Cards." *Card Technology*, November 1999.

Reardon, Marguerite. "MasterCard to Offer Virtual Credit." *Information Week*, 6 December 1999.

Redman, Russell. "Beware of Internet Card Appliers." *Bank System & Technology*, December 1999.

Rose, Sarah. "The Scoop on the New AmEx Blue." *Money*, November 1999.

Rutledge, Keisha. "Private-Label Credit Cards Spawn Loyalty, Drive Sales." *Discount Store News*, 17 April 2000.

Sanghera, Satham. "Teenage Revolution on the Cards." *Financial Times* (London), 18 May 2000.

"Senate Kills Credit Card Restrictions for College Students." *Human Events*, 3 December 1999.

Shermach, Kelly. "Permission-Based Telemarketing Poised to Ring in New Card Accounts." *Card Marketing*, December 1999.

Souccar, Miriam Kreinin. "Major Issuers' Sports Promotions Key on Fanatics' Fantasies." *American Banker*, 13 September 1999.

———. "Mass-Mailing Misfires Still Bedeviling Card Issuers Despite Technical Advances." *American Banker*, 16 February 2000.

———. "Visa Clinches Price Cuts to Get Chip Cards Moving." *American Banker*, 4 May 2000.

———. "Visa Sees B-to-B On-Line Buying as Next Frontier." *American Banker*, 15 March 2000.

Stock, Helen. "MasterCard's New U.S. Chief Vows to Wrest Industry Lead from Visa." *American Banker,* 10 March 2000.

Stock, Helen, and Lisa Fickenscher. "Card Execs See Trouble in E-payment Paradise." *American Banker,* 12 April 2000.

Svigels, Jerome. "Get Smart." *Credit Union Management,* January 2000.

Vickers, Marcia. "Big Cards on Campus." *Business Week,* 20 September 1999.

Weber, Joseph, and Ann Therese Palmer. "The Perils of Plastic." *Business Week,* 14 February 2000.

Wolcott, Rachel. "AmEx Unveils Exclusive 'Black Card' for Elite Clients." *Private Asset Management,* 20 September 1999.

Desktop Publishing

The desktop publishing rubric covers quite a wide breadth of workers, including those employed at large publishing companies, media outlets, nonprofit organizations, government agencies, small businesses inside and outside the publishing industry itself, independent writers and publishers, and hobbyists, producing everything from novels to newsletters, magazines to term papers. The emergence of desktop publishing (DTP) has completely transformed the publishing landscape. Conventional publishing requires writers, designers, typesetters, and artists, but sophisticated software and hardware afford a single individual the ability to perform all these functions on a personal computer to produce output for commercial printing. Books and newsletters sent directly to the consumer via the World Wide Web shift the cost of reproduction—paper, toner, printer wear and tear—to consumers who print or download the product on their own equipment.

DTP also fits in with the U.S. trend toward more flexible work schedules and work-at-home preferences. The U.S. Department of Labor predicted a growth rate of 74 percent in desktop publishing by 2006, making it one of the fastest-growing vocations. Desktop publishers can work at home, at an office for a DTP firm, or on-site for contracting companies.

Businesses, associations, and other organizations of all kinds are engaged in the frequent printing and dissemination of information for internal or external purposes, including annual reports, newsletters, manuals, research papers, brochures, books, and an almost unlimited number of other printed material. Many organizations carry their own publishing staffs and equipment to handle these tasks, while others contract out to DTP specialists, be they publishing companies or independent contractors.

The best desktop publishers have a feel for writing, since fitting text to a specific layout can often entail significant editing. Moreover, beyond just an ability to use the latest technology, they will have an understanding of design concepts so as to provide a design and layout that complement the information presented. Thus, desktop publishing is something of a confluence of technical skills and artistic vision. The ability to communicate with and understand a client's or employer's vision is equally important in order to deliver a product consistent with intentions, and often in order to help coax out an underformulated vision. While the $500 million market for DTP software continued to introduce ever more user-friendly publishing tools, the requisite skills resided primarily in the user, and not in the technology.

Desktop publishing has permanently altered the publishing and printing landscape. For example, according to *Electronic Publishing,* over 6,200 typographers, service bureaus, separators, and platemakers were in operation in 1990, employing a total of 83,000 workers. Just seven years later, those sectors dwindled to a combined 1,600 establishments and 13,000 employees lighter.

DTP is often associated with a single individual or small group of individuals who produce books, newsletters, or other types of written communication.

Desktop publishing is often performed by small- and medium-sized outfits to produce entire books or newsletters in camera-ready, or printable, form. Since the cost of software and equipment is low, large publishers also use DTP in-house for preparation of copy—including typesetting, graphics, layout, and other prepress activities—instead of outsourcing these tasks. In some cases, the intermediate film or paper copy used to produce a plate has been replaced in favor of a direct computer-to-plate process. In the case of direct computer-to-Web publishing, a printed copy may never come from the publisher.

The small publisher must be concerned with proofreading, editing, production of camera-ready copy for reproduction or printing, marketing, distributing, shipping, and all other tasks of a small business such as accounting and inventory control. The most common publications are generated by individuals or small businesses, and include flyers, newsletters, books, disk copies for use by a printer for processing, or CD-ROMs. Regardless of format, however, the publishing process is essentially the same, except for the medium of the final product.

The medium on which a product is printed largely governs the distribution method. Conventional paper books or newsletters are frequently distributed via a third-party book or news distributor who acts as a jobber, specialty bookstores direct from the publisher, or direct-mail order solicitation. A new medium for distribution and marketing is the World Wide Web, on which publications can be conveniently advertised to over 50 million users.

A number of companies print, bind, store, and ship final copies for desktop publishers. Seventy percent of books do not earn enough to cover the cost of a major distributing agent, so some distributors also assist small publishers in marketing or distribution to bookstores, providing a channel not otherwise available. Publishers Group, Publishers Group West, Book World, and the National Book Network are some of the distributors who help expand the small publishers market. While these distributors may charge a fee of up to $25,000 per book, some vendors enter collective exhibits at national conferences that are maintained by a single distributor that charges a modest one-time fee for display in an exhibit booth. Large book company royalties hover between 8 and 10 percent, while self-publishing and marketing via a distributor can yield a 35 to 65 percent return on the retail price. Organizations assisting small publishers include the Publishers Marketing Association, Small Publishers Association of North America, and Independent Publishers Network.

Industry associations also aid in DTP communications. The National Association of Desktop Publishers has 13,000 members and seeks to provide information, buying discounts, and other services to its professional and nonprofessional desktop publishers. The Publishers Marketing Association, a trade association of 3,100 independent publishers, including 200 foreign affiliates, was formed in 1983. Its purpose was to advance DTP professional interests, provide cooperative marketing programs, sponsor educational seminars about the industry, and make members' products visible to the trade and to the consumer. Each year it offers around 48 seminars on various facets of publishing.

BACKGROUND AND DEVELOPMENT

While the earliest mass printing technology dates back to second-century China, the movement to bring publishing technology to a wide audience began in 1450, when blacksmith Johannes Gutenberg invented the printing press, spreading literacy throughout Europe and further chipping away at the information monopoly enjoyed by the Catholic Church. Gutenberg's movable typeface was a long way off from the Adobe and Quark DTP tools of today, but it got the publishing ball rolling, as the production of books, newspapers, and pamphlets took off rapidly over the next several centuries and inched ever closer to the average person's desktop. The development of computers in the middle of the 20th century, and their introduction to households shortly thereafter, was the next leap forward.

In the late 1970s, when personal computers (PCs) had capacities of 640 kilobytes of memory and storage was approximately 120,000 bytes on a 5.25 inch diskette, word processing was available only if the author knew enough to write a crude program. Radio Shack's Scripsit was one of the first word-processing packages, and it was accompanied by Perfect Word. It was soon followed by Wordstar, WordPerfect, and some of today's more commonly known word processors. In a matter of less than a decade, however, especially following the introduction of the Macintosh computer from Apple Computer, Inc., all that changed, and by the early 1990s word processing gave way to full-scale desktop publishing.

Paul Brainard, founder of Aldus Corp., is generally considered the father of desktop publishing, since he first used the term in October 1984. He originally intended the term to describe the integration of text and graphics. Even after Brainard's first public use of the term, other terms such as personal publishing, self-publishing, electronic publishing, and computer publishing were still being used in 1985 to describe the same concept. Aldus used DTP to advertise Page-Maker software, and by the end of 1985, *Desktop Publishing* was an industry magazine. The next year it was sold and renamed *Publish*.

By 1987 a DTP software war emerged between Aldus, later known as Adobe Systems Inc., and Quark Inc. as Quark introduced the first edition of QuarkXPress, which went on to become the leading DTP package. In the early 1990s, Apple's QuickTime allowed developers to integrate multimedia. The Hewlett-Packard LaserJet printer series, with up to a 600 dots per inch printer, debuted at a cost of $3,000. In addition, direct computer to plate printing began, which made short-run color printing cheaper and faster; Pentium processors arrived; and QMS sold its ColorScript Laser 1000 for $12,449. The mid-1990s saw the introduction of new digital presses, the first Netscape Navigator Web browser, the release of Windows 95, Adobe's PageMill, a graphical HTML editor for Web publishing, and wide-format color ink-jet printers. These innovations contributed to the ease of production and subsequent growth of desktop publishing.

With all the functions of desktop publishing virtually at a publisher's fingertips, typesetting costs fell from between $110 and $150 per page to only $5 per page. DTP reduced the number of worker hours required, provided greater design flexibility at or near deadlines, and decreased or eliminated darkroom and chemical use for many newspapers. In addition to higher productivity, electronic file transfer also allowed employees more flexibility. Large corporations saw other benefits, as well, such as ensuring the secrecy of sensitive documents in the prepublication stage. DTP also facilitated the easier creation of informational graphics.

CURRENT CONDITIONS

Over the years, Adobe's PageMaker, once the industry king, increasingly assumed second-class status, having been deposed by QuarkXPress. By 2000, however, Adobe was poised to fight back with InDesign. InDesign, like QuarkXPress, utilizes frames to place text on pages, and was designed to facilitate not only a transition from the PageMaker model, but from QuarkXPress as well, signaling that Adobe very much hopes to win back some of its market share from Quark. In that spirit, analysts wittily dubbed InDesign "Quark killer." The first InDesign version met disap-

pointment with its page layout software, but the company quickly revamped the offending elements and brought out InDesign 1.5 in April 2000. At any rate, Adobe is in for a challenge, as the DTP software market has been notoriously resistant to change. About 80 percent of magazine publishers use Quark, and analysts expect many will be reluctant to overhaul their entire system in favor of InDesign.

Further integration of text-editing and layout capabilities and graphics editing tools is a primary focus of DTP software firms. The major DTP packages currently separate these applications, though they were beginning to move into this area. Moreover, DTP programs have begun to offer tools for creating design and layout for the printed page and for the World Wide Web.

Increasingly, however, as DTP tools and markets grow more sophisticated, so must desktop publishers' skills. Generalist-style desktop publishers were becoming less and less attractive, while technical knowledge and specialist skills grew more and more important. Since generalist knowledge is often under the purview of even the most low-end companies, firms seeking to contract out to a desktop publisher require more added value to make such an investment worthwhile. The ability to handle the different mechanics involved in various publishing media has become more of a premium, while other desktop publishers find themselves offering a more comprehensive publishing package, including writing, consulting, and even information gathering.

A report in *Mother Earth News* estimated total start-up costs for desktop publishers, including computer hardware and software, scanning equipment and other peripherals, and other overhead, at between $10,600 and $31,100, depending on the grade of equipment. In order to keep up with the latest developments, moreover, continuous training was a fact of life. Desktop publishing increasingly cropped up in college English curricula as well, though there often existed a degree of tension between the imparting of writing skills appropriate to the medium and the instruction of the mechanics of the DTP techniques, leading many teachers and researchers to consider the implications of the alteration of the word/print relationship inherent in the development of desktop publishing and other innovative technological publishing developments.

An increasingly prevalent DTP application is the miniature, self-produced magazine known as the zine. Zines are easy to produce and cost little or nothing to distribute, greatly relieving the pressure for financial success. Although the zine format traces its roots back to the 1930s when science-fiction fans began circulating pamphlets to share information and ideas on this relatively snubbed genre, the modern zine was born of underground publications associated with punk rock and related cultural scenes in the 1970s, and blossomed in the 1980s and 1990s to encompass any number of topics, from sports to politics to lifestyles. Many zines have grown to showcase extremely professional style and layout, thanks largely to the proliferation of DTP software. Since many zines were hand distributed and reached a limited audience, an exact figure was difficult to come by, though estimates ranged from 20,000 to 50,000 zines in the United States in 2000, with circulation reaching as high as 50,000 subscribers.

Despite the ballooning popularity and utility of the Internet, *Electronic Publishing* expected U.S. commercial printing shipments to grow to $57 billion by 2005. More and more of that printing business, however, will shift away from commercial printing specialists and into publishing offices, thanks largely to DTP innovation.

INDUSTRY LEADERS

The desktop publishing industry was highly diversified, though it was not without its rags-to-riches success stories within the publishing industry proper. Para Publishing, for example, was founded by Dan Poynter in 1978 on $15,000 borrowed from Poynter's parents. Poynter had no formal background or experience in publishing. After several successful releases, the company released its best-known, and highly reflexive, release, *The Self-Publishing Manual*. Pfeifer-Hamilton Publishers was established in 1983 by Donald and Nancy Tubesing to publish their training materials on stress management and wellness. Later, the company achieved notoriety for its wacky "duct tape" books. Bancroft Press expanded from Bruce Bortz's family Ping-Pong table to a successful outlet, which in the late 1990s released high-profile nonfiction books on the Marion Barry mayoral administration in Washington, D.C. and the John F. Kennedy assassination.

A pioneer in DTP software, Adobe Systems Inc. develops, markets, and supports software products and technologies enabling users to create information in all print and electronic media. Although the company retains its position as one of the leading software producers for the DTP industry, Adobe was gradually shifting its image to a Web solutions outfit, launching a multimillion-dollar advertising campaign to that effect in late 1999, noting that it has gotten little credit in this medium though Web designers use their tools every day. Adobe produces Adobe Acrobat, Adobe FrameMaker, Adobe PageMill, Adobe Illustrator, and Adobe Photoshop, among many others. Its top desktop publishing software, including Illustrator, Page-Maker, and Photoshop, accounted for 60 percent of all sales. In March 1999, Adobe introduced Adobe In-Design, a high-end page layout program designed specifically for graphics professionals and the publishing industry. Adobe created InDesign to compete with Quark's QuarkXPress, and repackaged its popular page layout program PageMaker to be more attractive to mid-size businesses. Based in San Jose, California, Adobe employs 2,760 workers. Sales in 1999 rebounded to $1.01 billion after falling to $894 million the year before.

Based in Denver, Colorado, Quark employs 600 workers and features the leading DTP software in its flagship QuarkXPress, which is geared toward publishers, graphic artists, and multimedia producers. Through successive editions, QuarkXPress increasingly featured tools geared toward specific publishing media, such as newspapers, catalogs, and magazines. Founded in 1981, the company made its first major splash when it introduced QuarkXPress in 1987, a move still reverberating throughout the industry as the company updates the product and maintains the lion's market share. Quark has increasingly moved into multimedia and Internet applications while maintaining its footing in its primary DTP market.

Apple Computer, Inc. is a key player in desktop publishing. Apple began the personal computer revolution with the first Apple II in the 1970s, and reinvented the PC with the creation of the first Macintosh in the 1980s. In August 1998, Apple reenergized its share of the computer market with the introduction of iMac, the low-cost, high-performance, all-in-one system. With nearly 10,000 employees, Apple achieved sales of $6.1 billion in 1999, up from $5.9 billion the year before.

AMERICA AND THE WORLD

U.S. firms have generally gone to much greater lengths to bring publishing operations in-house than have their foreign counterparts. Over 60 percent of the typesetter market in the United States was accomplished in-house by the late 1990s. One explanation for this statistic can be found in the heavy demand for full control of document production within many companies. Desktop publishing certainly capitalized on this psychology in the United States, although the picture is often different in other countries.

In Japan, for example, very few companies—with the exception of newspapers and catalog publishers—have such professional tools as typesetters and drum scanners. In Japan, a printer is usually a subcontractor for its client company and uses the services of a designer and a trade shop to do the work.

In the early 1990s, the potential for DTP in Japan greatly expanded, in part due to larger font libraries and more sophisticated composition software. In particular, QuarkXPress 3.11J stood out among composition software.

Although these developments had enormous ramifications for the Japanese publishing industry, a general downturn in the Japanese economy to some extent held back the progress of desktop publishing. Other reasons that desktop publishing has not caught on in Japan to the extent it has in the United States include: the traditional attitude of the Japanese graphic arts marketplace; the somewhat limited availability of superior-quality font designs; and the difficulties of managing two-byte characters. Hence, proprietary composition systems still controlled the Japanese market into the 2000s.

RESEARCH AND TECHNOLOGY

Digital asset management (DAM) was assuming greater importance in desktop publishing, organizing digital information in the manner of an electronic library for easy access. Quark's new Digital Media System (DMS), rolled out in early 2000, epitomized Quark's desire to branch out its publishing applications to encompass a more holistic media approach. DMS is a database management system designed to allow for easy retrieval of text, graphics, and photos as well as sound and video files in order to allow a publisher to focus on the editorial end of the project and leave it to the technology to integrate the finished product into whatever media form is desired. Still, the product was geared toward more sophisticated companies and publications, such as magazines, newspapers, and larger publishers, generally with a staff of 20 or more connected to a computer system, that were attempting to trim their staff and equipment costs. The bottom-level systems cost about $50,000, while the most advanced models run up to $1 million.

Xionics Document Technologies is a leading developer of embedded systems software for printing, scanning, copying, and transmitting documents to computer peripherals. They partner with original equipment manufacturers such as IBM. Embedded systems technology has allowed the continued convergence of desktop printers and copiers, creating a new category of multifunction peripherals that combine the functions of print, copy, scan, and fax in a single system. When embedded systems imaging equipment produces multiple original prints, it is called a "mopier."

Computer-to-plate (CTP) capability for off-set press production was emerging as an alternative to disk-to-film-plates press technology. While CTP is far from taking over desktop publishing processes, it has already exerted its influence on the entire print industry, and most observers agree that CTP is the future of the business. The intensive knowledge and capital investment required to implement CTP, however, will continue to stall its massive influx for the next several years. In addition, the ability for an organization to go to CTP is often only as strong as its weakest link; if advertisers or someone else in the relationship cannot handle the technology, it becomes less economical to make the switch.

Also, as printing becomes more a question of pre-or postdistribution, economics will favor postdistribution printing by end users on their own equipment. Eventually, a print shop could be in every home, and the desktop publisher could be both the producer and the consumer. As the economic barriers to home-generated publishing are lowered, individuals and small companies will have all the resources previously available only to larger print shops.

FURTHER READING

Asbury, Eve. "The DAM Revolution Heats Up." *Publishing & Production Executive,* August 1999.

Berman, Michael. "A New Desktop Publishing Contender." *Journal of Commerce,* 8 March 2000.

Eckel, Allison Schill. "Industry Report: The Status of CTP." *Publishing & Production Executive,* August 1999.

Edwards, Paul, and Sarah Edwards. "10 Surefire Home Businesses for the New Decade." *Mother Earth News,* December 1999/January 2000.

Frawley, Miriam O. "A Case for CTP." *Publishing & Production Executive,* August 1999.

Hafer, Gary R. "Making the Connection." *Technical Communication Quarterly,* Fall 1999.

Horrigan, David. "Publishing on a Shoestring Has Empowered the Masses." *San Diego Union-Tribune,* 28 March 2000.

Moseley, Bob. "InDesign 1.5: Adobe Fights for Market Share." *Folio,* May 2000.

Ott, Christopher. "Adobe Turns up Heat in Desktop Publishing Rivalry." *Washington Business Journal,* 23 April 1999.

"The Printed Word." *Times* (London), 29 December 1999.

Raabe, Steve. "Quark Adds Weapon to Publishing Arsenal." *Denver Post,* 4 February 2000.

Snyder, Beth. "Adobe Drive Aims to Build Image as a Web Company." *Advertising Age,* 4 October 1999.

Webb, Joseph W., and James R. Whittington. "Are You Ready for the 21st Century?" *Electronic Publishing,* March 1999.

DIGITAL IMAGING

Driven by voracious demand for digital cameras, digital imaging is swiftly becoming a mass-market phenomenon after years of languishing in the exclusive domain of imaging professionals and technophiles. Falling prices have fueled the market, as have technical strides and the wider use of the Internet for disseminating personal snapshots and the like.

In addition to digital still cameras, which in 1999 blossomed into a $1 billion market in the United States and a $3 billion market worldwide, digital imaging technologies include digital camcorders for capturing digital video; so-called personal computer or Web cameras, used mostly for live low-resolution video teleconferencing; and a range of still-image scanners for converting printed material into digital format. Most of these gadgets are designed for transferring ready-to-use, yet editable graphics to a computer, where they can be customized with graphics software and then shared with others via e-mail or over the Web.

An assortment of consumer-oriented digital imaging services have also sprung up. These include film-processing services that convert ordinary photographic images into digital format. Many traditional photo-processing labs now offer digitization as an option when developing film, and a number of companies have set up film-drop-off kiosks aimed specifically at customers who want digital output. After the film is dropped off and processed, the images are then given to the customer on diskette or compact disc, or made available to the customer over the Internet.

Businesses have discovered new applications for digital imaging as well. While such activities as creating image libraries, scanning forms, and publishing product catalogs have long relied on digital imaging, the technology has spread to new applications such as insurance claims verification and real estate marketing.

ORGANIZATION AND STRUCTURE

The traditional film photography market generates more than $30 billion annually in revenues. Film photography relies on tiny crystals of light-sensitive silver compounds suspended in a coating that surrounds a transparent film. As the shutter of the camera opens, light from the brightest parts of an image are thrown onto the film and the crystals start breaking down. In developing the film, a chemical called a "developer" changes the crystals exposed into black silver, while another chemical called a "fixer" dissolves the unexposed crystals. The resulting negative shows black silver where the scene was brightest and nothing where the film was left dark (no image was recorded). The wet chemistry required to develop photographs, however, has many disadvantages. It is messy and environmentally hazardous since most of the chemicals are toxic. In addition, the wet chemistry process is time-delayed—the entire developing process makes instant viewing and editing impossible. Finally, there is always a risk of spoilage; film that's over- or underdeveloped results in poor images.

Still images such as photos, slides, transparencies, and paintings have traditionally been converted to digital format using a scanner. The scanner "copies" the image and translates it to a binary format. Scanner accuracy is defined in two ways—by resolution and color information. Resolution is referred to as dpi (dots per inch) or ppi (pixels per inch). Color information is defined by the number of bits of information per color. For example, 24 bits per pixel (8 bits each of red, green, and blue) creates 1.6 million colors. The size of a pixel varies from one device to another and is, essentially, a single square unit of the same size. Digital cameras rely on the same measurements of resolution and color information.

Digital cameras don't require wet chemistry, lab processing, or scanning. Instead, digital imaging cameras create a binary image directly by recording the image on a charge-coupled device (CCD). The CCD sensor is an optoelectronic element that records light as a charge in a condenser. Developed originally by Bell Laboratories, the CCD contains an array of cells representing a picture element. Each cell converts light into an electrical charge. Pixels arranged in a straight row are called linear arrays. In the late 1990s, CCDs accounted for about half the cost of a digital camera. Together, CCDs and storage accounted for more than three-quarters of the cost. According to Nicholas van den Berghe, vice president and general manager of the consumer division at Live Picture Inc., the combined cost of the CCD and storage should be around 15 percent of the system cost before digital cameras take off with the consumer market. Digital images created by digital cameras measure resolution in the same manner as a scanner.

CURRENT CONDITIONS

Digital cameras are now sold in the mainstream, with everyone from Wal-Mart to high-end electronics stores offering them in some form. According to market research published by NPD Intelect, in 1999 digital still cameras made up fully 36 percent of all U.S. camera sales. By NPD's reckoning, some 1.8 million digital still cameras shipped that year—a steep 63 percent gain from the year before—and they were valued at more than $1 billion. More growth is expected: a study by InfoTrends Research Group predicted that North American unit shipments will soar to 7 million by 2003 for sales of $6 billion.

Digital camcorders, which tend to cost considerably more, posted an even more impressive rise in 1999, with sales weighing in at $532 million for the 524,000 units sold, NPD Intelect reported. Dollar sales of camcorders that year were up by about 472 percent from a year earlier.

DIGITAL CAMERA PRICES EASE, LOW-END NOT IGNORED

Although prices have dropped considerably since initial product launches, the typical digital camera still requires a hefty outlay. Based on industry-wide estimates by NPD Intelect, the average digital still camera in 1999 cost over $550. Digital camcorders averaged almost twice that, coming in at just over $1,000 apiece.

Of course, not all digital models sell at such a premium. Indeed, the low-end market is thriving, according to a study by International Data Corp. (IDC), accounting for nearly 28 percent of global digital-camera shipments as of 1999. IDC defined low-end as anything costing less than $250, but in fact some manufacturers have introduced models in sub-$100 territory as well, including low-priced toy models such as the

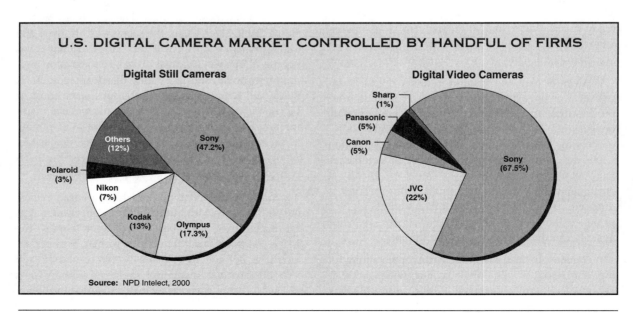

U.S. DIGITAL CAMERA MARKET CONTROLLED BY HANDFUL OF FIRMS

Digital Still Cameras

Sony (47.2%)
Others (12%)
Polaroid (3%)
Nikon (7%)
Kodak (13%)
Olympus (17.3%)

Digital Video Cameras

Sharp (1%)
Panasonic (5%)
Canon (5%)
Sony (67.5%)
JVC (22%)

Source: NPD Intelect, 2000

popular Barbie Photo Designer Digital Camera, which listed in 2000 at about $50.

Prices across the board are expected to continue creeping downward as shipments rise and as technically superior models are launched to supplant the present top tier. To some degree, the digital camera industry finds itself caught in the same cycles of product obsolescence that other high-tech manufacturers, especially personal computer (PC) makers, go through. Newer, flashier, best-ever devices are introduced, and the price of everything already on the market tends to get bumped down a few notches. Some of the leading producers, however, have foreseen the demand at the bottom of the food chain and have rushed out no-frills models specifically targeted to meet the limited needs—and budgets—of novices and penny pinchers.

WEBCAMS BRING VIDEOCONFERENCING TO THE MASSES

For transmitting real-time digital images, millions of PC users have been snapping up tethered PC cameras. Also known as Webcams or Netcams, these low-end input devices record a live video feed directly to a computer, most often through a cable connection, and usually have little or no storage capacity of their own. The video is then transmitted over the Internet to other computers, typically for videoconferencing with friends or coworkers. While the video's motion tends to be jerky and the resolution less than, say, that of a digital video disc movie, Webcams provide a modicum of visual telecommunications at a very reasonable price; the average Webcam cost only $69 in 2000. IDC reported about 1.4 million units sold in 1999, and predicted 2.5 million unit sales in 2000. InfoTrends was even more optimistic in its long-term expectations, estimating that the North American market for Webcams was more than doubling each year in the early 2000s, heading toward 38 million units by 2003.

SCANNER UNIT SALES TRENDING UPWARD, REVENUES FLATTENING

Meanwhile, in the more mature scanner market, unit shipments continue trending upwards as prices have fallen sharply. Between 1996 and 1999, consumer scanner sales jumped from 1 million to 8.3 million units. Mid-range and low-end flatbed models dominate the segment, and worldwide unit sales were expected to triple between 1998 and 2003, according to a forecast by IDC. A different projection from InfoTrends envisaged North American consumer-oriented scanner sales nearly doubling between 1999 and 2003, reaching 19 million units by the end of that period. With prices expected to continue tumbling,

though, InfoTrends warned that scanner revenues might top out around 2002.

High-end scanners for businesses aren't being left out of the boom, even though the difference between high-end and low-end machines has narrowed significantly thanks to improved technology. According to InfoTrends, the commercial publishing market for scanners was set to grow by more than a third between 1999 and 2004, surpassing 200,000 units in North America. Film scanners were expected to be one of the fastest-growing professional segments.

INDUSTRY LEADERS

Most digital imaging hardware is fairly sophisticated technology, and as such, the industry has been dominated by major international corporations specializing in consumer electronics, semiconductors, and other forms of photographic and imaging equipment.

Particularly in the digital camera segments, a handful of producers dominate the market. Foremost among them is Sony Corp. At the end of 1999 it controlled a ponderous 47 percent of the U.S. digital still camera market, according to NPD Intelect, and a stunning 67 percent of the digital video camera market. What's more astounding, in both categories Sony managed to strengthen its market share from year-earlier levels, despite the influx of new products from competitors and the vast increase in industry-wide sales during the ensuing year. Based on 1999 market share, other sizable makers of digital cameras for the U.S. market included old-guard photographic equipment makers Olympus Optical Co. and Eastman Kodak Co., and the consumer electronics developer Victor Co. of Japan, Ltd., better known as JVC. An underlying powerhouse in the digital camera business is Sanyo, which manufactures a large number of digital cameras for other name-brand companies.

In the Webcam segment, two well-established but very dissimilar firms control a preponderance of the market: Intel Corp. and Logitech International SA. Intel is the world's biggest semiconductor fabricator and the backbone of the PC industry through its market-leading production of microprocessor chips. It has also delved into computer peripherals manufacturing, which provides a captive side-market for its semiconductors. Logitech is a Swiss manufacturer of computer input devices, best known for its mice and other pointer devices. It bought its way into the Webcam business in 1998 when it purchased the Webcam operations of Connectix Corp. Logitech is regarded as the United States' top maker of Webcams. Intel and Logitech controlled upwards of two-thirds of that market as of 2000.

RESEARCH AND TECHNOLOGY

APS ATTEMPTS TO BRIDGE THE DIGITAL DIVIDE

The Advanced Photo System (APS) is a digital/print hybrid backed by Kodak, Fuji, Canon, Minolta, and Nikon. APS cameras, film, and processing equipment have the ability to "communicate" with each other and to compensate for conditions such as light and film speed. APS technology allows for switching between different size photographs on the same roll of film and imprints digital information about the shot, lighting conditions, date, and other data that facilitate the developing process. The cameras have the advantage of affordability; many models sell for between $100 and $300, and developing is available nearly anywhere offering 35mm processing. Kodak holds 60 percent of all APS camera patents.

DIGITAL IMAGING GROUP WORKS ON ADVANCED APPLICATIONS

The Digital Imaging Group (DIG) was launched in October 1997 with nine members—Adobe Systems Inc.; Canon, Inc.; Eastman Kodak Co.; Fuji Photo Film Co., Ltd.; Hewlett-Packard Co.; IBM Corp.; Intel Corp.; Live Picture Inc.; and Microsoft Corp. Two months after its formation, DIG more than tripled its membership, and currently has about 80 members.

The group is an open industry consortium whose mission is to communicate the benefits of digital imaging and digital technology and monitor market response and developer recommendations. Membership gives companies the opportunity to help define the future of digital imaging technology, promote solutions, and have the opportunity to collaborate in the DIG showcase Web site and future marketing and promotional activities sponsored by DIG. The first annual DIG Congress was held in Burlingame, California, in June 1998. DIG has launched international branches, first DIG Japan in 1998 and DIG Europe in 1999 with 11 founding members from eight countries. The branches will help DIG extend into local markets to ultimately spread its initiatives on a global scale.

Beginning early in 1998, DIG began the process of defining the next versions of the FlashPix and Internet Imaging Protocol (IIP) specifications. FlashPix is an incredibly powerful tool for users of digital im-

ages. It uses flexible compression and color management options to offer a universal storage and exchange platform for digital imaging. By transferring to random-access memory, or RAM, FlashPix reduces the amount of time it takes to manipulate and send a file.

FlashPix accomplishes this by using multiple-resolution versions of the image, each with half as many pixels (both vertical and horizontal) as the previous version. Each version of the image is also tiled or divided into squares measuring 64 pixels. To zoom in and out of the image, the FlashPix format allows for selection of the right resolution and tile display for each individual screen, eliminating the need to rebuild the image from scratch. FlashPix has the ability to add numerous extensions. Applications can add new storage, streams, and/or property sets that can be maintained across editing sessions of the file. Audio, for instance, can already be embedded in FlashPix images.

IIP transfers a FlashPix object and transports it over a network using a request-response protocol. IIP is extremely flexible and functional as well, and can transport any FlashPix image, including tiles, transform objects, and even metadata. It eliminates the need to create and store multiple files on a server. FlashPix and IIP create a bandwidth-efficient way to allow viewers to quickly receive rich, photographic-quality images online, as well as the ability to pan and zoom into the images. It allows images to appear rapidly on screen and has the ability to print very small images in the highest resolutions that the particular hardware permits. Advocates of FlashPix/IIP believe that its capabilities present new opportunities in areas such as electronic commerce and interactive communication. Over 100 products are now compatible with FlashPix/IIP.

DIGITA SOFTWARE ENABLES ON-CAMERA APPLICATIONS

A related innovation is a software application environment for digital cameras and related devices known as Digita. The software, developed by Flashpoint Technologies Inc., allows users to run mini-applications on specially equipped cameras. For instance, a photographer taking standardized pictures for a company catalog could instruct the camera to automatically modify the images to meet the project's needs, say, to automatically place the company logo in the right bottom corner of the image and adjust the color balance to remove the pallor of fluorescent lighting. More sophisticated uses might create a Web page directly on the camera using a template and a set of pictures. The applications rely on a scripting language that users can learn and program themselves, or predefined scripts can be purchased from developers.

FURTHER READING

Avalos, George. "California Firm Sees Bright Future in Photo Software." *Denver Post,* 12 May 1997.

Beale, Stephen. "FlashPix Format Gains Momentum." *Macworld,* December 1996.

Beardt, Cara. "Photo Sites Bulk Up amid Surge in Interest." *Advertising Age,* 21 February 2000.

Boyd-Merritt, Rick, and Margaret Quan. "Kodak, Intel Unroll Jointly Developed Imaging Products." *EE Times,* 29 September 1998.

Chakravarty, Subrata N. "How an Outsider's Vision Saved Kodak." *Forbes,* 13 January 1997.

Chinnock, Chris. "Low-End Digital Still Cameras Poised for Rapid Growth." *Electronic Design,* 17 December 1999.

Connor, Michael. "The Vital Lesson of Betamax." *Worldbusiness,* May/June 1996.

Day, Rebecca. "Pixel Puzzle—Building the Infrastructure for Digital Photography." *OEM Magazine,* 1 February 1997.

"Film vs. Digital: Can Kodak Build a Bridge?" *Business Week,* 2 August 1999.

Fulford, Benjamin. "Photo Finish." *Forbes,* 20 March 2000.

Glesi, Steve. "Kodak CEO Says Stock Is Undervalued: Photo Giant Eyes $1 Billion in Digital Revenue." *CBS Marketwatch,* 28 April 1999.

Grant, Linda. "Why Kodak Still Isn't Fixed." *Fortune,* 11 May 1998.

Heller, Laura. "Digital Imaging Catches On, Despite Glitches, Roadblocks." *DSN Retailing Today,* 19 June 2000.

———. "Mass Makes Room for Digital." *Discount Store News,* 20 March 2000.

Holstein, William J. "Can Kodak Refocus?" *U.S. News & World Report,* 9 November 1998.

Isaacson, Portia. "Who Will Emerge the Winner in the Business for Digital Cameras?" *Computer Reseller News,* 26 May 1997.

"IXLA Launches Major Marketing Initiative by Giving Away Digital Cameras." 14 April 1999. Available from http://www.digitalimaging.org/news/pr_04_20_99.

Jeffrey, Noel. "Getting a True Picture." *American Printer. Digital & Prepress Links Supplement,* June 1996.

Kay, Russell. "Apps Provide Lure for New Digicams." *Computerworld,* 17 April 2000.

"Kodak's Digital Direction." *Industry Week,* 19 May 1997.

Levy, Trudy. "Managing a Digital Image System—Choose the Ideal System to Archive and Access Your Valuable Images." *InformationWeek,* 25 November 1996.

McClelland, Deke. "The Personal Imaging Revolution." *Macworld,* September 2000.

Roberts, Bill. "Digital Cameras for the Masses." *Electronic Business,* March 2000.

Rossello, Rosanne. "Digital Imaging Pushes toward the Mainstream." *Seybold Report on Internet Publishing,* March 1997.

Ruber, Peter. "Digital Imaging Gets Real." *InfoWorld,* 1 December 1997.

Schoenberger, Chana R. "Candid Camera." *Forbes,* 18 September 2000.

Schwartz, Susana. "Digital Camera Highlights Kodak's New Image Strategy." *Insurance & Technology,* May 1995.

Stoffel, James. "New Imaging Pathways." *R&D,* June 1999.

Weber, Jonathon. "Photo Technology That Lens Itself to a Better Camera." *Los Angeles Times,* 23 June 1997.

DIGITAL MAPPING

A rapidly growing and widely diversified field, the digital mapping industry emerged in the late 1990s and almost immediately found ready application in industries as diverse as education, automobile navigation, agriculture, banking, railroading, and telecommunications. Though the idea of integrating and displaying complex data on digital maps was already several decades old at the time, the rapid increases in computer processing power in the 1990s brought business geographics (the use of digital mapping databases for business applications) into the mainstream business world.

By 2000, the number and variety of applications for digital mapping had grown by leaps and bounds compared to just a decade earlier, with an estimated 85 percent of all businesses having some geographic component able to be mapped and utilized. The maps created using these components are typically linked to large databases—often called geographic information systems (GISs)—making it possible to access, arrange, and view an ever wider range of information. With digital mapping's wide range of access and inherent flexibility, it remained poised to enjoy healthy growth in the 21st century.

ORGANIZATION AND STRUCTURE

Digital maps differ greatly from traditional paper maps. First, while printed maps are painstakingly hand drawn by patient mapmakers, digitized maps are made up of millions of pixels—the tiny colored dots that make up graphic images on computer screens. Sec-

ond, printed maps are static, based on a single interpretation of a single set of data, while digital maps are dynamic, created out of individually selected layers of data and images. The digital map used by a farmer, for example, might show an area's various soil types in one view and then, with a click of a mouse, layer the various types of crops being grown in the same area. The digital map for a railroad might at one moment display a map showing the signals, switches, and alternate routes along the track a train is traveling on and then call up a window showing the train's exact longitudinal and latitudinal location based on a satellite signal beamed to the train's cab. The user might even call up a recorded full-motion video image of the terrain and region of track the train is now passing. In short, then, the digital map is often interactive, an image that can be changed at the user's discretion.

MAPMAKING MODELS

Digital maps store data in layers of visual information that have been constructed using one of two models: the vector or the raster. The vector model uses standard geometry to plot a map's features—such as a building or road—using the specific longitudinal and latitudinal position in space each object occupies. This method is ideal for plotting discrete objects or features on a map, but it is also expensive. The raster model, however, is cheaper and more useful for mapping continuously and/or subtly changing features such as soil type. With this model, a map is created by dividing the terrain into equally sized cells and then combining scanned or photographed images of these terrain cells together into a grid. Simply put, the vector method builds maps out of individual points while the raster method builds them out of rectangular blocks of terrain images. With the advent of high-resolution satellites that photograph Earth in precisely this rectangular, cell-by-cell manner, the raster method has become the dominant method for digital mapmaking.

BUILDING A GIS

Building a GIS involves five distinct phases. First, and by far the most time-consuming part of the digital mapmaking process, the printed (or analog) map is digitized. This can be done using scanners, which create photographic images of the source map and then turn them into the binary ones and zeros a computer can understand, or by using a specialized digitizing table. In the latter process, the paper map is taped to the table, the operator selects an object on the map to digitize, and then traces it with a penlike instrument that reads or converts the object into digital information. Since a typical map has anywhere from 5,000 to 10,000 objects, digitizing is a laborious and expensive process that has traditionally been outsourced to countries in developing parts of the world.

The second stage in making a GIS is manipulating the newly digitized geographic data so it conforms to the needs of the mapmaker. For example, an analog map converted into digital data may need to have its scale (or degree of accuracy) adjusted, or the mapmaker may decide that some of the information included on the original analog map is irrelevant and can therefore be deleted.

In the third stage, a database management system (DBMS) is used to store, organize, and manage the digitized map data. The most popular DBMS is the "relational" method, which allows data to be stored in rows and columns of tables so different types of data can be compared and combined.

The fourth stage in the construction of a functioning GIS is the "query and analysis" phase: the posing of questions to the geographic database so that certain views or maps of information are displayed or hypothetical situations explored. It is at this stage that the digital map truly becomes a GIS, offering customized maps that answer or visualize the user's questions. Two common types of analysis are "proximity analysis" and "overlay analysis." In a proximity analysis, the user might ask the GIS how many switches or signals separate a train from the next station. In an overlay analysis, however, the user might ask the GIS to integrate two different types of data—or "data layers"—such as all the road crossings, as well as all the switches that separate a train from the next station. Once the analysis is complete, the final stage of the GIS process occurs—the requested information is displayed graphically.

RELATED TECHNOLOGIES

A GIS involves several related but distinctly different technologies, all of which may be used to create the GIS. "Desktop mapping" programs are GISs that have been tailored for the desktop personal computer (PC) and therefore have more limited data management and customization features than GISs. Computer-aided design systems are often used by architects, engineers, and builders to create designs and plans, but lack the data management and analytical features of GISs. Remote sensing and the Global Positioning System (GPS) are one aspect of the data-gathering arm of a GIS: using cameras or radar, for example, to generate digital images of Earth that can be used in a GIS. GPS is a network of orbiting satellites and earthbound receivers developed by the U.S. Department of Defense to provide users with pinpoint time and position information from anywhere on the globe. While the GPS can provide a GIS with the specific location data to create highly accurate digital map databases in real time, it cannot provide the context ("What's over the next hill?") that a good GIS offers. Another source of data for a GIS is photogrammetry—the use of aerial photographs to provide geographic images. GPS differs from photogrammetry in at least two important respects: GPS requires that the user actually be at the location whose coordinates the GPS satellites provide; photogrammetry does not provide location coordinates, but can provide remote imaging of inaccessible places.

INDUSTRY SEGMENTS

The digital mapping and GIS industry consists of four segments: services, hardware, software, and data. The services segment—which generates about one-fifth of the industry's revenues worldwide—is comprised of firms that offer GIS-related consulting, GIS integration, analog-to-digital conversion, photogrammetry and orthophotography, and satellite imagery. Consulting firms such as UGC Consulting and Plan-Graphics, Inc. provide project direction for companies trying to implement GISs, as well as project feasibility studies, GIS database design, and GIS project management. System integrators (Intergraph Corp., for example) design and build entire GISs by integrating the often proprietary or stand-alone GIS products of software, hardware, and database vendors: they make a customer's GIS components work together. The conversion services firms convert or digitize data so it can be used within the digital GIS environment. These firms may fix errors or omissions in the primary or analog data, or assure that the conversion is clean and accurate. Because it involves the snail-paced digitization process, this segment of the GIS services industry is highly labor intensive and therefore lucrative. Unfortunately for these firms, however, conversion generates little repeat business—data needs conversion only once. Moreover, as the world moves inexorably toward digital-only mapping, prospects for future growth in the data conversion market are slim.

The photogrammetry and orthophotography segments of the GIS services transform aerial photos into clean, sequenced map data. Photogrammetry might be considered "the science of surveying terrain from the air" and orthophotography as "the process of digitizing aerial photos." In particular, orthophotography involves smoothing out the distortions that inevitably arise from taking aerial photos of terrain so that the resulting image has a resolution of one meter (sharp enough, that is, to identify objects one meter in size or larger). Both photogrammetry and orthophotography firms must have expensive equipment and a highly skilled work force, and they generally offer services only in the geographic regions covered by their photo archives. Nevertheless, the photogrammetry segment (which includes firms such as Analytical Survey Inc. and Intera Information Technologies Corp.) is the most profitable sector of the GIS services industry.

The last segment of the GIS services industry is satellite imagery. A relatively new field, satellite imagery arose only after the conclusion of the Cold War made it possible for high-resolution spy satellites to seek commercial markets. By offering extremely fine-grained images for customers building digital maps, satellite imagery firms pose a threat to the aerial photo (photogrammetry) segment of the industry. The satellite segment was still rather small; according to Teal Group, only 43 Earth imaging satellites, or 3 percent of all satellites, were expected to built and launched between 2001 and 2010. (Also see the essay in this book entitled Satellites.)

The hardware—computers, workstations, and peripherals such as printers and scanners—used in the digital mapping and GIS industries is manufactured mainly by large computer equipment firms such as IBM, Hewlett-Packard, Digital Equipment, and Unisys. A few industry-specific firms, however, such as Intergraph and Trimble Navigation, also manufacture workstations and GIS-related hardware.

The software segments of the digital mapping and GIS industries produce design or mapmaking software used to create digital maps or to manipulate and display them. The customers of this industry segment have traditionally been the industries—energy, utilities, railroads, and governments—whose mapping needs were such a vital part of their businesses that

they had no choice but to buy the expensive, highly specialized software products that were once the sole niche of industry firms. With the rapid emergence of powerful desktop computers, however, the digital mapping software segment began to ply its wares to a wider marketplace: mainstream business and consumers. A host of software firms in the 1990s offered relatively inexpensive digital mapping products that allowed users to insert maps into their publications, multimedia presentations, animation, and Web sites. Among these firms were companies such as Autodesk, Inc.; Eagle Point Software; MapInfo Corp.; and Magellan Geographix. By 2000, some of these firms offered digital maps via the traditional CD-ROM format and through electronic-commerce sites on the World Wide Web. Similarly, high-quality maps were made available in such popular desktop graphics formats as Adobe Illustrator, Photoshop, Macromedia Freehand, and CorelDraw.

APPLICATIONS

As the industry developed, it became apparent that the range of applications for digital mapping and GIS was nearly limitless. In agriculture, for example, GIS technology is used to find the best soils for growing crops; to plan and optimize shipping routes for transporting food and agricultural chemicals and fertilizers; to monitor and analyze crop production trends; to rate and market crop insurance policies; and to plan the application of chemicals or pesticides. By 2000, more than 80 countries worldwide used GIS technology for agronomy and food planning purposes.

In banking and finance applications, GIS is used to ensure compliance with federal lending regulations; to maintain geographic distribution information on automated teller machines or competitors' locations; to create demographic profiles of existing and prospective customers; and to perform site analysis studies to locate branches at the best possible locations.

In police work and public safety, GIS is used to optimize the computer-aided dispatch of emergency vehicles through route planning and in-cab navigation systems; to track police and fire vehicles in real time as they respond to emergencies; and to analyze crime incidence records with map displays to learn and predict crime patterns. Firefighters also use digital maps to give them valuable information about hydrant and fire station location, hazardous materials hot spots, and building occupancy. Disaster planning agencies use GIS to create on-the-spot emergency action plans to help evacuate a region, track damaged structures for repair, or generate computer models to predict the behavior of natural disasters such as floods and tornadoes.

Electric utilities use digital mapping and GIS to manage their "call-before-you-dig" telephone systems for warning construction crews of buried power lines. They also use them to determine the appropriate rates for the sale of excess energy to other utilities, to automate equipment-inventorying procedures, and to map out the "joint use" of utility poles by telecommunications firms. Similarly, oil and gas pipeline firms employ digital mapping technology to perform market analysis, manage risk, and analyze complex pipeline routes so as to take into account environmentally sensitive areas and land-use conflicts, and to make appropriate decisions regarding terrain and geology.

The U.S. government, historically quick to adopt digital mapping technology, ran approximately 250,000 GIS applications annually between 1994 and 2000, from disaster planning and natural-resource preservation to traffic planning projects and the planning and tracking of census statistics. Other industries that have found uses for digital mapping include petroleum (analyzing the placement of filling stations), customer-service businesses (automating call-center responses), and railroads (tracking train deployment and safety).

BACKGROUND AND DEVELOPMENT

Although the science of mapmaking can be traced back to such pioneers as Ptolemy, Eratosthenes, Mercator, and Cassini, its modern development really began with the invention of the airplane at the start of the 20th century. To be sure, the invention of printing enabled maps to be widely disseminated for the first time, and the application of mathematical and statistical methods introduced greater accuracy, but the airplane enabled mapmakers to map previously unknown regions. Industrialist Sherman Fairchild (1896-1971) pioneered commercial aerial surveying after World War I. After the end of World War II, military surveillance techniques were adapted for use in civilian mapmaking and the science of photogrammetry began to come into its own.

In the 1960s the first rough computer maps came into use, and industries such as energy, utilities, and the railroads—as well as the federal government—employed computerized maps for such purposes as plotting pipeline routes, tracking population movements, and mapping the mineral content of geologic formations. Because computing power was still an expensive commodity, however, it took several millions of dollars just to create a customized map showing, for example, piping networks or infrastructure. Gov-

ernment offices and utilities could not afford to do without such mapping data, however, and still comprised three-quarters of the digital mapping industry's customer base well into the mid-1990s.

The U.S. spy satellite program of the 1950s and 1960s bore fruit for the digital mapping industry in 1972 when the National Aeronautics and Space Administration initiated the Landsat program to survey Earth with multispectral scanner technology, a development that marked the beginning of the systematic use of space-based remote sensing as a source of raw data for cartographers. With Landsat, mapmakers could create rapidly updatable, photo-based "thematic" maps for such specialized needs as mapping water pollution, mineral deposits, or crop health. For many years Landsat and its French counterpart were the only source of space-based imagery available to private mapping firms.

The birth of the desktop computer and advances in microchip manufacture and design in the late 1970s and early 1980s transformed the landscape of digital mapping. With computer processing power doubling every eight months (a phenomenon that came to be known as Moore's Law), previously impractical digital mapping applications were suddenly possible. By 1984 GIS-based vehicle navigation systems were already being used in marine and aeronautic applications, and companies such as Motorola and Rockwell Automotive were hard at work on navigation systems for automobiles. In 1985 digital mapmaker Etak introduced its Navigator map display and vehicle positioning system, and rival Navigation Technologies demonstrated a similar routing system, DriverGuide, the same year. By the mid-1990s such systems were already a reality at rental car companies such as Hertz and Avis.

By 1986 Thomas Bros. Maps, the largest mapmaker in California, sensed the change afoot in the mapping industry and began digitizing its entire map collection. With the launching of the new trade magazine *GIS World* in the late 1980s, it was clear that a new industry—digital mapping—had come into its own. For the first time in history maps were suddenly easy and inexpensive to make. By the late 1990s a typical government mapping project, such as mapping a state's population distribution, could be completed in a matter of weeks, or even days. Moreover, digital cartographers began systematizing the analytical foundations of the new GIS science by striving for standards for calculating distances and technical parameters such as terrain surface slope and aspect.

In 1990 the American Automobile Association, General Motors, the Federal Highway Administration, and the Florida Department of Transportation launched a project known as TravTek to develop one of the most important early demonstrations of on-board navigation and route guidance for the auto industry. The geographic data was provided by Navigation Technologies and Etak, both "street-level" digital map database providers. By 1995 Navigation Technologies had thoroughly mapped all the major metropolitan areas of the United States for the system, and Etak had completed a less detailed mapping of the rest of the country.

The collapse of the Soviet Union in the early 1990s opened a potentially major new niche for the digital mapping industry. As Russia began privatizing its military satellite system, its high-resolution Earth images suddenly became available to commercial mapmakers. Not to be outdone, the U.S. government responded by permitting U.S. firms to plan high-resolution satellite systems for commercial mapping purposes. In 1995 the U.S. Navy also declassified its secret radar charts, and two American entrepreneurs began preparing a comprehensive, high-accuracy map of the ocean floor for sale to nonmilitary markets. By the late 1990s three U.S. companies had announced plans to launch and operate small commercial satellites they claimed would deliver images at resolutions of three meters or less for a few hundred dollars an image and could be used for urban planning, agricultural and environmental monitoring, making and revising maps, and even vacation planning.

By the early 1990s major corporations such as McDonald's and Dunkin' Donuts were already using GIS technology to determine where to build restaurants. At the same time, Cincinnati began reducing mapping costs by sharing its GIS with local utilities. Furthermore, the U.S. Bureau of Land Management and the U.S. Forest Service each discussed allocating $1 billion to GIS public-land information services, and the U.S. Census Bureau sold a rough digital city block map of the United States for $10,000. By early 1992, map users in the United States could choose from 100 different geographic databases, plotting everything from streets to soil types, and from over 200 different software packages.

The emergence of the Global Positioning System (GPS; originally developed by the U.S. government to guide missiles) as a consumer product in the late 1990s enabled industry firms to offer real-time, high-precision mapping information for customers, and GPS receivers were quickly integrated into some auto navigation systems. At this same time, the former Federal Defense Mapping Agency had been reorganized as the National Imaging and Mapping Agency, with a new mandate to promote the application of formerly military mapping capabilities for the commercial market.

PIONEERS IN THE FIELD

Among the pioneering firms in the digital mapping industry are Etak Inc., Navigation Technologies, the Environmental Systems Research Institute, and GeoSystems Global. Founded in 1983 by Stanley Honey, Etak produced the world's first automated car navigation system, the Navigator, in 1985 and has licensed navigation technology to some of the biggest makers of automotive dashboard electronics. Though the sales of Navigator were limited to business customers such as restaurant guides, taxi companies, and vendors of PC mapping software, Etak (a subsidiary of Sony Corp.) was the only major company in the digital map business prior to 1985. By 1999 the company offered a GPS-based map generator to run on notebook computers with coverage across the United States, and traffic report services via cellular phones and cellular-phone connected screens.

A pioneer in the route guidance segment of the digital mapping industry was Navigation Technologies (NavTech), founded in Sunnyvale, California, in 1985. In 1988 NavTech partnered with Holland-based electronics giant Philips Electronics N.V. to develop its auto navigation system, in which it had invested more than $200 million. By the late 1990s it had accumulated detailed databases for North American and European metropolitan areas covering a population of 350 million, and less detailed coverage of submetropolitan areas representing another 270 million. The company supplies vehicle databases for factory or dealer installed systems on vehicles from such makers as Acura, BMW and Mercedes Benz. Aftermarket systems using NavTech databases include the Philips Carin Navigation System and Hertz NeverLost.

The Environmental Systems Research Institute (ESRI) was founded in 1969 in Redlands, California, by Jack and Laura Dangermond. In the 1970s, ESRI concentrated on developing GIS applications used in urban renewal projects. In the 1980s, ESRI became a digital mapping/GIS software company and, in 1981, released ArcInfo, the first modern GIS integrated into a single system. ArcInfo remained the company's flagship product and was modified to work in Unix, Windows NT, and network computer environments. In the early 1990s ESRI unveiled ArcView GIS, a mainstream desktop mapping and GIS tool; ArcData, to provide users with ready-to-use GIS data; and Arc-CAD, which integrated computer-aided design and

GIS technologies. ESRI released its first consumer mapping product in 1994. In the late 1990s it positioned itself to capitalize on the "live mapping" technology made possible by the Internet and, in 1999, enjoyed total sales of roughly $340.9 million and software revenues of $296.6 million for, commanding 35 percent of the GIS software market. That year the company began to contribute software and support to federal and local livability programs and to the National Oceanic and Atmospheric Sustainable Seas Expeditions project.

GeoSystems Global of Mountville, Pennsylvania, was founded in 1967 as the cartographic services division of publisher R.R. Donnelley & Sons. In the 1970s and 1980s it expanded into customized mapping services for textbook, atlas, travel, directory, and reference publishers, and became the largest custom mapping business in the United States. In 1989 Donnelley formed a joint venture with Spatial Data Sciences and two years later acquired selected assets of Spatial Data to form GeoSystems. In 1992 GeoSystems released GeoLocate, its flagship mapping and routing software program, and in 1993 Donnelley's Cartographic Services and GeoSystems were merged as GeoSystems to form a total GIS services company. In 1996 GeoSystems entered the online publishing business with MapQuest, the first interactive mapping service on the Internet. MapQuest immediately became a World Wide Web hot spot as consumers used the service to call up "zoomable" maps of locations throughout the United States. In 1999 the company changed its name to Mapquest.com and moved its headquarters to New York City, reflecting an increased commitment to the Internet.

CURRENT CONDITIONS

As early as 1991, the U.S. GIS industry enjoyed revenues of $3.5 billion, with Pentagon spending alone accounting for one-fourth of that figure. A 1992 estimate predicted that the demand for GIS products and services by utility companies and local governments alone ensured that the GIS industry would grow 25 percent annually through 2002—with even faster growth if applications could be found to entice corporate customers and consumers. By the mid-1990s the GIS market was one of the fastest-growing computer application markets, with an estimated value of $2 billion in 1995 and an 18 percent annual growth rate. In 1995 the remote-sensing arm of the digital mapping/GIS market (which included both satellite imaging and traditional aerial photography) was val-

ued at $550 million, and it was estimated that it would reach $2.7 billion by 2000. These estimates proved to be somewhat conservative, given that by that time the software segment alone garnered $1.5 billion in sales worldwide. Furthermore, the U.S. Department of Commerce projected worldwide sales of GPS-related products to exceed $16 billion by 2003.

Growth in the digital mapping and GIS industry is expected to be fueled by developing applications in banking, insurance, transportation, and telecommunications, and such traditional map-using industries as environmental monitoring, utilities, and resource management. For example, in 2000 the number of in-vehicle navigation systems totaled more than 100,000 in North America and nearly 1 million in Europe.

INDUSTRY LEADERS

Intergraph Corp., based in Huntsville, Alabama, is a diversified producer of hardware, software, consulting, and support services for the information technology field. Its Industry Solutions Division produces automated hardware, software, and consulting services to the process and building industries, to the infrastructure industry (including transportation, utilities, and state and local governments), and to the federal government. Its Computer Systems Division supplies high-performance graphics workstations and PCs, three-dimensional graphics subsystems, servers, and other hardware products. By 1999, Intergraph had added over $30 million in new contracts to its list of major contracts worldwide, and posted revenues of more than $914 million for the year.

Based in Troy, New York, MapInfo Corp. generated sales revenue of $74.7 million for the 1999 fiscal year. Its products, such as MapInfo and MapBasic, enable insurance companies and sales organizations to translate complex corporate data into easily understood maps to simplify the process of performing marketing analysis, selecting business sites, managing corporate assets and risk, and optimizing delivery routing and logistics. MapInfo sells its own digital maps to customers who can then overlay their own data on them for visual presentation and analysis, and manipulate it on any of the 400 software applications compatible with MapInfo's products. It also sells "geo-coding" products that assign latitude and longitude coordinates to corporate data containing geographic references so that data can be displayed accurately on a map. Its MapXsite, which was upgraded in mid-1999 to include additional features and applications, enables Web developers and Internet service providers to create Web pages in which a company's various locations can be displayed. Also in mid-1999, MapInfo partnered with Oracle, a leader in the information management industry. The company's software revenues of $46.7 million in 1999 made it the third-largest GIS software company.

Analytical Surveys, Inc. (ASI), produces high-accuracy digital maps that are integrated with databases in GIS applications to store, retrieve, analyze, and display information about the characteristics of utilities networks, natural resources, transportation systems, and residential and commercial communities. ASI creates maps using aerial photography, ground surveys, and existing printed maps. It also focuses on four aspects of the GIS business: digital mapping of physical plants such as power generation facilities; photogrammetric mapping for utilities using aerial photos that have been processed to remove distortions; cadastral mapping showing property lines, property zoning, and use restrictions for local governments; and digital orthophotography for creating high-accuracy maps that look like aerial photos. The company continued to grow as it signed record contracts in both the first and second quarters of 1999. In mid-1999, ASI was an integral player in the building of New York City's first photogrammetric land base. However, its many acquisitions that year caused some accounting turmoil, and the company was forced to restate its earnings and slash some of its workforce. In the end, ASI recorded revenues of $113.5 million and employed 1,225 workers in fiscal 1999.

AMERICA AND THE WORLD

At the end of 2000, the U.S. digital mapping industry remained the world's largest, and its long history of government and private initiatives in GIS, digital mapping, and satellite sensing technologies gave it a competitive edge in the world market. Nevertheless, the United States was estimated to account for only one-quarter of the total world demand for GIS-related products and services. Although the industry did not really begin to grow until inexpensive but powerful computer processors emerged in the 1990s, by the late 1990s it already employed more than 200,000 worldwide.

Despite the lead enjoyed by the U.S. digital mapping industry, however, several world regions were also at the cutting edge of GIS technologies. Japan, for example, quickly embraced auto navigation technology and by 1999 more than a million Japanese cars had already been manufactured with navigation sys-

tems. Europe was also a leader in the use of digital mapping to aid auto navigation, led by companies such as European Geographic Technologies and TeleAtlas. Germany was the first country in the world to complete a full mapping of its roadways for integration into in-vehicle navigation systems, and Germany's BMW was the first European car company to offer navigation technology as an option.

Great Britain played a major role in pushing digital mapping technology by launching, under the auspices of its Ordnance Survey (the national mapping agency), a complete digital database of all 70 million topographical features of the British Isles. When the mammoth project was completed, the British government explored the option of privatizing the Ordnance Survey—a clear reflection of the worldwide trend toward finding private, commercial uses for previously military or strictly governmental satellite technologies.

Russia also played a major role in the trend toward privatization. When the Soviet Union unraveled, its previously top-secret high-resolution satellite photos became available to commercial international mapmakers. Soon after, the private Russian company in charge of managing this satellite data reached an agreement with Sweden's Satellitbild to sell two-meter-resolution satellite images to Western buyers. About the same time, India's IRS-1 six-meter-resolution satellite images were also made available for commercial use. These developments prompted the United States to relax its restrictions on the commercial use of high-resolution satellite images, encouraging consortia of international companies to form ventures to launch commercial imaging satellites for the world market. The U.S.-based Lockheed and Raytheon teamed up with Mitsubishi to form Space Imaging, which promptly announced plans to launch a one-meter-resolution commercial satellite. A similar venture between the U.S. firm Ball Aerospace and Japan's Hitachi led to the formation of EarthWatch in the same period. EarthWatch had plans underway to launch its two high-resolution satellites in late 1999, backed by $50 million in investments, but slowness in the State Department's approval held the project up for over a year.

RESEARCH AND TECHNOLOGY

Advances in digital mapping technology center around the standardization of the map objects that comprise the content of digital maps, new applications for digital mapping technology, the growth of the Internet as a platform for "live" interactive mapping, and the likelihood that high-resolution military-quality satellite images will soon become available to consumers and businesses alike. The profusion of digital mapping platforms in the 1990s and concerns over how to ensure the integrity of digital maps spurred the digital mapping industry to undertake its largest research project ever in an attempt to find objective guidelines for communicating map data. Such guidelines would include standardized or codified classification techniques for grouping map data "attributes" and logic-based systems for selecting the right graphic symbols to represent different types of map data.

The Internet seemed to offer an increasingly natural environment for digital mapmakers, and the growing availability of such mapping technology on the World Wide Web was regarded as one of the key factors in the eventual emergence of a true "electronic yellow pages," in which users could not only search out addresses and phone numbers, but also detailed maps pointing out the best routes to a business. High-precision satellite images available for only a few hundred dollars came closer to reality in the late 1990s as 11 companies were given licenses for consumer GIS satellite systems, some with resolutions as sharp as 85 centimeters. A complete high-resolution mapping of the world, however, remained an unaccomplished goal by 2000 when, according to the National Imaging and Mapping Agency, less than 50 percent of Earth had been mapped with 10-meter or better resolution.

FURTHER READING

Barkow, Tim. "Ground Truth." *Wired,* December 1995.

Biederman, Patricia Ward. "Fans Hail Map-Making Revolution." *Los Angeles Times,* 26 January 1997.

Caceres, Marco. "Focus Sharpens for Imaging Satellite Market." *Aerospace America,* September 2000.

Caldwell, Douglas R. "GIS and GPS: A Marriage Made in the Heavens." *Map Report,* 1995. Available from http://www.maptrade.org.

"The Delight of Digital Maps." *Economist,* 21 March 1992.

"EarthWatch Forges Ahead without *EarlyBird 1* Satellite." Longmont, CO: EarthWatch Inc., 7 April 1998. Available from http://www.digitalglobe.com/company/news/pr/1998/04-07_ew_forges_ahead.html.

Enge, Per, and Pretap Misra. "Scanning the Issue/Technology: Special Issue on Global Positioning System." *Proceedings of the IEEE,* January 1999. Available from http://teaser.ieee.org/pubs/trans/9902/gps.html.

Fulghum, David A. "Digital Aircraft Camera Offers Cheap, Fast Images lion." *Aviation Week & Space Technology,* 31 July 2000.

"GIS Market Revenues Top $1.5 Billion." *Geospatial Solutions,* June 2000.

Ginsberg, Steve. "Digital Map Firm Finds Growth Path." *San Francisco Business Times,* 28 July 1995.

Green, Barry, and Erika Bauer. "All over the Map." *Publish,* April 1996.

Jacobs, April. "All Roads Lead to the Net." *ComputerWorld,* 8 July 1996.

"MapInfo Corp." 2000. Available from http://www.mapinfo.com.

Matzer, Marla. "A Digitized Future." *Forbes,* 24 April 1995.

Morton, Oliver. "Private Spy." *Wired,* August 1997.

"NavTech." Rosemont, IL: Navigation Technologies Corp., 29 September 1998. Available from http://www.navtech.com.

"Schott Consulting Services." 2000. Available from http://www.schott.com.

Schott Consulting Services. "GIS: What Is It?" 1999. Available from http://www.schott.com.

Sena, Michael. "In-Vehicle Map Display Systems." *Map Report,* 1995. Available from http://www.maptrade.org.

———. "In-Vehicle Navigation." *Map Report,* 1995. Available from http://www.maptrade.org.

———. "A Look Back to Future Technologies." *Map Report,* 1995. Available from http://www.maptrade.org.

Spicer, William. "Making Money with Digital Maps on the World Wide Web." *Map Report,* 1995. Available from http://www.maptrade.org.

Vantuono, William. "Mapping New Roles for GIS." *Railway Age,* March 1995.

Wagner, Mitch. "Mapping Software Heads in New Direction." *ComputerWorld,* 15 July 1996.

Wilford, John Noble. "Revolutions in Mapping." *National Geographic,* February 1998.

Young, Jeffrey. "Treasure Maps." *Forbes,* 18 November 1996.

DIGITAL VIDEO DISC

Digital video disc (DVD), or digital versatile disc as it is sometimes called, finally assumed its long-anticipated position atop the consumer electronics market in 1999, though the industry, still weary from a host of contentious setbacks, remained somewhat cautious about losing its head over the dramatic success. While an estimated 12 million U.S. households owned DVD players at the end of 2000, the machines still suffered from the high penetration of videocassette recorders (VCRs), estimated at about 90 percent of U.S. homes; a record 22.9 million VCRs were sold in 1999. Entertainment consumer electronics are generally upgraded more slowly than personal computers, but nonetheless analysts expected DVD players will have penetrated two-thirds of U.S. homes by 2009.

Skeptics cautioned that such predictions may be premature, as new technologies are being developed in consumer electronics at a record pace, and the infighting that hounded the industry in its early years has hardly been mitigated, potentially providing an opening for new products to move in and take the market share that DVD manufacturers have already claimed as their own. One such competing technology is on-demand video services delivered by cable television companies. The challenge for DVD companies is to penetrate enough homes and build enough momentum that on-demand presents a limited challenge in a niche market.

DVD compresses video signals, eliminating redundant information such as items not perceptible by the naked eye, into a format called MPEG-2, which turns out sharper and clearer video and audio signals to the television or computer screen. The five-inch, CD-like disc offers twice the resolution of VHS for video purposes, never wears out, doesn't need rewinding, and lets the user change languages at the touch of a button. The newest generation of product widely available offers a 24-bit audio-only format that can be played in a single audio/video unit, while emergent applications include recordable video.

By 2000, DVD was the fastest-selling new consumer electronics technology in history. In its first two years on the market place, over 5 million DVD-players were sold in the United States. By way of comparison, in their first two years, VHS players and CD players sold 450,000 and 960,000 units, respectively. By 2000, more than 100 models of DVD players were on the market. Nearly 7 percent of U.S. homes held DVD players, and industry experts expected to reach the magic 10 percent threshold—the percentage generally agreed upon as establishing a consumer-electronics product as a stable player—by the end of 2000. The average price of a DVD player has fallen steadily since its introduction, from $500 in 1997 to $275 in 1999, with some reaching as low as $170 by 2000. Meanwhile, in within three years of DVD's introduction, DVD shipments exceeded 190 million, while rentals gained significant market share at video outlets. Warner Home Video, for instance, derived about 30 percent of its revenues from DVD sales at the end of 1999.

The DVD industry produces both digital home-entertainment equipment and the software (i.e., movies) that is played on it. It is the software, in fact, that propels the sales of DVD players and discs. Consequently, electronics companies need the backing of Hollywood studios to sell their hardware. Many of the industry's leaders developed and now manufacture CDs and VCRs, the leading home-entertainment formats on the market today. Some are conglomerates with operations in both the electronics and the entertainment arenas. Time Warner Inc.'s list of holdings, including Time Inc., Warner Bros., and Home Box Office, made it the world's largest entertainment and information company, and was integrated into the robust online world via its 2000 merger with America Online. Sony Corp. manufactures consumer electronics and also owns Columbia Pictures.

Ever since it began, the DVD industry has been plagued with confusion over exactly who is developing which product. In April 1997, 10 major electronics firms created the DVD Forum for the purpose of agreeing on a single format for future-generation DVD. The forum also promotes the industry by defining DVD format specification, issuing DVD format and logo licenses, and providing certification laboratories.

The 10 original members of the DVD Forum were Sony, Philips Electronics, Toshiba, Time Warner, Hitachi, Matsushita Electric, Pioneer Electronics, Thomson SA, Mitsubishi Electric, and Victor Co., though by 2000 the forum had grown to include over 100 companies. But no sooner had members reached some unity on industry standards than Sony and Philips announced they were developing products that varied from the approved format. Thus, as a concession to those firms that wished to be free to pursue whatever avenue seems promising, forum members were not obligated to develop only those products that are compatible with the DVD format.

The industry also suffered as corporate players each strived to become the industry leader. A company can reap larger profits by inventing and owning the patent to the DVD format that ends up becoming the world's standard. As a result, many DVD products already on store shelves are incompatible with each other. This trend was nowhere more pronounced than in the market for DVD convergence with personal computers. Generally, DVD manufacturers work out specific deals with computer firms to develop specifications for DVD compatibility.

DVD-video (usually abbreviated to DVD) refers to the format for storage of video information. A DVD player, connected to a TV, can play movies from a DVD disc. Note that this format implicitly includes audio data as well, since movies need both video and audio data.

DVD-ROM, like any other technology dealing with personal computers, refers to a collection of related formats. DVD-ROM refers to any of the DVD formats that store computer data, but separate names distinguish the writable versions. The DVD-R (DVD-recordable) format refers to a write-once disc. DVD-RW (DVD-rewritable) refers to an erasable format. Another erasable format, DVD-RAM, works only for discs in a cartridge. Finally, the DVD+RW format is erasable, and is the most compatible of the DVD-ROM formats.

BACKGROUND AND DEVELOPMENT

The story of DVD began in the early 1990s with several different groups pursuing development of the new digital format. In search of new ways to release titles from its extensive movie catalog, Time Warner paired up with electronics giant Toshiba. The race began when a competing group formed between multimedia entertainment and electronics heavy-hitters Sony and Philips. Eventually, other big-name technology and computing companies such as Matsushita, IBM, Microsoft, and Intel joined the ranks. In 1995, fearing that the industry was heading toward a winner-take-all situation in the war over competing formats, IBM called for a solution. As a result, the Time Warner-Toshiba product became the industry standard, even though it wasn't necessarily better. Observers attributed Sony's failure to win the standard wars to its inability to win over major Hollywood studios to the format.

Hollywood, however, had mixed reactions to the new medium. Some entertainment companies, especially Paramount Pictures and Universal Studios, wanted the DVD format to have stronger antipiracy protection. Not surprisingly, Hollywood's strongest DVD advocates included Time Warner, Sony, and MCA, all companies with ties to electronics firms. Although manufacturers had hoped to market DVDs starting in 1996, those plans were delayed until the piracy issue could be resolved.

Meanwhile, Time Warner remained committed to the DVD format and was in the forefront of the movement to bring it to market. Concerns about piracy still left Hollywood uneasy, however. Finally, in July 1997 *Television Digest* reported that DVD encryption licensing issues were resolved to the satisfaction of Universal Studios. Consequently, Universal announced they would release 10 DVD movie titles between November 1997 and February 1998. In June 1998 Disney released several titles in the new Divx (short for "digital video express," a pay-for-view DVD) format, then made a

---

History THE FALL OF A FORMAT

After taking a beating for nearly a year, the DVD rival format Divx was mercifully laid to rest in June 1999. The Digital Video Express partnership between retailer Circuit City and Ziffren, Brittenham, Branca & Fischer, a leading Hollywood law firm representing producers, directors, and production companies, produced a loss of several hundred million dollars in its short life. The plan was designed to offer an alternative to customers reluctant to keep making the trek to the video store and worry about incurring late fees while offering the top-of-the-line video technology.

Divx offered customers a Divx movie for about $5 which, for two days, could be viewed without limit on a Divx-enhanced DVD player (which cost about $100 more than a regular DVD player). After the 48-hour viewing spree, the player was rendered inoperative, and the disc was either recharged through a modem hookup to a Divx service or simply disposed of. The player electronically reported viewing time to the Divx organization through the phone lines.

Divx players were released in select markets in June 1998, and a national campaign was launched three months later. The format was taken seriously enough as a contender that DVD manufacturers were forced into a competitive advertising blitz, hoping to stave off the competition before it began.

In the end, Divx was a washout, with minimal sales compared with DVD. Only 87,000 units were shipped between its release in June 1998 and the end of 1998, followed by only 115,000 more up to June 1999. Critics blasted the fatal combination of brand-new technology,

a modem hookup, and time restrictions as generating too much confusion for consumers to consider the products seriously. What's more, the technology gained a reputation for trying to milk consumers with its overzealous drive toward proprietary revenues. In the eyes of many consumers, the technology also imposed an intrusive monitoring of viewing habits.

Overall, by constraining the cutting-edge technology, analysts noted, the Divx scheme effectively tied the noose around its own neck, although proponents of the technology placed the blame on the lack of support from retail outlets and movie studios. DVD companies were much more savvy in wooing Hollywood studios, while video-rental companies, seeing a direct threat to their business, jumped behind DVD full force. Divx's ties to Circuit City also failed to endear the format to rival electronics retailers. Finally, DVD players enjoyed the advantage of providing the latest in digital video technology in a manner similar in style to the familiar VCR, thus avoiding information overload in the mind of the consumer.

The final bow of Divx was a $100 cash rebate offer to those customers who had already purchased Divx players before the format was rendered obsolete.

The elimination of the rival format further opened up the market for DVD competition, as manufacturers were no longer required to compete with alternative formats in addition to each other. Meanwhile, Zenith Electronics Corp., Matsushita, and Thomson Consumer Electronics all stated that it would be unproblematic to quietly phase out their Divx lines in favor of increased production of DVD players.

---

pact with Time Warner the following month for international distribution of its Buena Vista Home Movies.

Satisfied with the new encryption measures, Hollywood finally gave the go-ahead to the DVD format. In April 1997, DVD players and discs hit the stores in limited distribution. Retail prices for players generally ranged from $500 to $1,000, while discs cost between $20 and $30.

In August and September 1997, the industry was rocked by announcements from several core alliance members. First, Sony and Philips reported that they were designing a next-generation recordable DVD that deviated from industry standards. Then came word from retailer Circuit City that they would promote Divx, which was partly incompatible with existing players and discs.

Consequently, a struggle ensued reminiscent of the VCR wars of the 1970s between VHS and Beta formats. By mid-1999, the battle was over and DVD

had won. The 1999 industry explosion drove the nails into Divx's coffin. The much-feared and greatly hyped Divx failed to draw consumers to its plan to charge $3.25 per use of a disc and to require a modem hookup to the company to order another movie. In fact, reaction was often downright hostile, spawning a number of Divx-bashing Web sites. But the closure of that struggle simply refocused attention on the range of varying formats all vying for the commercial spotlight. The DVD battle is likely to continue as companies develop and manufacture machines with new formats.

CURRENT CONDITIONS

DVD finally emerged as the single fastest-growing entertainment format in the history of consumer electronics. Beginning in late December 1998, DVD hardware and software simply took over the electronics outlets. Analysts predicted that DVD shipments

---

would reach the 200 million mark in 2000, while some 6.5 million DVD players were expected to be sold. The technology took such a firm hold that the Consumer Electronics Association was delightedly humbled for its inaccurate player sales estimates for 1999; the organization forecast about 1.6 million sales, but by the end of the year, almost 4 million were purchased.

DVD manufacturers, realizing the awaited potential of their technology, pushed it in all directions. Adding multiple-disc capability, offering portable units, and even working with automobile manufacturers to install DVD players in the backseat of vehicles are just some of the ways industry players scrambled to command market share. Its commercial and institutional uses were also increasingly attractive; DVD players were used to read bar codes, access video clips for demonstrations, and administer computer-generated functions and programming.

Convergence was a key industry buzzword, as manufacturers integrated the technology ever more with personal computers (PCs) to allow for compatibility with e-mail programs, the World Wide Web, real-time video and audio, and computer games. DVD-ROM was installed in over 30 million computers. The wider presence in PCs rather than stand-alone sets follows from the frequent upgrading of PCs relative to home-entertainment centers. Hybrid technology was the order of the day for stand-alone DVD players that maintained software compatibility with PCs, including Internet access. DVD movie titles were increasingly released with direct hookups to the distributors' Web sites, allowing the companies to show preview clips of other films and peddle merchandise.

While sales finally met and exceeded expectations, the industry still faced a number of hurdles to ease customer confusion. Different DVD players offer their menus with varying degrees of control over the picture, audio, information access, and graphics controls, and some players allow only a linear transfer of the feature with no options available whatsoever. Much of the confusion still stems from the different alliances between DVD makers, computer companies, and media firms and the agreements they reach relating to the precise distribution method appropriate for DVD technology. Until the industries can establish a navigational standard for DVD players, analysts noted, the differing functionality was likely to result in more customers throwing up their arms in frustration.

DVD RECORDERS

Meanwhile, the familiar format wars followed the technology development into the DVD-recorder market as well. The DVD recorder features premium editing capability, allowing users to literally cut and paste clips in any arrangement they wish. These recorders are likely to prove quite popular among those who currently use VCRs to record programs off television; recordable DVDs allow users to record television-quality programs at DVD resolution, or about double the image quality offered by VCRs. Pioneer's DVD-RW was set to square off with Toshiba's and Matsushita's DVD-RAM. Not to be outdone, Sony and Philips were hard at work developing their own DVD-RW+. The primary differences will not be felt much by consumers who simply want to watch movies and record off the television, but for those wishing to utilize recordable DVDs with personal computers, a number of interoperability difficulties could arise.

Pioneer rolled out the first DVD recorders in December 1999. The units ran about $2,000, with blank disks that held up to 4.7 gigabytes selling for $30 a pop. These disks hold about the same amount of time as standard VHS tapes—about six hours—though with vastly superior quality. As a result of the inflated prices, production was limited to only 10,000 a month. Matsushita and Toshiba cranked out their own versions in 2000, but pricing were comparable, portending a long while before most VCRs are junked in favor of the new technology.

HACKER TROUBLES PUSH ENCRYPTION EFFORTS

While the DVD industry was hardly known for its ability to reach a consensus, major industry players Sony, MGM, Time Warner, and Universal all found common ground engaging in an intense battle with computer hackers who figured out how to crack the DVD code by reverse-engineering Windows player software, allowing DVD playback capability. A Norwegian father- and-son hacker team were arrested after cracking the code around late December 1999, and could face up to three years in jail for copyright infringement.

The Norwegian programmer, Frank Stevenson, claimed he essentially developed the DeCCS de-encryption system as a hobby to test the encryption code embedded in DVD technology. Internet activists, meanwhile, were busily encouraging people to download the software on the theory that it would be impossible to block with the technology in enough hands.

These dramatic events simply amplified a heated debate between the industry and consumer groups over the issue of DVD encryption coding. While industry leaders as well as the Digital Video Disc Content Control Association (DVDCCA) were adamant that the copyrights be protected to ensure ownership rights over their technology, consumer groups and Internet advocates insisted that such measures were not theft, noting that the reverse-engineering process was not illegal under the 1998 Digital Millennium Copyright Act, which specifically allows the process for interoperability between systems. They argued that the DVD industry has failed to support Linux and other non-Windows operating systems, and that interoperability was the reasoning behind the hacker actions to begin with.

The industry, however, was determined; DVD-CCA filed suit in a California state court against Web sites posting the de-encryption formula used by the hackers and even against the sites linking to them. Similar suits were filed in Connecticut and New York by the eight leading movie studios. The outcomes were difficult to predict, given the unsettled legal boundaries on the Internet, but the entire case lent some credence to long-standing Hollywood fears, as studios remained a bit reluctant to commit completely to a technology that appeared vulnerable to copyright infringement. Most analysts expected, however, that piracy fears will not be enough to keep movie studios away from DVD technology. The consensus of the DVD takeover is now significantly broad enough that the fear of lost market share and potential revenues trumps fears of copyright infringement.

DESPITE CONCERNS, HOLLYWOOD PUSHES FORWARD

Indeed, by summer 2000, motion-picture studios had released over 6,000 DVD titles in the United States, up from only 1,800 at beginning of 1999. Meanwhile, major video outlets such as Blockbuster and Hollywood Video maintained sizable DVD sections. By the end of 1999, Blockbuster offered DVD rentals at 3,800 of its 6,500 U.S. stores as well as in 1,000 foreign locations. Rental fees for DVDs are generally the same as for VHS. Video stores derived about 1 percent of their total revenue from DVDs in 1999, a figure expected to reach 5 percent in 2000.

INDUSTRY LEADERS

Matsushita Electric Industrial Co., Ltd. is the world's number-one consumer electronics company, with sales of $71.12 billion in fiscal 2000, up from 11.7 percent from the previous year. Its brand names include Panasonic, JVC, Technics, and Quasar.

Matsushita is a core member of the DVD Forum, the group of top electronics firms that is setting the format standards for future-generation DVD products, and along with Hitachi and Toshiba was a leading proponent of the new DVD-RAM recordable DVD format. Matsushita has nearly 283,000 employees and derives about 25 percent of its revenues from video and audio equipment. The company's net income skyrocketed in 2000, from $113 million to $971 million.

Koninklijke Philips Electronics N.V., a Netherlands-based firm, is the world's third-largest electronics company, with 226,800 employees. Revenues in 1999 totaled $31.75 billion, with healthy net income of $1.8 billion. Having spent most of the 1990s trimming the fat from its ranks, the slimmed-down electronics giant launched its first line of DVD players in 1997. The firm aggressively courted Internet firms, forging an alliance with Sun Microsystems and industry rival Sony for home-entertainment products that utilize the Web, a key step toward DVD-Internet convergence. Philips offers mid-range DVD equipment that includes features such as a built-in karaoke machine and a joystick-equipped remote. The firm has paired up with Sony to develop a second-generation recordable DVD that has a different format than the one key industry leaders had previously agreed to support.

Pioneer Corporation, headquartered in Tokyo, is a world leader in audio and audiovisual products. A pioneer in DVD technology, the firm generated sales of $5.63 billion in 2000, with net income of $123 million, while maintaining a payroll of 23,650 employees and deriving 93 percent of its sales from its range of electronics products. Its focus is on producing high-end DVD players that offer a variety of options. For example, Pioneer's model DV-700 can play DVDs, 12-inch laser discs, and CDs. Pioneer's long misfortune was to lead the way in new technologies, offering them at high prices, but fail to maintain market share when other competitors joined the market and drove down prices. Entering the 21st century, Pioneer was banking heavily on its DVD products, which included DVD-video, DVD-ROM, DVD-audio, and DVD-R.

Sony Corp., a multimedia powerhouse, has been a major figure in the DVD industry since its inception, aggressively promoting digital distribution networks to facilitate its movie and music operations. Early on, a DVD format developed by Time Warner and Toshiba was favored as the industry standard over one designed by Sony and Philips Electronics. For Sony, this was very much like the situation the company found itself in during the 1970s, when its Betamax VCR format lost to rival VHS after a prolonged struggle. In 1997 Sony and Philips joined forces to produce DVDs known as Super Audio CD. Sony's Electronics division generated $39.24 billion, or 63 percent, of total 1999 sales. The company, which has 177,000 employees, reported 1999 sales of $57.1 billion and net income of $1.5 billion. By continuing to promote formats incompatible with industry standards for future-generation audio and recordable DVD, Sony is clearly ready to do battle with its competitors; the company brought out eight new DVD entertainment systems in 2000.

Disney is a key player in the DVD industry because of the marketability of its movies, which include popular favorites such as *The Lion King* and *101 Dalmatians*. It has also managed to avoid committing itself to just one format by releasing titles for both regular DVD and the Divx format before the latter disintegrated, thus sidestepping one of the industry's most vexing problems. In 1999, Disney launched its own DVD Super-site on the Web to market animated classics upgraded to DVD format, provide previews of coming Disney DVD attractions, and raise consumer awareness of DVD technology. Disney has interests in Buena Vista Television, Miramax Film Corp., and Touchstone Pictures. The Burbank, California-based company has 117,000 employees and reported revenue of $23.4 billion in 1999, while net income dipped slightly to $1.3 billion from $1.85 billion in 1998.

Time Warner, one of the early proponents of DVD, was the world's largest entertainment and information company with 67,500 employees, and it got even larger in 2000 when it was bought out by Internet giant America Online in one of the largest merger deals in history. AOL Time Warner enjoys combined revenues of $30 billion. Among its holdings are Warner Bros., which produces and distributes movies and boasts the industry's largest film library, and Warner Home Video, where a good deal of its DVD earnings are focused. Time Warner helped develop DVD hoping to find a new release format for its vast catalog of movie titles.

Toshiba, based in Tokyo, developed the industry's standard DVD format in a partnership with Time Warner. In addition to DVD players and discs, Toshiba introduced a computer with a DVD-ROM drive in 1997. The company's product line also includes portable PCs, videocassette recorders, and electronic parts such as semiconductors. The company's consumer products division accounted for one-fifth of Toshiba's 2000 revenues of $54.5 billion. Toshiba employs 198,000 workers.

AMERICA AND THE WORLD

The DVD industry operates in a truly global marketplace. Not only are the key players mostly international conglomerates, but the product is expected to be available to consumers throughout the world. Early on, the industry divided the world into five regions, each with its own electronic code. Thus, discs purchased in one region cannot be viewed on players from another area. Since Hollywood releases movies in different countries on different dates, splitting the world into five incompatible regions allows Hollywood to maintain control over movie distribution. One company located in the United Kingdom has tried to thwart this system by offering DVD players over the Internet that have been modified with custom computer chips to bypass the electronic code so they can play DVD discs from any region.

Initially, there were problems synchronizing the audio hardware and software in the European market. By August 1997, however, companies had solved the problem with an alternative sound system that differed from the one used in the United States. In September 1997, *Television Digest* reported that DVD was set for an overseas launch in early 1998. In July 1998 Disney signed a pact with Time Warner to allow Warner Home Video to distribute 100 DVD movies from Disney's Buena Vista Home Video unit throughout Europe, the Middle East, Africa, and the countries of the former Soviet Union.

The large European and Japanese consumer electronics markets were generally deemed to be about one year behind the United States in DVD acceptance, a promising sign for DVD manufacturers in the early 2000s. True to form, domestic Japanese shipments of DVD players skyrocketed in 2000, making it the year that DVD technology broke through in Japan as it had in the United States.

The Chinese government invested in its own DVD development program to foster a domestic industry. Efforts have focused on laser diode technologies, MPEG-2 decoder development, and improved DVD manufacturing capabilities. Sales growth is expected to proceed slowly as Chinese consumers face the same problems over competing formats that characterize the U.S. market. Still, demand for the players is expected to increase in China, with sales reaching 10 million players annually by about 2002. As the Chinese market opens to outside involvement, moreover, Japanese firms have pushed their way into this neighboring market to produce and market DVD technology. Following the World Trade Organization deal negotiated between the United States and China in late

1999 that promises to alter the Chinese movie and music distribution structure, China promised to be a lucrative new field for DVD manufacturers to play in.

RESEARCH AND TECHNOLOGY

DVD offers high-resolution video. The five-inch disk, similar in appearance to a CD but with seven times the storage capacity, can hold up to 133 minutes of video in standard format, wide-screen format, and letterbox format. Other features include a choice of language soundtracks and subtitles as well as the ability to view scenes from different angles. DVD also has Digital Dolby surround sound for a theater-like experience.

The DVD and DVD-ROM format allows playback of music, video, and multimedia content. DVD-RAM, which is being developed by several competing groups, will go one step further and allow for recording. A forum composed of key industry electronics leaders established a standardized DVD-RAM format that had 2.6 gigabytes of storage on each side of the disc. Only a few months after that agreement was reached, however, Philips, Sony, and Hewlett-Packard Co. began development of a DVD-RAM format that contained up to 3 gigabytes of storage on each side.

DVDs became more playful even while the industry rapidly matured. At the 1999 Consumer Electronics Show, California-based VM Labs unveiled its NUON technology that, when utilized by DVD players, allows a vast range of interactive capabilities such as Web surfing and dazzling light shows to accompany audio CDs, a feature VM Labs CEO Richard Miller referred to as "a lava lamp for the new millennium." NUON technology-based DVDs also enable the viewer to zoom in on a picture in real time, and to divide the screen into nine frames and zoom in on any one. VM Labs won't offer NUON directly to consumers, but will license it to hardware and software manufacturers for integration into a range of products, much like Dolby Digital sound technology.

Almost ready for marketability is an audio-only format. Panasonic was set to roll out its first DVD audio player in summer 2000. Audio players generally will be marketed with video players until a sufficient number of audio titles are produced to warrant a separate unit. Audio DVD players, however, will unsurprisingly face the same challenges relating to copyright-infringement concerns giving pause to movie studios. To head off potential problems, representatives from the Recording Industry Association of America, the International Federation of the Phonographic Industry, and the Recording Industry Association of Japan created an International Steering Committee (ISC) to establish an industry standard for DVD audio. In order to set a technical standard, the ISC will listen to proposed formats developed by competing alliances. Given the history of the DVD industry, however, it is likely that whatever unified standard the ISC tries to enforce, some companies will nevertheless design and then market conflicting formats.

A standardized digital watermarking technology is being adopted by the major electronics companies to ease the entertainment industry's concerns about uncontrolled unauthorized copying of copyrighted materials. The electronic watermarks are invisible to the user but will be recognized by consumer digital recorders or PC systems to regulate the hardware's ability to make a copy.

Meanwhile, RCA and Thomson Consumer Electronics integrated high-definition television (HDTV) receiver technology with high-level Divx cryptographic technology, thus helping to secure high-resolution, superior-quality videos from video piracy. High definition supplies viewers with Dolby Digital surround sound in addition to the sharper definition. The Thomson RCA players read the encoded data bits and filter them through an interface port to the high-definition television. Once the data reaches the television, smart-card technology translates the encryption and produces the video and audio signal. The technology was quickly picked up by major DVD manufacturers.

FURTHER READING

"About DVD." Los Angeles: DVD Video Group, 5 April 1999. Available from http://www.dvdvideogroup.com/about/press/040599.html.

Alexander, Steve. "The Latest Spin on DVD." *Minneapolis Star Tribune,* 16 January 2000.

Bray, Hiawatha. "Web Sites Sued for DVD Piracy; Internet Users' Rights Debated in Controversy." *Boston Globe,* 29 December 1999.

Brull, Steven V. "DVD and Conquer: Why One Technology Prevailed." *Business Week,* 5 July 1999.

"Competitive Technologies Reports Increased Royalty Growth from Laser Diode Technology Used in DVD-RAM Drives." *Business Wire,* 15 April 1999.

"Decryption, Downloads Threaten Video Industry." *DSN Retailing Today,* 21 August 2000.

"DVDs Get a Big Play at the CES." *MMR,* 24 January 2000.

Horiuchi, Vince. "DVD Players Set Records in Electronics Sales." *Salt Lake Tribune,* 30 November 1999.

"Japan Jan DVD Players Domestic Shipments up 84.8 Pct Yr-on-Yr." *AFX European Focus,* 29 February 2000.

Lewis, Peter. "Consumer Electronics Show: Consumers Catch on, up to DVD Technology." *Seattle Times,* 7 January 2000.

Moffett, Sebastian. "DVD Players: Don't Toss That VCR Yet." *Business Week,* 6 March 2000.

Oldham, Jennifer. "Circuit City Ends Costly Venture into Divx Video Format." *Los Angeles Times,* 17 July 1999.

Palenchar, Joseph. "SACD to Battle with DVD-Audio: New Audio Format War Heats Up." *etown.com,* 23 April 1999. Available from http://www.e-town.com/news/articles/audio formats042399jpa.html.

Pinkerton, Janet. "DVD: Making It Recordable." *Dealerscope,* September 2000.

Pritchard, Robert. "Hollywood versus the Code Breakers." *Electronic Times,* 7 February 2000.

Schweber, Bill. "Nix Divx Pix: The Divx Failure Has Lessons for Anyone Involved in the Design of New Products." *Electronic Design News,* 22 July 1999.

Stoughton, Stephanie. "Circuit City's Slipped Disk; Firm Concedes Defeat, Abandons Divx Technology." *Washington Post,* 17 June 1999.

Thornton, Emily. "A Flash Flood of Japanese Goods?" *Business Week,* 29 November 1999.

"Video Wars: The Sequel." *The Economist,* 17 July 2000.

Waldrep, Mark. "Music on DVD: A Test for Terminology and Format." *Emedia,* August 2000.

———. "Status Check." *Sound & Video Contractor,* February 1999.

Direct Broadcast Satellite Television

The direct broadcast satellite (DBS) television industry was beaming with success in 2000. As the television broadcasting wars between cable companies and providers of DBS TV heated up around the turn of the 21st century, things began to brighten up for the latter. Major Congressional legislation greatly expanded DBS companies' access to local markets, leveling the playing field in this sector between the battling industries. And while DBS market penetration was still minuscule compared to cable's 60 million households, the total number of DBS subscribers jumped from 8.7 million at the end of 1998 to over 14 million the end of 2000. The research firm Yankee Group predicted that the subscription base could reach as high as 25 million by 2005, thus firmly establishing DBS as the fastest-growing technology for television content distribution and one of the most successful commercial applications of satellite communications.

Satellite signals are transmitted in a single digital stream to reception dishes mounted on rooftops, in backyards, and atop industrial buildings. Depending on the company and the exact viewing package a customer selects, one can expect to pay monthly fees ranging from $6 to about $100. Average fee revenues were expected to increase slightly in the early 2000s as the major DBS firms offered more and more local broadcast transmissions.

The industry's clear market leader, DirecTV, was the fourth-largest overall multichannel video provider in the United States, trailing only telecommunications giants AT&T, Time Warner Cable, and Comcast in total subscribers. As far into the future as any observer could see, DirecTV and its rival EchoStar would continue to easily dominate the DBS market.

ORGANIZATION AND STRUCTURE

Direct broadcast satellites orbit 22,300 miles above Earth. At this height, the orbital period coincides with Earth's daily rotation about its axis. The result is that the satellite seems to hang at a constant position in the sky, allowing subscribers to point their reception dishes at a fixed direction and reducing the cost and complexity of the home system.

The rights to telecommunications satellite orbital positions and transmission frequencies are assigned to individual nations by the Geneva-based International Telecommunications Union. The Federal Communications Commission (FCC), which controls U.S. slots, has reserved a portion of the broadcast spectrum and eight orbital positions for DBS. In order to allow higher-powered transmissions for interference-free reception by smaller dishes, the DBS orbital positions are spaced nine degrees apart, rather than two degrees as for conventional communications satellites.

Originally, four of the eight DBS orbital positions were intended to serve the eastern United States, with the others serving the west. With current technology, however, three of the positions (101, 110, and 119 degrees west longitude) can transmit to the entire continental United States. Abbreviated "Full CONUS" slots, they are by far the most coveted since they generate the greatest range for providers.

Each orbital slot is assigned 32 transponder frequencies. The number of channels a DBS provider can offer depends on how many transponders the FCC has licensed it to use; generally these rights are purchased at FCC auctions. Satellite owners buy slots in space and lease assigned transponder frequencies to service providers. Each transponder frequency can accommodate a number of channels, depending on how compactly the signal can be digitally compressed, which varies with the type of programming. Sports events, with small objects moving quickly against complex backgrounds, can only be compressed 7 or 8 to a transponder. Talk shows might be squeezed 9 to a transponder. Since film is shot at a slower frame rate than video, it can be compressed still further, up to 11 per transponder. High-definition television (HDTV), however, requires a great deal of compression, allowing only about 2 channels to a transponder. With the current mix of program types and compression technology, each orbital position provides about 200 channels from its 32 transponders.

The compression and processing of the signal happen before it ever gets to the satellite. DBS service providers maintain advanced, highly automated broadcast centers that receive programming via standard communications satellites, landlines, and videotape. From the broadcast centers, the material is encrypted for security and transmitted to the satellite using large uplink antennas. Taped programming goes through a careful editing and quality-control process before transmission, including optimization for digital compression. By contrast, live satellite programming received by the broadcast centers is generally retransmitted immediately, so the quality of the signal is dependent on that of the incoming "feed."

To receive a signal, the customer needs a small dish antenna and a set-top receiving/decoding unit, approximately the size of a VCR. This unit de-encrypts and decompresses the signal, usually for only one channel at a time; watching or recording multiple programs simultaneously requires multiple decoders. The receiver is individually addressable by means of a telephone connection and a "smart card" programmed with a unique serial number. With this capability, DBS providers can activate and deactivate programming options packages, track pay-per-view services, and implement electronic countermeasures to thwart unauthorized access, or "piracy." (Also see the essay in this book entitled Digital Imaging.)

INDUSTRY REGULATION

Congress and the FCC traverse tenuously between the competing interests of cable and DBS, and those industries' relationship with broadcast television. The Satellite Home Viewer Act of 1994 stipulated that

DBS providers could sell local service only to customers who could not receive acceptable broadcast television reception off the air and who were not cable television subscribers within the past 90 days. The loose definition of "acceptable broadcast" fueled no small amount of controversy between cable, broadcasting, and DBS companies, including a number of lawsuits to prevent DBS players from moving into local markets.

The problem was greatly alleviated, at least from the DBS industry's point of view, when in November 1999 Congress passed the Satellite Home Viewer Improvement Act allowing DBS to directly offer rebroadcast local network signals to customers. Cable companies were hardly impressed, given that this legislation dismantled one of the primary advantages they enjoyed over DBS providers. Knowing the legislation was likely to lead to a whole new round of fighting, the FCC ruled that after 29 May 2000, DBS carriers retransmitting local signals must obtain permission from the local station.

BACKGROUND AND DEVELOPMENT

Satellite dishes have been showing up in backyards for many years, as hobbyists set up receiving stations to intercept traditional analog satellite television downlinks transmitted on the "C-band" as feeds to local stations. But the 10-foot diameter antennas needed to pull in these signals, and the complications of swiveling the big dishes around to track the various satellites limited the appeal of this technology.

In 1986 the National Rural Telecommunications Cooperative (NRTC) was formed to address a need to provide reliable and affordable services to 25 million residents of rural communities across the United States. DBS was not yet feasible because of high costs and immature compression and encryption techniques. The NRTC approached GM Hughes, a leader in satellite communications, about a partnership. But Hughes was working on a deal of its own with Australian media mogul Rupert Murdoch, NBC, and Cablevision. Called Sky Cable, the project was to provide a 75-channel service, but the partnership collapsed.

Having worked out some of the bugs, Hughes launched the first DBS satellite in 1993, and negotiated a deal with NRTC that would attract more than 100,000 rural customers to Hughes' DirecTV service in its first year. These customers, spread out all over the country, received a basic package of 20 channels using 18-inch fixed dish antennas, and provided much wider exposure than DirecTV otherwise would have received in a few "rollout" test markets. Provisions in the Cable Act of 1992 assured that programming would be available to DBS.

Meanwhile, Primestar had established itself as the first direct-to-home service in 1990, operating from a conventional satellite and therefore requiring a larger (three-foot) dish antenna. In 1995 an improved compression scheme, MPEG-2, increased the number of channels available to provide viewers a full complement of offerings.

Since the signals are transmitted in digital packets, the medium is capable of sending signals as video, audio, and computer data, making it ripe for Internet and other interactive capabilities. In 1997, Hughes Network Systems launched DirecDuo, a service combining the company's 400 kilobit per second Internet service called DirecPC with its DirecTV offerings, using a single dish antenna. EchoStar developed similar technology shortly thereafter.

DirecTV scored its most successful offering in 1998. Nearly 700,000 DirecTV customers bought a Sunday Ticket, paying $159 for the chance to watch every National Football League game of the season. The company split the profits with the NFL.

DBS companies continued to aggressively pursue new business areas. America Online partnered with DirecTV, Hughes Network Systems, Philips Electronics, and Network Computer to work on developing "AOL TV." DirecTV and AOL worked together on a service to combine digital satellite television programming and AOL TV's enhanced interactive TV Internet service. EchoStar teamed up with WebTV Networks Inc. for similar purposes.

CURRENT CONDITIONS

DirecTV and EchoStar lost no time taking advantage of the Satellite Home Viewer Improvement Act to stake their claim in many local markets. DirecTV enjoyed early take rates of up to 55 percent in markets such as Washington, D.C., and Atlanta, and offered local channels in about 22 markets. DirecTV enjoyed an advantage over its rival in one key area pertaining to local broadcasts: in most of its markets, DirecTV subscribers did not need to acquire new dishes to receive the local signals. While EchoStar offered free hardware upgrades, the shipping time of about six weeks was a drawback in this rapidly growing market sector. Nonetheless, EchoStar was slightly better positioned in local markets, pitching its products in 35 cities in summer 2000. By that time, both DBS companies were wrapping up their first phase of local service launchings, and were busily signing carriage agreements with TV stations in mid-sized markets. Limited satellite bandwidth, however, will prevent the local signals from reaching all subscribers.

Following Congress's decision to allow DBS companies to sell local signals, major providers such as EchoStar expressed newfound interest in Capital Broadcasting Co., Inc.'s Local TV on Satellite (LTVS) division. LTVS has moved aggressively to develop satellites specifically for local-to-local broadcasts, which they expected to release by 2002 or 2003. LTVS has overcome some perceived problems with market penetration by designing dual encryption streams capable of interpreting both EchoStar's and DirecTV's unique encryption standards.

The industry remained embroiled in a battle with cable operators that was not likely to subside anytime soon. When news of the pending deregulation of the cable industry and expansion of the DBS franchise hit the public, a wave of customers canceled their cable subscriptions and set up satellite dishes in their yards. Yankee Group reported that 46 percent of all DBS subscribers, including 56 percent of new subscribers, received local channels as part of their DBS packages. Moreover, only 8 percent of DBS subscribers that received local channels maintained their cable subscriptions. Boston-based TechTrends Inc. found that, if customers carrying both DBS and cable were forced to choose between them, 70 percent would stick with DBS.

One area where DBS clearly has the advantage over cable is channel capacity; many DBS dishes can receive up to 300 channels, while dishes capable of receiving signals from more than one satellite at a time can get up to 500. To date, pricing wars between the industries have generally been avoided, much to the relief of both parties.

More broadly, however, the deregulated telecommunications marketplace featured DBS companies, cable providers, public utilities, phone companies, and others competing for a range of service markets dominated by integrated technologies. DBS companies positioned themselves in the market for Internet and telephone services among others, a key reason why the competitive atmosphere was particularly tense. The ability to establish a position in the DBS marketplace holds lucrative potential beyond the opportunity to receive revenues for beaming programs into homes.

More On   LONELY AT THE TOP?

When you're far ahead of the pack, your popularity can easily plummet. In the late 1990s and into 2000, DirecTV president Eddy Hartenstein earned the enmity of a number of organizations inside and outside the DBS industry his company dominates.

At the National Association of Broadcasters' annual "Futures" conference in 1998, where Hartenstein shared his vision of a future market in which broadcasters would gear their signals toward DirecTV's receiver-and-antenna combination, the reaction was described conservatively as lukewarm; one attendee remarked, "At least we didn't tar and feather him—and that was an option."

Hartenstein also failed to win friends in the broadcasting industry with his intensive lobbying in Congress leading up to the passage of the Satellite Home Viewer Improvement Act of 1999, which included pressing Congress to rule that secondary markets served by local carriers received "unacceptable pictures," thus justifying DirecTV's encroachment on these markets.

But broadcasters could not match DirecTV's rival EchoStar in distaste for the DBS leader. DirecTV faced a series of lawsuit allegations from EchoStar in 1999 and 2000. EchoStar decried what it saw as DirecTV's strong-arming tactics, including the company's exclusive contracts with consumer electronics retailers, claiming these deals amounted to monopolistic practices. In particular, EchoStar took offense at DirecTV's incentive fees doled out to retailers such as Best Buy and Circuit City that allegedly have the net effect of keeping EchoStar's Dish Networks equipment off the shelves.

The suit was born of retailer SoundTrack's decision to stop selling Dish in January 2000, a move that EchoStar claimed was forced by DirecTV's threat to cut off shipments of equipment if SoundTrack continued to sell EchoStar's products.

EchoStar further claimed that DirecTV's manufacturing partner Thomson Consumer Electronics threatened retailers with halted shipments if EchoStar's products were not boycotted, adding that Thomson followed through on the threat when Sears, Roebuck & Co. failed to comply.

DirecTV denies the allegations, and to date no charges have been proven in court. Some, including Hartenstein, dismissed the charges as sour grapes born of EchoStar's lagging market share. But whatever the reasoning, the animosity was indicative of an intensely competitive atmosphere in an emerging industry with explosive possibilities, yet overwhelmingly dominated by a single player.

INDUSTRY LEADERS

DIRECTV

DirecTV, an El Segundo, California-based subsidiary of GM Hughes Electronics, was the dominant player in the DBS industry, with 9 million U.S. subscribers in October 2000 and another 1 million in Latin America. The battle for market share grew increasingly bitter in 2000. DirecTV claimed 72 percent of the total DBS market, a fact that critics and competitors, including EchoStar, claimed the company was abusing to shut out competition. GM Hughes shed the last of its military contracting business in early 2000, selling its satellite manufacturing business to Boeing and paving the way for further expansion of DirecTV. By summer 2000, DirecTV was signing up about 150,000 new subscribers each month, a trend it expected to increase as it made further inroads in the local-to-local broadcast market.

To gain greater channel capacity and further seal its lead in the market, the company bought U.S. Satellite Broadcasting for $1.3 billion in 1998 and Primestar for $1.8 billion in early 1999. Immediately after its buying spree, DirecTV carried all three brand-name DBS services under its umbrella. In an effort to expand its subscriber base in 1999, the DBS giant signed marketing agreements with Bell Atlantic, GTE, and SBC Communications that allowed DirecTV to offer its satellite services to the companies' customers. The company further signed up electronics manufacturing giants Panasonic and Samsung to produce set-top boxes with DirecTV reception capability. Through its partnership with Wink Communications, DirecTV worked to create a sharper and more efficient broadcast signal, and it was working with America Online to develop a TV-based Internet service.

The DirecTV service provides 210 channels from a cluster of three high power DBS satellites. The company raked in revenues of $3.8 billion in 1999, more than doubling its 1998 total of $1.8 billion, and maintained a payroll of 1,400 employees.

ECHOSTAR COMMUNICATIONS

EchoStar, headquartered in Littleton, Colorado, was the only serious competitor to DirecTV's dominant market position, with 3,815 employees and a subscription list of 4.5 million in late 2000, up from 3 million a year earlier. The company started its Digital Information Sky Highway (DISH) Network in March 1996. In 1999 the FCC approved EchoStar's $1.46 billion purchase of its long-coveted property: News Corp.'s direct broadcast satellite. The firm also offers WebTV Internet access and moved into satellite-generated Internet data transmission with its purchase of Media4, now called EchoStar Data Networks. EchoStar transmits more than 500 channels from a Full-CONUS orbital slot, and also owns rights to East Coast and West Coast transponders from which it delivers local data services, foreign language programming, and other channels via an additional antenna dish. Sales rose 63 percent to $1.6 billion in 1999, up from $983 million in 1998.

AMERICA AND THE WORLD

Satellites orbit the globe and beam programming signals heedless of national borders. Among U.S. DBS providers, DirecTV has been by far the most active in pursuing joint ventures and other opportunities abroad, establishing a significant foothold especially in Latin American markets.

Canada, Mexico, and some South American countries hold some of the orbital slots over the Western Hemisphere that could service the United States. If any of these choose to auction off transponder rights, U.S. companies can bid for them. Likewise, U.S. companies can potentially service other markets in the Americas from their own slots. Nations may attempt to control the industry by regulating the sale of decoders; in 1998 Argentina temporarily halted DirecTV from competing in its market while it tried to get its own system in place.

In general, the European DBS market is well served by companies such as the Luxembourg-based Societe Europenne des Satellites S.A. (SES), which operates ASTRA, and British Sky Broadcasting (BSkyB). Thus, Europe does not represent a particularly attractive market for U.S. DBS firms. Americans wishing to keep up with hometown developments while traveling in Europe, however, welcomed the deal between European satellite operator Eutelsat and Virginia-based fiber-optic broadcast provider Teleglobe to beam Teleglobe's digital signal of North American news coverage to Europe and North Africa. The service, launched in February 2000, blends cable and satellite technology to feed Teleglobe's networked cable signals via satellite to Eutelsat's satellite.

Asia, home of 60 percent of the world's population, is a tempting target for telecommunications companies, but DBS growth there has been hampered by political and economic conditions. Japan, which can be completely covered from one orbital position and where cable television never really took off due to heavy regulation, has the most advanced satellite technology in Asia. As of spring 2000, SkyPerfecTV had more than 1.66 million subscribers in Japan, and DirecTV Japan had reached 401,000. Meanwhile, although reluctant countries such as China and India have shown signs of easing their restrictions against satellite broadcasts, piracy remains a central concern in Asia.

RESEARCH AND TECHNOLOGY

DBS was born of advanced compression schemes allowing multiple streams of programming, along with

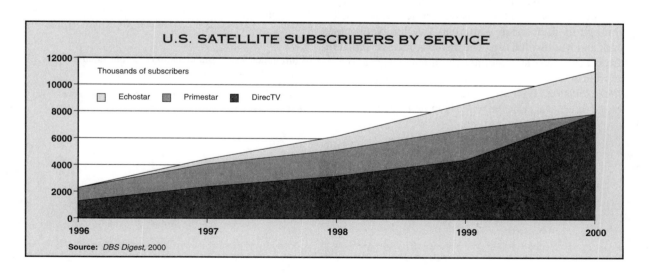

U.S. SATELLITE SUBSCRIBERS BY SERVICE

Thousands of subscribers

☐ Echostar   ▨ Primestar   ■ DirecTV

Source: *DBS Digest*, 2000

the ability to control information per transponder frequency. Still, one technological hurdle was to mitigate the trade-off between picture quality and the number of channels offered, since to date the heavy compression necessary to deliver a large number of channels can result in picture softness. Squeezing down the signal still further would be an advantage, but providers also want to eliminate the occasional blocky digital compression artifacts that some viewers find distracting. Moreover, both DirecTV and EchoStar have begun to offer a handful of HDTV channels, but were reined in somewhat by the massive compression required to deliver these signals.

Besides improving compression, other areas of technological development include higher-power transponders, which allow more information to pass through existing bandwidth because less error-correcting coding is required. Signal polarization, controlling the orientation of the electromagnetic wave transmissions, is used to isolate adjacent transponder slots and allow more of them within a fixed-frequency spectrum. Statistical multiplexing maximizes the use of existing bandwidth by assigning it upon demand, depending on the information density of a particular program being carried by a channel at a given time.

DBS providers also got personal in 2000. DirecTV capitalized on its partnership with Tivo Inc. to roll out its "personal TV" service featuring video storage capacity. The system competes with EchoStar's time-shifting technology developed through its partnership with WebTV Networks Inc.

Beyond just television delivery, however, the drive toward telecommunications integration was likely to be a prime area of research and competition in the early 2000s. EchoStar announced a new satellite dish, to be available by 2001, integrating two-way satellite Internet and television service, developed through its partnership with Gilat Satellite Networks Ltd. and Microsoft Corp. The dish can receive signals from three separate satellites simultaneously, allowing for interactive Internet capability as well as satellite television. Following the introduction of cable-based Internet access, the move heralded the next stage

in the battle between cable companies and the DBS industry.

FURTHER READING

"After Space, Hughes Battles Time." *New York Times,* 27 February 2000.

Conrad, Lee. "Cable Comes under Pressure to Roll out Digital, Phone Services: Satellite Broadcasters Coming on Strong." *High Yield Report,* 7 February 2000.

"DirecTV Personalizes, Defines Set-Top Strategy." *CED,* February 2000.

"DirecTV Sees Big Boost from Local TV." *Multichannel News,* 14 February 2000.

"Dish Dealer Drama." *Broadcasting & Cable,* 7 February 2000.

"EchoStar & Gilat Offer Satellite TV, Internet on 1 Dish." *Newsbytes News Network,* 23 February 2000.

George, David and Tom Ferguson. "EchoStar: A DBS Star Matures." *Broadcast Engineering,* June 2000.

Hancock, Amy E. "The Glitter of DBS Gold." *Satellite Communications,* April 2000.

"It's DBS vs. DBS in Suit." *Multichannel News,* 7 February 2000.

Larsen, Peter Thal. "BSkyB May Be Set to Dial up Radical Change." *Financial Times,* 10 February 2000.

Larson, Megan. "DBS Siphons Subs." *Mediaweek,* 25 September 2000.

"Local TV Birds May Fly." *Multichannel News,* 21 February 2000.

"Pegasus Amends DirecTV Lawsuit." *Multichannel News,* 21 February 2000.

Peterson, Richard R. "Satellite Television: A Consumer's Guide." 1 January 2000. Available from http://www.dbs-dish.com.

"Philippines Telecommunications Commission Targets TV Piracy." *Asia Pulse,* 31 January 2000.

"Teleglobe Beams America to Europe." *Newsbytes News Network,* 2 February 2000.

E-Commerce: Business-to-Business

B2B is the place to be, e-commerce mavens say. Although a good number of this industry's smaller players were battered by plummeting stocks and waning private funding, by most accounts business-to-business e-commerce still has heady growth in its future. In 2000, the commerce research firm Jupiter Research estimated the total value of B2B online commerce at $336 billion globally. Sizable as that seems, however, it's trifling compared to the $6.3 trillion Jupiter predicted by 2005. A similar forecast by AMR Research called for $5.7 trillion in B2B commerce by 2004. A more restrained prediction by Goldman Sachs placed the value of online business commerce in 2005 at $4.5 trillion.

To keep everything in perspective, it must be said that the lion's share of those trillions will be simply for the exchange of goods that is already taking place via non-electronic means; it will not be all new business. In other words, it doesn't mean that trillions of dollars will be lining the pockets of e-commerce software and service providers.

Still, all the anticipated business-to-business commerce will require substantial new infrastructure, and there a wide number of firms offering B2B products and services stand to benefit. For example, despite previous heavy investments and operational setbacks in online B2B exchanges, or online forums for buying and selling business goods, analysts expect continued heavy demand and new development for business-oriented exchanges and marketplaces. Sellers of software packages that run exchanges or other forms of e-commerce will also share in the bounty, as businesses continue to build and upgrade their own e-commerce ca-

pabilities into to integrate more closely with suppliers and customers.

Although a certain small percentage of all this spending may be attributed to fad-consciousness in business—the institutional inertia to copy what competitors are doing can be overpowering—the bulk of these outlays are for simple, practical reasons: B2B e-commerce can increase productivity, lower operating costs, and reduce time to market.

Such benefits are gleaned in several ways. For one, e-commerce can rid a company of any number of stages of manual order placement and tracking. Another is the ability to reach new suppliers, or at least old ones in new ways, so that the cost of merchandise is lower than what would have been paid otherwise. If these benefits seem abstract, consider that some large firms that only do a moderate amount of e-commerce with their suppliers have saved millions of dollars, and by some estimates, a few have already saved billions over time.

New technologies will also be fueling business commerce over the Internet. Mobile electronic devices, as one example, will be used increasingly to conduct commerce, and by 2005 are expected to be the portal to more than $200 billion in transactions, including both consumer and business commerce.

ORGANIZATION AND STRUCTURE

B2B e-commerce encompasses a curious mix of business models and activities. For purposes of this discussion, there are four main categories of B2B activities: (1) those who conduct some aspect of their normal line of work, whether it's manufacturing sprockets or providing astrological management consulting services, over the Internet; (2) online retail sites that cater primarily or exclusively to business clientele, such as office supply portals; (3) business exchanges or electronic marketplaces that provide a forum and tools to facilitate transactions among a range of participant companies; and (4) e-commerce software and services providers, which provide systems that enable other firms to engage in one of the other forms of B2B e-commerce, serving in a sort of meta-B2B role.

GENERAL E-COMMERCE

The "everything else" category, general B2B e-commerce is really not an industry unto itself so much as it is a new territory being settled by a host of different industries. In effect, it's merely an extension of those industries, often well established, into a new medium of transactions. What might be more interesting to consider is how they go about setting up their e-commerce. To the extent they buy software or use the services of e-commerce-oriented providers, they are providing revenues to e-commerce firms; otherwise they're simply conducting their usual line of business in a new way.

This is not to say what these firms do or don't do isn't important for the more narrowly defined B2B e-commerce industry. Quite the opposite, the route these firms take toward enabling electronic transactions has a dramatic effect on the fortunes of firms whose business it is to facilitate e-commerce. In other words, if ordinary firms go it alone and develop their own e-commerce systems without using the software and services of specialists, it will diminish opportunities for specialist firms. On the other hand, if ordinary businesses use e-marketplaces and e-commerce software packages extensively, it will mean tremendous growth for firms specializing in e-commerce products and services.

RETAIL B2B

Retail sites serving the business market are fairly easy to recognize and understand: they're often the online equivalents to the real-life storefronts providing similar products. In some cases, they're directly related, as in cases like staples.com, the online offering of office-supply giant Staples Inc. Likewise there are scores of Internet-only merchants that focus on various needs of businesses large or small, general or specific.

EXCHANGES AND E-MARKETPLACES

Electronic exchanges and marketplaces all share one goal: to bring together companies that are buying and selling some type of product or service. Exactly how they do it varies considerably.

Some e-marketplaces, for instance, VerticalNet, focus on establishing an online community that serves particular interests, say, food ingredients. They develop extensive Web content centered on that business with the aim of bringing people in the industry back regularly even if they're not coming to make a purchase. In addition, of course, they also provide software tools that allow firms to hold auctions, place orders, submit bids, and manage other aspects of the purchasing process.

B2B exchanges take a more utilitarian approach. They provide a Web-based forum and a mechanism for conducting online transactions, but don't attempt to make their sites destinations in their own right.

Most exchange venues have some reasonably well-defined focus, be it chemicals or metals or public utilities. These are commonly known as vertical segments or industries. Certain exchanges also focus on specific types of transactions, such as eliminating excess inventory, as opposed to general procurement activities.

Exchanges and marketplaces earn money in different ways. Some charge a per-transaction surcharge, occasionally as high as 20 percent of the selling price, for the privilege of using their system. However, this practice hasn't been received well, and there's some evidence that it's led to a loss of business for such services. Sellers who submit bids on the exchange are sometimes also charge a transaction fee. Other exchanges levy some type of annual fee or membership fee; still others are joint ventures run by the companies that use them.

E-COMMERCE SOFTWARE AND SERVICES

One of the fastest-growing and closely watched segments of e-commerce, software and service providers provide technical infrastructure for other firms' electronic endeavors. For example, vendors like Ariba and Commerce One develop software packages with predetermined functions that companies are likely to want for conducting business online. These packages are then customized for individual clients to fit their particular needs, giving them the look and functions that are appropriate for what the client does.

BACKGROUND AND DEVELOPMENT

Electronic commerce between businesses in the modern sense has its roots in a variety of earlier practices. One of the most important precursors was the development of electronic data interchange (EDI) systems, a breakthrough championed in the 1980s.

Using EDI, which was often complex and expensive to implement, two or more businesses would create an interface between their respective inventory and procurement systems. The network link would then be used to place orders for new supplies. In the more advanced EDI systems, the process would be highly automated so that when the customer's inventory dropped below a certain threshold, the system would automatically order an appropriate amount of new stock. For example, if a grocery store's inventory of paper towels fell below a certain level, the system might generate an order for 12 new cases of paper towels on a wholesaler or manufacturer's system. The system might also factor in other stock-depletion concerns, such as seasonal variation.

In practice, however, things were never quite so easy on a large scale. A big company gets its supplies from myriad vendors, so the task of integrating with everyone could quickly become daunting. Added to the challenge was the multitude of different software packages and data standards used by different firms in the supply chain. And this is to say nothing of the features needed from the EDI application, which differed by company.

All this spelled only limited success for EDI. Enterprises that implemented it successfully swore by it, but it certainly didn't fill everyone's needs and rarely even reached medium and small companies. As the Internet gained commercial viability in the mid-1990s, procurement visionaries began pondering—and some implementing—Internet-based commerce. One thrust of this activity was to adapt the old EDI model to an Internet-based system, which promised to be cheaper and faster to deploy than home-grown software and networking. But a more profound vision was that of using the Internet to completely revamp and simplify the business purchasing process.

Some important first attempts at Internet-based commerce between businesses began quietly in 1995 and 1996, when much attention was being paid to consumer applications and setting up business "brochure" sites—Web pages that described companies and their marketing messages, but didn't allow for any kind of transactions online. Meanwhile, fledgling companies like FreeMarkets, Inc. and VerticalNet, Inc., both founded in 1995, were charting new territory, trying to harness the vast public network to bring together disparate buyers and sellers into an efficient online exchange of goods, services, and information.

By 1997, billions of business-to-business dollars were flowing through the Internet. The majority of the activity then was concentrated in a handful of sites of very large companies like Cisco Systems Inc. that had seized on the Internet as an efficient conduit through which to conduct their already-thriving businesses.

Needless to say, B2B transactions of all types continued growing at a torrid pace, reaching $43 billion in 1998 according to an estimate by Forrester Research. Again, much of the dollar value was driven by relatively few companies, the Ciscos, Dells, Intels of the world.

By this time, industry watchers also grew increasingly enamored with B2B exchanges, which were expanding frantically and, ever important in the Internet economy, issuing public stock. The next year saw much of the same, with massive stock build-ups and soaring revenue projections bringing legions of new entrants into the business. E-commerce exchanges and so-called online vertical industries sprung up left and right, backed by venture capitalists, Fortune 500 companies, and existing players in the B2B arena.

By early 2000, though, things began looking a little dicey for smaller start-ups. The B2B exchanges, in particular, were doing paltry business compared to earlier growth projections and, for the publicly traded ones, compared to their stock valuations. As the general stock market reeled from sharp downturns in spring 2000, cash for smaller B2B operations dried up rapidly. Venture capital firms pulled back and stopped giving new money; public investors sold in droves. Within months, the shares of B2B high-fliers like Commerce One and VerticalNet lost 75 percent and even 90 percent of their value. Wrenching companies throughout the technology sector—and especially the Internet sector—a shakeout was underway.

The damage to Internet companies was considerable. By one estimate, over 200 Internet businesses of all types had failed in 2000, and another tally found 17 e-marketplaces shuttered. Layoffs abounded, and segments of the business had clearly not lived up to their optimistic growth predictions. For example, one jubilant estimate in 1999 had forecast 10,000 online B2B commerce sites in 2000, whereas the final tally peaked closer to 1,500, then dropped.

PIONEERS IN THE FIELD

In such a young business, it's little surprise that two of its trailblazers are still intimately involved in the industry. Mark B. Hoffman, CEO and chairman of Commerce One, and Keith Krach, his counterpart in both positions at Ariba, both have left an indelible mark on business-to-business commerce over the Internet.

Hoffman was already prominent in the software world when he founded Commerce One in 1997. More than a decade earlier he co-founded Sybase, Inc., an influential maker of relational database software. After being forced out of Sybase in 1996 amid declining revenues and rising losses, Hoffman, an ex-Army officer, quickly took an interest in an obscure, closely held electronic cataloging business. He saw in it potential to revolutionize the supply chain: using software and the Internet to connect buyers and sellers in a highly efficient marketplace. His venture, which originally concentrated on the vertical niche of selling business supplies, quickly obtained venture funding and began marketing a more generalized Internet procurement product in 1998. In another year, Commerce One, by that time publicly traded, had become a darling of Wall Street and grew its sales tenfold. Hoffman, who was separately involved in the publicly traded start-up Intraware, remained at the helm during a turbulent 2000, when sales rocketed more than tenfold again.

Keith Krach also had a noteworthy career before his e-commerce venture. With academic credentials in engineering and management, Krach had a successful tenure at General Motors, where he was something of a boy wonder. Later, he plied both of his talents at a software firm that sold innovative design automation applications. In 1996, Krach teamed up with several other entrepreneurs from engineering and venture funding backgrounds to form Ariba Inc., with the vision using Internet software to automate procurement. The firm swiftly developed a pedigreed clientele of Fortune 100 companies, thanks in part to Krach's contacts and stature, and by 1999 became another stock-market favorite following its public offering.

CURRENT CONDITIONS

Following the slowdowns of 2000 and 2001, B2B e-commerce initiatives were expected to return to a very high growth rate, and this time, more broadly based growth.

In early 2001 there were about 1,500 business-oriented exchanges and markets on the Internet. This was not as many as some had hoped, and was definitely fewer than had been in operation in the preceding year, in the wake of several high-profile shutdowns of faltering B2B sites.

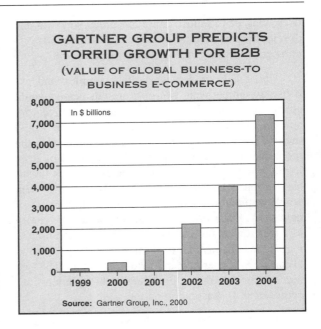

GARTNER GROUP PREDICTS TORRID GROWTH FOR B2B
(VALUE OF GLOBAL BUSINESS-TO-BUSINESS E-COMMERCE)

In $ billions

Source: Gartner Group, Inc., 2000

Some B2B failures were perhaps victims of their own marketing myths. Intoxicated by lofty market projections and by the popular folklore that, on the Internet, start-up companies can easily unseat entrenched corporations, executives at B2B ventures—and not a small number of their equity investors—plunged forth into the market with ill-defined products, unreal pricing structures, and inadequate buy-in from the big customers that could make or break their ventures.

Even though e-marketplaces took a thrashing during the 2000 shakeout, their prognosis isn't altogether gloomy. The bad news is that, by various estimates, somewhere between 5 and 30 percent of business-to-business marketplaces and exchanges will last. But the good news is that some will actually succeed, and new ones will also form. Analysts believe that in the no-so-distant future the typical company may belong to not one, but several, electronic marketplaces. For instance, a poll in 2000 by Forrester Research found that 71 percent of business leaders participating in a technology forum believed their companies would be part of electronic markets in 2001. Forrester predicted that by 2004 fully $2.7 trillion worth of business would be channeled through B2B online markets.

Analysts say B2B markets that withstand the industry's ups and downs are most likely to have solid backing by well-established firms. Often, these will be firms directly participating in the business of the exchange, rather than third-party start-ups. Businesses most likely to participate in exchanges, and in B2B e-commerce generally, are manufacturers (especially in electronics and technology) and large companies of Fortune 1000 stature.

Nonetheless, small- and medium-sized companies are also expected to assume rising importance in e-commerce spheres. Long denied the luxuries of highly efficient electronic transactions that very large enterprise can afford, smaller companies are likely to take advantages of exchanges and other e-commerce venues that can simplify their procurement processes and improve their bargaining power with suppliers.

In a broad study conducted in September 2000, researchers at Duke University and the Financial Executives Institute found that two-thirds of all companies made some form of purchase online. However, on average their level of purchase was only 4.5 percent of all spending.

INDUSTRY LEADERS

Based in Mountain View, Calif., Ariba Inc. is a leading provider of Internet procurement software and services. Founded in 1996, Ariba has alliances with i2 Technologies, a vendor of enterprise application software, and IBM to provide a suite of complementary products and services. The company also acquired in 2001 Agile Software Corp., a maker of software for managing manufacturing supply chains. That purchase was a sign of a potential rift between Ariba and i2 Technologies, which makes products similar to Agile's. In 2000 Ariba posted revenue of $279 million, up some 500 percent from the previous year, but on losses of $21 million. Based on its brisk sales and the Agile acquisition, Ariba executives expected revenue in 2001 to come in closer to $790 million.

Commerce One, Inc., of Pleasanton, Calif., is another top provider of software and services to run B2B exchanges and online procurement sites. With $402 million in sales during 2000, Commerce One has grown more rapidly than its arch-rival, Ariba, thanks to a few very large contracts and a greater emphasis on selling services, which represented about 44 percent of its revenues in 2000. A year earlier, the company had only brought in $33.6 million. It has a partnership with SAP AG, a major provider of enterprise applications. As of 2000 the company still was in the red, but its losses came in slightly less than most analysts expected. The investment bank U.S. Bancorp

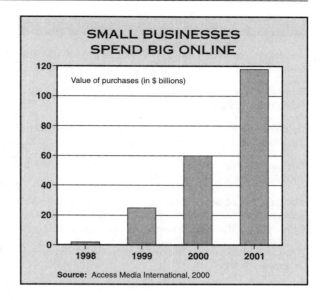

SMALL BUSINESSES SPEND BIG ONLINE

Value of purchases (in $ billions)

Source: Access Media International, 2000

Piper Jaffray forecast revenue in 2001 to exceed $800 million, and the company was expected to begin turning a profit during the year.

AMERICA AND THE WORLD

A growing share of business Internet commerce will come from outside the United States, particularly from Asia. B2B sites in Asia suffered some of the same setbacks as U.S.-based sites in 2000 and 2001. There was a build-up of new sites targeting the gamut of business interests, and gradually the start-ups faced tightening funding and increased competition from large, established firms. This trend was expected to play out similarly to the U.S. trend, where large, well-known players are most likely to survive. An estimate by Goldman Sachs called for B2B commerce in the Asia-Pacific region to represent about 14 percent of global e-commerce by 2005. According to Goldman Sachs, growth rates in Asia are expected to peak some two years after they peak in the United States. Other studies estimate the total level of Asian e-commerce even higher.

Europe also has a prosperous and growing market for B2B e-commerce, valued as of 2000 at 200 billion euros, according to Jupiter MMXI, the European affiliate of Jupiter Research. The firm predicted that B2B activities would rise ninefold by 2004, toward 1.8 trillion euros. The top sites were expected to originate from the United Kingdom, Germany, and Sweden.

FURTHER READING

Anders, Jason. "The Lessons We've Learned—B2B: Yesterday's Darling." *Wall Street Journal,* 23 October 2000.

Bermudez, John, et al. "B2B Forecast: $5.7T by 2004." Boston: AMR Research, April 2000.

Gallagher, Dan. "B2B Success Hopes Drop with Predicted Shakeout." *Business First-Columbus,* 17 November 2000.

"Japan B2B Net Market Forecast to Expand Fivefold by 2005." *AsiaPulse News,* 13 February 2001.

Mangalindan, Mylene. "Peering Ahead—Crystal Ball: Web Experts Offer Their Prediction for Where E-Commerce May Be Heading." *Wall Street Journal,* 23 October 2000.

"Optimistic Forecast for Internet Commerce." *Computimes,* 29 January 2001.

Pachetti, Nick. "A Little Guy's Marketplace." *Time,* 27 November 2000.

Paul, Brooke. "Opening Your E-Business Perimeter." *Network Computing,* 8 January 2001.

Perkins, Anthony. "Manager's Journal: New Hope for the New Economy." *Wall Street Journal,* 15 January 2001.

Petersen, Scot. "B2B Needs to Score." *eWeek,* 18 December 2000.

Seymour, Jim. "The Four Immutable Laws of B2B." *PC Magazine,* 5 December 2000.

Violino, Bob. "What Slowdown? E-Biz Spending Still Soaring." *InternetWeek,* 22 January 2001.

Wilson, Tim. "Heavy Hitters to Rule B-to-B." *InternetWeek,* 22 May 2000.

E-COMMERCE: CONSUMER PRODUCTS

Business-to-consumer electronic commerce (e-commerce) was the darling of the much-heralded New Economy in the late 1990s, and generated a flood of new business as well as a great deal of hype. It seemed as though everyone was setting up new dot-com enterprises to hawk virtually any type of good. And typically, once a new product category was established on the Web, a bevy of copycat vendors scurried to claim their share. This was certainly the case in the crowded sectors for consumer products such as computers, books, apparel, toys, and other retail items.

The highly publicized rush of cash to back new e-commerce ventures was one of the top stories on the covers of business pages throughout the late 1990s. Online retailers couldn't have avoided having money thrown in their direction by avaricious investors dying to join the rest of the market in its euphoria. According to Venture Economics Information Services, venture capitalists sank about $11 billion into online business-to-consumer retailers in 1999.

Consumers were no slouches when it came to giving money to online retailers. According to a report by Ernst & Young, about 39 million customers in the United States, amounting to about 17 percent of all households, did some shopping on the Web in 1999, and about half spent more than $500. Forrester Research reported total business-to-consumer transactions of $20.8 billion that year, with expectations that the figure could rise as high as $184 billion by 2004. The investment firm Goldman Sachs, meanwhile, suggested that online shopping could command up to 20 percent of all retail sales by 2010.

Nonetheless, by early 2000 it appeared that the honeymoon was over, particularly in the business-to-consumer sector, and online retailers became subject to the market discipline from which they were famously immune in the financing splurge of the late 1990s. The e-commerce market thus showed its first signs of maturity, as investors began to make solid distinctions between those online merchants that have established a durable presence and those that have not, and to evaluate prospective companies in terms of business plans rather than starry-eyed glamour.

Venture capitalists looked over their investment portfolios, now littered with fledgling or deceased dot-com start-ups, and tightened their belts. Most analysts expected that entrepreneurs will have to struggle much harder to secure funding for a new online retailing enterprise for some time to come.

DEVELOPMENT

One of the most inviting characteristics of the e-commerce world, and a major factor in the overcrowding that began to take its toll in 2000, is the exceptionally low barrier to entry. It may take as little as finding someone to create an attractive Web page, setting up an Internet domain, and attracting a retailer by emphasizing the importance of establishing an online presence.

But it is not always that easy, as many e-tailers found out to their dismay. Though there was an exceedingly wide range for development costs depending on innumerable variables—such as whether a company was an established retailer—a survey by the Gartner Group found that the cost of setting up an e-commerce Web site ran about $1 million, a cost that was expected to rise 25 percent annually in the early 2000s. The survey of mid-sized to large corporations also found, revealingly, that companies routinely underestimated the amount of money and time they would spend in setting up an e-commerce infrastructure, no matter whether their e-tail plans were modest or ambitious.

E-SHOPPING

There are a number of virtual outlets where consumer e-commerce takes place. The most basic is the direct, brochure-style corporate site, at which customers can order products directly from the company via e-mail or an online order form. This was often referred to as first-generation e-commerce, though many firms still enter into the online marketplace by this method.

The largest proportion of consumer products, however, are sold through large online retailers such as Amazon.com, Inc., which feature a number of departments for different product categories. These retailers develop deals with manufacturers to market and sell products through centralized Web sites, and the largest of these benefit from the vast interlinking network between various sites under their names.

There were also a number of sites designed to allow quick and easy comparison shopping. Junglee Corp. and MySimon.com Inc. made their mark by collecting pricing information from various Web sites and compiling them for their visitors, who could then assess prices across a broad range without having to hop from one Web site to another compiling lists of their own. Both of these companies were eventually bought by Internet behemoths—Junglee by Amazon.com and, more recently, MySimon by CNet. One of the largest remaining independent "shopbots," as they are known, was DealTime. While e-tailers originally resisted such sites, they have more recently begun to accept them as not only an inevitability, but even a positive force that can funnel more business their way.

Online auctions provided another avenue for online sales of consumer goods, whereby companies establish a deal with an auction site to provide a listing for their products, which customers then bid on. This method was particularly attractive to online merchants since they tend to generate higher selling prices, but they were not exceptionally lucrative for most consumer products that were widely available elsewhere. Since consumers generally hope to find the best bar-

gain they can, it made little sense to go to an auction site and bid up the price of a product they could purchase for a lower fee from a major retailer. Nonetheless, the auction site was a valuable supplement to business-to-consumer e-tailing operations, particularly in the collectibles market. Major online auction companies included eBay, Amazon.com, uBid, and Yahoo.com. (Also see the essay in this book entitled E-Commerce: Online Auctions.)

Finally, new sites were popping up by 2000 that enabled consumers to engage in online haggling with companies. Firms such as NexTag, HaggleZone, and Respond set up sites whereby customers could search for products in select categories, such as computers or consumer electronics. The site would then return a list of companies with whom the firm has established a contract. Customers could directly contact the prospective merchant suggesting a lower price, and the negotiation process would ensue until a satisfactory price was reached. Like shopbots, many companies originally saw these negotiation sites as a threat, but have since come to value them as a marketing tool.

TAXATION

At the political level, perhaps the most contentious issue was that involving state and national legislators, as well as both e-commerce and brick-and-mortar firms, regarding taxation of e-commerce sales. Despite pressure from the National Governors' Association, which drafted a resolution demanding the taxation of Web-based transactions, the U.S. Congress passed the Internet Tax Freedom Act in 1998, which prohibited discriminatory taxes—taxes implemented by brick-and-mortar businesses to discourage e-commerce—and established a moratorium on interstate e-commerce taxes through 2001, declaring that an appropriate and integrated tax policy would have to be in place before companies could be expected to apply taxes to online sales.

By May 2000, however, Congressional Republicans were already devising legislation to extend the tax ban through 2006, despite outcry from state governments and established retailers of all sizes. Democrats at the federal level also wanted to maintain a tax-free Internet. Opponents feared that such measures would leave state governments, which provide the bulk of government services, without crucial revenues, thus forcing them to scale back spending programs. Others simply contended that pushing back the end of the moratorium would provide a disincentive for state governments to streamline and coordinate their labyrinth-like tax policies so as to more easily facilitate e-commerce. California's state legislature, in late

2000, actually passed a bill to levy a 7.25 percent sales tax on online sales by companies that also maintain brick-and-mortar stores, but Governor Gray Davis was expected to veto the measure.

BACKGROUND AND DEVELOPMENT

In the early 1990s, the World Wide Web was just beginning to flower, and was touted as the new information superhighway that would spread knowledge and ideas to individuals at the click of the mouse. Up until the mid-1990s, the main users of the Internet were academic scientists and other tech specialists. It wasn't long, however, before talk of the information superhighway was drowned out by the buzz of e-commerce. By creating a stir over the potential windfall that online shopping could portend, venture capitalists poured billions of dollars into new firms, thereby essentially paying for the infrastructure to make online commerce a reality.

One of the first online retailers to make waves was Amazon.com, still the largest online retailer in 2000. The company's Web site went up in 1995 and the company, aware that most major bookstores and publishing companies maintained extensive electronic lists of titles, began selling books with a surprisingly good deal of success. In 1997 the company began to generate substantial revenues, much to the chagrin of established book retailers such as Barnes & Noble, which scrambled furiously to establish its own Web site to try to mitigate some of the damage.

In 1997, however, many companies were still weighing the prospective costs and benefits of establishing a Web site devoted to commerce, and an appropriate business model was far from resolved. As more and more new start-ups popped up in the late 1990s, though, companies were left with little choice but to either establish their own e-tail operation or align with an existing one. The frenzy also happened to coincide with, and contribute to, the sustained stock market boom of the period, and from there, the avalanche of dot-coms ensued.

CURRENT CONDITIONS

Books were the largest consumer-product category in terms of online sales, accounting for about 33 percent of online purchases, while computer equipment brought in 13 percent, according to a 1999 study

---

Trends — BREAKFAST AT TIFFANY'S.COM

Looking for the perfect diamond necklace for an upcoming anniversary? How about that divine new designer dress from the Paris fashion show? It may be only a click away. No more dealing with aggressive or snooty luxury-store sales representatives; new dot-coms such as Blue Nile Inc., eLuxury.com, and Ashford.com Inc., as well as luxury-industry staples such as Tiffany & Co., have set up shop on the Web. Marketing strategies vary widely; while Blue Nile concentrates heavily on advertising, other e-luxury merchants, such as Private Diamonds Inc., do little or no advertising, opting to generate sales primarily through online auction sites.

Luxury goods, which typically require a good deal of comparison shopping and scrutiny to obtain the item that's just right for the customer, were not initially seen as an easy entrant into the vulgar world of e-commerce. But in 2000 e-jewelers and other online luxury merchants began to make a dent, bringing in about $30 million over the 1999 holiday season, according to the *Wall Street Journal.* What's more, the research firm Forrester Research Inc., having surveyed 2,000 households with a net worth greater than $1 million in January 2000, found that about two-thirds had made an online purchase, while 12 percent had purchased jewelry. Forrester Research concluded that Web consumers were more common among the rich than among the general population.

---

by CDB Research and Consulting, Inc. These two categories, according to Boston Consulting Group, estimated that these categories achieved 10 percent market penetration in 2000.

Apparel manufacturers, meanwhile, continued to grow on the Web, though sales were expected to remain relatively modest, reaching about $6.7 billion by 2003, or about 4 percent of industry retail revenues, according to Jupiter Communications. The greatest difficulty facing apparel retailers was how to make clothing look as attractive on the Web as on a catalog page. In addition, customers remained wary of many dot-coms' shipping and return policies, a crucial element of this sector as customers search for the perfect look and fit.

Some of the fastest-growing product categories in 1999 were automotives—including automobiles sold directly to customers online—in which revenues leaped 2,300 percent; toys, which saw revenues increase 440 percent; and health and beauty products, which grew by 780 percent in 1999.

Entrepreneurs launching new shopping sites faced a number of profound challenges. First off, through the late 1990s such merchants had to face down the scads of competition in any given field. For instance, there were more than a half dozen commerce sites revolving around the "pets.com" theme in early 2000. In addition, the industry is particularly tied to the wax and wane of technology stocks now that reality has begun to assert its grip. Through the late 1990s, the industry largely floated itself on the copious flow of venture capital, but investors have grown weary of companies languishing for years without significant revenues.

Shakeout

Throughout 2000, the market finally registered the effects of what many analysts decried as over-exuberance on the part of investors and venture capitalists. For several years, the industry gained notoriety for its seemingly bottomless financing for firms that barely posted revenues, much less registered a profit. Market analysts chalked this behavior up to the feeling among financiers that something new, profound, and potentially lucrative was in the works in the economy, and investors scrambled to get in on the ground floor on most any venture that came their way. Moreover, this craze came at a time in the U.S. economy when investors had the disposable income to throw at new dot-com ventures, and the stratospheric trajectory of the stock market only encouraged these players that nothing could go wrong.

These rosy projections proved unfounded. The panic in the stock market's technology sector in the spring of 2000 crushed a good number of e-commerce firms, especially among the also-rans in the consumer-goods sector. Since, for most any given consumer-product category, the industry's successes tended to concentrate in one or two firms, the shakeout did away with much of the dead weight, the firms that many analysts expected had to go at some point.

As an illustration of the mounting difficulties, the 10 business-to-consumer firms that went public in the second quarter of 1999 brought in a combined net of $2.5 billion; the eight companies that did so in the same period in 2000 mustered only about $1 billion. Unfortunately for the industry, such trends were the rule rather than the exception for much of 2000.

But the damage was hardly limited to second-rate companies. Major e-tailers were forced to close their virtual doors as well. Boo.com, a leading sports-clothing retailer, announced its liquidation in May 2000 after several weeks of unsuccessful fund-raising. Even market linchpins were feeling the heat. Amazon.com and eToys watched their stock prices fall 60 percent between January and August 2000. With the future of capital financing in doubt, a large segment of the business-to-consumer e-tailing market was expected to either shut down or be absorbed by other companies by the end of 2000.

Still, many observers insisted that the shakeout was inevitable, and was in fact part of many firms' business plans all along. The idea was to build up a strong financial base by dramatizing the glamour and potential of the Web so as to position oneself for a buyout when push came to shove, as it did in spring 2000. In addition, the online retailing sector registered more real success stories than its reputation might indicate. Boston Consulting Group released a study in August 2000 reporting that nearly 40 percent of the 221 online retailers studied were already profitable.

Emerging Conditions

Still, predictions of the death of e-commerce are completely unfounded. A report issued by former Forrester Research analyst Joe Sawyer garnered a great deal of attention—in part due to its ominous title: "The Demise of Dot Com Retailers"—but Sawyer pointed out that about 40 million products would be sold online in 2000, and chalked up much of the industry's woes not to an inherent flaw with e-commerce but to the grossly inflated expectations investors had placed on the idea.

In general, much of the glamorous shine has worn off the business-to-consumer e-commerce sector, revealing the rough edges underneath. While no analysts expect that investors have grown completely cynical about the sector, and much of the industry's future financing will be drawn from its ability to woo investors with glitz and charm, the general consensus was that basic fundamentals and business practices will weigh much more heavily in investment decisions.

Meanwhile, traditional brick-and-mortar retailers, many of whom thought the end was near in the late 1990s as they eyed the onslaught of dot-com start-ups, have emerged as powerful online players in their own right. Companies such as Barnes & Noble, Wal-Mart, and Kmart all moved aggressively to mark out their territory on the Web, and many of the fledgling dot-coms were likely to turn to these retail giants for acquisition as the market consolidates into 2001. Kmart, for instance, announced the launch of BlueLight.com in December 1999 with the help of SoftBank Venture Capital; a month later Wal-Mart rolled out Wal-

Mart.com Inc. in conjunction with the venture outfit Accel Partners.

The Wal-Mart launch in particular was expected to put a dent in Amazon.com's dominance of the business-to-consumer market. Researchers at Sanford C. Bernstein issued a report in January suggesting that Wal-Mart.com could command up to 10 percent of the business-to-consumer e-commerce market. With Wal-Mart's enormous ability to absorb the kind of losses its new Web venture will entail, Wal-Mart.com will likely offer prices low enough to scare not only dot-com start-ups but other brick-and-mortar firms competing against Wal-Mart's seemingly limitless product line.

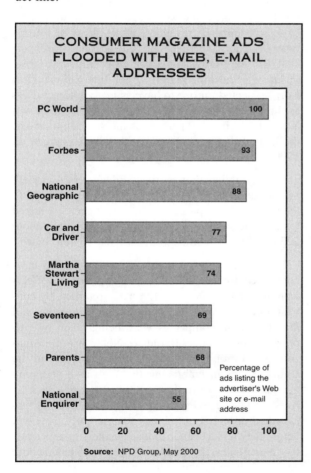

CONSUMER MAGAZINE ADS FLOODED WITH WEB, E-MAIL ADDRESSES

Magazine	Percentage
PC World	100
Forbes	93
National Geographic	88
Car and Driver	77
Martha Stewart Living	74
Seventeen	69
Parents	68
National Enquirer	55

Percentage of ads listing the advertiser's Web site or e-mail address

Source: NPD Group, May 2000

INDUSTRY LEADERS

AMAZON.COM

Amazon.com, based in Seattle, Washington, was one of the most recognizable names on the World Wide Web, and was nearly synonymous with e-commerce. One of the earliest Internet-related retail success stories, Amazon maintained a payroll of 7,600 employees in 2000. The world's leading online bookseller, Amazon expanded beyond that category in 1998, and by decade's end its retail lines were virtually without end, also leading the way in music and videos and including everything from jewelry to groceries to sporting goods. With its tremendous—and growing—leverage in the e-tailing market, Amazon.com was considered able to withstand market jolts such as those that hit the industry in 2000. Sitting at the center of a vast, diversified e-tail empire, Amazon.com can direct traffic through its disparate e-commerce operations, thus giving the company a leg up on competitors in those arenas. The company maintained an equity position in over a dozen online retailers, and that figure will likely increase as the industry hits a major wave of consolidation. The firm splurged on acquisitions in 1999, buying into a number of new categories with a series of start-ups, including Pets.com, the furniture outfit living.com Inc., luxury-goods e-tailer Ashford.com, gift registry Della.com, and Drugstore.com Inc. In 2000 the company inked a deal with Toys "R" Us to help the two compete against online toy giant eToys Inc. Amazon.com generated revenues of $1.64 billion in 1999, about 20 percent of which was derived from outside the United States. The firm also reported a net loss of $720 million.

ETOYS INC.

eToys Inc., based in Santa Monica, California, was one of the few online toy retailers that started out with no brick-and-mortar basis. Launching its Web site in time for the Christmas season in 1997 with a selection of 1,000 toys, eToys paid handsomely to get its name on the America Online page. The firm purchased market rival Toys.com in 1998, solidifying its dominance in the sector just in time for Toys "R" Us's entrance into the online toy universe. After going public in 1999, it purchased BabyCenter and moved into the United Kingdom market. The company maintained a stock of over 100,000 toys and other children's products, such as software programs and videos. eToys employed over 300 workers and brought in revenues of $30 million in 1999, generating a net loss of $28.6 million. By late 2000, faced with a mighty last-ditch effort to pull the Christmas shopping season out of a hat without repeating the delivery snafus it experienced in 1999, eToys's future looked exceptionally bleak; by late January 2001, the company was finally reading the handwriting on the wall.

BUY.COM INC.

Buy.com Inc. was a leading online superstore, second only to Amazon.com in overall Internet retailing. Its sales were concentrated particularly in computer hardware, software, and peripherals, but the firm also generated strong sales in books, consumer electronics, and a number of other product categories. Founded in 1997, Buy.com was based in Aliso Viejo, California. The company's portal provides links to its 10 specialty stores, selling products from leading manufacturers in each respective field. Buy.com posted revenues of $596.8 million in 1999 for a net loss of $130.2 million.

EGGHEAD.COM

True to its name, Egghead.com, Inc. of Menlo Park, California, was a leading online retailer in the market for computer hardware, software, peripherals, and accessories. Formed by the 1999 merger of the earlier Egghead.com and Onsale, the new company maintained a payroll of 560 employees by 2000. The Onsale sector sells computer equipment at wholesale and runs an online auction site, while Egghead.com, formerly a brick-and-mortar firm, engaged in a variety of computer-related retailing operations. Egghead's sales jumped from $356.5 million in 1998 to $514.8 million in 1999, when it registered a net loss of $154.9 million.

BEYOND.COM

The first company to offer software distribution online, by 2000 Beyond.com of Santa Clara, California, maintained over 6,000 software titles for electronic distribution. In addition, the company stocked about 50,000 software packages available for mailing. Beyond.com employed about 390 workers, and boasted the U.S. government as its best customer, accounting for nearly one-third of all sales. Beyond.com purchased competitor BuyDirect for $134 million in 1999, and that year recorded a net loss of $124.8 million on revenues of $117.3 million. By 2000, however, the company was refocusing its operations to concentrate more heavily on its business-to-business sector.

GLOBAL SPORTS, INC.

Based in Philadelphia, Global Sports catapulted to the top of the online sporting goods heap with its purchase of market leader Fogdog, Inc. in 2000. Fogdog was the leading online retailer of sporting goods apparel, footwear, and equipment. Amid mounting competition in the sporting-goods sector, Fogdog went public in late 1999, in the process granting Nike a 10 percent stake in the company in exchange for a special discount on Nike products, and an exclusive on-line-marketing deal with Nike. The technology-sector stock plunge in spring 2000 forced Fogdog to seek a partner. Global Sports also operates the online storefronts of leading sporting good chains such as The Sports Authority and The Athlete's Foot. Global Sports generated sales of $43.3 million in 1999.

AMERICA AND THE WORLD

The United States was the first market to really dive into e-commerce, and to date is by far the most immersed in online retailing. According to the Organisation for Economic Co-operation and Development, the United States commands about 80 percent of all e-commerce revenues, while Western Europe takes in about 10 percent and Asia accounts for 5 percent. But the European market, especially, was growing at an astonishing rate. By 2003, International Data Corp. expected Europe to have as many Internet users as the United States, while the European market will account for about 60 percent as much e-commerce as the United States, compared with only 15 percent in 1999.

U.S. e-tailers thus set their sights overseas, where foreign consumers were likely to start catching up to their U.S. counterparts. Forrester Research estimated total online sales of $454 billion in 2000, with about $233 billion derived from outside the United States.

While the United States enjoyed a leg up in e-commerce, for established retail companies the effects were not always pleasant. European retailers, by contrast, have the American precedent to learn from, and thus few giant companies were being taken by surprise as, for instance, Barnes & Noble was by Amazon.com. Europe was roughly two years behind the United States in embracing the Web as a shopping medium. Large European department stores such as Karstadt-Quelle AG got in on the ground floor and established an online retailing presence early, in 1996, before they had a chance to lose business to new startups. Nonetheless, by 2000 start-ups commanded about an equal share of the online-retailing market in Europe as did brick-and-mortar retailers, suggesting that these early entrants failed to take full advantage of their head start.

Among the biggest hurdles to international e-commerce were the differences between nations in privacy laws and restrictions relating to the Internet and commercial transactions. U.S. laws safeguarding consumer privacy are in general far more relaxed than those of European nations, allowing companies to engage in extensive trade of consumer data, and thus trans-Atlantic e-commerce was stuck in limbo through the late 1990s. In early 2000, however, the U.S. Department of Commerce negotiated a deal with the European Commission to guarantee European customers of U.S. online merchants the same privacy protections they expect under European laws, which decree that no company may share customer data with another firm without the customer's permission. U.S. retailers operating in Europe have the option of attempting to prove that U.S. laws are in sync with those of Europe in their sector of operation, placing themselves under the jurisdiction of a European regulatory authority, or participating in a self-regulating organization approved by the U.S. Federal Trade Commission. Meanwhile, however, U.S. officials were extremely critical of the European Commission's June 1999 decision to impose a value-added tax on Internet transactions, claiming that it would impede the development of international e-commerce.

Japan was the largest of the Asian e-commerce markets in the late 1990s, with business-to-consumer sales of $1 billion in 1999. That figure was expected to grow dramatically to $42 billion by 2003, according to a report by Andersen Consulting and Japan's Ministry of International Trade and Industry. About 20 million Japanese were hooked up to the Internet in 2000. The pending entrance of the People's Republic of China into the World Trade Organization will further open the massive Asian market to e-commerce. China and India were expected to spearhead growth in the Asian market, which, according to Morgan Stanley Dean Witter, would include about 150 million customers spending a total of $26 billion by 2003, up from about $2.5 billion in 2000.

The Latin American business-to-consumer market was facing many of the same oversaturation problems experienced in the United States. The years 1998 and 1999 saw intensive activity in this region with firms racing to establish a dominant presence in the region from the start. Other characteristics giving pause to new investors in Latin America are the relatively low penetration of personal computers, substandard phone-line infrastructure impeding Internet connectivity, and low credit-card usage.

RESEARCH AND TECHNOLOGY

While a number of firms have been established to allow customers to compare prices, one site made a killing by rating e-commerce firms on the much stick-

ier issues of customer service and shipping in addition to prices. BizRate.com of Los Angeles was the 12th most popular shopping site on the Internet by March 2000, according to the research firm Media Metrix. The company established a market for itself by convincing e-tailers that a positive listing on the BizRate.com site would be useful as a marketing tool. A few firms gambled on the idea, and BizRate.com compiled reports on companies' services, similar to those of Consumer Reports. Participating companies provide links to customers following a purchase asking them to grade the e-tailer's performance for BizRate.com, with the added incentive of winning up to $5,000. After the survey is completed and the product is delivered, the customer is asked to fill out a survey rating the e-tailer's delivery and return practices. BizRate then compiles the ratings and surveys across a broad spectrum and publishes overall site ratings.

These ratings have become increasingly important status symbols among online merchants; by summer 2000, some 4,000 companies participated in the program, while BizRate listed about 1,000 companies on its site. Also encouraging to e-tailers was BizRate's finding that its visitors were far more likely than the average Web surfer to make a purchase online. According to the *Wall Street Journal,* however, not all online retailers were thrilled about BizRate's growing power. Amazon.com, for instance, refused to participate in the program, claiming that it would pose a threat to Amazon's existing customer relationships.

The next structural development in e-commerce was the pending integration of internal and external business activities and data, which could then be linked with other firms, such as suppliers and co-marketers. Companies were developing infrastructures enabling them to quickly share databases, computer systems, and other information with related firms, and thereby make business decisions, such as yield-management pricing decisions, extremely rapidly. By reorganizing business models to more fully integrate Web retailing, many companies will begin to align their basic Web applications with behind-the-scenes applications, including market research programs and order-management systems.

FURTHER READING

Alexander, Antoinette. "E-commerce: Money, Money, and More Money." *Accounting Technology,* November 1999.

"B2B: The Hottest Net Bet Yet?" *Business Week,* 17 January 2000.

Chabrow, Eric. "Seeking the Deeper Path to E-success." *Information Week,* 6 March 2000.

"Chase Boosts B2B in Brazil." *Emerging Markets Report,* 22 May 2000.

"China, India to Lead Asian Internet Boom." *Singapore Business Times,* 8 May 2000.

Clark, Don. "Revamping the Model: Compare and Contrast." *Wall Street Journal,* 17 April 2000.

"Define and Sell." *Economist,* 26 February 2000.

"E-commerce Growth Forecast." *Retail Banker International,* 17 February 2000.

Fisher, Andrew. "Net Is Reshaping World Business." *Financial Times* (Surveys edition), 24 September 1999.

Gruner, Stephanie. "Boo.com's Collapse Further Darkens E-tailing Picture." *Wall Street Journal,* 19 May 2000.

Hamilton, David. "BizRate.com Lets Shoppers Rate E-tailers." *Wall Street Journal,* 18 May 2000.

Hunt, Ben. "Growth in Online Shopping Forecast." *Financial Times* (USA edition), 18 May 2000.

"It's a World Wide Web after All." *Interactive Week,* 8 May 2000.

Johnston, David Cay. "What Conservatives, Liberals, Stores and States Share." *New York Times,* 7 June 2000.

Khan, Mickey Alam. "Forrester Joins Chorus Singing Dot-Com Blues." *iMarketing News,* 17 April 2000.

Khanna, Vikram. "Asia Must Catch up Again—In the New Economy Now." *Business Line,* 11 May 2000.

Kroll, Karen. "The Great E-tailing White Sale." *Investment Dealers' Digest,* 29 May 2000.

Liebs, Scott. "World of Difference." *Industry Week,* 7 February 2000.

McGee, Marianne Kolbasuk. "Outlook 2000—E-business Initiatives Will Be IT Executives' Key Focus This Year." *Information Week,* 3 January 2000.

"Online Buying's Brave New World Emerges." *DSN Retailing Today,* 22 May 2000.

Pringle, David. "A Head Start." *Wall Street Journal,* 17 April 2000.

"Profitability is the New Priority for e-Retailers." *Chain Store Age,* August 2000.

Ramstad, Evan. "Too Good for the Web?" *Wall Street Journal,* 17 April 2000.

Rash, Wayne. "Don't Care About B2C E-Comm? Here's Why You Should." *Internet Week,* 28 August 2000.

Sacirbey, Omar. "Wal-Mart's Wrecking Ball Goes Online." *IPO Reporter,* 17 January 2000.

"Shopping around the Web." *Economist,* 26 February 2000.

Simpson, Glenn R. "U.S., EU Negotiators Reach Agreement on Electronic-Commerce Privacy Rules." *Wall Street Journal,* 15 March 2000.

Stockford, Paul. "E-nough Already." *VoicePlus,* January 2000.

Stone, Martin. "N. American Online Retailing Hit $33.1 Bil in 1999—Study." *Newsbytes News Network,* 17 April 2000.

Vincenti, Lisa. "The Party's Over, So Get Ready to Cry." *HFN,* 27 March 2000.

Walsh, Mark. "A Chill Hits the Alley." *Crain's New York Business,* 17 April 2000.

"We're off to the Online Mall." *Economist,* 26 February 2000.

Whiddon, Robert, and Stephen Lacey. "Fog Clears for Sporting Goods in Time for eChristmas." *IPO Reporter,* 29 November 1999.

Zbar, Jeffrey D. "E-tailing Fits in Upscale Niche." *Advertising Age,* 14 August 2000.

E-Commerce: Online Auctions

INDUSTRY SNAPSHOT

Garage sales may not yet be obsolete, but folks wishing to unload their attic collectibles have discovered a new way in which just about anything can be sold to anyone with an Internet connection. As a bonus, sellers were relieved of the ominous chore of hauling their wares to the flea market or to the driveway, and they could reach millions of customers rather than the handful they would attract in a physical setting, thereby assuring greater, and more lucrative, sales. Online auction sites, which put prospective buyers of virtually any product in touch with those with that item to sell, emerged as a cornerstone of the surging electronic commerce (e-commerce) market.

Whether searching for elusive Beanie Babies to complete one's collection or for the Mercedes of one's dreams, netizens helped place online auction sites among the most popular stops on the information superhighway by 2000, and the future seemed to promise nothing but happy days for the firms that ran them. E-commerce research firm Forrester Research expected online auction sales to jump from $1.4 billion in 1998 to $19 billion by 2003.

Individuals, businesses, and even traditional auction houses all acknowledged the benefits of conducting auctions on the Web rather than in a physical location where only a relative handful of people could attend. Since more potential buyers can participate in online auctions, the prices of the goods sold generally go up with more competing bids, generating enhanced revenues. Conversely, the sheer number of auctions taking place and the availability of comparative information on the Web help keep prices in check.

Not all that glittered on auction sites was in fact gold, however. The infant industry was beset with difficulties in 2000, not the least of which were dishonest sellers and legal liability uncertainties. A number of lawsuits and complaints against auction sites threatened to generate consumer distrust of the entire industry, and companies scrambled to meet the challenge of providing honest auction environments at which the consumer's rights and wishes were safeguarded.

ORGANIZATION AND STRUCTURE

There were thousands of online auction sites in 2000, including massive generalist sites as well as those specializing in certain kinds of products or certain forms of transactions, such as business to business. Typically, users register on a Web site and upload descriptions of the products they have to sell, which are then sorted into product categories. Often, these descriptions include photographs and a starting bid price. As prospective buyers roam around the site, they begin to register bids, which are continuously updated. The highest bidder at the time the auction closes is obligated to purchase the product. Sellers then contact the buyers directly via any communication method and work out payment and shipment plans. Some of the larger sites, moreover, maintain listings of recently completed auctions, detailing the number of bids and final sales prices so users can get a feel for what they can expect to spend or receive at an auction.

Sites typically charge a listing fee; market leader eBay Inc., for instance, charged based on the value of the item sold, ranging from 25 cents to $2, although other sites, such as Yahoo!, Inc., charge no listing fee, relying on advertising and other sources for revenue. Most sites also ask a small percentage—usually no more than 5 percent—of the final sale price, though configurations vary.

Although the large sites such as eBay promote themselves as enterprises more akin to swap meets than retail outlets, their huge stores of consumer products of all varieties effectively place them in direct competition with traditional retailers, a fact to which those retailers quickly awoke.

Unlike the major online auction sites, merchant auction sites do not provide space for individuals to auction off their products; instead they acquire items unsold by other vendors and then auction the merchandise for their own revenues. As a result, they open themselves to a great deal more liability, and indeed some have met with a tremendous share of controversy for taking money for products that never reached their buyers, issuing fraudulent bid-victory notices, or misplacing or short-changing shipments. In most cases, customers who encounter a problem with such sites are forced to take up the issue with the vendors, rather than the auction sites, who often fail to guarantee that the products are actually in stock.

BACKGROUND AND DEVELOPMENT

The online auction industry didn't exactly have the most dramatic or profound of beginnings. Pierre Omidyar apparently met with great frustration at his inability to locate Pez brand candy dispensers on the Internet, and decided that something had to be done. Thus he began Auction Web in 1995, which began charging fees for item listings a year later. By 1997 the company was known as eBay and was well on its way to becoming synonymous with online auctions, spreading its name around the Web with banner ads and overseeing some 800,000 auctions daily. Though the fees were miniscule, the sheer volume of activity raked in tremendous revenues, making other Internet companies, both established and fledgling, sit up and take notice.

Originally known for auction listings featuring mainly quirky collectibles, the online action industry grew in the late 1990s to include hundreds of specialized sites and subsites selling everything from jewelry to automobiles to real estate. By 2000, hundreds of online auction sites graced the Web, including some of the biggest and most established names in the New Economy, such as Amazon.com, Inc. and Yahoo! Inc.

CURRENT CONDITIONS

Forrester Research estimated sales of $3.3 billion at the 500 online auction sites in 1999, and predicted they would reach $8.5 billion in 2001. Moreover, contrary to many observers' assumptions, the market was hardly limited to those on a shoestring budget. A Harris Poll at the end of 1999 revealed that over half those engaging in online auctioneering lived in households pulling in more than $50,000 per year, compared with only 39 percent for all Internet users. In addition, about 46 percent of online auction patrons held at least a college degree. About 46 percent were women, a figure that escalated from 35 percent just six months earlier. Analysts estimated the total economic impact of online auctions at about 1 percent of all U.S. retail sales in 1999, which, while seemingly unthreatening to traditional retailers, represented astonishing prominence for an industry with such a short history.

Sellers, meanwhile, learned they could make a killing at online auction sites. According to eBay, its sellers included the casual player who pulled in under $2,000 in a month of trading, while others, known as "power sellers," sometimes rolled in as much as $500,000 in auction revenues each month. Over half of these power sellers, according to online-auction financial services firm Andale, Inc., were regular businesses that developed separate departments to focus on online auctions as an alternative to or in addition to direct e-commerce retailing operations. The remainder of this aggressive sector was comprised of individuals taking advantage of the extremely low barrier to entry, not to mention the return on assets estimated at between 5 and 15 times that of conventional small businesses.

True to the industry's reputation that one could acquire anything through an online auction, by 2000 fledgling entrepreneurs could even obtain start-up loans of up to $100,000 for small businesses at PrimeStreet's auction site. The company offered a location at which major banks such as Mellon Bank, Bank One Corp., and others could bid for loans to customers who uploaded their loan needs. In this manner, loan seekers were relieved of the need to shop around endlessly looking for the best financing deal. At the other end of the spectrum, online debt auctioning became a reality in 2000 when ereorg.com was activated to provide a forum for distressed debt and loan claims.

Even old-fashioned business giants got into the act. The business-to-business auction model was expected to assume increased importance in equipment and supply transactions, as it carried the benefit of reducing transaction costs for all parties. General Motors Corp. (GM) teamed up with the Canadian auction house Commerce One to launch TradeXchange, which GM used to sell off manufacturing equipment. Likewise, Ford Motor Co. conducted its first auction in early 2000 to purchase tires. The scheme brought together five tire manufacturers to bid on prices at which they would sell their products to Ford. Ford initiated the bidding with a price of just under $100 million, and tire suppliers, in reverse-auction fashion, competed with each other by offering progressively lower bids, which ended with a sale at $78 million.

Business-to-business auctions generated a great deal of hype in business circles, leading to proclamations to the effect that the practice would reconfigure the very matrix of supply and demand. Investors, meanwhile, took the news to heart and poured money into new online B2B auction start-ups. While the auction method for manufacturing-equipment and components purchases offered tremendous speed and efficiency, it not surprisingly worried many manufacturers who feared decreased returns and a diminished emphasis on the quality of the products auctioned.

The industry also managed to earn a darker image, gaining notoriety for online hucksters and snake-oil artists. The National Consumer League (NCL) reported that in 1999, online auction-related gripes were the number-one complaint of all Internet users, accounting for 90 percent of all NCL phone calls. Typically, the problems centered on damaged or unreceived goods, according to the Federal Trade Commission. Generally, it was up to the auction sites to check out their sellers, and many required credit-card numbers or other identification that could help stave off would-be scam artists.

Nonetheless, product and service complaints gave rise to a great deal of skepticism and dissatisfaction among consumers, and auctioneers attempted to shield themselves from these complaints and potential lawsuits by adding extensive disclaimers on their Web sites in order to preemptively wash their hands of any misdeeds related to products and shipments. Thus analysts advised caution, noting that, for the time being, the customer would have to maintain responsibility for assessing the validity of auction sites, the products they post, and the vendors and sellers from which they wanted to buy.

The level of responsibility placed on the shoulders of online auctioneers for the products that were auctioned on their sites was far from clear. In late 1999 eBay was slapped with a lawsuit by a San Francisco man alleging that the company failed to take adequate steps to prevent the trading of illegal bootleg music recordings. While all parties were agreed that bootlegs were in fact bought and sold through eBay, at issue was whether eBay had a right to conduct auctions for them. eBay's defense relied on its insistence that it was not an actual retailer, but rather more of a giant classified advertising collection, and was thus not responsible for the dealings between its customers.

In part to stave off such illegal trading on its site, eBay initiated its Verified Rights Owners Program in summer 1999, which invited over 200 interested parties, including companies, individuals, trade groups, and others to regularly log on and monitor the Web site for illegal or inappropriate activities. Some of the hardest-hit industries, including those for computer software, music, and movies, took eBay up on the offer to try to force pirates and scam artists off the site.

INDUSTRY LEADERS

eBay Inc.

The leading online auction company in 2000 was eBay Inc. Founded in 1995, the San Jose, California-based firm maintained a payroll of 138 employees by 2000, when the site listed nearly 3,000 product categories, generated about $8 million in auction sales each day, and laid claim to nearly 10 million registered users. In addition to listing fees, the company took between 1.25 and 5 percent of the final sales price of auctioned items. eBay's records indicated that over half of all its auctions generated sales. In addition to its flagship auction operations, the site housed chat rooms and bulletin boards. In order to make the purchase of bulky items such as automobiles simpler for customers, eBay also established about 50 local marketplaces throughout the United States. In the late 1990s, the company purchased a 6 percent stake in business-to-business (B2B) surplus retailer Trade-Out.com, and rolled out its own B2B unit, called eBay Business Exchange, for small businesses.

Though a series of technical setbacks ate into the company's prestige in 1999, the company maintained its dominance over competitors Amazon.com and Yahoo! eBay improved its technical capabilities later that year with the acquisition of Billpoint, which specialized in credit-card technology, and gained some posh notoriety with the purchase of the prestigious Butterfield & Butterfield traditional auction house. The company maintained several operations in Europe, Japan, and Australia. eBay's partnership with Wells Fargo allowed its customers to accept credit-card payments. With an estimated 90 percent of the person-to-person online auction market, eBay's 1999 revenues jumped 374 percent to reach $224.7 million, leading to net income of $10.8 million.

AMAZON.COM

Amazon.com's name, like that of eBay, was synonymous with a form of e-commerce, though Amazon.com earned its fame through book retailing. Nonetheless, Amazon.com was giving eBay a run for its money. Founded in 1994, the Seattle, Washington-based firm quickly established itself as one of the darlings of the Web's emerging commerce sector, and began its online auction operations in early 1999. With operations in about 150 countries, the company was poised to capitalize on the rapidly expanding global cyberspace auction market. Amazon.com achieved revenues of $1.64 billion in 1999 while maintaining a payroll of 7,600 employees.

YAHOO! INC.

One of the Internet's premier Web portals, Yahoo! Inc. moved into the online auction business in the late 1990s, attempting to take financial advantage of its positions as the most heavily trafficked sites on the Web. The company boasted a portfolio of over 1 million auction listings. Yahoo! employed 2,000 workers at the end of 1999, and that year generated revenues of $588.6 million, up from $203.3 million the year before.

UBID.COM

UBid.com, a Chicago-based merchant auction site with over 800,000 registered users, conducted some 1,000 auctions each day by 2000. UBid conducted auctions for a variety of products, with a particular focus on closeout and refurbished computer hardware and electronic items. Though criticized for its often-unpredictable merchandise availability, the company maintained a strong and loyal customer base; 70 percent of the company's business was generated by repeat customers. UBid was spun off from its parent company Creative Computers in 1999 after beginning its auction operations in 1997. The company expanded with a focus on specific B2B markets beginning in 2000 when it unveiled its new Ironmall.com, which conducted auctions of construction equipment. In 1999, UBid generated revenues of $204.9 million.

EGGHEAD.COM

Based in Menlo Park, California, Egghead.com specialized in computers, conducting auctions of hard-ware, software, peripherals, and accessories. The company added strength through its 1999 merger with Onsale, including the Onsale atAuction service, which focused on computers and electronics. Founded in 1994, Egghead was originally a bricks-and-mortar retailer before undergoing a complete overhaul in the late 1990s to become a dot.com giant. Onsale had slowly established itself as a respected online auctioneer in the meantime, even helping Yahoo! set up its auction operations. The merged companies, which took the Egghead.com name, brought in revenues of $514.8 million in 1999 and employed 560 workers.

AMERICA AND THE WORLD

The premier online auction companies were not particularly quick to move into foreign markets, and when they did, the moves were not without their complications. In France, for instance, the law stipulated that only a handful of certified auctioneers could operate. Similar cultural and legal barriers existed in other countries as well. Nonetheless, by 2000 the major companies, especially Yahoo!, eBay, and Amazon.com were spreading across the globe, setting up shop abroad by a variety of methods. eBay, for instance, bought its way into the German market by acquiring that country's Alando, and quickly surpassed Ricardo.de to achieve German dominance. In the United Kingdom, the company struck out on its own; in Australia, it established a joint venture, and in Japan it sold a percentage of its Japanese operations to its industrial partner NEC.

Some European companies already maintained a strong presence in that market by the time the U.S. firms arrived. The British online auction firm QXL.com, for instance, was established in 1997 and emerged as the strongest player in its home market and as a powerful presence on the continent as well, buying up rival firms throughout Europe.

RESEARCH AND TECHNOLOGY

As pressures mounted on online auction companies to protect customers from fraudulent sales pitches, the companies scrambled to implement measures that could perform that duty at a minimum of extra work and expense to themselves. eBay partnered with Austin, Texas-based InfoGlide to implement InfoGlide software to weed out auction fraud. Designed to sniff out similarities between different files and databases, InfoGlide acted essentially as an exceptionally scrutinizing search engine, turning up information such as whether a particular eBay user was previously barred from the site for prior shenanigans. As a bonus, the software also proved useful in tracking and organizing information relating to the site's sales and statistics, such as best-and-worst lists of sales and customers. Previous incarnations of InfoGlide's software were used by the U.S. military to track terrorist threats and by police departments to try to catch criminals by identifying similarities between seemingly disparate crimes.

Industrial suppliers were understandably concerned about the growing popularity of reverse-auction B2B transactions. Given the steamrolling proliferation of such sites, however, suppliers who failed to jump into the game risked being left behind completely. Out of this dilemma emerged Maxager Technology Inc.'s profitability-analysis software. The package was designed to help suppliers decide when the pricing neared its minimum level to generate returns, and thus when to cease its bidding.

FURTHER READING

Appin, Rick. "New Debt Trading Site Set to Launch." *Mergers & Acquisitions Report,* 20 December 1999.

Bechard, Theresa. "Junk Becomes Investment-Grade Collectibles with Online Auctions." *Business First-Columbus,* 28 January 2000.

"Beyond the E-auction Hype." *Purchasing Magazine,* 23 March 2000.

Boehlert, Eric. "Online and Off Limits." *Rolling Stone,* 2 March 2000.

Brown, Monique R. "Going Once, Going Twice, No Sale." *Black Enterprise,* March 2000.

Crockett, Roger O. "Going, Going, Richer." *Business Week,* 13 December 1999.

Doyle, T. C. "Who Put the E in EBay?" *VARBusiness,* 6 December 1999.

Echikson, William D. "Rough Crossing for EBay." *Business Week,* 7 February 2000.

Freedman, David H. "Can You Survive the EBay Economy?" *Inc.,* March 2000.

"GM Rings in Era of E-commerce." *Ward's Auto World,* March 2000.

Gutner, Toddi. "Going, Going, Click!" *Business Week,* 21 February 2000.

Hof, Robert D. "Will Auction Frenzy Cool?" *Business Week,* 18 September 2000.

"InfoGlide Will Be EBay's Cop." *Austin Business Journal,* 7 January 2000.

Kandra, Anne. "Merchant Auction Sites: Bidder Beware of the Fine Print." *PC World,* March 2000.

Kisiel, Ralph. "Ford Online Auction Worries Tire Maker." *Automotive News,* 28 February 2000.

"Online Auctions: A Shopper's Delight." *Inc.,* March 2000.

Saxe, Frank. "San Fran Man Sues EBay Web Site over Alleged Bootlegs." *Billboard,* 4 December 1999.

Wilder, Clinton. "Online-Auction Profitability Boost—Maxager Technology Software Lets Industrial Suppliers Analyze Profits at the Product Level." *InformationWeek,* 6 March 2000.

E-Commerce: Online Brokerages

Since the mid-1990s the sizzling U.S. stock market and the ease of Internet trading have lured millions of investors into opening online brokerage accounts. By late 2000, according to International Data Corp., online accounts housed more than $1.6 trillion in assets. What's more, analysts expect online brokerage assets to continue to burgeon in the early 2000s, potentially adding another $1 trillion by 2004. According to leading online brokerage Ameritrade, 11 percent, or 6.6 million, of U.S. brokerage accounts were online in 1998; by 2004, the company expected that online accounts would amount to half of the projected 80 million U.S. accounts. By year-end 2000, analysts generally expected 15 million online accounts to be activated.

The 160 or so U.S. brokerages offering online services as of 2000 are roughly divided into two camps. The first is comprised of online-oriented firms that focus primarily, even exclusively, on electronic accounts. Many of these are relatively young firms and include the likes of E*TRADE Group, Inc.; Ameritrade Holding Corp.; and Datek Online Holdings Corp. The second group consists of traditional brokerage houses and investment firms that have expanded into the online arena. Some, like Charles Schwab, the largest online brokerage in 2000, have done so on a monumental scale, amassing a million or more online accounts in just a few years. Big high-end houses such as Merrill Lynch have lumbered into the online business belatedly, but because of their size may readily capture huge shares of the online market.

Many online brokerages, including discounters, increasingly emphasize offering a range of content and services beyond simple online trading. For some, the ultimate prize will be to become a one-stop financial services site, offering banking, bill payment, retirement account management, and investment opportunities beyond stocks and mutual funds. In one high-profile bid, E*TRADE proposed in 1999 to merge with Telebanc Financial Corp., a consumer-oriented online bank. Although the deal was stalled because of regulatory hurdles involving E*TRADE's biggest shareholder, it took effect in 2000. That year E*TRADE also bought out Card Capture Services, an automatic teller machine (ATM) network. For its part, Charles Schwab & Co. agreed to acquire U.S. Trust, an entry for Schwab into the lucrative world of large asset management for wealthy individuals and estates.

Online brokerages function in much the same way as conventional brokerages and are governed by mostly the same laws and regulations. Customers often set up most aspects of their accounts by filling out and submitting forms electronically, and they fund their account by mailing a check or ordering a wire transfer to the brokerage. Most brokerages enforce a minimum balance, which can be as low as $1,000 at deep-discount outfits or as high as $100,000 or more for full-featured accounts. Basic accounts at discount brokerages may provide only the ability to place orders and monitor the account, whereas pricey accounts boast of such features as detailed research reports, stock recommendations, and access to financial advisers.

REGULATION

All online brokerages are subject to federal oversight and regulation, principally by the Securities and Exchange Commission (SEC), as well as state jurisdiction and self-regulation from bodies such as the National Association of Securities Dealers (NASD). Federal regulations, for instance, charge brokers with the duty of finding the best execution for a trade—a vague concept that means the broker should seek to maximize the customer's returns in market transactions, not simply its own. Brokerages must also take reasonable steps to provide timely execution of orders (although no time limit exists) and inform customers that delays are possible. Myriad regulations cover the kinds of communications and assertions a brokerage can make to its customers. These laws and regulations are aimed at curbing fraud and ensuring that investors have ample information before entrusting their money to a brokerage and its computer system.

A PRICE FOR EVERYONE

Online brokerages make their money in several ways and their pricing structures can be complex. Most obviously, they charge a commission on each trade their customers execute. Although customary commissions are a percentage of the dollar value being traded, easily amounting to hundreds or thousands of dollars on a single transaction by a larger investor, the battle cry of discount brokers has been flat commissions. Under a flat pricing structure, customers pay a fixed surcharge on each trade, ranging between $8 and $30 at the most popular brokerages. Some firms also levy account management fees, typically assessed on an annual basis, which are either a flat rate or a percentage of the assets in the account.

Even under flat pricing, though, there are often some exceptions. For one, different types of stock orders can yield different fees. The most common distinction is between market orders, where the customer agrees to buy or sell shares at the prevailing current price, and limit orders, which allow the investor to specify a maximum or minimum price that must be met for the transaction to be executed. Limit orders usually cost a few dollars more than market orders.

Recently, a number of online brokerages instituted a graduated flat-rate structure whereby people who trade more frequently pay lower fees. For example, E*TRADE gives its heavy traders a $5 rebate for each trade in excess of 29 per quarter, and a $10 rebate for each trade beyond the seventy-fourth. In effect, for the 75-plus share traders, the commission on trading popular Nasdaq stocks drops from $19.95 to $9.95—after completing 29 trades at $19.95 and another 45 at $14.95, at which point the brokerage has already collected $1,250 in commissions.

Other special pricing situations include trading in unlisted, over-the-counter stocks, which tend to be more speculative, thinly traded issues at very low per-share prices, and very large orders, such as moving more than 5,000 shares in one trade. These sorts of transactions often include a per-share surcharge. If a customer requires a broker to help complete a trade, typically an additional fee is charged.

MARGIN LENDING

Lastly, brokerages earn money by lending their customers investment funds through margin accounts. Use of margin has soared with the advent of online trading, with total margin debt leaping about 75 percent in 1999 alone. With these accounts, qualifying customers can buy or sell shares that are worth more than the total value of their own assets. In theory, if the customers get in on a profitable trade, they can reap most of the profits of having invested a greater sum. Of course, as does any lender, brokerages charge interest on the value of the margin trades, and margin transactions are regulated somewhat strictly to reduce the likelihood of investors losing too much money that isn't theirs. In a so-called margin call, the brokerage forces customers whose margin positions are losing money to either increase their own equity stake in the shares or sell the shares at a loss to pay back the brokerage. While this can be a setback for the investors, it tends to be profitable for brokerages, which may obtain 20 percent or more of their revenue from margin lending.

BACKGROUND AND DEVELOPMENT

The movement that ultimately gave rise to online brokerages in the 1990s dates to the mid-1970s deregulation of the securities industry. Until that time, full-service brokerages had a stranglehold on the business and their commissions were fixed by the securities exchanges they traded on. In 1975 the SEC deregulated the securities business, opening it up to new competition.

Originally a full-service brokerage like all the rest, Charles Schwab & Co., headed by its namesake, jumped on the opportunity to compete in the new era. The company is widely credited with launching the discount brokering business. The concept was simple: give customers access to affordable stock trades and let them fend for themselves (or simply pay extra)

About... **RAISING THE STAKES AT DAY-TRADING FIRMS**

An increasingly visible niche in the online brokerage industry is the portion catering to professional traders. Day traders are individuals who use electronic brokerage accounts to earn some or all of their income by executing frequent trades to take advantage of short-term price fluctuations. Die-hard day traders never hold a stock overnight: their credo is to take quick profits—often selling within minutes of buying—and cut their losses fast. By racking up dozens of trades in a day, day traders hope to come out ahead by limiting their risk and settling for incremental gains—along with occasional luck—that will earn them a living.

Day traders have fairly specific needs, and most serious traders rely on brokerages that cater to them. Typically they're not interested in stock research or a company's fundamentals—most traders know little or nothing about the stocks they trade, focusing instead on price and volume patterns. In order to get in on price movements, they demand breakneck executions and instantaneous feeds of prices and other market statistics.

Brokerages such as All-Tech Investment Group, CyBerCorp (now part of Schwab), Polar Trading, and Terra Nova Trading target the day-trading market heaviest, while larger firms such as Datek and Ameritrade also appeal to day traders. Often they provide custom software for monitoring stock charts and executing trades, and some operate trading centers where hoards of traders can congregate and use on-site computers to practice their craft.

Day trading is a controversial practice on a variety of grounds. Critics say that day-trading firms lure in gullible people who know little about the stock market and who subsequently lose most of their money. In the cultural sphere, day traders are perceived as young, brash, irreverent souls who care only about making a fast buck. Day traders have also been blamed for fomenting volatility in the markets, driving prices of technology issues—especially Internet stocks—up to unprecedented levels, only to ride them back down by short-selling the shares. Day-trading brokerages have been investigated for skirting federal margin-lending rules (they were accused of letting traders borrow more than the legal limit based on the traders' cash assets) and have contributed to a push by regulators to tighten cash requirements for margin traders.

For all of its controversies, though, the day-trading market isn't particularly large. Estimates placed the number of full-time, hard-core day traders in 2000 at just 7,000 nationwide. Most of the firms devoted to day-trading traffic are quite small; few, if any, had sales above $100 million as of 1999.

---

when it comes to researching investments and planning their portfolios. Schwab started offering no-frills investment services at deep discounts in 1974, and rapidly became the dominant player in that space.

By most measures, online brokerages didn't exist until 1995, although companies such as Schwab and E*TRADE offered some form of electronic trading since the mid-1980s. The rapid growth of online services such as America Online and, increasingly, Internet-based information accessed over the Web made for compelling market prospects. Using the eSchwab brand, Schwab was one of the first to set up shop online, quickly amassing 337,000 online accounts by 1995.

E*TRADE, which was founded in the 1980s as an electronic service for other brokerages, began offering retail online brokerage services in 1992 through the self-contained networks of America Online and CompuServe. Unlike Schwab, which had millions of accounts to draw on from its huge offline discount operation, E*TRADE was one of the first pure-play online brokerages. It launched its Web presence in 1996 and, taking a page from Schwab, began to compete on price with Schwab and other players in the nascent business.

As Internet use exploded and, relatedly, the U.S. stock market began a steep ascent, investors flocked to online brokerages. By 1997 more than a million online accounts had been opened, with nearly half at Schwab, and $50 billion in assets floated through cyber accounts. Swift growth continued through the late 1990s, with the number of accounts approaching 8 million and the size of assets surging toward $750 billion.

CURRENT CONDITIONS

At the end of 2000 the industry supported some 15 million online investment accounts, adding over a million new accounts each quarter. Already online brokerages were averaging as many as 500,000 trades each day, at times representing up to one-fifth of total market volume. Although brokerage revenues haven't grown as fast as the number of accounts, projections by Robertson Stephens, an investment bank,

---

showed revenues of top online players rising by more than 30 percent in 2000. However, to date, online trading consumers haven't maintained significant online financial resources. A study by McKinsey & Company showed that, while over one-third of all trades are made online, those trades represented only 5 percent of total assets invested.

Old-school brokerages such as Merrill Lynch & Co., Inc.; Morgan Stanley Dean Witter & Co.; and Donaldson, Lufkin & Jenrette, Inc. continue to lag in the online arena, but are expected to slowly grab a larger share of the market. Many of these full-service brokerages never quite took to the discounting revolution spearheaded by Schwab decades earlier, so they've considered mass-market online accounts unprofitable and outside their league. Still, all the major brokerages have online offerings, often with a mix of the traditional hand-holding of big firms and the self-empowerment of the start-up services. Their commissions and account fees have tended to be as large as ever, but some moved closer to the discount model while still insisting on substantial balances—easily $20,000 or more at a minimum. As a measure of the big firms' lag, Merrill Lynch's online accounts in early 2000 were at about the same number that Schwab had three years earlier.

The legions of online investors include many small investors who never had brokerage accounts before the online craze. The upstart brokerages have welcomed—and often depended on—this broadening of the investment market to build up their businesses. Because most of these firms charge flat rates for trading, their business depends on getting lots of customers who make lots of trades. Online trading has indeed surged, but even leaders such as E*TRADE are still finding profits elusive. The larger traditional brokerages are more wary of the low end, as they can potentially make significantly more money from one large account than dozens of small accounts.

Customer service has been the industry's albatross. In part victims of their own success, online brokerages have sometimes failed to invest adequately in their technical and corporate infrastructures. As a result, when trading activity surges, their systems have become sluggish and frustrating to use—a woeful liability in a fast-moving market—and have occasionally crashed. Online brokerages have likewise been inundated with technical support and general customer service requests that they've labored to keep up with, again often failing in their customers' eyes. Surveys report high levels of customer dissatisfaction with some aspects of online services and suggest that many

online investors contemplate switching brokerages because of perceived bad service.

INDUSTRY LEADERS

CHARLES SCHWAB

The biggest fish in the sea of online brokerages, Charles Schwab gained its position through its market leadership in the closely related discount brokerage business. In 2000 the company boasted about over 7 million online accounts, and daily online trades topped 310 million. Revenue from all sources in 1999 topped $3.9 billion with healthy net income. Although Schwab was able to command as much as half of the entire online brokerage business in the mid-1990s, by 1999 the flood of other entrants had trimmed its share to less than 20 percent. Even at that, however, it had more than three times as many online customers as its next-largest competitor.

E*TRADE

E*TRADE Group was the second-largest online brokerage based on 2000 accounts, which numbered topped 2.5 million. The company has advertised aggressively to make its site one of the premier finance destinations on the Web. It has likewise invested in a number of strategic acquisitions, including Telebanc, a fledgling Internet-only bank, and the ATM system Card Capture Services. The purchase of Card Capture was noteworthy in that it gave E*TRADE a vast infrastructure through which it can reach its clients electronically when they're not at their computers—including the potential to allow clients to fund their accounts by making ATM deposits, rather than mailing in a check, and withdraw money from their investment accounts at the ATM as well. E*TRADE's revenue in 1999 exceeded $750 million, but it failed to turn a profit due to heavy spending. In Internet-based polling, E*TRADE has been ranked frequently as the top brokerage in terms of customer satisfaction.

TD WATERHOUSE GROUP, INC.

Although its name isn't as well known as E*TRADE's, TD Waterhouse is a firmly established discount brokerage that has built an online business that increasingly rivals E*TRADE's in size. In 1999 TD Waterhouse had 1.3 million online accounts and more than 2 million accounts altogether. Controlled by Canada's Toronto Dominion Bank, TD Waterhouse held a 12 percent share of the U.S. market that year, still short of E*TRADE's 15 percent. TD Waterhouse, however, outshone E*TRADE in both revenue and profits, which totaled $945 million and $97 million, respectively. The company also had the distinction of having one of the lowest cost structures for obtaining new clients.

AMERITRADE

Ameritrade Holding Corp. is a smaller, deep-discount operation that usually ranks among the top five or six brokerages in terms of account numbers and trading volume. The company concentrates on providing no-frills, low-priced service to budget-minded individuals and frequent traders. In mid-2000 it had an estimated 1 million accounts. It brought in $327

million in revenue in 1999, but like E*TRADE, its copious spending on advertising and promotions to build market share left it in a loss position for the year.

DATEK

One of the more controversial players, Datek Online Holdings Corp., formerly Datek Securities, is another firm aiming at the no-frills and day-trading segments of the business. With 340,000 accounts in 1999, the privately held company was estimated to have an 11 percent share of the market that year. Datek has a majority stake in the stock-trading network The Island ECN, Inc. The company aborted its own public offering in 1998, and was pummeled in the late 1990s by several scandals involving an erroneous financial report and allegations of misusing investors' funds. Despite its troubles, Datek has been rated in several consumer surveys as the best online brokerage, mainly on the power and stability of its computer system.

AMERICA AND THE WORLD

The rise of online brokerages outside the United States has been subdued. The U.S. stock market in the 1990s vastly outperformed most other major world markets and Internet adoption was also faster in the United States than in most other places. These factors, as well as cultural and regulatory differences, have fed into the popularity of online investing in the United States as compared to elsewhere around the globe.

Nonetheless, regions such as Europe and Japan were forecast to have an online-brokerage boom in the early 2000s. Forrester Research, a technology market research firm, predicted that between 2000 and 2004 the number of people with online accounts in Europe would skyrocket tenfold, reaching 14 million by the end of the period. Germany and Scandinavian countries were expected to be the most fertile markets for online brokerage services. German-based brokerages were the Continent's largest in the late 1990s, although U.S. firms were attempting to break into the market as well.

Financial deregulation and a much-awaited economic recovery in Japan were expected to make the Japanese market more conducive to online investing. U.S. firms stand to make a bigger splash there, as Schwab; DLJDirect, Inc. (the online counterpart of Donaldson, Lufkin & Jenrette); and E*TRADE, which is part-owned by a Japanese company, all have been making overtures to Japanese consumers. Slower consumer adoption of the Internet has been a particular

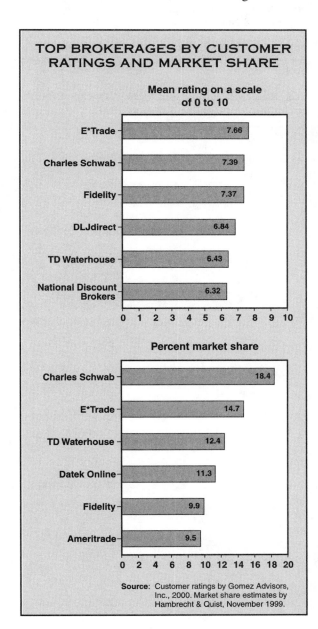

TOP BROKERAGES BY CUSTOMER RATINGS AND MARKET SHARE

Mean rating on a scale of 0 to 10

E*Trade	7.66
Charles Schwab	7.39
Fidelity	7.37
DLJdirect	6.84
TD Waterhouse	6.43
National Discount Brokers	6.32

0 1 2 3 4 5 6 7 8 9 10

Percent market share

Charles Schwab	18.4
E*Trade	14.7
TD Waterhouse	12.4
Datek Online	11.3
Fidelity	9.9
Ameritrade	9.5

0 2 4 6 8 10 12 14 16 18 20

Source: Customer ratings by Gomez Advisors, Inc., 2000. Market share estimates by Hambrecht & Quist, November 1999.

obstacle in Japan, but Internet use was expected to pick up in the early 2000s.

FURTHER READING

Anderson, Amy L. "Banks Seen Failing to Exploit Online Brokerage Surge." *American Banker,* 17 July 2000.

Appleby, Scott. "E*TRADE Group." New York: Robertson Stephens, 22 February 2000.

"Brokers." *Forbes,* 11 September 2000.

Carter, Adrienne. "Full-Service Brokers Hit the Web." *Money,* 1 February 2000.

Fugazy, Danielle. "Brokerage: Online Brokerage Activity Has Soared." *Web Finance,* 3 July 2000.

Gandel, Stephen. "Brokers Ready Big Offers for Day Traders." *Crain's New York Business,* 21 February 2000.

Gomez Advisors, Inc. "Internet Broker Scorecard." Lincoln, MA, spring 2000. Available from http://www.gomez.com.

Healy, Beth. "Battle of the Online Brokers Heats Up." *Boston Globe,* 3 April 2000.

———. "Heavy Volume Slows down Stock Traders." *Boston Globe,* 14 March 2000.

"Marginal Differences." *Economist,* 1 April 2000.

Minkoff, Jerry. "Brokerage: Online Trading Has Many Styles, Firms Report." *Web Finance,* 28 February 2000.

———. "Europe Is the Frontier for Online Stock Trading." *Web Finance,* 14 February 2000.

"The No-Name That's Shadowing Schwab." *Business Week,* 18 October 1999.

Schwab, David. "Iselin, N.J.-Based Online-Brokerages Operator Names New President." *Knight Ridder/Tribune Business News,* 8 November 1999.

Smith, Anne Kates. "One Heck of a Way to Make a Living—or Not." *U.S. News & World Report,* 27 September 1999.

Snel, Ross."Big Brokers Seen Making Net-Only Path Obsolete." *American Banker,* 7 October 1999.

E-Commerce: Online Grocery Shopping

The notion of ordering lettuce and peanut butter from home and having them delivered is nothing new, but online grocery services are beginning to build this convenience into a multibillion-dollar enterprise. Various firms made tentative forays into computer-based grocery shopping as early as the 1980s. But it wasn't until a decade later that a new breed of well-funded Web-based services held promise for tapping into the potentially massive U.S. market for online grocery services.

As of 2000 grocery retailing in the United States was a $450 billion business. Despite its size, though, it's also a mature business that's growing sluggishly—as little as 2 percent a year. Enter online grocers. They compete with both traditional supermarkets and, to a lesser degree, restaurants, especially takeout and delivery outfits. Some believe it will be an uphill battle to nab customers from either side, but online grocers can look forward to exponentially faster growth—at least in the short term—because of their newness and low market penetration.

Fat-cat supermarkets and pizza joints needn't hang the going-out-of-business signs just yet, however. In the early 2000s, according to a pair of market forecasts, online grocers were likely to be fighting over a fraction of 1 percent of annual grocery sales. Perhaps the most ambitious prediction was that of Forrester Research, which forecast sales of home-delivery Web grocers such as Webvan Group Inc. and HomeGrocer.com to skyrocket from $2 billion in 2000 to $20 billion by 2004, including sales of nonfood items. Other forecasts have been less sanguine in the short term. Still, even at a few billion dollars,

online grocery sales would be a far cry from the paltry $235 million Forrester calculated for 1998.

The biggest obstacle to running a Web-based grocery service is logistics—getting the product to the customer. This is manifoldly true when it comes to perishable goods.

At least four business models have been put forth to solve the problem: (1) some online services opt to sell only nonperishables and ship them via express delivery vendors such as FedEx; (2) some are affiliated with physical grocery stores in certain regions and thereby rely on the old-fashioned grocer to handle logistics down to the city or even neighborhood level; (3) some develop their own independent distribution systems complete with a system of regional and local warehouses and a fleet of delivery trucks; (4) some offer perishables and nonperishables, but only with very limited stock (often snacks or convenience foods), in limited distribution areas (often within one city), and accompanied by such nongrocery services as video rental and laundry services.

Nonperishables Offer Advantages

Firms as different as NetGrocer.com and Wal-Mart Stores, Inc. have embraced the first option with some success. On a logistics level, the business is akin to that of Amazon.com and many other nonfood consumer-oriented e-commerce ventures. Indeed, in 2000, the service claimed to have reached over 200,000 customers in less than 4 years of operation—twice as many customers as the oldest online grocer Peapod, Inc. had in its 11-year history.

Vastly lower overhead costs make this segment of the business easier to break into, and by some appraisals, potentially much more profitable than ordinary grocery retailing. Nonetheless, by limiting selection to nonperishable items and by relying on third-party couriers that can deliver the goods overnight at the earliest, online grocers that pursue this route have a more limited market than firms offering full-line groceries.

STORE AFFILIATIONS LOGICAL, BUT HAVE TARNISHED PAST

The oldest, and perhaps most obvious, way to organize a home-grocery-delivery service is around the ample infrastructure of the bricks-and-mortar grocery industry. This was industry founder Peapod's approach: it signed agreements with various supermarket chains and deployed its own delivery vans to cart groceries from the store to its customers' homes. A bevy of supermarkets, including Safeway, Shaw's, and Pink Dot, have themselves launched online order-and-delivery systems.

For the most part, though, store-affiliated online grocery ventures have done poorly thus far. A number of programs sponsored by stores were canceled in the mid-1990s because of slack demand. And Peapod, for all its perseverance, never turned a profit from 1989 to 2000, and was teetering on insolvency by the end of that period, though it managed to hang on by allying with Netherlands-based grocer Royal Ahold NV.

Part of the problem may be inefficiencies in store logistics, which are optimized for consumers to see, smell, touch, and squeeze their favorite groceries in stores. Some believe that if delivery is the object, a specially designed warehouse is better suited for rapid order assembly and shipment.

INDEPENDENT, FULL-SERVICE DELIVERY UNPROVEN

The third logistics option, creating a sprawling inventory and distribution system dedicated to home grocery delivery, is the riskiest. It requires heavy outlays to build and operate a network of warehouses. It requires a fleet of trucks. It's also more time-sensitive because some items in those warehouses can rot and spoil quickly.

Because of the high costs and risks involved, few companies have ventured into this territory; on any significant scale, it is one of the newer modes of business.

Pioneers include HomeGrocer.com and, most ambitiously, the Webvan Group. Webvan, formed in 1999, embarked on constructing a $1 billion infrastructure to support its full-line grocery service. The company has been by far the best-funded entrant in the online grocery contest, and its financial backers and management include top brass from the likes of Andersen Consulting and Borders bookstores. Such credentials and the sea of investment cash flowing into these firms make them a force to be reckoned with.

LIMITED, DIVERSIFIED SERVICES OFFER ALTERNATIVES

A number of Web-based firms have hedged their bets on groceries by offering limited selection and a variety of other products and services at the same time. Kozmo.com, for instance, offers basic groceries and snacks alongside video rentals, CDs, and magazines for speedy delivery—within an hour of the order. The logistics model here is much like that of a pizza-delivery chain; it covers a small territory, perhaps only part of a major city, and doesn't do anything too fancy. As of 2000, Kozmo operated only in parts of New York City and San Francisco. Streamline.com takes a different tack, offering dry cleaning, prepared meals, film processing, shoe repair, and parcel pick-up in addition to its groceries.

BACKGROUND AND DEVELOPMENT

Directly or indirectly, grocery stores have allowed people to place and receive orders at home for decades. Neighborhood grocers provided delivery service to customers since at least the 19th century. And, since at least the 1960s, third-party services have offered phone-in or dial-in ordering and delivery services in local areas.

More often than not, it seems, these services haven't caught on. They were often unavailable or unappealing to a wide number of consumers, and probably even more frequently they weren't profitable for the vendors. In the 1980s, for example, a number of delivery services sprang up claiming to be the solution for overworked, dual-income couples. With services couched in terms such as "teleshopping," they allowed consumers within local service areas to phone-in grocery orders and have them delivered at an appointed time.

By the middle and late 1980s, a number of local grocery delivery services also allowed consumers to browse listings and place orders by computer. Several of the familiar marketing strategies that would be revived in the late 1990s were articulated during this time, such as catering to suburban families and using price promotions to attract new customers. Some observers gushed about how common grocery delivery would be by 1990.

Out of this environment grew one of the more enduring services of this kind, Peapod, based in suburban Chicago. Founded in 1989, Peapod was one of the biggest and best-known services to rely solely on computer-based orders. Peapod subscribers used the company's proprietary software and a modem to dial into its local systems, originally in Chicago and San Francisco, where it had alliances with the Jewel and Safeway chains, respectively. Once an order was placed, Peapod staff would go to the local store, pick out the requested items, and deliver them to the customer.

Publicity over Peapod and similar services, perhaps along with fear of missing some great technological leap forward, caused many supermarkets to launch their own versions of home-based order and delivery. Safeway considered expanding its use of Peapod to cover a wider swath of northern California and even into Nevada. Other chains linked their catalogs to consumer online content services such as the Prodigy network and dispatched their own employees to fill orders.

But by the mid-1990s much of the promise had failed to materialize. Stores often found the arrangements unprofitable when their own workers were saddled with putting orders together. In some cases where both phone and personal computer (PC) orders were accepted, computer orders were negligible while the more labor-intensive phone orders predominated. Specialty services such as Peapod experienced growing demand, with sales about doubling each year; but costs kept mounting as well, leaving it with recurring losses and escalating debt.

Meanwhile, other competitors surfaced. Streamline Inc., of Westwood, Massachusetts, became one of the more aggressive players that didn't rely on existing supermarkets. The suburban Boston firm, founded in 1993, focused instead on developing its own warehouse and relationships with wholesalers and distributors in a bid to keep costs down and efficiency high. Streamline's model was also novel because it offered dry cleaning and other nongrocery services as well, which distinguished it from competitors. A separate innovation was its use of prepacked service boxes with freezer and refrigerator compartments, so delivery staff could drop off groceries in a customer's basement or garage without the customer there. In effect, Streamline created a blueprint that others would follow once the Internet was hammered into the model.

Companies such as Streamline, Peapod, and HomeRuns (operated by the Maine grocery chain Hannaford Bros.) began setting up shop on the Web in 1996. This came just as Internet use was skyrocketing and the Web was being targeted increasingly at ordinary consumers and families rather than technophiles. The Web provided a familiar and almost universal platform for firms to build their order-taking systems around, as contrasted with the murky world of proprietary software running on the customer's PC and dialing into a delivery service's computer.

Perhaps the final pivotal event influencing the nascent online shopping business was the Internet stock craze and the infusion of cash into "dot-com" companies. Emboldened by Netscape's phenomenal stock launch, venture capitalists and investors of all stripes in the mid- to late 1990s began combing for the next Internet—later, specifically e-commerce—wunderkind, while entrepreneurs sprang up to take a stab. Against this backdrop emerged competitors such as HomeGrocer.com and Webvan.

CURRENT CONDITIONS

VAST MARKET CREATES FAVORABLE OUTLOOK

The newer crop of companies, such as Webvan, NetGrocer.com, and HomeGrocer.com, have evoked guarded optimism from a variety of industry analysts. Wary of the glib and grossly overstated forecasts of the 1980s and early 1990s, recent observers have shown more restraint, if not consensus.

Estimates for 1998 placed online grocery sales in the $100-$200 million range, but forecasts diverged rapidly when it came to reckoning sales in the early 2000s. Forrester Research envisaged revenue in the van-based delivery segment of the business (thereby excluding perishable goods shippers such as NetGrocer.com) reaching $2 billion in 2000 and $20 billion by 2004. Jupiter Communications tended to offer more conservative valuations, suggesting that online groceries would represent a $6-$7 billion market by 2003. Another prognosticator, Zona Research, largely concurred with Jupiter's prediction.

Even at Forrester's high projection, online grocery sales in 2004 would likely represent less than 5 percent of all retail grocery sales in the United States, and a much smaller portion of all food sales. By contrast, rash predictions of earlier years suggested that as much as 20 percent of grocery sales would occur online by the mid-1990s or 2000.

Separately, a number of analysts have attempted to attach a price to the potential market for online grocery shopping. There is some agreement that the potential market is vast and will go untapped for some years, but the specific estimates again vary. Forrester believed the total market potential in the early 2000s was approaching $40 billion. Gazing further out, a senior executive at Streamline pegged the market's potential at $60 billion by 2007. To whatever extent the industry realizes this market potential, nearly all of its gains were expected to come at the expense of traditional grocery retailers.

One of the biggest challenges for online grocers is to tap into the peculiar customer attitudes toward online grocery shopping. A survey by PricewaterhouseCoopers in 2000 found that a full 21 percent of Internet users insisted that nothing could persuade them to buy their groceries online. And, interestingly, price seems to be a much bigger factor than convenience for online grocery shoppers. Only 11 percent of survey respondents said they would pay more for groceries even if ordering online saved them time. Nearly half wanted free delivery as an inducement to order online.

PEAPOD'S NARROW ESCAPE

As newer firms flush with capital have entered the online grocery arena, some of the old-timers such as Peapod haven't faired well. Some argue that Peapod's store-dependent model, one it was belatedly trying to break from in the late 1990s, was simply flawed. And although the company went public in 1997, it never achieved the levels of market capitalization and private funding that firms such as Webvan garnered. Things began to crumble in 1999 when Peapod admitted it had cash-flow problems. The announcement unnerved the stock market and sent Peapod's shares tumbling, just when it needed money most. By early 2000 Peapod had lined up a hefty $120 million deal with a group of corporate investors, but the deal caved in when Peapod's chief executive, William Malloy, fell ill and abruptly resigned in March 2000. On the brink of insolvency, Peapod stared at a dismal future. Then, in April, the Netherlands-based grocery firm Royal Ahold NV came to Peapod's rescue, throwing $73 million at Peapod in exchange for a 51 percent share of the company. Royal Ahold saw the move as an expansion of its domestic online grocery business into the United States.

INDUSTRY LEADERS

PEAPOD

With about 100,000 customers in 2000, Peapod, based in Skokie, Illinois, was the largest and one of the oldest firms in the online grocery industry. Founded in 1989 by brothers Andrew and Thomas Parkinson, Peapod was first rolled out in the Chicago area, where it teamed up with the large Jewel supermarket chain. Later Peapod expanded to the San Francisco Bay Area; Boston; Columbus, Ohio; and Dallas, Houston, and Austin, Texas. In 1999 it had the highest sales of all the online grocers, with $73.1 million, but it concomitantly suffered a $28.5 million loss.

In the middle and even late 1990s, Peapod was seen as the anointed grocer that would lead the charge into Web-based ordering and home delivery on demand. Slow to adapt from its inefficient store-shopping-service model, Peapod was blindsided in the late 1990s by mounting costs and competition. It failed to hold investors' imaginations the way feisty Webvan did, and as a result of its funding and management crises, Peapod in 2000 was forced into the arms of Netherlands-based Royal Ahold NV. Shortly thereafter, it purchased Boston-based online grocer Streamline.com.

WEBVAN

The Webvan Group Inc., of Foster City, California, took the online grocery business by storm when its service was launched in 1999. Serving only the metropolitan San Francisco area at first, Webvan sought to revolutionize the grocery business by simultaneously making it more profitable for the seller and more convenient for the buyer.

Louis Borders, of Borders bookstore fame, founded the company in 1996 as Intelligent Systems for Retail. No stranger to mass retailing, Louis Borders consciously set out to do the opposite of what Peapod had done: rather than trying to adapt the existing retail infrastructure to an online delivery service model, he designed a new system from the ground up. Between 1996 and 1999, Borders' team made grandiose—yet meticulous—plans for a supremely automated warehouse and distribution infrastructure that would receive orders over the Internet and deliver the goods to consumers' doors, all while delivering higher profit margins than old-fashioned retailers. Indeed, Borders claimed that unlike most of his e-commerce competitors, he expected regional segments of the business to be profitable within their first year.

Because of Borders' credentials and impressive plans, the company was able to tap into a huge influx of private investments from the likes of CBS, Goldman Sachs, and Knight-Ridder, among others. Renamed Webvan in 1999, by the time the company was preparing for a public offering, it had already landed a startling $4 billion in private capital. The company also attracted top-notch managers, including a surprise coup in the chief executive's office by recruiting George T. Shaheen, the influential CEO of Andersen Consulting. All the heavy hitters on Webvan's side added much credibility to its cause.

In September 2000, Webvan purchased Home-Grocer.com, one of its nearest competitors in terms of strategy. While it failed to charm as many white-shoe backers as Webvan, HomeGrocer was most prominently supported by Amazon.com, which in 2000 held a 28 percent stake in the company. Other funders included high-profile venture capitalists Kleiner Perkins Caufield & Byers, along with Netscape founder Jim Barksdale's investment group and Martha Stewart Living Omnimedia.

The company's approach is not without its skeptics. No less a logistics authority than Fred Smith, CEO of Federal Express parent company FDX Corp., questioned the viability of such services. Smith was quoted as saying online grocers would have "very tough sledding" because delivery logistics costs would likely price the services beyond what most consumers are willing to pay. Nonetheless, the company posted sales of $13.3 million in 1999.

NETGROCER.COM

NetGrocer.com Inc. followed a more proven method of making money on the Internet—letting third-party shippers—such as Federal Express—worry about getting the product to the customer. Although this practice limits NetGrocer's offerings and makes it something short of a one-stop grocery solution, the North Brunswick, New Jersey, company is one of the only to serve a nationwide market and reported having more than 200,000 customers as of 2000. A pair of late 1999 Internet surveys named NetGrocer the most trafficked grocery Web site. Closely held Net-Grocer's financiers include Cendant Corp., a troubled real estate, hotel, and car rental franchiser. The company's sales grew 200 percent in 1999 to reach $15 million.

KOZMO.COM, INC.

Based in New York, Kozmo.com was built by a handful of bicycle couriers in 2000 to offer one-hour delivery of grocery and entertainment items to New Yorkers who ordered service online. Since its inception in 1997, the company has expanded to over a dozen major U.S. cities and has attracted financing from the likes of Amazon.com and Chase Venture Capital. Kozmo.com raked in sales of $3.5 million in 1999 and registered a net loss of $26.4 million while employing 2,665.

OTHER ONLINE GROCERS

One source tallied a total of 31 online grocers as of 1999. Some of the others include Albertsons.com (affiliated with the store chain; delivery in Seattle to start), eGrocer.com (various areas), GroceryWorks (Dallas), HomeRuns.com (various areas), ShopLink.com (metro Boston), and WebHouse Club (New York).

FURTHER READING

Anders, George. "Co-Founder of Borders Is Planning to Launch an Online Megastore." *Wall Street Journal,* 22 April 1999.

Aragon, Lawrence. "FDX Chief Predicts Roadblocks for Webvan." *Redherring.com,* 11 November 1999. Available from http://www.redherring.com.

Bubny, Paul. "Not Yet Clicking." *Supermarket Business,* 15 July 2000.

Davey, Tom, and Sarah Lai Stirland. "Online Grocers: A Chicken in Every Tote?" *Redherring.com,* 17 March 2000. Available from http://www.redherring.com.

Dodge, John. "Harried Shoppers Are Ready to Buy Groceries on the Web." *Wall Street Journal,* 21 September 1999.

"Food." *Business Week,* 10 January 2000.

"Food Fight." *Chain Store Age Executive,* November 1999.

Guglielmo, Connie. "Web Grocer Weathers Storm." *Upside Today,* 11 July 2000.

Lindsay, Greg. "Will the Net Really Bring Home the Bacon?" *Fortune,* 22 November 1999.

Macht, Joshua. "Errand Boy." *Inc.,* November 1996.

Sandoval, Greg. "Pink Dot Takes Grocery Web Site National." *CNET News,* 10 March 2000. Available from http://www.cnet.com.

Satran, Dick. "NetTrends: A Scare for Online Grocers." *Reuters,* 22 March 2000.

Shao, Maria. "Shaw's Discontinues Electronic Grocery Shopping Service." *Boston Globe,* 26 November 1996.

Spurgeon, Bill, and Jim Carlton. "Peapod Weighs Sale, Options after Two Large Setbacks." *Wall Street Journal,* 17 March 2000.

Stoughton, Stephanie. "Hoping to Bag Busy Shoppers." *Washington Post,* 12 October 1999.

Wellman, David. "Are We On?" *Supermarket Business,* 15 December 1999.

E-Commerce: Online Music and Film Distribution

Online music distribution was ready to rock the entire music industry in 2000, ushering in the new millennium with a flurry of Internet music sales, as well as a great deal of controversy. Artists, retailers, and labels all came to embrace the industry as a welcome addition to the distribution market or, at least, as an unavoidable reality that was here to stay.

After years spent dragging their feet and resisting the new technology, major record labels quickly turned around by early 2000 and sought to play in tune with the exploding electronic commerce (e-commerce) market. These moves were perfectly timed to meet the avalanche of new high-speed Internet transmission technologies, including digital subscriber lines and cable modems, which were expected to achieve widespread popularity in the early 2000s.

Moreover, the rush to get online became an important defensive strategy for the music industry. Since music piracy using the popular MP3 digital format was so widespread, often flooding servers on college campuses, the major players had little choice but to get on board and outmuscle the pirates. (MP3 is a file format for storing audio files on a computer.) The new distribution market's faithful viewed this as an enormous opportunity for these companies, whose catalogs could skyrocket in value. Another maverick force in online music was Napster. An Internet application that allows users to swap music with other users over the Web free of charge, Napster was the scourge of music industry executives through the summer of 2000. Lawsuits were filed in which record companies likened the activity to theft, and Napster's future was uncertain. But whatever the industry's opinion of the

company, Napster was changing the face of online music distribution, forcing the industry to come to terms with the public's taste for downloadable music.

Due to the still-convoluted nature of the online music industry, precise figures were difficult to come by. For instance, two of the most prominent e-commerce research firms, Jupiter Communications and Forrester Research, offered extremely varied estimates of the industry's sales to date and projections for the future. According to Jupiter Communications, online music sales totaled $327 million in 1999 and were expected to jump to $586 million in 2000, which would amount to an estimated 3.8 percent of all music sales. Forrester Research, meanwhile, pegged the industry in 1999 at $848 million, and predicted total sales of $1.38 billion in 2000. Andersen Consulting estimated over 1 billion digital music downloads in 1999. Jupiter predicted that the market would reach $2.6 billion by 2003.

While nearly all new Hollywood film releases were accompanied by extensive Web-based promotion in 2000, film distribution remained a small, though rapidly growing, niche market. Concentrated heavily in the animation and experimental, independent short film spectrum, online film distribution faced even more hurdles than did music before it, both in technology and in industry dynamics.

ORGANIZATION AND STRUCTURE

The online music distribution industry includes a varied group of companies. Some, like MP3.com, Inc., offer space for the digital distribution of unknown or established artists. Others, such as CDnow, Inc., are retailing outlets similar to the online bookstore Amazon.com (which is also a major industry player) at which consumers order the physical products through a central online site. Especially by 2000, the major record labels ceased dragging their feet over online distribution and moved to offer both online retailing and digital distribution.

Some sites, moreover, offer "personalized" music packages, which come in a number of varieties. In general, the idea behind customized music is that customers can pick and choose from a catalog of music only those selections that they want, and have the compilation made and sent to them either digitally or as a physical compact disc (CD). CD-customization companies, however, were not given free rein to collage artists as they pleased. Most major artists' contracts, according to *Billboard,* include coupling clauses that grant the artists the final say on their music's appearance on compilations, typified by Ozzy Osbourne's insistence that, "You'll never put me on the same CD with Hanson!"

While one of online distribution's most profound impacts on the music industry was the inauguration of marketing schemes that directly targeted consumers, rather than radio and music-video stations and record stores, some Internet-based music companies offer their distribution or customization services to brick-and-mortar music retailers such as Best Buy, Tower, and Wherehouse.

Like most e-commerce industries, online music distribution carried no sales tax as of early 2000, a fact of great consternation on Capitol Hill and in state legislatures where lost tax revenues threatened to cut into government spending programs. The Advisory Commission on Electronic Commerce, created by Congress to study Internet taxation, issued a proposal in 2000 to temporarily eliminate the sales tax on CDs in order to create tax parity between tangible and digital music media. The proposal, warmly embraced by the music industry, constituted an effort to placate various industry sources as the precise taxation legalities of Internet sales were ironed out. Some analysts, however, insisted that the attempt to reach some kind of compromise on Internet taxation wasn't worth the effort, noting that sales-tax collection for mail-order distribution was barely enforceable, and Internet sales taxes would prove even more difficult to collect.

Though the traditional record industry was coming around to online music, tension was far from alleviated. The Recording Industry Association of America, while not hostile to online distribution itself, vigorously monitored the wide proliferation of digital downloads to try to mitigate the massive black market for online music. The RIAA's efforts culminated in its high-profile lawsuit against Napster in 2000 on behalf of the major record companies.

Film distribution, in general, is a far more complicated affair, since the movie industry's products pass through several layers of distribution, including theater, pay-per-view, video, cable, and so on, creating a complex web of contracts and methods that would require untangling before online distribution could become widely accepted in the mainstream.

BACKGROUND AND DEVELOPMENT

Music was one of the earliest commodities for which the Internet became a popular distribution medium, beginning especially in the mid-1990s. At first, however, the Internet hardly generated enthusi-

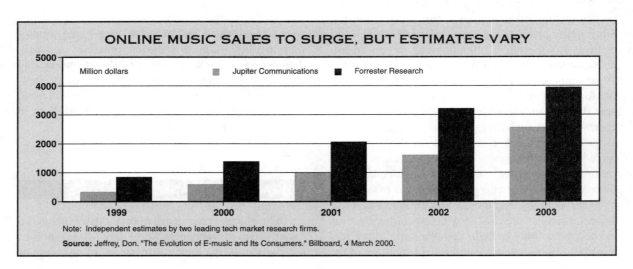

ONLINE MUSIC SALES TO SURGE, BUT ESTIMATES VARY

Note: Independent estimates by two leading tech market research firms.

Source: Jeffrey, Don. "The Evolution of E-music and Its Consumers." Billboard, 4 March 2000.

asm in the music industry. In fact, some of the earliest users of the Internet for music distribution were college students who figured out how to transfer CD-quality recordings to a digital format. Before long, people were sending artists' songs to their friend via e-mail.

Such digital music files, however, were generally so large and slow to transfer that mass distribution was nearly impossible. Not until compressed music formats, such as MP3, came along did digital music distribution become a viable activity, not to mention a burgeoning new industry. Quickly, sites popped up all over the Internet at which folks could download the latest releases by major music artists for free or for a cut-rate pirate fee, and "MP3" quickly became the most popular term for Internet searches.

Aside from piracy, one of the more positive uses of MP3 technology was by fledgling artists trying to get their music heard by promoting themselves on the Web. In this way, they hoped to generate an audience base that they could then use for leverage in trying to attract a label. MP3.com, the creator of the MP3 format, launched its Web site for this purpose, allowing artists to upload their songs for general distribution, while MP3.com kept half of the revenues for downloads.

Historically, the music industry has not earned a reputation as a leading supporter of cutting-edge technology. Prior to the advent of MP3, the common wisdom held that the Internet was of little concern to major record labels. As soon as their catalogs, however, appeared all over the Internet without their permission and without generating any revenues for the companies, they sprang into action, at first crying foul and calling for more stringent antipiracy measures, and then adopting the technology as part of their own marketing strategies.

CURRENT CONDITIONS

Music

Major labels, realizing that the Internet was an integral fact of music distribution, finally emerged from their shells. By 2000, nearly all the majors were engaged in some respect in online music distribution, and several planned to begin direct digital distribution. Ever wary of piracy of their copyrighted music, the majors simply decided to beat pirates to the punch. While the devices to ensure security were only beginning to hit the market, companies such as Sony and BMG Entertainment planned to offer digital music that was compatible with antipiracy safeguards.

One of the most obvious signs that the music industry planned to fully embrace online music distribution was the megamerger between America Online and Time Warner Inc., in 2000. Even in this deal, however, the tension between traditional and online distribution was rather apparent. In spring 2000, America Online placed downloadable software on its Web site that was ideal for music piracy, a move that got the Time Warner brass up in arms, causing AOL to then quickly remove the software. AOL also hoped to develop a subscription-based distribution system whereby consumers are granted access to entire catalogs for a flat monthly fee, which Warner feared would lead to diminished CD sales.

At any rate, with the major labels now in full online-distribution mode, established e-music sites were likely to depend for their survival on their ability to shore up their content and promote heavy traffic in an attempt to attract a major-label acquisition. Consolidation began to heat up in 2000, and several small distributors were swallowed by their larger counterparts. Some major sites, however, found it particularly difficult to find a suitor. Retail leader CDnow's proposed deal with Columbia House collapsed in early 2000, and the company's falling stock valuation made other potential investors nervous.

A series of lawsuits further sapped the industry's earlier luster. MP3.com and the music-trading Web site Napster were both slapped with copyright-infringement lawsuits by the record industry in early 2000. MP3.com was found guilty of copyright infringement and ordered to pay Universal Music Group $120 million in damages. The outcome of the Napster case was uncertain in November 2000, but Napster's 21.3 million users still enjoyed free music downloads, and the practice was so popular—between 12 million and 30 million songs downloaded a day—that the industry was considering ways to capitalize on it. In a surprise move, Bertelsmann A.G. even went so far in October 2000 as to announce its intention to partner with Napster to create a subscription-based Napster version. The deal included Bertelsmann's entire catalogue and measures to ensure premium quality sound, as opposed to the uncertain quality risked by Napster users. Bertelsmann promised to withdraw from the lawsuit once Napster developed the technology to get the system running, and invited the other major record labels to join it in creating such a service with Napster.

Online music retailers were also wary of the chilling effect of a sudden consumer or record-company panic related to security, particularly in light of a handful of high-profile computer hackings in 2000. Theft of credit-card numbers was a threat to all sectors of e-commerce, and thus a central concern for online music distributors was the development of adequate encryption technology and other security measures so as to stave off an erosion of consumer confidence.

Musical artists played a prominent role in promoting the Web as a viable music distribution source. While much of the original emphasis of online music was on generating interest in one's new garage band, by 2000 major label artists were taking the lead in offering creative ways to get their music to people online. The Beastie Boys, for instance, offered a custom two-CD promotion package in early 2000 whereby fans could compile up to 40 songs from a catalog of 150 tracks for about $18. The offer was fantastically successful, generating sales of 20,000 units in a two-month promotion, the largest of its kind to date. Other artists, such as David Bowie, Todd Rundgren, and Tori Amos, released download versions of songs or albums before their official real-world release.

Downloads constituted only a small portion of total online music sales in 1999, as relatively few record companies actually prepared their catalogs for digital distribution. Only about $300,000 in sales was attributed to direct downloads by Jupiter Communications that year. But record companies were quickly moving to digitize their artists' music in order to catch up with retailers' willingness to sell in this medium, and as a result downloads were expected to move out of their tiny niche and into the mainstream of music distribution. Jupiter Communications expected download sales of $3.1 million in 2000, followed by a leap to $16.5 million in 2001. Just two years later, Jupiter maintained, downloads alone could account for nearly 6 percent of online sales. Forrester, again, was more optimistic for the industry, estimating downloads of $1 million in 1999 and predicting an increase to $789 million, or 20 percent of the online music market, by 2003.

FILM

One of the major challenges to the online film distribution industry was to create added value that distinguishes the medium from and offers advantages over the burgeoning cable-based video-on-demand services. Imperfect transmission technologies, the still-large number of slow Internet connections, and the sheer size and popularity of traditional and emerging real-world film media will likely keep the industry's growth in check for the time being.

Moreover, since the movie industry is characterized by different copyright holders for different regional markets, ownership and distribution rights as pertain to the Internet were far from clarified, further stalling the industry's acceptance of online distribution.

Still, in much the way that online distribution allowed independent musicians a forum to have their music heard outside the confines of the massive music industry, online film distribution, with fast-improving technologies, gave independent film producers an entry into a market where they could acquire an audience on a budget (and with a level of artistic concessions) that doesn't even begin to compare with those working within the mainstream film industry.

Also in a replay of music distribution's path, pirate copies of *The Phantom Menace, Eyes Wide Shut,* and *The Blair Witch Project* cropped up all over the Internet, sending Hollywood into a panic over what the new medium will do to their copyrights. Hollywood nonetheless began to accept online distribution. In April 2000, Disney's Miramax unit struck a deal with SightSound.com Inc. to prepare 12 Miramax films for digital download.

Although the online film distribution market was only beginning to take baby steps in 2000, the industry already featured its own film festivals. The Yahoo! Internet Life Online Film Festival in March of that year showcased the films of such upstart film dot.coms as AtomFilms, SightSound.com, and IFILM.com, and previewed what was hailed as the first film produced specifically for online distribution, *Quantum Project,* starring John Cleese, Stephen Dorff, and Fay Masterson.

INDUSTRY LEADERS

MP3.COM

MP3.com, based in San Diego, specialized in offering downloadable music files for little-known artists, giving them a space to store and promote their own music. Established in 1997, MP3.com insisted that it was not a record label; rather, artists simply filled out forms and uploaded their tracks and artist information. The company's catalog included over 420,000 songs by some 67,000 artists. In 2000, the company generated a wave of industry controversy when it announced the introduction of My.MP3.com, a digital storage locker whereby customers with an account could log on and access music from any Internet connection, relieving them of lugging around bulky CD collections. While several sites offered such services, MP3.com's innovation was to save customers the time of uploading their CDs by reproducing CDs themselves to create a vast library of popular music, an activity that many record industry executives insisted amounted to copyright violations. The company lost a high-profile lawsuit in 2000 to Universal Music Group, to which MP3 was to pay $120 million for copyright violations. MP3 maintained a payroll of 800 employees in early 2000, and its 1999 revenues totaled $21.9 million.

CDnow, Inc.

New York-based CDnow was one of the leading online music retailers in the late 1990s, although the firm faced rough seas when the stock market for e-commerce companies soured in early 2000. The company searched frantically for major record labels with which to ally, but its proposed merger with Time Warner and Sony's jointly owned Columbia House fell through in March 2000. Moreover, the company was searching for ways to compete in a market in which downloadable MP3 files were gaining momentum. About 3.5 million customers used CDnow's site to mail order CDs by early 2000. CDnow's purchase of N2K's Music Boulevard moved them away from a simple retail-outlet model and into the provision of content, including music industry news. CDnow's sales reached $147.2 million in 1999, while the company employed over 200 workers. Cdnow's dreams of alliance with the record industry were answered when it was purchased by record-industry giant Bertelsmann in summer 2000.

Emusic.com Inc.

Emusic.com, based in Redwood City, California, offered digital downloads of both single tracks and entire albums, and was the leading distributor of MP3-format music, holding licensing deals with more than 500 independent record labels. The company's library boasted some 60,000 songs for customization. The firm purchased Tunes.com, operator of the Rolling-Stone.com and DownBeat Jazz.com Web sites, in December 1999. Emusic.com's sales reached $6.5 million in 2000, and the company employed 184.

Online Film Companies

A number of online film companies were beginning to establish a major presence by 2000. Atom Corp. was a leading online film distributor, offering short films to consumers and licensing them to other sites. Several major film-based Web sites, including @Home, Reel.com, and Film.com showcased Atom's shorts. Atom's catalog included about 1,000 titles, and its advisory board boasted acclaimed director Spike

Jonze. Atom moved to bolster its broadband capabilities by forming a partnership with Enron Broadband Services. IFILM.com, based in Hollywood, specialized in streaming full-length independent films. IFILM struck alliances with Kodak, Sony Pictures, Vulcan Ventures, and Liberty Digital to secure financing for improved broadband technologies. SightSound.com became the first online film distributor to strike a deal with Hollywood when it agreed to work with Disney to distribute 12 Miramax films online.

AMERICA AND THE WORLD

In both the music and film markets, international online piracy was of great concern to distributors. Since copyright laws and distribution rights often vary considerably between countries, the borderless world of the Internet posed particularly pressing difficulties. In the United States, the Digital Millennium Copyright Act granted the Recording Industry Association of America the authority to track and sue violators of copyright laws. On a global scale, the Secure Digital Music Initiative brought together 120 firms, including record companies and music publishers, to establish an open global standard for online music distribution and security.

But piracy was nevertheless eating into sales. Four members of the International Federation of the Phonographic Industry sued San Francisco-based Web portal MyWeb Inc.com in a Beijing court in 2000 for providing links to Chinese sites that sold pirated music. The suit was settled when MyWeb agreed to remove the links in question from its site, but the proliferation of sites offering pirated music worldwide greatly alarmed the music industry, and seemingly confirmed some of their early skepticism about the online medium.

FURTHER READING

Briody, Dan. "Big Record Labels Tune Into Digital Downloads." *Redherring.com,* 26 July 2000.

Clark, Don, and Martin Peers. "MP3 Chief Rocks and Roils Music." *Wall Street Journal,* 1 March 2000.

Cohen, Warren. "They Want Their MP3." *U.S. News & World Report,* 26 July 1999.

Fitzgerald, Michael. "Napster Sings the Blues." *Redherring.com,* 31 July 1999.

Fitzpatrick, Eileen, and Brian Garrity. "Wall St. Cools toward Web Cos." *Billboard,* 8 April 2000.

Flag, Michael. "Record Firms See Web as Threat to Sales in China." *Wall Street Journal,* 3 April 2000.

Gibeaut, John. "Facing the Music." *ABA Journal,* October 2000.

Gruenwedel, Erik. "Yahoo! Magazine Launches Premier Film Festival." *Brandweek,* 20 March 2000.

Harmon, Amy. "MP3.com Loses Copyright Case." *New York Times,* 7 September 2000.

Jeffrey, Don. "The Evolution of E-music and Its Consumers." *Billboard,* 4 March 2000.

Lardner, James. "The Record Industry Gives Peace a Chance." *U.S. News & World Report,* 20 September 1999.

Meyer, Lisa. "MP3.com Battle Brings Up Universal Issues." *Redherring.com,* 5 September 2000.

Murphy, Kathleen, and Jonathan Hill. "Digital Content Rights." *Internet World,* 1 April 2000.

"Net Music at Center of Latest Tax Debate." *Billboard,* 4 March 2000.

Peers, Martin. "Ex-Web Darling CDnow Hunts for a New Deal." *Wall Street Journal,* 3 April 2000.

————. "Sony Music, BMG Entertainment Plan to Start Selling Digital Music on Web." *Wall Street Journal,* 7 April 2000.

Peers, Martin, and Nick Wingfeld. "Seeking Harmony, AOL and Warner Music Hit Some Dissonant Notes." *Wall Street Journal,* 18 April 2000.

Schmuckler, Eric. "The Beat Goes On." *MediaWeek,* 18 October 1999.

Tice, Carol. "Movies on the Internet." *Puget Sound Business Journal,* 30 April 1999.

Traiman, Steve. "D-I-Y CDs: Online Sites Allow Customers to Compile Highly Personal Collections." *Billboard,* 8 January 2000.

Walker, Rob. "Between a Rock and a Hard Drive." *New York Times Magazine,* 23 April 2000.

E-Commerce: Online Travel Services

Spurred by consumer demand for convenience and value, the online travel services industry erupted into a multibillion dollar industry by 2000 after its inception in the mid-1990s. By 2000 online travel services garnered an estimated $6.5 billion in revenues—one of the leading categories of Internet commerce. According to *Mediaweek,* sales are predicted to reach $9 billion by 2002, but other industry monitors foresee even more exponential growth. While airline ticket sales accounted for 58 percent of the industry's revenues in 2000, up from 53 percent the year before, online hotel and car rental reservations are expected to represent a more substantial share of the industry's sales in the early 2000s.

Because online travel services represent a large share of overall electronic commerce (e-commerce), numerous Web sites offer these services in an attempt to cash in on the demand. Although a mid-2000 count placed the number at over 1,000, industry observers expect the number to decrease substantially to about 200 by the middle of the decade. Consequently, analysts anticipate a flurry of mergers and acquisitions as well as closings during the first half of the decade.

While many consumers use the Internet to gather travel information, a much smaller portion actually books flights or makes reservations online, due largely to continued concern about online security. In addition, many consumers prefer conducting business with people, instead of with machines, and others simply find online travel services too time consuming or confusing. Despite these sentiments, surveys demonstrate that most users of online travel services are satisfied and the number of converts from Internet lookers to Internet books continues to increase rapidly.

ORGANIZATION AND STRUCTURE

The online travel service industry, as used herein, refers to business transactions: that is, actually placing a reservation online and tendering payment for the service online. Therefore, simply using online travel services and Web sites for research and information is not included. The industry is made up of a melange of companies: traditional and upstart travel agencies, individual travel companies, and automated third-party booking sites. Traditional travel agencies such as AAA and Liberty Travel and their upstart online counterparts comprise companies that offer full travel services online, which may involve actual travel agents and hence commissions. Such online travel services emphasize convenience but necessarily lowest possible prices.

Individual travel company sites comprise individual hotel, car rental, and airline sites where customers can make reservations. Finally, automated third-party online travel services such as Travelocity and Expedia enable users to browse the offerings of many hotels, car rental agencies, and airlines. These services proved popular, accounting for significant shares of the industry's revenues.

Furthermore, Web portals such as Yahoo, Infoseek, and Lycos as well as Internet service providers such as America Online and CompuServe also offer online travel services. In addition, other types of Web sites indirectly drive the industry while not offering commercial services themselves over the Internet. For instance, tourism council Web pages, City.Net, World Travel Guide, and online travel magazines all help promote online travel services whether directly or indirectly.

Online travel transactions are often processed automatically by computers, which alleviates the need for travel agents and helps cut travel costs. Even though some online services still have travel agents, their commissions are less because their costs of business is less and because they can handle larger volumes of transactions.

Because of their automated structure, many online travel services do not require human agents for transactions, which helps reduce the price of travel arrangements made over the Internet. For example, while customers using traditional travel services may pay commissions as much as $50 per airfare ticket, those using online travel services pay a maximum of $10 per ticket, according to Tom Parsons, editor of Best Fares, a magazine that monitors the travel industry. Besides not having to pay commissions, airlines do not have to pay fees for computer reservation systems such as those provided by Sabre Inc., Galileo, Amadeus, and Apollo, which helps keep online travel service prices low. Online travel services also make it easy for users to comparison shop and find the best travel deals.

Services and amenities offered online vary depending on the market targeted. Most online travel services require users to register or fill out a user profile page. However, some sites have streamlined the process allowing users to research various travel arrangements and requiring registration only when booking. Some sites such as Biztravel.com will calculate flight mileage, keep track of frequent flyer miles, and negotiate discounts with hotels and airlines.

According to the Travel Industry Association of America, 92 percent of online travel service customers are between 18 and 55 years old. The majority (48 percent) of the customers are between 35 and 54 years old and 42 percent are between 18 and 34 years old. Better Homes and Gardens reported that 11 percent of family vacationers made reservations via Internet travel services.

BACKGROUND AND DEVELOPMENT

Online travel services grew out of telephone-based travel services and the development of the In-

ternet. The basic technology for online reservations and bookings existed at least since the early 1990s when a graphic browser was developed for the computer network known as the Internet. The graphic browser helped transform the Internet from a relatively obscure academic network to a commercial network, from a network of text only to a network of text and graphics. However, the industry faced an initial challenge because technology was not available to protect confidential user information such as credit card numbers. Therefore, while travel-related companies such as hotels and airlines set up Web sites during this period, they did not enable users to make reservations online.

At this point, the Internet served largely as an interactive brochure, which allowed users to view images and glean information such as price, availability, special offers, and so on. However, if users wanted to book a hotel room, a flight, or a rental car, they had to call a special number or a travel agent.

The lack of security not only kept consumers from using the Internet for making travel arrangements, but also businesses from even offering complete travel services online, since consumers are liable only for the first $50 charged to their accounts under federal law. Moreover, credit card companies frequently waive this amount if consumers notify them promptly of purloined credit card numbers.

Nevertheless, breakthroughs in online security technology began to occur in 1995 when Netscape Communications introduced its encryption technology, which scrambled confidential information such as credit card and social security numbers and which could be decoded only by the appropriate people. Major industry players such as Microsoft, IBM, Master-Card, and Visa quickly endorsed this technology, paving the way for its full-scale adoption and implementation.

As encryption technology improved and other online security measures increased, more consumers turned to Internet travel options for reservations and bookings. As a result, by the end of 1995, an estimated 5 percent of Americans made their reservations online, up from 3 percent in 1993. Nonetheless, this represented a small fraction of a wary market where 56 percent of the adult population was actually familiar with online travel services.

Despite the initial hesitant demand, online travel services constituted a significant segment of Internet commerce. In 1996 online travel transactions totaled $274 million—the number two electronic commerce category, trailing only computer hardware and software, according to Jupiter Communications. Sites such as Expedia and Travelocity tapped into consumer interest in convenience and savings, enabling them to research numerous fares and rates and select the best options to meet their needs. Nevertheless, consumers remained concerned about security, creating what the industry refers as "look, but not book" syndrome where many people—over 85 million—browse Internet for travel information, but most use other means for booking and tendering payment.

CURRENT CONDITIONS

In general, travel is big business in the United States, generating over $85 billion in revenues from global inbound travel and over $20 billion from business travel and constituting the country's third largest industry, according to *Business America*. Overall, the Travel Industry Association of America believes travel sales come to about $500 billion annually. Not surprisingly, therefore, the online travel services industry accounts for a substantial portion of electronic commerce revenues. According to a survey by PhoCusWright.com, 45 percent of online consumers patronize online travel services—second only to online book sales. While most other service industries have struggled to harvest sales through the Internet, the online travel services industry performed well after allaying business and consumer security concerns in the mid-1990s.

In 2000 the industry's sales reached an estimated $6.5 billion and were forecasted to climb to $9 billion by 2002, according to *Mediaweek*. Forrester Research expects even more spectacular growth, placing online travel service revenues at $29 billion for 2003. Of the 1999 total, online air reservations represented 77 percent and hotel bookings accounted for 16 percent, according to Jupiter Communications. Online car rental reservations accounted for the remaining 7 percent. The Travel Industry Association of America predicts that the share of revenues generated by hotel and car rental reservations will continue to surge, reaching a combined $2.4 billion by 2002.

Nevertheless, the industry still has enormous room for growth in that surveys report that under 10 percent of the population patronizes online travel services. However, Forrester Research predicted that 25 percent of U.S. households will make travel arrangement online by 2003. Other industry observers are more optimistic: Michael Shapiro, author of Net Travel, predicted 50 percent travel sales would take place via the Internet in 2000. Online user trends of the late 1990s support the optimism. According to *Computerworld*, traffic at online travel service sites rose by 175 percent between 1998 and 1999.

Use of online travel services for obtaining bargain rates continued to be a driving force behind the industry in the early 2000s. For instance, low-cost air carrier easyJet reported that 61 percent of its bookings came through the Internet and expected this number to reach 75 percent quickly. Furthermore, several online travel services specialize in bargain fares such as Lowestfare.com, Cheap Tickets, Inc., and Priceline.com. Moreover, major airlines such as Continental and British Airways predict comparable Web-based bookings. Continental anticipates 40 percent of its bookings to come through the Internet and British Airways foresees 50 percent of its bookings coming through its Web site by 2002. In pursuit of this goal, British Airways acquired a minority of Biztravel.com in 1999.

Besides bargain travel, business travel has been a key catalyst of the industry. A plethora of Web sites cater exclusively to business travelers and the more than $20 billion they spend annually. These sites include Biztravel.com, Sabre's Business Travel Solutions, and American Express Corporate Travel Online. In 2000 about 57 percent of all businesses made travel reservations through the Internet, but Forrester Research expects more than 77 percent to use online travel services later in the decade. According to Forrester Research, large corporations will lead the way and 70 percent of Fortune 1000 companies will rely on online travel services by 2002. As a result of this segment's high demand and overall competition in the industry, more online travel services are concentrating on this niche. In early 2000, Sabre announced it would offer a new online travel service in conjunction with Sequoia Software Corp. targeting employees of small and medium companies.

Due to the popularity of automated third-party online travel services such as Expedia and Travelocity, five leading airlines—United, Delta, American, Continental, and Northwest—pooled their efforts and launched such an operation of their own in early 2000. This company—dubbed T2—received significant regulatory scrutiny from the outset by the U.S. Department of Justice because of previous instances of anticompetitive conduct in the airline industry by major carriers. The airlines planned to sell discounted last-minute tickets through this site that would not be available elsewhere. Other online travel service providers such as Travelocity objected that not making these tickets available elsewhere would create a de facto monopoly for the five majors.

Furthermore, many e-travel sites sprouted in the late 1990s and early 2000s, because of the success of online travel services. eWeek reported in 2000 that over 1,000 online travel services vied for a share of the industry's revenues. Nevertheless, industry observers forecast wide-scale consolidation and exiting. Bear, Stearns & Co., for example, sees the number of online travel sites dropping to about 200 by 2005. Nevertheless, industry heavyweights such as Travelocity, Expedia, and Priceline.com are predicted to withstand the shakeout, according to *eWeek*.

As industry analysts expected, the online travel services industry saw a number of mergers, acquisitions, and spinoffs in the late 1990s and the early 2000s. The most notable merger was that between two industry leaders, Travelocity and Preview Travel, forming Travelocity.com, Inc., the industry's leading company. In addition, after creating one of the industry's leading online travel reservation sites, Microsoft announced it would spin off its Expedia in 1999. Selling a minority share of the company in a 1999 initial public offering, Microsoft retained control of 85 percent of the company's shares.

To cope with the glut of online travel services, some companies have turned to specialization, targeting niche markets. For example, Bedandbreakfast.com empowers users interested only in bed-and-breakfast lodging to bypass navigating through sites designed for other kinds of travel services. Instead, consumers can access information on bed and breakfasts directly.

Even with robust sales, online travel services still received criticism from industry researchers and analysts. Quidnunc North America Ltd., for instance, found that some online services simply put existing reservation systems on the Internet or use existing Web sites for e-commerce, instead of constructing reservations systems and Web sites designed to aid consumers and to foster online transactions. According to this analyst, online travel services should determine what users seek from their sites and build sites that will facilitate users in obtaining what they want.

Other complaints about online travel services tend to relate to the amount of time it takes to research travel options and finally make reservations. Activities such as registering, checking alternative arrangements, and comparing prices may take a while depending on the tools available on an online travel service Web site. In addition, some online travel services will initially show users only the companies that paid a premium on the first display page. To obtain lower rates, users must select options such to obtain more results. Such sites have the potential to deceive consumers and to slow down online travel research and booking. Nevertheless, customers of online travel services seem pleased with their experiences overall. According to PhoCusWright.com, 88 percent of the users surveyed indicated they were "satisfied" or "very satisfied" with online travel services.

Finally, the growth of online travel services has been blamed for the decline of traditional travel agencies. The American Society of Travel Agencies reported that in the first half of 1999 nearly 2,000 travel agencies closed their door because of flagging revenues. Furthermore, Bear, Stearns & Co. expects 25 percent of the smaller travel agencies to exit the business by 2002.

INDUSTRY LEADERS

Travelocity (Travocity.com, Inc.) was the most popular online travel service sites in that late 1990s and early 2000s. Founded by Sabre Inc., a company that developed ticket and reservation databases for the airline industry, Travelocity was ranked as the 138th largest travel agency in 1998 based on revenue, but by 1999 Travelocity cracked the top ten with sales of $90.9 million. Travelocity reached the apex of the industry with its 2000 acquisition of another major online travel service provider Preview Travel. Sabre still owned 70 percent of Travelocity after the merger.

Expedia, Inc. ranked among the top online travel services in 2000. Formed in 1994 by software behemoth Microsoft, the company began processing online transactions in 1996. By late 1999, almost 900,000 customers had used the company's Web site, making about $700 million worth of travel reservations, according to *Knight-Ridder/Tribune Business News*. In addition to offering online reservations and ticket sales, Expedia enables users to share information and travel experiences with its chat rooms and obtain maps. Microsoft spun off the company in 1999, while retaining a majority interest. The following year, Expedia posted sales of $134.9 million, an increase of nearly 250 percent over 1999, and posted a net loss of $118.3 million.

Cheap Tickets, Inc. purchases non-published fares from airlines and sells them at a discount through its Web site and by phone. Founded in 1986, Cheap Tickets has contracts with over 35 airlines around the world as well as with hotels, car rental agencies, and cruise lines. In 1999, the company's sales rose to $339.6 million.

Another dot-com, Lowestfare.com, Inc., also ranked among the leading online travel services. Through its Web site and its toll free number, the company markets discounted travel tickets, especially Trans World Airlines (TWA) tickets. Furthermore, Lowestfare has contracts with almost 400 air carriers, hotels, car rental agencies, and cruise lines. Moreover, Lowestfare acquired two tour operations: Jetset Tours and Maupintour. In 1999, the company had estimated sales of $300 million.

While not exclusively an online travel service, Priceline.com Inc. plays a major part in the industry. Priceline.com's approach allows users to bid on travel-related services, among other things, by selecting the maximum price they are willing to pay and attempting to find a match. The dot-com's travel selection includes airline tickets, hotel rooms, and rental cars. In 1999 the company brought in $482 million in revenues.

AMERICA AND THE WORLD

While online travel services are booming in the United States, they have been slower to catch on in other countries in part for many of the reasons that caused concern among U.S. businesses and consumers. For example, although 20 percent of the world's air travelers researched flights on the Internet in the late 1990s, only 1 percent actually booked flights. The timid demand has been attributed to reluctance to divulge credit card numbers over the Internet and preference for dealing with human travel agents.

Behind the United States, Europe constitutes the second largest market for online travel services. Europe's leading online travel service is Ebookers.com, the European counterpart to Travelocity.com and Expedia. In 2000 Ebookers operated in 10 European countries—the United Kingdom, France, Norway, Sweden, Finland, Ireland, Denmark, Germany, Switzerland, and the Netherlands—with plans to add two more, Spain and Italy. Ebookers secured its dominance over other European companies and over its U.S. rivals Travelocity and Expedia with an agreement to collaborate with America Online, the world's leading Internet service provider. In addition, Ebookers negotiated discount fares with 100 airlines. After a marketing blitz in 1999, Ebookers' users shot up from about 700,000 to 1.5 million. U.S. online travel ser-

vices attempted to establish a presence in the European market. However, by the end of 2000 Expedia was present only in the United Kingdom and Germany, and Travelocity only in the United Kingdom. Nevertheless, both companies planned to expand into other countries, including Sweden, Denmark, and France.

According to Denmark's Research Center of Bornholm, the European market for online travel services totaled $800 million in 1999 and is predicted to rise to $2 billion in 2000. The United Kingdom and Germany accounted for the majority of this business, representing 28 percent and 27 percent, respectively. Nevertheless, the industry's 1999 sales accounted for less than 1 percent of Europe's total travel sales.

Despite the wary consumers, travel-related companies around the world have adopted U.S. style tactics to market their services over the Internet and have developed their own techniques to appeal the demands of their specific markets. Air Canada, for instance, offers online ticket auctions. In addition, several Asian airlines have eliminated paper tickets and provide confirmation slips only on request in an effort to promote online ticket sales. Furthermore, Qantas and Lufthansa introduced smart cards to store flight reservations and frequent flyer miles.

Latin America also saw increasing demand for online travel services. The major computer reservation services—Sabre, Galileo, and Amadeus—have established a strong presence in Latin America. As a result, these companies are well positioned to provide and promote online travel services.

African firms also have begun to provide travel services online. Throughout the continent, tour companies—and even governments—have set up Web sites to enable users to book tours to national parks, casinos, and safaris. According to *African Business,* offering their services online frees companies from dependence on travel agents in other countries. Instead, the Internet allows African tour companies to court customers directly.

RESEARCH AND TECHNOLOGY

According to research by the Travel Industry Association of America, the leading reasons why consumers opt not to purchase travel services online are concern for security, preference for dealing with another person, the need for confirmation, lack of knowledge of computers and the Internet, and indefinite travel plans. Consequently, these represent some of the areas online travel services need to explore to continue to convert more people who seek travel information online to those who purchase travel services online. Addressing these issues involves enhancing online security and educating the public of it, making online travel service interfaces more user-friendly, and providing reassurance to concerned users and novice users.

FURTHER READING

Blank, Christine. "The Writing on the Wall." *Hotel & Restaurant Management,* 5 June 2000.

"Bookings by Computer." *Travel Weekly,* 27 November 1995.

Brady, Shirley. "Airlines Fight It Out on the World Wide Web." *Time International,* 22 March 1999.

Brown, Ann. "Is Booking over the Web Worth the Trip?" *Black Enterprise,* August 1999.

"Can the Internet's High-Flyer Remain Ahead of the Pack?" *New Media Age,* 11 May 2000.

Cohen, Sacha. "On the Modem Again." *Training & Development,* August 1998.

"eFiles." *eWeek,* 8 May 2000.

Flint, Perry. "Web of Ambivalence." *Air Transport World,* April 1998.

Harbaugh, Linda. "Travel and Tourism Hangs Ten on the Electronic Wave." *Business America,* January 1998.

Kong, Deborah. "Microsoft Will Spin Off Online Travel Service." *Knight-Ridder/Tribune Business News,* 24 September 1999.

Muellner, Alexis. "Online Offerings Change the Complexion of Travel Selling." *South Florida Business Journal,* 19 November 1999.

Mullins, Robert. "Competition Grows in Travel Agents v. Web." *The Business Journal-Milwaukee,* 10 September 1999.

Mulrine, Anna. "Window to the World." *U.S. News & World Report,* 4 December 2000.

Travel Industry Association of America. "Fast Facts: Travel and the Internet." Available from http://www.ita.org.

Vesely, Milan. "E-commerce Bonanza for African Firms." *African Business,* October 1999.

Warner, Bernhard. "Prepare for Takeoff: Airlines Ponder a Nation of Amateur Travel Agents." *Mediaweek,* 19 January 1998.

"Web Air Bookings To Rise in 2000." *TravelAge West,* 16 October.

"Why This New E-Biz Is Raising Trustbusters' Hackles." *Business Week,* 19 June 2000.

pen within seconds. When no match is waiting, the order remains on the system's list, often called a notebook or an order book, and in the case of Nasdaq shares, is sent for listing on the Nasdaq Level II quotation system. There anyone inside or outside the ECN can fill the open order.

Until recently most ECNs have been closed systems, meaning that only users of the same service are matched in the system's notebook. Archipelago has led the charge toward open systems. Given that market liquidity—access to buyers or sellers when you need it—is paramount to most traders, the trend toward open systems is likely to accelerate.

Setting up a basic ECN is relatively inexpensive, as far as capital expenses go. According to one estimate, a firm can build for less than $10 million a credible system that can support 15 transactions a second. It's not quite pocket change, but the fairly low entry barriers (others being mostly regulatory) have led numerous companies to seek a piece of the action. Although there were only a dozen functioning ECNs in 2000, several more were in the works and as many as 140 companies had approached the SEC about establishing an ECN.

UNMAKING THE MARKET MAKERS

ECNs are most similar to market makers and dealers on Nasdaq. These are brokerages, investment banks, and related firms that compete with each other to fill open orders at terms favorable both to themselves and the party that placed the order. (Whose interests come first is a matter for debate.) Market makers may keep an inventory of some companies' shares and engage in both buying and selling as the situation dictates. In effect, traders buy from or sell to market makers, who fill orders and provide liquidity to the market. Sometimes market makers have a particular interest in a company's shares, such as when they've underwritten the company's public offering, and because of their size they are able to manipulate a stock's price. Any market maker, however, can deal in any stock on Nasdaq, and on average there are 11 market makers per Nasdaq issue.

The premise behind an ECN is that in a large, reliable electronic environment buyers and sellers can find each other just fine without any go-between. If market makers function as wholesalers and retailers to the securities business, ECNs are akin to a trader cooperative, or perhaps a simpler brokering system in which buyers and sellers are brought together.

In order to compete with market makers, ECNs tend to make trading cheaper with the hope that heavy volume will keep them afloat. Whereas market makers, like retailers, usually skim a profit from the difference between what they pay for shares and what they sell them for, ECNs levy on every trade a very small surcharge, much as an exchange would. ECN commissions may run less than a hundredth of a cent to a few cents per share. Even so, some ECN fees have drawn criticism from SEC chairman Arthur Levitt, among others.

Nasdaq fought back with SuperMontage, a quote aggregation and execution system designed to draw market makers by displaying the top three quotes for best bid and ask price on a trading system. This would effectively match orders in the manner of an ECN, but with vastly greater liquidity. ECNs, of course, fiercely resisted this effort. They were aided in Congress by House Commerce Committee Chairman Tom Bliley (R., Va.), who sent a letter to Levitt expressing extreme concern over SuperMontage and the potentially unfair advantages it would afford Nasdaq.

NYSE COULD BE NICER

The comparison is similar with the New York Stock Exchange (NYSE), which has about twice the market capitalization of Nasdaq. On the NYSE each company's shares are delegated to a so-called specialist, a firm that exercises in effect a monopoly on making a market for a given issue. As a result, these firms tend to reap even richer profits when they deal. In heavy trading, though, it's possible for orders to be matched on the NYSE without bringing in a specialist; this kind of trading is executed at very favorable terms that ECNs would have trouble meeting.

For a long time, few ECNs needed to worry about meeting costs on the NYSE because they've been excluded from trading its shares. The NYSE's onerous Rule 390 forbade trading of shares that had been listed on the NYSE since before 1979. That made up about 30 percent of NYSE's shares, but half of its trading volume, including the IBMs and AT&Ts of the world. ECNs were thus restricted from trading many of the largest, most demanded stocks listed on that exchange. Rule 390, under heavy pressure from the SEC, was repealed in 2000, much to the delight of the ECN industry.

BACKGROUND AND DEVELOPMENT

ECNs trace their modern form to 1996, when the SEC meted out new order-handling regulations in the wake of a Nasdaq price-fixing scandal. In the mid-

1990s and earlier, Nasdaq market makers allegedly conspired to pad their pockets by not filling orders that weren't particularly profitable to them or by filling orders at less-than-optimal prices to the customer. All of this was fairly easy to pull off because market makers weren't required to publicize every order they received.

In its new Order Handling Rules, which took effect in 1997, the SEC forced market makers to publish all their orders to the Nasdaq or an ECN that would in turn post orders to the Nasdaq Level II bulletin board, an electronic queue of orders waiting for takers. This new order transparency, along with a weighty $1 billion civil settlement by the market makers, was intended to ensure fairer trading and better order executions for investors.

At the time, Instinet Corp., a unit of global news and financial data titan Reuters Group PLC, was about the only ECN around. Founded in 1969, Instinet was something of a private trading club for institutional investors, letting them trade after market hours and offering various other features. But part of the SEC ruling mandated that ECNs also post their orders to Nasdaq Level II, bringing Instinet's activities out in the open.

The order-handling rules created an easy opening for other ECNs to jump through: they were effectively guaranteed to be listed on Nasdaq. Provided that they could attract a loyal following of users to post orders on their systems, new ECNs could readily divert business away from traditional market makers and other intermediaries.

They wasted little time. Island and Bloomberg's TradeBook (later renamed B-Trade and merged with a service called Posit) set up shop in 1996, followed by Archipelago and RediBook ECN the next year. Companies such as Island, majority-owned by online brokerage Datek Online Holdings Corp., had roots in the day-trading business, which was resurgent around the same time and provided a natural user base for ECNs. By 1999 those four firms plus Instinet dominated the ECN turf, with an assortment of other players scrambling for their own niches.

CURRENT CONDITIONS

By 2000 ECNs were churning about a third of all Nasdaq share volume, and an even greater proportion of its individual trades. The higher number of trades indicates that the average ECN trade is still smaller

than the hefty institutional transactions that still rely on other channels. Still, for hotly traded stocks, such as those of Internet companies, the ECNs' share was even greater. Although estimates of ECN market share vary, the volume of shares trafficked through ECNs grew easily by 50 percent in less than a year.

Despite occasional insults lobbed by partisans of ECNs and traditional market players, the ECN business is heavily funded by mainstream Wall Street concerns. Archipelago, an innovative ECN, receives backing from Merrill Lynch, Goldman Sachs, and J.P. Morgan, among others. Spear, Leeds & Kellogg, majority owner of RediBook ECN, is an old-school NYSE market specialist. Several big-name brokerages, including Merrill Lynch and Morgan Stanley Dean Witter, have hedged their bets by investing in more than one ECN. All told, brokerages and investment houses may have poured into ECNs upwards of $200 million. Because the ECN model threatens comfy brokerage margins, though, cynics suggested that some long-time players would just as soon lose their investments.

Even as new ECNs were in the works, industry analysts predicted in 2000 that the increasingly crowded ECN field would soon be ripe for consolidation. Some of that has begun already. In late 1999 Bloomberg announced plans to merge its B-Trade system with Posit, a minor ECN for institutional investors, to create a "SuperECN." Soon after, BRUT and Strike, a pair of ECNs funded by a cadre of Wall Street bigwigs, made known their plans to merge. Some observers felt that as few as two ECNs could be left once consolidation sweeps through. In the meantime, however, market conditions are conducive to new entrants, and the number of functioning ECNs was expected to rise in the short term.

Experts also warned that ECNs could face extinction if major markets such as Nasdaq and the NYSE were to revamp their systems, creating a so-called supermontage or centralized system that in essence incorporates the functions of ECNs.

INDUSTRY LEADERS

INSTINET CORP.

The granddaddy of all ECNs, Instinet began operation in 1969, before the Nasdaq market even existed, when the trading system was known as Institutional Networks. While it was perceived as a maverick at points in its history, by the time new ECNs were being conceived amid the SEC's order-handling shake-up in the mid-1990s, Instinet seemed a stodgy near-monopoly. Under control of Reuters Group PLC since 1987, New York-based Instinet continued to serve its core institutional clientele through the late 1990s, gradually adding a number of additional services beyond basic trading. It continued to command the largest market share of any ECN, often double that of its nearest competitor. In 1999 the company decided to pursue a brokerage strategy and made plans to roll out an international retail brand in 2000. With $870 million in 1999 revenues, the service was projected to bring in $1.2 billion by 2003. It's also a minority stakeholder in Archipelago Holdings LLC. At year-end 1999, Instinet controlled an estimated 43.8 percent of the ECN market.

THE ISLAND ECN, INC.

A subsidiary of Datek, Island was the second-largest ECN in fourth-quarter 1999, with 19.5 percent of the market. Island was formed in 1996 and began trading as an ECN in 1997, supported by day-trading traffic through its affiliation with Datek. Just down the street from the NYSE, the company produced innovative software to help day-traders interact with the market and became the poster child for the new breed of ECNs. By 1999 it overtook Instinet in one key metric, number of trades, but the volume of shares traded over Island continued to lag behind. About one out of eight Nasdaq trades flows through Island. Nonetheless, Island has been a feisty innovator, extending its trading hours in 1999 and pressing for access to NYSE shares. Island is also noted for its young founders and management team, nearly all of whom were in their twenties when they joined the company, including the company's outspoken president, Matthew Andresen. The firm's strategy is to begin functioning as a full-fledged exchange, competing on cost with larger players. In 1999 more than 26 billion shares were traded on Island with total value of $1.5 trillion. The company's own take of that action was a bit more modest, estimated at less than $20 million.

ARCHIPELAGO HOLDINGS LLC

Archipelago had lagged behind several ECNs in terms of its share volume, but it one-upped Island's bid to become an exchange by merging with one in 2000. Archipelago agreed to merge with the ailing Pacific Stock Exchange to create a new national electronic exchange. While some viewed it as a dubious combination of two also-rans, Archipelago, whose private investors include Instinet; the online brokerage E*TRADE Group, Inc.; financial channel CNBC; and Wall Street pillars Goldman Sachs and J.P. Morgan,

has potentially a first-mover advantage in the electronic exchange arena, as the merged company is likely to avoid some regulatory hurdles that other ECNs will face. The company has courted both institutional and retail accounts, and was one of the first to adopt an open system. Formed in 1996, Chicago-based Archipelago held an estimated 7.9 percent of the ECN market at the end of 1999.

AMERICA AND THE WORLD

Securities regulations and practices differ markedly around the world, but U.S. ECNs have ties to a variety of international ventures. Europe is expected to be an important battleground for ECNs in the early 2000s, spurred by a boom in online trading mirroring that in the United States of the late 1990s. Instinet has interests in a number of European ECN projects, including Tradepoint, a U.K.-based system. Instinet itself has long been a member of over a dozen exchanges in various parts of the globe, and given its ambitions of becoming a global retail brokerage and moving into bond trading, the service was poised to offer a unique blend of services to world markets. Another European system, Posit, is being merged with U.S.-based B-Trade, operated by financial data supplier Bloomberg LP.

FURTHER READING

Barnett, Megan. "The Exchange Revolution." *Industry Standard,* 16 August 1999.

Barreto, Susan. "Trading Places." *Pensions & Investments,* 6 September 1999.

Birger, Jon. "Bleak Outlook for E-Markets." *Crain's New York Business,* 31 January 2000.

Fugazy, Danielle. "Online Brokerage Firms May Have to Consolidate to Stay Afloat." *Web Finance,* 27 March 2000.

Granfield, Anne. "Archipelago-Pacific Exchange Hopes to Compete with NYSE." *Forbes,* 16 March 2000.

Guerra, Anthony. "Nasdaq Rolls Back the Curtain on SuperMontage." *Wall Street & Technology,* October 2000.

Ip, Greg. "Archipelago Plans New Stock Market to Compete with Existing Bourses." *Wall Street Journal,* 15 March 2000.

———. "Electronic-Trading Firms Generate Buzz, Few Bucks." *Wall Street Journal,* 2 December 1999.

James, Sylvia. "From Trading Floor to ECN." *Information World Review,* June 2000.

Jovin, Ellen. "Fair Trades: Enthusiasts Say ECNs Level the Playing Field for Traders, but Many Others Remain Skeptical." *Financial Planning,* 1 June 2000.

Kosterlitz, Julie. "Market Forces." *National Journal,* 19 February 2000.

Minkoff, Jerry. "Market & Exchanges: ECNs Adapting to Rapidly Changing Environment." *Web Finance,* 28 February 2000.

Morais, Richard C. "Instihot." *Forbes,* 6 March 2000.

Moskowitz, Eric. "Matt Andresen vs. Wall Street." *Money,* July 2000.

"Rethinking Wall Street." *Business Week,* 11 October 1999.

Schack, Justin. "Cost Containment." *Institutional Investor,* November 1999.

Schonfeld, Eric. "Why Island Wants to Be an Exchange." *Fortune,* 15 March 1999.

Springsteel, Ian, and Michelle Celarier. "The ECN Dilemma." *Investment Dealers' Digest,* 6 March 2000.

Vinzant, Carol. "Do We Need a Stock Exchange?" *Fortune,* 22 November 1999.

Electronic Publishing

INDUSTRY SNAPSHOT

Though anathema to some literary purists, the explosive future of electronic publishing seemed etched in stone by 2000. With communication and commerce rapidly shifting to the Internet, publishers of all stripes were increasingly forced to look to this channel as a way of augmenting sales, or risk being left behind. By 2000, all major newspapers and magazines in the United States had an Internet strategy. Already, most of the world's classics, from Shakespeare to Virginia Woolf to James Baldwin, could be retrieved on the World Wide Web. Retail book giants such as Barnes & Noble were forced into the electronic-commerce market to hedge against market encroachment from such upstarts as Amazon.com. And by 2000, the market was poised for a booming new reading medium: the electronic book, or e-book.

Since readers quickly became accustomed to online news and magazines, the e-book was perhaps the most novel new development on the horizon. While only about 3,000 books were available commercially in electronic form, publishers and industry analysts expected the avalanche to ensue over the next several years. One target market that publishers were eyeing heavily as a potential early boon to sales was the high school and college sector. Since this group was already tech-savvy and comfortable reading information in electronic form, industry players hoped they would warmly embrace a searchable, compact, electronic medium that gave them a break from lugging around bags full of heavy books.

While customers feel comfortable purchasing books online, relatively few have delved into reading them in electronic format; only 1 percent of the $12 billion in online book purchases in 1999 was for e-books, according to Forrester Research. In their first year on the market, e-book readers were primarily used for periodicals, self-published works, and company documents. Still, several factors, including the rapid development of technologies, lowered costs, and the consolidation of the two leading manufacturers of e-book readers under the umbrella of Gemstar International Group, poised the e-book sector for strong growth in the early 2000s. By 2005, the e-book and e-periodical market was expected to reach sales topping $1 billion.

Although CD-ROMs remained popular, especially for reference books, they were in fact losing ground as publishers placed their sights on the World Wide Web as a new distribution channel. Still, a strong market was likely to persist for several years, since Internet access remained far from universal in 2000.

ORGANIZATION AND STRUCTURE

Generally, online publishers gain revenue from three sources: ad banners; subscriptions; and pay-per-view. Advertising revenue can be generated in several different ways. For instance, advertisers might pay a fee each time their banner is displayed on the publisher's site. Typically, these ads cost $0.005 for each exposure. In another method, publishers receive a payment—the going rate is five cents—each time one of their site-users clicks on an ad and is taken to the advertiser's Web site. Lastly, the publisher can receive a payment when the user buys an advertised product. This type of arrangement, which is becoming more popular, gives the publisher a percentage of the pur-

A SIZZLING ELECTRONIC SUCCESS STORY

There have always been more novelists than novels. Finding a publisher willing to give him or her a break is probably the most pressing concern of the average prospective writer. Electronic publishing, however, offers a glimmer of hope to self-styled Hemingways and Steels everywhere. The case of Melise Shapiro provides an inspiring example.

Shapiro shopped her erotic thriller, *Lip Service,* to a number of publishers, and was rejected at each turn. With little hope of a contract for the book, Shapiro uploaded her novel to the World Wide Web in 1998 under the pseudonym M. J. Rose. At that point, Shapiro set on the idea of writing a new book, which she would pitch to publishing houses with the ammunition of a demonstrated following from her online story.

But *Lip Service* turned out to be a significant success in its own right. After generating 150 download sales at $9.95 a pop, Shapiro invested in 3,000 print copies. The glowing praise from Amazon.com reader reviews won Shapiro a contract with Pocket Books, thus establishing her as the first electronic author to land a book deal. According to *Time, Lip Service* went on to sell over 40,000 copies, while Shapiro's follow-up, *In Fidelity,* was to be released by Pocket Books.

chase price. Online sellers using these kinds of programs include Amazon.com, Barnes & Noble, and Ticketmaster.

While print publishers routinely charge for their magazines or newspapers, subscription-based publications on the Web are unusual. With only a few publishing exceptions—notably the *Wall Street Journal* and *The Economist*—Web users have shown a reluctance to pay for online content. Publishers have another option to raise revenues in the form of pay-per-view, which requires readers to pay in order to download material. This method is commonly used for online fiction books and article archives, such as those of the *New York Times.* In the case of an archive, users can usually search for free but are charged a fee, running anywhere from 50 cents to several dollars, for each article they view.

BACKGROUND AND DEVELOPMENT

Modern publishing dates back to the 1440s and a German printer named Johannes Gutenberg, who is believed to be the first European to print with hand-set type cast in molds. For the most part, printing technology remained fairly static over the next centuries, but the rise of computers in the 1970s changed that. During the 1980s almost all printing functions—such as creating artwork, setting type, and scanning photographs—became automated. There were several electronic publishing advancements in 1984. That year saw the first computer-based CD-ROM (compact disc-read only memory); the first online magazine featuring short science-fiction and fantasy stories on the BITNET network at the University of Maine; and the appearance of desktop publishing systems that integrated high-quality images and graphics with text. The 1970s and 1980s also gave birth to the Internet—a global communication system composed of thousands of interconnected networks. In 1990 Tim Berners-Lee, working at CERN, a particle physics lab in Geneva, Switzerland, developed the World Wide Web. The accelerated growth of the Web in the 1990s can be attributed, in part, to its use of hypertext, the nonsequential form of writing created by Ted Nelson in 1968.

While much Internet activity has focused on trying to make money, at least one early Internet pioneer saw the value of providing online content at no charge. Project Gutenberg, which was founded in 1971 by Michael Hart of Urbana, Illinois, continues to this day making public-domain books available for free in an electronic format, boasting 2,500 titles by November 2000. Hart's goal is to have 10,000 books online before the end of 2001. The works of authors such as Leo Tolstoy, Rudyard Kipling, and Nathaniel Hawthorne are featured on the site.

Early electronic book publishers used diskette and CD-ROM formats. In 1994 there were five or six publishers, including Chicago-based Spectrum Press, which offered books on 3.5-inch and 5.25-inch floppy disks. Daniel Agin, who owned Spectrum, called these products "e-text" books. Even by 1994, however, disks were being replaced by CD-ROMs, which could hold 300,000 pages of text and had tracks for sound and motion pictures. Because of the vast amount of space available on CD-ROMS, reference publishers, such as Grolier Interactive, adopted the technology.

In 1995 U.S. newspapers were jumping on the Internet bandwagon. That year, 70 daily newspapers (three times as many as in 1994) established an Internet presence. As reported by Steve Alexander in a 12 June 1995 article in the *Minneapolis Star Tribune,* an American Opinion Research study found that 19 percent of newspaper editors and publishers believed that the Internet would be the main competitor for advertising revenue by 2000. Early on, the *San Jose Mercury News,* owned by Knight Ridder, and the *Raleigh News and Observer* were leaders in gaining an online identity. The *Mercury News* made use of on-screen graphics and hyperlinks to related Internet sites to build a national readership. The site received 250,000 to 300,000 hits a day in 1995.

The phenomenal growth of electronic publishing raised questions in the areas of copyright laws and pornography. Legislators, educators, citizens' groups, and Web site owners are grappling to find solutions to these complex issues. The enormity and easy access of the Internet makes its nearly impossible to regulate, much less monitor. Recognizing this fact, the Digital Millennium Copyright Act, passed by Congress in August 1998, provided immunity to Internet service providers, such as America Online, for the copyright infringements of its customers. Even so, the vastness of the Internet has not deterred some from believing that it needs controls. For instance, many people are bothered by the fact that children can readily find pornography on the Internet. The Child Online Protection Act, signed into law by President Bill Clinton in 1997, was designed to combat this problem by requiring commercial Web publishers of certain types of sexually explicit material to verify the age of Web site readers or face a penalty. Many mainstream Web publishers, however, were bothered by this federal law and challenged it in court. The publishers argued that the age-verification procedures would be too difficult and costly to implement, and as a result, many publishers would practice self-censorship—even if their material had not been intended to be prurient—to ensure that they did not break the law.

CURRENT CONDITIONS

As electronic publishing grew in the late 1990s early 2000s, virtually all sectors related to the publishing operations were forced to adapt to rapidly changing market conditions. Newsprint was slated to be the prime casualty of the electronic publishing boom. The online classifieds sector alone grew astronomically—240 percent in 1997 and 118 percent in 1998. By 2003, a full 15 percent of the U.S. classified market was expected to be online, according to the Boston Consulting Group. Online news services will similarly eat into the news printing market, as more and more customers look to the Internet rather than to the printed page to keep up with world developments.

Printed magazines and catalogs were expected to suffer a similar fate, though not to the same extent as newspapers.

After their much-heralded launch in late 1998, e-books enjoyed only lukewarm sales during their first years on the market, due in large part to their high costs, the limited number of titles available in electronic form, and entry-level technology making them difficult to read. E-book readers generally cost between $200 and $600. Moreover, the display is usually monochrome and fairly drab, while most high-quality texts require color capability. Many analysts noted that manufacturers hadn't done enough to create a market for e-books. While there were some modest success stories, e-book companies were forced to a realization: for the time being, authors, not technologies, sell books. Although the leading e-book companies were wary of offering projections, Jupiter Communications predicted e-book shipments to reach 1.9 million by 2005, while International Data Corp. expected e-book sales of just $500 million by 2004—fairly modest numbers. By October 2000, only about 20,000 to 25,000 e-book readers had been purchased.

Some market segments enjoyed sunnier projections. Electronic textbooks seem poised for growth in the early 2000s. Sales of electronic media to schools were growing at an annual rate of 10 percent and were expected to reach over $1 billion in 2001. Online courseware is the smallest segment of the industry, but it is estimated to increase at an annual rate of 31 percent, reaching more than $40 million in 2001. Reasons for this rapid rise include the increased use of the Internet in classrooms and the acceptance of electronic publishing in the learning process.

The e-book distribution method inched ever closer to the mainstream in early 2000. For instance, Stephen King, along with Simon & Schuster and Philtrum Press, released his short story "Riding the Bullet" electronically for $2.50. Given the size of King's following, the move was a momentous occasion for the electronic publishing industry, which expected to introduce a great many more customers to the e-book technology through King's release. About 550,000 of the author's devoted fans downloaded the story, and King estimated he would make about $450,000 from the 66-page story, compared with the $10,000 he might have garnered through a literary magazine. As a result, more authors and publishing companies were expected to look into this distribution method to capitalize on an online book-purchasing audience already primed for such methods after the success of online bookstores such as Amazon.com. The

Web and CD-ROM have afforded writers similar degrees of independence in recent years.

E-books are sold online through such specialty virtual shops as Fatbrain.com and, increasingly, through the traditional commercial online bookstores such as Amazon.com or Barnesandnoble.com. Other distributors include netLibrary, which offers 12,500 electronic books to over 120 publishers and to libraries, amounting to over 50,000 patrons. This field tightened considerably under the market pressures of 2000, however. In October of that year, Barnesand-noble.com purchased Fatbrain.com, which immediately turned around and formed a partnership with netLibrary to boost book sales to corporations.

The precise e-book format that will proceed to dominance remained unclear in 2000. The two leading formats were the Adobe Portable Document Format (PDF) and the Open e-Book (OEB) format. Although OEB was developed through the industry-wide Open e-book Forum, the transmission, display, and viewing formats were widely scattered and mutually incompatible. To date, the Adobe model clearly outpaced OEB, and was nearly a de facto standard, but the battle was expected to heat up as OEB's standard develops. Gearing up to challenge the established e-book formats, meanwhile, was the new Microsoft ClearType technology, which dramatically improved the text quality and readability that hindered early e-books. The Microsoft Reader, which employs the ClearType technology, was released for use with Pocket PCs in April 2000, to be followed by models fit for laptops and possibly on electronic tablets. Customers wishing to view e-books on handheld devices such as Palm OS, moreover, were restricted to titles released by publishers maintaining arrangements with Peanut Press.

Online periodical publishers are still trying to find out how to make their services profitable. By 2000 several thousand e-zines (electronic magazines) were on the Web, and most operated in the red. For one general-interest publication, the quest for profitability meant bucking the tide and doing something most other online magazines, no matter how hip and trendy, wouldn't dream of doing—going subscription only. That's just what Microsoft's online magazine, *Slate*, did in March 1998 when it asked readers to pay a $19.98 annual subscription fee. *Slate* received more than 17,000 orders within the first month. Subscription revenue, however, fell far short of *Slate*'s annual operating costs of $5 million. In February 1999 Microsoft had a change of heart and dropped the fee. Once again, *Slate* was free to Web users, and derived its revenue from advertising.

INDUSTRY LEADERS

CNET Networks, Inc., headquartered in San Francisco, is a leading content network in terms of audience size and revenues. The company operates a range of Web sites that offer information about computers, the Internet, and digital technologies. This portion of CNET's business accounts for over 90 percent of total revenues. In addition to its Internet presence, CNET produces several nationally syndicated television shows about the Internet. The company signed a deal in February 1999 to be the exclusive provider of computer-buying guides on American Online (AOL) and AOL.com. As part of the deal, CNET agreed to pay AOL a guaranteed minimal amount of $14.5 million over the two and a half years of the agreement. Over three-fourths of CNET's sales come from its Internet operations. CNET spent 2000 beefing up its international presence and developing technology to deliver content to non-PC devices, such as portable phones. The company, which maintains a payroll of 500 employees, reported more than $112 million in sales revenue for 1999, an increase of 95 percent from the previous year.

Competing against CNET is Waltham, Massachusetts-based Lycos, Inc., a leading Web portal company that propelled itself to the top of the electronic publishing industry with its 1999 purchase of Wired Digital. This purchase brought under the Lycos umbrella the Web site HotWired, which has articles on Web-related issues; Wired News; HotBot, an online search engine; and Webmonkey, a how-to site. The rest of the Lycos Network includes Quote.com, Gamesville.com, Tripod, and Angelfire. Lycos generated about 70 percent of its 1999 revenues of $135.5 million from advertising.

Dow Jones & Co., Inc.'s flagship publication, the *Wall Street Journal,* appears in both print and online form. The *Wall Street Journal Interactive Edition* is one of the few Web publications that charges a fee to access its site. The *Interactive Journal* was launched in April 1996 and was initially available free. By the end of 1996, however, the free access had been phased out and, by its first anniversary, Dow Jones announced that the site had a paid circulation of 100,000. Annual subscriptions are $49 and allow subscribers access to services such as business news articles, background reports on over 10,000 companies, and personal news and stock portfolios. The *Interactive Journal* site also features sports coverage and *SmartMoney Interactive,* a collection of personal finance and investment advice resources. The company joined its interactive business services with those of Reuters Group PLC in 1999 to form Dow Jones Reuters Interactive LLC, which jointly created Factiva. Factiva includes archived editions of the *Wall Street Journal*—though not the current editions—along with about 7,000 other sources in 20 languages. Dow Jones, which is headquartered in New York City, had sales revenue of $2 billion in 1999, down 7 percent from 1998, and employed over 8,000 people.

Knight Ridder was ahead of the times in 1993 when it launched its first Web site, Mercury Center, an offshoot of the its newspaper franchise, the *San Jose Mercury News.* Over the next four years, the company poured $70 million into online ventures without seeing any profit on its investment. Despite losses from Internet operations, Knight Ridder is committed to technology, and to that end, in 1998 the company moved its headquarters from Miami to San Jose to be closer to its new media division. Amidst declining stock value, Knight Ridder announced in March 2000 that it would launch KnightRidder.com, a collection of portals for cities in which Knight Ridder publishes and the home of all its online operations. The company operates 31 daily and 18 weekly newspapers across the United States, including the *Miami Herald* and the *Philadelphia Inquirer.* In 1997 the company launched the Real Cities network, which included 37 Web sites in association with its newspapers. Knight Ridder's sales reached $3.2 billion in 1999 while employing 22,000 workers.

Bill Gates, the chairman and CEO of Microsoft Corp., the world's number-one software company, has said that he wants industry-wide standards for electronic books. To that aim, Redmond, Washington-based Microsoft, which has a research and development budget of $3 billion a year, is working on e-book technology and is especially focusing on applications that will help foster greater acceptance of books in electronic form. In November 1998 Microsoft announced that it had created software that would vastly improve the appearance of fonts on color display screens. The new software, ClearType, could improve the resolution of displays, such as those on many notebook computers, by nearly 300 percent. In addition to its e-book research, Microsoft produces Encarta—an electronic encyclopedia—and has created content for the Internet, including the e-zine *Slate* and Microsoft Sidewalk, a network of local city guides. In April 2000, the company rolled out the Microsoft Reader for e-books. Microsoft employed 31,400 in 2000 and generated revenues of $22.9 billion.

Salon.com, a San Francisco-based online magazine, decided to go public in 1999. In April of that year, the publication announced an initial public offering of 2.5 million common shares. Salon is a media company that produces a network of 10 subject-specific Web sites and a variety of online communities, which Salon expanded in 1999 with its acquisition of The Well. In 1999 the firm struck a deal with Bravo Networks in which Salon traded over a million shares in exchange for $11.8 million in airtime on Bravo's cable television programming for Salon's news, interviews, and cultural coverage. The company also maintains distribution agreements with Lycos, CNET, and Reuters, among others. Like many online publications, Salon's main source of revenue comes from advertising. In 2000, Salon reported sales of $8 million, a 250 percent increase over the previous year, while maintaining a payroll of 150 employees.

In 1996 the Chicago-based Tribune Co., a newspaper and entertainment conglomerate, paired up with AOL to build Digital Cities, an online network providing services in cities across the United States. The Tribune Co. invested $20 million and owned 20 percent of the venture. The purpose of Digital City was to offer local content such as news, weather, and entertainment guides tailored specifically to each of its 88 U.S. markets. By 1998, however, the online city guide field had become so crowded and competitive that Digital City laid off 80 staff members. The Tribune Co. publishes four daily newspapers, including the *Chicago Tribune* and the *Orlando Sentinel.* Its Tribune Interactive operations maintain the Web sites for the company's newspapers and television outlets. The Tribune Co., which employs 13,400, reported total revenue of $3.22 billion in 1999, representing growth of 8 percent over the previous year.

In early 2000, the two largest e-book companies, NuvoMedia, Inc. and SoftBook Press, Inc. were purchased by Gemstar International Group, Ltd., owner of *TV Guide.* Combined, the companies enjoyed content-distribution arrangements with almost every major publishing house in the United States. SoftBook inked deals with *Newsweek* and the *Washington Post* to produce electronic versions of those periodicals in a format ready for the SoftBook Reader. It also carries over 1,000 book titles as well as a number of popular magazines and newspapers. The connections Gemstar built with consumer electronics manufacturers in order to license its VCR Plus technology neatly positioned the company to finance and develop its new e-book business. The company launched a massive advertising blitz to coincide with the release of Nuvo-Media's and SoftBook's new products in 2000 in order to raise consumer awareness of the new technology and establish it as a mainstream reading medium.

RESEARCH AND TECHNOLOGY

One of the biggest obstacles to e-books is that they lack the feel and appearance of printed books. To overcome this limitation, scientists at the Media Laboratory at the Massachusetts Institute of Technology (MIT) are developing electronic technology that will result in a finished product that has pages that can be turned or riffled through. Electronic ink, or e-ink, is the secret ingredient to make this possible, according to scientists at MIT. E-ink has the capability of erasing itself and redrawing new text and illustrations. Books that have e-ink will have a paperlike property but will also be able to store massive amounts of data. MIT assistant professor Joseph Jacobson, who heads up the e-ink research team, says the storage capacity for these books could be as much as the entire holdings for the U.S. Library of Congress, or 17 million volumes. For this reason, the e-ink project has been dubbed "the last book." "The last book," however, is still in the development stage and won't appear on the market until 2002, at the earliest. Two business consortia of 75 companies are funding the project.

Piracy remains a pressing concern for e-book makers and merchants. Since such books are downloaded from the Web, the potential for a sophisticated hacker to engage in unauthorized duplication is omnipresent. To assist in copyright protection, Adobe Systems developed its PDF Merchant to encrypt electronic content and distribute the certificates required for access to electronic documents. Adobe's product was likely to be especially well received since most electronic books already used Adobe's PDF format, thus making for easy conversions and, thus, faster market penetration.

There may come a day when consumers will go to the local grocery store to do their weekly shopping and have a favorite book printed while they wait. This book-while-you-wait concept is known as on-demand printing. Companies are taking several different approaches to developing this technology. The Ingram Lightning Print project will store paperback books on a disk at a large output facility and then print the books only when needed. Similar to this idea, some companies are designing kiosks that can be put into public areas such as airports and bookstores. The kiosks will have the equipment to print out books at a customer's request. Xerox is also developing on-demand printing technology that will use its existing high-speed copiers.

FURTHER READING

"Adobe Chooses CyberTrust for Secure Sale and Delivery of E-Books." *Information Today,* March 2000.

Albanese, Andrew Richard. "The E-Book Enterprise." *Library Journal,* 15 February 2000.

Alexander, Steve. "More Newspapers across the Country Are Launching Electronic Editions." *Minneapolis Star Tribune,* 12 June 1995.

"Boo! How He Startled the Book World." *Time,* 27 March 2000.

Campbell, Kim. "Scene Set for a Reading Revolution." *Christian Science Monitor,* 15 March 2000.

Cavanagh, Luke. "KnightRidder.com Builds Its Real Cities Infrastructure." *Seybold Report on Internet Publishing,* February 2000.

Haugan, Stephanie. "Digital Delivery Re-Engineers the Industry." *Publishers Weekly,* 21 February 2000.

Hilts, Paul. "Seybold Looks at E-book Market." *Publishers Weekly,* 18 September 2000.

———. "The Wait for an E-book Format." *Publishers Weekly,* 6 November 2000.

Lowry, Tom, and Neil Gross. "Will E-books be Real Page-Turners?" *Business Week,* 23 October 2000.

Lynch, Clifford. "Electrifying the Book, Part 2." *Library Journal,* January 2000.

Nicholls, Paul. "CD-ROM Is Still Rollin' Along: Pass It On!" *Computers in Libraries,* September 1998.

O'Brien, Keith. "Self-Publishers Turn to Online Vanity Presses to Get Their Works Out." *Gannett News Service,* 20 April 1999.

Peek, Robin. "Seybold Seminars Boston: Publishing 2000." *Information Today,* March 2000.

Peek, Robin, and Paula J. Hane. "Jump-Starting Electronic Books." *Information Today,* March 2000.

Quint, Barbara. "NetLibrary Offers 1,500 E-Book Titles to 100 Large Public Libraries in Trial Program." *Information Today,* March 2000.

Shaffer, Richard A. "The New Classics: E-Books Get Ready for the Mainstream." *Fortune,* 21 February 2000.

Siklos, Richard. "No Magic in This Dot-Com Idea!" *Business Week,* 20 March 2000.

Terrell, Kenneth. "E-Books Struggle to Replace Type on Paper." *U.S. News & World Report,* 31 January 2000.

———. "Writing the E-book Story." *U.S. News & World Report,* 11 September 2000.

Ward, Gareth. "Boston Gurus Predict Newsprint Will Suffer from Electronic Publishing." *Printing World,* 13 September 1999.

Wildstrom, Stephen H. "New Chapter for E-Books." *Business Week,* 27 March 2000.

ENCRYPTION SYSTEMS AND DIGITAL CERTIFICATES

Though for some it may bring to mind cereal-box decoder rings and sundry childhood sleuthing paraphernalia, data encryption is increasingly pervasive in the digital economy. Whether protecting wireless data from interception or vouching for a Web site's authenticity, digital certificates and encryption technologies are fast becoming staples of the networked life.

As just one example, the certification authority service VeriSign, Inc., a provider of digital certificates that vouch for a site's or a user's authenticity, at year-end 2000 had bestowed over 485,000 of its certificates—and supporting security infrastructure—on Web sites around the world. These certificates are used to verify that a site is being operated by the company that registered the site and to provide a channel for secure communications. In late 2000, VeriSign was churning out new site certificates at rate of 85,000 each quarter, Additionally, the firm, one of the largest in this market, has issued several million certificates to individuals.

As an economic enterprise, however, digital security software and services have a lamentable reputation for overpromising and underdelivering. In particular, public key infrastructure (PKI) systems, a widely used model of data encryption and exchange, have been alternately championed and lampooned. For several years running, industry soothsayers had proclaimed that PKI sales would skyrocket into the multi-billion-dollar stratosphere, with one forecast calling for 80 percent annual sales growth from 1998 to 2002. But, alas, estimates in 2000 by the Gartner Group pegged global PKI sales at $300 million, a "paltry"

sum to one observer. A dearth of widely accepted standards and the sheer cost and complexity of implementing PKI systems were to blame. Added to those troubles was a slowdown in corporate IT spending during 2000 and 2001, seen as another impediment to PKI's takeoff.

Setbacks aside, a number of industry watchers believe the market is ripening and point to mounting evidence. Quietly, PKI is becoming part of daily life. Transactions on secure e-commerce Web sites, for example, routinely use basic PKI behind the scenes. The rising popularity of technologies like virtual private networks (VPNs), used to securely access corporate networks from remote locations, likewise spells more sales of certificate-based technologies. New laws and government regulations are also easing the move toward legally binding digital transactions. In addition, mergers and partnerships are giving certificate issuers access to new customers and new business models. And market analysts continue their rosy financial forecasts.

Broadly speaking, data encryption is a branch of computer security that deals with the secure transmission of documents, authorizations, and other electronic communications. Companies active in the encryption field provide software and services, sometimes hardware as well, mostly to other firms. In many cases, encryption products are components used in other applications. They appear, for instance, in e-mail applications, Web browsers, networking applications, and on Web sites that require a secure exchange of information.

OF IDs, SIGNATURES, AND ALGORITHMS

Time was when a unique user name and a hard-to-guess password were considered a good security system. Today, however, a great number of security systems—especially for the Internet—are based on digital certificates and public key infrastructure (PKI). These technologies tend to provide multiple layers of encryption and authentication, compared with only one line of defense in simple password systems.

Although the implementation can be incredibly complex, at their core PKI systems are, in the words of one industry veteran, a "glorified messaging system." Public key system ncryption keys. In a typical configuration, the certificate is sent to the user as a digitally signed message. A digital signature adds another layer of encryption to ensure that the document—in this case, a certificate—wasn't altered between the sender and the recipient. If the document has changed, it's not valid. Once a certificate is issued successfully, it enables the user to send and receive communications—submitting online transactions, for example—within the secure system. Those of a technical persuasion call this process binding the certificate to the user.

PKI systems also involve certification authorities (CAs) and registration authorities (RAs), which are systems (often third-party services like VeriSign) that assign, validate, track, and revoke certificates for both individuals and Web sites. Once a PKI system is launched, CAs and RAs, which can be one in the same, provide the service backbone to keep it all running. RAs perform the initial certification, determining who should be allowed on the system and assigning unique certificates to users. They also usually determine who should no longer be using the system by revoking certificates. Meanwhile, CAs perform validation and authentication services on every transaction, making sure (via encrypted exchanges) that each user is who he says he is and has permission to do what he's trying to do. CAs and RAs must be highly trusted sources, because while they aren't giving away keys to the kingdom, they do give out security keys that could compromise a system's integrity if they fall into the wrong hands.

Equally important, the public key infrastructure contains policies for managing certificates. How long is a certificate good for? When can a certificate be revoked? Do different uses of the system require different levels of security? These are all questions that must be answered when defining a public key system. The answers typically take the form of rules or procedures the system follows under certain conditions or under all conditions.

ODE TO STANDARDS AND REGULATIONS

As with most new technologies, PKI and digital certificates suffer from a shortage of standards on how exactly the infrastructure should work, which elements of a system are essential and which are optional, what protocols should be used for transmitting information. Some progress has been made toward better standardization and consistent regulation of the system, but experts believe more work will be necessary before PKI can reach its potential.

The most widely acknowledged standard to date has been proposed by the International Telecommunication Union (ITU), a United Nations-affiliated body concerned with telecommunications standards and practices. Known as X.509, in perhaps a small tribute to cryptography, it defines what information a digital certificate should contain and how the different components of a PKI system should work together. For example, X.509 requires certificates to encode, among other things, who the issuer is, when the start and expiration dates are, and what algorithm was used to create the certificate.

While this is all good on paper, in practice different companies have implemented the standard in different ways. Web browsers of recent vintage, for instance, are capable of accepting and transmitting certificates; however, a Microsoft browser may not work with X.509 certificates designed for Netscape, and Netscape may choke on X.509 certificates created with Internet Explorer in mind.

Meanwhile, a pair of legal developments have begun to make it easier to use highly secure encryption systems and conduct authoritative transactions electronically. First, in September 1999, the Clinton administration announced an easing of the long-standing ban on exporting powerful encryption software. The ban, often decried by the software industry, had prevented firms from shipping abroad any software with encryption beyond a certain level. That level, according to security experts, was unreasonably low and impeded sales of products with state-of-the-art encryption. The new policy, while still restricting some activities, placed a much higher ceiling on the allowable level of encryption and reduced other burdens for selling strong encryption products.

Then, in June 2000, President Clinton signed into law—digitally—new legislation prescribing how electronic signatures may be used in legally binding transactions. The law, known as the E-Sign Act, or the Electronic Signatures in Global and National Commerce Act, essentially gives electronic signatures the same legal standing as paper signatures for transactions and agreements in the private sector. This was seen as a major milestone toward treating important and complex electronic transactions on equal footing with traditional paper contracts. Within the federal government a previous law allowed for a similar ability.

The problem is, some observers say, that the law barely defines what constitutes an electronic signature. Within some technical circles there's an understanding that an electronic signature consists of a digital signature, a mark or symbol with encoding to ensure no tampering after it's issued, coupled with some form of authentication that the issuer is not an imposter. As it turns out, you can have a digital signature that's not authenticated or an authentication without sealing it with a digital signature. In theory, an imposter could use someone's digital signature to authorize a purchase, and the rightful owner of the signature could deny responsibility.

But the law is silent about these issues. The implications are that individual businesses will have to decide for themselves what an electronic signature consists of, and absent further legislation to clear the air, the exact boundaries may be tested in court.

CURRENT CONDITIONS

By most measures the industry is poised to grow significantly in coming years. Looking at digital certificate issuing and management services, International Data Corporation (IDC) expected global revenues to reach $3 billion by 2004, according to a forecast issued in December 2000. By IDC's own numbers, that would be a tenfold increase from 1999, when the firm tabulated industry sales at $281 million. Separate estimates predicted a sixfold increase in PKI sales between 2000 and 2004. In the broader security software and services market, the Gartner Group anticipated 20 percent annual growth during the early 2000s.

BANKING ON CERTIFICATES

Some of the more interesting entrants to the digital security field are affiliates of banks. Led by Digital Signature Trust Co. (DST), a unit of Zions Bancorporation of Utah, banks have begun viewing themselves as potential facilitators and guarantors of secure financial transactions.

On the heels of a successful pilot program managing digital certificates for the Social Security Administration (SSA), which resulted in a larger digital ID contract with the SSA, DST is trying to build its presence in other certification services. For a small fee, a business or an individual can buy from DST a one-year certificate to use when conducting electronic transactions. DST requires various proof of identity (driver's license, corporate ID, and the like) before issuing a certificate. Upon verifying the applicant's information, the bank issues a public and private key to the individual. The digital certificate is designed to be compatible with popular Web browsers and e-mail programs.

On a larger scale, DST has worked with the American Bankers Association, a trade group for financial institutions, to broaden its endeavors into something of an industry standard.

OUTSOURCER'S DILEMMA

PKI and certificate management is so complex, not to mention expensive to build from scratch, that it would be nice to let someone else worry about the details. Firms like Baltimore Technologies, Entrust Technologies, and VeriSign are all eager to rise to the occasion, providing extensive outsourcing options for large-scale deployment of PKI systems.

But this poses a problem for applications that require the utmost security, such as government records and other sensitive information. If security is of the essence, some experts believe it's too much of a liability to allow outside firms to run the PKI system. For one thing, the outside service may not screen its employees as rigorously. Even riskier, if one part of the outside CA's system is compromised, say, its private key is cracked by hackers, the entire system may be vulnerable to attack or misuse.

Such concerns have made some companies and government agencies opt for doing part or all of it themselves. Going it alone is no small undertaking, as it costs easily $1 million or more to bring up a typical system. One compromise is to self-manage the most sensitive areas of the system, such as registering and revoking certificates, while leaving the authentication of certificates and other day-to-day tasks to outside contractors.

Still, outsourcing of PKI and certificate services is only likely to grow. Early on, the option is most likely to appeal to smaller organizations that don't have the resources or expertise to craft and run such a system on their own.

INDUSTRY LEADERS

Focusing on software that lets companies manage their own PKI systems, Entrust Technologies Inc., Plano, Tex., is one of the largest firms competing in the digital certificate and PKI arena. Originally part of Nortel Networks Corp., Entrust gained its independence in 1997 just as Internet use was skyrocketing. According to an estimate by International Data Corp., by 1999 Entrust controlled 46 percent of the PKI product market, which excludes services for managing certificates. In 2000 the company's revenues swelled 74 percent, reaching $148 million. The company projected its revenues would approach $240 million in 2001, driven by continued strong software sales and the company's push into certificate services.

Another big player is VeriSign, Inc. of Mountain View, Calif. The firm, founded in 1995, is a leading certification authority service, and also licenses its services through authorized resellers. The company also provides payment services to over 10,000 businesses online. But perhaps its boldest initiative was its purchase in 2000 of Network Solutions Inc., then a near-monopoly in the Internet domain name registration business. The purchase was seen as a strategic move into providing a suite of Web site life-cycle management services that extend from registering the domain name to the certifying the site operator and managing certificates throughout the site's operation. In 2000 the combined companies brought in almost $475 million in revenues.

Baltimore Technologies plc is a United Kingdom-based firm that has a sizable presence in the global encryption software market. Its offerings include software for secure e-mail, content security, access control, and cryptographic hardware. The company originated in 1976, but underwent a significant transformation in the late 1990s when it was bought out by a group of investors. More recently, it's been emphasizing outsourced PKI services. In 2000, based on an estimate by the brokerage Dresdner Kleinwort Benson, the company's revenues were set to reach 72 million British pounds, or about US$104 million. That would represent a threefold improvement over a year earlier; however, Baltimore was still expected to be operating in the red for the next couple of years. During that time, Dresdner projected revenues might rise nearly 300 percent, toward $400 million.

FURTHER READING

Chen, Anne. "Outsource Directories? Hmmm." *eWeek,* 30 October 2000.

Constanzo, Chris. "Enthusiast of the Year: Scott Lowry Digs Dig-Sig." *American Banker,* 1 February 2001.

Fonseca, Brian. "Authentication Services Come to the Fore." *InfoWorld,* 8 May 2000.

Fonseca, Brian, and Heather Harreld. "Users Inch to Security Outsourcers." *InfoWorld,* 29 January 2001.

Greenberg, Eric, and Carmin McLaughlin. "Real-World Security—Here's How Digital Certificates Can Secure Sensitive Transactions between Businesses." *PC Magazine,* 8 August 2000.

Higgins, Kelly Jackson. "Public Key Infrastructures—Few and Far Between." *InternetWeek,* 6 November 2000.

Israel, Robert. "Signed, Sealed and Delivered? A New Digital Signature Law Could Push PKI into the Mainstream." *Tele.com,* 5 February 2001.

Lewis, Jamie. "PKI Won't Hit the Mainstream Until Vendors Reduce Complexity." *InternetWeek,* 8 January 2001.

Raikow, David. "Who's Behind That Web Page?" *Sm@rt Reseller,* 31 January 2000.

Seminerio, Maria. "IT Considers Outsourcing Security Tasks." *PC Week,* 1 November 1999.

Streeter, Bill. "Will Banks Have a Role in E-Commerce?" *ABA Banking Journal,* September 2000.

"The Web's Virtual Vault: VeriSign." *Business Week,* 23 October 2000.

ENTREPRENEURIAL TRAINING AND ADVISORY SERVICES

INDUSTRY SNAPSHOT

Entrepreneurial training and advisory services focus on practical business skills and strategies, going beyond traditional theory-centered business classes. Entrepreneurial training courses are generally taught by instructors who have had substantial entrepreneurial success themselves—i.e., success starting and managing their own businesses. Therefore, they are able to provide guidance and mentorship to people starting or wishing to expand their own businesses, or seeking to apply entrepreneurial skills in a corporate environment.

While the number of U.S. college and university entrepreneurial training programs stood at only 16 in 1970, in the late 1990s it rose to over 400. The influx of entrepreneurial programs and the booming demand for them stems in part from the remarkable success of small businesses and computer-related startups, according to *Colorado Business Magazine*. The strong interest in entrepreneurial training has goaded colleges and universities throughout the country to revamp their business programs to instill and promote entrepreneurial skills more vigorously.

Furthermore, many consulting firms, including industry giants such as Andersen Consulting and PricewaterhouseCoopers as well as smaller outfits such as FastForward, began offering entrepreneurial advisory services in the 1990s as the trend of entrepreneurship began to pick up speed. These services provide guidance to entrepreneurs through various stages development, from planning to going public. Although entrepreneurs may receive general insights or confront specific business problems of other companies in entrepreneurial training programs, they receive help with specific problems they are facing with their business, such as expansion of obtaining financial backing, from advisory services.

Besides these primary forms of entrepreneurial training and advisory services, many government agencies and community organizations also offer an array services designed to teach entrepreneurial skills and help people plan, launch, and maintain businesses.

At the beginning of the 21st century, the outlook for the industry appeared favorable. During this period, entrepreneurship was on the rise. Reports indicated that twenty-somethings and babyboomers both were gravitating towards entrepreneurial ventures. Many members of the younger generation looked to starting their own businesses instead of taking traditional jobs, while large numbers of babyboomers are expected to launch their own businesses upon retirement. This interest in entrepreneurship created significant demand for entrepreneurial training and advising services in the 1990s and the early 2000s.

ORGANIZATION AND STRUCTURE

Generally speaking, entrepreneurial training concentrates on inculcating general real-world business skills and strategies, whereas entrepreneurial advising focuses on resolving specific entrepreneurial problems. Entrepreneurial education begins with the premise that entrepreneurship is a learnable skill, even though many renowned entrepreneurs had little formal training. Colleges and universities are the primary sources of entrepreneurial training. Nevertheless, some private training institutes and organizations offer entrepreneurial training, too.

Colleges and universities offer entrepreneurial training as part of undergraduate and graduate degree programs as well as part of continuing education programs. Some universities report, in fact, that entrepreneurship has become one of the leading majors in Master of Business Administration (MBA) programs, surpassing long-time favorites such as marketing and finance.

Some university entrepreneurial programs are even run as small businesses themselves. For example, the University of Colorado at Denver runs a self-funded entrepreneurial training program that operates without the aid of any state finances, according to the Colorado Business Magazine. The university established a $500,000 venture capital fund, which students can access after analyzing the merits of their investments.

Entrepreneurial training often consists of a mixture of class work and hands-on experience. As part of the class work, students attempt to solve real-world business problems with the help of other students and entrepreneurial veterans who teach the classes. In addition, entrepreneurial training courses and programs may require students to work at local small businesses, helping them solve real business problems and handle real business situations. For many entrepreneurial training programs, internships like these are an integral part of the education process.

Courses in an entrepreneurial degree program may include evaluating business and growth opportunities, developing a business plan, obtaining financing, and managing small businesses. Such courses frequently are supplemented by internships in startup businesses, offering students an opportunity to apply what they have learned and to learn new skills by solving actual problems that entrepreneurial ventures confront.

Entrepreneurial advising, on the other hand, is frequently provided by consulting firms. These services focus on the stages new businesses go through and the situations they encounter, addressing entrepreneurial problems such as how to obtain outside investment and how to expand.

These firms may provide advice in areas of entrepreneurship such as business, product, and financial planning; market analysis; and management assistance. In addition, such service providers also may offer transitional support to expanding startups, furnishing chief financial and technology officers to ensure that financial strategies and development plans are executed properly. In addition, since entrepreneurial advisory services tend to focus on the various business situations entrepreneurs face when starting a new business, they may render guidance during initial public offerings, mergers and acquisitions, business negotiations, and selecting investment banks.

Alternatively, organizations such as The Entrepreneurial Development Institute provide entrepreneurial training to low-income and otherwise disadvantaged high school students. The goal of such programs is to offer students an opportunity to transcend any setbacks they may have had by launching their own businesses. The Entrepreneurial Development Institute alone has had over 25,000 participants in its program—and 80 percent of these students went on to found their own businesses.

In addition, other entrepreneurial organizations promote the training of under-represented groups. For example, the Women's Network for Entrepreneurial Training strives to teach women entrepreneurial skills beginning in high school, and the National Minority Supplier Development Council as well as the U.S. Hispanic Chamber of Commerce offer various forms of entrepreneurial training and advice. Moreover, local community organizations, departments of commerce, and employment commissions also often offer entrepreneurial training. In particular, the U.S. Department of Commerce, the U.S. Chamber of Commerce, and the U.S. Small Business Administration all provide and promote entrepreneurial training, advice, and assistance.

Another form of this kind of entrepreneurial service is the business incubator. Business incubators offer entrepreneurs low-rent facilities to help them develop their products and services and offer them shared business services and equipment and management help. As a result, entrepreneurs have the accounting, computer programming, and other business services they need as well as the equipment necessary to develop their business ideas. The concept involves an entrepreneur moving into the incubator facility and working with the assistance of the incubator staff and co-tenants for a year or two before moving on and launching the business. Public, private, and public/private partnerships have established business incubators throughout the nation. This sector of the industry is served by the National Business Incubation Association.

CURRENT CONDITIONS

With ongoing corporate downsizing and the success of recent startup companies, entrepreneurship has become an increasingly popular career pursuit for people of all ages. Both college students and business veterans showed greater interest in entrepreneurship beginning in the early 1990s and extending through the early 2000s. Because of this interest in entrepreneurship, more schools, organizations, and training institutes started to offer entrepreneur training and advisory courses and services. Indeed, the period of the late 1990s and the early 2000s has been called the Entrepreneurial Age by some, and a survey by Ernst & Young LLP indicated that entrepreneurship would be a key trend in the 21st century. Moreover, the National Foundation for Teaching Entrepreneurship found that entrepreneurial training has been one of the fastest growing areas of education ever.

Moreover, federal and state governments have sponsored entrepreneurial training because entrepreneurship is an important source of job creation. During the mid-1990s, for example, small businesses accounted for about 85 percent of all new U.S. jobs, according to Fortune. During the late 1990s, about 4.5 million new businesses were launched annually, according to a study by Wells Fargo and the National Federal of Independent Business.

By the late 1990s and early 2000s, about 33 percent of all U.S. business schools offered concentrations in entrepreneurship, and U.S. colleges and universities have established some 100 entrepreneurship centers to promote entrepreneurial training. Each year during this period, more than 120,000 students enrolled in entrepreneurship courses, according to Business Perspectives. In addition, numerous entrepreneurial courses are offered as continuing education classes, enabling students to enhance existing skills or pick up some new skills quickly without devoting a substantial amount of time to obtaining a degree—a convenient option for people already running businesses.

According to a 1999 *Business Week* survey, the schools with the top entrepreneurial training programs were Babson College, the University of Pennsylvania's Wharton Business School, Harvard Business School, Stanford Business School, and Dartmouth College's Tuck Business School. The essential ingredients of a quality entrepreneurship program are mentoring, access to capital, and the ability to provide training that is easily applied to real world business situations, according to Robert H. Smith, director of the University of Maryland's Dingman Center for Entrepreneurship. To be sure, obtaining an MBA is the first step to starting a new business, as evidenced by the fact that 99 percent of the MBA applicants to Stanford indicated in their admissions essays that they

planned to pursue entrepreneurial ventures after graduation. Obtaining entrepreneurial training prior to starting a business helps new business owners avoid common mistakes made while running a new business or running a business for the first time.

The demand for entrepreneurial training and the need for it in the marketplace is also evident from the number of corporate donations business schools receive to start entrepreneurial centers. In the late 1990s, for example, Georgia Institute of Technology received $5 million from a benefactor who was a restauranteur and the president of Apple South; the University of Virginia received $10 million in donations from businesses and alumni; and Babson College received $30 million from the Olin Foundation to create programs in entrepreneurship.

Furthermore, university professors are playing an active role in helping entrepreneurial students obtain funding and manage their companies. Sometimes, the professors will even invest their own money in their students' ventures and sit on their companies' boards of directors. According to *Inc.,* business professors at schools such as Harvard, Stanford, University of California at Los Angeles, and Cornell frequently invest in their students' entrepreneurial ventures. Although some schools prohibit professors from directly investing in their students' businesses while they are in the professors' classes, they do not extend the prohibition to investments made after students have left professors' classes.

In addition, budding entrepreneurs in entrepreneurial training courses can obtain funding through search-funds. With this funding mechanism, entrepreneurs receive funding from investors—who might include university professors—for a few years while the entrepreneur looks for a business to purchase or start. After the new business is bought, the entrepreneur repays the search-fund investors by selling shares of the new company to them at an advantageous rate. During the late 1990s, this method increased in popularity among entrepreneurs, according to a study by Stanford University.

The Premier FastTrac training program, created by the Entrepreneurial Education Foundation of Denver and adopted by entrepreneurial foundations and organizations around the country, also played an important role in the education of entrepreneurs in the late 1990s and early 2000s. These training programs provide business neophytes with crash courses in business, allowing entrepreneurs to take courses at night while running their businesses by day. The program, however, encourages business planning in its first phase and then focuses on business expansion in its second phase.

Moreover, the late 1990s and early 2000s saw the growth of numerous private, for-profit schools specializing in business and entrepreneurial education, according to Eduventures.com, a research firm that monitors the education industry.

State governments also promoted entrepreneurship in the late 1990s and early 2000s. As of 2000, eight states—California, Delaware, Maine, Maryland, Oregon, New Jersey, New York, and Pennsylvania—offered programs where the unemployed could use their unemployment benefits to launch their own businesses. However, selection for these self-employment assistance programs is extremely competitive and those who qualify are required to attend entrepreneurial education classes as well as attending entrepreneurial counseling sessions. In addition to these basic requirements, individual states may impose other requirements.

Furthermore, with the Internet and advanced information services, entrepreneurs can obtain some training, advice, and information for free. Entrepreneurs can access this information at home or at a local library via a computer and a modem. Good starting points for this information include the Small Business Administration and local entrepreneurship centers, according to Barbara L. Wagner in the *Library Journal*. In addition, library reference staff usually can help entrepreneurs explore various sources of financing and research specific markets.

Besides appealing to people who want to start their own businesses, entrepreneurial education may also be sought by people wish to apply these skills and strategies to a corporate environment. Such people have been called "intrapreneurs." Intrapreneurs do not face some of the challenges entrepreneurs confront, such as obtaining funding. Instead, they may lead a team of a corporation's workers in a quasi-independent project funded by the corporation to launch a new product or service.

In the business incubator sector, the National Business Incubation Association reported that, in the 1990s, 80 percent of the companies started in business incubators remained in business after branching out on their own. In contrast, 80 percent of startup companies without business incubators failed within the first five years. Some of the success stories from this sector in the late 1990s and early 2000s included eToys, GoTo.com, and Peapod, Inc. At the beginning of the 21st century, they were over 600 business incubators in North America, a dramatic surge from only

12 in 1980. However, critics cautioned entrepreneurs to choose their incubators carefully because not all provide the kind of training, resources, and guidance entrepreneurs need.

INDUSTRY LEADERS

While colleges and universities are the leading providers of entrepreneurial training and education, large financial consulting and accounting firms such as Andersen Consulting and PricewaterhouseCoopers as well as specialty firms such as Euro Worldwide Investments, Inc. offer entrepreneurial advisory services.

Andersen Consutling is the largest consulting firm in the world. In addition to many other services, Andersen Consulting provides diverse advisory services of use to entrepreneurs and entrepreneurial companies, helping them secure financing, go public, outsource various functions, and develop and execute plans. Overall, the company had sales of $16.3 billion in 1999. As part of its split from Andersen Worldwide, the company will be renamed Accenture.

PricewaterhouseCoopers was formed after the 1998 merger of Price Waterhouse and Coopers & Lybrand, creating the second largest accounting and consulting firm in the country. Both Price Waterhouse and Coopers & Lybrand offered entrepreneurial advisory services. Through its nearly 850 offices worldwide, PricewaterhouseCoopers has a strong presence in the industry. In 1999, the company garnered $15.3 billion from all of its services, including entrepreneurial advisory services.

Based in San Francisco, Euro Worldwide Investments, Inc. (EWI) counsels entrepreneurs and small businesses at each step of the business development process. EWI's advisors can help take entrepreneurs from the planning of a product and market to target to executing those plans.

Sandler Sales Institute is one of the major non-college or university players in the entrepreneurial training industry with over 190 affiliates throughout the country. Founded by David Sandler in the 1960s, the company began franchising in 1983. Although the company's founder died in 1995, the Sandler Sales Institute continues to provide entrepreneurial and sales training via its network of trainers and consultants.

idealab! ranked among the leading business incubators in the late 1990s and early 2000s. The Pasadena, California-based company boasts of successful alumni such as eToys, Inc., GoTo.com. City-Search, NetZero, and Tickets.com. Bill Gross founded the company in an effort to launch his online business, eToys. The company provides funding, materials, working space, and other amenities in addition to its entrepreneurial advisory services. In 1999, idealab! booked sales of $21.2 million and in 2000 the company announced its plan to go public.

AMERICA AND THE WORLD

The United States is the leading provider of entrepreneurial training and education with an abundance of public and private colleges, universities, schools, organizations, institutes, and consulting firms offering such services. Nevertheless, other countries, particularly those in Europe and Asia, have adopted entrepreneurial training programs. For example, German business schools began offering classes on entrepreneurship in the late 1990s and established entrepreneurial departments. Despite efforts to teach entrepreneurship in Europe, critics contend that obstacles to entrepreneurship, such as business restrictions on where companies can operate and the timidity of European venture capitalists ,must be removed first.

Nevertheless, by the end of the century many Europeans were following the U.S. trend: quitting secure jobs and pursuing entrepreneurial ventures, especially in the technology industries. These conditions are fertile for the growth of entrepreneurial services in Europe.

In Asia, the financial crisis of the mid- to late 1990s brought increased entrepreneurial opportunity as well as greater interest in entrepreneurship. Entrepreneurs that could deliver products or services that helped cash-strapped consumers and companies faired well during this period.

African nations also turned to entrepreneurial training in an effort to combat high unemployment in the 1990s. Many of these programs were government-sponsored and focused primarily on training the younger generations to be economically self-sufficient.

RESEARCH AND TECHNOLOGY

Computer and information service technology holds the potential for facilitating the delivery of entrepreneurial training and advisory services. By the late 1990s, students could take a wide range of classes over the Internet and Internet universities began to crop up. Online entrepreneurial courses included degree program courses for undergraduate and graduate degrees as well as individual classes to acquire specific skills related to entrepreneurial ventures. In addition, with the high penetration of Internet access, the Internet looked to be a convenient tool for networking, sharing advice, querying other entrepreneurs, and communicating with advisory services.

In the business incubator sector, the Maryland Technology Development Corp. and the National Business Incubation Association teamed up in 2000 to research the best practices for incubating high-tech businesses. By studying the techniques of national and international incubation operations, the two organizations hope to determine the best approach for starting new high-tech business incubation facilities.

FURTHER READING

Aven, Paula. "Entrepreneurs in the Making: CU Boulder, Denver Centers Teach Art of the Small Business Startup." *Denver Business Journal,* 1 August 1997.

"Adventures with Capital: If only Europe Could Learn from America's Success in Nurturing New Business." *The Economist,* 25 January 1997.

Beck, Susan. "Professors Get Their Shares." *Inc.,* March 1998.

Curtis, Richard. "Mentoring with Realism Helps New Entrepreneurs Set Course." *Cincinnati Business Courier,* 22 October 1999.

Cutbill, David. "Incubators: The Blueprint for New Economy Companies." *Los Angeles Business Journal,* 27 March 2000.

Griffin, Cynthia E. "MBAs Aren't so Hard to Come By." *Entrepreneur Magazine,* March 2000.

———. "School Rules." *Entrepreneur Magazine,* August 1998.

———. "Silver Lining." *Entrepreneur Magazine,* July 1999.

Mallory, Maria. "Firm Helps Others Get Off to a Start." *Atlanta Constitution,* 5 July 2000.

Randall, Donna M. "School for Start-ups." *Business Perspectives,* July 1997.

Sommars, Jack. "Entrepreneurial Training." *Colorado Business Magazine,* October 1998.

Tartler, Jens. "Not the Best Place to Start." *Financial Times,* 8 December 1997.

Wagner, Barbara. "Getting Down to Business." *Library Journal,* January 2000.

"Where the Bigshots Learn to Think Like Hotshots." *Business Week,* 18 October 1999.

Williams, Geoff. "The Deliberate Entrepreneur." *Entrepreneur Magazine,* May 1999.

ENVIRONMENTAL REMEDIATION

Much of the American population lives within close range of sites that have been contaminated with hazardous materials. The U.S. government estimates that about one-third of all Americans live within four miles of a location federally designated as in need of environmental cleanup; in fact, 80 percent of all sites marked for cleanup under the Superfund, or Comprehensive Environmental Response, Compensation, and Liability Act (CERCLA), are located in residential areas. The process of removing harmful substances from the soil and water in such areas is known as environmental remediation. In addition, remediation efforts can also remove harmful substances such as asbestos from buildings. For decades, U.S. industries released a wide array of harmful or potentially harmful chemicals into the atmosphere with little or no monitoring. Among those substances are trichloroethylene (from dry cleaning and metal degreasing), lead (from gasoline), arsenic (from mining and manufacturing), tetrachloroethylene (from dry cleaning and metal degreasing), benzene (from gasoline and manufacturing), and toluene (from gasoline and manufacturing). Remediation efforts can require 10 years or more and millions of dollars to complete.

Environmental remediation has constituted a volatile political topic since the introduction of CERCLA in 1980 by the Carter administration. The state of the environment was a prominent topic in the Bush and Clinton presidential administrations and a focus of the 2000 election, which featured Democratic contender Al Gore, who wrote a best-selling book on environmental preservation, *Earth in the Balance: Ecology and the Human Spirit*. This persistent political attention helped foster the environmental remediation and protection industry.

Hazardous waste cleanup constitutes the industry's largest segment, generating 75 percent of revenues; nuclear waste accounted for the remaining 25 percent. By the late 1990s, the U.S. hazardous waste management market exceeded $15 billion in gross revenues annually. Federal, state, and local governments accounted for approximately 48.9 percent of the industry's revenues, while the private sector accounted for 51.1 percent. According to the U.S. Environmental Protection Agency (EPA), the average contaminated site costs $400,000 to clean up.

Environmental remediation services seek to remove hazardous substances that are toxic, corrosive, ignitable, explosive, infectious, or reactive, thereby making contaminated sites comply with state and EPA standards. Lead, arsenic, and metallic mercury rank among the leading hazardous substances found in the ground and in water, and all pose serious health risks. In addition, scientific literature is rife with examples of afflictions, such as lung disorders and cancer, that humans suffer as a result of exposure to noxious substances in the environment.

TYPES OF REMEDIATION

Environmental remediation operations rely on four general methods: thermal, chemical, biological, and physical remediation. Thermal remediation, which includes a variety of incineration techniques, subjects hazardous materials to high temperatures to decompose them. Traditional chemical remediation relies on the "pump and treat" technique for cleaning contaminated water. A remediation company pumps the water into a treatment tank where contaminants are removed or neutralized, then the water is pumped back into its natural basin. Newer techniques allow remediation services to treat the water chemically on site, thereby obviating transportation and storage and alleviating some of the costs. Biological remediation covers techniques such as using indigenous or genetically engineered insects or microorganisms to decompose hazardous materials. Physical remediation entails collecting and containing the contaminated or toxic substances and burying them in containers. This method, however, draws criticism from environmentalists who fear the containers could break, releasing dangerous substances into the ground and water.

EPA- and state-sanctioned remediation processes usually include three steps. First, the remediation contractor assesses the risks of the site and studies the soil and water contaminants. During this step, the investigator determines the site's possible hazards to the environment and to the public. Second, the remediation contractor decides which remedial method will adequately and efficiently purge the site, and considers which of the four general approaches to remediation will successfully accomplish the goal. Third, the contractor undertakes the cleanup of the site.

The EPA, along with state governments, sets contamination and pollution standards as well as criteria for establishing the risk posed by contaminated sites. The ranges reflect the different uses or locations of the contaminated areas. For residential areas, many states require that the probability of infection be 1 out of 1 million, whereas for an industrial site, states may require only 1 out of 10,000.

KEY LEGISLATION

The primary legislation governing and motivating environmental remediation includes the Comprehensive Environmental Response, Compensation, and Liability Act of 1980 (CERCLA); and the Resource Conservation and Recovery Act of 1976 (RCRA). CERCLA, also known as Superfund, established a list of high-priority industrial sites needing remediation. Environmental agencies and remediation firms refer to such locations as *brownfields*—contaminated sites no longer usable for industrial purposes that pose a risk to neighboring communities. CERCLA concentrates on the cleanup and redevelopment of already contaminated sites, not on creating contemporary environmental standards. Superfund constitutes the driving force behind environmental remediation. CER-

CLA entitles government agencies to several key enforcement prerogatives. They can use money from the Superfund Trust Fund to clean sites on Superfund's National Priorities List (NPL), require responsible parties to finance the necessary remediation, and pursue reimbursement for Superfunded cleanups from responsible parties.

Under Superfund, sites that are identified for possible hazardous substance releases are entered into a Comprehensive Environmental Response, Compensation, and Liability Information System (CERCLIS) database, a computerized log of all potentially hazardous sites. The cleanup process itself involves nine separate steps, from preliminary site inspections and assessments, through remedial investigation and feasibility study, implementation of cleanup plans, and post-operation evaluation. As of August 2000, a total of 1,238 uncontrolled hazardous waste sites were included on Superfund's NPL of sites.

CERCLA relies heavily on liability and the so-called polluter pays principle. Pollution-contributing past and present owners of a contaminated site bear the responsibility for cleaning the brownfield, and government agencies can pursue any or all of them for reimbursement of cleanup costs. With Superfund's scheme of strict liability, governments do not need to demonstrate negligence on the part of site operators. Furthermore, the government is not required to identify the exact source of the wastes located at a contaminated site. This joint-and-several liability forces companies to implement waste and pollution reducing technologies and to clean up any hazardous materials as soon as possible to avoid the escalating remediation costs. In 1986 the Superfund Amendments and Reauthorization Act was passed, which granted any potentially responsible party that settled with the U.S. government the right to seek contributions from other liable parties while obtaining contribution protection for itself.

RCRA amended the Solid Waste Disposal Act of 1970, which contains four key focal points: solid waste, hazardous waste, underground storage, and medical waste. This act regulates the usage, storage, and disposal of over 200 toxic substances, such as heavy metals, insecticides, and herbicides. With amendments in 1984, RCRA works in conjunction with CERCLA by imposing deadlines on brownfield remediation. In contrast to CERCLA, RCRA largely governs the management of waste substances so no further brownfields and Superfund priority sites are created. The act concentrates on companies that transport, treat, dispose of, and store potentially harmful forms of waste. Under the land disposal restrictions of

RCRA, the EPA establishes standards for wastes found in landfills. CERCLA and RCRA, however, overlap in some ways, which promotes confusion in enforcement of and compliance with these acts. In addition to these federal laws, each state develops legislation regarding environmental remediation and air, water, and soil cleanliness standards that work with the federal statutes.

The EPA also promotes remediation through initiatives such as the Brownfields Economic Redevelopment Initiative (BERI), which promotes the sustainable reuse of brownfields. Faced with a dwindling budget and congressional pressure to impose policies that do not inhibit economic growth, the EPA started a campaign to marry economic development to environmental remediation in the mid-1990s. By the late 1990s, BERI had funded 307 Brownfields Assessment Pilots and predicted it would select another 50 pilots by April 2000. Cleveland, Detroit, and Bridgeport, Connecticut, were among the recipients of loans under this initiative.

ENVIRONMENTAL REMEDIATION AND THE ECONOMY

As part of the growing link between the environment and economics, companies' environmental records play a role in their ability to borrow money. When environmental laws became tougher with the enactment of bills such as CERCLA, lenders started to avoid business with companies that frequently handle toxic substances, require thorough assessment of environmental liability prior to approving loans, and circumscribe their involvement in projects by companies dealing with toxic substances. While bankers' policies, however, curb the environmental degradation by companies prone to release hazardous substances, they also impede remediation since they approach such projects with caution or even refuse to finance them.

Other incentive packages designed to encourage environmental remediation and urban redevelopment include Community Development Block Grants (CDBG) offered by the U.S. Department of Housing and Urban Development. Cities eligible for CDBG can use the funds for hazard assessment and cleanup if the result of the remedial efforts promotes significant housing-related needs, such as benefiting lower-income households or eradicating slums and urban blight. The Economic Development Administration (EDA) also provides grants that can help stimulate environmental remediation. The EDA's public works grants, for example, allow cities to clean up and renovate contaminated or otherwise unusable industrial

sites. Finally, tax incentives, such as industrial development bonds, stimulate environmental remediation by offering private companies tax-exempt bonds to launch redevelopment and cleanup projects.

BACKGROUND AND DEVELOPMENT

Events such as the establishment of Earth Day on 20 April 1970 and the environmental disaster at Love Canal in New York state galvanized public awareness of the dangers of uncontrolled hazardous waste disposal. Over 40 pieces of environmental legislation, including laws governing air and water quality, hazardous wastes, chemicals, and pesticides were subsequently introduced. In December 1970, the Environmental Protection Agency (EPA) also was established to research environmental destruction, recommend policies to combat the contamination of natural resources, and prevent environmental degradation. The EPA estimated that by 1979 the United States contained between 30,000 to 50,000 abandoned hazardous waste sites.

Legislation enacted in the 1980s requiring hazardous site cleanups and limiting the release and disposal of harmful substances spawned a burgeoning industry, with companies vying to cash in on federally mandated and subsidized environmental remediation projects. Moreover, companies' environmental records slowly became associated with their financial capabilities. In 1989 the Securities and Exchange Commission (SEC) began requesting disclosure of environmental liabilities from companies, which forced businesses to exercise more caution and discretion when disposing of hazardous substances. As the industry's success continued in the 1980s, numerous companies offered remediation and consulting services, creating a glutted market in the early 1990s. Therefore, in the 1990s many environmental remediation operations competed for a limited number of contracts.

CURRENT CONDITIONS

In the late 1990s environmental remediation grew increasingly competitive as the industry started to slow down. Government gridlock impeded industry growth during this period. Since 1997, private sector projects have led the industry, accounting for slightly over half of all business. Federal, state, and local governments together represented the remaining industry sales. Industry players expected the private sector to continue expanding as government contracts dwindle. In addition, the water remediation sector is also slated to grow and industry analysts expected the discovery of methyl tertiary butyl ether (MTBE), a gasoline oxygenate, in drinking water to boost demand for environmental remediation services in the early 2000s. Despite the slowdown, the amount of remediation remaining to be done is colossal. In the next three decades, analysts predicted that between $373 billion and $1.6 trillion will be spent on environmental remediation, mostly funded by government agencies such as the U.S. Department of Energy and the U.S. Department of Defense.

The competitive industry climate forced companies to reduce fees; therefore, environmental remediation companies began operating with very slim profit margins. Smaller companies also started specializing in one area of remediation in an attempt to stand out. In addition, numerous mergers and acquisitions took place in the late 1990s, as companies attempted to achieve economies of scale necessary to win contracts from major clients such as chemical manufacturers and governments.

Because environmental remediation has grown less risky with the development of advanced technology, clients sought fixed-sum contracts instead of flexible-sum contracts. Furthermore, private sector companies realized in the mid- to late 1990s that their cleanup expenditures were greater than they anticipated, which made them more frugal, demanding lump-sum prices with no surprises.

To cope with the flooded market, many companies developed innovative practices, such as outsourcing, to stay ahead in the environmental cleanup business. Environmental operations started offering released waste testing and monitoring corporate compliance with environmental policies. In addition, they purchased sites requiring remediation, such as wastewater plants and oil wells, remediated and renovated them, then leased them back to operators. Environmental remediation companies also shifted their focus from the development of remediation plans—the sector of the industry that thrived in the 1980s—to the execution of remediation. They have also turned their attention increasingly to foreign markets, particularly Mexico, Eastern European countries, and the former East Germany.

Several factors hinder the industry's progress. For example, lawyers have advised some companies to postpone environmental remediation projects until Congress finishes haggling over the Superfund reau-

thorization, a process that has been ongoing for several years. Financing Superfund was a particular point of contention between the parties. Until 1995, an excise tax on the oil and chemical industries funded the project, but Congress subsequently refused to renew the tax. Superfund was up for revision in 2000, but analysts were confident reforms would fizzle prior to that year's elections before picking up again in the following legislative session. Nonetheless, President Bill Clinton proposed a $50 million increase in the Superfund budget for 2001, up to $1.45 billion, though House appropriators awarded only $1.27 billion. The political tone of the debates was typified by the two wildly differing reports of Superfund's performance in 2000, one of which was flaunted by Congressional Republicans as a sign of the program's failure, while the EPA pointed to the other as proof of the program's success.

Since its inception, Superfund has spent over $14 billion for site cleanups. Of all designated sites, cleanup was completed on 48 percent, underway on 44 percent, and not yet begun on 8 percent. In its July 2000 rulemaking, the EPA added 12 sites to its Superfund National Priority List (NPL) of sites requiring remediation, bringing the total to 1,238 at that point. As of August 2000, a total of 59 sites were proposed to the NPL. Despite the legislative hurdles, Superfund has demonstrated progress in identifying and remediating contaminated sites in the 1990s. The Government Accounting Office (GAO) estimated in a 1999 report on the status of Superfund that cleanups at 85 percent of all identified Superfund sites would be completed by 2008, and that total operations would cost from $8.2 to $11.7 billion more than had already been spent on the work. The EPA's estimate for time required to complete remediation of an average site was eight years; however, to pump and treat groundwater may require 30 years or more.

Recently, the efficacy of Superfund has come under increased scrutiny. In a study published in September 1999, Duke University public policy professor James Hamilton and Harvard law and economics professor W. Kip Viscusi calculated cancer risks associated with 150 Superfund sites and found that the actual risk of cancer being produced from exposure was relatively low. Hence, they concluded that Superfund cleanup costs were quite inefficient. They argued that Superfund site decisions were often determined by political exigencies, such as percentage of voters in a specific location or high levels of media attention, rather than by solid cost-benefit analyses. In the same year, researchers from the University of Texas at Austin evaluating three Superfund sites concluded that containment of on-site contaminants, rather than complete removal, would be far less costly and equally effective in reducing the health risks the contaminants posed. In 1999, the GAO reported that only 42 percent of the funds spent for Superfund actually went to hazardous waste cleanups.

The EPA also concluded an out-of-court settlement with environmental groups and hazardous waste treatment companies, with an arrangement that the EPA claimed will speed up waste cleanups under the RCRA. The settlement permits some facilities to handle and dispose of waste themselves without having to meet RCRA treatment and storage standards. The chemical industry is the largest single industry group to be affected.

The EPA also took steps to encourage more private investment in environmental remediation by removing 27,000 contaminated sites from its database of potential Superfund sites. At the same time, the EPA expanded its Brownfields Pilot Program by allocating $200,000 for 25 contaminated sites.

The U.S. Commerce Department's Office of Technology Policy in an industry overview—*Meeting the Challenge of the 21st Century*—characterized the industry as being in a state of transition from one focused on pollution control and waste remediation to one that should stress resource productivity and preventive measures. Average annual returns since 1991 of the 240 leading environmental companies listed by the *Environmental Business Journal* have hovered at about 6 percent, with investment in research and development very low. The Office of Technology Policy advocated "market-based" approaches to environmental management, such as environmental management systems, pollutant trading, brownfield redevelopment, and privatization, to combat the industry slump.

INDUSTRY LEADERS

Bechtel Group, Inc. ranked high with overall 1999 sales revenues of $12.6 billion; environmental remediation services accounted for 20 percent of sales. The construction company employs 30,000 workers and specializes in hazardous waste and nuclear waste remediation, including Chernobyl and Three Mile Island. About 63 percent of the company's clients were in the private sector and over 60 percent of Bechtel's sales came from international customers. Bechtel's construction division has also worked on the Alaskan pipeline, the Hoover Dam, and San Francisco's rapid transit system. The Bechtel family continues to control the private company, with Riley P. Bechtel as its CEO and chairman.

Waste Management, Inc. of Houston, Texas, was ranked at the top of the solid-waste industry, and served clients throughout North America. It collects, transfers, and disposes of solid wastes, and manages landfills and recycling services. Sales in 1999 equaled $13.12 billion and the company employed 75,000 people. Waste Management was divesting itself of the operations of Waste Management International, which it purchased in 1998, in an attempt to decrease its debt.

Safety-Kleen Corp. (formerly Laidlaw Environmental Services Inc.) specializes in environmental remediation and related services, with over 400,000 client companies. In 1999 the company reported sales of $1.7 billion, a one-year sales growth of 42.2 percent. The company has over 200 branches in the United States and Canada. Laidlaw Inc. owned 44 percent of the company in 1999, and forestalled plans to sell its holdings after Safety-Kleen's stock value decreased. An internal investigation of the firm's accounting practices was launched and three top officials, including CEO Kenneth Winger, were suspended.

The IT Group, with 70,000 employees worldwide, was designated as the number-one hazardous waste design firm by *Engineering News-Record* for seven consecutive years. It posted 1999 revenues of $1.314 billion and relied on government contracts for 57 percent of its business. It was, however, seeking to diversify its contracts with overseas markets. The IT Group has been active in brownfield remediation.

RESEARCH AND TECHNOLOGY

Environmental remediation firms seek more effective and cost-efficient technologies and methods of remediation. In the mid- to late 1990s, environmental engineers discovered they could use compact directional drilling—a horizontal drilling technique—for environmental remediation and testing for underground contamination. Unlike vertical drilling, it does not destroy surface objects and formations such as trees and sidewalks. It also lets workers access contaminated underground areas that cannot be reached by other means and facilitates bioremediation of leaking underground tanks and obviates bringing contaminated soil and water to the surface.

Engineers at Lawrence Livermore National Laboratory in Livermore, California, announced a new

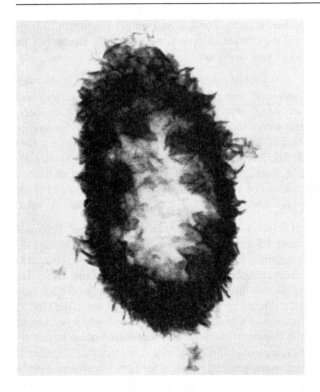

Sulphur-eating bacterium used in toxic waste treatment.
(Photo Researchers Inc./Jim Watson, Univ. of Southhampton, Science Photo Library)

technology that could reduce the time required for cleanup of underground contaminants from decades to months. Dynamic underground stripping uses steam to heat the soil and groundwater, thus freeing up pollutants. The technology was employed by Southern California Edison Corp. (SCE) at its Visalia pole yard, a four-acre Superfund site heavily contaminated with creosote and pentachlorophenols (PCPs). SCE reported that it removed about 1.2 million pounds of contaminants in only 30 months, a 1,500-fold increase in speed.

Older methods were also being exploited in new venues. For example, a pilot project was underway off the coast of southern California to install the deepest sea-floor cap of contaminated material ever attempted, in water up to 200 feet deep. The project was priced at $5 million and would begin the remediation of 11 million cubic yards of hazardous wastes.

Environmentally friendly approaches to remediation are gaining ground. The Federal Remediation Technologies Roundtable reported that the Idaho National Engineering and Environmental Laboratory was experimenting with an application of a potato, manure, and acetone compost mix to accelerate the cleanup of TNT-contaminated soil. Similarly, Envirogen, Inc. announced commencement of a National Science Foundation-funded project to research a bacterium that feeds on methyl tertiary butyl ether (MTBE), an oxygenated additive in gasoline that contaminates drinking water systems. MTBE captured public attention when it was featured in January 2000 on the television news magazine *60 Minutes*. It was also the focus of a class-action lawsuit brought by several environmental groups in the New York State Supreme Court.

Environmental remediation companies also used short-term crops such as alfalfa and sunflowers for cleaning up sites. Likewise, researchers experimented with using the bacterium *Deinococcus radiodurans* to clean up nuclear waste sites with radioactive and toxic contaminates. Researchers hope these genetically engineered bacteria will be able to degrade the toxins, yet withstand the radiation.

Some companies mix high- and low-tech options in their cleanup operations. At the Tibbetts Road Superfund site in New Hampshire, the cleanup effort directed by ARCADIS Geraghty & Miller Inc. involved "thyto-remediation," in which a pumped vacuum-enhanced recovery system extracted chemicals from the soil and water on the site. Afterwards, hybrid poplar trees were planted on the site, which acted as a natural filtration system to siphon the remaining low levels of chemicals from the soil and groundwater. The approach also reduced completion time for the project to three years, down from an estimated 22 years if more traditional methods had been used. U.S. Microbics employed its Bio-Raptor system to wash contaminated soil with microbially treated water in-situ, rather than hauling the soil off-site. The Bio-Raptor includes a mechanism for shredding and breaking up the soil so it can easily be treated on the premises. The procedure involves no gases, and is much quieter than traditional soil cleaning methods.

FURTHER READING

Bartsch, Charles. "The Color of Redevelopment." *American City & County,* November 1999.

Berg, David, and Grant Ferrier. "Meeting the Challenge of the 21st Century: The U.S. Environmental Industry." U.S. Department of Commerce, Office of Technology Policy, September 1998. Available from http://www.ta.doc.gov/reports.htm#mcs.

Bradford, Michael. "Cleanup Project Mixes Technology, Nature." *Business Insurance,* 24 May 1999.

Brown, Richard, Maureen C. Leahy, and Barry Molnaa. "Bioremediation: A Powerful and Resilient Companion Technology." *Pollution Engineering,* October 1999.

Canning, Kathie. "Beyond Compliance: Encouraging Top Performance." *Pollution Engineering,* August 1999.

Cohn, Jeffrey. "A Makeover for Rocky Mountain Arsenal." *Bioscience,* April 1999.

Franz, Neil. "EPA-Greens RCRA Accord." *Chemical Week,* 23 February 2000.

———. "EPA Proposes Funding Increases for Chemical Testing, Superfund." *Chemical Week,* 16 February 2000.

———. "Green Groups Press for Taxes." *Chemical Week,* 26 January 2000.

Hamilton, James, and W. Kip Viscusi. "Are Risk Regulators Rational? Evidence from Hazardous Waste Cleanup Decisions." *American Economic Review,* September 1999.

Koerner, Lizan, Lisa Blotz, and Robert Gilbert. "Remediation Lessons Learned." *Civil Engineering,* March 1999.

Kreuzer, Heidi. "Superfund Reforms: Satisfactory Advances or Stalled Progress?" *Pollution Engineering,* August 2000.

Lawlor, Matthew. "Super Settlements for Superfund: A New Paradigm for Voluntary Settlement?" *Boston College Environmental Affairs Law Review,* Fall 1999.

Licking, Ellen. "Is the Soil Polluted? Steam-Clean It." *Business Week,* 13 December 1999.

Maggi, Laura. "After Chafee." *American Prospect,* 20 December 1999.

McCrory, Martin. "Who's on First: CERCLA Cost Recovery, Contribution, and Protection." *American Business Law Journal,* Fall 1999.

Nash, James L. "Dueling Reports Re-Ignite Debate on Superfund." *Occupational Hazards,* August 2000.

"New Compound May Spell Doom for Deadly Water Pollutants." *Business Wire,* 17 April 2000.

"Reform Hopes Fade Again; Superfund." *Chemical Week,* 29 March 2000.

"Regulatory Watch: Chemical Industry Backs Changes Made by EPA and IRIS Procedures." *Chemical Week,* 7 February 2000.

Rosta, Paul. "Deep Water Cap to Cover DDT off Southern California Coast." *Engineering News-Record,* 24 April 2000.

Scott, Alex. "Industry Groups Opposed to European Draft Liability Law; Environment." *Chemical Week,* 1 March 2000.

Sissell, Kara. "Economics and Politics Drive Cleanup Trends; Environmental Services." *Chemical Week,* 12 January 2000.

"Superfund Tax Debate Resurfaces." *Chemical Week,* 8 March 2000.

U.S. Environmental Protection Agency. "The Brownfields Economic Redevelopment Initiative." October 1999. Available from http://www.epa.gov/swerosps/bf/html-doc/apappg00.htm.

———. "Superfund." November 2000. Available from http://www.epa.gov/superfund/.

Wood, David. "Superfund—Information on the Program's Funding and Status." *FDCH Government Account Reports,* 29 October 1999.

EXTREME SPORTS

INDUSTRY SNAPSHOT

Although sales of particular products, such as in-line skates, have been lethargic because of oversupply, sales of extreme sports products overall continue to outstrip those of more traditional sporting goods. Along with all the gear directly related to the sports, a slew of apparel, accessories, and media content is marketed to a willing audience of extreme sports enthusiasts, many of whom are in their teens and early twenties. And even as the growth of such well-established activities as in-line skating slows, newer extreme contests such as wakeboarding, freestyle motocross, and street luging are quickly amassing new followers.

According to statistics released by the Sporting Goods Manufacturers Association, tens of millions of Americans engage in extreme or alternative sports, depending how the category is defined. In-line skating is by far the most common, with nearly 28 million people slipping on a pair of skates at least once in 1999. Eight other sports associated with the extreme moniker, including skateboarding, snowboarding, wakeboarding, mountain biking, and rock climbing, claimed more than a million U.S. participants each during 1999.

The industry serving extreme sports devotees includes a diverse mix of companies. They range from multibillion-dollar mainstream sporting concerns such as Nike and Adidas-Salomon to scores of small startups run by fervent athletes. Brands marketed by the latter group tend to have more credibility with avid extreme athletes, who often identify with individualist and antiestablishment values.

ORGANIZATION AND STRUCTURE

As an industry, extreme sports tend to vary considerably in both structure and organization. In general, the sports player has four points of contact with the industry: purchase of basic equipment, purchase of safety equipment, training, and locating a place to practice the sport. The great explosion in extreme sports participation during the 1990s led to a proliferation of sport organizers and providers. Most new extreme sports business opportunities are in the service sector—providing equipment and opportunities for sports enthusiasts to practice and enjoy their pastimes.

Some aspects of extreme sports industries are regulated in part by government agencies. Bungee jumping from hot air balloons, for instance, requires a license from the Federal Aviation Administration. Bungee jumping from a crane requires licensing from the Occupational Safety and Health Administration to assure protection for the workers at the top of the crane. These sports have developed safety codes and organizations to ensure that safe practices are in place. The British Elastic Rope Sports Association and the North American Bungee Association both oversee safety standards within their industry.

ROCK CLIMBING AND WALL CLIMBING
Rock climbing and its manmade counterpart, artificial wall climbing, are among the most popular extreme sports. The television science program *Apple* reported that mountain and rock climbing, one of the oldest and most established of the extreme sports, experienced an annual growth rate of 50 percent in the mid-1990s.

Figures from the Sporting Goods Manufacturers Association (SGMA) for 1999 placed the number of U.S. rock and mountain climbers at 2.1 million, and almost a tenth of those enthusiasts were considered frequent participants, taking up the sport at least 15 times during the year. Artificial wall climbing attracted 4.8 million participants that year, but only around 5 percent of those who participated did so frequently.

There are two types of rock climbing practiced in the United States today. The first, and the most extreme, is called free climbing. Many rock-climbing enthusiasts prefer free climbing to all other forms of the sport. In free climbing, the climber uses only hands and feet for the actual climbing process. A rope is attached to pitons or chocks in the cliff in case of accidents. The second type of rock climbing is called direct-aid climbing; the climber attaches a rope ladder to pitons or chocks in the rock and uses the ladder to assist in the climb. Some climbers specialize in a particular type of ascent, such as vertical walls, while others specialize in different types of terrain, such as ice climbing, which involves ascending frozen waterfalls or glaciers. These types of climbs usually require additional equipment.

Of course, as rock climbing has become more mainstream, the definition of the sport has broadened. Many weekend adventurers enjoy walking on rocks on the weekends without necessarily scaling a 90-degree granite wall. Regardless of whether climbing straight up or walking on a slight incline, rock climbers need, and seem to love, the attendant gear. The rock-climbing industry has boomed in the last decade as demand for once specialty items such as climbing boots, backpacks, and dehydrated food are now available at the local Wal-Mart. The Outdoor Recreation Coalition of America, a trade organization, estimates that sales for rock-climbing and hiking equipment grew from just $1 billion in the early 1990s to over $5 billion by the end of the decade. Much of the industry's growth has relied on the proclivity that many consumers have for wearing hiking or climbing gear to the park or on a city stroll, even if they never intend to climb a mountain.

IN-LINE SKATING

In-line skating is one of the most popular modern sports. The SGMA estimated that participation in the sport has grown over 850 percent since the mid-1980s. Admittedly, the sport has grown so common that many of today's casual practitioners don't qualify as extreme athletes. Indeed, it has almost entirely eclipsed the traditional, subextreme pastime of roller skating.

The concept of in-line skates, in which the wheels are arranged in a single line like ice-skate blades, dates back to the 18th century. Around 1750, an enthusiastic Belgian skater named Joseph Merlin devised a set of roller skates by fastening wooden spools to the bottom of his shoes. In 1823 an Englishman named Robert John Tyers created the *rolito,* a set of skates with five wheels per shoe in a line. The idea of the *rolito* traveled to the Netherlands, where *skeelers* became popular for a period of 20 years. In 1863, an American named J.L. Plimpton developed the first roller skate using the pattern of two wheels in front and two in back. Plimpton's pattern dominated the market in the United States for almost 120 years. Hockey players Scott and Brennan Olson developed the first modern in-line skates in 1980. The sport has since attracted more than 30 million skaters around the world and has grown into a billion-dollar international industry.

In-line skaters vary from individuals interested only in skating as a hobby or an exercise, to serious aggressive skaters who compete by skating up vertical surfaces. Simple in-line skating, like traditional roller skating, can be performed on public streets and sidewalks. Aggressive skating, however, can require special surfaces. Both kinds of skating require safety equipment, including helmets, elbow pads, and knee pads. Manufacturers of skates usually also offer safety equipment geared to the interests of the people who buy their skates. Aggressive skating enthusiasts require different forms of protection than neighborhood skaters.

Many traditional manufacturers of roller skates turned to in-line skating when the craze began in the 1980s. The in-line skates manufactured and sold today generally have four wheels, arranged in a straight line, attached to a solid plastic or leather boot. The chassis, which holds the wheels, is usually made from aluminum, glass-reinforced nylon, or a composite. The wheels themselves are polyurethane.

Most advances in the field are technical innovations to the skate itself. Rollerblade introduced two important modifications: active brake technology (ABT) in 1994, and the Xtenblade in 1996. ABT allows the skater to brake simply by pointing a toe, while traditional skate brakes require the skater to press down with the heel. The Xtenblade is a children's skate that can be stretched through four sizes, allowing the skate to grow with the child.

In-line skating grew faster than any other for much of the 1990s. Although 1999 sales associated with the sport fell 30 percent to $305 million, the market for in-line skating equipment still exceeded those of more traditional sports such as baseball, tennis, bowling, and downhill skiing.

BUNGEE JUMPING

Bungee jumping remains one of the most controversial of the extreme sports, and one of the least widely practiced. The inspiration for it came from Pentecost Island, in the New Hebrides chain in the South Pacific. According to legend, a woman tried to escape from her abusive husband by climbing to the top of a banyan tree. When he started to climb after her, she tied vines to her ankles and jumped from the top of the tree. The vines kept her safe, but her husband fell to his death. By the time the first *National Geographic* article appeared in 1955 describing the islanders' practice of diving from the top of a tower, the practice had changed into a ritual performed by the men of the tribe, partly as a rite of manhood and partly as a fertility ceremony to ensure a good crop of yams.

On 1 April 1979, the modern sport of bungee jumping was born when members of the Oxford Dangerous Sports Club jumped from Clifton Bridge in Bristol, England. A member of the same group set a world record in 1980 by dropping from the Royal Gorge Bridge in Colorado. Although bungee jumping overall has a low total number of fatalities, the sport has attracted a lot of notoriety because of the inherent danger involved. For instance, an exhibition jumper named Laura Dinky Patterson died in preparation for a jump at the 1997 Super Bowl in New Orleans.

The Kockelman brothers were among the fathers of bungee jumping in the United States. John and Peter Kockelman, engineering graduates of California Polytechnic State University in San Luis Obispo, formed Bungee Adventures Inc. in 1998. Bungee Adventures was North America's first commercial bungee operation, according to the company's Web site, which popularized the sport of bungee jumping by leaping from bridges over deep ravines in the Sierra Nevadas. The brothers have jumped from many diverse structures, including redwood trees, indoor coliseums, office atriums, the Golden Gate Bridge, and hot-air balloons. In 1993 Bungee Adventures released the Ejection Seat, a patented human slingshot ride. The Kockelman brothers have also been active in planning safety regulations for the industry.

By and large, though, bungee jumping is a fairly unregulated sport. Jump sponsors can range from unlicensed pirate jumpers to large companies. The sites of the jumps also vary widely. Jumping from public

---

About...	**EXTREME WEB SITES**

The Web is awash with sites dedicated to alternative sports. They include offerings from traditional publishers and media outlets, content from manufacturers, and of course, eclectic pages posted by fans and practitioners. Below is a sampling of 10 sites.

- Burton.com is the flashy home page of the world's top snowboard maker.
- Climbing.com is a Web version of a popular rock and mountain climbing magazine.
- EXPN.com is ESPN's site devoted to several of the most popular extreme sports.
- ExtremeSports.com is a general site dedicated to the subject.
- Liquidforce.com contains product information and news from a large wakeboard manufacturer.
- Quiksilver.com is the interactive home page of a leading surf apparel company.
- Skater.net packages a wide array of information of interest to skateboard enthusiasts.
- Sportlink.com contains statistics and other information from the Sporting Goods Manufacturers Association.
- Streetluge.com bills itself as the official site of professional street luging.
- Vans.com pitches shoes and other gear to skaters.

---

bridges is perhaps the most popular because the sites require little preparation and are plentiful. Safety concerns, however, have made bungee jumping from public bridges legal only in the states of Oregon and Washington. Jump sponsors can legally work from privately owned bridges, but the regulations against public bridge jumping have led to many illegal pirate jumps. Hot-air balloon jumps are also popular, but they are dependent on weather and time of day. Balloons can fly safely only in relatively still air, usually in the early morning or evening. A third option is crane jumping; however, cranes that can support the repetitive shock caused by bungee jumping are expensive and hard to find. A jump sponsor can spend between $70,000 and $150,000 for a used crane and then has to obtain permission from local agencies to set it up and use it for the business of jumping.

SNOWBOARDING AND SKIBOARDING

Snowboarding is arguably the fastest-growing extreme sport. Ski resorts, once hesitant to allowing snowboarders in, are now embracing them, especially during the off-season. Since the snowboard course tends to be smaller, resorts manufacture the snow (usually shaved ice) during periods of limited snowfall—much like ski resorts. In the late 1990s, nearly two-thirds of ticket sales at Southern California ski resorts came from snowboarders. A recent variation called skiboarding, which involves smaller boards that allow higher speeds and more tricks, has gained popularity as well. A late 1990s estimate pegged the U.S. snowboard market at $2 billion a year, while the number of participants grew from 1.4 million in 1990 to 4.72 million in 1999.

WAKEBOARDING

Wakeboarding, performed in the wake of power-boats, is the fastest-growing water sport. The sport is similar to water skiing, only a board is used rather than skis. The board makes it easier for daring athletes to perform flips and jumps, and wakeboarding shares some techniques with surfing, skateboarding, and snowboarding, making this newer sport a popular warm-weather substitute for those more established extreme activities. A number of leading wakeboard manufacturers are snowboard makers that branched into the wakeboard business.

STREET LUGING

Another of the newer entrants to the world of extreme sports, street luging is inspired by the winter sled-based luge. In the street variety, the lugers, sometimes called "riders," lie face-up and feet first on a board similar to a skateboard. Donning helmets and other protective gear, riders race each other on downhill courses, steering with subtle body movements and braking with their feet. Street-luge boards, which are specially engineered, can reach speeds up to 90 miles an hour.

FREESTYLE MOTOCROSS

Freestyle motocross is an amalgamation of various motorbike stunt and race events that have been around for decades. The version that has gained favor lately, as featured in such competitions as the Gravity Games and the X Games, usually involves a dirt track with large ramps and obstacles. Motocross bikers attempt to pull off high jumps and other difficult and original tricks while maintaining style and continuity in their performance.

CURRENT CONDITIONS

Many small entrepreneurial companies market trips to exotic locations specifically for the purpose of pursuing extreme sports. Adrenalin Dreams Adventures, a worldwide company based in Pittsburgh, Pennsylvania, creates adventure vacation packages both in the United States and abroad. Many foreign countries have fewer regulations than the United States for governing extreme sports. In addition to two bridge bungee-jumping sites in Pennsylvania, the company offers an African vacation that includes sky-diving, bungee jumping, whitewater rafting, tiger fishing, and wild-animal encounters. Adrenalin Dreams Adventures, according to its promotional material, has trained and supplied sites in the United States, Colombia, Brazil, Norway, Japan, and Israel, and it supplies cord, equipment, and training to bungee-jumping programs worldwide.

Most rock-climbing companies tend to be small, local outfits run by climbing enthusiasts trying to make a living by introducing their sport to newcomers. Many provide training and equipment for novices and advanced instruction for more experienced climbers. A typical outing costs between $75 and $100, usually with equipment included. As with most extreme sports, there are no national companies capitalizing on rock climbing as a corporate enterprise.

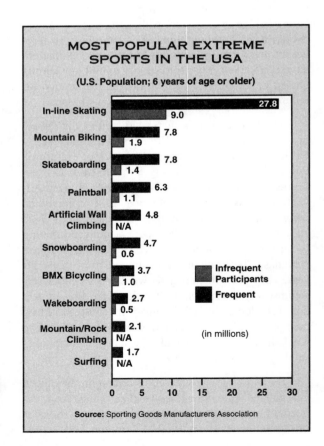

MOST POPULAR EXTREME SPORTS IN THE USA

(U.S. Population; 6 years of age or older)

Sport	Infrequent Participants	Frequent
In-line Skating	27.8	9.0
Mountain Biking	7.8	1.9
Skateboarding	7.8	1.4
Paintball	6.3	1.1
Artificial Wall Climbing	4.8	N/A
Snowboarding	4.7	0.6
BMX Bicycling	3.7	1.0
Wakeboarding	2.7	0.5
Mountain/Rock Climbing	2.1	N/A
Surfing	1.7	N/A

(in millions)

Source: Sporting Goods Manufacturers Association

The most extreme rock-climbing adventure requires not only professional equipment and training, but professional guides as well. Mt. McKinley, once the most feared mountain in the world and only touched by the most skilled climbers, is now something of an extreme sports tourist attraction for the very wealthy. The *Los Angeles Times* reported that, in the late 1990s, the mountain received more than 1,200 climbers a year, leaving behind an estimated several thousand pounds of trash. Professional guides for mountains such as McKinley, which are highly recommended even for skilled climbers, average between $2,800 and $3,500 for a standard climb. The most challenging climbs can cost up to $10,000. One in 200 climbers who steps onto Mt. McKinley never step off again.

The sale of safety equipment accounts for a greater percentage of sales in the extreme sports market. One reason for this is the increased awareness of the safety hazards associated with snowboarding. According to the U.S. Consumer Product Safety Commission, injuries among snowboarders have tripled since 1995.

The increasing popularity of extreme sports, both from a participant and spectator standpoint, is evidenced in the continued media coverage devoted to such ventures. Snowboarding got a strong boost in 1998 with its debut at the Nagano Winter Olympics. In 1999 the fifth annual Summer X Games, sponsored and covered by ESPN, drew 270,000 spectators and were watched internationally by millions of viewers on ESPN, ESPN2, and ABC. ESPN also backs the annual Winter X Games and in 2000 launched the alternative sports Web site EXPN, with highly graphical content devoted to five extreme categories: skateboarding, in-line skating, surfing, snowboarding, and skiing. Viacom's MTV Sports and Music Fest and NBC's Gravity Games are other recent additions to the extreme games viewer market. Meanwhile, a spate of other Web sites and magazines cater to enthusiasts of the full range of alternative sports.

INDUSTRY LEADERS

RETAILERS

On the retail side of the business, Recreational Equipment, Inc. (REI) is among the leaders. The member-owned cooperative retailer, which markets many general-line sporting goods as well, posted sales of $621 million in 1999, up 5.8 percent over 1998, and employed 6,000.

Another influential player, The North Face, Inc., is both a manufacturer and a retailer. The California-based company makes everything from hiking gear for frigid polar expeditions to backpacks for use on an afternoon stroll. In 1999 sales fell to $238 million, a 3.7 percent slide from the previous year.

Known as much for its trendy style and chic designs as for its high quality equipment, Lost Arrow Corp. is another retailer with manufacturing ties. Perhaps best known for its pricey Patagonia-brand retail outlets and merchandise, Lost Arrow took in $182 million in sales in its fiscal 1999, a 7.1 percent improvement over the previous year.

Vans, Inc. is one of the more visible apparel and accessory maker-retailers catering to the extreme sports crowd. Its main product line is a diverse selection of athletic shoes, mostly targeted at skateboarders. Vans also operates a few skateboarding parks in California and sponsors extreme sporting events. In its fiscal 2000 Vans recorded $273.5 million in sales, up 33.3 percent from the previous year.

MANUFACTURERS

Manufacturers devoted to alternative sports include the fast-growing Ride, Inc., which had $39.7 million in sales in fiscal 1999, up 8.8 percent from the year before. Ride made its name in snowboards, which account for almost a third of its sales. The company is rapidly expanding into other extreme sports domains, such as wakeboarding.

The world's biggest snowboard maker, though, is Burton Snowboards, founded by Jake Burton, one of the pioneers of snowboarding. In addition to snowboards, Burton Snowboards also produces apparel and accessories. In 1998 the privately held company had estimated sales of $150 million.

For in-line skating equipment, the leader in the field is still its founder, Rollerblade. In 1996, a survey by *In-Line Retailer & Industry News* named the company first among the 25 major manufacturers of in-line skating equipment, but the company does not release financial information.

First Team Sports is the number-two company in the in-line world. As with other in-line skate companies, First Team lost ground in the late 1990s as the market for skates grew saturated. Its sales grew 6.1 percent in 2000 to reach $45 million. With hockey great Wayne Gretzky as its chief spokesperson, First Team is especially popular among young skaters.

Variflex, Inc. produces more than 25 different kinds of in-line skates as well as snowboards, skateboards, and other sporting equipment aimed at more casual participants. Because of the slowdown in inline skate demand, the company's sales dropped to $37.4 million in fiscal 1999, marking its second year in a row of double-digit revenue declines.

Rock climbing and bungee jumping use similar equipment, and major manufacturers for both sports overlap. One of the most prominent manufacturers of climbing and jumping equipment in Europe is Petzl Ltd. Petzl makes and sells harnesses that are used by both private individuals and service companies. Its Crux harness is among the most popular and most copied safety devices used in sports today.

FURTHER READING

"ESPN Showcases Alternative Sports." *Knight-Ridder/Tribune Business News,* 29 June 1999.

"Extreme Sports Focus Has Company on Road to Success." *Emerging Company Report,* 10 July 1998.

Forstenzer, Martin. "On and Off the Beaten Path." *New York Times,* 16 May 1998.

Frase, Nancy. *Bungee Jumping for Fun and Profit.* Merrillville, IN: ICS Books, 1992.

Garcia, Irene. "The Height of Adventure." *Los Angeles Times,* 11 September 1997.

Hochman, Paul. "Street Lugers, Stunt Bikers, and—Colgate-Palmolive!" *Fortune,* 22 November 1999.

Johnston, Turlough, and Madeleine Hallden. *Rock Climbing Basics.* Mechanicsburg, PA: Stackpole Books, 1995.

Kroichick, Ron. "X Games Finds Snow, Beach Don't Mix." *San Francisco Chronicle,* 27 June 1998.

Luo, Michael. "As Snowboarding Popularity Soars, Injuries Multiply." *Los Angeles Times,* 23 March 1999.

Murphy, Kim. "To Some, the Height of Lunacy." *Los Angeles Times,* 1 April 1998.

Ruibal, Sal. "Going to the Extremes Surfers Turned Alternative Tide." *USA Today,* 12 August 1998.

Spiegel, Peter. "Gen-X-tremist Pitchmen." *Forbes,* 14 December 1998.

Sporting Goods Manufacturers Association. "2000 State of the Industry Report." North Palm Beach, FL: Sporting Goods Manufacturers Association, February 2000. Available from http://www.sportlink.com.

———. " In-Line Skating Rolls Out Initiatives to Counter Market Woes." North Palm Beach, FL: Sporting Goods Manufacturers Association, 13 March 2000. Available from http://www.sportlink.com/press_room/2000_releases/inline2000-001.html.

———. "Whassup... With Extreme Sports?" North Palm Beach, FL: Sporting Goods Manufacturers Association, 30 October 2000. Available from http://www.sportlink.com/press_room/2000_releases/m2000-032.html.

"What's Hot and Why." *Inc.,* July 1998.

FERTILITY MEDICINE: PRODUCTS AND SERVICES

Use of drugs and clinical procedures in the pursuit of bearing children has been on a steady incline in the United States for two decades. Although such treatments lead to successful childbirth in only a minority of cases, technological advances have edged up the success rates of assisted reproductive techniques. Likewise, sales of fertility drugs have flourished.

Estimates vary on exactly how much is spent on fertility medicine, but figures from the late 1990s place it between $1 and $2 billion a year. Statistics suggest that more than 6.1 million U.S. couples are faced with infertility, often defined as the inability to conceive after one year of unprotected intercourse, and about a fifth of them seek out treatment of some sort. In fact, while the percentage of couples who are infertile is believed to remain stable over time, the proportion of those obtaining treatment has possibly doubled since the 1980s as treatments became more widely available.

Not surprisingly, social trends have also influenced demand for infertility treatments. For decades many U.S. couples have been waiting longer to have children, and the evidence is unambiguous that the older women are, the harder it is to get pregnant. And as the general public has grown more comfortable with the idea of procedures such as in vitro fertilization (IVF), institutional support for infertility treatments has risen. Private health-insurance plans increasingly cover infertility treatment, and over a dozen states have passed laws that require insurers to cover it under certain conditions.

Despite the improvements in technology, the overall failure rate for fertilization procedures is somewhere between 70 and 80 percent. Yet another downside to fertility treatment has become apparent. Now that baseline data have accumulated for more than two decades, research is beginning to show correlations between fertility drugs and certain cancers, such as breast and ovarian cancer in women. Other potential drawbacks with some infertility treatments include a greater chance of multiple births and the risk of passing on infertility to children.

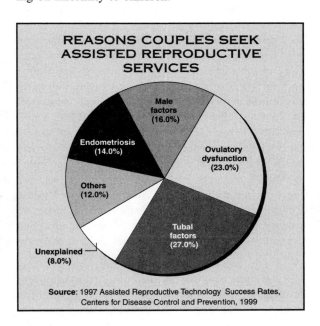

REASONS COUPLES SEEK ASSISTED REPRODUCTIVE SERVICES

Male factors (16.0%)

Ovulatory dysfunction (23.0%)

Endometriosis (14.0%)

Others (12.0%)

Tubal factors (27.0%)

Unexplained (8.0%)

Source: 1997 Assisted Reproductive Technology Success Rates, Centers for Disease Control and Prevention, 1999

ORGANIZATION AND STRUCTURE

The fertility industry can be divided into two broad sectors: pharmaceutical and medical. The pharmaceutical sector is dominated by two companies,

Serono Laboratories, Inc. and Organon, Inc. Both firms manufacture drugs used primarily to stimulate or regulate ovulation. The drugs can be prescribed on their own, as a low-tech treatment, to assist conception. More and more, however, they are used in conjunction with a high-tech procedure such as IVF in which the drugs stimulate ovulation and then eggs are collected and fertilized in vitro before being implanted in a woman's uterus or fallopian tubes.

Selling fertility drugs is an extremely profitable undertaking for pharmacies. A typical prescription for a woman undergoing IVF includes 12 different products, including as many as eight drugs, prenatal vitamins, and paraphernalia such as syringes and swabs. Profit margins are also higher in infertility care than for other categories of drugs pharmacists dispense. While most pharmacies make a 20 to 22 percent profit on drug sales, they earn 30 to 35 percent on infertility products.

The medical sector of the industry is far more complex. It includes private obstetrics and gynecology (OB/GYN) and urology practices, fertility clinics, hospitals, and laboratories. Statistics on fertility clinics are difficult to come by. One reason is the lack of agreement as to what constitutes a "fertility clinic." The American Society for Reproductive Medicine (ASRM), which for years has single-handedly assembled statistics on fertility in America, prefers the term "ART (assisted reproductive technology) practice." ART encompasses high-tech methods of fertilization such as IVF, gamete intrafallopian transfer, and intracystoplasmic sperm injection, all of which arose after the first test-tube babies were born in the late 1970s and early 1980s. ASRM's professional organization, the Society for Assisted Reproductive Technology, had nearly 360 member practices. That figure, according to ASRM, accounts for about 90 percent of the ART practices in the United States. The Centers for Disease Control and Prevention has released annual reports on fertility clinics, giving consumers, researchers, and lawmakers access to success rate rankings of over 300 clinics that provided data for its studies.

ART practices can be small or large, independent or affiliated with other institutions such as hospitals or universities. The larger practices have staffs of physicians, embryologists, andrologists, nurses, lab technicians, and advanced laboratory facilities where the latest techniques of micromanipulation can be performed. A small ART practice might consist of just one or two reproductive endocrinologists, a staff of a few nurses and technicians, and a small lab capable of basic fertility analyses. When it performs high-tech treatments, such a clinic generally uses a hospital lab.

Fertility treatments can be classed as low tech and high tech. Low-tech treatments might be relatively new—fertility drugs, for example, have been in use only 30 years or so—but they rely on traditional medical techniques. The most common treatments include artificial insemination, surgery, and basic drug therapies. They have varying success rates, generally lower than high-tech treatments. Success in fertility is defined as a cycle of treatment that results in the birth of a live baby.

Artificial insemination is the oldest and most common low-tech treatment. Semen, either from a woman's partner or an anonymous donor, is inserted into the vagina through a catheter; insertion is timed to occur just after ovulation to maximize the chances of fertilization. Since the 1970s, most donor sperm has been supplied by sperm banks, where it has been cryogenically preserved.

Surgery has been most often used when a woman has no fallopian tubes or when they have been blocked or damaged. Until the advent of IVF, surgery was the only possible treatment for tubal infertility. Surgery, however, is more costly and invasive and less effective than IVF, and during the 1990s its use declined by 50 percent.

Fertility drugs are one of the simplest low-tech methods. They can be taken orally, by injection, or subcutaneously (under the skin), and they work by stimulating the ovaries to produce eggs. After approximately 36 hours, fertilization is attempted via sexual intercourse or artificial insemination. The use of fertility drugs is complicated by their powerful effects on the endocrine and reproductive systems, as well as their link to ovarian cancer. Furthermore, a large percentage of pregnancies stemming from fertility drugs result in multiple fetuses. Nationwide, about 38 percent of the live births from fertility-enhanced pregnancies in 1996 involved more than one fetus.

As a means of achieving pregnancy and birth, these low-tech methods when used on their own seem to be unpredictable. Statistics for the U.S. population as a whole are not available, but studies on small sample groups suggest that simple artificial insemination has a success rate of around 6 percent; when accompanied by fertility drugs, that rate can nearly triple. Fertility drugs alone have a success rate of approximately 10 percent. There are conditions when neither drugs nor artificial insemination can be used, such as when a woman has tubal problems or when a man has a low or nonexistent sperm count.

ART is at the high-tech end of the fertility treatment scale. The most common treatments are IVF, gamete intrafallopian transfer (GIFT), zygote intrafallopian transfer (ZIFT), and increasingly, intracytoplasmic sperm injection. Freezing of sperm and embryos (known as cryopreservation) and drug therapies are often used in tandem with these techniques.

IVF is the most common high-tech assisted reproductive technology. In this procedure, eggs are removed from the prospective mother's ovaries, usually after stimulation with fertility drugs, or donor eggs are obtained. The eggs are then fertilized in a laboratory dish with sperm from the partner or a donor. Two to four of the resulting embryos are implanted in the woman's uterus. Other embryos can be cryogenically preserved for use in future IVF if the first attempt at conception is unsuccessful. IVF can be used in practically all cases of infertility, though at first it was used primarily for women with fallopian tube disorders or endometriosis, a condition in which tissue from the lining of the uterus exists and functions elsewhere in the abdomen.

In GIFT, gametes (sperm and eggs) are collected and the sperm prepared as in IVF. They are introduced separately, however, into the fallopian tubes rather than the uterus and fertilization takes place in vivo, that is, in the body. It was believed that a large number of eggs and high concentrations of sperm at the natural site of fertilization would increase the likelihood of conception. As IVF is refined, use of GIFT is dropping. Its slightly higher success rates do not seem to outweigh the more difficult surgical intervention that is required.

ZIFT is a hybrid of IVF and GIFT. Fertilization takes place in vitro as in IVF. The zygote is introduced immediately into the fallopian tube, as in GIFT, where the normal cycle of conception then runs its course. ZIFT is most often used when a male's sperm count is low or when antisperm antibodies are present in the woman.

Nonsurgical embryonic selective thinning and transfer (NEST) is a new technique that helps IVF embryos live a day or so longer. This allows extra time to determine which one is the strongest and healthiest for implantation. The embryonic shell is then hatched to make it easier to attach to the uterine lining. Some experts believe this process may boost IVF success rates from about 24 percent to as high as 80 percent.

Intracytoplasmic sperm injection (ICSI), first used successfully in Belgium in 1992, is one of the latest high-tech procedures to be used on a mass scale. A single sperm cell is injected directly into an egg. ICSI enables men with very low sperm counts or inactive sperm—80 percent of infertile men—to father their own children. The procedure also allows men who have had vasectomies to have genetic offspring. ICSI is seen as a useful tool for many conditions because it largely eliminates sperm as a factor in fertilization and allows physicians to concentrate on the conditions for pregnancy in a woman's body. By 1999, tens of thousands of babies had been born through ICSI.

The chance that a healthy, reproductively normal couple will conceive a child in a given month is estimated at around 20 percent. Success rates of assisted reproductive technology procedures are as good as or often better than that, ranging from about 22 to 28 percent.

Fertility treatment is expensive. A single attempt with artificial insemination usually costs between $300 and $500. One cycle of fertility drug treatment, which typically involves multiple drugs, can cost $2,500, and patients typically need drug treatment for two to four monthly cycles. ART procedures typically cost between $8,000 and $12,000 per treatment. Given that the most effective treatment results in a child barely one in four times, a high percentage of infertile couples inevitably go through more than one round of treatment. According to Kiplinger Online it is not unusual for a couple to spend at least $30,000 trying to have a child.

Only about 25 percent of traditional insurance plans and 37 percent of health maintenance organizations (HMOs) cover infertility. Even when they do, reimbursements are often limited to diagnostic costs; when they cover treatment, coverage is frequently limited to treatments that are ineffective for some patients or less cost-effective than others. As of 2000, 13 states mandated insurance for infertility, but coverage varies widely. Some states require a round of low-tech treatments before IVF can be attempted. Some exclude HMOs from providing coverage. Hawaii mandates nothing more than a one-time outpatient diagnostic visit. In Texas, a couple must try unsuccessfully for five years before they are considered infertile, although most physicians consider one year the defining period. Lack of insurance combined with high costs has made ongoing infertility treatments a realistic option for only the well-to-do.

But this may be changing. Infertility treatment has long been something of a gray area with insurers, but increasing demand coupled with lawsuits by those without insurance coverage seems to be leading to a more standardized approach. In June 1998, the U.S. Supreme Court issued a ruling stating that reproduction is "a major life activity." This cleared the way for patients denied infertility coverage by insurers to sue

About **FERTILITY CLINIC SUCCESS RATES:
A FECUND SUBJECT FOR RESEARCH**

National statistics indicate that, on average, just under 30 percent of assisted reproductive technology (ART) procedures, mostly in vitro fertilization (IVF), lead to pregnancy. That percentage has crept up slowly since comprehensive statistics were first compiled in the mid-1990s, but otherwise success rates have been fairly stable on the national level. Data for individual clinics and practitioners, however, reveal a wide range of variation, not all of which is easily explained.

In fact, a pair of large clinics in urban areas can have dramatically different success rates, according to figures published in an annual study by the Society for Assisted Reproduction Technology and the Centers for Disease Control and Prevention. One such pair is the New York University Medical Center (NYUMC) of New York City and the Greater Cincinnati Institute for Reproductive Health at the Christ Hospital (GCIRH) in Cincinnati. Both initiate hundreds of ART cycles each year (in 1997 NYUMC performed 818 procedures using fresh, nondonor eggs, while GCIRH did 564), and each performs IVF almost exclusively.

Their live-birth rates differed significantly. For women under 35 who were using fresh, nondonor eggs (the largest demographic group for IVF procedures nationally), the Cincinnati clinic recorded a 1997 average rate of 32.8 live births per 100 cycles, whereas patients at NYUMC succeeded in having live births 50.7 percent of the time. Both initiated over 200 of that type of cycle. To allow for statistical error, the actual rates were probably between 27.2 percent and 38.5 percent for

GCIRH and between 44.1 percent and 57.3 percent for NYUMC, based on a 95 percent confidence interval reported in the survey analysis. Thus, even after factoring in random error, it would appear that NYU's clinic had a significant edge over GCIRH.

Size doesn't appear to be a deciding factor. Indeed, the much larger Boston IVF clinic in Brookline, Massachusetts, which did 2,200 fresh, nondonor IVF procedures that year, had a lower average than the Cincinnati facility. Of the 837 cycles involving women under 35 with fresh, nondonor eggs, just 27.7 percent (24.7 to 30.8 percent including the margin of error) resulted in live birth. Even worse, the Glenview, Illinois, Center for Human Reproduction averaged just 21.7 percent live births for its 598 cycles of that kind—less than half the success rate at the NYU Medical Center.

Separate research specifically on success rates at the Center for Human Reproduction (CHR), an affiliate of the University of Illinois, highlights the disparity in ART success even among doctors at the same facility. A 1998 study by Vishvanath C. Karande, a clinical OB/GYN professor at the university, found that pregnancy rates (which are higher than live-birth rates) of individual doctors' patients ranged from 14.3 to 37.4 percent within the same clinic. Although Karande believed that some of the variation could be explained by different doctors' willingness to take on difficult cases, he suggested that the so-called physician factor might also be caused by differing choices of medication, dosage, and timing. As a result of this research, CHR began a program to improve the success rates of below-average doctors.

---

under Title VII of the Civil Rights Act of 1964 or under the Americans with Disabilities Act of 1990.

Patients find fertility services in a variety of ways. Many are referred by personal physicians. Some clinics advertise. Consumer groups are a valuable source of information. The most important one in the fertility area is Resolve. Besides having over 50 local offices throughout the United States, Resolve maintains a National Helpline and compiles a referral list of over 800 fertility specialists in the United States and Canada. Another important source of information is patient support groups. Members share the names of doctors and their experiences, suggest solutions to those with problems, and help newcomers navigate the complex and often impersonal medical bureaucracy.

The Internet has become an important resource as well, enabling individuals to gain access to information about new techniques and medications that their own doctors may be unwilling to share. The num-

ber of fertility-related chat rooms is growing, and a few fertility doctors have set up Web pages to answer questions and discuss the latest medical developments. Some pharmacies sell fertility drugs online. The Web site for the International Council on Infertility Information Dissemination also provides a wealth of material.

The field is beginning to see the development of a market for donated eggs. From 1989 to 1994 the number of births that resulted from the implantation of donated eggs grew from about 120 to nearly 1,300. Cumulatively, by 1999 upwards of 10,000 babies were produced from donor eggs. In an extraordinary example, 63-year-old Arceli Keh gave birth in 1996 to a healthy baby that grew from a donor egg. As these successes multiply, donor eggs will be in increasingly high demand. It can be a lucrative business; donors can earn up to $5,000 for donating eggs, and an egg that is suitably matched to an infertile couple may cost the couple as much as $6,000 or more.

REGULATION AND LEGISLATION

The Food and Drug Administration (FDA) regulates the manufacture and sale of all fertility drugs in the United States. Like other pharmaceuticals, such drugs must undergo a series of stringent clinical trials and reviews before they are approved for use. According to the Pharmaceutical Research and Manufacturers of America, it takes an average of 15 years for a drug to move from the experimental stage to pharmacy shelves, a long process that contributes to high costs. Drugs are usually available in other countries years before they reach the United States but remain unavailable to American consumers. Occasionally the FDA will relax restrictions on foreign drugs. When two common American fertility drugs, Pergonal and Metrodin, were in very short supply between February 1996 and February 1997, the FDA allowed the import of substitutes from foreign suppliers.

Andrology laboratories, which work with sperm, are regulated on a federal level by the Clinical Laboratory Improvement Amendments of 1988 (CLIA-88). The law spells out strict standards of specimen control and technical supervision for labs performing "high complexity" procedures and tests, such as those connected with sperm handling. Labs are required to register with the Health Care Financial Administration and are subject to inspection by that body or an equivalent such as the College of American Pathologists. Embryology labs, where in vitro fertilization takes place, do not fall under CLIA-88 regulation.

The American Society for Reproductive Medicine (ASRM), together with the College of American Pathologists, has drawn up andrology and embryology lab guidelines for its member clinics. There are also attempts in Congress to include andrology labs under CLIA-88, a move ASRM opposes because CLIA was written for diagnostic facilities and their specific conditions. Embryology labs, the ASRM argued, engage in treatment rather than diagnosis and should be regulated accordingly.

The Fertility Clinic Success Rate and Certification Act of 1992 (FCSRCA) directed the U.S. Department of Health and Human Services, in cooperation with the Centers for Disease Control and Prevention (CDC), to develop a model program for the certification of embryology labs. Unlike CLIA-88, such programs would be voluntary and would be made available to the states to adopt at their discretion. Lack of funding has prevented the model program clause from ever being implemented.

FCSRCA also includes a provision requiring fertility clinics to report success rates for IVF, GIFT, ZIFT and other procedures to the CDC. The CDC issued its second such report in 1999, based on data collected in 1996. (Previously, ASRM collected and distributed this information itself.) The 1996 data show that nationwide IVF had a 26 percent success rate, GIFT 28.7 percent, ZIFT 30 percent, and ICSI 28 percent (where success is live-birth rate per retrieval procedure). Despite the above-mentioned federal policies, the use of assisted reproductive technology by physicians and clinics is largely unregulated, and a variety of doctors dabble in fertility treatments. Since 1978 the number of clinics has increased from about 30 to over 300. Although the drug therapies are approved by the FDA, the actual practice of fertility medicine is unstructured and highly variant.

BACKGROUND AND DEVELOPMENT

The first documented case of artificial insemination in humans was in 1790. The development of infertility treatment as a discrete sector of the contemporary economy is directly linked to technological development. The most important clinical practices of the 1990s have their roots in the discoveries of the past 40 years.

The 1950s and 1960s were largely a period of research advances that only slowly made their way into practice. The first of the modern fertility-inducing substances were discovered and developed during the 1960s, when gonadotropins (hormonal substances that stimulate ovulation) were extracted from human pituitary tissue. Mass scale production was made possible when researchers learned they could also be produced from the urine of postmenopausal women. So-called menotropins are the active ingredients in the most widely used fertility drugs such as Pergonal, Humegon, and Metrodin.

Clomiphene citrate was also first introduced in the 1960s. Unlike menotropins, however, which had to be injected, it was an oral medication. Another advantage of clomiphene citrate was the considerably lower incidence of multiple births that resulted from taking it—about 8 percent as opposed to between 25 and 50 percent for the menotropins. In 1977, Andrew V. Schally and Roger Guillemin won the Nobel Prize in physiology for their discovery of gonadotropin releasing hormone (GnRH), a substance that enables the pituitary to secrete gonadotropins, which in turn stimulate the gonads. GnRH restored ovulation in women in whom it had apparently ceased completely.

Cryopreservation techniques date from the late 1940s, and the first successful artificial inseminations using sperm that had been frozen were reported in 1954. An increase in oral contraception and legalized abortion decreased the number of babies available for adoption during the 1970s, helping create a demand for donor sperm. As a result, sperm banks, which could preserve sperm cryogenically, proliferated.

The major landmark in the history of fertility was achieved in England's Bourn Hall clinic on 25 July 1978, when Patrick Steptoe and Robert Edwards delivered the world's first "test-tube baby" conceived via in vitro fertilization (IVF). The first IVF baby in the United States was delivered in 1981 by Drs. Howard and Georgiana Jones. The 1980s were subsequently marked by breathtaking progress. Among the new developments was transvaginal ultrasound, a procedure that involved inserting a wand vaginally to collect eggs needed for IVF. It required only a local anesthetic, and no laparoscope was necessary. The first pregnancies were achieved using frozen embryos, and the first births were from donor eggs. Late in the decade, the first GIFT and ZIFT babies were born.

During the early 1990s, intracytoplasmic sperm injection (ICSI) was developed, and further refinements of the procedure continue. With this method, if there is no sperm in a man's semen, it can be surgically removed from testicular tissue and implanted using ICSI. New technologies are also being perfected that enable physicians to recognize a potent, live sperm cell among sperm that are apparently dead.

The impact of these new technologies can be seen in the growth of assisted reproductive technology (ART) since the early 1980s. In 1985, four years after the first American IVF baby, the Society of Assisted Reproductive Technology had 30 member clinics. By 1993, that number had grown to 267 clinics, and by 1999 the figure climbed to more than 335.

The fertility industry has suffered occasional embarrassments. During the summer of 1996 a scandal erupted when it was revealed that three doctors at the University of California at Irvine were suspected of having taken eggs and embryos from patients without their consent. As many as 10 babies may have been delivered from the "undonated" eggs and embryos. The physicians were sued by 39 patients, and the incident led to the closure of the university's Center for Reproductive Health. In Virginia, another fertility doctor inseminated nearly 75 patients with his own semen and not with semen from anonymous donors as he had told them. He was sentenced to a five-year prison term for fraud.

Cloning is a result of ART. In 1997 a sheep named Dolly was cloned from a single adult cell. While this was a tremendous milestone in the annals of science, it was also a development fraught with ethical and moral issues. For instance, doctors are researching the transfer of the nucleus from an older woman's egg into a younger donor egg whose nucleus has been removed. The donor egg would then be transferred to the uterus of the older patient for gestation. Using denucleated eggs is very similar to the process that led to Dolly the sheep, and this kind of ART makes the cloning of humans very possible. President Bill Clinton responded to the controversy surrounding such procedures by calling for a five-year ban on any experiments related to human cloning.

CURRENT CONDITIONS

A growing number of infertile couples opt for drugs or procedures that may help them produce children. The number of clinics devoted to high-tech assisted reproductive technology (ART) jumped from only 30 in 1985 to over 400 in 2000. IVF continues to be the most common form of ART, accounting for more than 70 percent of all procedures, while the more invasive GIFT and ZIFT methods are on the decline. IVF has been shown to yield live-birth rates similar to those of the other two procedures.

An ironic side effect of many infertility treatments is the prevalence of multiple births: couples who had trouble conceiving a single child find themselves rearing twins, triplets, or even greater numbers of multiple siblings. Overall, couples using ART procedures, for example, experience multiple births in 38 percent of all pregnancies—10 times the rate of the general population.

Newer procedures such as blastocyst transfer, a refined form of IVF that allows an embryo to develop in vitro a few more days than ordinary IVF before transferring it to the uterus, greatly reduce the likelihood of more than two births per medically assisted pregnancy. Blastocyst transfer, which has been practiced since only the late 1990s, also reportedly may lead to higher live-birth rates than other IVF techniques. Some observers believe improving success rates and falling multiple-birth rates will win infertility treatments greater protections under the law and better coverage by health-insurance plans.

Improved pharmaceuticals also play a significant role in infertility treatment. Some are used alone and others are used in conjunction with artificial insemination, IVF, or other medical procedures. In the late 1990s two follitropin-based drugs, Gonal-F from

Serono and Follistim from Organon, rapidly gained market share as they made it easier for women to take follicle-stimulating hormone to enhance egg production. The follitropin compounds are easier to administer and reduce certain side effects that can impair embryo development. Another promising new drug is Antagon, a gonadotropin-releasing hormone (GnRH) antagonist that helps ensure eggs develop properly by regulating a woman's hormone levels. Antagon, produced by Organon and approved by the FDA in 1999, represents a new generation in GnRH antagonists that are easier to control and administer.

Another new fertility aid employs high-frequency sounds to determine whether a woman is in ovulation. Fertility Acoustics Inc., with backing from consumer-products giant Kimberly-Clark, was developing in 2000 a hearing test that lets women know if they're ovulating. The technology is based on a finding that women's sound perception changes during ovulation. The company believed the family-planning product could eventually be used in homes without a prescription, but the test kit had yet to be approved for marketing by the FDA.

INDUSTRY LEADERS

Two pharmaceutical companies dominate the fertility drug industry: Serono Laboratories and Organon, Inc. Serono Laboratories is the leader in the field with a wide range of products, primarily for reproductive medicine, but also in the areas of growth, metabolism, and immunology/oncology. Serono's parent company, the Swiss firm Ares-Serono, sold $591 million worth of reproductive health medications in 1999, led by its $349 million Gonal-F line. Altogether, the company was believed to control as much as 65 percent of the global fertility drug market. In 2000, the company purchased the marketing rights to Asta Medica's fertility treatment Cetrotide, which is used to prevent premature ovulation for women using other fertility medicines. Its infertility treatment franchises were expected to gain 8 percent in sales during 2000, including a 12 percent boost for Gonal-F.

Serono has an impressive list of research achievements. They launched the world's first human menotropin, Pergonal, in the 1960s; the first gonadotropin containing only follicle stimulating hormone, Metrodin, in the 1980s; and the world's first gonadotropin that could be injected subcutaneously instead of intramuscularly, Fertinex, in the late 1980s. In 1995 the company developed the world's first recombinant menotropin, Gonal-F. With this revolu-

tionary discovery, the active ingredient in the most important fertility drugs can be synthesized. Thus, production is no longer dependent on world supplies of human menopausal urine, a fact that should ultimately bring the drug's price down. Gonal-F (follitropin alpha) is a hormone that stimulates follicle development, which leads to egg production. Gonal-F was the first drug approved by the European Union, and the FDA approved its use in 1997. In 2000, the company purchased the marketing rights to Asta Medica's fertility treatment Cetrotide, which is used to prevent premature ovulation for women using other fertility medicines. Ares-Serono also licenses drugs to other manufacturers, including Organon, its leading competitor in the fertility field.

Organon, Inc. manufactures Humegon, a gonadotropin, as well as a wide range of drugs for contraception, anesthesiology, central nervous system disorders, and immunology. The company is part of the Pharma health-care group of Akzo Nobel, with holdings in over 50 countries and annual sales of over $500 million.

Organon was founded in Europe in the early 1920s to develop human pharmaceuticals from the hormones present in animal organs. In addition to creating the world's first fast-acting insulin, Organon was the first to isolate and identify the male hormone testosterone in 1935 and the first to standardize the hormone progesterone in 1939. Humegon was introduced in Europe in 1963; FDA approval was not granted until 1994. Organon also received FDA approval in 1997 for its Follistim (follitropin beta), a hormone that helps stimulate the growth of follicles. In 1999 Organon beat out its larger competitor by gaining the FDA's blessings on Antagon, the first of a new generation of GnRH treatments.

One of the leading American fertility clinics is the Jones Institute for Reproductive Medicine in Norfolk, Virginia. The Jones Institute was founded in 1981 by Drs. Howard and Georgiana Jones. They delivered America's first IVF baby at the institute in 1981 and have delivered over 1,700 more since then. The institute offers a full range of fertility techniques. In June 1993 the institute delivered the first baby that had been screened for Tay-Sachs disease, a fatal condition, using pre-implantation genetic testing. Jones Institute prides itself on attracting sizable research funds from private sources and the pharmaceutical industry.

Another leading American fertility clinic is the Genetics and IVF Institute (GIVF) in Fairfax, Virginia. GIVF was founded in 1984 and has achieved over 1,400 pregnancies utilizing assisted reproductive

A microscopic image of IVF, showing the needle and pipette. (*Photo Researchers, Inc./Hank Morgan*)

technology (ART) procedures. In 1984 GIVF conducted its first prenatal genetic testing, and it does ongoing research on sperm separation, DNA testing, and other advanced technologies. GIVF was the first clinic to use nonsurgical transvaginal ultrasound for the retrieval of eggs for IVF in 1985. In the early 1990s, they became the first fertility center in the United States to offer cryopreservation of ovarian tissue.

The assisted reproduction industry is also seeing the growth of smaller, more consumer-friendly companies that focus on regional markets. For example, Matria Healthcare, Inc., of Marietta, Georgia, in addition to operating standard IVF clinics, also offers in-home obstetrical care and infertility treatment, including IVF services.

WORK FORCE

There are no reliable statistics on precisely how many American physicians currently treat infertility. The American Society for Reproductive Medicine (ASRM) has 8,800 members, 90 percent of whom are obstetrician-gynecologists and 7 percent of whom are urologists. Most of these members have general practices rather than fertility clinics and offer reproductive

services together with other related treatments. Such practitioners provide most first-tier fertility treatment.

Various reproductive specialists work in ART practices. The most common are reproductive endocrinologists (REs), specialists who treat female infertility. An RE completes a normal medical school education, usually as an obstetrician/gynecologist, followed by a two-year fellowship in a certified RE program. A reproductive urologist diagnoses and treats male-factor infertility and completes a similar two-year, postmedical school fellowship program on reproductive medicine. According to ASRM, in June 1997 there were 650 board-certified reproductive endocrinologists and medical doctors enrolled in RE fellowships. Larger clinics often have a reproductive immunologist on their staff who is also a medical doctor and whose presence—considering the growing importance of immunological factors in fertility—can be critical to treatment.

Other specialized clinic personnel include embryologists, who may be medical doctors or have advanced degrees in biology, biochemistry, or a related science. The embryologist is responsible for preparing embryos before and after cryopreservation. Andrologists prepare sperm for freezing and fertilization procedures; these are lab technicians with degrees in biochemistry, endocrinology, or physiology. Geneticists advise couples with potential genetic abnormalities and generally have an advanced degree in biology or genetics.

AMERICA AND THE WORLD

In general, American reproductive science lags behind that conducted in Europe due to the stringent U.S. regulation of pharmaceuticals and the financial and societal restrictions placed on research. Drugs are usually available overseas 10 to 15 years before they can be purchased by American patients, and when they finally become available for sale in the United States, they are frequently much more expensive than in Europe or Latin America. Because of high fertility drug costs, a certain percentage of Americans prefer to buy them abroad (in Mexico, for example) despite the risks involved in smuggling them back into the country.

American fertility research also comes up short versus its European counterpart because so little of it is publicly funded. The most imposing foreign presence in the American fertility industry are the two drug companies, Serono and Organon, whose parent companies are both European. Another European company, Cryos, based in Aarhus, Denmark, is considered one of the world's largest sperm banks—it even exports to a number of countries, including the United States.

Differences in health insurance between the United States and other countries also account for differences in reproductive technology. For example, medical insurance in Sweden pays for numerous cycles of IVF and allows doctors to transfer just one embryo as opposed to the two to four (or even more) typically transferred in the United States. This gives Swedish clinics a lower success rate of births per egg transfers. But it greatly reduces the risk of multiple births, the rate of which some observers find disturbingly high in the United States.

RESEARCH AND TECHNOLOGY

In the mid-1970s, federal funding of research on human embryos was halted in the United States when the Congress failed to fund an ethics board to review research proposals. Although the law was nullified by later legislation, it still prompted the National Institutes of Health (the major source of federal funding for medical research) to deny financial support for human embryo research. Therefore, such research must depend on private funding, some of which comes from grants established by two drug companies, Serono and Organon. Much of the research is conducted at fertility clinics and is paid for from clinic revenues.

Research conducted at the University of Pennsylvania School of Veterinary Medicine showed that sperm stem cells, or spermatogonia, can be transplanted successfully from fertile mice into sterile mice. Spermatogonia are the cells that manufacture sperm. The once-sterile mice can then have healthy offspring. These sperm stem cells can also be frozen, thawed, and transplanted. The initial success in these animal trials holds promise for reversing fertility problems in men.

Some techniques are being perfected in clinical research. A handful of clinics can perform pre-implantation genetic diagnosis, which is used when a couple is at risk for X-linked recessive diseases such as cystic fibrosis or spinal muscular atrophy. In this procedure, researchers do a single-cell genetic analysis on cells taken from embryos until they find one that does not have the genetic defect. Some clinics are able to perform clinical sperm separation, distinguishing sperm by the X or Y chromosome they carry. When perfected, this treatment will enable physicians to control over 350 X-linked recessive disorders such as hemophilia, a disease that strikes primarily males. Fewer than 100 children have been born using this process, but it has allowed parents to avoid passing along serious genetic disorders.

An even more revolutionary advance will be the ability to remove immature eggs from a woman's ovaries (or ovary tissue itself), maturing them in the lab, and then performing IVF on them. As of late 1999 it was not possible to freeze human eggs, though it has worked on mouse eggs and embryos. The technique, if perfected, would have various applications. It would eliminate the need for fertility drugs, lowering the cost of IVF by approximately one-third, and it would eliminate the risk of side effects from the drugs. It would also enable women about to undergo cancer therapy that could conceivably destroy ovary function to bear their own children in the future or even regenerate ovaries with reimplanted tissue.

An interesting breakthrough reported in the fall of 1998 was the ability of one clinic, the Genetics & IVF Institute in Fairfax, Virginia, to ensure their patients an 85 percent chance of conceiving a girl. The clinic announced it had adapted a technique used on agricultural animals for more than a decade to select sex by relying on a sperm-sorting technique before artificial insemination. The clinic was unable to produce results for selection for boys, but it predicted that such a development was on the horizon and that many other clinics would soon offer sex selection services.

The safety of ICSI, the technique in which individual sperm are injected directly into eggs to fertilize them, has spurred a good deal of new research. ICSI was discovered accidentally by a Belgian doctor in 1992 and has since blossomed into a treatment that can allow 99 percent of infertile men to father children. A study published in the journal *Nature* in March 1999 warned that the injection of sperm into eggs can damage egg proteins that move chromosomes. The study involved rhesus monkeys, and it did not show any apparent genetic damage to the monkey offspring resulting from intracytoplasmic sperm injection. But it indicates that there is a great deal that is still unknown about the technique.

Another advance was in the use of laser technology to aid fertilization. Noting that many IVF failures occur because the fertilized embryo doesn't get embedded in the womb, researchers based in Hungary and Belgium explained to the European Society of Human Reproduction and Embryology conference in Bologna, Italy their laser-aided fertilization technique. In this process, lasers were used to precisely drill the membrane surrounding the human egg to allow for easier implantation of the embryo.

FURTHER READING

Abma, Joyce C., et al. *Fertility, Family Planning and Women's Health: New Data from the 1995 National Survey of Family Growth.* Hyattsville, MD: U.S. Department of Health and Human Services, May 1997.

American Society for Reproductive Medicine. "A Brief History of Assisted Reproduction." January 1998.

———. "Results of Joint SART/ASRM, CDC and RESOLVE 1996 Assisted Reproductive Technologies Success Rate Report." 1999. Available from http://www.asrm.org.

Aronson, Diane D., and Merrill Matthews. "Q: Should Health Insurers Be Forced to Pay for Infertility Treatments?" *Insight on the News,* 8 February 1999.

"Assisted Reproductive Technology in the United States and Canada: 1995 Results." *Fertility and Sterility,* March 1998.

Beavers, Norma. "Pharmacists Offering New Drugs and Procedures to Help Infertile Couples Realize Their Dreams to Reproduce." *Drug Topics,* 7 June 1999.

Bridger, Chet. "Buffalo, N.Y., Firm Gets Funding to Develop Family-Planning Tool." *Knight Ridder/Tribune Business News,* 31 March 2000.

Centers for Disease Control and Prevention. National Center for Chronic Disease Prevention and Health Promotion. "1997 Assisted Reproductive Technology Success Rates." Atlanta, GA, December 1999. Available from http://www.cdc.gov.

"Contribution of Assisted Reproductive Technology and Ovulation-Inducing Drugs to Triplet and Higher-Order Multiple Births—United States, 1980-1997." *MMRW Weekly Report,* 23 June 2000.

"Disposition of Abandoned Embryos." *Fertility and Sterility,* May 1997.

"Fertility Technology: Lasers to the Aid of Embryos." *Health & Medicine Week,* 10 July 2000.

Gross, Jane. "The Fight to Cover Infertility." *New York Times,* 7 December 1998.

Ince, Susan. "'Physician Factor' May Influence IVF Pregnancy Rate." *Medical Tribune* 5, no. 5 (1998).

"Infertility: A Fertile Niche for R.Phs." *Drug Topics,* 21 September 1998.

"Infertility Treatments: Weighing the Risks and Benefits." *HealthFacts,* February 1999.

Kolata, Gina. "New Questions about Popular Fertilization Technique." *New York Times,* 30 March 1999.

Larkin, Marilynn. "Male Reproductive Health: A Hotbed of Research." *Lancet,* 15 August 1998.

Lewis, Pete. "Boomers Fight Infertility." *Denver Business Journal,* 12 February 1999.

Mulholland, Megan. "Americans Spend Billions on New and Costly Infertility Treatments." *Knight Ridder/Tribune Business News,* 26 January 2000.

"New Technologies Prevent Multiple Births." *Drug Topics,* 7 June 1999.

Norderberg, Tamar. "Overcoming Infertility." *FDA Consumer,* January/February 1997. Available from http://www.fda.gov.

Phillips, Donald F. "Reproductive Medicine Experts Till an Increasingly Fertile Field." *Journal of the American Medical Association,* 9 December 1998.

Van Voohis, Bradley J. "Cost Effectiveness of Infertility Treatments: A Cohort Study." *Fertility and Sterility,* May 1997.

FIBER OPTICS

Intense jockeying for share in the high-speed communications markets is driving the breakneck roll-out of fiber-optics technology as demand continues to outstrip supply in many segments. In 1999 alone, according to a study released by Corning Inc., a leading manufacturer of optical fiber, companies around the globe installed 35 percent more optical fiber than in 1998, reaching 70 million kilometers (about 43 million miles) deployed worldwide. In North America, the growth rate has been even more furious, registering around 45 percent in 1999. Another 20 million or so kilometers were expected to be tacked on worldwide by the end of 2000.

Demand was so torrid, in fact, that hardware suppliers such as Lucent Technologies Inc. and Nortel Networks strained to ramp up supply. Lucent was keenly aware of the pressure in late 1999, when it posted lower-than-expected earnings because it failed to keep up with orders. In that case much of the impact was merely a delay in getting the associated revenue. But for some fiber-optic vendors, there's a profound sense of urgency in keeping up with demand, because many industry luminaries believe that whoever captures the market first will have decided advantages over the Johnny-come-latelies.

Local access—the so-called last mile of fiber-optic networks—is fast becoming one of the most important frontiers in fiber-optic telecommunications. Rigging homes and small businesses with fat-bandwidth fiber-optic cabling was once considered an extravagant and excessively costly proposition, but it's one an increasing number of firms are entertaining. Indeed, local exchange carriers in the United States were expected to boost their residential-access installations from just 322,000 miles annually as of 1999 to 2.2 million miles by 2003. As they do so, more and more homes will be equipped for converging high-speed data, voice, and multimedia communications.

Still, demand for fiber optics in long-haul telecommunications hasn't yet abated. In 1999, the Corning study reported, fiber-optic deployment by long-haul carriers, whose networks traverse regional, national, and even international boundaries, surged a whopping 80 percent. Although it includes some local installations by such firms, that figure is particularly interesting because long-haul is a segment that's already deployed fiber optics extensively. Behind much of that growth is the rampant growth of independent high-speed national network operators, such as Qwest Communications International Inc. and Level 3 Communications, Inc. These independents, along with utility companies and others that aspire to run high-speed networks, have broken the stranglehold of such established long-haul carriers as AT&T, Sprint, and WorldCom on the long-distance fiber-optic infrastructure.

ORGANIZATION AND STRUCTURE

Fiber optics for telecommunications can be broadly cleaved into two industry segments: cable and equipment. While it's not exactly inexpensive compared to other transmission media, fiber-optic cable is largely a commodity and in 1999 represented just 16 percent of the world's fiber-optic hardware market. The equipment side, which includes devices for transmitting, multiplexing, switching, amplifying, and decoding optical data, accounted for the other 84 percent. The larger segment also includes relatively low-tech wares such as connectors and adapters. Companies that manufacture cable and equipment are usually separate from those that install fiber-optic networks and operate them.

Fiber-optic technologies are likewise used in a host of special instruments and other devices. These include medical instruments, industrial sensors, testing equipment, and a variety of other industrial applications.

FIBER FABRICATION

The manufacturing of optical fibers consists of coating the inner wall of a silica glass tube with 100 or more successive layers of thin glass. The tube is then heated to 2,000 degrees Celsius and stretched into a thin, flexible fiber. The result is called a clad fiber, which is approximately .0005 inches in diameter (by comparison, human hair typically measures .002 inches).

Optical fibers operate on the principle of what is called total internal reflection. Every medium through which light can pass possesses a certain refractive index, the amount by which a beam of light is bent as it enters the medium. As the angle at which the light strikes the medium is decreased from the perpendicular, a point is reached at which the light is bent so much at the surface that it reflects completely back into the medium from which it originated. Thus, the light will bounce back rather than escape.

In an optical fiber, total internal reflection is accomplished by a layer of material known as cladding, which has a lower refractive index than glass alone. Once light enters the fiber, it is internally reflected by the cladding. This prevents light loss by keeping the beam of light zigzagging inside the glass core.

MARKETS AND APPLICATIONS

The manufacturers sell their products to organizations that use fiber-optical equipment to supply a service, such as telecommunications or cable television stations; to run an information/communication network, such as that used by the U.S. government; or to other industry segments for various uses. Businesses are slowly turning to fiber optics when they install in-house computer networks, and at least one local government started wiring an entire city with fiber. For the most part, however, high-volume applications such as these are still too expensive.

Since the invention of the telegraph in the 19th century, most data sent along lines has consisted of electrical impulses transmitted along copper wires. Fiber optics differ in two fundamental respects—the medium of transmission is a line of glass or plastic, not copper, and pulses of light, not electricity, are the means. Lasers send pulses of light down the glass strand in an information stream that can be either analog or digital. The stream is slightly faster than an electrical current on copper, and it is unaffected by electrical disturbances that can create static in the line.

Different information streams travel down the same fiber strand separated by their wavelengths. The number of wavelengths available on a line determines how much information can be transmitted. That amount is referred to as the medium's bandwidth, and the essential difference between fiber-optic line and copper line is fiber optics' enormously higher bandwidth. A fiber strand can transmit 4,200 times more information than copper at one time—and transmit it thousands of times faster due to the higher volume of data that can be packed into the higher frequency wavelength. Copper relays, for example, can handle 24 simultaneous phone calls per second. By 2000, laser- and fiber-optics systems were nearing a capacity of 320,000. This capacity is increasingly important as videos, sound, and other space-hungry files get transmitted back and forth across the Internet. Copper can transmit a mere 64,000 bits per second compared to fiber optic's 10 gigabits per second, or 10 billion bits. Higher bandwidth means not only more information, but faster information. For example, a Web page that takes 70 seconds to load by copper will be nearly instantaneous by fiber, and an X-ray that requires two and a half hours by conventional lines takes only two seconds on fiber.

BACKGROUND AND DEVELOPMENT

Medicine was the first application of fiber optics. In the late 1950s, Dr. Narinder S. Kapany hit upon the idea of building an endoscope capable of seeing around twists and turns in a patient's body by using fiber-optic bundles. His device, which came to be called the fiberscope, consisted of two bundles of fiber: one incoherent bundle, where there is no relationship between the order of fibers from one end of the bundle to the other; and one coherent bundle, in which the individual fibers have the same position at both ends of the bundle, to carry a color image back to the physician.

Optical fibers were first used in telecommunications in the late 1960s when it became apparent that data transmitted by laser light could be broken up and absorbed by uncontrollable elements such as fog and snow. The first optical fibers produced contained flaws that resulted in significant amounts of light loss. To boost the range of the light signal, energized atoms from rare elements were used to amplify the signal at 1.54 micrometers—the wavelength at which the fibers are able to transmit light the farthest.

Paul Henson of United Telecommunications in Kansas was perhaps the first to gamble on fiber optics in the telecommunications field. He invested $1 billion in the late 1970s; by 1982 United Telecom had one of the largest fiber-optic networks in the world, outstripping even AT&T.

The technology took off with the first deregulation of the telephone industry in 1982. Carriers competing with AT&T for long-distance business, such as MCI and Sprint, began planning their own state-of-the-art fiber-optic phone networks. By 1984 Henson was chairman of Sprint, which announced plans for a 100 percent fiber-optic long-distance network. The same year MCI laid its first fiber-optic line from Washington, D.C., to New York. By 1988 Sprint's entire network was fiber optic and, in 1989, the company made the first transatlantic phone call along fiber-optic line. Currently fiber-optic technology forms the backbone of the long-distance telephone industry.

Full implementation of the Telecommunications Act of 1996 was expected to stimulate the industry. Passed in February, the law completed the deregulation of the telecommunications industry that started with AT&T's breakup in the early 1980s. The law did away with the monopoly of local phone service that had been in place since 1934 and allowed anyone to compete in the market, including long-distance servers, local companies, cable television companies, and utility companies. The law also reversed the AT&T consent decree that forbade regional Bell companies from providing long-distance service or manufacturing telephone equipment. The law was intended to stimulate competition and the quick implementation of new technology. Fiber-optic companies were expected to benefit from the new situation.

Optical fibers have also been demonstrated as an ideal method of transmitting high-definition television (HDTV) signals. Because its transmissions contain twice as much information as those of conventional television, HDTV allows for much greater clarity and definition of picture; standard transmission technology, however, is not capable of transmitting so much information at once. Using optical fibers, the HDTV signal can be transmitted as a digital light-pulse, pro-viding a near-flawless image reproduction that is far superior to broadcast transmission.

A few cities have taken an active role in ensuring the successful rollout of fiber optics in their areas. In the late 1990s Anaheim, California, started converting to full fiber, investing $6 million in a basic system and contracting with SpectraNet International of San Diego to run it. The cost for the city of 300,000 people was expected to total $70-$90 million before the project's completion in 2004. This was the first-ever attempt to link every building in a city by fiber optics.

CURRENT CONDITIONS

While the conversion to fiber optics first began in earnest during the 1980s, spending on fiber and equipment escalated sharply in the 1990s and remains on a steady uptick today. According to the *2000 Multimedia Telecommunications Market Review and Forecast,* the world market for fiber-optic cable and equipment advanced threefold between 1990 and 1999, rising from $4.1 to $14.6 billion. The report, an annual publication put out by the Telecommunications Industry Association and the MultiMedia Telecommunications Association, valued global spending on cable at $2.4 billion and equipment outlays at $12.2 billion in 1999. While cable revenue growth has been somewhat subdued because of declining prices, equipment revenues were predicted to hit $28 billion by 2003. Investors, meanwhile, were giddy about the sector in 2000; in the first half of the year, venture financing for optical technologies more than tripled to $1.6 billion.

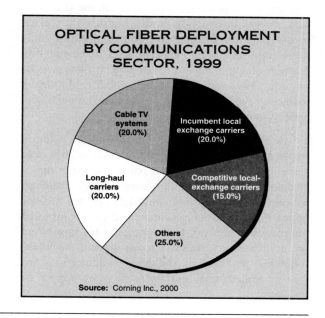

OPTICAL FIBER DEPLOYMENT BY COMMUNICATIONS SECTOR, 1999

Cable TV systems (20.0%)

Incumbent local exchange carriers (20.0%)

Competitive local-exchange carriers (15.0%)

Long-haul carriers (20.0%)

Others (25.0%)

Source: Corning Inc., 2000

Every segment of the fiber-optic manufacturing industry is growing. From 1987 to 1997 fiber-optic cable was laid at a rate of about 4,000 miles a day and, by the late 1990s, more than 25 million miles of it had been installed. Nonetheless, 60 percent of that was "dead fiber," which is completely unused fiber-optic line. The remainder was used at only a small fraction of its total capacity—a reflection of fiber's enormous potential. KMI, a market research group, predicted that transmitters and receivers, which make up the bulk of fiber-optic sales, would reach $1.1 billion in sales by the year 2000; the market for erbium-doped fiber amplifiers was also expected to rise as networks convert to 100 percent fiber optics.

LOCAL ACCESS MOVING TO CENTER STAGE

As both national and local network build-outs continue, metropolitan areas are where most of the world's fiber cable is being laid. Statistics released by Corning Inc. cited that as much as 70 percent of all cable deployment in 1999—about 3 million miles— was for metropolitan area networks, including access lines for businesses and homes. A range of carriers has been targeting this market, including cable operators, local Bell companies, and independent phone and data carriers. Fueling the expansion has been the insatiable appetite for Internet bandwidth as well as heightened interest in integrated communications packages.

BUT THE ROAD MAP ISN'T CLEAR

The challenge is for the fiber-optics industry to replace the old cumbersome copper line systems with a faster, more powerful type of electronic transmission without interrupting or slowing down a service people have come to expect. Communications companies must also weigh the cost, load, and signal differences of upgrading and revamping obsolete switching equipment from copper to optical cable versus replacing everything with a completely new fiber-optic system.

A hybrid approach was considered the solution by the telecommunications industry. The plan was to use copper at one level and patch into fiber optics at another level. Later, the copper lines could be removed, and the system could be upgraded to fiber optics. Fiber-optic equipment is rapidly being installed for computer network backbone infrastructure based on asynchronous transfer mode optical switches, following the lead of the telecommunications industry. Nonetheless, not everyone sees copper as obsolete.

LOCAL ACCESS ALTERNATIVES WILL DIE HARD

Costs and competitive dynamics will no doubt affect the rate and extent that fiber optics penetrate local access markets. Cable operators use fiber optics as the backbone of their TV systems, but generally use metal coaxial cables to connect individual customers to the network. They've already made significant strides toward offering cable Internet service and most of the big operators are planning to unveil some form of digital interactive TV or similar service in the first years of the 2000s. (See the essay in this book entitled Internet Service Providers.)

Some industry insiders believe a union between cable and copper-wire phone carriers would be ideal; cable companies would possess bandwidth-rich "dumb" networks, or networks unencumbered by complex switching equipment. Phone companies, on the other hand, have extensive two-way networks— and money. Upgrades to digital cable in many metropolitan areas has narrowed the communications gap, affording some cable systems two-way capabilities, but the process has demanded vast sums of cash. AT&T has been the biggest proponent of this approach, investing billions in the late 1990s to snatch up several large cable systems.

Meanwhile, phone companies and several independent carriers are aggressively pushing an alternative high-speed data format that relies on old-fashioned copper phone wires. Known as digital subscriber line (DSL), the service involves upgrades at phone companies' central offices but lets consumers access high-bandwidth service using just a DSL modem and a phone line.

Added to these moderately high-speed alternatives is a new generation of wireless data services that eliminate the need to be physically tethered to a network port.

Still, as much of an improvement as cable and DSL are over regular telephone lines for high-speed data, they're no match for optical fiber where bandwidth is concerned. Whereas cable's ideal throughput is measured in millions of bits per second, fiber rates in the billions. When it comes to streaming high-definition digital movies off the Internet, all those extra bits matter.

In addition to the advantage of raw speed, several other factors militate in favor of fiber. Chief among them are continued declines in pricing, which has regularly occurred in the fiber-cable segment and is expected to be felt increasingly in the fiber-optic components and equipment segments. Increased compatibility with high-speed local area network standards will also hasten the acceptance of fiber over metal wire. And even if standards such as DSL win out in the short term, some analysts believe that the backbone traffic needed to support wider high-speed data services will almost certainly require investment in optical fiber for the infrastructure—even if it's not yet reaching the end users.

INDUSTRY LEADERS

CORNING

Corning Inc., one of the founders of fiber optics, remains the world's leader in the production and sale of fiber-optic cable. In 2000 the company solidified its lead in that market with the purchase of Siemens AG's fiber-optics units, with the combined businesses christened Corning Cable Services. The newly formed unit had sales of $2.2 billion in 1999 and employed 12,600 people.

Based on 1999 sales, Corning provides about 36 percent of the world's fiber-optic cable. The company, which has deep roots in the glass industry, has been averaging nearly 20 million miles of cable annually. To meet anticipated demand, the company invested more than $1 billion in plant construction and expansion in 1999. The acquisition of Rochester Photonics Corp. (with 1998 revenue at $3 million) gave Corning access to new fiber-optic technology, such as "microlenses," which increases network performance through improved in-fiber laser focus and has transmitters and receivers that are more temperature-resistant.

LUCENT TECHNOLOGIES

Lucent Technologies Inc., of Murray Hill, New Jersey, was split off from AT&T in November 1995. It took with it about three-quarters of the world-famous Bell Labs and is now one of the leading designers and manufacturers of conventional and wireless telecommunications equipment, as well as fiber optics. Employing approximately 153,000 workers in its diverse operations, Lucent is the world's second-leading producer of fiber cable, producing about 16 percent of the cable purchased for the U.S. domestic market. The company also produces a variety of other fiber-optic components, systems, and fiber/copper telecommunications systems. Corporate sales in 1999 topped $38 billion, although only a portion of that was from fiber optics.

Despite a downturn in 1996, Lucent's fiber-optic production grew fivefold between 1991 and 1999. In 1999 the company agreed to supply its TrueWave RS fiber for Viatel Inc.'s European Network, an ambitious project to link several major European cities. That endeavor was followed in 2000 with Lucent's hefty $3 billion purchase of Ortel Corp., a producer of optoelectronic components that allow speedy two-way communications over cable TV systems. Analysts viewed the latter move as a strategic commitment to serving the fiber-optic needs of the cable TV broadband market.

CIENA

Ciena Corp. of Savage, Maryland, is a smaller developer of optical networking gear. The company's primary products are dense wavelength division multiplexing (DWDM) systems for such companies as WorldCom, Sprint, and Teleway Japan. DWDM systems give optical fiber the ability to carry up to 40 times more data, voice, and graphic information than usual. The company is also a major supplier of erbium-doped fiber amplifiers—one of the key technologies in the change to a 100 percent optical system. Sales slipped to $482 million in 1999 because of falling equipment prices, but the company made two major acquisitions that year, Omnia Communications Inc. and Lightera Networks Inc., two other fiber-optic equipment makers. In 1999 Ciena employed 1,928 workers.

ADC TELECOMMUNICATIONS

ADC Telecommunications Inc. of Minnetonka, Minnesota, is a leader in the design and manufacture of fiber-optic connectivity products, including transmitters, receivers, couplers, patch cords, panels, and Internet working products. The company has customers in the public, private, and government sectors, as well as foreign nations building telecommunications infrastructures. Net sales in 1999 increased 40 percent to $1.93 billion. Growth was driven by heavy demand for fiber-optic components, among other products. In addition to sales to the regional Bell companies, ADC has made acquisitions and has entered the wireless and international markets.

JDS UNIPHASE

Formed in the 1999 merger between Uniphase Corp. and JDS FITEL Ltd., JDS Uniphase Corp. is a major manufacturer of both passive and active fiber-optic components. Its line includes lasers, switches, transmitters, and amplifiers. The company has been on a buying spree in the wake of the 1999 merger, with the biggest deal coming in 2000 with the $15 billion acquisition of E-Tek Dynamics, another equipment maker. The rich price was made possible by JDS Uniphase's high-flying stock, which had been a favorite on Wall Street because of the industry's expected growth rate. The company's own operations are a bit more modest, with total sales registering at about $283 million in 1999. The company's acquisitions pushed sales in 2000 up 406 percent to reach $1.4 billion.

METROMEDIA FIBER NETWORK INC.

On the installation side of the business, Metromedia Fiber Network (MMFN) is constructing a fiber-optic network to lease out to carriers. With services starting in the eastern United States, the wholesaler has designs on 67 cities throughout North America and Europe by the time its network is complete. It was expected to have more than a million miles worth of cable deployed by the end of 2000.

MMFN, a subsidiary of Metromedia Co., a conglomerate with sundry telecommunications holdings, lays fiber cable and sets up most of the system, but its fiber isn't used (hence it's sometimes said to sell "dark fiber") until a wholesale customer such as a local phone company purchases access and links into its system. The company's management believes this approach keeps the company focused and improves its costs relative to competitors. Its niche is in cable with extraordinary fiber capacity. MMFN's sales in 1999 were modest, at $75 million, but were expected to grow at better than 100 percent a year in the early 2000s.

AMERICA AND THE WORLD

The United States has a significant lead on foreign companies in the fiber-optics race. The American companies Corning and Lucent sell over 80 percent of the world's fiber cable, and companies such as Ciena and ADC are at the cutting edge with erbium-doped fiber amplifiers (EDFA) and dense wavelength division multiplexing technology. Two European companies, Pirelli of Italy and Alcatel Telecom of France, are involved in development and production to the same extent as the leading American firms. Pirelli introduced the first commercial EDFA through its North American subsidiary in North Carolina. It has formed a partnership with MCI to install wavelength division multiplexing (WDM) technology on a fiber-optic line from St. Louis to Chicago. Alcatel produces EDFA and WDM as well, but its penetration into the American market has not been as pronounced. The annual revenue growth for optical transmission

systems in Europe was estimated at 40 percent in the early 2000s.

Countries that have virtually no existing telecommunications networks are a major market—perhaps the primary market—for fiber optics. In the late 1990s, the People's Republic of China was a major consumer of optical cable and required millions of core-kilometers of fiber optics, buying WDM systems from Lucent and Japan's NEC. In Russia, Lucent Technologies has more than $30 million invested. In 1999 Lucent joined with SviazStroy-1 (Russia's largest construction company) to form a joint-venture fiber-optic cable manufacturing company called Lucent Technologies SviazStroy-1 Fiber Optic Cable Co. Lucent retained a 51 percent share of the Voronezh, Russia, company. In 1999 Alcatel and Fujitsu Ltd. were preparing an 18,000-mile undersea WDM cable that would run from Australia and New Zealand to the United States, then loop back through Hawaii and Fiji to Australia.

RESEARCH AND TECHNOLOGY

Two technological breakthroughs recently transformed fiber optics—the erbium-doped fiber amplifier (EDFA) and wavelength division multiplexing (WDM). EDFA grew out of the fundamental incompatibility of electronics and fiber optics. The optical pulses must be amplified as they travel along the fiber or else they dissipate and no longer register as signals. In the past, because they could not match fiber optics' larger bandwidth, electronic amplifiers acted as a bottleneck on the fiber-optic flow. Bell Laboratories demonstrated that a short length of fiber treated with the mineral erbium and excited with a laser acted as an optical amplifier. With the use of this type of system, electronics are no longer necessary; fiber optics' huge data capability can be exploited in full.

WDM was developed at Bell Labs in the mid-1980s. In WDM laser signals generate light pulses that can be as short as a billionth of a second in length. Each wavelength opened can be used to transmit data. The first WDMs opened transmission lines that could carry up to 2.5 gigabits per second (Gbps). They were integrated into the standard fiber-optic systems. In the early 1990s researchers discovered dense wavelength division multiplexing, which squeezes more pulses into shorter wavelengths. At the decade's end, amplifier design advances, such as Lucent's WaveStar Optical Line System 400G, expanded the operating region, thus bringing more than 40 channels operating at 10 Gbps each.

Some analysts believe WDM is the foundation of all future fiber-optic technology. It enables a network to increase its bandwidth significantly without installing any new lines. One problem is that the technology is so advanced that the monitoring and diagnostic tools have not been developed to trace failures. The International Telecommunications Union has started outlining a standard for the industry, however. Insight Research Corp. projected the market for WDM components to reach $4 billion by 2002; the market analysis firm Electronicast predicted that number would rise to $10 billion by the year 2005.

The development of plastic optical fiber brought a number of advantages over glass. It is cheaper to produce and easier to work with, as well as being equal to glass in performance, flexibility, and reliability. An industry standard was established in April 1997. Landmark discoveries continue to flow from the laboratory to the marketplace. Where most were impressed by the terabit (one trillion bits) speeds reached in 1996, Alastair Glass, head of photonics research at Bell Labs, envisioned the day when one fiber-optic cable carries thousands of WDM beams with a capacity of 200 terabits per second—enough to transmit all the contents of the Library of Congress within one second.

FURTHER READING

Biancomano, Vincent J. "All Optical Net Takes Next Steps." *Electronic Engineering Times,* 23 December 1996.

———. "Communications: Optical Nets Start Seeing the Light." *Electronic Engineering Times,* 31 March 1997.

Carey, Bill. "Demands for Optical Fiber, Photonics Soar." *New Technology Week,* 13 March 2000.

Dobbin, Ben. "Fiber Optics Change, Speed Up World's Flow of Information." *Los Angeles Times,* 16 December 1996.

"Fiber-Optic and Optical Cable Market Demand to Mount." *China Daily News,* 21 July 1997.

"Fiber Optics Market Tripled in the '90s." *Business Communications Review,* March 2000.

Flanagan, Patrick. "Fiber Frenzy Is on in North America." *Telecommunications,* February 2000.

Fleck, Ken. "Fiber Optic Growth." *Electronic News,* 1 May 2000.

Gilder, George. "Fiber Keeps Its Promise." *Forbes,* 7 April 1997.

Lindstrom, Annie. "Unmasking the Fiber Barons." *America's Network,* 1 March 2000.

Montgomery, Jeff. "Annual Technology Forecast: Fifty Years of Fiber Optics." *Lightwave,* December 1999.

Pearson, Eric R., and Elizabeth Goldsmith. "Ten Reasons Fiber Is Becoming More Cost-Effective in Horizontal Applications." *Lightwave,* January 2000.

Price, Richard. "Fiber Optics to Entwine Anaheim-Network to Link Homes, Businesses." *USA Today,* 18 July 1997.

Schmidt, Eric. "Communications Components: POF Extends Network Reach." *Electronic Buyer News,* 23 June 1997.

Schonfeld, Erick. "Divide the Wave." *Fortune,* 9 October 2000.

Shinal, John G. "At the Speed of Light." *Business Week,* 9 October 2000.

Sweeney, Dan. "Optical Illusions?" *America's Network,* 1 September 2000.

Weinberg, Neil. "Wired and Restless." *Forbes,* 7 February 2000.

Wirbel, Loring. "Signal Scheme Pushes Terabit Rate—Sonet Transport Catches a Wave." *Electronic Engineering Times,* 16 September 1996.

Woolley, Scott. "Sewer Rats and Billionaires." *Forbes,* 3 April 2000.

FINANCIAL PLANNING SERVICES

Financial planning is a holistic approach to personal financial management that has flourished since the mid-1980s. Rising levels of wealth and consumer sophistication about finances have fueled the upswing, as has deregulation of the financial services industry. Experts predict the pace of growth will remain brisk, and even increase, as baby boomers near retirement and as large institutions target planning services at middle- and lower-income people.

SCOPE OF ACTIVITIES

Financial planners, sometimes called advisers, analyze a person's complete financial situation and develop a strategy to optimize personal resources and meet life goals. They consider a number of factors, including income, assets, present and future expenses and investments, as well as personal data such as age, health, and number of dependents. Planners use the detailed information they get from meeting with clients to make financial recommendations, including advice on budgeting, saving, insurance, taxes, investments, and retirement planning. They often assist customers by directly managing assets. Some financial planners focus on only one financial issue, but most work on many.

Financial planning services originated in the early 1960s; it wasn't until 1970, however, that the first fee-only planners—now a quasi standard—appeared. As an industry, financial planning came of age as America's corporations gradually replaced traditional corporate-managed pension plans with employee-managed 401(k)s and other retirement savings alternatives, forcing individuals to take on more responsibility for long-term fiscal planning. Concerns about the viability of Social Security and Medicare, coupled with growth in the number of small businesses and the self-employed, have forced many individuals who had given very little thought to retirement planning to become more knowledgeable about estate plans, insurance, home ownership, taxes, and the multitude of new financial products and investments.

BRISK GROWTH

The number of firms and individuals offering various forms of consumer financial advice has skyrocketed since the late 1980s. Because there is neither a single definition of what a financial planner is, nor a consistent set of boundaries between the profession and related activities such as investment advising or accounting, estimates of the industry's size vary considerably. A 1997 *Barron's* report pegged the count of financial planning firms at 25,000, while more recent estimates entertain figures as high as 300,000 for the total number of professionals offering financial advice. The number of those with formal accreditation is much smaller: the Certified Financial Planner Board of Standards, one of the largest and most visible professional licensure bodies for the industry, reported over 35,400 active licensees in 2000, a figure triple that of the mid-1980s.

The growth of the financial planning industry parallels the increasing accumulation of assets by Americans and greater sophistication about investments. The change in saving patterns illustrates the trend. The 61 percent of personal savings that were held in banks, savings and loans, and credit unions during the 1970s had declined to less than 38 percent by the mid-1990s. Through pension and mutual funds, households and businesses increasingly participate in huge, diversified portfolios of stocks, bonds, real estate, and even commodities. As reported in the *Washington Times,* pollster Peter Hart said that it took 25 years for stock ownership among Americans to double, from 10.4 percent in 1965 to 21.1 percent in 1990. It took only seven years for stock ownership to double again. By 1997 43.2 percent of Americans owned stock. Other data reveal, according to the *Times* article, that U.S. households now hold more wealth in the form of stocks than home equity.

As rising wealth widens demand for financial planning, large financial services firms are jockeying for shares of the highly fragmented market. Such captains of finance as Citigroup and American Express launched new financial planning services in the late 1990s, and tax-preparation giant H&R Block was readying a major retail thrust that could make planning-service outlets as ubiquitous as its tax centers. Even discount broker Charles Schwab has forayed into planning-related territory by rolling out a planner referral service for its investment clients. Meanwhile, some smaller firms that have specialized in planning have begun to merge and consolidate in hopes of building a more recognizable presence in this traditionally localized business.

COMPETENCY CONCERNS

Increasing apprehension over the competency and legitimacy of individuals practicing financial advising has accompanied the industry's growth. As a *Barron's* writer quipped, "Can't cut it as a hairstylist? Try financial planning." In the absence of universal professional or legal credentials distinguishing financial planners, several professional organizations and recent laws have sought to impose a baseline of competency and heighten public awareness of the meaning of a bewildering array of financial planning credentials.

ORGANIZATION AND STRUCTURE

Financial planning is the process of establishing financial goals and creating a way to realize them. The process involves taking stock of all personal resources and needs, developing a plan to manage them, and systematically implementing the plan to achieve financial objectives. Financial planning is an ongoing process. A plan must be monitored and reviewed periodically so that adjustments can be made to assure that it continues to meet individual needs.

The profession involves expertise (or access to experts) in various disciplines such as estate planning,

taxation, benefit plans, pension plans, insurance, investments, and real estate. Thus the consumer financial planning market has come to be fragmented across several disparate service professions in addition to those just practicing planning, and many of these services specialize in certain aspects of financial planning to the exclusion of others.

The Certified Financial Planner (CFP) Board's Web site (www.cfp-board.org) provides a wealth of information for those confused by the many definitions of "financial planner." There were some 36,000 CFP licensees working in the U.S. in 2000. According to the CFP Board, the following list of professions may provide financial planning services:

- Accountant
- Broker/Dealer
- Certified Financial Planner Licensee or CFP Practitioner
- Chartered Financial Analyst (CFA)
- Chartered Financial Consultant
- Estate Planning Professional
- Fee-based Financial Adviser
- Fee-only Financial Adviser
- Financial Adviser
- Financial Consultant
- Financial Counselor
- Financial or Securities Analyst
- Financial Planner
- Insurance Agent
- Investment Adviser
- Investment Adviser Representative
- Investment Consultant
- Money Manager
- Personal Financial Specialist
- Portfolio Manager
- Real Estate Broker
- Registered Investment Adviser
- Registered Representative
- Stockbroker

Adding to the confusion about the variety of financial planning services, a CFP Board survey showed consumers still have many misconceptions about the role of a financial planner. The survey, conducted in February 1999 by Bruskin-Goldring Research for the

CFP Board, was nationwide and included 1,016 adults. Among the misconceptions, 36 percent of those surveyed believed that financial planners would automatically put their assets into the best-performing stocks and mutual funds; 17 percent expected assurances from a financial planner that they would become rich; another 16 percent expected that they would be asked to pay up-front for a financial planner's services.

FEES AND COMMISSIONS

Financial planners are paid in a variety of ways, usually depending on the planner's affiliations. The methods are fee only, commission only, fee-offset, combination fee/commission, and salary. Ethical standards mandate that planners disclose who pays them if they're earning commissions, but this isn't always observed.

Aside from fee-only, the balance of these payment schemes imply that financial planning is being offered in conjunction with other products or services such as investment brokering, banking, accounting, or underwriting. These planners are often described as product-driven, as opposed to fee-only planners who are called process-driven. Less delicately, critics of financial planners who accept commissions call them salespeople, not advisers.

Because fee-only planners are paid by the client and don't receive commissions, they have fewer conflicts of interest when they recommend investment vehicles and thus are sometimes considered more impartial than other types of planners. Still, despite a major push in the industry toward fee-only compensation, the most common pay structure among CFP certificate holders is combination fee and commission.

The problem of identifying a planner's potential conflicts of interest is aggravated by a dearth of openness and clarity about many planners' compensation. Guy Halverson, writing in the *Christian Science Monitor,* described the results of a study released in 1997 by the Consumer Federation of America and the National Association of Personal Financial Advisors, the trade association for fee-only planners (which has trademarked the phrase "fee only"). Of 288 Washington, D.C.-area planners and firms in a random survey, "two-thirds claimed to offer fee-only services. Of those, three out of five were earning commissions or other financial incentives from undisclosed third parties, such as mutual-fund companies or insurance firms." Consumer wariness about conflicts of interest may be part of the reason for a planner's reluctance to reveal sources of income, the study suggested. The organization has been perhaps the most aggressive advocate of true fee-only planning, and has developed visibility programs such as its Fiduciary Oath and the fee-only trademark to make consumers aware of the distinction.

Regardless of the type of planner retained, fees can vary widely. *Money* magazine, in a piece by Ruth Simon, reported that fee-only advisers often charge a flat fee to develop a plan, typically from $500 to $6,000, depending on complexity. Hourly fees range between $75 and $225, and the average in 1999 for CFP holders was about $120. Some use a sliding scale, charging more to customers with higher incomes or greater assets. Many also charge an annual fee equal to .5 percent to 1.5 percent of total assets to manage a portfolio.

REGULATION

In part reflecting the fragmented market, government regulation of financial planning has been uneven and complex. That, however, is changing. A law amending federal securities laws, the National Securities Market Improvement Act, effective 8 July 1997, divided regulation between the federal government and the states. Firms with $25 million or more in managed assets remain under the jurisdiction of the U.S. Securities and Exchange Commission (SEC) while the remaining investment advisers—an estimated 16,500—revert to state regulation.

In the past some states, but not all, licensed advisers. Financial planners weren't required to register with the SEC unless they recommended specific stocks or bonds, in which case they had to be registered investment advisers. The SEC required no test, however, with the result that registration reflected little about the adviser's competency. Applicants simply paid a fee and submitted a form listing their disciplinary history, educational background, and investment philosophy. Even as many states don't require licensure of financial planners, most state securities agencies don't regulate individuals associated with investment of financial planning firms, whether or not those firms are registered with the SEC or with a state agency.

Under the new regulations, the SEC retained jurisdiction within any state that had not enacted its own regulations, but had no plans for testing or enforcing competency requirements. Many states, however, have begun to coordinate some testing requirements for new entrants to the field. As of June 1998, the American Institute of Certified Public Accountants reported that 15 states had a 150-hour education requirement for planners in effect, with another 29 scheduled to follow suit on a future date; in addition, 22 states prohibit commissions and contingent fees.

The states present a mixed picture. David Weidner wrote in a *Wall Street Journal* report that some are adapting faster than others to the new order of things: "Pennsylvania, along with [Connecticut and Washington], is considered a model in dealing with the new responsibility." Like them, the state had an active regulatory agency that worked with the SEC before the act went into effect, he said.

ASSOCIATIONS

Professional associations have been key to developing standards of ethics and raising the bar for who qualifies as a financial planner. A number of associations have emerged to promote education, expertise, professionalism, and ethics in the field. These groups provide professional financial planners with information and continuing education. Many will also recommend reliable firms and individuals who are knowledgeable in financial planning. The most important include the following:

- Financial Planning Association (FPA; www.fpanet.org). The FPA was formed in 2000 through the merger of two of the industry's foremost associations, the Institute of Certified Financial Planners (ICFP) and the International Association for Financial Planning (IAFP). Although the two organizations, which were roughly the same size, had previously disagreed on licensing and other matters, in 1999 they agreed to merge. The combined entity had 27,400 members in 2000. The ICFP had allowed only members who held the CFP designation or were in the process of getting it, whereas the IAFP consisted of a more diverse group. Under the merger, FPA was opened to non-CFP holders as well, although members were encouraged to seek the designation.

- Association for Financial Counseling and Planning Education (AFCPE; www.hec.ohio-state.edu/hanna/afcpe/index.htm). Headquartered in Phoenix, Arizona, the AFCPE is a nonprofit professional organization comprised of researchers, academics, financial counselors, and planners. AFCPE administers certification programs for financial counselors, including the national Accredited Financial Counselor program, as well as certification programs for housing counselors, including Accredited Housing Counselor and Certified Housing Counselor. It offers education and

training programs at an annual conference and publishes a professional journal devoted to financial counseling and planning as well as a newsletter with a guide to resources, including Web sites, publications, and industry trends.

- Association for Investment Management and Research (AIMR; www.aimr.com). AIMR has more than 36,000 members in 87 affiliated societies and chapters in 80 countries. The organization sets the highest standards in education, ethics, and advocacy for investment professionals, their employers, and their clients. Through the Institute of Chartered Financial Analysts, AIMR grants the prestigious Chartered Financial Analyst designation.

- Certified Financial Planner Board of Standards (www.cfp-board.org). Founded in 1985, the CFP Board administers the CFP exam and regulates professional behavior for holders of that credential. The board creates professional and ethical standards and disciplines CFP holders who violate its tenets.

- National Association of Independent Public Finance Advisors (NAIPFA; www.naipfa.com). Members include firms that specialize in financial advice on bond sales and financial planning to public agencies. Headquartered in Washington, D.C., the NAIPFA seeks to build credibility and recognition of financial advisory firms and maintains high ethical and professional standards. It maintains a board of review to ensure members' compliance to standards, provides education materials to independent financial advisers, and responds to legislative needs of member firms and the public agencies they serve.

- National Association of Personal Financial Advisors (NAPFA; www.napfa.org). Founded in 1983, NAPFA is headquartered in Buffalo Grove, Illinois. With more than 640 members and affiliates in 50 states, it serves as a network for fee-only planners to discuss practice management, client services, and investment selections. The association works to encourage and advance the practice of fee-only planning by developing the skills of members, increasing awareness of fee-only financial planning, and fostering interaction with other professional groups.

- Registered Financial Planners Institute (RFPI; www.rfpi.com). Headquartered in Amherst, Ohio, the institute promotes professionalism in financial planning for individuals and businesses. RFPI offers classroom seminars and correspondence courses and sponsors a research program and referral service. The institute bestows the designation of Registered Financial Planner (RFP) on qualified members.

- The Society of Financial Service Professionals (SFSP; www.asclu.org). Headquartered in Bryn Mawr, Pennsylvania, SFSP was formerly the American Society of CLU & ChFC. It is a national membership organization representing 33,000 financial services professionals who have earned the chartered life underwriter or chartered financial consultant designation from the American College (www.amercoll .edu), also located in Bryn Mawr. Members specialize in estate planning, investments, tax planning, wealth accumulation, and life and health insurance.

CURRENT CONDITIONS

The overall market for financial planning services is expected to continue growing quickly in the early 2000s. In a *US Banker* report, Louis Harvey, a consultant for the industry, forecast the number of households seeking financial advice to climb from 11 million in 1999 to 60 million by 2015. Much of this growth, he said, will be fueled by investment-savvy baby boomers as they approach retirement.

INDUSTRY REACHES MOSTLY THE WEALTHY—FOR NOW

The industry's client base continues to be weighted heavily toward those in upper-income brackets. Among respondents in a 1999 survey of practicing CFPs, the average net worth of an individual client was $13 million and the median was $390,000. Only 26 percent of the CFPs studied had an average client net worth below $250,000. The survey also found the vast majority of financial planning customers are over age 45.

To some observers, these skewed demographics point to market opportunities to provide planning and advising services to middle- and lower-income earners, as well as younger people who have assets to manage. This gap hasn't been lost on H&R Block, which is aiming to target planning services at people earning $30,000-$60,000. Citibank, part of Citigroup, has taken a different tack: it's been experimenting with a program directed at middle-income customers who already hold one of its credit cards. The bank asks customers for copies of common financial documents such as pay stubs and tax forms, then produces a detailed report for the client free of charge. With this approach, Citibank hopes to strengthen its existing customer relationships, and in the process, find opportunities to pitch new products and services to those customers.

STOCKS TRUMP FUNDS

Long versed in recommending mutual funds to their clients, many experienced financial planners have had to adapt to the fervent demand for direct ownership of stocks. Dramatic gains in the U.S. stock market during the late 1990s drew considerable attention from consumers, who increasingly view mutual funds, which tend to be less volatile than individual stocks, as too conservative. As well, the popularity of stock options as employment compensation has caused planners to ponder options strategies for their clients. To keep up with demand, some financial planners have gone as far as setting up their own portfolio of stocks, a sort of home-grown mutual fund, that meets clients' goals and saves them money on mutual-fund fees. Other planners are skeptical, however, citing that picking stocks isn't their forte and that client interest in stocks is often more speculative than the kind of disciplined investment planners should advocate.

ELECTRONIC ADVICE

Another trend that's likely to affect the industry is online advising. Many of the bigger financial services companies have begun dispensing routine advice via the Web. Often this takes the form of a free automated system that guides consumers through a common financial decision-making process such as choosing a mutual fund or obtaining a mortgage. A study released in 2000 by Forrester Research found the quality of early entrants to be lacking, but the research firm nonetheless predicted that the market for online advice will expand rapidly in the early 2000s, reaching 23 million households by 2005, up from less than 2 million as of 2000. Demand was expected to be driven by the rising number of employees with 401(k) plans and increased availability and sophistication of online services.

Related to online advice is an older crop of software programs aimed at helping consumers do their own planning. Financial planning programs can calculate tax projections, net worth, cash flow, education funding, retirement savings requirements, survivor benefits, and estate taxes. Many also offer investment and cash management analysis. They cost anywhere from $40 to over $1,000; some entail more than $100 annually for maintenance of current interest and inflation rates. The ease of using online advice services is expected to curtail demand for such stand-alone programs, though, and major developers have staked out territory on the Web instead, as Intuit has done with its Quicken product line.

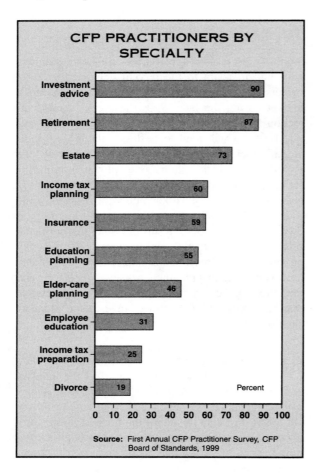

CFP PRACTITIONERS BY SPECIALTY

Specialty	Percent
Investment advice	90
Retirement	87
Estate	73
Income tax planning	60
Insurance	59
Education planning	55
Elder-care planning	46
Employee education	31
Income tax preparation	25
Divorce	19

Source: First Annual CFP Practitioner Survey, CFP Board of Standards, 1999

RESEARCH AND TECHNOLOGY

Beyond impersonal online-advice systems that dish out recommendations based on prefabricated problems and solutions, some planning-services companies envision a future where they will videoconference with customers over the Web via home personal computers and public kiosks. Indeed, some firms are making these services a reality. H.D. Vest Inc., of Irving, Texas, was testing in 2000 a videoconferencing program that would put its 8,000 financial planners on computer screens throughout the country. Equipped with a Web camera, conferencing software, and a high-speed connection, clients would be able to inter-

face with their financial planners over the computer much as they would in person. Another possibility for the service would be to bring together several specialists, say, a lawyer, an accountant, and an insurance broker, to work together with a customer instead of making the client visit each one separately. American Express Financial Advisors was eyeing a similar program, and a number of consumer-oriented investment brokerages were reportedly considering the same. Early customers for these services were expected to include tech-savvy consumers and busy professionals who don't have time for an in-person visit.

FURTHER READING

Arndorfer, James B. "Adviser Growth Taxes H&R Block." *Investment News,* 23 August 1999.

Barrett, William P. "Bedlam." *Forbes,* 15 June 1998.

Barry, James A., Jr. "Playing Favorites." *Financial Planning,* 1 October 2000.

Carey, Theresa W. "Beyond Cool: Online Trading Goes Mainstream as Quality Rises and Commissions Plunge." *Barron's,* 16 March 1998.

Certified Financial Planner Board of Standards. *First Annual CFP Practitioner Survey.* Denver, summer 1999. Available from http://www.cfp-board.org.

———. "1999 Edition Media Guide to the Financial Planning Profession." Denver, 1999. Available from http://www.cfp-board.org.

Cross, Margaretann. "Getting Personal with Fiscal Health." *Crain's Chicago Business,* 3 February 1997.

Curtis, Carol E. "The Next Hot Product: Advice." *US Banker,* May 1999.

———. "A Plan for Building Sales." *US Banker,* April 1998.

Edwards, Franklin R. *The New Finance: Regulation & Financial Stability.* Washington: AEI Press, 1996.

Fickenscher, Lisa. "Citibank Pushes Financial Planning for Indebted Mid-Income Customers." *American Banker,* 14 December 1999.

Foust, Dean. "For the Good Life, Hit 'Enter.'" *Business Week,* 21 July 1997.

"Full Speed to $1 Billion?" *Business Week,* 15 November 1999.

Haas, Donald Ray. "To Fee of Not To Fee?" *Advisor Today,* August 2000.

Halverson, Guy. "Warning: Few Planners Are Really 'Fee Only.'" *Christian Science Monitor,* 14 January 1997.

"IAFP, ICFP Boards Approve Framework of Combined Organization: The Financial Planning Association—Final Approval Awaits ICFP Member Vote," 22 March 1999. Available from http://www.iafp.org.

Meece, Mickey. "For Financial Advisors, a Pledge on Payments." *New York Times,* 10 May 1998.

Minkoff, Jerry. "Research: Firms Offering Online Advice Will More Than Double This Year, Study Says." *Web Finance,* 13 March 2000.

Molis, Jim. "Few Problems Reported in Merger of Trade Groups." *Denver Business Journal,* 21 January 2000.

"More Capital Gains, Less Urge to Tax Them." *Washington Times,* 7 July 1998.

Most, Bruce W. "When Science Clashes with Art: The Financial Planner's Dilemma." *Journal of Financial Planning,* June 1996.

"New Survey Shows Consumers Continue to Have Misperceptions about Financial Planning Process," 19 February 1999. Available from http://www.cfp-board.org/index .html.

Ozer, Jan. "Investment Tools and Advice." *PC Magazine,* 15 May 1998.

Simon, Ruth. "The Big Bad News about Fee-Only Financial Planners: Some Are Wolfing down Commissions on the Products They Recommend." *Money,* December 1995.

Toonkel, Jessica. "Videoconferencing's Next Wave to Wash over Customers' PCs." *American Banker,* 17 March 2000.

"Trends in Financial and Estate Planning." *Taxes,* January 1996.

Vestner, Charlie. "E-Mazing." *Individual Investor,* July 1997.

"Web-Based Financial Planning Generates Actionable Advice." *ABA Banking Journal,* September 2000.

Weidner, David. "Oversight of Financial Planners Is Mixed." *Wall Street Journal,* 15 September 1997.

Zarowin, Stanley. "The Elusive Holy Grail." *Journal of Accountancy,* October 1996.

FUEL CELLS

As the curtain rose on the 21st century, consumer demand for large trucks and sport-utility vehicles was on the rise, but so were gasoline prices. The energy industries were undergoing rapid deregulation, and the dust had yet to clear on the precise direction they would take. Meanwhile, environmental consciousness was on the upswing, and with it consumer and regulatory demand for efficient, ecologically sound energy sources. Fortunately, at a number of research laboratories and companies around the globe, help was on the way.

The late 1990s brought huge advances in fuel-cell technology, which was rapidly being readied for commercial deployment in vehicles, power plants, homes, and even electronic devices as the solution to our dependence on fossil fuels and dirty or inefficient energy sources generally. The market for fuel cells was well charged in the late 1990s, reaching about $355 million and growing over 30 percent annually. At that pace, which was expected to continue, and most likely accelerate, the market was projected to total $1.3 billion by 2003. But the biggest questions remain unanswered, and harbor all the real excitement. Most prominently among these was the degree of technical and commercial viability of fuel cells in the short term. Bear Stearns predicted that if fuel cell stacks prove as economical as industry players expect, fuel cells will constitute a $100 billion market by 2010.

Fuel cells produce electricity from the electrochemical interaction of hydrogen and oxygen, resulting in a clean and efficient energy source fit for a wide variety of applications. While the exact method of extracting hydrogen varies and can influence the emission composition, the most efficient fuel cells produce only clean—even drinkable—water as a by-product.

Though the modern fuel-cell industry reaches back a few decades, auto companies began intensive development of the technology for their vehicles in the early 1990s; by 2000, automakers and fuel-cell specialists had spent about $1.5 billion on research and development to bring fuel-cell vehicles to market, according to *The Economist*. A handful of models were on the road that year, though they were not expected to hit the commercial market en masse until the middle of the decade. Although plagued by prohibitively high production costs because mass-production facilities were scarcely outfitted for fuel-cell infrastructures, analysts predicted that, through the cooperation of fuel-cell manufacturers, auto companies, and governmental agencies, such problems would be sufficiently overcome within decades. Between one-third and one-half of the entire U.S. vehicle population was projected to be powered by fuel cells by 2030.

Fuel cells also began to shake the utility industries, promising "grid-busting" power distribution whereby customers need only make a trip to their local appliance store to acquire the only energy source they need. The turnover to stationary home power systems was likely to be gradual, however, with fuel cells first emerging as a niche market, particularly in areas with troubled grid reliability and excessive peak loads at power plants.

ORGANIZATION AND STRUCTURE

The introduction of fuel cells to the mass market was stalled somewhat by ambivalence over the proper configurations for their various applications. Fuel cells use one of a number of possible electrolytes, including phosphoric acid, solid oxide, molten carbonate, polymer, and alkaline, which determine the operating temperature and, thus, the efficiency of the fuel cell. Electrolysis is the process whereby water's component elements—hydrogen and oxygen—are physically separated by an electric current shot through the molecule. After electrolysis, the elements are shuttled toward battery-style electrodes—the hydrogen toward the anode and the oxygen toward the cathode. A catalyst then kicks the hydrogen atom, forcing it to release its electron into the cathode, while the remaining, positively charged hydrogen proton is also shot toward the cathode. The electrodes then run through an external circuit, such as a motor, to yield an electric charge. When the current returns to the cathode, the hydrogen electrons recombine with the oxygen to generate heat and water. As long as a stream of fuel is provided, the fuel cell can run indefinitely, requiring no recharging.

There are four major types of fuel cells. Solid-oxide fuel cells (SOFCs) and molten-carbonate fuel cells (MOFCs) pull hydrogen out of methane, which requires particularly high operating temperatures (in this case, reaching 600 degrees Celsius and 1,000 degrees Celsius, respectively). As a result, these fuel cells necessitate dangerous and expensive materials to build component parts capable of withstanding such temperatures. Mainly for that reason, these types of fuel cells receive relatively little practical attention.

Phosphoric-acid fuel cells (PAFCs) find their most extensive use in stationary power systems, and indeed were the only type of fuel cells in significant commercial use in the late 1990s. Like SOFCs and MOFCs, PAFCs utilize methane rather than pure hydrogen, but PAFCs operate at only 200 degrees Celsius, and thus are practical for stationary use. Such temperatures, however, still require heavy components, thus making PAFCs of limited use for vehicles. ONSI Corp. of Connecticut sold about 60 200-kilowatt power-plant model fuel cells worldwide by 2000.

For vehicles, proton exchange membrane (PEM) fuel cells are the order of the day. With comparatively quick power conversion at temperatures of 80 degrees Celsius, PEM fuel cells are the crown jewel of the auto industry's fuel-cell research, although they still pose significant difficulties. The membrane that gives the fuel cell its name is a thin, Saran Wrap-like electrolyte coated with a catalyst and is permeable to hydrogen protons. Such cells, however, result in only about .6 volts of electricity. In order to effectively power an electric motor, a series of cells are stacked

together. PEM fuel-cell stacks are also finding increasing favor among manufacturers devoted to stationary power systems.

Hydrogen is the most widely used fuel for fuel cells, although it poses its share of difficulties. The low energy density of hydrogen calls for a great deal of storage space, which can be impractical in an automobile. Liquefied hydrogen, moreover, necessitates cryogenic storage, resulting in significant energy losses. As a result, great strides must be forthcoming in hydrogen storage before such vehicles can hit the mass market. A temporary solution favored by oil companies and automakers is to generate hydrogen inside the vehicle by reforming methanol or light hydrocarbons, though such methods continue to result in dirty emissions. While reformers will likely provide manufacturers with a more immediate market-entry strategy, most analysts expect that the ability to implement effective and practical direct hydrogen fueling is just around the corner.

Fuel cells have been nurtured by a regulatory climate increasingly aimed at curtailing U.S. dependence on foreign energy supplies and reducing pollutant emissions. A host of laws, regulations, and initiatives are in place fostering the development of fuel cells in one way or another, including the Clean Air Acts of 1963, 1970, and 1990; the Energy Policy Act of 1992; the Omnibus Budget Reconciliation Act of 1993; the National Appliance Energy Conservation Act of 1987; the Tax Payer Relief Act of 1997; the Federal Highway Bill of 1998; and the Climate Change Action Plan. The U.S. Department of Energy (DOE) aims to eliminate 10 percent of all petroleum-based vehicle fuels by 2010 and 30 percent by 2030, while the international Kyoto Protocol calls for the United States to reduce greenhouse-gas emissions.

The Congressional Climate Change Technology Initiative is a massive project aimed at reducing emissions, improving air quality, and reducing U.S. dependence on foreign energy supplies. The initiative received $227 million from Congress for fiscal 2001. The 2001 budget included over $1.6 billion in funding for various programs, including tax credits for implementing efficient, renewable energy technologies in buildings, automobiles, and power plants. The program currently provides for a 10 percent tax credit for the purchase of fuel-cell or other highly efficient electric vehicles. Proposed measures include tax credits ranging from $1,000 to $2,000 for the purchase of new homes running at over 30 to 50 percent greater efficiency. The Department of Energy received over $100 million in the 2001 budget specifically for fuel-cell programs.

Technicians assembling a hot module fuel cell. (Photo Researchers Inc./Volker Steger/Science Photo Library)

The DOE also runs the Vision 21 program, designed to streamline power-plant operations toward more ecologically sound practices. The DOE began dispersing money to fuel-cell companies and research centers in 2000, with an eye toward completing a clean Vision 21 power-plant infrastructure for commercial use by 2015. Another key DOE program was the Partnership for a New Generation of Vehicles, which joined the federal government with the three largest automakers (DaimlerChrysler, Ford, and General Motors) to develop low-emissions vehicles. The partnership's participants promised the introduction of five-passenger sedans that can get up to 80 miles per gallon. By 2000, the U.S. government had doled out $1.5 billion in contracts for the development of fuel-saving technologies.

BACKGROUND AND DEVELOPMENT

While fuel cells were touted as one of the most significant emerging energy technologies, they have had an extremely long shelf life in the laboratory. The principle of deriving electricity from hydrogen was discovered as early as 1839, but since generating an electrochemical current proved especially problem-

atic, the principle failed to yield any significant breakthroughs, and was put back on the shelf for a century. With the rise of the internal combustion engine and its reliance on fossil fuels, the discovery was simply written off.

Not until the U.S. National Aeronautics and Space Administration (NASA) employed General Electric to develop alkali fuel cells for its Gemini and Apollo spacecrafts did the technology reemerge. While the fuel cells proved successful on these missions, only an enormously resourceful organization such as NASA could afford to use them, because in order to generate high power at an appropriately low weight, the fuel cells were outfitted with high amounts of platinum and gold.

Spurred by the energy crisis of the 1970s, the American Gas Association and the Institute of Gas Technology set out to study the possibility of a hydrogen-based energy infrastructure. The next major breakthrough came in the early 1980s, when researchers at the Los Alamos National Laboratories eliminated the need for much of the precious metals in fuel-cell components, thus paving the way for the popular PEM cell that stood at the industry's forefront in 2000.

Meanwhile, the range of fuel options for fuel cells was expanded with breakthroughs in the reforming process. Working with the U.S. Department of Energy, industry leader Plug Power Inc. in 1997 found a way to capture sulfur from gasoline before it reached the fuel cell. Gasoline had been considered unusable for fuel cells since sulfur acts to poison the cells. With a specialized catalytic converter, the company worked to expand reformer capabilities to facilitate multiple fuel sources.

While the immediate impetus behind the search for alternative energy sources was the pending depletion of the world's oil supplies coupled with the jolts to the nation's economy generated by foreign political turmoil, recent years have witnessed a gradual shift of rationale. With oil reserves currently deemed stable for decades to come, perhaps the most pronounced motive for the development of new fuel technologies is the evolving public attitude toward environmental sustainability. The high cost, in terms of political initiative and military security, of the nation's foreign oil dependence further spurred calls for improved energy technologies in the United States.

PIONEERS IN THE FIELD

The principle underlying fuel cells was first uncovered in 1839 by the colorful British physicist Sir William Grove while he was experimenting with electrolysis. Grove found that not only can these elements be broken apart, they can be combined in a sort of reverse electrolysis to yield water and electricity. Despite his insistence that he had no interest in the potential uses of his discovery, Grove described in great detail exactly how the reverse electrolysis would generate electricity.

Nearly 150 years later, a Canadian geologist named Geoffrey Ballard propelled the technology into the industry we know today. After the General Electric/NASA fuel-cell successes, Ballard worked in a government laboratory in the United States as well as on various government-subsidized alternative-energy products before settling in Vancouver, British Columbia, to work on the development of lithium electric car batteries. Ballard Power Systems Inc. built on the early PEM technology by General Electric to develop fuel-cell stacks with sheets of graphite, thereby generating increased power output. Ballard's research team's big break came from the Canadian military, which found that the team's PEM fuel cells could be of use in battlefield communications equipment.

CURRENT CONDITIONS

In light of increasingly pressing concerns regarding air quality, climate change, and environmental sustainability, and with the expectation that consumer travel habits were unlikely to undergo any substantial alteration in the near future, the adaptation of vehicles to more efficient fuel technologies was expected to constitute the primary focus of the automotive industry well into the 21st century. While consumer demand for cleaner, more efficient-burning fuels rose through the late 1990s into the 2000s, natural-gas fuels, such as methanol and ethanol, and hybrid vehicles combining such fuels with standard gasoline were the most common alternatives by 2000. (See the essay in this book entitled Alternative Vehicle Fuels.)

FUEL CELLS MARKED AS THE FUTURE OF THE AUTO INDUSTRY

Analysts were virtually unanimous, however, in their prediction that by the middle of the 2000s fuel cells would be on their way to dominance of the alternative-fuel market, to be followed within decades by dominance of the auto market itself. Emitting only water vapor, fuel-cell vehicles were about 50 percent more efficient and 90 percent cleaner than gasoline-powered vehicles. The most common projections held that by 2004 fuel-cell vehicles would be widely available. In the meantime, fuel-cell cars and trucks will find their most extensive deployment in federal, state, and local government fleets, such as postal-delivery trucks, buses, sanitation trucks, and so on.

Ballard's PEM fuel cells were widely hailed as the automotive industry's standard model, and automakers were quick to jump on board. DaimlerChrysler and the Ford Motor Co. combined purchased about half of Ballard and set about developing engine infrastructures around the Ballard core. The fruits of the respective automakers' partnerships with Ballard were Ford's P2000 HFC (hydrogen fuel cell) and DaimlerChrysler's Necar 4, both of which rolled out in 1999. Other manufacturers followed suit, either partnering with Ballard or initiating their own development projects. So certain was the future of fuel-cell technology that even oil giant Royal Dutch/Shell created a new division, Shell Hydrogen, whose head, Don Huberts, fully expected fuel cells to eventually replace traditional energy sources in power plants and automobiles.

BUT THE CONVERSION PROCESS FACES HURDLES

A number of factors will determine how quickly the transition to fuel cells takes place. First of all, the level of pressure applied to companies by consumers will have the most immediate impact on the industry's willingness to invest heavily on the commercialization of fuel-cell vehicles. The world's oil and gas prices, which skyrocketed and garnered considerable attention in 2000, are subject to dramatic fluctuation and political wrangling as well, which could in turn affect the pace at which companies are inclined to speed fuel cells to market. These factors also influence, and be influenced by, progress in implementing processes and facilities capable of delivering low-cost mass production of fuel-cell vehicles.

The nation's fueling infrastructure must also be factored into the fuel-cell equation. A complete overhaul of refueling stations to include hydrogen pumps would undoubtedly be prohibitively expensive, and smaller gas stations feared that such a restructuring would put them out of business. Methanol was touted as an intermediary solution to this problem, although methanol's ecological deficiencies sparked many environmentalists to argue against this remedy. Alternatives included the installation of small electrolysis centers alongside traditional gasoline pumps, or even the implementation of photovoltaic cells—which produce electricity directly from sunlight and yield no pollutants—atop service stations to facilitate the local production of hydrogen. While such solutions would mitigate some of the environmental impact, cost and technology hang-ups remain.

The reforming process is pivotal to the choice of fuel. Since reformers add weight to an automobile, the more refined the process, the more feasible the technology. Down the road, reforming will likely be unnecessary, but if companies want to start to introduce fuel cells to the automotive marketplace, some compromise will have to suffice. For this reason, the earliest fuel-cell cars will not be completely devoid of pollutant emissions, either, as the on-board conversion of methanol, the most common alternative, into hydrogen will release some carbon dioxide.

Other problems associated with methanol seeped to the surface in early 2000 when studies found that the fuel's oxygenation derivative methyl tertiary-butyl ether (MTBE) found its way into California's groundwater supply, leading to the state's banning of the substance, which was followed by similar legislative actions around the country. Though the oxygenation process achieved considerable success in improving air quality, regulators felt that such improvements should not come at the cost of water contamination.

Standard gasoline, a possible reforming source thanks to recent innovations, could take advantage of both filling stations' and vehicles existing infrastructures. This, however, was a dubious benefit in the eyes of environmentalists, since gasoline is so laden with carbon dioxide. In that respect, methanol is greatly preferred, but then the infrastructure difficulties reemerge—although outfitting the nation's filling stations with methanol pumps poses nowhere near the costs associated with the implementation of pure hydrogen pumps.

Reformers are also problematic because they typically require up to a minute to warm up after starting, and add time between a driver's action, such as flooring the gas pedal, and the engine's response. With performance demands at an all-time high, such restrictions are not likely to win over many customers. While reformers could instead be installed at filling stations, thereby eliminating many of the size and time restrictions (since these reformers could run continuously), in the end the problem of on-board storage won't go away.

BUILDINGS AWAIT ENERGY CONVERSION

Meanwhile, households and businesses prepared to be taken off the grid by fuel cells. Plug Power noted that about 75 percent of all U.S. homes incorporate a natural-gas infrastructure, and are thus tailor-made for an efficient conversion to stationary built-in distributed power. Energy companies and fuel-cell manufacturers positioned fuel cells to facilitate what is known as "distributed generation"—an industry buzzword signifying the production of energy at or near the location of use. The applicability of fuel-cell technology to public utilities heated up in the late 1990s. The King County, Washington, Department of Natural Resources, in conjunction with the U.S. Environmental Protection Agency, Washington State Energy Office, M-C Power Corp., Bechtel Corp., and Puget Sound Energy, invested $17 million in a pioneering test of the feasibility of fuel cells for use in the conversion of digester gas into electricity and heat.

According to the U.S. Fuel Cell Commercialization Group, when fully developed, fuel cells will provide household efficiency levels (measured by the amount of power generated as a percentage of fuel consumption) of over 50 percent, possibly reaching as high as 70 percent if the steam and heat outputs are also harnessed for productive use. By way of comparison, traditional coal-burning sources yield efficiencies of about 30 to 40 percent.

Still, at current production costs, fuel-cell stacks for an average-sized home would run about $20,000, a steep investment for the average household. Plug Power, however, in conjunction with General Electric, set out on an ambitious project to bring its stacks to the consumer market by 2001 for only $7,500, with plans to cut that price in half by 2005. While competitors, such as Ballard, thought such projections were a bit wishful, most industry players expect the technology to take hold rapidly after their widespread commercial debut in 2001. Within five years of their introduction to the market, analysts expected home fuel-cell stacks to emerge as a billion-dollar industry.

PROHIBITIVE COSTS

The biggest, most immediate obstacle for fuel cells in both the transportation industry and utilities was capital costs. A PEM fuel-cell unit for a mass-produced vehicle cost an estimated $30,000 in late 1999, thereby doubling the price of the car. A host of government-industry-research partnerships took off in the late 1990s to figure out a way to mitigate this nagging problem. The Department of Energy doled out millions of dollars in grants to teams working to bring costs down. These projects have already met with considerable success. PEM fuel cells have significantly lowered costs, primarily by reducing the amount of platinum required to sustain the conversion process from about $30,000-worth in the mid-1990s to about $500-worth by the turn of the century.

ADJACENT INDUSTRIES A MAJOR FACTOR

Competing industries will play a prominent role in the course of fuel-cell proliferation and in the precise materials they incorporate. For instance, adding to the debates over the most viable fuel source for fuel cells were the interests of oil companies, who feared that the quick transition to pure hydrogen could undermine their operations before oil firms could effectively adapt to the new technology. Thus, many oil companies pushed methanol as the fuel of choice. The debate was far from a clear-cut, fuel-cell-versus-oil-companies battle, however; British Petroleum's Bernie Bulkin, according to *The Economist,* stressed that promoting the less efficient methanol will only necessitate further infrastructure redevelopment for hydrogen a few years down the road. Ballard, meanwhile, felt that fuel cells could get a jump start into the market by deploying the methanol-based devices in the short term until pure hydrogen is more viable.

INDUSTRY LEADERS

BALLARD POWER SYSTEMS INC.

A pioneer in fuel-cell technology and the acknowledged world leader in the development of PEM fuel cells, Ballard Power Systems specialized in the cells, their systems, and their related components. The company maintained partnerships with most of the world's major automakers to produce the fuel cells around which they develop vehicle infrastructures. DaimlerChrysler and Ford Motor Co., in fact, were major Ballard shareholders, and worked directly with the fuel-cell manufacturer to bring the technology to market. Ballard also built relationships with the municipal governments in Chicago and Vancouver, which have incorporated Ballard's PEM fuel cells into their bus fleets. Ballard developed its fuel cells both for stationary power systems and for the transportation market. Ballard's first released product was its 1995 275-horsepower fuel-cell bus engine. Its Mark 900 fuel cell was rolled out in 2000 in Ford's TH!NK FC5 prototype, a stepping stone to future automobile fuel-cell commercialization. Based in Vancouver, British Columbia, Ballard employed 675 workers and achieved revenues of $22.9 million in 1999, up 41.4 percent from 1998.

PLUG POWER INC.

Plug Power of Latham, New York focused on distributed power systems for commercial and residential buildings with its PEM fuel-cell stacks. The company signed a worldwide distribution agreement with General Electric Power Systems in February 1999 to help bring its washing-machine size fuel-cell stacks to the consumer market as early as 2001 through a project called GE Fuel Cell Systems. Plug Power was born of the joint venture between a subsidiary of DTE Energy Co. and Mechanical Technology Inc., and

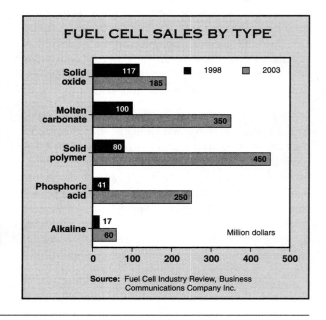

FUEL CELL SALES BY TYPE

1998 / 2003

Type	1998	2003
Solid oxide	117	185
Molten carbonate	100	350
Solid polymer	80	450
Phosphoric acid	41	250
Alkaline	17	60

Million dollars

Source: Fuel Cell Industry Review, Business Communications Company Inc.

went public in late 1999. The firm tested over 500 more residential fuel systems during 2000 in preparation for their commercial release the following year. With a payroll of 280 employees, Plug Power's sales jumped 69 percent in 1999 to reach $11 million.

FuelCell Energy Inc.

FuelCell Energy of Danbury, Connecticut—formerly Energy Research Corp.—focused on fuel-cell stacks with a generating capacity of over 250 megawatts, mainly for power plants. In its hometown in 1999, the company commissioned its first commercial plant, which supplied power to its own manufacturing facilities and the local power grid. By 2000, the bulk of FuelCell's revenues derived from Department of Energy grants for a number of development projects, including the company's Direct FuelCell, which generated hydrogen from natural gas without needing an external reactor. The electrochemical technologies firm Energy Research Co. spun off its batteries operations in 1998 before renaming itself FuelCell Energy Inc. FuelCell achieved revenues of $20 million in 1999 while employing over 100 workers. That year, the company partnered with Mercedes-Benz, Southern Co., and Alabama Municipal Electric Authority to build a Mercedes-Benz fuel-cell power plant.

Avista Corp.

Avista, based in Spokane, Washington, was an energy, information, and technology firm employing 2,900 workers. The firm developed PEM fuel cells through Avista Labs, which received a U.S. Department of Commerce grant of $2 million. In addition to its fuel-cell operations, Avista—formerly Washington Water Power—was engaged in telephone services, fiber-optic network construction, energy trading, and other services, primarily in the western United States. Sales in 1999 reached $7.9 billion, an increase of 114 percent from the year before.

AMERICA AND THE WORLD

Western Europe has for years heavily taxed fuel as a way of raising revenue and safeguarding the environment by cutting consumption and emissions. In recent years, the United Kingdom, moreover, announced that it would continue to increase gasoline and diesel taxes at a rate of 6 percent annually above the rate of inflation. The European Union as a whole, meanwhile, planned to reduce its emissions by 8 percent from their 1990 level by 2010, in keeping with the Kyoto Accords to which the United States was also

bound, though of which the United States fully expected to fall short.

Toward these ends, in summer 1999 the British energy firm BG plc and fuel-cell developer Alstom, which is engaged in a joint venture with Ballard, signed a memorandum of understanding to help commercialize PEM fuel cells for stationary power systems in the United Kingdom and throughout Europe. Germany has also made great use of PEM fuel cells and natural-gas reformers in early tests for home heating and power-generation systems.

Meanwhile, Iceland took the leading role on the world's fuel-cell stage in 1999 when it announced its plans to become the first hydrogen-powered economy, immediately attracting the likes of DaimlerChrysler, Shell's new hydrogen division, and the Norwegian energy firm Norsk, all hungry to test their newest fuel-cell vehicles in what is seen as a dress rehearsal for the future. Daimler's first fuel-cell buses hit the Reykjavik in late 1999. Iceland hopes to eventually replace its entire automotive population with fuel-cell vehicles.

Increased international cooperation was on the horizon for fuel-cell development as well. Mitsubishi Motors Corp., with plans to roll out its first generation of fuel-cell vehicles by 2005, suggested that research into fuel cells should reside in the hands of a neutral, third-party association or government rather than be relegated to free-market proprietary forces so as to better facilitate the widespread implementation of the energy-saving technology.

RESEARCH AND TECHNOLOGY

Environmentalists cheered the 2000 discovery by researchers at the University of California at Berkeley of a process by which green algae, or "pond scum," can be made to produce hydrogen rather than oxygen. By literally starving the algae of its requisite sulfur, the research team halted its oxygen production, forcing the algae to substitute hydrogen as its protein of choice. Moreover, if timed properly, the process can be run over and over with the same algae by simply reintroducing sulfur into its diet after a few days, thereby allowing the algae to regenerate the carbohydrates necessary for protein production. While the implementation of this process into a viable commercial system was a ways off, it gave hope for the ecologically sound use of "biomass" for fuel-cell technology.

The production of hydrogen for use in fuel cells was becoming more practical as well. In 2000 researchers at the University of Pennsylvania reported success in preventing carbon buildup by using copper and cerium oxide, rather than nickel, as the catalyst for the oxidation process.

In an attempt to avoid being outdone by adventurous balloonists, NASA was busily developing PEM fuel cells to store solar energy so as to allow for perpetual flight (up to six months or so) of its Helios solar-powered plane. The cells ideally will convert its electrolyzed hydrogen and oxygen into water and electricity during the night before reconverting it during the day. The plane was reportedly intended for use as a high-bandwidth communication outpost, an observation platform, or for atmospheric research. NASA charged its Environmental Research Aircraft and Sensor Technology program with the development of the fuel cells' components, which pose particular difficulty because they must be significantly lighter for an airplane, especially one of such endurance.

FURTHER READING

Chambers, Ann. "Fuel Cell Market Escalates." *Power Engineering,* November 1999.

Cuthbert, Nigel R. "Auto and Oil Industries Improving Quality, Efficiency of EU Fuels." *Oil & Gas Journal,* 12 July 1999.

"DOE Launches Research for Efficient Power Plants." *Engineering News-Record,* 13 March 2000.

Dornheim, Michael A. "Special Fuel Cells Key to Months-Long Flight." *Aviation Week & Space Technology,* 28 February 2000.

Dukart, James R. "Power Plants of the Future." *Utility Business,* August 1999.

Dye, Lee. "You'll Never Look at Algae the Same Way Again—Or So Some Researchers Hope." *Los Angeles Times,* 28 February 2000.

Energy Information Administration. "Analysis of the Climate Change Technology Initiative—Executive Summary." Washington: U.S. Department of Energy, 2000. Available from http://www.eia.doe.gov/oiaf/climate99/execsum.html.

———. "Annual Energy Outlook 2000." Washington: U.S. Department of Energy, 2000. Available from http://www.eia.doe.gov/oiaf/aeo/index.html.

Ford, Tim. "Fuel-Cell Vehicles Offer Clean and Sustainable Mobility for the Future." *Oil & Gas Journal,* 13 December 1999.

"Fuel Cell Future Remains a Gamble, But Inroads Continue." *Consulting-Specifying Engineer,* Summer 2000.

"'Fuel Cell-Powered Cars Will Be on the Road in Five Years,' Report Says." *Design News,* 5 July 1999.

"Fuel Cells Meet Big Business." *Economist,* 24 July 1999.

Koppel, Tom. "As Pure as Driven Snow?" *Economist,* 15 January 2000.

Lamb, Marguerite. "Power to the People." *Mother Earth News,* October/November 1999.

Lavers, Bill. "The Place of Fuel Cells in Power Supply to Take Off?" *European Power News,* December 1999.

Lewis, Tony. "A Call for Open Access to Fuel-Cell Technology." *Automotive News International,* 1 November 1999.

Malloy, Gerry. "Workings of 21st-Century Power Source Baffle Many." *Maclean's,* 25 October 1999.

McLean, Bethany. "Fuel Cells: They Bring Good Things to Life." *Fortune,* 12 June 2000.

Motavalli, Jim. "Harnessing Hydrogen." *E Magazine: The Environmental Magazine,* March/April 2000.

Pearce, Fred. "Power House." *New Scientist,* 18 March 2000.

Port, Otis. "The Key to Cleaner Fuel Cells? It's in the Water." *Business Week,* 23 October 2000.

"Project to Examine Potential of Fuel Cell Power." *Water World,* January 2000.

Robinson, Aaron. "Automakers Design 'Green' Cars: American Motorists Yawn." *Automotive News International,* 1 February 2000.

Swanekamp, Robert. "Distributed Generation Seeks Market Niches." *Power,* November/December 1999.

GAMBLING RESORTS AND CASINOS

The United States was fast becoming a nation of high rollers by 2000. While Americans wagered over $640 billion on all forms of gambling in 1999, the gambling industry itself was worth about $58.2 billion, the gross amount taken in by gambling operations after doling out winnings and before paying expenses. Casinos took in about $24.9 billion of this total; however, with growing competition among casinos, industry revenues grew more slowly in the late 1990s than they did earlier in the decade. By 2000, 33 states had passed legislation allowing for some form of casino gaming, be it land-based, on riverboats, or run by Native American tribes, led by Nevada, New Jersey, Mississippi, and Louisiana. The National Indian Gaming Commission reported that, as of 2000, about 195 reservation casinos operated in 28 states, earning annual revenues of $8.4 billion.

Gambling has received increasing, though hardly universal, acceptance as a mainstream form of entertainment over the years, with about 85 percent of Americans holding that the practice is a matter of personal choice and is acceptable for themselves or for others, according to a national survey by pollsters Peter Hart and Frank Lutz. As legalized gambling spreads, the industry faces a period of transition, its structure yet to be ironed out as of 2000. The biggest, glitziest names were consolidating in order to boost efficiency and secure market position, while the smaller gambling houses and riverboat casinos have tried to boost their image and diversify their services to attract high rollers to their niche market.

Casinos are the biggest moneymakers and the driving force in the gambling industry. They have completely changed from their inception—moving from purely gaming houses to adult theme and fantasy parks, often with such services as childcare and video arcades. Casino gambling is now interlaced with 24-hour shopping malls and visual attractions such as talking statues, erupting volcanoes, and mock ocean battles with pirate ships. Slot machines are generating mounds of new business; slots appeal to novice gamblers because they are easily understandable and fast-paced. Originally, casinos devoted only about 30 percent of their space to slot machines; now it's about 90 percent.

Casino gambling stretches well beyond the havens of Las Vegas, Nevada, and Atlantic City, New Jersey. Shortly after New Jersey approved gambling in 1976, Native American tribes, exempt from local laws as sovereign nations, realized that they too could profit. Gambling also spread to several waterfront and river states such as Iowa, Mississippi, and Illinois after state legislatures authorized gambling on cruise ships and paddlewheel riverboats.

Casinos are subject to federal, state, and local regulations. Before operating a casino, gambling companies must acquire a license or reach an agreement with a state. Some states, such as Illinois, limit the number of licenses they issue, while other states simply conduct reviews and background checks on all applicants for casino licenses. The Indian Gaming Regulatory

Act (IGRA) of 1988 is the key piece of legislation governing casinos run by Native Americans. This act led to tremendous growth of such facilities, especially in states such as North Dakota, Iowa, New York, South Dakota, and North Carolina. IGRA permits Native American tribes to engage in and regulate gambling on their lands if their lands are located in a state that allows gambling and if federal law allows for such gambling.

The industry's primary organizations are the American Gaming Association (AGA) and the National Indian Gaming Association (NIGA). Based in Washington, D.C., AGA provides the industry with statistics and information on the gambling industry around the country. Besides promoting the economic success of the industry, AGA also promotes casino safety and responsible gambling. Providing its members with national representation, AGA pushes for legislation to stimulate the gambling industry.

NIGA comprises 168 Native American nations and strives to protect and advance the Native American casino industry. The broader, stated purpose of NIGA is to propel advancement of the economic, social, and political lives of all indigenous Americans, promoting the gaming industry as one remedy for the crippling poverty suffered by Native American communities. Also based in Washington, D.C., NIGA trains tribal members to run casinos and offers seminars on improving casino business and safety.

BACKGROUND AND DEVELOPMENT

According to Dr. John Findlay, author of *People of Chance,* gambling in America really evolved in the 1800s during the westward migration. With little other entertainment and a belief in luck and risk taking, many American pioneers embraced all forms of gambling. Between 1800 and 1840, towns along the Mississippi River became ports for the riverboats transporting goods and people. The riverboats were transformed into moving gambling parlors. Further west in the mining camps and small towns, public, organized systems of gambling evolved. Most of the gambling involved such card games as monte and poker, but some wheel games existed.

As emerging cities in the Midwest, South, and West became bigger, wealthier, and more sophisticated, they sought acceptance from the East by tackling their "problems." Since the East viewed gaming as vulgar, many cities passed ordinances banning dealers and gamblers, and those caught were arrested.

While American cities started turning against gambling in the mid-1800s, a new, elegant, upscale form of gaming evolved in Europe among the aristocratic classes—casino gambling. Casinos were different because they used large tables and machinery, such as roulette wheels. Casinos were found in elegant vacation resorts and mineral spa areas such as Baden Baden and Bad Homburg, Germany, along with Nice, Cannes, and Monte Carlo on the French Riviera.

In 1863 Francois Blanc—a successful Parisian casino manager who was jailed for stock fraud—arrived in Monaco to build and run a casino there, despite wavering and resistance from his patron, Prince Charles II. Blanc brought wealth to Monaco and is considered the father of today's casinos. His management theories and rules for customer relations are used in Las Vegas casinos as faithfully as they were in the 1850s.

While casino games such as baccarat and roulette became popular and gained wide acceptance in Europe, a series of irregularities in U.S. lotteries and horse racing caused national scandals in the late 1800s. By 1910 almost all American forms of gambling had been outlawed.

Regulated betting on horses, overseen by strict state laws, eventually returned in the 1930s. During Prohibition, private clubs in cities offered various forms of illegal gambling—crap pits, poker, blackjack, and slot machines. After World War II, Las Vegas started using its gambling resorts to attract tourists. During the 1950s, Benjamin "Bugsy" Siegel, a known gangster, saw an opportunity to elude California's strict ban on gambling and quench its citizens' thirst for gaming.

Siegel traveled to Nevada, since the state had tolerated gambling in the 1930s during the construction of the Hoover Dam, and built a luxury Caribbean-style hotel and casino called the Flamingo. Siegel contributed to Las Vegas' reputation as a rough town operated by organized crime from New York and Chicago but, with his casino, he had started something that would eventually contribute to the development of a new reputation. To attract gamblers, Las Vegas began offering inexpensive hotel rooms, food, free drinks, and famous entertainment. Soon, Las Vegas became one of the regular stops for such performers as Frank Sinatra and Elvis Presley.

Howard Hughes became an investor in Las Vegas after he and his entourage moved into the Desert Inn in 1976, renting an entire floor of the hotel to stay out of range of photographers and the public. The Desert Inn management decided Hughes and his crew were a detriment to the business since they didn't gamble, so management evicted him; Hughes responded by buying the hotel. He then began buying land on the Las Vegas Strip, which prompted large East Coast corporations such as Hilton to do the same.

In 1978 casinos spread to Atlantic City; they later cropped up in states such as Colorado, Louisiana, and South Dakota. The early 1980s saw casino resorts become more popular for guests and businesses alike, and casino growth increased dramatically by the decade's end. Casino gambling was approved in South Dakota, Iowa, Illinois, Mississippi, Missouri, and on many Native American reservations. In 1989 Iowa became the first state to officially allow gambling on riverboat casinos.

Also in the late 1980s, Stephen A. Wynn almost single-handedly changed Las Vegas by taking gambling to its next step when he built the Mirage resort. The casino resort boasted a shark tank, a wild-animal haven, and an artificial erupting volcano. Other major casino operators soon followed suit. Old casinos such as the Sands, the Hacienda, and the New Frontier were demolished. New casinos like the Luxor—a glass version of the great pyramid with copies of Egyptian monuments and statues of pharaohs—were built to attract tourists looking for entertainment.

Although many new casinos were introduced in various cities in the early to mid-1990s, Las Vegas and Atlantic City still claimed approximately two-thirds of 1994's gross revenues. To attract visitors, these casino resorts were becoming ever more elaborate; some even had features such as malls, roller coasters, and golf courses.

Casino companies spent the early 1990s scaling back operations and plunging themselves into serious debt in an effort to rebuild their operations with an eye toward a more lucrative late-1990s market, a gamble that paid off.

CURRENT CONDITIONS

Following the release of the National Gambling Impact Study Commission report, a good deal of heated political debate ensued in Washington and in state legislatures on how to properly regulate the casino industry and the activity of gambling itself. Proposals included everything from a legal gambling age of 21 nationwide to banning automatic teller machines (ATMs) from casinos to cigarette-style warning labels on all gambling products about the potential risks of addiction.

The commission, initiated in 1997 by President Bill Clinton, recommended a federal ban on Internet gambling and wagering on college sports. The report also urged a limit on casino-industry political contributions at the state and local levels. Overall, however, analysts expected that the report was unlikely to lead to any drastic changes to the industry, and thus casino companies' widespread worries upon creation of the commission would prove unwarranted.

Perhaps the most significant element of the report was its call for a moratorium on the expansion of legal gambling in the United States. Particularly concerned were Native American casino industries, which noted that casinos constitute a cornerstone of their

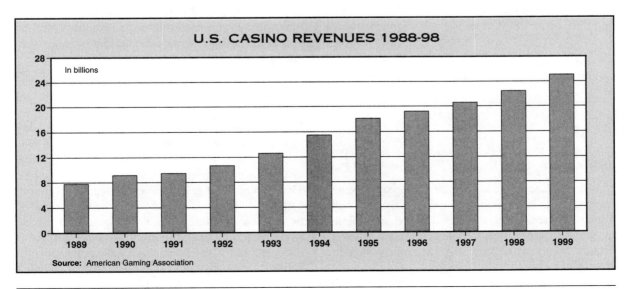

U.S. CASINO REVENUES 1988-98

In billions

Source: American Gaming Association

Trends BECAUSE WE CARE

In light of intensifying criticism of the gambling industry and concerns over the harmful effects of gambling itself, some of the industry's major players invested money into research aimed at understanding and mitigating gambling addiction. Leading gambling researchers, such as Harvard Medical School's Howard Shaffer, added casinos to their list of research supporters.

The American Gaming Association, in conjunction with Station Casinos, Inc. and Boyd Gaming Corp., established the National Center for Responsible Gaming in 1996 to disperse grants to academic studies. With casinos' and other gambling interests' contributions projected at $7 million over 10 years, the center has supported studies at Harvard, the University of Missouri, the University of Minnesota, and Washington University, among others. These studies engaged in a variety of research programs: devising tests and surveys to discover the extent of problem gambling in the United States, performing genetic research aimed at isolating the biological factors of gambling addiction, and so on.

Critics' reactions have been mixed. While some, such as the National Council on Problem Gambling, welcome the financial support, noting that any research will help address the issue, others, such as the Compulsive Gambling Center Inc. of Baltimore, criticize the studies as concealing a broader agenda, claiming the industry has no stake in the neurological problems associated with problem gambling but do have a responsibility to address the social costs that casinos contribute to.

The industry doesn't deny that a problem exists; they estimate that roughly 1 percent of the nation's population has a serious gambling problem. By directing funds toward academic studies, the casino industry hoped to keep criticism at bay.

While some critics fear that the funding of research by the industry itself could compromise the integrity and results of the studies, some of the earliest studies sponsored by the center, such as Shaffer's, revealed findings that were not particularly favorable to the industry, including a higher number of compulsive gamblers found by other studies as well as trends toward more addiction in recent years.

economies and that a ban would entail a drastic cutback in social services.

The release of the commission's report nonetheless had the industry claiming victory. AGA President Frank J. Fahrenkopf Jr. trumpeted the report's failure to validate concerns over the gambling industry's connection to organized crime or casino-propelled increases in crime rates.

In efforts to stave off compulsive gambling and the massive losses that accompany it, several proposals cropped up aimed at restricting the ease of cash access. In light of growing awareness of gambling addiction and its dangerous social side effects, critics argued that the presence of ATMs in or near gaming facilities greatly increases the likelihood that individuals will get in over their heads. The industry was heartened, however, when Illinois state legislators struck down an attempted ban on the installment of ATMs inside the state's casinos.

In 2000 AGA released its report, "The State of the States: The AGA Survey of Casino Entertainment," polling 54,000 U.S. households on their gambling activities and assessing the economic impact of the gambling industry. According to the study, the industry paid over $3 billion in state and local taxes, bolstering some of the arguments of supporters who claim that the industry is a stimulus to local economies. The survey also compiled a profile of the average gambler and gambling household. The composite gambler is a college-educated white-collar worker belonging to a household bringing in about $46,000 a year, well above the national average household income of $39,000. Overall, 45 percent of the nation's gamblers work in white-collar occupations, while 27 percent are blue collar and 13 percent are retirees. About 30 percent of all U.S. households were home to someone who made a trip to the casino in 1998.

The survey reported that most Americans accept casino gambling as an acceptable fact of life, with only 25 percent holding that such activity is "morally wrong." Interestingly, 82 percent of those surveyed agreed that "casino gambling can be a fun night out." While the survey unsurprisingly unearthed widespread support for legalized gambling, it also reported enormous public acceptance—at about 80 percent—of the notion that casinos have a responsibility to actively combat compulsive gambling.

Other national surveys focused on this latter aspect of gambling, sounding alarm bells by noting that gambling is becoming less an activity engaged in for leisure and more an avenue chosen by those hoping to reap financial rewards. Meanwhile, two Congressional studies, one in 1975 and the other in 1998, found disturbing patterns in the nation's gambling habits. The percentage of gamblers who wagered in order to earn money jumped from 44 percent to 66 percent between the two studies, while those gambling for entertainment fell from 70 percent to 49 percent. AGA President and Chief Executive Frank J. Fahrenkopf, however, took exception to these findings, claiming that the Congressional research methods of combining television surveys with random interviews at casinos couldn't yield accurate data.

Despite all the continued debate and controversy, the industry's financial supporters were apparently feeling lucky. Bank of America Corp., the leading casino-lending operation in the late 1990s, closed the biggest bank financing deal the casino industry had ever seen in 1999 when it agreed to lend $3 billion to Park Place Entertainment for the latter's purchase of Caesar's World and other gaming operations from Starwood Hotels and Resorts Worldwide, Inc. The major casino operators, meanwhile, with more leverage to invest, continued to offer new resorts in efforts to capture the broadest number of customers.

After years of fighting in Atlantic City, Las Vegas, and other cities, the casino industry scored a major victory in June 1999 when the Supreme Court struck down a 65-year-old prohibition against broadcast advertising of casino gambling. Resting on First Amendment provisions, the court stated that the ban "sacrifices an intolerable amount of truthful speech about lawful conduct." Casinos were particularly eager to be rid of the ban following a 1988 amendment in Congress legalizing such ads for Indian tribes pitching their resorts as vacation spots.

Tribal casinos found some friends in the federal government in the late 1990s. The Department of the Interior issued a controversial ruling in April 1999 under the Indian Gaming Regulatory Act allowing alternative procedures for gaming compacts between states and Native American tribes. The alternative proposal mandates judicially supervised mediation in the case of a state's failure to negotiate gaming compacts in good faith. Since tribes can claim sovereign immunity under the 11th Amendment to the Constitution, states had little incentive to negotiate compacts with Native American gaming interests. The ruling gives equal footing to tribes in negotiations by reinforcing them with the possibility of a federally enforced nonnegotiated compact with the state, thus putting it in the interests of the state to engage in good-faith bargaining. Some states, however, such as Alabama and Florida, where casino gambling has been rejected, decried the ruling as an usurpation of states' rights.

INDUSTRY LEADERS

Perhaps the biggest news in the casino industry in 2000 was the $6.4 billion takeover of Mirage Re-

sorts, Inc. by MGM Grand, Inc. The resulting MGM Mirage Inc. emerged as the world's largest gaming company, with 18 properties and some of the most high-profile and glitzy resorts in the business. MGM Grand ran casinos in Australia and South Africa in addition to its U.S. strongholds in Detroit and Atlantic City, and operated Nevada casinos through its subsidiary, Primadonna Resorts. But MGM's pride and joy was its flagship 5,000-room MGM Grand Las Vegas hotel and casino. Its famous New York-New York Hotel and Casino apes the Manhattan skyline. Mirage Resorts featured everything at its Las Vegas casinos from tigers and dolphins to fine art galleries to themes of pirate ships and a tropical paradise. Under the leadership and colorful personality Steve Wynn (who chose not to stay on board after the purchase), Mirage grew into one of the largest casino companies in the world. Shortly after uniting the two firms, MGM Mirage announced plans to expand its presence in Las Vegas and Atlantic City. Both companies relied extensively on their hotel operations and entertainment events. About half of each companies' revenues flowed from gaming operations,

Park Place Entertainment Corp. boasted about 30 casinos nationwide, including such behemoths as Caesar's Palace and the new Paris Las Vegas. Park Place employs 42,000 worldwide and garnered revenues of $3.18 billion in 1999. The company's purchase of Starwood Hotels & Resorts' gaming operations that year brought Caesar's Palace under its empire, adding to its high profile operations like the Flamingo, Bally Entertainment Casinos, and Hilton Casinos. Park Place derives about 70 percent of its revenue from its casinos, with the remainder spread out over hotel rooms, food and beverage sales, and other sources. Park Place's gambling operations include resorts in Las Vegas, Atlantic City, New Orleans, Indiana, and Mississippi, as well as Australia and Canada.

Harrah's Entertainment, Inc. operated casinos and gambling resorts in 10 states, garnering revenues of $3.02 billion and employing about 37,400. The company was wired to encourage repeated visits; its Total Gold program features a database tracking frequent visitors and offering perks for accumulated expenditures. Park Place derives three-fourths of its revenue from its casinos, which boast 32,000 slot machines, 11,600 hotel rooms, and 90 restaurants. Harrah's operates over 20 casino resorts in Nevada, New Jersey, Illinois, Indiana, Kansas, Louisiana, Missouri, Mississippi, and Arizona, as well as in Australia and New Zealand. In 1999 the company announced that it would merge with Rio Hotel and Casino, and then purchased riverboat casino operator Players International.

Trump Hotels & Casino Resorts, Inc. featured another colorful personality at the helm; the notorious billionaire Donald Trump owned 40 percent of the company, which raked in revenues of $1.41 billion in 1999. The company employed 12,700 and derived over 80 percent of its revenue from casinos, especially from Trump Plaza Hotel and Casino, Trump's Marina, Trump World's Fair, Trump Taj Mahal in Atlantic City, and Trump Indiana, a riverboat casino on Lake Michigan, operating out of Gary. Together the Trump Hotels have approximately 3,700 rooms, 11,900 slot machines, and 500 table games.

WORK FORCE

Excluding Native American casinos, the industry employed some 355,000 workers in 2000 in occupations as diverse as poker dealers, slot attendants, cocktail waiters and waitresses, security guards, and hospitality workers dressed in novelty costumes. According to the American Gaming Association and the National Gambling Impact Study Commission, the average salary for these workers was $23,200 a year. About 46 percent of these employees worked in the casino portion of the operations, while the rest worked in food, lodging, and other divisions. Tribal casinos employ an additional 150,000, with an average annual salary of about $18,000.

In some markets, at least, union representation can have a significant impact on wage levels. In two cities in the casino-heavy state of Nevada, Las Vegas and Reno, studies revealed significant wage differentials between the highly represented Vegas hotel, gaming, and recreational employees and those in the less unionized market in Reno, with wages substantially higher in the former.

RESEARCH AND TECHNOLOGY

Online gamblers numbered an estimated 25 million in 2000, a figure expected to leap to 300 million by 2005. Though there was extensive support for a ban on Internet gambling in the United States, the boundary-less Internet created difficulties in enforcement, especially since most countries in the world had no laws against the practice. The U.S. House of Representatives narrowly rejected a proposed Internet

Gambling Prohibition Act in July 2000. The benefit of online gambling, as Internet casinos see it, is the anonymity and round-the-clock access afforded by the medium. Critics cite the same features as its dangers.

Skeptics likened the efforts to ban Internet gambling to Prohibition; that is, to an impractical and largely unenforceable restriction that would cause more harm than good. Since gambling legality differs from state to state and from country to country, and since regulatory agencies already have difficulty keeping pace with the sticky issues of online retailing and credit-card use, opponents of a ban insist on its futility, even if it were desirable. Many further decry what they see as a restriction of liberty on the Internet that doesn't exist in everyday life. Supporters counter that minors are prohibited from casinos, but would face no such restrictions if Internet gambling were legal.

In 2000, Australia was the only developed country regulating Internet casinos, maintaining strict compliance measures designed to cradle the integrity of the infant online gaming industry before its reputation collapses. Bear Stearns estimated global revenues of $1.2 billion from Internet casinos in 1999, with projections of $3 billion in 2002.

Online gambling was not necessarily seen as a threat to gambling resorts and casinos, however. Cosmoz Online Ltd.'s online casino network features Las Vegas directories, casino-news updates, events schedules, and a casino-industry stock-monitoring site in addition to its online games.

Meanwhile, systematization and networking of casinos and resorts received a welcome boost with the marketing of new proprietary software by a partnership between Advanced Casino Systems Corp. (ACSC) and Lodging Management Systems (LMS) that integrates hotel and casino management programs. The LMS component includes property management software and credit-card processing, while ACSC's package features its slot marketing system and casino management system. By marketing the two companies' products together, they hope to capture the market for resorts trying to gain competitive advantage by streamlining and integrating their information and management systems.

According to a report by the consulting firm KPMG, the casino industry has never been especially quick to embrace the latest technology, opting instead to invest in new buildings and resorts with the old technology and new frills. This lag feeds on itself, since KPMG noted that casino executives in charge of the companies' computer information divisions generally earn about 20 to 30 percent less than their counterparts in other consumer marketing industries. As a result, the industry often fails to attract quality personnel in this field.

FURTHER READING

"Advanced Casino Systems Corporation and Lodging Management Systems Strengthen Marketing Relationship Offering the First Integrated Casino/Hotel Software Package." *PR Newswire,* 17 November 1999.

Alm, Rick. "Aiming for Mainstream: Casino Industry Striving for Greater Acceptance." *Kansas City Star,* 15 September 1999.

The American Gaming Association. "The State of the States: The AGA Survey of Casino Entertainment, 2000." Available from http://www.americangaming.org/survey2000/sur_index.html.

Findlay, John M. *People of Chance.* New York: Oxford University Press, 1986.

Greenhouse, Linda. "Justices Strike down Ban on Casino Gambling Ads." *New York Times,* 15 June 1999.

McDermott, Kevin. "Illinois Rejects Proposed Ban on ATMs in Riverboat Casinos." *St. Louis Post-Dispatch,* 17 February 2000.

McLendon, Deanna R. "Industry Questions Proposed Ban on Internet Gambling." *Sun Heral d,* 29 April 1999.

Melmer, David. "States Litigate to Stop New Rules on Gaming Compacts with Tribes." *Indian Country Today,* 27 April 1999.

Pascual, Aixa M. "Offshore Betting: The Feds are Rolling Snake Eyes." *Business Week,* 28 August 2000.

"Penthouse Teams with Veteran Casino Developer and GET Group to Launch Worldwide Online Gaming Site to be Licensed by Australian Government." *Business Wire,* 24 January 2000.

Peterson, Molly M. "It's Snake Eyes for Gambling Ban ." *The National Journal,* 22 July 2000.

Waddoups, C. Jeffrey. "Union Wage Effects in Nevada's Hotel and Casino Industry." *Industrial Relations,* October 1999.

Weidner, David. "B of A Closes $3B Credit to Finance Deal for Nev. Gambling Properties." *American Banker,* 2 September 1999.

Young, Virginia. "Casinos Fund Scientific Research on Problem Gambling, Addiction." *St. Louis Post-Dispatch,* 10 February 2000.

Genetic Engineering

INDUSTRY SNAPSHOT

The embattled genetic engineering (GE) industry stood at a crossroads at the turn of the 21st century. While many scientists and companies pushed aggressively ahead in a number of fields related to genetic engineering, the public mood was far less enthusiastic. Particularly hesitant in light of health, environmental, and ethical considerations related to such high-profile developments as cloning, genetically modified foods, and human gene experiments, many in the United States and around the world demanded that the pace slow down so such concerns could be addressed.

GE transfers a gene from one or more cells to another cell, thereby transforming the original cell's genetic makeup. While genetic engineering often conjured visions of mad scientists, more sober analysis still yielded a number of serious concerns. The physical jiggling of genes offers humans a heightened degree of control over life, posing the potential to alter the metaphysical outlook of humankind, including how humans view themselves and their relationship to their surroundings. According to Dr. W. French Anderson, a pioneer in the field of genetic engineering, the ability to alter a human's genetic blueprint could theoretically afford interested parties the ability to alter genes related to any human characteristics, including, intelligence, hair loss, docility, or aggression. While the ability to make sweeping changes to the human infrastructure was years away, concerns were already pronounced by 2000, and many scientists, ethicists, and others hoped to generate more discussion of the possibilities and their consequences before the issue was beyond remediation.

Human genetic engineering was touted as the fourth major medical revolution of the modern age, on a par with the discovery of the cause of cholera infection that led to remodeled sanitation systems in the 1850s, the use of anesthesia in surgery, and the development of vaccines and antibiotics to treat infections. Unlike these remedies, however, genetic engineering proposes to solve the underlying human biological causes of diseases and ailments. Gene therapy is built on the knowledge that human genes play a pivotal role in the body's ability to withstand and adapt to conditions forced on it by nature, such as diseases. Understanding genes, the logic goes, will help us to understand and control our susceptibility to diseases and infections.

The complete mapping of the human genome, the first draft of which was completed in summer 2000, promises to produce some of the most dramatic and influential discoveries in modern biological science. By translating the entire human genetic code, scientists will gain an understanding of the precise nature and function of human genes, including the isolation of malfunctioning genes that can then either be replaced or directly modified to resume functioning.

Genetic engineering also held the promise of increased food production and pest-resistant crops, and indeed supermarkets were flooded with products composed of genetically modified ingredients, such as soybeans and corn. But this application met with vociferous criticism of many kinds throughout the world. Critics of GE foods questioned their safety to human health and natural ecosystems, while scientists produced conflicting data about genetic engineering's stated benefits, such as improved crop yields. The backlash against GE foods forced many food companies to retreat from their forays into genetically engineered products.

ORGANIZATION AND STRUCTURE

REGULATION

Genetic engineering research, development, and marketing are highly regulated in the United States. For genetically engineered foodstuffs, direct oversight is primarily the responsibility of the manufacturers, who are then required to consult with the U.S. Food and Drug Administration (FDA), which retains the authority to issue a recall of products it deems unsafe. In 1999 the FDA maintained a policy of strictly monitoring and testing genetically engineered food products if they varied in nutritional value or genetic makeup. The FDA also reserves the right to require labeling of any genetically engineered food product that contains allergens that the conventional food product does not contain or any product whose nutritional content is altered via the GE process. In light of heating protests, both foreign and domestic, against genetically engineered crop production, the U.S. Department of Agriculture (USDA) issued tightened rules to scale back the latitude it had afforded marketers of genetically engineered foods for employing the organic label on products. Most of the policies pertaining to genetically engineered food products stem from the federal Food, Drug, and Cosmetic Act of 1938 (and its amendments), which stipulates the type of labeling various kinds of products must have.

Furthermore, a USDA branch, the Animal and Plant Health Inspection Service, monitors the research and testing of genetically engineered products such as seeds and livestock. The U.S. Environmental Protection Agency (EPA) also plays a role in regulating the industry: it establishes standards for the performance of genetically altered products in conjunction with the USDA. These last two government agencies try to ensure that genetically engineered products do not pose any environmental risks such as introducing undesirable characteristics to naturally occurring plants and wildlife. These agencies have a particular concern for the possibility that a genetically modified plant might outcross with wild plants, creating new weedlike species.

PATENTS

In 1995 President Bill Clinton helped open new financial doors for the industry by amending the U.S. code of patents with the Biotechnology Process Patent Act, extending its scope to include the development of a novel product from a specific gene in a specific cell line. Although gene patents were first issued in the mid-1970s, a former ruling contended that a process for creating biotechnological materials could not be patented. The 1995 policy allowed the patenting of procedures that yield genes and genetic materials.

This policy has subsequently met with controversy, however, since it unleashed a rush of patents as geneticists face pressure to patent the general section of genetic code they are sequencing before that section was patented by someone else and the work lost. The issue heightened a step in early 2000 when Human Genome Sciences, Inc. received a patent for a new gene that human immunodeficiency virus (HIV) exploits when it attacks a cell. While major biotech firms held that such intellectual property rights were necessary to protect research and maintain the incentive to engage in expensive research, opponents of more liberal patent rules charged that such protection would actually slow innovation as companies are prohibited from entering into areas of research patented by other companies. More broadly, some ethicists were concerned over the right to own discoveries related to the human genome.

BACKGROUND AND DEVELOPMENT

Genetic engineering of sorts has taken place for centuries: breeding of plants and animals traces back many centuries as farmers have often experimented with various crossbreeding and grafting techniques to create hybrids with more desirable features. Wheat, for example, is a hybrid of several wild grasses. Yet as a discipline of modern science it emerged around the end of the 19th century, becoming more pronounced and codified throughout the 20th century. Early interest and later motivation for interest in genetics came from the work of Gregor Mendel, an Austrian botanist who studied the hereditary features in peas, pumpkins, beans, and fruit flies. In 1865 Mendel established laws of genetic traits, characterizing those most likely to be transferred through breeding as dominant, while those less likely to be transferred as recessive. His work led to theories and methods of crossbreeding.

Before genetic engineering proper could come about, scientists needed an understanding of genetics itself. In *The Epic History of Biology*, Anthony Serafini reported that genetics pioneer, T. H. Morgan in-

Newborn transgenic cows. (AP/Wide World Photos)

troduced the formal study of genetics to the 20th century. Beginning with the work of his predecessor, William Bateson, Morgan ascertained that chromosomes were the bearers of genetic data. In 1911 Morgan and some colleagues published the first substantive article on chromosomes and genes. Morgan made other crucial discoveries including sex-linked (male and female chromosomes carry different information) and sex-limited (certain genetic characteristics are realized only in one sex, not both) genetic information. In 1926 Morgan sketched an early picture of how parents passed traits to their offspring in his book *The Theory of the Gene.*

The 1920s brought discoveries of ribonucleic and deoxyribonucleic acids, RNA and DNA, which are essential to genetic communication. RNA holds the genetic information for some viruses, while DNA carries it for most organisms. In the 1940s scientists proved that genes carried genetic information, not proteins as some had believed. In the 1950s researchers James Watson and Francis Crick used X rays to photograph DNA, leading to further understanding of the acid. As a result, they determined that DNA contained four kinds of smaller molecules hooked together in spiral chains. At this point, genetic engineering began to accelerate. Max Delbrück, of Vanderbilt University,

---

Trends   MAPPING OWNERSHIP RIGHTS

Gene patenting presented a number of sticky issues to the genetic engineering (GE) industry by 2000. The issue of who gets to own and profit from information about the building blocks of human life unsurprisingly spurred a good deal of controversy, particularly as scientists closed in on the decoding of the human genome. Biotech firms, genome researchers, pharmaceutical companies, ethicists, and the public all weighed in with their own answers.

The U.S. government, of course, had some answers too, though their footing was much more tenuous. In 2000 Human Genome Sciences, Inc. was awarded a patent granting commercial ownership of a gene that is manipulated by human immunodeficiency virus (HIV). Rival firms worried that the patent could inhibit similar research and development of the virus most scientist believe causes acquired immune deficiency syndrome (AIDS). But these concerns were a mere microbe under the intense microscope that has centered around the mapping of the genome. Each of the several hundred gene patents that had been awarded by mid-2000 were open to similar challenges.

Court rulings dating back several years decided against the idea that only specific *uses* of the genetic code—such as certain treatments—could be patented, insisting that the data itself was also protected. As scientists move closer to deciphering the entire human genome, however, those rulings present enormous difficulties.

Some interest groups were more or less settled on the issue of *whether* genes should be patentable, and were simply focused on *when*. Pharmaceutical companies, who pick up on gene research later in the process, insisted that patents were being awarded too early in the process, before scientists could really have made much progress in discovering the efficacy or novelty of the studies, and when the gene's functions are merely hypothesized. The use of high-speed computers, for instance, greatly accelerated the pace at which the code itself was revealed, but also far outpaced scientists' understanding of what the newly discovered gene sequences actually did. The biotech firms, of course, stand the most to gain from liberal patent laws, since such laws provide those companies with greater leverage in their negotiations with drug makers.

Beyond that, however, ethicists questioned the right of *anyone* to control and profit from such sensitive information, as well as the implications posed by leaving the crucial data about inherited human traits to market forces.

---

and Alfred Hershey created a hybrid virus by combining the chromosomal material from two different viruses—a creation that had a powerful impact on genetic engineering research as other scientists began to attempt more arduous genetic manipulations, according to Serafini.

By 1977, a gene manufactured by researchers was used for the first time to create a human protein in bacteria. This procedure used a recombinant gene—one made from the combination of the genes from two separate organisms—to clone the protein. This feat helped to launch the industry: biotech companies and universities began to flood the field with attempts to produce marketable products. Consequently, the flurry of interest in genetic engineering provoked Congress to attempt regulating the industry by forcing researchers to concoct specimens that could not escape from their laboratories, though none of these legislative proposals ever passed.

This discovery led to the development of many recombinant DNA (rDNA) projects throughout the country in the mid- to late 1970s. One of the first was in 1978, when Genentech, Inc. and The City of Hope National Medical Center created a center for developing human insulin for diabetics, using the rDNA technology. The FDA approved of the sale of genetically engineered insulin in 1982. A wave of gene and protein clonings also took place within this period, such as proteins from hepatitis B, in pursuit of a cure or treatment, and genes for human growth hormones in hope of unlocking the door to growth and development.

In the 1980s the genetic engineering industry received the patent support it needed when the U.S. Supreme Court decided that genetically engineered products could be patented. Thus businesses could pursue years of research and investment without the worry that other companies could capitalize on their research by producing a similar product. Also in the 1980s, Kary Mullis and others at Cetus Corp. in Berkeley, California, created a technique for multiplying DNA sequences in laboratories, called polymerase chain reaction. In 1986 the FDA approved of the first genetically engineered crop: genetically modified tobacco, while in 1990 Calgene Inc. began testing modified cotton, which was designed to have a genetic structure resistant to herbicides. That year, GenPharm International Inc. developed the first transgenic cow, which produced human milk proteins for infant formulas.

Criticism and controversy steadily grew through the 1990s. A 1997 EPA ruling raised the ire of Greenpeace and other international environmental activist organizations, as well as EPA scientists, for what they saw as a systematic leniency toward the GE industry at the expense of consumer and environmental protection. The EPA's approval of the genetically engineered bacteria *Rhizobium meliloti* ignored the advice of its own Biotechnology Scientific Advisory Committee (BSAC), resulting in the resignation of one BSAC biologist, Dr. Conrad Istock, who decried the relegation of the committee's research to a mere formality. Shortly after, a release from EPA scientists criticized the lack of objectivity in the EPA's final release, which, the white paper concluded, amounted to a de facto endorsement of the bacteria.

Researchers from countries around the world banded together in 1990 in an effort to develop a map of all the human genes. Known as the Human Genome Project, this grand endeavor was backed by the U.S. government with $3 billion. By the late 1990s, profit incentives had spurred the race, with pharmaceutical companies and even some private laboratories competing with the federal project. Completion of the map of human genetic information entails identifying the 23 pairs of chromosomes, then sequencing all the DNA contained in the chromosomes to discover the protein each gene produces and for what purpose. The first draft of the basic map was completed in summer 2000 by the U.S. National Human Genome Research Institute and Celera Genomics. A polished version was expected before 2003.

CURRENT CONDITIONS

GENETICALLY MODIFIED FOODS

In 1999 genetically engineered crops covered 72 million acres of U.S. farmland, and were grown on an additional 16 million acres throughout the rest of the world. Roughly two-thirds of U.S. soybeans, one-third of corn, and 60 percent of cotton was genetically modified, thus finding their way into a mountain of food products from soft drinks to pasta to ice cream, as well as livestock products from animals fed with genetically engineered crops. Livestock, for instance, consume about 75 percent of the nation's corn production. Market leader Monsanto Co. rolled out a number of new genetically engineered products, including the development of a bruise-resistant potato and heart-healthy canola oil.

Genetically engineered food traditionally was not required to carry any labeling distinguishing it from other foods. In January 2000, however, the United States bowed to pressures and, for the first time, agreed to officially acknowledge a difference between genetically modified and natural foods when it signed an international trade agreement in Montreal. The ruling was expected to lead to tightened regulations on food labeling and safety. By the end of 2000, two proposed bills—the Genetically Engineered Food Safety Act (GEFSA) and the Genetically Engineered Food Right to Know Act (GEFRKA)—in the U.S. Congress addressed these issues. The former would subject all genetically modified food components to premarket review by the FDA, while the latter would require food products with any genetically modified materials to be labeled as such.

Controversy over genetically engineered crops in the United States began to catch up to that of Europe in May 1999 when a study at Cornell University found that corn engineered to withstand pesticides, carrying a gene producing *Bacillus thuringiensis* (Bt) toxins, killed monarch butterflies and caterpillars, validating some environmentalists' fears that such technology posed a threat to natural ecosystems. The Cornell team, while clarifying that such findings were preliminary, advocated that seed companies encourage their client farmers to plant a buffer zone of traditional corn around their genetically engineered crop fields, thus preventing pollen-carrying Bt toxins from finding their way into butterfly habitats. Furthermore, the most comprehensive research study to date, by the Economic Research Service of the U.S. Department of Agriculture, failed to confirm one of the GE-crop industry's most persistent claims: that such crops result in significantly increased yields.

Critics also decried the de facto centralization of the world's food supply that could result from continued dominance of seed technology by a handful of large biotech firms. Not only would such centralization afford such firms an alarming degree of influence over the world's population, protesters contended, but it could also expose the food system to more drastic catastrophe should mishaps occur within such a tightly systematized production process.

While maintaining the overall safety of genetically engineered crops and food products, a number of major food companies, including Frito-Lay Inc., Seagram Co., Gerber Products Co., and H.J. Heinz Co. took the threat of declining sales to heart, announcing they would refrain from using genetically engineered crops in their products. Militant environmental and consumer activists, meanwhile, perturbed at what they saw as the cozy relationship between the Clinton administration and the biotechnology industry, took to trashing a number of research labs. The future earnings prospects in light of the rising backlash against genetically engineered crops proved dim enough to induce some major players to call it quits: Novartis spun off its agribusiness unit, and DuPont opted to return to its traditional chemical operations.

GENE THERAPY

Gene therapy faced similar difficulties. Gene therapy involves the injection of one or more genes as a replacement for absent or failing genes in the human body. Scientists discovered that inserting genes into cells can also be used to change cell function, broadening the range of disorders that can be treated genetically. Another technique, usually known as small-molecule therapy, alters the gene's functions by adding molecules via drugs into the patient's system. By 2000, gene therapy was mired in the experimental stage and was fraught with controversy and complications, though the first treatments were expected to be publicly available by the middle of the decade.

Gene therapy's troubles intensified significantly following the September 1999 death of 18-year-old Jesse Glesinger in an experiment at the University of Pennsylvania. Mr. Glesinger's untimely passing spurred the FDA to issue new rules requiring researchers to submit more detailed information on their experiments, acknowledging that monitoring had been "less than adequate." The National Institutes of Health (NIH) reported in January 2000 that only 39 of the 691 "adverse events," including deaths, in gene therapy experiments were reported to the NIH, despite requirements to do so. Mr. Glesinger, who suffered from a rare hereditary disease, was injected with an experimental gene carried by adenovirus, a weakened cold virus, the safety of which has been questioned. Monitors will be required to review experimental processes to ensure that patients' rights and safety are protected.

The industry also faces additional problems: genetic research requires persistent effort and funding even though a marketable product may not automatically result from this effort and funding. Therefore, universities often carry out initial GE and general biotechnology research projects and later sell findings to companies. Also, companies that do engage in this kind of research may show only marginal profits and may go many years without producing any product at all, let alone a wonder drug or super gene. Of the few genetically engineered products that make it through clinical study, the FDA approves only about 10 percent for public sale.

As such tribulations mounted, the gene therapy sector welcomed experiments that successfully kick-started failing livers in rats with the aid of newly grown cells transplanted via genetic manipulation. The results offer hope of wider application in humans awaiting liver transplants. The process involves the injection of a cancer gene into a liver cell, thus allowing the cell to reproduce perpetually, while treating the cell with an enzyme to prevent it from reproducing out of control and taking over the body. While all the rats in the control group died, the 60 percent who received the therapy went on to live normally.

CLONING

Following the success, and furor, over Dolly the sheep, the first successfully cloned large mammal, scientists at the University of Hawaii cloned several mice in June 1998. The copying of large mammals, however, seemed to be somewhat of a fluke. That changed in late 1999 when a research partnership between the University of Connecticut in Storrs and the Prefectural Cattle Breeding Development Institute in Kagoshima, Japan, cloned four calves from skin cells derived from a bull. The cells were allowed to grow in a dish before gene DNA was pulled from their nuclei, and were then injected into cows' egg cells before being inserted into the cows' uteri. The use of skin cells, rather than cells from reproductive organs, offers a far more practical method of deriving the genetic material for cloning. In addition, since the cells were preserved for several months instead of injected freshly into the host animal, the new techniques offer greater possibilities for genetic manipulation of the material to be injected.

Meanwhile, just two-and-a-half years after the creation of Dolly, her parents at Scotland's PPL Therapeutics moved closer to genetically copying a human being by creating cloned triplet piglets, which scientists had been attempting for years. Pigs are more difficult to clone than sheep or mice. The most widely publicized purpose for cloned animals, particularly pigs, is for the development of xenotransplantation, or the transplant of animals' organs into humans. Such organs would require genetic manipulation to survive in a human being. Another purpose is for drug treatments; Dolly the sheep was engineered with human genetic data, thus allowing her to produce human proteins through milk that can then theoretically be used to treat human illnesses.

OTHER APPLICATIONS

The actual creation of artificial life from scratch came closer to fruition with the discovery of the minimal number of genes required to maintain a living organism. Using scientifically created genes and chromosomes, researchers at the Institute of Genomic Research (TIGR) in Rockville, Maryland, successively knocked out genes until they isolated those necessary to sustain the world's simplest known organism, the *Mycoplasma genitalium* bacterium. Though ethical and technical questions abound, the next step was to synthesize a new life form from scratch building on this knowledge.

Some GE discoveries, moreover, could prove pleasing to environmentalists. Michael Daly at the Uniformed Services University of the Health Sciences in Bethesda, Maryland, genetically enhanced the bacterium *D. radiodurans,* known to withstand an enormous level of radiation, to help break down nuclear waste by reducing the toxicity of ionic mercury. The development offers the potential to help in the bioremediation of the nation's 113 federal nuclear-waste sites, which cover a combined area about the size of Delaware and Rhode Island and have contaminated alarming amounts of water and soil, according to the U.S. Department of Energy. By stabilizing the metal compounds, the bacteria can alleviate the spread of contamination. While early tests revealed no adverse effects to humans, it has yet to be actively tested in the field, and researchers suggested it would take at least five or six years before testing could be completed and the bacteria modified to effectively treat the waste at the different sites.

INDUSTRY LEADERS

GENENTECH, INC.

Founded in 1976, Genentech, a biotechnology company, develops and markets pharmaceuticals made from recombinant DNA. Genentech markets eight drugs in the United States, including Protropin, a hormone for children suffering from growth impediments; Nutropin, a hormone for children with renal trouble and growth insufficiency; and Activase, an agent that dissolves blood clots in heart attack patients. In 1998 the company launched Herceptin, an antibody for certain breast cancer patients. That year was also a profitable first full year of sales for the non-Hodgkin's lymphoma drug Rituxan. In the late 1990s Genentech suffered legal difficulties, reaping a $50 million lawsuit settlement following charges that it sold human growth hormone for improper purposes. The San Francisco-based company has 3,900 employees and reported 1999 sales of $1.14 billion in 1999, but suffered a net loss of the same amount. Swiss drug giant Roche Holding, whose subsidiary Hoff-

mann-La Roche, Inc. markets Genentech's products internationally, owns about two-thirds of the company. Genentech develops some of its drugs in partnership with Pharmacia Corp., the product of the merger between genetic-engineering leader Monsanto and the drug company Pharmacia & Upjohn.

AMGEN INC.

Amgen, the world's largest biotech firm, has also led the genetic engineering industry with its two products that exploit GE recombinant DNA technology: Epogen, the world's leading antianemia drug, and Neupogen. Epogen simulates red blood cells and is used to treat the kidney problems of renal dialysis patients, while Neupogen simulates white blood cells and is used by cancer patients undergoing chemotherapy. In 1999 Epogen accounted for 55 percent of sales, with Neupogen bringing in 44 percent. Another drug on the market was Infergen, a treatment for hepatitis C; in Amgen's pipeline were products for AIDS, rheumatoid arthritis, and bone marrow disorders. Its research into the human genome also yielded the discovery of material that aids the spread of cancer cells. Based in Thousand Oaks, California, Amgen's product sales reached $3.04 billion in 1999, up from $2.7 billion the year before, and a net income of $1 billion, while maintaining a payroll of 6,400 workers.

MONSANTO COMPANY

In late 1999 Monsanto announced it would merge with drug giant Pharmacia & Upjohn to become one of the largest biotechnology firms in the world. With many other major GE agriculture firms backing out of the business, Monsanto remained the world's leading player in this field in 2000. The new firm, under the name Pharmacia Corp., turned Monsanto into a separate subsidiary in an attempt to insulate the firm from Monsanto's mounting negative publicity. Though Pharmacia owns 86 percent of Monsanto, it took the company public in 2000. Roughly one-third of Pharmacia's sales derived from Monsanto's agricultural products.

A former chemical firm, St. Louis-based Monsanto Co. spent the 1990s transforming itself into a leading life sciences company. In its agricultural sector, the potential to patent seed technology spurred Monsanto to spend over $8 billion in the late 1990s buying up seed companies. Monsanto is best known for its flagship chemical Roundup, a leading herbicide. Monsanto also has developed a variety of genetically engineered agricultural products. Roundup Ready brand soybeans, canola, and cotton are genetically resistant to Roundup brand herbicides. Seeds genetically designed to prevent insect damage include Bollgard and Ingard brands of cotton, Yieldgard and Maisgard brands of corn, and NewLeaf brand potatoes. The company weathered controversy in 1999 to generate revenues of $9.15 billion and net income of $575 million, while employing 31,800 workers. Agricultural products accounted for about half of total sales, while pharmaceuticals raked in 33 percent.

AMERICA AND THE WORLD

In what amounted to the first global legal challenge to genetically engineered crops, an international coalition of farmers and activists filed a class-action lawsuit against Monsanto in Washington, D.C., in 1999 for allegedly failing to conduct the necessary tests to ensure that its genetically engineered foods were safe for consumers and the environment, and for attempting to develop a worldwide cartel to monopolize trade in genetically engineered foods through patent protections. The lawsuit charged Monsanto with trying to force farmers into restrictive planting contracts whereby they could not to save seeds for the next year's planting, a traditional practice for farmers. Moreover, included in Monsanto's Terminator project was the attempt to render seeds sterile, forcing farmers to purchase Monsanto seeds each year. As a result of this and other mounting criticisms, Monsanto dropped its Terminator project in late 1999.

The United States found itself embroiled in a number of GE-related battles on the international scene in the late 1990s. In early 1999 the United States worked to block an agreement at the 130-nation Protocol on Biosafety to the Convention on Biological Diversity in Cartagena, Colombia, an extension of the 1992 Earth Summit. Along with Canada, Australia, Chile, Argentina, and Uruguay, all major GE-crop exporters, the United States rejected the treaty, which would have required exporting nations to receive permission from importing countries before such products could enter the market. Specifically, the United States, which agreed to the provisions over genetically engineered seeds, objected to the measures as they applied to GE-food products.

Shortly thereafter, an embittered trade war ensued following the European Union's decision to slap import restrictions on genetically engineered U.S. crops out of health and environmental concerns. Meanwhile the United Nations Food Safety Agency in September 1999 endorsed the European Union's moratorium on bovine somatotropin, a genetically engineered hormone injected into cattle to stimulate milk production that was banned by the European Community in 1990. Approximately 30 percent of U.S. dairy cattle received the hormone treatment, according to Monsanto.

Farmers in the developing world, moreover, were beginning to take matters into their own hands. In India, home to one-quarter of the world's farmers, a coalition of 2,000 organizations representing farmers, environmentalists, scientists, and religious groups initiated Operation Cremate Monsanto, digging up cotton fields and setting Monsanto-brand seed crops afire. Long-suffering Indian farmers were furious over Monsanto's perceived attempts to dictate their farm production.

By 2000, however, the controversy cooled as 130 nations met in Montreal to set a worldwide agenda for genetically engineered foods. The treaty signed grants all countries the right to prohibit the import of genetically engineered foods if they feel it poses a health risk. The United States, with the most stake in GE agriculture, had vigorously opposed such agreements in the past as barriers to free trade; thus the Montreal agreement signaled a change of course. The treaty also increases the likelihood that such products will have to be physically separated from other foods for export purposes, which further propels the chance that domestic products will carry labels.

European countries, as a result of their own ambivalence toward genetic engineering, own very few genetic patents. Even patents issued by the European Patent Office (EPO) are primarily the property of the United States and Japan, since U.S. and Japanese researchers prefer the EPO's processing procedures—which are quicker and more efficient—to those of their own countries.

RESEARCH AND TECHNOLOGY

By 2000 GE researchers were scurrying to find new ways to propel their technology forward while circumventing the negative publicity. Scientists at the Center for the Application of Molecular Biology to International Agriculture in Canberra, Australia, built on the knowledge of naturally occurring mutations, noting particularly the overwhelming similarity of the genes that produce the proteins giving corn and rice their distinct characters. Because of the great genetic overlap, which research leader Dr. Richard A. Jefferson said generalizes to all living things, actual gene swapping may actually be unnecessary. Dr. Jefferson surmised that the same effects, such as resistance to

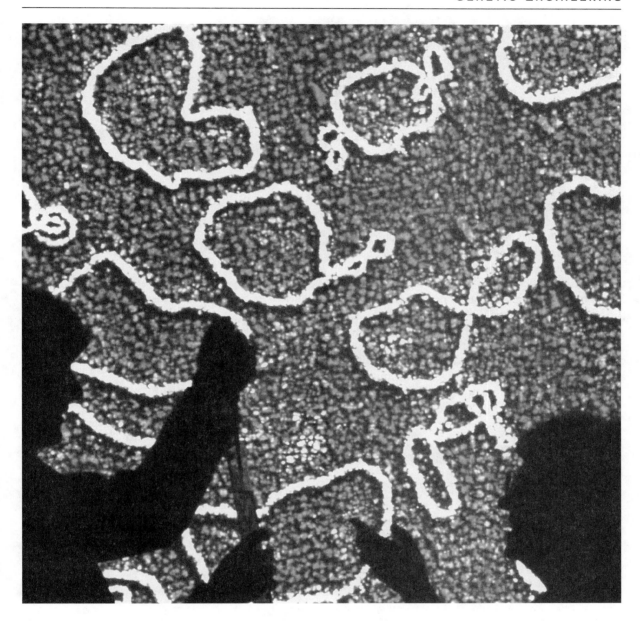

Genetic researchers viewing a transmission electron micrograph of DNA plasmids. *(Photo Researchers Inc./Dr. Gopal Murti/ Science Photo Library)*

cold, achieved by gene transfers could be generated by spurring genetic mutations inherent in the original crop or species.

Essentially, this process, which the group called transgenomics, involves the rapid shuffling and mutating of genes, thus speeding the process of evolution in order to bring desired inherent traits into prominence centuries before natural processes would bring them about. As a result, the transfer of genes that has protestors up in arms is avoided altogether in favor of

a controlled acceleration of evolution and genetic mutation. In a way, this simply brings farmers' traditional practice of selective breeding to the molecular level, letting nature do most of the work, albeit egged on by scientists. Dr. Jefferson claimed that, in addition to helping third-world countries meet their food necessities, the process would also help small seed and biotechnology companies sidestep the overwhelming obstacle of patents produced by the seed-acquisition frenzy at Monsanto, DuPont, and other large corporations.

Computer-generated research, meanwhile, not only analyzed genetic material, but made use of it. In a development fitting of Silicon Valley, researchers developed microarrays, or biochips, which use genes or gene fragments and their DNA in the manner of computer-chip semiconductors to power computerized biochemical experiments. The chips were beginning to find extensive use at companies engaged in research related to the genomics industry.

After all the difficulties surrounding gene therapy, scientists were intent on building the field's experimental sector on studies of hemophilia, widely viewed as the simplest illness to treat with gene therapy. In March 2000, researchers at the Children's Hospital of Philadelphia, in conjunction with the biotech firm Avigen Inc., announced success with two of three hemophiliac patients who received gene treatments based on the spherical adeno-associated virus (AAV). For years thought impossible to manufacture, AAV was genetically engineered by Avigen and Targeted Genetics and readied for testing in humans. Though the experiment proved both safe and successful, the researchers stressed that results were preliminary, and the research required further trials.

FURTHER READING

Adams, Chris. "Gene Therapy to Be Given Tougher Rules." *New York Times,* 8 March 2000.

Anderson, W. French. "A Cure That May Cost Us Ourselves." *Newsweek,* 1 January 2000.

Connor, Steve. "Blueprint for Creating Artificial Life Is Discovered; Minimum Genes to Support Living Organisms Found." *Independent* (London), 10 December 1999.

"E.U. Watches Monsanto GM-Seed Case." *European Report,* 18 December 1999.

Feder, Barnaby J. "New Method of Altering Plants Is Aimed at Sidestepping Critics." *New York Times,* 29 February 2000.

"Genetic Work on Liver Cells Shows Promise for Therapy." *Los Angeles Times,* 18 February 2000.

Goldenberg, Suzanne. "Indian Peasants Torch Crops amid Fear of Losing Home-Grown Seed." *Guardian* (London), 6 October 1999.

Goldman, Karen A. "Bioengineered Food—Safety and Labeling." *Science,* 20 October 2000.

Jaroff, Leon. "Fixing the Genes." *Time,* 13 January 1999.

Licking, Ellen. "Evolution on Fast-Forward." *Business Week,* 27 September 1999.

Luoma, Jon R. "Pandora's Pantry." *Mother Jones,* January/February 2000.

Marshall, Eliot. "Rival Genome Sequencers Celebrate a Milestone Together." *Science,* 30 June 2000.

Pollack, Andrew. "Concerns on Human Testing Don't Seem to Faze Biotech Investors." *New York Times,* 19 February 2000.

————. "U.S. and Allies Block Treaty on Genetically Altered Goods." *New York Times,* 25 February 1999.

Roosevelt, Margot. "Taking It to Main Street." *Time,* 31 July 2000.

"The rBST Ban Plays On." *Food Ingredient News,* June 1999.

Serafini, Anthony. *The Epic History of Biology.* New York: Plenum Publishing, 1993.

Simon, Stephanie. "Bioengineered Crops on Shaky Ground." *Los Angeles Times,* 5 March 2000.

Simon Moffat, Anne. "Can Genetically Modified Crops Go Greener?" *Science,* 13 October 2000.

"Strict Rules to Limit Genetic Engineering on Organic Foods." *New York Times,* 5 March 2000.

Wade, Nicholas. "Skin Cells Bring Cloning a Step Nearer to Efficiency." *New York Times,* 5 January 2000.

Waldholz, Michael. "Right to Life: Genes Are Patentable; Less Clear Is If Finder Must Know Their Role." *Wall Street Journal,* 16 March 2000.

"What Labels Don't Tell You (Yet)." *New York Times,* 9 February 2000.

Whitman, David. "Michael Daly." *U.S. News & World Report,* January 2000.

Winslow, Ron. "Benefits of Gene-Based Heart Therapy in Doubt." *Wall Street Journal,* 13 March 2000.

HANDHELD COMPUTING DEVICES

After a decade and a half of false starts and sputters, the handheld computing industry has finally come of age as features and performance have been paired with true portability. At year-end 1999, between 8 and 9 million handheld computing devices had been sold worldwide, just under half in the United States alone. That's up from less than a million three years earlier. What's more, analysts expected even greater gains in the early 2000s, when worldwide shipments could top 30 million as early as 2003. Business users, who accounted for up to 80 percent of sales in 1999, will continue to form the dominant market for handhelds, but demand was expected to broaden as prices come down and features stabilize.

At the center of much of the attention is Palm, Inc., the spin-off from 3Com Corp., whose eponymous personal devices have captured a leading share of the market. The company's older devices were known as PalmPilot but more recently have been redubbed simply Palm. The Palm product line was responsible for nearly 40 percent of all handheld computer sales in 1999, and about two-thirds of the personal digital assistant (PDA) segment within handhelds. Despite its comfortable lead heading into 2000, Palm is expected to face keen rivalry from both larger and smaller competitors, including an ambitious start-up called Handspring run by Palm's founders.

While early handhelds were little more than glorified calendars and organizers, both the software and hardware have come a long way. Today's top-of-the-line PDAs come equipped with modems and are capable of sending e-mail and receiving basic information from the Web. They're easier to synchronize with desktop machines and do a reasonable job at reading handwriting, since many models rely on an electronic pen instead of a keyboard.

Besides PDAs, the other main segment in the handheld industry is a class of more powerful, notebooklike computers sometimes called palmtops or simply handheld computers. These machines have their own minikeyboards and often run Windows CE, a lightweight version of Microsoft's omnipresent operating system. Whereas some PDAs might still be mistaken for low-tech electronic calendars, some palmtops, such as Hewlett-Packard's Jornada line or IBM's Workpad, might well be mistaken for a full-fledged notebook personal computer (PC). Typically housed in a so-called clamshell case—one with a flip-up display like a notebook computer—they tend to have much larger screens than Palms, for example, and boast significantly faster processors and bigger memory chips. As a result, they also tend to cost two or three times the price of a Palm or similar device, putting them at the premium end of the scale.

Handheld and palmtop computers are the lightest and smallest computing devices for the mass market. Features common to these devices include flat-panel display screens; built-in touchpads or other pointing devices in lieu of a separate mouse; specialized versions of software; and expansion slots for Personal Computer Memory Card International Association (PCMCIA) cards, the credit-card sized devices that supply fax modem capability and extra memory. Some handhelds and palmtops use PCMCIA slots for disk drives as well. Most PDAs use a stylus or pen instead of a keyboard for input.

Screens in handhelds are flat liquid crystal displays (LCDs), which can be either passive matrix or active matrix, and may be backlit for clarity. Passive matrix displays have grids of horizontal and vertical wires, the intersections of which are LCD elements, single pixels that either admit or exclude light. Active matrix, or thin-film transistor displays, have much better resolution but are more expensive to produce. LCD technology was developed in the United States; however, Japan, Korea, and Taiwan produce almost all of the world's LCD screens. (See the separate essay entitled Video Displays.)

Distribution patterns in the handheld business have been changing as the machines have gained wider acceptance. In previous years retail and catalog sales dominated the business, but by 1999, according to International Data Corp. (IDC), the Internet and direct orders to manufacturers had become the biggest channels. IDC attributed the shift to better pricing in those channels, among other factors. Unlike in other segments of the computer business, resellers haven't had a large role in handheld distribution.

BACKGROUND AND DEVELOPMENT

SHORT HISTORY OF PORTABLE COMPUTING

The Osborne I, developed in 1980 by Adam Osborne of Osborne Computer Corp., included innovations that led the way in the evolution of truly portable computers. Weighing 17 pounds, it had a detachable keyboard, a five-inch black-and-white display, and two floppy disk drives. It used a Zilog Z-80 microprocessor chip, an improved clone of Intel's 8080. The Osborne I not only pioneered portability, it was also credited with being the first to bundle software packages with the computer—an idea that became fundamental to selling hardware in the industry. Tens of thousands of the Osborne I portable computers were sold before it became the victim of the company's own success. In 1983 the company announced that it would build an IBM-compatible portable called the Vixen, causing buyers to stop buying the Osborne I in anticipation of the new machine. The announcement, however, was premature and, without incoming orders to fund the new product's manufacture, Osborne was forced to file for bankruptcy protection. By the time the Vixen was ready to market, consumers had been wooed away by the products of a new leader, Compaq, which had been able to meet their demand.

According to Les Freed's *The History of Computers,* Compaq's opportunity to successfully take the portable computer market lead was largely due to a gaping hole in IBM's product line. In 1983 Compaq shipped the Compaq Transportable and Compaq Plus, both fully functional, IBM-compatible, portable PCs weighing a not-so-svelte 30 pounds. During its first year in business, the company sold 53,000 portables and took in revenues of $111.2 million, giving Compaq the highest first-year sales in the history of American business.

In 1984 Gavilan Computer developed a truly portable machine that did not have to be plugged in. Industry commentator Tim Bajarin wrote, "The computer's clamshell design and battery-power capability made it the first serious mobile computing system." Gavilan, however, could not manufacture them in sufficient quantity, and went out of business.

Apple Computer's PowerBook models, introduced in 1991, set a new standard for portables. They combined long battery life with excellent display quality and a built-in pointing device. The PowerBook 170 contained an optional internal modem slot, again redefining the meaning of a mobile office computer. Apple's Duo 210, released in 1992, featured the DuoDock, an innovation that allowed hookup to a docking station that might contain more system RAM, a larger hard drive, or more video RAM for a color monitor. The Duo could thus function fully as a desktop computer when in the DuoDock, and as an excellent portable at other times.

EMERGENCE OF HANDHELDS

In 1993 another Apple innovation was the Newton MessagePad, a new type of portable known as a personal digital assistant (PDA). It was the first mass-market handheld computer and was offered as a personal information manager. The Newton solved the problem of keyboard size by using a stylus for input, but it promised more of this new pen-based technology than it could deliver. Apple promoted the Newton's ability to interpret handwriting, with disastrous results, because at the time its capability was relatively primitive. By 1997 when the next-generation Newton, the MessagePad 2000, reached the market, its handwriting recognition was much improved. Reviewers praised the revamped MessagePad for its robust communication and computing features. But with Apple mired in losses and profits from the Newton not imminent, in 1998 Apple dropped the curtain on the Newton line—the MessagePad, eMate (a Newton-based clamshell notebook for the education market), and the Newton operating system.

A man using a handheld computing device with a stylus. *(Kelly Quinn)*

In the meantime, another competitor with greater staying power was emerging. In 1994 inventor Jeff Hawkins came up with a design for a new kind of PDA that would become the PalmPilot. At the time he was working at a software firm developing handwriting-recognition technology for handheld devices. But the sparse handhelds at the time lacked many useful features, and to Hawkins, an engineer, were poorly designed. He believed an effective handheld device should be extremely light and portable, ought to synchronize readily with desktop computers, and should be simple in features and purpose. With his innovative design and support from the company's management, Hawkins helped transform the company into a hardware designer and maker—Palm Computing.

In 1995 the private company was sold to modem manufacturer U.S. Robotics in order to finance the product's debut. The first PalmPilot shipped in early 1996, and by year's end they had sold over 350,000 units. Within another year, over a million PalmPilots had been sold, and the product began attracting a devoted following of users, software writers, and corporate partners. Palm became part of 3Com Corp. with its 1997 purchase of U.S. Robotics, and by that time

Palm was becoming entrenched as the market leader in the nascent PDA category.

By then Palm wasn't alone, though. Numerous models of handhelds, palmtops, and other PDAs came on the market around the same time. These included computers running Microsoft's Windows CE operating system. Windows CE, although less functional than desktop Windows versions, was easy to learn for those familiar with the PC versions. Windows CE devices included modified versions of the popular Microsoft Word and Excel software, along with Microsoft's Internet Explorer browser. The Casio Cassiopeia, for instance, was able to transmit faxes, access e-mail, and receive information via a one-way pager, in addition to being able to link and synchronize data through a docking station to a Windows 95 desktop computer. Hewlett-Packard introduced its 1000CX palmtop PC; and Philips Electronics North America Corp. unveiled the Velo 1, in early 1997.

Still, others resisted the Windows product: the Toshiba Libretto, the ill-fated Newton, and most importantly, PalmPilot. Although some Palm devices were capable of running CE, for strategic and other reasons Palm preferred to use its own operating system, Palm OS.

CURRENT CONDITIONS

After surging past $1 billion for the first time in 1998, worldwide handheld sales continued their sharp uptick in 1999, when sales reached an $2.3 billion, according to estimates by Dataquest. The U.S. market is believed to account for about 45 percent of global handheld sales. In 1999 handheld shipments were estimated at 5.7 million units, and Dataquest forecast a nearly sixfold increase in annual production by 2003, when it pegged unit sales to reach 21 million. By that time, the market research firm predicted, some 32 million handhelds were expected to be in use throughout the world.

Besides continued technological innovation and product enhancement, probably the biggest issue facing the industry is the shift toward wireless communications. In that domain handhelds will increasingly compete with smart phones and other specialized gadgets that offer basic access to e-mail and limited Internet content. Palm embarked on the wireless path in 1999 with the introduction of its topflight Palm VII model, which included built-in wireless connectivity through the company's Palm.net subscription service. Until the Palm VII, most handhelds could gain access to Internet communications only through expensive add-on devices. Other high-end handhelds are beginning to include modems as well, but a bevy of phone-based wireless Internet devices are being positioned to provide comparable and even more advanced services.

Elsewhere on the technical front, advancing performance and versatility of handhelds is another key trend. As a gauge of technical advancement, in 1999 the higher-end handhelds had the processing speed and memory capacity of midrange desktop PCs about three years earlier. Technical hurdles for handheld makers include improving battery life, which can be woefully short as features get added, increasing speed and processing power, and upgrading graphics. A regular gripe about Palm PDAs, for instance, has been that their monochrome screens don't fare well in dim light (or in very bright light, for that matter). Palm's answer was its first color-screen model, introduced in 2000, which featured a very modest, low-resolution screen despite its premium price. Of course, even small improvements in graphics tend to boost power consumption noticeably—making improvements in battery life all the more pressing and, in the meantime,

leaving handheld makers on the horns of a dilemma as far as existing technologies go.

Meanwhile, Microsoft has been struggling in the scrimmage for handheld operating systems, thanks in large part to Palm. Its Windows CE, first released in 1996, has been roundly criticized for being cumbersome and bug-laden. Although it enjoys wider adoption in the palmtop segment, Windows CE has been trounced in the PDA market by the Palm OS, which controlled 80 percent of the market as of 2000. Indeed, Palm OS market penetration is greater than that of Palm's own devices, as even some competitors prefer to use Palm software over Microsoft's. Notably, in 1999 several PDA manufacturers abandoned Windows CE as their software of choice. In 2000, however, Microsoft unveiled a new version of Windows for handhelds called Pocket PC that it hoped would begin to close the gap. On Microsoft's side was an array of heavy hitters in the hardware business, including Casio, Compaq, and Hewlett-Packard, who were committed to using Microsoft's product for the foreseeable future.

INDUSTRY LEADERS

Major players in the handheld market include several of the top computer makers as well as specialists. In addition to the vendors discussed below, leading manufacturers include Compaq, IBM, NEC Corp., Sharp Electronics, Casio Computer, Oregon Scientific, Vadem, and Psion PLC (developer of the Epoch handheld operating system).

PALM, INC.

Almost since its first product debut in 1996, Palm has been the handheld maker to beat. Palm had an uneasy relationship with its parent, 3Com Corp., which acquired Palm through the 1997 buyout of U.S. Robotics. To give Palm greater autonomy and value, separate from that of 3Com, primarily a networking equipment company, Palm was spun off from 3Com in 2000. In 2000 Palm's sales jumped 87 percent to reach $1.06 billion, and the company boasted 65 percent of the handheld market.

Despite its commanding lead, Palm has been criticized for a lack of innovation since its first products were introduced. It was slow to adopt color displays and other new features that competitors have rolled out. Part of Palm's strategy has been to keep its brand clear and devices simple, but skeptics suggest it may be vulnerable to losing customers based on its limited product offerings. At any rate, Palm's generous lead in the market is all but guaranteed to diminish as new competitors ship handhelds that have more features, and in some cases are cheaper, than Palm's line.

HANDSPRING, INC.

One visible competitor taking Palm head on is Handspring, a start-up led by two of Palm's founders, Jeff Hawkins and Donna Dubinsky. Chafed by 3Com's heavy-handed corporate management after its acquisition of Palm, Hawkins and Dubinsky departed the company in 1998 to form Handspring. Handspring maintained some ties with Palm, though, by licensing Palm OS instead of Windows CE to run its PDAs.

The new company's mission was strikingly similar to Palm's: create an inexpensive, feature-rich, easy-to-use, well-designed personal computing device. It received start-up funding from the venerable venture capital firm Kleiner Perkins Caufield & Byers, and unveiled its first product, the Visor, in 1999, with wide-scale retail introduction in 2000. Visor models are priced sometimes below comparable Palms and can offer more flexibility to interface with other devices through the firm's Springboard add-on modules. Visors also come in an assortment of bright colors, borrowing another successful tactic of Apple Computer. Handspring plans to close in on the consumer side of market, which is less developed than the business market. By mid-2000, Handspring commanded 21.6 percent of the U.S. market for personal digital assistants, according to NPD Intelect. It also introduced VisorPhone, an add-on cartridge for its Visor model that turns it into a cell phone. The company generated revenues of $101.9 million in fiscal 2000.

HEWLETT-PACKARD CO.

Hewlett-Packard (HP) has been a leading contender in the handheld arena mainly through its Jornada line. Aimed at higher-end users, Jornada machines deliver color graphics and fast processing speed relative to PDAs. Increasingly, they also support multimedia and wireless communications. The Windows CE (Pocket PC)-based devices, which look like tiny notebook computers, have been some of the highest rated in terms of performance and versatility, and are considered one of the bigger challengers to Palm's market dominance.

RESEARCH AND TECHNOLOGY

Given the industry's intense focus on adding wireless communications capability to handheld com-

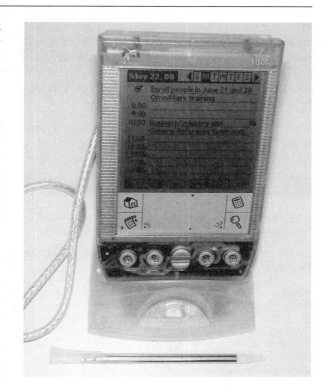

The Handspring Visor Deluxe, a product of Handspring, Inc. (Kelly Quinn)

puters, many industry analysts are banking that a new wireless standard will be a key part of the picture. The curiously dubbed Bluetooth wireless standard for so-called personal area networks is predicted to have sweeping ramifications for many areas of personal computing, including handhelds. Named after a tenth-century Danish king who united disparate Nordic provinces, Bluetooth technology attempts to do the same with portable electronics by providing a lingua franca for high-bandwidth wireless data exchange over short distances. The standard was first proposed in 1998 as a result of a collaboration by the same name between computing and electronics giants such as IBM, Nokia, Ericsson, and Intel. Since then, about 2,000 companies have joined the Bluetooth effort.

Bluetooth competes with the nascent Infrared Data Association (IrDA) infrared communications standard, which offers less bandwidth. Whereas Bluetooth may be used in everything from cell phones to digital cameras to handhelds, IrDA has been used mainly to link handhelds, peripherals, and desktop computers.

Early products relying on Bluetooth were released in 1999, and wider offerings were rolled out in 2000, including forays by Palm and other handheld makers.

Market researcher International Data Corp. predicted massive adoption within a few years, citing that upwards of 450 million electronic devices worldwide—a quarter of them in the United States—would use Bluetooth by 2004. So-called smart phones were expected to lead the migration.

FURTHER READING

Bournellis, Cynthia. "Platform for Windows CE Added to Intellisync Family." *Electronic News,* 31 March 1997.

Deckmyn, Dominique. "Bluetooth." *Computerworld,* 12 June 2000.

Freed, Les. *The History of Computers.* Emeryville, CA: Ziff-Davis Press, 1995.

"GartnerGroup's Dataquest Says Worldwide Handheld Shipments to Surpass 5.7 Million Units in 1999," 27 May 1999. Available from http://gartner3.gartnerweb.com/dq/static/about/press/pr-b9924.html.

Gimein, Mark. "Palm and Handspring To Hand to Hand." *Fortune,* 18 September 2000.

Hagendorf, Jennifer. "1999 Market Leaders: Mobile PCs—New Form Factors Give Vendors a Boost." *Computer Reseller News,* 17 May 1999, 96.

International Data Corp. "Bluetooth Bares Its Teeth with 448.9 Million Devices Enabled Worldwide in 2004." Framingham, MA, 5 April 2000. Available from http://www.idc.com.

Kutler, Jeffrey. "Un Wired: Banks Again in Catch-Up Mode as Wireless Devices Widen Net." *American Banker,* 6 August 1999.

Nobel, Carmen. "Win CE Aimed at Embedded." *PC Week,* 3 April 2000.

"Palms Together." *Economist,* 18 September 1999.

"The Parents of the Pilot Try for an Encore with Handspring." *Fortune,* 22 November 1999.

"Pen Touch Sensitive Screen Featured in Casio Handheld." *Computing Canada,* 3 February 1997.

Pittelkau, Jeff. "The Newton Weighs In: Apple Newton MessagePad 2000." *MacUser,* June 1997. Available from http://www4.zdnet.com/macuser/mu_0697/features/newton/newton.html.

Rae-Dupree, Janet. "PalmPilot Has a Cult Following." *San Jose Mercury News,* 10 November 1997.

Schwartz, Ephraim. "Palm OS vs. Win CE for Business-to-Business: Which to Choose." *InfoWorld,* 28 August 2000.

"U.S. Robotics Plans Palm Pilot Upgrade." *Computerworld,* 10 February 1997.

"Worldwide Handheld Market Grew 65 Percent in 1997." *EDP Weekly,* 1 June 1998.

HEALTH SPAS

There are those who feel that Americans are just a bit too pampered and comfortable. The health-spa industry would love to contribute to that reputation, and by 2000 was playing no small part in making it so. Health spas enjoyed booming popularity throughout the 1990s. The spa industry was estimated at about $12.5 billion in 2000, and was expected to double by 2004. During that period, the general character of health spas shifted dramatically from the strict and vigorous emphasis on strength and fitness training of yesteryear. These days, while such aspects remain a vital component of the health-spa experience, they are couched within a broader emphasis on relaxation and holistic health and therapy. Many spas have dispensed with gymnasiums altogether, instead offering expansive outdoor retreats for exercise in a more natural and, presumably, less stressful environment.

Spas address a wide range of concerns related to human health and fitness—or wellness, in modern parlance—including skin care, muscle relaxation, weight loss, fitness, stress relief, energy boosting, and others. Even more than the pampering, clients rated relaxation as the chief reason for their spa attendance, according to the International Spa Association, followed by pampering, stress reduction, weight loss, and exercise.

For those desiring the full spa experience, the "destination spa" will provide a personal schedule for mind, soul, and body needs. A hotel or resort with spa facilities allows guests to enjoy spa treatments, cuisine, and advice during their vacation. A "day spa," the fastest-growing segment of the industry, provides consumers with access to the spa experience at a fraction of the cost of a traditional destination spa.

Analysts attributed the explosion of spa popularity in the mid- and late 1990s to a variety of factors: the increasingly technological setting of the workplace; the greater number of individuals reaching middle age; the strong U.S. economy creating more leisure spending; and the growing acceptance of alternative therapies and treatments combined with awareness of health and fitness. Spas are increasingly used as a retreat from job-related stress and a fast-paced culture. Many companies take it upon themselves to send their employees to day spas, and some even take advantage of spas as a way to combine meetings with relaxation.

ORGANIZATION AND STRUCTURE

Spas draw from techniques used by ancient peoples as well as those from the modern world. Ideally, the spa experience focuses on a client's total physical, mental, and spiritual well-being. Many spas actually request that patrons leave all "necessities" at home, including clothing, makeup, cellular phones, and hair dryers. The resorts provide loose, comfortable clothing and products for personal hygiene.

Destination spas focus on varying themes and specialties. While some offer assistance in dealing with specific health concerns, such as smoking cessation or weight loss, the health benefits offered at most destination spas are relaxation, fitness, and stress reduction. Spas slow time for clients in a secure environment devoid of demands. A rhythmic pace is set, with most spas alternating treatments and fitness classes. Destination spas also generally take on a parenting role, in which they assume responsibility for the clients' eating, sleeping, and exercise activities and schedules. The itinerary may not be completely filled; time is left for meditation, walks, reading, or naps. Menus are designed to nourish the body, maintain energy levels, and relax moods, without adding unnecessary calories. Destination spas offer a wide variety of rigorous fitness routines such as aerobics, boxing, cycling, walking, jogging, horseback riding, aquatics, and martial arts. These routines are balanced by relaxation techniques such as meditation, massage, hydrotherapy, journaling, and reading.

Cruise-ship spas and hot springs are other forms of destination spas. The increasingly popular cruise-ship spa experience typically lasts from three days to two weeks, depending on the destination. Spas developed around natural hot springs are currently undergoing a resurgence in popularity. As generations of people have known, therapeutic minerals such as sulfur, iron, calcium, and magnesium found in these waters can alleviate discomfort from arthritis, sore muscles, and chronic back pain.

Many luxury hotels and resorts are adding spas and outdoor recreation facilities to their properties. Surveys reveal that vacationers and business travelers who patronize higher-end hotels and resorts have come to expect spa amenities and treatments. Hotel and resort owners unanimously agree that having full spa facilities gives them an edge over the competition in attracting clients. Fitness facilities with saunas, whirlpools, steam rooms, and juice bars are usually available, not to mention salons for pampering, and rooms for massage, aromatherapy, and other treatments.

Day spas were the industry's hottest sector in the late 1990s. Affluent clients leading hectic lifestyles shared the public's growing interest in alternative-health therapies, and many beauty salons offered these spa services in conjunction with traditional beauty services. At a day spa clients may purchase full- or half-day packages, or selected services à la carte. Along with manicures, pedicures, and hair styling, the day-spa client can experience facials, yoga, various types of massages, aromatherapy, hydrotherapy, acupuncture, meditation, light and sound therapy, and other treatments that are offered at destination spas.

Health spas offer many differing types of treatment. Aromatherapy employs oils, herbs, and flowers for relaxation or stimulation. Ayurvedic relaxation treatment combines oil and massage, dripping oil in energy centers while massaging it in. Body wraps consist of the application of herbs, seaweed, or mud, followed by a wrap as the substance penetrates the skin. Hydrotherapy may include any treatment that

takes place in water or milk; since a hydrotherapy tub can cost up to $20,000, the presence of one indicates the availability of advanced treatments. Underwater music frequently accompanies these treatments. Shower hydrotherapy includes the Vichy shower with seven nozzles that hit nerve spots along the spine, and Scotch hose therapy that hits the skin in a high-pressure massage.

Reflexology is the massage of the feet; practitioners believe pressure points on the foot relate to systems throughout the body. Massage is the manipulation of the skin and underlying muscles; practitioners believe it improves circulation, rids the body of toxins, and relieves stress. Lymphatic massage manipulates the muscles to drain the lymph nodes and move waste out of the system. Reiki uses healing touch to direct universal healing energy into the body's energy centers. Swedish and sports massage get blood flowing for relaxation and get lactic acid out of the system. Acupuncturists use needles, finger pressure, or electrodes to stimulate different points on the body. These points are said to release energy flow and correspond to different body systems.

Some spas also address the specific needs and desires of teenagers and young adults. For instance, as young people become a more powerful spending demographic, spas have begun to offer special acne treatments and similar services. Moreover, for younger adults, some day spas provide day-care facilities.

All the success of the health-spa industry in the 1990s, however, was not without its consequences, the most prominent being competition—not only within the industry, but outside it as well. Techniques traditionally reserved for spas have cropped up in new places. Barbershops increasingly offered back massages, gymnasiums featured mud treatments, and department stores offered aromatherapy.

BACKGROUND AND DEVELOPMENT

Today's spas evolved from public baths, a tradition going back over 4,500 years. The Dead Sea Scrolls reveal that the site around Qumran, Jordan, was famous for its hydrotherapy and herbal medicines. Hydrotherapy was used by Hippocrates and incorporated into the healing practices of Greeks, Romans, and Egyptians. Public baths have also been found in Pakistan and in Babylonian ruins. Massage therapy has been an important aspect of Chinese and Ayurvedic healing for 3,000 years. The popularity of the public baths declined in the Middle Ages; in the seventeenth and 18th centuries physicians began prescribing baths, and their popularity rose again. Spa popularity continued to rise with the endorsement of Vincent Priessnitz, often referred to as the father of the modern hydrotherapy movement, and wealthy Europeans in the 1800s visited spas for months, both for treatments and for socializing.

Spa-going was introduced to the United States in the 1840s by Robert Wesselhoeft and became more popular as prices began to fall and day spas began to open, allowing those with more modest means to try the spa experience. By the 1930s, the American Medical Association maintained a committee devoted to spas. Spas benefited from the growing acceptability of alternative medicines and therapies in the 1980s. Some baby boomers reported that doctors seemed unreceptive to treating creeping complaints—such as arthritis, back pain, and high blood pressure—in nontraditional ways. Since many people preferred not to be on long-term medication or to undergo surgery, they turned to massage therapy, acupuncture, biofeedback, hypnosis, and reflexology.

CURRENT CONDITIONS

Some 30 million people visited spas in 1999, about 14 million of whom attended day spas, while the rest went to resorts and hotels, destination spas, and cruise spas. Contrary to many perceptions, moreover, the majority of those attending spas considered themselves to already be in reasonably good shape, and the practice was becoming increasingly popular among athletes, a group that traditionally scorned such delicate treatment.

While traditionally, health spas have been a feminine retreat, the current trend leans toward men as clients. Men are more educated and concerned about their own health and well-being than they were in the past and are dedicating more time to improving their health. In 1999, 28 percent of spa-goers were men, up from 9 percent in 1987. Spas attached to fitness centers are particularly attractive to men. As introductory advertising, spas encourage businesses to reserve their facilities for meetings and offer group prices and incentive packages for men who attend these meetings. According to the International Spa Association, 45 percent of spa-goers were between the ages of 34 and 52, while 87 percent were white and only 8 percent were black. Sixty-one percent were married, and 56 percent had at least some college education.

Modern health-spa regimes have moved from extreme vigorous exercise in favor of a more balanced rejuvenation escape, combining exercise, treatments, nourishment, relaxation, and pampering. Various forms of massage, aromatherapy, and hydrotherapy are designed to improve circulation, relieve stress, release endorphins, and eliminate toxins. New alternative therapies that achieved popularity in the late 1990s included the hay-flower sack, in which a thin, paperlike sack is filled with hay flowers and wetted and heated, and then placed on the client's back. The resulting aroma is purported to combine with the heat to act as a sedative, enhancing blood flow and allowing the body to heal itself.

Day spas were the hottest commodity in the industry through the 1990s, catering to the business community and others seeking a quick one-day getaway without necessitating an entire planned vacation. The boom in day spas was tremendous throughout the decade, growing from only 30 such outfits in the United States in 1989 to about 860 in 1998. The fastest growth, however, was saved for 1999, when the total nearly doubled to reach 1,600. According to Spa Finder, the leading industry reservation and marketing firm, the day-spa craze could be traced to the fitness boom of the 1980s. As baby boomers slowed down from their vigorous high-impact aerobics regiments, they increasingly looked to spas to help keep in shape and relieve stress on a regular basis. Though precise figures were unavailable, many observers held that day spas were the fastest-growing sector of the beauty industry. Day spas do not relax the pocketbook, however; the average visit cost about $350.

Day spas typically offer many of the same exotic treatments as resorts and destination spas, albeit minus the lavish outdoor settings. Day spas often include massages, facials, hair and scalp treatments, acupressure, and a host of other services in addition to exercise facilities. The gender gap among day-spa visitors, however, was greater than the slowly closing gap among destination- spa and resort visitors. About 85 percent of day-spa goers were women, while nearly half were between the ages of 34 and 52.

According to an industry study, 82 percent of resort owners felt having a spa on the premises increased perceived value of the room rate, 57 percent felt it increased their occupancy rates, and 100 percent surveyed felt having a spa gave them a marketing advantage over competitors. The survey also asked guests who did not take advantage of spa services why they did not do so. For 86 percent of such respondents, time was noted as a factor, while 30 percent were discouraged by the fees. Almost 65 per-

WHERE THE NAME FITS THE MEN

One of the most exclusive and well-known health spas in the United States took advantage of, and hoped to further, the trend toward increased male patronage of the industry's facilities by devoting one week entirely to testosterone. Men's Week at the Golden Door, the glitzy and expensive 377-acre retreat for the leisure class in Escondido, California, offered men a week to come and receive pampering and indulge in the boyhood fantasy of wandering free from the adult world's burdens of scheduling golf meetings and building portfolios. According to *Fortune,* the average Men's Week client was at least a multimillionaire, usually in midlife.

For a week, the clients are basically programmed to follow a precise regimen. Basic ground rules include no: alcohol, nicotine, butter, salt, cologne, or sex. And lest anyone try to sneak a cell-phone call in their rooms, the signals are deliberately weak in the guest rooms, and such calls can be made only in the public labyrinth. The clients are not entirely shut off from the real world, however. The resort's television flashes CNBC so the visitors can track the latest stock movements.

To help the men return to their primal nature, they are forced to confront the rugged elements with a brisk hike first thing in the morning, followed by strength training, power cycling, and even archery, among other exercises. The Men's Week activities are not entirely about sweating and grunting, however. The troupe is also treated to yoga exercises and a fashion show. After this hard day's work comes the reward, in the forms of massages, facials, manicures, herbal wraps, and other soothing treatments. After a week, the men are relaxed, fresh, and ready to return to the daily grind of the real world.

tomers have also begun creating their own mini-spas at home, buying massage tables, electric massagers, hot tubs, whirlpool baths, and a whole array of spa products to relieve stress and build relationships in privacy.

As doctors came increasingly to acknowledge the benefits offered by spas, spa treatments were recognized as viable medical treatments, though usually as a supplement, rather than a replacement, for traditional medicines and therapies. Some spa proponents, for instance, hold that the body's immune system is greatly influenced by the mind, and thus that spa relaxation techniques and aromatherapies can help stimulate the immune system by reducing the stress that inhibits the immune system's optimal function. Unfortunately, the insurance industry generally remained more skeptical of spa treatments than did the medical community, and thus most spa therapies usually must be paid for out of pocket.

The spa industry had even gone to the dogs by 2000. Some retreats, such as The Common Dog in Boston, were designed especially for the canines of the well-to-do, and offered the pups a place to run free of a leash in an enormous yard and lounge on couches. Such facilities generally cost the owner about $25 a day, while special treatments, such as hairstyling and pedicures, were extra.

INDUSTRY LEADERS

Conde Nast Traveler magazine, a leading resource for the spa industry, conducted a poll of vacationers, published in April 2000, to discover the most popular international day spas and spa resorts. The 10 most popular resorts, in order, were the Golden Door of Escondido, California; Canyon Ranch in the Berkshires, Lenox, Massachusetts; Miraval Life in Balance of Catalina, Arizona; Four Seasons Resort Hualalai of Big Island, Hawaii; Grand Wailea Resort Hotel & Spa of Maui, Hawaii; Rancho La Puerta of Tecate, Mexico; Las Ventanas al Paraiso of Los Cabos, Mexico; Canyon Ranch Health Resort of Tucson, Arizona; The Greenbrier of White Sulphur Springs, West Virginia; and the Centre for Well-Being at the Phoenician of Scottsdale, Arizona.

Canyon Ranch, one of the best-known spas in the world, offered an enormous array of services, from aquatic therapy to exotic massage treatments to dance classes to fitness training. Canyon Ranch's men-only fitness classes, outdoor-sports classes, and medical treatments geared toward men made it the most pop-

cent of the participants said they would have used the spa facilities had these factors been eliminated. Hotels also found that spas helped their operations maintain a healthy stream of customers through the most depressed months, when weather or other tourism-related variables are usually not conducive to drawing clients.

Although the popularity of the spa concept is steadily growing among the public, many destination spas had some difficulty attracting clients, simply because of the costs involved. With a typical one-week stay at a destination spa running $3,000-$4,000, many people sought out good quality day spas to get a taste of the spa experience. Prices for services at a day spa varied greatly depending on the geographical location of the spa and the services rendered. Cus-

ular spa among men in the United States. The company also opened the largest day spa in the United States, covering some 61,000 square feet, at the Venetian Resort Hotel Casino in Las Vegas.

The Golden Door was among the most exclusive destination spas, with a tradition of catering to the extremely wealthy. Those who could afford the price tag of $5,375 for a week's visit were provided with everything they might need, and thus little luggage was necessary. The Golden Door's expansive property afforded visitors the opportunity for a range of outdoor activities, including kayaking and hiking, in addition to its streamlined indoor facilities featuring most of the industry's premier treatments.

WORK FORCE

As with other segments of the hospitality and services industry, all types of people work for health spas. In the hotel/resort/destination end there are managers, marketers, salespeople, human resource specialists, receptionists, maids, concierges, and maintenance people. Professionally, chefs, nutritionists, massage therapists, acupuncturists, reflexologists, fitness trainers, cosmetologists, and other treatment specialists all contribute to and make their living from the spa industry.

In 2000 the American Massage Therapy Association claimed a membership of 40,000. The National Certification Board for Therapeutic Massage and Bodywork (NCBTMB) has certified over 35,000 professionals through its exam as of December 1999. While all do not work in the spa industry, the industry tends to hire licensed or certified therapists. The NCBTMB also accredits massage-therapy schools, which require 500 or more hours of course work. Recertification requires 200 hours work experience and 50 hours of appropriate continuing education. The national exam requires proficiency in the following areas: human anatomy, physiology, and kinesiology; clinical pathology and recognition of various conditions; massage therapy and bodywork theory, assessment, and application; and professional standards, ethics, and business practices.

Reflexologists are increasingly subject to state regulation. Most of these states require the practitioners to obtain massage-therapy licenses. Some state codes call for venereal disease and AIDS testing, the purchase of an adult entertainment license, and make such businesses subject to surprise inspections by law enforcement. Several industry associations have formed to bring increased awareness, respectability, and standards to reflexology.

Cosmetologists perform a variety of functions at health spas including facials, manicures, pedicures, waxing, and other pampering treatments. Cosmetologists are regulated by states, most of which require graduation from a cosmetology school, successful completion of an exam, and continuing education. Other professionals employed by health spas may or may not be regulated under state or local laws. There are, however, a growing number of professional societies, such as the American Alliance of Aromatherapy, and the Awareness Institute Reiki Certification, attempting to self regulate with ethical and professional standards.

AMERICA AND THE WORLD

As the spa industry moved closer to the mainstream in the international arena, spas watched their revenues skyrocket. According to the International Spa Association, about one-third of their registered spas brought in revenues between $5 and $10 million in 1999, while that year alone the number of visitors leaped 16 percent.

Women and men around the world are rediscovering the many advantages of spa treatments. More Asian women are taking advantage of spas that traditionally catered to male clientele. The most popular spa treatments in Asia are: Thailand, massage; Japan, bathing; Korea, exfoliation; China, herbal medicine and acupuncture; and Indonesia, herbal body treatments.

In Europe, spas were once the province of the wealthy, who might spend months on end at their retreat. In the late 1990s, however, European spas were increasingly taking on the role of vacation and health destinations rather than physician-prescribed government-subsidized visits. As a result, the customer base was getting younger and more mainstream. European spas, then, were increasingly taking on the look and feel of U.S. spas, which themselves blended European and Asian practices and augmented them with particularly American features. Still, the cultural differences were apparent among the clientele. In the United States, Americans expect results and tend to over-schedule, partaking in treatments, fitness, and classes back-to-back. European spas encourage a slower pace, one with little or no exercise, the emphasis being terrific cuisine and pampering treatments such as facials, massages, and body wraps.

FURTHER READING

Bronikowski, Lynn. "Queen (or King) for a Day." *ColoradoBiz,* January 2000.

Edwards, Tamala M., and Laird Harrison. "A Day at the Spa." *Time,* 18 October 1999.

Fetto, John. "Queen For a Day." *American Demographics,* March 2000.

Foxman, Ariel. "Behind the Golden Door." *Fortune,* 18 April 2000.

Glock, Allison. "Spa Handbook." *Women's Sports & Fitness,* January/February 2000.

Green, Leslie. "Day Spas Massage Their Way into Booming New Business." *Crain's Detroit Business,* 6 December 1999.

Johnson, Hillary. "Alamo Plaza Spa Uses Old Ideas to Treat Modern-Day Stress." *San Antonio Business Journal,* 31 March 2000.

Levine, Joshua. "The Way to Okay." *Forbes,* 4 October 1999.

Naversen, Laurel. "Comfort Zone." *Women's Sports & Fitness,* January/February 2000.

Serviss, Naomi. "Spa Treatment." *WE Magazine,* September/October 1999.

Svetcov, Danielle. "Lapdog of Luxury." *Mother Jones,* 31 March/April 2000.

"Top 40 Spas." *Conde Nast Traveler,* April 2000. Available from http://www.concierge.com/traveler/spapoll/intro.html.

Zeiger, Ari, and Joan M. Steinauer. "Don't Worry Be Happy." *Incentive,* October 1999.

High-Tech PR Firms

Even (or perhaps especially) in the world of high-tech wizardry, it is often how a product is portrayed rather than how it works that makes or breaks a company. With the surge in high-tech industries in the late 1990s, more and more companies came to realize this essential truth, and in so doing gave a dramatic boost to the high-tech public relations industry. The rush of dollars into high-tech start-ups flooded the industry with new business, as companies sought to grow at an accelerated pace while scrambling to differentiate themselves from competitors through the employment of public relations (PR) firms. The high-tech sector of the PR industry easily outpaced other major sectors, such as finance and health care, during this period.

Meanwhile, those traditional PR agents who specialized in high-tech issues and who felt confident enough to brave the rapidly consolidating high-tech PR environment struck out on their own, setting up their own PR boutiques catering to dot-coms and other sectors.

Public relations firms create a buzz around a new product, getting media, and thus customers, talking and thinking about the item. At the same time, PR firms devote themselves to digging up sales leads. In addition to product placement, high-tech PR firms are often called on for crisis management, investor relations, publicity related to mergers and acquisitions, and a range of other tasks.

ORGANIZATION AND STRUCTURE

PR firms sell their services to clients in the high-tech industry, and work with those clients to develop public relations strategies that are then implemented by the PR firm itself. In effect, then, PR firms act as consultants and as media concierges. Companies contract with PR firms to acquire the kind of specialized knowledge of product placement and media savvy they may not be able to muster within their own organizations.

Of course, not all agencies are right for all firms all the time, and a good deal of specialization exists even within the high-tech sector. The selection of a PR agency is often a major undertaking in itself, and many companies bring in outside consultants to aid in the selection process.

Generally, a well-prepared company will draw up a precise outline of the problems and deficiencies in their internal public relations efforts, a clear and specific list of the objectives and expectations they hope to realize with the PR firm, and a team of internal contacts to work with the PR firm on an ongoing basis.

For their part, high-tech PR firms maintain inside contacts with the media and analysts, sending e-mails, attending trade shows, initiating meetings, and generally keeping the public abreast of goings on within client firms regarding new products and business developments, and placing the desired spin on the events to create a positive image of the company in the public mind.

BACKGROUND AND DEVELOPMENT

When the high-tech PR industry first began to take off in the 1970s and 1980s, it was a world of glitz and glamour centering around highly publicized trade shows featuring the latest gadgetry. By the late 1980s,

More On WALKING DOWN
THE AISLE

An oft-repeated quip in the high-tech community is that choosing a PR firm is quite like choosing a spouse. This adage, however, sends some industry insiders, such as Catherine O'Rourke—who ran her own PR agency, O'Rourke & Co., from 1988 to 1998 before selling it to Manning, Selvage and Lee and taking up a career consulting for companies on their selection, recruiting, and training of PR firms—into fits; she insisted that choosing a PR firm appropriate for a long-term relationship is far more difficult than finding a soul mate.

While eschewing any sort of strict formula for settling on an agency, such analysts held that several broad selection guidelines apply pretty much across the board, and that the rigorous screening process required to secure the ideal PR firm makes the spousal selection process seem like a haphazard and frivolous undertaking.

Above all, clients are advised not to adopt any one company's proven strategy for agency selection, as every company has its unique needs and capabilities, and the often-subtle differences between similar companies can make the same PR firm that was so successful for one firm a disaster for the other.

To begin with, firms are advised to have a clear understanding of what kind of internal organization they have and how it could accommodate a PR firm. If this step is not carefully taken, a PR firm can add significantly to the workload with little or no benefit derived for its trouble.

Most people would not marry a suitor without some sort of outside opinion on the matter, and likewise PR firms often obtain the services of consultants who specialize in agency selection. Consultants, according to O'Rourke, take over the more unpleasant tasks of courtship, when tough questions must be raised and the PR firm's most vulnerable areas are exposed.

The courtship itself, according to O'Rourke, typically begins with a Request for Proposal, which announces what the company wants out of a PR firm and for what price, and an Evaluation Check List, which the company uses to gauge how well the potential PR mate measures up to those standards.

After a few weeks of intensive evaluation, during which the company ideally has perused the PR firm's Web site, visited its headquarters, and gotten a feel for its personality and habits, the big decision can finally be made. If the PR firm is accepted as a new partner, the marriage date is set, and the two begin to build a life together.

Sadly, however, somewhere in this process, most companies end up fooling themselves; the average company's marriage to a PR firm ends in divorce after 18 months.

however, things began to cool off as the economy slowed, the industry matured, and its customer base became more fragmented.

Partly as a result, the mid-1990s were characterized by furious merger activity. Beginning with Porter/Novelli International's high-profile purchase of Waltham, Massachusetts-based Brodeur & Partners in 1993, the industry's leading firms consolidated over the next several years, reshaping the high-tech PR market in the process. GCI Group acquired Jennings & Co.; Manning, Selvage & Lee bought up Rourke & Co.; and other leading firms were forced into similar deals in order to keep up with these competitors. Smaller firms, meanwhile, were continually squeezed by the industry giants, and scrambled to make themselves attractive for larger suitors to acquire them.

Propelling the trend was the realization that PR companies were beginning to outgrow the niche markets to which smaller PR firms catered, and needed a more integrated, holistic PR approach that only the larger players could generate. And as high-tech gadgetry and services increasingly became a part of the average consumer's daily life, clients demanded a more consumer-oriented PR approach.

The development of the Internet and the World Wide Web through the early and mid-1990s had a twofold effect on the high-tech PR industry. First, the Web brought about a flurry of new businesses—as dot-com start-ups began popping up in droves—that demanded the services of PR firms. At the same time, the Web gave PR firms a new medium to consider in their PR strategies, as companies used the Web for advertising and product placement and generally quickened the pace at which the crucial PR-related information moved throughout the market.

CURRENT CONDITIONS

In the start-up-crazy New Economy of the late 1990s and early 2000s, high-tech PR firms found a gold mine. So firmly established were these agencies that it was not unusual for a high-tech start-up to pay between $20,000 and $40,000 in monthly fees to their PR firms. And since the nature of the Internet fostered the faster movement of information, PR firms were able to procure clients by convincing them that they needed outside, professional help in getting the latest information and spin to media outlets.

As the news cycle speeded up and media outlets deployed fewer reporters to cover regular beats, meanwhile, reporters increasingly requested packaged news stories containing the bulk of the information they required to complete an article. High-tech companies, of course, were often too strapped for time, cash, or personnel to get such information to the press in the most articulate, timely, and favorable fashion.

Still, the high-tech PR industry was in a somewhat dubious position at the start of the 2000s. As the New Economy continued its meteoric ascendancy and money poured into Internet and high-tech start-ups, the demand for high-tech PR firms was by all accounts at a stratospheric level. While this was obviously good news for those with a stake in the industry, demand far outpaced the industry's ability to supply quality people and services, alarming many industry players who were caught between the desire to capitalize on the booming market and the need to foster knowledge and skills among their employees. In leaning toward the former, firms were forced to speed new recruits through the training process, generating calls for greater training resources for PR firms. In particular, the industry was inundated with pleas for a greater number of face-to-face meetings between PR trainees and reporters as well as heightened knowledge among PR agents of the contours of the media itself.

Indeed, one of the crucial relationships in the PR industry, that with the media, was far from intimate. A poll conducted by *Softletter* in late 1999 revealed that journalists specializing in high-tech issues were displeased with the service they were getting from PR firms, and many journalists and analysts registered a sense of alienation stemming from a lapse in PR quality. Some respondents, such as Michael Vizard at *Infoworld,* concluded that PR clients were not actually receiving the access to the media that they thought they were when they contracted with PR firms. Denny Arar of *PC World* added that PR reps typically failed to acquire a good sense of the publications and the kinds of issues and products they covered before trying to do business with those publications.

Other complaints were based on the industry's growing client list and subsequent inability to accommodate all the demand at premium levels of quality. For instance, much of the personal nature of the PR process was lost to mass e-mail distributions that failed to differentiate between publications, much less between writers of varying specialties.

For every negative report, however, there was a PR firm insisting that their agents did their homework, were articulate, and were knowledgeable about the product and the media outlet. Sure enough, the high-tech PR industry, though clearly not without its difficulties, was in strong shape in 2000, and the market for such services was expected to prove exceptionally lucrative well into the decade.

One hitch in this projection, however, was that the air was finally let out of the dotcom tire in 2000, and PR firms were forced to sift through the rubble to find viable clients. No one felt that the sudden grounding of the dotcom industry was going to have a devastating effect on PR firms, of course; the Internet is here to stay, and companies will always need agents to help with their images. It does, however, mean that the "can't miss" feeling PR agencies had with Internet startups is long gone. In some ways, the shakeout was viewed as a healthy development; Internet companies, facing greater skepticism from investors, required even stronger PR efforts than before.

INDUSTRY LEADERS

Porter/Novelli International was one of the world's leading public relations firms, and its Brodeur Porter Novelli technology division sat at the top of the high-tech PR industry. The company grew about 25 percent each year in the late 1990s, bringing in annual fees of $85 million. Brodeur Porter Novelli wrote its own software, designed extranets for clients, and built and maintained Web sites. In January 2000, Porter/Novelli International merged with Copithorne & Bellows Public Relations to form the Porter/Novelli Convergence Group, which was one of the world's largest high-tech PR operations, working in Europe, Asia Pacific, and the Americas.

Edelman Public Relations Worldwide, based in Chicago, Illinois, was a privately held company spread over the PR sectors, including health-care, financial, and consumer firms in addition to its high-tech operations. Founded in 1952, Edelman maintained a client list that included AT&T, IBM, Microsoft, the Gartner Group, NCR, Samsung, Texas Instruments, and other heavy hitters. About 20 percent of Edelman's revenues derived from technology communications work for Apple Computer and other tech firms, while the rest came from its wide array of PR services, including crisis management, marketing, interactive services, public affairs, and investor relations. In 1999, the firm acquired Wham Communications of Seattle and finished the year with fees of $75 million, while maintaining a payroll of 1,400 employees.

Waggener Edstrom, one of Silicon Valley's last independent PR agencies, worked with such companies as Amazon.com, GTE New Media Services, and Hewlett-Packard in the late 1990s, but its meal ticket was its role as Microsoft's public relations agency, which was responsible for about half the company's annual fees of over $40 million—aided, no doubt, by Microsoft's high-profile fight with the Justice Department over alleged antitrust violations. The company's relationship with Microsoft made it a coveted object for the larger PR firms, which were increasingly eyeing the firm for acquisition. Founded in 1983, the Lake Oswego, Oregon-based company employed 450 workers by 2000, and brought in revenues of $52.7 million in 1999.

Blanc & Otus, founded in 1985 in San Francisco, focused its high-tech expertise primarily on the software industry. The company maintained a client list of over 60 high-tech firms segmented into Internet, eBusiness, Mainstream, Convergence, and Impact divisions. Blanc & Otus merged with the PR giant Hill and Knowlton in 1999, but retained its name, operating as a Hill and Knowlton subsidiary. The firm employed 75 people and boasted clients such as Vitria, Ariba Technologies, and Xerox Scansoft.

Shandwick International was another leader in the high-tech PR industry through its Miller/Shandwick Technologies operation. Miller/Shandwick maintained clients in the fields of electronic commerce, telecommunications, and computer hardware and software. Alexander Ogilvy Public Relations Worldwide of San Francisco, California, counted among its clients such giants as Hewlett-Packard, Qwest, and Merrill Lynch. The company, founded in 1987, employed 150 workers in 1999.

WORK FORCE

High-tech PR agents, ideally, are personable folks with a good inside knowledge of the relevant media. Not only should PR agents command extensive knowledge of their clients' products, but they're charged with knowing which media outlets are appropriate placement venues for those products and services, the precise nature and editorial slant of those outlets, and even which editors or contacts are the best in a given situation or for a given type of product.

As a result of the enormous demand for PR firms, however, the reality was often far short of the ideal.

Such chores were increasingly left to interns, and were characterized as grunt work rather than the specialized and valued knowledge and functions of PR agents. This very trend has been at the heart of some of the media's negative reaction to the high-tech PR industry in recent years. *Computer Dealer News'* Michelle Douglas complained that the PR agents she dealt with didn't even understand what a reseller was.

Still, PR salaries were healthy, especially at the largest firms. According to *PRWeek*'s Salary Survey in 2000, PR salaries rose 8 percent in 1999—more than four times the national average—and were expected to experience similar growth in 2000. At the leading agencies, salaries shot up 12 percent in 1999. Salaries in the high-tech sector, moreover, yielded the fastest growth in the entire PR industry, at a national average of 10 percent. In 1999 the average national salary for a high-tech PR flack was $69,957. Moreover, with all the demand for PR services in the high-tech sector, there were exceptionally few unemployed high-tech PR agents.

AMERICA AND THE WORLD

A survey of international public relations firms conducted by Virtusio Public Relations of Manila, Philippines revealed that the PR industry expected the high-tech sector to generate the greatest levels of client demand and fee revenues in all of PR until the mid-2000s. Two-thirds of the survey's 62 respondents, however, predicted that recruiting and maintaining top-level employees would remain the most pressing challenge, and highest priority, during that period.

The Chinese high-tech market inched ever closer to an open international position when InfoEx-World Services Ltd., the co-organizer of the China Computerworld & NetChina Expo '99 contracted with the international high-tech PR firm the Hoffman Agency to handle public relations for the event.

The event, the largest of its kind in China, drew some 50,000 Chinese high-tech executives and government officials. The decision to bring in the San Jose, California-based firm to handle PR highlighted the growing international convergence of the PR industry. As the high-tech world, especially the Web-based market, blurs borders and as the PR firms grow larger through mergers and acquisitions, high-tech PR firms will likely place greater emphasis on international networking, and agents will find their tasks increasingly specialized so as to facilitate the smooth and successful placement of products in foreign markets, taking account of cultural and marketplace variations.

RESEARCH AND TECHNOLOGY

The PR industry has come a long way from the standard tool kit of yesteryear, which basically included a press release, press kit, and white paper along with the old-fashioned face-to-face schmoozing. By 2000, PR had gone high tech, especially those PR firms in the high-tech sector. To fully integrate themselves into the digital era, such PR firms have supplemented these industry standbys with digitized response systems that allow interactions with media outlets and clients to be customized quickly. For instance, some analysts may focus more on a broader market overview and competition while others may specialize in technical innovations or business models. Much of the tailored innovation has been streamlined for the World Wide Web, where analysts can simply download the data for their specialization directly from the PR firm's Web site. Activities such as this, which help make analysts' jobs easier, can make all the difference in an industry as increasingly competitive as high-tech public relations.

One of the crucial selling points that PR firms use to differentiate themselves from competitors is the level of continuous communication with clients. In that spirit, in the late 1990s PR firms, led by Pat Meier Associates PR, began offering in-house audio and video Webcasting services to allow for live, personal consultation between the firms and their clients, as well as between PR firms and the media outlets they targeted. The systems were also useful in video-based training programs, internal communications, and news releases.

FURTHER READING

"China Computerworld & NetChina Expo '99 Partners with the Hoffman Agency, Silicon Valley High-Tech Public Relations Firm." *PR Newswire,* 14 July 1999.

Cuthbert, Wendy. "High-Tech PR Expertise in Short Supply." *Strategy,* 10 April 2000.

Gove, Alex. "Heads Up." *Redherring.com,* 14 July 1999. Available from http://www.redherring.com/insider/1999/0714/vc-vcps.html.

"How Digital Tools and Audiences Are Changing High-Tech PR." *Public Relations Tactics,* November 1999.

"Journalists Rap High-Tech PR Firms." *O'Dwyer's PR Services Report,* December 1999.

"Labor Shortfall May Crimp High-Tech PR." *O'Dwyer's PR Services Report,* May 1999.

Merll, Richard. "PR Firms Sort Through Wreckage of Dot-Coms." *O'Dwyer's PR Services Report,* July 2000.

Messier, Anne Marie. "Hiring, Retaining Staffers Is Art in Fast-paced High-Tech PR." *O'Dwyer's PR Services Report,* November 1999.

"Newsletter Shakes up High-Tech PR Industry." *Public Relations Quarterly,* winter 1999.

O'Rourke, Catherine. "Selecting a High-Tech PR Firm: It's Easier Finding a Spouse." *O'Dwyer's PR Services Report,* November 1999.

"PR League Tables: High-tech Sector is Swiftly Evolving." *Marketing,* 25 May 2000.

"PR Means Pay Raise: Industry Paychecks Grew 8% in '99—Nearly Four Times the National Average, Outpacing Growth of Advertising Salaries." *Business Wire,* 30 March 2000.

Rojas, Peter. " Gotta Have It: What to Look for in a PR Firm, and When." *Red Herring Supplement—Guide to Professional Services 2000,* 2000. Available from http://www.redherring.com/mag/issue71S/news-gotta.html.

"SF High Tech PR Firm Launches In-House Webcasting Service." *PR Newswire,* 10 June 1998.

"Trends & Ideas." *PR News,* 29 May 1999.

HOLOGRAPHY

INDUSTRY SNAPSHOT

While folks could not yet use holography to reenact scenes from their favorite novels as promised on *Star Trek: The Next Generation,* by the 21st century holographic technology was boldly going where no one had gone before. The technology was expanding into numerous alien territories, such as solar-weather forecasting, three-dimensional (3-D) information storage and sound projection, and the production of lifelike images of objects that exist only in virtual reality. Such applications move light years beyond the more familiar holographic uses on credit cards, packaging, compact discs, and in fields such as computer-aided design, medical imaging, and security.

Holography permits the recording and reproducing of 3-D images called holograms. This can be achieved via two methods. Transmission holograms are created by splitting a laser beam into two sections. The first, or reference beam, is bounced off a mirror and strikes a photographic plate, but the waves of the reference beam remain unchanged. The second, or object beam, encounters the holographic subject, before also striking the same side of the photographic plate. The intervening object alters the object beam's waves, and the plate records the difference between the two beams. Known as the interference pattern, this difference is accounted for by the shape of the holographic subject, which is imprinted on the photographic place in three dimensions. A laser shone through the film permits the image to be viewed.

The newer, and more common, reflection holograms are generated in much the same manner. The laser beams, however, strike the opposite sides of the holographic plate. Reflection holograms can be seen in white light without the aid of an additional laser. The interference pattern recorded on the plate distorts the silver material within the film, creating varying depths within the image. Unlike the stereoscopic views created by toy View Masters, holographic images are genuinely three-dimensional. The viewer's eyes refocus on different depths; rotating the image permits one to see around and behind the object.

ORGANIZATION AND STRUCTURE

Characterized initially by individual artistic shops and museum marketers, the holography industry has continued to be dominated by private companies. Like most new industries, it experienced some volatility among its corporate players. The most active industry leaders are in the areas of advertising, engineering, medicine, mass storage media, and security. Several other companies have found specialty niches in producing holographic foil supplies or equipment.

More than 2,800 companies were involved in the production or distribution of holographic products or services in the United States in the late 1990s. The industry tends to be grouped largely by function: design, origination, production, utilization, distribution, and marketing or sales of holographic products—although several companies are vertically integrated.

There are several working research groups concerned with the development of holography, some with spin-off or affiliated corporations. The Holography Working Group is involved with computer-generated holography, materials, processing, and nondestructive testing, as well as optical elements, commercial applications, and standardization. The group meets at the annual International Society for Optical Engineering annual conference. The Holography and Optical Data Storage Group includes five postdoctoral and research associates as well as more than a dozen other researchers. Activities include investigation of photorefractive materials and devices, volumetric holographic data storage in a crystal, optical tomography, and computer-generated graphics.

ADVERTISING AND PACKAGING

Advertising holograms have eye-catching appeal that results in an exceptional rate of retention as compared with other advertising media. Universal Studios commissioned a custom- made hologram watch to commemorate the 100th anniversary of Alfred Hitchcock's birth. The face of the watch contained a holographic version of the director's unmistakable silhouette surrounded by birds. McDonald's full-page hologram on the back of *National Geographic*'s centennial anniversary issue cost more than $1 million for space that normally sold for $200,000. The ad ran worldwide in 10.5 million copies.

In 1995 Ford Motor Co. began generating full-size, full-color, photographic quality holograms of new cars directly from computer images that allowed a clinical view without the historic clay model. As early as 1973 General Motors Corp. used holography for measuring clay models prior to making press dies. Virtual reality will allow test drives without prototypes in the future. In 1999 Ford used stereograph technology to display a full-blown prototype car, the P2000, at the Detroit Auto Show. The impressive P2000 appeared on the display floor in living color, a demonstration of future innovations planned by the auto manufacturer. The P2000 was generated exclusively from an array of holographic images that created the illusion that a solid object (the car) was on display. Zebra Imaging of Austin, Texas, which assembled the resource- intensive P2000 display, processed approximately three terabytes of digital data for nearly two weeks to create the final image. Zebra Imaging predicted that pending technology improvements will reduce that time-consuming process from 300 hours to a mere five minutes in the foreseeable future.

SECURITY DEVICES

The production of holograms requires expensive, specialized, and technologically advanced equipment, so they are considered a good security device. Holograms cannot be easily replicated by color copiers, scanners, or standard printing techniques since they are governed by light diffraction as opposed to light

reflection. Visa and MasterCard have used holograms for more than a decade. They are also used on passports in several European countries and on some government bonds and certificates in the United States. The market for optically variable devices, such as those used on credit cards, is anticipated to be expanding by 30 to 40 percent a year. The sector is highly fragmented, with over 350 producers worldwide.

Microsoft adopted an anticounterfeiting label, the 3M Authentication Label, which first appeared on MS-DOS 6.0 packages in 1993. In 1996 the holographic seal on Microsoft's MS-DOS and Windows software helped break up a $4.7 million counterfeit operation, the largest ever in the United States. The Windows 2000 software contained a full-surface, holographic security image generated by Applied Optical Technologies.

U.S. military applications included the development by the U.S. Department of Energy's Pacific Northwest Regional Lab in Richland, Washington, of a holographic 3-D radar camera. The device can record images of fighter planes before and after repair work to verify that radar- absorbing material that coats stealth bombers (to help them remain stealthy) has not been damaged, thus jeopardizing their security.

DATA STORAGE

Holographic storage developments reached a watershed by 2000. Holographic data storage surpasses magnetic storage technology because of its ultrahigh storage density, rapid data transfer, short data access times, and exceptional reliability. In 1995, to develop the holographic storage technology, the U.S. Department of Defense funded half of a $64 million joint industry, academic, and government venture that consisted of two branches. The Holographic Data Storage System Consortium, with participants including IBM, Rockwell, and Stanford University, was to investigate hardware development for a commercially viable storage system in which (ideally) a gigabyte of data would fit on a pencil eraser and could be retrieved at 1 billion bits per second. The Photorefractive Information Storage Materials project worked on materials research.

MEDICAL FIELD

In 1998 Voxel announced that it had filed a voluntary Chapter 11 petition in response to a 5 May arbitration ruling that ordered Voxel to pay $1.9 million to General Scanning, Inc. (GSI). The two companies entered into a contract in 1994 in which GSI was to engineer and manufacture the Voxcam imager, equipment used to produce film-based, hard-copy images of the internal structure of the body. Voxel claimed that GSI had breached its obligation under the contract. Voxel converted to Chapter 7 bankruptcy on 8 August 1998 and agreed to continue development of the Voxcam imager, pending acquisition by hologram technology giant, Holographic Dimensions, Inc.

The Voxcam is part of a system designed to interface with existing medical scanners to produce 3-D X rays, and consists of a camera to convert computerized axial tomography or simply computerized tomography (CT) and magnetic resonance scans into holograms that provides an accurate interactive "road map" for physicians prior to surgery. The system converts complicated conventional CT or X rays, which normally require a radiologist's interpretation, into a virtual model that is readily understandable by any physician. The hologram enables the physician to interact in, around, and through the image as if it were a real specimen. It allows doctors to peer inside blood vessels and assists in treating brain tumors, carotid arteries, and pelvic surgery since the viewer moves around within the image.

BACKGROUND AND DEVELOPMENT

A theoretical procedure for holography (which comes from the Greek *holo,* meaning "whole," and *gram,* meaning "recording") was originally conceived by Dennis Gabor in 1948 as a means of improving the resolution of electron microscopes. Where conventional photography captures only the amplitude or brightness of reflected light, a hologram also records the interference of light waves between a single coherent light split into two beams of light waves that converge on a recording plate or film. The reference beam travels directly to the recording medium and the other beam is reflected off the object. The recorded intersection of straight unreflected light waves and the light waves reflected from an object allow a hologram to reproduce a virtual image that includes parallax (an apparent change in perspective or viewpoint that occurs with different angles of viewing).

The invention was ignored for several decades except for attempts by Albert Baez and Hussein El-Sum at Stanford University to use X rays to make holograms in the 1950s. Interest in holography ebbed because of the lack of a coherent light source of consistent, unvarying wavelengths with the equal crests and troughs essential to the success of the process. In the 1960s, Emmett Leith and Juris Upatnieks at the

University of Michigan produced several holograms by combining Gabor's principles with Theodore Harold Maiman's laser. But it was not until 1991 that physicists were able to use electron holography to reconstruct a crystal's structure, fulfilling Gabor's original goal.

In 1994 Lambertus Hesselink, John Heanue, and Matthew Bashaw developed the first holographic storage system to store digital data. Initially, commercialization was expected to take three to five years, but that outcome has yet to be achieved. The combination of the storage of millions of data bits per page, fast retrieval rates, and rapid random access make this a highly practical storage method.

Sources for holograms include light waves, X rays, electron beams, and microwaves. Waves other than light waves have successfully used holographic principles in an increasing variety of applications. In 1994 a new holographic system for displaying 3-D images of internal anatomy was developed. Microwaves that penetrate a variety of media have been used to detect unseen flaws in layered metal parts. X-ray technology, using the same principles, allowed 3-D imaging of live organisms. A new family of organic materials such as peptide oligomers appears promising in offering erasable holographic storage. Energy X-ray holography, which was developed by Charles Fadley and Dietlef Bahr, relied on fluorescent atoms as detectors rather than sources to look at the structure of minute materials to make the first hologram of an atom in a solid.

Engineering applications of holography include stress analysis, checking for cracks or voids in layered or composite surfaces such as aircraft fuselages or wings, and vibration analysis. Acoustic holography is applied to geophysical and underwater explorations. Microwave holography can also provide detailed surface maps. A heterodyne Mach-Zehnder interferometer was first built by students to show the feasibility of detecting sound waves in a small cell.

Other applications include a digital scale, developed by Sony Magnescale, Inc. in 1995, which can measure plus or minus .0086 micrometers by monitoring and measuring the phase change of a laser beam as it passes through a hologram grating. IBM Corp. introduced its 3687 holographic supermarket checkout station that could read universal-product-code information on standard and irregularly shaped articles in 1982. HoloScan introduced its first holographic barcode scanner in 1994.

Scientists are now examining the possibility of using holograms to display 3-D images, creating true

VIRTUALLY
YOURS

The hot holographic trend of the late 1990s was the custom-tailored hologram. With production costs and time requirements dropping significantly, more companies turned to 3-D to enhance the advertising and packaging of their products. The shimmering, fluid effects created by holographic additions lend eye-catching appeal to containers and also help create lingering impressions on consumers as they wander through increasingly crowded store aisles or flip through ad-laden magazines.

Developments such as direct-to-plate holographic technology introduced by International Holographic Paper Co. of Glenside, Pennsylvania, reduced the time required to generate holographic masters from weeks to only a matter of hours. From the mid-1990s to 2000, the total cost for custom-designing a hologram plunged from $20,000 to $1,000—and as prices decreased, the size of holograms increased.

Customers have a menu of options to choose from when ordering their custom holograms. Registered multicolor printing can be incorporated with images, or wallpaper-style patterns can be used as an underlay for printed graphics, so that the hologram emerges from portions of the packaging. Colgate Total toothpaste's carton is emblazoned with such an arrangement. Even Colgate's toothbrushes come encased in hologram-enlivened clamshell packages.

The sparkle and festivity of the holiday season seemed an especially appropriate time for a little extra packaging glitter, especially in the beverage industry. Stolichnaya Vodka unwrapped a noteworthy custom-hologram package for its 1998 Christmas gift-packaging that combined rotogravure-printed graphics and a customized holiday design on its cartons. The move proved successful enough that Stoli repeated the tactic the following year. Likewise, Zima Co., a division of Coors, promoted its beverages in a hologram-decorated bottle carrier for the 1998 holiday season.

3-D television and movies. In fact, Gabor himself began such research late in his life. The fruits of these efforts can be found in the appearance of holographic goggles and even a hologram-simulation video game.

PIONEERS IN THE FIELD

Dennis Gabor studied in Berlin, earning his doctorate in engineering in 1927. After World War II, Gabor turned his attention to the electron microscope. His earlier attempts to develop the instrument had failed and he was determined to make a comeback in the field. His goal was to be able to "see" individual atoms by taking an electron picture. In initial attempts the image was distorted by problems with the lens. Gabor theorized that this could be corrected by optical means using light. He published his theory in scientific papers in 1947, in which he first coined the term *hologram*. Its implications for beams of light, however, awaited only the invention of the laser.

The invention of the laser in 1960 sparked renewed interest in holography, since a constant narrow light source where all waves were in phase was now available to experimenters. The first laser hologram in 1962 ensured Gabor's reputation. In 1967 he retired from the Imperial College of Science and Technology, where he had worked since 1949, but continued his research. He was able to show the application of holography to computer data processing, where it has been particularly useful in data compression. He received his highest honor in December 1971, when he was awarded the Nobel Prize in physics for his work in holography. His Nobel lecture concerned the issues that dominated his later years—the role of science and technology in society.

After Gabor was awarded the Nobel Prize, Lawrence Bartell of the University of Michigan set out to develop a holographic electron microscope. He shared his work with Gabor in 1974, and Gabor immediately began designing his own holographic electron microscope. In the summer of that year, however, Gabor suffered a stroke that left him unable to read or write. Despite this he was able to maintain contact with his colleagues. He even visited the Museum of Holography in New York City when it opened in 1977. He died in a London nursing home in February 1979.

CURRENT CONDITIONS

By the late 1990s, Business Communications Co. valued the global holography industry at $2.8 billion. An accurate total value, however, is difficult to ascertain, because once a holographic application becomes successful it is usually absorbed by another segment, such as printing or X ray.

In 2000, several Holographic Data Storage System (HDDS) Consortium partners proclaimed they were pursuing technical developments that would speed holographic storage to market. The IBM Almaden Research Center, Rockwell Science Center, and Jet Propulsion Labs were developing optical associative memories that combined holographic storage capacities with optical correlation, which permits the retrieval of data by association performed in parallel for a speedy perusal of large volumes of information. It would also enable complex queries involving multiple variables. Any holdups in debuting the system were credited to insufficiencies in available storage media.

Imation, meanwhile, was designing modestly priced, read-only holodiscs, which could store the equivalent of six digital video discs' worth of data. They faced competition from German Bayer, which expected to introduce a similar product by 2004. Imation hoped to beat Bayer to market by two years.

INDUSTRY LEADERS

Holographic Dimensions, Inc., a vertically integrated manufacturer of holographic imagery, produces a variety of security devices for credit cards, negotiable documents, event tickets, and transit passes. It claims to have delivered more than 2 billion units throughout the Northern Hemisphere, including to companies such as Merck Pharmaceutical and General Electric. Its holograms are used on transit passes in Eastern Europe to authenticate bank checks for Citibank. Holographic Dimensions also produces the online *Holography Digest: Featuring People, Companies, Technology & News of the Holographic Industry,* which is available on its Web site. In 1999, the company announced that it purchased exclusive rights to direct digital holographic printer technology, which reputedly doubles the dot matrix image resolution from previous generations of holographic printers. Printer-write speeds will increase by a minimum factor of five in the first iteration, and will increase by a factor of 1,000 in future iterations. The firm completed the printer prototype development phase in March 1999 and began commercial production of the printer, which is marketed to the packaging industry.

Holographics North, Inc. produces some of the world's largest holograms and claims to be the only U.S. company capable of producing large format (42 by 72 inch), color, high- resolution holograms. They are generally used in trade shows, museums, space

centers, and educational centers. The firm also creates animated stereographs, which include computer graphics, reduced or enlarged images, and on-site recordings. Their work is custom-produced. The company is located in Burlington, Vermont.

Applied Optical Technologies is a U.K.-based company that was created when Applied Holographics acquired the American companies Optical Security Group and Bridgestone. Optical Security specialized in security laminates and it counted the U.S. National Football League and several state driver's license issuers among its customers. The company's customer strongholds were based in Europe and the Far East. Applied Optical Technologies projected annual sales of $42 million, which would place it at the front of its industry sector.

An international presence in the manufacture of holographic packaging materials was CFC Holographics, a separate division of the U.S. chemical-coating producer CFC International. Like Applied Optical Technologies, CFC's holographic offerings cut across several industry sectors, though they center primarily in the high-security and premium-packaging arenas. The packaging group had production centers in Chicago Heights, Illinois, and Oeser, Germany, and the company has designed materials for such industry heavyweights as Colgate-Palmolive Co. and Glaxo SmithKline.

New York-based American Bank Note Holographics (ABNH), a spin-off of American Bank Note, specialized in holographic images for security and promotional applications. The firm hit rough waters in 1999 when it admitted that it had to restate earnings for half of 1998 due to "financial misstatements." Both ABNH and its parent company had delayed filings with the Securities and Exchange Commission, for which they are under investigation. Approximately 20 class-action suits were also pending against the two companies. At the time of its initial public offering, ABNH boasted a 75 percent share of revenues in the credit-card hologram market. Among its customers are MasterCard, Europay, Discover Financial Services, and Citicorp Diners' Club. Despite its troubles, the company achieved revenues of $21.2 million in 1999.

Zebra Imaging is an Austin, Texas-based company that devises large-format, full-color holograms. For its first commission it created Ford's virtual P2000 for the Detroit Auto Show. In 1999 Ford acquired an equity interest in the firm, whose customers also include the Walt Disney Co., DuPont, Starbucks, and Warner-Lambert.

Taiwan's K Laser Technology Corp., established in 1988, was the world's third- largest producer of holographic products by 1998. In 2000 it added a new optical instruments department and would begin production of liquid crystal display projectors in 2001. About 90 percent of its 1999 revenue derived from laser products and the remainder from optical products. It hoped to achieve income parity, however, between the two branches by 2005. K Laser reported an annual growth of 50 percent, 20 percent more than industry growth overall. It also targeted mainland China as an emerging market and had set up a production plant in Shanghai in 1994.

Nimbus CD International, part of Carlton Communications PLC's Technicolor unit, was one of the first companies to digitally record music on CDs. In conjunction with Applied Holographics PLC, Nimbus developed a 3-D I*d antipiracy hologram, which functions without any loss of digital information, disc capacity, or playback quality. Based in Charlottesville, Virginia, Nimbus distributes optical discs throughout North America, the United Kingdom, and Europe. In May 1998 Nimbus initiated a $22 million upgrade to expand its capacity for the production of digital video disc and Divx, at the time the newest digital disk formats. When finished, the company will be able to produce 28 million discs a year.

WORK FORCE

Due to the diversity of applications, unique niche products, and the private nature of many of the companies, it is difficult to estimate the total size of the work force in the holography industry with any degree of accuracy. Like all new and emerging industries, however, holography will likely create jobs that do not exist today. The growth of affiliated medical and computer fields is well documented. Trends for employment in areas associated with holography products in medicine, manufacturing, research, and advertising appear to be strong and growing. The skill level and compensation ranges from that of engineers, physicists, and optical scientists in research and development with salaries varying from $45,000 to $75,000 to machine operators at $15 to $17 per hour to minimum wage clerks in holography stores.

AMERICA AND THE WORLD

The *Holography Marketplace* lists more than 700 businesses connected with holography in more than

30 countries: 350 U.S. firms, 70 German firms, 68 in the United Kingdom, 43 in Japan, and 25 in Canada. Several U.S.-U.K. partnerships have developed to market holographic products.

In 1999 researchers led by P. S. Ramanujam at Denmark's Riso National Lab reported the development of instant holography, which reduces production time of holograms from several minutes to 5-billionths of one second. A single five-nanosceond pulse of blue-green laser records the image on the surface of a photosensitive azobenzene polymer film without the need for chemical processing. Heating the film to 80 degrees Celsius erases the surface for reuse.

Opstostor, a German company, was devising a read-only memory system for holographic archives. The technique centers on a 50mm x 50mm x 4mm photorefractive crystal on which the images are embedded through heating. The company expected to bring the technology, which could be compatible with personal computers, within two years.

Hologram-projecting home televisions formed the focus of several research agendas. The Dutch electronics firm Philips Electronics N.V. and Korea's Samsung Electronics each were bringing to market holographic televisions that don't require viewers to wear the special glasses to perceive 3-D images. Early consumers of the flat-screen TVs were expected to be medical educators and security firms.

RESEARCH AND TECHNOLOGY

Breakthroughs were being reported in many sectors of the holographic industry by 2000. North American Products Corp. announced it had designed a holographic cloning amplifier technology (HCAT) to reconstructs sounds, distortion-free, in acoustic holograms. The technology creates a "virtual map" of the physical locations from which sounds were generated during recording, which are embedded deep in audio signals. With HCAT, sounds seem to the listener to come out of the surrounding air, rather than being projected from speakers. HCAT has promising applications in 3-D movies, videos, and high- definition television (HDTV) in theme parks, movies, military simulations for training exercises, and home-entertainment systems.

In 1999 JVC announced the first commercial application of photopolymer-based holographic materials, developed by DuPont, in a display of color filters for HDTV projection. The process uses the materials in a hologram color filter for direct-derived image light amplifier in liquid crystal display (LCD) projection TV. The holographic optical elements involved don't record images; instead they move light around by turning or directing it. This enables brighter and more efficient displays. The technology could also be adapted for lightweight reflective and transmission color filters for laptop computers.

Researchers at the Massachusetts Institute of Technology (MIT) developed a working prototype of a holographic videoconferencing system. This sci-fi staple, which was at least a decade away from commercial in-home use in 2000, according to the head of MIT's Spatial Imaging Group Stephen Benton, uses holographic data storage and fiber optics to create real-time, three-dimensional, computer-generated holograms. Having mastered the reduction of information and image scanning, the next trick for scientists is to take the compressed digital signals and scale them up to a practical size. Researchers expect to tackle this problem with micro electro mechanical systems (MEMS), or micromachines, which combine sensors, actuators, electronics, and mechanical components on a tiny silicon substrate. (Also see the essay in this book entitled Micromachines/Nanotechnology.)

New holographic probe technology to take non-contact measurements of 3-D cross sections from any angle of complex objects and parts that contain many blind spots and holes was under development by Optimet. The Conoscan 3000 used a laser probe technology, called conoscopic holography, to produce finely detailed analysis of angles, radii, and the distance between points on objects made of most opaque materials even under low-light conditions. A laser beam is shot into a blind hole and bounced off a mirror to gauge the piece's internal angles. Measurement precision equals more than 1/8,000 of the working range. The technology would benefit quality- control operations for clients such as the auto industry, which must inspect engine blocks, and the plastics industry.

Even predicting the weather on the far side of the solar surface emerged as a holographic application. Physicists Charles Lindsay of Solar Physics Research Corp. and Douglas Brown of Northwest Research Associates, Inc. announced in 2000 that they had devised a means using seismic holography to track the path of sound waves as they travel through the inside of the Sun. Though under normal conditions sound waves make the interior journey in about three and one- half hours, when they bump into areas of high magnetic activity, their path is distorted and they advance about six seconds out of synch with the undisturbed waves. Following the wave paths permits space weather fore-

casters to predict the emergence of solar storms that are brewing on the far side of the Sun, which is hidden from normal viewing, about one week before they would appear. Though the researchers proposed the forecasting technique a decade earlier, it was only with the construction of the Michelson Doppler Imager at the Solar and Heleospheric Observatory that a sophisticated enough device was available to register the recordings. Routine tracking is not yet possible, but is anticipated to be so by 2006. Knowing the solar weather report in advance would help earthlings prepare for the damage solar storms can inflict on power grids, telecommunications systems, and space-station workers.

An unlikely pair of inventors—two London sculptors working in a deconsecrated church- turned-studio and bar—developed a highly effective auto-stereoscopic, holographic display device that can produce a remarkably impressive image for little more than $5 over the costs of a conventional LCD. Working on a virtually nonexistent budget, artists Edwina Orr and David Trayner developed the technology to create their holographic art at their studio 291—which they so christened for both the former-church's address and in homage to pioneering photographer Alfred Stieglitz's pathbreaking gallery at 291 Fifth Avenue in New York. They also founded a company, Reality Vision Ltd., and intended to market a scaled-up version of their device that was produced using an LCD module from IBM. One of the device's greatest strengths was its compatibility with ordinary two-dimensional viewing. Adding the modestly priced holographic optics to a conventional LCD module permits the user to turn it off for normal viewing, then switch it on for use in computer-aided design, medical imaging, or computer games applications.

Atomic holography, which was first demonstrated in 1997 at the Massachusetts Institute of Technology, was taken a step further in 1999 when researchers at the NEC Fundamental Research Lab, in conjunction with the University of Tokyo, directly imprinted complex material patterns onto a substrate using holographic gratings. According to Jabez McClelland of the Electron Physics Group at the National Institute of Standards and Technology (NIST), atomic holography could create a new means for controlling atomic motion, shaping a beam of atoms into a complex image. With further refinements, the technique could permit the creation of circuits over large areas that are deposited in a single step.

It may soon be possible to create holograms of objects that never existed in reality. A new high-performance computing holography (HPCHolo) algorithm was developed by Hesham Eldeib and reported in May 1999 in *Computer Modeling & Simulation in Engineering*. HPCHolo, when implemented on parallel processing hardware, greatly decreased the computation time required for hologram generation and resulted in much-improved virtual image quality. The algorithm was intended to facilitate the generation in real time of 3-D virtual images—holograms of objects that never existed in reality.

One example of a successful NIST-funded program the emergence of Accuwave. The fiber-optics telecommunications firm received funds to pursue research on an innovative holographic system that would allow several communications channels to simultaneously share the same optical fiber. The company is now selling three spin-off products developed with their own funds in the United States, Japan, and Europe. It is also developing a wavelength multiplexing system based on the core results of the Advanced Technology Program project funds it received from NIST in 1992. The projected market for multiwavelength multiplexing capable of transmitting holograms was expected to grow from $50 million in 1997 to $2 billion by the end of 2000.

Pacific Northwest Laboratories developed a handheld scanner capable of producing high- quality holographic images. Potential uses include detecting radar reflective leaks in stealth aircraft, augmenting airport security, and checking cross sections of aircraft components.

FURTHER READING

"Acoustic Holograms." *Poptronics,* March 2000.

Andreeva, Nellie. "Saturday Night at the Holograms?" *Business Week,* 28 June 1999.

Bains, Sunny. "Holographic Data Storage Merges with Optical Correlation—Emerging Optical Technologies Fight Bottlenecks." *Electronic Engineering Times,* 15 May 2000.

Bains, Sunny, and Chappell Brown. "NEC-University Team Achieves Atomic Holography." *Electronic Engineering Times,* 3 April 2000.

Bertrand, Kate. "Custom Holograms—High-Tech, High-Glamour, Lower Cost." *Brand Packaging,* September 1999.

Boztas, Senay, and Jonathan Leake. "TV Leaps from Box in 3D-Vision." *London Sunday Times,* 27 February 2000.

Clarke, Peter. "Sculptors' Holography Rolls 3-D LCD." *Electronic Engineering Times,* 22 February 1999.

Cowen, Ron. "Spacecraft Sounds out the Sun's Hidden Self." *Science News,* 18 March 2000.

Dye, Lee. "Instant Holographic Images Make 3-D Movies a Possibility." *Los Angeles Times,* 21 June 1999.

Eldeib, Hesham. "A High-Performance Computing Algorithm for Improving In-Line Holography." *Computer Modeling & Simulation,* May 1999.

Forster, Barbara. "Virtually There." *Computerworld,* 2 October 2000.

Fox, Barry. "Plumbing the Depths." *New Scientist,* 15 April 2000.

Fruscione, Ela. "How'd They Convert That?" *Converting Magazine,* February 2000.

"Has Holography Died Aborning?" *Technology Review,* January/February 2000.

Hellemans, Alexander. "Holograms Can Store Terabytes, but Where?" *Science,* 19 November 1999.

———. "Supersmall Structure Created by Holography." *Science Now,* 3 March 2000.

"Holographic Deal Brings a New Global Leader." *Label & Narrow Web Industry,* January 2000.

Irion, Robert. "Solar Physics on the Far Side." *Science Now,* 9 March 2000.

"K Laser Technology Corp. Excels in Holography Technology." *Central News Agency,* 6 May 2000.

"Laser-Based System Gives a 3-D Look to Nooks and Crannies." *Quality,* April 2000.

Lindsey C., and D. C. Braun. "Seismic Images of the Far Side of the Sun." *Science,* 10 March 2000.

Mahoney, Diana Phillips. "Ford Drives Holography Development." *Computer Graphics World,* February 1999.

Murphy, Patricia. "The Mess at Holographics." *Credit Card Management,* June 1999.

Nicholson, Leslie. "Data Crunch." *Houston Chronicle,* 1 October 1999.

Pidgeon, Ron. "Holography: The Race Is On." *Packaging Magazine,* 9 March 2000.

"Pump up the Volume." *Economist,* 31 July 1999.

Quan, Margaret. "Final Exams Loom for Holographic Memories." *Electronic Engineering Times,* 6 September 1999.

Schewe, Phillip. "Physics Update." *Physics Today,* July 1999.

"Science and Technology: A Trip Down Memory Lane." *The Economist,* 17 June 2000.

Stein, Nicholas. "Office Fantasies of the Future." *Fortune,* 6 March 2000.

Tighe, Chris. "Expanded and Keen to Make Its Mark." *Financial Times* (London), 24 February 2000.

Toupin, Laurie Ann. "Holographic Radar Keeps Fighter Planes Stealthy." *Design News,* 21 June 1999.

Vasilash, Gary S. "Forward to Holography. . .and Back to Clay." *Automotive Manufacturing & Production,* August 1999.

Yoshida, Junko. "Projection TV Casts Light on Holograms' Potential." *Engineering Times,* 13 September 1999.

Wu, Corinna. "Peptide Packs in Holographic Data." *Science News,* 22 May 1999.

HOME HEALTH-CARE SERVICES

INDUSTRY SNAPSHOT

Health-care organizations recognized a number of advantages in offering home health-care services. First and foremost, such services offered significant cost savings compared with similar services conducted inside hospitals. Patients, moreover, tend to prefer to receive treatment in the comfort of their own homes rather than in a hospital or nursing home, provided adequate and appropriate care is maintained. Thus, the home health-care services industry grew dramatically in the 1990s.

Home health care, however, faced a grim reality in the late 1990s, as a number of setbacks rocked the industry and caused its players to seriously rethink their home-oriented operations. A number of players simply abandoned the practice altogether, while others were forced to streamline services or focus on a niche that fit comfortably with the organizations' existing specialties. Increasingly, companies devoted only the resources necessary to cure a specific medical problem. Patients must show progress toward goals or their home health services may be withdrawn. An agency thus had to focus on successfully completing a treatment within a prescribed number of visits.

Home health-care services were devastated by the implementation of the Balanced Budget Act in 1997, which included a measures to slash Medicare and Medicaid reimbursements to home health-care providers. In part this was seen as an effort to reduce the levels of fraud—a charge leveled frequently at the industry—and in part the move was emblematic of Congressional leaders' calls for reduced government spending. But no matter what the intentions, the effect on the industry was clear. More than 1,000 agen-

cies closed their doors between January and August of 1999 alone, according to the National Association for Home Care. Home health-care officials screamed about the spending caps, claiming that they unfairly punished efficient and honest health-care providers for the wasteful or dishonest practices of a few agencies. While some alterations and relief packages were in the works, the industry stood at a crossroads at the start of the 21st century.

Still, the demographic realities ensured that home health-care services would likely remain popular well into the century. At the end of 1999, over 6.25 million of the nation's elderly received home health care, up from only 4.6 million just 20 years earlier. As the population continues to age, the demand will only grow. According to the Health Care Financing Administration, home health care amounted to 9 percent, or $10 billion, of all Medicare benefit payments at the end of 1999, up from only 3 percent in 1990. Total spending for home health-care services exhibited similar expansion, approaching $20 billion by 2000 from only $4.7 billion in 1997.

ORGANIZATION AND STRUCTURE

Home health-care service is generally administered by a nurse or aide, and can include part-time or intermittent skilled care, physical therapy, the administration of medicine, rehabilitation, durable medical equipment and supplies, home health-aide services, family and patient education, and other services. Supported by technology, home care is considerably less expensive than institutionalized or hospital care. Home care agencies providing health-care services fall into three main categories: private or proprietary, hospitals, and public or not-for-profit. Services are differentiated by the type and level of activity, such as home health aides, nursing care, and physical therapy. The home health-care services industry is structured along the lines of prevention, diagnosis, infusion therapy, skilled and unskilled care, and durable medical equipment. The three largest of these segments are infusion therapy, skilled care, and durable equipment. Infusion therapy consists of intravenous products and services such as antibiotics and immunoglobulins. Skilled care includes nurses, home health aides, and therapists, all under the direction of a physician. Durable medical equipment includes ventilators, respirators, and wheelchairs.

If a person is homebound and requires skilled care, Medicare pays for medically necessary home health care, including part-time or intermittent nursing care; physical, speech, and occupational therapy; medical social services; and equipment and supplies. For terminally ill patients, Medicare will pay for care provided by a Medicare certified hospice, where specialized care includes pain relief, symptom management, and supportive services in lieu of curative services.

To qualify for Medicare home health care, a patient's doctor must determine medical care is needed in the home; care must be intermittent; and the patient must be homebound, except for infrequent trips of short duration. Skilled nursing for wound care or injections; home health aides for personal care and physical assistance; physical, speech, and occupational therapy; and medical social services, supplies, and equipment are all included. A maximum of 28 hours

per week, including a mix between all of the various providers, is allowed to qualify as part-time care.

The Joint Commission on Accreditation of Healthcare Organizations serves as the accrediting body for home care agencies. Participation is voluntary, but agencies must still meet accepted industry standards. State and local governments also serve to regulate the industry.

Nearly every segment of home health-care services is determined heavily by public policies and funding, and there is a growing need to reconcile the aging population with the call for reduced government expenditures. Some states are now imposing bans on new nursing home construction, which should channel more patients to home care.

BACKGROUND AND DEVELOPMENT

Beginning in 1965, the federal government funded Medicare for home health-care services, structured primarily to cover short-term services following hospital discharge. Since this home health coverage allowed health-care organizations to shift some of the fixed hospital overhead to cost-based services, home health-care services sprouted up in droves in the 1970s and 1980s. By 1994 it was the fastest-growing segment of health care, and the second-fastest growing segment of the economy at large. Contributing to this growth were new advances in medical devices and high technology that made home care a viable alternative to institutional care. For example, respiratory patients who previously would have been hospitalized or nursing homebound were able to conduct normal working and living activities with the aid of portable oxygen systems. In addition, cancer patients, who were once confined to hospitals, could live at home and even return to work.

The industry's fortunes changed suddenly in 1997 as Medicare, mandated by the Balanced Budget Act, began implementing massive cuts in reimbursements to home health-care companies. The federal agency planned to decrease home care spending by $16 billion over five years. Between 1989 and 1996 the number of beneficiaries receiving home health care and the number of visits per user more than doubled. In an effort to hold down costs, Medicare changed its payment system. Before October 1997, the agency reimbursed home care companies on a visit-by-visit basis with no limitations. The new system paid on an average cost basis. Depending on the service, payment reductions to home care agencies ranged from 15 to

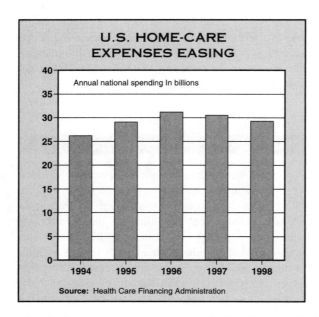

U.S. HOME-CARE EXPENSES EASING

Annual national spending In billions

Source: Health Care Financing Administration

50 percent. The decreased payments devastated home health agencies, leaving the industry in a state of crisis. Critics argued that that method didn't adequately cover chronically ill patient care.

Home health-care appeals to insurance companies. The Medicare cuts of 1997 created a market for supplemental home health-care benefits in addition to, or coordinated with, long-term care benefits. When the baby-boom generation reached 50 years old they began taking care of their parents; therefore they were aware of the need for insurance to cover some of the cost. Few in that generation wished to move into nursing homes as they aged. They wanted to stay in their own homes as long as they could and use home care policies. Insurance companies moved into this niche market. Bankers Life and Casualty, along with long-term-care insurance companies, pursued the home health-care segment of the market.

CURRENT CONDITIONS

The Health Care Financing Administration (HCFA) noted that, while the number of home health-care providers receiving Medicare benefits jumped from 5,656 in 1990 to 10,500 in 1997, a significant proportion of that increase was attributed to wasteful practices and fraud, a factor that contributed heavily to the implementation of the Balanced Budget Act. In addition to the new Medicare fee restructuring, therefore, the HCFA took several steps to reduce Medicare and Medicaid fraud. In response to the increasing home health-care share of Medicare expenditures, the HCFA worked to cut costs, implementing rulings establishing salary equivalency guidelines for physical, occupational, respiratory, and speech therapists providing home health services. These rulings were projected to save Medicare $1.7 billion from 1997 to 2001. The HCFA also proposed revisions to regulations that would require Medicare home health providers to conduct criminal background checks on home health aides.

Meanwhile, legislative help was on the way in the form of the Medicare Balanced Budget Refinement Act, which was signed into law in late 1999. Both houses of Congress and the White House even reached a tentative agreement in advance of the bill to pass reform legislation. The act restored about $1.3 billion in federal funding to home health-care agencies. In addition, the further 15 percent Medicare payment reduction was delayed another year, scheduled to be enacted in October 2001.

HCFA is also shifting from open-ended reimbursement for home care agencies based on numbers—rather than the nature of the service—to a prospective payment system (PPS). The PPS plan sets regional limits on reimbursement rates based on the cost history of providers in a given area. Thus, for more severe cases, the agency receives greater set amounts for administration of care services to that patient. In this way, agencies have a precise idea of their incoming funding and can schedule costs accordingly, although it was not yet determined exactly how much money would be offered up-front.

Under the PPS system, companies can no longer count on their home health programs to produce revenues, and as a result, the industry was likely to see a large-scale shakeout. Those companies opting to remain in the game can still use home health care as a way of reducing overall costs, and such services can still contribute to health-care profitability provided the services are effectively integrated into the organizations' cost-based hospital departments.

Moreover, if health-care organizations do opt to get rid of their home health-care operations, those patients will have severely restricted options. Most local home health operations shy away from patients requiring higher cost and longer-term care, and as a result many such patients may simply wind up in long-term care inside the organizations' hospitals, which would severely boost the organizations' costs and would defeat the purpose of divestiture.

The new PPS was implemented nationwide in October of 2000. Until then, agencies were reimbursed

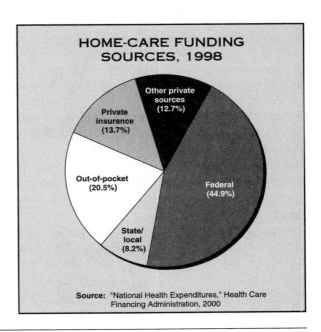

HOME-CARE FUNDING SOURCES, 1998

Other private sources (12.7%)
Private insurance (13.7%)
Out-of-pocket (20.5%)
Federal (44.9%)
State/local (8.2%)

Source: "National Health Expenditures," Health Care Financing Administration, 2000

on the interim payment system (IPS), which is a flat sum per patient and involves a yearly per-patient cap. One problem with the IPS is that payment is not adjusted by the severity of the illness. If the cost of care goes over the cap, the agency loses money. If the cost is under the cap, however, the agency does not get the difference. A number of analysts contend that the IPS policy was the primary reason many home health-care agencies have failed. While the PPS system was expected to force companies to make difficult decisions, it was largely seen as an improvement over IPS, precisely because companies will have a more specific idea of the kind of funding they can expect against a detailed indication of what kinds of costs they can expect to accrue.

Health-care companies will be able to keep their home health-care operations afloat if they streamline their structures, institute innovative programs, and in some cases, merge with other agencies to create larger, more effective units. Clinical programs must be adapted to serve the patients who have the greatest needs for their services and deal with the most prevalent diseases in the areas they serve.

Innovative programs are seeking to improve quality while maintaining costs. One program ensures early dismissal of new mothers from the hospital by sending a registered pediatric nurse to the home to check on both the mother's and child's progress soon after they are discharged. Another innovative program has a specialist on phone duty 24-hours-a-day to talk with congestive heart failure patients, which sometimes solves the problem without a nurse's visit or hospital admission. Lastly, a study by researchers at Rush University in Chicago involved two groups of older patients: one group watched a series of eight two-hour videos and another group attended eight two-hour classes. The classes covered meditation and relaxation training, anxiety and depression management skills, and nutrition and exercise counseling. The patients using the videos received follow-up phone calls to check their progress. A third group received neither. Results of the study, which appeared in *JAMA, The Journal of the American Medical Association*, proved that videotapes with phone follow-up worked as well as live presentations.

LEGAL WOES

The home health-care industry was rocked by a series of lawsuits and scandals in the late 1990s, and the industry was trying diligently to dust itself off for the new decade. But the damage to the industry's reputation, and to the leading players, was likely to be felt for some time.

Coram Healthcare was embroiled in a bitter legal battle with Aetna U.S. Healthcare. In the meantime, Coram plowed through three chief executive officers in less than one year, and also lost its chief financial officer and chairman, laid off over 100 employees, and tried to stay afloat amidst plummeting stock valuations. The dispute originated in 1998, when the two firms reached a contract whereby Coram was to provide home health care to Aetna members. Coram charged Aetna with withholding proper reimbursement for Coram's services, which the company contended were provided to 2 million Aetna members at a utilization rate far greater than that which Aetna recognized. For its part, Aetna countersued Coram, claiming that Coram had no intention of fulfilling its contractual obligations. The contract was terminated in June 1999. The charges of fraud and negligent misrepresentation against Aetna were dismissed five months later, though the companies' respective breach-of-contract suits against the other were still raging on until June 2000, when the companies finally settled on undisclosed terms.

Moreover, Coram's R-Net subsidiaries, which manage contract providers for managed care organizations, filed for bankruptcy protection, an action that also contributed to Coram's legal imbroglio, according to *HomeCare Magazine*. A number of the subsidiaries' providers, including industry leader Apria Healthcare Group, filed an involuntary bankruptcy petition against R-Net to force payment for services rendered. Coram held that it couldn't withstand the losses from such payments until its legal battle with Aetna was resolved. The subsidiaries eventually folded.

Apria itself met with trouble at the U.S. Attorney's office in Sacramento, California, stemming from suspicions regarding Apria's Medicare and Medicaid billing practices, though the government closed the case without taking action in summer 1999.

Columbia/HCA (also know as HCA-The Healthcare Co.) faced perhaps even more serious difficulties in the late 1990s. In 1997, federal officers raided the company's hospital facilities in El Paso, Texas, seizing billing records and other documents on suspicion of fraudulent billing practices, including for home health-care services. In the wake of this drama, the company was completely remade, highlighted by a boardroom coup that did away with the chairman and other chief company officers. The federal suit was settled in May 2000, when Columbia/HCA agreed to pay $745 million to the U.S. government, but in the meantime, the company was forced to restructure entirely, selling off its home health-care business.

EMERGING NICHE MARKETS

Behavioral home care began to emerge in the late 1990s and was expected to come into its own as a powerful market niche at the start of the 21st century. Behavioral or mental health home care is a short-term rehabilitation service for recently discharged psychiatric patients. In the critical weeks following hospital discharge, behavioral home care was designed to ensure that patients received their medication on schedule, thereby preventing relapse or complications. Moreover, the practice facilitates a smoother readjustment to daily life and generates significant cost savings to the health-care organization by reducing the necessity for rehospitalization and emergency-room visits. Since the average stay in psychiatric hospitals has been reduced from 23 to 6 days or less, the need for close follow-up care has become increasingly obvious. According to the Treatment Advocacy Center in Arlington, Virginia, at least 1,000 people are murdered each year by mentally ill individuals who went off their medication.

INDUSTRY LEADERS

American HomePatient, Inc. headquartered in Brentwood, Tennessee, reported sales of $357.6 million in 1999, down from $403.9 million the year before, and a net loss for the year of $99 million. Reeling from the Balanced Budget Act, the company froze its acquisitions schedule and trimmed its staff. American HomePatient had 3,600 employees and maintained 350 branches in 40 states. It increased its vertical integration and geographic expansion through the acquisition of a specialty retail pharmacy and four home health service firms.

The Costa Mesa, California—based Apria Healthcare Group had over 8,600 employees and provided home care services in 350 locations across the United States. It was the largest national home health-care service provider in the United States. Services included home respiratory and infusion therapy services and the rental and sale of home medical equipment. The firm agreed to pay the government $1.7 million to settle a claim filed in 1995 charging that the company improperly paid physicians for patient referrals. Apria's sales dropped 1 percent in 1999 to $940 million, while registering a net income of $204.1 million. Over one-third of its business was derived from contracts with managed care operations, including Aetna and Human Health Plans.

Coram Healthcare Corp. (CHC) specialized in serving chronically ill patients suffering from asthma,

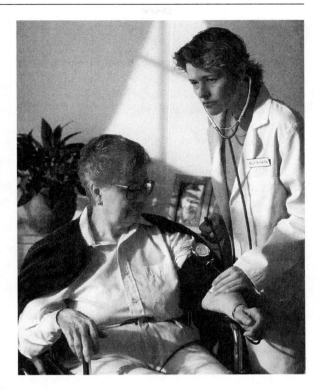

A home-care nurse checks her patient's blood pressure.
(Stock Market)

diabetes, cancer, cystic fibrosis, or AIDS. CHC was based in Denver, Colorado, and maintained a payroll of 3,600 employees, along with about 90 home care sites in 44 states. Despite its legal difficulties, the company was gearing up for significant growth by investing heavily in overhauling its facilities to implement more efficient technologies and creating electronic-commerce operations for its prescription drug subsidiary. Coram reported sales revenue of $521.2 million in 1999, down from $526.5 million the year before.

Lincare Holdings Inc., an aggressive provider of oxygen and other respiratory services in the home, is one company that has not been severely hurt by the recent Medicare cutbacks. Serving 250,000 patients through some 300 home care sites in 42 states, it is one of the largest respiratory services in the nation. The company also offered infusion therapy and sold and rented home medical equipment. About 60 percent of the company's business comes through Medicare and Medicaid payments. In 1999, the company purchased the nursing firm Healthcor Holdings. That year, Lincare raked in $581.8 million in revenues, up from $487.4 million in 1998. Lincare, too, faced legal troubles; in 1999 and 2000 the company was the subject of a federal investigation relating to Medicare billing practices in some of its local operations.

With more than 5,000 employees, the Norcross, Georgia-based Pediatric Services of America (PSA) found a niche in providing home pediatric nursing and therapy to medically fragile children, along with adult respiratory therapy, infusion therapy, and other home services and equipment. PSA has 110 offices in 30 states. Since January 1997, it has acquired more than 10 health-care companies, including a New Jersey nursing company, a Florida pediatric company, a North Carolina home health agency, and an Illinois pharmacy. It relies on Medicaid and Medicare for 37 percent of its revenues. In 1999 PSA suffered a net loss of $55 million, its second-straight year operating in the red, on sales revenue of $214.4 million.

Olsten Corp. was the third-largest temporary staffing agency, with 700,850 employees and over 1,400 offices worldwide. The company offered a full line of nursing, speech, and occupational therapies, pediatric care, and drug infusion. Approximately 15 percent of Olsten's revenues come from Medicare. In 1999, Olsten's Health Services business maintained about 500 home care sites in the United States and Canada, servicing over 500,000 patient/client accounts.

WORK FORCE

According to the U.S. Bureau of Labor Statistics, there were about 746,000 home health and personal care aides in the United States in 1999. About 90 percent of home health aides were female, most under the age of 45. Home health aides were listed among the fastest-growing occupations from 1994 to 2008. According to some estimates, the industry will require over half a million more aides by the middle of the 2000s.

As a result, calls to make employment in home health care more attractive were growing louder. Workers are usually paid minimum wage and generally visit two clients a day; however, they are not paid for commuting time while traveling to homes of clients. Largely due to such conditions, the industry was characterized by heavy personnel turnover, a factor that industry analysts warned could damage public perception of service quality. Efforts toward organizing home health-care workers were beginning to pay off by the end of the 1990s. The Service Employees International Union, for instance, won the right to represent 74,000 home care workers in Los Angeles, bringing those workers into the reach of collective bargaining activities.

The National Association for Health Care Recruitment, a 1,400-member organization, seeks to provide information, education, and networking for facility-based health-care center recruiters and human resources professionals. Additionally, the Cooperative Home Care Associates assists home health aides in finding above minimum-wage jobs.

RESEARCH AND TECHNOLOGY

With expenditures expected to continue their rise over the next several years, health-care organizations were under increasing stress to effectively implement information technology strategies into their home health-care operations. The Outcome and Assessment Information Set (OASIS) data collection requirements sponsored by the HCFA systematizes the key data that factor into the assessment of home patient care and outcomes. Home health-care agencies are required to report OASIS data to their state survey agencies, typically by electronic means. These requirements may in fact benefit the industry in ways that extend beyond basic accountability. As health-care organizations assess the future of their home health-care operations, such streamlined, automated data sets can be used to determine which aspects of those operations integrate on a cost and service level with their core operations.

"Nursing informatics,"—the application of information and computer science to the field of nursing—will allow a home health-care nurse to remotely check on patients' progress in their homes. For example, by using Cornell University's free CUCME (pronounced see you/see me) videoconferencing software, nurses will be able to watch patients perform certain tasks and to give instructions directly.

FURTHER READING

"Apria, Other Providers Sue Coram Resource Network." *HomeCare Magazine,* October 1999.

Auer, Tonie. "Home Healthcare Industry Shrinks Due to Federal Regulations." *Business Press,* 12 November 1999.

"Behavioral Home Care: New Industry Finds Its Niche." *LI Business News,* 15 January 1999.

"Coram, Aetna Resolve Legal Dispute." *HomeCare Magazine,* June 2000.

"Coram Gets New CEO, Grapples with Fallout from Aetna Suit." *HomeCare Magazine,* January 2000.

DeParle, Nancy-Ann. "Implementation of Medicare Changes." *FDCH Congressional Testimony,* 4 May 2000.

Dodd, Kathleen. "Home Health Heals Both Patients and Hospitals." *Baltimore Business Journal,* 19 November 1999.

Field, Anne. "The Best Old-Age Home May Be at Home." *Business Week,* 22 November 1999.

Galloro, Vince. "Embracing PPS: Home-Care Providers See Opportunity Under New System." *Modern Healthcare,* 25 September 2000.

Hopkins, Suzanne. "Relief in Sight? House Approves BBA Reform Bill." *HomeCare Magazine,* December 1999.

Kane, Robert L. "Examining the Efficiency of Home Care." *Journal of Aging & Health,* August 1999.

Keener, Ronald E. "Home Care Looks Toward Technology." *Health Management Technology,* September 2000.

Lagnado, Lucette. "Columbia/HCA to Pay the U.S. $745 Million." *Wall Street Journal,* 19 May 2000.

Lugar, Dick. "Lugar Supports Legislation to Help Home Health Care Patients." *FDCH Press Releases,* 6 April 2000.

Malveaux, Julianne. "Fair Pay for Home Health Aides." *Essence,* April 2000.

Martin, Jeannee Parker, and Kathleen J. Dodd. "Home Health Programs Will Continue to Add Value under PPS." *Healthcare Financial Management,* April 2000.

Nugent, Dempsey. "Providing Solutions for the Growing Trend toward Home Healthcare." *Health Management Technology,* September 1999.

"Provider News." *HomeCare Magazine,* August 1999.

Rocks, David. "Columbia/HCA: Showing Signs of Health." *Business Week,* 6 March 2000.

Shaw, Robert. "Ailing Home Health Looks to Reg Changes for Relief." *Memphis Business Journal,* 26 November 1999.

Shea, Biff. "There's No Place Like Home: Despite the IPS, Home Health Agencies Can Survive If They Do Research and Tailor Their Services." *Modern Healthcare,* 8 March 1999.

Stone, Deborah. "Care and Trembling." *American Prospect,* March/April 1999.

Voelker, Rebecca. "Wellness Works at Home." *JAMA, The Journal of the American Medical Association,* 24 February 1999.

HOME NETWORKING EQUIPMENT

In the digitized 21st century, U.S. households are expected to place a premium on connectivity. Home networking equipment, as a result, is finally emerging out of its "someday" mind-set and into the mainstream. Home networking electronically links devices throughout the home in an integrated, seamless network. Networked computers share peripherals, file storage, and Internet connections over a single system. As home offices flourish and the Internet becomes increasingly central to daily activities, from news to research to shopping to communication, home networks are expected to fill households at a rapid pace in the first decades of the 2000s.

The research firm Yankee Group's 1999 Networked Home Survey found that some 660,000 homes were wired for networking in the United States by late 1999. Based on that survey, the group estimated that up to 10 million households in the United States would undergo digital remodeling by 2003, representing an annual growth rate of 95 percent. An estimated 1.6 million homes were wired for networking by the end of 2000. Cahners In-Stat Group of Scottsdale, Arizona, meanwhile, expected the worldwide market for home networking equipment to reach $5.7 billion in 2004 from only $600 million in 2000.

Most of the biggest names in computers, electronics, and communications have thrown themselves full force into the home networking era, and some currently reside atop the home networking equipment industry's list of leading companies. As a result, products in virtually all high-tech home consumer product categories will be manufactured with the integrated home network in mind.

Still, by 2000 the variety of installation methods and networking products did not make for seamless transition to networked households, thus holding market growth somewhat in check. In the long run, visionaries see home networking equipment leading to the advent of smart homes, in which appliances will speak to each other to generate maximum household efficiency and even talk to the household's members, sensing their presence to optimize lighting and upgrade home security. Eventually, analysts claim, personal computers (PCs), stereos, telephones, digital video recorders, and even refrigerators will be in constant communication with each other.

ORGANIZATION AND STRUCTURE

At its most basic (and, with current technology, practical) home networking is simply the connection of several computers to a central workstation that includes everything from a printer, fax machine, scanner, server, and so on all connected to the Internet. Such integration is assuming increasing priority; about 24 million homes will contain two or more PCs by 2002, and most of those will have more than one computer requiring Internet access at the same time. With a home network, no one has to wait turns to use the modem.

Networks are activated by plugging an interface card into a computer and then connecting the system's requisite power source, such as plugging into a phone jack. Since most home networks utilize existing infrastructures, they can be quite simple to set up. Still, a variety of configurations exist, and choosing the appropriate systems for one's home poses a great many challenges, depending on the household's current equipment and the users' specific needs, exacerbated by the uncertainty over developing standards.

The most common home-networking method involves channeling data signals through the home's existing phone lines, typically resulting in data transmission speeds of 1 megabit per second (Mbps), though since speed is a primary concern, companies were fast at work trying to outdo one another in this area. The phone-line network configuration, however, suffers from the limitation of phone-jack locations throughout the house, and the quality of phone-line data transmission can be highly erratic. Phone-line networks generally cost about $75 to set up.

Home networks can also be installed by routing signals through the house's existing electrical wiring, at a cost of about $100. While this makes for easy adaptation to the infrastructure, as of 2000 the electrical-wiring method was problematic due to signal interference from large electrical appliances, limiting data speeds to only about 400 kilobits per second (Kbps).

Another prominent network method involves wireless communication of networked appliances over radio frequencies. Wireless systems, not surprisingly, find their greatest utility in households relying extensively on battery-powered notebook computers and handheld electronic devices. The data transmission speed is typically on par with phone-line systems. The most prohibitive drawback for wireless systems thus far is the high costs necessitated by the sophisticated transmission system, which can rise to about twice those of phone-line networks.

Universal serial bus (USB) networks connect two or more computers via specialized cables to USB ports, which are generally included on newer model computers. The setup, which includes the cables and a USB hub, costs about $75.

The final configuration is the Ethernet local-area-network protocol, which offers speeds of 10 to 100 Mbps and exceptionally clear signals. Ethernet, however, requires some infrastructure alterations in the form of new wiring between each network node, which can prove prohibitive to most potentially networked households.

BACKGROUND AND DEVELOPMENT

Perhaps the earliest home networks were the intercom systems of the early 1900s, developing even-

tually into the novelty of centrally controlled distributed systems of the 1950s that handled light, climate, and audio and video appliances. But the modern home network, featuring the transmission of digital information between household locations, did not emerge until the massive influx of PCs into the mainstream household in the 1980s. A handful of companies at that time developed central security systems and electronics controls within reach of only the extremely wealthy. However, such systems were generally clunky, communicating awkwardly with the components since the various technologies were nowhere near a universal communication standard. At that time, the emphasis lay more on home automation than home networking as it is conceptualized today. By the mid-1990s, home offices and Internet connections fueled the transformation of the industry into a viable and mass-marketable commodity.

CURRENT CONDITIONS

Home networking equipment was in its gestation stage in early 2000, and as such the optimal home network for computers and peripherals did not yet exist. But all industry players expected the market to take off over the next decade, and were jockeying for position in hopes of gaining a name, and a standard, that will resonate with consumers as the market matures.

Like many emerging high-tech industries, home networking equipment was evolving rapidly. Whereas in the late 1990s it seemed that power-line networks were poised to rise to market dominance, by 2000 several formats offered a host of advantages and disadvantages, and there were no set criteria by which a broad market could base a sound decision.

Moreover, since nearly all major electronics manufacturers maintained some kind of commitment to home networking, a number of competing standards developed that threatened to contain the market's potentially explosive emergence into the mainstream consumer market.

Phone-wire networking teetered between two competing standards. The Home Phone Networking Standards Association (HomePNA) standard used a device that plugged into a phone jack and transmitted information to all connected home phone lines. Developed by Tut Systems, the HomePNA standard was modeled on the digital subscriber line (DSL) and was endorsed by such leading firms as Intel, 3Com, Compaq, and Hewlett-Packard. The MediaWire standard, created by Avio Digital, required additional wiring but featured data speeds up to 100 Mpbs and its own application interfaces. Though Microsoft co-founder Paul Allen invested in Avio, MediaWire's standard enjoyed only limited support throughout the industry. The increasingly common USB ports installed on PCs had their own standard, but as of 2000 it was not widely supported by other electronic devices, except for cable modems. Wireless home networking enjoyed a fairly stable and widely supported standard in Home RF, which utilized an Ethernet-based protocol developed by Proxim Inc. Its most recent incarnation, however, failed to provide for broad multimedia support. Such confusion was expected to maintain many consumers' ambivalence about diving into home networking until a clear, lasting standard was accepted.

While the smart-home dream remains vivid in the mind of developers, most networking, at least in the short term, will likely center around PCs. The steamrolling proliferation of the Internet may prove to be just what this long-heralded "industry of the future" needed to finally become the explosive industry of the moment. While industry observers long held that home automation would propel home networking into the mainstream, it is the desire for perpetual Internet connectivity, the preponderance of information and commerce on the Web, and the proliferation of multiple-PC households that will take the home networking equipment industry to a wide audience. One of the developing Internet technologies spurring the growth of home networking was high-speed broadband connection, which offered 24-hour Internet access and thus served as a justification for a home network setup allowing the simultaneous connection of two or more PCs to the Internet. Moreover, as PC and peripheral prices fall, more homes will inevitably house the equipment for which a home network becomes practical, and even necessary.

Because each home's setup and equipment are unique, using components from a variety of vendors, networked homeowners are generally on their own to troubleshoot bugs and difficulties. To get around such problems, many companies have embarked on the development of systems that stand behind a simple principle: no new wires.

Security is also a concern for home networks, because most networks involve sending the data through systems outside the home. Since hacking into a broadband-based modem is fairly simple for anyone so inclined, many people remain hesitant to invest in home networking equipment.

INDUSTRY LEADERS

3Com Corp. of Santa Clara, California, poured extensive research-and-development resources into home networking equipment in the late 1990s, and to great effect; the firm was well established as a major force in the young industry. Its Personal Connectivity unit built interface cards that enabled the connection of computers to a network, while the Network Systems units produced the structural equipment, such as routers, switches, and network management software. The firm also specialized in handheld computing equipment. Founded in 1979, 3Com employed 11,000 workers by 2000, maintaining a partnership with software giant Microsoft to create home networking products. 3Com was the second-largest overall manufacturer of networking equipment after Cisco. In March 2000, 3Com sold off its modem business and ceased to manufacture high-end networking equipment for large businesses so as to focus networking production on the home and small-business market. Largely for this reason, the company's sales dropped from $5.7 billion in 1999 to $4.3 billion in 2000.

Cisco Systems, Inc. of San Jose, California, was the leading manufacturer of computer networking equipment, although its main area of concentration was the high-end business networking market. In addition to its top-selling routers and switches, the firm also developed servers and network management software. By 2000, Cisco was focusing increased attention on the growing home networking market in hopes of winning market share from its rival 3Com. Cisco spent the mid- and late 1990s on a buying spree, acquiring dozens of companies to expand its product lines, and maintained partnerships with top computer-industry players Microsoft, IBM, and Sun Microsystems. In 1999 the firm acquired fiber-optic network equipment maker Cerent as well as routing software producer GeoTel. Cisco was developing gateways with GTE, Whirlpool, and Sun Microsystems and was working toward the integration of home appliances into high-speed networks. The firm's revenues totaled $18.9 billion in 2000, up from $12.1 billion in 1999, and employed 21,000 workers.

Intel Corp., based in Santa Clara, California, produced computer microprocessors that were used in about 80 percent of all PCs. By 2000, however, Intel had also emerged as a leader in the networking market, building hubs, servers, and routers. Founded in 1968, Intel maintained a payroll of over 70,000 employees in 2000. The firm invested heavily in networking in 1999 with its purchase of Shiva Corp., which it renamed Intel Network Systems, and the subsequent acquisitions of Dialogic, DSP Communications, and Level One. Intel's AnyPoint system used existing phone lines to send data signals at such a high frequency as to render the interruption of phone calls nonexistent. The company boosted revenues 12 percent in 1999 to reach $29.4 billion.

Lucent Technologies Inc. of Murray Hill, New Jersey, centered its home networking operations on the development of wireless systems. Lucent also purchased its way to networking prominence in the late 1990s, acquiring the networking firm Ascend Communications, local-area-network switch developer Madge Networks' Lannet unit, International Network Services, and Excel Switching. The former AT&T unit brought in revenues of $38 billion in 1999.

Other leading computer industry names figured prominently in home networking equipment as well. Compaq Computer Corp., the world's leading PC manufacturer, developed portable systems and corporate servers. Apple Computer Inc.'s Airport product line, developed in collaboration with Lucent Technologies, was a leader in the wireless technology market. IBM Corp., meanwhile, spun off its Home Director networking product into its own separate company in late 1999.

FURTHER READING

"Home Connectivity No Longer a Niche—Market to Reach $5.7 Billion by 2004." *Business Wire,* 29 February 2000.

"Home Networking Market Finishes 1999 with a Bang!: In-Stat Research Reveals State of Market and Identifies Early Leaders." *Business Wire,* 3 April 2000.

Knisley, Joseph R. "Wiring Today's Homes for Tomorrow." *CEE News,* July 2000.

LaGesse, David, and Janet Rae-Dupree. "Home Networks: A Party Line to the High-Speed Web." *U.S. News & World Report,* 4 September 2000.

"Market Research." *EDP Weekly's IT Monitor,* 25 October 1999.

"The Network in Your House: Easy to Set Up, Home Networks Give Every Member of the Family a Connection to the Internet." *Fortune,* 1 December 1999.

Rubenking, Neil J. "Network Your Home Painlessly." *PC Magazine,* 4 April 2000.

Seymour, Jim. "The Home Network Problem." *PC Magazine,* 16 November 1999.

Starr-Miller, Elizabeth. "Keeping Up With the Jetsons." *Sound & Video Contractor,* September 2000.

Sweeney, Daniel. "Arrested Development, Part 1 of 2." *Business and Management Practices—America's Network Telecom Investor Supplement,* 1 December 1999.

Thurm, Scott. "3Com to Sell Modem, Networking Lines in Bid for Growth." *Wall Street Journal,* 21 March 2000.

Walford, Lynn. "From Cables to Wireless Systems, Here's the Latest in Home Networks." *Investor's Business Daily,* 16 March 2000.

Webb, Warren. "Home Network Contenders Steer a Collision Course." *EDN,* 24 November 1999.

INFANT AND PRESCHOOL PRODUCTS

The infant and preschool products industry is no child's play. In fact, the various sectors comprising this industry amount to an enormous and fiercely competitive market. In general, the industry can be broken into two large, diversified sectors: toys and non-toys.

Toys was the more high-profile sector, generating sales of $1.5 billion in 1999, up 7.1 percent from 1998, according to the Toy Manufacturers of America. The increase in sales however, outpaced the increase in unit sales, which were up 5.3 percent in 1999 to reach 231 million units. The most notable trend in the infant and preschool toy industry was the shift toward more educational and high-tech items. In addition, toy manufacturers were beating each other over the head with their checkbooks bidding on licensing rights for the latest media characters and brands, such as *Star Wars* and *Teletubbies*. At the same time, there were growing fears related to product safety, and firms were scrambling to meet consumer demands for toys that posed no threat whatsoever to their children.

The market for non-toy products aimed at infants and preschoolers includes children's furniture, such as child seats, high chairs, and bedding; "functional" items such as strollers, baby carriers, and similar accessories; and everyday items such as bath toys, bibs, and diapers. This sector was growing up quickly, totaling $4.86 billion in the United States in 1999, up from $1.7 billion in 1980, according to the Juvenile Products Manufacturers Association, Inc. In this sector, too, however, ever-heightening safety concerns were among the chief factors driving innovation and competition.

ORGANIZATION AND STRUCTURE

By far the leading retail outlets for infant and preschool products were mass merchandisers. In 2000, the NPD Group reported its findings for the top toy sellers of the past year, in which Wal-Mart Stores, Inc., for the second consecutive year, topped the longtime leader Toys "R" Us, Inc. to claim the pole position, with 17.4 percent of the retail market. Toys "R" Us finished second, although its share slipped from 16.5 percent in 1998 to 15.6 percent in 1999. Rounding out the top five were Kmart Corp., with 7.2 percent of the market; Target, with 6.8 percent; and K-B Toys, commanding 5.1 percent of retail toy sales. Approximately two-thirds of the total toy industry sales occur in the fourth quarter when many toys are bought as holiday gifts. This is beginning to level out, however, as toy manufacturers market products year round through movie and fast-food chain tie-ins.

These retail giants were also leaders in the baby-care category, which includes baby soaps, ointments and bath powders, oils and lotions, bottles and nipples, and nursing accessories. By the end of the 20th century the largest percentage of nursing accessories, bottles and nipples, oils and lotions, and baby bath soaps were sold through mass merchandisers, as opposed to baby powder and baby ointments, which had the heaviest sales in supermarkets.

Baby superstores were another way to sell juvenile products. In the latter part of the 1990s Toys "R" Us introduced its new Babies "R" Us stores focusing on juvenile products, furniture, apparel, and toys. Through these stores, Toys "R" Us was expected to become an even larger retailing force for young families. By the end of the 1990s Toys "R" Us had about

Trends

SAY, ARE THOSE NIKE BOOTIES?

In the old days, babies and preschoolers, too young to have formed a social identity or to feel the crushing weight of peer pressure, never felt compelled to sport the hippest trends and hottest brand names. All they needed were the essential items: diapers, clothing, bibs, rattles, and the like. Design, labels, fashion—these words rarely entered into these tots' heads, nor were they factored into spending decisions in this category.

The times they are a-changing. By 2000 parents were rushing to supermarkets and large retailers not just to find disposable diapers and t-shirts, but disposable diapers and t-shirts with Nike swooshes and pictures of Barney, that lovable Triassic puppet. Baby clothing has thus gone from functional to fashion statement.

Although few infants were interviewed for their take on this hot trend in toddler fashion, parents, particularly younger parents, were driving the first major shift in the infant-wear market since the introduction of the disposable diaper 30 years ago, according to America's Research Group.

120 Babies "R" Us stores throughout the country. Baby Superstore, with outlets in 18 states, was another large infant-products chain.

Juvenile products and toys are also sold through catalogs. Many parents found this an easy and convenient way to shop. There were also parent information and resource centers on the Internet as well as World Wide Web shopping directories pointing online shoppers to products for children.

The late 1990s saw the rise of the Internet as an avenue for toy sales. The online toy market totaled about $30 million by 2000. Toys "R" Us launched an online site, and Santa Monica-based eToys opened its virtual doors in 1997. eToys claimed to be the largest online store for children's products, and carried more than 10,000 items, all priced at or below prices of traditional toy retailers. By 2000 over 2 million people had ordered from eToys. K-B Toys started KBkids.com Inc., which was quickly gaining a presence for online toy retailing. Online retailing giant Amazon.com also threw its hat into the ring, establishing its Toy & Games site.

LICENSING

Toy licensing began during the 20th century, when Richard Felton Outcault's design of the comic character "The Yellow Kid" was placed onto toys. Since then, toy licensing has become increasingly sophisticated and is reaching ever deeper into children's lives. Licensed products, such as Disney and Winnie-the-Pooh, contributed greatly to sales in such areas as baby bottles and toys. In 1999 the Toy Manufacturers of America estimated that over 40 percent of all toys sold were licensed products. Even youngsters under the age of three are affected by the onslaught of commercials and characters they encounter as part of daily television viewing, and companies continue to initiate new ways to reach these youngsters through electronic media.

Almost anywhere children go, they find products reflecting the characters they know from popular television shows and movies. *Barney,* the *Teletubbies, Blue's Clues, Sesame Street,* Winnie-the-Pooh, and many other Disney characters are among the most universal and there are many more. In the late 1990s Hasbro, Inc. entered into a fierce bidding war with Mattel, Inc. to maintain Hasbro's longtime license for *Star Wars* products, which Hasbro finally won in 1997 for $600 million plus a 7.4 percent share of Hasbro for *Star Wars* mastermind George Lucas. Mattel, meanwhile, managed to secure the licensing rights to the 2002 Olympic games, allowing the company to produce toy mascots for the events.

But not all vendors agree that licensing is the best avenue; some juvenile bedding vendors pinned products on nonlicensed looks and patterns that stayed clear of major films or cartoon and comic-book characters, believing that licensing is becoming a high-risk proposition.

PRODUCT SAFETY

Safety is the primary concern of parents with infants and young children. The Juvenile Products Manufacturers Association developed a Certification Program that tests products for compliance with the American Society for Testing and Materials (ASTM) standards and issues a certification seal after the product passes rigorous testing. The ASTM Certification Program covers high chairs, play yards, walkers, carriages and strollers, gates and enclosures, full-size cribs, and portable hook-on chairs. They continue to develop standards for additional categories including toddler beds, bath seats, bedding products, and nonstandard sized cribs.

As with other juvenile products, child safety is fundamental to the development and manufacture of toys. Together with the U.S. government, the Toy Manufacturers of America leads the world in the development of toy safety standards by investing heavily in child development research, dynamic safety testing, quality assurance engineering, risk analysis, and basic anthropometric studies of children.

Toys are closely monitored and highly regulated by the federal government. The basic law covering toy safety is the federal Hazardous Substances Act and its amendments, notably the Child Protection and Toy Safety Act of 1969. This legislation was supplemented by the Consumer Product Safety Act in 1972. These regulations were incorporated by reference in the industry's voluntary standard, ASTM F963. While toy makers are not compelled to abide by ASTM F963, many retailers require compliance with voluntary standards, and many manufacturers, especially the larger ones, have in-house testing laboratories that ensure that all products meet or exceed government standards for safety.

BACKGROUND AND DEVELOPMENT

There is archeological evidence that simple toys were made thousands of years ago in Greece, Rome, and ancient Egypt. Later, during the Middle Ages, the colorful world of knights and fair ladies was reproduced for the pleasure of medieval children. From the end of the Middle Ages on, toy production increased rapidly, and by the middle of the 18th century central Europe had become the heart of the world's toy industry. Germany, particularly the city of Nuremberg, was the established toy-manufacturing center of the world. In the early 20th century, Japan, Great Britain, and the United States also began to manufacture toys on a large scale.

Toys are an important part of every child's life starting in infancy. Children learn through play, and today we know that a child's education begins long before he or she enters school. Babies become familiar with shapes and sounds by playing with rattles and bell toys. They learn to distinguish colors by watching mobiles. Toddlers enjoy and learn from pull toys, pegboards, puzzles, and blocks. And the preschooler uses paints, crayons, and clay to express emotions.

Revolutionary educational methods, such as those of Maria Montessori (1870-1952) and Friedrich Froebel (1782-1852), with their precepts of learning by doing, have taught that an interested child is a happy one. Each year, more and more toys are designed to educate as well as to amuse. For example, wooden clocks with movable hands teach children how to tell time, and alphabet blocks help them learn

to spell. In addition, new methods of teaching in kindergarten influenced the pattern of toys and introduced building blocks, constructor sets, educational puzzles, and many of the toys we now take for granted. In the 20th century, soft toys also became popular. The teddy bear made its debut in 1903 and remains a favorite. Advanced technology in vinyl, plastic, and foam rubber also helped to revolutionize the toy industry.

CURRENT CONDITIONS

INNOVATIVE NEW JUVENILE PRODUCTS

By the end of the 1990s, traditional toy sales were beginning to level off in favor of more sophisticated alternatives, such as advanced computer programs and other electronic equipment, even for preschool children. As technology assumes an ever-increasing role in American daily life, and thus in children's education, parents increasingly seek out toys that provide educational content and early familiarity with gadgetry in addition to entertainment.

High-tech toys were all the rage at the start of the 21st century. The 2000 International Toy Fair featured such high-profile items as robotic dogs from Mattel's Fisher-Price and the MGA Entertainment's My Dream Baby, a doll that progresses from crawling to walking and interacts with emotional responses to users via proprietary technology.

Toy manufacturers' high-tech efforts geared for tots often tie in their existing successes. For instance, in order to jump on the interactive computer-based market for preschoolers, Mattel Interactive rolled out Elmo's Deep Sea Adventure and Ernie's Adventure in Space, two CD-ROMs packaged with small toy spaceships or submarines. These were the follow-ups to Mattel's successful Reader Rabbit and Baby & Me, the company's first ventures into the interactive baby market. Hasbro, meanwhile, created an interactive Barney, called My Barney, which plugs into the Internet. Parents can download specific activities and games from the My Barney Web site. Once My Barney is programmed, children can play with it without the computer. Fisher-Price and other companies had similar products in the works, and industry analysts expected such toddler products to get even more whizbang in coming years.

The increasingly tech-savvy toddler was forcing a major revitalization effort among the industry's leaders and prospective entrants alike. Toy manufacturers have leaped on top of new market possi-

Two preschoolers playing a developmental game. (FieldMark Publications/Robert J. Huffman)

bilities stemming from the latest research contending that children can take steps toward becoming better learners and get a leg up on their peers by starting younger. Industry players stepped up their efforts to pitch their products to parents not only as entertainment but also as a means toward helping children reach their full potential. Interactive toys typically targeted at older children were being adapted for use by their younger siblings.

Another important innovation in juvenile products was the proliferation of toys designed for children with disabilities. Advances in medicine, ironically, have led to a dramatic increase in the number of children with disabilities as mortality rates for premature babies and babies with severe ailments have plummeted. The American Academy of Pediatrics estimated that at least 6 million children had some form of disability, a figure that rose 20 percent from 1989 to 1990. The handicapped toy industry was led by such familiar names as Mattel, which introduced a Barbie doll in a wheelchair in 1997, and smaller toy makers such as People of Every Stripe in Portland, Oregon, which began making dolls with hearing aids and prosthetics in the early 1990s. Toy manufacturers were also offering modified versions of standard toys for use by children with disabilities.

MARKETING

By far the most radical innovation in juvenile products during the late 1990s was the very controversial extension of packaged entertainment, in the form of television shows and video games, for children under the age of two. The lovable purple dinosaur Barney got the ball rolling by appealing to youngsters from two to five years old in the mid-1990s, but by the late 1990s the British import *Teletubbies* was marketed to infants under the age of one. Along with television programs came computer programs, such as Jump Start Baby, which offers children as young as nine months their first formal introduction to the Sun, bears, shapes, and capitalism.

The extension of marketing to babies spawned a great deal of controversy, with some arguing that it was unethical to market products to children who cannot even speak the name of the item they are being encouraged to desire. Still, marketers themselves argued that infants watch television anyway, and they are simply filling a market niche with appropriate material. There were as yet no figures available for how large a market the three-and-under set represented, but it was certain to draw the attention of toy and entertainment producers for the next few years.

In the earliest stages of product development, many designers use information from sources that include parents, psychologists, educators, and other child-development specialists. This background provides valuable clues to what consumers are looking for when they purchase toys and how children learn through play. Some toy manufacturers maintain in-house year-round nursery school facilities for this purpose, while others establish relationships with universities or other research facilities.

Meanwhile, although the industry increasingly rushed to attach itself to highly recognizable media phenomena, the practice didn't always pay off to the extent anticipated. Hasbro poured money into its truckloads of new *Star Wars* action figures and related products—the largest product-line rollout in the history of manufactured toys—in anticipation of a rush to toy stores following the May 1999 release of the film *Star Wars: Episode I-The Phantom Menace.* But sales of Jar-Jar Binks, Darth Maul, and friends disappointed, falling far short of the expected $800 million to $1 billion for 1999.

CHILD SAFETY

Of concern to the industry during the late 1990s was a claim made by some public interest groups that polyvinyl chloride (PVC), a vinyl used in toys and infant products such as teethers and pacifiers, posed environmental hazards as well as dangers to children, who could ingest lead, cadmium, and phthalates into the bloodstream if they chew on these products.

In 1998 the U.S. Consumer Product Safety Commission requested that toy manufacturers eliminate the use of phthalates in teethers and rattles in favor of less risky alternatives. The Toy Manufacturers of America stands by the safety of vinyl toys. Still, many large retailers pulled all soft rattles and teethers from their shelves, and some toy manufacturers began to phase out the use of phthalates in products for young children. A study released by the National Environmental Trust in December 1999, however, found that teethers appearing in U.S. stores, especially those manufactured by foreign companies, still contained phthalates. The study also reported that while U.S. companies had eliminated phthalates from teethers, phthalates were still present in bath toys.

The European Union also took consumers' fears to heart, issuing a formal ban in late 1999 on phthalates from PVC-based toys that manufacturers expected children to chew on. Meanwhile, Mattel announced that it would phase out production of toys containing PVC, switching instead to plant- and vegetable-based plastics, which the company planned to roll out in the early 2000s.

Car-seat safety was also of concern in the late 1990s. A study by the National Safe Kids Campaign found evidence that eight out of 10 child-safety car seats were used incorrectly. Infants under 20 pounds and one year of age were required to be placed in a rear-facing seat at a 45-degree angle to best support their necks. From 20 to 40 pounds, children could be seated in forward-facing car seats, and from 40 to 80 pounds they could use booster seats. Adding to the problems were the sheer proliferation of car-seat styles and automobiles, making it difficult for manufacturers to ensure a proper fit. In hopes of correcting some of these problems, federal laws began requiring auto manufacturers to add special bars, bolts, and tethers to make it easier for parents to secure the car seats. Automakers and the government also teamed up to offer roadside clinics and seat-checks to verify child-safety seats were correctly installed.

INDUSTRY LEADERS

MATTEL

Headquartered in El Segundo, California, Mattel, Inc. was the world's leading toy manufacturer. Mattel's second-largest core brand (after Barbie) is Fisher-Price, the leader in the infant and preschool market with a history that spanned more than 70 years. Mattel also includes Disney infant and preschool See 'N Say talking toys; Tyco Toys, which has an infant preschool line based on *Sesame Street* characters; and Magna Doodle and View-Master toys.

Barbie's popularity in the late 1990s culminated with the celebration of the doll's 40th birthday in 1999. According to the company, 1 billion Barbie dolls were sold in the last four decades, making Barbie the best-selling fashion doll worldwide. Barbie software continued to expand in 1999 to meet the new demands of Barbie fans. In addition, the company's Barbie Web site allows its mostly preteen customers to design Barbie dolls online. According to Mattel, about 40 percent of its sales are generated internationally, and most of its manufacturing is done in Asia and Mexico. Fisher-Price, meanwhile, announced in 2000 that it would sell children's clothing online and via direct mail.

In 2000 Mattel introduced a new interactive games and education portal on the Web, allowing users to play and purchase such games online, as part of its efforts to dramatically boost its online presence, which will include more of its own electronic-commerce sites. The company also planned the release of products related to the Harry Potter book sensation. Mattel's revenues jumped to $5.5 billion in 1999 from $800 million the year before, and the company derived $1.63 billion from the sale of infant and preschool products. Mattel maintained a work force of 31,000 employees.

HASBRO

Hasbro, Inc., the second-largest toy company, raked in revenues of $4.2 billion in 1999, up from $3.3 billion the year before. Hasbro began as a family-owned company in 1923. In more than 70 years it has grown from eight family members to a company with more than 9,500 employees in facilities around the world. By 1985 Hasbro was the world's largest toy company, gaining access to the European market and uniting four strong divisions: Hasbro Toy, Milton Bradley, Playskool, and Playskool Baby. In the late 1990s the entire line of infant products was part of the well-recognized Playskool division. The Playskool line offers fun and educational items ranging from baby-care products to clothing and preschool toys, including such classics as Mr. Potato Head, Play-Doh, and Lincoln Logs. The company also maintained industry staples such as the Nerf, Tonka, and G.I. Joe lines. The 1998 purchase of Tiger Electronics gave Hasbro one of the biggest hits of the late 1990s in the talking Furby doll, which was slated to turn multilingual in the early 2000s.

About 15 percent of Hasbro's revenues come from *Star Wars* products. Although *Star Wars* product sales disappointed in 1999, its Pokemon, Furby, and Teletubbies toys came through in fine style. The firm underwent a major restructuring around the turn of the century, with major job cuts in 1997 and again in 2000 in an effort to reduce many of its lower margin products, including some of its preschool line. The company hoped to streamline its operations to focus on its big-name products such as Furby dolls and computer games. Following the latest cutbacks, the company will outsource some 70 percent of all manufacturing operations.

WORK FORCE

Toy production is labor intensive, requiring procedures such as painting, assembly, inspection, packaging, and detailing for authenticity. The costs associated with this type of production in the United States are often very high. Since the early 1950s, American manufacturers have combined domestic operations with overseas production in developing countries (where labor is inexpensive) to lower costs. It was estimated that 75 percent of toys sold in the United States were manufactured either wholly or in part overseas.

By the late 1990s, activist pressure was brought to bear on major toy manufacturers such as Mattel for what was decried as abusive labor practices in factories overseas. Mattel responded by dismissing several of its Chinese contractors for harsh treatment of workers and poor working conditions, including low wages, child and prison labor, and unsanitary and unsafe working environments. Mattel also was a cosignatory, along with apparel manufacturers Levi Strauss and Reebok, of a "bill of rights" for foreign factory workers. Such actions were not quite enough to placate critics of these companies' labor practices, however, arguing that such gestures were primarily formal and provided for little substantive change.

AMERICA AND THE WORLD

The United States is the largest market for toys in the world, representing about 47 percent of total toy revenue, followed by Japan and Western Europe. Approximately 5,000-6,000 new items are introduced annually at the American International Toy Fair. The United States also led the world in toy development and in such sales support areas as marketing, advertising, and special promotions.

Some European countries were much more vigilant than the United States in combating toy advertising aimed at small children. Greece, Sweden, and Norway restrict at least some forms of toy advertising, and Sweden even announced its intention to propose such a ban throughout the entire European Union when it assumes the European Union presidency in 2001. In summer 1999, the European Commission dropped its attempts to fight Greece's advertising ban, as little progress had been made to repeal the Greek government's decision, which the commission feared would spread to other countries. Denmark was also considering a toy-advertising ban in 1999.

Global alliances have proven an attractive option for leading toy makers seeking a competitive edge in new markets. The leading manufacturer in the $8.4 billion Japanese toy industry, Bandai Co., partnered with Mattel in 1999 to market the latter's products in Japan, while Mattel agreed to market Bandai's products throughout Latin America. In the future, the two companies' planned to collaborate on the development of new toys.

FURTHER READING

"Bandai's Alliance with Mattel Could Prove to Be a Turning Point." *Wall Street Journal,* 27 July 1999.

Birger, Jon. "Toys R Cheap." *Money,* September 2000.

Christie, Rebecca. "Manufacturers Sign up to Foreign Workers' Bill of Rights: The U.S. Code Is a Good Start but Lacks Teeth to Improve Factory Standards, Say Critics." *Financial Times,* 3 June 1999.

Corral, Cecille B. "The Customer Connection: Baby's World, Newborns to 3 Years." *Discount Store News,* 25 October 1999.

Dunfield, Allison. "Licensing of Infant Merch a Must." *Kidscreen,* 1 December 1999.

"EC Drops Fight against Greek Toy Ad Ban." *Euromarketing via E-mail,* 2 July 1999.

"Estimated Manufacturers' Shipments by Product Category, 1999 vs. 1998." New York: Toy Manufacturers of America, 2000. Available from http://www.toy-tma.com/industry/statistics/nsp99/national.html.

"Hasbro's *Star Wars* Line Fails to Bring in Expected Billion-Dollar Sales." *Providence Journal-Bulletin,* 23 January 2000.

"Juvenile Products Manufacturers Association." Available from http://www.jpma.org.

Leccese, Donna. "Baby Steps." *Playthings,* October 1999.

"Mattel Signs up for 2002 Olympics." *Playthings,* November 1999.

"Mattel Will Phase out Petroleum-Based Products." *Industrial Maintenance & Plant Operation,* February 2000.

Morton, Anne. "Kids Turned on by Intelligence: Children Are Abandoning Traditional Toys and Games in Favor of More 'Intelligent' Toys." *Brand Strategy,* March 2000.

Priel, Ross. "PC Software, Videos Propel Toys." *MMR,* 20 March 2000.

Prior, Molly. "New Batch of Toys Reflect Growing Computer Age." *DSN Retailing Today,* 24 July 2000.

"Rhode Island-Based Hasbro Cuts 2,200 Jobs Worldwide." *Providence Journal-Bulletin,* 8 December 1999.

Stanley, T. L., and Becky Ebenkamp. "In Search of the Magic Formula." *Brandweek,* 14 February 2000.

"Toy Biz: Glad All Over." *Playthings,* March 2000.

"Toy Industry Fact Book, 2000." New York: Toy Manufacturers of America, Inc., 2000. Available from http://www.toy-tma.com/industry/publications/fb2000/contents.htm.

"Toy Sales up 8.8% in '99; Almost Half Are Licensed Properties." *Entertainment Marketing Letter,* 15 May 2000.

"Toy Stories Grabbing Attention of Industry: Mattel Turns from Traditional Plastics." *Plastics News,* 13 December 1999.

INFOMERCIALS

The infomercial industry has generally grown away from its often tacky late-night spots hawking novelty items and get-rich-quick schemes, though its former tendencies still periodically manifest themselves. Production values have grown slick and sophisticated, products have become mainstream and functional, and the medium's reputation was by 2000 considered stable enough for well-established giants in major industries. Consumer confidence in infomercial products likewise grew through the 1990s, though not without glitches and setbacks.

The most intensive and "intimate" of the more than 500 commercial messages absorbed by the average American each day, infomercials comprised a $1.5 billion industry in the late 1990s, drawing some 6.8 million consumers. An increasingly familiar sight on the tube, infomercials flooded the broadcast and cable television airwaves with about 2.5 million broadcasts in the United States and Canada during 1999. The Infomercial Monitoring Service reported that about 800 to 1,000 infomercials hit the airwaves annually, with about 10 to 15 debuting each week.

Infomercials also leaked increasing sales into supermarkets and discount stores, where "as seen on TV" sales, though down 10 percent from their peak in 1999, hovered around $1.5 billion in 2000. Analysts noted that while only 10 percent of consumers actually buy directly from an infomercial or other television advertisements, the infomercial medium develops pent-up demand that releases itself in standard retail channels. In fact, "as seen on TV" has developed from an occasional novelty promotion to a standard in-store marketing scheme, with some outlets even opening entire departments devoted to "as seen on TV" products. But while the industry was well poised in 2000, producers had reason to remain humble: only about one in 20 infomercials prove financially successful, though a hit can have producers rolling in money.

An infomercial is usually a 28.5 minute block of programming that resembles a television show, designed to explain and sell anything from kitchen gadgets to advice from psychic friends. An infomercial's purpose is to show consumers how a product would satisfy a need, benefit their lives, motivate them, or solve a problem. Fitness devices are among the most successful infomercial products because they are easily demonstrated by fit, photogenic people. The more sophisticated infomercials often have a celebrity spokesperson, testimonials from satisfied customers, location shooting, a musical soundtrack, and a well-developed script. Production costs vary widely, depending on the amount and quality of special effects, talent salaries (which for celebrities can be astronomical), and a host of other considerations. Infomercials cost a minimum of about $150,000, but the price could rise as high as a million dollars.

The industry's history is littered with its share of hucksters, prompting the creation of an organization to regulate itself and project a professional image. The Electronic Retailing Association (formerly known as NIMA International and the National Infomercial Marketing Association) represents the electronic retailing industry in the United States and overseas.

ORGANIZATION AND STRUCTURE

Most electronic retailers do not invent products themselves, but instead scout trade shows and fairs—or accept submissions—for easily marketable, new inventions. For instance, the two biggest industry firms, Guthy-Renker Corp. and e4L Inc., often buy the rights to a product from inventors and pay them a 10 percent (or less) royalty fee. In return, infomercial producers assume all the financial risk—and most of the payoff—for launching a product.

After finding a prospective product, the company produces an infomercial. Costs vary widely, depending on quality, but general estimates run between $100,000 and $600,000. These costs could include: $4,000-$20,000 for the script and the same range for a director; $3,000 for props; $30,000-$60,000 for editing; and $25,000-$50,000 for crew and equipment. For kitchen items, a chef and a food stylist are also necessary, and live audiences add even more expense. Costs for location and a host (who may be a celebrity) are vastly divergent, and can run into the hundreds of thousands of dollars.

Industry firms usually test finished ads on focus groups before airing infomercials in specific markets. If the product generates enough response, industry firms buy more media time in diverse markets. Because response is so rapid—customers either call in or the phones are quiet—industry firms know within days if the infomercial is working or if it needs rewriting and reshooting. If the product receives positive responses, it eventually goes to home shopping channels, the Internet, and, finally, traditional retailers. If the product receives negative responses, industry firms often pull it from the air and move on to promoting other products. Due to expanding television markets, the largest firms had plenty of media time available and could launch 30 or more products per year.

While major success stories are few and far between, the potential payoff can be juicy. Once an infomercial's product generates good sales, electronic retailers display the product on television, usually on the home shopping channels. Some products may also be shown on channels related to the product, as when a fitness machine and exercise video are featured on sports channels. The final sales venue is the retail store, where the original infomercial runs on a store's videocassette player, repeating and reinforcing the product's benefits to potential buyers.

Fortune 500 companies, such as Lexus, Microsoft, Apple Computer, Magnavox, Sears, AT&T, Volvo, Fannie Mae, and Fidelity Investments, added infomercials to their marketing strategies during the late 1990s, but they worked with industry firms differently than did struggling entrepreneurs. Major corporations typically contract with a direct-response marketer to produce the infomercial or spot, establish both the supporting telemarketing and fulfillment structure, and buy media time and provide operational management. Or the marketer might provide just one or a group of these services. The advantage of this approach is maximum flexibility and control of the project while still retaining all the upside potential. The disadvantage, of course, is that the investor's capital is at risk.

The infomercial production industry reaches consumers by purchasing air time on broadcast, satellite, and regional and national cable television. Infomercials are not tracked by Nielsen ratings in the manner of traditional broadcast programs, so the number of viewers is unknown. About 4 percent of the U.S. adult population, however, purchased items from an infomercial in 1999, according to the Infomercial Marketing Service.

In order to revive the infomercial sector and make broadcasters more comfortable after years of eating the costs of infomercial ad time after producers' low returns made them unable to foot the bill, Colorado-based Product Information Network rolled out its Pin-Point Response initiative. The program estimates the per-inquiry response revenues for each infomercial it handles, and then distributes the infomercials by videotape to broadcasters along with a check for that amount, thus securing broadcasters up front. Traditionally, infomercial producers dispersed a percentage of the per-inquiry profits to broadcasters after the numbers are processed, situating the risk with the broadcasters. The PinPoint Response program affords broadcasters complete autonomy over scheduling of the products; they can choose to wedge them into productive time slots if they feel the infomercial is promising in order to meet or surpass the original check amount, in which case Product Information Network issues another check. By offering broadcasters greater incentive to air infomercials, it was hoped that revenues would be enhanced all around and a renewed relationship of trust would be forged between producers and broadcasters, in effect helping to alleviate the ghettoization of the infomercial.

Beginning in 2000 all infomercials longer than 10 minutes are required by the Telecommunications Act of 1996 to be close-captioned. Direct marketers generally viewed this as a welcome development, noting that the inclusion of closed-captioning will open the door for about 24 million new consumers who were untapped by the infomercial industry due to hearing impediments. The National Captioning Institute further noted that such consumers are often influenced in their purchasing decisions by the drive to include them in marketing campaigns; 66 percent of this market are more likely to purchase from captioned advertisements, and 35 percent will devote brand loyalty to a company that offers captioning over a company that doesn't. The investment was attractive to many infomercial producers; captioning a 30-minute spot cost an average of $520 and usually no more than $1,000, a pittance when factored into a $400,000 production budget.

Infomercials, and the products they sell, stand or fall on consumer reaction. Gene Silverman, president of Hawthorne Communications, advised prospective electronic retailers that at virtually every moment, an infomercial must grab the viewer's attention and convince that viewer that it is necessary to continue watching. That is because only about 1 percent of viewers will actually call the toll-free number to place an order or request information, so a company must reach a large audience to keep the response level high. Some suggested tips include: avoid telling the whole story right up front—consider how to tease an audience; use a "grabber" that keeps an audience watching, such as "In the next half hour you will. . ." or "Stay tuned to witness an amazing. . ."; and give the viewer an opportunity to think subconsciously, "I want to see this." The formula for success can be summed up in a few words: first, engage a viewer emotionally, then convince the viewer intellectually that buying the product is a smart deal.

The Electronic Retailing Association (ERA) member firms must agree to comply with all laws, from federal to local, that cover advertising and selling consumer goods. In addition, they must portray their own business operations, including revenues and profits, accurately and avoid libel or slander of competitors. Most importantly for consumers, member firms must promise: "To honor all warranties and money-back guarantees, and to establish and maintain a fair and equitable distribution system for handling customer complaints." Unlike the Federal Trade Commission (FTC), however, the ERA cannot really punish violators.

BACKGROUND AND DEVELOPMENT

Infomercials began during the 1950s when television grew popular. In those days, television had lit-

tle regulation, and some shows became intertwined with the sponsors. For example, some analysts believe the late 1990s corporate infomercials owe a debt to 1950s shows such as the *Bob Hope Texaco Star Theater*. The show featured the Texaco logo prominently throughout, and Bob Hope interrupted the program with commercial breaks pitching Texaco's products.

In 1963 the Federal Communications Commission set a two-minute limit on television ads, which effectively killed the infomercial. The two-minute limit, however, allowed marketers to refine the short form to pitch straightforward items such as K-Tel records.

When the Reagan administration deregulated the broadcast and cable television industry in 1984, cable subscriptions expanded and infomercials reappeared. From 1984 to 1987, few federal guidelines existed, and this sometimes led to misleading ads and fraudulent claims. FTC guidelines issued in the late 1980s halted most deceitful ads by forbidding false claims and misleading presentations, noting that such regulatory measures were necessary since so many infomercials constituted deliberate attempts to fool customers into believing they were watching regular programs. From 1987 to 1997, the FTC charged over 100 people or companies with false advertising in an infomercial. Joel Winston, an assistant director of the FTC's division of adversting practices, commented that the FTC filed fewer charges each year because the industry had "matured" and become more mainstream.

The prestige of the Fortune 500 found its way into the infomercial industry in the 1990s: their products accounted for 10 percent of infomercials on television. In the mid-1990s, Microsoft Corp. anointed the genre by using an infomercial to help launch Windows 95, using actor Anthony Edwards from television's *ER* to explain the new operating system to consumers. High-tech and financial products lent themselves especially well to the 28-minute television format since their features were not easily summed up in a 30-second television spot. The motive was to educate consumers, fix the brand name in their minds, and point potential customers to the nearest retailer. The aim of Fortune 500 spots is to generate sales leads rather than to sell products over the phone. For example, the Lexus infomercial explained its used car program and included a toll-free number. Over one year, the infomercial generated 40,000 phone calls, and 2 percent of those callers eventually bought a used Lexus. Sears, Roebuck & Co. also ran infomercials during the mid-1990s and claimed to have doubled in-store sales on items featured in the spots.

PIONEERS IN THE FIELD

One industry trailblazer is Ron Popeil, who began as a television pitchman for his father's kitchen inventions, the Chop-O-Matic and the Veg-O-Matic, during the 1950s. These products made over $1 million and drew Popeil into a career marketing his own inventions on television. Under the Ronco brand name, Popeil marketed such gadgets as the Ronco Spray Gun, the Pocket Fisherman, and Mister Microphone. Considering himself an inventor, Popeil is indeed acknowledged to have invented the new advertising medium. The highly successful Chop-O-Matic spot is today considered the first infomercial. After a series of financial setbacks, Popeil rebounded with a new 30-minute spot hawking his Ronco Electric Food Dehydrator. By the late 1990s, Popeil was back at it, reaping rewards from his infomercials for GLH Formula #9 Hair Spray, a tinted spray used to conceal men's bald spots, and for Ronco Showtime kitchenware.

Other industry pioneers started during, and have survived, the unregulated days of the 1980s. For example, Tyee Productions of Portland, Oregon, a private company headed by John Ripper, produced a very successful infomercial for Soloflex in 1987. By 1999 Tyee had clients such as Philips Magnavox, Home Depot, and Target and generated sales of $60 million. Another 1980s pioneer was Tim Hawthorne, of Fairfield, Iowa-based Hawthorne Communications. Hawthorne represented the infomercial's first mainstream client when the company brought Time Life Music to the air in 1986. By the late 1990s, Time Life had grown so comfortable with the genre that it sold ad time within its infomercials to other companies.

CURRENT CONDITIONS

An estimated 5 percent of the $2.67 trillion in total retail revenue in 1999 was generated by electronic retailing; direct-response television (DRTV) accounted for about 3 percent while the remaining 2 percent was derived from radio and the Internet. The future portends a massive expansion of the Internet's share, and as a result the line between DRTV and Internet commerce is likely to blur.

In that spirit, the Television Executives Council of the ERA was formed to foster continued integration of interactive capability on television and cable stations and to teach production of infomercials to electronic retailers directly. The entire process was a massive preparation for the pending day in the future when purchases will be made directly through the television.

The infomercial industry was expected to be buoyed somewhat by demographic luck in the 2000s. One of its largest sales demographics was empty-nest baby boomers, especially those reoutfitting their homes to suit changing lifestyles. This market will grow about 19 percent by 2009, while similar growth will occur in nontraditional households of childless couples and singles, another prime infomercial target.

Infomercials owe a good deal of their strength to health and fitness products, including training equipment, exercise videos, and dietary and nutritional supplements, which combined accounted for half of the top 10 infomercials produced in 1999. American Telecast's Total Gym, Cyclone Cross Trainer from Quantum/Direct.America, and the Tae-Bo video series all placed near the top of the *Greensheet Annual Review* in 1999. The market for such products generally coincides with general societal levels of prosperity, one clue to their success in the late 1990s. The combination martial arts and aerobics Tae-Bo series was in fact such a knockout that the infomercial graduated to pay-per-view status in late 1999. While cosmetic infomercials suffer from the consumer's inability to actually try on the products, infomercials promising consumers a quick route to a healthy and beautiful body flourish. With more than one-third of all Americans qualifying as overweight according to the National Center for Health Statistics, and with most of them opting for self-treatment, the direct "one-to-one" nature of infomercials fits perfectly. For the future, the continued increase in fitness-consciousness among more affluent older audiences offers the infomercial industry a promising future in this longtime staple category.

Jordan Whitney, Inc. tracked the top selling infomercials each week, and published the top 100 infomercials in the *Greensheet Annual Review*. The 1999 review listed the top infomercials as follows: Billy Blanks' Tae-Bo exercise video series placed first, followed by Popeil's Ronco Showtime kitchenware; the Carlton Sheets real estate investment system; the Enforma System weight-loss program; the Video Computer Store; Proactiv skin-care products; exercise machines the Ab Rocker, Total Gym, and Torso Track; and the North American Slim Down diet.

Amalgamating diverse demographic studies reveals two major groups dominating the infomercial consumer profile: well-off starting families with young children and affluent new empty nesters. Infomercial producers are increasingly following the money, focusing on more affluent customers, whom

Billy Blanks's Tae-Bo exercise video tapes. (Kelly Quinn)

time has shown to be more likely to buy products from infomercials. While about 4 percent of the U.S. population made an infomercial purchase in 1999, that figure rose to 7 percent among those earning between $75,000 and $99,000. Women were slightly more likely to buy from an infomercial, at 4.3 percent compared with 3.7 percent for men.

Despite years of effort to improve the image and integrity of infomercials, the medium remains one of the least trusted in the eyes of consumers. A survey conducted by Wirthlin Worldwide in July 1999 found that only 9 percent found infomercials to be "very believable," and 48 percent figured them to be "some-

what believable." An unfortunate 42 percent completely distrusted infomercials as an advertising medium. By way of comparison, 27 percent found product information in news articles to be very believable and 68 percent found it somewhat believable. Interestingly, however, infomercials ranked just above regular TV commercials in the eyes of the public.

INDUSTRY LEADERS

The leading U.S. infomercial producer, Guthy-Renker Corp. employed 200 and pulled in revenues of

$350 million in 1999, generating particularly lucrative business from the fitness and motivational-tape markets. Founded in 1988 by Bill Guthy and Greg Renker, the Palm Desert, California, company was at one point 38 percent owned by TV mogul Rupert Murdoch after Murdoch purchased World Communications, with whom Guthy-Renker had formed an alliance in 1993. In 1999, however, the company repurchased its stock from Murdoch, and is currently once again 100 percent privately owned. Guthy-Renker also operates the Guthy-Renker Television Network, which runs commercials on cable around the clock. A series of strategic alliances over the years have afforded Guthy-Renker privileged access to a number of consumers and resources, from which it has helped build its reputation as a leading producer of winning infomercials. In 1999 the firm allied with San Francisco-based Internet firm Looksmart. Some of their infomercial products included Personal Power by Tony Robbins, which has generated $250 million in sales over the years, and the Power Rider fitness machine. Greg Renker, incidentally, moonlights as chairman emeritus of ERA.

The largest publicly held direct-response television company was e4L (Everything4Less), Inc. In 1999 the company entered into an alliance with BuyIt Now, Inc. and Clear Channel Communications to form BuyItNow.com LLC. Formerly known as National Media, e4L banked on its hit "Body by Jake" Ab Rocker infomercial in 1999, which generated over 350,000 direct-response sales and earned Infomercial of the Year honors from Jordan Whitney, Inc. Other major products included the Great North American Slimdown, the PowerWalk Plus treadmill, Frankie Avalon's Zero Pain pain reliever, the Instant Fisherman, GOO Gone, and Tony Little's Target Training System. e4L employed 250 workers in 2000 and posted sales of $251.1 million, representing a decline of 26 percent from the previous year. The company airs its products with TV and cable companies, on satellite broadcasts, and even directly over the Internet. Over 6,000 half hours of e4L infomercials were broadcast to 370 million households in 70 countries all over the world, including 100 percent of the U.S. market.

AMERICA AND THE WORLD

Industry observers are optimistic about the global potential of infomercials. ERA held a conference in Venice, Italy, in 1998, that outlined the spread of infomercials into European markets. European customers likewise signaled their increased receptiveness to direct-response television and Internet commerce. The Scandinavian DRTV firm TV-Shop already has an established presence in much of Europe with its infomercials that, thanks to the more flexible European broadcasting slots, run sometimes only 15 minutes or less. ERA discussions with more than 50 local television stations throughout China also were underway. Finally, Japan's biggest trading company purchased an almost 20 percent stake in the Asian subsidiary of Guthy-Renker.

RESEARCH AND TECHNOLOGY

Enhanced interactivity and convergence were the buzzwords in the infomercial industry in 2000, both of which pointed to further integration with Internet commerce. With this thought in mind, the ERA recognized as crucial and logical the integration of all electronic retailing, including DRTV and Internet-based commerce, launching the Electronic Commerce Online Info Link through its Web site. The database acts as a central research and tracking portal for electronic retailing news and trends for producers, retailers, and suppliers. The ERA was further busy shoring up its relationship with the Internet industry as a whole, creating an Internet-industry liaison to help familiarize the Internet community with direct-response retailing and vice versa.

The Internet-infomercial cooperative efforts were mutual. Florida-based Reliant Interactive Media Corp. launched a global computer marketing concern called "As Seen on TV PC," while one of the most common new features in infomercial campaigns is the inclusion of retail Web sites, specifically designed to supplement traditional direct-response sales. Less directly, the Internet has aided the infomercial industry by providing a whole new spectrum of market research focusing on nontraditional shopping venues.

Meanwhile, the infomercial industry greeted a new research organization in 1999 called Atomic Direct. The Portland, Oregon-based company utilizes focus groups, trade shows, and prototype research to determine the likely success of infomercials. While companies wishing to invest in this research pay top dollar—a focus group costs $18,000, prototype research and trade show research cost $4,000 each, and qualitative surveys run $10,000—the largely hit-or-miss nature of the industry coupled with the high production costs could turn many companies on to the idea.

Profile KICKING HIS WAY TO INFOMERCIAL STARDOM

A former personal trainer for a host of Hollywood celebrities, by the end of 1999 Billy Blanks was poised as the next Jane Fonda—a fitness guru whose name was synonymous with the exercise-video world. Blanks's Tae-Bo video series generated the most successful infomercial on the market in the late 1990s. The 45-year-old star's workouts—a blend of tae kwon do, aerobics, and boxing—generated enough popularity to make Blanks one of the most recognizable faces on late-night television, and perhaps the only actor to have graduated from infomercials to prime time; Blanks was invited to appear in an episode of the popular television drama *ER*. Blanks also inked a book deal with Bantam Books, and planned a string of additional videos to add to his lucrative catalog.

The Tae-Bo workout dates back to the early 1980s, when Blanks began integrating karate maneuvers into a regular aerobic exercise, specifically considering ways to draw more women into martial arts training. Over the next 15 years, he drew such celebrity students as Sinbad, Shaquille O'Neal, and Carmen Electra to his program.

The Tae-Bo phenomenon as we know it today was born of Blanks's meeting with Ohio-based infomercial producer Paul Monea, who originally intended to hawk yet another exercise gadget before Blanks convinced him of the viability of a Tae-Bo infomercial, tipping the scale by securing free celebrity endorsements from Blanks's friends.

Recognizing a hit when they saw it, the infomercial's producers had few qualms about the weekly investment of about $1.5 million for cable television broadcasts. Thanks largely to the infomercial, over 1.5 million Tae-Bo videos were sold through direct response and at retail, amounting to revenues topping $100 million.

The infomercial was not completely free of taint, however. Boxing champion Sugar Ray Leonard filed a lawsuit over unauthorized use of his name in the spot after he pulled a testimonial endorsement following a dispute with Monea, though Leonard insisted that he and Blanks remain friends.

Despite such glitches, Blanks offered his analysis of the long-tenuous public perception of infomercials to the *Los Angeles Times*: "Most infomercials are cheesy." Blanks was consciously positioning his Tae-Bo infomercial as the honest and useful approach customers desire.

FURTHER READING

Cantanese, Sam. "IMS Top-100 Infomercials of 1999." *Response,* December 1999.

Collins, Scott. "Tae-Bo Infomercial Kicks up Success—and Legal Disputes." *Los Angeles Times,* 3 March 1999.

"DM Is Phat for Diet." *Direct,* 15 November 1999.

Foley, William F. "ERA to Debut New Online Database." *DM News,* 17 January 2000.

————. "Response Program PinPoints Broadcasters." *DM News,* 31 January 2000.

Gaw, Jonathan. "Media Firm Testing Infomercials On-line." *Los Angeles Times,* 23 November 1998.

Hawthorne, Timothy R. "Closed-Captioning Can Be DRTV Boon." *DM News,* 17 January 2000.

Laman, Justin. "The Next Big Thing As Seen On TV." *Drug Store News,* 14 August 2000.

McCrea, Bridget. "Mixing Television with the Web." *Response,* January 2000.

Nagel, David. "Atomic Goes Ballistic over DRTV Marketing Research." *Response,* October 1999.

Sexton, Sean. "FTC Charges Firm with Slippery Claims." *DRTV News,* 17 May 1999.

"Supers Rack up Biggest Gains in Growing Category." *MMR,* 10 January 2000.

Swartz, Jon. "Infomercials Slop over to the Net." *San Francisco Chronicle,* 25 January 1999.

Wellner, Alison. "Demographics Analysis: Trends Signal Boon for Home Products." *Response,* January 2000.

————. "Research Shows Untapped DRTV Potential." *Response,* October 1999.

INFORMATION MANAGEMENT SYSTEMS

The field of information management systems, like so many industries based on computer technology, is characterized by consistent change. Whether the result of improvements in hardware and the underlying software, the evolution of the World Wide Web as a medium of information delivery, or fundamental shifts in thinking about the role and use of information in business and industry, information management and the systems used to implement it function in an environment that is rarely the same from one day to the next.

Information management is the means whereby information is collected, identified, and analyzed, then distributed to the points within an organization where decisions are made and customers are served. Information management systems streamline and automate the often complex processes of coordinating a company's many activities with employees, suppliers, and customers.

The field is populated at once by computer industry giants such as IBM Corp. and Microsoft Corp.; smaller but powerful companies such as PeopleSoft, Sybase, and Oracle; and as-yet-unknown start-ups with large doses of technological savvy and the fierce desire to reap the benefits of redefining the possibilities of what can be accomplished through technology.

Ours is an increasingly global society wherein rapid, accurate access to vast amounts of disparate information is not only demanded, but increasingly taken for granted. Employee output in the United States is 40 percent higher than it was just 10 years ago; businesses, however, still feel the need to reduce costs and move with increasing efficiency in the marketplace. What fills the inevitable gaps created by the necessity to do more with less? Information: timely, accurate information. In that context, information management systems will continue to assume greater prominence while businesses, governments, and individuals become increasingly reliant upon them.

An industry study estimated sharp growth in the document technologies market through the year 2003. The study, a joint project of the Gartner Group and AIIM International, an information management trade group, projected that the market would grow from about $17.5 billion in 1999 to $21 billion in 2000, to more than $40 billion in 2003. The study emphasized the relationship between core document technologies and such emerging technologies as electronic commerce (e-commerce), Web content management, and knowledge management. Among the recommendations that might be drawn from the study is the vital importance of using document technologies in all phases of an operation, whether it's corporate, government, or nonprofit in nature.

An information management system is built on workflow software, groupware, and reporting tools. Workflow software automates the division and assignment of work and removes unnecessary steps along the way. Examples of workflow software include project management, billing, or integrated payroll systems. Groupware incorporates a variety of software, including e-mail and World Wide Web browsers, and hardware, including fax machines and voice mail, to allow employees direct access to the information management system and each other. Reporting tools enable users to retrieve information from the information management system. Examples of reporting tools include online analytical processing tools associated with data warehouses.

With the rise of the Internet and the World Wide Web as ubiquitous and fundamental research tools, issues related to retrieving and organizing information have become increasingly important to a wider and more varied population of information consumers. Libraries, once the primary users of information management systems, no longer have exclusive claim to the need to manage vast pools of wide-ranging data. Businesses, governments, and similar institutions have developed an unrelenting need to use the tools available for controlling a steady, massive inflow and output of information.

Data warehousing and online analytical processing (OLAP) are information repositories and reporting tools that enable users to convert raw data to valuable information. Data warehousing is a variation of data migration that involves moving and transforming data from a variety of systems into a single repository. OLAP software provides interactive access to multidimensional analysis of the data. There is a symbiotic relationship between the data warehouse and the OLAP tools used to mine the information since the repository structure and querying tools operate interdependently.

A data warehouse in essence is a large collection of data with the tools to sort and analyze the data—or, as defined by founding father William H. Inmon, it centers around a subject orientation, includes normalized data, and incorporates nonvolatile content (archival data that does not change once recorded). The subject orientation of a data warehouse may include, for example, products, customers, and inventory. The data warehouse receives information on these subjects from a variety of operational databases within the organization such as transactional (invoice databases) or records (marketing databases). The data received from these different databases is frequently coded and described in different ways and must be normalized prior to use. Disparate databases, data types, and data elements can be handled by a gateway within the information management system to integrate enterprise-wide knowledge into one usable whole. Structured query language (SQL) translators accomplish the task of interpreting a variety of database types, elements, and messages from standard relational databases. Essentially, a database begins by

talking to an SQL server such as Oracle 7 or IBM's DataJoiner. The SQL server provides the necessary translation using a global data dictionary and passes the information on to the next database. The internal formats of different databases vary according to the business concepts behind the database design. Thus, while the translation may be technically accurate, the SQL solution means data may require additional manipulation. Because of the substantial potential of data warehouses, about 90 percent of Fortune 2,000 companies have implemented or plan to implement a data warehouse.

Alternately, Web-based information management systems rely on the system architecture of the client-server and a common user interface to integrate information between disparate databases. A client-server system consists of a server (a computer that contains information and serves it up at the request of a client computer) and a client (a computer that asks for information from a server). Client-server solutions can result in a lack of data cohesiveness. While operational databases are updated regularly with deletions and insertions, the data warehouse is a read-only environment in which information is loaded, then read through a series of snapshots. As the snapshots are stacked together, it becomes possible to examine data across layers of geography or time, as well as across the traditional two-dimensional columns and rows of the single snapshots. The content of the data warehouse includes integrated data, detailed and summarized data, historical data, and metadata. Metadata describe the context of the information.

OLAP tools extend the architecture of the data warehouse by reading and aggregating large groups of diverse data. Richard Finkelstein, president of Performance Computing Inc., noted that the objective of OLAP is to analyze these relationships and look for patterns, trends, and exceptional conditions. The key characteristic of an OLAP is that it provides a multidimensional conceptual view of the data. Variations of OLAP include relational online analytic processing (ROLAP) and desktop online analytical processing (DOLAP). Data mining, another form of online analysis, creates a model from current information and projects this model onto another scenario where information is nonexistent. One drawback to an OLAP system is that it often requires the use of a proprietary OLAP database or warehouse without the same capacity as a standard relational database. ROLAP software allows users to make queries of a relational data warehouse.

Decentralized data and different databases abound in corporate America. Information management systems piece together information from disparate sources. Simple component information management systems link databases together based on their involvement with a part or product. For example, an inventory reorder system is a kind of information management system that tracks inventory stock and updates all databases for reorder, shipment, and payment. Because component information management systems are based on a preexisting product or need, such as the search for a part, gateways and search engines are precoordinated. Evolving from these product-based systems, a more complex information management system emerges to allow employees to postcoordinate their information retrieval needs. Workflow software, groupware, and reporting tools share information with each other so that, for example, employees can specify what kind of information is desired and in what format it will appear. This integration of information represents a progressive movement from piecemeal business data toward business knowledge for employee, supplier, and customer alike.

TRENDS

Many companies have already embraced Internet technology, and many more are now looking to one of the spin-offs of that technology: intranets. An intranet is an internal information system based on Internet technology such as Web services, transfer protocols, and the Hypertext Markup Language (HTML). Although intranets use technological concepts that are prevalent on the Internet and World Wide Web, the information contained on an intranet stays securely within the company or organization managing it. Intranets are private business networks based on Internet and World Wide Web standards, but they are designed to be used internally. In other words, random Internet users cannot access a company's intranet; only those individuals granted specific access to an intranet can use it.

Like the Internet, intranets often require little or no training, as people who are familiar with navigating the Internet can usually become equally proficient at using intranets. Intranets can be easily maneuvered within graphics-based Web browsers, which are standard on every hardware platform in the intranet. This facilitates greater remote access without the use of wide area networks.

The connection between intranets and information management systems is twofold. First, information management systems are fundamental for any company trying to take advantage of intranets, since they provide the freedom to fine-tune access to data, facilitate the targeting of specific information to specific people, simplify delivery of information, and incorporate databases. Second, using intranets in conjunction with information management systems reduces the costs of software, hardware, and maintenance. Indeed, the two systems are so well-suited that most information management vendors are now adapting their products for intranet use; with ever more information to manage and share, it is a trend that is sure to continue.

Emerging from the use of intranets is the trend toward the next level: extranets. Extranets are business-to-business networks operating over the Internet. When two companies allow each other access to parts of their intranets, they have created an extranet. Extranets can provide regulated and secure communications between companies, and are frequently used to aid in customer service, to facilitate transaction processing, and as an adjunct to marketing.

A number of software applications making it easier to set up and use extranets were introduced in the late 1990s. With increased ease of use and the convenience to customers and business partners of unimpeded access to a company's communications and information core, it is expected that extranet use will continue to increase dramatically until extranets become as prevalent in corporate information management systems as networks. The ease with which they let companies and customers interact will be a dominant factor in the increased use of extranets. For example, no more than 5 percent of Motorola, Inc.'s computer group customers used the company's extranet in January 1998. Company executives, however, reported that well over 50 percent were utilizing the extranet by the spring of 1999. Business-to-business use of extranets will also be crucial to their wider acceptance. For example, some companies, such as wood products maker Boise Cascade Corp., are moving their supply chains to the extranet.

Leading software manufacturer Lotus Corp. predicted that "the Internet/Intranet phenomenon will continue to reshape how people play, work, and interact in all conceivable (and maybe some inconceivable) ways. A wired world of global networks is fast replacing the world-in-a-desktop computing model." IBM's Network Computing Framework, integrated through Lotus's Domino Web Server, is an example of such an interconnected system.

APPLICATIONS

Information management systems appear in a variety of ways and for a variety of reasons. A human resource information management system, for example, concentrates its focus on payroll, benefits, and status information. Laboratory information management systems (LIMS) are typically designed specifically for the analytical laboratory. LIMS connect the analytical instruments in the lab to one or more workstations or personal computers (PCs). When data are collected by these instruments, they are forwarded by an interface to the PC where the data are stored, sorted, and organized into reports and other meaningful forms of output based on the type of information requested by the system users. Financial institutions benefit greatly from information management systems when customer account data and transaction histories are integrated. Coeur Business International offers an information management system for value-added resellers called VARoffice. VARoffice features a knowledge-base navigator to find solutions to common problems, a technical support log, and a marketing events management system. The program can be customized with Microsoft Access, VisualBasic, and an SQL server. Businesses that rely heavily on statistical analysis, such as real estate investment firms, also benefit from information management systems. Many buy-sell decisions are made according to a wide variety of market indicators. Viewing data multidimensionally across time and geography can provide invaluable information for investment decisions using an information management system. The Security Capital Group uses a multidimensional OLAP database for critical budgeting and analytical tasks.

Among their advantages, information management systems provide quick access to multiple databases holding information such as engineering parts, financial transactions, textbook titles, and customer contacts. Information management systems also encourage design reuse and reduce the time necessary to set up a new part, coordinate schedules, or change workflow processes. The Internet and the World Wide Web have spurred innovation and development of information management systems by capitalizing on the inherent network functionality of the Internet and the universality and ease of the Web browser. It is possible for all workers, suppliers, and customers to enjoy the same common interface without regard to physical location or time. Reduced hardware and software costs are prime benefits of a Web-based information management system. The formerly separate processes of document management and workflow are two applications now merging into one larger system on the World Wide Web.

BACKGROUND AND DEVELOPMENT

The first functioning document retrieval system to use electronics was demonstrated in Dresden, London, and Paris in 1931, according to Michael Buckland, a professor at the University of California-Berkeley's School of Information Management and Systems. Well before digital computers, Emanuel Goldberg's "statistical machine" combined photocell, circuitry, and microfilm for document retrieval.

But even if Goldberg's machine provided the first hints of what an electronic information management system could do, it was not until the advent of the computer that information management began to evolve and increasingly complex systems became necessary to handle the large amounts of data generated.

The first prototype of a working business computer, the 409, was introduced in 1951. Information was fed to the 409 via a refrigerator-sized punch-card unit. Punch cards—stiff cards in which holes were actually punched via machine—provided the programming and data for early computers as they "read" the sequence of holes. This physical means of introducing data to a computer, however, created an environment in which an error could result in many lost hours of work. Early computer operators did not have the convenience of a backspace or delete key.

Yet information management systems evolved from the punch-card machines to mainframes and spools of magnetic tape. Structured query language (SQL) was introduced in the 1970s via a database system called System R. The Multics Relational Data Store was released in June 1976 and is believed to be the first relational database management system offered by a major computer vendor, in this case, Honeywell Information Systems, Inc.

In the 1970s, IBM mainframe computers were the prevalent systems found in business usage, whereas minicomputer platforms such as AS/400 and VAX/VMS dominated in the 1980s. The 1980s also saw the rise of the personal computer as both an individual and business tool.

It is, however, the evolution of the Internet and World Wide Web in the 1990s as a medium of information archiving and dissemination that continues to have the greatest impact upon the field of information management systems. In 1970 the average Fortune

500 company might house 8 billion characters of data in its electronic storage banks. By the year 2000, it was predicted that a similar organization will have the need to control and manage 400 trillion characters of electronic data. Current trends strongly suggest that much of this information will be manipulated by Web technology on the Internet and through corporate intranets and extranets.

CURRENT CONDITIONS

The information management systems industry experienced rapid growth in the late 1990s and this growth is forecasted to continue through the beginning of the new decade. According to an AIIM International and Gartner Group study, the market grew from about $10 billion in 1997 to $17.5 billion in 1999. The study indicated that this expansion should increase through 2003, when the market is expected to top $41 billion. Of the 1999 total, workflow technologies accounted for $3.2 billion and by 2003 they are expected to grow to $8.5 billion. Despite the increase in revenues, however, use of information management systems is expected to outpace sales because the technology is becoming more of a commodity with greater competition among producers, which may cause prices to drop or remain stagnant, according to AIIM International and the Gartner Group.

The financial services and manufacturing industries led the information management systems boom in the late 1990s with heightened demand for information technology and services. According to AIIM International and the Gartner Group, these industries, along with utilities and telecommunications industries, will drive the information management systems industry at the beginning of the new century.

During the late 1990s, the leading applications of information management systems included record and archival, accounts payable and receivable, customer service, human resources, and litigation information management. Furthermore, some of the leading motivations for implementing information management systems included the growth of e-commerce, the need for greater efficiency, the influx of information and data, and the popularity of the Internet.

The growth of e-commerce also spawned a new segment of the industry: applications services providers (ASPs) that create Web-based systems for providing information on product availability and current customer orders, processing orders and payments, arranging delivery, and storing names and addresses.

While smaller companies such as Digital River Inc. were some of the first providers of this technology, industry giants such as Oracle and SAP AG formed ASP divisions. This segment garnered about $296 million in revenues in 1999, but sales are predicted to balloon to $7.7 billion by 2004, according to International Data Corp.

To combat the information overload, a growing technique used for Web-based information management systems during the late 1990s and the early part of the new decade was the development of portals. Similar to Web sites such as Yahoo!, the portal organizes information on a Web page replete with graphs, images, tables, charts, and other objects to make the tangle of information on the Web more accessible and manageable. Portals are often used with intranets, integrating and organizing applications, files, and data from throughout a company and its departments. In 1999, only about 16 percent of companies had implemented portals, but by 2001 more than 80 percent are expected to use portals, according to the Delphi Group, an information technology consulting firm. In 2000, portal software ran from $50,000 to $500,000. Roughly 40 companies offered portals during this period, including Plumtree Software, Viador, SAP AG, and PeopleSoft Inc.

Furthermore, companies and information management systems vendors began working more closely together in the late 1990s in order to achieve greater efficiency in information management. For example, IntelliCorp, a leader in the information management industry, announced the formation of an industry leadership council made up of executives from companies active in information management. Council members were drawn from such prestigious companies as Andrews Inc., Deere & Co., Coca Cola Co., Fluoroware, TRW, and Nestlé USA. The group held a two-day meeting in November 1998 to consider some of the more pressing challenges facing the industry as the millennium neared an end. Assessing IntelliCorp's initiative after the council's first meeting, Marie Fuggle of Nestlé USA concluded that it "was an excellent forum to discuss today's pressing business process management issues, such as application integration, data integrity, and cleansing." Of data cleansing, which the council found to be one of the most costly and least anticipated expenses during implementations, Fuggle said: "I've seen double-digit man years spent to cleanse fewer than 100,000 records; there is tremendous potential to dramatically reduce these costs."

IntelliCorp suggested that another critical issue facing the industry is the need to stage global system rollouts in a manner that is cost-effective but that still ensures continuity of corporate objectives and business processes. "Given today's requirements for daily information management between divisions and sites, corporations are looking for ways to save time and resources," according to Colin Bodell, IntelliCorp's chief operating officer. "We are developing tools and training that reduce the time and resources required to manage and control enterprise resource planning systems throughout their life cycles—and make data easy for nontechnical managers to use." Elaborating on IntelliCorp's rationale for setting up the leadership council, Ken Haas, president and CEO, said, "It's vital for us to review industry trends and the direction in which we are moving with leaders in the information management industry." He remarked that hosting the meeting of the council helped the company to uncover "some new areas where we can add value to our customers in today's business climate."

INDUSTRY LEADERS

Oracle Corp., Sybase Inc., and IBM all provide SQL gateways and OLAP software for use in an information management system. Oracle, based in Redwood City, California, posted revenues of $10.1 billion in fiscal 2000. The company employed about 43,800 worldwide. Sybase, headquartered in Emeryville, California, and the employer of nearly 4,200, reported a net profit of $62.5 million on sales of $871.6 million in 1999. Giant IBM, based in Armonk, New York, posted net income of $7.7 billion on sales of $87.5 billion in 1999 and employed more than 307,401 worldwide.

PeopleSoft, Inc. is another major player in the industry, providing human resources and enterprise resource planning applications. In 1999 PeopleSoft had $1.42 billion in revenues from offices in the United States, Canada, Europe, the Pacific Rim, Central and South America, and Africa. The company is headquartered in Pleasanton, California, and employed 6,929 people in 2000.

Other players in this market niche include Informix Corp.; Cognos, Inc.; and Hyperion Solutions. Informix produces Metacube, while Cognos offers PowerPlay and Impromptu (a reporting and querying package), and Hyperion Solutions makes Essbase. In 1996 Arbor Software (which merged with Hyperion Software in 1998 to form Hyperion Solutions) integrated Essbase with a reporting tool called Crystal Info and Crystal Reports from Seagate Software Co. Ora-

cle revised and renamed its reporting software to incorporate OLAP functions into the Oracle relational database. Oracle's renamed product is called Discover. In April 1996 PeopleSoft Inc. began bundling Cognos PowerPlay and Impromptu OLAP tools and Arbor's Essbase with its applications software.

A number of companies offer component or parts information management systems. Empart Technologies offers a product called EMPART. Other industry leaders in the area of component information management systems are Aspect Development Inc. and Information Handling Services. Aspect Development offers a product called Explore, while Information Handling Services produces a component information management system called CapsXpert. Both cover more than a million parts and offer specialized search capabilities. In July 1997 Aspect introduced a new search tool called SmartMatch that allowed users to search through large databases and find parts under different naming conventions. Another company, Team Corp., offers EDA-Bridge, a Windows-based component information management system. In contrast, other companies such as OrCAD Inc. offer a component information management system without a centralized database. OrCAD features Capture Enterprise Edition, offering parts management, parts searching, and links to online corporate databases.

Information Handling Services Group Inc., the U.S. subsidiary of Netherlands-based Information Handling Services, is based in Englewood, Colorado. The company, which is privately held, generated estimated sales of $450 million in fiscal 1999. Worldwide the company employs about 3,200. In January 1997 Information Handling Services and Team Corp. agreed to jointly develop and market an interface between CapsXpert and Explore. By 2000, Information Handling Services boasted of 900,000 users in almost 100 countries. OrCAD, based in Beaverton, Oregon, in April 1997 purchased the EDA Bridge from Team Corp., significantly expanding its leadership in the worldwide component information management systems market. In mid-1999, Cadence Design Systems, Inc. acquired OrCAD for $121 million.

Computer Associates International Inc., characterized by chairman and CEO Charles B. Wang as the world's leading developer of client-server solutions and a world leader in mission-critical business software, offers financial and human resources management, products for Internet and Web development, and multiple-access database management systems, among many other offerings. Computer Associates, headquartered in Islandia, New York, reported net income of $696 million on sales of $6.7 billion for the fiscal year ending 31 March 2000. The company employed more than 14,650 worldwide. IntelliCorp, based in Mountain View, California, is one of the nation's leading providers of enterprise resource planning life-cycle management products and services. The company reported for fiscal year 2000 a net loss of $7.1 million on revenue of $22.7 million. IntelliCorp employed 137 people as of late 2000.

AMERICA AND THE WORLD

The United States accounts for roughly 50 percent of the global information management market, while Europe makes up about 30 percent and Asia 10 percent. Further, although many of the major players in the information management systems industry have headquarters in the United States, these providers also maintain an extensive worldwide presence. Cognos, for example, has corporate headquarters in Ottawa, Canada, with U.S. sales headquarters in Burlington, Massachusetts. Cognos also has more than 32 offices worldwide in such countries as Australia, France, Germany, Hong Kong, Japan, and the United Kingdom. Lotus maintains offices in several different countries, while Sybase has its world headquarters in Emeryville, California, but has other departments located in 63 countries, including France, Canada, Italy, Germany, and the People's Republic of China.

One of the industry's major software providers, SAP AG, is headquartered in Walldorf, Germany, but also maintains several international offices. SAP's products are used by thousands of companies throughout the world, including Microsoft and General Motors. In 1999 SAP posted sales of $5.1 billion.

Testimony to the growing internationalization of the information management industry came in April 1999 with the announcement of the merger of the world's leading information management trade groups. AIIM International and the International Information Management Congress announced their merger on 14 April 1999. The combined organization carried the name of AIIM International. In announcing the merger, AIIM President John Mancini said, "this combination creates a single international resource to develop more effective and timely industry events, reports, studies, and standards."

RESEARCH AND TECHNOLOGY

In February 1998 the World Wide Web Consortium approved the Extensible Markup Language (XML) as a standard. XML, a metalanguage that provides information about data, comes from the same common background as HTML, but is considerably more powerful and permits more efficient structure and easier exchange of data than HTML.

The advantage of XML is that it is expected to streamline e-commerce, making it easier for companies to conduct business in the online world. XML will ease existing difficulties in sharing information on an intranet, and will allow Web searches to become more detailed and sophisticated. In addition, whereas HTML allows users to only view data, XML will allow the manipulation of data inside a browser. Microsoft included XML support in Internet Explorer 4.0, and Netscape Communications plans for Navigator 6.0 to be equipped with XML support.

A number of vendors are already producing products that use XML as a basis. For example, Sequoia Software Corp. provides an XML transaction server that allows different applications to share data. Marquette Medical Systems of Milwaukee, Wisconsin, plans a Web-enabled version of its cardiovascular monitoring system that will use XML tags to consolidate and post information from various departments on a hospital intranet. (Also see the essay in this book entitled XML.)

Lotus Corp. also sees other technological trends that will continue to shape the world of information and information management. For example, e-commerce, based on the 64 percent annual growth rate of the Internet as a business medium and perhaps fueled by the expansion of XML, will require increased delivery of electronic catalogs and customized shopper information. Lotus predicted that improved levels of Internet security and the merging of messaging, groupware, and the Web will allow e-commerce levels to grow to an annual volume of $300 billion within the first decade of the 2000s. Lotus also believed that three-dimensional data will soon be available over the Web via Virtual Reality Modeling Language.

Intranets and data warehouses will continue to proliferate, Lotus predicted, and push technology will make it easier to establish customized methods for delivering exactly what information a person wants from the vast store of material available electronically, even if a customer does not really know what might be available.

Other technologies will continue to aid the evolution of information management systems, particularly in Web-based applications. Java, Sun Microsystems's platform-independent programming language, is being used for several intranet applications (such as

Novasoft's NovaWeb) and in document management systems (IntraNet's Intra.doc! 3.0). Intra.doc!, for example, permits the immediate building and posting of custom Web pages based on a customer's unique requests. The pages contain the requested information, appropriate links, and ordering information. Lotus reported that more than 1,000 IBM and Lotus programmers are working full-time on integrating Java technology, "Designed from the start for networked applications, this new programming language builds bridges where barriers used to be." Being platform-independent, Java applications can run on any computer and will not be hindered by the perpetual PC vs. Mac obstacles. The phrase to remember, Lotus said, is "Write once, use anywhere."

At the turn of the century, information management researchers focused on issues such as record-keeping software, electronic records retention, and archiving electronic records, according to John T. Phillips in *Information Management Journal.* Since e-mail and computer-generated documents constitute the major business records, companies require information management systems that are designed to organize and store these kinds of documents, not paper documents. Electronic documents also create a problem of how long they should be stored, and so information management applications must address this problem, too. Some methods being explored to solve this problem include developing retention schedules for different departments (for example, ones for accounting, human resources, and production) so that certain types of documents are retained for specific periods, depending on the department. Finally, given the potential for loss of electronic documents through computer malfunctioning, viruses, and environmental factors, researchers are exploring issues of media compatibility, data transfer rates, and data recording methods, while simultaneously considering their effect on information retention.

FURTHER READING

AIIM International. "AIIM International and IMC Combine." 14 April 1999. Available from http://www.aiim.org/events/pressroom/aiim_imccombine.html.

Buckland, Michael. "Emanuel Goldberg and His Statistical Machine, 1927." Available from http://www.sims.berkeley.edu/~buckland/statistical.html.

———. "Emanuel Goldberg, Pioneer of Information Science." Available from http://www.sims.berkeley.edu/~buckland/goldberg.html.

Carrillo, Karen M. "PIM for the Enterprise Lotus Integrates Personal Information Manager with Notes and Domino." *InformationWeek,* 19 May 1997.

Castelluccio, Michael. "Data Warehouses, Marts, Metadata, OLAP/ROLAP, and Data Mining: A Glossary." *Management Accounting,* October 1996.

Dalton, Gregory. "XML Becomes a Standard; Vendors Ready Products-Language Likely to Boost E-commerce, Ease Web Searches." *Information Week,* 16 February 1998.

Darrow, Barbara. "Client/Server Software." *Computer Reseller News,* 3 June 1996.

David, Julie, and Paul Steinbart. "Drowning in Data." *Strategic Finance,* December 1999.

"EDA Software System Manages Parts Data." *EETimes,* 16 December 1996.

"EDA Software Uses Indexed Fuzzy Matching Aspect Spins a Smart Tool to Broaden Search for Parts." *EE Times,* 14 July 1997.

"EDA-Tool Users Can Tap CapsXpert Component Database IHS, Team Forge Access Deal." *EETimes,* 20 January 1997.

"Empart Technologies Delivers World's Most Powerful Parts Information Management System: Company Announces Availability of EMPART Viewer and EMPART Publisher." *Business Wire,* 27 August 1996.

Georing, Richard. "Acquisitions Involve Pioneers of Windows-Based Tools, OrCAD, PADS Make Small but Strategic Buys." *EE Times,* 21 April 1997.

Greengard, Samuel. "Making Sense of the Information Storm." *Industry Week,* 20 September 1999.

Gupta, Vivek R. "An Introduction to Data Warehousing." System Services Corp., August 1997. Available from http://system-services.com/dwintro.asp.

Henson, Row. "HRIMS for Dummies: A Practical Guide to Technology Implementation." *HR Focus,* November 1996.

Hinrichs, Randy J. *Intranets: What's the Bottom Line?* New York: Sunsoft/Prentice Hall, 1997.

Hise, Phaedra. "Human Resources: Hitting Pay Dirt." *Inc.,* 15 June 1998. Available from http://www.inc.com/inc-magazine/archives/16980891.html.

Horowitz, Alan S. "Year of the Extranet at Last?" *Information Week Online,* 5 January 1998.

Inmon, W. H. "The Data Warehouse and Data Mining." *Communications of the ACM,* November 1996.

"IntelliCorp Leadership Council Highlights Trends in Business Process Management." *M2 PressWIRE,* 20 November 1998.

"An Introduction to LIMS." *LIMsource.* Available from http://www.limsource.com/intro.html.

Leon, Mark. "Query, Reporting Tools Offer Data Access, OLAP Functions." *InfoWorld,* 21 October 1996.

Liebs, Scott. "Think before You Link." *Industry Week,* 17 April 2000.

Linder, Jane C., and Drew Phelps. "'Design' Critical in Information Age." *Computerworld,* 14 February 2000.

Patel, Jeetu, and Clark Brady. "Architecture Fit for an Intranet." *Information Week Online,* 23 March 1998.

Phillips, John T. "Technology: Tools for Managing Information." *Information Management Journal,* July 1999.

Richman, Dan. "Oracle Develops OLAP." *Computerworld,* 11 March 1996.

Ryan, Bill. "The Computer Age Began in a Barn." *New York Times,* 29 March 1998.

Spinner, Karen. "Unlocking the Data Warehouse with OLAP." *Wall Street & Technology,* winter 1997.

Stein, Tom. "JumboSports Inventory Problem Stores Flooded with Excess Products." *Information Week,* 14 July 1997.

Taft, Darryl K. "CBI Aims to Make a VARs Day." *Computer Reseller News,* 9 June 1997.

Walsh, Jeff. "Document-Management Products Unveiled at AIIM." *InfoWorld Electric,* 12 May 1998.

Waltner, Charles. "Up-to-Data Publisher Uses Information Management System to Centralize Product Data." *Information Week,* 26 May 1997.

INTERNET SERVICE PROVIDERS

The Internet service industry is maturing rapidly even as the customer base continues to swell at double-digit rates. Slim profit margins and changing competitive dynamics are forcing many Internet service providers (ISPs) to merge—dragging the total count of ISPs down—but the Internet user base is nonetheless expected to rise by as much as 50 percent in the early 2000s.

In the consumer market, basic Internet access has grown rapidly into a commodity service, and a rising number of consumers even opt for ad-driven free access services. Meanwhile, ISPs are stumbling over each other in a mad rush to ramp up high-bandwidth services using digital subscriber line (DSL) or cable networks. Along the way, a cadre of broadband operators has emerged that has begun tapping into revenues that previously went to conventional ISPs and telecommunications companies, although cable operators and phone companies have been getting in on the broadband action as well.

Many observers believe the future of ISPs lies solidly in broadband and value-added services. Broadband is essential for users who wish to download large files, such as music and video applications. The number of broadband households in the United States was expected to rise from just over 2 million in 1999 to more than 15 million by 2003, according to projections by Jupiter Communications, a high-tech market research firm. By the end of that period, upwards of 68 million U.S. households are expected to be online, giving broadband just over a fifth of the market. The

rest will still use customary phone lines and modems to dial into ISPs' networks, Jupiter predicted.

To differentiate themselves and to mine for new revenue streams, ISPs of all stripes are looking for new value they can bring to customers beyond getting them connected and delivering their e-mail. Because they're usually less pedestrian than basic access service, value-added services can offer greater opportunities to profit. Different approaches include offering unified messaging (receiving voice, fax, and e-mail messages all from one source), instant messaging (text-based chat with others online), online security software and software applications for rent, and unique content by partnering with media and entertainment outlets.

In a related trend, the distribution structure for Internet services is changing. To wit, there's a growing specialization of retail marketers and wholesale service providers. This distinction has existed to some degree since the early commercialization of the Internet, but increasingly firms with no infrastructure of their own are able to project a massive retail presence while leaving the logistics to someone else. These so-called virtual ISPs often have a well-known brand identity, such as Wal-Mart or Alta Vista, but don't have expertise or resources to run a national network of their own. Instead, they depend on behind-the-scenes wholesalers, sometimes called Internet service distributors (ISDs), to handle the back end. In effect, the retailer leases network resources and technical support from the ISD. This trend is expected to continue as ISPs realign around new value propositions, with some ISPs with strong brands taking the retail path

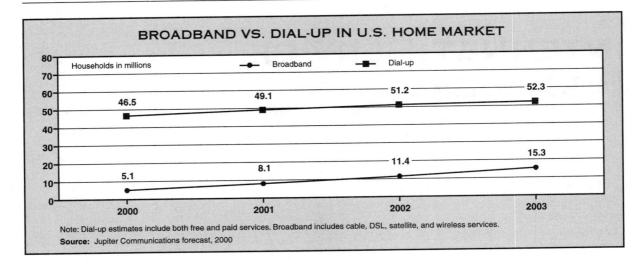

BROADBAND VS. DIAL-UP IN U.S. HOME MARKET

Households in millions — Broadband — Dial-up

Note: Dial-up estimates include both free and paid services. Broadband includes cable, DSL, satellite, and wireless services.

Source: Jupiter Communications forecast, 2000

and others exploiting their technical prowess in the wholesale arena.

ORGANIZATION AND STRUCTURE

SLOW PHONE LINES

Internet service is delivered in myriad ways and is required by several distinct markets. Mode of access often varies by market. For consumers, by far the most common method is analog dial-up service over standard phone lines. This supports download speeds up to 56 kilobits per second (Kbps) and is usually both the slowest and cheapest way to reach the Internet. In 2000, over 95 percent of U.S. online households used dial-up services.

Speed limitations, however, have rendered dial-up access ineffective at transmitting the vast pools of data that popular Internet applications increasingly require. Downloading high-resolution graphics, animations, sound files, and video clips are all problematic over a 56 Kbps line, not to mention trying to download large software application files. And upload speeds are typically worse.

CABLE HAS EARLY LEAD IN BROADBAND

As a result, there's been a veritable race to launch services that rely on faster, higher-capacity technology—collectively known as broadband. The most common of these in 2000 was using coaxial cable and a special cable modem. Cable system operators and specialized partners such as Excite@Home are usually the service providers. These services, run through the same wires that supply cable television programming, can support speeds up to 1 megabit per second

(Mbps), although the norm is considerably lower. Cable Internet services effectively connect households to a local area network that's shared with other subscribers in their area. This allows consumers to maintain a constant connection—no dialing in—but as marketers of competing broadband services are quick to point out, if too many people in the same neighborhood are using cable Internet services simultaneously, performance can suffer markedly. The cable network structure also makes the medium one of the least secure, leaving the average subscriber's personal computer (PC) vulnerable to hacking unless the subscriber takes special measures to shore up security. In early 2000, just over a million U.S. households subscribed to cable Internet services.

DSL CATCHING UP

Cable's main broadband challenger is a collection of technologies known as digital subscriber line (DSL). DSL variants include symmetric DSL (SDSL), where upload and download speeds are the same, and asymmetric DSL (ADSL), where downloads are faster than uploads. DSL sends a digital signal over ordinary telephone lines and requires special equipment at the local phone switching center and a DSL modem for the subscriber's computer. DSL services are offered by local phone companies as well as specialty distributors, such as Covad Communications Group, that have deployed DSL infrastructure in metropolitan areas. The technology can support speeds up to 800 Kbps, but the common consumer speed is closer to 128 Kbps. Unlike cable, DSL service doesn't degrade as quickly when more users are on the local system—and ISPs are able to guarantee a minimum level of service—but it faces some of the same security and local overload issues. There were only about 900,000

DSL subscribers by the end of 2000, according to Yankee Group, but the number was growing more quickly than that of almost any other medium.

SATELLITE AND WIRELESS OPTIONS, TOO

Other consumer options include satellite and terrestrial wireless services, although neither have yet garnered large followings. Satellite services such as DirecPC offer fast downloads, but the leading providers can't accommodate high-speed uploads. Wireless is likely to be a major growth category, especially as Internet service and mobile phone serve begin to meld, but so far the services are fairly underdeveloped. In addition to cellular service carriers that offer some form of Internet messaging and limited content retrieval, a handful of general-purpose wireless ISPs such as Metricom, Inc. have launched services aimed at users with mobile computing devices.

BUSINESS MARKET NEEDS HIGHER PERFORMANCE

All the connection types available to consumers are options for businesses, but usually medium and large companies require even greater bandwidth to support Internet connectivity for legions of employees and to accommodate electronic commerce (e-commerce) needs.

Some of the most common formats are leased lines such as T-1 or T-3 connections, which can achieve transfer rates of 1.5 Mbps and 45 Mbps, respectively. The technology is similar to that of DSL, only these connections have much greater capacity, and consequently, cost more. Indeed, T-3s are what connect much of the Internet backbone, the core high-speed network that forms the central nervous system of the Internet. T-1s and T-3s can also be bundled or divided to tailor the amount of bandwidth available. Fiber optics, even faster and more costly, provide another alternative.

One possibility for smaller organizations is an integrated services digital network (ISDN) connection, but this may be a dying standard because conventional ISDN tends to be slower and more expensive than DSL services (although a faster version exists). For small businesses, though, DSL is likely to become the connection of choice as it becomes more widely available.

SERVICE PROVIDERS VARY

Just as connection types vary, so do the companies offering them. The industry can be segmented broadly into three types of carriers. Consumer-oriented ISPs such as America Online (AOL) and EarthLink focus on residential service and frequently offer their own content. Business-oriented providers such as PSINet and many local phone companies, meanwhile, provide high-speed connections along with such services as Web hosting and network consulting. Finally, wholesale providers such as PSINet and Microportal sell Internet access and related services to resellers rather than end users.

BACKGROUND AND DEVELOPMENT

THE HISTORY OF COMPUTER NETWORKS

Forbears to the Internet began as limited network systems for organizations to communicate either internally over short distances or externally over long distances by using computers. In the late 1970s computer networking started to grow. Organizations could afford to use this technology due to the advent of microcomputers that had the power to support several user terminals at once. With local area networks (LANs), companies or organizations could connect a cluster of microcomputers because the technology was relatively inexpensive and easy to install. LANs, however, had their disadvantages, too: they required expensive hardware to transmit large quantities of information quickly, and certain kinds of LAN systems could not work with others. Therefore, if an organization had a special LAN for its warehouse and another for its accounting department, they would not be compatible. Moreover, LAN cables could extend only about 500 meters without harming performance.

The LAN counterpart, wide area networks (WANs), existed since the late 1960s and early 1970s and used modems to send messages through regular telephone lines instead of through directly linked cables such as LANs. WANs also required a host computer at each participating site that was devoted to connecting transmission lines and maintaining the operation of the system. The host computer, often called a server, functioned independently of computers using the WAN. On the other hand, WAN technology cost substantially more than LAN technology because WANs required transmission lines, modems, a special computer, and WAN software, whereas LANs simply required cabling and software. Furthermore, as with LANs, most WANs were incompatible with other WANs and with LANs.

This background created a need for a less expensive, long- and short-range, expandable networking system. The U.S. Department of Defense's Advanced Research Projects Agency (ARPA) endeavored to resolve the problems with existing networking technology and developed a working model of what came to be called the Internet. ARPA interconnected LANs and WANs using this model to provide the features of each computer networking system. In the mid-1970s, commercial computer companies began to develop their own closed, or proprietary, networks, which would work only with the vendor's software and hardware, although ARPA had conceived of the Internet as an open network that could allow users to communicate no matter whose software and hardware they used. Companies changed their minds, however, as computer hardware technology advances spurred new sales. The cost of computers also decreased, so companies could expect an expanding customer base, as well.

By 1982, researchers had a working version of the Internet in operation, and some major technological universities and industrial research organizations began using it. Computer science departments, in particular, led a campaign to connect all researchers in computer science via the Internet. In addition, the U.S. military also started to rely on the Internet as a standard means of communication and information transmission. At this point, the Internet became an actual tool for communication as opposed to being just an experiment. After the military began using the Internet, the number of computers connected doubled to about 500, though the amount was small relative to the number of computers connected to the Internet in the 1990s. By 1984 the number of Internet users doubled again as more government agencies, including the U.S. Department of Defense and the National Aeronautics and Space Administration, started to take advantage of computer network communication.

Researchers, however, realized that the existing system was becoming flooded and could not hold many more connections. Consequently, the National Science Foundation (NSF) launched an effort to renovate the Internet. Although the NSF could not fund the campaign itself, it served as a clearinghouse by devising a plan and soliciting the help of IBM Corp., the long-distance carrier MCI, and MERIT, a Michigan school consortium that had developed its own computer network. By 1988, the cooperative effort of these companies and organizations laid the foundation of the Internet. Yet in 1991, this network reached its capacity, too.

The same participants plus Advanced Networks and Services (later ANS Communications, originally a nonprofit company until bought by AOL in 1995) set out to revamp the network once more, expanding it to hold substantially more connections. This renovation also took the majority of the funding away from

the federal government, turning over to private industry instead. Between 1983 and 1993, the number of computers connected to the Internet increased from 562 to 1.2 million. By 1994 the number soared to 2.2 million. Around this time, the Internet became a means of communication and information transmission for private individuals because of the expanded network and the decreasing prices of PCs.

EMERGENCE OF INTERNET ACCESS SERVICES

In the mid-1980s online services that would provide a model for ISPs began to emerge. CompuServe, an H&R Block subsidiary, had accommodated businesses with proprietary information services since 1969. Prodigy, a joint venture between Sears, Roebuck & Co. and IBM, began offering proprietary online services to the general public in 1984, and AOL (under the name Quantum Computer Services, a network for Commodore computers) went online in 1985. Netcom On-line Communications Services, Inc., one of the first true Internet services, emerged in 1988, originally providing Internet service to university students and later expanding to include residential and business clients. PSINet, Inc., founded in 1989, was one of the early Internet services to focus on business and commercial users and sold Internet access to residential providers to resell to their clients. General Electric also launched an online venture called GEnie, although the company later divested itself of the service when it failed to capture a wide following.

Technological advances in 1993—particularly the introduction of graphical Web browsers—brought mass appeal to the World Wide Web, an area of the Internet that was previously navigable only via text-based browsers. As a result, small ISP operations cropped up all over—in major cities as well as in rural areas that the larger companies neglected. Phone companies also wanted part of the action; the regional Bell operating companies petitioned the Federal Communications Commission to allow them to participate. Long-distance phone carriers Sprint and MCI also vied for customers in the booming market of the mid-1990s.

As use of the Web expanded, proprietary online services such as AOL came under pressure to offer general access as other companies started offering this service. The closed network was becoming obsolete because the Web featured more diverse content, and its access wasn't dependent on a captive subscriber base. As a result, companies moved away from this format. IBM jettisoned its share of Prodigy and offered general Internet access instead called Internet

Connection. Finally, in 1995 Microsoft introduced the Microsoft Network (MSN), which at the outset provided proprietary services in addition to general access. It briefly opted to abandon the proprietary service and focus exclusively on World Wide Web service; however, MSN later decided to stay with exclusive content offerings and to expand them to distinguish its service from that of other companies. Most of the proprietary networks, most notably AOL, followed a similar hybrid approach, keeping some unique content and a distinct user interface but also allowing general access to the Internet.

Before the advent of relatively low monthly fees for unlimited access, providers such as AOL and MSN charged a base monthly fee ranging from $5 to $10 per month that included 10 or 15 hours of access. After the monthly hour allocation was spent, these services charged additional fees for each subsequent hour. In 1994 these rates ranged as high as $9.80 per hour; by 1995 many were closer to $2.95 per hour; and in 1996 the flat rate of $19.95 for unlimited hours became widespread.

CURRENT CONDITIONS

Internet service revenues have soared as more households and businesses get connected. In 2000 there were an estimated 46.5 million U.S. households and 6.3 million businesses online, according to analysis by the Strategis Group. Industry revenues in 1999, reported Strategis, approached $18 billion, and separate estimates by International Data Corp. foresaw industry sales in 2001 topping $34 billion when value-added services are included in the equation.

Although new ISPs continue to spring up, the total number has been heading south because of stiff competition and increasing consolidation. Although estimates vary, Infonetics Research estimated the head count at just over 4,200 at the end of 2000, down from 4,500 a year earlier, with further declines in following years. Indeed, the research firm forecast that by 2004 there might be only 3,500 ISPs, as the biggest players increase their penetration and as smaller players are absorbed or exit the business.

FREE ISPs WEIGH IN

Free dial-up service for consumers has been one of the fastest-growing segments of the industry, not to mention one of the most controversial. Such services, which include among their ranks Alta Vista, NetZero, Juno, and Freeinternet.com, let consumers access the Internet for free after filling out a detailed registration form. Advertisers then use information gleaned from subscribers to target well-defined consumer groups with their sales pitches.

In addition to feeding subscribers a heavy dose of advertising, some free ISPs require users to click on an ad every so often, say, once an hour, in order to stay connected. Free ISPs may also track what sites users visit and store that information in marketing profiles of the users. These practices gall some consumers, who feel their privacy is being compromised, but given that access is otherwise completely free and voluntary, their grumbling thus far has fallen on deaf ears.

Consumer worries seemingly haven't slowed the migration to free ISPs, either. In 1999 free services logged an estimated 1.5 million subscribers, and that figure was expected to double in 2000 and surge to 15 million by 2003, based on forecasts by Jupiter Communications. About half of free ISPs' subscribers, however, are reportedly infrequent users who may use the service only as a backup when their primary carrier is down.

BROADBAND RAMPING UP

Cable and DSL services are becoming a major thrust of many ISPs serving the consumer and small business markets. Both broadband options only began to be offered widely in 1999, and upgrading cable and phone networks to support these services in all areas will continue into the early 2000s. Cable-based services, which hit a wider market sooner than DSL, had just over a million U.S. subscribers in early 2000, whereas DSL claimed just 300,000. Analysts predicted the gap will narrow in short order, though, as DSL makes strides in awareness and availability. The Yankee Group forecast DSL subscriptions to reach 2.7 million by 2002, by that time only slightly behind cable at 3 million users. Mounting competition between cable and DSL carriers, as well as among different DSL carriers in the same markets, has brought prices down and will help stimulate demand. And as in the dial-up market, a few maverick ISPs have toyed with offering free DSL service to build market share.

Because it's based on phone lines, DSL favors local phone companies as ISPs since they already own much of the hardware needed to make the system work. Indeed, when independent DSL providers such as Covad Communications, Rhythms NetConnections, and NorthPoint Communications move into a new market, they must secure the cooperation of the local phone company in order to add their equipment to its local switching offices. And whereas phone companies tend to perform both the retail marketing and technical development, many independent DSL outfits specialize in one or the other, relying on a distributor-retailer arrangement.

ISPs PARTNER WITH NON-ISPS TO REACH AFFINITY GROUPS

Large employers have begun arranging for Internet service for their workers, and this may signal a shift in some ISPs' business models. Ford Motor Co. and Delta Air Lines were two of the early adopters. In 2000 Ford signed a contract with the business/wholesale ISP UUNET, a subsidiary of MCI WorldCom, to wire an undisclosed number of its employees for Internet service. Under the arrangement, Ford subsidizes part of the monthly fee and employees get uniform service at a lower cost than they would likely get through an independent ISP. Delta entered a similar agreement with AT&T. For the company, such a partnership could make it easier to manage remote connectivity for employees, since there would be fewer variations in workers' home services. The voluntary programs also serve as an employee benefit. The ISP, on the other hand, gains access to a large pool of potential customers for its add-on services, which may include Internet telephony and customized content.

This is all part of a broader trend of directing Internet services at recognizable affinity groups, whether they be employee groups, social organizations, or neighbors. This tactic can make the Internet service more relevant to specific consumers, and may help improve customers' loyalty to their ISPs. Deals of this kind may also be on the rise with large apartment- and office-building management firms, which have shown strong interest in wiring their buildings for Internet access and offering such services to well-heeled tenants.

INDUSTRY LEADERS

AOL TIME WARNER, INC.

Founded in 1985, America Online (AOL) is the United States' biggest consumer ISP, with customers numbering 25 million in late 2000. The company, which is merging with media conglomerate and cable operator Time Warner, has held a commanding lead in the U.S. market since the mid-1990s, when it launched a massive campaign to recruit ordinary consumers who weren't necessarily technology mavens. AOL originated as a closed network with proprietary content, and it remains a hybrid between an online content provider and an ISP.

Since then, AOL has fashioned itself as the blue-chip ISP, a reference to its vaunted stock traded on the New York Stock Exchange, and has made numerous acquisitions worldwide. In 1998 it took over rival CompuServe (with 2.2 million customers of its own as of 2000) and bought Internet-browser developer Netscape later the same year. AOL has also been a major force in international markets, with millions of subscribers in Europe and a growing base in Latin America. In spring 2000 the company purchased Bertelsmann's half-interests in AOL Europe and AOL Australia. AOL has been actively pursuing broadband opportunities, which its merger with Time Warner, the United States' second-largest cable operator, will undoubtedly benefit.

Stephen M. Case has led the company as CEO since 1991 and will become the chairman of AOL Time Warner when the merger is complete. His counterpart at Time Warner, Gerald Levine, will serve as chief executive. In 2000 AOL posted $6.9 billion in total sales, up 44 percent from 1999, over 85 percent of which derived from subscription fees, with the remainder spread out over advertising and e-commerce sources. The combined media and communications behemoth is expected to have more than $30 billion in sales.

EARTHLINK

Created by the 2000 merger between EarthLink Network and MindSpring Enterprises, the new EarthLink, Inc. weighed in as the second-largest U.S. ISP in 2000, with 4.5 million subscribers, only slightly ahead of free ISP NetZero and established player MSN. EarthLink and MindSpring were both founded in 1994. MindSpring had gone through a series of mergers and acquisitions before; some of the ISPs it absorbed included Netcom On-Line Communication Services, SpryNet, and a consumer unit of PSINet. The new company is part owned by Sprint Corp., the long-distance phone carrier, and has ties to Apple Computer Inc., which has invested in EarthLink and uses the service as the default ISP for some of its computer models. The merged company reported 1999 combined revenues of $670 million, 87 percent of which came from its conventional dial-up subscriptions. EarthLink bolstered its subscription base in 2000 by acquiring OneMain.com and its 700,000 subscribers located in small cities and rural areas.

EXCITE@HOME

Officially known as At Home Corp., the Excite @Home service is the pairing of an Internet search engine and portal (Excite) and a cable-based ISP

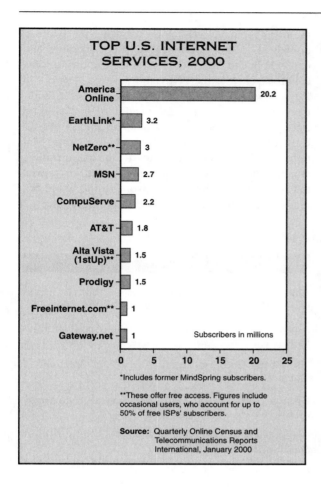

TOP U.S. INTERNET SERVICES, 2000

	Subscribers in millions
America Online	20.2
EarthLink*	3.2
NetZero**	3
MSN	2.7
CompuServe	2.2
AT&T	1.8
Alta Vista (1stUp)**	1.5
Prodigy	1.5
Freeinternet.com**	1
Gateway.net	1

*Includes former MindSpring subscribers.

**These offer free access. Figures include occasional users, who account for up to 50% of free ISPs' subscribers.

Source: Quarterly Online Census and Telecommunications Reports International, January 2000

(@Home and @Work service brands). Controlled by AT&T, Excite@Home is the largest U.S. cable ISP, with about 2 million cable Internet subscribers in 2000. It has partnered with several cable operators to provide its services, including the former Tele-Communications Inc. (TCI), now known as AT&T Cable Services, as well as Comcast, Cablevision, and Cox. About 24 million households in regions covered by its cable alliances were able to receive Internet service, and twice that number were in its regions but not yet wired for two-way digital cable. In 1999 the company brought in $337 million in revenue, about 40 percent of it from subscription fees, but took a whopping loss on paper related to the Excite acquisition that year. Heavy investment continued in 2000, when the firm was readying a new package of services aimed at linking cable Internet access with the other signal flowing through cable—TV—for interactive consumer applications.

NETZERO

The biggest of the free ISPs, NetZero, Inc. was founded in 1997 and began offering service in late 1998. Advertisers pick up the tab for its free, unlimited access, but the catch is that users must divulge details about themselves and have ads streaming onto their computer screens the entire time they're online. The formula has proven successful, however, as by 2000 the ISP had racked up 3 million users, half of whom were considered active. The company had $55.5 million in sales for fiscal 2000, but was still far from turning a profit.

MSN

Despite its powerful backing by the world's largest software company, the Microsoft Network (MSN) has amassed only about as many customers in its lifetime as AOL tacks on in a few good months. In late 2000 its count stood at 3.5 million, although the company's management hoped to jump-start its languishing consumer business by offering consumers free service for their first six months. MSN was positioned as the flagship operation in the Microsoft.NET division. The company, which was again gearing up to compete with AOL, was working to play to its strengths in the software market by offering software services along with its subscriptions. MSN was rated as the fourth-largest ISP in 2000. Separately, Microsoft has interest in WebTV, another consumer service that delivers Internet access through TV sets.

PSINET

PSINet Inc. is a long-standing powerhouse in the wholesale ISP market, recently dubbing itself a global supercarrier in an effort to raise its profile. Founded in 1989, PSINet sells access to other ISPs, for example, EarthLink, and large corporations. PSINet is focusing increasingly on offering a comprehensive range of services to multinational organizations. To that end, it has acquired a number of international and specialty ISPs, and in 2000 it acquired the information technology services firm Metamor Worldwide, in a bid that was expected to make PSINet an able contender in the emerging application service provider and e-commerce services markets. The company's total sales reached $554.7 million in 1999, including $362.9 million from its access services and another $129 million from carrier services.

COVAD COMMUNICATIONS GROUP

One of several national DSL specialists, Covad wires metropolitan areas for its high-speed network and distributes access to front-end firms that in turn sell DSL to consumers. One of the largest independent DSL providers, Covad served over 100 metro regions by late 2000. The company, founded in 1996, had revenues of $66.5 million in 1999, but took a hefty $195 million loss because of heavy technical and marketing investments. Covad's resold services reached only an estimated 50,000 subscribers by 2000.

AMERICA AND THE WORLD

Although the United States is the world's largest market for Internet services, other regions are proving significant markets as well. In 2001, the top four Western European countries were expected to have more than 45 million Internet users. Germany was expected to remain the biggest European market, with over 16 million users, followed by France (12.4 million), Britain (12.2 million), and Italy (5.6 million). Meanwhile, Eastern Europe has been catching up, with its estimated 4 million Internet users as of 2000 expanding to 15 million by 2002.

The Latin American Internet market was surging at the turn of the century, posting the fastest growth rate in Internet hosts, according to the International Telecommunication Union. From only 56,000 hosts in 1995, the figure jumped to nearly 2 million by year-end 2000. The number of Internet users in this market was expected to grow about 47 percent annually between 1998 and 2003. The largest markets as of 2000 were Brazil, with 3.8 million; and Mexico, with 3.6 million. Frost & Sullivan predicted revenues from the Internet services market to skyrocket to $17.4 billion in 2005 from just $1.1 billion in 1999.

Meanwhile, in Asia, Japan and South Korea are the largest markets for Internet services, with 18 million and 14 million users, respectively, as of 2000. And while penetration rates are much lower in China, that country nonetheless recorded about 9 million people on the Internet at year-end 1999. China's user base, moreover, was expected to swell to more than 60 million by 2002.

Human Rights Watch argues that since the Internet has the potential to unite thousands and thousands of people from all over the world, allowing them to engage in political discussion among other things, some countries see the Internet as a threat to their autonomy and their policies. Hence, some countries have enacted strict regulations. For example, China requires all Internet service providers to register with the government, while Saudi Arabia and Vietnam provide only government-controlled access.

Although affluent citizens of countries such as the United States, Japan, and Germany can afford PCs and the other requisite technology for using the Internet, elsewhere in the world access is considerably less common due to cost. Nonprofit organizations in some countries, such as the Peruvian Scientific Network in Peru, however, have created public computer facilities that offer Internet access in addition to classes on Internet navigation for $15 a month, according to Calvin Sims in the *New York Times*. The United Nations provided initial subsidies to the organization, which at the time had 22,000 members and was ranked the fourth fastest-growing network in the world behind Brazil, Mexico, and Chile, according to Sims.

FURTHER READING

Ahles, Andrea. "Cable Access Is Faster, but Has Drawbacks." *Fort Worth Star-Telegram*, 23 August 1999.

Albiniak, Paige, and Price Colman. "High-Speed Demands Fast Action." *Broadcasting & Cable*, 11 May 1998.

"Broadband Goes Full Speed Ahead." *PC Magazine*, 7 March 2000.

Dickson, Glen. "Cable Leads Broadband Race." *Broadcasting & Cable*, 17 January 2000.

Gates, Dominic. "Raising the White Flag." *The Industry Standard*, 30 October 2000.

Gerwig, Kate. "Will Web Surfers Play Favorites?" *Tele.com*, 6 December 1999.

Graham, Rusty. "Small-time Connections." *Tele.com*, 30 October 2000.

Human Rights Watch. "Silencing the Net: The Threat to Freedom of Expression On-line." *New York Times*, May 1996.

"Internet Providers at War." *Economist*, 7 November 1998.

Junnarkar, Sandeep. "New Phone Rules Will Have Mixed Effect on Net." *New York Times*, 8 May 1997.

Katz, Frances. "Shareholders of Atlanta-Based MindSpring Approve Merger with EarthLink." *Atlanta Journal and Constitution*, 7 February 2000.

Krause, Jason. "In Flat Market, ISP Says 'We're Not Dead Yet.'" *The Industry Standard*, 18 September 2000.

LaBarba, Liane H. "Battle of the Bands." *Telephony*, 9 August 1999.

Ladley, Eric. "Behind Every Good ISP Is@el3Another ISP." *ISP Business*, 10 April 2000.

———. "Ford, Delta Contracts Provide ISPs with Ripe Market." *ISP Business News*, 20 March 2000.

———. "Survival of the Fittest." *ISP Business News*, 3 April 2000.

Lake, David. "No Deposit, No Return." *Industry Standard,* 27 March 2000.

LaPolla, Stefanie. "Internet Outages Strain Corporate Networking." *PC Week,* 21 April 1997.

Lewis, Peter H. "An 'All You Can Eat' Price Is Clogging Internet Access." *New York Times,* 17 December 1996.

Lubove, Seth. "Mom and POPs Thrive." *Forbes,* 22 February 1999.

Murphy, Jamie, and Charlie Hofacker. "Explosive Growth Clogs the Internet's Backbone," 30 June 1996.

Nairn, Geoff. "Industry's Transformation Poses Tough Challenges." *Financial Times,* 15 March 2000.

Rodriguez, Karen. "Internet Providers Gird for Long-Distance Service Battle." *Business Journal,* 23 March 1998.

Schonfeld, Eric. "The Exchange Economy." *Fortune,* 15 February 1999.

Stuck, Bart, and Michael Weingarten. "Has High Tide Come for ISPs?" *Business Communications Review,* September 1997.

Suarez, Ruth. "ISPs Offer More Enhanced Services to Bolster Sales." *ISP Business News,* 18 October 1999.

Swisher, Kara. "Now Poised to Challenge AOL Online: MSN." *Wall Street Journal,* 6 November 2000.

Walsh, Mark. "High-Speed Chase." *Crain's New York Business,* 14 February 2000.

Wertheim, Peter Howard, and Dayse Abrantes. "International Fiber-Optic Companies Scramble to South America." *Lightwave,* October 2000.

Zalud, Bill. "DSL: Good, Bad, Ugly." *SDM,* June 2000.

IT CONSULTING

Only one segment of the larger information technology (IT) services continuum, IT consulting is the weighty and highly competitive business of telling companies what technologies to buy and how to deploy them. Paradoxically, though IT consulting has relatively few entry barriers—largely just having some expertise in an area of technology—serving top-tier clients like the Fortune 500 is an opportunity usually accessible to only a handful of consultancies, themselves often among the Fortune elite.

The consulting side of IT has evolved with the onset of e-business, or Internet-enabled business processes such as e-commerce, supply-chain integration, and sales force automation. Early on, large firms like Andersen, KPMG, and EDS were perceived sometimes as old-school vendors who weren't proficient in cutting-edge Internet technologies. This was a boon in the late 1990s for emergent e-business specialty houses like MarchFirst and Razorfish and Scient, which quickly racked up revenues in the hundreds of millions and stock valuations in the billions.

By 2000, however, as dot-com stocks toppled and high-flying upstart consultancies teetered on insolvency, momentum began shifting back to traditional vendors serving traditional clients. The shakeout proved a double-edged sword, since Internet companies can be both providers and sizable customers of IT consulting. In the meantime, the big, established vendors had gone to great lengths to prove their relevance in the changing market. Many of the big operations set up specialized e-commerce units, sometimes treating them as independent companies, as if to un-

derscore how much things were changing. And that's not to mention the wave of separations and mergers among top-tier consulting firms in their efforts to maximize their market power and to quell rising fears that integrated accounting and consulting firms have intrinsic conflicts of interest.

All these changes played out against a backdrop of tremendously strong sales, at least until 2000. Demand for IT consulting was hard to sate, propelled by Internet-related projects, year-2000 preparations, and generally strong business conditions that left many corporate budgets replete with funds for technology consultation. According to published projections by International Data Corp. (IDC), a prominent technology-market-research firm, the red-hot market for consulting services worldwide was on course to approach $125 billion by 2004, more than twice the level in 1999. Using different methodology, another estimate by the Gartner Group envisioned e-business services alone being worth $160 billion globally by 2004. Both forecasts were issued in 2000.

Still, buoyant sales at the macro level couldn't hide the tumult facing some of the industry's finest. The revenue decelerations of 2000 were devastating, as were the bitter losses in market capitalization. By one estimate, based on government filings, publicly traded Web services firms laid off some 5,000 employees during the latter half of 2000 in the wake of financial shortfalls. As a result, consultancies on shaky financial footing lay prey to acquisition or worse. Thought to be most vulnerable were firms focusing on sleek designs and simple e-commerce deployments rather than meat-and-potatoes competencies like legacy-system integration and large-scale process reengineering.

ORGANIZATION AND STRUCTURE

IT consulting encompasses many types of computer work and its boundaries with other industries are often vague. Although the name "consulting" may suggest primarily an advisory role, in practice IT consultants are usually likewise the implementers of technology development, deployment, and training.

The field ranges from large multinational management consulting firms with billion-dollar budgets to one-person shops that bring in $100,000 or less a year. What they all have in common is a client who contracts them as outside service providers to work on a computer problem on a project basis. A project may be a day or two in length to a year or longer. Some contracts are renewed indefinitely until a consultant becomes, in many respects, indistinguishable from a normal full-time employee.

The most visible side of the industry consists of large firms. Traditionally these included the so-called Big Six accounting firms and big hardware and software producers like Hewlett Packard and IBM.

In the late 1990s, however, a series of mergers, spin-offs, and acquisitions changed the character and form of the industry, particularly the independent consulting firms. Price Waterhouse, for example, merged in 1998 with Coopers and Lybrand, another Big Six firm, to become PricewaterhouseCoopers (PwC). Later, as fears arose about conflicts of interest, PwC was actively considering spinning off its IT consulting business, possibly even selling it to another large player in the business.

Other large consulting firms also transformed themselves. The consulting arm of Ernst & Young LLP, another member of the remaining Big Five, was sold in 2000 to Cap Gemini SA of France, forming Cap Gemini Ernst & Young. Also in 2000, KPMG LLP, for its part, spun off its consulting business as KPMG Consulting LLC. KPMG Consulting received major funding from networking giant Cisco Systems Inc., which also had a financial stake in the Cap Gemini Ernst & Young venture. Meanwhile, after a bitter and drawn-out separation, Andersen Consulting, later renamed Accenture, gained its independence from Arthur Andersen (but, confusingly, Arthur Andersen has another internal IT consulting practice that was not spun off with Andersen Consulting).

These firms are distinguished from the thousands of smaller consultancies, which often provide only a fraction of the breadth of services offered by a top-tier firm. Nonetheless, in the United States a major share of IT consulting is performed by small companies, partnerships, or individuals. Companies often begin as one-or-two person operations and grow as their reputation builds. They are offered more work than they are able to handle alone and then expand to take on extra employees. These smaller operations generally have from 1 to 10 employees and tend to specialize in a few particular types of projects. They can be in a particular business sector, or involving specific applications, computer languages, and operating systems that are within their expertise.

Staying current or even ahead of technology is a critical ongoing process for IT consultants. Consultants' fees relate directly to the demand for the skills mastered, and it is the new and uncommon abilities that are in greatest demand. Familiarity with SAP software, a popular but relatively new set of business applications in the United States, brings significantly higher fees than a familiarity with UNIX, a system that is important, but with which a great deal of consultants are conversant. Consultants frequently accept work outside their skill set at a fraction of the rates normally paid in order to get experience in a new application. According to the Software Contractors' Guild, the software side of consulting alone encompasses numerous abilities: 171 different applications, 55 computer languages, and 24 operating systems, in all more than 500 skill classifications.

Consultants find clients in different ways. Some advertise or have Web pages, however word of mouth plays an important role. A sizable number of consultants get new clients only through referrals. Once consultants or companies have completed an impressive job, they can rely on new client referrals because there are so few consultants in relation to the amount of work at any given time. One group of independent consultants, known as contractors, does not organize its own jobs; they rely instead on placement agencies, similar to temporary employment agencies, to find work for them. Contractors provide a resume to an agency that describes in depth their skill set, conduct an interview, and indicate their availability. When work is available, usually within a few days, the agency notifies the contractor. Clients pay the contractor's fee, which has been specified or negotiated in advance, plus an additional 30 to 60 percent to the agency.

Staffing agencies play a large role in the consulting business. All of the major temporary staffing firms, including Adecco, Kelly, Olsten, have technical units geared to placing consultants and other technical specialists in interim positions.

The Software Contractors' Guild acts as a job clearinghouse for contractors, consulting companies, agencies, and clients. For a $12 annual membership, contractors can post resumes online, noting their skill-set items and relocation options. According to observers, listing with the Guild brings more work offers than most members can single-handedly manage, and the organization has steady turnover. Contractors frequently have their own Web pages to advertise their special skills.

Although both are self-employed and work for clients, a few rough distinctions can be drawn between contractors and consultants. Contractors, in general, work through agencies, at least while they are getting started in the business; they tend to work exclusively on-site at the client's place of business; their projects range from a day to indefinite renewal; the projects they work on tend to be more clearly defined, and of more limited scope; and they tend to spend more time "writing code," that is, creating computer programs. Contractors, who number in the tens of thousands, constitute the majority of the consultant labor force. Consultants tend to work on a project between 3 to 9 months. Often, they are required to take an active role in client's problem definition and needs analysis. The first weeks or even months of a project at a mid- to large-sized company, usually involve a series of meetings and interviews with different members of staff. Only afterwards can the technical problems be approached.

The technical work performed by IT consultants varies. Sometimes older software is modified to run in a different system or in an ensemble of different applications. Other times programs are written from scratch, or may be patched together from routines a consultant keeps in his or her "tool kit."

The decision to outsource an IT function is increasingly viewed not just as a quick fix, but as an integral part of a company's long-term business strategy. According to Frank Casale, executive director of the Outsourcing Institute of Jericho, New York, "an organization needs to analyze its core competency. Anything from that point on could be a candidate for outsourcing." Among the reasons for increased outsourcing is the need to be able to react quickly to market shifts, to have access to highly skilled personnel, and—most importantly—to cut costs. Companies considering the outsourcing of an IT function are cautioned to carefully determine the cost of that function. "Estimating cost is more complicated than people think," Casale says.

For corporations that outsource IT functions, the benefits may be either obvious or difficult to quantify. Some of the benefits, such as improved performance, the ability for the company's full-time staff to concentrate on its core competency, and a reduction of operating costs, can readily be seen and measured. However, some of the more subtle benefits of outsourcing may take time to become apparent. "If four years ago you had told someone you could use outsourcing to increase morale, you would have been laughed at," Casale says. Today, however, most top IT executives realize that outsourcing one or more functions can reduce the pressure on an overtaxed staff, creating a more hospitable working environment for full-time employees in the IT department. "Then it becomes a tool to create a good work environment," says Casale. "It's tough enough to keep these people as it is. It becomes a perk."

REGULATION

Section 1706 of the Internal Revenue Code is the most troublesome regulation for consultants because they fall into three tax classes: 1099 workers, W-2 workers, and those who have incorporated. The latter two are legally uncomplicated, however, the former falls into the IRS's gray zone. W-2 workers are paid by the placement agency for which they work. The agency collects the fees from the client and cuts the contractor a paycheck with income tax already deducted. The advantage of not having to keep track of taxes is offset by the numerous tax breaks not available to W-2 employees. Self-employed consultants who have not incorporated are considered 1099 workers. Although they are ostensibly independent, by working on-site and using the client's equipment, they may be considered for tax purposes regular employees of the client, i.e. as workers who should be in the W-2 class. As such, 1099 contractors risk being audited and forced to repay deductions made as self-employed workers. Their clients are also at risk of litigation for unpaid benefits or failure to withhold income taxes.

Thus, it is to an independent consultant's advantage to incorporate, even if he or she works completely on their own. Incorporation as a business sidesteps these problematic income tax questions. The Software Contractors' Guild expressly advises clients looking for contractors to hire only those who have incorporated, or who are W-2 employees of a contract placement agency.

There are certain contractual restrictions on software consultants. Because of the sensitive client information to which they have access, consultants are usually required to sign confidentiality agreements. Their placement agency contract requires them to wait a year after the conclusion of such a contract before accepting independent work with the same client. Professional ethics require that when a contractor is offered the same job by different agencies, the first offer is accepted.

BACKGROUND AND DEVELOPMENT

The rise of technology consulting as a profession parallels the expansion of computers throughout the business world. Not long after this expansion began, computer manufacturers began to realize that they had to provide many more services to the companies installing their computers than was possible for them. The in-house programming and computer department soon realized they were incapable of maintaining the cutting edge skills necessary to adapt to the swiftly evolving computer industry.

Led by pioneers like Jerry Weinberg and Ed Yourdan, the first independent software consulting firms opened in the 1960s. They arose in response to software packages that were difficult to use, and to software vendors that offered inadequate support for complex projects. Software consulting began mediating between inflexible software and the increasingly helpless software user.

IT consulting services also grew out of the support businesses run by leading hardware vendors like IBM and Hewlett Packard and Unisys. Firms like these developed extensive support and maintenance services because their systems were usually proprietary and outsiders often lacked the knowledge needed to manage them on their own. Later, these services grew into full-fledged consulting and systems integration operations, often handling machines and software produced by their competitors. Indeed, by the mid-1990s, services became key to sustaining business growth and profitability at large hardware makers like IBM and Compaq, which faced declining margins on their hardware sales due to falling computer prices.

CURRENT CONDITIONS

IT consulting has turned into a phenomenal growth industry, and yet one that continues to transform itself. One of the biggest growth drivers, not surprisingly, has been Internet-related technology. Barely on the consulting map in the mid-1990s, business initiatives involving the Web or derived technologies have funneled billions of dollars into consulting, and by all expectations, that trend will continue, even if not at such a frenzied pace.

Related, and perhaps equally profound, is an altered paradigm regarding technology's role in business. Technology, once the means toward implementing the corporate strategy, or perhaps merely the mundane but necessary infrastructure for operating the business, has become ever more strategic. In the most visible examples, the famous and infamous Web startups of the 1990s, superior technology was sometimes the entire strategy. The implications were—and still are—unparalleled productivity and efficiency, the forging of new markets, and formidable competitive advantage.

All this translates into significant yet shifting opportunities for the consulting world. IT consultants are hired increasingly because they bring to bear expertise about business strategy and execution, not simply coding expertise and cost-efficiency. This has boded well for the large accounting-consulting firms, which have traditional strength in management consulting as well as in nuts-and-bolts technology deployment. Observers expect demand for consultants with business acumen to continue trending upward as companies further embrace technology as critical to their strategies.

Another perennial source of new business is, of course, new technology. Just as the initial embrace of the Internet and e-commerce was a major thrust during the mid- and late 1990s, new applications like wireless networking and the melding of computing and communications promise to spur new growth well into the 2000s. Some analysts expect that the delivery of consulting services entirely online, rather than in person, will present another large growth opportunity in the near future.

ENTERPRISE APPLICATIONS STILL PROVIDE DEMAND FOR CONSULTING

Still another trend benefiting consultants has been the rise of so-called enterprise software. These heavy-duty systems, often aimed at companies with many thousands of employees, attempt to provide the advantages of off-the-shelf software, yet with sufficient customization to meet a company's unique requirements. They're designed to serve enterprise-wide functions like human resources, accounting, inventory management, and sales management. The software category is commonly known as enterprise resource planning (ERP) because one of the bigger selling points is the software's ability to give management detailed information about corporate resources. Authored by such vendors as SAP, PeopleSoft, J.D. Edwards, and more recently, Oracle, these programs have predefined features and their own development environments for customizing the software.

While profitable for consultants and software vendors alike, ERP packages gained an unsavory reputation in the late 1990s because their deployment cycles were often drawn out and, frankly, some were bad products that were hard to use and lacking in obvious features. At times the systems took so long to install that the software was deemed obsolete by the time it was operational. Coupled with fears about year-2000 readiness, ERP sales lagged in 1999 and some analysts believed the category was doomed.

But since then ERP vendors have shored up their products, emphasizing Web-enabled versions, smoother and faster implementations, better features, and nicer interfaces. The truth is, many big and medium-sized corporations still have pent-up demand for these kinds of systems—and they'll need consultants to carry them through the sometimes harrowing process. A number of industry watchers believe that these deep-pocketed (albeit perhaps less exciting) customers are exactly what the industry needs in the aftermath of the dot-com woes.

Dot-Com Fallout

The burst of the dot-com stock bubble in 2000 has left the industry in a state of flux. Up-and-coming e-business consultancies were severely impacted by the stock downturns and sharp pullback in spending by upstart Web companies. One of the more pessimistic forecasts was that only a quarter of Internet-strategy consulting firms would survive. Among others, there was some consensus that consolidation would continue to reduce the number of major players in the business.

Revenue shortfalls and layoffs have only been part of the e-business firms' problems. They've also been mired in low morale and high employee turnover as the remaining workers fear the worst.

The surviving firms, some analysts say, will be those that court Fortune 500 accounts and develop deep competencies in complex projects. Increasingly, the simpler, front-end Web work is being done in-house at big companies, so consultants will have to distinguish themselves as strategic visionaries and as experts with in-depth knowledge of particular industry problems.

Large, established firms like the KPMGs and the Andersens may continue down their own consolidation paths, but in general were expected to have an

easier time in a slowing market. In some respects they'll benefit from the smaller firms' misfortunes, as they may be able to nab talented employees and clients have greater confidence dealing with established service providers.

INDUSTRY LEADERS

Numerically speaking, the industry is dominated by small firms, which typically cater to small businesses or highly specialized, low-volume needs of larger businesses. However, much more visible are the large companies active in the industry.

Successors to the reconfigured Big Five accounting/consulting firms form a major part of the industry at the top tier. These include Accenture (formerly Andersen Consulting), KPMG Consulting, PricewaterhouseCoopers, and Cap Gemini Ernst & Young. These firms, and others like them, are distinct in that they are very well established, multinational enterprises, and are largely independent of any hardware or software vendor (although some, like KPMG, have financial ties to hardware concerns). They're also unique in their extensive offering of management and technical consulting services. All of them have (or had) ties to financial and accounting services, but most have taken great pain to distance their consulting businesses from their accounting and auditing responsibilities.

Another group of large players consists of firms with ties to the hardware and software sectors. Examples include IBM Global Services, the world's biggest IT services firm, Hewlett Packard, and Compaq. Each of these does billions of dollars in IT services each year, but sometimes they're seen as not being independent enough and as being too focused on pushing their own platforms. They're also perceived more as technical experts rather than comprehensive consulting firms that can advise on strategy, branding, or other business issues.

Consulting is also done by a number of large, independent IT outsourcing firms like Computer Sciences Corp. (CSC) and Electronic Data Systems (EDS). These firms may perform anything from operating a data center to deploying very large custom systems for corporations or governments. Companies like CSC and EDS are often chosen for long-term, highly complex projects involving legacy systems and scads of data.

Finally come the Web-oriented consultancies. The largest of these in 2001 included MarchFirst, Sapient, Razorfish, and Scient; also Organic and iXL

Enterprises. Most of these were born in the mid-1990s and styled themselves as young, dynamic, cutting-edge firms. Sometimes known as Web boutiques, they concentrated on building high-profile Web sites and brands for the multitude of Internet start-ups, as well as a large number of traditional business clients. Following the crash of the Internet stocks, not to mention the tightening of venture capital, many of the boutiques struggled. MarchFirst, iXL, Sapient, and their cohorts laid off thousands of employees in an effort to control costs. They've also redoubled their efforts to focus on Fortune 1000 clientele, but some analysts predicted this group would still be extremely vulnerable to failure or consolidation.

WORK FORCE

Precise statistics regarding the number of active IT consultants are scarce, but the work force is large and growing rapidly. The U.S. Bureau of Labor Statistics reported in the late 1990s around 500,000 information technology/information systems consultants, which includes hardware as well as software consultants. Insiders at some of the placement firms estimated the number at around 2.2 million; *Contract Professional*'s unofficial estimate was around 1.5 million.

Technology consultants usually have a college degree, and often an advanced degree as well, in computer science, engineering, or business. Independent consultants generally require about two years experience working in a company before they generate work on their own. Some have professional engineering licenses issued by the states, but clients do not generally expect such licensing. A large number of consultants also have systems certification issued by software companies like Novell, Inc. or Microsoft or Oracle.

One of the main challenges for consultants and contractors is keeping up-to-date with the rapid changes in the computer world. To this end, many read the latest computer periodicals and maintain personal reference libraries of the latest computer manuals. A great deal of information is available from the Internet. All of the major computer magazines have Web sites and all of the businesses associated with computers and software maintain an online presence where they publish press releases and other updates. Many seek out work that will bring them into practical contact with technologies and systems of interest, and many also complete training or certification courses to develop new skills.

It's not unusual for a qualified consultant to earn $100,000 or more per year. Even contractors who work primarily through agents do not find it difficult to earn a six-figure income. Average income for newcomers to independent practice—consultants or contractors who have put their time in with a firm and struck out on their own—is around $55,000 per year. In addition, because consultants tend to work on short-term projects, usually no longer than nine months, they have more flexibility to schedule vacations. On the other hand, as self-employed persons, consultants have to take responsibility for their own taxes, health insurance, and retirement plans.

AMERICA AND THE WORLD

Being a profession where so much work is distributed by referral and personal reference, consulting depends on establishing face-to-face, individual relationships with clients. For that reason, domestic workers do most software consulting in the United States. What foreign competition does exist is as yet unorganized and poses little threat to Americans, if only because of the serious shortage of qualified personnel that currently exists in the United States.

However, the Internet has made it easier for international consultants to work for U.S.-based customers. For instance, some consultants come from India, Indonesia, or eastern Europe. These consultants find clients that transmit the work electronically, which is becoming easier to do. It is then distributed to a crew of workers who finish the job much more quickly—and for a much lower price—than domestic manpower. Software workers in India, as an example, do extremely high-quality work, and many charge much less than U.S. consultants.

U.S. consulting firms also have a tremendous global reach. Top providers like Accenture and KPMG have large international operations that serve multinational corporations and government agencies throughout the world. Likewise, European firms like Cap Gemini have global presence as well.

FURTHER READING

Caruso, David. "Command Performance." *Intelligent Enterprise,* 5 January 1999.

Gow, Kathleen. "PeopleSoft Consultants Thrive in Sellers' Market." *Contract Professional,* May/June 1997, 12-14. Available from http://www.iscg.com.

Greenberg, Ilan. "Consultants See Action." *InfoWorld,* 27 April 1998.

Hayes, Ian S. "E-Services Strategy Shift." *Software Magazine,* October 2000.

Hicks, Matt. "The Big Five: A Safe E-Biz Harbor?" *eWeek,* 11 December 2000.

Isaacs, Nora. "Call in the Outsiders." *InfoWorld,* 17 May 1999.

"IT Consulting: Risky Business." *Economist,* 16 September 2000.

Jastrow, David, and Jerry Rosa. "Make or Break Year?" *Computer Reseller News,* 8 January 2001.

Moran, Nuala. "A Big Rethink Is Underway as Systems Converge." *Financial Times,* 5 July 2000.

Murdock, Michelle. "Who Ya Gonna Call?" *InfoWorld,* 10 March 1997.

National Association of Computer Consultant Businesses (NACCB). Available from http://www.naccb.org.

"Old Consultants Never Die: They Just Go 'e'" *Fortune,* 12 June 2000.

"Professional Services." *Business Week,* 8 January 2001.

Weil, Nancy. "Oracle Setting Up Consulting Centers, Ships Enterprise Bundle." *InfoWorld,* 29 April 1998.

Juice Bars

INDUSTRY SNAPSHOT

It's been smooth sailing for vendors of raw juices and smoothies as juice-bar chains have spurted up and established retailers have sloshed out their own made-to-order juice concoctions. With estimated sales of $647 million in 1999, juice bars have grown mainstream as franchise chains such as Jamba Juice Co. and Smoothie King amassed hundreds of outlets each throughout the United States. While juice bars were enjoying surging popularity, industry players were busily working to make sure the concept proved more than just a fad. In the late 1990s juice-bar sales rose at a torrid 30 percent annual clip, convincing some observers that the concept has staying power. Indeed, leading chains such as Jamba Juice, which hired a former Burger King executive as CEO in 2000, hope to make juice bars as ubiquitous and prosperous as fast-food restaurants—on par with such other successful specialty retail concepts as the Starbucks coffee chain. By 2000, there were over 2,300 juice bars in the United States, about 300 of which were located in Southern California.

Juice bars owe their prosperity to at least two trends: (1) consumer interest in fruits and healthful eating and (2) consumer demand for convenience foods. Raw juices and smoothies satisfy both trends. With ample fruit, yogurt, and supplemental nutrients, juice-bar offerings serve as breakfast, lunch, or snack fare. Juice-bar beverages also allow customers to get recommended fruit intake by just consuming one drink, instead of several pieces of fruit. Besides containing vitamins from fruits and vegetables, juice-bar products may also include other essential nutrients, such as calcium and protein, when low-fat dairy products or fortified soy products are part of the mixture.

Eyeing juice-bar chains' success, a number of other food stores have moved in on the fresh-juice territory in a bid to tap into the sales boom that specialty retailers have enjoyed. Entrants as diverse as supermarkets, coffee shops, and bottled-juice producers have all offered beverages that rival those found at juice bars. With competition mounting, more of the juice-bar market is going to larger chain players and small independent operators are getting crowded out—or simply bought out. In 1999 Juice Gallery, a market-research consultancy, estimated that fully 70 percent of U.S. juice-bar revenue went to the top nine chains.

ORGANIZATION AND STRUCTURE

The juice-bar industry's key companies include those that concentrate on selling fresh blended juices and smoothies. These juice bars, however, may also offer products such as low-fat muffins, snacks, sandwiches, soups, and bottled water. In addition, operations such as cafes, restaurants, and supermarkets provide juice-bar services to augment the primary selection of products. Many gyms, fitness centers, and health clubs offer customers juices and smoothies, often augmented with extra protein from sources such as eggs, soy, or whey. Also, some operations focus on being "beverage bistros," selling nearly equal amounts of gourmet coffees, sodas, and juice-bar offerings.

Primary concoctions sold by juice bars include a spate of mixed fruit and vegetable juices such as apple, orange, banana, guava, papaya, carrot, cucumber, and beet juices, as well as smoothies. Smoothies are shakes made of fresh fruit juice, ice, and either frozen yogurt, sherbet, or soy milk, and are often fortified by wheat grass, ginseng, protein powder, vitamin C, spirulina, bee pollen, and/or wheat germ. Juice bars frequently market these nutritional supplements as enhancers of the immune system and energy boosters, based on research on the effects of homeopathic substances. Some juice bars use only fresh fruit juice, while others use a combination of prepared and fresh juice. Using only fresh juice creates a number of difficulties for juice bars, in that the price of fresh fruits—especially exotic produce—fluctuates throughout the year; fresh fruit is highly perishable, and employees may have a hard time extracting juice from fruits without the appropriate consistency. Consequently, smaller operations, experimental juice bars, and sideline juice bars often opt for canned and bottled juices to avoid these problems.

In *Restaurants & Institutions,* Beth Lorenzini recommended that juice-bar operators display plenty of fresh fruit at all times, even if they use prepared juices, and that they should install three compartment sinks in the juice-preparation area to promote frequent cleansing of equipment and utensils. Moreover, Lorenzini urged entrepreneurs to invest in top-quality blending and extracting accoutrements. She argued that heavy-duty blenders capable of emulsifying at 32,000 revolutions per minute (rpm)—not the standard 16,000-rpm blenders—work best for juice bars. Though these blenders bear a high price of $800 to $1,200, they can endure frequent, high-output use, and produce the best emulsions. Since juice bars often must run blenders and extractors from open to close, juice-bar owners should consider having a spare blender and maintaining a stock of spare parts as well. Lorenzini also contended that in many regions of the United States operators should couple a juice bar with other offerings such as bakery, vegetarian, and health-food products.

BACKGROUND AND DEVELOPMENT

The food-bar phenomenon of recent business history began in the 1970s with the salad bar. Restaurants sprouted up that centered on the salad-bar concept, and supermarkets began offering salad bars in addition to regular items, according to Bob Ingram in *Supermarket Business.* With demand for convenient and healthful food, salad bars caught on quickly by providing products to meet both of these needs.

Shortly after the introduction of the salad bar, restaurants and stores began adding other services such as pizza bars, coffee bars, olive bars, fruit bars, and sandwich bars. Furthermore, establishments started focusing exclusively on one or more of these products, as witnessed by the influx of cafes and coffeehouses in the 1990s. Nonetheless, with the exception of the salad bar, many of these concepts did not offer particularly healthful fare, thereby alienating a significant segment of the potential customer base.

In addition to these forebears, the juice-bar industry has antecedents in the soda, ice cream, and frozen yogurt parlor and coffeehouse crazes of earlier years. Many juice-bar operators in the 1990s strategically placed units near high schools and universities, as well as near businesses and stores, hoping to attract a crowd interested in healthful beverages and a pleasant atmosphere for socializing. Like its predecessors, the juice bar provides what sociologists have termed "third places" in contrast to the primary and secondary places of home and work. Third places offer environments where people can meet for casual conversation, according to Gerry Khermouch in *Brandweek.* Khermouch also reported that scholars attribute the popularity of such places to the suburbanization of the United States, and to the emerging numbers of people who work out of the home. Because of these factors, cafes, juice bars, and other such places provide venues for renewed social connection. To function as third places, juice bars must emphasize atmosphere and location in addition to convenient and healthful products. That is, they must be within walking distance of target customers and provide a relaxed, gregarious environment.

In the 1980s, health-food stores began to flourish, offering not only organic and low-fat foods, but also a particular style of deli service. Many of these health-food stores, particularly those on the West Coast, pioneered the juice bar, bringing in blenders and juice extractors and mixing up assorted fruits and vegetables along with nutritional supplements. As these kinds of beverages grew more popular, California entrepreneurs realized that demand was strong enough to start launching stand-alone juice bars in the late 1980s and early 1990s.

Driven by healthful eating habits and the demand for convenient food, raw juice bars began springing up in the United States in the 1990s. Although health-food stores offered such concoctions as low-fat fresh fruit and vegetable mixtures and "smoothies" (shakes with fruit and added nutrients) since the 1980s, they did not begin to penetrate the mainstream market un-

More On BACTERIA THREAT GIVES JUICE MAKERS PAUSE

Juice bars may be enjoying sweet success but regulations by the U.S. Food and Drug Administration (FDA) could sour the industry. After a batch of fresh apple juice contaminated with *E. coli* bacteria led to the death of one child and the illness of 66 people in three western states and Canada in 1996, a nationwide debate erupted over the safety of fresh juice.

The FDA took subsequent steps to prevent future contamination, including suggesting warning labels for juices that were not pasteurized. According to the FDA, unpasteurized juice can contain bacteria that make people ill. Those at high risk include children, older adults, and people who have weakened immune systems. The various microorganisms that can cause food-borne illnesses have been found in apple juice, apple cider, orange juice, and frozen coconut milk, according to the FDA.

A 1997 assignment by the FDA to inspect unpasteurized-cider operations generated eye-opening data. While the agency detected no pathogens in a finished product to be sold to the public, it found that one firm's apples tested positive for *Salmonella*. The assignment also uncovered fecal coliforms and *E. coli* in the wash water used at several of the companies.

Though industries have contended that good manufacturing practices and increased inspections should be enough to ward off contaminants, the FDA said more needs to be done. In 1998 the agency began requiring warning labels on most packaged fresh juices that weren't pasteurized or otherwise treated, and it was considering further controls over fresh-juice production to control pathogens.

Pasteurization, a process of briefly heating the juice to reduce harmful pathogens, is an option many fresh-juice makers eschew. They believe it saps nutrients and distorts the flavor. Others have engineered so-called flash pasteurization systems that they claim provide the benefits of pasteurization without detracting from flavor. Fresh-juice processors have also experimented with other means of rooting out pathogens short of pasteurization, including exposure to ultraviolet light.

Food-borne pathogens are naturally a concern to juice bars, as well. But because their beverages are usually prepared in small quantities right at the time of consumption, juice bars are considered less risky and aren't subject to the warnings and processing scrutiny that packaged-juice makers are.

---

til the following decade. Achieving initial success and popularity on the West Coast—primarily in California—they soon began to spread across the country. Only large cities and university towns with residents of diverse tastes, however, tended to sustain stand-alone juice bars, that is, operations functioning mainly as juice bars. In other areas, stores, restaurants, health clubs, gyms, and coffeehouses integrated juice-bar amenities into other food services.

CURRENT CONDITIONS

By 2000 juice-bar revenues nationwide were growing 30 percent a year, accelerated by scores of new store openings and wider consumer awareness. Although skeptics questioned whether it's all just a fad, perhaps as frozen yogurt was a decade earlier or as bagel shops were until the market grew oversaturated, industry insiders believed juice bars still have substantial untapped market potential.

Analysts and industry executives argued that fresh-juice mixes and nutritionally fortified smoothies reach a market that is both deeper and broader than those of faddish foods. The health benefits of fruit, they argued, appeal to a wide swath of customers and

demographics—even wider than coffee retailing, which has done remarkably well—from teens to baby boomers. Likewise, the convenience of grabbing a healthful drink at shopping centers or near workplaces makes it an effective, long-term alternative to other food and drink. At least one smoothie vendor reported in 1999 that many of its customers visit five or six times a week, and some more than once a day.

Juice bars still have vast stretches of territory to conquer geographically. For example, Jamba Juice, the largest chain in 2000 based on number of locations, began to make serious forays outside its West Coast stronghold only in 1999, in part through its partnership with the Whole Foods produce chain. In early 2000, Jamba still had only two outlets on the East Coast. Similarly, Smoothie King, another top chain, was concentrated heavily in southern and southeastern states, with almost nothing in the West or Northeast.

One juice-bar distinction likely to sharpen in the early 2000s is that between vendors offering "plain," unfortified juice blends and those with nutrient-enhanced potables. Firms in the latter category are already apt to market their drinks as meal replacements or as solutions to specific health needs or problems. One of the older players in the business, Louisiana-based Smoothie King, has positioned itself this way and draws a contrast to others such as Jamba Juice, a potentially formidable competitor, which Smoothie King views as mere beverage purveyors. Such positioning may signal a trend toward niches within the juice-bar business.

While franchises accounted for most of the growth in the juice-bar industry in the late 1990s, juice-bar consultancies have also cropped up to help those entrepreneurs choosing to go it alone. Juice Gallery owner Dan Titus offers a comprehensive package as a franchise alternative that takes prospective juice-bar owners through all the steps to opening and running a successful business. Chris Cuvelier, owner of Juice & Smoothie Bar Consulting helps clients in the United States as well as overseas avoid some of the common industry mistakes. These consultants draw from their own experiences as juice-bar start-ups, including successes and things they could have done better, to lead others to successful ownership.

INDUSTRY LEADERS

Jamba Juice Co. was the biggest juice-bar chain in 2000, with 350 stores in 18 states and plans to add dozens more. Founded as the Juice Club in 1990 by Kirk Perron, the San Francisco-based juice seller has gradually expanded from its California base by franchising outlets and acquiring other retailers. Perron created the company to offer consumers an alternative to both fatty fast foods and to insipid health foods. "Jamba" is a west African word meaning celebration, according to Perron, who wants his Jamba Juice units to offer customers a festive atmosphere as well as exciting, healthful drinks. In 1999 the company bought out Utah-based Zuka Juice, which broadened Jamba's coverage in western states. To ready the company for further expansion, including a possible initial public offering of its stock, in 2000 Jamba Juice hired Burger King's former North American unit president Paul Clayton as its chief executive. Also in 2000, Jamba contracted teamed up with Waiter.com to provide online ordering and delivery services in the San Francisco Bar area. The company has begun offering soup and other items in addition to juices.

Smoothie King, based in New Orleans, has expanded its franchises across the United States. In 2000 Smoothie King operated or franchised over 225 outlets in 22 states and was continuing to place franchises in various locations throughout the country. Smoothie King was founded in 1973 by Stephen and Cynthia Kuhnau and began franchising in 1989. Stephen Kuh-

nau develops all of the company's emulsions and studies nutritional trends and findings to provide up-to-date products for his health-conscious customers. In addition to smoothies, Smoothie King offers health products, such as vitamins and minerals, and competes with general health-food stores. In 1999 the company recorded total sales of $65 million. *Entrepreneur* magazine acknowledged the success of Smoothie King in 1995, ranking the juice-bar operation the number-one specialty-beverage franchiser in its annual "Franchise 500" list.

Atlanta-based Planet Smoothie vied with Smoothie King in the race to bring juice bars to the East Coast. Founded in 1995, Planet Smoothie operated nearly 140 outlets by the end of 2000 and continued adding new ones at a furious pace. In 2000 it opened several stores in Singapore. Most of its stores are located in shopping centers, and like most of its competitors, Planet Smoothie relies on franchising to expand its presence. The chain also sells vitamins, nutritional supplements, soups, and sandwiches in addition to its drinks. Under its policies, the corporation subsidizes the opening of new Planet Smoothie outlets and unit operators share profits with the Planet Smoothie corporation. In 1999, the company estimated it cost between $82,000 and $146,000 (including leasing fees) to start a new Planet Smoothie unit.

Juice Kitchen Inc. is an up-and-coming player. The Denver-based company was formed in 1999 to buy the ailing Juice Stop chain, which went into bankruptcy protection in 1998. Juice Kitchen was leaving the Juice Stop brand name on many of the acquired outlets; it planned to position the Juice Kitchen brand as a higher-end vendor. The company reduced some of the Juice Stop sites to kiosks to make them more cost-efficient, and it planned to open 70 percent of its new stores as kiosks. As of early 2000, the combined operations consisted of about 70 stores scattered in parts of New England, the Central Plains, and the company's home state of Colorado. The juice chain sells soups and prepackaged snacks in addition to its juices and smoothies.

Other leading smoothie and juice-bar operations include Edina, Minnesota-based Orange Julius's Just Juice concept; Juice It Up of Irvine, California; San Diego-based Fresh Blend Smoothie and Juice Bar; Surf City Squeeze, based in Scottsdale, Arizona; and Freshens Smoothies of Atlanta. Dairy Queen International, Blimpie International (through the Smoothie Island chain), and TCBY Enterprises (through its Juice Works unit), have also made inroads into the juice-bar market.

AMERICA AND THE WORLD

Overseas expansion is on the minds of many of the companies growing in the United States. Analysts agree that there is room for everyone both here and in the international market. To date, however, no U.S. chain has made any significant foray into foreign markets and foreign companies are all but absent from the U.S. market. In 2000, Planet Smoothie was one of the few venturing into international markets thus far, with agreements to open five test outlets in Singapore. Other players such as Blimpie International, primarily a fast-food sandwich chain, were well-poised to introduce the juice and smoothie concepts through their existing international franchising relationships.

FURTHER READING

Adams, Michael. "Smoothie Operator." *Restaurant Business,* 10 October 1996, 80.

Brack, Elliott. "Innocent-Sounding 'Juice Bars' Can Drive Their Neighborhoods to Drink." *Atlanta Journal and Constitution,* 1 November 2000.

Castagna, Nicole G. "Smoothing Out the Juice Bar: Extract Profits from Growing Interest in Produce-Based Beverages." *Restaurants & Institutions,* 15 September 1997, 110.

Clancy, Carole. "Smoothie Bars: Serving Up the Next Food Fad?" *Tampa Bay Business Journal,* 30 May 1997, 1.

Gibson, Richard. "Jamba Juice's Deal for Zuka May Result in a Profitable Blend." *Wall Street Journal,* 19 February 1999.

———. "Smoothie Barons Dream of Fast-Food Empires." *Wall Street Journal,* 6 August 1999.

Holleran, Joan. "Squeezing Fresh, Healthy Profits." *Beverage Industry,* April 1996, 25.

Khermouch, Gerry. "Third Places." *Brandweek,* 13 March 1995, 36.

Krummert, Bob. "A Growth Bonanza for Smooth Beverages." *ID: The Voice of Foodservice Distribution,* June 1998, 66.

Lempert, Phil. "Do Smoothies Give You a 'Real' Boost?" *Los Angeles Times,* 21 August 2000.

Lorenzini, Beth. "Turn up the Juice." *Restaurants & Institutions,* 1 February 1995, 113.

Phillips, Debra, et al. "Entrepreneur Magazine's 12 Hottest Businesses for 1999: Juice Bars." *Entrepreneur Magazine,* 1999. Available from http://www.entrepreneurmag.com/entmag/hotbiz99/juice.html.

"Planet Smoothie Blends Nutritious Quick Fix." *Shopping Center World,* December 1998.

Plotkin, Hal. "Seeking Quality, Juicer Squeezes out Franchisees." *Inc.,* July 1997, 25.

Quail, Jennifer. "Squeezing the Profits." *Supermarket News,* 28 February 2000.

Rohland, Pamela, et al. "SmartPicks Top Businesses for 1999: Juice Bars." *Entrepreneur Magazine,* 1999. Available from http://www.entrepreneurmag.com/startup/topbiz99/juice.html.

Rousseau, Rita. "Squeezing Profits from Juice." *Restaurants and Institutions,* 15 October 1995, 142.

Ruggless, Ron. "Juice Kitchen, after Juice Stop Takeover, Taps 2-Brand Strategy." *Nation's Restaurant News,* 14 February 2000.

Scarpa, James. "Be Fruitful." *Restaurant Business,* 15 January 1997, 93.

"Squeeze to Please." *Restaurant Business,* 1 July 1996, 147.

Strauss, Karyn. "Perron: Jamba's Juiced for Growth, Plans IPO." *Nation's Restaurant News,* 24 January 2000.

———. "Planet Smoothie Orbits New Growth Strategy." *Nation's Restaurant News,* 22 November 1999.

———. "Report: Smoothie Indies Face Rocky Road as Chains Slurp up Market Share." *Nation's Restaurant News,* 14 June 1999.

Teague, Elaine W. "Juice Bar Franchises Pour into the Global Marketplace." *Entrepreneur International Magazine,* March 1998. Available from http://www.entrepreneurmag.com.

———. "Virgin Versions: Smoothie Operators Sweet Talk Customers into Alcohol-Free Concoctions of Fresh Fruit Juices." *Restaurant Business,* 20 November 1996, 103.

KNOWLEDGE MANAGEMENT SOFTWARE AND SERVICES

The knowledge management movement began in the late 1980s and early 1990s, as knowledge management become one of the key buzzwords of the decade. Although the concept suffers from ambiguity, at the core of knowledge management is the sharing of knowledge and information. By the turn of the new century, knowledge management software and services had blossomed into a strong and rapidly growing industry, because businesses sought to capitalize on the greater efficiency promised by knowledge management. As the Information Age inundated companies with information and the movement towards a knowledge-based economy placed greater import on efficient use of knowledge and information, the knowledge management software and services industry experienced strong growth in the late 1990s—and this growth is expected to accelerate in the early 2000s. In 2000, worldwide industry sales were an estimated $3.1 billion. By 2004, revenues are forecast to balloon to between $12 and $41 billion, according to forecasts by various industry analysts.

During this period some of the industry's first-wave software products began to hit the market led by software powerhouses such as Lotus and Microsoft as well as by smaller concerns such as Abuzz and Hummingbird. These applications typically facilitated e-mail communication and collaboration as well as access to vital company information and documents.

ORGANIZATION AND STRUCTURE

Knowledge management, or KM, seeks to solve common problems such as one employee developing a solution to a problem that an employee in another department has already solved. Knowledge management strives to pool a company's knowledge and best practices to promote greater efficiency, avoid redundancy, and retain knowledge and practices within the company after key employees and officers leave. Furthermore, knowledge management also encompasses adopting successful business practices of other companies—even of competitors. Knowledge management theorists distinguish knowledge from information and data. Unlike information and data, which have not been processed, knowledge—or know-how—has been processed and has a particular use. For example, knowledge or know-how can be used to solve problems, whereas information cannot until it is converted to knowledge. Consequently, knowledge management is not simply compiling a database. Instead, knowledge management involves creating knowledge repositories where company know-how can be accessed and reused.

The key participants in the industry include software companies such as Microsoft and IBM and consulting firms such as Andersen Consulting and KPMG—as well as their smaller counterparts. The goal of knowledge management software is to categorize information in an easily accessible format and to facilitate the exchange of information. The foundation of many knowledge management software applications is the use of portals, or pages similar to Web sites such as Yahoo! that organize information into different categories. Knowledge management consultants, on the other hand, help companies achieve similar results by recommending software or cultural and structural changes, or a combination of the two, to bring about a more manageable organization of knowledge that can be readily shared with others.

Knowledge management applications usually are accessible, searchable, and shareable repositories of knowledge. To create such repositories, companies often create a centralized network where all this knowledge and information is stored and can be accessed by all employees. The benefit of knowledge management is the reusability of knowledge and information: a solution to a specific problem is developed only once (unless a better solution is needed). In addition, knowledge management is frequently characterized as "leveraging" information to new applications or uses. However, most industry observers agree that knowledge management involves more than just technology: corporate culture also plays a role in the exchange of knowledge. Hence, knowledge management ultimately is a meld of information-sharing practices (accessing and retrieving information) and technology that facilitates this process.

Ultimately, a knowledge management effort might look something like the following scenario. A company installs a communications application such as Lotus Notes or Microsoft Outlook on its computers, which enables employees to communicate with each other easily over the company network or intranet. A company might also take inventory of how it operates and how it solves various problems and handles various situations, identifying who has specific expertise in what areas. In addition, a company might develop a universal library of all its documents so that employees from throughout the organization can locate and access them quickly.

BACKGROUND AND DEVELOPMENT

In 1992, before the knowledge management hype of the late 1990s, Buckman Laboratories, a chemical manufacturer based in Tennessee, set up private forums via CompuServe to enable its 1,200 employees around the world to share successful business practices and information, according to Workforce. The forums and their interconnected databases and online bulletin boards allowed employees to pose questions and receive prompt answers, share information, and swap proposals and presentations for feedback. This information exchange ultimately enabled the company to leverage the knowledge and information of the many to help the few so that a single employee could accomplish tasks involving input and expertise from several departments quickly. Other companies also had what now would be called knowledge management procedures and technology in place before the explosion of interest in the field.

Nevertheless, the theoretical history of knowledge management began in the 1970s with research on information transfer at Stanford University and Massachusetts Institute of Technology, according to Rebecca O'Barclay and Philip C. Murray in "What Is Knowledge Management?" These studies examined how knowledge was produced, used, and transferred in organizations. With this foundation, companies started to realize knowledge was a vital asset, and that it needed to be managed properly, in the mid-1980s. By the end of the decade, researchers were using artificial intelligence technology for knowledge management purposes called at the time "knowledge engineering" and "knowledge-based systems," according to Barclay and Murray.

At the end of the 1980s and the beginning of the 1990s, "knowledge management" became of bona fide term in the business lexicon. In 1989, a group of companies established the Initiative for Managing Knowledge Assets in an effort to develop technological solutions for knowledge management. Simultaneously, consulting firms began offering knowledge management services. Likewise several influential articles and books were written around this time, which addressed knowledge management issues, including Ikujiro Nonaka's article "The Knowledge-Creating Company." All these factors combined to create a thriving trend in management by the mid-1990s, which included the creation of chief knowledge officers or chief intelligence officers as new corporate executives.

The knowledge management software and services industry also is a product of computer and information technology innovations and the movement to a knowledge-based economy in the 1990s. Advances in computer and information technology brought about the rapid-fire transmission of information. During the mid- to late 1990s, businesses could easily access prodigious quantities of information via the Internet and massive databases. Unstructured data on the Internet is particularly problematic for companies because of the labor needed to locate and analyze it. Employees who then bring information in off the Internet tend to keep it for personal use, even though it may be of use to others in the company. These varied developments and events all contributed to the growth of knowledge management as an industry, and not just an academic theory.

CURRENT CONDITIONS

According to a study by International Data Corp., the 500 largest U.S. companies squandered about $12 billion in 1999 because of inefficiencies in their use of and access to knowledge resources. The business monitoring firm also projects that such losses will rise $31 billion by 2003. In addition, a Korn/Ferry International survey showed that 88 percent of workers do not have access to knowledge resources from other parts of their companies. Further, the Gartner Group reported that U.S. business generate 5.5 billion documents annually and generally these documents are filed and retrieved by hand.

Consequently, the market was rife with opportunities for knowledge management software and services. The information overload of the late 1990s and early 2000s proved to be fertile ground for the industry, which saw spectacular growth in the late 1990s and anticipated even greater growth in the early 2000s. Ovum, an industry analyst, estimated that knowledge management software sales for 2000 reached $515 million and that knowledge management service revenues climbed to $2.6 billion worldwide. By 2004, Ovum expects software sales to hit $3.5 billion and services to reach $8.8 billion worldwide, creating a $12.3 billion industry. However, a survey by the Gartner Group found that the industry was much larger and would grow much faster. This study indicated that worldwide revenues totaled $13.2 billion in the late 1990s and that they would soar to $41.6 billion by 2003. Furthermore, the U.S. Bureau of Labor Statistics predicts that there will be about 10,000 knowledge management workers by 2006. Research by Teltech Resource Network Corp. indicated that companies invested most of their knowledge management dollars in their production (30 percent) and product development (25 percent) departments. Other key departments included customer service (15 percent), strategic planning (10 percent), and sales (5 percent). International Data Corp. research demonstrated that 50 percent of U.S. corporations with over 500 employees planned to implement some form of knowledge management program in the near future.

The change from a manufacturing-based to a knowledge-based economy also spurred the knowledge management services and software industry. In the New Economy, knowledge or intellectual capital is the crucial asset and must be properly managed. Without adequate management of knowledge, companies spend greater resources locating and exchanging information or recreate knowledge unnecessarily, all of which increase costs.

KNOWLEDGE MANAGEMENT SOFTWARE AND TECHNOLOGY

Software makers began to roll out knowledge management applications in earnest around 2000. Industry big boys such as Microsoft and IBM (especially

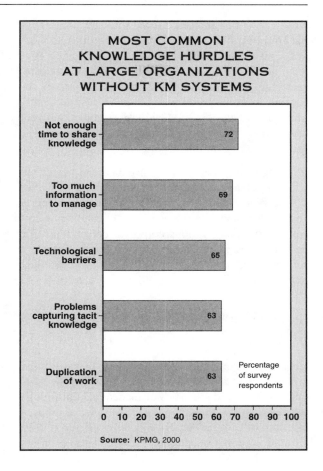

MOST COMMON KNOWLEDGE HURDLES AT LARGE ORGANIZATIONS WITHOUT KM SYSTEMS

Not enough time to share knowledge: 72
Too much information to manage: 69
Technological barriers: 65
Problems capturing tacit knowledge: 63
Duplication of work: 63

Percentage of survey respondents

Source: KPMG, 2000

through its Lotus subsidiary) all entered the knowledge management fray. Lotus touted its knowledge management software, code named Raven, as the first genuine knowledge management application. Raven's innovations included discovery engines that categorize data and user profiles, which facilitates moving important information into prominent areas. Raven complements earlier IBM/Lotus efforts to promote knowledge sharing, including their Lotus Notes client and Domino server.

However, critics were more skeptical of the value of these and other knowledge management applications, arguing that knowledge management is still too theoretical, according to *PC Week*. Others contend that knowledge management is often specific to a given company. In response, Lotus announced its intention to offer Raven via Lotus Professional Services and IBM Global Services, which would adapt the application to the specific needs of each company. Moreover, Lotus maintained that the versatility of Raven made it adaptable to a wide range of businesses.

Microsoft's venture into knowledge management included the Digital Dashboard of its Outlook 2000 as well as its Office and BackOffice software suites. Digital Dashboard technology integrates various applications and functions according to user preferences. Digital dashboards combine personal, department, corporate, and outside information and resources according to user specifications. As an easy example, Microsoft's Outlook 2000 Digital Dashboard delivers users news, weather, stock quotes, calendar entries, and task entries on one page.

Knowledge management also has been associated with corporate intranet, or computer networks within a corporation. Some companies consider intranets a key tool for knowledge management by facilitating collaboration among various corporate departments. To make intranets more effective, knowledge management software and services try to create portals where key information organized and prominently displayed.

KNOWLEDGE MANAGEMENT AND ITS CRITICS

However, some industry observers caution that technology is only part of the solution; that is, access to information alone is not enough to avoid the inefficiencies and redundancies of inadequate knowledge sharing. Instead, they emphasize the need of companies to assess their corporate cultures to see if they promote information sharing. Hence, these observers suggest that companies should first examine their management style and corporate culture before investing in knowledge management software and services, which may be of little use if the management style and culture do not encourage or outright inhibit knowledge sharing.

In a *Workforce* article, Samuel Greengard identified three primary obstacles in corporate cultures that might impede knowledge management efforts. First, workers tend not to share their best ideas. Second, people often fail to use others' ideas because they fear using them would make them appear less knowledgeable. Third, workers are inclined to view themselves as experts and hence shun collaboration. According to Greengard, eradicating or at least lessening the effect of these obstacles is an essential first step to implementing any knowledge management program, which can be achieved through incentives as well as accountability programs.

INDUSTRY LEADERS

This industry's top companies includes some of the world's leading consulting and software firms.

Nevertheless, smaller concerns also play an important role in providing knowledge management counseling and in developing knowledge management software.

The world's largest consulting firm, Andersen Consulting ranks among the leading providers of knowledge management services. Andersen specializes in knowledge management of the pharmaceutical, chemical, energy, food, automotive, and financial services industries. The company strives to help clients identify best practices, expedite innovation, reduce risk, and increase value. Andersen's clients have included British Petroleum, MCC, and the U.S. Department of Housing and Urban Development. Andersen Consulting has a strong global presence in business and technology fields with offices in over 40 countries. In 1999, Andersen's parent company, Andersen Worldwide, posted revenues of $16.3 billion.

KPMG Consulting, Inc. is another major provider of knowledge management services. KPMG customizes its services based on particular business needs and focuses on helping companies optimize the use of Microsoft products such as Office and Outlook as knowledge management tools. Its primary services included Program Management Office, designed to aid information technology departments in sharing their knowledge, and Customer Management, developed for creating knowledge warehouses of customer information. In addition, the company plans to expand its offerings to include advisory services on knowledge management in research and development, supply-chain management, and mergers. KPMG services six primary industries: the public sector, financial services, communications, technology, health care, and consumer and industrial markets. In 1999, the private company brought in $1.9 billion.

Other knowledge management service providers include Sopheon plc and MeansBusiness. Sopheon, which merged with the KM firm Teltech Resource Network Corp. in late 2000, concentrates on supplying companies with systems for organizing and sharing their knowledge. The firm launched Intotaa, a Web-based knowledge resource to facilitate business-to-business knowledge transactions in the technical and scientific fields, in 2000. That year, Sopheon brought in revenues of $20 million. MeansBusiness's take on knowledge management is a bit different: the company sorts through various resources such as newspapers and periodicals and extracts parts it considers important, such as key ideas. The company then makes these resources available to subscribers in a searchable format. With over 20,000 resources to their name, MeansBusiness sought to expand in 2000 with the signing of an extensive deal with 25 of the largest

English-language business publishers to acquire full, verbatim extracts from their publications.

In the software sector, IBM's Lotus Development Corp. and Microsoft are two of the most prominent companies. Lotus considers itself the first mover in the knowledge management software sector with its Lotus Notes and more recently with Raven. Lotus Notes—a communications application—dominates the business intranet market, with some 56 million users. Lotus Notes features e-mail, calendar, scheduling, and Web access functions. In addition, Lotus makes the intranet messaging application Domino. Nevertheless, Lotus believes its latest knowledge management application, Knowledge Management Suite, or Raven, is the first true set of knowledge management software tools. Raven features user profiling, content tracking and analysis, and a knowledge portal for organizing individual and group information. Furthermore, Lotus has a division, Lotus KM Products Group, devoted to developing knowledge management solutions. Lotus is one of the world's largest software producers, having achieved initial success with its spreadsheet software Lotus 1-2-3.

IBM has a presence of its own in the industry with its software and its consulting services. Some of IBM's knowledge management applications include IBM Enterprise Information Portal and Visual Warehouse. In addition, the company provides knowledge management services through its IBM Global Services KM Consulting, which focuses on three primary aspects of companies to bring about improved knowledge management: content, infrastructure, and culture. In 1999, IBM reported overall sales of $87.5 billion and net earnings of $7.7 billion. Software sales, including Lotus's, accounted for 14 percent of the company's total sales.

As the largest software maker in the world, Microsoft, Inc.'s approach to knowledge management is not to create a bunch of new applications, but to use existing software. Microsoft contends that some of its core products, including its Office suite, BackOffice, and in particular its Outlook application, are all knowledge management tools. Company founder and chairman Bill Gates considers Microsoft Outlook a quintessential knowledge management application with its Digital Dashboard, which facilitates communication among employees and the organization of critical company knowledge. In addition, Microsoft manufactures programs such as Visual Studio that allow users to develop knowledge management applications to augment its Office suite. Moreover, Microsoft plans to continue integrating functions, enabling users to combine information and applications according to their needs.

This vision includes continuing production of software with collaboration, searchability, information management, and data warehousing capabilities.

In 2000, the company's revenues continued to climb rapidly, reaching almost $23 billion—up over 10 percent from 1999. Microsoft also remained highly profitable with $9.4 billion in profits for 2000. On the dark side, Microsoft was embroiled in antitrust litigation in the late 1990s and early 2000s. Having found Microsoft had engaged in anti-competitive conduct regarding its Web browser, Internet Explorer, the court ordered that Microsoft would have to split into two companies. Microsoft appealed this decision.

Besides these industry giants, a host of smaller software firms are key participants in the industry. Among these companies are Tacit Knowledge Systems Inc. with its KnowledgeMail and KnowledgeMail Plus, which comb through company e-mail in search of knowledge and make such information available company-wide. In addition, former IBM and Lotus executives teamed up to form Energia Software Inc., which plans to provide knowledge management software that solves problems not dealt with by Lotus and Microsoft applications. One of the company's first products was Unity NT. Other important KM companies include Abuzz Inc. with its Beehive, WisdomWare with its Sales Coaching, Open Text with its Livelink, and Hummingbird with its portals such as the Enterprise Information Portal.

AMERICA AND THE WORLD

As some industry analysts frequently point out, knowledge management practices are not new. In fact, some of the theories and practices were developed in the United States after observing the structure of Japanese companies. While researching their customs, Ikujiro Nonaka discovered that some Japanese companies were structured so that information and knowledge of different departments overlapped, which circulated company know-how among a broad range of employees, as described in the article "The Knowledge-Creating Company." The advantages these companies experienced included faster product development and more efficient problem solving.

Furthermore, European companies have followed U.S. ones, implementing knowledge management initiatives. These efforts mirror their U.S. counterparts with a combination of technology and business practices to promote the exchange of knowledge and best practices. Global U.S. companies such as IBM also have taken their knowledge management practices abroad. Like U.S. companies, European companies found that information sharing is not an intuitive employee activity and instead it must be taught and induced with incentives.

RESEARCH AND TECHNOLOGY

According to Ovum, a central area of research and expansion in the knowledge management industry will be creating virtual communication within and without corporate intranets. Achieving this kind of communication would involve converting intranets to extranets, which enable people outside of a company to communicate with those inside. Hewlett-Packard introduced its Silicon Space application to promote this kind of exchange. To maintain the confidentiality of information, however, companies must ensure that adequate security measures are taken so that only the appropriate users can access the networks.

In 2000, Microsoft added a learning function, IntraLearn 2000, developed by IntraLearn Software, Inc. to its knowledge-management solutions. This integration marked the first time knowledge management and learning software had been blended together. IntraLearn provided Microsoft's Digital Dashboard with capabilities for aiding online educators and corporate trainers and integrating online lesson plans with e-mail, discussion groups, and examinations.

FURTHER READING

Berry, John. "Employees Cash In On KM—Knowledge Management Programs Pay Rewards to Share Ideas." *InternetWeek,* 22 May 2000.

Blake, Paul. "The Future of Knowledge Management." *Information Today,* March 2000.

Bonner, Dede. "Enter the Chief Knowledge Officer." *Training & Development,* February 2000.

Caton, Michael. "ASP's Fate Tied to Definition of Knowledge Management." *PC Week,* 8 November 1999.

Deckmyn, Dominique. "New Niche: Finding Experts." *Computerworld,* 15 November 1999.

"Footnotes." *Business Week,* 26 June 2000.

Greengard, Samuel. "Storing, Shaping and Sharing Collective Wisdom." *Workforce,* October 1998.

———. "Will Your Culture Support KM?" *Workforce,* October 1998.

Harvard Business Review on Knowledge Management. Cambridge, MA: Harvard Business Review, 1998.

"Intellectual Capital" *Inc.,* 15 September 1999.

"KM Market Grows." Computer Dealer News, 7 January 2000.

"Know Thyself." *Industry Week,* 24 January 2000.

"Knowledge Resource Launch." *Regulatory News Service,* 4 December 2000.

Krogh, Georg von, and Johan Roos, eds. *Managing Knowledge.* London: Sage Publications, 1996.

Nobel, Carmen. "Lotus, Autonomy Hawk Knowledge." *PC Week,* 14 February 2000.

Petersen, Scot. "IntraLearn Turns On Dashboard Learning." *PC Week,* 13 December 1999.

Ruber, Peter. "Keep the Knowledge You're Paying For." *Information Week,* 30 October 2000.

"Smart Starts." *Inc.,* 15 September 1999.

Strugatch, Warren. "Angst in the Info Age." *LI Business News,* 4 February 2000.

Verespej, Mike. "Knowledge Management: System or Culture?" *Industry Week,* 16 August 1999.

Wareham, Elynn. "Knowledge Management Spending to Skyrocket: IDC." *Computing Canada,* 29 October 1999.

LASERS AND LASER APPLICATIONS

The very same qualities that made lasers so potently frightening in grade-B sci-fi flicks from the 1950s—their speed, precision, and ability to vaporize anything in their path—are precisely the things that have given them such versatility. Their applications span the fields of medicine, the military, electronics, machine processing, and cosmetics, to name a few.

The term "laser" is an acronym for *l*ight *a*mplification by *s*timulated *e*mission of *r*adiation. A laser is a narrow, extremely focused, powerful beam of monochromatic light that can be used for a variety of functions. For instance, lasers etch information onto the surface of compact discs. Lasers used in the production of CD-ROM disks condense large amounts of information, such as a set of encyclopedias or the New York metropolitan phone book, onto one disk. Another example of laser etching is in video discs, which in the 1990s promised to give videocassettes significant competition, if not replace them, as the means of providing home movie entertainment. Holograms, three-dimensional images, are also examples of laser technology at work. By the 1990s many credit-card companies affixed holograms to their cards to discourage would-be counterfeiters. Public speakers employ laser pointers when giving presentations. Laser light shows abounded in entertainment, often as an alternative to fireworks displays at public events.

On the forefront of laser-oriented research are attempts to perfect high-speed, high-density storage of digital data using the newly discovered blue or violet laser. In the realm of medicine, promising procedures for the quick diagnosis of cancer and highly accurate methods to target tumors in treatment have emerged. Scientists at the University of Wisconsin-Madison discovered that infrared lasers could image not only molecules, but even the smaller bonds that hold them together. At the opposite end of the scale, astronomers scanned the skies for laser pulses as a clue to the existence of extraterrestrial life and physicists attempted to control the weather with lasers by issuing preemptive laser strikes at storm clouds to generate lightning bolts on demand. Breakthroughs in the field occurred more quickly than technology could evolve to support laser's many promising new applications.

ORGANIZATION AND STRUCTURE

Lasers have become indispensable. Fiber-optic communications use pulses of laser light to send information on glass strands. Before the advent of fiber optics, telephone calls were relayed on thick bundles of copper wire. With the appearance of this new technology, a glass wire no thicker than a human hair could carry thousands of conversations. Lasers are also used in scanners, in price-code checkers at supermarkets; in tags to prevent book thefts from libraries or clothing thefts from stores; and in inventory systems in company warehouses. Heating lasers can drill through solid metal in an industrial setting. They remove gallstones in operating rooms and cataracts in outpatient surgery. They are able to precisely remove an oxidized outer layer and thus restore an art object to its original beauty. In the late 1960s and early 1970s, measuring lasers assisted scientists in calibrating the distance between Earth and the Moon to within two inches. They continue to provide surveyors assistance in making much smaller measurements as well. Lasers are used for guiding missiles. They aid building contractors to assure that walls, floors, and ceilings are in proper alignment. (See the essay in this book on Fiber Optics.)

Several interest and advocacy groups foster technological advances. These organizations include: the Laser Institute of America (formerly the Laser Industry Association); the Laser and Electro-Optics Society; and the Institute of Electrical and Electronics Engineers. Many significant laser manufacturers belong to the Laser and Electro-Optics Manufacturers' Association (LEOMA). LEOMA plays a key role in representing the industry in Washington and in settling disputes between companies. For example, LEOMA lobbies in Washington to maintain funding for laser research. LEOMA also possesses an alternative dispute resolution agreement, whereby members agree not to initiate legal action against one another without first attempting to resolve the conflict with the help of a mediator. According to LEOMA, its 40 member companies represent 90 percent of the industry's annual North American sales.

While the federal government oversees laser research through the Technology Reinvestment Program, the National Institute of Standards and Technology has an interest in the laser industry, especially through its Advanced Development Program. The U.S. Department of Energy, the National Institutes for Health (NIH), the Food and Drug Administration (FDA), and the National Aeronautics and Space Administration (NASA) are also interested in various laser applications.

BACKGROUND AND DEVELOPMENT

Laser light is produced by the process of stimulated emission, which involves bringing many atoms into an excited state. When light travels through a normal material containing more ground- state atoms than excited-state atoms, it is more likely to be absorbed than amplified. To make a laser, energy must be delivered to produce more excited-state atoms than ground-state atoms. This situation is called a population inversion. If light traveling through the material is more likely to collide with excited atoms than ground-state atoms, it causes stimulated emission. The material or medium then becomes an amplifier.

A laser consists of three components: an optical cavity, an energy source, and an active medium. The optical cavity, two mirrors facing one another, contains the active laser medium. One of the mirrors fully reflects light from the stimulated emission, whereas the other is only partially reflective. Light, generated and amplified by the medium, resonates back and forth between the mirrors in a constant flux between the background and excited energy states. Some of the light transmitted by the less reflective mirror is diverted as a highly focused beam, the laser. Generally, electricity is the energy source. The active medium can be solid-state, semiconductor, gas, or dye. One example of a solid-state laser is a ruby crystal.

PIONEERS IN THE FIELD

Albert Einstein (1879-1955) first considered the idea of stimulated emission, a key element in laser technology, in 1917. In 1954 Charles H. Townes (1915-) supplied another key element by producing population inversion in a microwave device, which he called a *microwave amplification by stimulated emission of radiation*, or maser. During the 1950s, the United States and the Soviet Union entered into a technology race to develop a laser, and on 16 May 1960, Theodore Harold Maiman (1927-), a U.S. scientist, operated the first solid-state laser. In 1964 Townes and two Soviet physicists shared the Nobel Prize in physics for their work in laser development.

The gas laser also made its appearance in 1960. That was the creation of Ali Javan, a Bell Laboratories engineer working in New Jersey. In 1962 semiconductor lasers were developed. The dye laser made its first appearance in 1966.

During the 1960s, some people within the scientific community called lasers "a solution without a problem," because they could not conceive of a practical use for them. Lasers began having commercial applications in 1961 when Maiman formed the industry's first laser company, Quantatron. Other laser companies also made their appearance, primarily producing ruby solid-state lasers. In 1999 Bell Labs in Murray Hill, New Jersey, created the first bidirectional, semiconductor laser, which can emit two beams of light of widely divergent wavelengths—a feat previously accomplished using two different lasers.

The military took a keen interest in the use of lasers for missile guidance and other applications such as the development of nuclear fusion. The federal government became a major player in laser development

An industrial carbon dioxide laser used for welding and cutting metal. (Photo Researchers Inc./Maximillian Stock Ltd./Science Photo Library)

during the 1970s and 1980s as it tried to augment laser's existing uses. One of the most famous plans for a military application of lasers was the highly publicized Star Wars Defense system, championed by President Ronald Reagan, which did not come to fruition during his administration. By the 1990s, laser applications were rapidly expanding in both the military and automotive fields for vehicle position sensing, crash avoidance, and profiling object surfaces from long distances. The military used laser guidance systems in smart bombs during the Persian Gulf War of 1991.

CURRENT CONDITIONS

The laser and laser applications industry in the late 1990s continued to grow quickly. The computer industry needs to etch increasingly complicated circuit patterns onto increasingly smaller microchips, requiring something more effective than the mercury light process that had sustained the microchip industry throughout the late 1980s.

Lasers are used in many types of surgery because of the precision they guarantee. The cauterizing effect of the beam greatly reduces blood loss during procedures. Laser eye surgery continued to be one of the most widely implemented applications of laser medical technology, although medical insurance frequently does not cover it. A laser "smart scalpel" was presented by the U.S. Department of Energy's Sandia National Laboratories. The instrument—a biological microcavity laser—identifies the presence of cancerous cells while a surgeon operates, by shining a laser beam on a stream of cells as they are pumped from the operation site into a spectrometer. Cancerous cells, which contain a higher density of protein than regular cells, change speed when the laser illuminates them, thus alerting the surgeon when all the malignancy has been removed.

Doctors at Emory Hospitals in Atlanta began treating cancer patients with photodynamic laser therapy (PLT) in 2000. Patients receive a cancer-fighting drug, photofrin, by injection; while healthy tissues excrete excess amounts of the drug, cancerous tissues absorb it. A nonthermal laser beam is then introduced into the patient's throat via an endoscope and aimed at the tumor. The light activates the drug, which destroys the cancerous cells. PLT was initially approved for use only on patients with esophageal and lung cancer, though the treatment will probably be extended for use on other cancers as well.

In 1996 the FDA approved lasers for the removal of facial wrinkles. Since then, use of lasers for cosmetic treatments has boomed. Applications included the removal of unwanted hair, tattoos, and spider veins. An estimated 3.2 million such procedures were performed in 2000, up from about 1 million in 1996. Laser skin resurfacing remained a popular cosmetic laser procedure, with approximately 170,000 people exposing their faces to laser beams in 1999. Dental whitening and the sterilization of infected tooth tissue constituted the newest, and fastest-growing, applications in this segment.

Just as lasers are used to resurface humans, they also find applications for treating industrial surfaces. They can harden, anneal, and alloy surface materials in targeted areas with great precision. Laser cutting of manufacturing parts creates a milled-quality edge and eliminates the need for secondary operations, such as grinding and deburring, thereby reducing production costs.

Laser printers, CDs, and other products featuring lasers continue to be fast-selling items. By 2000, network-ready, color laser printers were on the market. While the machines approached ink-jet printers' color performance and delivered much faster results, their prohibitive prices kept them out of the reach of most consumers for home use.

The world of high fashion also benefited from laser's precision. The Civilian American/European Surface Anthropometry Resource group launched a $6 million project to measure the exact dimensions of 8,000 volunteers in the United States and Europe by 2001. The project used a laser-scanning system to create 3-D templates for a database of human sizes. The data will be used by designers, from Parisian couture to the U.S. Air Force, to create well-fitting clothing. Eventually, more ordinary customers might be able to be scanned for a perfect fit.

Not all laser applications were benign. Throughout the 1990s, anti-optic laser weapons were deployed. Though intended to confound the opposition's surveillance systems, they also can be used to blind human beings, often permanently. And America's first military aircraft of the 21st century—the Boeing-manufactured, 747-400 freighter numbered 00-0001—flaunted an antimissile laser beam mounted on its nose.

The search for extraterrestrial life also became laser-oriented. The Search for Extraterrestrial Intelligence (SETI) project expanded its focus beyond radio waves to start scanning for laser signals that might be directed at earth. Astronomers will monitor the sky for laser pulses from Oak Ridge Observatory at Harvard University, Leuschner Observatory near Berkeley, and an observatory at San Francisco State University.

The abuses of the laser are also rampant. Hoops fans even use them to distract players on the free-throw line. More seriously, police worry that they're the target of snipers when they see the laser light on their chests. Lasers are banned or restricted in Philadelphia; New York City; Dearborn, Michigan; Virginia Beach, Virginia; Ocean City, Maryland; Chicago Ridge, Illinois; Westchester County, New York; and in Seattle's public schools.

INDUSTRY LEADERS

The Laser and Electro-Optics Manufacturers' Association includes most of the major players in the North American laser industry. Many laser manufacturers produce a wide variety of instruments for industrial to military to medical operations. Lucent Technologies Inc., a spin-off of AT&T located in Murray Hill, New Jersey, is the nation's largest manufacturer of telecommunications equipment. Many of its devices use laser technology developed by Bell Laboratories. Most of Lucent's customers are in the telecommunications industry, with AT&T accounting for 12 percent of total sales. Rated number 22 in the Fortune 500, Lucent had 1999 sales of $39.3 billion and approximately 153,000 employees.

Among other firms are PRC International of McLean, Virginia, a subsidiary of Litton, which makes lasers particularly for governmental purposes. Federal agencies make up about 85 percent of its clients. Laser Corp. of Salt Lake City derives 95 percent of its sales from its subsidiary American Laser. About 70 percent of its $3.8 million 1999 sales were to customers outside of the United States. Semiconductor Laser International Corp., based in Binghamton, New York, is another company that produces a broad variety of lasers, with clients in the fields of medicine, weaponry, and telecommunications, among others. It posted $1.5 million in sales in 1999, down 30.7 percent from 1998.

Several companies specialize in the manufacture of lasers for the medical and dental markets. Prominent among these are Coherent, Inc. and Candela Corp. Coherent, of Santa Clara, California, produces 150 kinds of lasers and its models are especially popular for cosmetic medical applications. Coherent reported 1999 sales of $468.9 million, a 143 percent increase from the previous year. About 58 percent of Coherent's sales are to foreign customers. Candela, of Wayland, Massachusetts, is another manufacturer known for dermatological lasers. It posted sales of $75.4 million in 2000. Medical lasers for noncosmetic procedures form the basis of BioLase Technology Inc.'s production. BioLase registered a 366.7 percent rise in sales for 1999, to $7 million. Surgical Laser Technologies, Inc., whose lasers are adapted specifically for otolaryngology, posted 1999 sales of $8 million, for a one-year loss of $1.9 million.

Nortel Networks Corp. manufactures extremely high-precision lasers for high-speed fiber-optic transmission of traffic on the Internet. In 1999 the company reported that it had to triple its production capacity, adding 5,000 new jobs worldwide, to keep pace with demand. That year it posted revenues of $22.2 billion and employed 76,000.

Symbol Technologies, Inc. was the leading maker of laser bar-code scanners. Among Symbol's innovations are a handheld laser scanner, a scanner-integrated computer, and a portable self-checkout shopping system. Symbol generate revenues of $1.14 billion in revenue in 1999, with about one-half of its sales occurring overseas.

RESEARCH AND TECHNOLOGY

In January 1997 physicists at the Massachusetts Institute of Technology (MIT) made an astonishing announcement: the development of a single-atom laser. The MIT laser emits atoms and employs a type of matter first discovered in 1995. It was called "Bose-Einstein condensate" in honor of Satyendra Nath Bose, an Indian physicist whose work stemmed from Albert Einstein's hypotheses. This form of matter consists of a gas that is so dense and cold that atoms lose some of their individual properties and fuse into a giant superatom. These superatoms are cooled to a temperature just a few billionths of a degree above absolute zero, and at that temperature, the atoms assume some of the characteristics of light waves. The new laser, which the head of the MIT scientific team described as "a dripping faucet," emits pulses of Bose-Einstein condensate droplets. The single-atom laser is expected to be a valuable research tool in studying atomic and subatomic properties of atoms. Among the practical applications for this technology was microchip etching, a field where it may represent as much of an improvement over the semiconductor laser as that was over the old mercury light process.

The search to employ lasers for enhanced digital data storage remained on the cutting edge of developments in laser-enhanced technology. This promising application could permit storage densities of 1 trillion bits per cubic centimeter and increase the speed of data loading and retrieval to over 10 gigabits per second. Several organizations pursued this line of development, among them SRI International in Menlo Park, California, which announced its coherent time-domain optical memory. This technology, which incorporates semiconductor processing techniques and dye lasers, was being overseen by the Defense Advanced Research Projects Agency.

Shuji Nakamura, of the small Japanese firm Nichia Chemical Industries, unveiled the first blue semiconductor laser adaptable for commercial use in 1998. Since it sports a shorter wavelength than the conventional infrared lasers used for decades, the blue laser permits digital data to be packed much more densely on storage media such as digital video discs. Blue lasers could also turn up in longer-lasting, more energy-efficient lights; large-scale, high-precision video displays; and extremely accurate medical instrumentation.

Medical laser developments on the horizon in the late 1990s were equally encouraging. Dr. Harry Whelan and his colleagues at Milwaukee's Children's Hospital successfully adapted light emitting diode (LED) light to treat brain cancer. The procedure, FDA-approved for clinical trials, is called photodynamic therapy (PDT). The surgeon directs LED light with a pinhead-sized diode onto the tumor, which has been treated with the anticancer drug photofrin. The light activates the drug, which destroys the malignant cells but leaves surrounding healthy tissue unaffected. Interim trials of a similar PDT for age-related macular disintegration, which causes loss of eyesight, were underway at Johns Hopkins. In those studies, doctors activated the drug verteporfin with lasers; the drug slows the growth of choroidal blood vessels in the eyes that leads to sight impairment. In ophthalmology, laser scanning was also introduced to map the contours of the eye in three dimensions, thus enabling physicians to identify retinal diseases much earlier than with previous diagnostic methods. Researchers at Dartmouth College discovered that cancerous cells fluoresce more quickly, but less brightly, than normal cells. This aid for early detection was 5 percent more accurate than the surgical biopsies it's intended to replace and was expected to be in use, pending clinical trials, in 2001.

In Chicago, physicians at Rush-Presbyterian-St. Luke's Medical Center pioneered a new, if somewhat controversial, laser-based treatment for angina, the pain that accompanies heart disease. The researchers reported that drilling tiny holes into the heart muscle with a laser—a process called transmyocardial laser revascularization—improved blood flow to the heart muscle, thus greatly reducing pain and increasing mobility in 72 percent of the patients treated, compared with 13 percent of patients given only drugs to treat the condition.

Scientists at the University of Wisconsin-Madison revealed that twin infrared lasers, when trained on clumps of molecules, cause them to vibrate. The unique signature of the vibration indicates the nature of the chemical bond between the molecules. The finding should help with the development of new drugs.

Scientists even wanted to tame the weather with lasers. A team at the Canadian power company Hydro-Quebec investigated firing lasers into storm clouds to trigger lightning strikes in storms and direct them away from power lines and plants. In 1997 Japanese scientists at the Institute for Laser Technology successfully generated two outdoor bolts in this manner.

Industry observers in the late 1990s hoped for a breakthrough in the area of nuclear fusion as well. Nuclear fusion promised to provide cheap and abundant power without the dangers associated with nuclear fission, the conventional form of nuclear reaction. In May 2000, the federal budget for development of this technology was increased when $245 million was earmarked for the National Ignition Facility at Livermore Lab. The project, which involves the world's largest laser, is intended to aim 192 laser beams at a target the size of a pellet. If achieved, that would permit scientists to test the possibility of generating fusion energy and to simulate nuclear weapons without actual detonation. Though originally scheduled for completion by 2003, the project deadline was pushed back to 2008.

One development generated as much skepticism as excitement. A Seattle start-up called Terebeam touted its program for wireless optics, a system it claimed would banish fiber-optic cables to technology textbook history. Terebeam's founder, C. Gregory Amadon, heralded the development of its laser teletransmitters, with which he expected to erect a wireless laser network to beam communications at 1 trillion bits per second. Although Merrill Lynch backed the endeavor, previous attempts at wireless communications have been hampered by the difficulty of getting laser transmissions to land reliably on-target over distances of more than a mile. While most other attempts have used one laser per customer, Amadon predicted he could handle up to 96 accounts on a single laser transmitter. Birds and raindrops can hamper transmission, while fog grinds it completely to a halt. As of 2000, Terebeam had only one trial involving one client in operation. Meanwhile, industry hulk Lucent was investigating wireless transmission on its own.

FURTHER READING

"At-Home Laser for Diabetics." *Consumer Reports on Health,* August 1999.

"Beam Me Up." *Electronics Now,* July 1999.

Booth, Cathy, et al. "Light Makes Right." *Time,* 11 October 1999.

Comarow, Avery. "Healing the Heart." *U.S. News & World Report,* 13 March 2000.

Greeley, Alexandra. "Cosmetic Laser Surgery." *FDA Consumer,* May/June 2000.

Hara, Yoshiko. "Blue/Violet Laser Nears Use for High-Definition DVD." *Electronic Engineering Times,* 7 June 1999.

Henderson, C. W. "'Smart Scalpel' Detects Cancer Cells in Seconds." *Cancer Weekly,* 4 April 2000.

Johnson, Douglas. "Laser Threats to Law Enforcement." *FBI Law Enforcement Bulletin,* May 1999.

Jones, Judy, and James E. Morgan. "Using Lasers for Early Detection of Retinal Disease." *British Medicine Journal,* 13 November 1999.

Kopel, Andrew, and Wayne Reitz. "Laser Surface Treatment." *Advanced Materials & Processes,* September 1999.

Koselka, Rita. "Into the Blue." *Forbes,* 14 June 1999.

"Laser-Guided." *Economist,* 25 March 2000.

Littman, Dan. "Fast Color Lasers? Sorry, Not Quite Yet." *PC World,* January 2000.

McCall, Jack H. "Blinded by the Light: International Law and the Legality of Anti- Optic Laser Weapons." *Cornell International Law Journal* 30, no. 1 (1997).

Normile, Dennis. "The Birth of the Blues." *Popular Science,* February 2000.

Ohr, Stephen. "Color Laser Printers Gain on Inkjets." *Electronic Engineering Times,* 10 January 2000.

"Prototype." *Technology Review,* January/February 2000.

Samuel, Eugenie. "Look, No Fillings." *New Scientist,* 16 September 2000.

Saunders, Stephen. "Hot Air." *tele.com,* 17 April 2000.

Senior, Kathryn. "Photodynamic Therapy Slows Vision Loss in Macular Degeneration." *Lancet,* 30 October 1999.

"SETI Shifts from Radio to Lasers." *Astronomy,* June 1999.

"The Shape of Clothes to Come." *Consumer Reports,* January 2000.

Somasundaram, Meera. "New Treatment Eases Pain of Heart Disease." *Crain's Chicago Business,* 8 November 1999.

"Tuning in to Tunable Lasers." *Lightwave,* December 1999.

Voss, David. "Nanomedicine Nears the Clinic." *Technology Review,* January/February 2000.

Weiss, P. "Pushy Lasers Sweep into Ion Race." *Science News,* 4 December 1999.

Woolley, Scott. "Shameless in Seattle." *Forbes,* 1 May 2000.

Wright, Karen. "Lightning Tamers." *Discover,* September 1999.

Logistics Outsourcing Services

Logistics refers to supply-chain services such as the transportation of goods from manufacturers to retailers and distributors. Logistics outsourcing services enable companies to dispense with their own fleets and rely on third-party shipping services to transport their goods. Outsourcing logistics tasks can reduce logistics costs by over 20 percent, according to late-1990s surveys.

In 1999, the industry's sales reached $45.3 billion and sales were estimated at about $53 billion in 2000. Logistics outsourcing was expected to continue growing by about 20 percent annually in the early 2000s. Despite the industry's high revenues, its profitability has been less spectacular, averaging about 5 percent. Nevertheless, logistics outsourcing services anticipated higher profitability in the early 2000s as a result of increased efficiency and technological advances.

ORGANIZATION AND STRUCTURE

Logistics outsourcing services provide an array of supply-chain services including warehousing, transportation, and inventory management. Warehousing refers to the storage and management of products usually in the third-party service provider's warehouse. Typically, these warehouses have information technology in place that enables both parties to monitor inventory. Transportation services include the shipment of goods from warehouses to customers, such as the shipment of goods from manufacturers to distributors or retailers. Third-party logistics (or 3PL) transportation services include truckload, less-than-truck-load (shipping freight that does not completely fill a truck), intermodal (truck, train, air), dedicated contract carriage (dedicated fleet for a contract) and express delivery services.

Finally, inventory management involves keeping track of customers' inventories, often using inventory-control software. Logistics services manage freight and information about freight for everything from raw materials to finished products.

Most companies that use logistics outsourcing services rely on bidding processes to determine which logistics service will be awarded a contract. A minority negotiate with individual logistics companies to reach an agreement on outsourcing logistics tasks.

BACKGROUND AND DEVELOPMENT

The modern logistics outsourcing services industry grew out of warehousing and shipping services of Europe. Venice was the home to the first major European commercial warehouse and transportation nexus, according to James A. Tompkins in "Logistics: A Challenge for Today." As trading spread out from the Mediterranean, port cities cropped up with their own warehouses. By storing goods at port city warehouses, transportation time decreased because ships spent less time at each port.

In the United States, Tompkins points out that the growth of the railroad industry spurred the development of the logistics industry. Freight-train cars themselves served as warehouses, but the dearth of cars led to the construction of warehouses throughout the country. Since the railroads controlled both transportation and warehousing, it had a monopoly on logistics services. To court large corporations, the railroads would offer them free warehousing to use their transportation services.

The American Warehousing Association, formed in 1891, fought to end free warehousing by the railroads, lobbying for the Hepburn Act of 1906. The Hepburn Act terminated warehousing by railroads, facilitating the development of the separate warehousing businesses.

The Industrial Revolution also contributed to the growth of the early logistics industry. Companies started to using mass-production techniques, creating a large supply of goods that had to be shipped around the country. While companies initially stored their products in their own warehouses, they started to move their products closer to the markets for them and to use warehousing services to achieve this goal.

Advances in transportation technology such as the development of the truck and the airplane also drove the industry, as it evolved from just railroads and warehouses. Although companies tended to handle their own warehousing and transportation, they frequently began to outsource these tasks beginning in the late 1980s and early 1990s, spawning the logistics outsourcing services industry. During this period and in subsequent years, companies determined what their core competencies were. If these competencies did not include logistics, then they outsourced these tasks to third-party service providers.

CURRENT CONDITIONS

At the turn of the century, outsourcing logistics tasks had become a significant trend among U.S. companies. Although the logistics outsourcing services industry had not skyrocketed into the colossal industry some forecasted in the early 1990s, it had become a strong and growing industry that etched a permanent place in the economy. In the late 1990s, total U.S. logistics costs reached $862 billion annually, according to *Transportation & Distribution*. Logistics outsourcing services saved the companies an estimated $5 billion in 2000, according to Cass Information Systems and Armstrong & Associates. Total revenues for the industry were an estimated $50 to $55 billion, according to the *Journal of Commerce and Commercial*, up from $45.3 billion in 1999. In 1999, dedicated contract carriage services accounted for $7.2 billion, other domestic transportation services for $6.6 billion, warehousing for $16.6 billion, international services for

$12 billion, and logistics software for $3 billion, according to Armstrong & Associates. During the late 1990s, the industry grew at a rate of roughly 20 percent annually, which is expected to continue in the early 2000s.

The outlook for the logistics outsourcing services industry also appears favorable because most customers seem pleased with these services according to various surveys. For example, a survey by University of Tennessee's Center for Logistics Research, Exel Logistics, and Ernst & Young found that nearly 100 percent of the customers surveyed believed objectives such as asset reduction, strategic flexibility, employee reduction, and expanded global presence were being fulfilled. In addition, over 90 percent felt they were accomplishing their goal of supply chain integration via logistics outsourcing services and about 90 percent of those surveyed indicated overall satisfaction with third-party logistics companies. However, respondents were less satisfied with logistics services in meeting objectives such as facilitating e-commerce and implementing changes and new technology quickly. Nevertheless, the survey revealed several key benefits of outsourcing: reduced logistics costs, shortened order cycles, and reduced inventories.

Surveys and reports indicated that 80 percent of the Fortune 500 companies outsourced at least some of their logistics tasks. Nevertheless, a study by the industry publication *Logistics Management Distribution Report* found that many companies only farmed out a portion of their logistics functions, thereby failing to realize greater savings achieved when entire logistics functions are outsourced. A report by the University of Maryland's Best Practices Group demonstrated that companies that outsource their entire logistics functions save approximately 21 percent the first year. Furthermore, their savings increase proportionately with the number of tasks they outsource: the more they outsource, the more they save. The report also revealed that about 10 percent of all major U.S. companies outsource their entire functions and that the savings these companies realized did not dilute the quality and reliability of warehousing and transportation.

Nevertheless, while companies that outsourced their entire functions garnered the greatest savings, those that retained oversight of their relationship with the logistics outsourcing services reported the most successful outsourcing experiences.

In pursuit of more customers, logistics services began courting clients with yearly logistics bills of $1 to $10 million, according to *Purchasing*. Previously, the majority of the major third-party logistics companies had a cut-off point at $10 million. New entrants expanding into this market and startups initiated and are expected to continue to drive this targeting of the mid-market.

Recent trends have included the movement towards one-stop logistics services, the increased profitability of third-party logistics companies, and greater global expansion. One-stop logistics or integrated logistics companies provide a host of services and oversee the entire logistics process. If they are unable to provide particular services they form partnerships with other third-party providers to offer their clients a single outsourcing solution with one contact, bill, and computer interface. These bundled services may include packaging, assembly, warehousing, transportation, and information systems. Nevertheless, integrating services has led to rising costs among third-party logistics services, which forces them to increase their rates. However, logistics services have been wary of raising rates too high out of fear the customers will shop around to find lower rates.

With the aid of improved technology and greater internal efficiency, industry observers expected greater profitability from logistics outsourcing services, according to *Logistics Management Distribution Report*. Furthermore, companies have become more amenable to paying higher fees for value-added logistics services. Armstrong & Associates reported that overall net profitability stood at 5 percent in 1999. As logistics services obtained more clients and larger contracts for transportation and warehousing, they grew increasingly able to use their resources more efficiently by consolidating loads and shipments.

In addition, logistics outsourcing services began to go global during this period. Because companies seek one-stop logistics services, third-party providers started to expand their services overseas. With the increase in global commerce and trade, logistics companies responded by creating global information networks for inventory, tracking, and dispatch, according to *Industrial Distribution*.

The Internet was an important tool for third-party logistics services in the late 1990s and early 2000s. The Internet enabled logistics services to provide their customers with access to information and pricing, online dispatch and ordering of services, online tracking systems, and expedited communication via e-mail. During this period, the Internet and software expenditures constituted one of the most substantial investments of the industry, driven by customer demand for real-time information and easy accessibility to it.

Finally, the industry witnessed heightened merger and acquisition activity in the late 1990s and early 2000s. The industry's leading company, Exel Plc, came about via the merger of Ocean Group Plc and NFC Plc. Exel went on to acquire over 12 other logistics service providers. In the United States, UPS acquired Rollins Logistics and Finon Sofecome, FedEx bought Caliber Logistics and GeoLogistics, and Schneider added Tranzact to its portfolio. Furthermore, six logistics outsourcing services, including J.B. Hunt Logistics and Covenant Logistics, pooled their efforts together to form Transplace.com.

INDUSTRY LEADERS

Exel Plc is one of the world's largest logistics service providers based on revenue. The company formed after the merger of Ocean Group Plc and NFC Plc and is a global player with strong sales from e-commerce. The company has over 500 offices in 112 countries and provides air courier, trucking, warehousing, and express courier services. In 1999, Exel booked sales of $2.8 billion, over 90 percent of which derived from logistics services, and employed 16,700 workers.

Menlo Logistics, a subsidiary of the transportation giant CNF Inc., is another major player in the logistics outsourcing services industry. In addition to managing the logistics tasks of other companies, Menlo Logistics also develops logistics software. In 1999, the company's parent reported revenues of $5.5 billion.

Ryder System Inc.'s Ryder Integrated Logistics also ranks among the leading logistics outsourcing companies. Operating on both the domestic and global fronts, Ryder specializes in distribution management and transportation management. In 1999, Ryder System had overall sales of $4.9 billion from its commercial leasing, rental, and logistics services. Of these total sales, Ryder Integrated Logistics accounted for approximately $1.8 billion.

Schneider Logistics, a division of Schneider National, Inc., plays a key role in the industry. The company's core services include freight management, supplier management, inbound freight conversion and control, and express shipment services. In 1999, the private parent company posted sales of $3 billion.

J. B. Hunt Logistics, a subsidiary of J. B. Hunt Transport Services, Inc., was another industry leader in the late 1990s. However, in 2000, J. B. Hunt merged its logistics arm with the logistics units of five other companies—Covenant Transport, Inc., Inc., M.S. Carriers, Inc., Swift Transportation Co., Inc., U.S. Xpress

Enterprises, Inc. and Werner Enterprises, Inc.—to form Transplace.com. Transplace.com is a Web-based platform for shippers and carriers to work together to plan logistics services including truckload, less-than-truckload, intermodal, and express delivery services worldwide.

Other major logistics outsourcing services include Airborne Logistics Services, FedEx Logistics, UPS Worldwide Logistics, Emery Worldwide Global Logistics, and Skyway Freight Systems, all of which specialize in domestic and international airfreight distribution.

AMERICA AND THE WORLD

A late-1990s survey by Mercer Management Consulting, Cranfield University, and Northeastern University indicated that logistics outsourcing services in Europe still were more advanced and had a greater penetration than in North America, although the gap has grown significantly smaller. In North America about 80 percent of the companies surveyed said they used third-party logistics services, up from 60 percent in the mid-1990s, and 30 percent in the early 1990s. In contrast, 80 percent of the European companies surveyed reported that they used these services in the late 1990s, up from 75 percent in the mid-1990s. The survey also revealed that European companies tend to outsource tasks such as fleet management, shipment consolidation, warehouse management, product returns, and carrier selection most often, according to a report published in *American Shipper*.

RESEARCH AND TECHNOLOGY

One of the oft-cited reasons for not using logistics outsourcing services is that companies do not want to lose control of their logistics tasks. Hence, a crucial research area for the industry is how to provide logistics services while providing their customers with control and input.

Furthermore, computer network and information technology have been areas of significant research by the logistics outsourcing services industry. Collaborative Planning Forecast and Replenishment (CPFR) software, for example, enables manufacturers and retailers to share their forecasts on the production of and demand for certain products and to develop sales targets together. This software, referred to as advanced planning and scheduling (APS) software, allows manufacturers and retailers to respond to fluctuating demand by alerting each other of possible changes in demand through computer software.

Other computer networking and Web-based software, such as transportation management software (TMS) and warehouse management software (WMS), lets companies purchase products and arrange shipping via the Internet. With this software, companies can also monitor the inventory of their trading partners. In addition, some developers of Web-based logistics software rent their applications for a monthly fee or service charge, making it possible for small and medium logistics outsourcing services to employ this kind of supply, scheduling, and inventory software. Besides these kinds of Web-based applications, logistics companies were developing new programs in the early 2000s that allow users to create custom contracts, execute these contracts, and automatically pay for services online.

FURTHER READING

Armstrong & Associates, Inc. "Contract Logistics Market." 18 July 2000. Available from http://www.3plogistics.com/Logmkt.htm.

Cooke, James. "Software Driven Change." *Logistics Management & Distribution Report,* 1 April 2000.

Damas, Philip. "Survey: What Customers Think of 3PLs." *American Shipper,* February 2000.

Gettings, Paul. "Top Three Trends in Logistics Today." *Industrial Distribution,* November 1997.

Gooley, Toby B. "Growth Spurt." *Logistics Management and Distribution Report,* 1 November 2000.

Harrington, Lisa H. "Cost Creep and What to Do About It." *Transportation & Distribution,* July 1998.

———. "Mr. Toad's Wild Ride." *Industry Week,* 18 October 1999.

Johnson, Gregory S. "Brooks Sports Turns to Fritz to Handle Its Logistics." *Journal of Commerce and Commercial,* 25 March 1998.

MacDonald, Mitchell E. "Time to Swing for the Fences." *Logistics Management Distribution Report,* August 1998.

Miligan, Brian. "Service Providers Under Pressure to Control Rates." *Purchasing,* 20 April 2000.

"Outsourcing: Europe Ahead of U.S." *American Shipper,* February 1997.

Thomas, Jim. "12 Trends That Will Shape 3PLs." *Logistics Management Distribution Report,* January 1998.

Tompkins, James A. "Logistics: A Challenge for Today." 30 July 2000. Available from http://logistx.dartgc.com/LToday/fall96-3.htm.

Mail-Order and Catalog Shopping

The U.S. catalog business has enjoyed vigorous growth at the industry level, but not all of its most established merchants have been sharing in the bounty. While U.S. Census Bureau numbers reported mail-order and catalog house sales growing by a solid 17 percent in 1999, well-known catalogers such as L.L. Bean, Inc.; Lands' End, Inc.; and J.C. Penney Co., Inc. lagged in the late 1990s, with sales flat or even declining. The apparel market, long a staple of the catalog industry, has been particularly soft. Nonetheless, other segments such as computers, electronics, gifts, office products, and health products have sustained the catalog industry's momentum. And the near future portends steady overall growth; the Direct Marketing Association predicted annual catalog sales growth of 6.5 percent.

Catalog and mail-order firms are uniquely affected by the tremendous growth of electronic commerce (e-commerce) over the Internet. About three-fourths of all catalogs conduct online transactions, according to the Direct Marketing Association. On the one hand, traditional catalog companies have generated hundreds of millions of dollars in sales via the Internet, including many purchases by first-time customers. Indeed, in retail categories such as clothing, traditional catalog houses are some of the biggest online retailers. But on the other hand, the Internet presents a whole new crop of Web-only challengers that are sometimes better equipped to compete in the electronic arena.

To a large degree, in fact, Web retailing simply brings the traditional catalog and mail-order business model into a new electronic medium. Like old-fashioned mail-order outfits, Web-based sellers rely on direct marketing and in-home (and at-work) shopping to transact with their customers. Also like traditional nonstore retailers, e-tailers often don't maintain a physical retail infrastructure, which lets them keep overhead down and potentially offer a greater selection of merchandise than would be feasible in a store. All of this means the distinction between e-tailers and print-based catalogers is far from clear. With most large traditional catalog merchants mounting an Internet strategy, the main differences are media used and perhaps whether a company is rooted in traditional catalog marketing or originated as an Internet-based retailer.

Given the similarities, perhaps it's no surprise that the two have been converging. A number of old-style catalogers have dived headfirst into e-tailing, some by acquisitions of fledgling Web companies. Analysts believe this is an effective pairing because old-line catalog retailers have the discipline and techniques for growing and maintaining a large customer base. Meanwhile, upstarts have an online presence as well as innovative ideas about technology and the retail value proposition for customers. The symbiotic relationship goes both ways: other observers point out that stagnant print catalogers are likely targets for acquisitive Web-based merchants.

ORGANIZATION AND STRUCTURE

Mail-order and catalog retailers usually do not maintain an inventory warehouse; instead, the retailers purchase products directly from manufacturers or wholesalers once orders for specific items have been received. The manufacturers or wholesalers then ship the merchandise either directly to the end customers or to the mail-order catalog companies. This system allows retailers to avoid the overhead costs unavoidably incurred by maintaining vast on-site inventories. Many companies, such as Williams-Sonoma, Inc.; J. Crew, Inc.; and J.C. Penney, also have retail stores in addition to their mail-order operations.

The mail-order and catalog shopping industry includes two primary sectors: consumer and business sales. Of these two, the consumer sector tends to garner more sales than the business sector, typically between 60 and 75 percent, leaving the business sector with about 25 to 40 percent of industry revenues. The consumer sector comprises a spate of products and services such as apparel, books, food, health-care products, toys, home furnishings, and sporting goods. Key business products and services include computer hardware, data-processing products, and general office supplies.

BACKGROUND AND DEVELOPMENT

In the late 1400s, a Venetian book merchant named Aldo Mannucci (1449-1515) provided one of the first mail-order services, selling Greek and Latin books via catalog, according to Ronald Vanderwey in the *Journal of Lending & Credit Risk Management.* In the United States, Benjamin Franklin (1706-1790) used catalogs to sell scholarly literature in 1744. As people moved across the country and settled in rural areas, catalog shopping offered a convenient alternative to traveling long distances to shop at general stores. In the mid-1800s catalogs, such as Orvis and Montgomery Ward, sprang up and started to flourish. Orvis has been marketing fishing gear since 1856. Montgomery Ward began selling general merchandise in 1872. As railway transportation improved, connecting the East Coast with the Midwest, Richard Sears (1863-1914) and Alvah Roebuck (1864-1948) teamed up in 1897 to offer what would become perhaps the best-known American general merchandise catalog.

Technological advances of the 20th century propelled the industry forward. In 1913 the U.S. Postal Service began offering parcel post delivery and, in 1928 it introduced third-class bulk mail, creating an inexpensive method for sending packaged goods. The Diners Club offered the first credit card in 1950, ushering in increased demand for mail-order and catalog shopping, by providing users with a convenient and safe means of payment. Later, AT&T made mail-order shopping one step easier by introducing toll-free phone numbers. More recently, the widespread use of personal computers (PCs) has made possible catalogs via CD-ROM, and especially, over the Internet.

CURRENT CONDITIONS

While they still represent just 6 or 7 percent of all U.S. retailing, catalog and mail-order revenues continue to outpace those of the broader sector. The U.S. Census Bureau reported for 1999 that retail sales through catalog and mail-order avenues gained 17 percent from the year before. Estimates by the Direct Marketing Association, a leading trade group for the industry, placed 2000 sales at $104.3 billion, and predicted sales of $142.9 billion in 2005. For perspective, catalog sales in 1990 were just $47 billion.

The business-to-business catalog sector was predicted to outpace, albeit slightly, the consumer sector in the first half of the 2000s. In 2000, the consumer segment totaled $63.8 billion, and was expected to grow 6.3 percent a year to reach $86.4 billion by 2005. The B2B segment, meanwhile, was pegged to grow from $40.5 billion in 2000 to $56.4 billion in 2005, for an annual growth rate of 6.9 percent.

In general, catalogs are downsizing. Without careful management, catalog operations can quickly become unwieldy and unprofitable. This realization caused many of the industry's largest and best-known merchants to trim their catalogs, and in few cases, exit the business entirely.

For instance, using the measure of the number of catalog pages distributed in a year, Spiegel Catalog Inc. reduced the number of pages it distributed from 1996 to 1997, going from 197 to 154 million. In fact, by the mid-1990s most retail catalog companies were no longer developing huge general merchandise catalogs. Instead, they used demographics and marketing research to create small specialized catalogs. Sears discontinued its "Big Book" catalog in early 1993 and has since relied on 18 specialized catalogs—ranging from automobile parts to clothing for women size 14 and up—catering to the diverse tastes of its 24 million customers.

With escalating postage and catalog production costs, general catalogs have struggled to compete, and in many cases, simply can't. Instead, mail-order houses have sought to make their products stand out or closely match the buying needs of their catalog recipients.

CATALOG CUSTOMER PROFILE

According to a 1999 survey conducted by the trade journal *Catalog Age,* 46 percent of U.S. consumers said they bought something from a catalog within the past year. Catalog shoppers are most often women, and the most common reasons they cite for purchasing by catalog include convenience, unique product selection, and good prices.

The annual survey's results also reiterated the overall level of satisfaction most catalog shoppers have for the medium. When asked to compare catalog shopping to other forms of retailing, a decisive majority of respondents, almost 62 percent, answered they found it comparably satisfying to other modes of shopping. Another 30 percent of respondents said they thought catalog shopping was more satisfying. That left fewer than 9 percent of respondents who compared catalog shopping unfavorably to other forms of retailing.

Certainly some people have gripes about catalog shopping, or simply no interest in it. The *Catalog Age* study found that the biggest reason consumers choose not to shop by catalog is that they want to see the merchandise, literally, before they pay for it. Some consumers likewise report a lack of interest in what's being sold by catalog. Other deal-breakers include security concerns over placing orders by phone (the same for the Internet), dissatisfaction with prices, and unwillingness to wait for the goods to be delivered.

CHALLENGES FOR THE MAIL-ORDER INDUSTRY

Most mail-order purchases are discretionary or optional. This means if the economy heads south, customers tend to abandon these expenditures first. When recession hit the U.S. economy in the early 1990s, mail-order sales slumped. Successful mail-order and catalog companies bear this economic fact in mind and manage their businesses accordingly.

As with Internet retailers, conventional catalog and mail-order companies are faced with ambiguous and inconsistent tax obligations, particularly regarding state sales taxes. Numerous state and local governments claim they have lost revenue from taxable products purchased by customers in their areas from mail-order companies in other states. The state of Maryland, for example, estimates a loss of $35 million a year in sales tax revenue. Some mail-order companies allegedly don't apprise their customers of tax

Consumers have a huge assortment of catalogs to choose from. (FieldMark Publications/Robert J. Huffman)

obligations, prompting some U.S. senators to call for a Federal Trade Commission mandate that mail-order houses must disclose their customers' tax responsibilities. On the other hand, if mail-order companies collected and tendered the taxes themselves, then they would be exempt from the mandate.

The issue is much the same for Internet retailers, although they enjoy special protections—at least for the time being. Various state and local tax agencies have clamored over the potential loss of sales tax revenues as more merchandise is sold over the Internet.

A federal law passed in 1998 placed a moratorium on any new Internet taxes, including state sales taxes, through at least 2001. Over states' objections, that law was likely to be renewed for at least a few more years, leaving most online retailers out of the tax-collection racket for the short term.

INDUSTRY LEADERS

DELL COMPUTER

One of the world's largest PC makers, Dell Computer Corp. is customarily considered a catalog retailer because it sells its systems through direct channels. These days, the $25 billion company gets most of its orders from its popular e-commerce site, which generates tens of millions of dollars in sales every day. The box builder's legendary operations then assemble computer systems to order, allowing Dell to keep its inventory low and its business lean. Dell serves primarily the business and government markets, but since the late 1990s has been making overtures to the general public as well. Industry rankings such as those compiled by *Catalog Age* magazine usually cite Dell as the world's largest catalog retailer, although admittedly it's in a completely different league from most others.

FINGERHUT COMPANIES

Minnetonka, Minnesota-based Fingerhut Companies, Inc., is another major catalog retailer in the United States. Fingerhut sells private-label and brand-name products and its catalogs include items such as electronics, crockery, and housewares. In 1999, Federated Department Stores, Inc. purchased Fingerhut and its prized database of 30 million customers. Federated hoped to realize synergies between Fingerhut and its other mail-order units, Macy's by Mail and Bloomingdale's by Mail. Before the acquisition, Fingerhut had proven somewhat of an industry visionary by courting the Internet markets more aggressively than most old-line catalogers. To that end, it made several site acquisitions to shore up its online reach, which no doubt made it all the more attractive to Federated. The parent company doesn't report Fingerhut's sales separately, but the mail-order unit had sales approaching $2 billion in the late 1990s. However, in late 2000, the company announced plans to slash its workforce in an effort to make up for recent losses.

J.C. PENNEY

J.C. Penney Co., Inc., located in Plano, Texas, is the leading U.S. general catalog retailer. Penney's catalog includes such products as clothing, furniture, housewares, and luggage. Although J.C. Penney is the fourth-largest U.S. retailer and has 1,150 department stores in North and South America, the retailer has struggled as smaller niche competitors and large discount chains have eroded its sales base. Penney's catalog business, which includes its e-commerce site, has fared slightly better than the retail outlets, but still struggled to gain sales. In 1999 the company's catalog business brought in $3.9 billion, essentially flat with the previous year. That amount included an infusion of $100 million in online sales, which were up sharply from 1998. Housewares and home furnishings have been Penney's strongest categories, while apparel has been especially disappointing.

J. CREW GROUP

J. Crew Group Inc., headquartered in New York, markets casual and professional wear for men and women. The company has 120 retail and factory outlet stores across the United States and another 70 outlets in Japan. Like several other top apparel catalogers, J. Crew suffered in the late 1990s from stagnant sales and greater competition from other channels. It formerly produced a pair of specialty branded catalogs, but sold them off in a bid to focus on its core brand. This move seemed to pay off, with its core catalogs exhibiting renewed growth in 2000. That year the company recorded sales of $716.6 million, about 40 percent of which derived from its 30 catalog editions.

LANDS' END

Dodgeville, Wisconsin-based Lands' End, Inc., focuses on monthly catalogs featuring its casual and outdoor apparel for men and women. In addition, Lands' End provides specialty clothing for children, as well as housewares. About 60 percent of the company's sales result from catalog marketing. The firm also markets its products in Japan, the United Kingdom, and Germany. In January 1999 three of the company's outlet stores were closed and 94 jobs were cut because of tepid sales and mounting overhead costs. Later that year Lands' End eliminated one of its holiday-season catalogs and shed some pages from others, in yet another effort to rid itself of unprofitable operations. As a result of its catalog cuts and a weak apparel mail-order market generally, Lands' End suffered a sales decline in 2000, with sales dropping almost 4 percent to $1.32 billion. Still, the company distributes about 250 million catalogs a year. Although Lands' End's Web site has been named one of the Internet's biggest apparel sellers, online sales accounted for only 10 percent of the company's sales in 1999.

L.L. BEAN

Leading apparel retailer L.L. Bean, Inc., based in Freeport, Maine, issues 50 catalogs a year and operates a 24-hour, year-round retail store in Freeport. The company specializes in outdoor wear, household furnishings, and sporting goods. L.L. Bean also gained a reputation for its strong customer service. Its sales, however, have been largely flat since the mid-1990s at just over $1 billion. In 1999 L.L. Bean employed 4,000 workers in its operations, which included 10 U.S. factory outlets and 20 retail stores in Japan.

WILLIAMS-SONOMA

Williams-Sonoma, Inc. is a leading U.S. retailer of housewares. The company, based in San Francisco, issues four different catalogs and has over 350 stores in nearly 40 states. It sells cookware, housewares, furniture, and storage items through its namesake catalog and two other divisions: Hold Everything and Pottery Barn. Its other catalog, Chambers, offers bed and bath items. The company posted revenues of $1.4 billion in fiscal 2000, of which about $515 million came from catalog sales.

AMERICA AND THE WORLD

According to *Advertising Age,* Germany purchased more catalog products than any other country. The U.S. mail-order industry, however, has remained one of the strongest in the world, earning billions of dollars per year and penetrating international markets. Nonetheless, several European companies have not only done well in their respective countries, but they have also captured part of the U.S. market.

Germany's Otto Versand GmbH & Co., controls 8.4 percent of the international mail-order market, making it the largest mail-order company in the world, with about 600 catalogs. The company plans to expand its catalog business into Asia, specifically targeting the People's Republic of China, Korea, and Taiwan. The company posted sales of $18.6 billion in 1999 and employed more than 63,000 workers. Otto Versand owns brands popular in the United States such as Eddie Bauer and Spiegel, Inc., both sizable catalogers and retailers themselves.

Britain's The Great Universal Stores P.L.C. (GUS) is another one of the world's leading mail-order houses. GUS's Kays and Marshall Ward catalogs sell more products than any others in Britain. GUS markets its wares throughout Europe and South Africa. Less than one-eighth of its sales come from North America. It also holds financial and information services units in various countries. For fiscal 2000, the company recorded $9 billion in sales.

Mail-order shopping has increased by about 11 percent per year in Japan since it was first introduced to the country in the 1970s, according to *Nikkei Weekly.* Although 10 large Japanese companies control about 50 percent of the market there, they continue to employ somewhat antiquated marketing techniques such as sending out large general catalogs. More efficient international companies, however, such as Lands' End Japan KK and J. Crew have begun to flourish using niche marketing tactics as practiced in the United States.

RESEARCH AND TECHNOLOGY

Emerging database and statistical analysis technology can aid mail-order and catalog retailers in targeting consumer tastes and purchase habits. Artificial intelligence already played a decisive role in the success of some mail-order companies in the mid-1990s and promises to have an even more vital impact in the coming millennium as competition increases and technology progresses. In particular, neural networks—artificial cognitive systems that replicate the functioning of the human brain and are capable of learning—allow mail-order retailers to accurately track what products specific consumers buy, when they buy them, and how much they spend. Though they require training or "learning" time, ultimately neural networks can identify patterns in complicated sets of data. The data provided by neural networks facilitates the development of a special catalog designed specifically for individual customers or for a group of customers with similar tastes and habits. Even though using neural networks to analyze consumer data may require some training, mail-order companies can still take advantage of this technology by enlisting the help of consulting agencies. Such technology should benefit both small companies that cannot afford a bevy of statisticians and large companies that want fast, accurate, and manageable information.

FURTHER READING

"Cashing in on Catalogs." *WWD,* 8 May 1997.

"Catalog Age's 1999 Consumer Catalog Shopping Survey." New York: Primedia, May 1999. Available from http://www.catalogagemag.com.

Chandler, Susan. "For 1st Time, Lands' End Turns to Layoffs; 3 Stores to Be Closed." *Chicago Tribune,* 13 January 1999.

Chiger, Sherry. "The High & the Mighty." *Catalog Age,* 1999. Available from http://www.catalogagemag.com.

Devine, Michael D., and Faye Musselman. "E-tailing Gaining Steam, but Print Catalogs Still Tops." *HFN,* 29 November 1999.

Direct Marketing Association. *The DMA State of the Catalog Industry Report.* New York, 1999. Available from http://www.the-dma.org.

Johnson, Kelly. "Internet Spurs Widely Varying Predictions for Retail." *Sacramento Business Journal,* 31 December 1999.

Kiener, Sigmund. "The Future of Mail Order." *Direct Marketing,* February 1995.

Kletter, Melanie. "Catalogs Lose Teen Appeal." *WWD,* 2 March 2000.

O'dell, Patricia. "Catalog Sales Up $100 B." *Direct,* August 2000.

Miller, Paul. "The Catalog Age 100: The Heavy Hitters." *Catalog Age,* August 2000.

Vanderwey, Ronald. "Lending to Mail Order Companies." *Journal of Lending & Credit Risk Management,* September 1996.

Yamamoto, Yuri. "Mail-Order Companies Home in on Markets." *Nikkei Weekly,* 7 April 1997.

MANAGED HEALTH-CARE SERVICES

Managed care organizations (MCOs) were the dominant force in the health-care industry in 2000, and enrollments continued to grow at a rapid pace. The three primary types of MCOs—health maintenance organizations (HMOs), preferred provider organizations (PPOs), and the hybrid point-of-service (POS) plan give their members health coverage and emphasize cost savings via preventive care. MCOs represented an $80 billion per year market share at the end of the 1990s. Under the managed care arrangement, MCOs facilitate the financial and contractual arrangements between the various parties involved, which include the payer (often an employer or union), the member or enrollee, the doctor or health professional, and the MCO itself.

Still, MCOs faced a public relations crisis in 2000 that was likely to result in a severe overhaul of the industry via government legislation. The popularity of managed care organizations was registered by the prominence of evil MCO managers on popular television dramas such as *ER*. While the evils perpetrated by these characters may be only a caricature of the worst elements in the MCO industry, it was clear that the managed care industry was braced for significant restructuring at the start of the 21st century.

Publicity struck at the very heart of the managed care concept, which holds that a board of managers can best oversee the health-delivery process by forcing restraint on medical consumption, rather than leaving the task to patients and their doctors. An overriding ideological issue being hashed out in political and business circles alike was the extent to which U.S. health care should be relegated to the orthodoxy of

most of the U.S. economy—that is, to market forces alone—and to what extent regulatory controls and protections should be implemented to ensure the greatest amount of social equity. In other words, customers, officials, legislators, and companies alike were struggling with the tension between health care as a commodity and as a social exchange. In the meantime, various sectors were scrambling to position themselves for the future. Legislators on Capitol Hill wrangled over new health legislation, doctors were beginning to unionize, and MCOs themselves were trying new tactics to placate increasingly frustrated members, health practitioners, and payers.

The American Association of Health Plans reported that, as of 1999, more than 160 million Americans were enlisted in a managed health-care plan, the largest share of which were in HMO plans, which enrolled about one-fourth of all Americans. The nation's 650 MCOs provided health coverage for 86 percent of workers and their families in 1999, up from 55 percent only six years earlier. As of 2000, however, there were still over 44 million uninsured Americans, particularly concentrated among people of color, a fact that was placing increasing pressure on politicians to make health care more accessible.

ORGANIZATION AND STRUCTURE

Health insurance in the United States is paid for by individuals who either contract directly with indemnity (fee-for-service) insurers, by their corporate employers who pay or co-pay the premiums, or by governments who may contract either with indemnity insurers or pre-paid MCO plans. The federal government insures its employees and those eligible for Medicare (people 65 years of age and over). State governments increasingly contract with MCOs for workers compensation insurance; for example, state and county governments began turning to MCOs to provide insurance for those receiving public assistance.

MCOs are managerially organized as corporate staffed, contracted group practice, affiliated networks, or individual practitioners contracted through an independent practice association (IPA). The driving force behind MCOs is the elimination of duplicated services. HMOs are grouped by one of the above organizational structures. Staffed HMOs employ their physicians directly on salary and services are typically provided in a single location. Group-practice HMOs contract with several medical groups according to the type of service provided. A network system provides services in two or more distinct geographical units.

Traditional fee-for-service insurance plans typically allow the individual the freedom to visit any doctor or specialist and be reimbursed for around 80 percent of the total costs. As a consequence, the patient could, for example, be given several separate prescriptions that, combined, could be redundant at best and harmful at worst. Coordination is designed to reduce this risk and lower costs. The lock-in features of HMOs mean that patients going outside the system have no benefits and are responsible for all bills incurred with these providers. Nearly all HMOs require a gatekeeper or primary care physician who screens, evaluates, and redirects patients to participating specialists if necessary. Traditional health care has been declining since 1985 at roughly the same rate that managed care has been growing in terms of population insured.

Several MCOs use a pharmacy benefit manager and have formularies (lists of approved drugs and accepted equivalents). There are also open-ended HMOs that allow patients to go outside the defined network to obtain care from any provider in the network without first going through a primary care physician or gatekeeper but at a higher co-payment.

Doctors are paid by the contracting MCO. HMOs typically contract with a local IPA, usually for a capitation fee (per-capita average cost per member). Such a fee is variable and dependent upon demographics and local health-care costs. HMOs typically pay doctors one-half to one-third the amount they would receive from fee-for-service patients and either pay on a flat-rate-per-month-per-patient basis or on a per-visit basis. Physicians hoping to improve revenues have started up physician friendly MCOs. Some HMOs withhold a percentage of the service fee for payout as bonuses to physicians at the end of the year if they save the HMO money by ordering fewer tests, defer visits, or cut back on procedures. MCOs also sometimes hire physicians directly or enter into strategic alliances.

PPO plans allow members to move in and out of networks and to see specialists without a gatekeeper's approval, but the member's co-payment will be higher outside the network. Health-care providers in such plans are bound to certain procedures and reimbursement structures. As many as 30 percent of PPO member patients go outside the network in the first year of membership, but this number typically drops considerably by the third year.

POS plans combine the independence of traditional plans with managed care plans by allowing members to get care inside or outside the network, with or without permission, with maximum benefits. Health Partners of Minneapolis pioneered POS plans in 1961 under the name Group Health Plan Corp., but it took 25 years for POSs to become widely accepted. Health-care providers in POS plans coordinate patient care, directing patients toward other providers within the network, and are reimbursed at a fixed monthly rate. Outside the network, the POS plan functions in the guise of basic insurance, in which the member is responsible for paying only a set deductible, while the MCO makes up the difference. In the late 1990s, POS plans were one of the fastest-growing segments of MCOs since they provided a popular mix of freedom and cost containment. They appealed to small firms because they were a less expensive option than indemnity insurance even though they cost more than HMOs. People were willing to pay for flexibility. A growing number of HMOs began offering POS plans that allowed the patient to go outside the network for service with the understanding that the co-pay may increase quite significantly.

In the late 1990s, some MCOs dropped their managed care programs for the poor and elderly. Industry leaders such as Aetna U.S. Healthcare, Kaiser Permanente, and United HealthCare Corp. ended many of their Medicaid services in states such as New York, New Jersey, Florida, Massachusetts, and Connecticut. Such companies claimed that cuts in government payments caused the service cutbacks. Nevertheless, the number of Medicaid beneficiaries enrolled in a managed care program of some kind continued to increase through the latter half of the decade and was expected to reach 50 percent of all Medicaid enrollees.

MCOs have grown more diverse over time, especially in the late 1990s, when competition forced players to expand their services to differentiate themselves from their competitors. Many MCOs currently offer comprehensive coverage tailored to those with severe mental and physical disabilities, unlike MCOs of yesteryear, which were usually geared toward healthy customers. Managing health care for people with disabilities, however, was somewhat problematic for the MCO structure. Since MCOs maintain a pool of physicians for their patients, chosen so as to facilitate the most cost-effective care across their entire enrollee list, it was difficult for MCOs to retain physicians who could adequately attend to the more detailed and specific health concerns of those with disabilities.

The quality of MCO service is controlled in several ways. The National Committee for Quality Assurance (NCQA), started in 1991, serves as an accrediting body and seeks to measure the organization's ability to provide quality service by evaluating its structure and procedures based on a uniform set of criteria and statistics. The media, such as *Consumer Reports,* base their evaluations on consumer satisfaction. Watchdog groups, such as the Coalition for Accountable Managed Care and the Center for Health Care Rights, are concerned with patients' rights as well as client satisfaction with services. Congress aims at consumer protection through legislation and cost containment via budget reductions, especially in the Medicare-paid programs. MCOs themselves put new doctors through a credentialing process and a re-credentialing every two years, although the process is not always considered thorough.

NCQA, an independent, nongovernmental, not-for-profit organization, collects standardized data from MCOs and compiles it into the Health Plan Employer Data and Information Set. Fifty standards in six categories (quality improvement, physician credentials, members' rights and responsibilities, preventive health services, utilization management, and medical records) are applied in evaluating an MCO. Accreditation status based on the degree to which a set of standardized criteria are met is designated as full three-year, one-year, provisional, under review, or denied. Participation is voluntary for nongovernment MCOs but mandatory for Medicare-funded contractors. Large private and public companies increasingly require their health contractors to be accredited.

Among the major concerns was whether services should be MCO driven, physician driven, or end-consumer driven. Formularies, definitions of emergencies, and the general lack of provision for mental-health care were some of the prevailing issues. According to one project, there was a clear correlation between formulary restriction and increased physician and emergency-room visits, sicker patients, and longer hospitalizations. HMO formularies—lists of approved drugs including substitute and/or generic brand drugs—proved problematic as well. Mental-health benefits were another issue of concern, particularly in regard to limitations on the number of sessions or treatment allowed by some carriers.

BACKGROUND AND DEVELOPMENT

The term "health maintenance organization" was coined in the early 1970s. Although numerous bills introduced in the 1970s to institute a national universal health insurance law failed, Congress did pass the Health Maintenance Organization Act of 1973. The act defined the requirements for a health maintenance organization, including physician service arrangements, contracts, fiscal requirements, and safeguards to insure solvency. Prepaid group-practice plans, renamed health maintenance organizations, had already emerged in some areas of the country. Employers, in particular, welcomed managed care as the method to curtail double-digit health insurance premium hikes.

The emergence of HMOs as a major force in the health-care industry in the 1980s was directly related to the explosion in health-care spending in that decade, when health care accounted for about 15 percent of the gross domestic product and total spending reached $1 trillion. While a modest number of HMOs have been around since the 1970s and 1980s, they received a big boost when President Bill Clinton's proposed "managed competition" health-care plan failed in 1993. The industry quickly responded with a more aggressive program. Many states even began contracting with MCOs to handle health care for some or all of the states' major social welfare recipients, such as those receiving Aid to Families with Dependent Children or Supplemental Security Income. In 1995 the U.S. Department of Defense replaced its traditional insurance with an HMO/PPO hybrid and the government implemented its Civilian Health and Medical Program of the Uniform Services reform initiative.

Several major changes occurred in HMOs during the 1990s: the growth of for-profit plans and the decline of nonprofit plans; the shift from vertically integrated staff and group models to vertically integrated individual practice associations and networks; increased patient cost sharing; and the shift to capitation as a means of payment to primary care physicians.

There were also notable abuses, as evidenced by the U.S. General Accounting Office's claim that Medicare overpaid California HMOs by $1 billion in 1995. The HMOs were accused of selecting the healthier Medicare beneficiaries, thus leaving the more costly patients in the fee-for-service plan. Nonprofit organizations were rated more highly than for-profit plans.

Time has shown that the enactment of the Employee Retirement Income Security Act of 1974 (ERISA) has had the single greatest effect on health plans in the United States. ERISA's employee benefits statements have been broadly interpreted by the federal courts as relating to insurance mandates, medical high-risk pools, and uncompensated care pools. The Health Insurance Portability and Accountability Act of 1996 increased the portability of health-care coverage, limited preexisting-condition limitations, and established a program for tax-free medical savings accounts for health-care purchases.

As one might expect in the health-care industry, managed care has never strayed far from the political arena. Nearly every state has passed a law regarding some facet of managed health care, and new bills are continually pending. An important decision by the Eastern Court of Arkansas ruled that MCOs were not required to take any willing provider who agreed to their terms and met their conditions on the basis that it was preempted by ERISA and the federal HMO Act of 1973. Dozens of bills were introduced in Congress alone that would regulate either managed care providers or insurers, cover minimum hospital stays for breast cancer patients, and allow patients greater freedom when choosing physicians. One bill would eliminate the "gag clause" imposed by MCOs on physicians to prohibit them from discussing fiscal arrangements. In 1997, legislation was also drafted to eliminate the use of drug formularies, and a panel of legislators from nine states developed the Managed Care Consumer Protection Act to protect the rights of managed care plan enrollees.

The merger fever in the industry in the 1990s was driven by increasing competition, with regional firms acquiring plans on opposite sides of the nation to establish a national presence and increasing demand for value (quality of service for premium charged). Mergers and acquisitions resulting in megacompanies were commonplace in the late 1990s.

By the end of 1996, HMOs in the United States were recovering from higher medical costs experienced earlier in the year. POS plans, intended as a temporary hybrid to lead people to HMOs, appeared to be taking on a life of their own as a substantial number of MCOs added them to the list of options. Meanwhile, HMO growth began to slow considerably.

The proliferation of MCOs caused increased competition between companies and fewer rate increases than analysts had predicted. Insurers low-balled prices to gain new contract bids, especially with medium-sized firms. As a result, midsize companies saw their health-benefit costs reduced by nearly 2 percent in 1997. One possible response to this trend would be for HMOs to look more like traditional insurance and for the inclusion of self-funded plans in which the employer bears some of the financial risk for employees' health-care costs.

In mid-1997 President Clinton proposed a budget savings of $25 billion by reducing Medicare reimbursements over the proceeding five years. This new legislation, which went into effect in October of that year, lowered the per capita Medicare payments to HMOs. Proposed cuts in MCO payments could result in the elimination of prescription drug coverage by Medicare plan providers.

CURRENT CONDITIONS

While national health-care costs stabilized somewhat in the early and mid-1990s, the decade between 1997 and 2008 was expected to see U.S. health-care spending double from $1.1 to $2.2 trillion, accounting for 16.2 percent of the gross domestic product, according to the Health Care Financing Administration. Premiums, meanwhile, were slated to rise about 6.5 percent each year. The precise effects of these hikes were difficult to determine given the uncertain fate of regulatory measures, but many analysts expected that employers would find themselves less capable of floating expensive, comprehensive plans as part of a benefits package. In the late 1990s, 80 percent of employees at companies offering health coverage were engaged in a managed care plan, up from 29 percent from a decade earlier.

Some of these effects were already being felt. The 2000 Towers Perrin Health Care Cost Survey found that the costs of health plans at large corporations were likely to increase 12 percent in 2000 as a result of an aging population, slashes in Medicare coverage, and skyrocketing drug prices. Companies were thus taking a second and third look at their health plans to determine if they could afford to continue on their present course. At the National Managed Health Care Congress in Atlanta in April 2000, managed care representatives cautioned employers that they may have been doling out more for employee illnesses than they realized. In addition to direct costs, such as inpatient and outpatient care and medicines, additional costs added up when employees were operating on the job at less than full capacity following an illness. Employers looking to streamline their managed care plans were thus advised to implement a more integrated cost analysis that accounted for all aspects of employees' illnesses and their related expenses. According to Analysis Group/Economics in Cambridge, Massachusetts, for instance, the average cost to an employer for an employee's depression illness in 1997 was $11,096, but less than half that amount was attributed to direct costs. Costs that generally went untallied in depression cases included those for related medical and mental-health problems, including alcoholism. Thus, by concentrating on the medical costs only, employers end up losing a good deal more money than they recognize.

The hottest issue on the political table was the Patients' Bill of Rights, discussed for several years on Capitol Hill and in the White House. Both the House of Representatives and the Senate passed different versions in 1999. The House version would enable customers to file lawsuits against HMOs chartered under ERISA and would expand medical savings accounts, which were maintained by 45,000 Americans at the end of 1999, according to the Internal Revenue Service. The Senate version originally did without the litigation provisions. A joint House-Senate conference committee spent summer 2000 amalgamating the two versions in preparation for a final legislative run, but the issue stalled before the 106th Congress adjourned.

The Patients' Bill of Rights was ostensibly designed to allow the growing numbers of customers frustrated with their managed health plans more autonomy in deciding their precise care arrangements. While polls showed the public was extremely squeamish of any plan that boosted the ranks of the uninsured and raised health-care costs, many employers insisted that a bill that allowed patients to sue their providers would force prices upward. Thus, some analysts cautioned that the Patients' Bill of Rights would carry severe consequences. The Heritage Foundation released a report, "The Patients' Bill of Rights: A Prescription for Massive Federal Regulation," in which it was estimated that such a bill would cost as many as 15.4 million Americans their health coverage and put employers at risk of potentially crippling amounts of litigation.

As Congress struggled to complete the Patients' Bill of Rights, many states moved ahead with their own

initiatives. States such as Missouri offered residents a wide range of protections, including the right to sue, make external appeals, see out-of-network providers, and obtain prescriptions not covered by their plan. By 1998 all states required HMOs to set up grievance procedures for patients who'd been denied treatments. Given the widespread, bipartisan support behind the concept, many MCOs warmed to the practice.

Several factors could have contributed to the diminishing health of MCOs' bottom lines, including increased competition between insurers, employers participating in self-insurance plans, and the fact that the managed care industry was failing to cut expenses as it once did. In a survey conducted by the Managed Care Information Center, respondents ranked "increasing efficiency/profitability" as the third-most important health-care industry concern in 1999. The top-two concerns were "complying with health-care legislation/regulation" and "keeping customers satisfied."

One area MCOs were particularly eyeing for cost savings was the emergency room. The research firm Sachs Group of Evanston, Illinois, reported in 1999 that as many as 60 percent of the 94.9 million emergency-room visits in 1997 were unnecessary and could have been handled at other care facilities. According to the National Hospital Ambulatory Medical Care Survey, 16.6 percent of all visits were made by HMO members.

At the end of the decade the "Medicare Fairness Gap" was another major issue that the managed care industry faced. The American Association of Health Plans (AAHP) urged Congress in 1999 to make Medicare reform a top priority. Medicare recipients in managed care plans received more benefits at lower costs than seniors in traditional insurance plans, but the government projected that by 2004 MCOs would receive only 75 percent of the reimbursement rate of fee-for-service plans. The AAHP warned that, as a result, many MCOs might reduce benefits to Medicare patients or cease participation in the program.

In considering ways to boost productivity, cut costs, and improve customer service, many industry analysts looked to the Internet as a resource just waiting to be exploited by MCOs. Noting that the most popular health-care Web sites welcome 3 million hits a day, players sought ways to tap into the growing consumer demand for information by establishing a constant exchange and updating of information for dissemination to customers over the Web. In this way, MCOs can better establish one-to-one relationships with their enrollees while streamlining their burdensome administrative bureaucracies.

More On TO SUE OR NOT TO SUE?

The tension between cost cutting and effective care provision was near the breaking point at the turn of the century. The industry's growing reputation for allegedly encouraging physicians to deny proper care reached the Supreme Court in spring 2000. Appendicitis patient Cynthia Herdrich sued her health plan physician for failure to properly diagnose and treat her illness, and won a $35,000 malpractice suit before pushing on with claims that her care plan broke its contractual duties under ERISA by financially encouraging the physician's actions. The Supreme Court heard oral arguments in April 2000 in the case of *Pegram v. Herdrich,* which was watched closely by managed care observers on all sides of the issue.

Attorneys for the defense argued that Dr. Pegram was only acting in accordance with a plan that encouraged cost savings, and the Supreme Court held that, while MCOs are indeed structured for that purpose, for the time being, it was not the Court's place to make decisions as to whether particular types of incentives were or were not appropriate.

The stakes in the case were high, and the decision was expected to carry a great deal of weight for the managed health-care industry's future. Coming as it did at a time of great political debate over the future of managed care, specifically the role of market forces in providing adequate care, any decision was likely to stir things up for MCOs. Were the court to rule in favor of Pegram, the public outcry could press into action legislators who are more likely to implement legislation allowing MCO members to sue. If Herdrich were to win, many analysts contend that efforts by MCOs to minimize costs would be greatly undermined.

Finally, in July 2000, the Supreme Court ruled in favor of Dr. Pegram, arguing that HMOs are not to be punished for rewarding doctors who help keep costs down. Thus, the MCO industry scored a victory in the short term, but all sides expected the battle at the political level to intensify, with no certain implications for the managed care industry.

INDUSTRY LEADERS

AETNA U.S. HEALTHCARE

One of the titans of the managed care industry, Aetna U.S. Healthcare maintained a payroll of 55,900 employees in 2000. After acquiring NYLCare Health Plans in 1998, the MCO increased its member base by 2.1 million enrollees. That same year, Aetna acquired Prudential Healthcare for $1 billion. This move added another 6.6 million members to Aetna's rolls, making it the country's largest MCO with a total of about 18.4 million members. About half of Aetna's health-plan members were registered in HMO plans, though the company also offered PPOs and indemnity insurance. Aetna's revenues increased 28 percent to reach $26.5 billion in 1999, resulting in net income of $716.9 million. However, a realignment aimed at stemming the tide of financial difficulty and negative publicity may result in a splitting of the company into publicly traded Global Health and Global Financial Services firms.

In 1999 Aetna U.S. Healthcare became the first national MCO to voluntarily submit to external review of coverage. As a result, members gained the right to appeal denials of coverage to a panel of independent physician reviewers. The decision to allow external reviews was an expansion of the company's policy of permitting internal reviews. Aetna also poured $30 million into an advertising campaign to promote its Web site so as to establish an Internet presence. Aetna was marred, however, by a class-action lawsuit filed in Mississippi and Pennsylvania that charged the company with fraud and deliberate efforts to "limit, delay, or deny medical care to its members."

CIGNA

CIGNA Corp. is another leading provider of health-care insurance and related financial services. CIGNA operated one of the largest HMOs in the U.S. at the end of the 1990s, with 6 million enrollees, and all in all provided managed care for about 15 million people. CIGNA was a major life insurance company both in the U.S. and in about 30 countries around the world. CIGNA reported net income of $1.8 billion in 1999 on revenues of $18.7 billion. The firm in 1999 shed its property/casualty operations to focus on employee benefits packages.

WELLPOINT HEALTH NETWORKS

WellPoint Health Networks Inc. was one of the largest publicly traded MCOs in the United States by 2000. The company served more than 7 million medical members and 32 million specialty pharmaceutical and dental members with its HMO, PPO, and POS plans. WellPoint was formed in 1996 by the merger with Blue Cross Blue Shield of California. The firm initiated a public offering of 10 million shares in March 1997. The company reported net income of $278 million on revenues of $7.3 billion in 1999, and maintained a payroll of 10,600 employees.

COVENTRY HEALTH CARE

Nashville-based Coventry Health Care Inc. had over 1.5 million members enrolled in its HMOs and

PPOs throughout the Midwest and Southeast in 2000. Of that number, almost 110,000 were Medicaid members. Emerging as a leading MCO following its merger with Principal Health Care in 1998, revenues increased 2.5 percent to $2.16 billion in 1999, generating net income of $43.4 million. Coventry employed some 2,900 workers.

UNITEDHEALTH GROUP

In 1998 the United HealthCare Corp. changed its name to UnitedHealth Group Inc. after a year marked by the acquisition of HealthPartners of Arizona and the decision to terminate a previously announced merger with Humana Inc. By 2000 UnitedHealth Group provided health coverage to 14.5 million people, offering its services in 150 markets in the United States and Puerto Rico. The company also had an international presence, providing management services in South Africa and Hong Kong.

The company offered HMO, PPO, POS, Medicare, Medicaid, and other plans. In a move that perhaps foreshadows a new trend in the health-care industry, UnitedHealth granted their physicians a great deal more autonomy in 1999 when it announced it would no longer second-guess their decisions. UnitedHealth's revenues jumped from $17.1 billion in 1998 to $19.3 billion in 1999, when it registered net income of $568 million.

KAISER PERMANENTE

Kaiser Permanente, founded in 1945, is the largest nonprofit HMO in the United States. The Oakland, California-based company had a membership of 8 million voluntarily enrolled members in 2000, and a network of over 10,000 group-practice physicians. The HMO served members in 11 states and the District of Columbia, having shed its unprofitable Texas and Northeast operations in 1999, and had 100,000 employees in 2000. About 60 percent of Kaiser's members are private-sector employees, while public employees and individuals make up the remainder.

WORK FORCE

There were an estimated 11.3 million persons employed in the health services industry in 2000, according to the U.S. Bureau of Labor Statistics (BLS). The BLS reported that occupations in the health services field were expected to increase more than twice as fast as the entire economy. Between 1998 and 2008,

the bureau expected about 14 percent of all wage and salary jobs to be in the health service industry, which would be home to 12 of the 30 fastest-growing occupations in that period.

The late 1990s were not a good time, however, to be employed in an upper-level MCO management position. In a study conducted for the National Directory of Managed Care Organizations, and reported by the Managed Care Information Center, it was found that during 1997, more than 46 percent of MCOs' senior management experienced personnel changes.

FURTHER READING

Arnett, Grace-Marie. "Better, Not Bitter, Medicine for Managed Health Care." *Puget Sound Business Journal,* 24 March 2000.

Carey, John. "Managed Health Care Isn't Healthy After All." *Business Week,* 24 July 2000.

Connor, James L. "How to Heal Managed Care." *Puget Sound Business Journal,* 25 February 2000.

Davidson, Tim, and Jeanette R. Davidson. "Managed Care: Satisfaction Guaranteed...Not!" *Health & Social Work,* August 1999.

Donegan Shoaf, Lisa. "Defining Managed Care and Its Application to Individuals with Disabilities." *Focus on Autism & Other Developmental Disabilities,* winter 1999.

Gardner, Jonathan. "The Great Compromise." *Modern Healthcare,* 14 August 2000.

Gorham, John. "Train Wreck in Hartford." *Forbes,* 6 March 2000.

Knight, Wendy. *Managed Care: What It Is and How It Works.* Gaithersburg, MD: Aspen, 1998.

"Managed Care Facts," May 2000. Available from http://www.aahp.org.

McCue, Michael T. "The Grinch Paid a Visit to MCOs in 1999." *Forbes,* 6 March 2000.

Murray, Shailagh. "Managed-Health-Care Bill Is Step Closer after Negotiators Agree on Three Items." *Wall Street Journal,* 10 March 2000.

Prince, Michael. "More to Cost of Illness Than Doctor Bill." *Business Insurance,* 24 April 2000.

"Providing Healthcare in the Age of Consumerism." 4 May 1999. Available from http://managedcareinfocenter.com.

"Second Class Medicine." *Consumer Reports,* September 2000.

Shapiro, Joseph P. "Giving Doctors the Final Word." *U.S. News & World Report,* 22 November 1999.

———. "Seeking a Second Opinion." *U.S. News & World Report,* 8 March 1999.

"A Trial Run for HMOs." *U.S. News & World Report,* 22 February 1999.

U.S. Bureau of Labor Statistics. *2000-2001 Occupational Outlook Handbook.* Available from http://www.bls.gov/oco/ocos173.htm.

Waid, Mary Onnis. "Brief Summaries of Medicare and Medicaid." 11 May 1999. Available from http://www.hcfa.gov/stats/NHE-Proj/hilites.

Walker, Tracy. "HMO Patients in the ER: Not an Urgent Issue Yet." *Managed Healthcare,* September 1999.

———. "Legal Issues Will Intensify If MCOs Can't Satisfy Members." *Managed Healthcare,* February 2000.

Wechsler, Jill. "MCOs Face Heightened Scrutiny from Employers." *Managed Healthcare,* February 2000.

MASS MERCHANDISING

INDUSTRY SNAPSHOT

Mass merchandising (or tie-ins), which may have begun as a technique to bolster sales on occasion, has become a veritable industry in its own right. With advertising costs increasing, competition heating up, and markets peaking, companies turn to ties-ins—whether movie, television show, recording artist, or sports star tie-ins—to revitalize aging products and brands and to propel new ones. Entering the new century, Disney stood as the paragon of tie-in campaigns, releasing a slew of blockbuster movies coupled with cross-promotions in the fast-food, toy, apparel, and other industries. Despite the success of this technique, tie-ins can backfire, as companies in the late 1990s found when, for example, a melange of *Star Wars: Episode I—The Phantom Menace* paraphernalia failed to sell briskly as expected and had to be substantially discounted. Moreover, some aggressive tie-in tactics end up putting the cart before the horse: companies planning tie-ins will pressure moviemakers to modify their films for the sake of tie-in promotions.

Nevertheless, mass merchandising—such as spin-offs, tie-ins, cross-promotions, and merchandise licensing—plays an increasingly important role in the entertainment industry. Licensed entertainment properties, such as action figures, clothing, and plush dolls, along with marketing campaigns tied to fast-food chains and soft-drink companies—not to mention musical soundtracks, books, and computer games—have become just as important as the original source material. Some high-profile blockbuster films, including director Steven Spielberg's *Jurassic Park,* have even earned more in merchandise revenue than in ticket sales, while successful movie soundtracks often stay on the charts months after the films disappear from theaters.

In the last two decades, the licensing practice of licensing—when companies pay a fee to use the image of a sports team or an animated character, for example—has exploded. Businesses as diverse as fast-food restaurants and T-shirt makers discovered the benefits of aligning themselves with high-profile characters and images that literally sell themselves. Meanwhile, entertainment companies have discovered a vast new revenue source to help offset rising production costs. By the end of the 20th century, the U.S. and Canadian market for licensed products fermented into a $74.2 billion industry, with entertainment-based tie-ins accounting for $15.9 billion, according to *Promo Sourcebook Supplement.* Worldwide, according to *Brandmarketing,* the market booked revenues of about $143.5 billion during this period.

ORGANIZATION AND STRUCTURE

Generally, after a product, movie, television show, recording artist, or athlete achieves fame or popularity, companies attempt to tap into this popularity with tie-ins (although many movie tie-ins are hatched before the movies are released). In doing so, companies create a network of brands, each capitalizing on the strength of the other—in theory at least. For example, toy-maker, Hasbro, Inc., ties different toys with different quick-eats restaurants, which allows the restaurants to get Hasbro toys and Hasbro to use the chain names on its toys.

Because of the explosive popularity and substantial revenues of Disney movies, for example, doing a tie-in with a Disney movie means the likelihood of a successful centerpiece promotion. The soaring revenues have come with greater expectations and some growing pains. Some critics worry that movies are being made simply to sell more licensed gadgets, rather than the other way around. Meanwhile, advertisers with a growing stake in the promotion of movies have even been known to propose script changes to maximize tie-in potential or press for earlier release dates.

Conversely, high-profile box-office releases such as *Godzilla* and *Babe: Pig in the City* proved disappointing when it came to tie-ins. Even before the film was released, merchandisers were griping because the makers of *Godzilla* did not want the famed monster's image used in advertising campaigns. With licensing costs rising, such promotional ventures have become more risky. Rising costs on both sides of the licensing fence might push movie studios and restaurant chains into unprecedented alliances, enabling chains to consider films while they're still in the development stage.

Meanwhile, manufacturers who pinned hopes on a product as seemingly solid as sports merchandise—shirts, hats, and trash bins with team logos—faced losses when the major sports organizations experienced labor trouble, such as the baseball strike of 1994 and the National Basketball Association lockout during the 1998-99 season. Nonetheless, for both large and small businesses, mass merchandising in its various forms continues to offer important benefits to firms that spend wisely, whether it be to put the latest Disney character on a pair of socks or a *Star Wars* character on a pencil sharpener. So, as media companies continue to merge and expand, and books and soundtracks based on film and television become increasingly popular, marketing such spin-offs using different media is likely to become more frequent and sophisticated.

BACKGROUND AND DEVELOPMENT

Mass merchandising has been around for quite a long time, though the industry was not always as lucrative as it has been since the late 1970s. In the early 20th century, actors and baseball players often appeared on cigarette cards, while children looking to purchase chewing gum would also get free trading cards.

Upon analysis, it was the cards, not the gum or cigarettes, that collectors came to crave. A famous

Honus Wagner cigarette card from 1909—rare because the Hall of Fame player quickly demanded his image be yanked from the package because he didn't want to encourage smoking—has an estimated worth of $500,000.

Toy executive Cy Schneider asserted in his book *Children's Television* that the first licensing agreement arranged with a toy manufacturer came in 1913, when the Ideal Toy Co. introduced the world to the "teddy" bear, having first sought permission from former president Teddy Roosevelt. Companies would later use popular radio characters from the 1920s and 1930s to sell products and licensed goods. Ralston cereals, for example, offered the "Ralston Straight Shooter Manual," which told readers—presumably young boys—about the real adventures of the popular cowboy character Tom Mix. It even included the "Tom Mix Chart of Wounds," which illustrated 12 bullet wounds and nearly 50 bone fractures the cowboy purportedly suffered. The General Mills cereal company, meanwhile, organized several promotions around the *Lone Ranger* radio series, as did Quaker Oats with the famed detective Dick Tracy.

Ovaltine, meanwhile, targeted girls with "Little Orphan Annie's Very Own Shake-Up Mug," based on the famous character who got her start in the Sunday comics, then moved to radio, and later was found in movies and on Broadway.

PIONEERS IN THE FIELD

It was television and film that spurred real growth in this area. The first big success is familiar enough. In 1928 Walt Disney brought the character Mickey Mouse to life for the first time in a picture called "Steamboat Willie," costarring Minnie Mouse. Within five years, Pluto, Goofy, and Donald Duck joined Mickey and Minnie in notoriety. By the mid-1930s, 1 million Mickey Mouse watches were sold annually, and 10 percent of Disney's revenues came from licensing its cartoon characters, according to *The Disney Touch*, by Ronald Grover. *Snow White and the Seven Dwarfs*, the first full-length animated film, released in 1937, was a huge licensing success as well.

Into the 1940s and 1950s, animated films such as *Pinocchio, Fantasia, Dumbo,* and *Bambi* all came with a line of products and cross-promotions, such as books and music. The new Disneyland theme park in California, which had fledgling television network American Broadcasting Co. (ABC) as a big investor, added to Disney's already considerable ability market its own products.

With ABC backing it up, Disney was also one of the first companies to use television to sell related products. The *Davy Crockett* series, part of ABC's *Disneyland* series, inspired a famous national craze for coonskin caps, and the song "The Ballad of Davy Crockett" sold 10 million copies. Building on the success of *Disneyland,* the *Mickey Mouse Club* hit television airwaves in 1955. A small toy company, Mattel, also jumped on the Disney bandwagon. They advertised on the *Mickey Mouse Club* and later marketed successful tie-in products, such as "Mousegetars," a musical instrument for kids. Such early successes helped Mattel become the nation's top toy manufacturer.

Warner Brothers cartoon characters—Bugs Bunny, Porky Pig, Daffy Duck, and others—also proved to be licensing and tie-in hits for their creators. Disney hit it big again in 1964 with the mostly nonanimated feature *Mary Poppins,* which produced not only inexpensive trinkets, but entire clothing lines and even shoe polish.

Nonetheless, despite Disney's success, "licensed products coming from hit movies had not been big winners" into the 1970s, Cy Schneider wrote. But the release of George Lucas' *Star Wars* in 1977 changed that. The *Star Wars* trilogy, as well as the later Indiana Jones productions, generated billions in licensed product sales. In 1976 licensed toys accounted for 20 percent of all toy sales. By the mid-1980s, that figure rose to 80 percent. According to the Toy Manufacturers of America (TMA), that figure has settled at about 40 percent—although in his 1999 annual address, TMA president David A. Miller predicted an upswing "with the introduction of the new *Star Wars* series."

Before the release of the original *Star Wars,* Kenner toys signed an exclusive deal to produce toys, games, and other products based on the film for $100,000 annually, a fairly risky venture at the time. The deal made Kenner hundreds of millions of dollars through the 1980s.

The effect of this on the entire toy industry should not be underestimated. By 1991, Hasbro bought Kenner; there had not been a *Star Wars* movie in nearly a decade, and merchandise sales lagged. Yet Lucas was still receiving $100,000 every year. Hasbro ended the relationship. A year later, San Francisco-based Galoob Toys was able to launch its own *Star Wars* line, and it was a success. Hasbro later returned to the *Star Wars* fold. Some industry analysts have speculated

though that Galoob's successful marketing of older *Star Wars* merchandise spurred Lucas' decision to reissue the original trilogy in theaters, thus kicking off the anticipation, and marketing frenzy, for *The Phantom Menace.*

For a large company such as Hasbro, which earns over $3.5 billion annually, the *Star Wars* line represents a significant but not overwhelming portion of its revenue. Galoob, on the other hand, earns up to one-third of its $360 million annual revenue from *Star Wars* merchandise. Although licensing fees for *The Phantom Menace* were around the once unthinkable 15 percent of wholesale revenues from the goods sold, the involvement with Lucas seemed to help Galoob's stock rebound from earlier losses. Hasbro's purchase of Galoob in 1998 may have helped as well, since it consolidated the nation's second- and third-biggest toy makers, not to mention each major *Star Wars* toy license holder.

CURRENT CONDITIONS

High marketing costs and market unpredictability still fueled the tie-ins and cross-category promotions in the late 1990s and early 2000s. Because tying a product in with a universally recognized character such as Mickey Mouse can substantially reduce the need for advertising, companies continued to launch tie-in campaigns. By the same token, however, tie-ins proved not to be fail-safe as some tie-ins don't strike a chord with consumers and hence result in losses. For example, many companies put their advertising eggs in the *Star Wars: Episode I-The Phantom Menace* basket in 1999 and the movie was not the cornucopia they anticipated. While action figures sold well, the numerous other products concocted to capitalize on the movie—such as clothes, linens, and cookware—had flaccid sales, according to *Entertainment Weekly.* Moreover, the houses of fast food that did tie-ins— Tricon's KFC, Pizza Hut, and Taco Bell—realized only a 1 or 2 percent increase in revenues—which amounts to somewhat of a phantom flop.

Nevertheless, one company has persistently done well with tie-ins, namely Disney. Continuing its legacy of churning out hit after hit, Disney remained on the vanguard of the tie-ins industry at the beginning of 2000. With its May 2000 release *Dinosaurs,* Disney positioned itself to reap the benefits of another tie-in campaign, which included licensing rights to McDonald's for its Happy Meals. These rights are so important to McDonald's that it considered the *Di-*

nosaurs promotion the crux of its summer 2000 marketing program, according to *Advertising Age*. In addition to providing dinosaur toys with its Happy Meals, McDonald's offered its "Hatch, Match, and Win" game, which featured prizes such as a $25,000 diamond, $1 million in cash, and Hawaiian vacations.

McDonald's wasn't the only company to climb aboard Disney's gravy train. Many a company tries to set a Mickey Mouse trap to bolster its sales. General Mills, for example, struck a two-year deal with Disney in 2000 to fortify its Betty Crocker fruit snacks. The agreement enables General Mills Mickey Mouse Peel-Outs, Winnie-the-Pooh Fruit Snacks, and *Dinosaur* fruit rolls. With this agreement, General Mills hopes to cut advertising costs and continue to dominate the fruit snack market. In 1998 General Mills spent $6.6 million on marketing its Betty Crocker fruit snacks, whereas it spent only $26,000 in 1999 thanks to tie-ins, which generally require less advertising because the tie-ins make the product easily recognizable. In 1999, sales of Betty Crocker fruit snacks totaled $272 million.

Because of tie-in campaigns such as these in previous years, a *Nation's Business* writer said Disney "sets the gold standard," when it comes to success in the area of mass merchandising. Mickey Mouse, as Cy Schneider wrote, remains "the greatest salesman of them all." Disney's track record is impressive. Nearly every year in the 1990s Disney produced a lucrative animated film, from 1992's *Aladdin,* which made about $500 million worldwide at the box office alone, to *Hercules* in 1997. *The Lion King,* released in 1994, has taken in an estimated total of $1.5 billion in theaters, merchandise, and related products. Animated films are secure foundations for a wide variety of marketing possibilities and revenue sources since they appeal to the whole family and tend to include characters that can easily become cute toys or other licensed properties.

Disney has easily shown itself to be the top player in the animation game. "Aside from extensive use of the usual avenues of publicity, Disney finds promo tools through toy store displays, record albums, and merchandising and fast-food tie-ins: It's impossible to troll the mall without multiple exposures to the Disney blitz," reported *Variety* in an article entitled "High Noon for Toon Boom," which described increasing competition in the animation field.

Indeed, other entertainment companies are jumping into the animation business. After decades spent watching Disney run away with the animation market, rival companies decided to invest heavily in an effort to wrest some of the market from Disney's grip. While this was an expensive and risky maneuver, the potential rewards for a successful campaign are almost too tempting to ignore; each company realizes that any opportunity it fails to jump on is one some other company will.

In an effort to keep up with Disney and McDonald's, Universal Pictures teamed up with Burger King with a tie-in deal for Universal's *The Flintstones in Viva Rock Vegas,* which opened in May 2000. The $20 million promotion included Burger King commercials with footage from the movie and Flintstone toys in its Kids Meals. Later in 2000, Burger King put its efforts into tie-in promotions with *Rugrats in Paris—The Movie* and *Pokemon 2,* while the latter also drew in such heavy-hitters as Target, Kmart, Sears, Kellogg, Clorox, and others. Moreover, the fast-food mogul agreed to sponsor the fall 2000 tour of the Backstreet Boys, which included the release of a compact disc (CD) with five new songs and a video.

Television has been another important catalyst for the tie-in industry. Animated television shows in particular perform well as vehicles for creating and promoting tie-ins. As Cy Schneider wrote, "Television can do what movies cannot by virtue of its enormous reach and frequency of exposure." This has been reversed completely. As *Advertising Age* reported, these days, "most TV properties don't have the revenue potential of feature film blockbusters." Consider MTV's raunchy cartoon characters Beavis and Butt-head. Paramount Pictures expanded on the cartoon's television popularity and created a blockbuster film, *Beavis and Butt-head Do America,* which then led to several profitable tie-ins, from books to a successful soundtrack. Still, while generally not as lucrative as blockbuster films, successful TV shows are typically a much safer gamble for tie-ins than the uncertain movie market.

Moreover, there is growing potential in television for selling everything from computer games to clothes to videos, especially to and for children. From the *Mickey Mouse Club* to *Sesame Street,* television has had its long-term lucrative franchises. The Tickle Me Elmo doll, which rocked the toy industry, was a *Sesame Street* spin-off. Almost all popular television shows from the 1970s and 1980s produced tie-ins such as lunch boxes, comic books, and toys. In the late 1980s, *The Simpsons* brought television merchandising possibilities to a higher level, and the scale has only grown since then.

A leader in the field, not surprisingly, is the children's network Nickelodeon. Popular shows such as

Rugrats and *Blue's Clues* have become spin-off bonanzas for the network. *Rugrats* even made the transition to the big screen in 1998. Two years earlier, meanwhile, Paramount Home Video—Nickelodeon's sister company—released a home video based on *Blue's Clues*, a "detective show" for kids aged two to six. The video release attracted 7,000 fans to the FAO Schwarz store in Manhattan, and 480,000 videos sold in just nine days. Two CD-ROM titles based on the show were also highly successful. *The Rugrats* show, meanwhile, spun off a CD that can be used for music and computer activities. Of course, each of these Nickelodeon-based products line the shelves of toy and children's clothing stores.

As with blockbuster films, the success of television cartoons has also raised the stakes in the industry. Many "competitors have been trying to imitate Nickelodeon's success. The Fox Family Channel, for one, will spend some $500 million to reach into this market using, among other things, the Fox Kids Network." Fox even hired a prominent executive away from Nickelodeon, Rich Cronin, to become chief executive officer of the Fox Family Channel.

The competition has even led marketers to target younger and younger children. British exports of the *Teletubbies* have spurred a "Beatlemania for 2-to-5-year-olds," according to *Advertising Age*. The Teletubbies—four, teddy-bear-like, live-action figures who speak like infants and have televisions for stomachs—are designed for children as young as 18 months. Again, typical products such as videotapes, bath toys, and puzzles have proven lucrative. Tie-ins stretch all the way to TubbieCustard, a ready-to-eat, yogurtlike product based on what the Teletubbies eat on the show.

The president and CEO of Itsy Bitsy Entertainment, which licenses *Teletubbies* for broadcast in the United States, outlined the keys to a successful children's entertainment product. "For a hit, you need a property that children really like, parents approve of and that retailers will support, plus a little innovation," Ken Viselman told *Advertising Age*.

Of course, that's not as easy as it sounds. Already the increasing competition of the tie-in merchandising market has claimed casualties. For years, Equity Marketing made promotional items that were given away free by other marketers, such as Coca-Cola and Exxon. Equity produced toys based on *Small Soldiers* and *The Rugrats Movie*, for example, which were given away free with the purchase of children's meals at Burger King. Looking to expand, Equity attempted to directly sell products based on the films *Godzilla* and *Babe:*

Pig in the City, both of which failed to generate big merchandising sales and were viewed as critical and commercial failures. Equity subsequently announced it would drop out of the movie-licensing business. Equity's "misfortunes are an example of the risks smaller marketers are forced to take in hopes of riding the coattails of potential blockbusters," according to *Advertising Age*. "Such marketers as Hasbro and Mattel, for instance, do a broader array of license and nonlicense toy making, which enables them to sustain the ups and downs of the film business." This also suggested that, despite worries that the quality of films will suffer in the zeal to snare tie-in deals, it appears that it still takes a good movie to sell products. As one analyst told *Advertising Age*, "If you don't succeed on the silver screen, it's very hard to have merchandise jump off the shelves."

Some feel that the advertisers and merchandisers are tinkering excessively with what, in the end, may be the most important product—the movies themselves. According to *Time*, Universal's 1996 summer movie *Flipper* was ready for theaters when studio executives approached the film's writer and director with concerns that there were only three main animal characters in the film. Toy manufacturers wanted a fourth, to round out a line of dolls. The director said it was simply too late to add another character. A compromise was forged when the studio found a turtle who appeared literally in one shot, turned it into Sam the Turtle, and then shipped him out to toy stores nationwide.

Similarly, when McDonald's expressed strong interest in the Disney film *George of the Jungle,* the studio promptly doubled the film's budget to increase the special effects and the number of animals that could be turned into toys.

As Pat Wyatt, president of licensing for Fox, acknowledged to *Time*, "Not every film is a great merchandising opportunity." Importantly, *Time* added, "not all spin-offs are aimed at junior."

Indeed, almost everyone eats candy and cereal, also popular tie-in products. Hershey Foods ran a theater-concession promotion with the Dreamworks film *Antz* and launched five dinosaur-themed products to go with *The Lost World: Jurassic Park.* A mass-merchandising opportunity was also taken advantage of by Estée Lauder; the company produced a line of women's makeup as a tie-in with the film *Evita.*

Substantive tie-in growth for all ages has also occurred in publishing, especially with musical soundtracks. While acknowledging that "most movie tie-in books are crass rehashings of the films," *U.S. News and World Report* highlighted a trend towards higher-quality tie-in volumes during the 1998 holiday season.

Meanwhile, a front-page headline for a *Billboard* article announced: "Soundtracks Spark Chart Heat." As reporter Catherine Applefeld Olson wrote, "the staying power of soundtracks in [the 1990s], which kicked off with *The Bodyguard* in 1992 and has gained momentum with *Waiting to Exhale, Space Jam,* and *Titanic,* to name a few, has given record companies a new perspective on the potential of film music." Most recording companies now have departments dedicated to soundtracks, Olson explained, and "several are even outperforming the films from which they were culled." Soundtracks also serve as useful venues to debut a record company's new bands. Even television shows such as *Ally McBeal* have spawned successful albums.

The *Billboard* report continued, "With this popularity has come escalated bidding wars," as well as "increased cooperation between record labels and film studios." This is where mass merchandising seems to be headed. Cooperation, synergy, or convergence—call it what you will. Larger and larger media companies, not to mention online technology, have made marketing and selling tie-in merchandise increasingly sophisticated. The Web site for the hit Warner Brothers network television show *Dawson's Creek* has a complete list of songs played on the show, many available through the Warner Brothers recording arm. A media empire such as Time Warner can promote a movie and soundtrack using print media, cable television, and books since it has its own film, recording, publishing, and broadcasting arms. Feature stories and interviews on entertainment products can even pop up on a network's newscasts.

WORK FORCE

Importantly, mass merchandising is not a game merely for Hollywood movers and shakers and global fast-food chains. Many small and mid-size clothing manufacturers, for example, do a large portion of their business through licensing and other mass-merchandising methods. "The opportunities for small companies in licensing are bigger than ever," the executive editor of *The Licensing Letter* told *Nation's Business* in 1995. Indications suggested that this industry remains "driven largely by small firms." This article highlighted several success stories in its cover story on licensed entertainment products—among them Zak Designs Inc., based in Spokane, Washington, which launched a generic children's dinnerware line in the mid-1980s. Business took off when the company obtained a license for Disney's Little Mermaid character in 1989, and revenues "increased 20-fold and employment 10-fold, to about 100 people."

There are potential pitfalls, of course. Disney, for example, can bring manufacturers profits but, according to *Nation's Business,* they can be a very demanding licenser. You may also tie your product to a character suffering from overexposure, as many who invested in a license for the purple dinosaur Barney eventually discovered. Sports merchandise has also been a fickle investment given that three of the major four sports experienced labor troubles in the 1990s.

RESEARCH AND TECHNOLOGY

What's a prospective licensee to do? *Nation's Business* made several suggestions. "Make the initial contact," to find out a licenser's requirements. This inquiry might involve hiring a consultant or attorney who specializes in the field. Be prepared to "document your qualifications," since licensers may not want to risk selling their product to an unsound firm. Knowing the market and finding a niche are important, according to *Nation's Business,* which also suggested that potential players "consider taking a risk." Being in on the ground floor of an unproven property could be lucrative.

A less costly way to play this game is to "try a knockoff." That is, if a film such as *Jurassic Park* hits it big, rather than license characters from the film itself, look into products related to dinosaurs. *Nation's Business* noted that generic wildlife products did well following the release of Disney's *The Lion King.*

As the 20th century closed, participants in the mass-merchandising industry began researching the tie-in capabilities of the Internet. As part of a plan to cash in on the projected $2.4 trillion e-commerce industry by the middle of the decade, television producers experimented with marketing wares seen in their shows via the Internet. Through the site As-SeenIn.com, viewers can obtain the clothes and furniture beheld in popular shows such as *Melrose Place* and *Friends.* The site also featured links to other sites; for example, clicking on a game in a *7th Heaven* room will transport users to eToys, according to *Variety.* In a parallel endeavor, TVStyle.com will empower users to search for clothing they've seen worn by their favorite actors on television shows.

FURTHER READING

Britt, Bill. "Teletubbies Are Coming: Brit Hit Sets U.S. Invasion." *Advertising Age,* 19 January 1998.

Buss, Dale B. "Hot Names, Top Dollars." *Nation's Business,* August 1995.

"Evergreen Appeal." *Promo Sourcebook Supplement,* October 2000.

Fierman, Daniel. "Toy Crazy." *Entertainment Weekly,* 9 July 1999.

Friedman, Wayne. "Saying Goodbye to Hollywood." *Advertising Age,* 11 January 1999.

Graser, Marc. "E-Commerce Boots up TV Tie-Ins." *Variety,* 24 May 1999.

Grover, Ronald. *The Disney Touch: How a Daring Management Team Revived an Entertainment Empire.* Homewood, IL: Business One Irwin, 1991.

Gunther, Marc. "The Rules According to Rupert." *Fortune,* 26 October 1998.

Handy, Bruce. "101 Movie Tie-Ins." *Time,* 2 December 1996.

Jensen, Jeff, and Judann Pollack. "Bug Flicks Will Feast on Candy." *Advertising Age,* 29 June 1998.

Karon, Paul, and Leonard Klady. "High Noon for Toon Boom." *Variety,* 15 June 1998.

MacArthur, Kate. "Burger Giants Dig up Dinos for Summer Movie Tie-Ins." *Advertising Age,* 17 April 2000.

Miller, Cyndee. "TV Networks as Brands." *Marketing News,* 9 October 1995.

Morris, Kathleen. "Bated Breath in Toyland." *Business Week,* 15 February 1999.

"The Movies Go Pop." *U.S. News and World Report,* 14 December 1998.

Olson, Catherine Applefeld. "Soundtracks Spark Chart Heat." *Billboard,* 11 July 1998.

Schneider, Cy. *Children's Television: The Art, The Business and How It Works.* Chicago: NTC Business Books, 1987.

Snyder, Beth. "Rivals Attracted to Nickelodeon's Sweet Success." *Advertising Age,* 9 November 1998.

Thompson, Stephanie. "General Mills Adds Disney Characters to Fruit Snacks Line." *Advertising Age,* 8 May 2000.

MEDICAL SELF-TESTING PRODUCTS

INDUSTRY SNAPSHOT

Medical self-testing products are quietly usurping the doctor's office as the checkup of first resort. With an increasingly health-conscious populace more at ease with technology, and with prohibitive medical costs forcing individuals to consider health from a preventive standpoint, the market for home diagnostic test kits emerged as a powerful industry by the turn of the 21st century, growing from $747 million in 1992 to $2.1 billion in 1999, according to the San Jose, California-based research firm Frost & Sullivan. Over the next five years, Frost & Sullivan expected the market to double.

With the growth of general medical knowledge, consumers have become far more aware of the importance of early disease detection. Using the large—and growing—number of medical self-testing products currently on the market, preventive-minded "patients" could test themselves for a wide range of ailments and conditions, including high cholesterol and glucose levels, HIV, high blood pressure, and pregnancy.

Industry proponents noted that, while medical self-testing cannot replace a visit to a doctor altogether, it does offer individuals the opportunity to assume a proactive role in the physician-patient relationship, allowing patients to catch a problem early in the process and come to the doctor's office with an idea of what's in store. Most importantly, however, the industry players pitch their products as a cost-saving medical strategy. While the cost of medical kits is often as expensive as an actual checkup, the benefits of early detection can drastically cut massive medical expenses that would result from late-stage detection.

ORGANIZATION AND STRUCTURE

There were over 300 U.S. Food and Drug Administration (FDA)-approved over-the-counter home diagnostic tests on the market in 1999, and they came in many shapes and sizes.

Blood-pressure monitors could be purchased in the old-fashioned model, which featured a stethoscope and inflating armband, while the newer models were diminishing in size and encompassed digital technology. Diabetes tests involve obtaining a small blood sample and placing it on a strip of paper, which can then be monitored by a small electronic device to determine glucose levels.

Diagnostic tests for colon cancer and for urinary tract infections involve placing a specially designed strip into the toilet after using. The strip will then change color to denote a potential problem. Doctors stress, however, that a colored strip for a colon-cancer test does not necessarily mean that the user in fact has colon cancer, only that there is something wrong with the stool sample, and that a potential problem may exist.

Meanwhile, home diagnostic tests for HIV infection, approved by the FDA in the mid-1990s, actually involve outside input. Users simply send a dried sample of their own blood to a laboratory and await the results, usually delivered by a trained counselor over the telephone. Hepatitis C tests function in much the same manner.

In many cases, customers are encouraged by their physicians to purchase home diagnostic equipment as part of the treatment for a particular condition. Manufacturers, however, while recognizing the importance of this outlet, have attempted to reduce their reliance on this aspect of distribution in recent years.

Although pharmacies remain the primary retail outlet for medical self-testing products, a growing proportion of total product sales were garnered through specialty stores, including Sharper Image and Brookstone, which carry everything from body-fat monitors to cholesterol tests. In addition, general retailers such as Walgreen's and Safeway have cleared off shelf space for diagnostic kits. In 1999 about 46 percent of all home diagnostic kits were sold through drugstores and pharmacies, while discount stores accounted for 28 percent; supermarkets for 6 percent; and mail order for 3 percent. The remainder were sold through a variety of channels, primarily through doctors' offices.

Manufacturers have also received some aid at the distribution level in the form of patient education campaigns, which were administered at an increasing number of pharmacies in the late 1990s. Correspondingly, manufacturers have taken great strides to make their products easier to use, and many provide literature comprehensively explaining the product and the importance of monitoring the particular condition.

Medical self-testing products are subject to approval by the FDA before they hit the market. The extensive clinical tests each product must wade through to meet approval generally mean that product accuracy is rarely a problem once it hits store shelves. The much more pressing difficulty for manufacturers of home medical self-testing products is generating significant enough margins on their sales. Typically, manufacturers thus concentrate on the mass production of a small number of products, usually in the same general health area. By 2000, firms were devising all sorts of creative marketing strategies to bolster margins, and their efforts were beginning to pay off.

BACKGROUND AND DEVELOPMENT

While some home diagnostic equipment, like the thermometer, has been around for ages, the modern medical self-testing product industry dates back to the early 1970s, when home testing kits for diabetes were introduced. Medical self-testing's sharp rise through the late 1980s and 1990s was closely tied to the growth of managed health care, which strongly encourages preventive medical practices as a way of trimming medical costs. Meanwhile, the movement of many baby boomers into middle age—a time at which health concerns such as blood pressure and cholesterol begin

to assume crucial proportions—along with the aging of the population in general and an enhanced understanding of preventive medicine, provided a natural marketplace for home diagnostics.

Home diagnostic kits originally were sold almost exclusively through doctors' offices or, occasionally, behind the counter at pharmacies. In general, pharmacies were reluctant to carry such items because they tended to be bulky and sales were so slight. Through the mid- and late 1990s, the technology and production of medical self-testing products improved dramatically, thus bringing costs down and causing over-the-counter sales to skyrocket. By the late 1990s, revenues for manufacturers of home diagnostic tests were growing between 10 and 15 percent each year, according to Frost & Sullivan.

A high-profile breakthrough came when the first home access tests for HIV were approved by the FDA in the mid-1990s. This development was part of a massive effort to boost the numbers of individuals who tested their HIV status. At the time, U.S. surveys found that 60 percent of Americans engaged in behavior that put them at risk of infection, but only a small minority had actually been tested. With the relatively high degree of anonymity of home testing, it was hoped that more people would be inclined to keep track of their sero-status.

CURRENT CONDITIONS

The market for medical self-testing products was exceptionally fertile at the dawn of the 21st century, and manufacturers began to engage in sophisticated marketing strategies to capture a share of the potentially lucrative market. With the baby-boomer generation spanning middle age, and possessing a relatively high level of education and income, concern over health and fitness was at an all-time high.

This represented a profound change in the demographic market for home diagnostic kits. Traditionally, such products were pitched toward individuals over 55 years of age suffering from chronic medical conditions. In addition, due to the high costs of self-testing products, most of those customers brought in annual incomes exceeding $60,000, according to AC-Nielsen Corp. Most such customers also made their purchases on the recommendations of their doctors. By 2000, all that had changed. Home diagnostic kits were geared especially for baby boomers, but also toward individuals as young as 25.

As the market grows more sophisticated, so do merchandising strategies. It was commonplace to see diagnostic kits and health monitors marketed in conjunction with over-the-counter treatments for the respective condition. In this way, manufacturers hoped to lure more customers who had not been advised by a doctor to seek out diagnostic kits. Omron Healthcare markets its products with brochures, on display in the aisles, explaining the benefits of routine blood-pressure monitoring for overall health maintenance.

But analysts surmised that perhaps the most basic factor affecting the growth of the medical self-testing product industry is the convenience such products afford their customers. These days, it's rare to find someone who doesn't take at least some active interest in his or her ongoing health maintenance, and routine testing is becoming a central part of that process. With prices lowering to within reach of the average consumer, home diagnostic kits provide a simple, quick way of keeping abreast of one's vital signs, be it for personal appearance or for acute medical conditions.

Blood glucose monitors comprised the leading industry category in 1999, with sales totaling $386 million, according to ACNielsen. Product innovation in this sector was a leading factor in its strong sales; by 2000, glucose test kits capable of measuring blood sugar in a matter of seconds were beginning to hit the market.

Blood-pressure monitors were another strong category for medical self-testing products, with sales topping $330 million by the late 1990s as the technology was refined, producing more accurate readings and eliminating a lot of the guesswork that characterized earlier models. Competition in this sector was heating up, with new players such as Panasonic and Braun throwing their hats into the ring. Meanwhile, the American Heart Association reported that about one-quarter of all adults in the United States suffer from hypertension, but about 32 percent of those are unaware of the condition. The challenge for blood-pressure-kit manufacturers, then, was to create greater awareness of the extent and severity of this problem while positioning their products as a part of the arsenal to combat it.

Home pregnancy tests were another mainstay in the medical self-testing product industry, generating annual sales of about $220 million by the late 1990s. Home pregnancy tests first went on the market in 1977, courtesy of Warner-Lambert. More recently, ovulation-monitoring kits emerged as a significant market sector, worth about $30 million by the end of 1998. Ovulation kits are designed to test fertility to denote when a couple is most likely to get pregnant,

and thus were marketed, unlike pregnancy tests in recent years, toward women who hoped for positive results. Meanwhile, a growing number of women over 35 years of age were attempting to get pregnant for the first time, and thus the industry predicted growing demand for ovulation testing kits.

Industry reports suggest that diagnostic kits do in fact aid significantly in personal medical monitoring. One-third of home-diagnostic customers reported that the kits led to early detection of a disease or condition, according to a national survey of over 1,000 such customers by LifeSource. Forty-two percent answered that the kits spurred them to take their medications on a regular basis. The two biggest factors in the purchase of home diagnostic equipment seemed to be convenience and cost; 64 percent responded that their primary reason for their purchase was that using such kits was easier than going to a doctor, while half said that the affordability of testing kits makes them a practical monitoring method.

INDUSTRY LEADERS

Roche Diagnostics, based in Indianapolis, Indiana, is a subsidiary of the Basel, Switzerland-based Roche Holdings Ltd., one of the world's leading pharmaceutical companies. Roche's Accu-check blood glucose monitor was one of the largest-selling items in the home diagnostics industry. While its diagnostic-products business was traditionally a lower priority for Roche, the firm bought its way to the position of the world's largest diagnostics company with the $10.2 billion purchase of Corange in 1988. Though the company was rocked by a massive federal lawsuit accusing the company of participation in a vitamin price-fixing cartel, Roche managed to increase revenues from $15 billion in 1998 to $16.8 billion in 1999.

One of the largest manufacturers of health-care products in the world, employing some 97,800 workers in 2000, Johnson & Johnson was home to several brands in the medical self-testing market. LifeScan, purchased by Johnson & Johnson in 1986, produces One Touch Strips, a blood glucose diagnostic kit that was the industry's top-selling product in 2000 and that constituted about 70 percent of LifeScan's revenues. LifeScan also manufactures palm-sized monitors for blood-glucose levels. Advanced Care Products, another unit of Johnson & Johnson, produces a line of cholesterol screening kits. The company's Confide home HIV test was another major product. In 1999

A wide range of self-testing products are available. (FieldMark Publications/Robert J. Huffman)

Johnson & Johnson's total sales reached $27.5 billion, up from $23.6 billion the year before, while about 25 percent of its revenues were derived from the consumer-products division. In 2000 LifeScan Inc. lost a lawsuit it brought against Home Diagnostics, Inc. for patent violation.

Based in Abbott Park, Illinois, Abbott Laboratories, a diversified drug and nutritional product manufacturer, is engaged in the production of a wide range of noninvasive monitoring technologies. In all, the firm employed about 51,700 workers in 1999. Founded in the home of Dr. Wallace Abbott in 1888, Abbott Laboratories dived headfirst into the home diagnostic products market in 1996 with the purchase of MediSense, a manufacturer of blood-sugar tests. The company was embroiled in controversy in the late 1990s, culminating in a $100 million fine from the FDA, which ordered that Abbott pull 125 diagnostic products from the shelves as a result of serious questions of quality assurance at its Chicago manufacturing plants. Nonetheless, Abbott was able to boost its overall sales in 1999 to $13.2 billion from $12.5 billion in 1998.

Omron Healthcare, based in Vernon Hills, Illinois, was the medical-products division of the giant Omron Corp. of Japan, and generated about $100 million in annual sales. The division expected to achieve revenues of $300 million by 2004. Omron's Body Logic Pro fat analyzer was geared especially toward younger consumers as a fitness product. The firm was expanding its marketing efforts by developing new diagnostic kits and monitors, such as its wrist blood-pressure monitor, for sale in sporting goods stores and health clubs. Its wrist blood-pressure monitor features the company's patented IntelliSense technology, which enables the monitor to adjust itself to the user's optimal compression setting, thereby reducing discomfort and speeding the time before a reading is obtained.

Home Access Health Corp. of Hoffman Estates, Illinois, produces home HIV and hepatitis C tests. Through the late 1990s, Home Access maintained an agreement with Abbott Laboratories to collaborate on the manufacturing and marketing of a range of new diagnostic kits using Home Access's Telemedicine technology. Telemedicine, pioneered by Home Access in the late 1990s, provides anonymous test information and professional consultation from the customer's home via the telephone, and allowed for the rapid sales of their Home Access HIV Test System. Abbott also bought a minority interest in Home Access as part of the agreement.

Health-Mark Diagnostics, L.L.C., a subsidiary of Technical Chemicals and Products, Inc., produces a line of home diagnostic products, including tests for diabetes, urinary tract infections, cholesterol, pregnancy, ovulation, and the development of skin abnormalities for signs of melanoma and other skin cancers. The company claims about a 25 percent share of the market for private-label home pregnancy test in the United States with its One-Step One Minute test kit. In January of that year the Technical Chemicals and Products, Inc. announced the launch of a new electronic-commerce site specifically for direct consumer sales of Health-Mark products.

Unipath Diagnostics, a division of Unilever, manufactures home pregnancy and ovulation tests. In 1999 Unipath received FDA approval for its ClearPlan Easy Fertility Monitor, which earmarks a six-day span for high fertility, as opposed to the usual two for ovulation tests.

RESEARCH AND TECHNOLOGY

Size and speed were among the key realms for innovation of medical self-testing products, whereby companies scrambled to create smaller, more lightweight products that can perform their tasks in less time. Thus, medical self-testing products have grown more user friendly over time. In the old days, kits and monitors tended to be bulky and not especially mobile. These days, a number of products are designed to fit in the user's palm. This is especially true for monitors of blood pressure and heart rates, with which customers can keep tabs on their readings while they are working out on the exercise bike or treadmill.

Another new development, which received FDA approval in 1997, was the home screening test for drug abuse, which detects traces of narcotics such as marijuana, cocaine, heroin, amphetamines, codeine, PCP, and other controlled substances. Most drug-abuse test kits require the user to send in a urine sample or piece of hair to a laboratory for analysis. Some tests, however, such as Pharmatech's QuickScreen at Home Drug Test, which the FDA approved in late 1998, could determine the results almost instantaneously. Instant home drug tests were particularly popular among suspicious parents of teenagers.

The Internet has also played a subtle but significant role in boosting the popularity of medical self-testing products. The sheer level of information widely available as a result of Internet distribution affords customers with an abundance of health and medical knowledge, thereby encouraging greater sales of products designed to monitor personal health.

Innovation among some of the industry's leading product sectors, especially blood-pressure and blood-glucose monitoring kits, is directed toward the integration of monitoring and treatment, often via high-tech means. For example, several companies, such as Lifescan and Roche, developed software packages to supplement their diagnostic monitors by tracking trends over time for use in the development of treatment plans.

FURTHER READING

"At-Home Testing: Beyond the Basics." *Drug Store News,* 3 March 1997.

"Boomers Embrace Home Testing Kits." *MMR,* 18 September 2000.

"Consumers Take Charge of Health Care." *Research Alert,* 15 January 1999.

"Health-Mark Gives Consumers More Control." *Chain Drug Review,* 7 June 1997.

"Home Test Kits: The Category Hits Its Stride." *Chain Drug Review,* 10 August 1998.

"Home Testing Probably Saved Lives: LifeSource Survey." *Drug Stoe News,* 26 June 2000.

Ignelzi, R. J. "Do-It-Yourself Diagnoses Offer a Way to Find out What Ails You." *San Diego Union-Tribune,* 8 May 2000.

Key, Sandra W., and Daniel J. DeNoon. "Home Diagnostic Telemedicine Products Agreement Announced." *AIDS Weekly Plus,* 15 September 1997.

Kyriakos, Tina. "Consumers Buy into Home Testing." *Drug Store News,* 17 May 1999.

———. "Self-Care, Innovation Boost Today's Home Health Offering." *Drug Store News,* 20 March 2000.

Littman, Margaret. "Home Health Tests." *Marketing News,* 5 July 1999.

Marquez, Rachelle C. "Home Self-Testing Market Grows as Medical Costs Rise." *Business Journal Serving San Jose & Silicon Valley,* 3 November 1997.

Merson, Michael H., and Eric A. Feldman. "Rapid Self-Testing for HIV Infection." *Lancet,* 1 February 1997.

"O-T-Cs: Diabetes Test Kits: Educational Efforts Spur Diabetes Cure." *Chain Drug Review,* 4 January 1999.

Rodriguez, Alex. "More Kids Face Home Drug Tests: Parents' Demand for Kits Soars." *Chicago Sun-Times,* 2 January 1999.

Roller, Kim. "Retailers Are Optimistic about Solid Growth in Blood-Pressure Monitor Sales." *Drug Store News,* 10 April 2000.

Sauer, Pamela. "Finding the Green in OTC." *Chemical Market Reporter,* 25 October 1999.

"Self-Care Has Arrived." *About Women & Marketing,* March 1999.

"Supplier Buzz." *Drug Store News,* 23 November 1998.

MICROMACHINES AND NANOTECHNOLOGY

Broadly speaking, micromachines and nanotechnology refer to gadgetry and systems on a lilliputian scale. While the market penetration of such technology has been slight up to 2000, major research efforts over the previous few decades were beginning to pay off, and most analysts agree that the pintsized technology could usher in a new era in a wide range of fields, including medicine, computing, energy, mechanical design, manufacturing, and others. In medicine, for example, micromachines have been employed for invasive surgery, and the future of nanotechnology promises molecule-sized robots that can be trained to enter and repair internal bodily systems.

Micromachines have their roots in the miniaturization processes that lead to the development of the transistor in the 1950s, to be followed later by the integrated circuit and the microprocessor. The potential benefits of micromachine technology include vastly expanded functionality and, eventually, dramatic savings in production costs, although, to date, production is relatively expensive since the processes and system architecture are so varied throughout the industry.

The field of nanotechnology grew out of increased scientific understanding of the way in which tiny structures, such as atoms and molecules, come together and interact to form highly complex systems. Nanotechnology refers specifically to materials, devices, and systems built on the scale of a nanometer, which is equal to one ten-millionth of a centimeter, or 500 times smaller than the width of a human hair. Nanotechnology involves manipulating and harnessing chemical reactions and the molecular processes of living cells in a design aimed at a specific technological function. One of the most stifling roadblocks in nanotechnology development is that, at the nano scale, different laws of physics must be taken into account. Instead of everyday forces such as gravity, researchers working with nanotechnology must be able to negotiate quantum variables.

By 2000, there was basically no commercial market for nanotechnology, while only a few micromachine applications, such as inertial and medical sensors and automotive systems, had begun to reap significant rewards. Annual microelectrical mechanical systems (MEMS) growth was hovering around 6 percent in the late 1990s. According to Cahners In-Stat Group, the MEMS market was ready for take-off, from \$3 billion in 1999 to an expected \$7 billion in 2004. The driving force behind this market growth was the demand for optical networking applications.

Companies in the automotive and medical sectors accounted for by far the largest part of MEMS sales as the 20th century drew to a close. Established industries in the United States barely recognized the potential impact of MEMS technology on its products—micromachine producers still have to prove themselves in the market against entrenched conventional products. Characteristics that should make MEMS products profitable in the long run are size, weight, ability to solve "unsolvable" problems, and extremely low cost. As new, viable microtechnologies develop in the first decade of the 2000s, the industry is expected to expand into the profitable areas of consumer electronics, data storage, and microinstrumentation, and to buttress its hold on the auto and medical industries.

By 2000, the realms of micromachines and nanotechnology were moving toward marriage, whereby the tiny chemical processes of nanotechnology will be precisely guided by MEMS-based machines.

ORGANIZATION AND STRUCTURE

About 80 U.S. companies were active in the MEMS area in the late 1990s. About 20 of them were large organizations of international scope. MEMS usually comprise a very small percentage of the total production of these larger firms, though some, notably Motorola Inc. and Texas Instruments Inc., have been working in the field since the 1970s. The remaining U.S. MEMS companies were small businesses with an annual production of less than $10 million, or in most cases less than $5 million per year. These companies, in general, focused exclusively on MEMS and a small number of products. A significant number of small to mid-sized MEMS companies, about 30 in all, were located in the Silicon Valley. The majority have been financed with venture capital, are still doing research, and have yet to bring a product to market. In the MEMS industry it is the norm for a company, big or small, to focus on a single micromachine technology to the exclusion of all others.

Despite the enormous success of the silicon integrated circuit (IC) industry, mounting a circuit on a MEMS chip has been a low priority. In 1995, only about 12 percent of the accelerometers and 8 percent of the pressure sensors sold featured on-chip integrated circuitry. Most industry observers are convinced, however, that integrated systems with on-chip electronics will play a determining role in the future of MEMS, particularly given the availability of the IC industry's existing infrastructure. Analog Devices, among others, has produced commercially successful examples of such devices.

The most common MEMS production techniques are essentially the same as those used to produce ICs—material is deposited on a silicon disk. A pattern is imposed lithographically, and material around the pattern is removed, revealing the mechanism. Companies use this process to mass-produce large numbers of inexpensive micromechanisms—including micromachines with moving parts. Because the scale of MEMS production is larger than that of ICs, start-up companies are often able to purchase obsolete production equipment from IC manufacturers. As the MEMS industry has begun to grow, a small group of satellite concerns has grown around it—businesses from other sectors devoted to the specific needs of MEMS. A small group of marketing professionals, for example, specializes in the area. More significant is the computer software industry where new computer-aided design software and other design tools are being developed for MEMS. Microcosm and Tanner EDA are two companies that have produced such products.

Products of the micromachine industry are sold to other manufacturers for use as components in the fabrication of more complex systems. According to *Design News,* air-bag accelerometers and disposable blood-pressure transducers together accounted for 30 million MEMS devices sold in 1996. The rest of the market is small enough to be virtually nonexistent. Other microtechnology applications—gas, chemical, and rate sensors, microrelays, microdisplays, and micromachined parts—are expected to reach full commercialization only within the next five to 10 years and, by the year 2000, sensors' share of the total market hovered around 50 percent.

The university, government, and company laboratories where most of the industry's leading-edge research takes place are the vital engines powering the micromachine and nanotechnology industries. Research is critical to the development of the new technologies and products that MEMS will require to become a niche market. Funded university research is critical, because the broad interdisciplinary nature of MEMS and nanotechnology uses technologies from electrical, chemical, biomedical, and mechanical engineering, as well as from chemistry, biology, physics, and materials science. Assembling the equipment and expertise required to undertake such a wide-ranging research program is beyond the means of any but the largest multinational companies. Some insiders see the "pure" research of the university lab as a potential brake on the drive toward commercial applications that are so crucial currently, and consider it essential for companies to continue their own product-oriented research.

In the middle ground are working agreements that exist between industry and academia. A model for this type of work is the Berkeley Sensor and Actuator Center (BSAC) at the University of California-Berkeley. Founded in 1987, the BSAC is the foremost MEMS center in the world. It is an Industry-University Cooperative Research Center funded by the National Science Foundation, a 21-member cooperative including such major companies as Motorola, Honeywell, Texas Instruments, and IBM; major government labs, such as Lawrence Livermore and Sandia National Laboratories; and most of the major MEMS companies.

Members contribute $55,000 per year to the center and in return get access to labs, graduate students, and expertise. Some members also enter into private contracts to do targeted research at the center, entitling them to preferential licensing rights to any technology developed.

An important recent development at the center was I-MEMS—integrated MEMS—developed in conjunction with Analog Devices. I-MEMS are an array of linked microdevices, gyros, accelerometers, and other sensors built around a chip that is linked to a computer. Other current research includes work on computer-aided design for MEMS, a MEMS mass spectrometer, and micromirrors to miniaturize scanner technology.

Important MEMS and nanotechnology research is also being conducted at the University of Utah, the University of Wisconsin, the University of Michigan, Washington University, and Case Western Reserve University. In the late 1990s, Cornell University established the Center of Nanobiotechnology to study the integration of silicon technology with biology. Government labs active in the field include Sandia National Laboratories in Albuquerque, New Mexico; the Jet Propulsion Labs in Pasadena, California; and Lawrence Livermore Laboratories near Berkeley, California.

A measure of the industry's importance to governments throughout the world is the amount of research dollars earmarked for micromachine research. The Defense Advanced Research Projects Agency, renamed the Microsystems Technology Office in 1999, funded more than $131 million worth of research in the late 1990s. Government spending on nanotechnology in 1999 totaled $232 million and was broken down as follows: National Science Foundation, $80 million; Department of Defense, $60 million; Department of Energy, $54 million; National Institutes of Health, $5 million; Department of Commerce, $12 million; and the National Aeronautics and Space Administration (NASA), $18 million. Total federal spending on nanotechnology research and development just two years later, in fiscal year 2001, more than doubled to $497 million. Funding, albeit in significantly lower amounts, is available from other federal agencies, including the Small Business Innovative Research program of the Technical Reinvestment Program.

REGULATION

Aside from the restriction of high-technology exports the president of the United States could impose for national security reasons, the only regulation of micromachines required is FDA approval for material used in medical applications. On the other hand, federal regulation of the auto industry presented opportunities for the micromachine industry. Federal fuel economy and pollution standards in the 1970s led to the development of the micromechanical manifold air pressure sensor, a critical element in the system that regulates a car's fuel to air ratio. Similarly, air-bag laws created a market for the small, accurate accelerometers used in passenger-safety systems. Finally, the increasing development of fuel-cell systems in automobiles provided a new opportunity for MEMS sensors.

BACKGROUND AND DEVELOPMENT

The first real impetus toward the development of the micromachine and nanotechnology came from physicist Richard Feynman in a talk at the California Institute of Technology in 1959. But the industrial world was already moving in this shrinking direction. The first technological advance toward the micromachine was the discovery of a piezoresistive effect—a resistance charge created in silicon when it is under stress—at Bell Labs in 1954, a factor that made silicon an ideal candidate for sensors and accelerometers. Development continued apace throughout the 1960s and 1970s. Spurred mainly by funding from NASA, the first silicon pressure sensors were created. The National Science Foundation provided funding as well in the 1970s, albeit on a limited scale. Fairchild spawned a number of spin-off companies in the Silicon Valley that pursued silicon sensor technology: ICTransducers (now Foxboro/ICT) and National Semiconductor Sensor Group (now SenSym) were founded in 1972, Cognition (now Rosemount) in 1976.

A major turning point in the micromachine field was the publication in 1982 of *Silicon as a Mechanical Material* by Kurt Peterson, called "the father of MEMS." The paper described the unique mechanical-structural properties of silicon. (Metals such as iron, steel, and aluminum have too many structural irregularities at a microscopic level to be viable micromachine materials.) The paper was followed by the first two MEMS start-up companies in Silicon Valley: Transsensory Devices (1982) and NovaSensor (1984).

Pressure sensor designs were modified throughout the 1980s, with a great deal of impetus for these modifications coming from the automotive and medical industries. Full commercialization was finally

NANOVISIONARIES

It stands to reason that one of the earliest visionaries of nanotechnology would be a major thinker in the world of quantum physics. Richard Feynman (1918-1988), the Nobel laureate and physics giant, symbolically ushered in the age of nanotechnology in 1959 when he delivered his speech entitled "There's Plenty of Room at the Bottom" at the annual meeting of the American Physical Society at the California Institute of Technology. Feynman discussed matters that until then were purely the stuff of scientific fiction, such as building machines at the quantum level.

One of the most basic ideas in Feynman's speech was the novel notion that the microscope, that staple of the scientific laboratory, be expanded from its traditional role of simple observer of the molecular world into a creative instrument. That is, he suggested that scientists find ways to build from the "bottom up" at the molecular level rather than simply viewing the molecular level from the "top down."

The speech was a feat of prescience that described the possibility of computing, mechanical production, and information storage, as well as the unique characteristics of materials and machines on the molecular level.

Over 20 years later, in 1981, Eric Drexler had taken Feynman's vision to heart and produced the first scientific paper presenting a plausible, theoretical program for nanotechnology. Ten years after that, Drexler paved the way for the field in academia by receiving the first doctorate in nanotechnology from the Massachusetts Institute of Technology. In his 1987 book, *Engines of Creation,* Drexler spelled out his vision for nanotechnology, setting the industry on its present course. The book, a study of molecular machines, explained that simple, tiny "machines" work to build complex objects and systems as a mater of course throughout nature; in a sense, everything was a product of micromachines. Simply by mimicking the manufacturing processes that take place on the molecular level in nature, it was theoretically possible to create useful, man-made machines. Drexler went on to found the Foresight Institute to disseminate nanotechnology information on a mass scale.

reached around 1990. Sales of micromachine pressure sensors increased from about 3 million units a year in 1983 to over 50 million units by 1995, and continued to grow at double-digit rates. There were expectations that 125 million units will be sold in first decade of the new century.

Micromachined accelerometers, used primarily as crash sensors in automotive air-bag systems, are the other micromachine application brought to market on a mass scale, though nowhere near the degree of the pressure sensor. First developed between 1985 and 1990, sales grew from about $200,000 in 1992 to $13 to $15 million in 1995. A few other micromachined products have begun to enter the marketplace, including ink-jet heads for printers, read/write heads for magnetic hard drives, fuel-injection nozzles for autos, and video chips for high-resolution television. The impact of these products has thus far been minimal.

CURRENT CONDITIONS

In the late 1990s, the micromachine industry ended a childhood characterized by a long period of research "push," and began an adolescence where a growing commercialization—it is hoped—will create market "pull" and will draw the industry into a period of sustained growth. The lithography-based techniques of silicon batch processing developed by the integrated circuit (IC) are considered to be the key to low-cost micromachining by the industry in the United States. The present infrastructure—adapting old IC production facilities to MEMS needs—is seen as advantageous for small firms wishing to enter the market. This infrastructure is not considered optimal for generating or supporting the manufacturing energy needed to push beyond the prototype stage to the mass production stage. It is seen as a potential brake on MEMS manufacturing technology. With MEMS's limited effect on IC manufacturers, there is no need felt in those quarters to create new solutions to the problems facing the MEMS industry. With relatively low revenues, most of which are tied up in applications research and product development, the micromachine industry is at present unable to pursue those solutions on its own.

Optical and magnetic sensors were to receive even further refinement following a grant by the U.S. government's Small Business Innovative Research program awarded to NanoSciences Corp., which aimed at the development of micromachines for burrowing holes in silicon so as to convert light rays. This technique is intended for the creation of self-contained position sensors for MEMS devices, using a magnetic field to get a precise position fix by reading the system's voltage. Such systems find use in medical, security, and industrial applications.

As research projects developed, many remarkable science-fiction fantasies began to turn into reality. A team of Japanese electronics firms developed microscopic plumbers, rolling out micromachines designed to probe pipes, especially in power plants, and isolate and repair them. Expected to experience their first duties in Japanese power plants, these robots, at a weight of about 1/70 ounce each, will invade leaky pipes and end up acting as component parts by connecting to the pipes with couplings affixed to their sides.

At the University of Southern California's Information Science Institute, a production process was developed that could make the fabrication of micromachines far more efficient. The process, known as Efab, for "electrochemical fabrication," employs a unit, small enough for a desktop, that accepts images from a computer to reproduce three-dimensional (3-D) complex shapes for the production of new micromachines. A similar process has been used for years for the 3-D design of planes and automobiles.

Carbon nanotubes, which were nearly ready to move into industrial production in early 2000, offer a wide range of potential uses. Carbon nanotubes conduct electricity and heat highly efficiently through tiny strips of graphite with unpaired electrons. Some applications for carbon nanotubes include acting as wires for micromachine computer components, flat-screen televisions, and computer monitors, and as hydrogen-storage units in fuel cells.

The U.S. government saw enough promise in nanotechnology to increase its funding for its development 84 percent to $497 million in the 2001 budget. In addition, President Bill Clinton called for the creation of a National Nanotechnology Initiative (NNI) in January 2000 to integrate nanotechnology and information technology. While most of the bulk of this money will go toward basic research, approximately $100 million was earmarked for "grand challenges," as the White House called them, including such pet projects as cancer-treating nanobots, machines to clear water pollution, boosted computer speed by a factor of millions, and "shrinking the entire Library of Congress into a device the size of a sugar cube."

New MEMS and nanotechnology applications were likely to be heavily concentrated in the sciences. By 2000, MEMS technology itself had created a laboratory of sorts in which biotechnology researchers could test biochemical reactions for the study and manipulation of DNA strains. Moreover, one of the most ambitious nanoprojects is DNA computer technology, and data storage in general. DNA computing was hailed as a new and ultrapowerful development intended to rival high-speed supercomputers in the storage and processing of large amounts of complex information.

CHALLENGES

Difficulties lie in finding new applications for MEMS, creating a group of basic products that can be simply and easily modified to meet a broad range of customer needs, and establishing a manufacturing infrastructure to support a large market. In short, establishing the silicon-based MEMS techniques in the market will depend upon volume production.

The outlook for MEMS is strong, although estimates of near-future growth vary. In early 1999 experts at Sandia National Laboratories, a major center of micromachine research, projected the entire MEMS industry at as much as $30 billion early in the 21st century. Gary Title, a technology manager at 3M Corp., projected it at $10 to $14 billion by 2001. European estimates of the world market for micromachines in the year 2002 range from $15 to $38 billion, according to *Electronic Times*.

There are a few specific areas that MEMS need to develop in order to lay a foundation for commercial success:

- The lithographic and etching methodologies of the IC industries will have to be modified to reflect micromachining's need for greater 3-D focus (in contrast to integrated circuitry's drive toward ever-greater degrees of miniaturization).

- MEMS need their own specialized design tools in order to continue product development. New firms are already creating computer-aided design software specifically for the micromachine industry, and a major contract was awarded in 1998 by the Defense Advanced Research Projects Agency for the development of an engineering kit to enable design engineers not expert in MEMS fabrication methods to create workable designs.

- Micromachine companies will have to develop low-cost, accurate, and implementable product testing techniques on a mass scale if potential clients are to be convinced of the reliability of MEMS products.

- One of the most serious questions to be addressed by the industry is micromachine packaging—the outer case of the micromachine that must insulate its sensitive inner workings from external factors (e.g., chemicals or electrical conductivity), without interfering with other operations of the machine.

Even when MEMS overcome these problems, manufacturers will have to compete with the "macro" products already established in the marketplace. This means not only being smaller than the competition, but better and more versatile, with improved performance, and above all cheaper.

The production process was a limiting factor for mass-market availability of nanotechnology at the turn of the century, since the customization process required for each design necessitated extensive research and production costs. The standard micromachining technique involves the application of a series of layers of materials on silicon in a high-temperature setting, and requires a great deal of intensive labor from skilled technicians. Typically, the entire process of physically creating a new micromachine typically takes over two months. In total, it typically takes two to three years to develop a prototype, and another one to three years to design the larger system for which the microcomponent is intended.

As with many highly advanced scientific developments, nanotechnology and MEMS were not immune from fears of misuse and ethical violations. The science-fiction overtones of some of the potential developments, particularly medical nanobots, arouse concerns over the ability of these tiny machines to carry viruses or other destructive materials. Such fears were not limited to the fringes of society or to technophobes, moreover. The cofounder of Sun Microsystems, Bill Joy, announced his concerns that such technology, if not properly controlled, could find its way into the hands of extreme individuals, affording them too much capacity for mayhem. Still, most scientists held that such fears were grossly overstated and premature, contending that for the time being most of the research was invested in simply learning how the technology really works in the first place, and thus the ability to unleash Armageddon was a long way off.

INDUSTRY LEADERS

Involvement in microelectrical mechanical systems (MEMS) is spread across a wide range of companies, all with varying degrees of involvement in the industry. Three large electronics companies for which involvement in commercial micromachine production is a small but growing part of their businesses are Motorola Inc., Texas Instruments Inc., and Analog Devices Inc. Major breakthroughs have also come from companies such as Lucent Technologies Inc.'s Bell Laboratories. In addition, there are a number of companies that began specifically as MEMS developers.

THREE DIVERSIFIED ELECTRONICS COMPANIES

Motorola has been engaged in MEMS research since the late 1970s but did not release its first product, a pressure sensor, until the mid-1980s, when it formally founded a sensor product division, called Senseon. Motorola's primary MEMS products are pressure sensors for the automotive and medical markets and accelerometers for auto air-bag systems. Research for the pressure sensor and accelerometer was conducted in-house, and technology for Motorola's new chemical sensor was licensed from a small independent company—a trend the company intends to continue in order to cut new product development time. In the future, Motorola will move toward more integrated sensor/actuator systems, and many of those will be aimed at the auto industry, an area of large potential growth and one that can spin off numerous applications into the industrial sector. The company expects sensors to be the next hot commercial product and have named them as one of four key initiatives for future growth, with a commitment of future funds and manpower.

Texas Instruments (TI) has been doing MEMS work since 1977, but its first commercial application was not released until 1987—a print chip with 840 mirrors designed to print tickets and boarding passes for the airline industry. Fewer than 1,000 were sold, but out of that research grew TI's big micromachine application, the digital micromirror device (DMD). The DMD was designed as a video component for home television, teleconferencing, and projection theaters. DMD is based on a million fluctuating mirrors that act to project an image onto the screen. Each mirror, only 16 microns square, represents a single pixel, and serves as a viable solution to many of the problems associated with image projection. The company positioned it as a key technology in the high-definition television market. The DMD is TI's only current or projected MEMS product, and can be modified by adding more mirrors to increase brightness and resolution. TI has set up an advanced MEMS production facility in which 600-800 people work on developing and producing the DMD. Competition comes from manufacturers of traditional liquid crystal displays and cathode ray tubes, primarily in Japan, which can still be manufactured and sold much more cheaply than DMDs. TI currently sells about 100,000 DMDs a year, which amounts to about 20 percent of the projection display market. TI's total sales for 1999 were $9.47 billion, but micromachined products were only a minuscule part.

Analog Devices, a leading manufacturer of micromachined accelerometers, is one of the mid-sized members of the MEMS world. Founded in 1965 as an electronic module company, its first MEMS product was an air-bag crash sensor that was first integrated into the 1994 Saab 900. The company produces five accelerometer models currently; five others are about to go into production. Analog had about one-third of the world air-bag accelerometer market in 1998, with a corporate clientele list that included Ford and Volkswagen. Analog's sales in 1999 were estimated at $1.45 billion, of which the Micro Machines Products Division accounted for a small but growing portion. The company announced plans to sell $320 million worth of MEMS by the year 2002, amounting to 10 percent of total revenue. Three hundred Analog employees, about 25 percent of them engineers, are currently active in the MEMS division. In 1998 Analog announced that its fourth-generation accelerometer had been designed into computer-game pads, the first MEMS application in the realm of consumer products. By 2000 it had also been designed into an earthquake sensing device, a vehicle security system, navigation devices, computer peripherals, and a device to guard against back injuries. Analong's purchase of the Irish firm BCO Technologies plc in 2000 highlighted its heightened focus on micromachined components for optical switching.

MEMS START-UP COMPANIES

EG&G IC Sensors' products are spread across the MEMS market; medical, industrial, and automotive are its leading market sectors. A special area of involvement for the company is custom silicon micromachining: applying its special MEMS expertise to meet the special requirements of particular customers. Custom microstructures have included detection cantilevers for atomic force microscopes, pressure arrays for noninvasive blood-pressure monitoring, electrostatically driven microrelays, microcoolers for high-power electronic components, and read/write coils for optical disk drives. EG&G IC Sensors employs over 275 workers at two manufacturing facilities, one in Milpitas, California, the other in Santa Clara, California. The company was collaborating with Perkin Elmer Corp.'s Applied Biosystems Division to develop MEMS for genetic analyses and detection.

Lucas NovaSensor, a division of the high-tech firm TRW, Inc., produces more silicon sensors every year than any other company. Founded in 1985 by Kurt Peterson, NovaSensor's first product was a micromachined disposable blood-pressure sensor monitor. In 1990 LucasVarity purchased NovaSensor. At the end of the decade more than half the company's total sales were made to the medical industry for use in invasive and noninvasive procedures. The majority of their business is in pressure sensors, but they produce proportional valves, optical switches, DNA analyzers, and microchips for use in various consumer and industrial applications. Lucas NovaSensor employs about 150 employees, 25 percent of whom are engineers. Key research is now underway on deep ion reactive etching, work begun under federal contract.

BEI Technologies, Inc. was already a leading supplier of conventional sensors when it became involved in MEMS in the mid-1980s. Its first commercial micromachined product, an automotive gyroscope originally developed under government contract, was used in 1997 Cadillacs and Corvettes as part of an antiskid device. General Motors Corp. was its largest customer for this gyro, which was the first of its kind anywhere. Thus far BEI has been the only company that has been able to produce it reliably and repeatably. The automotive industry is BEI's primary market, although it has customers in the aerospace and industrial sectors as well. In addition to the gyros, the company produces a line of micromachined mechanical sensors, position sensors, pressure sensors, and accelerometers. In 1999 the company's total sales increased 28 percent to reach $159.4 million, and it employed 1,110 workers.

Breed Technologies, Inc., is a leading supplier to the automotive industry, supplying steering wheels and other plastic components as well as air bags and air-bag components. Its sensor products are also used in nonautomotive applications. In 1998 it opened a 126,000-square-foot plant dedicated to the manufacture of micromachined sensor devices. It was equipped to produce 10 million sensors annually, with expansion possible to 50 million. Breed maintained a payroll of 16,300 employees in 1999, although that year it went on the market, having worked itself into debt through a series of acquisitions and filing for Chapter 11 bankruptcy protection. In 2000 the company was picked up by the auto components firm Harvard Industries.

AMERICA AND THE WORLD

So far international competition in the production of micromachines and nanotechnology is very slight, if only because the market is so underdeveloped. U.S. companies accounted for 45 percent of world pressure sensor production and sales in the late 1990s. Small start-up companies, which lead the drive in bringing new technologies to the marketplace, are a far smaller market force in Europe and Japan, which accounts partly for what insiders see as a slow pace of commercialization in the MEMS arena. There were about 75 companies in the MEMS industry in Japan, about

35 in Germany, and a few more in other Western European countries and Korea.

New international competition was announced in 1998 by South Korea's Daewoo Electronics in the form of a micromirror array similar to Texas Instruments' DMD, except that it is controlled by analog signals rather than digital. According to Daewoo, the analog circuitry is simpler and cheaper than digital, and enables finer adjustments to the mirrors and a brighter image.

But while market influence was minimal, research investments in nanotechnology have escalated rapidly in the last few years, notably in Japan, where nanotechnology is geared primarily toward semiconductors. Companies such as Hitachi, Toshiba, and NEC were all engaged in the development of a silicon nanocrystal memory device. Japanese industry is pursuing approaches similar to those in the United States, but the 10-year, $250 million program in micromachines sponsored by the Ministry of International Trade and Industry (MITI) emphasizes miniaturizing more traditional machining methods, which has not been pursued in the United States. MITI's Atom Technology Project also funded the analysis of DNA base sequences on the nanolevel.

Meanwhile, the European Commission established a new program to promote research and development in MEMS. Nexus, the Europe-wide organization established to promote micromachines under the initiative to increase the competitiveness of European industry (called Europractice), has set up what it calls a "distributed Silicon Valley." The effort spans 12 countries and involves dozens of companies and research institutions organized into a number of clusters, with members of each cluster sharing expertise and facilities, even manufacturing facilities. The hope is that this infrastructure will enable the microsystems market to fulfill its potential in Europe.

RESEARCH AND TECHNOLOGY

Innovative production processes also boosted the efficiency and usefulness of MEMS. Sandia National Laboratories pioneered a production process whereby nanotechnology components assimilate five layers of polysilicon, the highest number of layers yet allowed attainable. The benefits of more layers include the ability of micromachine components to perform more complex tasks. According to *Machine Design,* three layers allows for the creation of gears with hubs, while four layers can generate linkage arms throughout the plane of gears. With the five-layer process developed by Sandia, complex, interactive components can be manipulated on moving platforms. Adding layers of polysilicon is tricky because each new layer inherits the textural qualities of those underneath it, thereby adding surface protrusions that can interfere with the gears if not factored into the design. Sandia solved this problem by implementing a process that smooths out the protrusions with chemical oxide before each new layer is added.

Durability was another serious concern among micromachine manufacturers, and research efforts were spearheaded to find more wear-resistant materials that were also compatible with the precise functions for which they were intended. In that spirit, Sandia National Laboratories pushed research on amorphous diamonds, the second-hardest material on Earth after crystalline diamond. Researchers have long coveted diamond as a nanotechnology material due to its durability and biocompatibility. In 2000 Sandia announced that it had successfully developed the first diamond micromachine, which added the benefit of compatibility with existing manufacturing techniques. Amorphous diamond, essentially a form of chemically benign carbon, was slated as a potentially useful material in medical nanotechnology, as it would not generate allergic reactions.

According to *Electronic Design,* researchers speculated that amorphous diamond could enhance durability in wear applications by a factor of 10,000. Moreover, since the material was compatible with silicon chips already in production, Sandia even suggested that silicon micromachines with diamond layers could wind up replacing polysilicon machines. Sandia's premier diamond micromachine was a diamond comb driver to be used in a microengine piston.

Scientists were also harnessing the information-storage capabilities of DNA molecules for use in micromachine technology that could potentially generate information systems far more powerful than the current generation of supercomputers. Researchers at the University of Wisconsin pushed this technology ahead several steps toward the production of DNA-based computers, which will harbor hundreds of millions of DNA molecules each carrying tremendous amounts of data and memory. In DNA computing, any specific problem can be solved by a process of elimination, in which the molecules, each identified as carrying a possible answer to a particular problem, are weeded through until only the DNA molecule with the correct answer is left standing. To spur this process, the molecules are exposed to catalysts designed to execute a particular operation.

The University of Wisconsin team successfully employed hybridization chemistry to facilitate this identification process. Initial tests found that the DNA chips were capable of solving multistep mathematical problems, and as the technology is further refined, it was expected to tackle far more complex problems than can currently be solved by digital technology. The full potential of such tiny DNA supercomputers, in the form of tiny supercomputers, will not be realized, however, until researchers discover an appropriate architecture in which to store the millions of molecules.

FURTHER READIN]G

Allan, Roger. "Diamond Micromachines Could Be a Designer's Best Friend." *Electronic Design,* 3 April 2000.

Appenzeller, Tim. "The Chemistry of Computing." *U.S. News & World Report,* 1 May 2000.

Belsie, Laurent. "Nanotechnology's Descent into Matter's Minuteness." *Christian Science Monitor,* 13 April 2000.

Bender, Bryan. "Miniaturization." *Jane's Defence Weekly,* 25 October 2000.

Brown, Chappell. "Materials Scientists Tap Micromachining to Aid Sensor Performance." *Electronic Engineering Times,* 3 January 2000.

Burggraaf, Pieter. "Microelectronics' Nanotechnology Future." *Solid State Technology,* January 2000.

Hart, Matthew, and Meng-Hsiung Kiang. "MEMS Enhance Optical Switching." *Electronic Engineering Times,* 17 July 2000.

Johnson, R. Colin. "DNA Computing Finds New Life." *Electronic Engineering Times,* 14 February 2000.

———. "Sandia Builds the First Diamond Micromachine." *Electronic Engineering Times,* 13 March 2000.

Johnson, R. Colin, and Chappell Brown. "Frontiers of Nanotechnology, MEMS Converge." *Electronic Engineering Times,* 24 April 2000.

Koucky, Sherri, and Stephen Mraz. "Sophisticated Layering Will Usher in More Complex Micromachines." *Machine Design,* 24 February 2000.

Longman, Phillip J., Janet Rae-Dupree, and Charles W. Petit. "The Next Big Thing is Small." *U.S. News & World Report,* 3 July 2000.

Marshall, Sid. "Nanotech Moves Forward." *R&D Magazine,* February 2000.

McDonald, Glenn, Cameron Crotty, and Michelle Campanale-Surkan. "The Digital Future." *PC World,* January 2000.

"Microbots Fix Pipe Leaks." *Popular Mechanics,* December 1999.

Murphy, Tom. "Switching Light at the Speed of Light: MEMS Poised for Explosive Growth in Fiber Optic Networks." *ENEWS,* 23 October 2000.

"Nanotechnology and the Future." *Poptronics,* April 2000.

"Nanotechnology Overview." *Advanced Materials & Processes,* May 2000.

Quan, Margaret. "USC's Efab Could Become Standard for MEMS." *Electronic Engineering Times,* 3 May 1999.

Rotman, David. "Intelligent Self-Assembly." *Technology Review,* March/April 2000.

"Silicon Valley Killjoy." *U.S. News & World Report,* 3 April 1999.

Swaine, Michael. "Atom by Atom." *Dr. Dobb's Journal: Software Tools for the Professional Programmer,* March 2000.

"Tanner EDA and Sandia National Laboratories to Deliver New Design Kit for MEMS Technology." *Business Wire,* 1 March 1999.

Thibodeau, Patrick. "White House Seeks More Money for Nanotechnology." *Computerworld,* 14 February 2000.

MICROWAVE APPLICATIONS

Microwave technology applies to many industries other than the most obvious one—food preparation. Radar, medicine, chemistry, and telecommunications have increasingly relied on this form of electromagnetic energy. The entire electromagnetic range (in order of increasing frequency) includes: radiowaves, infrared radiation, visible radiation (light), ultraviolet radiation, X rays, and cosmic radiation. Within the telecommunications industry, microwave technology is used for some conventional mobile radios and telephones, all cellular telephones, all television broadcast channels above channel 13, satellite communications systems, and high-speed computers. In the late 1990s and the beginning of the new decade, this segment of the industry expanded quickly because of heightened demand for high-speed Internet access.

Microwave energy has been applied to food preparation since 1950. Conventional heating combines two disadvantages—slowness and inefficiency—because it warms food gradually with heat entering from the outside. In contrast, microwaves create heat only when absorbed by the object they cook, resulting in rapid, even heating. Microwave technology works best on materials that hold some water and don't conduct electricity particularly well. Since microwaves focus energy, much less floor space is necessary in comparison to conventional heating and drying equipment.

Many other industries have reaped the benefits of microwave technology for heating and drying purposes. The chemical industry employed microwave technology in curing coatings, cross-linking polymers, and plasma polymerization. Printers and photographers have used microwave drying of film and ink curing to work more efficiently. Also, a microwave kiln for processing of ceramic raw materials has also been successful. Despite its success, however, microwave energy to heat materials is not as widespread as some of its proponents believe it should be. One reason is that radio-frequency heating, a related and more established technology, was more popular than microwave technology in such processes as plastics welding and wood gluing. Second, there are a great variety of microwave uses, and most use different kinds of equipment. Some companies are understandably reluctant to invest in one microwave-related product, only to realize they should have chosen another.

ORGANIZATION AND STRUCTURE

Microwave applications are found in a number of industries including telecommunications carriers, electronic device and component manufacturers, and the appliance industry. Certain firms, generally smaller companies, focus more exclusively on microwave applications, but large electronics firms, such as Matsushita, and telecommunications giants, such as Motorola and WorldCom, have a great impact on the industry overall.

The wireless cable industry in the United States in 2000 had about 250 systems serving more than 1 million customers. Although the first systems appeared in 1984, the industry never took off as expected. Most of these systems used an analog signal to provide multiple television channels to consumers, competing with wireline cable providers, or filling gaps where conventional cable was not available.

These systems primarily operated in the 2.1-2.3 gigahertz (GHz) spectrum. At the end of the 1990s, the Federal Communications Commission (FCC) ruled that two-way communication could be used in this spectrum, and the new spectrum became available in the 24 GHz spectrum, which opened up new possibilities. Also, manufacturers and software developers continued to make improvements that increased the capabilities of microwave systems. The industry looked toward broadband communication of data such as Internet access as the future of the industry, and these developments attracted the attention of the broader telecommunications industry.

By 1999 microwave ovens had reached the status of a household necessity in the United States. According to a report cited in *Forecast* magazine, 93 percent of homes in the United States had a microwave. All major appliance lines included microwaves of various sizes, wattage, and features. Larger and sometimes more sophisticated models were made for commercial kitchens.

REGULATION

Like the rest of the telecommunications industry, regulation of wireless cable companies was drastically reduced by the Telecommunications Act of 1996. Most radio frequencies, however, including most microwave frequencies, are licensed by the FCC, although some telecommunications companies operate on unlicensed frequencies. This gives them easier access to the frequency, but also makes interference more likely. The FCC continues to regulate the telecommunications industry to some degree in order to promote orderly development and proper competition.

Microwave ovens have been regulated by the U.S. Food and Drug Administration (FDA) since 1971. Medical devices that use microwave energy are also regulated by the FDA.

BACKGROUND AND DEVELOPMENT

The term "microwave region" is generally defined as falling in the upper section of the radio frequency range of the electromagnetic spectrum, under that of infrared radiation. Microwave is defined differently by different groups. The FCC identifies the lower end of the range at a frequency of 890 megahertz (MHz), or 890 million cycles per second; the Institute of Electrical and Electronics Engineers defines microwave frequencies beginning at 1000 MHz. More general definitions extend the range from 300 MHz to 300

GHz—equivalent to 300 billion cycles per second. Regardless of the definition, the term "microwave" in general pertains to one segment of the whole electromagnetic spectrum.

German physicist Heinrich Rudolph Hertz (1857-1894) was the first person who intentionally generated electromagnetic energy at microwave frequencies in his experiments to verify the existence of electromagnetic waves. By 1920 other scientists were generating frequencies exceeding 3700 GHz; these relatively low energy levels, however, could not be easily controlled. In 1931 the first microwave-radio link for telephone use connected Dover, England, and Calais, France.

During World War II, major microwave innovations began in earnest. Microwave technology generated the higher frequencies necessary for the use of radar in airplanes. In 1947 the first point-to-point microwave-radio relay system began, connecting Boston and New York City. By 1951 the first coast-to-coast system was in effect. By the 1960s microwave technology (specifically, two-way wireless communications) manifested itself in the citizens-band radio trend. Eventually, though, because of its reputation for undependable analog transmission quality, microwave technology faced tougher times in the 1980s. Many local telephone companies also deployed high bandwidth digital services around this time.

By the 1990s, however, microwave communication technology made something of a comeback. With access to an electromagnetic spectrum formerly reserved to the military sphere, many established and start-up companies took advantage of the digital compression of video channels in the telecommunications industry. This development allowed wireless cable systems to deliver up to 200 virtual channels of video. From 1980 to the mid-1990s, the total number of licensed microwave-radio stations in the United States rose from about 22,000 to more than 100,000.

The telecommunications landscape in the 1990s appeared very different from that of any other time in history. In 1996 nearly two-thirds of all long-distance telephone calls were delivered via microwave. Pager and cellular telephones represented two of the most successful examples of wireless technology. The widespread application of both products prompted many telephone companies to worry about exhausting their supply of telephone number exchanges. (Also see the essay in this book entitled Wireless Communications.)

The microwave spectrum is an enormous domain with 100 times as much frequency space for communications in the microwave range as in the whole spectrum beneath that bandwidth. A wireless cable is a broadband service that may deliver addressable, multichannel television programming, access to the Internet, data transfer services, and other interactive benefits. The wireless cable system has three main components—the transmit site, the signal path, and the receive site. These systems receive their programming from satellites that transmit a signal downward to the cable operator's receiving station. The operator then converts that signal to a microwave frequency and broadcasts it to subscribers from a transmitting tower. These signals can travel up to 50 miles.

Wireless cable customers have a rooftop antenna, a piece of equipment that receives the signal and transforms it into a cable frequency. The rooftop antenna may be installed on a single dwelling unit or on a multiple dwelling unit. These antennas generally fall into two categories—microwave antennas to capture the wireless cable signals and VHF/UHF antennas to receive the local broadcast channels. The signal is then decoded and unscrambled for viewing. Some analog wireless cable systems use microwaves to deliver local channels.

The FCC set up rules and regulations for wireless cable operators in 1983, and the first wireless cable system emerged in 1984. For several years, the wired cable industry thwarted its program subsidiaries' attempts to sell on fair and nondiscriminatory terms to new competitors. That changed in 1992 when Congress passed the Cable Competition and Consumer Protection Act, which allowed fair access to programming for cable rivals.

Until 1996 the FCC gave each wireless cable licensee the legal right to operate particular multipoint multichannel distribution service channels within a protected service area (PSA). Generally, a PSA's radius was 15 miles and was shielded from signal interference from other close transmissions. In 1996 the FCC overhauled this system and divided the United States into 493 basic trading areas (BTAs), each of which was auctioned to the greatest bidder. Under the new rules, each licensee operated as before, although with the implementation of BTAs, the incumbent PSAs were enlarged to cover 35 miles.

In July 1996 the FCC issued a declaratory ruling that allowed wireless cable operators to digitize their licensed channels as long as neighboring wireless cable systems suffered no interference from the analog-to-digital conversion procedure. One result of this ruling was that wireless cable could transmit up to 200 digitized channels of video, a considerable improvement over the original 33 analog channels per market.

In the United States, the wireless cable industry ballooned from about 200,000 subscribers in 1992 to 1 million by the mid-1990s. According to the Wireless Cable Association International, by 1997 roughly 5 million people in 80 countries subscribed to wireless systems. At the same time, more than 200 wireless cable systems existed in the United States. Mexico City, Mexico, particularly thrived on wireless cable with more than 600,000 subscribers in its service area.

MICROWAVE COOKING

In 1946 the Raytheon Co. filed a patent applying microwaves to cook food. An oven that heated food with microwave energy was put in a restaurant in Boston, Massachusetts, for testing. The original weighed more than 750 pounds and cost more than $5,000. Given its bulkiness and expense, initial sales were not impressive.

In 1962 Dr. Roberta Oppenheimer perfected the world's first Underwriters Laboratories-approved microwave oven. While unsophisticated by the standards of the new century, it could prepare a 12-pound turkey in slightly less than two hours, as compared to six hours in a conventional oven. With this development making international headlines, the U.S. government proceeded with plans to install the new ovens in homes and restaurants.

The U.S. Department of Health and Welfare eventually took responsibility for production of microwave ovens, while many scientists worried about the potential abuse of other nations latching onto microwave cooking. By the mid-1960s the Soviet Union had its own microwave ovens. By the late 1960s, many more countries were producing microwave ovens of their own.

In 1972 the North Atlantic Microwave Organization (NAMO) was founded in an attempt to prevent franchised microwave ovens produced in communist countries from infringing upon models made in the Western world. NAMO also created standards for maximum power levels and radioactivity. By 1975 sales of microwave ovens outdistanced that of gas ranges. By the 1980s the United States and Europe were manufacturing microwave ovens in record numbers.

CURRENT CONDITIONS

TELECOMMUNICATIONS

Entering the new decade, the telecommunications segment of the microwave application industry experienced expansion and consolidation. The explosive popularity of the Internet during this period drove the expansion of microwave-based telecommunications, leading many in the telecommunications industry to recognize the need for the capability to transmit large volumes of data without the use of landlines. With the newly granted right to use two-way digital signals, existing wireless cable companies took steps to move into this market by converting their systems to digital, an expensive proposition. Many of them found themselves in debt beyond their capability to maintain.

By the late 1990s, the FCC helped wireless cable operators branch out into high-speed digital data applications, including Internet access. In 2000 some of the U.S. cities that offered such access included Washington, D.C.; Las Vegas, Nevada; Lakeland, Florida; Colorado Springs, Colorado; Dallas/Fort Worth, Texas; Santa Rosa, California; New York City; Seattle, Washington; Rochester, New York; San Jose/Silicon Valley, California; and Nashua, New Hampshire. Hence, by 2000 wireless cable telecommunications providers had garnered over 1 million subscribers in 250 U.S. systems and 5 million subscribers in 90 countries.

By 1997 a new group of products applied microwave technology to connect local area networks (LANs) at speeds of 10,000 bits per second and at distances of up to 15 miles. Companies such as Southwest Microwave, Inc. and Microwave Bypass Systems, Inc., in particular, capitalized on this relatively low-risk, low-cost trend. Unfortunately, some shortcomings in using microwave technology to connect LANs exist. These include forests, which, like highrise buildings, can obstruct communication; poor weather; and long distances, all of which can create similar problems.

At the end of the 1990s, the FCC put up for auction 986 licenses for local multipoint distribution service systems. These licenses for frequencies in the 28 GHz range opened up still more possibilities and attracted the interest of wireless entrepreneurs such as Craig McCaw, called "the father of cellular." Given the very large amount of transmission capability of these frequencies and their fiberlike reliability, the primary use of these licenses was expected to be for high-speed data transmission and Internet access.

The possibilities of broadband wireless communication in the lower frequencies used by the older wireless cable operators also attracted the interest of telecom giants, goading a spate of consolidations at the brink of the new century. In 1999 Sprint Corp., the third-largest U.S. long-distance company, agreed to acquire People's Choice TV, American Telecasting, Wireless Holdings, Transworld Telecommunications, Inc., and Videotron USA, all wireless cable companies. At the same time, MCI WorldCom (which became known as WorldCom in mid-2000) agreed to purchase CAI Wireless Systems and Wireless One. Besides Internet access and data transmission, these assets could be developed to enable these companies to bypass the local telephone company to reach the individual home or business for regular telephone service. In early 2000, MCI WorldCom proposed a merger with Sprint, which shareholders of both companies approved. This merger would have created a global wireless telecommunications powerhouse. The merger was shot down by the antitrust team at the U.S. Justice Department; the proposed marriage also sparked harsh criticism from the European Commission.

MICROWAVE OVENS

According to a survey by the Harris Corp., U.S. consumers ranked the microwave among the five most important household technologies. In addition, consumers were getting more value for their money when purchasing a microwave oven in the late 1990s and the beginning of the new decade. New models of microwaves had more features and more power, at nearly the same prices as earlier models. According to *Appliance* magazine's shipment statistics, 1999 shipments of household and commercial microwaves in the United States reached 11,421,900 units, up 10 percent from 1998. Consequently, microwave ovens represented the best-selling major cooking appliance. Over 90 percent of U.S. households stored a microwave oven, and demand throughout the rest of the world was climbing. Worldwide microwave oven shipments were expected to climb another 3.7 percent in 2000 to reach 31 million units.

MEDICINE

By the late 1990s medicine increasingly used microwave applications. In 1996 the Prostatron became the first microwave device to treat an enlarged prostate (benign prostatic hyperplasia) in men. Manufactured by EDAP Technomed Group, this piece of machinery uses microwaves to eradicate excess prostate tissue. Restricted to medium-sized prostate glands, the procedure usually lasts an hour and can be done on an outpatient basis with local anesthetic. The FDA has approved of this procedure, which provides people suffering from benign prostatic hyperplasia a third treatment option. While medications sometimes cause substantial side effects and surgery requires anesthesia, an extended stay at a hospital, and a longer recuperation period, the microwave therapy can often be performed in a doctor's office without side effects, an extended stay, or a long recuperation period, according to *RN*.

In the late 1970s, Augustine Cheung, a microwave engineer, was exploring possibilities in microwave hyperthermia (heat therapy) to eventually cure cancer. Undeterred by the lack of research funds, he started Cheung Laboratories in the early 1990s to sell microwave hyperthermia systems. Even though his company experienced a $1.3 million loss on revenues of $157,618 in 1995, Cheung remained committed to his own original purpose, encouraged by studies that indicated a 90 percent response rate in applying extreme heat to destroy cancerous cells. The side effects caused by burning surrounding tissue, however, often outweighed the technology's benefits. To eliminate such side effects, Cheung began applying an adaptive focusing technique called adaptive phased array, developed by the Massachusetts Institute of Technology.

A third medical microwave application in the 1990s was for dissolving varicose veins. In 1996 Dynamic Associates Inc., a holding company that contains two subsidiaries—P & H Laboratories Inc. and Microwave Medical Corp.—owned the patent for a technology in which a metal wand is employed to focus microwave energy on varicose veins. The procedure disintegrates the tissue, then collapses the vein. It is generally less painful than the more established practice of relying on a needle to insert a saline or acidic solution in the vein.

Microwave technology was also used in the late 1990s to treat menorrhagia, a form of abnormal uterine bleeding. A *Lancet* article described a study in which microwave therapy was compared to laser, diathermy, and radio frequency electromagnetic waves. With the latter three therapies, the failure rate ranged from 19 to 56 percent, and many complications ensued. By contrast, microwave therapy achieved an 83 percent success rate six months after treatment. In terms of safety, microwave proved superior to the other therapies, and medical staff found it easy to learn and perform.

In the mid-1990s Drs. Theodore and Wendy Guo, both employed by Potomac Research Inc., received a patent for microwave-imaging technology that could eventually replace the much more expensive CAT scans and magnetic resonance imaging. The National Institutes of Health and the U.S. Department of Energy have funded some of Potomac Research's efforts. Until the mid-1980s, microwaves, with relatively massive wavelengths, were considered ineffective for probing the human body. Since X rays and CAT scans had shorter wavelengths, they were the preferred technology of choice. After the Guos helped to produce an algorithm to decipher microwaves' images, however, a new microwave application seemed imminent.

By 2000, microwave therapy emerged as a possible long-term cure for those suffering from symptoms of hepatitis: hepatocellular carcinoma. Researchers at Ehime University's School of Medicine in Japan conducted a study that indicated "microwave coagulation therapy can cure some patients with multiple bipolar hepatocellular cancer," according to Charles Henderson in *Hepatitis Weekly*. For one patient, after her tumors were removed with microwave therapy, none had recurred four years later.

INDUSTRY LEADERS

In 1999 the consolidation that had been going on in the broader telecommunications industry began to grip the wireless cable segment as well. Heartland Wireless Communications, Inc., which had been the largest operator with almost 160,000 subscribers in 58 U.S. markets, emerged from bankruptcy proceedings with a new name, Nucentrix Broadband Networks Inc. Since bankruptcy proceedings, Nucentrix has concentrated on wireless Internet access service, with over 140,000 subscribers in 90 markets throughout the central United States. Nucentrix had 1999 revenues of $52 million. American Telecasting, which had been the second largest, was purchased by Sprint for $449 million. Sprint went on to purchase other industry players, including People's Choice TV, Videotron USA, Wireless Holdings, and Transworld Telecommunications. MCI WorldCom expanded its microwave communications portfolio by acquiring CAI Wireless Systems, with over 73,000 subscribers, and Wireless One, with over 100,000 subscribers, in the late 1990s. Nevertheless, despite their years of competition, Sprint and MCI WorldCom agreed to a merger subject to regulatory approval in 2000. This development would have completely overhauled the telecommunications sector, but the U.S. Justice Department's antitrust regulators effectively blocked the deal in summer 2000.

A relative newcomer, Teligent, Inc., was founded in the early 1990s. Using broadband microwave technology, it began service in 15 cities in 1998 and owned spectrum in 74 of the U.S. markets in 2000. By late 2000, Teligent had begun providing services in 42 major markets throughout the country. It offered local telephone service, Internet access, and other services, bypassing the local telephone companies through its wireless systems. It was certified as a competitive local-exchange carrier rather than a wireless cable company, but it was doing what many wireless cable companies were moving toward. In 1999 the company recorded sales of $31.3 million from its more than 15,000 subscribers.

RESEARCH AND TECHNOLOGY

ENVIRONMENTAL RISKS IN TELECOMMUNICATIONS

From the mid-1970s to the mid-1990s, there were thousands of journal articles and research studies on the subject of the correlation between electromagnetic field (EMF) exposure and cancer in human beings. Although the research data were not conclusive, several studies in different countries indicate the possibility that EMF may at least contribute to some cancers in humans. The studies that explore a possible link between cancer and EMF are entirely different from other studies that focus on whether the microwave radiation can contribute to cancer. According to the Electromagnetic Energy Association, there were more than 100,000 microwave-radio stations in the United States in the mid-1990s. Harmful exposure of the public and the worker to microwave energy from these sources was extremely low. The output power of the average transmitter employed for microwave radio is fairly comparable to that of a citizens-band radio.

By the early 1980s U.S. measurements done in close proximity to microwave towers and on the rooftops of buildings near microwave antennas indicated a very positive scenario. Even in the most troubling cases, the recorded microwave levels were thousands of times below exposure limits set by the American National Standards Institute and the National Committee on Radiation Protection. There are several epidemiological studies, however, of people who have been exposed to above-average levels of radio-frequency/microwave radiation in their jobs. Through their medical records and other health-related data, researchers have found some correlation between high radiation exposure and physical symptoms such as heart disease, cancer, birth abnormalities, and miscarriages. To what extent these workers' problems are due to radiation exposure or to other factors (such as work or stress), however, was not always easy to ascertain.

With the worldwide popularity of cellular telephones in the 1990s, scientists began studying whether the radioactive effects of these devices actually posed a health threat to users. In 1994 Australian researchers concluded from their experiments that cancer-susceptible mice that had been exposed to cellular phones' radio-frequency/microwave radiation experienced two times the number of cancers as other mice. Since the Australian cellular phone industry participated in this study and had not anticipated its disturbing results, other scientists praised the validity of the study—many of them following up on its results. In the late 1990s, however, it was still not known whether the study's results and conclusion are applicable to the health of humans.

In 1995 Debbra Wright, a 42-year-old mother of three children and an employee of Bell Atlantic Mobile, sued Motorola, Inc., claiming that the cell phones she had used since the late 1980s had caused a brain tumor. The cancer, diagnosed in 1993, was close to her left ear. While at the time there were at least eight other lawsuits seeking to tie cellular phones to cancer, *Microwave News* claimed Wright's was reportedly the first by a service provider employee.

While many environmental concerns about microwave energy have been completely resolved, many, if not most, of its applications have been proven reasonably safe. While microwave technology's most traditional purposes revolved around heating and drying, some of its most innovative uses have been in telecommunications and medicine.

MICROWAVE COOKING

At the end of the 1990s and the beginning of the new decade, many other applications of microwave technology were emerging. For example, a group of scientists at Boston-based Invent Resources were working on such innovations as a microwave clothes dryer that tackles metal zippers and buttons and a microwave cooking device that allows for a crispier texture.

A Cornell University study demonstrated how moisture, heating rate, and food's porosity interact during microwave cooking. By understanding these interactions, scientists hope they can improve microwave technology to produce tastier foods. Ashim Datta, an associate professor of agricultural and biological engineering at Cornell, explained, "The microwave is grossly underused. Up until now, we haven't really understood much of the physics that occur during the microwave processing of food. This research shows us the quantitative physics as to why microwave food can be soggy and sometimes unappealing and also why sometimes excessive amounts of moisture can be lost."

According to Datta, previous research on microwave technology did not calculate the interrelationship between porosity and the internal pressures that develop because of evaporation of water inside food. With the impact of internal pressure, much more moisture reaches the food's surface, while air inside a microwave oven stays at room temperature. This sometimes causes sogginess in foods. "Through understanding the true physics of microwave cooking, companies can use this information to provide better tasting and better texture of food, as well as to provide more convenience to consumers by promoting increased use of microwave cooking," said Datta.

In 1999 General Electric Co. introduced a new method of browning and achieving crispier food via the microwave: the Advantium, which featured a 950-watt microwave coupled with 4,500-watt halogen bulbs. This combination not only browned food but also cooked it quickly. The Advantium was also pre-programmed to cook more than 100 recipes.

Packaging for microwavable meals was increasingly important in the late 1990s and the early 2000s. The most sophisticated packaging used susceptors (surface layers) to minimize the flaws of microwave cooking. These devices consisted of a plastic film metalized usually with aluminum and laminated to paper or paperboard. They often made foods crispier by improving their texture. Since producers of packaging materials continually explore methods to improve the design of susceptors, monitoring of high temperature materials is extremely important.

In 1998 Microwave Science LLC, a Georgia software company, received a patent for a system that would allow microwave ovens to prepare food to consistent standards. This system used software and sensors in the oven, which would enable the user to input simple codes that would adjust the oven during cooking to match the actual conditions of voltage, altitude, type of food, and other factors.

Manufacturers were beginning to add capabilities to microwaves that provided some of the benefits of conventional ovens, such as hot-air circulation to brown foods and steamers to supply additional moisture. Another microwave oven available to consumers has true variable control. The power control on a typical microwave causes the magnetron, which generates the microwave energy, to turn on and off at appropriate intervals, but the power control on these new ovens actually varies the amount of electricity going to the magnetron, thus giving more precise control of the microwave energy.

Developers also created more portable microwaves at the turn of the century. For example, Samsung rolled out its battery-operated microwave oven in 2000 for the trucking, recreational vehicle, and marine markets. By 2001, the company planned to introduce a lighter model for use in family cars and sport-utility vehicles.

Sharp Corp. launched a trendier innovation in microwave oven technology in the late 1990s in Japan: the Internet-ready microwave, which connects to a computer through a special adapter and enables users to locate recipes on Sharp's Web site. The oven's video display then shows the recipe and the oven automatically adjusts itself for the preparation of the selected dish.

FURTHER READING

Bartlett, Stephen. "Unlicensed Microwave: Blessing or Curse?" *Mobile Radio Technology,* October 2000.

"The Browning Version." *Business Week,* 20 December 1999.

Cahoon, Jim. "How Does Wireless Cable Work?" *Wireless Cable Association International,* 1999. Available from http://www.wcai.com.

Cheremisinoff, P. N., O. G. Farah, and R. P. Oullette. *Radio Frequency/Radiation and Plasma Processing: Industrial Applications & Advances.* Lancaster, PA: Technomic Publishing Co., Inc., 1985.

"Communities and Telecommunications Corporations: Rethinking the Rules for Zoning Variances." *American Business Law Journal,* winter 1995.

Dagani, Ron. "Molecular Magic with Microwaves." *Chemical & Engineering News,* 10 February 1997.

Electromagnetic Energy Association. "What Is Microwave Radio?" 1996. Available from http://www.elecenergy.inter.net/eeaindex.html.

"Electromagnetic Radiation and Health Risks: Cell Phones and Microwave Radiation in New Zealand." *Journal of Environmental Health,* July/August 1996.

Everything You Always Wanted to Know about Wireless Cable but Were Afraid to Ask. Washington: Rini, Coran & Lancellotta, P.C., 1996.

"First Microwave Device to Treat Enlarged Prostate." *FDA Consumer,* July/August 1996.

Henderson, Charles W. "Microwave Coagulation Technique Provides Chance for Cure." *Hepatitis Weekly,* 21 February 2000.

Hodl, James J. "Samsung to Debut Portable Microwave Oven at Retail." *HFN,* 3 April 2000.

Kirkpatrick, David. "Electricity, Cellular Phones, and Cancer." *Fortune,* 15 May 1995.

McVicar, Nancy. "New Studies Fuel Debate on Cellular Risks Signals May Damage Tissues." *Fort Lauderdale Sun-Sentinel,* 13 May 1997.

Meyers, Jason, and Joan Engebretson. "Wireless Networks: The Other Side of Wireless." *Telephony,* 8 March 1999.

Rodger, William. "Microwave Imaging May Be Wave of the Future." *Washington Business Journal,* 21 April 1995.

Sharp, Nicholas C., et al. "Microwaves for Menorrhagia: A New Fast Technique for Endometrial Ablation." *Lancet,* 14 October 1995.

Throop, John. "Cable Alternative Sees Business Upswing." *Peoria Journal Star,* 14 December 1996.

"Waiting for Wireless." *Forbes,* 13 January 1997.

Wireless Cable Association International. "Wireless Cable Statistics." July 1997. Available from http://www.wcai.com.

Zimm, Angela. "A Hot Opportunity: Cheung Labs Adapting Microwave Technology to Treat Cancer." *Warfield's Business Record,* 29 July 1996.

Minimally Invasive Technologies

Players in the field of minimally invasive technologies would like to offer surgery patients a helping hand that isn't a hand at all. Minimally invasive technologies include a wide array of medical devices designed to perform complex surgeries that forego traditional medical procedures relying on massive incisions. Also called keyhole surgery, minimally invasive surgery (MIS) has proven successful in a wide range of operations, from the removal of gallbladders—one of its most common procedures—to kidney transplants, and new applications for these technologies were found at an increasing rate in the early 2000s. Among doctors who routinely use minimally invasive technologies are gastroenterologists, internists, gynecologists, cardiovascular surgeons, plastic and reconstructive surgeons, orthopedic surgeons, and veterinarians.

Some of the equipment used in minimally invasive surgery are: guidewires, which connect the surgical devices with their operators and help guide the instruments to their proper location; steerable catheters, soft-tipped devices designed to offer greater maneuverability within the body; sutures, the tiny materials used to sew together small incisions; micro-sized needles, staplers, scissors, and similar surgical tools; and supplemental equipment such as monitors, cables, lighting equipment, and computer consoles. Perhaps the most developed sub-market, however, is that of endoscopes. An endoscope is a medical instrument, typically a hollow tube with a tiny video camera inside, or with light-transmitting glass fibers, that allows a live picture of the patient's insides to be viewed in the operating room during surgery.

By making two small holes in the patient's body, rather than the large incisions used in traditional open surgery, minimally invasive surgeons greatly simplify the procedure. In one hole, they insert the endoscope, and in the other they maneuver their tiny medical instruments. The internal images are projected and magnified by the endoscope onto an operating room video screen, on which doctors monitor progress and manipulate their instruments. This high-tech procedure offers a number of advantages to patients, particularly the speeding of recovery times, since patients needn't heal from large incisions. In addition, MIS drastically reduces patient pain and scarring, cost of surgery, and post-surgical complication.

At this early stage in the development of minimally invasive technologies, the competition revolves primarily around bringing out new tools, systems, and equipment that simply make operations easier for the surgeons to perform, while keeping cumbersome costs to a minimum. However, by the early 2000s, most equipment was still fairly expensive and primitive, greatly limiting MIS's applicability over a wide range of conditions. Still, competition in this area was heating up, as more and more open surgeries were converted to MIS procedures. Indeed, every few weeks it seemed a new type of operation marked its first use of minimally invasive technologies. As of 2001, doctors used MIS technology to perform such minute tasks as reconnecting ligaments in the knee, operating on infected sinuses, performing tubal ligation, repairing heart valves, and removing gall bladders. Companies sell their equipment to hospitals and research laboratories by emphasizing not only the efficiency of the operating process itself, but also the savings in administrative and logistic costs as well.

The leading manufacturers of minimally invasive technologies were either large, multinational firms (often specializing in both medical and optical instruments) or smaller specialty companies engaged in partnerships with larger medical and diagnostic firms. Johnson & Johnson's subsidiary Ethicon Endo-Surgery was a long-time market leader, as was Tyco International's United States Surgical Corp. Three multinational Japanese firms produced many of the top-selling endoscopes: Olympus Optical Co., Inc., Fuji Photo Optical Co., Ltd., (also known as Fujinon), and the Pentax Corp. These companies enjoy the built-in credibility of their established lines of scientific instruments as well as their expertise in camera equipment, research that can easily be applied to endoscopic technology. Other significant players in the industry included Boston Scientific Corporation, Endoscopic Technologies, Inc., and endoscopy pioneer Karl Storz GmbH & Co.

ENDOSCOPY PROVES FLEXIBLE

Endoscopes have been adapted to enter many regions of the body that were previously accessible only via large incisions. Endoscopy can be performed for diagnostic or therapeutic reasons. These might include evaluating a source of pain, taking biopsies, removing foreign bodies and abnormal growths, arresting bleeding, reshaping or reconstructing tissue, and placing tubes or stents.

Endoscopes may be either rigid or flexible. Rigid endoscopes contain a solid rod lens developed by Harold Hopkins, a physicist who was largely responsible for making modern medical endoscopy a practical reality. Flexible endoscopes use a fiber-optic bundle, also developed by Hopkins, that maneuvers around curves and bends, but provides poorer resolution than the solid rod lens. The most common endoscopes are called colonoscopes, cystoscopes, fiberscopes, gastroscopes, hysteroscopes, laparoscopes, peritoneoscopes, sigmoidoscopes, and proctosigmoidoscopes.

Although MIS is considered the "gold standard" in diagnosing and treating some diseases, it is nonetheless still an invasive technique that carries risks and requires a level of training that is not yet standardized. Although benefits to the patient can include shorter hospital stays, reduced pain, and fewer complications, these advantages can be offset by other risks. Because

the manual and visual skills required for these procedures can be very different from those required for conventional surgery, the surgeon's skill and experience, as well as careful patient selection, are especially important to a successful outcome.

BACKGROUND AND DEVELOPMENT

Minimally invasive technology traces its roots back to the earliest endoscopes, employed in the early 20th century, that were basically small telescopes, with a light on the front end, through which doctors peered. Two problems challenged endoscopy's widespread use: how to safely get enough light into a body cavity and how to transmit realistic visual images. These considerations served to limit the earlier scope of application for endoscopic procedures, and kept many old-school physicians skeptical. Karl Storz is recognized as the father of cold light endoscopy, developed in the 1960s, which made incandescent bulb mounting obsolete. Storz's discovery opened the door for capturing diagnostic findings in images, and he also built the first extracorporeal electronic flash. Eventually, as the hardware developed, so also did the attitudes of the collective medical community, who eventually came to accept the technology not only for diagnostic, but also for therapeutic application.

In 1988, the field finally got onto its present course, when doctors first used a tiny endoscopic camera and tiny medical tools to remove a gall bladder, after which MIS took off. Though the procedure spread quickly, the established medical community was slow to accept it. A meeting of leading professionals called by the National Institutes of Health (NIH) in 1992 resulted in a rather hesitant go-ahead for laparoscopic invasive surgery, and this early statement still held that traditional, open surgery "remains a standard against which new treatments should be judged." Moreover, despite the boom in demand in the late 1980s and early 1990s, the onset of managed care pushed pricing considerations to the forefront, thus holding industry growth in check as firms struggled to get their latest products to the market at affordable prices, and driving out many smaller competitors in the process.

Because of such economic pressures, claims were made asserting the superiority of some MIS techniques that were later disproved by long-term studies. For example, in the rush to offer laparoscopic gall bladder removals in the early 1990s, surgeons attempted the procedures after attending a weekend course, and nu-

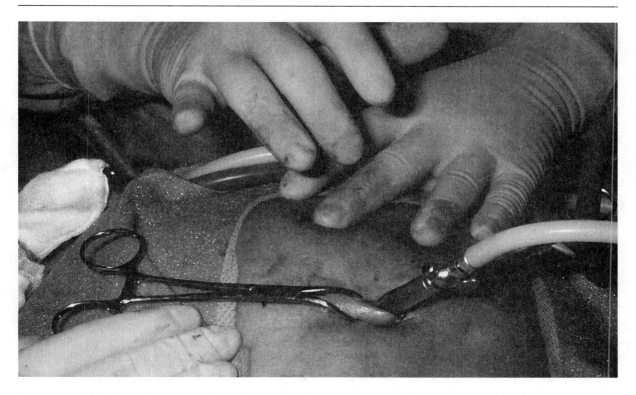

A surgeon performing a laparascopic procedure on a patient. *(Custom Medical Stock Photo, Inc./Michael English, M.D.)*

merous complications occurred as a consequence of inadequate training. Minimally invasive appendectomies didn't reduce the length of hospital stays or complications, and many arthroscopic orthopedic procedures continued to be less successful than their open equivalents.

However, as medical schools began adding MIS procedures to their clinical programs, the level of skill and experience in the medical community greatly changed in the 1990s. In 1997, the American Gastroenterological Association (AGA) issued a policy statement to guide hospitals in making decisions about extending endoscopic surgery privileges to physicians. In the late 1990s, many metropolitan hospitals and clinics were well equipped with both hardware and knowledgeable professionals who were well seasoned in multiple areas of minimally invasive surgery.

PIONEERS IN THE FIELD

Endoscopic technology pioneer Karl Storz founded his medical instrument firm, Karl Storz GmbH & Co., in 1945. In 1960, he discovered that he could use a fiber optic light cable to send light through an endoscope into the body. (Fiber optics involves transmitting light through extremely thin fibers or rods.) Storz patented this process, called "cold light endoscopy." Next, inventors developed a remote electronic flash unit to enable endoscopes to take pictures inside body cavities. According to his company, Storz built the first extracorporeal (outside the body) electronic flash for endoscopy. In 1966, Storz teamed with Harold H. Hopkins to develop the Hopkins rod lens system, which an industry source called "the most important breakthrough in optics since the development of the conventional lens system by Max Nitze in 1879." That allowed inventors to reduce the endoscope's diameter while maintaining its photographic resolution. Years later, Storz's company improved the design with the Hopkins II optics system.

CURRENT CONDITIONS

HOSPITALS EMBRACE MINIMALLY INVASIVE TECHNOLOGIES

Since minimally invasive technology exploded in the early 1990s, the amount of equipment required to support it has turned operating rooms into obstacle courses of computers, monitors, lighting equipment, and other gadgetry. In large part, this was due to hospitals adding minimally invasive technologies piecemeal to their facilities as the equipment became available, rather than overhauling hospital infrastructure from the start to more easily and efficiently integrate the new equipment.

In order to reduce the crowding and clutter, some hospitals began to take ambitious steps toward constructing entirely new operating facilities that seamlessly integrate the array of minimally invasive medical technologies. One of the most advanced facilities was opened at ValleyCare Medical Center in Pleasonton, California in summer 2000. This MIS center highlighted an added benefit of such integration, which is the ability to access medical records, files, and data, from both inside the hospital and from across networks outside the hospital, for use and referral right inside the operating room. This convenient access for doctors can save valuable time during the operation, while contributing to the overall efficiency of the hospital. The technology facilitates research and educational procedures as well, as the procedures can be viewed by teleconference in remote locations, providing surgeons and students with a first-hand look inside the operating room irrespective of location.

ROBOTS MOVE INTO THE FIELD

On the cutting edge of MIS technologies in 2000 was robotic surgery employing highly sensitive surgical consoles and 3-D imaging. The U.S. Food and Drug Administration (FDA) in summer of that year gave the okay to a system developed by Mountain View, California-based Intuitive Surgical Devices Inc. that was immediately used to remove a gall bladder. The system builds on the science of "haptics," derived from the Greek word meaning "to touch," which builds the sense of feeling into computer consoles. Since one of the biggest drawbacks of minimally invasive surgery was the negation of surgeons' physical contact with the patient's organs, developers were hopeful that such technology could breathe new life into MIS. Already, robotic MIS devices coupled with non-invasive imaging that show tissue in three dimensions allow surgeons to attempt intricate procedures in previously inaccessible places and to target tissue more accurately. In addition, streamlined approval procedures for new medical devices have made it easier for manufacturers to develop and bring new products to market in step with the pace of technological changes.

One potentially invaluable haptics device under development in the early 2000s was the CyberGlove, engineered by Dr. Mark Cutkosky of Stanford University's Dextrous Manipulation Lab. The CyberGlove is linked to a robotic arm that mimics the user's movements. The arm, in turn, returns a tactile sensation to the fingers. While the device is still fairly primitive—it will take much stronger impulses to convince the fingers they are actually feeling the objects under operation—such technology promises to greatly enhance the surgeon's remote command of the operating room.

Some see such developments as moving inevitably toward surgical practices in which the surgeon is in fact several hundred miles away from the operating table, controlling the robotic surgical tools by remote control. While such prospects make some observers queasy, most analysts agree that, while such projections may be partly true, it is more likely that only the most difficult and specialized procedures will be performed by doctors from afar, while more basic work will be the jurisdiction of a doctor in the operating room. Thus, the patient will not be entirely severed from a competent surgeon.

MORE AND MORE APPLICATIONS

One of the most promising new applications of endoscopic technology is the treatment known as endoscopic photodynamic therapy, which technically involves the use of light-activated chemotherapeutic reactions to destroy abnormal tissue. In trial applications during the latter 1990s, it was used to halt, and in some cases cure, early gastrointestinal cancers. Despite some initial problems with systemic photosensitization (untoward patient reaction), the future of endoscopic photodynamic therapy in contrast with the more conventional thermal (heat) laser therapy remained promising.

By the start of the 21st century, use of minimally invasive technologies in cosmetic surgery, especially for the brow and eye area of the face as well as for breast augmentation, was considered state-of-the-art technology, and demand for such procedures was growing steadily. Again, the advantages were that endoscopic surgery offered faster healing, less surgical invasiveness, and was less harmful to surrounding tissue, all of which is of particular concern for patients undergoing cosmetic surgery. For example, an MIS brow lift requires just a few half-inch incisions in the scalp behind the hairline, rather than larger incisions directly on the face in the brow area. After threading an endoscopic tube through one of the small incisions, the tiny instruments are inserted in another incision. Through remote viewing on a monitor, the surgeon then pulls brow muscle and tissue taut, splices them internally, and exits.

Another growing application of MIS is in the area of organ transplants. Minimally invasive technology has advanced from simple exploratory laparoscopy followed by conventional surgery, to actual surgical intervention during laparoscopy. This greatly reduces patient risk. In 2000, Canadian doctors performed a successful MIS kidney transplant on a married couple, with healing times cut to a matter of days. Kidney transplants previously required 12- to 18-inch surgical incisions through the abdominal muscles of the donor. With laparoscopic surgery, a small incision is made above the navel (where the kidney will be channeled out), and four small holes are also made into the skin to insert the laparoscope and surgical instruments.

OBSTACLES

Still, a number of factors keep the growth of minimally invasive technology in check. Many surgeons remain resistant to use it, insisting that hands-on surgery of the kind in which they were trained is both practically and ethically superior. This is most true in the general surgery arena, in which surgeon skills are the most lacking, since most early MIS products were geared toward specific procedures. In addition, the high costs of many MIS systems limit their marketing possibilities. And research and development still create a long pipeline. Thus, companies must wait several years to realize profits from new products—a wait that not all companies are able to withstand.

INDUSTRY LEADERS

The two leading firms devoted to minimally invasive surgical technologies were Cincinnati-based Ethicon Endo-Surgery, an operating company of Johnson & Johnson, and Norwalk, Connecticut-based United States Surgical Corp. (USSC), which was purchased by Tyco International Ltd. in 1998 for $3.3 billion. Ethicon's disposable surgical stapler, rolled out in 1978 to compete against a similar USSC product already on the market, sparked the long rivalry between these two firms. Johnson & Johnson was able to make great use of its vast product lines in conjunction with its Ethicon Endo-Surgery subsidiary to market bundled packages to hospitals and other customers. This critical mass gave the firm a great advantage in moving MIS products to market.

To compete with Ethicon, USSC began bundling its products with Tyco's line of supplemental equipment, including electrosurgical generators and stereotactic tables. Whereas USSC used to focus on the surgeon in the customer relationship, the heated competition has changed the company's tactics, and the firm now promotes itself as catering to the "whole-hospital customer." USSC's minimally invasive surgical tools were especially strong in the field of women's health care. Indicative of the rivalry between these two firms was a lawsuit filed by USSC in 1993 charging Ethicon with patent infringement. After years of legal maneuvering, the issue was finally settled out of court in 1999.

The endoscope segment's giant is Olympus Optical, of Tokyo, Japan, which controls 70 percent of the world market in that sector. It was the leading maker of flexible fiberscopes and videoscopes used for examining the upper and lower gastrointestinal tract or the bronchial tubes. In the late 1990s and early 2000s, the company rolled out a series of new products to complement its line of minimally invasive and endoscopic technologies, including its EVIS EXERA 160-Series Video System, and the integrated information and management system EndoWorks. Olympus also makes endoscopic peripherals, including video monitors, computer support equipment, light sources, and video processors. Sales in 2000 totaled $4.06 billion for an increase of 17 percent over the previous year. Olympus maintained a payroll of 19,000 employees.

Based in Natick, Massachusetts, Boston Scientific Corporation produced a range of minimally invasive surgical devices, including guide wires, steerable catheters, and stents, which are used to hold open arteries. The company want on a purchasing spree in the mid- and late 1990s, greatly expanding its size and product line and propelling it to the industry's top ranks. Despite legal and financial difficulties in the late 1990s—partly caused by its numerous acquisitions—the company began the 21st century on strong ground, finishing 1999 with sales of $2.8 billion, up from $2.3 billion the year before. In 2000 the company employed 12,600 workers.

Fujinon, part of Fuji Photo Optical Co., Ltd., of Omiya, Japan, makes a complete line of endoscopes including video endoscopes, panendoscopes, laporoscopes, fiberscopes, duodenoscopes, colonoscopes, and sigmoidoscopes. The company claims to make the thinnest and most flexible instruments, qualities of particular importance in pediatric procedures. Fujinon also makes a top-selling processor to carry the images gathered by its scopes. The company's major products include the Ultra Vision Sigma (SIGMA) 400, a high-resolution, high-magnification endoscopic system.

A major international player is Karl Storz GmbH & Co., of Tuttlingen, Germany. The company, with a history deeply rooted in MIS history as its founder, Karl Storz, was a pioneer in the development of endoscopes, remained family owned in the early 2000s. A few of the firm's major subsidiaries were Karl Storz Endoscopy-America, Inc., of Culver City, California, with some 1,800 employees and 18 worldwide affiliates; and Karl Storz Veterinary Endoscopy of America, Inc., which was a leader in expanding MIS to the veterinary services industry. Karl Storz Endoscopy designed the state-of-the-art, integrated operating facility at ValleyCare Medical Center in Pleasonton, California, described above. In addition to its endoscopic devices, the company was a leader in video documentation and surgery illumination technologies, such as monitors, lights, cables, and video cameras.

Stryker Corporation, of Kalamazoo, Michigan, has enjoyed at least a 20 percent profit growth for each consecutive year since 1977, and maintained a payroll of 11,000 employees worldwide by 2000. In 1999 worldwide sales reached $2.1 billion, up from $1.1 billion the year before. The company researches, designs, and manufactures endoscopes through a California subsidiary called Stryker Endoscopy. Stryker operates in over 100 countries worldwide, deriving about 40 percent of its sales from overseas. The firm also manufactures a wide range of surgical tools and devices.

The largest U.S. firm specializing in endoscopic technology is Circon Corporation of Santa Barbara, California, a subsidiary of Maxxim Medical, Inc., which acquired the company in early 1999. This followed Circon's solicitation in August 1998 of proposals for strategic partnerships or mergers, and the defeat of a hostile takeover attempt by United States Surgical Corporation in September 1998. The firm specializes in minimally invasive surgical instruments for urology and gynecology, and employed 1,200 workers in 2000.

A smaller U.S. firm forging ahead with innovative new products was Intuitive Surgical Inc. Based in Mountain View, California, the firm designs and manufactures the da Vinci Surgical System, which corresponds a surgeons's manipulation of manual controls with operating tools inside the patient. The company achieved revenues of $10.2 million in 1999, and had 120 employees.

Smith & Nephew Endoscopy Inc. of Andover, Massachusetts (formerly Smith & Nephew Dyonics Inc.), is a worldwide healthcare company specializing in products to facilitate arthroscopy, visualization, and minimally invasive surgery. Its parent company, the diversified manufacturer of medical products Smith & Nephew plc of London, employs about 11,200 workers and generated revenues of $1.8 billion in 1999.

RESEARCH AND TECHNOLOGY

Not only is minimally invasive technology a field ripe for research, it also facilitates research, not only into ever-greater technologies but also into more accurate understandings of anatomy and physiological disorders. The internal images provided by high-powered endoscopes offer researchers invaluable data from which to devise new treatments.

The educational applications of minimally invasive technologies were taken advantage of by Saint Peter's University Hospital in New Brunswick, New Jersey, which added a virtual training center specializing in minimally invasive surgery to its cutting-edge surgical center. In partnership with the University of Medicine and Dentistry of New Jersey-Robert Wood Johnson Medical School, Saint Peter's outfitted the facility with interactive workstations and teleconferencing equipment for easy consultations between students and their instructors. In this way, students can watch live feeds of MIS procedures and practice on models, both physical and in 3-D images, at their workstations.

One of the most important developments of the latter 1990s was the successful use of computer-enhanced robotic instruments to perform intricate microsurgical procedures. Using the ZEUS system developed by Computer Motion Inc., surgeons at the Cleveland Clinic reconstructed the small vessels of the fallopian tubes with a voice-controlled endoscope and robotically operated instruments directed by the surgeon from a console. In 1998 French surgeons used the similar Intuitive(tm) System from Intuitive Surgical Inc. to perform the first closed-chest, minimally invasive coronary artery bypass graft.

Improvements in miniaturization techniques and chip circuitry greatly expanded the applicability of minimally invasive surgeries in contemporary operating rooms. Due to promising research in miniature video cameras and miniature flexible endoscopes, endoscopy also holds much future potential for neurosurgery. Endoscopic methods of shrinking and tightening herniated disks in the upper spine and neck were successfully demonstrated in 1998, and endoscopes are being used to relieve pressure on the brain and to assist in microsurgery by revealing structures hidden from the microscope.

Patients suffering from gastrointestinal difficulties, by the luck of sheer anatomy, will even be spared the travails of having long cables maneuvered through their system during minimally invasive surgery, a procedure that results in discomfort. A team of British and Israeli scientists in 2000 announced the creation of a micro-sized camera that is simply swallowed like a pill. As the camera moves through the digestive system, it takes pictures through the entire 20-foot pathway to the colon. The wireless capsule endoscope, as it's called, thus provides a detailed map of the gastrointestinal tract, the second-leading location of cancers, which doctors can thus store and access for more precise diagnosis and, eventually, surgical plans.

Microelectromechanical systems (MEMS), also called micromachines, and nanotechnology, which were under extensive development in the late 1990s and early 2000s, also carried great promise for the medical industries. These tiny devices, embedded with circuitry, cameras, and programmable computer chips, could be designed to target specific areas of the body and, eventually, perform the surgery themselves, controlled by computer from outside the body entirely. (Also see the essay in this book entitled Micromachines/Nanotechnology.)

In April 1999, Endoscopic Technologies, Inc. (ESTECH), a company less than three years old) received a major U.S. patent for its "Multi Channel Catheter," to be used in minimally invasive cardiac surgery. Technically referred to in the field as a "Remote Access Perfusion (RAP)" cannula, it will take the place of the several catheters previously needed in any cardiac surgery. For example, prior to RAP, several different catheters and multiple incisions were needed to perform the separate but simultaneous functions of delivering oxygenated blood to the body, stopping blood flow to the heart with a balloon, and delivering drugs to the heart. RAP allows all of this to be done, using a single easily inserted catheter, without opening up the chest. All that is needed are small "window" incisions through the ribs. These permit remote access approaches including direct aortic, femoral, sub-xiphoid, or other trans-thoracic approaches.

The field of minimally invasive technology continues to be a very dynamic area of advancement. With each new innovation in equipment comes a commensurate increase in breadth of application. The possibilities are seemingly endless.

FURTHER READING

Abate, Tom. "Cutting Edge Operating Room Opens." *San Francisco Chronicle*, 8 June 2000.

"Advances in ENT Surgery." *The Practitioner*, February 2000.

Barr, Hugh. "Gastrointestinal Tumors: Let There Be Light." *Lancet*, 17 October 1998.

Becker, Cinda. "Students Can Learn at High-Tech Surgery Lab." *Modern Healthcare*, 6 November 2000.

Borzo, Greg. "Minimally Invasive Surgery: Can It Be Physician Friendly?" *American Medical News*, 13 April 1998. @SRC:"Companies Team Up on Robotic System Instruments." *Medical Industry Today*, 26 June 1998.

DeMeis, Rick. "Miniaturization: Not Just Electronics Anymore." *Design News*, 17 April 2000.

Frieling, T., and D. Hussinger. "Endoscopy as a Research Vehicle: Potentials and Pitfalls." *Endoscopy*, March 1998.

Gerzeny, Michelle, and Alan R. Cohen. "Advances in Endoscopic Neurosurgery." *AORN Journal*, May 1998.

Hamilton, Kendall, and Julie Weingarden. "Lifts, Lasers, and Liposuction: The Cosmetic Surgery Boom." *Newsweek*, 15 June 1998.

Hellwig, D., and B.L. Bauer, eds. *Minimally Invasive Techniques for Neurosurgery: Current Status and Future Perspectives.* New York: Springer, 1998.

Hercz, Robert. "Seeking Computers That Can Feel." *New York Times*, 9 November 2000.

"Imaging Technology: Tiny Camera Allows Inside Tour of Intestines" *Health & Medicine Week*, 12 June 2000.

"Keyhole." *Toronto Star*, 19 July 2000.

Mestel, Rosie. "Pill-Size Gastro-Cam is Just a Swallow Away." *Los Angeles Times*, 1 June 2000.

Montori, A. "Minimally Invasive Surgery." *Endoscopy*, March 1998.

Lucier, James P. "Future is Now for Robotic Surgery." *Insight on the News*, 14 August 2000.

Okada, Shinichiro, Yoshiaki Tanaba, et al. "Single-Surgeon Thoracoscopic Surgery With a Voice-Controlled Robot." *Lancet*, 25 April 1998.

"Robotics: Desktop Biofactories?" *Genomics & Genetics Weekly*, 14 July 2000.

Satava, Richard M. *Cybersurgery: Advanced Technologies for Surgical Practice.* New York: Wiley-Liss, 1998.

"Scientists Design Tiny, Wireless Camera to View Digestive Tract." *St. Louis Post-Dispatch*, 25 May 2000.

Svitil, Kath A. "Robotic Surgery." *Discover*, July 1998.

Todd, Joanne M. "J&J, U.S. Surgical Maintain Product Market Dominance." *Health Industry Today*, August 1998.

MOLECULAR DESIGN

Molecular design is a big bag of tricks comprised of the principles of biochemistry, medicinal chemistry, molecular biology, and computerized molecular modeling, with a pinch of mathematics and computer science thrown in for good measure, aimed at isolating a novel chemical compound, assessing its beneficial uses, and finding a means to synthesize it in a form optimal to the target use. Enormous advances in high-performance computing and visualization techniques have pushed molecular design to the forefront of biotechnology research. In place of random laboratory screening of chemical compounds, molecular design uses computational chemistry to produce research chemicals aimed at synthesizing new compounds for employment in a commercial market. The leading companies in the pharmaceutical, chemical, and agribusiness industries all make use of molecular design for integration into new products.

Molecular design greatly streamlines the painstaking and time-consuming process of weeding through enormous chemical "libraries" to find molecules appropriate for a specific application, a process that requires screening molecules one at a time. Scientists are now able to cut their time and effort considerably by using molecular-design screening processes to isolate in minutes the precise chemical compounds that interact appropriately with their target. Meanwhile, software tailored to the process is employed to create a simulation of the chemical compound's action in its target situation, be it a pharmaceutical medicine or an agricultural crop. Molecular design allows many of these advances to take place through genetic research. This is an area of rapidly increasing importance in med-

icine and industry—in part because extraordinary advances in computing make it possible to conduct accurate theoretical and experimental studies of enzymes, nucleic acids, and biomolecular assemblies.

Biological activity is dependent on the three-dimensional geometry of specific functional groups. Biomolecular research has traditionally required synthesis and screening of large numbers of molecules to produce optimal activity profiles, producing an average of one compound a week. Combinatorial chemistry allows researchers to amass libraries of large populations of molecules (100,000 in a matter of weeks) for screening compounds. Similarly, advancements of modern computers, which have become fast, small, and affordable, allow researchers to visualize molecular structure and activity on screen rather than in a test tube. Moreover, advancements in chemical models and program interfaces allow researchers to describe the mechanisms of biomolecular activity. Finally, high throughput robotic screens identify which compounds exhibit desired activity against the target. These potential lead candidates are then sold or licensed as information to the subsequent biotech companies for further product development and marketing in the individual sectors.

While computers allow the visualization of chemical interactions and large information databases, they have not entirely replaced experimentation in the lab. The final key to the technology that has made possible the massive libraries of potentially profitable biotech molecules each year is the process of combinatorial chemistry. First developed as a scheme to save time in drug research, the approach has evolved into the ability to create large numbers of organic compounds with the ability to tag them in such a way that those with optimal properties can be screened and identified. Combinatorial chemistry has reduced the time required to profile an optimum form of the compound from years to weeks.

College and university departments and institutes traditionally accounted for the majority of molecular design and research, although successful business applications attracted a tremendous amount of attention in the late 1990s and early 2000s and have enabled industry growth. The genetic engineering sector is responsible for much of this attention, with its promise of powerful new superdrugs and boosted agricultural yields, although the latter generated a storm of controversy in the late 1990s. (Also see the essay in this book entitled Genetic Engineering.) Major changes in molecular-design technique have enabled numerous small research companies to operate with specialized core technologies and computer programs. Design companies then lease their software and technology. Alternately, they can carry out the molecular design that fuels the rest of the industry, working closely with international pharmaceutical companies such as Hoechst Marion Roussel and Bristol-Myers Squibb Co.

Within the molecular-design industry, individual molecular-design companies tend to center on a patented specialized technology that can speed the search for compounds with properties that react favorably with a desired target. Once fully established, large corporations often acquire all or part of the smaller companies and their discovery processes.

The discovery and analysis of genes and their manifestations has come to be known as genomics. Coupled with other major technological advances in molecular design, the use of genomics to identify molecular targets revolutionized the molecular-design industry in the 1990s. Giant undertakings, such as the Human Genome Project, offer an abundance of information accessible on highly sophisticated computerized databases. Having identified the biological target—an enzyme, hormone, growth factor, or other protein—the researcher has a point of entry for chemical manipulation.

Efficient and productive realization of molecular-design techniques allows the biotech industry to profit from small molecule development and discovery in each of these areas. The pharmaceutical industry entirely depends upon the discovery and selective development of molecules possessing characteristics that

may become profitable drugs. Also, genetic engineering continuously uncovers interesting gene activity and needs large arrays of compounds to screen against gene products for potential activity. Developers of bioremediation processes use molecular design to discover advanced synthetic treatments and accessory compounds, such as nitrification inhibitors, to optimize conditions for microorganism activity.

BACKGROUND AND DEVELOPMENT

Humans have been using naturally occurring compounds to their benefit for thousands of years. Plants and animals provided food, medicine, and lubricating oils. New products were limited by traditional methods of screening naturally occurring substances. In contrast, the development of new substances based on knowledge of chemical properties could rarely be realized in practice. Once a novel compound with beneficial properties is isolated, it is often in a form that is unacceptable for its application, say, as a drug. It is beneficial to have access to knowledge about hundreds or thousands of chemicals that display similar beneficial properties and, among those, one form just possibly will be free from any undesirable properties.

The ability to do accurate theoretical and experimental studies of enzymes, nucleic acids, and biomolecular assemblies is inherent to "designing" a molecule, but the idea of using living things for human benefit is far from new. The use of living organisms to make cheese and bread has been practiced since 7000 B.C. Modern molecular design grew out of this larger field of molecular biotechnology. (The term "biotechnology" was coined in 1917 by Hungarian engineer Karl Ereky to describe "all lines of work by which products are produced from raw materials with the aid of living things.")

The greatest problem facing molecular biotechnicians is the development of microorganisms and compounds into marketable products. Naturally occurring microorganisms rarely produce the results scientists need for commercial application. By exposing organisms to other factors, such as ultraviolet radiation, scientists induce genetic changes that might or might not produce a desired by-product. With the recognition in 1944 that DNA (deoxyribonucleic acid, a chemical component of most living cells) held all the genetic material needed for a cell to reproduce itself, scientists began to think about creating organisms that would produce waste products that could serve as useful substances.

It was not until the late 1970s that researchers were able to apply genetic engineering techniques to molecular design. Due to the tedious nature of testing, the traditional genetic improvement regimens were time consuming and costly. In addition, the best result that this traditional approach could yield was the improvement of an existing inherited property, rather than the expansion or creation of the certain genetic capabilities. Molecular design, combined with genetic engineering, allowed these improvements to be made more efficiently.

The emergence of powerful microcomputers in the late 1970s allowed great advances in molecular biotechnology. In terms of molecular design in particular, computers proved to be important tools in the production of new chemicals. Computer databases allowed easy tracking and interpretation of huge numbers of characteristics. As microcomputing technologies improved during the 1980s, new computer programs were developed that allowed individual molecules to be displayed graphically on computer monitors. In the late 1990s, most advanced computer programs could create, edit, and print depictions of chemical molecules on the atomic level. (Also see the essay in this book entitled Molecular Modeling.)

In 1978 the genetic research company Genentech, Inc. used a genetically modified *E. coli* bacterium to produce human insulin. The bacterial host cells acted as biological factories for the production of human insulin that was then purified and used by diabetics who were allergic to the commercially available porcine (pig) insulin. Genentech's product also made human insulin cheaper and more readily available to diabetics throughout the world.

Genentech was one of the most successful leaders in the molecular and genetic design industry in the 1980s. Its success inspired many imitators, only a few of which prospered. Promoters dreamed of a world in which genetically and molecularly engineered microorganisms would produce petroleum, clean up wastes, cure diseases, and repel pests. According to reports that appeared in newspapers, magazines, and television at that time, the applications of molecular design were limitless. Many of those applications were being realized in the late 1990s, and while the field was rife with success stories, reactions were not so universally euphoric as predictions might have led some to expect.

CURRENT CONDITIONS

The early 2000s will produce a great deal of fertile ground on which to expand the application of molecular-design techniques. Along with the mapping of the human genome will arise intricate new understandings of the classification and function of proteins, resulting, according to some analysts, in a complete dictionary of protein families and their functions. As a result, the molecular foundations of genetic variation will come increasingly into focus, spurring more accurate and streamlined molecular-design applications.

About | MOLECULAR DESIGN: THE AGRICULTURE QUESTION

Robert B. Shapiro, the former chief executive of Monsanto Co., is a man whose name stirs emotions in and around the agriculture industry. Having popularized NutraSweet while working at G.D. Searle in the 1980s, Shapiro helped pioneer the introduction of molecular design and state-of-the-art genetic engineering to food crops, under the motto "food, health, hope." Some industry players thus heralded Shapiro for revolutionizing agribusiness.

Shapiro's aggressive promotional style and novel new technology, however, eventually rubbed a lot of people the wrong way. Especially in Europe, beginning in the late 1990s consumers raised their voices in outrage at Monsanto's attempts to infiltrate their markets with what activists came to refer to as "frankenfoods." Monsanto's staple product, genetically engineered soybeans that are resistant to the company's powerful Roundup brand herbicide, became the virtual symbol of what activists perceived as attempts to dominate world food markets with a product whose health and environmental impacts remained clouded in uncertainty. Shapiro, in particular, became notorious among activist groups, who put his human face on the ills they were fighting.

By the end of 1999, the protest had spread from Europe to the United States and throughout the world, to the point that farmers and agribusinesses were wary of devoting their fields too heavily to genetically engineered crops that may have difficulty finding a market. Partly as a result of the negative publicity, which seemed to hit Monsanto the hardest, the firm merged with the Swedish-American drug company Pharmacia & Upjohn to form Pharmacia Corp., which split the troublesome agribusiness unit into a separate subsidiary before spinning it off into a public company in October 2000. Pharmacia maintained 85 percent ownership over the new company. Shapiro, meanwhile, departed Monsanto, and the novel agriculture concept he nurtured, within months of the merger. Thus, while molecular design offered lucrative potential in a number of different fields, some applications came with the warning: "proceed with caution."

Meanwhile, efforts were underway to systematize the mountains of new data pouring out of the world-wide effort to decode the entire human genome, a project that was expected to reach its conclusion by 2001. The first incomplete draft was released in summer 2000. The Institute of Medicinal Molecular Design developed a new technique, known as Eigen-ID, which runs the genetic sequences through an encryption system and compresses the data, often with as many as several billion nucleotides, into strings of only 20 characters. Using these packaged, identifiable data sets, scientists can quickly scan the genomic sequences to identify potential genes that match those in their own databases, to which molecular screening can quickly be applied and new chemical compounds formulated for drugs.

Since a protein's shape determines whether and how it will interact with a molecule, pinpointing protein structures is a sort of holy grail for molecular-design firms. Crystallography and nuclear magnetic-resonance imaging have proven enormously helpful in "protein-structure prediction." Such techniques probe the crystals formed by proteins, thus revealing their structure. Scientists, however, have grown increasingly anxious for more reliable ways to determine the shape of proteins.

Three new types of software have been developed to try to pinpoint the protein structure in more accurate and less painstaking fashion. The first begins by assuming no prior knowledge of the protein, except for its amino-acids sequences, and starting from scratch, or *ab initio,* as it's called. Building on the knowledge of amino-acid sequences derived from genomic technology, the software tells the computer to reconstruct the protein one atom at a time. The forces between each atom are then measured to determine the way in which the protein folds and, thus, the shape it assumes.

Comparative modeling, meanwhile, builds on the protein structures that have already been identified, comparing their amino-acid sequences for similarities with the target protein. This results in an educated guess at the protein's structure, which is then augmented with further comparisons, producing an iterative process of protein-structure prediction.

The final method proceeds from similar beginnings as comparative modeling, but the amino-acid sequence of the target protein is graphed onto the known protein and compared with its sequences throughout its structure, at each point yielding comparative data. At the end of this process, the final composite-comparison data is measured against other known protein structures.

Several companies offer molecular-design services tailored to suit clients' needs. For example, Pharmacopeia, Inc. performs research services to develop drug discovery programs. The company generates large libraries for pharmaceutical research that offer structure-activity data, the likelihood of rapid discovery of a suitable compound, and broad patent protection of identifiable libraries, thus slowing competitors' attempts to develop similar drugs. Indeed, the trend throughout the molecular-design industry is collaboration. Chiron Corp. produced leads for corporate partners such as Pharmacia & Upjohn, Inc. and Novartis AG, while Tripos, Inc. specializes in software that creates virtual combinatorial libraries, and pins its hopes for its strongest future growth on software and consulting. In the realms of genetic and molecular medicine, Orchid Biocomputer and the University of Washington School of Medicine announced their collaboration to form the Institute for Qualitative Systems Biology.

Molecular design also alters the relationship between the various industries it touches. For instance, firms employing the most advanced molecular-design techniques are no longer required to purchase enormous volumes of chemicals in order to conduct molecular research. As a result, firms specializing in combinatorial chemistry may find themselves compelled to form strategic alliances with companies and laboratories engaged in computerized design and structural biology.

INDUSTRY LEADERS

Specialized molecular-design research services are carried out in both academic and commercial environments, with many partnerships and alliances formed between the two. For example, the Molecular Design Institute (MDI) at the University of California-San Francisco (UCSF) advances molecular-design methods and works closely with industry. The National Institutes of Health have awarded MDI several grants covering structure-based molecular design. MDI also works to further drug discoveries.

Widely recognized as the leader in molecular design, Tripos, Inc. is a publicly owned company founded in 1979. Based in St. Louis, Missouri, the company has a history of success in the field of molecular imaging and design software, and also offers software consulting and chemical compound libraries. The firm also occasionally offers collaborative research services to life sciences companies. Tripos's product line includes more than 50 drug-discovery research software products, the largest inventory of molecular design and analysis packages currently available. Its SiteID software, for instance, isolates and identifies binding areas within proteins. The firm will continue to roll out new software in coming years, with several new offerings in its pipeline. Practically every pharmaceutical company uses its patented comparative molecular field analysis technology. Customers include scientific research organizations as well as biotech companies such as Genelabs Technologies, Inc. and Cell Pathways, Inc. Tripos is involved in a research collaboration with the Central Research Division of Pfizer, Inc. to generate novel new software products geared toward pharmaceutical research, and also works with Hewlett-Packard Co. to broaden its range of hardware and operating systems. In summer 2000, Tripos agreed to utilize its discovery technologies to discover candidate drugs for metabolic and related diseases in conjunction with the Merck pharmaceutical subsidiary Lipha, S.A. With a payroll of over 200 employees, Tripos boosted its revenues 6.2 percent in 1999 to reach $27.2 million. About half of its sales are garnered outside of North America, mostly in Europe and the Pacific Rim.

Pharmacopeia, Inc., together with its San Diego subsidiary, Molecular Simulations Inc., combines three platform technologies of combinatorial chemistry, high throughput screening, and molecular-modeling software to aid the development and discovery of life and material sciences products. Revenue is generated through software sales and service, chemical compound leasing, internal drug discovery, and collaborative drug discovery. Headquartered in Princeton, New Jersey, Pharmacopeia has utilized its proprietary ECLiPS encoding technology to synthesize over 5.9 million small molecules. The company, which was founded in 1993, has collaborative agreements with agricultural and pharmaceutical companies such as Bayer Corp., Novartis AG, and Schering-Plough Corp. In addition to the San Diego facility, the company runs a drug discovery services segment—Pharmacopeia Labs—and operates major operations in Cambridge, England, and Tokyo, Japan, to distribute software. In 1999 the company had 510 employees and reported total revenues of $104 million, up from $92.2 million the previous year.

Chiron Corp. is one of the world's largest biotechnology companies, founded in 1981. The company conducts much of its research on cancer and cardiovascular and infectious diseases in collaboration with partners from industry and academia. Swiss pharma-

ceutical company Novartis AG owns approximately 44 percent of its outstanding common stock. Headquartered in Emeryville, California, Chiron spent much of the late 1990s reorganizing its product lines, selling off bits and pieces to various pharmaceutical companies in order to concentrate on its core businesses of biopharmaceuticals, blood testing, and vaccines. The company uses its gene-mapping technology to design treatments for hepatitis, HIV, meningitis, coronary artery disease, and osteoarthritis, and in 1999 began testing a hemophilia gene treatment. That year, Chiron employed 3,110 workers, and its sales reached $762.6 million, up from $736.7 million the year before.

RESEARCH AND TECHNOLOGY

A few companies use molecular-design software strictly to develop new commercial products. A great many more colleges and universities, however, use molecular design primarily to train students in chemistry. Still, there is some overlap between the two. The Department of Chemistry at the University of Houston, for instance, sponsors the Institute for Molecular Design (IMD), which exists to promote the exchange of information between field researchers. This information exchange helps with researching new computer tools for molecular design, attracting funds to support molecular design, and promoting computer-aided molecular design. Students as well as professional chemists utilize the programs and resources of the IMD. It is not a commercial program, however, and is therefore supported by grants from the government, private foundations, and companies in the industry.

The Molecular Design Institute (MDI) at the University of California-San Francisco (UCSF) is another example of the overlap between academia and commerce in molecular design. MDI was established in 1993 as an academic research institute to promote the discovery, design, and delivery of pharmaceutical agents. MDI seeks innovative partnerships between businesses and universities to expand their basic and applied research efforts and works closely with different agencies in the university, including the School of Medicine, the School of Pharmacy, and the biophysics program. It is also associated with the UCSF Computer Graphics Laboratory (CGL), which developed the MidasPlus program for use in molecular design. MidasPlus, an acronym for "molecular interactive display and simulation," is used both for training and for commercial applications.

The UCSF CGL has also introduced a number of other programs for use in molecular design. One program is AMBER, a suite of programs for performing a variety of molecular mechanics-based simulations on machines ranging from workstations to supercomputers and designed for researchers working with proteins and nucleic acids. DOCK/BUILDER/MOLSIM, is a suite of three programs also distributed by the UCSF CGL that provides a way to screen large databases of chemical compounds that have features in common with receptor targets.

Other areas of UCSF associated with the MDI have also produced software aimed to support their specific interests and needs. The UCSF Magnetic Resonance Laboratory, for instance, offers CORMA and MARDI-GRAS, two programs designed to reduce error in creating molecular models. The Department of Cellular and Molecular Pharmacology, which works extensively with models of proteins, has developed four programs to help researchers working with amino acids and other protein structures. The MDI at UCSF also offers a corporate scholars program to disseminate information about molecular design and provides sabbatical positions for corporate chemists in UCSF laboratories.

Meanwhile, the push for faster, better screening technologies plunges forward. Protherics Molecular Design Ltd., a subsidiary of the U.K. firm Protherics PLC, completed its new DockCrunch project, which teamed Protherics with high-performance computing manufacturer SGI. DockCrunch analyzed over 1 million chemical compounds for their effectiveness in treating a number of diseases associated with the female hormone estrogen. This represented a far more powerful application of computational analysis for a screening library than had previously been attempted, and the results portend significant cost savings for drug discovery.

FURTHER READING

Baldwin-Gilbert, Virginia. "Monsanto Trudges Along After Spin-Off, as CEO Promises Improvement." *St. Louis Post-Dispatch,* 10 November 2000.

"Bioremediation." Birmingham, NJ: Sybron Chemicals, Inc., 1999. Available from http://www.sybronchemicals.com/biochem/bio.htm.

"Center for Molecular Design and Recognition." University of South Florida, 2000. Available from http://dendrimers.cas.usf.edu.

"Combinatorial Chemistry: What Is Combinatorial Chemistry?" Princeton, NJ: Pharmacopeia, 1999. Available from http://www.pcop.com/chemistry.html.

"DockCrunch: Large Scale Virtual Molecular Screening for Drug Discovery Comes of Age." *Business Wire,* 26 January 2000.

"Grim Reaper." *Economist,* 25 December 1999.

Hadlington, Simon. "Faster Pace in the Hunt for Drugs." *Financial Times,* 12 November 1999.

"Lab Uses Encryption Technology to Compress Genetic-Code Data: DNA Sequence Containing Billions of Nucleotides Coded as 20-Byte String." *Nikkei Weekly,* 24 January 2000.

Milmo, Sean. "Europe's Drug Biz Embraces Virtual Research." *Chemical Market Reporter,* 7 February 2000.

"Molecular Design Institute." University of California-San Francisco, 2000. Available from http://mdi.ucsf.edu/.

"Molecular Origami." *Economist,* 4 September 1999.

Studt, Tim. "Raising the Bar on Combinatorial Discovery." *Drug Discovery & Development,* January 2000.

Thornton, J. M. "Protein Folds, Functions, and Evolution." *Journal of Molecular Biology,* 22 October 1999.

MOLECULAR MODELING

A powerful tool, molecular modeling uses computers to help predict the three-dimensional structures of molecules and elucidate their other physical and chemical properties. Its goal is to aid the rational design of compounds, including medicinal drugs, by bridging the gap between theoretical chemistry and synthetic chemistry. Theoretical chemistry employs concepts that do not always translate smoothly from the scratch pad to the bench top, and synthetic chemistry often relies on painstaking trial and error. Molecular modeling allows the display of 3-D models of molecules that can be rotated on screen so users can perceive atomic and molecular interactions. In the hands of highly skilled professionals, molecular modeling can provide significant insight into chemical structures and processes.

Molecular modeling complements analytical and experimental work. But just as power tools alone are not enough to build a house, computational methods alone are not enough to replace experimentation. No molecule has ever been conceived and created "from scratch" using molecular modeling alone. And all molecular modeling relies on data first obtained from experiments. Still, molecular modeling serves an essential role. Time and money limit the number of experiments scientists can run, and simulations guide their research efforts and aid their interpretations.

The chemical, pharmaceutical, and biotechnology industries use molecular modeling extensively for materials research and drug development. The chemical industry, for instance, has used molecular modeling to create better catalysts, which make chemical reactions possible even under harsh conditions, as well as to synthesize substances from new fuels to industrial lubricants. Medicinal chemists, on the other hand, have used molecular modeling to design drugs that are more potent and less toxic than their precursors.

Computational chemistry was a $2 billion industry in 1996 and experienced 25 percent annual growth through much of the 1990s. As computers get faster and scientists familiarize themselves with the software, the predictive power of molecular modeling will only grow. Commercial software for this field generates annual sales of about $50 million.

More than 50 percent of molecular modeling efforts are applied in pharmacology or biotechnology. Additional applications include polymers (about 30 percent) and general materials such as metals, clays, and cements (less than 20 percent).

The major worth of molecular modeling is its predictive value. Acting as a scratch pad to test ideas and graphically display molecules, it allows scientists to predict the properties of hypothetical compounds. It also can facilitate the analysis of experimental data and suggest useful trends. For example, in 1992 Hoechst Celanese of Somerville, New Jersey, began a program to bring molecular modeling to its bench chemists to get chemical insights in the shortest possible time. When chemists there used molecular modeling to develop polymers, they were able to reduce from 300 to 30 the number of chemical pairs they needed to examine. Similarly, guidance from molecular modeling helps the pharmaceutical industry streamline and accelerate the discovery and development of new drugs, making these processes less expensive.

Molecular modeling software treats molecules as a 3-D system of balls interconnected by springs. It applies mechanical constraints to the system to show the conformation (shape) that takes the least energy to maintain, to calculate the angle between two atoms bonded together in the molecule, or to reveal the location of electrostatic charges within the molecule.

Medicinal chemists may use this information to predict the biological performance of a compound, which guides the drug-discovery process. Drugs work by interacting with biological molecules in the body, such as nucleic acids (DNA and RNA), enzymes, and receptors. How well a drug interacts with its biological target depends on a concept called complementarity: just as a key must properly fit a lock to open a door, a drug must bind correctly at a specific site. Complementarity, the degree of "stickiness" of the drug to the target, influences the biological activity of the drug.

Molecular modeling aids drug design by facilitating two processes: lead generation and lead optimization. Lead generation is analogous to finding the key that can fit the lock; it determines the correct chemical structure that can bind to the desired biological target. To generate lead compounds, molecular modeling takes advantage of knowledge of the 3-D structure of a biological target. This knowledge is obtained experimentally: the target molecule is isolated, purified, and characterized using X-ray crystallography or nuclear magnetic resonance spectroscopy.

To find new lead compounds, scientists search 3-D databases of known chemical structures. These include commercial databases, such as those from Chemical Abstracts Service, of Columbus, Ohio, and Cambridge Crystallographic Data Centre, of Cambridge, United Kingdom, as well as databases available in the public domain, and in-house databases maintained by drug and chemical companies. Using technologies established by Sun Microsystems and Netscape Communications, scientists can now access chemical databases through the World Wide Web. With the Human Genome Project underway, a large database of information is becoming available on the Internet. San Diego—based Molecular Simulations Inc. released in March 1999 its WebLab Version 1.5 with improved features that, among other enhancements, allow the biotech researcher to locate reading frames in a DNA sequence and translate them into protein sequences.

De novo drug design is an approach by which experimentally obtained knowledge of molecular properties is used to generate a lead compound. Based on the molecular properties of the region to which the drug binds, scientists can devise a chemical structure that will fit into the binding region. Molecular modeling can play an important role in creating a structure with a good fit. The chemical is then synthesized in the laboratory, tested, and optimized.

Lead optimization, the second method of designing drugs, is analogous to cutting a key to the exact shape needed to turn a lock; it fine-tunes the degree of the interaction between the drug and the biological target. To optimize lead compounds, researchers try to correlate the relationship between a chemical structure and the biological effects it produces. This area of research is called *structure-activity analysis*. It is the main focus for present-day drug design, as it does not require knowledge of the biological target or its structure. First the chemist makes a series of analogs—compounds that are structurally similar to the lead compound—and tests them in the laboratory. It is necessary to use a family of analogs that range in biological activity from inactive to active. The idea is to observe how changes in molecular properties, such as size, shape, electronic charge, or solubility, affect biological activity. Molecular modeling helps scientists decide what chemical modifications to make.

Optimizing the lead compound means maximizing its potency, minimizing its toxicity, and enhancing its delivery. Potency refers to how well a drug interacts with its biological target molecule. Toxicity and side effects result when drugs interact with biological molecules other than the desired target. (In the lock and key analogy, the key opens more than one lock.) Delivery deals with issues including the ability of the drug to reach its biological target in a large enough quantity to produce the desired effect. Sometimes, as when crossing the blood-brain barrier, this task is daunting. Molecular modification of the drug can affect all these properties, and modeling helps scientists decide what modifications to make.

It is important to note that molecular modeling seeks not to replace experimentation, but to improve it. Virtually every aspect of drug design still depends on data obtained through experimentation. To build a structure-activity model, compounds have to be synthesized and tested. Biochemical studies must be conducted to identify the biological target molecules. Many molecular properties that drug designers need to explore are better measured experimentally than calculated.

BACKGROUND AND DEVELOPMENT

The pharmaceutical industry was at the forefront of, and remains the driving force behind, computational chemistry. Traditional drug discovery relied on trial and error: extracts of natural substances were tested for their useful properties. In 1910, for example, Paul Ehrlich used a compound he obtained from a dye to create a drug for treating syphilis. Later, chemists made and tested large numbers of compounds and, when they identified an active compound, attempted to fine-tune it into a substance that was clinically useful. This approach has been enormously successful in finding thousands of substances that turned out to be biologically active when tested in model systems. Since the 1970s, however, this approach has grown more expensive and less successful in yielding new medicines. The cost of synthesis and testing, especially in animal studies and human clinical trials, has risen sharply. Competition among drug companies to be the first to the market with a new product is intense, and any tool that can facilitate that process is indispensable.

In 1965 the Massachusetts Institute of Technology introduced the first molecular modeling graphics system. By 1974 at least 19 universities and institutes had independently developed their own systems. Since then, many other organizations have developed systems, some of which are commercially available: The National Institutes of Health (NIH) and the Environmental Protection Agency created the Chemical Information System; Brookhaven National Laboratories introduced Crystnet; NIH and Bolt, Beranek, and Newman produced Prophet; Washington University in St. Louis completed MMS-X. These systems help scientists search chemical databases, display and analyze molecular structures, study chemical interactions with their biological targets, and design drugs. To aid drug-design efforts, Searle Co. of Chicago created the Moloch-2 molecular modeling system. Similarly, DuPont of Wilmington, Delaware, produced Tribble, and Rohm & Haas of Philadelphia introduced Moly. These are but a few of the many modeling systems on the market.

CURRENT CONDITIONS

Although molecular modeling is far from being able to simulate complex chemical reactions from A to Z, it is a powerful research tool. Unfortunately, several factors hinder its performance. One of the biggest challenges faced by the industry is training those without computational backgrounds to get reliable results on computers. People need extensive training to use molecular modeling properly and to familiarize themselves with strengths and weaknesses of various methods. Compounding the problem is that the computers themselves may be slow: it can take a month to perform a single calculation. In medicinal chemistry, a major limitation is the inability of modeling programs to calculate the energetics of the binding of molecules to their biological targets.

Still, molecular modeling is making headway. Computers are getting faster, cheaper, more powerful, and more accessible. Software programs are able to yield more accurate information, as well as analyze bigger molecules—some having more than 20,000 atoms. Hybrid computers that emerged in the mid-1990s combined the power of supercomputers with newly developed massively parallel machines to solve big chemical problems. Greater accessibility and quickly expanding databases, such as Brookhaven National Laboratory's protein data bank, are helping researchers build upon the modeling efforts of others. Consortia formed with researchers in areas as diverse as pharmaceuticals, catalysts, and polymers has facilitated the spread of modeling knowledge. The result for chemists has been more quality time at the computer, which in turn allows for more quality time in the lab.

New technologies in the life sciences allow researchers to generate enormous libraries of molecular data through both computer programs and new laboratory methods. These molecular libraries provide starting points for experiment design in the development of compounds showing promise of usefulness and profitability in the biotech industry. For example, Pharmacopeia, Inc., a leading provider of drug discovery technologies and services, has generated more than 4.5 million diverse, small molecules. DuPont Pharmaceutical Research Laboratories' Universal Informer Library, a virtual library, has approximately 10,000 compounds. Compounds with similar chemical properties can take on many forms, and molecular libraries must be sifted through to find the optimum form of the compound for its ultimate use as, say, a drug or fertilizer. New software tools allow scientists to organize such massive amounts of data and exchange information. Novel compounds and processes can be simulated, developed, and analyzed. Researchers can interpret the properties of the molecular forms within those libraries in order to direct research efforts toward the most profitable results before they even enter the lab.

To tackle the massive undertaking of analyzing all of the chemical building blocks in terms of the rules of chemical behavior, screening vast numbers of compounds for activity with a target protein, and delivering the information in a form manageable by human scientists, many of these programs rely on high power systems. The intricate interactive graphics displayed require high-resolution systems such as Silicon Graphics Onyx2, Octane, and O2. Such powerful systems are costly and may not be available in every lab, much less for every chemist. Continued advances in personal-computer hardware coupled with low cost and greater availability allow molecular modeling applications to be run under Windows NT. Software providers for the industry have responded by directing their efforts toward producing specific programs with high visualization in a standard Windows NT desktop environment. According to one DuPont Pharmaceutical Research Laboratories representative, the most important direction of the industry is the increasing availability of the Windows software at the workplace for each chemist.

While a great number of companies and learning institutions offer software programs and computational services designed to meet specific applications, sometimes it has been advantageous for pharmaceutical and biotechnology companies to build their own molecular modeling systems. These firms include Bristol-Myers Squibb, Upjohn, DuPont, Novo, Glaxo, and Merck. For example, Merck decided to develop its own molecular modeling system to help its scientists study the geometry and reactivity of certain antibiotics. Scientists have successfully used this to design novel drug candidates, and the system has also aided the understanding of drugs' mechanisms of action.

INDUSTRY LEADERS

The dominant trend among the leaders in the molecular modeling industry is that of mergers and acquisitions. Smaller start-up firms, once they've established a valuable product and a strong customer base, are often acquired by larger drug behemoths. These large companies have more money for research and development as well as advanced distribution and marketing systems, both of which are appealing to any "small" firm interested in the further scientific pursuit of molecular modeling.

Molecular Simulations Inc. (MSI) offers molecular design services to pharmaceutical, chemical, biotech, petroleum, and gas companies. MSI develops and distributes software to aid in all aspects of the chemical compound discovery process. MSI's customer base is made up of research and development facilities of corporations from diverse industries, and as of 2000, no single customer accounted for more than 10 percent of its annual revenues. In 1998 Pharmacopeia, Inc. acquired MSI as part of its software segment, and in March 1999, purchased the remaining 50 percent of MSI's Asian joint venture. That year, Pharmacopeia's software segment (MSI) posted revenues of nearly $61 million, and the division accounts for roughly two-thirds of Pharmacopeia's revenues.

DuPont Pharmaceutical Research Laboratories, formerly CombiChem Inc., offers services to accelerate the chemical compound discovery process for customers and collaborators in the pharmaceutical and biotech industries. The company's proprietary design technology can generate, evolve, and optimize new lead molecular candidates to be developed, manufactured, and marketed by collaborators. The firm is collaborating with Novartis for crop pesticides, and also works with Athena Neuroscience, Inc.; ICOS Corp.; ImClone Systems Inc.; Ono Pharmaceutical Co., Ltd.; Roche Bioscience; Sumimoto Pharmaceuticals Co., Ltd.; and Tejin Ltd. CombiChem completed its initial public offering in May 1998, raising $18.9 million. That same year, the company had revenues of $15.1 million, and posted revenues of $6.1 million for the first six months of 1999. In late 1999, however, CombiChem was acquired by DuPont for an estimated $95 million. In 2000, the company began operations—from its original California location—under the name DuPont Pharmaceutical Research Laboratories.

Tripos, Inc. is a publicly owned company founded in 1979. Based in St. Louis, Missouri, the company has a history of success in the fields of molecular imaging and design software. Tripos supplies software, sells third-party hardware, and offers research services and molecular libraries to the pharmaceutical, biotech, and other life-science industries. In 1998 the company experienced a 15 percent decrease, as anticipated with the termination of its joint venture with MDS Penlabs and investments to initiate internal chemical laboratory operations. Net sales for 1999 were listed at more than $27 million, an increase of over 6 percent from the previous year. The company expected continued high returns into the 21st century as a result of combining its computer software technology with chemical synthesis.

RESEARCH AND TECHNOLOGY

One of the most active areas of research in which molecular modeling is being applied is medicinal chemistry. In a path of chemical reactions that ultimately ends in the development of a disease, many biological molecules that can act as potential targets for drug intervention are involved. Molecules that interact specifically with receptors or enzymes, for instance, can act as leads for creating new drugs. Molecular modeling plays an important role in this process. For example, by using molecular modeling to study a small protein in snake venom that binds to and inactivates an enzyme that helps regulate blood pressure, an angiotension-converting enzyme, scientists have been able to create better drugs to treat hypertension. Molecular modeling reduces the time and cost of drug discovery dramatically. For example, in the late 1990s, researchers at the Eli Lilly Co. screened an average of 75,000 molecules per week for drug potential, compared with 75,000 per year prior to the introduction of molecular modeling software.

AIDS researchers have also used molecular modeling to study proteases—protein-cutting enzymes required for the function of the human immunodeficiency virus (HIV). When developing protease inhibitors, drug designers used computers to generate a 3-D structure of a related protease in order to model the smaller HIV protease. They compared the structure of the active site to that of other biologically important molecules. Medicinal chemists often compare different structures with similar biological activities to detect nonobvious likenesses. These computer simulations provided enough insight into the probable features of the enzyme's active site to be useful in designing effective inhibitors.

Correlating the 3-D shape of a molecule with its performance is also a useful activity in many research arenas. Scientists at Sandia National Laboratories in Albuquerque, New Mexico, developed their own molecular modeling system and used it to create synthetic substances that mimic natural enzymes' abilities to catalyze reactions. At Procter & Gamble, molecular modeling is used to develop enzymes that make detergents fast-acting. Other organizations have used it to study superconductors. Amoco uses molecular modeling to find better fuels. The use of this technology is also growing in fields as diverse as electronic, optical, and magnetic materials. Indeed, the possibilities may be endless.

FURTHER READING

Borman, Stu. "MEDLA Technique Calculates Electron Densities." *Chemical & Engineering News,* 14 August 1995.

———. "Military Research on Cubane Explosives May Also Lead to New Pharmaceuticals." *Chemical & Engineering News,* 28 November 1994.

———. "Problems and Pitfalls of Molecular Modeling Cited." *Chemical & Engineering News,* 29 May 1995.

Bozman, Jean S. "From Supercomputers to the Desktop; Workstations Reach New Heights with Increase in Speed, Drop in Price and Off-the-Shelf Applications." *Computerworld,* 21 March 1994.

Brown, Maxine D. "Visualization Applications." *Byte,* April 1993.

Cronin, Mary J. "Getting Drugs to Market Fast." *Fortune,* 24 November 1997.

Challener, Cynthia. "Broader Horizons for Computational Chemistry." *Chemical Market Reporter,* 31 July 2000.

Krieger, James H. "Computer-Aided Molecular Design Teeming with Change." *Chemical & Engineering News,* 11 April 1994.

———. "Molecular Modeling Technology Is Dynamic and Changing." *Chemical & Engineering News,* 1 May 1995.

———. "New Software Expands Role of Molecular Modeling Technology." *Chemical & Engineering News,* 4 September 1995.

Moad, Jeff. "Building a Better Life." *Datamation,* 15 November 1987.

"Molecular Modeling." *Industry Week,* 16 September 1996.

"Molecular Modeling Software Debuts." *PC Week,* 6 April 1992.

Rotman, David. "Computers in the CPI: Designing Tomorrow's Profits." *Chemical Week,* 20 May 1992.

Seiter, Charles. "Alchemy III." *Macworld,* September 1993.

———. "MacSpartan Plus 1.1 (Molecular Modeling Program from Wavefunction)." *Macworld,* October 1996.

———. "Sculpt 2.0 (Interactive Simulations Molecular Modeling Tool)." *Macworld,* September 1997.

Siam, Khamis S., Rick D. Gdanski, Bruce E. Landrum, and David Simon. "Molecular Modeling Aids Design of Downhole Chemicals." *Oil and Gas Journal,* 19 August 1991.

Singletary, Lynda. "Molecular Modeling Refines Genencor's Lipases." *Chemical Marketing Reporter,* 4 May 1992.

Studt, Tim. "Molecular Modeling Makeover." *R&D,* February 1997.

———. "Molecular Modeling Software Changes Research Techniques." *R&D,* February 1995.

———. "Promise of Rich Payoffs Drives Computer-Aided Chemistry." *R&D,* September 1993.

———. "Scientific Visualization Comes down to Earth." *R&D,* November 1992.

"The Ultimate Science Story." *Economist,* 21 August 1993.

Weber, Irene T., et al. "Molecular Modeling of the HIV-1 Protease and Its Substrate Binding Site." *Science,* 17 February 1989.

Wilson, Eve J. "Molecular Modeling: Computer-Assisted Innovations in Drug Design." *Alcohol Health & Research World,* fall 1992.

Zirl, David M. "A New Tool for Chemists." *ChemNews.com,* 1999. Available from http://www.chemnews.com/art. cfm?S=37.

MORTGAGE COMPANIES

The American Dream is intricately tied to home ownership, which by 2000 was intricately tied to mortgage companies. While calling mortgage companies the gatekeepers of the American Dream may be a bit hasty, it is safe to say that mortgage companies represent a central component of the nation's housing and loan markets, and increasingly resemble players in other financial sectors in their behavior. By 2000, 70 percent of all mortgages were originated by lending brokerages rather than by banks and thrifts, up from 20 percent in the early 1990s. Closely tied to the nation's interest rates, mortgage companies experienced wild swings in their operations in the late 1990s as the Federal Reserve tinkered with rates to stem the effects of global economic crisis and inflation. Through it all, however, the mortgage market remained robust.

Companies in this industry are generally subsidiaries of large financial institutions, but mortgage companies themselves do not engage in banking functions such as accepting deposits or offering checking accounts. They concentrate specifically on mortgage loans, but within that market there is a great deal of variation, a factor that was becoming more pronounced as industry competition heated up. Whereas mortgage companies traditionally focused on providing mortgages to customers with credit difficulties, that business was by 2000 simply a hot niche market in an industry increasingly dominated by mortgage specialists. In 1999, the U.S. Bureau of Labor Statistics reported there were about 376,000 mortgage bankers and brokers, a figure that has had its share of ups and downs in this immature industry. While the business is growing, heightened competition has led to consolidation, which was likely to continue through the early 2000s, although smaller niche players, involved in Internet marketing and high-risk lending, will also have their place in a dynamic market that is so responsive to consumer demand.

ORGANIZATION AND STRUCTURE

In the 1990s, numerous new companies entered the industry because of low entry barriers. Mortgage companies' share of loan originations more than doubled between 1988 and 2000, when mortgage firms accounted for about two-thirds of all originations. The second most important group by volume of mortgages was that of commercial banks, followed by the thrift industry (such as savings and loan associations), which as recently as 15 years earlier had dominated the industry. Other mortgage lenders included credit unions and life insurance companies.

Many consumers may still be confused by the plethora of lending sources. Basically, however, people who shop for mortgage loans can go to one of three different types of lenders. First, there are the traditional financial institutions and their affiliates. These include most banks, thrifts, and credit unions, nearly all of which make mortgage loans. Sometimes the financial institution itself offers the loan; sometimes the loan is offered via a mortgage company owned by the institution. If a bank directs a customer to a loan office somewhere else, chances are that it will be to a mortgage company owned by the bank. Financial institutions generally underwrite their own loans, i.e., they use their own assets to fund the loan. Banks and thrifts may hold the new loan in their own portfolio until it is paid off (sometimes as long as 30 years), or they can sell the loan into the broader secondary market for mortgage loans.

Mortgage bankers and mortgage companies are more specialized. They offer the same sort of mortgage loans as financial institutions but without any other banking services. They, too, underwrite their own loans. The national mortgage companies in particular are fairly innovative about creating mortgage products with varying terms, floating interest rates, and other features to attract a wider range of customers.

According to the Mortgage Bankers Association of America, mortgage banking companies are the largest group of home mortgage lenders, followed by commercial banks and savings and loans. Mortgage banking companies operate mainly in the secondary mortgage market, using government institutions such as Fannie Mae, Freddie Mac, and Ginnie Mae.

Finally, there are mortgage brokers, which are mortgage banks in that they're not financial institutions, and can be part of national companies. But there is one important distinction: mortgage brokers don't provide the money to make their loans. Instead, they play a matchmaking role by putting borrowers in touch with loan sources for a fee. Especially if a borrower has had credit problems in the past, a broker can be helpful in locating more flexible lenders. A broker makes its money by collecting a fee from the lender, the borrower, or both. In the best of circumstances, the lender and the broker will split the points (the fees the borrower pays), so it shouldn't cost more to borrow through a broker.

Banks and thrifts may hold or sell newly originated mortgages, but mortgage companies generally sell their new loans almost immediately, often at the end of each month. This process involves what is known as the secondary mortgage market, in which large numbers of individual loans are bundled together according to characteristics such as their term in years and their interest rate. This large bundle is then used as the basis for a security or bond that is backed by the predictable payoff schedules of the underlying mortgages. These securities are then sold on the open market, normally to pension funds and other institutional investors who consider them a reliable long-term investment. This process of "securitization" of mortgages has two profound effects on the market. First, since the secondary market makes cash available to buy up mortgage loans, it permits the influx of more money into the mortgage market. This, in turn, frees up more money for loans to the consumers, and is particularly helpful in financing loans at the lower

end of the market where credit histories may be suspect. The other great effect of securitization has been the growth of mortgage companies. Since these firms lack the deep pockets of banks and thrifts, they could not possibly bear the risks involved in maintaining each of these loans in their own portfolio. By selling off the loan (and the attendant risk) to the secondary market, mortgage companies can provide a vital service to the consumer at little or no risk to themselves. This has fueled the rapid growth of private mortgage companies, which in turn has meant more choices for consumers.

The volume of mortgages sold into the secondary market varies with changes in the volume of fixed-rate lending (as opposed to variable rate loans). The higher the percentage of fixed-rate loans being made (such as in periods of low interest rates when consumers want to lock in good rates for the long term) the easier it is to secure such loans. By 2000, with interest rates on the upswing, the secondary market was seeing less and less mortgage activity.

As in other industries experiencing soaring growth rates, mortgage companies come in all sizes and shapes. The cost of entry into loan origination continues to be low, and many of the smallest brokers are mere mom-and-pop storefronts. But the financial sources necessary to compete and succeed as a full-service mortgage banker have increased dramatically. As a result, in terms of dollar volume the industry is increasingly dominated by the largest players, major lenders such as Wells Fargo & Co., Chase Manhattan, Countrywide, and GMAC Mortgage, which together account for tens of billions of dollars in home loan originations each year.

The low barriers to entry also generated some controversy in their own right. In 2000, the mortgage industry began to crack down on itself in an effort to eliminate fraud through a toughened self-regulatory program. Weary of declining consumer confidence amid increasing reports of fraud, the industry, led by the National Association of Mortgage Brokers, aimed to require national registration for all mortgage brokers by 2005.

CURRENT CONDITIONS

The mortgage industry braced for an expected moderate rise of inflation and a tailing off the U.S. housing market in 2000, though housing price appreciation, which averaged about 5 percent in the late 1990s, was predicted to remain healthy. In light of expectations of a slowing economy in 2000, the Mortgage Bankers Association predicted loan originations of $940 billion, down from $1.29 trillion in 1999. Later estimates pegged 2000 originations at just under $1 trillion. While the decline discouraged some players, it was still the 4th-best year ever for originations; the record of $1.55 trillion was set in 1998. With interest rates on the rise, however, refinancings become less attractive, and so lenders will likely see less flight of their clientele; the drawback is that loan performance will likely diminish. Refinancing was expected to account for 18 percent of originations in 2000, continuing their downward trend from 35 percent in 1999 and 50 percent during the 1998 refinancing boom.

Delinquency rates, meanwhile, reached a 28-year low of 3.72 percent in early 2000 following the wave of refinancing activity in the late 1990s. Loan refinancings are less likely to face delinquency problems, and thus the delinquency fears of a few years before were considered well hedged against by 2000, at least for a few years. As rates increase, however, new loans pose a greater delinquency risk of which mortgage companies were especially cognizant. Analysts expected delinquencies to shoot up rapidly in the event of an economic downturn. Furthermore, the country's bankruptcy level continued to reach new heights in the late 1990s, despite the nation's economic prosperity.

Rising interest rates are not without their blessings for mortgage companies, however. Since the cost of new loans rises with interest rates, refinancings diminish, resulting in lesser portfolio runoff. Moreover, servicing charges tend to rise with rates as well, leading to an improved revenue stream. Both these trends favor the larger lending companies who maintain greater economies of scale to hold onto customers and maintain viability. Indeed, through 2000, mid-sized lenders were having difficulty generating revenues from their portfolios in proportion to their larger counterparts. The Mortgage Bankers Association reported that lenders servicing between 50,000 and 150,000 loans reaped about $405 in revenues per loan, while those servicing 150,000 to 350,000 generated only $369 per loan. Those servicing between 350,000 and 750,000, by contrast, enjoyed $474 per loan, and those servicing over 750,000 loans brought in an average of $491. As a result of such imbalances, mergers and acquisitions are likely to continue their fevered pace.

While mortgage processing no longer takes weeks, as it did in the past, the industry nevertheless faced calls for speeding processing in order to keep up with the fast-paced marketplace. Automated underwriting, which received a boost with the onset of electronic signature imaging in 1999, can reduce the cost and speed of processing, but it can just as easily reduce the level of service, especially for customers less familiar with the mortgage process and who may desire face-to-face service. Moreover, although processing costs, to the tune of about $4,600 each, were considered inflated throughout the industry, electronic imaging remains too costly at present to pose a viable alternative.

Mortgage companies also explored the subprime and "no equity" niche for a new avenue of growth, by offering loans for debt consolidation, paying off existing loans, and home improvement. These companies cater to borrowers who do not qualify for Federal Housing Administration, Fannie Mae, or Freddie Mac mortgages because of poor credit history and bankruptcy. With low profit margins in the traditional mortgage market, companies turned to the subprime and "no equity" market where profit margins—and

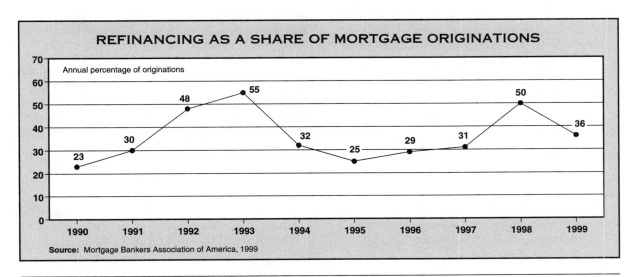

REFINANCING AS A SHARE OF MORTGAGE ORIGINATIONS

Annual percentage of originations

Source: Mortgage Bankers Association of America, 1999

risks—are much higher. Typically, subprime lenders charge interest rates about 6 percent higher than traditional mortgage companies. Furthermore, instead of using traditional mortgage criteria for determining credit worthiness, these mortgage companies often rely on criteria more akin to the finance industry, where the age of the previous debt, not just the amount, is considered. In the early days of subprime lending, mortgage companies provided loans to people with poor credit that did not exceed 60 percent of the value of their homes. Lenders, however, increased these loans to as much as 70 percent of the value of their homes by the late 1990s.

The $140 billion subprime sector, after emerging as the superstar segment of the mortgage industry in the mid- and late 1990s, took a bath in late 1998 and the following year when "risky" became a dirty word on Wall Street in light of the Russian debt default and the world financial markets' dizzying volatility. Many subprime lenders flowed out of the business in a hurry, while others simply collapsed altogether and filed for bankruptcy. The blow was attributed to several factors exacerbating the social causes, including the overexuberance of lenders descending on the storied subprime market in hopes of cashing in quickly, leading to mispriced loans. The dark days of subprime lending, however, had light on the horizon for the financial industries' larger players; the price of subprime lenders was cheap, and major banks, thrifts, and mortgage companies were buying them up fast.

The mortgage industry became even more competitive in the late 1990s as companies operated with very low profit margins to remain competitive. The industry's emphasis on volume fueled the competition, which also began to lead to waves of consolidation within the industry. Most of the industry's profitable companies were large mortgage brokers who could slash their profit margins and glean their profits from the plethora of loans they issued. Smaller companies, on the other hand, struggled to stay afloat or exited the business as competition started to escalate in the mid-1990s.

Meanwhile, as the online lending market heated up, international servicing was expected to pose significant competition to U.S. mortgage companies. In particular, lenders were under increased pressure to simplify the lending process and to make it more consumer-friendly, as opposed to the more intensive grilling customers traditionally received. Mortgage companies were thus faced with the competing demands of making the process simpler while hedging against potential delinquencies.

Moreover, the greater competition in the industry gave rise to greater innovation as companies sought ways to differentiate their services from those of other companies. Online mortgage sites such as E-Loan Inc., Mortgage.com Inc., MortgageSelect.com, and Homestore.com, Inc. took off in the late 1990s and early 2000s. These sites allow home buyers to search for rates, compare rates, receive recommendations, and apply for mortgages over the Internet while saving up to 80 percent of traditional fees. Web-originated loans are expected to become even more popular. Forrester Research predicted online-originated loans to reach $40.5 billion by 2001, while the January 2000 U.S. Bancorp Piper Jaffray survey estimated that up to 20 percent of all originations will be applied for online by 2003.

Less technical concerns also threatened the industry's reputation. Gaining considerable attention in the late 1990s were increasing reports, confirmed by the findings of separate studies conducted by the Association of Community for Reform Now (ACORN) and the Urban Institute, of lingering racial bias in mortgage lending practices. The latter study reported that lenders in 1999 were less likely to provide minorities with information about loan products, and generally quoted higher interest rates on mortgages to minorities than to white customers. The ACORN study, meanwhile, reported that blacks were denied loans 217 percent as often as whites, a trend that worsened in the late 1990s from 206 percent in 1995. Latino customers, likewise, were far more likely to be rejected for conventional mortgage loans than were whites, at a rate of 183 percent as often, up from 169 percent in 1995.

INDUSTRY LEADERS

Wells Fargo & Co., the seventh-largest bank in the United States, moved to the top of the industry through its acquisition of Norwest Co. in 1998. By early 2000, Wells Fargo dissolved the Norwest name entirely, but had expanded its mortgage operations, forming a joint venture with American Financial Corp. and agreeing to sell most of its originations to Freddie Mac while focusing on its approval expertise. Wells Fargo provides banking, insurance, investments, and mortgage and consumer finance through 6,000 locations in North America and abroad. The company generated net income of $3.75 billion in 1999 on sales of $21.8 billion. Its mortgage assets totaled $11.7 billion.

Countrywide Home Loans, Inc. of Pasadena, California, was the nation's largest independent residential mortgage lender and servicer. Countrywide is a subsidiary of Countrywide Credit Industries, Inc., which has more than 10,600 employees in 550 offices in the United States. The mortgage company has about 350 branches around the country and manages over 2 million loans annually, over which the company retains all servicing rights. Countrywide's focus is the traditional retail and wholesale loan origination market, though it has built an extensive online presence as well. Moreover, the company moved into the European market in 1999 when it agreed to service loans for the United Kingdom's Woolwich PLC. Founded in 1969, Countrywide Home Loans achieved its prominence in the industry by focusing solely on mortgages. Among Countrywide Credit Industries' other subsidiaries is Full Spectrum Lending, Inc. of Pasadena, California, founded in 1996. Full Spectrum Lending features options for borrowers with less-than-perfect credit, and operates out of 40 offices and its Web site. The Full Spectrum Web site was launched specifically to ease the loan process for borrowers who are self-employed and have a harder time verifying their income, and those who have suffered financial hardships such as job loss, debt, or divorce. In 1999 Countrywide sold most of its loans to Fannie Mae, but continues to approve those loans through its automatic underwriting system. Countrywide Credit Industries achieved sales of $3.4 billion in fiscal year 2000, up from $2.9 billion the year before. Loan servicing generated sales of $1.2 billion and the company collected origination fees of $406 million.

The Principal Financial Group, a diversified financial services corporation with insurance and banking divisions based in Des Moines, Iowa, ranks among the leading mortgage companies through its Principal Residential Mortgage, Inc. arm. This division was founded in 1936 and grew into one of the country's industry leaders by the late 1990s; the acquisition of ReliaStar Mortgage in mid-1998 helped the company's growth in revenues and assets. In 1998 the company reorganized as a mutual insurance holding company. Mortgage loan assets reached $12.3 billion in 1999, amounting to 15 percent of the company's total assets. The company has 16,800 employees in over 250 offices throughout the world in the Americas, Europe, Australia, and Asia.

The Money Store, acquired in the late 1990s by First Union Corp., is another key player in the mortgage industry. The majority of the company's revenues come from mortgages, although the company also provides student loans and Small Business Administration-guaranteed loans. The Money Store, based in Union, New Jersey, began offering mortgages in 1967 and is also the country's largest provider of home improvement loans. The transition to First Union was a bit rocky, knocking down originations significantly, though they were beginning to rebound by 2000.

GMAC Mortgage Group, based in Horsham, Pennsylvania, is a subsidiary of General Motors Acceptance Corp. (GMAC), one of the largest financial services companies in the world. GMAC Mortgage Corp. formed in 1985 and specializes in single-family and commercial loans. With over 27,000 employees, GMAC maintained 900 offices in 35 countries, and by 1999 the company had built a portfolio of 1.5 million customers and originated more than $12 billion in residential mortgages. In 2000 the company launched its online mortgage broker MortgageRamp.

The government-mandated companies, Fannie Mae and Freddie Mac, also play a significant role in the industry by ensuring that lenders have sufficient funds for low- and moderate-income, minority, and immigrant borrowers. These companies do not lend directly to home buyers, but make sure mortgage companies have enough money to lend home buyers, by purchasing mortgages from lenders. Fannie Mae, the one-time Federal National Mortgage Association, has helped over 30 million Americans buy homes since 1968. In 1999 Fannie Mae reported earnings of $3.91 billion, up from $3.4 billion in 1998, on sales of $37 billion, of which $32.7 billion derived from mortgage interest. The company purchased a record $195.2 billion of mortgages in 1999, compared with $188.4 billion the year before.

Congress created Freddie Mac in 1970 to ensure the availability of low-cost mortgages. Like Fannie Mae, Freddie Mac—formerly the Federal Home Loan Mortgage Corp.—serves the low- and middle-income market as well as borrowers with special needs. Because of Freddie Mac, borrowers can take advantage of long-term, low-down-payment, and fixed-rate mortgages. Throughout its history, the company has implemented new services and technologies to make obtaining mortgages easier; its loan approval time was cut to as little as two minutes in some circumstances. For example, Freddie Mac introduced automated underwriting, Loan Prospector, to expedite the application process in 1995. Freddie Mac maintained a payroll of 3,500 employees and generated revenues of $23.8 billion in 1999. Freddie Mac financed homes for about 3 million families that year.

RESEARCH & TECHNOLOGY

Technological advances continued to help the mortgage industry grow throughout the 1990s. By 1997, consumers who applied for loans for the first time in several years found that instead of dealing with a loan officer, they more than likely would confront a computer program. Computers and office automation software converted the paper-heavy and labor-intensive underwriting process into a much faster and more cost-efficient process.

Yet to be resolved was how much of a role traditional lenders would play in the online lending industry. While major lenders typically maintained their own online lending operations and some of the online specialists counted the traditional lenders among their clients, the precise levels of interaction, competition, or cooperation remained unclear. All observers agreed, though, that online lending was here to stay and would assume increasing importance. By 2000, online lending was beginning to outgrow its residential-loan focus and emerge into commercial real estate. Still, practically and legally, not all mortgage underwriting could be handled online.

Some observers felt that online mortgage lenders had done little to build brand loyalty, and thus could easily lose investors with new waves of refinancings. Countrywide Home Loans chairman Angelo Mozilo noted that online lenders' strategy of providing online originations without retaining serving rights would eventually undercut their burgeoning success. When the origination business slows, as it is wont to do, online lenders could face a severe shortage of business. Many analysts, however, remained skeptical of Mozilo's analysis. Servicing ownership can be expensive and volatile, and thus not the most effective means for maintaining life in the face of a cooling origination market. Moreover, without the costly overhead of branch office systems, online lenders could actually find themselves in a favorable position when a downturn hits.

FURTHER READING

Bergsman, Steve. "Bricks and Clicks." *Mortgage Banking,* August 2000.

Cornwell, Ted. "Mid-Size Servicers Fall Short on Revenue Collection Efforts." *Mortgage Servicing News,* November 1999.

———. "Online Lenders Survive without Servicing." *Mortgage Technology,* 2000.

"Economic Forecast 2000." *Mortgage Servicing News,* December 1999.

Hackett, John. "Higher Rates May Stem Run-Off but Also Pose Delinquency Threat." *Mortgage Servicing News,* December 1999.

Marshall, Jeffrey. "Great Numbers While They Last." *U.S. Banker,* October 1999.

Mattson-Teig, Beth. "CMBS Market Dampens Real Estate Cycles." *Promo,* January 2000.

"Mortgage Delinquency Rates Fall to 28-Year Low." *Community Banker,* September 2000.

Muolo, Paul. "Getting Back in at Low Tide." *U.S. Banker,* September 1999.

———. "Only $1 Trillion—What a Shame." *U.S. Banker,* October 1999.

"Processing: Lighting a Fire under the Mortgage Business." *Mortgage Technology,* 2000.

Quinn, Lawrence Richter. "Regulating Mortgage Brokers; Industry to Back National Registration." *Washington Post,* 4 March 2000.

Strickberger, Matt. "Making Sense of the Internet." *Mortgage Technology,* 2000.

"Studies Find Race Bias in Mortgage Process." *Los Angeles Times,* 12 March 2000.

MUTUAL FUNDS

As one of the most popular investment vehicles in the United States in the 1990s, mutual funds take money from public investors and invest it as a collective institution. Investment decisions are made by a fund manager chosen by the board of directors; the fund manager is responsible for making the right picks to deliver strong returns to investors. While there are mutual funds for every type of investor, from the tycoon to the neophyte, they can be particularly attractive to inexperienced investors, not only because fund participants are not charged with direct control over investment, but also because funds limit risk exposure. Since funds are spread out over a number of different investments, a washout in one will not deplete the entire investment pool.

But that doesn't mean fund investors are excused from doing their homework. Funds come in a variety of shapes and sizes. There are three main categories: stock, money market, and bond and income funds. But under these broad rubrics, variation is rampant. Some stocks funds are devoted to specific industries or to stocks of a specific size; bond funds can devote themselves exclusively to Treasury bills or municipal bonds. Others are devoted to specific regions or to companies embodying certain ethical standards. Finally, fund personalities differ, with aggressive funds pursuing risky investments and conservative funds playing it safe. Each of these carries its specific advantages and drawbacks, depending on shifting market conditions, investors' needs and wishes, and social and cultural developments.

In large part due to the progressive influx of 401(k) and other company retirement plans into mu-

tual funds, 49 percent of U.S. households were active in the stock market either directly or through mutual funds in late 2000, up from 19 percent in 1983, according to a survey by the Investment Company Institute and the Securities Industry Association. By late 2000, the combined assets of all U.S. mutual funds totaled $7.1 trillion, compared with $4.5 trillion in 1997.

Investors, however, were creating a rift in the mutual-fund market between growth funds and value funds—the market tilting heavily in favor of the former into early 2000. Growth funds focus on the fastest-growing companies, hopping on the latest trends to generate quick returns at high risk. High-growth funds in 2000 were focused on such hot industries as Internet "dot.com" start-ups and biotechnology. Value funds are favored by conservative fund managers and are concentrated on "old economy" sectors such as automobiles. Hardened analysts advised caution, however, noting that Wall Street's herd mentality could reverse such balances in a matter of days; a quick jolt to the market could quickly send investors scurrying into funds resting on tried and true companies. Indeed, that's just what occurred in spring 2000 when the technology markets floundered.

ORGANIZATION AND STRUCTURE

There are three broad categories of mutual funds. Money-market funds normally invest in securities maturing in one year or less and are known as short-term funds. Stock funds and bond and income funds invest in securities to be held for the long term. Each category is further broken down depending on investors' goals. Money-market mutual funds invest in either taxable or tax-exempt securities including Treasury bills, municipal securities, certificates of deposit of banks, and commercial paper. Bond and income funds look for growth of principal and/or income from bonds, Treasury bills, mortgage securities, company debt, municipal securities, and stocks. Stock or equity funds look for a combination of growth in the price of stocks and other securities and income, or dividends, of stocks.

There are also funds of funds—funds that pool money to invest in other mutual-fund groups. These funds can be divided into the same categories as the funds they invest in; thus there are funds that invest only in funds that invest only in technology stocks, and so on.

Mutual funds are managed professionally by those in the securities industry. They perform research on companies and securities, plus keep tabs on general market conditions. Based on their research, managers decide which securities to add or delete from a fund to achieve investors' goals. An individual investor is known as a shareholder. A principal underwriter sells shares to shareholders, who include individuals and companies engaged in institutional investment, such as through 401(k) plans. The precise services a fund offers is determined by the board of directors. While a mutual fund in theory spreads risk, risk is still associated with investing, including a possible loss of the principal investment. Just as with funds invested directly in the stock market, in bonds, or other securities, money invested in mutual funds is not insured by any federal agency.

Most mutual funds list their prices with the Nasdaq Stock Market (formerly the National Association of Securities Dealers Automated Quotations System) in daily newspapers. The price of a fund must be calculated every day by law. The price is the net asset value (NAV) plus any front-end sales charges. The NAV is determined by market value of the securities owned by the fund, minus the liabilities, divided by the total number of shares owned by shareholders.

All U.S. mutual funds are regulated by the U.S. Securities and Exchange Commission (SEC) and by federal laws. Mutual funds must provide investors with a prospectus and shareholder report free of charge. A prospectus educates a prospective investor on how to buy and sell shares; states the goals, strategies, and risks of the fund; and gives information on fees and expenses. The shareholder report contains financial statements and reviews the performance of the fund.

Four main laws also govern mutual funds. The Investment Company Act of 1940 requires twice-yearly filings with the SEC, while the fund administrators must keep detailed financial records. The Securities Act of 1933 states that mutual funds must offer prospectuses to investors and must register the offerings of fund shares. The Securities Exchange Act of 1934 requires sellers of mutual funds, such as brokers, to register with the SEC and dictates seller and buyer relations. The Investment Advisers Act of 1940 details record-keeping requirements, requires registration of investment advisers, and includes antifraud provisions.

In 1996 the U.S. Congress passed the National Securities Markets Improvement Act. This legislation calls for uniform regulation for mutual funds. While preserving states' regulatory powers, mutual funds are regulated on the federal level as far as structure, operation, and review of prospectuses and advertising. The law lowers fees paid to the SEC by the securities industry and gives the SEC exclusive oversight of mutual-fund advisers.

Individual investors can buy shares in mutual funds through brokers, financial planners, bank representatives, insurance agents, or other investment professionals. Professionals can recommend funds based on clients' needs and goals, and are compensated by commissions or fees. Investors may also buy shares directly, making decisions based upon their own research.

The SEC was intensifying its focus on funds' pricing valuations at the turn of the century. Since some funds specialize in thinly traded holdings, funds often calculate their valuations themselves, a practice that some observers insisted was leading funds to succumb to the temptation to use those holdings to pay down debts, thus altering the fund's value without the knowledge of observers. As a result, valuations were increasingly seen as inaccurate, leading buyers to pay too much and sellers to make a killing. While the degree of latitude provided by SEC rules for such practices was unclear, the SEC expected to refine pricing rules to better reflect the emerging popularity of such funds.

BACKGROUND AND DEVELOPMENT

In 1868 the Foreign and Colonial Government Trust in London, England, set up the first mutual fund. It promised those of modest means the same chance at making money in securities as wealthier people. In the United States those who invested in capital markets were still only the wealthiest few until the 1920s.

Until then, middle-income people put their money into banks or bought stock in specific companies. The first mutual fund in the United States appeared in 1924 as the Massachusetts Investors Trust. The fund contained stocks of 45 companies and had $50,000 in assets. The stock-market crash of 1929 forced Congress to act to protect investors. While risk is part of the industry, Congress passed laws to enable investors to gather as much information as possible about all types of securities, including mutual funds.

Once the country began recovering from the Great Depression of the 1930s, people turned to mutual funds as an alternative to investing directly in the stock market. The Investment Company Act of 1940 provided for the protection of investors through a fund's board of directors, charging the directors with ensuring a smooth convergence between the interests of the fund's investors and those of its managers. At the same time, the first international stock fund was offered. Funds remained relatively the same, containing mostly stocks, until the 1970s when funds began adding more bonds. Money-market mutual funds were also created, and tax-exempt funds offered. By the 1990s there were mutual funds for almost any investor's goals, including very specialized industry funds.

The choices facing investors have exploded since the creation of the first mutual fund. In 1940 there were fewer than 80 funds; in 1960, 161 funds; in 1980, 564; and in July 2000, 7,929. Assets have grown from $500 million in 1940 to $7.1 trillion at the end of the third quarter of 2000.

Investment professionals have added many services for investors over the years. Investors now receive information beyond the prospectus and annual report. Professionals provide tax information, retirement and general financial planning, toll-free 24-hour telephone service, newsletters, and facsimile and Internet access.

CURRENT CONDITIONS

By fall 2000, the Investment Company Institute reported that about 88 million Americans invested mutual funds, representing an increase of 5 million shareholders from 1999. Company retirement plans garner mutual funds about half their business, while 34 percent of shareholders work primarily through a broker, insurance agent, financial planner, or bank representative. The rest seek out funds themselves or through a discount broker. Generationally, baby boomers accounted for 51 percent of mutual-fund shareholders, while those born prior to 1946 accounted for 27 per-

Trends

OUT OF THE CLOSET

While mutual-fund popularity continues to soar, a number of skeptical observers contended that the brilliance of fund managers was overstated. By 2000, many managers were seemingly engaged in a practice called "closet indexing." Actively managed funds were putting greater quantities of stock in the major firms that comprise the key indexes, even doubling up on many of them, yet still charging the regular service fees to shareholders, which are generally 3-10 times as high as those for index funds. The net result, in some critics' eyes, is that such fund managers were reaping huge rewards by skimming off the top. Since the funds' fees theoretically pay for the managers' expertise and market research, investors in such funds were losing returns relative to what they could rake in from index funds.

The financial publisher Morningstar, Inc. monitors a figure known as R-squared that measures the percentage of a fund that is tied directly to an index; that is, how much of a fund's performance can be attributed to like movement on the index. Between 1996 and 1999, the average R-squared of all U.S. mutual funds rose 74 percent. The trend was particularly pronounced among large-capitalization funds, which averaged an R-squared of 86, up from 71 just three years earlier. This means that an average of 86 percent of a large-capitalization fund's movement was based on an index, usually the Standard & Poor's 500. Moreover, about 40 percent of large-capitalization funds had an R-squared of 90 or higher.

In light of surging stock performance overall, many analysts attributed this trend to an increasing unwillingness to suffer the swings in performance generally associated with actively managed mutual funds relative to index funds. More precisely, investors themselves were impatient when it came to poor returns, and were thus quick to jump ship if managers' decisions resulted in too little gain. To stay competitive, then, mutual funds found an easy solution in the safer stocks that keep pace with the major benchmarks. Nonetheless, many viewed this practice, as Oakland Fund manager Robert Sanborn put it bluntly, as "a big rip-off."

cent and generation X-ers for 22 percent. The average shareholder in 1999 was 44 years old, married, and employed, with total mutual-fund investments of $25,000. Median household income for the average shareholder was $55,000. In a little over half the U.S. households owning mutual funds, investment decisions were shared between men and women.

Mutual funds faced competition, however, from bankers and insurers who were fast encroaching on their territory. The repeal of the depression-era Glass-Steagall Act with the late-1999 passage of the Gramm-Leach-Bliley Act, also known as the Financial Services Modernization Act, accelerated the pace at which such firms could engage in retail investment. To capitalize on their financial-services business, banks and insurers have gobbled up brokerage firms with an eye toward the creation of financial supermarkets, at which customers will conduct most or all of their financial business, including institutional investing. Wells Fargo Securities, for instance, rolled out a mutual-fund marketplace in 1998 that generated over $500 billion in assets by 2000. In part related to these developments, the early 2000s promised a wave of consolidation among mutual funds, as competition heightens and firms strive to remain competitive.

Index funds became all the rage in the late 1990s. Indexes are basically little mirrors of the market in general, or at least of a segment of the market. Well-known indexes include the Standard & Poor's 500 and Nasdaq, although a bevy of novelty indexes have cropped up in recent years. Since the companies making up these funds are relatively static, index-fund performance is generally a bit more stable than that of actively managed funds, which must continually look for new movement, pulling money in and out of stocks and reinvesting elsewhere. As the markets and overall economy surged in the late 1990s, so did index funds.

Emerging-market funds also took off in 1999, reversing the previous year's dismal performance, which was largely due to the shockwaves from the Asian financial crisis. Having fallen 27.1 percent in 1998, emerging-market funds shot up 70.8 percent in 1999 on fund flows totaling $702 million, led by the Lexington Worldwide Emerging Markets Fund, with $300 million. Austerity programs and structural adjustment in developing countries, which lower the costs of doing business there, spurred terrific growth in this often-risky sector, which remains subject to political and economic turmoil overseas. As the global financial system grows increasingly integrated, however, emerging-market funds are likely to see a diminishment of their independence from domestic stock performance, as volatility in the United States reverberates around the world. By July 2000, emerging-market fund assets totaled $141.3 billion, compared with only $14.3 billion ten years earlier. According to *Barron's,* global funds accounted for about half of total assets, while Asian regional fund assets amounted to $30.1 billion.

Those investors hoping to make a profit without having to contribute to the economy's more heartless activities welcomed the rise of "ethical funds." As government deregulation flourishes, the responsibility to enforce business practices consistent with social welfare, environmental efficiency, and ethical standards was being relegated increasingly to market forces. Ethical funds thus allow investors' money to speak their minds, as well as their consciences. Ethical funds are concentrated primarily on equities, and have generally favored smaller or new firms, though that trend has grown less pronounced. As a recognized investment practice, socially responsible investment is fairly new, though some investors have long tried to remain cognizant of the social consequences of their investment patterns.

Meanwhile, diversification reigned among mutual-fund investors. The Investment Company Institute and the Securities Industry Association survey found that 22 percent of fund investors owned shares in seven or more stock funds, while an additional 26 percent maintained portfolios with four to six funds. Only 19 percent were invested in only one fund.

Although they've maintained a slightly more modest profile than the raging stock market, U.S. equity mutual funds have outperformed all U.S. stocks over the three, five, and ten years up to 2000, when assets in such funds totaled $3.95 trillion, up from $3.1 trillion the year before. Funds that invested heavily in large-capitalization U.S. companies continued to capture the lion's share of the new cash inflow, compared with the flow of funds to small-capitalization funds. By far the most popular type of fund, 90 percent of all fund investors put some money into equity funds, which generated an average return of 18 percent in 1999.

The close of the 1990s reversed long-standing trends in the bond markets, however, largely as a result of the Federal Reserve's attempts to hedge against inflation through a series of interest-rate hikes. Investors thus raced away from Treasuries and other bonds. While 42 percent of all mutual-fund shareholders invested in bond funds, assets tailed off in 2000 to reach $781 billion from $831 billion just two years earlier. This figure amounted to only 11 percent of all mutual fund assets, down from 31 percent in 1992. In all, about 16 percent of U.S. households were invested in bond funds in 2000. Meanwhile, 35 percent of fund investors, and 12 percent of U.S. households, maintained money in hybrid funds, which invest in a mixture of stocks and bonds. Assets in such funds inched up slightly in 1999 to $367 billion from $365 billion in 1998.

Money-market mutual funds, both taxable and tax-free, ended 1999 with assets of $1.7 trillion, up a record $350 billion from 1998. Fueling the sharp increase in money-market fund assets was the favorable interest-rate climate, though by 2000 it seemed that such robust growth was at an end as that climate changed. Money-market funds were home to about 48 percent of all mutual-fund investors.

The market for 401(k) plans stood at $1.41 trillion in the late 1990s, accounting for about 13 percent of the U.S. retirement market, according to the Investment Company Institute. For mutual funds, this translated into 401(k) assets of $593 billion. By early 2000, 401(k) plans accounted for up to one-half of sales at the larger fund families.

INDUSTRY LEADERS

Fidelity Investments, known officially as FMR Corp., is the world's leader in the mutual-fund industry, maintaining over 290 funds with some 17 million investors. Based in Boston, the company in recent years has taken steps to streamline its operations and performance. Having shed some of its nonfund assets, Fidelity focused increasingly on picking the best stocks instead of concentrating on operational issues. The performance of Fidelity's funds has shown steady improvement since 1996 when its flagship fund Magellan was lagging behind the Standard & Poor's 500. Fidelity aggressively expanded its online presence, including its Powerstreet online brokerage where investors can trade and monitor their investments. The fund family's assets totaled $351.1 billion, and led the market in 401(k) assets. With a payroll of 28,000 employees, Fidelity raked in profits of $1.01 billion in 1999 on revenues of $8.85 billion, more than doubling its lackluster 1998 margin.

Vanguard Group Inc., a notoriously conservative fund family, focuses overwhelmingly on investments of more than three years. Based in Malvern, Pennsylvania, outside Philadelphia, Vanguard has managed to attract a high level of investment largely by word of mouth, sharply cutting advertising and marketing costs. In another novel management twist, Vanguard outsources management on some of its funds to other companies. The company employed 11,000 people worldwide as of 2000, and generated 1999 revenues of $1.5 billion.

A major force in the mutual-fund business worldwide is AMVESCAP PLC, headquartered in London. Although it is based in the United Kingdom, AMVESCAP generates almost 90 percent of its revenue in the United States, with additional sales derived from operations in Europe, Japan, Hong Kong,

Australia, and Latin America. The company was formed in 1997 by the merger of INVESCO and AIM Management Group. AMVESCAP manages about 100 mutual funds for individuals and corporate and state institutions. With more than 5,545 employees worldwide, AMVESCAP posted net income of $140.1 million on revenue of $1.7 billion in 1999.

Franklin Resources Inc. remained a major player in the mutual-fund industry, managing over $200 billion in assets spread over 230 funds, despite difficult times in the late 1990s. The firm was aided by its heavy investment in international markets, amounting to one-third of all investments, which recovered well from their 1998 levels. With worldwide employees numbering about 6,700, Franklin Resources reported net earnings of $427 million on revenue of $2.2 billion in 1999.

WORK FORCE

In addition to a college degree, a good bit of stamina will usually serve a securities representative well. Early in one's career, long hours, cold calling, and rejections can be expected as a client base is built. Many people drop out of the industry due to the tough nature of sales. Those who persevere usually stay in the field until retirement because of the amount of training and education undertaken and the large amounts of money that can be made.

As of 1998 about 240,000 people were securities sales representatives in the United States, with the greatest concentration in New York and other large cities. The U.S. Bureau of Labor Statistics (BLS) stated that securities brokers and dealers earned a median annual income of $57,700 in 1998. New employees go through a training period while studying for licensing exams and waiting to become registered representatives of their firm. During this period the pay is low, usually an hourly wage or small salary, but after licensing and registration, employees will earn commissions against sales. The BLS predicted that employment in the securities industry will grow much faster than average through 2008. Factors in this prediction include strong economic growth, rising personal incomes, and more inherited wealth.

AMERICA AND THE WORLD

Over 45,000 mutual funds were in operation around the world in late 2000, up from 22,000 in 1992, led by the United States with 7,929. By 2000 mutual funds were present in 36 countries around the world, including Argentina, Finland, New Zealand, and Taiwan, and several countries seemed ripe for growth of institutional investment. For example, venture-capital funds were eagerly eyeing India's burgeoning pharmaceuticals and information-technology industries. Meanwhile, the bilateral agreement between China and the United States for China's entry into the World Trade Organization (WTO) included provisions to open up China's asset-management market to foreign firms. In particular, U.S. firms may own up to one-third of joint-venture asset-management firms upon China's entry into the WTO, and up to 49 percent three years later.

RESEARCH AND TECHNOLOGY

The technological advances that have helped the mutual-fund industry have mostly been in the area of computers. Computer hardware and software development assists the industry with trading by making it quicker and more accurate. Computer technology has enabled brokers to buy or sell securities closer to the price their clients want. The proliferation of computers in the home and the development of the Internet and the World Wide Web allow investment companies to reach more potential investors than ever before. Potential investors can access a company's Web site to find information about the firm's history, past performance, future strategies, and the types of funds offered. Once an account with a company is set up, investors may be able to access it through the company's Internet site. Those investors who trade online were found to be considerably more affluent than the average old-fashioned trader, a significant factor spurring firms' aggressive moves to establish online brokerages.

FURTHER READING

Arnold, Catherine. "Mutual Fund Flows Solid, Analysts Say." *National Underwriter,* 18 September 2000.

Barney, Lee. "Lower Margins, More Mergers Predicted." *Mutual Fund Market News,* 20 September 1999.

Barney, Lee, and Mike Garrity. "Conference Coverage: Fund Industry Said to Face Major Layoffs." *Mutual Fund Market News,* 28 February 2000.

Browning, Lynnley. "After 1990s Peak, Mutual Fund Industry May Have Nowhere to Go But Down." *Boston Globe,* 9 January 2000.

Damato, Karen, and Laura Saunders Egodigwe. "Only Two Months Old and Already 2000 is Wild." *Wall Street Journal,* 6 March 2000.

Eveillard, Jean-Marie. "Benchmark Tyranny: Closet Indexing and Shooting for the Stars are Exposing Investors to Undue Risk." *Financial Planning,* 1 November 2000.

Hancock, John. "Greens Will Do You Good." *Money Marketing,* 2 March 2000.

Hayes, Michael. "How Profitable is the Mutual Fund Business." *Registered Representative,* August 2000.

Healy, Beth. "Web Activity Lifts Fidelity Investments' Earnings to Record $1.01 Billion." *Boston Globe,* 3 March 2000.

Henwood, Doug. *Wall Street: How It Works and for Whom.* New York: Verso, 1997.

Hughes, Amy. "Emerging-Markets Funds Are on a Roll." *Wall Street Journal,* 28 February 2000.

"Investment Company Institute." March 2000. Available from http://www.ici.org.

Israelsen, Craig L. "Pick Funds, Not Stocks." *On Wall Street,* 1 March 2000.

Laderman, Jeffrey M. "Investing 101 for Twentysomethings." *Business Week,* 28 February 2000.

Oppel, Richard A., Jr. "The Index Monster in Your Closet." *New York Times,* 10 October 1999.

Thomas, Trevor. "ICI Study Finds Surge in Fund Ownership." *National Underwriter,* 18 September 2000.

U.S. Bureau of Labor Statistics. "Securities and Financial Services Sales Representatives." *1998-99 Occupational Outlook Handbook,* March 2000. Available from http://www.bls.gov/oco/ocos122.htm.

Wiles, Russ. "The Death of Bond Funds." *Registered Representative,* October 2000.

New Age Products and Services

INDUSTRY SNAPSHOT

Akin to the alternative medicines, the philosophies and practices behind the New Age movement have been active in many forms worldwide for centuries. In the Western Hemisphere, the New Age movement draws much of its inspiration from Native American practices, Asian and Indian beliefs and customs, and the 19th-century Utopian movement. The New Age industry draws its revenues from several diverse markets including products and services ranging from incense and crystals to yoga and meditation classes. With the Internet allowing for increased awareness of and access to New Age methodologies and medicines, and with major insurance providers beginning to offer partial coverage of New Age treatments, the New Age industry has gone mainstream.

In the 1990s, major "traditional" food, beverage, and pharmaceutical manufacturers introduced their own versions of New Age products. Even the political arena felt the movement's influence: founded on New Age principles, the Natural Law party appeared on the ballot in 48 states for the 1996 elections. It's clear that while the philosophies behind the New Age movement are often centuries old, the burgeoning industry resulting from this movement is indeed only beginning to emerge, and the likelihood of its success in the 21st century appears great.

ORGANIZATION AND STRUCTURE

For the most part, the New Age industry consists of numerous small businesses that furnish products and services to interested consumers. Excluded from the mix are those large, traditional firms (such as the Coca-Cola Co.) that came out with New Age products only after they became popular with a substantial segment of the market. By the mid- to late 1990s, many big stores sold trendy New Age products that were once available only in New Age establishments. The major exceptions were health-food and grocery stores that carried New Age foodstuffs and food supplements. In the service sector, some consolidated meditation and yoga schools emerged on the scene in the late 1990s.

In 1986 the publishing sector of the New Age industry established its own trade association called New Alternatives for Publishers, Retailers, and Artists (NAPRA). It functions as a communications network for publishers and retailers of New Age books, helping them run their businesses with integrity and sell products with life-affirming intent. In 1990 NAPRA launched a New Age journal called the *NAPRA Review*. By 2000, NAPRA distributed more than 10,000 issues on a bimonthly basis to bookstores, health-food stores, practitioners, and subscribers. Among the subscribers are retailers, publishers, wholesalers, distributors, agents, authors, musicians, and producers of music, audiotapes, videos, and gift items.

CONFERENCES, SEMINARS, AND OTHER GATHERINGS

The rapid growth of the New Age industry can be attributed in part to the many conferences and seminars that characterize the movement. Featured speakers address topics such as the environment, dreams, nutrition, yoga, meditation, and spirituality. Among the most popular gurus on the circuit are author/physician Deepak Chopra and spiritual writer Marianne Williamson; cost of attendance at one of their programs may well run into the hundreds of dollars. The Whole Life Expo, a three-day event held twice yearly in major cities such as San Francisco and Los Angeles, brings together hundreds of vendors, speakers, and practitioners of multiple New Age disciplines. Participants learn about the latest in everything from enzyme therapy to hair regrowth products, peruse the newest books, and go to seminars conducted by well-known personalities. Some New Age events are held at the same time as celebrations marking Earth Day and the spring and fall equinoxes, while others take their inspiration from ancient religious holidays of the Druids and Native Americans and include attempts to re-create the old rituals.

BACKGROUND AND DEVELOPMENT

The sensibilities propelling the New Age industry developed from a host of different sources. Helena Petrovna Blavatsky, founder of the theosophical movement, is often credited with inspiring the New Age movement as well. When she died in May 1891, an editorial writer in the *New York Daily Tribune* declared that, "No one in the present generation, it may be said, has done more toward reopening the long-sealed treasures of Eastern thought, wisdom, and philosophy. . . . Her steps often led, indeed, where only a few initiates could follow, but the tone and tendency of all her writings were healthful, bracing, and stimulating." The Theosophical Society, which has followers around the world, espouses a doctrine that emphasizes direct and mystical contact with a divine power through meditation incorporating elements of Buddhism and Brahmanism.

The New Age movement also has some historic antecedents in the hippie and counterculture movements of the 1960s. These movements did not constitute the largest or most consistent segment of New Agers, wrote Elliot Miller in his book, *A Crash Course on the New Age Movement.* He observed that New Age principles share some similarities with the 1960s movements. Yet the respect for and appreciation of nature; the movement away from materialism; the interest in non-Western thought, culture, and medicine; and the desire to create a better way of living have not been embraced by all participants in the New Age industry. Miller also argued that Asian Hinduism and Buddhism have been key influences on the New Age movement, as are the concerns about health, personal growth, and environmental conservation and protection that germinated during the 1970s.

Even those ideas had first surfaced in the United States as early as the mid- and late 19th century. Philosophers and writers such as Henry David Thoreau and Ralph Waldo Emerson of New England, wellness advocate Dr. John Harvey Kellogg of Battle Creek, Michigan, and the founders of the various Utopian communities across the country foreshadowed much of the later New Age movement. Around the same time, the mineral water springs in such places as Hot Springs, Arkansas, and Saratoga Springs, New York, led to the construction of resort complexes that became gathering places for many of the early progressive thinkers. All of this in turn stimulated an interest in organic foods (those free of chemicals and preservatives), recycling used materials, reducing natural-resource consumption, fighting pollution, and cultivating respect for the environment.

Eventually, people began seeking spiritual fulfillment and self-authenticity outside of the traditional secular and religious channels. Miller noted that the people involved in these early movements also wanted to take responsibility for themselves and the planet, concerns similar to those that later prompted the environmental and spiritual quests on which New Agers embarked.

Some practices of the New Age movement became quite common in the United States during the 1960s and 1970s; yoga and meditation, for example, had many devotees. Miller contended that the movement received very little attention until the mid-1980s when actress Shirley MacLaine began promoting her New Age beliefs on television and in her books. The mass media also took note in August 1987 after the Harmonic Convergence brought together approximately 20,000 New Agers to sites considered sacred worldwide for activities that included meditation, channeling, and rituals with crystals. The event prompted innumerable articles and programs exploring the New Age movement, culminating in a *Time* magazine cover story that appeared in December 1987. The press coverage introduced a larger section of the public to the ideas, wares, services, practices, and foodstuffs associated with the New Age movement.

The confluence of these forces spawned the New Age industry. As more people started to share some of the beliefs and concerns of the original members of the New Age movement, the industry surrounding it grew. Demand for New Age-oriented products and services hit the market in full force during the late 1980s and continued to expand throughout the 1990s, especially as the millennium drew near. Consequently,

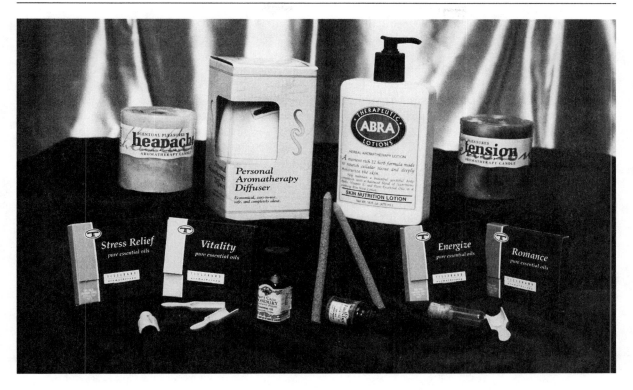

Aroma-therapy items are among the many New Age products available to consumers. (FieldMark Publications/Robert J. Huffman)

many traditional businesses started offering New Age-related products, hoping to profit from the public's fascination with the not-so-new trend.

CURRENT CONDITIONS

Since private service providers and small business operations make up such a large part of the New Age industry, it is nearly impossible to come up with a sales figure for the entire market. In 1996 revenues from New Age industry products and services combined were estimated at nearly $22 billion, but in 1999 analysts estimated the global market for natural and organics products (a major component of the industry) at about $65 billion.

Health-related products in particular have boomed since the early 1980s. According to the National Center for Homeopathy, annual sales of homeopathic remedies in the United States were more than $200 million between 1997 and 1999 and were projected to increase by 12 percent per year. Alternative medicine as a whole earned about $11 billion per year as early as 1990, by the late 1990s sales of all alternative medicines were estimated at between $21 bil-

lion and $34 billion. As reported by the National Center for Homeopathy, the complementary and alternative medicine marketplace exhibited an annual growth rate of close to 15 percent.

The sales of books and food products classified as New Age were estimated to amount to as much as $9 billion by the late 1990s. New Age music sold well, too. Labels such as Windham Hill and Narada made up a significant part of the $86 million music industry in the late 1990s, according to *Forbes*.

MARKETING NEW AGE PRODUCTS

Typically, New Age products and services were marketed in small shops in major cities and towns. The distribution network for such items was limited and, for most vendors, expansion was an option they could not afford. During the mid- to late 1990s, however, the Internet emerged as a major marketing tool for New Age vendors. Hundreds of sites offering candles, crystals, astrolites, incense, and other products have made their debut on the World Wide Web, thus enabling New Age suppliers to market their merchandise virtually everywhere without incurring significant additional expenses. Besides electronic New Age shops, the Internet hosts a number of sites advertising New

Age services such as yoga, meditation instruction, and massages. Various New Age organizations also promote themselves on the Internet and provide links to related sources of information. Of course, this trend is not limited to the New Age products market. It is similar to the experience of many other industries as the Internet becomes an international shopping center.

BOOKS

Sales of New Age-oriented books dealing with religion and spirituality began to soar during the late 1980s, making it the fastest-growing publishing category of the decade. The Book-of-the-Month Club even launched a New Age book club in 1995 called One Spirit that quickly became the most successful specialty book club in the firm's history. The genre remained on top during most of the 1990s, especially among female readers. In fact, between 60 and 70 percent of such titles are bought by women.

Quite a few U.S. best sellers fall within the New Age genre, according to the trade magazine *Publishers Weekly,* including *The Celestine Prophecy, The Seven Laws of Spiritual Success, Simple Abundance,* and *Conversations with God.* Books linking creativity with spirituality also did well in the United States. Upon its release in 1992, for example, *The Artist's Way* had only 5,500 copies in print; by 2000, nearly 1 million copies had been sold.

Titles that publishers once promoted as New Age have since been reclassified as psychology, philosophy, religion, health, or fiction, thus marking the assimilation of New Age ideas into mainstream culture. Yet some authors shun the New Age label, seeing it as a liability that could lead to lower sales on account of some consumers' prejudices. For instance, *Publishers Weekly* reported that Bantam created a New Age label in 1980 but began to shy away from it by the mid-1990s because some authors did not want the New Age association. Alternative terms subsequently began to come into fashion, including "spiritual growth" and "personal growth," even if these covered only certain aspects of what was typically regarded as New Age. Since no one has been able to come up with another name for New Age books, it remains the only inclusive label available for such literature.

As the 1990s drew to a close, the industry was undergoing some changes. Sales flattened, publishers of New Age materials consolidated, and alternative bookstores were facing a number of challenges, including increased competition from large chain operations and Internet booksellers.

BEVERAGES AND FOOD

Alternative beverages and natural foods are closely identified with the New Age movement. (Natural foods are those deemed free of pesticides, preservatives, and artificial sweeteners, and are produced without being cruel to animals.) As with most other New Age products, they were often available at first only in smaller markets and specialty stores. By the year 2000, however, they enjoyed much wider distribution and acceptance.

New Age beverage manufacturers encountered several obstacles when they tried to tap into existing distribution networks or create new ones. According to John N. Frank in *Beverage Industry,* they had trouble getting their products into stores and, if they managed to do so, the stores would often neglect New Age products in favor of traditional brands. Moreover, the well-established companies began developing their own products (such as Coca-Cola's Fruitopia) to take advantage of the growing demand for New Age products.

To address this problem, purveyors of New Age products had to choose from among several less than satisfactory options. They could, for instance, do business with small beverage distributors that served a strictly local market and thus lose out on national exposure, or they could seek out big beer distributors knowing that their products would not reach many convenience outlets and other small stores that did not sell beer. On the other hand, if they opted to go with food distributors instead, they risked bypassing the smaller stores that did not offer a large array of food items. No matter which option they chose, Frank argued, they also needed to come up with a niche marketing strategy or their products would not move quickly. Yet most New Age beverage and food operations were small and could not afford to promote their products on television or with other popular, expensive forms of advertising.

Despite these problems, New Age beverages managed to do extremely well during the 1990s. According to the trade publication *Beverage World,* so-called alternative beverages—such as fruit juices, ready-to-drink teas and coffees, and sports drinks—together reported sales of nearly $7 billion in 1999. From 1993 to 1999, the category experienced a 14 percent compound annual growth rate.

Retail sales of natural products experienced a 26 percent compound annual growth rate between 1994 and 1999, growing from $7.6 billion in 1994 to $19 billion by 1999. The total sales of natural products were estimated at $25.4 billion in 1998. This included Internet sales, sales by practitioners, and mail-order sales.

Natural and organic foods have also been a hit with consumers. According to *Supermarket News,* many traditional food stores are expanding their natural- and organic-food sections, and natural-foods retailers such as Whole Foods Market and Wild Oats Markets have grown by leaps and bounds during the 1990s. Furthermore, organic food producers have increased the diversity of their products with some companies even manufacturing organic baby and pet food. In 1995, for example, 1,015 new products debuted—compared to only 512 in 1991. As Cyndee Miller observed in *Marketing News,* beginning in 1991 organic-food sales nearly doubled. She estimated that this portion of the industry earned $3 billion in 1996, and analysts estimated sales growth for the sector at over 20 percent throughout the 1990s. Sales of all types of organic products, a mere $178 million in 1980, blossomed into more than $6.6 billion by 2000, while sales of natural products exceeded $12 billion.

Mainstream businesses feverishly pursued the organic- and natural-foods market by way of mergers and acquisitions during the 1990s. Investor Roy E. Disney bought organic frozen vegetable pioneer Cascadian Farm in 1996. H.J. Heinz Co. purchased Earth's Best, a rapidly growing organic baby-food company. Such expansion moved this emerging industry "off the natural foods screen and onto the global agribusiness screen," noted Bob Scowcroft, executive director of the Organic Farming Research Foundation in Santa Cruz, California, in a *Los Angeles Times* article.

HEALTH AND HEALING SERVICES

Health and healing services such as yoga, Tai Chi, and meditation have constituted an important element of the New Age industry since its beginnings. Yoga in particular has become very popular. According to *U.S. News & World Report,* the Clinton White House made yoga classes available to staff members. Large law firms and investment banks commission yogis to teach their employees. Many physicians recommend yoga to patients afflicted with diseases such as arthritis and diabetes, as well as those with cardiovascular ailments. Also, some health insurance providers have started covering expenses related to yoga and meditation. Health-care facilities have even started offering yoga and meditation classes, as do some private practitioners.

Paul L. Cerrato and Aria Amara reported in *RN* that one of every three people in the United States relied on some kind of holistic or non-Western therapy in 1997. Another study conducted that same year by a different researcher put the number at about 40 percent and observed that more than half of the patients were between 30 and 50 years of age. Not surprisingly, the number of professional practitioners of nontraditional medicine in the United States rose from 200 during the 1970s to 3,000 in 1998. Even national drugstore chains such as CVS, Kmart, and Walgreen's started carrying homeopathic products in the late 1990s.

The New Age trend has even been reflected in the policies issued by several major insurance firms. By the end of the 1990s, for instance, Mutual of Omaha was covering chiropractic care, Prudential was paying for acupuncture, and Blue Cross of Washington and Alaska was offering a plan called "AlternaPath," which covered licensed naturopathic doctors. In addition, a growing number of hospitals and health maintenance organizations are including alternative medical services in the treatments provided for their patients. The book *New Choices in Natural Healing,* a publication of *Prevention* magazine, noted that at the end of the 1990s the insurance plan that covered the widest array of alternative medicine practices was one offered by American Western Life Insurance Co. of Foster City, California. It reimbursed patients for homeopathy, Ayurveda, nutritional counseling, massage, and physical therapy as part of its wellness plan. The company also offers a full-time "Wellness Line" with naturopathic doctors on call for their patients.

Much of what has come to be known as New Age or alternative medicine (increasingly referred to by the acronym CAM, for complementary and alternative medicine) is not really new, nor did it all originate in Asia. Homeopathy developed in 18th-century Germany. Chiropractic and naturopathy began in the United States, and people have been using herbs for healing all over the world for centuries. Practices such as homeopathy, herbalism, and midwifery were, in fact, part of mainstream medicine until the early 20th century, when members of the medical establishment began rejecting what they viewed as "nonstandard" practices. Yet as of the end of the 1990s, reported David Plank in *Vegetarian Times,* the World Health Organization estimated that 65-80 percent of what is regarded as standard health care elsewhere in the world would be defined by Americans as "alternative."

Homeopathic medicines remain very popular in Europe. For years they have been sold on drugstore shelves in France and Germany and, in the United Kingdom, the government's national health insurance plan covers the cost of purchasing them. The use of herbal medicine is especially common in Germany; German physicians are far more willing than their American counterparts to recommend herbal medications to patients.

The growing popularity of other New Age-oriented health regimens has prompted close scrutiny from the Western medical establishment. The results of their investigations have so far proved favorable to holistic medicine. For instance, meditation has been found to lower blood pressure, chiropractic care can eliminate certain kinds of back pain, and massage alleviates stress, anxiety, and pain, according to Cerrato and Amara in *RN*. In 1996 medical research revealed that acupuncture stimulates the excretion of analgesic and nerve-healing substances, wrote Doug Podolsky in *U.S. News & World Report*. That same year the U.S. Food and Drug Administration (FDA) decreed that acupuncture needles could be considered medical instruments.

As herbal remedies increased in popularity, however, the FDA began to subject them to intense examination. Some of the claims made by dietary supplements, for instance, have been found to be false. Consequently, manufacturers have become more careful about what they claim their products can do.

INDUSTRY LEADERS

WHOLE FOODS MARKET

The largest retailer of natural foods in the United States is Whole Foods Market, based in Austin, Texas. Beginning as a tiny natural-foods store in 1980, it went on to pioneer the concept of selling natural foods in a supermarket-style atmosphere, and it posted sales of nearly $1.6 billion for 1999, an increase of more than 20 percent over the 1998.

In 1998 the chain operated more than 90 stores in more than 20 states. In early 1999, it added 22 new and acquired stores to its ranks, and expected to have more than 120 stores by 2001. Its growth can be traced in part to its aggressive expansion drive during the 1990s, which saw Whole Foods Market acquire several successful independents and smaller chains in major markets characterized by numerous well-educated and affluent consumers. In March 1999 it became the first grocery chain to launch a national online shopping service, beginning with nonperishable goods. Future plans include expanding the online service to include perishable items if customers demand it.

WILD OATS MARKETS

Wild Oats Markets, headquartered in Boulder, Colorado, is the second-largest natural-foods retailer in the United States. In 1999 Wild Oats acquired 17 stores through cash acquisitions and completed two stock-for-stock transactions with Henry's Marketplace, Inc. and Sun Harvest Farms, Inc., thereby adding another 24 stores to its store base. With a total of 110 stores in the U.S. and Canada, sales for the 1999 fiscal year stood at almost $721 million, a 36 percent increase over the 1998 total of $530.7 million.

NEW LEAF DISTRIBUTORS

New Leaf Distributors is the largest and oldest wholesale distributor of New Age books and periodicals. Founded in 1975 and originally called Shakti Distributes, New Leaf started out by distributing the fledgling *New Age Journal,* as well as Dr. Ann Wigmore's books on dietary medicine, to health-food stores and food co-ops in the Atlanta area. By 1976 the firm was bringing in only about $500 per week. Then a store was opened to supplement the distribution service, and in 1979 the company changed its name and sales began to rise. New Leaf posted a profit for the first time in 1983; by the late 1990s annual sales topped $35 million.

THE RED ROSE COLLECTION

The Red Rose Collection is a leading distributor of such New Age products as incense, candles, crystals, and books. Using mail-order catalogs and the Internet, Red Rose also offers New Age apparel and home decorations with New Age motifs. In addition, Red Rose sells meditation and yoga paraphernalia, inspirational and instructional video and audio recordings, and an assortment of novelty gift items. According to *Catalog Age,* Red Rose has about 425,000 customers.

AMERICA AND THE WORLD

The New Age industry has won over many Americans, and people worldwide have embraced some of the movement's ideals and practices. According to *Marketing in Europe,* German demand for organic food started increasing during the 1980s, climbing 20 percent per year through the end of the decade. The market then slowed during the mid-1990s, posting gains of only about 10 to 15 percent per year. Organic food was also attracting a growing base of customers in France. A writer for *Eurofood* reported that the market increased by 15 percent each year beginning in the 1980s as French customers sought higher quality food and adopted healthier eating habits. The lack of an organized distribution system has hindered the industry's ability to expand even more, though.

As Yumi Kiyono noted in *Nikkei Weekly*, Japanese citizens have also heartily embraced the New Age movement. Spiritual books and other wares have done well, as have so-called power stones, which facilitate meditation.

Sumit Sharma reported in the *Wall Street Journal* that in India—especially in Bombay—yoga, meditation, and other indigenous practices for health and stress reduction were prospering in the late 1990s. In 1996 some physicians were turning to classical yoga breathing exercises and laughing postures for their patients in the belief that they relieved stress. This spawned more than 100 laughing clubs across the country.

FURTHER READING

"The Age of New Age." *Beverage Industry,* March 1997.

"Americans Mingling Alternative and Traditional Medical Services." *USA Today,* February 1999.

Brotman, Barbara. "Finding Personal Growth in Abundance." *Dallas Morning News,* 14 January 1998.

Chillot, Rick. "Homeopathy: Help or Hype?" *Prevention,* 1 March 1998.

Condor, Bob. "Americans Increasingly Trying Alternative Medicine, Study Shows." *Knight Ridder/Tribune News Service,* 11 November 1998.

Garrett, Lynn. "Fifth New Age Trade Show Thrives." *Publishers Weekly,* 10 July 2000.

Garrett, Lynn, and Bridget Kinsella. "New Age is All the Rage." *Publishers Weekly,* 10 March 1997.

"Going Outside the Mainstream." *U.S. News & World Report,* 23 November 1998.

Grossman, Cathy Lynn. "Religious Retail Stores Have Strong Faith in Sales Soaring to Heaven." *USA Today,* 12 March 1998.

Gwynne, S. C. "Thriving on Health Food, Whole Foods Has Grown into the Biggest Organic Supermarket Chain by Feeding on Weak Competition." *Time,* 23 February 1998.

Kinsella, Bridget. "New Leaf Adds a New Leaf." *Publishers Weekly,* 27 January 1997.

Langone, John. "Challenging the Mainstream." *Time,* fall 1996.

McCracken, Samuel. "The New Snake Oil: A Field Guide." *Commentary,* June 1999.

Miller, Elliot. *A Crash Course on the New Age Movement.* Grand Rapids, MI: Baker Book House, 1989.

Plank, David. "Alternative Medicine Comes of Age." *Vegetarian Times,* April 1999.

Podolsky, Doug. "Nature's Remedies." *U.S. News & World Report,* 19 May 1997.

"Seeking Organic Growth." *Snack Food & Wholesale Bakery,* August 2000.

Sharma, Sumit. "Stressed? Inhibited? Grumpy? Join the (Laughing) Club, Indians Say." *Wall Street Journal,* 12 September 1996.

Smith, Stephen. "National Study to Examine Effectiveness of St. John's Wort." *Knight Ridder/Tribune News Service,* 12 March 1999.

Warner, Bernhard. "Whole Foods Market Joins Online Rush." *Industry Standard,* 22 March 1999. Available from http://www.thestandard.net/articles/display/0,1449,3870,00 .html.

Wind, Edgar. *Pagan Mysteries in the Renaissance.* England: Faber & Faber, 1958.

NEW FOOD PRODUCTS

The cozy scene of families gathered around the table each evening to share a home-cooked, made-from-scratch meal has been vanishing from the American dining horizon for some time. The reality of meal preparation is in flux. At the end of the 20th century, almost one-half of all U.S. food expenditure went for meals prepared outside the home and only one-third of meals included at least one dish made the old-fashioned way. Americans don't want to invest more than 15 minutes in preparing their food, according to a Food Marketing Institute report. Seventy percent of households buy takeout at least once a month. Even the definition of food is changing rapidly. Meals can be prepared in minutes, since many packaged foods now eliminate the need for washing, slicing, and dicing. Functional foods, which contain extra beneficial effects for "targeted" functions in the body, promise to rival medicines in their disease-fighting and -resisting capacities. In 2000, the U.S. functional foods market was estimated to be worth $17 billion, according to *Nutraceuticals World.*

Organic and ethnic food items continued to retain consumer interest, though media attention focused increasingly on so-called functional foods, or "nutraceuticals," and on the controversies surrounding genetically modified foods. Low-fat products, which had slipped in recent years, also showed a bit of a resurgence. Among ethic foods, Asian specialties—particularly prepackaged sushi made fresh on the premises in supermarkets— joined the ranks of the perennially popular Mexican and Italian cuisine.

ORGANIZATION AND STRUCTURE

Before new food products hit stores nationwide, producers usually test-market them in a limited geographical region. Companies monitor the success of the new products and determine whether they have market-staying or trend-setting power. If the products are deemed successful during the trial period, the companies then begin more extensive marketing. In order for new products to thrive once they are introduced, analysts note that companies must fortify them with a robust barrage of promotional strategies. Unless companies support new food products, they will never gain much attention from consumers, and if businesses let up on promoting new products prematurely, sales will start to flag and the new product will fade out of the market. After launching a new product, developers must track it—scrutinize the movement of the product and ascertain who buys it and why. Developers must also anticipate consumer reactions to the product and alter promotional campaigns to accommodate consumer response.

The U.S. Department of Agriculture (USDA), U.S. Food and Drug Administration (FDA), Center for Food Safety and Applied Nutrition, National Organic Standards Board, and an array of state, county, and municipal organizations that oversee the growing, production, and sale of foods all play a role in the regulation of new food items. The industry itself has an array of related trade organizations and groups such as the American Crop Protection Association and the Food Marketing Institute. Many commodities boast their own lobbying and marketing groups. The produce industry, for example, has the International Fresh-cut Produce Association, United Fresh Fruit and Vegetable Association, Texas Produce Association, Produce Marketing Association, Florida Fruit and Vegetable Association, Northwest Horticultural Council, and Western Growers Association protecting its interests and marketing its products nationally and regionally.

Perhaps the most rigorous industry oversight involves the certification and monitoring of organic foods. As early as 1974, the USDA called for policies to govern the growing, processing, and marketing of organic foods, but no hard-and-fast rules resulted from these early exhortations. But the USDA did provide a working definition: "organically grown food" refers to produce not treated with chemical pesticides or fertilizers, and "organically processed food" includes produce not treated with synthetic preservatives, according to William Breene in *Prepared Foods*. Farm organizations started certification programs throughout the country beginning in the 1970s and 1980s. In 1990 Congress finally passed legislation towards creating standards for certifying organic food. The Farm Act of 1990 established the National Organic Standards Board, which tried to develop official standards for the organic foods industry. A host of certification agencies all over the country, however, still bear the brunt of the certification task using standards they create. By 1999, the USDA had issued guidelines for the certification of organic meat and poultry, but no final regulations to establish standards for all organic products. Further complicating issues related to the standards were whether foods genetically engineered, irradiated, or grown in soil fertilized with sewage sludge could be considered organic.

CURRENT CONDITIONS

Market emphasis on convenience and health food continues. With a slew of popular products, such as the widening variety of home-meal replacements on the market, food producers largely expanded or remarketed existing lines and did not launch many revolutionary products in the mid- to late 1990s. A growing problem at the end of the decade was dwindling shelf space in stores. New product introductions slowed, but organic and all-natural products showed significant gains. Meal kits and convenience foods continued to dominate, however.

DINNERS, ENTRÉES, AND MIXES

The drive to create products that capture market share for convenience, and at least seemingly health-ful food, often resulted in the release of hundreds of new dinner, entrée, and mix offerings each year. Leading this category were frozen pizzas; analysts predicted sales of $2.5 billion by 2000. Most new products, however, were merely extensions of existing lines of entrées, such as Stouffer, Lean Cuisine, Healthy Choice, and Budget Gourmet.

For traditional supermarkets home-meal replacement was the hottest item in the late 1990s, according to *Food World,* an industry newspaper. But many stores moved away from offering fully prepared meals, stressing preprepared meals in the refrigerated or frozen sections, meals that require only heating. Among the items located in these sections are meats that are already marinated, and packaged meals, such as Skillet Sensations or Voila! one-dish dinners that include pasta, vegetables, and meat.

Interest in international cuisines remained strong, led as usual by Mexican and Italian. But Asian, Mediterranean, and Middle Eastern food products increased as well. One fully prepared meal item that did enjoy notable success was sushi. Larger supermarket chains, such as Jewel, Dominick's, and Wegman's, introduced to-go sushi rolled, packaged, and placed on ice right before the shoppers' eyes. It proved to be a popular lunch option for office workers. Alongside traditional maki and California rolls, more adventurous combinations appeared. Sushi House offered Philly rolls (salmon and cream cheese), and Whole Foods featured shiitake rolls (shiitake mushrooms, avocados, and carrots encased in rice and seaweed). Prices ranged from $5 for a simple tuna-maki to $8.45 for a deluxe assortment of eel, tuna, salmon, swordfish, and shrimp.

Mexican items featured one particularly unusual offering—the Dilberito. Based on the main character in the "Dilbert" comic srip, it was a $2.50 vegetarian burrito containing 100 percent of the daily value for 23 vitamins and minerals.

BABY FOOD

Due to the possibility of babies suffering harmful effects from farm chemical residue after consuming food processed with toxic chemicals, parents have grown more wary and cognizant of what they feed their children and how it is grown and processed. In addition, parents want healthful natural food for their babies, not food adulterated with unnecessary ingredients and treated with preservatives. Health-food companies launched products to compete with the traditional baby-food producers. Growing Healthy and Earth's Best are two of the most prominent alternative producers, offering unalloyed organic foods. Sales, however, slumped for these new contenders and baby health food never fully caught on. Furthermore, even though the Center for Science in the Public Interest reported that Gerber Products Co. diluted its products, the center failed to pique the public's interest, and Gerber retained a majority market share. Nonetheless, Earth's Best has had moderate but improving success, becoming the country's fourth-leading producer of baby food. The key problem organic baby-food producers face is offering competitive pricing. Yet Gerber began to market organic foods in its Tender Harvest line in order to retain market domination.

PACKAGED PREPARED PRODUCE

A trend that started in the early 1990s and fared well by catering to both sensibilities of convenience and health consciousness was packaged salad. Its success led to the creation of numerous other new packaged produce releases. Introduced in 1994, salad kits continued to sell well throughout the decade. One of the most successful food categories in the 1990s was packaged produce. Although supermarkets traditionally offered many of these value-added products in order to promote or use up produce that neared its maximum storage limit, producers and distributors now want to participate in the market. The newest additions to packaged salads were edible flowers: marigolds, lavender, and rose petals.

In an effort to garner more fresh fruit sales, companies have begun to launch washed, sliced, and otherwise prepared fruits. For example, Fresh Express introduced Grape Escape—washed red seedless grapes removed from the stem in four ounce packages. Fresh World Farms brought out its Necta Fresh Pineapples in a few different varieties—whole cored, chunked, and sliced. Some producers also offered prepeeled fruit. Fruit of Groveland introduced the Heart Garden Fresh Cut Fruit, providing an assortment of melons, as well as grapes and pineapple. Global Fresh began marketing Fresh Cut Apples with Dip, which includes slices of Granny Smith or Fuji apples and reduced-fat caramel dip. Ready Pac Produce also introduced its ready-to-eat Fresh Melon Chunks featuring watermelon, cantaloupe, or honeydew.

LOW FAT

Though they declined in popularity in the late 1990s, the food industry created over 5,600 low-fat foods. Advances in food technology and the FDA's approval of Olean increased consumer options for fat-modified foods. A 1996 survey revealed 88 percent of Americans eat low-fat, reduced-fat, or fat-free foods.

Rather than invent new fat-free foods, the recent trend moved toward the reformulation of fat-free foods into better-tasting low-fat foods. Even small amounts of fat improve the sensory appeal of food, including texture and flavor.

Three types of fat replacers are used in the new reformulations, according to American Dietetic Association spokesperson Cindy Moore—carbohydrate-based, protein-based, and fat-based. Most are carbohydrate-based and include such ingredients as cellulose, gums, dextrins, fiber, starches, maltodextrins, and polydextrose. Pureed prunes and applesauce can also be used in baked goods. A new fat replacer, NuTrim, made from soluble oat fiber, helps lower high blood levels of LDL-cholesterol and risk for heart disease. Carbohydrate-based replacers are used in processed meats, frozen desserts, baked goods, dairy products, salad dressings, sour cream, gravy, sauces, and soups. In contrast, protein-based fat replacers are usually made from egg white or skim milk. Some examples include Simplesse, Veri-lo, and Dairy-lo. Since protein-based replacers stabilize fat emulsions and add creaminess, they appear in cheeses, mayonnaise, butter, sour cream, bakery products, sauces, frozen dairy desserts, and salad dressings. Protein-based fat replacers contribute only one to four calories per gram of fat and usually can't withstand high temperatures. Therefore, they can't be used in baked goods, because the protein coagulates. But some fat replacers are made from chemically altered fats, such as Salatrim (Benefat) and Olestra (Olean). Olestra is made from vegetable oils and sugar (sucrose polyester), and contains no calories, because its bulk prevents it from being digested. It is also heat-stable, and therefore can be added to baked goods and snacks.

VENDING MACHINES

The convenience and speed of vending-machine cuisine has traditionally outranked its taste, but that appeared to be changing. New lines of pizza, Mexican favorites such as burritos and chimichangas, and soups and sandwiches edged out the usual coffee and chocolate-bar fare traditionally provided by the machines. Shelf-stable entrées were introduced by DeLuca, Inc.; Hormel Foods Corp.; International Home Foods, Inc.; and Jimmy Dean Foods. DeLuca, a subsidiary of Perdue Farms Inc., featured 12 different entrées, including meat lasagna; eggplant lasagna; meatballs in meat sauce; macaroni and beef; sausage, peppers, and onions; American meat loaf; and baked ziti. Hormel and Dinty Moore extended their well-known canned products such as chili, beef stew,

Innovative milk products are among the new foods available to consumers. (FieldMark Publications/Robert J. Huffman)

corned-beef hash, scalloped potatoes, and beans and wieners to the vending-machine venue as well. Among soups, Maruchan, Inc. of Irvine, California, provided instant ramen noodles and instant wonton in Styrofoam cups. Hormel and others also have soups available in ovenproof paper or foam cups. Oscar Mayer Lunchables and Charlie's Lunch Kit by Starkist Tuna rounded out the category.

NUTRACEUTICALS

Americans have been eating fortified foods since 1924, when manufacturers started adding iodine to salt to prevent the nutritional deficiency that causes goiters. But the aging of the health-conscious and often affluent baby boomers has focused increasing attention on the development of nutraceuticals, also known as functional foods. Though a precise definition of functional foods is hard to pin down, they are often described as complete food items that provide an enhanced health benefit beyond the usual nutritional properties normally found in a food item. Products fitting this description raked in an estimated $12.7 billion in 1999. Nutraceuticals continued to eclipse low-fat, no-fat, and sugar-free products. They are promoted as remedies or preventives for common ailments, such as high cholesterol and osteoporosis, which predomi-

nantly strike people as they age. Many of these products competed with pharmaceuticals and were designed to replace vitamins or other diet aids.

On average, women exhibited greater awareness of the value and the health-related benefits of functional foods, yet consumed them less frequently than men. And widespread appreciation of nutraceuticals has yet to penetrate the U.S. populace at large. According to a 2000 survey by the American Dietetic Association, 79 percent of those surveyed hadn't heard of functional foods, 68 percent defined them simply as "healthy" foods, while 17 percent felt that they either boosted energy or improved athletic performance. Leading consumers of functional foods had a high awareness of health topics and nutrition news. In addition, about 44 percent were 55 and over. The physical and performance benefits of some nutraceuticals, however, appealed most strongly to those at the ends of the age spectrum: 18- to 29-year-olds and healthy seniors 70 and older. In contrast, consumers in the 40- to 65-year-old group and seniors in poor health sought the medical and preventive functional benefits, according to Linda Gilbert, the president of HealthFocus Inc. of Des Moines, Iowa.

Antioxidants received particular attention for inclusion in functional foods. Clinical trials of the benefits of vitamins E and B are underway. Also under consideration were n-3 fatty acids found in fish and certain vegetable oils, since they may prevent ventricular fibrillation and sudden death. Pharmaceutical makers view functional foods as a way to help their products cross over from the pharmacy to the grocery store. For packaged-goods companies, nutraceuticals seem to be the next hot-selling, high-margin products in a traditionally very flat industry sector.

Among notable functional-food releases were Benecol, a Johnson & Johnson margarine-like spread touted as lowering cholesterol levels by as much as 10 percent with regular use. In the first few months after its introduction, it had captured 2 percent of the market. It was joined by Unilever's Take Control, a similar spread with slightly lower performance abilities. Mead Johnson Nutritionals premiered Viactiv, chocolate-flavored, calcium-enriched chews, and EnfaGrow, a series of vitamin-fortified cereals and snacks for children. Novartis debuted its Aviva line in Europe, which consisted of orange drinks, biscuits, and muesli intended to strengthen bones and aid digestion. The company introduced the line in the U.S. in 2000. Cooke Pharma developed the first functional food for the management of vascular disease—the HeartBar. It contains the amino acid L-arginine, which, the company says, relieves angina, or heart-related chest pain, by dilating the coronary arteries. Gerber was developing a preschoolers' snack fortified with docosa hexaenoic acid, which is claimed to boost concentration. The additive is already in use in Japan.

Phytochemicals, which are extracts from plants, appeared in increasing numbers in functional foods. For example, Kellogg introduced its Ensemble line of frozen foods, desserts, and cereals that contain psyllium, a fiber that lowers cholesterol. Take Control spread featured soybean extract to lower cholesterol levels.

Functional foods don't lack for critics, however. The Center for Science in the Public Interest has charged that some functional foods don't live up to their health claims, often because they don't contain a great enough amount of their "functional" ingredient to deliver promised benefits, or because the products require sustained consumption to achieve results, just as ordinary medicines do. Price constitutes another basis for complaint, as well as a barrier to widespread adoption of functional foods by U.S. consumers. Frequently nutraceuticals cost five or six times the amount of nonenhanced counterparts.

Like dietary supplements, functional foods are not regulated by the FDA. The agency, however, established 12 health claims that manufacturers could feature in their promotional efforts, based on the general health-enhancing properties of key ingredients in the food items.

ORGANICS AND NATURAL FOODS

Organic foods continued to draw strong interest from consumers. Sales grew nearly 20 percent annually through the 1990s, topping $6.6 billion in 2000. In contrast, ordinary grocery sales experienced only a 1-2 percent growth over the same period, according to the Grocery Manufacturers of America.

Organics also caught the eye of major food and pharmaceuticals manufacturers, who rushed to acquire prominent producers in this segment. For example, H.J. Heinz Co. formed an organic and nutritional foods unit through investment in Hain Food Group. Kraft Foods, Inc. bought Boca Burger, the producer of soy-based meat alternatives. General Mills, Inc. purchased Small Planet Foods, which makes a line of frozen and canned organic produce. While such acquisitions boost the visibility of organic items, they also probably threatened the market presence of the smaller, independent producers that traditionally characterized this sector.

GENETICALLY MODIFIED FOODS

Undoubtedly the most controversial new foods were genetically modified (GM) foods, which continued to create vigorous debate in Europe, although they appeared to be less problematic for U.S. consumers. Critics broadcast fears of newly created viruses and allergens as a result of tampering with the genetic structure of food items, whose long-term consequences were as yet unknown. Opponents also charged that patenting GM foods would lead to the domination of the world's food supply by a handful of large manufacturers.

Nevertheless, developing countries such as the People's Republic of China and India are heavy users of GM crops created by industry giants such as Monsanto and Novartis. China intended to put one-half of all its harvest of rice, tomatoes, peppers, and potatoes into GM varieties within the next five to 10 years, citing both its lack of arable land and the lower pesticide and herbicide requirements of GM crops. In the United States about 60 percent of all supermarket products contained GM canola oil, soybeans, or corn.

European representatives have called for labeling on all GM foods and advocate the establishment of an international supervisory panel to police the development and dissemination of GM foods. While the United States, with an enormous stake in GM foods, was traditionally resistant to labeling, by the end of 2000 the proposed Genetically Engineered Food Right to Know Act (GEFRKA) was making its way through the U.S. Congress.

Fans of GM foods may have found their champion in the form of "golden rice," a GM strain developed by Swiss professor Ingo Potrykus in Zurich. The rice, named for its golden hue, contains beta carotene (vitamin A), which the body needs for vision health. Potrykus developed the rice in an effort funded by the Swiss government and the Rockefeller Foundation to help combat vitamin A deficiency in the developing world, which kills about 2 million children each year and causes blindness in many others. Growers will be given the rice free.

PET FOODS

New food items aren't limited to human consumers. The $1 billion U.S. pet-food market encompasses many novel products that resemble the special foods intended for pets' human counterparts. Since nearly as many pets as owners are overweight, for example, "lite" foods are included in most pet-food brand lines. In 1999 the American Animal Feed Control Officials established standard calorie references for reduced-calorie pet foods.

Other special pet foods include formulas adapted for particular stages in the pet's life cycle, such as puppyhood, old age, or pregnancy. Gourmet pet foods feature "human grade" ingredients and no fillers or artificial byproducts. Medical foods, such as low-protein mixes for pets with kidney ailments and dental products to reduce plaque on teeth, are regulated as foods, not drugs.

The next wave in specialty pet foods will be nutraceuticals for pets. These include dietary supplements, herbals for the stressed dog, and canine probiotics to aid digestion. Pet snacks constitute a popular product with pet owners; according to the Pet Products Manufacturers' Association, eight out of every 10 dog owners and five of every 10 cat owners regularly buy pet treats. Like other consumers of specialty foods, however, pet owners must exercise caution in their purchasing decisions. The long-term health effects of many pet products are not well known, since very few manufacturing guidelines have been established for these items. In addition, some dietary supplements may be entirely unnecessary for pet health or may even have negative effects.

INDUSTRY LEADERS

Nestlé S.A., based in Vervey, Switzerland, was the world's leading food company at the end of the 1990s, with over 8,500 products spread over several food categories. Founded in 1843, the company was a long-established brand in the food industry, with 231,900 employees by 2000. The firm's new foods operations focused on production of dietary supplements to boost the function of the immune system. Nestlé spent the late 1990s buying and selling companies and brands, acquiring Berkeley, California-based Power Bar Inc., and selling off its European frozen food business. Nestlé's sales reached $43.04 billion in 1999, up from $41.36 billion the year before.

The New York-based Philip Morris Companies Inc. was the world's leading cigarette maker, but augmented its operations in that troubled industry with food products, where it followed Nestlé in the world market. The company, started as a London tobacco store in 1847, leaped to the top of the food industry with its purchase of Kraft Foods in 1988. In summer 2000 the company purchased Nabisco, which it planned to combine with Kraft to form the world's leading food company. Although rocked by lawsuits stemming from its tobacco operations as political and legal battles in that industry heated up, Philip Morris continued to bring in healthy revenues. In 1999, sales reached $78.6 billion, up from $74.4 billion in 1998, and derived about 34 percent of its revenues from its food businesses. The company employed some 137,000 workers.

The Minneapolis, Minnesota-based Pillsbury Co., with its cuddly Pillsbury Doughboy, was another leader in the new foods industry. The company, which maintained a payroll of 17,610 employees, was the subsidiary of the foods giant Diageo, and was the U.S. leader in refrigerated foods. Since the 1970s, Pillsbury has been at the front of the convenience-food movement, starting out by developing microwave dinners, baking mixes, and refrigerated products. After a series of acquisitions in 1999, Pillsbury's revenues tailed off slightly, totaling $5.92 billion, down from $6.09 billion the year before. In 2000, Pillsbury's parent company, Diageo, sold Pillsbury to the cereal giant General Mills.

ConAgra Foods, Inc., based in Nebraska, was another leading frozen-food producer in the United States. The diversified food company produced some of the leading prepared-food products in the United States. The company manufactured products for agriculture and prepared-food items under various brand names such as Hunt's, Healthy Choice, Wesson, Rosarita, La Choy, Chun King, Peter Pan, Knott's Berry Farm, Orville Redenbacher's, Armour, Butterball, Hebrew National, and Van Camp's. ConAgra formed the CAG Functional Foods Division to take advantage of projected growth in that category. About half the company's revenues derive from its refrigerated-foods operations, while packaged foods brought in about 30 percent. ConAgra also ran one of the country's largest flour- and corn-milling operations. In 1998 ConAgra rolled out its Advantage 10 vegetarian entrée line, and purchased meat-snack maker GoodMark Foods. In 2000 the firm picked up high-profile brands Chef Boyardee and PAM cooking spray with its purchase of International Home Foods. The ConAgra, which employed 80,000 workers and announced a major restructuring in 1999, finished fiscal 2000 with $25.4 billion in revenues, up from $24.6 billion in 1998.

Novartis AG of Basel, Switzerland, with 81,845 employees, was a leader in the functional-foods sector. The firm was hard hit by controversy in 1999 related to its use of genetically modified foods. Partly as a result of these difficulties, Novartis planned to spin off its agribusiness unit to focus on health-care products. But its foods business was just gearing up for growth. In 1999 the company announced an equally owned joint venture with Quaker Oats Co., to be known as Altus Food Co, to produce nutraceuticals. The company's total sales in 1999 reached $19.98 billion, down from $23.05 billion in 1998, and its nutrition unit accounted for about 18 percent of that total.

AMERICA AND THE WORLD

Many U.S. food trends and products originate elsewhere in the world. In many Asian cultures, diet and health are considered integrally linked, and herbal enhancements are routinely incorporated into everyday cuisine. Unique Japanese functional products include chewing gums and soft drinks that claim antiallergy properties, a throat candy packaged in antibacterial film bags, and health/beauty drinks that contain collagen—an ingredient used in external skincare products.

The number of new food products launched in Europe by 2001 will increase by 15 percent, according to market research firm Datamonitor. As in the United States, desire for convenience or indulgence combines with a concern for quality and health. In the United Kingdom, a cultural preference for snacking is creat-

ing a greater market for breakfast bars and other "on-the-go" foods. In Europe, functional foods include vitamin-fortified frozen vegetables from Agro, a division of Unilever, and "smart fat" Maval yogurt that contains appetite-suppressing palm-oil extract. Spanish manufacturer Union Tostadora produces lines of coffee enriched with fiber, vitamins, and ginseng. According to analyst David Jago and others, European interest in natural, organic, and artisanal food is developing in tandem with increasing ethical concerns about animal welfare and environmentally responsible food production. This was especially evident in the well-publicized European opposition to GM foods. The European functional food market totaled $14 billion in 2000.

FURTHER READING

Austin, Sarah, and Alison Demos. "We Pop Our Pills with Our Meals, Why Not in Them?" *Civilization,* October/November 1999.

Bertagnoli, Lisa. "From Sushi Bar to Supermarket." *Crain's Chicago Business,* 10 January 2000.

Clark, Jane Bennett. "Washed, Cooked and Priced to Go." *Kiplinger's Personal Finance Magazine,* January 2000.

"Designer Foods." *Consumer Reports,* January 2000.

Dwyer, Paula, Amy Borrus, and Lorraine Woellert. "The 'Frankenfood' Monster Stalks Capitol Hill." *Business Week,* 31 December 1999.

Ebenkamp, Becky. "The Food of the Future." *Brandweek,* 17 January 2000.

Eder, Bob. "Understanding the New Natural Health Customer." *Drug Store News,* 29 November 1999.

Fulmer, Melinda. "Food Firms Heat up Health Trends." *Los Angeles Times,* 1 March 2000.

Gruenwald, Joerg, and Alexandra Pearl. "The European Approach to Functional Foods." *Nutraceuticals World,* October 2000.

Hunter Trum, Beatrice. "That Special Diet for Fido, Fluffy." *Consumers' Research Magazine,* May 1999.

Katan, Martijn B. "Functional Foods." *Lancet,* 4 September 1999.

Knowlew, Francine. "Quaker Joins Effort to Tap Health Market." *Chicago Sun-Times,* 10 February 2000.

"Kraft Foods Agrees to Buy Boca Burger, a Soy-Products Firm." *Wall Street Journal,* 19 January 2000.

Leighton, Peter. "Up-and-Coming Markets." *Nutraceuticals World,* October 2000.

Margen, Sheldon, and Dale Ogar. "Shedding Light on Nutrition's Gray Area." *Los Angeles Times,* 10 May 1999.

Moore, Stephen. "Novartis-Quaker Venture to Market 'Functional Foods.'" *Wall Street Journal,* 10 February 2000.

Morrow, David. "A Medicine Chest or a Grocery Shelf?" *New York Times,* 12 December 1999.

Mott, Gregory. "Functional Illiteracy." *Washington Post,* 8 February 2000.

Neporent, Liz. "Foods Containing Many Promises." *New York Times,* 13 June 1999.

"The New Foods: Functional or Dysfunctional?" *Consumer Reports on Health,* June 1999.

Potter, Mitch. "Rhetoric Rules in Altered Food Debate." *Toronto Star,* 5 March 2000.

Rubins, Karen Wilk. "For a Healthier Diet: Fat Replacers." *FoodService Director,* 15 January 2000.

Sheldon, Silver. "New Foods, Technologies Hit the Spot: Vending 'Round the Clock." *FoodService Director,* 15 August 1999.

Squires, Sally. "FDA Clears a Medicinal Margarine; Drug-Like 'Designer Foods' Proliferate." *Washington Post,* 1 May 1999.

Stevenson, Seth, et al. "Wrapping Up." *Newsweek,* 17 January 2000.

"Too Many Calcium-Fortified Foods?" *Tufts University Health & Nutrition Letter,* February 2000.

Vierhile, Thomas R. "Functional Foods or Modern-Day Snake Oils?!" *Health Products Business,* September 2000.

"The World of Nutraceuticals." *International Food Ingredients,* July 2000.

Wrong, Michela. "Field of Dreams." *Financial Times* (London), 25 February 2000.

Noise Control and Technology

Noise pollution is endemic in modern society. Antinoise technology, also known as active noise control, active noise cancellation, or active structural-acoustic control, is a promising approach to coping with the overload of objectionable noise. For example, one noise-control solution is to use speakers that silence disturbing noises by emitting an opposing noise. If the device works correctly, the new sound and the offensive one will have wavelengths that counter each other so that nothing is audible, or at least the offending noise is reduced.

Noise control has far-reaching applications ranging from aircraft and machinery to communications devices and office electronics. Because of so many uses, this quiet industry is also a fragmented one, with such diverse participants as Bose Corp. (of high-end speaker notoriety), IBM Corp., Lucent Technologies, Matsushita Electric, and Owens Corning, as well as specialists such as Andrea Electronics, NCT Group, Industrial Acoustics Co., and Sennheiser Electronic.

SOURCES OF NOISE, WAYS TO DEAL WITH IT

Technologies are needed to cope with various types of noise, particularly those connected with aircraft, trains, and motor-vehicle traffic. Some solutions are of the more passive type, along the lines of soundproofing. Redesigning passenger compartments in cars and airplanes in order to cut down on noise for their occupants is an example of such methods, as is finding new materials effective in blocking noise within buildings and residences. Active noise cancellation technology can also be effective in such situations. An example is Barry Controls Aerospace's Active Tuned Mass Absorbers, which resonate at the same frequency as the engine compressors in a DC-9 airplane and thereby reduce cabin noise.

Airplanes and helicopters are among the most serious sources of noise in the United States, in urban settings and even in wilderness areas of national parks. Excessive noise emanating from airports often spurs years-long battles with city residents and institutions over building projects. Noise regulations adopted in the early 1990s stipulated that older planes must be modified and new aircraft were to be designed with quieter engines by 1999. Lucent Technologies and Sikorsky Aircraft, in conjunction with the U.S. Naval Research Laboratory, are studying the use of smart materials to reduce helicopter rotor noise. *Flight International* reported that Bell Helicopter Textron Inc. is developing a noise-reduction plan in its Quiet Cruise system to meet new federal guidelines for aircraft that fly over national parks.

Cars and trucks are another racket to contend with, as anyone living near a freeway can attest. Proposed solutions include highway barriers of concrete, dirt, and even waterfalls to muffle noise. Alternative tire designs and on-vehicle silencing equipment have been explored. Researchers have likewise pondered new road building materials, such as porous asphalt, to reduce the din of traffic. One noteworthy project is that of the Institute for Safe, Quiet, and Durable Highways at Purdue University. Backed by federal and private industry dollars, the Institute has focused on complementary tire and pavement designs to eradicate noise.

Household appliances and power tools also add to environmental noise. A combination of reengineering, noise regulations, and antinoise protection, such as headsets, are among the ways being used to tone down the clatters, whirrs, whines, and buzzing produced in residential areas. At Owens Corning, for example, acoustic engineers record the sounds of an appliance going through its operating cycles and then use different sound-control systems to modify the noises. After the sounds are digitally edited, they are played to humans to get feedback on which have been most successfully quieted. Using this method—along with computer simulation—as part of the prototyping process, saves half the time needed to develop a noise-control system for an appliance.

BACKGROUND AND DEVELOPMENT

Antinoise technology is far from new. In 1936 Paul Lueg patented one of the first working active noise-control systems. His process of silencing sound oscillation received patents in the United States and Germany. Another pioneer in antinoise technology was H. F. Olson, whose 1953 article on electronic sound absorbers was published in the *Journal of the Acoustical Society of America.*

The Noise Control Act of 1972 was passed to protect Americans from noise that threatened their health and well-being. It was amended by the Quiet Communities Act of 1978, Public Law 95-609, which required the administrator of the U.S. Environmental Protection Agency (EPA) to disseminate educational materials on the effects of noise on public health and the most effective means of noise control; to conduct or finance specified research projects on noise control; to administer a nationwide Quiet Communities Program designed to assist local governments in controlling noise levels; and to provide technical assistance to state and local governments in implementing noise-control programs.

The Airport Noise and Capacity Act of 1990, Subtitle D of Public Law 101-508, required the establishment of a national aviation noise policy and issuance of regulations governing airport noise and access restrictions for stage two aircraft (weighing under 75,000 pounds). The act provided for the phaseout of older, noisier planes and for noise reduction to specified levels for new aircraft to go into effect in 1999, and it set civil penalties and reporting requirements for aircraft operators. It prohibited operation of certain domestic or imported civil subsonic turbojet aircraft unless such aircraft complied with Stage III noise levels. Subtitle B of the same law, known as the Aviation Safety and Capacity Expansion Act of 1990, called for environmental reviews before air traffic could be rerouted during an airport expansion.

The Office of Noise Abatement and Control Establishment Act of 1996 sought to reinstate the EPA's role in noise control after funding for it was eliminated in 1982. The primary duty of the office would be to coordinate federal noise-abatement activities with state and local activity and other public and private agencies. It would also be responsible for updating and developing new noise standards, providing technical assistance to local communities, and promoting research and education on the impact of noise pollution. Initially, the Office of Noise Abatement and Control would study the physiological effects of airport noise in major metropolitan areas and surrounding communities in order to propose new measures to combat the impact of aircraft noise.

The National Park Scenic Overflight Concession Act of 1997 set guidelines for air traffic over national parks in order to eliminate intrusive noise. It proposed rules for use of quiet aircraft and minimum flight altitudes within national parks, flight-free zones, and, if necessary, flight bans to prevent commercial air tours in a park to preserve, protect, or restore the natural quiet of the park. It also created a schedule for any commercial air tour operator operating within a national park to convert the operator's fleet to quiet aircraft.

Because of the 1 January 1999 deadline for implementation of restrictions on aircraft noise, much activity in the aviation field was directed toward meeting the new noise-control requirements, called the Stage III rules. Older airplanes, such as DC-8s and 727s, would be grounded if they weren't retrofitted with "hush kits" to decrease noise. The Boeing Co. and Raisbeck Engineering, both of Seattle, Washington, were two companies developing solutions to the problem of retrofitting older aircraft and redesigning new ones to bring them into compliance with the Stage III regulations. In 1996 Raisbeck recertified the Boeing 727 to meet federal requirements. In January 1997 the Federal Aviation Administration (FAA) approved the installation of Lord Corp.'s NVX Active Noise and Vibration Control System in DC-9 models, making it the first active noise and vibration control system to receive FAA approval on a large commercial jet.

Trends

NOISE IN PARKS IS NO PICNIC

In recent years U.S. parks have been bombarded with noise of all kinds as Americans enjoy the outdoors in the company of motorized vehicles and recreation equipment. In different national parks at various points in the year, visitors may be greeted with the clamor of Jet Skis, snowmobiles, cars and sport-utility vehicles, or aircraft full of tourists. Engine noise from Jet Skis and other brands of personal watercraft can alone approach volumes of 115 decibels—louder than a jackhammer—according to one critic.

The National Park Service has tightened its regulation of noise pollution, increasingly opting for outright bans on the offending machines rather than seeking technological solutions. In response to earlier criticism and regulation, aircraft operators and makers of personal watercraft had devised ways to reduce the noise their equipment emitted.

In 2000 the park service drastically cut the number of parks and recreation areas where personal watercraft could be used. Separately, the federal government took measures that year to restrict automobile traffic in Yosemite National Park, including removing roads and requiring more people to ride special shuttles into the park. Meanwhile, activists pressed for a ban on snowmobiles and further curtailing of sightseeing overflights.

CURRENT CONDITIONS

The noise-control industry is still in its infancy, so much work is being done in researching and developing new methods and applications. The difficulties lie in blocking various noise patterns—sometimes unpredictable ones. Until that's accomplished, the noise from a source such as moving traffic can't be easily dampened. And when the technology is relatively new or rare, cost is also a factor. While household appliances and products, such as dishwashers, are noisy, consumers may not be willing to pay the additional cost to control the clatter.

Noise-control headphones can block everyday noises—lawn mowers, leaf blowers, weed whackers. Noise Control Technologies is one of several manufacturers that produce headphones available through retail outlets such as Sharper Image. Bose Corp., based in Framingham, Massachusetts, manufactures higher-end headphones that have been used on the space shuttle.

In automotive applications, a few manufacturers have introduced new products to attack auto noise at various levels. Most common have been enhanced mufflers that can either cancel noise or at least curtail it some. For example, in 2000 DaimlerChrysler AG announced a partnership with Owens Corning to produce high-end mufflers for some of DaimlerChrysler's European cars. The Owens Corning product, called Silentex, is a highly engineered glass-fiber filling for the mufflers. Others have attempted noise-cancellation mufflers with mixed success; they have tended to be costly and temperamental. Others, such as European components maker Freudenberg-NOK, have focused on reducing noise and vibration under the hood.

Aircraft remains a major source of noise pollution, and thus a great deal of resources continue to be channeled into reducing aircraft noise. By 2000 hundreds of Boeing 727s and DC-9s had been fitted with hush-kit mufflers. For the European Union (EU), however, this was not an aggressive enough step toward noise muffling. In February 1999 the European Parliament approved a ban on airplanes that use hush kits—primarily those of U.S. carriers. Some interpreted the row between the EU and the United States as more a political and economic dispute than a scientific or environmental disagreement; each side advocated technology that its companies had already embraced. In response, the United States threatened to ban Concorde flights into the country, and won in late 1999 at least a temporary reprieve from the EU ban.

But the activity pushed cool-headed observers to take more constructive action. Realizing that a lack of a global standard would only hinder all players in the long run, over 50 airlines worldwide—including all North and South American outfits and a rising number of Asian, African, and European players—joined engine and aircraft manufacturers in establishing the Coalition for a Global Standard on Aviation Noise. The coalition works to build a reasonable consensus to be approved by the International Civil Aviation Organisation (ICAO) as the global standard, which the coalition hopes will be adopted by September 2001.

INDUSTRY LEADERS

The NCT Group, Inc., formerly Noise Cancellation Technologies, Inc., is a leading provider of noise and vibration reduction technology, and it is one of the most innovative companies. The firm holds rights to over 300 inventions, including applications in active noise reduction, active vibration reduction, active mufflers, active headsets, and multimedia audio. NCT has executive offices and product development facilities in Linthicum, Maryland; sales and marketing offices in Stamford, Connecticut; product development and marketing facilities in Cambridge, England; and marketing and technical support offices in Tokyo. In 1999 NCT reported revenue of $7.1 million, a decrease of 112.5 percent from the previous year.

The company uses patented active sound and signal wave management technology to reduce noise and improve sound quality. NCT focuses on headsets, communications, microphones, audio systems, and fans. Product innovations include NoiseBuster and NoiseBuster Extreme! headphones, which won a Discover Award for Technological Innovation in 1994 and the Innovations '96 award, respectively. The company also developed Earpeace active noise-control technology, used in in-flight passenger entertainment systems, and ProActive industrial hearing protection. Its ClearSpeech technology removes background noise from speech and transmits signals through telephones and radios, and it holds promise in the development of speech recognition programs. Its patented flat panel transducer technology creates a surround sound effect without the use of traditional speakers and is being produced and marketed as the automotive Top Down Surround Sound system with Johnson Controls, Inc. With other business partners, NCT is working to develop markets for industrial and vehicular mufflers, technologies for quieting vehicle and aircraft cabins, and noise-reduction methods for air ducts and power transformers. Licensing accounts for roughly half of NCT's revenues.

Another industry leader and maker of noise cancellation headsets is Andrea Electronics, based in Long Island City, New York. Its Anti-Noise product line is led by its best-selling NC-50 PC headset, which uses patented technology to reduce the distortion associated with many voice-activated personal-computer applications. Other devices include the Active Noise Reduction car phone and the Active Noise Cancellation near-field microphone. In 1997 Andrea introduced the QuietWare 1000 antinoise stereo headset for the computer market. Andrea Electronics's key customers and resellers include IBM, Microsoft Corp., Kurzweil, Dragon Systems, and NEC. In 1999 Andrea Electronics announced that it had received a patent for a head-mounted microphone. The company's products are used in pay phones and commercial, industrial, and

military equipment. Andrea reported 1999 revenues of $17.1 million, of which 78 percent derived from its Anti-Noise line and 22 percent came from industrial and military communications operations.

Other firms trying to make the world a quieter place include Acoustical Solutions Inc.; Empire Acoustical Systems; Industrial Acoustics Co., Inc.; Industrial Noise Control, Inc.; Sennheiser Electronic; and Ultimate Technologies, Inc. (UTI). Products ranged from acoustical windows, diffusers, and foams to UTI's telecommunications product that allows phone users to have a private conversation, even when other people are present.

RESEARCH AND TECHNOLOGY

Controlling the noise from jet engines is a major problem, but engineers at Georgia Tech may have found one possible solution, according to Mark Hodges in *Technology Review*. By filling a liner with ceramic beads of assorted sizes and wrapping this liner around the engine, both low- and high-frequency noises were lessened, and the ceramic beads were able to withstand the high temperatures generated by the engine. This discovery could be used to reduce the noise of commercial jet liners traveling at supersonic speeds.

Pennsylvania State University's Center for Acoustics and Vibration, the National Aeronautics and Space Administration, and the Anti-Vibration Control Division of PCB Piezotronic announced the creation of a self-regulating vibration absorber that tracks changes in the frequency of undesirable noises and adjusts itself in response. This invention will have applications for noise control in industrial machinery, cars, and household appliances.

Professor Dimitri Papamoschou of the University of California-Irvine, created a new technology to quiet supersonic jets, such as the Concorde, which have been permitted to land at only a few airports throughout the world because of the amount of noise they produce. His invention, the Mach Wave Eliminator, reduces the exhaust noise output of these aircraft.

FURTHER READING

"The Active Assault on Cabin Noise." *Business and Commercial Aviation,* September 1995.

"Andrea Electronics Corp." Melville, NY: Andrea Electronics Corp., 2000. Available from http://www.andreaelectronics.com.

"California Professor Reduces Supersonic Jet Noise." *Flight International,* 29 January 1997.

Chamberlain, Gary. "Vibration Absorber That Tunes Itself in the Works." *Design News,* 7 April 1997.

"Cincinnati Airport Gets New Aircraft Tracking System to Deal with Noise Complaints." *Cincinnati Enquirer,* 18 July 1997.

"Company Releases New Anti-Noise Headset for Computer Use." *Newsday,* 30 June 1997.

Cox, Jeff. "Good Vibes Noise-Control Gizmos Go for Quieter World." *Denver Post,* 17 May 1998.

"Curtains for Noise." *Industry Week,* 20 September 1999.

Doke, Deedee. "Aircraft Noise: The Next Chapter in a Global Saga." *Flight International,* 18 July 2000.

Greenman, Catherine. "Ah! The Sounds of (Almost) Silence." *New York Times,* 18 March 1999.

Hodges, Mark. "The Anti-Music of the Aerospheres." *Technology Review,* January/February 1998.

"Illinois Airport Gets New Holding Apron Designed to Reduce Noise for Nearby Residents." *Chicago Tribune,* 17 July 1997.

Isidore, Chris. "Leaders in Air Industry Disagree about Impact of New Noise Regulations." *Journal of Commerce,* 16 February 1999.

Kilian, Michael. "Jet Skis, Boats Banned from Most National Parks." *Chicago Tribune,* 21 March 2000.

Langston, Jennifer. "Park Service Proposal to Ban Snowmobiles at Yellowstone Worries Idahoans." *Knight Ridder/Tribune Business News,* 21 March 2000.

Lavitt, Michael O. "Active Absorbers Cancel Aircraft Engine Noise." *Aviation Week & Space Technology,* 24 February 1997.

Masi, C. G. "Putting 'Quiet Shoes' on Household Appliances." *Research & Development Magazine,* November 1996.

NCT Group, Inc. "Corporate Overview." Linthicum, MD: NCT Group, 2000. Available from http://www.nct-active.com.

"New Technology Quiets Supersonic Jets." *Tulsa World,* 5 January 1997.

"Noise Control Technology Now More Affordable." *Air Conditioning, Heating, and Refrigeration News,* February 1994.

"The Noise Pollution Clearinghouse." Available from http://www.nonoise.org.

"Quieter Helicopters Designed for National Parks." *Flight International,* 29 January 1997.

Staples, Susan L. "Human Response to Environmental Noise: Psychological Research and Public Policy." *American Psychologist,* February 1996.

Syarto, Marilyn Zelinsky. "Sound Solutions." *Home Office Computing,* October 1999.

"Writer Reviews New Noise-Reduction Headphones on Airplane." *Buffalo News,* 11 April 1997.

NONMEDICAL SENIOR CARE AND PERSONAL SERVICES

INDUSTRY SNAPSHOT

Nonmedical senior care includes an enormous range of services, including consulting, day-to-day assistance with routine chores and personal care (such as eating and bathing), and more general welfare and social services. In the final decades of the 20th century, such tasks were increasingly handed over by family members to professional service providers. One of the most widespread sectors in this industry in that period was the adult day-care center, which followed the child day-care model to provide social and medical attention to the elderly. According to the National Council on Aging, the number of adult day-care centers operating in the United States jumped from 2,000 in 1989 to over 4,100 by 2000. Another strong sector was geriatric care management, in which consultants met with families to design a care strategy for loved ones that was tailored to particular needs and financial capabilities.

The future portended a voracious market for such services. According to the Health Insurance Association of America, some 7 million seniors required long-term care in 1997, a figure expected to rise to 9 million by 2005. For seniors not yet at the stage of needing long-term care, but in need of some daily attention, day-to-day care was increasingly viewed as an intermediary step in a smooth transition to old age. Moreover, as baby boomers moved into retirement years and began to require nonmedical care, a smaller percentage of those requiring such services would have family members capable of providing for them, since about one-quarter of baby boomers were childless in 1990. Thus, the professionalization of nonmedical senior care was likely to continue its strong upward trend.

ORGANIZATION AND STRUCTURE

Adult day-care programs are offered in senior centers, community centers, and churches. These programs are sometimes attached to hospitals, nursing homes, or other health-care institutions. In addition, residential care facilities might provide these services should the client's care needs extend to mental and other chronic care concerns. The 1989 *National Adult Day Center Census,* compiled by the National Council on Aging's National Adult Day Services Association (NADSA), found that the adult day-care centers that responded served a high proportion of individuals with disabilities who preferred to stay in their homes rather than enter nursing homes. In 1997 NADSA compiled updated statistics based on its 1989 survey. The latter survey indicated that approximately 80 percent of the country's adult day-care facilities were nonprofit, 10 percent were state-run, and 10 percent were for-profit institutions. The average adult day-care attendee was 76 years old, while two-thirds were women. One-quarter lived alone, while the remainder lived with a spouse, children, or other family and friends. Adult day-care centers gave participants opportunities for social interaction and exercise along with hot meals. Adult day-care operations offer a range of services, including transportation to and from home; counseling and social services; grooming, hygiene, and laundry services; social activities; physical, occupational, and speech therapy; and others, to those seniors with cognitive or functional impairments.

Intergenerational day-care facilities, where both children and elders are cared for, were on the rise by the end of the 1990s in the United States. These programs often began with intergenerational programming ventures in nursing homes and continued to expand. At a time when it was not uncommon to live across the country from other family members, grandparents and grandchildren often missed out on the interaction that was taken for granted only a generation or two ago. Older adults and children through school age were all beneficiaries of these expanded services. According to the American Association for Retired Persons, by 2000, about 280 facilities in the United States housed intergenerational care services, up from only about 50 in the early 1980s. A handful of these centers placed seniors and children in the same activities and areas for the entire day.

As this concept continued to evolve, an increasing number of care programs across the United States reconsidered their options. The baby boomers, often caught between caring for young children and aging parents, were also referred to as the "sandwich generation," with little time and busy careers of their own. Intergenerational day-care sites showed promise to alleviate the burden of the situation. On-site corporate adult day-care programs, such as the one formerly housed at Stride-Rite in Cambridge, Massachusetts, were not successful in the early stages. But as the population of aging and retired workers grew, more businesses were expected to consider starting them as a benefit for employees.

Adult day-care centers were transformed as the accompanying services of speech, physical, occupational, and drug therapy became more available, attracting Medicare and private-pay patients. Another development was the expansion of outpatient care and rehabilitation to complement nursing home services. Adult day-service centers focused on assisting seniors with either minimal or extensive needs. Some centers specialized in certain types of patients, namely those with early onset dementia or Alzheimer's. Typical adult day-service centers provided transportation, routine health care, meals, activities, and assistance with daily chores. The demand for more intense services is expected to increase in the 21st century as the U.S. population ages, and as changes in technology permit the delivery of medical services outside traditional hospitals.

The bulk of the nation's adult day-care centers were small facilities based in the community they served, and statistics on regional growth were difficult to determine accurately. Adult day-care centers were run as for-profit, nonprofit, or state-run operations. Expenses were paid by various sources such as Medicaid, the participants, donations, grants, and private long-term care. Centers were typically run by a director, usually a nurse or social worker, with the assistance of administrative and office personnel, recreation and activity personnel, case managers and social workers, therapists, nurses, and medical staff. In centers run by non-profit organizations such as community groups or churches, volunteers were crucial to providing services.

Adult day-care facilities were often one component of a larger-scale continuum of care for senior adults. One example is a program operated by Adventist Healthcare in Takoma Park, Maryland, and also in the suburban Washington, D.C., area, which grew out of a subacute-care nursing home. For a balance in the services, the nonprofit Adventist opened the day-care center in Takoma Park in 1987. Such services were generally not exceptionally profitable, but they offered strong growth opportunities. Since for many people day care was only a first step for seniors in failing health, many assisted-living and other continuing care facilities began day-care centers with a view to the future business they could provide. If one was familiar with a long-term care center affiliated with the day-care center, that long-term facility would become a reasonable choice when further care was chosen.

BACKGROUND AND DEVELOPMENT

The 1970s were flush with funding for older adult services in the United States. Federal and state monies flooded local areas as a result of the establishment of the National Institute on Aging in May 1972, during the administration of President Richard Nixon. Americans of the World War II generation were beginning to retire. People were living longer, though not always without health problems. Many older women, especially, had not worked outside the home and lived on very small retirement pensions or minimal Social Security benefits. Many of these men and women came from rural backgrounds and moved to factories in the city where they had limited incomes, forcing them to live at or near poverty level. A new awareness of age—both its problems and its joys—swept the country. Money was made available for senior nutrition programs and senior centers, among them adult day care. Most adult day-care centers were run by nursing homes for both social activities and medical rehabilitation that would prove a cost-effective alternative to long-term inpatient care.

Special library outreach services grew out of the needs of older adults who were homebound or hearing- or sight-impaired. Funds for large-print books and other arts-related programs for older adults were made available. Senior high-rise apartment buildings, many of them government-subsidized, went up in small towns and big cities. Local agencies on aging were set

A personal aide assisting an elderly client. (Stock Market)

up under the auspices of state and federal programs. Church denominations started building retirement homes, along with private corporations. The dated notion of sending the aging population to "rest homes" was fading away. Better health and more leisure time were cutting through stereotypes.

In addition, the demand for adult day-care services developed as more people, especially women, tried to balance the demands of jobs with the needs of family members. For those living near and caring for aging parents, adult day-care services provided a way to be sure of elders' safety and supervision during the workday. American Association of Retired Persons statistics indicate that about three-fourths of caregivers to older people are women, more than 50 percent of whom are in the labor force, and 41 percent of whom also care for children. Day-care facilities equipped to care for individuals with certain conditions, such as Alzheimer's disease, also provided a needed respite for their caregivers.

CURRENT CONDITIONS

About 40 percent of families have to care for their aging parents, according to statistics gathered by the

Associated Press from the Families and Work Institute. In fact, contrary to many presumptions, families care for their elderly members far more often than nursing homes or other care facilities. As a result, the demand for nonmedical senior care was accelerating rapidly by 2000. To help potential patients and their families decide what type of care to seek out, the federal government funded the Eldercare Locator, which provides information and referral services regarding local care agencies.

In order to alleviate some of the burdens on their employees—and to attract employees in a tight labor market—more and more firms began to offer elder-care programs as part of their benefits packages. Among larger corporations, especially, this often involved establishing on- or off-site adult-care programs of their own, sometimes in conjunction with existing child day-care facilities. In addition, firms provided coverage for geriatric care managers and home health-care services. According to a study by MetLife Mature Market Institute in fall 1999, the number of employees responsible for care of at least one adult was expected to rise from 11 million to 15.6 million by the end of the 2000s, representing about 10 percent of the work force. Companies reported that the assistance also helps boost productivity for their workers, who don't have to spend their working hours on the phone to various care companies.

The National Adult Day Services Association's (NADSA) latest survey revealed that adult day-care services averaged 14 participants per program, with an average ratio of one staff person to six participants. About 80 percent of the respondents were nonprofit programs, 10 percent were for-profit, and 10 percent were public or government-funded. The majority provided some type of nursing services. State licensing, certification, and accreditation standards for adult day-care services vary, but most states require adherence to at least one category of such criteria. NADSA serves as a national clearinghouse for information on state-by-state licensure requirements.

The cost of attending such centers varied. Typically, adult day-care centers run about $40 to $60 per day. Medicare and Medicaid do not cover such expenses, but most long-term health-care policies do. One adult day-care center, housed in a Baptist church in the small Arizona community of Peoria, offered basic services for $6.80 an hour, and adjustments could be made on an ability-to-pay basis. As with other such centers, this one was licensed to serve people under the Department of Developmental Disabilities. Additional charges were added for: transportation, $3.50 one-way; a shampoo and shower, $12; toenail trim, $12; in-home care, $12 to $13 an hour; overnight stay at the center, $105 for a 24-hour period; and, evening care from 5:30 until 9:30 P.M. was also available at the $6.80 an hour rate. The character of adult day-care centers also varies considerably. Some concentrate mainly on the provision of medical or therapy services, while others simply arrange social activities so as to keep seniors active and engaged.

A growing trend in the late 1990s was the short-term care center geared toward families needing to take care of loved ones while the family goes on vacation. Some day-care facilities take on seniors while their adult children or other caregivers get away from it all. The Fairfax Nursing Center, for instance, offered respite care along with its long-term services. The facility featured such spa-like amenities as manicures and massages, along with frequent visits from child-care groups. Other companies, such as Healthquest Travel Inc., aid travelers by arranging for adequate services to be provided at their destinations, thus allowing elders to more comfortably travel along with younger family members. For example, after meeting with clients and arranging precise needs and logistics, such companies will arrange for doctors or oxygen to be available at the point of destination.

Other services allow seniors to care for each other. California Blue Shield runs a program called CareX-change, in which seniors volunteer to provide basic services, such as running errands or driving others to the doctor's office. Seniors thus offer those services they are capable of in exchange for the provision of tasks they cannot accomplish themselves.

Unfortunately, the nonmedical senior care industry was blackened by findings of corruption. According to the *New York Times,* the federal inspector general of the U.S. Department of Health and Human Services reported in 1998 that about 90 percent of the nation's mental-health centers simply provided social activities while billing for acute outpatient care.

The industry also sprouted a new type of service, known as the geriatric care consultancy. Such consultants provided seniors and their families with information and expert advice on juggling the bevy of legal and financial concerns associated with senior care, including Medicare and Medicaid concerns. Consultancy agencies, such as Next Step Elder Assist and Elder Care and Cost Consultants Inc., analyze family members' financial situations and help them determine an effective care strategy, be it home health care, nursing homes, day-care services, or some other care arrangement. Consultants also help the family secure placement into a care service, such as a nursing home or day-care program, and arrange bookkeeping services for the family.

Many managers were certified through the National Academy of Professional Geriatric Care Management Association, which was founded in Connecticut in 1994 and began administering a certification program in 1997. Rona Bartelstone, a clinical social worker in south Florida, was the founder of that program, as well as the National Association of Professional Geriatric Care Managers, based in Tucson, Arizona. The latter organization began in 1986 and grew to 1,200 members out of the estimated 4,000 private-care managers across the United States.

Geriatric care managers typically don't come cheap, charging between $200 and $500 for a consultation of about two or three hours. Typically a nurse or social worker, a geriatric care manager will consult with all the parties involved and help resolve differences based on detailed knowledge of different services and an assessment of financial situations. Customers turn to geriatric care managers to gain an objective, expert, outside opinion, and to help relieve the tension that can stem from such emotional decisions. Geriatric care managers thus help adult children resolve a crisis effectively rather than hurriedly, or, in a best-case scenario, provide solutions before a crisis ever occurs.

Geriatric care management programs around the country often emerge as part of a municipal program. One such program in Stark County, Ohio, operates as "Family Connections" through the county's Family Services department. Local programs operate under the guidance of the National Geriatric Care Management Association. The cost of such services was usually about $45 an hour.

INDUSTRY LEADERS

According to the National Adult Day Services Association, the vast majority of the 4,100 adult day-care centers were still primarily private or not-for-profit institutions by 2000. There was significant growth in the number of day-care centers operating over the previous decade, and this was expected to continue over the next 10-15 years. In 2000, Catholic Charities was one of the largest nonprofits in the category. Asbury Methodist Village in Gaithersburg, Maryland, opened in September 1998, and it launched a day-care center for older adults in March 1999. Many church-related facilities such as these were leaders in the nonprofit sector for adult day care.

Two of the largest for-profit companies in adult day care in 2000 were Almost Family, Inc. and American Retirement Corp. Formerly known as Caretenders Health Corp., Almost Family, based in Louisville, Kentucky, employed some 3,900 workers. The company operated 25 adult day-care centers and 12 home health agencies, and also provided housekeeping services and skilled home nursing. The company's revenues in 1999 totaled $44.7 million in 2000, over one-third of which derived from insurance and private payments. American Retirement, based in Brentwood, Tennessee, was primarily engaged in the operation of assisted living communities for the elderly, but also offered a variety of nonmedical senior care, such as grooming, laundry services, and skilled nursing. The company's sales grew 23 percent in 1999 to reach $175.3 million.

WORK FORCE

Residential care workers increased from 683,000 to 746,000 workers between 1996 and 1998, and the occupation was expected to be one of the fastest growing through 2008, according to the U.S. Bureau of La-

bor Statistics (BLS). Opportunities for adult day-care workers would continue to expand as the aging population demanded more such facilities and services. The BLS reported that the average hourly earnings for home health and personal care aides was $7.58 at year-end 1998. Because the field of for-profit adult day care was relatively new at the end of the 20th century, opportunities had not been fully evaluated. The professional field of gerontology, in the areas of medicine and social work, was expanding as well. The number of geriatric social workers, geriatric nurses, and physicians who specialized in geriatrics continued to grow at the start of 21st century.

FURTHER READING

Elliott, Suzanne. "Senior Care Niche—To Go." *Pittsburgh Business Times,* 30 July 1999.

Field, Anne. "The Best Old-Age Home May Be at Home." *Business Week,* 22 November 1999.

Goldman, Melanie D. "Employers Can Help Boomers Find Care for Parents." *Washington Business Journal,* 23 April 1999.

Guthans, Sandra. "Geriatric Care Managers Can Help Ease the Burden." *Times-Picayune,* 6 February 2000.

Lee, Karen. "Eldercare Benefits Are Gaining More Attention." *Employee Benefit News,* 1 May 2000.

Martin, Claire. "Young, Old a Compatible Combo Intergenerational Programs on the Rise." *Denver Post,* 4 November 1999.

Murphy, Kate. "Day Care for Kids—And Grandparents, Too." *Business Week,* 22 November 1999.

National Council on the Aging. "National Adult Day Services Association." Available from http://www.ncoa.org/nadsa.

Pearson, Robert L. "Long-Term Care: Addressing the Real Issues." *Compensation & Benefits Review,* September 1999.

"The Profiteers of Elder Care." *New York Times,* 12 February 2000.

Redfearn, Suz. "Day Care for Seniors Becoming Popular Niche." *Washington Business Journal,* 26 March 1999.

Rimer, Sara. "The Growing Business of Helping Elders Cope." *New York Times,* 4 March 1999.

U.S. Bureau of Labor Statistics. *2000-2001 Occupational Outlook Handbook.* Available from http://www.bls.gov/oco/ocos173.htm.

Votava, G. Joseph. "Preparing for the Long Haul." *Financial Planning,* 1 September 1999.

NUTRITIONAL SUPPLEMENTS

Despite a diet rich in soft drinks and oversized fast-food burgers, the American public has increasingly consumed products that promote dietary health. These nutritional supplements include well-known vitamins and minerals, as well as formerly counterculture herbal remedies and phytochemicals, and futuristic nutraceuticals. The annual worldwide market for dietary supplements was estimated to be worth about $46 billion in 2000. That year, the vitamin and mineral market alone was valued at $17.8 billion, herbal and homeopathic products at $19.4 billion, and sports and specialty supplements at $8.8 billion, according to *Nutraceuticals World.* Americans comprise the largest national market for nutritional supplements; the *Nutrition Business Journal* projected overall supplement sales in the United States to reach $15.7 billion in 2000. It was estimated that about 40 percent of all Americans took a vitamin supplement regularly.

Though overall sector sales growth was slowing, household penetration by the industry equaled 71 percent in 1999, up from 68 percent in 1998, according to the Hartman Group. Leading products included those that strengthened bones and joints, antidepressants, energy boosters, sports supplements, and diet aids. Vitamins and minerals alone comprised 63 percent of all supplement sales. The overall category was revived by interest in products such as glucosamine, SAM-e, and creatine.

According to the *Nutraceuticals World,* herbals experienced the greatest overall segment growth between 1994 and 1999, though that trend slowed in 2000. Sales of herbal formulas increased about 8 percent that year, roughly on par with vitamins and minerals. There was little change in product leaders from the previous year, as interest in vitamins C and E, gingko biloba, St. John's wort, ginseng, echinacea, and saw palmetto remained strong. In general, the field became more competitive as the presence of major pharmaceutical firms expanded and leading supplement makers merged. Among such ventures were those involving American Home Products Corp., Warner-Lambert, and Bayer Corp., all of which targeted providing greater offerings in mass-market outlets.

Consumer direct means, such as direct marketing, catalogs, sales representatives, the Internet, and infomercials, account for the majority—42 percent—of supplement sales. Sales in food, drug, and mass-market stores contribute another 30 percent and specialty health-food stores, 20 percent. The remainder are generated by sales through physicians, dieticians, and other professionals.

ORGANIZATION AND STRUCTURE

Nutritional supplements are produced by more than 1,000 private manufacturers, as well as major drug and chemical companies. Sales have been especially strong over the Internet. About 95 percent of all companies, however, sell less than $20 million in products per year. The American Herbal Products Association (AHPA) is a national trade association that includes among its members thousands of companies that are importers, growers, manufacturers, and distributors of therapeutic herbs and herbal products. Located in Washington, D.C., the AHPA was founded in 1983.

The definition of nutritional supplements is broad and encompasses such diverse categories as phytochemicals, herbals, and nutraceuticals. The Office of Dietary Supplements describes dietary supplements as "products intended to supplement the diet, which contain one or more of the following: vitamins, minerals, amino acids, herbs, or other botanicals; or dietary substances used to supplement the diet by increasing total dietary intake; or concentrates, metabolites, constituents, extracts, or combinations of the above." In addition, supplements are "intended for ingestion as capsules, gelcaps, powders, or softgels." Supplements do not constitute conventional foods or the sole item of a meal, however.

Phytochemicals overlap the vitamin field and are defined as plant substances used as food fortifiers and dietary supplements, including garlic, I3C, spices, soy, and herbal teas. About 4,000 different phytochemicals have been identified, but fewer than 200 have been carefully investigated for their health-giving properties. Well-known phytochemicals include indoles (in vegetables such as broccoli), protease inhibitors, and isoflavones in soybeans.

Nutraceuticals are loosely defined as foods that promote health or medical benefits, including disease prevention. The market's vague parameters make estimating its value and scope difficult. Often called functional foods, leading products in the market include soy isoflavones, tocotrienols, lutein, lycopene, gingko biloba, and St. John's wort among their ingredients. Other popular nutraceuticals are creatine monohydrate, androsteniodene, DHA (omega-3 fatty acid from fish), peptidase, and calcium citrate maleate.

Historically marketed through health-food stores, direct mail, and network marketing, nutritional food supplements were also distributed through retail stores, pharmacies, discount stores, catalogs, multilevel marketing, and the Internet. The thousands of Kmart, Target, and Wal-Mart stores regularly selling nutritional supplements began installing displays adjacent to their pharmacies to expand herbal lines. Other chain stores such as Sam's Club and Costco installed pharmacies or nutritional supplement centers to take advantage of the booming market. With the visibility gained through chain stores, the relatively obscure herbals market caught the attention of many large over-the-counter brand companies. Bayer Corp., among others, is using extensive marketing efforts as well as nationally known and trusted brand-name recognition to attract nonusers to its line of herbal products.

INDUSTRY REGULATION

The dietary supplements industry is regulated only loosely. Dietary supplements are considered a subset of foods under federal law and are regulated by the U.S. Food and Drug Administration (FDA) pursuant to the U.S. Food, Drug, and Cosmetic Act of 1938. The FDA has the authority to take action against any dietary supplement product found to be unsafe or making unsubstantiated or unapproved drug claims. The agency can also take action against supplements presenting significant risk of illness or injury. In addition, the Nutrition Labeling and Education Act of 1990 mandates that no health claims be allowed on food labels or advertisements unless the FDA finds "significant scientific agreement" for such claims. The U.S. Pharmacopoeia, a nonprofit group, was established to test supplements and assure compliance with scientific standards.

Informative point-of-purchase displays and the ability to make general claims about products were enabled by the 1994 Dietary Supplement Health and Education Act (DSHEA). The act defines dietary supplements—vitamins, minerals, and herbs—and the limits of information about them. A supplement must contain a premeasured amount that is in the form of a soft gel, powder, tablet, capsule, or liquid. DSHEA also permits substantiated, truthful, nonmisleading statements on labels and in advertising. These statements may include claims about how the product benefits body structure and function, but not any specific assertions that it prevents or cures disease. Supplement makers are supposed to send all labels to the FDA for review before using them; many, however, don't do so. The FDA recently estimated that it had scrutinized only about 10 percent of the 22,500 labels it should have reviewed.

The limited regulatory framework established under DSHEA has been widely criticized. Companies have avoided the extensive testing requirements of over-the-counter drugs by distributing their products as supplements. The FDA's vague definitions found within the dietary supplement category have prompted numerous manufacturers to challenge the 1994 act. The FDA treats herbs as food, which means they do not need to be proven effective if they are safe. In 1995 the vitamin supplement industry was not heavily regulated because vitamins were considered neither a food nor a drug, and few standards regarded truth in advertising.

Regulatory activities regarding supplements are split between the FDA, which oversees product safety, manufacturing, and information, and the Federal

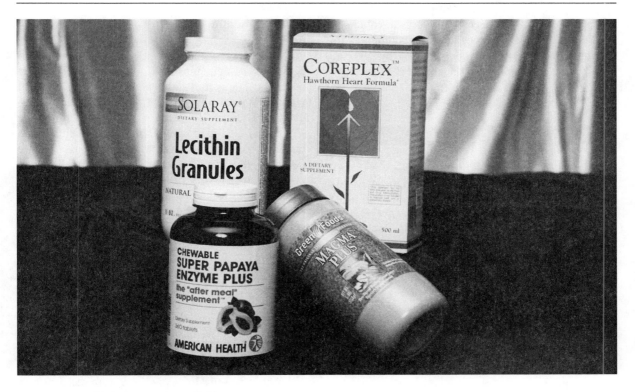

A wide array of supplements is available to consumers. (FieldMark Publications/Robert J. Huffman)

Trade Commission (FTC), which regulates product advertising. In late 1998, the FTC issued advertising guidelines for the first time for the dietary supplement industry. The guidelines were posted on the FTC Web site on 18 November 1998 and also sent to industry trade associations. The guidelines dictate that supplement claims be truthful, not misleading, and that advertisers be able to back those claims up with research. They also explain what kind of claims supplement manufacturers can and cannot make. Action taken by the FTC was in part due to the industry's rapid growth during the late 1990s, and also due to confusion on the part of supplement manufacturers after the Dietary Supplement Health and Education Act of 1994 limited the FDA's authority to regulate the industry.

New labels, mandated by the FDA in 1998, began to appear on supplement packaging in March 1999; all products manufactured after that date must bear them. The new labels contain Supplement Facts panels similar to the Nutrition Facts labels required on most packaged foods since 1994. The Supplement Facts panels include dosage information on 14 essential vitamins and other nutrients, as well as definitions of such terms as "high potency." They also must mention the presence of any additional ingredients, such

as herbals and botanicals, which currently lack recommended daily intake guidelines.

Much important information, however, won't appear on the Supplement Facts panels. Maximum safe dosages, dangerous interactions with other substances and medications, and cautions for people for whom the supplements might be unsafe still aren't required. Thus, the guidelines are far from complete. Also, the panels can list ingredient amounts in relation to Daily Values (DVs) limits established in 1968, instead of Recommended Dietary Allowances (RDAs), because the RDAs are being revised; the project won't be completed until 2005. Even spokespeople for the supplement industry advised caution and the need for a high level of education about supplements when consumers use the new labels. John Hathcock, vice president of the Council for Responsible Nutrition, warned that the consumer has to "be inherently skeptical" when reading the Supplement Facts panels.

The industry itself is promoting the adoption of Good Manufacturing Practices guidelines for the industry, which industry groups feel would bolster consumer confidence in product quality and help stave off further governmental regulation. The National Nutritional Foods Association, a California-based trade group, urged its members to undergo a voluntary, third-party certification procedure as a requirement for continued membership. It predicted that by 2002 all of its members should have undergone the audit.

BACKGROUND AND DEVELOPMENT

The use of herbals and other botanicals as dietary supplements predates written history. In the West, the first known study on medicinal plants was produced by the Greek scientist Dioscorides in the first century A.D. Among modern early proponents of vitamins and micronutrients was the German chemist Hans von Euler-Chelpin (1873-1964), whose first work centered on fermentation. After World War I, Euler-Chelpin began his research into the chemistry of enzymes, particularly in the role they played in the fermentation process. Apart from tracing phosphates through the fermentation sequence, he detailed the chemical makeup of co-zymase, a nonprotein constituent involved in cellular respiration. In 1929, Euler-Chelpin became the director of the Vitamin Institute and Institute of Biochemistry at the University of Stockholm.

In more recent times, food supplement companies often originated from their founders' responses to physical adversity or from the personal discovery of a new product. These companies then grew phenomenally through multilevel marketing. For example, as the result of curing a stomach ulcer with capsicum, a spicy red-pepper powder, Eugene Hughes and his wife began making gelatin-filled red-cayenne capsules and selling them to local health-food stores in the mid-1960s. He added chaparral, for digestion, and goldenseal, a natural antibiotic. In 1972 they founded Hughes' Development Corp., which became Nature's Sunshine Products.

In the 1970s and 1980s the United States witnessed a resurgence of general interest in herbal remedies. More than 50 percent of all pharmaceuticals were made from natural sources or synthetic analogs of natural products. Beginning in the mid-1990s, an increasing number of physicians started to recognize the medicinal value of herbs and foods in curing ailments.

Nutrition drinks and energy bars became popular in the mid-1990s. Boost, by Mead Johnson Nutritionals, debuted as an energy drink for active adults without the time to eat properly. Together, ReSource, Ensure, and Boost represent the leading liquid nutritional supplements, a category that has grown to account for $330 million in retail sales.

Rapidly growing sectors of the nutritional supplement market have been mineral supplements, single vitamins (especially vitamins C and E), and combinations of vitamins and minerals targeted at particular population segments, such as menopausal women or those involved in athletic pursuits. Popular (and often controversial) supplements in the late 1990s included glucosamine and chondroitin, which claimed to combat the symptoms of arthritis; SAM-e (s-adenosylmethionine), naturally found in all human cells and which was touted as a joint lubricant and antidepressant; creatine and the steroid androstenedione, which gained national prominence as athletic-performance enhancers when baseball stars Mark McGwire and Sammy Sosa admitted to using them after their famous home-run hitting battle in 1998; and cholestin, made from fermented rice and argued to lower cholesterol levels.

CURRENT CONDITIONS

About one-third of Americans turn to herbals to treat medical or physical conditions. In response, the National Institutes of Health launched the International Bibliographic Information on Dietary Supplements database. The database includes published international, scientific literature free of charge via their Office of Dietary Supplements Web site.

Growth of supplement sales in the late 1990s was spurred by increased consumption by older consumers, the rising number of pharmacies in supermarkets, more display visibility, and health benefits substantiated by medical research. For example, because numerous studies verified that saw palmetto helps the prostate gland, its sales increased significantly. The herbal market also experienced a number of shifts in market share among various herb products. Sales of vitamin E, whose health benefits were also supported by scientific studies, grew by about 5 percent per year. Calcium, meanwhile, remained the leading components of the nutritional supplement market, with sales of $361 million in 2000.

Some popular herbs were selling so well that their natural supply was becoming endangered. Specifically, echinacea, goldenseal, American ginseng, and wild yam were becoming scarce and more expensive. What was becoming more dangerous was that some products touted to have these ingredients were adulterated, sometimes containing none of the ingredients listed on their labels. Demand for St. John's wort and kava was also exceeding supply.

In May 1999, Roche Holding AG of Switzerland and BASF AG of Germany agreed to pay $725 million to the U.S. government to settle charges that alleged they participated in a nine-year global cartel that fixed prices for human and animal supplements. Roche had previously paid fines for fixing the price of critic acid. Assistant U.S. attorney general Joel Klein described the situation as the "most pervasive and harmful criminal antitrust conspiracy ever uncovered." Rhone-Poulenc SA of France was instrumental in revealing the cartel; its cooperation led to immunity from prosecution for participation in the scheme.

INDUSTRY LEADERS

Among industry leaders is General Nutrition Corp. (GNC), with 1999 sales of $1.4 billion (18 percent growth from 1998) and almost 16,900 employees. GNC is the number-one specialty retailer of nutritional supplements distributed through almost 4,400 company- and franchise-owned stores. About two-thirds of the company' sales stem from its sports nutrition and vitamin and mineral lines. The company planned for a total of 5,000 stores by the year 2002. Retail outlets are operated under the names GNC Live Well, Nature's Fresh, Nature Food Centres, and Amphora in the United States. GNC Live Well planned to open 1,500 outlets within Rite Aid drugstores between 1999 and 2002. The Dutch Royal Numico acquired GNC in July 1999, creating the world's largest firm devoted to human nutrition. Its Internet affiliate is drugstore.com.

Nature's Bounty employees grew from 400 to 2,000 people, and sales increased from $33 to $281 million in just 10 years through aggressive automation, acquisitions, new product development, and advanced marketing, making it one of the country's leading nutritional supplement manufacturers. In May 1999, the company announced its acquisition of Dynamics Essentials Inc., a distributor of nutritional supplements and skin-care products, for $1 million. It markets more than 1,000 products under the brand names Nature's Bounty, Vitamin World, Puritan's Pride, Holland & Barrett, Nutrition Headquarters, and American Health. Sales for fiscal 2000 totaled $721 million, an increase of 14 percent over the previous year. The company operates some 500 stores, but scaled back plans for new openings in the early 2000s and planned to shed unprofitable outlets.

Cyanotech Corp. produces natural products from microalgae, including Spirulina nutritional supplement, which it markets to a Hong Kong natural-products company. Sales in 2000 totaled about $7.4 million, a healthy recovery from the firm's slump in 1999, which it attributed to the costs of optimizing its NatuRose production facility. Cyanotech generates about 90 percent of its revenues from its Spirulina Pacifica nutritional supplement.

Nature's Sunshine Products, Inc., one of the major U.S. manufacturers of alternative health-care products, posted 1999 sales of $289.2 million, a decline of 2.3 percent. Herbal products make up about two-thirds of the company's total sales and are sold through a network of approximately 500,000 distributors and members worldwide.

Rexall Sundown sells the Sundown, Rexall, and Thompson brands of vitamins and supplements to mass-market stores, drug stores, health-food stores, supermarkets, and through mail order. In February 2000 it agreed to buy Worldwide Sport Nutrition Supplements, Inc., a maker of sports bars and shakes, to broaden its product offerings. Along a similar line, it agreed in December 1999 to purchase MET-Rx Nutrition of Irvine, California.

Herbalife International, Inc. of Los Angeles swam against the industry tide by announcing its attempt to go private. Its 1999 sales equaled $956.2 million and it employed 2,170 people. A manufacturer of about 130 natural and herbal products, it operated through independent distributors in about 45 countries worldwide. About half its sales stemmed from its food and dietary supplements.

AMERICA AND THE WORLD

Global demand for bulk herbals increased by 13 percent per year, according to a Freedonia Group report. Domestic vitamin producers faced competition from foreign producers, particularly those located in China; these chemical makers have undercut U.S. producers of bulk pharmaceuticals by 50 percent. For example, due to pressure from Chinese imports, vitamin C prices were falling in the mid-1990s, and they hit an all-time low in mid-1997 at $4.50 per kilo, half its value a year before. Big Western producers of vitamin C such as Hoffmann-La Roche, Inc. will spend about $200 million by 2002 to upgrade facilities, improve production, and lower costs to become more competitive. BASF and Takeda, also world leaders, are also expanding their operations in response to overseas competition; Takeda expanded its production of vitamin C by 15 percent.

Asia is an escalating market for vitamin-enriched animal feed because of increased meat consumption in Asian countries. Deregulation in Japan is making vitamins more easily available to the public. Roche and BASF are formulating joint ventures in China to manufacture vitamins and fortified animal feed.

Among the most closely regulated supplement industries is that of Germany, where nearly 40 percent of medicines are based on phytochemicals. The German government hosts Commission E, a special committee on herbals that checks information about products from clinical trials, field studies, and medical literature. It issues product monographs about product identification, risks, and dosages. The European Scientific Co-operative on Phytotherapy planned to create similar monographs, and the World Health Organization launched two series of plant monographs.

Metabolife announced that it was devoting $11 million to a three-year effort to developing Chinac, a line of herbal remedies that it would market simultaneously in both the United States and China.

RESEARCH AND TECHNOLOGY

Research is continuing to define the health benefits of vitamins, other micronutrient supplements, and phytochemicals. A great deal of work was focused on the anticancer properties of vitamin E, vitamin C, and folic acid. A number of studies have shown these are useful in fighting Alzheimer's disease, cancer, heart disease, and birth defects. Vitamin E was proving to have an important role in cognitive function, respiratory health, immune response, and the prevention of heart disease.

Research at Cyanotech included development of an antioxidant supplement based on the microalgae asta xanthin, whose antioxidant properties the company claimed as up to 550 times more effective than vitamin E.

Lycopene, an up-and-coming phytochemical of the beta carotene group that occurs naturally in red tomatoes, attracted attention as a promising antioxidant. Both BASF and Roche were developing lycopene products, which were believed to help prevent macular degeneration, prostate cancer, and heart disease. The world market for the product was estimated at $6 to $8 million annually.

FURTHER READING

Adams, Chris. "Hair-Splitting Distinctions Guide World of Herbal Supplements." *Wall Street Journal,* 2 March 2000.

"AHPA: Association Information." Washington: American Herbal Products Association, 1999. Available from http://www.ahpa.org.

Apgar, Barbara. "Do 'Health Products' Really Help Athletic Performance?" *American Family Physician,* 1 April 1999.

Babcock, Charles. "Stimulant Propels Diet Empire; Herbal Coalition Fights FDA's Proposed Safety Regulation." *Washington Post,* 24 May 1999.

"Bad Mix: Roche, Avon in Vitamin Products Pact." *Natural Health,* September 1999.

Bassett, Sarah. "Herbal Drugs: Medicines or Food Supplements?" *Manufacturing Chemist,* January 2000.

"Battle over Dietary Supplement Heating Up." *Chemical Marketing Reporter,* 16 August 1999.

Beach, Andrew. "Big Isle Biotech Firms Race to Market New Antioxidant." *Pacific Business News,* 24 December 1999.

Birchard, Karen. "Body-Building Supplement Fails to Strengthen Muscle and May Harm Health." *Lancet,* 5 June 1999.

"Caveat Emptor: Dietary Supplements." *Economist,* 28 August 1999.

Chen, Ingfei, and Elizabeth Kreiger. "Supplements Win— For Now." *Health,* June 1999.

Cowley, Geoffrey, Jamie Reno, and Anne Underwood. "Mad about Metabolife." *Newsweek,* 4 October 1999.

"Don't Use Dangerous GHB-Related Product, Agency Warns." *FDA Consumer,* May/June 1999.

Eder, Rob. "Understanding the New Natural Health Customer." *Drug Store News,* 29 November 1999.

"Educated Consumers Keep Demand High." *MMR,* 24 January 2000.

"FDA Will Set New Manufacturing Standards." *MMR,* 24 January 2000.

Gottlieb, Scott. "U.S. Relaxes Its Guidelines on Herbal Supplements." *British Medical Journal,* 22 January 2000.

Gugliotta, Guy. "FDA Takes Aim at Ephedra; Agency Renews Effort to Show Extract Poses Risks." *Washington Post,* 19 March 2000.

———. "Health Concerns Grow over Herbal Aids; As Industry Booms, Analysis Suggests Rising Toll in Illness and Death." *Washington Post,* 19 March 2000.

Gruenwald, Joerg. "The Supplement Markets in the U.S. and Europe." *Nutraceuticals World,* July 2000.

Hall, Carl T. "Critics Find Stimulant Difficult to Regulate." *The San Francisco Chronicle,* 26 October 2000.

Hunter Trum, Beatrice. "The New Dietary Supplement Label." *Consumers' Research Magazine,* September 1999.

Key, Sandra, and Michelle Marble. "Popular Diet Supplement May Be a Cancer Risk." *Cancer Weekly Plus,* 19 April 1999.

Kupper, Thomas. "Heavy Scrutiny Follows Metabolife Diet Product." *San Diego Union-Tribune,* 30 May 1999.

LaValle, James B. "Unlocking the Potential of Dietary Supplements." *Drug Store News,* 2 November 1999.

Lindner, Lawrence. "The Growing Case against Antioxidants; New Research Questions the Value of America's Favorite Supplements." *Washington Post,* 29 February 2000.

Mirasol, Feliza. "Lutein Emerges as a Leading Carotenoid Food Supplement." *Chemical Market Reporter,* 13 September 1999.

———. "Synthetic Lycopene Offers New Supplement Growth for Roche." *Chemical Market Reporter,* 16 August 1999.

Nagourney, Eric. "6 of 13 Herbal Brands Fail a Label Test." *New York Times,* 28 March 2000.

"NBTY Sets Acquisition Accord." *Wall Street Journal,* 15 November 1999.

"Now on Store Shelves: New Labels for Supplements." *Tufts University Health & Nutrition Letter,* May 1999.

"Price-Fixing: Vitamin Firms to Pay Record Fine." *American Health Line,* 7 September 1999.

Rafi, Natasha. "Herbs and Supplements: What You Need to Know before You Buy." *Money,* April 2000.

Reno, Jamie, et al. "Heavy Meddling." *Newsweek,* 18 October 1999.

Ritter, Stephen K. "Faster, Higher, Stronger." *Chemical & Engineering News,* 6 September 1999.

Roan, Shari. "SAM-e Tests Show Some Labels Mislead." *Los Angeles Times,* 27 March 2000.

Rubin, Karen Wilk. "How They Compare to Real Foods: Dietary Supplements." *Food Service Director,* 15 May 1999.

"SAMe for Depression." *Medical Letter on Drugs & Therapeutics,* 5 November 1999.

Sauer, Pamela. "Is the Bloom Fading for Dietary Supplements?" *Chemical Market Reporter,* 8 November 1999.

Scalise, Annette. "Echo Boom Generation New Target for Calcium Market." *Drug Store News,* 25 September 2000.

Schwartz, Harry. "Beware of What You Read." *Pharmaceutical Executive,* May 1999.

Squires, Sally. "High Irony; New Supplement Labels Are Short on Facts." *Washington Post,* 7 March 2000.

"Supplement Makers Consolidate." *Chemical Market Reporter,* 16 August 1999.

Waslien, Carol. "Support Builds for Good Manufacturing Practices for Dietary Supplements." *Chemical Market Reporter,* 23 August 1999.

Webb, Marlon. "Metabolife to Appeal Court's Defamation Ruling." *San Diego Business Journal,* 22 November 1999.

"What Makes SAM-e Run?" *Consumer Reports,* October 1999.

Wise, John A., and Robert O. Voy. "The Science of Supplementation." *American Fitness,* January/February 2000.

OPHTHALMIC LASERS

Nearly 1 million pairs of eyes underwent laser surgical procedures in the United States in 1999 to correct nearsightedness, astigmatism, and farsightedness. The number was projected to fall slightly to about 900,000 in 2000 and rebound strongly in 2001 to 1.2 million. Those numbers, however, represent only about 3 percent of the estimated 57 million prospective candidates suitable for the procedures, a figure perhaps not surprising given both the squeamishness many people feel about putting their eyes in the path of a laser beam and the still-high cost of doing so—almost $2,000 per eye, though competition was beginning to force prices downward by 2000. One procedure in particular, laser in-situ keratomileusis, or LASIK, dominated optical laser surgeries, accounting for more than half of all those performed. LASIK operations were projected to reach 750,000 in 2000, constituting a $3 billion market.

ORGANIZATION AND STRUCTURE

The two primary manufacturers of the ophthalmic lasers used for corrective vision surgery in North America are: VISX Inc. of Santa Clara, California, and Summit Technology Inc. of Waltham, Massachusetts. Summit was the first laser maker to get U.S. Food and Drug Administration (FDA) approval in 1995 for photorefractive keratectomy (PRK), a surgical procedure. The company advertised laser eye surgery directly to the public, owned vision centers that performed the procedure, and offered financing to patients for the surgery. It also ran print ads in popular magazines, and

"category development" ads for the procedure on cable television, which included a toll-free number where operators referred callers to the nearest vision center using a Summit laser system. Some industry analysts criticized this marketing approach, saying medical device makers should not perform procedures themselves but should concentrate only on producing their instruments.

An FDA-mandated training program is required for those performing laser eye surgery. Ophthalmologists usually perform the procedure, but some states allow optometrists to perform laser eye surgery. Some doctors have formed groups that own or control the eye-surgery centers using the lasers. Other vision centers allowed doctors to use the lasers on a rental basis. Summit Technology located their vision centers in prestigious institutions such as Tufts University, Stanford University, George Washington University, and the Cleveland Clinic. Start-up costs are high for laser eye surgery, with excimer lasers costing $525,000 and up to 10 percent of that amount in yearly maintenance fees. Virtually no insurance plan covers the surgery, which is usually considered a cosmetic procedure, so consumers wanting optical laser surgery often pay from $2,000 to $2,500 per eye.

The procedure takes less than 30 minutes to perform, with less than a minute of that time spent under a laser whose firing pulses last less than a second. The surgery requires only local anesthetic and some drops to deaden the blinking impulse for a short time. Patients usually notice immediate vision improvement, with the final corrected vision taking a few days to develop. Industry statistics report that the vast majority of patients' vision improves to at or better than 20/40—enough to pass a driver's license exam with-

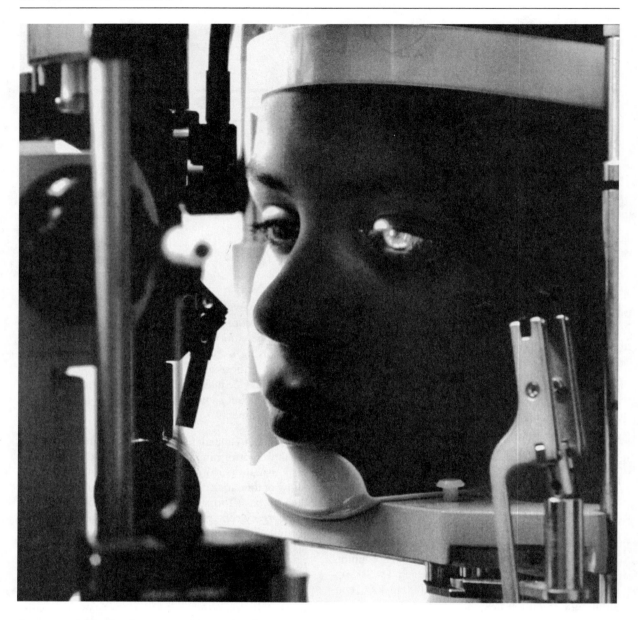

A woman undergoing laser eye surgery. (Photo Researchers Inc./John Greim/Science Photo Library)

out glasses—and that most patients achieved 20/25 or even 20/20 vision. Ophthalmologists recommend that patients be between the ages of 21 and 50, since patients older or younger than that might not get optimal results.

Laser vision correction does entail some risks and negative side effects, however. None of the available procedures correct for presbyopia, the gradual loss of lens flexibility that affects nearly everyone after age 40. Thus, most laser patients will still require reading glasses at some point. Side effects encompass an increased halo-effect from lights, especially at night,

which can interfere with driving; double vision; or ocular infections. In some patients, vision is overcorrected; in others, the improvements aren't sufficient to obviate the need for corrective lenses. LASIK carries a small risk that the corneal flap will not reseal properly, but instead will heal in a wrinkled fashion.

BACKGROUND AND DEVELOPMENT

Refraction describes the way in which light is focused by the eye. Factors affecting eyesight acuity are the curvature of the cornea, the strength of the lens, and the length of the eye. Variations in these factors can result in myopia (commonly referred to as nearsightedness), hyperopia (farsightedness), or astigmatism.

Although lasers may be used to correct opacities and other problems resulting from diseases of the eye, they have been most aggressively marketed and developed as a means of lessening dependence on glasses and contact lenses in healthy people.

Refractive surgery began in the mid-1800s, when some claimed that the cornea could be flattened with a spring-mounted mallet through the patient's closed eyelid. L. J. Hans, of the Netherlands, devised the basic principles of incisional surgery, or keratotomy, in 1898. Clinical work by the Japanese doctors T. Sato and K. Akiyam in the 1940s and 1950s demonstrated that transverse and radial incisions in the rear of the cornea caused it to flatten, thus altering refraction. The degree of visual correction depended on the number, depth, and length of incisions.

In the 1960s, S. Fyodorov of the U.S.S.R. performed keratotomies with multiple incisions on the anterior surface of the eye to yield greater safety and control over the degree of refractive correction. Interest in the new radial keratotomy led to a large study of the procedure in the late 1970s by the National Eye Institute. Although the technique was found to be effective, many patients experienced complications.

Ophthalmology was the first medical specialty to use lasers extensively, and clinical research on the use of excimer lasers for eye surgery began in the early 1980s. The excimer ablates rather than cuts tissue and thus is an ideal technique for precisely sculpting the corneal surface. After years of clinical trials, the FDA approved the use of lasers for moderate myopia in 1995, and industry giants Summit Technology and VISX were formed in 1985 and 1986 to introduce lasers into clinical practice in the United States.

LASIK, the newest available laser corrective procedure, evolved from a procedure introduced in the 1970s in which a thin wafer of tissue was removed from the cornea, reshaped, and reinserted into the eye. A Greek physician who used a laser to treat tissue underlying a thin flap of the cornea's surface first described in 1989 the procedure now in wide use. LASIK's dramatic results and absence of postoperative pain soon created worldwide demand, and in 1997 the FDA ruled that it was an "off-label" procedure that could be used by any licensed medical professional if it was judged to be in the best interest of the patient. In June 1998 the FDA recommended approval of LASIK using a system developed by researchers at the Emory Vision Correction Center—the first time approval has ever been granted to a physician team for a surgical system.

In late 1998 and early 1999 VISX excimer laser systems were approved to treat hyperopia and astigmatism, greatly expanding the availability of the procedure.

RADIAL KERATOTOMY

Radial keratotomy (RK), the original incisional technique, has been performed since the late 1970s but is no longer widely used. It is still sometimes recommended for patients with mild myopia for whom cost represents a persuasive factor. RK involves making radial cuts with a diamond-tipped knife along the cornea to weaken the sides of the eye. Ocular pressure then flattens the cornea's surface and reduces myopia. The procedure leaves scars on the cornea, however, and cuts through almost 90 percent of the cornea's thickness, which tends to weaken the eye. Up to half of all RK patients experienced mild farsightedness five years after the procedure. The process also left the cornea's surface too bumpy to wear contact lenses and involved a relatively painful healing process. Despite the drawbacks, an average of 275,000 patients per year opted for RK treatment before it was largely replaced by safer and more effective methods. RK is the only procedure that had been practiced for enough time to yield long-term clinical data; a study released in 1994, based on 10-year evaluations of results, revealed that about 85 percent of patients investigated retained vision of 20/40 or better.

PHOTOREFRACTIVE KERATECTOMY

The photorefractive keratectomy (laser PRK) procedure uses short pulses from an excimer laser to sculpt only 5 to 10 percent (25 to 50 microns) of the cornea's front surface, producing a flattening effect that slightly reshapes the eye to dramatically improve vision. The entire procedure takes less than 40 seconds per eye. Excimer lasers use a specific wavelength of ultraviolet light that cannot penetrate the cornea completely or harm the eye's internal tissue. The protective outer layer of the cornea, however, must first be scraped off before the laser reshaping is done, a process that increases postoperative pain while the cornea heals. Performed under local anesthetic eyedrops, laser PRK is appropriate for mild to moderate visual distortions. A two-year follow-up study published in 1997 in the journal *Ophthalmology* indicated an ongoing success rate of 20/40 vision or better in 92.5 percent of patients. The FDA's Center for Devices and Radiological Health, however, reported that about 5 percent of laser PRK patients will still require corrective lenses on a continuous basis and an additional 15 percent will need them for driving or other specific visual tasks.

LASER ASSISTED IN-SITU KERATOMILEUSIS

In 1997 the FDA approved an even more sophisticated technique, which uses a two-stage process (popularly known as "flap and zap") to expose the top layer of the cornea and remove a minute amount of corneal tissue with a high degree of precision. Laser assisted in-situ keratomileusis (LASIK) involves greater surgical skill and somewhat greater risk during the procedure itself than PRK; LASIK patients, however, experience more rapid recovery and dramatic improvements in their vision. In LASIK, the surgeon uses a very thin surgical blade, or microkeratome, to slice a hinged flap of the outer corneal tissue and then flips it away from the eye, exposing the corneal surface to a computer-guided laser beam for reshaping. The surgeon then repositions the flap, which quickly adheres to the eye and bonds back in place in a few moments. LASIK results in less eye trauma, less post-op discomfort, and almost immediate improvements in vision. Preliminary reports indicate a success rate similar to that of PRK, with about 60 percent of patients enjoying 20/20 vision and nearly all experiencing sight-enhancement to at least 20/40. About 10 to 15 percent of all LASIK patients require a secondary procedure to fine-tune their vision.

PIONEERS IN THE FIELD

IBM Corp. developed the excimer laser in the early 1970s to etch microchips. A so-called "cool" laser, it cut through most substances without generating heat. An industry pioneer, Stephen L. Trokel, theorized that the laser could also be used to successfully sculpt the cornea. Working with IBM physicist R. Srinivasan, Trokel patented his idea for using excimer lasers in eye surgery in 1983. In 1985, Theo Seiler performed the first excimer laser procedure in Germany, and the first PRK was performed in the United States on a blind eye in 1987. In 1988, Marguerite McDonald performed the first PRK in the United States on a sighted person with myopia. From 1987 to 1989, several companies experimented with excimer lasers based on Seiler's work, and Trokel got the first investigational device exemption from the FDA.

Another important industry pioneer was Dr. Stephen N. Joffe, president and CEO of LCA-Vision Inc. Joffe earned his medical degree in South Africa in 1967, and spent 15 years at the University of Cincinnati Medical Center. He started Laser Centers of America in 1985 as a private company, doing ophthalmic laser surgeries. He also helped found the International Nd:Yag Laser Society. (YAG referred to Yttrium Aluminum Garnet lasers, a photodisruptive laser.) LCA-Vision performed the first FDA-approved laser eye procedures in the United States, in late 1995, and did thousands of the procedures from 1990 to 1995 in Canada.

CURRENT CONDITIONS

Few could fail to foresee the momentous growth in the refractive surgery market during the few years since ophthalmic lasers became available; the expanded range of procedures is bound to accelerate growth even further. The high demand for refractive surgery has resulted in many ophthalmologists switching to full-time refractive surgery.

The expenses incurred for equipment generated a volume-geared business whose focus has been criticized for its heavy and aggressive advertising. Because patients must usually pay for laser correction themselves, many surgeons have actively pursued this patient pool with the help of large vision-care ventures as a highly profitable source of income free of the administrative obstacles posed by managed-care plans. Other ophthalmologists, however, decline to perform the surgeries at all and consider them cosmetic procedures whose benefits may often be exaggerated.

The preference for LASIK refractive surgery over PRK procedures continued. In studies with patients receiving PRK in one eye and LASIK in the other, LASIK was preferred for generating less post-op pain, faster visual recovery, and greater visual acuity. Some experts predict that refinements in LASIK technique will permit the procedure to correct vision for better than 20/20 within the next decade. As the number of both patients receiving surgery and surgeons providing it has escalated, so has the variety of accessory instruments for cutting the flap (microkeratomes), as well as spatulas, forceps, and others to maneuver it. Despite the popularity of LASIK, PRK is indicated in some situations, such as when the cornea is too thin to safely cut a flap, or if there is likelihood of physical contact with the eye, as in sports, where the flap could be lost before healing properly.

Cost-cutting trends were sighted on the horizon by 2000. In addition to a February 2000 statement by Summit and VISX that they would reduce their licensing fees from $250 to $100, competition surged as new players entered into all segments of the industry. Also in early 2000, Bausch & Lomb announced that it had won FDA LASIK approval for its Technolas 217, and that it would match Summit and VISX's reduced licensing fee. To reduce the price of laser surgeries, thus enticing new customers, increasing numbers of laser eye centers began permitting optometrists or technicians, rather than only ophthalmologists, to carry out pre- and post-op checkups. Some also relied on less-skilled surgeons fresh from training to perform the actual surgeries. Medical experts charged that some laser centers occasionally relaxed the patient-acceptability screenings, to permit greater numbers of borderline cases to undergo the operations. Although most health-coverage plans did not reimburse for optical laser correction, by 2000 at least two of the nation's largest managed-care vision benefits firms, Vision Service Plan and Cole Managed Vision, offered discounts for laser surgeries to members and their dependents who elected to undergo the procedure at one of The Laser Center Inc.'s centers. This placed the per-eye cost at $1,800 or less.

Logically, the growth potential of the market is limited by the number of available candidates for surgery, since many Americans who require corrective lenses are not suitable for optical laser surgeries. These include persons with greater than moderate visual distortion, with larger-than-average ocular dimensions, those suffering from autoimmune diseases or who have corneal scarring. Ideally, of course, the procedure should be performed only once. It is estimated that perhaps 44 million Americans would be eligible for these procedures.

INDUSTRY LEADERS

LASER MANUFACTURERS

The two industry giants, Summit Technology Inc. and VISX, dominated the manufacture of ophthalmic lasers approved to perform PRK for myopia and astigmatism in the United States. In March 1998, however, federal authorities charged the two with price-fixing in a complex patent-pooling venture that had allowed them to share revenues in effectively blocking competition. They were also accused of overcharging consumers—by more than $40 million—the $250 royalty fee that surgeons were required to pay them per procedure. Of such royalties VISX received 56 percent, and Summit received 44 percent. Under pressure from

the Federal Trade Commission (FTC), VISX paid Summit $35 million in a settlement that dissolved the joint venture. In July 1998 the FTC prohibited any further license fee agreements and required fuller disclosure to consumers by both companies.

Meanwhile, in spring of 1999 VISX filed a patent infringement suit against the Japanese laser manufacturer Nidek, Inc., in an attempt to block its importation of lasers into the United States. Nidek denied any patent infringement and added that Nidek does not charge per-procedure fees. In March 2000, the International Trade Commission agreed with Nidek and VISX stock plummeted.

Summit Technology, Inc. of Waltham, Massachusetts, makes the Apex Laser Workstation used for PRK surgery, and its corneal disc has been approved for the treatment of astigmatism. The company acquired Autonomous Technologies Corp. as a subsidiary and in November 1998 the FDA approved Autonomous' LADARVision, the only excimer system that tracks and compensates for involuntary eye movement. Summit's 1999 sales were $111.1 million, representing 21.3 percent yearly growth. Summit employed 425 workers, down 19.7 percent from 1997. Summit also owns Lens Express, the nation's most successful contact lens replacement service.

VISX, Inc. of Santa Clara, California, had 1999 annual sales of $271.3 million, up 102.8 percent from 1998, and employed 280 people. VISX, the world's leading manufacturer of optical surgical lasers, manufactures its own excimer laser surgical system, complete with operating software and a system for managing patient data. Operators must purchase single-use key cards imprinted with the software to run the laser, and also pay a $100 usage fee. VISX lasers were used in about 80 percent of all U.S. laser eye surgery. In March 2000 a securities class-action suit was filed on behalf of stockholders against the company in the U.S. District Court of Northern California. The suit alleged that VISX had disseminated deliberately misleading statements concerning the revenues its laser system was expected to generate and that limited industry competition would permit it to maintain its then-$250 licensing fee. Initially VISX seemed in a very strong position, since the value of its stock increased from $20 per share in early 1999 to $102 by July of that same year. Increased industry competition and the adverse ruling involving Nidek, however, "cast doubt on the company's competitive position," the suit asserted. Although poor earnings for the fourth quarter of 1999 led to another drop in stocks, VISX didn't reveal it would reduce its licensing fee until February 2000.

Leading optical-products giant Bausch & Lomb of Rochester, New York, entered the optical laser production arena as part of its refocusing on the eye-care industry after William Carpenter took over the company in 1995. In 1999 its surgical division posted total sales of $433 million, and constituted the fastest-growing segment of the company. It won FDA LASIK approval for its Technolas 217 scanning excimer laser in February 2000. Its entry coincided with the Summit and VISX decision to lower their licensing fees to $100, an amount Bausch & Lomb said it would match. The clinical studies that led to FDA approval claimed that 99.7 percent of all patients treated experienced vision correction to 20/40 or better. Bausch & Lomb bought Chiron Vision in late 1997, which controlled 80 percent of the domestic microkeratome market. In March 2000, Bausch & Lomb unveiled its Zyoptix integrated laser system for personalized optical laser correction at the Video Refrattiva 2000 Satellite Congress.

A much smaller entity, LaserSight, Inc. of Winter Park, Florida, which employed only 131 people, experienced sales of $21.7 million and a net loss of $14.4 million in 1999. The company, which manufactures the Astra lasers, is undergoing clinical trials in the United States. LaserSight operated in 30 foreign countries and had previously completed 3,000 patient treatments at 13 centers in Italy of what was believed to be the largest application of customized laser vision correction conducted thus far.

OPHTHALMIC LASER SURGERY PROVIDERS

Laser Vision Centers, Inc., headquartered in St. Louis, Missouri, operates both fixed-site and mobile excimer lasers, both independently and through joint-operating agreements. Laser Vision Centers' locations span 44 U.S. states, Canada, the United Kingdom, Ireland, Sweden, and Greece. With 270 employees, the company generated sales revenues of $88.1 million in 2000, and net income reached $13.9 million. Laser Vision constitutes 9.3 percent of the total U.S. laser surgery providers, and 22 percent of large corporate sites. Case volume increased 78 percent from January 1999 to January 2000.

The largest network of laser eye-surgery centers in the United States is operated by The Laser Center Inc. (TLC) of Mississauga, Ontario, which brought in annual revenues of $188 million in 1999, for net income of $2.72 million. In the twelve months ending 31 May 2000, over 134,000 patients underwent laser procedures at TLC refractive centers. The company employed 750 individuals and managed 45 refractive laser clinics, including four in Canada (in British Co-

lumbia and Ontario) and 26 in the United States. The firm builds alliances with local doctors, who receive fees for pre- and postoperative care if they refer patients to TLC laser facilities.

In April 1999 TLC announced plans to restructure to focus on its core laser correction business. The corporation will use TLC Capital Corp., a wholly owned subsidiary, for strategic investments, and negotiations are underway for the sale of Partner Provider Health, TLC's managed-care division. Targets for further expanding its core business include agreements with major corporations and health maintenance organizations as a source of revenue. In 1999 TLC formed agreements with Southern California Edison Co., making available discounts on services for the utility's 600,000 employees, and with the Oakland, California-based health-care organization Kaiser Permanente, which serves 8.6 million people in 17 states and the District of Columbia.

The forecast for TLC seemed blurry, however, when stocks fell in late 1999. Cofounders Elias Vamvakas and Dr. Jeffrey Machat had dumped 1.61 million of their own shares, more than 20 percent of their combined holdings, earlier in May of the same year. The move might have foreshadowed a cloudy future for the industry, with increased competition at home and mounting pressure from Canadian upstarts such as Lasik Vision Corp. of Vancouver—"budget" operations that charge less than $1,000 an eye for laser surgical correction.

LCA-Vision of Cincinnati, Ohio, provides clinical application of laser technology for optical correction. It operates 30 laser vision correction centers, including two in Canada and one in Europe. Revenues rose 63 percent in 1999, to reach $57.4 million. The company had over 200 employees.

WORK FORCE

As of 1997 only ophthalmologists could actually use ophthalmic lasers on patients. Ophthalmologists are medical doctors specifically trained in the branch of medicine dealing with the structure, functions, and diseases of the eye. After four years of medical school, ophthalmologists spend another year as medical interns and three years as residents. In 1997 some of these doctors clashed with optometrists over who had the right to perform ophthalmic laser surgery, since so much of the process was guided by computer instead of by the human hand. In contrast to ophthalmologists, optometrists go through four years at a college of optometry, and have to pass a state exam. Optometrists prescribe glasses and contact lenses and are not licensed to write drug prescriptions or perform surgery. Some optometrists, however, began training to use ophthalmic lasers during the mid-1990s.

In 1997 the state legislatures of Alaska, California, Colorado, New Jersey, and Virginia considered letting optometrists perform the laser procedures. Idaho already permitted some optometrists to perform such operations. Although ophthalmic laser surgery was something done in the caregiver's office rather than a hospital, some ophthalmologists insisted that optometrists should not be allowed to do the procedure. Other analysts claimed that as more people trusted the laser procedures, traditional optometry (selling glasses and contact lenses) could disappear unless these professionals could compete with medical doctors. By 2000 the battle was becoming increasingly heated, and no end was in sight.

AMERICA AND THE WORLD

Ophthalmic lasers have been used in Europe since the 1980s. Because of international differences in the regulation of medical devices, many lasers for medical use are sold and widely used first outside the United States. By the late 1990s, perhaps 1,700 ophthalmic lasers were in operation worldwide and over 1 million laser eye surgeries were performed, of which 40-45 percent were LASIK procedures. Estimates of annual world market sales hover around $3 billion.

RESEARCH AND TECHNOLOGY

Many clinical studies are in progress to broaden the applications of laser techniques, but some analysts believe future innovations will not be as dramatic as those made in recent years. New techniques are being investigated for treating macular degeneration (an age-related scarring of the retina), glaucoma, and cataracts. Innovative microkeratomes, the device that creates the corneal flap, are also undergoing large-scale evaluation. Multifunction products such as Coherent's EPIC system—a three-in-one apparatus that uses a standard slit lamp to treat diabetic retinopathy, open-angle glaucoma, and cataracts—may further reduce surgeons' operating costs.

In March 2000, the Ophthalmic Devices Panel of the FDA recommended the premarket application for Autonomous Technologies' treatment of hyperopia

using its LADARVision LASIK system, which is owned by Summit. If Autonomous gains final FDA endorsement, it would possess the widest range of application approvals for any excimer laser. In January of the same year, Intralase Corp. won FDA clearance to produce the first laser technical system that would replace mechanical cutting devices. Its Femtosecond Laser Keratome System offers a laser alternative to the microkeratomes, whose movement can halt in mid cut and which occasionally becomes tangled with corneal tissue. Lasers had been avoided previously for such cuts, because of dry eye tissue. But the speed of the Femtosecond—one-millionth of one-billionth of the second—eliminated the problem. The device was already at work in Europe.

New nonlaser technologies may affect the market as they emerge. The FDA has approved Intacs, which are insertable discs and rings that slightly alter the cornea's curvature to treat myopia. The procedures are considered permanent but reversible; and modifications to treat myopia are being investigated. Also under development are intraocular lenses, which promise better correction for more severe vision distortion and which leave the cornea intact. Another technique, radio frequency keratoplasty (RFK), uses radio-frequency energy to shrink the intra-stromal collagen fibers deeply within the cornea. The procedure is approved for sale in Canada and has received the CE mark of approval in Europe; it will be marketed as less invasive than lasers to treat hyperopia, presbyopia, astigmatism and overcorrections by laser treatments.

FURTHER READING

"Apex Excimer Laser Will Complement LASIK Procedure, FDA Says." *Medical Industry Today,* 22 October 1999.

"Autonomous Gets Approval Recommendation for Hyperopic LASIK." *Eyeworld Week Online,* 27 March 2000.

"Barracks Rodos Files Suit against VISX, Inc. Alleging Misrepresentations and Insider Trading." 25 February 2000. Available from http://www.barrack.com.

Bellantoni, Christina, Monique Martinez, and Lucila Naranjo. "Largest Medical Device Companies." *Business Journal Serving San Jose and Silicon Valley,* 21 January 2000.

Brody, Jane. "Promise and Risks of Laser Eye Surgery." *New York Times,* 14 September 1999.

Bulkeley, William. "Bausch & Lomb Gets FDA Approval for Vision Laser." *Wall Street Journal,* 25 February 2000.

Chaudhry, Iftikhar, et al. "Advances in Refractive Surgery." *Post Graduate Medicine,* September 1999.

Chang, Kenneth. "Laser Eye Surgery's Turf War." *New York Times,* 1 August 2000.

Comarow, Avery. "A Visionary Quest—Bad Eyes, Good Candidate?" *U.S. News & World Report,* 27 March 2000.

"Corneal Surgery for Correction of Refractive Errors." *Medical Letter on Drugs & Therapeutics,* 17 December 1999.

Cullen, Lisa Reilly. "Battle of the Eyeballs." *Money,* December 1999.

"Eye Lasers and 'Black Boxes.'" *Medical Update,* April 1999.

"FDA Panel Backs Summit Eye Laser for Broader Use." *Medical Industry Today,* 27 July 1999.

"FTC Drops Charge of Price-Fixing for Laser Eye Surgery." *American Medical News,* 17 August 1999.

Gerber, Paul, and Marjolijn Bijlefeld. "Do Managed Care and Refractive Surgery Mix?" *Eye World Online,* 8 January 2000. Available from http://www.eyeworld.org.

Gilbert, Virginia Baldwin. "Cost of Laser Eye Surgery May Head Lower." *St. Louis Post-Dispatch,* 25 February 2000.

Gorman, Christine, Dan Cray, and Alice Park. "R U Ready to Dump Your Glasses?" *Time,* 11 October 1999.

Johannes, Laura. "U.S. Says Japanese Firm Doesn't Infringe on VISX." *Wall Street Journal,* 8 December 1999.

————. "VISX Wins Dismissal of Case by FTC Alleging Deception of the Patent." *Wall Street Journal,* 7 June 1999.

Knestout, Brian. "Myopia over Laser Surgery." *Kiplinger's Personal Finance Magazine,* February 2000.

Krieger, Elizabeth. "A Clear-Eyed View." *Health,* October 1999.

"Laser Eye Surgery." *Mayo Clinic Health Letter,* December 1999.

"Laser Eye Surgery: Price Wars Mean Lower Costs." *American Health Line,* 25 February 2000.

"LaserSight Provides Company Update and Comments on Industry Developments." *PR Newswire,* 24 February 2000.

Lawrence, Donna. "Second Sight." *Forbes,* fall 1999 Supplement.

Manning, Margie. "Klobnak Says Short Sellers Selling Company Short." *St. Louis Business Journal,* 14 February 2000.

Marcus, Mary Brophy. "Before You Get Lasered, Squint at the Fine Print." *U.S. News & World Report,* 27 March 2000.

Marsh, Ann. "A Poke in the Eye." *Forbes,* 18 October 1999.

McLean, Bethany. "Why So Few Saw the Warnings on VISX." *Fortune,* 21 February 2000.

"Medical Bausch & Lomb Gets FDA Approval for Laser System to Correct Vision." *Investor's Business Daily,* 25 February 2000.

Middleton, Otesa. "A Laser-Surgery Procedure for Eyes Clears Hurdle with Federal Panel." *Wall Street Journal,* 23 July 1999.

Monroe, Linda Roach. "Refractive Surgery Update: Custom Cuts for Better Vision." *Eyenet Magazine,* January 1999.

Moretti, Michael. "Manufacturers Race to Improve LASIK Instruments." *Eye World Online,* 23 August 1999. Available from http://www.eyeworld.org.

Moukheiber, Zina. "Eye Strain." *Forbes,* 4 October 1999.

O'Neil, Sean. "Eyes on the Price." *Kiplinger's Personal Finance Magazine,* September 2000.

Portman, Robert. "Marketing LASIK: Between a Regulatory Rock and an Ad Space." *Eye World Online,* 11 August 1999. Available from http://www.eyeworld.org.

Rajpal, Rajesh. "How to See Clearly before Eye Surgery." *Washington Business Journal,* 17 December 1999.

"RFK Is Still a Less Expensive Option for Low Myopia." *Primary Care Optometry News,* January 1999. Available from http://www.slackinc.com/eye/pcon/199901/rk.asp.

Schwartz, Bruce, and Bruce Zagelbaum. "Refractive Surgery for Active Patients." *Physician and Sportsmedicine,* 1 October 1999.

van Tine, Julia, et al. "Laser Eye Surgery at 40+." *Prevention,* February 2000.

Vedel Kessig, Sven, Jannik Boberg-Ans, and Steffen Heegaard. "Intrastromal Holmium Laser Keratostomy: Long-Term Results." *Ophthalmic Surgery and Lasers,* January/February 2000.

"Zap Your Myopic Eyes?" *Consumer Reports,* June 1999.

Optical Data Storage

New digital entertainment media and ceaseless demand for gigabyte upon gigabyte of removable computer storage have created a booming market for optical storage devices and recording media. The industry's offerings range from digital video disc read-only memory (DVD-ROM) gadgets for playing full-length digital movies to various compact disc (CD) audio and compact disc read-only memory (CD-ROM) data drives for storing and retrieving music, software, and other digital miscellany. Specialized optical storage is also on tap in corporate and government settings as part of high-end storage systems for network servers and mainframes.

Optical storage boasts three big advantages over other formats:

- It uses physical space efficiently by compressing a lot of data into a relatively compact storage medium, namely, an optical disc.

- Discs are durable, portable, and cheap to produce.

- Technical standards have been fairly stable and nearly universal, so cross-brand compatibility is generally high.

Although most optical drives' read and write speeds tend to lag behind those of magnetic hard disk drives, optical has fast become the mode of choice for relatively permanent storage uses, such as archiving movies, music, and data for periodic retrieval. CD-ROM drives became standard gear on personal computers (PCs) sold in the mid-1990s, and by 2000, DVD players had grown commonplace on new machines as well. Demand for storage flexibility has likewise produced robust sales of CD-rewritable and minidisc drives.

So many choices mean the plain old CD-ROM drive may be on its last leg. According to an estimate by Disk/Trend Inc., a market research group, CD-ROM drive shipments peaked in 1999 at about 95 million units. The market research firm predicted unit sales in 2000 to tumble to 83 million, and several observers expected that in 2001 more DVD-ROM drives would be sold than CD-ROM devices. Freeman Associates, another research firm, forecast the total number of optical ROM drives hitting the market in 2001 to approach 128 million, including 68 million DVD drives.

The optical storage industry includes companies that manufacture optical discs and cards and record data on them, along with those that make the drives and other devices that read data stored on them. Consumer optical storage products are sold in retail computer and electronics stores, via mail-order catalogs and television shopping programs, and over the Internet, while other devices such as mass storage towers and optical memory cards are sold to government agencies and businesses through resellers and other channels.

Types of Optical Discs

Optical discs are the most common kind of optical storage devices. One of the first optical discs was produced in 1978 in a joint effort by Philips Electronics N.V. and Sony Corp. This audio compact disc used CD technology to deliver digital sound and music to consumers. Philips and Sony continued to work together throughout the 1980s developing CD technology standards to store computer data. As the technology advanced, new standards were adapted industry-wide. These standards evolved into the CD-ROM technology used today.

Among the types of optical discs used for data storage are compact disc read-only memory (CD-ROM), on which data are permanently written and cannot be altered; write once, read many (WORM), on which data can be written once before it is unalterable; and erasable (EO), on which data can be both written and erased.

Recordable CDs (CD-R) are another type of optical storage disc; they allow individuals to create their own CDs. One of the drawbacks to CD-R discs, however, is that although a user can write to different sections of the disc over several sessions, the user can write to them only once, after which time the data are permanently encoded on the CD-R.

In 1986 Philips and Sony joined forces and developed compact disc interactive (CD-I). CD-I was unique for that time because of its ability to store text, images, sound, and graphics and through "interleaving" these types of data, presenting them to the user seamlessly and simultaneously. CD-I was created for the consumer market, which made it virtually incompatible with other CD-ROM drives. For this reason, CD-ROM/XA (extended architecture) was developed, thus serving as a bridge between traditional CD-ROMs and CD-Is. CD-ROM/XA allows textual data, audio, and video on the same tracks of a CD, but is compatible with both CD-ROM and CD-I drives.

Erasable optical discs include magneto-optical (M-O), rewritable (CD-RW), and the most advanced, phase-change (PD). M-O discs can be written and erased in much the same way as a traditional magnetic disc—through the use of heat and an electromagnet. With CD-RW discs, today the most popular optical recording format, users can both write and erase data many times, much like with a traditional floppy disk. PD discs were developed as an alternative to M-O discs. PD technology is unique in that it uses multiple layers on which data can be stored. With this technology, data can be both written and erased with a single laser, thus eliminating the need for an electromagnet. Interest in this technology is fading.

Digital versatile discs or digital video discs (DVDs) represent the latest technological advance in optical storage. These types of discs deliver exceptional video and audio quality and can store vastly greater amounts of data than CD-ROMs. What's more, most DVD-ROM drives are backwards compatible with ordinary audio CDs and CD-ROMs. Various forms of recordable and rewritable DVD have also begun to reach the market, but standards are still being hashed out among the major producers.

STORAGE CAPACITY

Optical data storage is ideal for multimedia applications that include sound, images, and text because optical discs can hold scads more information than old-fashioned floppy diskettes. The typical floppy disk holds just 1.4 megabytes of data, whereas CD-ROMs appeal to users because they can hold between 600 and 700 megabytes of data. For comparison, a floppy disk can hold about 10 seconds of CD-quality audio data; the typical CD can fit 74 minutes or so.

The advent of DVDs, with their tremendous storage capacity—4.7 to 17 gigabytes—takes capacity to a whole new level: a single DVD can accommodate an average-length movie along with a high-quality multichannel soundtrack and even extra scenes and peripheral content. DVDs also provide much sharper images than VHS videotape—at more than twice the resolution—and thus, as with audio CDs, DVDs can be played from a PC drive or from a stand-alone player as part of a home entertainment center.

HOW OPTICAL DATA STORAGE WORKS

Optical data storage technology uses lasers to write data to disc and later to read it. Because lasers can encode data in smaller areas than magnetic storage technology, optical storage discs can hold much more. The laser beam of an optical disc reader, or player, strikes the disc's reflective surface and either scatters the light or reflects it back through a prism, then to a light-sensing diode that generates a small electrical voltage. This voltage, in turn, produces the binary code—a series of ones and zeros—that the computer understands and translates into meaningful information for the user.

For the record, standard CDs and DVDs are 4.75 inches (130 mm) in diameter with a small hole in the middle and are made of a thin wafer of clear polycarbonate plastic and metal. The metal layer is usually pure aluminum that is sputtered onto the polycarbonate surface in a layer that is only a few molecules thick. The metal reflects light from a tiny infrared laser as the disc spins in the CD player. The reflections are transformed into electrical signals, and then further converted into meaningful data for use in digital equipment.

Information is stored in pits on the CD-ROM that are one-to-three microns long, approximately .5 microns wide, and .1 microns deep. There may be more than three miles of these pits wound about the center hole on the disc. The CD-ROM is coated with a layer of lacquer that protects the surface. Usually a label is silk-screened on the back.

THE MANUFACTURING PROCESS

Compact discs are made in multiple steps. First, a glass master is made using photolithographic techniques. An optically ground glass disc is coated with a layer of photoresistant material that is .1 microns thick. A pattern is produced on the disc using a laser; then the exposed areas on the disc are washed away, and the disc is silvered to produce the actual pits. The master disc is next coated with molecular layers of nickel, one layer at a time, until the desired thickness is achieved. The nickel layer is then separated from the glass disc and used as a metal negative.

In the case of low production runs, the metal negative is used to make the actual discs. Most projects require several positives to be produced by plating the surface of the metal negative. Molds or stampers are then made from the positives and used in injection molding machines.

Plastic pellets are heated and injected into the molds, where they form the disc with pits in it. The plastic disc is coated with a thin aluminum layer, for reflectance, and a protective lacquer layer. The disc is then labeled and packaged for delivery. Most of these operations take place in a "clean room" since a single particle of dust larger than a pit can destroy data. Mastering alone takes about 12 hours.

The smallness of the pits and the pattern in which they are applied give optical discs their tremendous storage capacity. In contrast to magnetic disks, where data are stored in concentric sectors and tracks, data are stored on optical discs in a spiral pattern originating at the small hole in the center and reaching to the outer edges.

The primary unit of data storage on a CD-ROM is a sector. Each sector on a CD contains 2,352 bytes of data, and is followed by 882 bytes of error detecting and correcting information and timing control data. Thus, a CD actually requires 3,234 bytes to store 2,352 bytes of data.

The disc spins at a constant linear velocity, which means that the rotational speed of the disc may vary from about 200 revolutions per minute (rpm) when the data being read are located at the outer part of the disc, to about 530 rpm when the data are located at the center.

CDs are read at a sustained rate of 150 kilobytes per second, which is sufficient for good audio, but very slow for large image files, motion video, and other multimedia information. Newer drives spin at up to 52 times this rate. Still, CD access speeds and transfer rates are much slower than those from a hard disk.

Optical storage is stable and reliable, and the discs are very durable. The surface of a CD is basically transparent. It has to allow a finely focused beam of laser light to pass through it twice, first to the metallic layer beneath the plastic where the data resides, then back to the receptors. While dirt, scratches, fingerprints, and other imperfections may interfere with data retrieval, improvements in error correction rates allow for some margin of error.

BACKGROUND AND DEVELOPMENT

Optical data storage technology was first used commercially in the 1960s when Philips Electronics N.V. developed laser discs known as LaserVision. Video and audio, stored together on 12-inch discs, were read from a laser light beam's reflections as the disc rotated. Variations of the reflections were translated into analog electrical impulses.

This laser disc storage technology played an important role in the development of compact disc audio (CD-A) for the consumer market. The information was stored in digital, rather than analog, format. In 1980 Philips and Sony jointly created the standard for audio CDs technology known as the "Red Book." The Red Book was the first in a series of CD technology standards that are still used.

In 1984 Philips and Sony followed the Red Book with the "Yellow Book," which defined standards for the storage of large volumes of computer data on compact discs as read-only memory in addressable sectors. The Red Book defined standards for audio only. The CD-ROM discs and drives were similar to the audio CDs and drives, though with a better error correction rate and without a digital-to-analog converter. The Yellow Book provided the structure for the High Sierra Agreement published by Philips, Sony, and Microsoft in 1985. This agreement became the ISO 9660 standard governing the presentation of data on CD-ROMs that were developed and first shipped during the mid-1980s, and continued to serve as the governing standard for all CD-ROM manufacturers throughout the 1990s.

In 1989 Philips and Sony again joined to develop the software and hardware standard known as the "Green Book" for compact disc interactive (CD-I). Although the technology failed to gain wide acceptance, the Green Book was adopted as a standard way of providing images, sound, and other multimedia functions on CD.

CURRENT CONDITIONS

In 2000 Disk/Trend Inc. estimated the optical storage drive market worldwide at over $10.6 billion, a modest improvement over $10.2 billion in 1999. Those figures don't include sales of optical discs and stand-alone CD audio and DVD players. Within the PC-based optical storage market, DVD is fast becoming the most important format. Disk/Trend predicted that DVD-drive revenues would overtake those of conventional CD-ROM drives in 2001, when DVD-ROM was expected to become the top-selling format in the entire optical storage category. Rewritable CDs (CD-RW) and DVD-recordable drives were also expected to amass a growing share of the market as consumers bypass CD-ROM drives for more versatile devices. Indeed, in the short run, International Data Corp. (IDC) expected CD-RW sales to rise faster than DVD-recordable purchases because of wider familiarity with CDs and lingering compatibility problems with DVD-writing devices.

Unit sales of optical drives continue on an upward track. In 1999, by one estimate, there were about 110 million optical drives sold around the world. A separate calculation by Freeman Associates placed the growth rate at 8 percent a year category-wide. The newer segments, though, have been growing much more briskly. IDC forecast global CD-RW shipments to nearly double in 2000, amid falling prices, and DVD-ROM shipments to advance 55 percent the same year. The fledgling DVD-recordable segment, IDC predicted, was likely to surge more than 200 percent, but on unit volume of still less than 1 million.

Not surprisingly, declining prices are—and will continue to be—both a boon to unit growth and a damper on revenue growth. DVD-ROM prices have already fallen considerably. According to one source, the difference in wholesale prices between DVD-ROM and CD-ROM drives was likely to be cut in half by the end of 2000. CD-RW prices have also fallen, while the old standby CD-ROM drives are at rock bottom. Because of such conditions, IDC predicted that revenues for the greater optical and removable storage industry would stall in 2000 at 2 percent growth, even amid double-digit advances in unit shipments. Disk/Trend took a slightly more optimistic view, forecasting growth to register between 3 and 4 percent on the year.

One segment that has carved out only a marginal existence within the industry is the minidisc (MD) format. The format, pioneered by Sony, is targeted as a portable digital music alternative to conventional CDs. MD players have been available in the U.S. market since the early 1990s, but by 2000 the segment was still struggling to top 1 million units in sales. The two-inch rewritable discs can accommodate roughly the same amount of music as a conventional CD, and the format has been touted as more tolerant of bumps and jarring when used on the go. But while Sony holds out hope that MDs will catch on in the United States as they have in Europe and Japan, the popularity of MP3

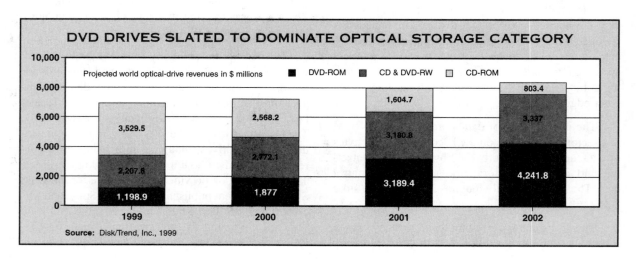

DVD DRIVES SLATED TO DOMINATE OPTICAL STORAGE CATEGORY

Projected world optical-drive revenues in $ millions — DVD-ROM — CD & DVD-RW — CD-ROM

	1999	2000	2001	2002
CD-ROM	3,529.5	2,568.2	1,604.7	803.4
CD & DVD-RW	2,207.8	2,772.1	3,180.8	3,337
DVD-ROM	1,198.9	1,877	3,189.4	4,241.8

Source: Disk/Trend, Inc., 1999

players—digital audio devices for playing music files downloaded off the Internet—may keep MDs on the sidelines indefinitely.

Competitive pricing forced industry consolidation in late 2000. First Quantum Corp. and Maxtor Corp. agreed to combine their disc-drive operations. Immediately after that, market leader LG Electronics teamed up with DVD-ROM giant Hitachi to form an enormous optical data storage partnership. The latter move, especially, was a signal to analysts and industry players that industry competition was too intense even for the market leaders to weather profitably, and accelerated consolidation was expected to follow.

INDUSTRY LEADERS

As with most of the electronics and computer manufacturing industries, the optical storage industry is thoroughly internationalized. It's dominated by highly efficient, cost-competitive multinational concerns based in Asia, particularly in Japan and South Korea. As a result, there's not a U.S. company to be found on the industry's top-10 list, as ranked by International Data Corp. (IDC) based on worldwide CD-ROM and DVD-ROM drive market share.

LG Electronics, of Seoul, South Korea, is a major producer of semiconductors as well as finished electronic goods. According to IDC estimates, LG Electronics was the world's largest maker of CD-ROM and DVD-ROM drives in 1999. The firm formerly marketed its electronics under the Gold Star label, but began phasing out that name in favor of LG, its corporate identity. LG Electronics also owns the U.S.-based television maker Zenith.

Toshiba Corp. of Japan makes everything from cutting-edge notebook computers to massive industrial power-generation equipment. In between all that, it's carved out a handsome niche in the optical storage drive business, commanding 13 percent of the world market as of 1999. Sagging profits forced the company to restructure in 2000. Nonetheless, Toshiba continues rolling out innovative optical storage products, such as its well-received combination CD-RW and DVD-ROM drives, which offer users access to the two most popular optical storage formats through a single device.

Japan's Matsushita Electric Industrial Co., Ltd. is another of the world's biggest electronics manufacturers. In the optical storage arena, Matsushita rolled out the very first DVD player in 1997, and its Panasonic brand claimed third place in 1999, with an estimated 11 percent of the global CD/DVD drive market. Matsushita's JVC, Quasar, and Technics brands are also mainstays of the consumer electronics market.

AMERICA AND THE WORLD

In 1996 the Japanese Technology Evaluation Center (TEC) released a report comparing the optoelectronics industries in Japan and the United States. The TEC noted that annual sales of optoelectronics (optical storage discs and drives) in Japan were $40 billion, while sales in the United States were only $6 billion. This discrepancy was largely due to the fact that during the 1980s companies in the United States concentrated their efforts and interest on further developing magnetic hard disk drives instead of optical storage; the hard disk market is where a majority of sales in the United States is centered. Meanwhile, Japanese companies invested heavily in optical technology. In recent years, however, U.S. companies and universities have invested significantly in optical storage research.

According to Disk/Trend, of the 53 companies that made optical disc drives in the late 1990s, 44 were headquartered in Asia. Among the 64 manufacturers of optical disc libraries and towers, used for mass storage for mainframes and computer networks, 36 were headquartered in the United States.

Many of the major users of optical storage technology are located in the United States, and they are collaborating with Japanese manufacturers to define new formats and standards for the medium. For example, Time Warner Inc. and Thomson Multimedia were part of the DVD Forum that produced the DVD standard, in which the U.S. movie, cable TV, video, and multimedia software industries had strong opinions and large stakes.

In spring 1997, nine companies with major investments in high-density, rewritable optical storage (Fujitsu Inc., Hitachi Ltd., Hitachi Maxell Ltd., Imation Corp., Olympus Optical Co. Ltd., Philips Electronics N.V., Sanyo Electric Co. Ltd., Sharp Electronics Corp., and Sony Corp.) formed another group, the Advanced Storage Technical Conference. Their goal was to develop the MO7 specification, which will use magneto-optical technology to store up to seven gigabytes of data on these single-sided removable discs.

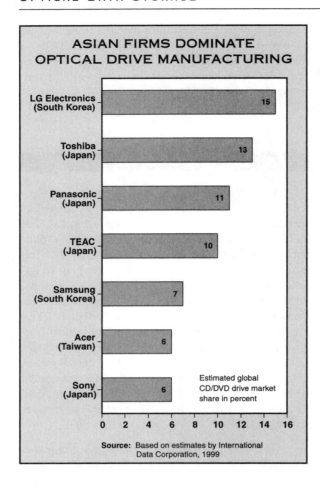

ASIAN FIRMS DOMINATE OPTICAL DRIVE MANUFACTURING

LG Electronics (South Korea) — 15
Toshiba (Japan) — 13
Panasonic (Japan) — 11
TEAC (Japan) — 10
Samsung (South Korea) — 7
Acer (Taiwan) — 6
Sony (Japan) — 6

Estimated global CD/DVD drive market share in percent

0 2 4 6 8 10 12 14 16

Source: Based on estimates by International Data Corporation, 1999

RESEARCH AND TECHNOLOGY

HOLOGRAPHIC STORAGE

As the use of computers grows, the demand for more and more memory continues unabated. So far conventional technologies have been able to satisfy the demand, but there is evidence that there are physical laws that put a cap on what current technology can accomplish. Therefore researchers continue to search for new and possibly unconventional ways to meet the increased memory demands. Holographic three-dimensional methods seem to hold the greatest promise, although other approaches are also being researched and studied.

Holographic data storage has attracted a great deal of research support. A large consortium funded by the U.S. Defense Advanced Research Projects Agency, which includes such industrial partners as IBM, Optitek, Rockwell, Kodak, and Polaroid, has been working on it, as well as Bell Labs and start-up companies such as Holoplex. A significant amount of progress has been reported, though problems remain, particularly in the area of suitable materials for recording media.

A hologram is a recording of the interference pattern formed where two coherent beams of light cross. Light from a single laser is split into two beams. One of the pair picks up and carries the information, while the other, the reference beam, is reflected across the path of the first. Where they cross, an optical interference pattern forms, which is recorded on the media. In playback, a similar beam of light is shined on the recorded media along the path of the reference beam, and the holographic image is generated. If the angle at which the playback beam of light strikes the recorded media is not the same as the angle of the reference beam when the hologram was recorded, the hologram will not appear. This makes volume recording of holograms possible. If a thick recording material is used (1 mm is thick in this context), many different holograms can be recorded and played back from one location by very slight variations of angle of light.

Another aspect of holographic data storage that enables large amounts of data to be stored is that each hologram is a two-dimensional image and can contain a million bits of digital data. Because of the limitations of the material available and the need for a reasonable read-out rate, the maximum number of holograms in one location is 1,000. This means that each location can hold one gigabit of data, and data can be retrieved at the rate of one gigabit per second. A DVD has a read-out rate of about 10 megabits per second (Mbps).

Several different configurations of holographic storage are being studied. Erasable write once, read many (WORM) drives are envisioned with the capability of storing terabytes of data and reading out data at the rate of one gigabit per second. These would be suitable for applications in which data change rarely but fast access to large volumes of data is required, such as video-on-demand and large Web servers. Write-once 3-D disks the size of DVD could hold more than 100 gigabytes, with fast access and read-out rates of 500 Mbps could be used where data require permanent storage but fast access, such as with medical data and satellite images. Prerecorded 3-D disks holding 100 gigabytes per disk could be used for distributing software, movies, and multimedia programs.

At the end of 1998 researchers at Bell Labs reported the development of a new holographic material that "appears to constitute a commercially viable medium with archival lifetime, shelf life, and thermal stability being the critical (nonperformance) parameters." They noted that until recently other components necessary for a holographic storage system were not commercially available but that now they were, having been developed for other applications. They suggested that the nearest-term product would be a write once, read many times drive. The goals for such a device would be 125 gigabytes of data on a 5.25-inch removable disk, with read-out rates of 30 to 50 megabytes per second.

Other researchers are working on a variation of holographic storage using a technique called spectral-hole burning. Spectral-hole burning takes place when certain materials reach a state in which they cannot absorb any more light energy. At this point the electrons of the atoms that make up the material are boosted to a higher energy level. Usually the electrons quickly lose this energy, but some materials, at very low temperatures, do not. This means that any more light at the same wavelength is not absorbed, so the material acts on the full spectrum of light as if it had a hole burned in it at a certain point in the spectrum. Using the right materials, researchers have found that they can use the phenomenon to store vast amounts of data in a very small area. Combining this with holography offers the possibility of multigigabyte capacities with both random-access and data-transfer rates a thousand times faster than those of magnetic hard drives, according to Tom Mossberg, of Templex Technology, which is developing an optical dynamic random-access memory using this method. The major obstacle is finding material that can function at higher temperatures.

Another approach to holographic storage being worked on in France proposes recording reflection gratings—a simple form of hologram—within an array of microfibers formed vertically in a disk. The interference patterns are produced along the fiber by introducing the light from each end. The wavelength of the recording light is varied, the variations containing the data. To read back the data, another light, containing every available wavelength, is introduced into one end of the fiber, and each wavelength that was recorded previously is strongly reflected. The data are decoded by analyzing the reflected spectrum. Work on this approach is in the early stages and the ideal materials and light sources have not yet been found, but patents have already been taken out on the microfiber disk and the polychromatic laser that the research has inspired.

OTHER DEVELOPMENTS

Quinta Corp., a San Jose, California, company bought by Seagate Technology Inc., the leading hard-disk drive manufacturer, has developed a system that it calls optically assisted Winchester (OAW) technology. It combines Winchester-type hard-disk technology, such as what is used in standard hard drives, with

higher capacity optical storage. The laws of physics appear to limit magnetic drives to about 40 gigabits per square inch, which Quinta says OAW will be able to surpass, at a lower price. Quinta aimed to announce its first products by the end of 1998 but was unable to.

At the other end of the capacity spectrum, but important for a growing part of the computer industry, is a new technology being developed by Ioptics Inc. called optical read-only memory (OROM). A credit-card-size OROM module can store 128 megabytes per cartridge, enough for many portable applications that have low memory requirements, and much more than Drexler Technology's LaserCard. The device has no moving parts, which makes it rugged enough for portable devices, and will sell for about two cents per megabyte, much less than current technologies for similar applications. Despite a $9.5 million financing package from Microsoft and others for development, by March 1999 the company had not been able to produce a product suitable for the handheld market with its constant demand for smaller and smaller components. Lane DeCamp, president of Ioptics, said they were exploring a number of possible steps, including a larger round of funding to modify the OROM device. Sale of the technology was also being considered.

FURTHER READING

Alaimo, Dan. "DVD on Fast Track to Mass Market: Group Exec." *Supermarket News,* 31 January 2000.

Bains, Sunny. "Holographic Films on Disk Hold Hope for Ultra-Dense Memories—Fiber Storage Reaches for Terabytes." *Electronic Engineering Times,* 13 April 1998.

———. "Novel Frequency Technique Supercharges Holographic Recording—Spectral 'Holes' Promise Optical Storage to Burn." *Electronic Engineering Times,* 4 May 1998.

Curtis, Kevin, William L. Wilson, Lisa Dhar, and Adrian Hill. "Holographic Data Storage, Finally. . . ." *Computer Technology Review,* fourth quarter 1998.

Del Prete, Crawford, Robert Amatruda, Danielle Levitas, and Wolfgang Schlichting. "Industry Outlook: All's Well That Ends Well." *Data Storage,* January 1999.

Hanan, John. "Digital Audio Discs Seek to Replace Music CDs." *Dallas Morning News,* 25 May 1999.

Hara, Yoshiko. "Competing Rewritable-Drive Formats Aim to Usurp DVD-RAM: Upstarts Challenge DVD-ROM's Heir Apparent." *Electronic Engineering Times,* 23 March 1998.

Hara, Yoshiko, and Terry Costlow. "Japan Leaps into DVD-RAM." *Electronic Engineering Times,* 5 May 1997.

Hachman, Mark. "Storage Industry Consolidates." *Electronic Buyers News,* 9 October 2000.

Holsinger, Erik, and Rex Farrance. "The Fastest Drives Alive." *PC World,* July 1997.

Hutchinson, Roger. "Digital Versatile Disc: The Next Generation of CD-ROM." 25 January 1997. Available from http://www.ecomedia.org/sigcat/97w/dvd.html.

Japanese Technology Evaluation Center. "Optical Storage Technology." February 1996. Available from http://itri.loyola.edu/opto/c3_s1.htm.

Jasco, Peter. "Looking Back: CD/DVD-ROM in 1999." *Information Today,* February 2000.

"Optical and Removable Disk Drives." Mountain View, CA: DISK/TREND, Inc., July 1999. Available from http://www.disktrend.com.

"Optical Storage Overview." *HP: The Optical Storage Primer.* Available from http://www.esrf.fr/computing/cs/nice/impl/optical/optical-overview.html.

Parker, Dana J. "DVD-RAM Finalized, High-Density Contenders on the Way." *EMedia Professional,* July 1997.

Psaltis, Demetri, and Geoffrey W. Burr. "Holographic Data Storage." *Computer,* February 1998.

Thompson, Brad. "The PD Combo: A New Palimpsest?" *CD-ROM Professional,* March 1996.

Verna, Paul. "MiniDisc Still a Niche Format in U.S." *Billboard,* 24 July 1999.

Wiley, Lauren. "Analysts See Bright Future for DVD." *EMedia Professional,* July 1999.

OPTICAL SENSING AND INFRARED SENSORY DEVICES

INDUSTRY SNAPSHOT

Bolstered by greater penetration of commercial markets, increased defense spending, and heightened demand from emerging economies, the optical and infrared sensing industry entered the 21st century with strong prospects. Although scientists originally developed optical sensing devices for the aerospace and defense industry, the technology ultimately crossed over many industry lines, finding applications in the medical, electronics, and automotive industries, among others. The ever-popular and ever-present television remote control, which uses an infrared sensor, shows the mass-market potential of an optical sensing device that clicks with users. While the military continues to develop innovative and improved uses for optical sensing devices through government-funded research, other industries have developed and continue to develop their own commercial applications geared and priced for the masses. Sensors continue to pop up in a slew of consumer products—such as cars, phones, pagers, watches, cameras, and computers.

Paul Saffo, a leading futurist, characterized the start of the 21st century as the decade of the sensor, just as the 1980s were the decade of the microprocessor. According to Saffo, sensors will eventually penetrate most aspects of life, making possible so-called intelligent homes and cars. But the realization of this vision depends on the development of micromachining processes, which will enable the cheap mass production of more highly efficient and compact infrared sensors.

ORGANIZATION AND STRUCTURE

Infrared sensors, the most common type of optical sensors, detect objects or conditions by identifying the heat they emit. Infrared radiation (IR) is transmitted constantly through the atmosphere and is, in varying degrees, reflected or absorbed by objects. IR energy, which is absorbed, raises the temperature of the objects. The heat humans feel from a fire, sunlight, or a radiator is infrared.

Infrared sensors have a variety of applications—military, commercial, and otherwise. The guidance systems in heat-seeking missiles, for example, depend on infrared sensors, and sensors are the key technology in night-vision systems, which the military was also instrumental in developing.

Sensors have also made a difference to ground troops. Soldiers on night guard duty at a camp during the North Atlantic Treaty Organization peacekeeping mission in Bosnia, for instance, often came outfitted with compact radios, night-vision goggles, infrared sniper sights, and global positioning satellite range finders.

Infrared sensors have many civilian uses as well. Weather satellites carry IR sensors to track meteorological systems. They also track pollution. Polluted water, for example, has a higher temperature gradient, which satellite sensors easily detect. Earth- and space-based telescopes integrate infrared sensors. Infrared systems are also integrated onto helicopters for finding people lost in wilderness areas; law enforcement agencies have modified versions designed to track criminals or escaped convicts. More and more, optical sensors are making their way into consumer markets. Digital cameras were made possible by optical sensors; the imaging system relies on optical sensor technology. "Smart" consumer devices, such as automatic light switches—lights that turn on automatically when someone enters a room—are smart because IR sensors "know" when someone is there.

Optical sensors are produced by a variety of company types. Historically, the biggest producers have been defense contractors that manufacture sensors for specific purposes—missile guidance systems, for example. Companies such as Northrop Grumman Corp. and Rockwell International Corp. continue to produce components for government projects, often in cooperation with other firms, while at the same time are expanding into broader industrial applications such as robotics. Companies that make electronics for the industrial and consumer markets also produce sensors. These firms sell their sensors to other original equipment manufacturers for use in a broad variety of industrial and consumer applications.

As the technology becomes more highly developed and less expensive, specialist companies as well as smaller start-up firms are becoming involved in the development and manufacture of sensors. Camera companies, such as Olympus Optical and Polaroid, have made important advances in sensor technology, which led to the sophisticated auto-focus devices so popular with consumers. These firms continue to be an important force in the industry as they develop digital cameras that are dependent on optical sensors. Other smaller companies, often working with proprietary technology, produce sensors for diverse, highly specialized purposes as varied as night vision, environmental monitoring, or infrared telescopy.

BACKGROUND AND DEVELOPMENT

Because infrared sensors measure heat in objects, the first ones developed were essentially thermometers that relied on a change of temperature in the measuring device itself. These early devices led to the development of bolometers, which are still used to detect infrared radiation.

The first practical infrared sensor was developed in Germany during the 1930s when research capitalized on the IR sensitivity of lead sulfide. After World War II, American researchers followed suit, abandoning the materials they had been studying and instead concentrating on lead sulfide sensors. Early IR sensors were limited to the short end of the IR spectrum. Other infrared-sensitive materials, however, soon helped extend sensitivity into the medium, and eventually into longer wavelength ranges. The introduction of semiconductor alloys, such as mercury cadmium telluride, enabled infrared sensors to be fine-tuned to a specific wavelength for specific purposes.

In the early 1960s, photolithography—the repeatable imprinting of chemical or electronic patterns on silicon or other materials—made possible the first complex arrays of infrared sensors, some with focal planes of more than 1,000 elements. The refinement of such arrays would eventually make possible the focal systems for digital cameras. High-volume production of IR sensor arrays using mercury cadmium telluride took off in the 1970s and have been the dominant technology ever since. They are used in a number of applications, including missile systems and weather satellites. Eventually silicon was used and it was discovered that IR-sensitive chemicals could be "grown" on a silicon substrate and used as sensors. Other advantages of silicon included its ready availability (deriving from sand), limited frequency response, and low thermal expansion quotient.

The first generation of IR sensors is represented by the arrays developed in the 1960s; the second generation began with electronic signal readouts that could integrate output from the many elements of an infrared array. That capability was first developed in the 1970s, and reached maturity in the 1990s with large, fully integrated two-dimensional arrays. Such massive arrays are common on sensor-bearing satellites, and work was underway in the late 1990s to create miniature arrays on silicon chips using microelectrical mechanical systems technology. Since the 1970s, the development of the infrared sensor has directly followed upon the development of the silicon integrated circuit. (Also see essays in this book on Astronautics, Micromachines, Satellites, and Semiconductors.)

In 1993 the Infrared Data Association (IrDA) formed to establish a low-cost universal standard to enable all infrared-based cordless data communications to work together. IrDA envisioned a walk-up, point-to-point user model, with data flying back and forth between a broad range of appliances from a variety of makers.

By 1998, IrDA reported that the IrDA standard port was rapidly becoming the most common cordless connection in the world. IrDA boasts more than 150 members—including 3Com Corp.; Canon Inc.; Dell Computer Corp.; Hewlett-Packard Co.; Motorola, Inc.; IBM Corp.; Sony Corp.; and Xerox Corp. The

IrDA port can be found in pagers, watches, cell phones, pay phones, printers, cameras, organizers, photo kiosks, communicators, and laptop and hand-held computers.

Two basic types of infrared sensors have been developed: one detects energy (heat), the other detects photons (light). The energy sensor detects temperature changes caused by infrared radiation. An electrical current is monitored for changes, which results in proportion to external temperature. Energy type IR sensors are relatively inexpensive and are used in various applications—from fire detection systems to automatic light switches. One technical limitation of energy sensors is that they must be insulated from the external environment to increase their sensitivity, while at the same time be able to dissipate heat rapidly in order to respond quickly to changes.

The most recent development in energy-type sensors involves micromachining on silicon. Manufactured using photolithography, such sensors have extremely low power requirements, yet match traditional sensors in performance. Microbolometers, devices that compare current and voltage in order to measure infrared radiation, have been developed. Micromachined IR sensors have, by and large, not moved from the laboratory into commercial production, but one foreseen application is in night-vision systems for military and civilian use.

Photon-type sensors react to the interaction of light with a semiconductor. Because they react to light rather than temperature, they respond to changes much faster than energy-type sensors. Photon sensors are easily manufactured in large two-dimensional arrays, a feature that has led to their application in advanced IR detection systems such as satellites. A major limitation to photon-type IR sensors is sensitivity to their own infrared radiation. To reduce such interference, they must be cooled to cryogenic temperatures, which requires added power and equipment. A focal point of IR sensor research is the development of sensors that don't require cooling. In 1996, after a year's work, Amber, a division of Raytheon, produced Sentinel, the world's first commercially available, microbolometer-based, uncooled, infrared imaging system. The development is eventually expected to revolutionize future production of infrared sensors.

CURRENT CONDITIONS

In the past, most of the aerospace and defense industry's sales were to the government, primarily the U.S. Department of Defense, whose sensor purchases were symbolized by heat-seeking missiles and the "smart" weapons that burst into public view during the Persian Gulf War. Nevertheless, defense spending receded significantly in the 1990s: by about 50 percent between 1989 and 1998—and even more when compared to its height during the Reagan years. Consequently, aerospace and defense industry firms turned their focus to the civilian market. As a result, these manufacturers and developers sought civilian applications for technologies already developed for the military as well as completely new sensors specifically for the civilian market.

A turnaround in defense spending, however, was heralded in 1999. U.S. expenditures on the military increased by 8 percent in 1999, ending a 12-year period of decline. Defense spending in 2000 totaled $300 billion, and was expected to continue rising through the middle of the decade. The Electronics Industry Association predicts that defense spending on weapons electronics will grow by $7.4 billion over the next 10 years. Procurement of electronics including sensors for guidance and control systems will increase from $18.5 billion in 1998 to $23.8 billion in 2007. Spending in this sector will be greatly bolstered by an aggressive push to develop a strategic defense system, which, despite technical hang-ups, was politically popular in 2000. According to another forecast by research firm Frost & Sullivan, the commercial and military infrared imaging and sensors systems market will grow by a compound annual rate of 31 percent through 2003. Sales of infrared focal point array sensor systems were approximately $1.25 billion in 1999. Frost & Sullivan further forecast that emerging infrared technologies such as microbolometer, ferroelectric, and multiple quantum sensors would fuel the industry's future growth. Moreover, the firm expected the significant trends affecting the infrared sensor market to be upgrades of infrared sensors by the military, the expansion of the commercial market, and corporate consolidation among large defense contractors. Despite the increases in military spending, Frost & Sullivan expected the percentage of infrared sensors sales from military contracts to decrease to about 67 percent by 2001.

In the late 1990s, a research consortium called ULTRA—Uncooled Low-Cost Technology Reinvestment Alliance—was formed by Honeywell, Texas Instruments, and Inframetrics to develop uncooled focal plane array (UFPA) sensors. This technology has greater cost advantage over cryogenically cooled sensors, plus higher reliability, instant operation, and decreased systems costs. The sensor includes a signal conditioning circuit, analog-to-digital conversion, and signal processing functions, all arrayed on silicon chips—all the capabilities that define a smart IR sensor. The sensors are made from barium-stontium-titanate, which is a ferroelectric material. Ferroelectric materials are characterized by being crystalline materials having spontaneous electric polarization. Overseen in part by the Federal Aviation Administration, an initial application of the technology was for infrared-based inspection of aircraft hangar environments. Furthermore, the automotive and photography industries quickly adopted this technology.

Work continues on standard IR technologies and materials, as well as on micromachined IR sensors. Infrared sensors are increasingly being used to monitor environmental conditions such as oil pollution, forest fires, combustible vapors, and leaks. A new generation of household smoke detectors uses an infrared sensor to detect the presence of lethal carbon monoxide. Development also continues on linear image sensors, the primary component of color scanners, and on new complementary metal oxide semiconductor (CMOS)-based image sensors for digital still cameras, whose sales are expected to exceed $1 billion by the year 2002. CMOS sensors use low-power semiconductor microchips, which help conserve energy in battery-powered devices. By 2000 CMOS sensors accounted for about 5 percent of the imaging sensor market, according to *Electronic Design*. A new generation of high-resolution infrared cameras also emerged in the late 1990s and the early 2000s for use in machine vision systems.

The automotive industry is one of the first big customers for infrared and optical sensing devices as they become available at a competitive price. Infrared sensors are being integrated, for example, into automotive air-bag systems to detect the presence of a child or small adult in a car seat, thus avoiding the inappropriate and dangerous deployment of an air bag. Other applications on the horizon include warning systems and adaptive cruise control. Unlike normal cruise control, which maintains a constant speed, adaptive cruise control would sense the presence of cars on the road ahead—by means of infrared sensors in one plan—and slow the car down to maintain a safe distance.

Furthermore, General Motors Corp. (GM) gave the public a peek at its new night-vision system—based on UFPA technology—at the 1999 North American International Auto Show. The automaker became the first to offer night-vision technology with the 2000 Cadillac Deville. GM touts the feature as a way to improve driving safety by enhancing the nighttime driver's ability to detect potentially dangerous situations beyond the range of the headlamps without taking the driver's eyes off the road. In addition, this technology enables drivers to see 3-5 times farther down the road. GM mounted the infrared sensor on behind the car's grille with a display for it integrated into the dashboard. The 2000 Cadillac Evoq, a two-seat luxury roadster, sports both night vision and a rear obstacle detection system. The back-up aid uses three sensors in the back bumper—one radar and two ultrasonic—to help avert back-up collisions.

Honda Motors and other automobile companies are also testing forward-drive systems, which use optical and infrared sensors to center the vehicle, change lanes, and avoid obstacles. Lockheed Martin is testing a forward-looking infrared camera adapted from its driverless military vehicles, and forward-looking radar systems are also being developed. Some engineers predict that basic sensors could become standard automotive equipment in three to five years.

INDUSTRY LEADERS

The most important companies in the optical sensor market are defense contractors that have been involved in cutting-edge research for the government. Recent consolidation of the aerospace and defense industry, tied to federal spending cutbacks, has left only four major players in the industry—The Boeing Co., Lockheed Martin Corp., Raytheon Co., and Northrop Grumman Corp. Citing a concern about the lack of competition for military contracts, federal regulators barred further consolidation in 1998, when they protested the proposed merger of Lockheed Martin and Northrop Grumman.

THE BOEING COMPANY

Boeing is the world's largest aerospace firm. The Seattle-based company manufactures planes, missiles, rockets, helicopters, space-faring vehicles, and advanced communications systems. After a series of acquisitions in the late 1990s, including McDonnell Douglas in 1997, and Hughes Electronics' satellite division in 1999, Boeing became the leading aerospace company. Buoyed by the acquisition of the space and defense unit of Rockwell International Corp. in 1996, Boeing also serves as the largest contractor to the National Aeronautics and Space Administration. The defense giant racked up sales of $57.9 billion and employed nearly 200,000 people in 1999.

In 1999 the U.S. Department of Defense started launching a distributed, low-Earth orbit satellite constellation that uses infrared and visible optical sensors to detect ballistic missile attacks anywhere in the world. Boeing acts as the prime contractor for the first phase of the Space-Based Infrared Surveillance System (SBIRS) and subcontracts under Lockheed Martin for the second phase of the project, to be up and running by 2007. Boeing will provide all sensor payloads for the SBIRS.

LOCKHEED MARTIN CORPORATION

Lockheed Martin, the world's second largest aerospace and defense firm, is also developing a remote sensing satellite that will provide high resolution black-and-white imagery, as well as multispectral images, to highlight chlorophyll content, chemical composition, surface water penetration, and other environmental features. The satellite's main advantage is a digital imaging sensor that can provide images with a resolution of one meter from 680 kilometers in altitude.

The Maryland-based company also builds warplanes, rockets, and fire control systems and manages government projects—and government contracts make up about 70 percent of the company's sales. Total sales for Lockheed Martin stood at $25.5 billion in 1999 and the company had 147,000 workers the same year.

RAYTHEON COMPANY

Raytheon was the third-largest aerospace and defense company in the late 1990s, specializing in aircraft and electronics. Its electronics account for the majority of the company's sales. Raytheon doubled in size when it bought the defense electronics division of Texas Instruments Inc. for $3 billion and the aerospace and defense division of Hughes for $9.5 billion from parent company GM in 1997. Also that year Raytheon supplied a major sensing system for the refurbished Hubble Space Telescope. In 1998 the company began a major joint initiative with the U.S. Army to reduce the cost of night-vision sensors and broaden their commercial applications. The Massachusetts-based company expects to sell 6 million units of its uncooled infrared sensor devices over a 10-year period in military, police, automotive, and consumer markets. In 1999 Raytheon posted sales of $19.8 billion and employed 105,000 workers.

The Santa Barbara Research Center (SBRC), recently acquired by Raytheon, is one of the most innovative producers of infrared sensors. SBRC specializes in integrated focal plane sensing, and for 10 years their focal plane arrays have been used in telescopes and other astronomical instruments. Basic research and development of multielement detector arrays covers a wide range of the spectrum, from the visible to longwave infrared. In the late 1990s the company was developing multispectral sensors that could be used for emissions sensing, process control monitoring, chemical processing, and explosive detection. They have been in the forefront of the development of uncooled infrared sensor technologies. Raytheon's sensor technologies have been widely adapted for other industrial and consumer purposes, including wireless communications, satellite imaging, and airport operations.

NORTHROP GRUMMAN CORPORATION

The fourth-largest aerospace firm, Northrop Grumman, became a powerhouse in defense electronics and systems integration with two acquisitions: the 1996 purchase of a defense and electronics arm from Westinghouse Electric Corp.; and the 1997 acquisition of Logicon, Inc., an information and battle-management systems maker. After its merger with Lockheed Martin was blocked, Northrop Grumman began to refocus its operations to remain competitive, which included putting some of its aircraft parts units up for sale. In 1999 Northrop Grumman reported revenues of nearly $9 billion for the California-based company, which had 44,600 employees the same year. The electronic division of Northrop Grumman accounted for about 30 percent of its revenues in 1999.

With the increased defense expenditures and the prediction for continued increases, defense applications will continue to fuel innovation as missile guidance and detection systems are upgraded and existing night-vision and electronic sensor technologies are refined. Significant progress has been made in developing real-time imaging systems for satellites and high-altitude surveillance aircraft. The Global Hawk, an autonomous prototype aircraft built by Teledyne Ryan Aeronautical and Raytheon, is equipped with electro-optical and infrared sensors that can provide high-resolution images of large geographic areas in near-real time.

AMERICA AND THE WORLD

The United States and Europe represent the largest consumers of infrared and other optical sensors, and U.S. companies manufacture the majority of the sensors used in the United States. Foreign companies have little visibility in the U.S. market, except perhaps in the area of digital camera sensors, a market segment in which Japanese companies such as Mitsubishi and Olympus Optical are very active. Nonetheless, innovative sensor technologies are being produced by small firms such as Bureau Etudes Vision Stockplus, a French company that has developed an advanced visual recognition chip that mimics the human eye and can accept infrared, video, or radar signals.

Despite its economic downturn in the late 1990s, Asia remained a key target for U.S. and European makers of optical sensors, as they anticipate strong growth as these economies continue to recover, according to Frost & Sullivan. In addition, the Electronic Industries Association noted that Asia "will continue as the world's premier growth market." Furthermore, a study released by Georgetown University estimated the market in Asia—not including China—for imported U.S. defense and civil electronics was $125.8 billion in the late 1990s. Frost & Sullivan expected China to become a significant player in the world sensor market in the early 2000s. Other important markets for the 21st century include Argentina and Brazil.

Overall, the global sensor market fetched about $15 billion at the close of the 20th century, according to Frost & Sullivan. In addition, the worldwide market for industrial machine vision systems totaled $4 billion in the late 1990s, according to the Automated Imaging Association, as demand for image capture and analysis in manufacturing processes grew in Europe, Japan, and other industrialized countries. Machine vision sales in North America were $1.5 billion in 1997 and were expected to exceed $2 billion by 2000.

RESEARCH AND TECHNOLOGY

Like most high-tech fields, research is the lifeblood of the optical sensor industry. Two key fields are microelectrical mechanical systems (MEMS) and uncooled infrared sensors. The most important area of research affecting the optical sensor industry is the miniaturization/digitalization of sensor technology. Pressure sensors and accelerometers are already being micromachined on silicon chips, and research is underway to extend micromachining and its extremely cheap batch-processing capabilities to infrared sensors.

Although commercial applications are still several years away, MEMS devices are being actively investigated in 10 projects sponsored by the Defense Advanced Research Projects Agency. Development

continues on uncooled, large array, and multispectral focal point array sensors as well as on a number of new technologies. Using uncooled microcantilevered sensors developed at Oak Ridge National Laboratories, Sarcon Microsystems is developing a line of infrared imagers, which may be inexpensive enough to be included on a wide scale in process monitoring and safety devices for cars, boats, and trains. Subminiature photoelectric optical sensors, which are more durable than fiber-optic devices and less expensive than laser sensors, were being used in a variety of manufacturing operations in the late 1990s.

Bell Labs developed the world's first laser-based, semiconductor sensor. The sensor operates at room temperature and can detect minute amounts of trace gases or pollutants (potentially parts per billion). Its power and range are unprecedented for the mid-infrared region of the spectrum. It has been called a revolutionary development for sensor applications because it opens up a new field of uncooled tunable infrared sensors.

In the late 1990s researchers at San Diego State University developed infrared sensors for detecting defects in computer chips. These sensors use technology similar to that used in some of the world's best telescopes, such as the Hubble Space Telescope. Attached to microscopes, these sensors pass over computer chips and then generate images of the chips, revealing the slightest flaws in the chips, including flecks of dust or debris. Consequently, these sensors are an inexpensive way for chip manufacturers to cull bad chips and improve design to avoid defective chips.

FURTHER READING

Costlow, Terry. "Emerging Markets—Automotive: Safety, Comfort Drive Electronics." *Electronic Engineering Times,* 31 March 1997.

"Electronics: Honda's Automated Highway System Research." *Asia-Pacific Automotive Report,* 5 April 1998.

"Electronics Industries Association Says U.S. Defense Spending Will Rise by $7.4 Billion over Next 10 Years." *Defense News,* 6 October 1997.

Flanagan, Dennis. "Infrared Machine Vision—A New Contender." *Sensors,* 4 April 1998.

Flanders, David. "Airborne Infrared and Ultraviolet Remote Sensing for Oil Spill Detection." *Advanced Imaging,* April 1997.

Graham, David. "Go for the Glow." *MIT's Technology Review,* March/April 1998.

Hara, Yoshiko. "CMOS, CMD Parts Promise to Cut Power, Ease Integration—Sensors Jockey for Role as Successors to CCDs." *Electronic Engineering Times,* 3 March 1997.

"Innovative Technology Could Make Driving Safer." *Minneapolis Star-Tribune,* 13 January 1998.

"ITT Industries Gets $35.7 Million Satellite Contract." *Newsbytes News Network,* 1 August 1997.

"Lockheed Martin: Commercial Sensing System Program Profile." *M2 PressWIRE,* 1 October 1996.

"Lockheed's Vision of the Road Ahead." *Industries in Transition,* September 1997.

"MEMS Get Lift from Pentagon." *Electronic Buyers News,* 9 March 1998.

"Microcantilever-Based Devices." *NDT Update,* April 1998.

"Motorola Eyes Imaging Shift—Continues Push from CCDs to Less Costly CMOS-Based Sensors." *Electronic Buyers News,* 6 April 1998.

Shelley, Suzanne. "Proper Surveillance Can Keep a Minor Leak from Becoming a Major Event." *Chemical Engineering,* February 1998.

Siuri, Bill. "Night Vision for Your Car." *Electronics Now,* June 1999.

"STM Optimizes Optical Sensing." *Vital Publications,* 1 May 1998.

"Team to Reduce Cost of Night Vision Sensors." *Defense News,* 9 February 1998.

"Uncooled IR Detectors: Their Time Has Come." October 1996. Available from http://www.spie.org/web/oer/october/oct96/uncoolir.html.

"U.S. Gives Go-Ahead to Merger Creating Giant Defense Company." *Tampa Tribune,* 4 October 1997.

"U.S. Global Hawk Completes First Flight." *M2 Presswire,* 3 March 1998.

Useem, Jerry. "It's Payback Time for Defense Stocks: Their Shares Are Bombing, but Armsmakers' Long Retreat May Be Over." *Fortune,* 22 November 1999.

Oxygen Therapy

Having emerged from its long-term obscurity and shaken off much of its huckster-riddled image, oxygen therapy was an established, if shaky, market by the turn of the 21st century, used by doctors for intensive therapies; by New Age enthusiasts seeking new sources of energy, strength, and health; and by those trying to fend off aging and remain beautiful. Thus, that simple, universal element, oxygen, became the focus of a multibillion-dollar health-care industry that captured the imagination of healers and charlatans alike. In all, the United States is home to over 250 hyperbaric oxygen therapy (HBOT) facilities. The research firm Frost & Sullivan forecast annual growth in the oxygen therapy industry at about 5 percent through the mid-2000s.

Perhaps the most common form of oxygen therapy was the hyperbaric chamber. Within small pods that look like something out of a science-fiction movie, a person could sit and breath enhanced oxygen for 15 minutes to an hour to quicken the healing process for wounds or injuries or simply to receive a boost of energy. Regular air is composed of 21 percent oxygen, and even if a person breathes pure oxygen, the body will consume only 21 percent unless the person is placed inside a pressurized chamber.

From a medical standpoint, HBOT floods the body's cells with oxygen carried through the body's fluids, rather than via the blood's hemoglobin, thereby stimulating the cells in area's of compromised blood supply. Upon sustaining a wound, for instance, oxygen levels in the blood near the wound are altered, thereby kicking bodily enzymes into action to attract cells appropriate for healing the wound. By applying extra oxygen, these cells are given enhanced energy to accelerate the healing process.

Oxygen therapy grew up in large part outside the realm of established medical practice. As a result of that alienation as well as inconclusive and varying assessments of the treatment's effectiveness, the medical community still maintained a great deal of skepticism, though HBOT has won increasing acceptance in recent years for specific ailments and treatments. Among the public, at any rate, the popularity of oxygen therapy was on the rise in 2000, with no signs of slowing.

Oxygen therapy is a segment of three major industries: health care, alternative medicine, and cosmetics. Oxygen therapy became the general term for any method by which oxygen was introduced into the human body in order to effect some manner of healing. For traditional medicine, hyperbaric oxygen chambers became standard equipment in many hospitals. After decades of seeing oxygen therapy work for decompression sickness and resulting air embolism, physicians began to experiment with other uses. Burns, carbon-monoxide poisoning, and serious flesh wounds benefited from these pressurized treatments. Other oxygen therapies for use in medicine became more advanced in such treatments as those for emphysema, asthma, and respiratory complications of newborn infants, to name a few. With the rise in the use of these therapies, the manufacture of new medical equipment surged to meet demand.

In the area of nontraditional medicine, or what came to be known as alternative medicine, oxygen therapies became popular, even if they were not medically advised. Hyperbaric therapy crossed over to alternative medicine. In fact, even before it received widespread acceptance in the medical community, hyperbaric therapy was promoted in health spas and sports clubs for serenity, skin rejuvenation, and other "miraculous" treatments. In addition, nutritional supplements said to purify blood, stabilize the body's metabolism, reduce stress, and remove toxins from the body were developed for oral use. Perhaps the most remarkable trend began with the opening of the first oxygen bar in Toronto, Canada, during the mid-1990s. And the cosmetics industry also got into the business of selling oxygen for skin treatments, whereby customers apply oxygenated moisturizers and breathe pure oxygen to maintain healthy skin.

Whatever the outcome of the debates over medical and health benefits, oxygen therapy is universally eyed as potentially dangerous if improperly administered. Hyperbaric chambers require extensive and precise monitoring as well as cleaning and maintenance.

Alternative medicine encompasses a broad spectrum of nontraditional practices using oxygen therapy. They might include the modern technology of the more widely accepted HBOT medical procedure adapted for nonlicensed homeopathic purposes. Or they might include other oxygen therapies such as orally ingested nutritional supplements, ozone therapy, chelation therapy, hydrogen-peroxide therapy, and forms of exercise therapy. In 1992, under the auspices of the National Institutes of Health (NIH), Congress established the Office of Alternative Medicine. That year, NIH provided $14.5 million in research to explore alternative medical options not recognized by the established medical community. No specific regulations governing such practices or medicines were established, however. In 1994 the Dietary Supplement Health and Education Act offered even more freedom to alternative medical providers by determining not to regulate this area through U.S. Food and Drug Administration (FDA) standards.

INDUSTRY REGULATION

The health-care system in the United States is highly regulated. The FDA sets national standards and guidelines for any medical treatment. Any oxygen therapy for use in an approved medical setting is subject to regulations regarding the licensing of qualified personnel, the safety and effectiveness of the equipment used, and the authorization of any medicine that might be used in administering treatment.

The American Medical Association also offers its discretion in approving medical practices. In addition, professional societies for physicians, researchers, and other medical personnel set standards for conduct in the practice of utilizing the technology. Health maintenance organizations and major insurance companies, too, provide monitoring when determining appropriate oxygen therapies. Continued medical research into various therapies expands the market for these products and services annually. Finally, the licensing of cosmetologists under state testing programs also offers additional regulation of industry practices.

BACKGROUND AND DEVELOPMENT

In 1664 the first experiment using compressed air in a specially designed chamber was conducted in England, reportedly by a British physician by the name of Henshaw. Over a century later, after British scientist Joseph Priestley published his own discovery of oxygen in 1774, its utilization remained primarily the domain of physicians and scientists. The first reported use of oxygen as a therapy was by a doctor named Caillens in France in 1783. Details of this case were unknown. For most of the next 150 years, the use of oxygen for therapeutic purposes suffered from inconsistent research and trendiness, which earned it a reputation for quackery.

In 1874 in Geneva, Switzerland, however, a scientist named Jurine published his results of the daily oxygen inhalation treatments of a young woman in failing health due to tuberculosis, or a condition causing similar deterioration. Throughout the entire 19th century, research and experimentation continued. Nothing proved significant until 1917, when physicians J. S. Haldane and J. Barcroft began to administer oxygen therapeutically, primarily to relieve respiratory illnesses.

In 1928 the progress of oxygen treatment in the form of hyperbaric oxygen therapy (HBOT) suffered a severe blow. Wealthy industrialist H. H. Timken of Canton, Ohio, known for his worldwide production of roller bearings, entered into a million-dollar venture with Dr. O. J. Cunningham of Kansas City, Missouri, to build a primitive chamber, called a "million dollar sanitarium," in the form of a giant steel ball. It was Cunningham's theory that diabetes, pernicious anemia, and cancer were due to an anaerobic form of pathogenic bacteria, and could be cured with the use of concentrated oxygen therapy.

However much he made these claims, Cunningham offered no proof of his theories. After a few years without success, the property fell into further disrepute, changing owners several times throughout the 1930s. In 1941 the huge steel ball was dismantled for use as scrap metal in the war effort. While advances continued in the use of bedside oxygen tanks and tents for varying degrees of life support, hyperbaric therapy would not begin recovering from the Cunningham folly for some time.

In 1939 the U.S. Navy began to treat deep-sea divers suffering from decompression sickness, also known colloquially as "the bends," with this specialized therapy. Different from the Cunningham experiment and others that simply used compressed air, these chamber treatments involved only compressed pure oxygen. During World War II, studies in high-altitude sickness were also conducted using hyperbaric and other oxygen therapy technology. Acceptance of HBOT was slow to emerge. Studies continued into the 1960s and 1970s with claims that it could treat anything from hair loss to senility, claims that were never fully supported. Other studies indicated that the therapy showed some measure of success in the treatment of burn patients, wounds, and serious infections, such as gas gangrene.

The use of the hyperbaric oxygen chamber as a crossover between the worlds of traditional and alternative medicine became a widespread phenomenon in the 1980s. Famous pop star Michael Jackson reportedly slept in a hyperbaric chamber, a practice he continued long after treatment for facial burns he suffered in an accident while filming a television commercial. Beginning in the late 1980s, professional athletes used HBOT on a routine basis for treatment of charley horses, deep bruises, and even torn ligaments. Following right behind this development was the appearance of hyperbaric chambers known as hypoxic rooms in major gym facilities throughout the country. The claim by Nicholas Cohotin, vice president at Hypoxico, Inc. where the machine was made, was that his machine "will give you a 30-minute workout in just 15 minutes." He also made the claim that the machine could be effective simply by sitting inside of it. Another example was the Hyperbaric Oxygen Clinic in Santa Monica, which offered sessions in their chambers to those recovering from plastic surgery, adding further to the miracle claims of the treatments.

The origin of oxygen therapy in the world of alternative medicine is more difficult to pinpoint, although it did grow out of authentic medical research. The "wellness movement" that began in the 19th century throughout Europe and America gave birth to much of what eventually became known as the New Age Movement that emerged during the 1960s social revolution. European spas for health treatments were a centuries-old tradition. The ancient health and beauty treatments of China and the Far East, Egypt, and along the Mediterranean for everything from mud baths to breathing in mountain air were well-established, revered traditions long before anyone ever set sail for the new world of the Americas. The movement of the 1950s and 1960s toward eastern religions provided an opening to reconsider the western traditions by which many Americans were raised, particularly after World War II. The prevalence of tuberculosis sanitariums, often placed in rural or mountain settings for the purer air, prompted the experimentation into the uses of oxygen.

Dietary herbal supplements were offered for better circulation—and that involved getting oxygen to flow more freely throughout the body. Into 20th-century America people amassed vast fortunes from tonics and treatments that offered no verifiable medical validity. Some treatments were harmless; others were not. Even as late as the 1980s the FDA reported death and injury from the ingestion of hydrogen peroxide. Industrial strength hydrogen peroxide was illegally promoted to treat acquired immune deficiency syndrome (AIDS), some cancers, and at least 60 other conditions. The product was sold as "35 percent Food Grade Hydrogen Peroxide," which was diluted for use in "hyper-oxygenation therapy." The formula proved to be fatal to one child in Texas in 1989, and was particularly toxic to several other children due to its highly corrosive qualities.

Despite warnings of the harmful aspects of such nontraditional practices, the industry managed to grow into an $18-billion market by 1996, as reported by the *Nutrition Business Journal*. Even insurance companies began to look at various alternative treatments as viable and offered some reimbursement for certain procedures. A significant 35 percent of Californians polled in 1998 admitted to the use of high-dosage vitamins, once only a bastion of the alternative arsenal. The market for homeopathic remedies in California alone totaled $3.65 billion, up 100 percent from 1994 to 1998. California was long considered the forerunner in such experimentation.

Two interesting commercial venues opened for oxygen therapy by the 1990s. One was that of the oxygen bars opening first in Toronto, Canada, shortly thereafter gaining serious popularity in Hollywood and New York. When *Science World* magazine first reported on the opening in Toronto in December 1996, customers could stop in for 20 minutes of pure oxygen, pumped in through the plastic plugs in their noses, for a mere $16. In January 1999, *Parade* magazine reported the latest celebrity craze. Actor Woody Harrelson and his wife, along with holistic physician Dr. Richard DeAndrea, opened an organic-food restaurant on Sunset Boulevard in Hollywood. A 20-minute serving of oxygen there was available for $13. Other well-known television and film stars carried oxygen tanks with them to their sets.

Another area where oxygen therapy began to climb into prominence was in the cosmetics industry. The theory went that aging skin was a product of insufficient oxygen flowing to the cells in order for them to perform at a healthy, youthful rate. Geared especially for the rich and famous or otherwise well-to-do, an oxygen facial could cost $120.

Physicians remained skeptical of such treatments, however, warning that they relied on deceiving the customer into believing, contrary to available evidence, that the oxygen that is so necessary for life could actually provide a direct benefit to certain parts of the body, such as skin, if applied directly. Vendors of these treatments remained convinced, however, and their popularity seemed to bear out their claims, at least as far as business was concerned.

The industry's escalating popular support at the end of the 20th century was largely attributable to two collective psychological factors. One was the general, and rising, distrust the population held for government and its regulations. Another was the progress medical researchers made throughout the 20th century, helping people imagine that all diseases were curable and that the aging process itself was not as inevitable as it used to be.

PIONEERS IN THE FIELD

A list of the earliest pioneers in the discovery of oxygen's therapeutic benefits would include Haldane and Barcroft, certainly, in the area of traditional medical treatments. The U.S. Navy itself was unparalleled in its use and investigation of hyperbaric oxygen therapy (HBOT), and that paved the way for other medical doctors and researchers to further its use. Authors of the book *Hyperbaric Oxygen Therapy*, Richard A. Neubauer, M.D. and Morton Walker, D.P.M. were devoted to the ongoing study of the benefits of that form of oxygen therapy. In his foreword to the book, well-

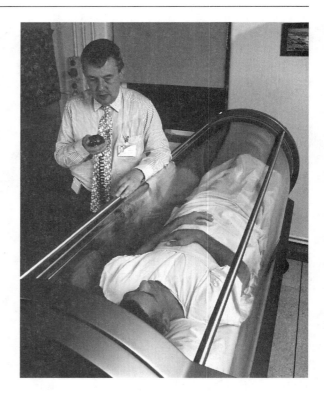

A man undergoing hyperbaric oxygen therapy as his doctor observes. (Photo Researchers Inc./James King-Holmes/Science Photo Library)

known scientist Dr. Edward Teller, director of the Lawrence Livermore Laboratory in California, offered enthusiastic support for HBOT, and for the physicians' efforts in promoting its use. Teller was also critical of the United States for dragging its feet on the technology, and held that lives and bodies could be saved by administering HBOT to patients after major surgery.

One of the best-recognized authorities on oxygen therapy as an alternative medicine is Ed McCabe. Known as "Mr. Oxygen" because of his book, *O2xygen Therapies—A New Way of Approaching Disease*, he traveled the world promoting various forms of oxygen therapy. His activities were curtailed on 7 April 1998 when he was arrested by the U.S. Justice Department on counts of tax fraud.

CURRENT CONDITIONS

A number of new potentially useful applications for oxygen therapy cropped up in the late 1990s and early 2000s. About 100,000 patients were treated with hyperbaric oxygen therapy (HBOT) yearly. With increased exposure of the benefits of this therapy, and increased research findings, the future of HBOT held promise. For example, HBOT proved effective in slowing the swelling of nerve tissues, which led many industry hopefuls to conclude that it helps to slow the progress of such diseases as multiple sclerosis in which internal scarring causes the body's immune system to disrupt signals to the brain by attacking those tissues.

Another area in which researchers have increasingly accepted oxygen therapy is infection-prevention for postsurgery patients. A study performed by anesthesiologist Daniel I. Sessler and colleagues at the University of California-San Francisco tested 500 patients undergoing major surgery. Half were treated with 80 percent pure oxygen during postsurgery anesthesia, while the other half received 30 percent pure oxygen. Only half as many, however, in the 80 percent group developed postsurgery infections. The researchers found that the higher oxygen doses enabled those patients' immune cells to capture and destroy infectious bacteria more effectively.

Having successfully tested his research on cats, Dr. Steven K. Fisher, director of the Neuroscience Research Institute at the University of California-Santa Barbara, concluded that oxygen therapy can reduce eye damage to patients with retinal detachment. Administered to patients as they await remedial surgery, Dr. Fisher held, oxygen can help save the eye's photoreceptor cells. The process was being further researched for its application to humans in 2000.

Meanwhile, long-term oxygen therapy has won increasing acceptance among medical researchers, especially for patients with chronic obstructive pulmonary disease and for those who have stopped smoking.

A particularly cautious yet emerging field for oxygen therapy was pediatric care. A number of products were developed especially for postnatal infants. One such product provided long-term patient-triggered synchronized assisted ventilation in infants. A case study during the early 1990s by a team led by Nadarasa Visveshwara, M.D. of Valley Children's Hospital of Fresno, California, proved the procedure to be safe and effective in very low birth weight infants with uncomplicated respiratory failure. More recently, the National Institutes of Health Supplemental Therapeutic Oxygen for Prethreshold Retinopathy of Prematurity Trial found that liberal uses of oxygen resulted in decreased likelihood of surgery requirements for infants by limiting the harmful effects of postnatal injuries.

Soon, however, large hyperbaric chambers may prove unnecessary for many injuries and conditions for which HBOT is currently employed. A partnership between Sandia National Laboratories and Numotech aimed at the production of a new oxygen therapy vehicle known as topical hyperbaric oxygen treatment (HTOT), which captures hyperbaric oxygen in a small, disposable plastic bag. Simply placing the bag around the affected wound or body part requiring attention allows the patient to breathe normal air while the area is bathed in high-pressure oxygen. The Sandia team will incorporate their patented internal pressure sensors in HTOT to enable easy readings and build in an automatic system shutdown if pressure levels rise to dangerous levels.

Outside the strictly medical field, a health- and image-conscious society looked for ways to deter the aging process, especially among the baby boomers. Oxygen therapy as realized through alternative medicine options was driven by market demand for products that promised benefits to health and well-being.

Oxygen facials, for instance, were purported to enhance cell-production and repair, thereby improving the health and glow of skin. Cells take about 28 days to reach the skin's surface, though as people grow older, an increasing number of those cells do not survive that journey, leading to less healthy, drier skin. One cause of this general decay is the diminished oxygen load the body allows to enter the cellular system. Through oxygen therapy, proponents suggest that individuals can literally stave off the skin's aging process, retaining moisture and improving cell performance to produce youthful, glowing skin. Many salons therefore sell and use skin-care products, such as cleansers, face lotions, and masks, with encapsulated oxygen molecules.

Oxygen therapies in alternative medicine included specially designed deep breathing exercises (often followed with the assistance of a personal trainer), hydrogen-peroxide therapy, oxidative therapy, oxone therapy, ionization, and the ingestion of oral stabilized oxygen products. Many of the oxygen compounds for ingestion, in the form of dietary supplements continued to flood the market.

More socially oriented oxygen enthusiasts popped into oxygen bars to inhale oxygen cocktails, or quick bursts of pure oxygen, to receive a boost of energy and a general feeling of vigorous health. Oxygen cocktails combine about 40 percent strength oxygen with water and a fruit extract, which is then inhaled for 15 minutes to an hour through a mask or nasal prongs. While, again, doctors tended to ridicule the trend and deny the cocktails' efficacy, a number of customers continued to swear by it.

In addition to the often-questionable health benefits, medical researchers warned of the still-pervasive dangers of improper casual oxygen therapy, especially of the self-administered variety. Deaths resulting from patients falling asleep inside a chamber or other improperly supervised oxygen administration were not unheard of.

The major challenge that faced oxygen therapy in traditional medicine was research and development. Since the techniques remain so awash in controversy and skepticism, research grants were relatively hard to come by. Private companies, such as Sechrist Industries, Inc., a leader in the field of hyperbaric therapy equipment and other respiratory products, provided much of the funding for further experimentation.

The challenges of HBOT extend further. The field of HBOT was relatively young by medical standards even at the close of the 20th century. Only since the 1960s had valid research and results been followed. Consequently, many doctors were graduated from medical school knowing little about this therapy. They might come to accept HBOT for certain conditions, such as wounds, burns, air emboli, carbon-monoxide poisoning, and chronic bone infections. But the medical profession as a whole did not yet accept its use for many other conditions that hyperbaric doctors already recognized. These treatments included coma related to head injuries, bruising of the spinal cord, stroke, and multiple sclerosis. Other conditions that Neubauer and Walker noted were treatable with HBOT included cranial nerve syndromes, peripheral neuropathy, various orthopedic conditions, gangrene, frostbite, diabetic retinopathy, cirrhosis, and Crohn's disease, to name a few.

The Internet was inundated with sales of oxygen therapy products. Established businesses and new start-ups appeared on the Internet and offered consumers thousands of products involving oxygen therapy. Among them were Crossroads' The Oxystore and Bio-Karmic Technologies, both California companies. Crossroads offered books, video and audio tapes, testing kits, oral oxygen, and a range of other products relating to oxygen and detoxification. The health value of these products was considered questionable, and many thus came with warnings even by the businesses themselves.

Another impact felt by this market was the unprecedented growth of health spas. The number began to grow so rapidly into the 1990s that it was nearly impossible to calculate. These spas included holistic health centers that could offer one-day, one-week, or extended stays for treatments. Americans patronized many of the clinics that had opened in Mexico offering cancer treatments not approved in the United States. Even department stores began to cash in on the business of in-store therapeutic facials. As the world welcomed high-technological advances, an American public began to turn to health products that were born often of ancient health practices.

INDUSTRY LEADERS

The business of oxygen therapy is part of a diverse number of professions, occupations, and industries. It includes medical professionals and trained technicians, academic researchers, cosmetologists, alternative-health practitioners, medical-equipment manufacturers, health-spa owners, hospitals, and business owners who sell related products. Still, the key manufacturers of hyperbaric oxygen chambers are important to note. They include: Environmental Tectonics Corp. of Southampton, Pennsylvania, which brought in revenues of $29.2 million in 1999; Mediscus Group of Trevosie, Pennsylvania; Reneau, Inc. of Stafford, Texas; Tampa Hyperbaric Enterprise, Inc. of Tampa, Florida; and Sechrist Industries, Inc. in Orange County, California.

Research and development of hyperbaric treatments is the focus of several laboratories and companies around the United States. They are: the Ocean Hyperbaric Center in Florida, also operating the American College of Hyperbaric Medicine from that facility; Biopure Corp. of Cambridge, Massachusetts; Baptist Medical Center in Jacksonville, Florida; Lifeforce, in Baltimore, Maryland; Texas A & M University Hyperbaric Laboratory at College Station, Texas; and the Undersea Hyperbaric Medical Society, Inc. of Kensington, Maryland.

Other standard oxygen equipment, such as monitors, analyzers, and transmitters, were products of a multitude of medical-equipment companies and companies that dealt simply with oxygen-related products. The Alpha Omega Instruments Corp. of Rhode Island is a rising company in this area of the industry, as is Sandia National Laboratories of Albuquerque, New Mexico.

WORK FORCE

As in many other aspects of the alternative-medicine market, true projections for oxygen therapy were difficult due to the nature of the business. Workers from chiropractors to herbal-supplement specialists to health-bookstore staff to production factory employees reaped the benefits of this multibillion-dollar business. Because those who seek out alternative care tend to be affluent, well-educated members of the population with the resources to experiment, the economic implication was growth in exponential increments. This was true of the work force in the cosmetics industry, too, as oxygen therapy facials and similar body therapies became a central source of oxygen therapy profits.

AMERICA AND THE WORLD

While America lagged behind the rest of the industrialized world in the use of hyperbaric therapy and alternative medicine, it was catching up near the end of the 20th century. American wealth, education, and growing travel options helped to create more options in seeking health and beauty care. While many Americans continued to seek treatment at spas in Europe and Mexico, the growth of similar facilities in the United States had begun to offer them such opportunities closer to home. Because of the country's continued dominance in traditional health-care services, the United States was considered likely to dominate the field, particularly in the manufacturing of equipment, as the possibilities for HBOT grew from increased research.

In many countries, meanwhile, oxygen therapy was finding a market embracing the treatment with open arms. Nearly all Japanese are within practical distance of one of Japan's 200 hyperbaric chambers. In Italy, doctors can even be sanctioned for failing to administer oxygen therapy for appropriate conditions.

Still, skepticism continued to hold the industry somewhat in check overseas as well, and will likely continue to do so for some years to come. In the United Kingdom, for instance, approximately 90,000 people suffer from multiple sclerosis (MS). Over 11,000 of these have experimented with a hyperbaric oxygen chamber since the mid-1980s, but in light of the U.K. Multiple Sclerosis Society's judgment that the treatment was risky and expensive, doctors still often did not even bother to report the existence of oxygen therapy alternatives to those diagnosed with MS.

FURTHER READING

D'Arrigo, Terri. "An Air of Healing." *Diabetes Forecast,* February 2000.

Grimaldo, Bradie. "Are You Injured? Try an Oxygen Bath." *Electronic Design,* 9 August 1999.

Henderson, C. W. "Oxygen Therapeutic Restores Brain Oxygenation." *Blood Weekly,* 23 March 2000.

Jackson, Nancy Beth. "Vital Signs: Treatment; Oxygen May Help Save Threatened Eyes." *New York Times,* 10 August 1999.

Leach, R. M., P. J. Rees, P. Wilmshurst, and Richard M. Leach. "Hyperbaric Oxygen Therapy." *British Medical Journal,* 24 October 1998.

Lewis, Carol. "Every Breath You Take." *FDA Consumer,* March/April 1999. Available from http://www.fda.gov.

McLean, Candis. "Waking Up Sleeping Cells." *Report/ Newsmagazine* (Alberta edition), 28 February 2000.

Neubauer, Richard, M.D., and Morton Walker, D.P.M. *Hyperbaric Oxygen Therapy.* Garden City, NY: Avery Publishing, 1998.

"Oxygen & Ozone Therapies." 2000. Available from http://www.oxytherapy.com.

Park, Richard. "Market Analysis." *HomeCare,* October 2000.

Prentice, Eve-Ann. "Can Pure Oxygen Help MS Sufferers?" *Times* (London), 21 December 1999.

Prisi, Angela. "Oxygen Therapy: Does It Make Sense to Pay for Air?" *Gazette* (Montreal), 23 November 1999.

Seppa, Nathan. "Oxygen Limits Infections from Surgery." *Science News,* 22 January 2000.

Swinglehurst, Deborah. "Questions Answered by Evidence-Based Medicine." *Pulse,* 29 January 2000.

"What Is Hyperbaric Oxygen Therapy?" Thousand Oaks, CA: Hyperbaric Chamber Systems & Management, 2000. Available from http://www.hyperbaric.com/over.htm.

PARALLEL PROCESSING COMPUTERS

The ongoing parade of ever faster personal computers (PCs) may cause some to overlook the true high-performance computer market—tremendously powerful, often multimillion-dollar machines—but demand for massively parallel processing (MPP) computers, supercomputers, and other ultra-high-end computers certainly hasn't dried up.

Scientists, engineers, and other researchers depend on such rarified machines for a host of processing-intensive applications. Common high-end applications range from predicting hurricane movements to modeling nuclear warfare to exploring the human genome. These applications have a need for speed. It would literally take years—even decades—to run the same kinds of analyses on a single-processor system. For example, in a recent record-setting demonstration, a supercomputer at the Los Alamos National Laboratory ran in three days a series of engineering simulations that would have taken a single processor almost 18 years to muddle through. To put it another way, each hour of the supercomputer's time was worth 90 days of computing by lesser machines.

Not surprisingly, the majority of the world's most powerful computers are used for research applications. According to the June 2000 edition of a semiannual report on the world's fastest computers, 56 of the top 100 computers were used for various types of research, including weather and energy research. Another 20 superfast machines were specified as academic systems, which tend to be used for research as well. Ten of the top 100 were used in commercial applications, and the remaining 14 were used for classified government pro-

jects and by computer makers themselves as part of their development programs.

Sales of high-performance computers have been mixed. In the late 1990s revenues from traditional supercomputers and MPP systems actually declined, while sales of technical servers and so-called midrange systems experienced modest gains. In an effort to shore up sales, makers of high-end systems are increasingly targeting business applications rather than their mainstay academic and government markets.

ORGANIZATION AND STRUCTURE

Parallel computing simply means delegating a computing task to multiple processors (central processing units, or CPUs), each of which performs part of the operation in tandem with the rest. Parallel processing computers are of two basic types: vector and multiprocessing. In vector computers, a single, specialized processor can perform more than one operation at a time. Multiprocessing computers, by contrast, use many processors simultaneously to break difficult operations into pieces and complete those operations collectively. Multiprocessing systems are today by far the most common.

A rudimentary form of parallel processing is available on relatively inexpensive network servers (some costing less than $10,000) equipped with two or more microprocessors. These common devices, however, aren't considered part of the high-end market. High-performance systems often use hundreds or even thousands of microprocessors, and perhaps more importantly, rely on specially designed connectivity hardware and software to achieve dramatically faster speeds and greater capabilities.

The structure of the parallel and supercomputing market is driven, in large part, by hardware advances. While it is processor architecture that defines parallel processing, leaps and bounds in processor speed and miniaturization have made supercomputers much more compact and powerful than the room-size computers of the 1960s and 1970s. The power of the supercomputers of the early 1960s was available on many desktops at the end of the 1990s.

On the hardware side, parallel processing computers fall into several categories: supercomputers, often called "heavy iron"; clusters of small computers linked together to act as a single computer; and technical servers. These high-flying machines are produced by a small number of U.S. and Japanese companies, such as Silicon Graphics Inc., Cray Inc., IBM Corp., Hitachi Ltd., Fujitsu Ltd., and NEC Corp.

Most software used by supercomputers is developed by manufacturers specifically for their machines. Generally, the investment in a supercomputer is for a particular purpose or range of purposes, and the software and hardware are chosen together to accomplish that purpose. Still, in some cases off-the-shelf software is available for certain applications such as graphics, mathematical simulations, and database applications.

BACKGROUND AND DEVELOPMENT

The first parallel computer architecture appeared in 1959 with the delivery of the IBM 7030, affectionately known as "Stretch." With a performance measurement of approximately 1 megaflops ("flops" being short for floating-point operations), or 1 million instructions executed per second, the 7030 was the most formidable computing machine of its time. It was comparable in speed to the average desktop personal computer of 1992. It was delivered to Los Alamos National Laboratory to model nuclear explosions, but only eight 7030s were ever manufactured. Other government labs, such as Lawrence Livermore and the National Aeronautics and Space Administration (NASA) competed for high-speed computing machines to perform complex aeronautical and fluid dynamics calculations. The birth of the first single processor CPU, the Intel 4004, was another 12 years away.

Control Data Corp. (CDC), founded in the late 1950s, developed the CDC 6600 in 1964 and the CDC 7600 in 1969, both exceeding a megaflop. Other giants of the early parallel processing supercomputing field included Burroughs, Sperry-Rand, and Texas Instruments. CDC was the starting place of a man who was later referred to as the father of the supercomputing industry—Seymour Cray (1925-1996), who left the company in 1972 to found Cray Research. Cray Research dominated the supercomputer scene of the 1980s with its freon-cooled Cray-1, Cray-2, and X-MP models. Soon new competitors arose to capture some of Cray's dominant market share. Convex, Sequent, and Alliant developed competing systems, but for those who could afford the million-dollar price tags (mainly government laboratories and engineering departments at major research universities), a Cray computer was the first choice.

The late 1980s saw the production of the first non-American parallel processing supercomputers for the general market. Companies such as Hitachi, NEC, Meiko, and Fujitsu began marketing computers to compete with Cray and CDC. The breakup of the former Soviet Union and the end of the Cold War caused a marked decline for supercomputers during much of the 1990s. University research that depended on heavy number crunching, such as oceanography and meteorology modeling, plus the growth of commercial applications such as power generation and transmission, securities and stock market data modeling, high-definition television, and even virtual reality, kept the market alive. These and other high-bandwidth applications relied on parallel rather than serial processing of data.

By the mid-1990s, led by the parallel and multiprocessing hardware of Intel Corp. and its P6, or PentiumPro chip, computer manufacturers such as IBM, Silicon Graphics, and Sun Microsystems, Inc. began to develop architectures to take advantage of greater throughput. Database giants Oracle Corp. and Sybase Inc. also used parallel architectures to quickly manipulate and retrieve records in relational databases. Their products represented the first forays of parallel processing and supercomputing into software products for standard to high-end business applications. This meant that parallel processing was nearing the desktop of the average personal computer.

CURRENT CONDITIONS

Demand for high-performance computers has been somewhat weak for traditional dedicated supercomputers and massively parallel processing (MPP) systems. Part of the slowdown stemmed from uncertainty surrounding the Cray computer line, one of the pillars of the supercomputer business. Cray floundered under several years of uneasy ownership by Silicon Graphics, but Tera Computer's 2000 purchase of Cray was expected to revive sales and marketing of Cray machines.

Nonetheless, a broader market shift may help account for the softness in some high-performance computer sales—and the strength in other segments. Universities and government agencies have long been the core users of many types of supercomputers, and demand in those markets, particularly in the post-Cold War era, simply hasn't been rising very quickly.

The fastest-growing segment of the high-performance market was for so-called technical servers. These are high-end network servers, often running Unix, that are devoted to a range of specialized tasks. An example is an image server for storing and transmitting medical images within a hospital system. Technical servers are more likely to be deployed in commercial and industrial settings rather than in pure research settings, which is probably why they're in greater demand than highbrow supercomputers.

Indeed, businesses represent a large and growing share of the high-performance market. Commercial sales made up about 68 percent of the nearly $6 billion high-performance market in 1999. By 2002, businesses were expected to provide 75 percent of sales. Factors driving business use include heightened interest in data mining, especially for scouring electronic-commerce numbers for trends, and data visualization. International Data Corp.'s conservative estimate pins the total market's growth rate between 8 and 10 percent per year in the 2000s.

FASTER AND FASTER

The world's fastest computer in operation, at least as of late 2000, is an Intel-designed system known as ASCI Red. This one-of-a-kind system can summon 9,632 processors to achieve theoretical speeds of more than 2.3 trillion floating-point operations per second (teraflops). Installed at the Sandia National Laboratories in Albuquerque, New Mexico, ASCI Red was unveiled in 1996 as part of the U.S. Department of Energy's Accelerated Strategic Computing Initiative (ASCI) for modeling of the effects of aging on nuclear warheads. Since its debut, when it was noted for breaking the teraflops barrier, upgrading has boosted ASCI Red's performance by more than 75 percent in just a few years.

Continued development aims to push supercomputing into quadrillion-flops (or petaflops) territory.

Trends   RECONFIGURE YOUR SUPERCOMPUTER

Most computers, whether high end or low end, come with a fairly fixed system architecture. Sure, you can add and remove memory, swap storage devices, and tack on countless peripherals, but the underlying processing architecture remains the same. Yet some architectures are more efficient at certain problems than others—and in high-end applications every little efficiency counts because of sheer volume.

So for years, computer engineers have sought ways to harness different architectures within the same system to perform different tasks. One recent endeavor, for instance, was the merging of vector computing with massively parallel processing (MPP), such as Cray Inc.'s government-funded SV2 project, slated for completion in 2002. Ideally, this approach gives users the benefits of the traditionally separate vector and MPP machines all in one system.

An obscure company called Star Bridge Systems has a less modest proposal: why not have system hardware that configures itself on the fly based on software commands? Coining the phrase "architecture-on-demand" and branding the technology as hypercomputing, Star Bridge officials suggested that such a system is possible and have begun taking steps to bring it to market.

In 2000 the Midvale, Utah, company introduced its HAL-300 system, billed as a general-purpose, reconfigurable supercomputer. Short for hyper-algorithmic logic, HAL, like its science-fiction namesake, is a very capable device. It uses Star Bridge's hypercomputing approach to reprogram its chips as the software directs—potentially thousands of times per second. The processor uses a field-programmable gate array (FPGA) and MPP features to deliver performance that is blazingly fast and highly adaptable to changing conditions. The special silicon FPGA chips are supplied by Xilinx Corp.

Ultimately, the company says, its model could revolutionize computing from the very fastest supercomputers down to ordinary desktop PCs. It remains to be seen whether HAL and hypercomputing will take root, though. The HAL-300 was reportedly 60,000 times faster than a typical PC, and the company has made claims of speeds surpassing those of most, if not all, supercomputers. The problem so far is that Star Bridge doesn't measure speed like anyone else, making it hard to interpret its claims. Many experts remain skeptical, however, deferring judgment until the machines can be run through independent tests. Star Bridge shipped its first HAL models in August 2000 to the Salt Lake City telecommunications firm CeriStar, Inc.

Leading new development efforts is an ambitious project announced in 1999 by IBM. Nicknamed Blue Gene, the venerable computer maker's project is intended to produce a system that will vastly outpace all existing computers. IBM's goal is to make Blue Gene, a successor to its celebrated Deep Blue of the mid-1990s, 2 million times faster than a conventional PC and faster than a few hundred present-day supercomputers combined. The gargantuan computer will boast something near 1 million processors and reportedly would have enough power to download the entire Internet in a second. If that's not enough, Blue Gene is supposed to have self-healing abilities that allow it to recover from errors and breakdowns on its own.

Costing an expected $100 million to develop, Blue Gene was expected to be completed in about five years. While computer enthusiasts needn't expect to see IBM taking orders for Blue Gene models off the Web any time soon, the company does plan to leverage technological breakthroughs from the development process eventually in its commercial devices.

A brief note on speed: many manufacturers claim on different grounds that their machines are the world's fastest. Some measure theoretical speeds that are never attained in practice; others measure peak operating speeds that are only rarely reached; still others gauge sustained operation speeds, but tend to measure the speed during operations that their machines are particularly well-suited to handle. That's not to address the morass of processor capability versus specific interconnect capacities, which can dramatically affect end performance. In short, there are many variables that determine actual performance, so most observers are likely to encounter contradictory claims about speed and performance, particularly when coming from the manufacturers.

Clustering Inexpensive Computers for High Performance

A significant trend in the supercomputing market is a series of initiatives that has combined ordinary PCs and network servers into a surprisingly powerful high-performance system. In 1998 a team at Los Alamos announced their "supercomputer," which was actually a cluster of 68 PCs that could operate as a single computer and reach speeds up to 47 gigaflops. What was most noteworthy about it was the cost—approximately $313,000, roughly 10 percent of the cost of a conventional supercomputer. This computer, called Avalon, was a "Beowulf-class" computer, a development in parallel processing that began in 1994 among NASA scientists. Thomas Sterling and Don Becker, working

at the Center of Excellence in Space Data and Information Sciences, a NASA contractor, put together 16 desktop computers using Ethernet connections and called it Beowulf. It was an instant success, and a movement began, first among government researchers but soon moving toward commercialization.

Beowulf clusters used off-the-shelf hardware and publicly available software, most significantly the Linux operating system (a version of Unix that is available free), but requires considerable knowledge of computer networking to put together. In May 1999 EBIZ Enterprises, Inc. demonstrated a fully configured Beowulf Clustered Super Computer, a 16-node cluster that was priced at under $15,000. This machine ran a standard test problem in 12 seconds, compared to the three seconds required by the Cray T3E, which cost $5.5 million. According to the company, this made supercomputer power available to many people and organizations without the funds for a conventional supercomputer or the knowledge to build their own cluster.

Other groups, mostly affiliated with universities and research centers, have experimented with cluster configurations as well. In one interesting case, researchers at a South Korean university used parallel processing software over the Internet to simulate supercomputing functions on a group of 64 PCs.

Still, a clustered system may not be the answer to all supercomputing needs. Experts distinguish between high-performance systems that meet capacity needs, or large but relatively straightforward tasks, versus those that meet capability needs, which involve both large and complex tasks. In short, cluster systems tend to fare better meeting capacity needs, whereas more traditional (and expensive) machines with specialized chips are considered better candidates for capability needs. This distinction, however, has been played up by traditional manufacturers such as Cray, which stands to lose the most if cluster computing catches on in a big way.

Chips

At the other end of the computing scale, individual chips were also being developed incorporating parallel processing instruction within the chip. Making the most news at the end of the 1990s was the Merced IA-64 chip being jointly developed by Intel and Hewlett-Packard. A 64-bit processor, as opposed to a 32-bit such as the Pentium, it was designed with explicitly parallel instructions computing, or EPIC. This parallel processing within the chip would make it at least twice as fast as previous Intel chips, according to the designers. It would also incorporate previous generation instruction sets for backward compatibility.

Merced was not the first 64-bit processor, though. Digital Equipment Corp. introduced its 64-bit Alpha processor for its servers and workstations in 1993, but it did not make the impact on the industry that is expected of the Intel chip when it takes hold. In the meantime, Elbrus International, a Russian computer company, announced in May 1999 the design of a processor that it claimed would operate faster than Merced. It also used internal parallel processing. Elbrus had taken out 70 patents on its design and was looking for a Western firm to help manufacture the chip.

INDUSTRY LEADERS

The high-performance computing industry is largely dominated by a handful of companies. Most of them are large, integrated computer companies with far-flung operations in other segments, such as IBM, Fujitsu, Compaq, Sun, and Hewlett-Packard. Other more specialized players include Cray and Silicon Graphics.

According to a semiannual report on the 500 fastest supercomputers in the world, IBM and Cray models accounted for 57 of the top 100 as of June 2000. Three Japanese firms, Fujitsu, Hitachi, and NEC, supplied another 28 of the top 100. Looking at the broader 500, IBM topped the list with 28.8 percent, followed by Sun (24.2 percent), Silicon Graphics (12.4 percent), Cray (10.8 percent), and Hewlett-Packard (9.4 percent). Systems made by just seven other firms rounded out the remaining 14.4 percent of leading supercomputers in operation.

CRAY

Seattle-based Cray Inc. has a long and colorful history in the supercomputing business, which it helped pioneer in the 1970s under the leadership of its eccentric and brilliant founder, Seymour Cray. Cray Research, operating out of Eagan, Minnesota, became a dominant leader in the 1980s, but saw its supercomputer and parallel computer market share slide in the 1990s as government spending declined. Financial strife and indecision at Cray's helm left the company a willing target in a 1996 purchase bid by Silicon Graphics Inc. (SGI). Later that year Mr. Cray, who had formed a separate entity called Cray Computer Corp. a few years earlier, died at age 71 from injuries sustained in a car crash.

The marriage of Cray Research and SGI proved an unhappy pairing, although arguably SGI profited more than from the arrangement than did Cray. The two companies' cultures didn't mesh, and SGI never fully appreciated Cray's product line and marketing. Finally, in 1999 SGI made known its plans to sell Cray. It found a buyer named Tera Computer Co., a little-known publicly traded designer of multithreading high-end systems. The buyout was completed in spring of 2000, with the new entity taking the name Cray Inc.

In 2000 the new Cray Inc. was expected to have revenues of about $200 million and some 900 employees. Its early sales, however, will be a far cry from the company's revenue heyday in the mid-1990s, when the former Cray Research achieved peak sales of $922 million before its decline. The new company is focusing on bringing out a new line of scalable supercomputers with both vector and MPP capabilities, backed by heavy funding from the U.S. Department of Defense. It is also rebuilding a sales force to sell its machines, after having its sales channels all but ignored at SGI.

IBM

Armonk, New York-based IBM Corp. was still the world's largest computer company at the end of the 20th century. Practically synonymous with large computers for years, IBM built a market share of almost 80 percent in the 1960s and 1970s. It introduced the PC in 1981, but failed to capitalize on the growth of the low-end computer market and went into a steady decline as interest in mainframes stagnated and prices declined.

By the mid-1990s, though, IBM had regrouped, returning to profitability and rejuvenating its product and service lines. In 1997, Deep Blue, IBM's enormous parallel processing computer, defeated world chess champion Garry Kasparov in a six-game match. The feat was mostly symbolic, of course, but it helped set the tone for the company's ambitious research and development program that would close out the 1990s with the massive Blue Gene project (see above). All told, IBM is responsible for more of the world's supercomputers than any other company. According to a June 2000 ranking, IBM claimed 144 of the fastest 500 machines, largely through its SP Power3 and SP PC604e models.

SUN MICROSYSTEMS

Sun Microsystems, Inc. is a major producer of technical servers and cluster systems using symmetric multiprocessing (SMP) technology. The Palo Alto, California, company was formed in the 1980s, when it earned a reputation for producing powerful, speedy Unix-based workstations for scientific and engineering applications. It also branched into servers, and got a big boost from SGI in the mid-1990s when SGI sold off part of Cray Research's server business for a relative pittance. In subsequent years Sun earned a hundredfold return on its investment. Sun also manufacturers its own line of microprocessors (UltraSPARC), some of which are used by other high-performance system manufacturers, and other system components such as storage devices. Its top-notch offerings are its HPC line, including the Starfire brand, but Sun has been very successful in the general high-end and midrange server markets, which include systems costing $100,000 or more. Sun machines accounted for 121 of the top 500 supercomputers in mid-2000.

HEWLETT-PACKARD

Hewlett-Packard Co., also of Palo Alto, California, is a top producer of computer systems for all markets. In the high end, it acquired Convex Computer in 1996 to offer the Exemplar line of parallel processing computers. Hewlett-Packard also participates in the high-end market through its N-Class and V-Class servers and its HyperPlex clustering platform, all of which run on the company's own chips.

INTEL

Intel Corp., well-known for its dominance of the processor market, has been selling parallel computers since about 1985. It built the multiteraflops ASCI Red for the Sandia National Laboratories, but its Paragon line of parallel computers is its standard business offering. It also began shipping its Merced and Itanium 64-bit parallel processing microchips in late 2000. Some expected the Merced development to eventually bring parallel processing to the ordinary desktop computer. Aside from chip making, however, Intel is not a sizable producer of finished high-performance computers.

COMPAQ

A world leader in sales of PCs and low-end servers, Houston-based Compaq Computer Corp. has gradually bought its way into the high-performance market through its acquisitions of Tandem and Digital Equipment Corp. Although a couple of former Digital products (souped-up AlphaServer models) ranked among the world's top 30, overall Compaq's machines don't compete on a world-class basis. Indeed, only six of the top-500 supercomputers were attributed to

Compaq. Its diverse high-end AlphaServer line includes the SC (supercomputer) series, based on SMP technology. Compaq is also noted for its production of high-end Alpha chips, which run all high-end Compaq servers as well as those of other manufacturers.

WORK FORCE

Employees in the supercomputing and parallel processing computer industry mainly come from engineering or computer science backgrounds. Due to the theoretical work involved, a small percentage may come from mathematics or other hard science fields. Nonetheless, the growing multidisciplinary perspective used by many university research centers affects the work in parallel processing as well. According to the Caltech Concurrent Computation Project, which researched parallel computing from 1983 through 1990, a wide range of disciplines were recruited to tackle different aspects of the technology. It was also noted that the traditional interdisciplinary field for the project, computational science, is not well understood or implemented either nationally or within the university structure.

According to the *Occupational Outlook Handbook,* published by the U.S. Bureau of Labor Statistics, computer scientists, computer engineers, and systems analysts held approximately 1.5 million jobs in the late 1990s, including 114,000 who were self-employed, and these were expected to be the three fastest-growing occupations through 2008. Median earnings of this group were about $52,180.

RESEARCH AND TECHNOLOGY

There is much relevant research on parallel processing computers. While a significant amount of research considered hardware architecture, a growing body of research looked into the complexity of writing software for parallel hardware architectures. Scalability of parallel architectures varied, and some architectures handled certain mathematical problems (such as algorithms) better than others.

Research was being done on three basic parallel architecture types at the end of the 1990s: symmetric multiprocessing (SMP), massively parallel processing (MPP), and clustering technology. SMP uses a number of CPUs but they share one memory. This approach is good for large databases, for example, which are continually updated. Because the memory is shared, it is easier to update. MPP, on the other hand, utilizes many processors, each of which has its own memory and copy of the operating system. This approach works well for massive problems that can be broken into pieces that can be worked on simultaneously. Clustering architectures are similar to MPP except that they are in fact many separate machines linked together in a high-speed network and running special software.

Described by one programmer as "fiendishly difficult" and something that "should be considered illegal at most sites," parallel software programming was still in the early stages of development at the end of the 1990s. Software testing is often difficult to execute due to the lack of repeatability and dependence on the relative timing of one processor versus another. Writing software for parallel systems often involves mathematical proofs rather than brute testing, something beyond the scope of many programmers. Also, different types of parallel architectures support different types of software—what works on one may not work on another. Significant research has begun on a standard communications protocol in parallel processing computers. A standard for a "message-passing interface," the parallel computing version of an operating system, is being developed by international forums and computer groups.

Open MP, an applications programming interface (API) standard announced in December 1997, was intended to ease some consternation on the part of applications programmers developing code for parallel processing systems. APIs afford portability between hardware platforms by shielding the programmer from the idiosyncrasies of the proprietary machine codes. Open MP, developed in tandem by SGI and software developers Kluck & Associates, received endorsement from Digital Equipment, IBM, Intel, and others. Representatives from Dow Chemical and DuPont also voiced optimism regarding the potential of the new standard.

While supercomputers tend to be evaluated based on their CPU throughput, input/output (I/O) requirements are a major consideration as well. Mapping the human genome, for example, requires just as much I/O throughput as CPU brute force due to the massive amount of data needed for input. Meteorological modeling can have billions of data points. Such "grand-challenge applications" push the frontiers of parallel processing research and development.

Fiber optics may offer a solution for both I/O and processing limitations. Researchers struggling with scaling problems in parallel architectures are working with light rather than electrical signals to transmit signals. For instance, a conventional electronic connection of 10 processors requires 100 wires, and the number of wires rises exponentially as the number of processors increases. Fiber-optic technology, by contrast, has a theoretical potential of 2 terabits per second. The implementation, however, is expensive and daunting. Positioning systems for light pulses must be micro-accurate. Light beams through fiber-optic wires also suffer attenuation, or weakening of a signal over longer distances; lasers solve the problem, but with huge costs. Honeywell, Lucent Technologies, and Motorola, among others, have already invested research dollars into developing marketable optical computing solutions.

Research centers involved in the performance computing industry include the Center for Research on Parallel Computation (CRPC), a consortium of universities led by Rice University in Houston, Texas. The CRPC is a National Science Foundation Science and Technology Center. Other research centers include the Institute for Parallel Computation at the University of Virginia, the Center for Applied Parallel Processing at the University of Colorado-Boulder, and the Parallel Architecture Research Laboratory at New Mexico State University.

FURTHER READING

Adams, Charlotte. "SMP Clusters Offer Low-Cost Alternative to Supercomputers." *Federal Computer Week,* 19 October 1998.

Babcock, Charles. "A New View of the Parallel Universe." 18 December 1995. Available from http://www.computerworld.com/home/print9497.nsf/all/SLsuperD3EE.

———. "Software Lags Hardware's Fourfold Leap." 17 June 1996. Available from http://www.computerworld.com/home/print9497.nsf/all/SLfourIA26A.

Bains, Sunny. "'Fully' Connected." *OEM Magazine,* 1 February 1997.

Brown, Chappell. "FPGA Blends Parallel Architectures." *Electronic Engineering Times,* 22 April 1996.

Brownstein, Mark. "A $1000 Supercomputer?" *PC World,* 10 June 2000.

"Capability Computing: In the Eye of the Beholder." *New Technology Week,* 20 May 2000.

Copeland, Ron. "IBM: Supercomputing's Top Gun." *Informationweek,* 13 November 2000.

Dicarlo, Lisa. "Big Blue Outlines Power Plays." *PC Week,* 20 December 1999.

Dongarra, Jack, Hans Meuer, and Erich Strohmaier. "Top 500 Supercomputer Sites." Mannheim, Germany: University of Mannheim, June 2000. Available from http://www.top500.org.

Halfhill, Tom R. "Inside IA-64." *Byte,* June 1998.

Hall, Mark. "Supercomputer Revival." *Computerworld,* 22 November 1999.

———. "Supercomputing: From R&D to P&L." *Computerworld,* 13 December 1999.

Hunt, Laura. "Massively Parallel Processing." *Computerworld,* 15 February 1999.

"Interconnect Contract Kicks off Quest—U.S. Starts Path to 30 TFLOPS Computer." *Electronic Engineering Times,* 5 January 1998.

Jones, Christopher. "The Super-Duper Hypercomputer." *Wired,* 11 February 2000. Available from http://www.wired.com.

Lubove, Seth. "Megaflop." *Forbes,* 3 April 2000.

Manchester, Philip. "FTIT: New Generation of Supercomputers Now Emerging." *Financial Times,* 6 September 2000.

Mason, Scott. "SMP Provides a Mirror into Your Server." *Network Computing,* 1 May 1997.

McGrath, Steve. "Supercomputing Gets a New Hero." *Communications News,* August 1998.

Nance, Scott. "Sale Price Shows Diminished Cray." *New Technology Week,* 10 April 2000.

Nash, Kim S. "Behind the Merced Mystique." *Computerworld,* 6 July 1998. Available from http://www.computerworld.com/home/features.nsf/all/980706rc.

"Open MP API Created for Cross-Platform Parallel Apps." *Computergram International,* 29 October 1997.

Pickering, Carol. "Blue Mountain." *Forbes ASAP,* 22 February 1999.

"The Power of Multiprocessing." *VAR Business,* 15 November 1996.

Robertson, Jack. "Intel Goes to 1 Trillion Ops." *Electronic Buyers' News,* 23 December 1996.

"Russia: A New Super-Fast Microchip Designed by Elbrus International." *Moskovskie Novosti,* 23 March 1999.

Santo, Brian. "Team More Than Doubles the Speed of Chess-Playing Computer." *Electronic Engineering Times,* 24 March 1997.

Sharp, Oliver. "The Grand Challenges." *Byte,* February 1995.

U.S. Bureau of Labor Statistics. *2000-2001 Occupational Outlook Handbook.* Available from http://www.bls.gov/oco.

Watterson, Karen. "Parallel Tracks." *Datamation,* May 1997.

Wilck, Jennifer. "Chemical Makers Welcome Open MP Interface." *Chemical Market Reporter,* 1 December 1997.

Young, Peter. "Programming for Parallel Processors Too Often Is a Problematic Procedure." 8 May 1995. Available from http://www.computerworld.com/home/print9497.nsf/all/SL16para.

PASSENGER RESTRAINT SYSTEMS

Consumer demand for safe autos, tight competition among car makers, and technological advances have proven a potent mix where advanced passenger restraint systems are concerned. Going far beyond those old standbys, seat belts, newer restraint mechanisms such as various kinds of air bags and child restraint equipment attempt to harness researchers' knowledge of crash physics in order to make safer cars, minivans, and sport-utility vehicles (SUVs). Demand for advanced restraint systems was brisk in the late 1990s and was expected to continue climbing rapidly well into the 2000s.

Air bags work as a supplement to lap-and-shoulder belts in the event of an accident that propels the driver or passenger toward the steering wheel, dashboard, or windshield. Deployed by electronic sensors at the moment of a crash, air bags inflate in a fraction of a second and cushion the forward-hurtling passenger.

Even though air bags have been available commercially since at least the 1970s, it wasn't until the 1990s that their popularity surged. Some of this was due to federal regulations, which first mandated driver-side air bags in the 1993 model year and later expanded the requirement to passenger-side air bags in vehicles made during or after 1998. But competition in the auto industry and consumer demand have fueled additional growth, especially for the newer side-impact systems, which in 2000 were installed on only 9 percent of cars in the United States. That amount was forecast to reach 50 percent by 2005. Indeed, air-bag production worldwide was expected to skyrocket 120 percent between 1999 and 2005. The restraint manufacturer Autoliv projected that in 2001 the global market for all forms of passenger restraint technology, from seat belts to electronic sensors, would approach $14 billion.

Children are a special consideration when it comes to auto safety, and their needs have been of increasing concern to both manufacturers and safety regulators. Early air bags were notorious for being designed only with adults in mind, making them less effective—even harmful—for children. A series of purportedly air-bag-induced deaths of children in the 1990s sent the industry backpedaling on air bags, belatedly offering switches that allowed parents to turn them off. Meanwhile, parents and safety experts groused that add-on equipment such as child-safety seats was often ineffective because of poor design and improper use. In response to those complaints, progress was made in the late 1990s toward standardizing child-seat hardware and developing other child-centric safety features such as weight-sensing air-bag systems, so-called smart air bags, which react differently based on the passenger's weight and position in the seat.

Despite years of debate throughout the 1980s, it wasn't until 1993 that the federal government mandated that automobile manufacturers begin installing air bags in all vehicles. Prior to that, air bags were installed in some European models and in a few domestic cars, usually in pricey models.

Air bags seized the public's imagination and soon car makers, after years of avoiding any mention of safety issues for fear of scaring consumers, began to sell safety in their advertisements. Less than 1 percent of American-made cars contained an air bag in the mid-1980s; by 1997, however, virtually all new vehicles sold in the United States had at least one, and 60 percent also had a passenger-side air bag. As of 1 September 1998, government regulations required all passenger cars, vans, and light trucks to contain dual front air bags. Several states, including New York, Ohio, Arizona, Indiana, and Texas, ruled that consumers can sue car manufacturers for failing to equip cars with air bags, even if the cars were produced before laws were passed requiring them to be installed. Pennsylvania, Mississippi, and Idaho, however, have since ruled that car manufacturers cannot be sued in such cases.

Government and industry figures indicated that air bags were saving lives. Crashes resulted in roughly 1.4 million air-bag deployments through 1996, including 1.2 million on the driver's side and 200,000 on the passenger side. Since 1986 an estimated 2,000 lives have been saved by air bags. Significantly, some 520 of those lives were saved in 1996 alone, indicating that as air bags became universal, their benefits grew.

Intense debate continued, however. First, safety experts maintained that side-impact air bags were needed to save even more lives. Secondly, the occurrence of several deaths apparently due to air bags deploying so fast that they killed occupants, led to questions about whether air bags needed to be depowered or even disengaged at the owner's request.

It was clear that while an air bag mounted on the steering wheel or dashboard saved lives in head-on collisions, it did little for side-impact crashes. Indeed, the sensors telling an air bag to inflate were mounted on the front of the car and would not be activated in the event of a side crash. The idea of a side-impact bag also ignited consumers' imaginations, and soon all the major car companies and their suppliers were rushing to develop systems. A variety of side-impact systems were proposed, but by 1998 only expensive luxury vehicles had them as standard features, and few people were requesting them as added options. Some side-impact bags inflate near the driver's or passenger's knees; others pop out from near the headrest or from a door panel. Volvo was among the first car manufacturers to actually offer such a system.

The second key question in the air-bag debate involves whether air bags should be depowered or even switched off at the consumer's request. This question arose out of reports that air bags were deploying at minor low-speed bump crashes, and striking occupants with such force as to injure or kill them. A review by

the Centers for Disease Control and Prevention (CDC) looked at 32 such deaths that had occurred between 1993 and 1996. Young children and small or elderly women seemed to be at particular risk.

The CDC reported that of the 32 deaths, 21 had occurred among children who were not properly restrained. Nine were children who had been in rear-facing child-safety seats in the front seat. The CDC found that while only one death occurred in 1993 when fewer than 1 percent of all vehicles had dual air bags, there were 18 such deaths during the first 11 months of 1996 when the percentage of dual air bags had risen to 11.4 percent. In addition, small or elderly women sometimes sat so close to the steering wheel that the inflating bag struck them, instead of merely cushioning them as they fell forward.

As media reports of such incidents mounted, the safety industry rushed to placate fears. Air bags, they pointed out, had saved far more lives than they had cost. There is confusion and there is concern about air bags. Unfortunately, most of the concerns are misplaced, Brian O'Neill, president of the Insurance Institute for Highway Safety, told the *Washington Post*. The simple act of buckling up eliminates the risk of serious injury from an air bag for almost all adults, and putting children in the back seat eliminates the risk entirely for children. The benefits of air bags, particularly if one follows those instructions, greatly outweigh any risks.

Two solutions have been offered to eliminate the potential problems air bags can cause. One is to "depower" air bags so that they inflate 25-35 percent slower (first-generation air bags deploy at a rate of 200 miles per hour). The answer to the question lies in determining the type of accident the industry hopes to guard against. Air bags were originally designed to save lives in high-speed head-on collisions, during which occupants are thrown forward at such speeds that a bag needs to inflate almost instantaneously to do any good. But a bag can inflate at a slightly slower rate—with less potential for injury from the bag—if the accident is a slower fender-bender type. Either option involves engineering compromises and trade-offs.

There was also discussion of a cut-off switch, which would allow an operator to disengage the passenger-side air bag. Safety regulators, however, feared that consumers would switch off air bags due to unfounded worries about their defects and, thus, compromise their own safety. In 1997 the Big Three automakers said they were installing cut-off switches on the passenger side of some, but not all, two-seaters and pickups, where babies or small children may be at risk in deployment. A few manufacturers, such as Subaru and Volvo, have refused to produce cut-off switches, insisting that their cars are safest with the air bags fully operational.

In late 1997 the government's National Highway Traffic Safety Administration (NHTSA) began allowing Americans who met certain narrow height or age requirements to have a cut-off switch installed in their cars. The process is cumbersome, however, requiring a formal application and approval procedure with the NHTSA itself. By the middle of 1998 the federal government had issued 30,000 cut-offs for approvals, but consumers soon found that government permission was not enough: many auto dealers refused to install cut-off switches, afraid they'd be held liable should an injury occur as a result. According to the NHTSA, of the estimated 25,000 auto dealerships nationwide, only 400 were willing to install cut-off switches in 1998. The Automotive Service Association advised its members not to install the devices, out of safety and liability concerns.

By spring 1998, Ford Motor Co. announced that all of its cars, as well as the Ford Windstar minivan, would be outfitted with side air bags over the following two years. Side air bags were initially offered as an option on the Mercury Cougar coupe, then became standard on the Lincoln sedans and other Ford luxury models. The company promised that by 2000, side bags would be added to all other models.

While the air-bag debate continued to be the loudest in the passenger restraint field in the late 1990s, renewed attention was also returning to earlier mechanisms such as head restraints and seat belts. Starting in 1969, the federal government had required head restraints—a primary defense against whiplash injuries—to be installed in all automobiles. Two studies by the Insurance Institute for Highway Safety, however, found that, by the late 1990s, head restraints had morphed into more comfort oriented "headrests," thus losing much of their protective function. In 1998 the NHTSA was considering new regulations that would raise the height of head restraints, and require them to lock in position so as to stay in place during an accident.

Car manufacturers in the late 1990s were also revisiting the idea of head restraint systems. In 1998 Saab became the first car maker to offer "active" head restraints, which actually cradle a passenger's head in the event of an accident. Unlike air bags, the system—developed in part by General Motors Corp. (GM) and expected to become more widely available in GM cars—does not require professional repair or resetting after a crash.

With all the technological advances, however, simply "buckling up" remained the primary and most effective passenger restraint system in any vehicle. The NHTSA estimated that using seat belts can reduce the risk of death in an accident by 45 percent for front-seat occupants. Unfortunately, less than three-quarters of passengers reported wearing seat belts, even though every state but New Hampshire required it by law.

Child-safety seats also provoked intense public debate in the mid- to late 1990s. This debate grew out of concerns that improperly restrained children, such as a baby placed in a rear-facing child-safety seat in the front seat, were at greater risk from inflating air bags, as well as from a crash itself. The CDC report noted that children were more likely to move around or lean forward in the front passenger seat, and that adult-sized shoulder belts may not fit properly. Also, because children are shorter than adults, they may be more likely to have their heads or necks struck by inflating air bags. Smart bags would likely reduce this danger, but in the meantime, the NHTSA and other safety groups endorsed the recommendation that all children ride restrained in the back seat in appropriate safety seats or wear safety belts.

These safety concerns were a boon to manufacturers of child-safety seats. Laws in all 50 states and the District of Columbia required that young children ride in safety seats. As consumers who rushed to buy the equipment soon learned, however, child-safety seats could be confusing and easily misused. The *Wall Street Journal* reported that nearly 80 percent of child-safety seats in cars and vans were used improperly, resulting in an estimated 600 deaths annually for children under the age of five. Further adding to the confusion was the multiplicity of models—dozens of child-safety seats were on the market in 1999.

To correct such problems, in 1997 the NHTSA proposed rules backing a General Motors design that would change the ways child-safety seats are attached to vehicles. The new design requires vehicle makers to install fixtures that anchor child-safety seats, through a series of straps and buckles, to the automobile. A drawback of the system is that it would raise the price of child-safety seats, from approximately $55 to more than $100, which could discourage some consumers from buying them.

Some vehicle manufacturers responded to safety concerns by building child-safety seats directly into the rear passenger seat of their vehicles. This, too, led to confusion. The *New York Times* reported that in July 1997 Chrysler Corp. was forced to send instructional videos to some 135,000 customers after receiving complaints that child seats built into its minivans malfunctioned. Complaints focused on whether restraints could retract and trap, or even choke, young children in their seats. No injuries or deaths were reported, but some parents were reported to have cut the belts away to free their children. Chrysler maintained there was no defect in the seat, and hoped that the videos would help resolve the problem. In 1998 General Motors produced a video called "Precious Cargo—Protecting the Children Who Ride with You" and offered it free to anyone at 4,000 Blockbuster Video stores around the country. The video showed parents how to correctly install various child-safety restraint systems.

The NHTSA reported that child-safety seats, when properly installed, reduce the risk of death in automobile accidents by 69 percent for children, and 47 percent for toddlers. In 1996 alone, the agency asserted, an estimated 365 lives were saved by child-safety restraint systems. More than half of all the children who died in car accidents in 1996 were completely unrestrained.

In addition to the proliferation of child-safety seat regulations, a number of states in the late 1990s began requiring children to ride in the back seat. Children in Florida and Minnesota must ride in the back seat until they are 16; in Tennessee they cannot ride in the front until they are 13. As often happens in the safety industry, cautionary steps taken by these states will likely domino throughout the country in the coming years.

Child-safety seats also figured in a long-running debate in the airline industry. For decades, airlines permitted children under age two to ride for free, if held in a parent's lap during flights. The National Transportation Safety Board had long recommended that aircraft restraint systems for toddlers be made mandatory. The Commission on Airline Safety and Security agreed with the recommendation and forwarded it to the Federal Aviation Administration (FAA). In the late 1990s the FAA reviewed the proposal, but expressed doubts about making such a requirement, saying that the benefits gained from child-safety seats might not outweigh the cost to airlines and passengers.

CURRENT CONDITIONS

Building on their growth during the 1990s, air bags remain the fastest-growing vehicle restraint systems. According to market research conducted by Providata Automotive Consulting, in 1999 about 81 million air

bags of all types were produced worldwide. Providata estimated that the number would approach 180 million by 2005, driven by continued deployment of side-impact devices and other newer air-bag systems.

Recent innovations include multistage air bags and so-called smart air bags that rely on sensors to determine the size and position of the seat occupant, as well as the speed of the collision, and adjust deployment accordingly. By 2004 just about every automaker will install smart air bags. For minivans and SUVs some manufacturers are also introducing air curtains that drop out of the vehicle's headliner to cushion occupants during a rollover accident.

Supplementing the smart air bags are smart seat belts. Armed with an array of sensors and other gadgetry, these belts instantly tighten upon collision to snug passengers into their seats, and then loosen slightly to prevent whiplash and rib injuries. In this way, the seat belts, many of which are equipped with small air bags of their own, serve to cradle the occupant throughout the duration of the accident.

Figures compiled by the Insurance Institute for Highway Safety suggested that 48 percent of cars and light trucks on U.S. roads in 2000 had driver-side air bags, and 35 percent had passenger air bags. Federal regulations have required passenger vehicles to come equipped with both driver-side and front-seat passenger-side air bags since 1998 (or 1999 for light trucks). Thus shipments of these air bags track closely with overall auto sales, and are not expected to grow as rapidly as those of optional devices. Side-impact bags, which aren't mandated by the federal government, are expected to supply most of the growth, rising from just 9 percent penetration in the U.S. new-car market to nearly 50 percent by 2005. Other optional air bags, such as for back seats, are expected to gain market share as well.

AIR BAGS SHOWN EFFECTIVE

Despite the small number of troubling mishaps with air bags, their overall benefits are well documented. As of 2000, the National Highway Traffic Safety Administration (NHTSA) reckoned that air bags saved about 5,300 lives in the United States since the agency first began monitoring their use in 1990. Most of the people saved—nearly 85 percent—were drivers, and the vast majority of them weren't wearing seat belts. Still, seat-belt statistics highlight why air bags are considered supplemental restraints: while air bags saved somewhere between 750 and 1,000 people a year in the late 1990s, seat belts were credited with saving 11,000 lives each year.

DANGERS REDUCED, NOT ELIMINATED

Fatalities associated with air bags remain a source of unease. As of early 2000 the NHTSA had confirmed 153 deaths attributed to air bags since 1990. Over half the victims were children, mostly young children who weren't adequately restrained by seat belts or child-safety seats. There were signs, however, that public outcry since the mid-1990s was helping reduce air-bag deaths. From a 1997 peak of 23 fatalities, the number of deaths of children who weren't in rear-facing child-safety seats fell to 11 in 1998 and 8 in 1999. Heightened public education on the dangers of air bags and on proper vehicle safety precautions for young children were believed to be factors; regulators also believed redesigned air bags with less forceful deployment helped bring the count down. The threat of side-impact air bags to children is comparatively unstudied, but they are believed to pose similar dangers and will require the vigilance of parents and automakers as the air bags enter the mainstream.

STANDARDS REACHED ON CHILD-SAFETY SEATS

Separately, a few initiatives have attempted to improve vehicle safety for children and address the weak points of existing child restraint equipment. Perhaps the biggest problem has been lack of standardization of child-safety products and a dearth of information about how best to use them. The NHTSA's Uniform Child Restraint Anchorage (UCRA) ruling was aimed at standardizing some features and restraint techniques so that parents have an easier time understanding the best kinds of restraints and so that children are optimally protected. Issued in 1999, the UCRA ruling decreed a standard set of three anchorages (two seat-level bars and an upper ring) in all new vehicles by September 2002. Makers of the seats themselves were told to produce compatible units. In a similar vein, the International Organization for Standardization (ISO), a United Nations affiliate that promulgates nonbinding standards for private industry, has adopted safety-seat standards under the stewardship of Volvo, which led an ISO working group on the matter.

INDUSTRY LEADERS

AUTOLIV

Autoliv Inc., based in Sweden, is a major supplier of air bags and seat belts in the United States (where it gets almost a third of its sales) and around the world. Founded in 1956, the company was originally a seat-belt manufacturer and gradually branched out into air bags and other restraint systems and components. It received a huge boost in the air-bag market in 1996 when it merged its air-bag business with that of Morton International, a top producer at the time. Autoliv now controls all of Morton's former air-bag operations. As of 1999, air bags were responsible for 70 percent of Autoliv's $3.8 billion in sales. Its air-bag sales that year were up 12 percent, driven by solid demand for front and side air bags. Autoliv has also been a trailblazer in the market for air-curtain devices, which are specialized side-impact air bags. With most of the world's largest automakers as customers, including the U.S. Big Three, the company produced more than a quarter of the world's air bags in 1999, including 24 million front air bags and 13 million side air bags.

BREED TECHNOLOGIES

Breed Technologies, of Lakeland, Florida, manufactures seat belts, air-bag systems, air-bag inflators, and electronic crash sensors. Through a joint venture in the late 1990s with Siemens AG, Breed was working on "intelligent" restraint systems that would "provide optimum protection for all occupants in every crash scenario," according to company literature. A string of acquisitions and mounting debt, however, forced the firm into Chapter 11 bankruptcy in 1999 as it struggled to restructure its finances. In 2000 the company agreed to be acquired the auto parts manufacturer Harvard Industries.

TRW INC.

Another longtime leader in the passenger restraint business, TRW Inc., of Cleveland, Ohio, is a diversified manufacturer of motor vehicle and defense systems. Its Occupant Safety Systems operations brought in just over $3 billion in 1999, essentially flat with the two previous years because of lower prices. Passenger restraint systems accounted for almost 18 percent of TRW's $17 billion in corporate revenues in 1999.

The first vehicle to feature TRW's complete occupant restraint system was the 1998 Mercedes-Benz M-Class. The company was able to draw on the technical expertise of its aerospace and defense lines to keep its air-bag technology on the cutting edge. TRW also enjoyed a healthy cash flow, which was expected to help as the company worked toward a totally integrated passenger safety system. The 1998 purchase of technology specialist Magna International, which specializes in air-bag and steering wheel operations, helped to solidify and extend TRW's position in the field.

In 1999 TRW signed 12 production contracts with six different automakers worldwide to develop advanced, integrated safety systems. These systems will feature enhanced pretensioners, energy management systems, buckle switches, dual-stage inflators, an inflatable "tubular torso restraint," and head and knee air bags.

FURTHER READING

"Agency Checks on a Problem with Air Bags." *New York Times,* 24 February 1998.

Autoliv Inc. *Annual Report 1999.* Stockholm, Sweden, 2000. Available from http://www.autoliv.com.

Brown, Warren. "Car Dealers Refusing to Switch off Air Bags." *Washington Post,* 1 June 1998.

———. "How to Buy a Safe Car." *Washington Post,* 22 February 1998.

Chartrand, Sabra. "Patents." *New York Times,* 22 September 1997.

Chew, Edmund. "Autoliv Diversifies as Airbag Profits Shrink." *Automotive News,* 8 November 1999.

DeMeis, Rick. "Seat Standard Boosts Child Safety." *Design News,* 20 March 2000.

"Ford to Offer Side Air Bags on All Models." *CNN Interactive,* 8 April 1998. Available from http://www.cnn.com/US/9804/08/ford.side.airbags.

"Government Sets Standards for Head Air Bags." *CNN Interactive,* 30 July 1998. Available from http://www.cnn.com/US/9807/30/new.air.bags.

Harler, Curt. "The Great Air Bag Cut-Off Debate." *AutoInc. Magazine,* March 1998.

Huelke, Donald F. "An Overview of Air Bag Deployments and Related Injuries." *Society of Automotive Engineers,* 1995.

"Inflatable Seat Belts Could Prove the Safest System." *Car Today,* April 1997.

Jensen, Cheryl. "Safety Devices That Can Save Your Neck." *New York Times,* 29 May 1998.

MacDonald, Sue. "You Need to Be a Savvy Consumer When Selecting a Car Seat." *Gannett News Service,* 29 May 1997.

Mateja, Jim. "Despite Critics, Airbags, Antilock Brakes Save Lives." *The Toronto Star,* 10 June 2000.

Meredith, Robyn. "Chrysler Sends out Videos after Child-Seat Complaints." *New York Times,* 26 July 1997.

Miel, Rhoda. "Side Bags Create Need for Plastics." *Automotive News,* 28 February 2000.

Naughton, Keith, and Joan Raymond. "Safety First." *Newsweek,* 30 October 2000.

Nomani, Asra Q. "Autos: Regulators Plan Safety Rules for Child Seats." *Wall Street Journal,* 13 February 1997.

"Operation ABC '98: Mobilizing America to Buckle up Children." *National Safety Council,* 18 May 1998.

Perez-Pena, Richard. "Albany Court Allows Suits over the Lack of Air Bags." *New York Times,* 17 June 1998.

Reed, Donald. "Child Occupant Protection a Priority." *Automotive Engineering International,* May 1999.

Russell, Christine. "Keeping Them Safe: With the Controversy over Air Bags, How Can Parents Protect Their Children?" *Washington Post,* 17 December 1996.

"Safety of Airbags Becomes Explosive Issue." *The Toronto Star,* 4 October 2000.

"Sensor for Smart Air Bags and Parking Assistance." *Automotive Engineering International Online,* December 1998. Available from http://www.sae.org/automag/top-prod/1298p11.

Sherefkin, Robert. "Financial Woes Close in on Breed." *Automotive News,* 14 June 1999.

"Some Importers Delay De-Powered Air Bags." *Ward's Automotive Reports,* 7 July 1997.

Wingo, Walter. "Depowered Airbags Appear Safe for Big Adults in Minor Crashes." *Design News,* 15 February 1999.

Pet Products and Services

Each year Americans lavish tens of billions of dollars on their animal companions. U.S. spending on pet-care products and services was expected to soar by 26 percent between 1997 and 2001, according to the Pet Industry Joint Advisory Council, hitting $28.5 billion by 2001.

Some attributed this growth to the rise in the 1990s of such pet superstores as Petco Animal Supplies Inc. and PETsMart, Inc., which offer thousands of pet items at each location, including many premium and specialty products unavailable in supermarkets and general discount stores such as Wal-Mart. PETsMart has also delved into the service market in a bid to create a national brand for the traditionally localized market for animal shots, grooming, training, and the like. More recently, the Internet has emerged as a key battleground for retailers, launching several start-ups that hope to give chains such as PETsMart a run for their money.

The expanding market for pet products and services has been broadly based. Such industry mainstays as pet food, which amounts to a third of industry sales, have racked up handsome gains in sales and profits, especially among premium brands. Meanwhile, new products and services promise to widen the sales base further. Some of the most encouraging new categories include dog litter and pet insurance.

ORGANIZATION AND STRUCTURE

The pet products and services business can be divided into three major segments—manufacturers, retailers, and services.

MANUFACTURERS

The manufacturing side is dominated by food makers such as Ralston Purina Co. and Iams Co. Food accounts for around 70 percent of all pet product sales, and more than a third of total pet spending in the United States. Other important manufacturing niches include cat litter, aquarium equipment and supplies, bird supplies, pet cages and transporters, leashes and collars, and of course, toys.

RETAILERS

The pet-retailing business has three subdivisions: large national superstore chains, independent pet stores, and general-line retailers such as supermarkets that carry pet supplies in addition to many other things. The first two subdivisions are sometimes collectively known as pet specialty retailers to distinguish them from supermarkets and general merchandise stores.

PETsMart Inc. and Petco Animal Supplies Inc. are the largest national retailers of pet supplies. Using a superstore format that may include more than 10,000 different products, these stores can often charge lower prices than others because of their negotiating power with manufacturers and because of efficiencies in their inventory and distribution systems. Indeed, they even boast their own brand of products that are specially made for them, often by manufacturers of familiar branded pet products. In the late 1990s and early 2000 both chains were still expanding rapidly, opening dozens of new outlets each year.

The industry also has numerous independent specialty retailers that operate on a local or regional level. These pet stores may be found in downtown shopping centers as well as in the smaller regional malls throughout the country. In general, these stores don't fare as well when the big chains roll in, but because of the generally buoyant market for pet goods, many have been spared from demise. Independent retailers also include in their ranks a handful of offbeat endeavors such as restaurants and bakeries for pets.

Competing with the large pet retailers for consumers' pet supply dollars are supermarkets and the giant discount retailers, such as Kmart and Wal-Mart, most of which aggressively market pet foods and a modicum of other basic pet supplies. In the past, specialty retailers have had an edge on such stores based on a wider breadth of offerings and, sometimes, on price. Because pet products are more profitable, however, than some of their other product lines, retailers such as Wal-Mart have been trying to move in on this territory, offering better prices and more selection.

SERVICES

Pet services include veterinary and health services, kennel and boarding services, and sundry minor activities such as pet grooming, training, walking, and sitting. Veterinary care is by far the biggest service category, representing about 48 percent of all pet expenditures. Most veterinary business is conducted by local operators, although one major national chain, Veterinary Centers of America, exists. That company's share, though, is less than 3 percent of the total veterinary services market. The American Veterinary Medicine Association reported 22,400 U.S. veterinary practices in 1997; the average practice grossed less than $480,000 per year.

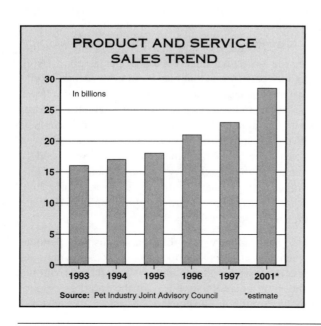

PRODUCT AND SERVICE SALES TREND

In billions

Source: Pet Industry Joint Advisory Council   *estimate

BACKGROUND AND DEVELOPMENT

Although American companies have been meeting the needs of American pet owners for decades, the major forces in the pet supply industry at the close of the 20th century were all of relatively recent vintage. Small independent retailers had been the norm until the build-up of nationwide chains and megastores in the 1980s and 1990s.

PETsMART WISES UP

PETsMart, headquartered in Phoenix, is the country's number-one retailer of pet supplies. It traces its origins to the vision of a California-based pet supply wholesaler who decided in the 1980s that he could make a lot more money if he opened his own retail outlets.

The wholesaler opened his first retail store in Las Vegas, Nevada, and hired Jim and Janice Dougherty to operate it. Called the Pet food Supermarket, the Las Vegas outlet did a booming business, leading soon to the opening of four more stores in the Phoenix area. The Doughertys, managing the fledgling chain of Pet food Supermarkets, met Ford Smith, a graduate of the Harvard Business School, and the trio decided to introduce the superstore format into the pet business. Using Toys "R" Us, Inc. as their model, they opened two PetFood Warehouses in Arizona in 1987. The following year another seven stores were opened in Arizona, Colorado, and Texas.

PetFood Warehouse was redubbed PETsMart in 1989. At about this time, Jim Dougherty left the company for health reasons, followed a short time later by his wife. PETsMart brought in Sam Parker, who had previously worked for Jewel Supermarkets, as chief executive. Parker redesigned the company's strategy as well as the layout of its stores. In the early 1990s the chain added a new range of services at its outlets, including grooming, veterinary services, and obedience classes. It also broadened its product range to include birds and fish. The company went public in 1993. In the late 1990s it operated more than 500 stores in the United States, Canada, and the United Kingdom.

PETCO TAKES A SLOWER PATH

Petco Animal Supplies, the number-two U.S. retailer of pet supplies, evolved from a San Diego-area veterinary supply store called Upco, which opened in 1965. When it decided to market a full range of pet supplies in the late 1970s, the company changed its name to Petco. By 1988 the company had grown to

Trends ONLINE PET STORES VIE FOR SPACE AT THE TROUGH

Several companies took pet wares to the Web in hopes of becoming the Amazon.com of the pet-products business. In the late 1990s venture capitalists and other investors poured hundreds of millions of dollars into such consumer sites, but as with many e-tailing ventures, early results were decidedly mixed.

The three leading Web contenders in early 2000 were Petopia.com, Pets.com, and PETsMart.com, but the market was quickly getting overcrowded. Despite its name, PETsMart.com is only partly owned by its namesake; in addition to a large stake owned by Idealab, an Internet business incubator, the site had planned a public offering in 2000, but backed off when the online pet market stumbled mid-year. Meanwhile, Petopia.com was aligned with Petco, which held a minority stake in it, and Pets.com was backed by none other than Amazon.com. A fourth site, Petstore.com, which had ties to pet-oriented content providers, was reportedly facing an uncertain future until it merged with Pets.com under the latter's name, and a fifth site, Allpets.com, was already retreating from the consumer side of the business. Some analysts believe that too many players got in too quickly.

According to one estimate, the online market for pet products could reach $700 million in the early 2000s, still only a nibble out of the estimated $15 billion market for pet products. A study by the NPD Group and Media Metrix found that only 14 percent of all pet owners made a purchase online, though almost all were aware of their online options. While food is the dominant product category in the overall market, nonfood items were expected to drive more growth in Web-based sales, particularly in the shorter term. According to the NPD Group, pet toys were the most common item purchased in late 1999, followed by staple food, treats, and accessories.

As of 2000 PETsMart.com appeared best positioned to dominate Internet pet retailing, much as PETsMart Inc. has done in the traditional marketplace. The NPD survey found that PETsMart.com handily attracted the largest audience, outdistancing the next-best site by 16 percentage points. Pets.com, which waged an aggressive TV ad campaign, was second, trailed at a distance by Petopia.com, and Petswarehouse.com.

In a sign of how heated the competition had become, in early 2000 PETsMart announced a sweeping competitive refund and credit program. The new policy allowed consumers to return goods bought from any Web site or traditional retailer in exchange for cash or credit toward a PETsMart purchase. The material impact of this strategy was expected to be negligible for all parties, though. It came on the heels of a series of generous discounts, cash giveaways to new customers, and other gimmicks by pet sites aimed at leashing greater market share.

Later that year, however, the market shakeout that many analysts insisted had to occur finally hit the online pet products market. One of the most dramatic foldings was that of Pets.com, which enjoyed exceptional brand recognition due to its successful television commercials featuring the popular Socks hand puppet. Spectacularly high shipping costs, heated competition, and lack of consumer commitment to online pet shopping finally forced this industry powerhouse out of the game. Also, despite its powerful backing, Pets.com lacked the strong bricks-and-mortar support enjoyed by its surviving competitors. By the end of the year, only two players—Petopia.com and PETsMart.com—maintained a significant presence online.

---

about 40 stores and was purchased jointly by the Spectrum Group and the Thomas H. Lee Co. Shortly after the takeover, Petco acquired two pet supply chains, more than tripling its number of stores.

By early 1990, however, the company found itself in financial hot water with mushrooming advertising costs. Under a new management team, headed by Toys "R" Us veteran Brian Devine, the company launched a new policy of everyday-low-prices for its premium pet foods, which increased traffic and stimulated sales of other products as well. The company stabilized financially and in 1994, with nearly 200 stores, went public.

VCA FINDS HEALTH IN THE SERVICE MARKET

One of the largest networks of full-service animal hospitals in the United States is operated by Veterinary Centers of America, Inc. (VCA). Founded in 1986, VCA's goal from the start was to become a leader in the field of veterinary services. In its second year, VCA acquired the West Los Angeles Veterinary Medical Group. VCA has continued to grow through the acquisition of leading veterinary hospitals across the country. To finance its expansion, the company successfully completed its initial public offering of stock in October 1991.

The company joined with Heinz Pet Products in early 1993 to introduce a premium line of pet food called Vet's Choice. In 1996 VCA merged with Pets Rx and the Pet Practice. That same year the company set up the largest veterinary diagnostic laboratory in the United States. Nine veterinary diagnostic laboratories across the country were consolidated to form Antech Diagnostics. VCA's laboratory services are available to veterinarians across the country, who also are encouraged to consult with VCA's staff of more than 50 board-certified veterinary specialists.

CURRENT CONDITIONS

In the late 1990s Americans owned about 120 million cats and dogs, although estimates vary on whether there are more cats or dogs. This figure, staggering as it is, does not include the hundreds of thousands of other pets, including tropical fish, birds, reptiles, and amphibians that Americans have taken to their hearts.

The Pet Industry Joint Advisory Council, a trade group, estimated that American spending on pet-related goods and services would reach $28.5 billion in 2001. This would culminate a decade of solid growth, with industry sales soaring a total of 80 percent between 1993 and 2001. On an annual basis, that works out to a compound average of nearly 7.5 percent a year for the entire period. Industry experts expected growth would ease in the early 2000s, sliding to an average of 5 percent a year. Those figures don't include the market for horse products, which was estimated at another $8 billion in the late 1990s.

FOOD AND SUPPLIES REMAIN STRONG, INNOVATIVE

The array of pet products and services available to pet owners in the United States and abroad continues to grow. Among the products that debuted at the annual Pet Products Trade Show in Atlanta in the summer of 1998 were a number of interesting items likely to turn up soon on the shelves of pet stores across the country. These included Wordy Birdy, from Wordy Birdy Products, a $30 tape recorder that plays continuously (or until the tape wears out) a bird owner's recorded message of the phrase or phrases he would like his pet to learn. Another product sure to gladden the hearts of cat owners everywhere is CatFinder, offered by Pet Friendly for $40. This product is a radio-remote device that attaches to the collar of a cat so that its owner can track it down in a pinch. Pet-Ag introduced its $7 Emergency Feeding Kit that contains everything one might need to feed an orphaned raccoon, kitten, porcupine, or other small mammal.

With the growing market in pet foods, specialized segments such as pet bakeries and herbal supplements for dogs and cats have emerged in the late 1990s. A gourmet dog food manufacturer, Canine Caviar Inc. of Anaheim, California, went into business in 1996 and two years later had franchises all over California expected to bring in $3 million in 1999. Several ca-

nine bakeries chains operate in California and the West, with business expected to grow nationally and internationally. Along with the late 1990s obsession with alternative medicine for people came homeopathic and herbal veterinary medicine. While the number of nontraditional veterinarians is not known, the practice seemed to be growing, according to a 1999 article in the *Arizona Republic*. High-tech medicine such as organ transplants, laser surgery, chemotherapy, and insertion of pacemakers is increasingly being used on animals as well.

RETAILERS CLAW FOR MARKET SHARE

For the pet superstores such as PETsMart and Petco, a significant percentage of their revenue is derived from the sale of pet foods. The competition for the pet food dollar tightened considerably after 1994, when Wal-Mart introduced a premium brand of pet food at a price notably lower than the major brands. Many of the other major discounters followed Wal-Mart's lead. From mid-1997 to mid-1998, sales of pet food at the major discount chains rose more than 16 percent. Regular supermarkets, which until the 1990s had been the primary source for U.S. pet food purchases, took note of the competition from the discounters and began introducing their own brands of pet food and sharply discounting some of the name brands they carried.

Perhaps the most surprising phenomenon in the pet supply market has been the resilience of the small, independent pet shops. Although many were predicted to fold under the pressure of competition from the pet superstores, most of these independent pet shops have demonstrated amazing staying power. The superstores generally don't deal in the sale of dogs and cats, although some of them participate actively in pet adoption programs. The small neighborhood pet shops almost all sell cats and dogs, in addition to fish, birds, and other small pets. Many pet owners, it turned out, felt more comfortable dealing with the pet stores from which they had originally acquired their pets, guaranteeing these smaller retailers a decent level of repeat business.

SERVICES CONTINUE GROWTH

Veterinary Centers of America (VCA) by the late 1990s had become the largest provider of pet care in the United States. In addition to its network of freestanding veterinary hospitals and its chain of clinical laboratories, VCA owned an interest in Vet's Choice, a joint venture with Heinz Pet Products, and an interest in Veterinary Pet Insurance Inc., the nation's biggest pet health-insurance company.

Facade of the Three Dog Bakery in Rochester, MI, specializing in canine treats. *(Kelly Quinn)*

PET INSURANCE ON AN UPTREND

Pet insurance is a relatively new business and one that is expected to show growth as both the scope and the cost of veterinary care climbs sharply.

A small but growing number of American companies have begun offering pet-related benefits to their employees. American Management Systems, an information consulting firm based in Virginia, pays the kennel bill for its employees who must board their animals when they are sent out of town on business. Many companies offer to pay a portion of employees'

veterinary bills. Though less than 1 percent of all pets in the United States—including 3 percent of all dogs and cats—were covered by insurance as of 2000, this seems to be a growing market, as evidenced by increasing business at several firms that specialize in veterinary insurance.

INDUSTRY LEADERS

Although supermarkets and the large discount chains compete in segments of the pet supply market, particularly pet foods and the most basic pet maintenance products such as collars, leashes, and flea sprays, the specialty pet-retail segment is divided between two large superstore chains and hundreds of independent stores.

PETsMART HOLDS LEAD

The industry leader is PETsMART, headquartered in Phoenix, Arizona. After going public in 1993, it began to expand rapidly through acquisition, adding 40 stores in 1993, 50 more in 1994, and acquiring a Midwest chain of pet superstores, Westheimer Companies. PETsMART moved into Europe in 1996, but its stores didn't fare as well in that market.

As of 2000, PETsMART operated 525 outlets in the United States and Canada, with plans to open some 50 more in 2001. For its fiscal 2000, its sales stood at $2.1 billion, unchanged from the previous year due to the sale of its troubled U.K. stores, which the company finally sold to Pets At Home for $40 million. Same-store sales in the United States posted a modest increase on the year. To jump-start growth, PETsMart has been rolling out new equine departments at dozens of stores to tap into the horse-care market, which has been traditionally ignored by many pet retailers. Pet food accounts for nearly half the company's revenues, and its vast array of pet supplies and services makes up the rest.

PETCO CATCHING UP

Number two in the pet supply market is Petco Animal Supplies Inc., headquartered in San Diego. With more than 500 stores throughout the United States, Petco gets a little better than 40 percent of its total revenue from selling premium pet foods. The company's selection of products numbers about 10,000, including pet toys, grooming supplies, collars, leashes, aquariums, pet bedding, and pet enclosures. Like its larger rival, Petco does not sell cats and dogs, although it does offer fish, birds, and rep-

---

About... A FEW OF THE INDUSTRY'S LESS COMMON OFFERINGS

A Chinese pug named Frodo was the first canine ever to be neutered and implanted with a solid silicone testicular implant. The procedure took place in Castro Valley, California, where Dr. Cynthia Edelman performed a three-minute procedure on the 16-month-old pug. Implants, made of solid silicone, have the texture and feel of a gummie bear, according to Gregg A. Miller, inventor and president of Missouri-based CTI Corp.

Neuticles, as they are called, are 100 percent safe and will never flake, leak, or cause adverse reaction, Miller said in a press release. Five sizes of the false testicles are available for canines. They are sold to veterinarians for $89 to $129 per pair for the silicone models, and $25 to $32 a pair for the polypropylene version. Neuticles are also available for horses and bulls.

Pets can also be pampered with gourmet pet food: how about pasta for dogs? Thompson's Pet Pasta Products, Inc., owned by Coldwater, Kansas, native Richard Thompson, specializes in making dog food out of pasta that resembles meatballs and ziti. Thompson knows about pasta, having built up the American Italian Pasta Co., 74 percent of which he and investors sold in 1991 for $50 million, according to a 1998 article in *Food Processing*. When traveling in Italy, he conceived of the idea to cook pasta for pets when he saw Italians cooking pasta for their dogs.

Though the company lost $13 million in 1996, according to *Forbes,* Thompson's Pet Pasta Products had grown to $20 million in 1998. Some of the products include beef-flavored and bacon liver-flavored Woof-a-Roni, which are chewy pasta bones; Labonies, which are crunchy bones flavored with real lamb; and Petzels, chewy beef-flavored twists.

Avid Canada, a microchip company, has invented PETtrac, a worldwide computerized tracking system for companion animals. To activate the system, a chip is injected in the animal. Then the microchip number is entered into the patient's records and is recorded on a patient identification sheet that is forwarded to the company. Each participating animal is registered in the PETtrac database, using the clinic as a tracking site. The company has numerous back-up systems to guarantee continuous tracking.

sales, helped restore it to profitability after taking a $2.3 million loss a year earlier. In May 2000 the company agreed to be bought out by Leonard Green & Partners and Texas Pacific Group.

VCA TOPS SERVICES

In health care for pets, Veterinary Centers of America Inc. (VCA) leads the U.S. market with more than 200 animal hospitals in 29 states. VCA's hospitals account for over 70 percent of the company's revenue. The hospitals' services range from basic services such as vaccinations, sterilization, and routine exams to specialized surgeries for most household pets.

In addition to its hospitals, VCA operates the country's largest network of veterinary laboratories. Its 14 diagnostic labs provide services to more than 13,000 animal hospitals in 49 states. The labs provide a full range of diagnostic services, including blood, urine, and tissue testing.

Headquartered in Santa Monica, California, VCA owns a 50 percent interest in the Vet's Choice premium pet food brand, a joint venture with Heinz Pet Products. The company also owns a share in Veterinary Pet Insurance Inc. VCA posted net income in 1999 of $22.4 million, a gain of over 37 percent from the previous year. Revenue in 1999 totaled $321 million, up 14 percent from 1998.

PROCTER & GAMBLE: A NEW GRAVY TRAIN?

The diversified consumer products behemoth Procter & Gamble Co., based in Cincinnati, made a startling entry into the premium food business in 1999 with its purchase of Iams Co., a leading premium food maker. Dayton, Ohio-based Iams, under the Iams and Eukanuba labels, controlled an estimated 27 percent of the premium foods market and had sales of more than $800 million. Procter & Gamble's strategy was to expand the Iams distribution channel to include mass-retailers such as Wal-Mart. Previously, Iams was distributed only through veterinarians and pet stores.

Cutting Iams's prices was expected to be part of the equation, as Procter & Gamble calculated it could make up the forgone unit revenue with volume. Mass-merchandising Iams was expected to unsettle the lucrative and fast-growing premium segment, where Procter & Gamble faces its longtime rival in the soap business, Colgate-Palmolive, maker of the market-leading Hill's Pet Nutrition line. Eukanuba, Iams's

---

tiles. It also follows PETsMart's lead in sponsoring pet adoption programs.

For the year ended 29 January 2000, Petco reported net income of $22 million on revenue of $990 million. The chain's impressive 18 percent gain in revenue, underlined by an 11 percent rise in same-store

---

top-notch label, was expected to remain in the specialty distribution channels.

WORK FORCE

Employment opportunities in the pet supply business range from entry-level sales jobs and main-office clerical positions through top-level management positions with the leading superstore chains. Within the veterinary-care segment of the pet industry, jobs range from support personnel through veterinary surgeons and specialists.

As of 2000, PETsMart employed 19,800, an increase of more than 25 percent from its employee rolls of 1997. The number-two pet superstore chain, Petco, employed 10,200, up by almost 75 percent from just years earlier. Veterinary Centers of America reported a total payroll of just over 3,465 employees, up over 45 percent from 1997.

AMERICA AND THE WORLD

The pet industry is alive and well outside the United States, particularly in Canada and the United Kingdom. Britons, in particular, have been noted for their obsession with their pets. Of the two big pet superstore chains, only PETsMart has ventured outside the United States, and it apparently regretted doing so. In 1998 the company had 84 retail outlets in the United Kingdom and 12 in Canada. Two years earlier it had acquired Pet City Holdings PLC, which operates more than 50 stores throughout the United Kingdom; amid sluggish sales, however, PETsMart sold its U.K. holdings in 1999.

Pet insurance, a concept that has begun to catch on in the United States, is also making headway in Canada and the United Kingdom. So far, however, fewer than 1 percent of Canadian pet owners have opted to insure their pets. In the United Kingdom, with a total of more than 50 million pets, about 15 percent of pets have been insured by their owners, according to 1998 data from Euromonitor.

Pet Healthcare Services, a U.K. pet insurance specialist, in early 1999 launched an online information service for pet owners. The Web site offers a wide range of information about caring for one's pets and provides an e-mail notification service to remind pet owners when vaccinations or flea control treatments are due for their pets. The market for pet products and services is booming in the United Kingdom and was estimated in 1998 at about $3.2 billion annually. The market for pet food reportedly grew by about 20 percent between 1994 and 1998.

RESEARCH AND TECHNOLOGY

The pet industry, like almost every segment of the economy, is turning to high technology to develop products for pets and pet owners. One product certain to appeal to any pet owner who has ever been traumatized by the loss (temporary or permanent) of a pet that strayed away is offered by a Canadian firm. The PetNet microchip, barely larger than a grain of rice, is implanted under the skin of a pet for identification purposes. Pets that have been "chipped" are registered with PetNet, a registry of all pets that have been implanted with such a microchip. Anitech Enterprises Inc. of Markham, Ontario, which developed the PetNet microchip, said the technology makes it much easier to locate lost pets, sparing both pet owners and pets a lot of grief.

FURTHER READING

Barker, Colin. "Dot-Coms Must Pull Their Socks Up." *Computing,* 23 November 2000.

Biddle, Frederic M., and Khanh T. L. Tran. "PETsMart Widens Refund, Credit Policy to Include Goods Bought from Rivals." *Wall Street Journal,* 14 February 2000.

Bidwell, Carol. "Furry Friends, Big Bucks: Pets Generate Billion-Dollar Industry; Doting Owners Eager to Make Animals' Lives the Cat's Meow." *Arizona Republic,* 2 March 1999.

Branch, Shelly. "Procter & Gamble Plans to Expand Pet food Distribution for Iams Brand." *Wall Street Journal,* 6 January 2000.

Cheng, Kipp. "Best of Breed." *Mediaweek,* 22 November 1999.

Earnest, Leslie. "Dogs Collar the Market in Pet Pampering: Animals: From Bakeries to Veterinarians, Businesses Increasingly Are Catering to Pets, Especially Canines." *Los Angeles Times,* 12 November 1998.

Eig, Jonathan. "Inside Scoop: Behind the Race to Make a Dog Litter with the Right Stuff." *Wall Street Journal,* 23 February 2000.

Garber, Joseph R. "Albums and Alpo." *Forbes,* 26 July 1999.

Gribble, Roger A. "Pet-Store Sales Leave Room for Large, Small Shops, Industry Council Says." *Wisconsin State Journal,* 7 October 1999.

Harrison, Bette. "New Gadgets May Be Useful to Your Faithful Pampered Pet." *Atlanta Journal and Constitution,* 26 June 1998.

Hof, Rob. "Pets.com: Putting a Sock On It." *Business Week,* 20 November 2000.

Hunter, George. "Owners Increasingly Pampering Pets." *Gannett News Service,* 22 March 1999.

Kellner, Tomas. "Fido's Insurance." *Forbes,* 30 November 1998.

Marks, John. "Tail of the Pampered Pooch." *U.S. News & World Report,* 17 May 1999.

Polsky, Carol. "Beyond the Goldfish Bowl: Today's Elaborate Home Aquariums Include Everything from Shark Tanks to Mini-Coral Reefs." *Newsday,* 19 November 1998.

"Sock It To Me: Pet Lovers Know Their Sites, But They're Not Buying." *Internet Retailer,* July 2000.

White, George. "Like Cats and Dogs; Pet Supply Superstores Have Got a Fight on Their Hands." *Los Angeles Times,* 24 July 1998.

PHARMACOGENOMICS

The newest and hottest sector of the pharmaceutical industry takes offense at the notion that, deep down, all humans are pretty much the same. In fact, of course, about 99.9 percent of the DNA strands spelling out an individual's genetic code is identical to that of the next person. But it is on that tiny .1 percent variation in the human genetic makeup that those in the field of pharmacogenomics have pinned their hopes for the key to a revolution in health care.

Pharmacogenomics is the study of how human genetic variations, known as polymorphisms, affect the way in which pharmaceuticals react with patients suffering similar illnesses. Understanding that different patients with similar ailments or symptoms respond differently to the same drugs, pharmaceutical companies, acting in concert with firms busily working on uncovering the complete human genome, have certainly come to recognize a potential gold mine when they see one.

The pharmacogenomics revolution promises an avalanche of new drugs, often referred to as tailor-made medications, targeting smaller and smaller markets. Investment money has poured in from a variety of sources, especially pharmaceutical firms, on the hunch that this burgeoning field will completely overhaul the way in which medicines are researched, developed, and prescribed.

Combining the research of the pharmaceutical industry and the rapidly expanding body of knowledge surrounding the human genome, pharmacogenomics works toward the development of predictive medicine—treatments that identify the genes in question for the patient's condition and determine the nature of the patient's response, with an eye toward improving future medicines to more specifically target a patient's genetic profile.

Thus, pharmacogenomics constitutes a radical shift from the one-size-fits-all approach traditionally employed to treat diseases, often with high failure rates, and is thus highly favored by drug companies. The hit-or-miss nature of the pharmaceutical industry results in millions of dollars and years of time lost to doomed drug developments that fail to succeed in clinical trials and never receive regulatory approval. Moreover, even the best drugs on the market yield successful results in about only 80 percent of all targeted patients, while some are effective in as little as 20 percent.

Pharmacogenomics, however, promises to change all that. Since pharmacogenomics has as its starting point the particular genetic data that can end up causing the problems for drugs later (in the form of failed patient responses or adverse side effects), drug companies can be more assured of betting on a sure thing right from the start, realizing dramatic cost savings, and expanded profit margins, in the process. While pharmacogenomics will reduce development costs, retail prices will likely increase significantly compared with traditional generalist medicines.

The field itself was poised for significant growth alongside these developments. Pharmacogenomics data gathering was worth about $1 billion in 1998, according to *Medical & Healthcare Marketplace Guide,* and by 2002 was expected to reach $3.5 billion.

ORGANIZATION AND STRUCTURE

The most important fact of life for the pharmacogenomics industry is that different people's bodies respond differently to the same drugs. Absent that, the industry would not exist. People's systems metabolize and react to drugs differently, in some cases resulting in uncomfortable, harmful, or even fatal side effects. In fact, drug side effects constitute one of the leading causes of death in the United States, at approximately 106,000 fatal cases each year, according to the *New York Times,* and result in an additional 2.2 million nonfatal reactions. The primary regulatory oversight for pharmaceuticals, including those developed through pharmacogenomics, is performed by the U.S. Food and Drug Administration, which rigorously reviews new drugs developed for specific genetic groupings.

Building especially on the massive Human Genome Project, genomics involves identifying and determining the function of specific genes. Pharmacogenomics simply takes this knowledge to the next step, applying it to the development of novel chemical compounds geared toward accommodating individual patients' specific genetic configurations, thereby accounting for defective or mutated genes that vary from what is considered a "normal" genetic profile.

Using the latest pharmacogenomics techniques, firms, based primarily within the biotechnology industry, develop DNA profiles of patients that can be stored and displayed on an electronic chip or similar platform in order to determine who will benefit from a specific drug. Generally, such companies are devoted either to the direct development of new drugs based on such information or to the storing and selling of the information itself, or both. Several leading pharmacogenomics firms maintain extensive databases storing details on genetic sequences and their precise meaning. Drug firms then pay for access to the database, and use the information to more accurately target specific patients in their research and development programs.

One of the most commonly employed techniques in pharmacogenomics involves the identification of tiny variations in DNA strains located in the minuscule DNA units called single nucleotide polymorphisms, or SNPs (pronounced "snips"). SNPs determine whether an individual is predisposed to certain diseases and whether he or she will respond positively, negatively, or not at all to a particular drug.

For example, some immunosuppressive drugs developed for the treatment of cancer, including aza-thioprine and 6-mercaptopurine, can generate a potentially fatal toxin when they interact with mutant forms of the thiopurine methyltransferase gene. Pharmacogenomics can help drug makers take such factors into account before the development process. By understanding the nature of the mutant genes, drug firms can alter the chemical composition of the drugs so as to render them harmless to the system. Diagnostic tests for such genes therefore hold some of the earliest commercial promise for the genomics industry as a whole.

Research and development is the most important, and the most frustrating, component of the pharmaceuticals industry. Success stories are few and far between. Only about one out of every 10 drugs entering clinical trials ever sees the marketplace, while the remaining 90 percent either fail to attain regulatory approval or stall in unsuccessful clinical trials.

Drug companies also pay top dollar for the privilege of success. The average research and development expenditure as a percentage of sales for drug companies rose from 12 percent in 1980 to 20 percent in 2000, totaling about $240 million per drug, a figure that they would obviously like to slash considerably. Analysts expect pharmacogenomics to be a key element in these efforts. By streamlining the development and regulatory process, pharmacogenomics could result in cost savings of about $60 to $85 million for each approved drug. Furthermore, some analysts expect that genomics, combined with advances in combinatorial chemistry and molecular-design techniques, could cut the duration of the preclinical development stage by as much as half.

The prescription process will be similarly altered. For example, the most popular and successful cancer drugs available in 2000 resulted in only about a 30 percent success rate, while doctors prescribing an appropriate treatment to an individual patient are generally forced to rely on a good deal of guesswork based on sorely inadequate information about a patient's predisposition to certain side effects. With a streamlined database of drug compounds and genetic details, however, combined with the patient's genetic profile, the guesswork can be greatly reduced, if not eliminated altogether.

BACKGROUND AND DEVELOPMENT

For decades, it has been well understood that genes underlie patients' reactions to medicines, and scientists known as pharmacogeneticists devoted themselves to the study of variations in drug responses between patients. Such studies, however, were generally confined to one gene at a time. It wasn't until the mid-1990s, when research into the human genome began to yield dramatic results, that pharmacogeneticists had a real solid grounding on which to base their studies of a system's reaction with chemical compounds. Once the methods for studying the entire genome set, rather than only specific genes, were developed, the new field of pharmacogenomics was born, taking off around 1997.

The broadest back on which the pharmacogenomics industry has hitched a ride is the Human Genome Project, the enormous, government-funded global effort to decode the entire 3-billion-digit sequence of the human genetic code. Begun in 1990, the project really bore fruit in the mid- and late 1990s as high-speed computers revealed ever-larger bits of the code, and research began into what exactly the code meant. A first, incomplete draft was released in summer 2000; the genome was expected to be entirely decoded by 2001, with a comprehensive map to follow in 2003.

In the meantime, however, dramatic new developments were underway. In the mid-1990s, the French genomics firm Genset S.A. mapped approximately 60,000 SNPs over the human genome, shortly thereafter teaming up with Abbott Laboratories Inc. to pinpoint variations aimed at eliminating the side effects of Abbott's Zyflo asthma drug. The development of DNA chips by Affymetrix, Inc. of Santa Clara, California, propelled the industry ahead forcefully with the chips' ability to act as tiny laboratories capable of picking up microscopic variations in genetic data contained within a small sample of DNA.

One of the first practical applications of pharmacogenomics rolled out in the late 1990s when Judes Poirier at McGill University in Montreal isolated the cause of inconsistent reactions to drug treatments for Alzheimer's disease in inborn genetic variations. The risk of developing Alzheimer's disease is marked by variations of a gene known as ApolipoproteinE (ApoE), a fact determined years ago. Poirier, however, noted that variations in responses to drug treatments were rooted in the same genes. Patients carrying the E4 variety (ApoE4) failed to show rates of improvement from the Parke-Davis drug Cognex that were as successful as those patients with the non-E4 versions (ApoE2 and three-gene complexes), and indeed often experienced worsening conditions. In early 1998, Poirier augmented his findings with the discovery that gender added to such variation, whereby women with non-E4 showed dramatic improvements while men of the same type experienced little change. These discoveries coincided with rapid developments in combinatorial chemistry and genetic screening, leading to a number of new applications for genomics in the pharmaceuticals industry.

CURRENT CONDITIONS

Since the latest techniques and technologies in this young industry are scattered widely, strategic alliances flourished in the late 1990s and early 2000s. Pharmaceutical companies have bought or partnered with biotechnology firms in droves. While many such deals are for a fairly long duration, usually three to five years, the erratic nature of the biotech industry has given due pause to some pharmaceutical giants, which have insisted on clauses enabling them to exit the deal in a hurry if the development seems destined to fail. Moreover, as the euphoria over the emerging developments subsides, drug companies are likely to become significantly more selective in their strategic alliances.

As a result, most analysts expect that biotechnology firms specializing in pharmacogenomics are in for a sustained wave of consolidation in the early 2000s. To attract the investment of increasingly choosy pharmaceutical companies, such firms will likely seek to generate economies of scale, expanded pipelines, and thicker technology portfolios by merging with and acquiring each other. Moreover, such alliances may prove necessary in order to gain leverage in negotiations with drug firms.

So far, however, cooperation has been far-reaching. In 1999, 11 pharmaceutical companies announced the formation of a $45-million-public, nonprofit genome-mapping consortium in an effort to facilitate the pharmacogenomics revolution and get information on the crucial single nucleotide polymorphisms (SNPs) into the public domain. The SNP Consortium was originally devoted to the development of a map made of 300,000 SNPs, with an eye toward streamlining the process of bringing tailor-made drugs to market. By late 2000, the consortium was well underway, having identified over 1 million SNP variations—not bad considering its original was goal to reach 700,000 SNPs by early 2001. The first fruit to develop out of the SNP Consortium's SNP discoveries was the collaboration between Third Wave Technologies, Inc. and Novartis Pharmaceuticals Corp. to develop a panel of 10,000 SNP assays, which will be used to better understand genes and SNPs to target specific diseases and develop therapies.

SNPs act as signposts on the genome map, occurring once every thousand nucleotides throughout the 3-billion-nucleotide human genome. Thus there are approximately 3 million SNPs in the genome. A small proportion of SNPs produce amino-acid alterations that carry some observable functional weight, and are thus the focus of pharmacogenomic attempts to isolate variations.

In order to study the function of SNPs, a physical genomic map of a healthy individual is compared with that of an individual suffering from a particular ailment. In this way, researchers can pinpoint differences in SNPs. Any conspicuous SNPs may tip researchers off to a potentially varied gene near the SNP that could be at the root of the ailment.

Once troublesome genes are identified, pharmacogenomists can either target the gene directly with new drug compounds or can build on knowledge of the gene's function to alter existing compounds so as to better facilitate a patient's metabolism, absorption, or excretion of the medicine, thereby staving off harmful side effects.

Pharmacogenomics could provide an added benefit to the pharmaceuticals industry by bringing back to life drugs that were shot down in clinical trials for their negative side effects on certain patients, under the recognition that the drugs could in fact be marketed to patients with genetic profiles that were not at risk.

Still, while the pending pharmacogenomics revolution in health care attracted scores of research projects and mountains of investment dollars, as of late 2000, only a small handful of human genes had been specifically defined as to function. Furthermore, patient testing remains an expensive undertaking, to the tune of about $2,000 per test.

Moreover, some critics contended that pharmacogenomics would result in a market full of "orphan" drugs—defined as medicines reaching markets of fewer than 200,000 people. Traditionally, such minuscule drug markets were so unattractive to pharmaceutical firms that the Food and Drug Administration was inclined to offer tax breaks to firms producing them. The market may not become as fractured as that, however, as some proponents note that, for any particular family of drugs created through pharmacogenomics, there may be only a handful of potential genetic profiles, since, despite variation in DNA even among identical twins, human beings share almost all the same genetic information housed within the 100,000 or so human genes.

CONCERNS OVER IMPLICATIONS AND POTENTIAL FOR MISUSE

Like the wider study and implementation of gene technologies, however, pharmacogenomics makes some squeamish. Ethical considerations abound, and some critics fear what such technology could potentially lend itself to. For instance, Glaxo SmithKline announced its plans to bring to market a treatment for patients suffering from HIV that combines a newly licensed drug, known as Ziagen, with DNA chips—tiny particles laced with a sample of the patient's blood that will ideally determine the extent of the patient's genetic responsiveness to the drug. Such a treatment was heralded as a sort of new paradigm whereby the effectiveness of drugs is enhanced and the likelihood of harmful side effects reduced. The ethical debate, however, centers on the control of the findings of such genetic testing, known as medical response profiling. The range of access and ownership of such personal information will likely spur heated debate for years to come.

While early pharmacogenomics developments will require genetic testing primarily only for significant drug reactions, a series of such tests could result in the amassing of a great deal of genetic data on an individual, at which point very crucial privacy concerns arise. Critics fear the potential for such information to be used to label persons as "genetically deficient" and discriminate along those lines.

To guard the privacy and genetic information of patients, Arthur L. Holden, the chairman and chief executive of the SNP Consortium, launched a new company called First Genetic Trust Inc., which will act as the first "genetic bank," storing DNA in individual accounts. The genetic data in those accounts can only be released to medical researchers with the account-holder's permission. Now that pharmacogenomists require DNA samples for research, the time was ripe for setting up an institution to help individuals overcome their reluctance to hand out their genetic makeup.

INDUSTRY LEADERS

Based in Cambridge, Massachusetts, Millennium Pharmaceuticals Inc. is one of the top firms engaged in the race to complete the map of the human genome, and is a leader in the pharmacogenomics sector, maintaining scores of development deals with large drug companies. The firm entered into a $32-million research alliance with Bristol-Myers Squibb Co. in 1999 by which Millennium's subsidiary, Millennium Predictive Medicine, will develop drugs to improve the response level of cancer patients by focusing the drugs on the genetic makeup of specific tumors. In addition to cancer remedies, Millennium works on treatments and diagnostics for a range of conditions, including diabetes, obesity, and asthma, and has research and development deals with Bayer, Eli Lilly and Co., and Hoffmann-La Roche, Inc. The company augments its research into single nucleotide polymorphisms (SNPs) with a focus on genetic intermediaries, such as proteins and RNA, for variations that can be targeted for treatment. With a payroll of 950 employees, Millennium boosted sales 37 percent in 1999 to reach $183.7 million.

Incyte Genomics Inc. of Palo Alto, California, provides databases of gene sequences and related analytical software to drug companies and research firms by subscription. The company aims to develop databases cataloging polymorphisms for every single gene, to be used in the development of individually tailored medicines. Incyte counts among its clients virtually all of the world's major pharmaceuticals firms, which maintain subscriptions for access to Incyte's databases, such as LifeSeq. Founded in 1991, the company also works on deciphering the human genome through Incyte Genetics, a separate business formed in 1998. Also in 1998, Incyte acquired DNA-chip manufacturer Synteni. Employing 1,100 workers, Incyte generated revenues of $157 million in 1999, up 16.5 percent from 1998. With patents on 300 genes and over a thousand new patents pending, the company has a large insurance policy for future growth.

Human Genome Sciences, Inc. (HGS) of Rockville, Maryland, was founded in 1992 and both develops drugs and proteins and provides data to fuel its partners' drug discovery programs. HGS's proprietary portfolio includes drugs for cancer, heart disease, and other diseases. The firm maintains partnerships with SmithKline Beecham and Merck & Co., among others, and uses its gene-sequencing technology to develop its database of human and microbial genes, generating royalties when pharmaceutical firms manufacture drugs based on information derived from the database. By 2000, the company had no products on the market, but it boasted a substantial pipeline, including three drugs in clinical trials. It also received a patent in early 2000 for a gene that could play a vital role in understanding how HIV attacks and exploits human cells. HGS saw its revenues decline 17.2 percent in 1999 to $24.5 million, and employed over 500 workers.

Genset S.A. of Evry, France, was a leading pioneer in pharmacogenomics, building on its 1994 mapping of all the human chromosomes to develop a more comprehensive mapping of genes aimed at drug development in early 1998. The firm formed a partnership with Abbott Laboratories Inc. of Abbott Park, Illinois, in 1997 to run pharmacogenomics tests for companies with drugs in clinical trials. With a payroll of 475 employees, Genset focuses primarily on the information side of pharmacogenomics, contracting with drug companies to provide data to assist in the development of medicines for cancer, heart disease, mental illness, osteoporosis, and other illnesses. The company's NetGene database of about 60,000 DNA sequences fuels its research and development services. In 1999 Genset raked in revenues of $27.9 million, up from $27.1 million the year before.

The world's major pharmaceuticals firms play a pivotal role in the pharmacogenomics industry, representing the primary customer base for the genomic research and often working in collaboration with pharmacogenomics specialists to bring drugs to market. For example, Glaxo SmithKline, a product of the pending merger of drug giants Glaxo Wellcome and SmithKline Beecham, was an early investor in pharmacogenomics, including its 1993 investment of $125 million in HGS in exchange for access to the HGS's database of genetic sequences. Glaxo upped its involvement by forming a partnership with Incyte Pharmaceuticals four years later, this time aimed at the production of gene-based diagnostic products. Bristol-Myers Squibb, meanwhile, announced its intention to apply pharmacogenomics throughout its therapeutic operations. In November 1999, the firm partnered with Millennium Predictive Medicine to develop pharmacogenomic tests aimed at the treatment of cancer and the tailoring of therapeutic products for specific tumor populations. Nearly all the other big pharmaceuticals firms, including Hoffmann-La Roche, Novartis, Merck, and Pfizer Inc., also partner with pharmacogenomics firms for drug development.

AMERICA AND THE WORLD

The overwhelming bulk of the pharmacogenomics industry's development has taken place in the major industrialized countries, especially the United States. The increasing specialization and more focused targeting of drug treatments promised by pharmacogenomics, however, has many critics sounding alarm bells about the industry's relationship with less-developed countries. As the pharmaceutical industry positioned itself for a massive shift toward pharmacogenomically developed tailor-made drugs, some observers feared that, since research and development of general, lower cost drugs will inevitably decline in favor of more expensive target-market drugs, simple economics could lead companies to direct their efforts to particular genetic profiles in the wealthier nations where there exists a greater potential return. Meanwhile, critics fear that those in poorer nations could face a diminished supply of quality medications.

RESEARCH AND TECHNOLOGY

Developments in information technology are the cornerstone of advances in genomics and pharmacogenomics. To make for smoother, more efficient information flow, information technology networks and, especially, bioinformatics, have been quickly developed, in the process integrating information on an industry-wide and cross-disciplinary scale. Bioinformatics is the computer data management that systematizes the discovery and analysis of pharmacogenomics research. Generally, huge databases of genetic sequences and descriptions allow for quick and easy access available over intranets for easy comparison and cross-referencing with emerging discoveries. Robot and computer technology have also been deployed to scan the genes of patients in drug trials.

Bioinformatics integrates and simplifies the vast overflow of new information provided by such diverse fields as combinatorial chemistry, throughput sequencing and screening, DNA-chip technology, and structure-function analysis through the implementation of an industrial-scale information-technology platform. In this way, pharmacogenomics can further strip down the research, development, and regulatory processes. By installing intranets to integrate research and development databases, Datamonitor estimated that the average amount of time a drug spends in research and development could drop from the current 14 years to 10.5 years.

Research technology for pharmacogenomics also got a boost in March 2000 with the licensing by Intergen Co. of its Amplifluor technology to Amersham Pharmacia Biotech, which will use it to augment Amersham's Sniper SNP scanning platform. The Sniper system, set to launch in late 2000, can process some 500,000 genotypes per day, far surpassing any previous technology. The Amplifluor system injects some muscle by allowing for SNP detection directly from genomic DNA.

FURTHER READING

"Agreement Entered for First High-Density Set of Gene Markers." *Genomics & Genetics Weekly,* 28 July 2000.

Becker, Cinda. "Advances in Genetics Give Physicians Ability to Tailor Drugs to Patients' Unique Makeup." *Modern Healthcare,* 28 August 2000.

Bhandari, Man, Rajesh Garg, Robert Glassman, Philip C. Ma, and Rodney W. Zemmel. "A Genetic Revolution in Health Care." *McKinsey Quarterly,* Issue 4 (1999).

"Bioinformatics." *Medical & Healthcare Marketplace Guide,* 1999.

Brewer, Richard B. "You Bet!" *Forbes,* 31 May 1999.

"Bristol-Myers Squibb Companies Establish Unique Pharmacogenomics Alliance in Cancer Treatment." *Biotech Week,* 29 November 1999.

Carey, John. "This Drug's for You." *Business Week,* 18 January 1999.

Fischer, Joannie. "Snipping Away at Human Disease." *U.S. News & World Report,* 23 October 2000.

Fisher, Lawrence M. "The Race to Cash in on the Genetic Code." *New York Times,* 29 August 1999.

———. "Smoother Road from Lab to Sales; DNA Technique Aims to Predict Whom a Drug Will Benefit." *New York Times,* 25 February 1998.

"Gene Test Drugs Pose Ethics Dilemma." *Guardian* (London), 14 April 2000.

Griffith, Ted. "Mapping the Way." *Boston Business Journal,* 17 December 1999.

"Pharmacogenomics—A New Discipline." *Chemist & Druggist,* 9 October 1999.

Philipkoski, Kristen. "Closer to Tailor-Made Meds." *Wired News,* 1 March 2000. Available from http://www.wired.com/news/print/0,1294,346600,00.html.

Pollack, Andrew. "New Venture Aims to Guard Genetic Data." *New York Times,* 9 October 2000.

Rosenberg, Ronald. "Millennium in $32m Pact with Bristol-Myers; Predictive Medicine Will Be Focus of Research Alliance." *Boston Globe,* 11 November 1999.

Saltus, Richard. "Tailor-Made Drugs: Genome Research May One Day Allow Doctors to Prescribe the Medicine That Best Fits Each Patient's Genetic Profile." *Boston Globe,* 20 April 1998.

"Single Nucleotide Polymorphisms and the New Drug Discovery Paradigm." *Medical & Healthcare Marketplace Guide,* 1999.

Stix, Gary. "Personal Pills." *Scientific American,* October 1998.

Stokes, Rob. "I-Biology: The Next Drug Discovery Tool." *Pharmaceutical Technology Europe,* September 1999.

Wade, Nicholas. "Tailoring Drugs to Fit the Genes." *New York Times,* 20 April 1999.

Weiss, Rick. "The Promise of Precision Prescriptions: Pharmacogenomics Also Raises Issues of Race, Privacy." *Washington Post,* 24 June 2000.

PHOTONICS

Much as in the field of electronics before it, the applications for photonics technology were poised to kick start a minor technological revolution at the start of the 21st century, extending from telecommunications to computers, from energy generation to imaging systems, and from home entertainment to optical storage. And as the research is refined and the technology matures, a robust market was predicted to arise. The photonics industry as a whole was expected to reach $15 billion by 2004, according to the Photonics Development Center.

The most explosive growth and widespread application of photonics technology is in the field of telecommunications, specifically in optical fiber systems. Thanks largely to developments in photonics, telecommunications providers have expanded carrying capacity at a dramatic pace over the last several years, with even greater gains expected in the near future as the vast potential of photonics begins to be realized. Most analysts fully expected telecommunications operations, in the near future, to forsake electronics entirely in favor of photonics. In the meantime, however, most photonics technologies have both electronics and photonics technologies working in harmony, with photons picking up the slack in those areas where electronic technology is sluggish.

ORGANIZATION AND STRUCTURE

Photonics generates and harnesses light and other radiant energy forms, measured in photons, to power technological operations. The science of photonics re-

places the electron, now dominant in electronics, with the photon. Photons are uncharged particles of light; they are thus not affected by electromagnetic interference. Where electrons require barriers such as wires to keep them from interacting with one another, the photons in streams of light can cross paths with no adverse consequences. Scientists see in them an opportunity to move bits of data at speeds greater than anything previously known in the world of electronics. Photonics uses light for information processing and communication; light is emitted, transmitted, deflected, amplified, and detected by sophisticated optical and electro-optical instruments and components, lasers, fiber optics, and sophisticated hardware and systems.

Photonics research in the late 1990s was geared toward communications, computer processing, and the generation of energy. Researchers experimented with optical memory, storage devices, computer buses, optical network interfaces, and photon-based processors, all of which could drastically speed up communication and computing processes.

Though they are often passed through fiber-optic cable, photons can be beamed in all directions, thus providing a great number of parallel, interconnected data channels. Data transmission is "clean," with information traveling unhindered on independent channels of light. Given the neutral nature of photons, nonoptical techniques are required for putting data onto these beams of light, and so-called photonic circuits still depend on electronic technology. Photonics also means more bandwidth, with photonic processes measured in trillion hertz (terahertz), as opposed to the fewer than 10 billion hertz (gigahertz) reserved for electronics. Given this high bandwidth and capacity for interactivity and parallel information processing, photonics researchers envision devices that are cheaper, faster, and lighter than anything ever delivered by electronics.

Of those firms specializing in photonics technology, the vast majority were very small, distinguishing themselves primarily through technological differentiation. From there, the most common practice to date has been to appeal to the major companies opening themselves to photonics operations in specific fields, such as telecommunications, and enter into a strategic alliance or position the company for acquisition. New photonics start-ups were finally emerging as a Wall Street trend by early 2000.

BACKGROUND AND DEVELOPMENT

In the 20th century, electronic technology revolutionized areas as varied as medicine, manufacturing, and defense, and sparked new industries such as computer science and telecommunications. By harnessing the electron, scientists are able to store, process, and transmit information through wires. Electrons are interacting, charged particles whose power—electricity—is manifested in electronic products such as the computer. The electronic integrated circuit (the chip), which often contains millions of rapid information-processing transistors, is the foundation for all electronic products—everything from computers to missiles to videocassette recorders. While the advances wrought by electronics have been nothing short of revolutionary, electrons do have their shortcomings. Given the charged nature of electrons, the transmission of data runs the risk of "cross talk," noise sparked by their unwanted interaction. To be effective, electrons must pass through wires and, while a chip might hold millions of transistors, it can only accommodate hundreds of wires to transport the information they contain. In essence, there is more information being produced than there is capacity to transport it, so information traffic "clogs up." In order to overcome such "bottlenecks" in electronic processing, scientists are integrating photonics and optoelectronics (a hybrid technology combining electronics and photonics) into electronic products.

Researchers first explored photonics in the early 1950s, but experiments using light from the Sun and from mercury arc lamps proved unsuccessful. Laser and the transistor were born a scant decade apart, yet it was the transistor that would triumph from the 1960s on. Early laser experiments for optical computing led many scientists to conclude that high heat dissipation and inadequate materials made photonics an improbable endeavor; but advancements in laser technology (in particular the use of room-temperature laser) encouraged more vigorous research into optics. With the advent of semiconductor lasers and optical fiber in the early 1970s, photonics research gathered momentum, particularly in the communications industry, where industry leaders saw the implications for high-speed data transmission. That need for speed, accompanied by the growing view that electronic computers left little room for evolution, sparked a renewed photonics industry that began to flourish only in the mid- to late 1990s.

In 1999, the Holy Grail of many photonics researchers remained the perfected "photonic crystal." Much as semiconductor chips can manipulate electricity, this artificial structure can transmit light, bend it, and make it turn corners with a minimal loss of light. Scientists have already been able to bend light in the laboratory, but photonic chips are still on the workbench. Despite the revolutionary applications of photonics in telecommunications, current communication systems require electronic circuits at either end; light signals must pass through these circuits to be converted to electrical signals—a process that slows down the communication process. The development of all-photonic circuits was expected to bring tremendous increases in speed and efficiency.

CURRENT CONDITIONS

Perhaps indicative of the industry's imminent success was the launching by several entrepreneurs of Incubic LLC in Mountain View, California, in spring 2000. Recognizing the shortage of incubators for the photonics industry, the partnership, incorporating the resources and know-how of photonics, telecommunications, and laser-technology interests, was established to provide initial capital and management resources to photonics start-ups, whose numbers were snowballing by 2000. A number of industries were beginning to register the effects of photonics research, none more so than telecommunications.

TELECOMMUNICATIONS

The rush toward fiber-optic networking will be the main impetus for the rapid expansion of photonics technology in the 2000s. The market for photonics switches and switch matrices was expected to jump from $119.1 million in 1998 to $4.11 billion in 2008, according to a report from the market consultancy ElectroniCast Corp. Telecommunications applications spearheaded the movement of photonics technology out of the laboratory and into the commercial market.

Demand for high-performance optical switches pushed communications firms into strategic alliances with firms grounded in photonics research. Nortel Networks Corp., for instance, bought the Sunnyvale, California-based Xros Inc., maker of the X-1000 optical cross-connect switch, in March 2000 just a week after that product was rolled out. Other firms developed their own teams to introduce optical switches tailored to their existing systems, as when Siemens AG of Munich, Germany, rolled out the TransXpress Optical Service Node, which the company boasted could handle the connection of up to 2,160 wavelengths, according to *tele.com* magazine.

Optical fiber is small, light, durable, resistant to corrosion, and difficult to tap. In addition, its broad bandwidth makes it the media of choice among long-distance carriers. Among the crucial advances in photonics has been the development of the optical fiber amplifier and error correction; with this technology, electrical impulses are sent to a local phone office where a switch modulates a laser to convert those impulses into optical form. Wave division multiplexing (WDM) is another technology helping to augment the capacity of optical fibers; with this technique, multiple laser pulses of different hues are sent simultaneously down a singular tiny fiber, increasing a fiber's capacity dozens of times.

In 1999 Lucent Technologies Inc.'s Bell Laboratories unveiled a single-laser, time division multiplexing system that would quadruple information transmission to 40 gigabits per second—enough to send 500,000 phone calls per second over a single fiber-optic cable. At a time when companies were pushing toward a record of 1,000 fibers per one-inch cable, this meant radically faster and cheaper data transmission, which the industry needed to keep up with a growing number of consumers and their demands for high bandwidth capable of sending data, voice, and video on demand. (Also see the essays in this book entitled Telephony and Voice Mail Systems.)

With demand for high-speed optoelectronic integrated circuits expected to grow, greater sales of photonic switches won't be far behind. Given the ubiquity of the technology, individual consumers would receive a double advantage: drastically reduced communications charges and radically improved data throughput speeds. The most optimistic of photonics proponents contended that, with the expansion of bandwidth to almost unthinkable levels, the cost of overseas telephone calls could be reduced to that of calls down the street, while users could even project entire holographic images of themselves into others' living rooms.

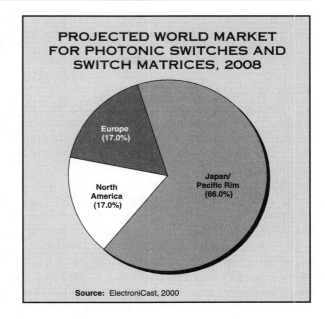

PROJECTED WORLD MARKET FOR PHOTONIC SWITCHES AND SWITCH MATRICES, 2008

Europe (17.0%)

North America (17.0%)

Japan/ Pacific Rim (66.0%)

Source: ElectroniCast, 2000

While the optical switches facilitating the capabilities of WDM were improving all the time, however, that very improvement was beginning to generate a sort of technological arms race that, observers surmised, the switches were destined to lose. Vendors, recognizing these advancements in switching capabilities, will be forced to expand their bandwidth continuously until the point when their demand outpaces the photonic switches' abilities to deliver. Ironically, then, a bottleneck is likely to develop as a result of the implementation of the optical switches. Analysts expected this crunch to occur as the current generation of switches was overwhelmed by about the middle of the 2000s.

The existing generation was mainly dependent on the conversion of optical light to electricity in order to send signals to an outward-bound port. While innovative new technologies were on the drawing board, a number of obstacles impeded their rush to market. For instance, according to the director of the photonics research laboratory at Lucent's Bell Labs, Dr. Alastair Glass, the amount of cable worldwide increases about 15 percent each year, but by the end of the 1990s bandwidth on a single fiber doubled annually.

Still, researchers were doing their best to stave off a gap between demand and delivery. Dense WDM (DWDM) and ultra-dense WDM refined the process and dramatically boosted the amount of traffic that could be accommodated by a single fiber. In addition, optical amplification alleviated the periodic electronic conversion necessary for most fiber-optic systems. The North American market for DWDM was set for takeoff in 2000, expected to jump from $3.5 billion to

$7.7 billion that year, and reaching sales of $26 billion by 2004, according to the telecommunications consulting firm RHK.

OPTICAL STORAGE

The more photonics research translates into affordable consumer products, the more individuals and institutions can expect to see revolutions in the way they store their information. Optical storage technology has grown considerably since the early 1980s. Among the most ubiquitous optics products available today is the compact disc. With the growing presence of personal computers, consumers in the late 1990s were using CD-ROM (compact disc read-only memory) on a regular basis and increasingly were receiving computer software on CD-ROM, capable of holding hundreds of megabytes of data. WORM (write once, read many) disc technology postdated the CD-ROM and has a storage capacity measured in billions of bytes (gigabytes). In the late 1990s many institutions began replacing paper and microfilm storage with optical storage. Digital video disc (DVD) technology also materialized commercially, along with stand-alone DVD players and DVD computer peripherals. In late 1998 Fujitsu Computer Products of America unveiled the world's first 1.3 gigabyte 3.5 Magneto-optical drive. Magneto-optical media is resistant to moisture, shock, dust, and other dangers and can be rewritten more than 10 million times, making it an appealing long-term storage option. In late 1999, Blue Sky Research of San Jose, California, introduced a new photonic design known as Super Seek Time (SST) Optical Actuator that promised to afford CD and DVD players a level of performance on par with a magnetic hard drive, but with a higher degree of durability since the photonic system eliminates physical contact. The SST actuator was expected to find use in interactive video games played directly through a DVD or CD in real time, and eventually in Internet servers. Some predict that erasable optical memory will eventually replace magnetic disks as the storage medium of choice. (Also see the essay in this book entitled Optical Data Storage.)

PHOTONIC COMPUTERS

For computers, optical photon switching holds a degree of promise commensurate with the fiber-optics revolution in telecommunications. The most attractive potential was in the realm of speed, of which there seems never to be enough when it comes to computing. For that reason, next-generation optical switching was a potential gold mine for the computer industry. *PC Magazine* suggested that by 2005 a standard desktop computer could run at a clock speed of 10 gigahertz, while featuring data storage and resolution far greater than anything currently offered. Inspired by the possibilities of light, researchers dream of the day where computers consist of several processors communicating and connecting with one another in massive parallel interconnections based on photonics. The final goal of such technology was to refine it to the point that computations are performed at the speed of light. In addition to computer-to-computer fiber-optic links, photonics research is evolving to provide solutions at increasingly minute levels: links between circuit boards inside computers, chip-to-chip connections on individual circuit boards, and optical connections within the chips themselves.

The ultimate success of all-optical computing will likely rest in the successful development of all-optical processors. In 1999 there were already patents on the world's smallest laser, photonic light-emitting, and microresonator devices; jointly, these three devices are the basis of a light-based "photonic" logic circuit expected to revolutionize computers. Photonic devices are similar to current semiconductor integrated circuits, so thanks to microcavity technology and the devices' planar structure, they can be built into current semiconductor wafers, integrating more high-speed features on a single chip than electronics ever could. With the use of lenses, lasers, and holograms, some organizations are currently developing optical computers. The ultimate success of all-optical computing, however, will likely rest in the successful development of all-optical processors. (Also see the essays in this book entitled Holography, Lasers and Laser Applications, and Parallel Processing Computers.)

TELEVISION

Electro-optic technology may also transform television, with the traditional boxy television set being replaced by the flat panel display; this technology is also applied to computer monitors. The billion-dollar flat panel display industry exists thanks to beam-steering applications, a key component derived from photonics research. Electro-optics may also mean greater consumer choice and freedom from the restrictions of local cable television providers: with photonics technology, electrical TV signals turn into optical signals capable of traveling through fiber optics over long distances. If the industry's plans to deliver high-definition television with two-way communication pan out, many buildings and homes may see their traditional copper wire replaced by fiber cable—an expensive proposition that will require tearing out old network lines. (Also see the essay in this book entitled Video Displays.)

MILITARY

In addition to providing commercial products based on photonics technology, researchers are combining light beams and electrical pulses in various military-related applications. Given the durability of cable, and light's immunity to electromagnetic interference, weapons systems-based photons rather than electrons may be more reliable in battle conditions. A proposed high-speed optical digital computer network will have effects on avionics, satellites, and ground platforms. The fiber-optic, high-speed Synchronous Optical Network has been adapted for military data and voice transmission. The U.S. Air Force and AT&T worked toward perfecting a ruggedized optical connector for potential use in helicopters and tactical fighters. The military has also shown an interest in photonic memory as a means of creating databases of interactive battlefield visualization systems; the current synthetic aperture radar technology requires equipment so large that the electronics and their power supply must be carried in separate trucks. With photonic technology—particularly dense, system-on-a-chip photonics and free-space optical components—such battlefield tools could conceivably fit in one's hand. Such companies as VLSI Photonics currently work toward achieving such computing density. The U.S. Defense Advanced Research Projects Agency was in charge of the Photonic Wavelength and Spatial Signal Processing program, which aimed at developing photonic technologies that cut down on the enormous data sets returned by existing sensing and spectral imaging techniques.

MICROSCOPY

With the aid of photonics technology, scientists are better prepared to view the world at the microscopic level. At Hamamatsu Photonics, Dr. Hiroyasu Itoh developed the framing streak camera in 1992. With a shutter speed of 50 billionths of a second and capabilities for taking pictures at less than a millionth of a second, this photonic camera allowed him to capture clear, detailed photos of the process by which the pores of different types of cells open and close. Physicists at Cornell University have successfully applied photon physics to monitor the cellular presence of serotonin, a primary brain chemical. This new microscopy has revolutionized biochemistry, allowing biologists to track molecular movement deep inside living cells, without destroying or damaging the cell. Whereas previous microscopy precluded the study of certain molecules, this new method gives visibility to previously unobservable molecules by employing the additive energies of multiple photons

to spark fluorescence in them. Multiphoton instruments were previously the sole creations of researchers, but Bio-Rad Laboratories, Inc. received license from Cornell to commercialize the instrument. In 1999 physicists learned to determine the position of fluorescent molecules in a solid matrix with a resolution finer than a light wavelength; by probing with an ultraprecise frequency laser, they could study how chemically identical, adjacent fluorescent molecules react to light.

INDUSTRY LEADERS

There are literally thousands of companies using photonics, though not all are engaged exclusively in the field. Lucent Technologies Inc., Telcordia Technologies, and Corning are some of the major players in the photonics industry. Despite the presence of giant corporations dedicating part of their research and development costs to photonics, a substantial share of the cutting edge research was carried out by smaller photonics specialty firms, which were starting up in droves by 2000.

Lucent Technologies, with 153,00 employees and 1999 sales of more than $38.3 billion, was a telecommunications powerhouse. Locally, the U.S. company was the top producer of software and telecommunications equipment, providing everything from wireless networks and switching and transmission equipment to telephones and business communication systems. Globally, Lucent was a leading developer of telecommunications power systems and digital signal processors. The company sold primarily to telecommunications network operators such as AT&T. Its products were chiefly the result of technology provided by Bell Labs. Bell Labs had among its laboratory projects an ultra-dense wave division multiplexing system that will use only a single laser to open up thousands of channels at a time. The company's LambdaRouter, which incorporates microelectrical mechanical systems technology, was rolled out in late 1999. The Lucent/Bell Labs optical switch reflects the photons with 256 tiny mirrors situated on a silicon chip.

Telcordia Technologies, formerly Bell Communications Research, was created after the breakup of AT&T in 1984 as a research institution for the so-called Baby Bells. The company changed its name to Telcordia in 1999, the year after it became a subsidiary of the defense contractor Science Applications International Corp. Telcordia provided software to about

80 percent of U.S. telecommunications networks and was a key provider of telecommunications software globally. Annual sales jumped 20 percent in 1999 to reach $1.2 billion. The company dedicated one-tenth of its efforts to research, with its 6,000 employees engaged mainly in consulting and software programming, though its focus was broadened in the late 1990s to include Internet-based technology.

Despite its reputation for consumer glass products, Corning Inc. was the world's leading producer of fiber-optic cable, having sold all but 8 percent of its glassware and cookware operations. In 1999, the company's 17,000 employees (down from 20,500 in 1997) produced $4.3 billion in revenue, of which nearly 10 percent derived from photonics and another 43.6 percent came from optical fiber. Through its Specialty Materials unit, the company manufactured laboratory equipment and emission control substrates. The company invested heavily to secure its strength in photonics components, merging with Oak Industries and purchasing Siemens AG's optical fiber and cable unit. The company also purchased British Telecommunications' Photonics Technology Research Center for $66 million. Corning's optical switches use liquid crystals to split wave division multiplexing (WDM) streams and deflect them into separate channels.

CIENA Corp. was a rapidly growing telecom equipment maker, providing dense wave division multiplexing (DWDM) systems, such as its Multi-Wave model, for giants such as WorldCom, Sprint, and Teleway Japan; its DWDM systems give optical fiber the ability to carry up to 40 times more data than usual. CIENA more than doubled its work force in the late 1990s, maintaining a payroll of 1,930 employees by 2000. Revenues in 1999 totaled $482.1 million, of which 45 percent were derived from sales overseas.

Nortel Networks, based in Brampton, Ohio, was the dominant player in the DWDM field, controlling about 57 percent of the North American market. In addition, Nortel boasted 38 percent of all North American optical transport sales. With 76,700 employees, the firm was the second-leading overall manufacturer of telecommunications equipment, after Lucent. A string of acquisitions in the late 1990s and early 2000s propelled Nortel to the top of the optical telecommunications industry. The company boasted that roughly three-fourths of all Internet traffic is funneled through its equipment. Nortel achieved revenues of $22.2 billion in 1999, up from $17.6 billion the year before.

Pioneer DR. DAVID PAYNE

Though photonics is largely the business of research teams at universities and giant corporations, there are individuals who stand out for their contribution to the field. In 1997 *Forbes* called Dr. David Payne "perhaps the leading scientist behind two key inventions in photonics over the past decade and a half."

A physicist at Britain's University of Southampton, Payne was a key force behind the optical fiber amplifier and error correction. The former facilitates the magnification of a light pulse's reach, amplifying light without having to convert it to electrical pulses and back again, and tripling data transmission speeds yearly. The latter is an enhancement to the amplifier that corrects distortions that may occur when light pulses are stretched to their limit in distance and speed. Both of these technologies can be implemented in fiber already buried underground. Thanks largely to Payne's work, the university's Optical Research Center (ORC) enjoyed a reputation as one of the world's leading photonics research centers. Payne went on to help launch Southampton Photonics Ltd., a U.K. startup that designs and manufactures fiber-optic components for DWDM and telecommunications firms.

AMERICA AND THE WORLD

The United States is one of the world's largest consumers of photonics technology and has been researching photonics for nearly half a century. In some areas, however, the United States lagged far behind sales in other regions. For instance, of the $119.1 million worldwide photonic switch and switch-matrices market in 1998, the United States accounted for only 14 percent, commensurate with Europe's share but far behind Japan and the Pacific Rim's 70 percent share. Ten years was expected to show little difference in this area, with the U.S. and European shares each rising to only 17 percent as the enormous East Asian population overhauls its telecommunications infrastructure.

European companies operating through the Advanced Communications Technologies and Services (ACTS) program, meanwhile, formed the ACTS Photonic Domain, through which 30 separate research efforts were underway by 2000. Projects ranged from the broad implementation of massive optical networks to experimentation with new technologies for photonic switches. The United Kingdom, in particular, produced a number of companies devoted to expanding bandwidth for fiber-optic telecommunications, including Bookham Technologies and Kymata.

In Texas, the STARTech technology business development center announced the creation of the Photonics Development Center, meant to be a key global center for the optical communications market for attracting capital and personnel to the photonics industry. The $3 billion in funding came from the University of Texas at Dallas, industry giants such as WorldCom, Nortel Networks, Alcatel, ADC Telecommunications, and Fujitsu Network Communications, and a group of venture capital firms.

RESEARCH AND TECHNOLOGY

Despite nearly a half-century of related research, the photonics industry was basically in its infancy at the end of the 20th century. While many photonic products were already on the market, much research remained to make photonics a more viable commercial option in the future. Researchers were investigating in many different areas, with many different techniques. Photonic crystals, photonic switches, photonic processors, and quantum information technology were just a few of the technologies brewing in laboratories worldwide.

PHOTONIC CRYSTALS

The appeal of photons is also their handicap. Despite the greater freedom of movement that photons enjoy, they are not as easy to channel as electrons. Microelectronics researchers have been able to control electrons with the help of semiconductors: by using an electric field, scientists can control the movement of electrons across a semiconductor's "band gap." This technology has provided the base for minute solid-state transistors and for the advancement of electronics in general. Photonics research, on the other hand, has lacked a similar light "semiconductor" and spent most of the 1990s looking for a way to isolate and manipulate certain wavelengths of light.

One of the major barriers to developing photonics crystals was size; an effective crystal would have to be several times smaller than the ones used in integrated circuits. Researchers at Bell Communications Research used a drilling technique to design a crystal that filtered out certain wavelengths of microwave radiation. Others built photonic crystals from colloids (fine solid particles suspended in liquid). In 1997 electrical engineers and physicists at the Massachusetts Institute of Technology used X-ray lithography to build the first photonic crystal to function at an optical wavelength. By drilling strategically spaced, micro-

scopic holes in a silicon strip, they were able to trap light of the infrared wavelength—just what the telecommunications industry uses in fiber optics. With this new technology, light can be bent and controlled much in the way electrons are in integrated circuits. In March 2000, the Santa Clara, California-based firm SpectraSwitch Inc. introduced its WaveWalker photonic switch that incorporated liquid crystal cells to polarize light signals and direct them with an optical device.

PHOTONIC SWITCHING

As internetworking capabilities become a primary concern among telecommunications service providers, the demand for optical backbone equipment will flourish. Companies such as NEC and Lucent took the lead in developing photonic routers to integrate into an open-switched core network. Speed, of course, remains the central concern for manufacturers of photonic switches. The most advanced optical switches in production in 2000 routed traffic on a packet-by-packet basis in a matter of milliseconds, but that was still far too slow for the expected demand in the coming years, according to the New York consulting firm Light Reading Inc., which contended that the process would need to be accomplished in nanoseconds.

Meanwhile, the purely photonic optical switch became a more practicable reality. The start-up Calient Networks developed an architecture known as scalable control of a rearrangeable and extensible array of mirrors, through which the company planned to roll out an all-photonic network that bypasses the need for electronic infrastructure. Astarte Fiber Networks Inc. of Boulder, Colorado, likewise marketed its Star*Switch all-photonics switch, installing it within the MCI WorldCom (which became known as WorldCom in 2000) network in 1996.

Most optical switches produced as of 2000 incorporated microelectrical mechanical systems (MEMS), or micromachine technology, which redirect light signals via tiny mirrors. According to the research firm System Planning Corp., the market for MEMS-based optical devices was one of the key growth sectors in optical switching, with sales expected to grow from nothing in 1999 to $950 million by 2003. (Also see the essay in this book entitled Micromachines/Nanotechnology.)

For the time being, the competition between emerging all-optical photonic switching and the traditional optical-to-electrical-to-optical conversion will continue, with the potential benefits promised by an all-optical technology forestalled by the immature stage of development so far attained. There was universal agreement among industry players and analysts, however, that all-photonic switching technology would eventually emerge as the dominant format in fiber-optic telecommunications.

QUANTUM INFORMATION TECHNOLOGY

In 1998 applied physicists at Stanford University reached a long-sought goal: they developed a "single-photon turnstile device," the first device capable of creating a beam of light composed of a steady stream of photons. By overcoming the noise caused by microscopic variations in ordinary light, the device paved the way for scientists to advance in such nascent, cutting-edge fields as quantum information technology. This new research area brings new computation and encryption techniques with major implications for the future of mainstream computers and telecommunications devices. Quantum computers, for example, could solve problems millions of times more quickly than the most powerful supercomputer currently on the market. A research team from IBM Corp., the Massachusetts Institute of Technology, the University of California-Berkeley, and Oxford University has reportedly built the world's first computer modeled on the principles of quantum mechanics.

Photonics advocates dream of the day when information processing is entirely optical, whereby light is used to define the transmission of a signal beam. The final result, once again, is greater speed; with all-optical processors, computers, telecommunications equipment, and other devices will be able to operate without having to translate between electrons and photons. The main barrier to all-optical signal processing continues to be the properties of the materials it requires. Increasingly, laboratories are recognizing the strengths and weaknesses of both photonics and electronics, and are working toward a hybrid technology called optoelectronics, whereby electricity is used to manipulate the transmission of light through a material. Some laboratories, such as Telcordia Technologies, have already made progress in the development of photonic integrated circuits (these chips are also known as "optoelectronic integrated circuits" or "optical integrated circuits"). In 1999 Nanovation Technologies, Inc. patented its functional, fully integrated optical circuit based on photons. The company claimed that a photonic chip would be up to 1,000 times smaller than semiconductor circuits based on electrons, and could multiply chip speed and data capacity by up to 1,000 times.

FURTHER READING

Anscombe, Nadya. "UK Takes Global Lead in the Booming Photonics Sector." *Electronics Times,* 28 February 2000.

Biagi, Susan. "Eye on Optics: Photonic Routers Coming of Age with Solutions from NEC, Lucent." *Telephony,* 22 May 2000.

Brown, Chappell. "Bell Labs: Riding a Photonics Wave." *Electronic Engineering Times,* 31 January 2000.

———. "Light Hot: Optical Networking Picks Up (Even More) Momentum." *Telephony,* 22 May 2000.

———. "Technology: DARPA Program Seeks Next-Generation Chip-Level Interconnect—Optics Tackles VLSI Data Bottleneck." *Electronic Engineering Times,* 1 June 1998, 41.

"Complex Switch-Matrix Systems to Dominate Photonic-Switching Market Revenues." *Lightwave,* April 2000.

"Corning Acquires Rochester Photonics Corporation; Company Is a Technology Leader in Diffractive Optics and Microlens Technology." *Business Wire,* 14 February 1999.

Daigle, Lisa. "Optical Actuator Design May Cut Access Times Tenfold." *Data Storage,* January 2000.

Day, John. "Corning Strengthens the Fiber of Its Being." *Electronic Buyers News,* 6 March 2000.

"Fiat Lux." *Economist,* 5 February 2000.

"First Device That Produces Light—One Photon at a Time." *Business Wire,* 11 February 1999.

Griffiths, Andrew. "Money-Go-Round: Race Starts for a New Generation of Microchips below the Salt." *Daily Telegraph,* 10 April 1999.

Hardy, Stephen. "Meanwhile, Back at the Lab. . . ." *Lightwave,* October 1999.

Hecht, Jeff. "Hot Fibre Optics." *Electronics Times,* 28 February 2000.

Hernon, Monta Monaco. "As DWDM Market Grows, So Does Nortel's Share." *Fiber Optics News,* 13 November 2000.

Johnson, R. Colin. "Device Turns Photons On and Off—New Optical Switching Method Comes to Light." *Electronic Engineering Times,* 27 March 2000.

Pease, Robert. "New Resource Enables Photonic Startups to Get 'On the Air' Faster." *Lightwave,* April 2000.

"Photonic WASSP Stings at Light Speed." *International Defense Review,* 1 October 1999.

"Photonics Development Center." Available from http://www.photonics-center.com.

"Photonics Spectra." Available from http://www.photonicsspectra.com.

Regalado, Antonio. "Intellectual Capital." *Technology Review,* 1 January 1999.

Salamone, Salvatore. "An Awful Lot of Vendors and Providers Are Seeing the Light, and It's Coming from Photonic Switches." *tele.com,* 1 May 2000.

Van den Berg, Rob. "Microscopy: Molecular Imaging Beats Limits of Light." *Science,* 31 July 1998.

Wirbel, Loring. "Technology: Photonic Circuits Easing into Silicon Optical Benches." *Electronic Engineering Times,* 8 March 1999.

PHOTOVOLTAIC SYSTEMS

While the efficiency of electronic components for electrical systems improved rapidly through the 1990s and into the 2000s, the amount of power drawn from electric utilities continued to escalate, and the solution to the increased energy demand was far from certain by 2000. Renewable energy sources have become enormously popular, both among the public and among researchers, in an effort to reduce the reliance on energy sources that cause pollution, such as fossil fuels. One of the most highly touted remedies was solar energy. The untapped energy potential of the Sun was enormous. For instance, scientists surmised that a single day's worth of sunlight, if properly harnessed and converted, could supply the entire energy needs of the United States for two years, and the daily dose of solar energy outpaced that of the world's entire fossil-fuel energy by a ration of 1,000 to one.

Photovoltaic (PV) systems thus lie at the heart of the movement toward efficient energy, acting as the mediator between the Sun and the desired energy by converting sunlight directly to electricity. Research and development in the closing years of the 20th century pushed the technology within the grasp of those wishing to market it to a mass audience in the consumer and industrial worlds. PV systems were finding increasing employment in households, automobiles, and remote power systems, and for telecommunications, lighting systems, and a range of other applications.

Renewable energy was certainly on its way by 2000, accounting for as much of the total U.S. energy consumption (7 percent) as nuclear power, despite massive obstacles in the forms of production costs and political barriers. Though solar power was among the most hotly anticipated of all renewable energy sources, by the late 1990s the Sun accounted for only 1 percent of all the renewable energy consumed in the United States. Viewed from another angle, however, PV systems were doing quite well. According to the Solar Energy Industries Association, over 10,000 homes in the United States were powered completely by solar energy in the late 1990s, and an additional 200,000 homes incorporated some form of photovoltaic system. At any rate, energy researchers and analysts were nearly universal in their prediction of a sunny future for the photovoltaic systems industry.

The term "photo" stems from the Greek *phos,* which means "light." "Volt" is named for Alessandro Volta (1745-1827), a pioneer in the study of electricity. "Photovoltaics," then, could literally mean light-electricity. Solar power has long been recognized as a potentially inexhaustible, inexpensive source of energy. Within solar power, there are active and passive systems that include solar thermal and solar heating, cooling, and lighting; and photovoltaic, or solar electric, systems. Although both systems gather and contain energy, they distribute it in different ways. PV cells, panels, and arrays consist primarily of silicon, the second-most abundant element on Earth, or other semiconductor materials. When these are combined with other materials, it exhibits electrical properties in the presence of sunlight, generating direct current (DC) electricity. Electrons are charged by the light and move through the silicon. This is known as the photovoltaic effect. Photovoltaic systems typically carry a life span of about 20 years, during which time maintenance and servicing are minimal, as there are no moving components. The typical PV panel was about two feet by five feet and generated about 75 to 100 watts of electricity.

Of equal importance, there are few power-generation technologies as environmentally friendly as PV systems. During operation, PV systems generate no noise, hazardous waste, or pollution. These systems are used in a wide variety of applications, including wireless and cellular communications, recreational vehicles and boats, off-grid homes, and crop irrigation systems. In developing countries, PV systems are used for water purification, water pumping, and vaccine refrigeration.

The overwhelming bulk of federal research funding for solar energy passed through the U.S. Department of Energy (DOE), particularly the National Renewable Energy Laboratory and the National Center for Photovoltaics (NCP). The latter was created to facilitate cooperative research efforts between the industry, government, and universities, and established guidelines to help bring about a solar-power industry that, by 2030, would enjoy an annual growth rate of 25 percent and would maintain a central position in the U.S. and world energy markets. Most of the government funding went to universities and industry players to develop cheaper and more efficient semiconductor materials and components, while at the same time boosting total capacity and production rates. Moreover, to bring about commercial success, and thus ensure U.S. leadership of the PV industry, the NCP fostered the development of PV-product standards and simplified maintenance procedures and called for the elimination of legislative and regulatory obstacles to the development and promotion of PV technology.

Technology Experience to Accelerate Markets in Utility Photovoltaics (TEAM-UP) is a program designed to assist in developing commercial markets for a wide range of solar photovoltaic technologies. TEAM-UP, managed since 1994 by the Utility PhotoVoltaic Group, is in partnership with the utility industries and the DOE. It provides cost sharing for selected PV business ventures in the United States, and because funding is provided by the U.S. government, TEAM-UP support is restricted to U.S. firms.

The Utility PhotoVoltaic Group is a nonprofit association of 90 electric utilities and electric service organizations in the United States, Canada, Europe, Australia, and the Caribbean, cooperating to accelerate the commercial use of solar electricity. The DOE's $5 mil-

lion grant in 1998 was awarded to 14 solar electric businesses in the Utility PhotoVoltaic Group, and also helped attain an additional $27 million in private funding, to be used to support 1,000 systems in 12 states and Puerto Rico.

The industry has its share of concerns, however. Although efforts are being made to reduce costs, solar energy systems are still rather expensive. Nonetheless, by building upgraded, innovative photovoltaic systems and equipment, manufacturers are providing jobs and reducing the rate of consumption of polluting fossil fuels. Extensive use of solar energy technology will have a beneficial impact on air pollution and global climate change. PV technology can also help generate ethanol and methanol, which are themselves quickly gaining popularity as alternative-fuel sources.

BACKGROUND AND DEVELOPMENT

The first experimenter to successfully convert sunlight into electricity was French physicist Edmond Becquerel (1820-1891), who noted the PV effect in 1839 when he built a device that could measure the intensity of light by observing the strength of an electric current between two metal plates. For over 110 years following the initial discovery of the PV effect, scientists experimented with different materials in an attempt to find a practical use for PV systems. In the late 19th century, scientists discovered that the metal selenium was particularly sensitive to sunlight, and during the 1880s, Charles Fritts constructed the first selenium solar cell. His device, however, was inefficient, converting less than 1 percent of the received light into usable electricity.

The Fritts selenium solar cell was mostly forgotten until the 1950s, when the drive to produce an efficient solar cell was renewed. It was known that the key to the photovoltaic cell lay in creating a semiconductor that would release electrons when exposed to radiation within the visible spectrum. During this time, researchers at the Bell Telephone Laboratories were developing similar semiconductors to be used in communication systems. By accident, Bell scientists Calvin Fuller and Daryl Chapin found the perfect semiconductor: a hybridized crystal called a "doped" cell made of phosphorous and boron. The first solar cells using these new crystals debuted in 1954 and yielded a conversion efficiency of nearly 6 percent. Later improvements in the design increased the efficiency to almost 15 percent.

In 1957 Bell Telephone used a silicon solar cell to power a telephone repeater station in Georgia. The process was considered a success, although it was still too inefficient to penetrate the general marketplace. The first real application of silicon solar cells came in 1958, when a solar array was used to provide electricity for the radio transmitter of *Vanguard 1,* the second American satellite to orbit Earth. Solar cells have been used on almost every satellite launched since.

The oil crisis in the early 1970s and the nuclear accidents at Three Mile Island and in Chernobyl greatly enhanced the public's desire for alternative and renewable energies. As environmental consciousness grew, solar energy became the darling of the renewables category. It was not until the late 20th century that solar energy became practical and economical enough to warrant its broadscale marketing as one of the primary energy sources of the future. In the 1990s alone, the price of solar energy dropped 50 percent as technology continued to advance. It was during that period that PV applications went from a niche source of electricity to bringing solar technology to the threshold of big business. The market of photovoltaic systems began to take off in the late 1990s, expanding 42 percent in 1997 and another 21 percent in 1998, and by 2000 the worldwide market was well over $1 billion.

Cities such as Santa Monica, California, began programs to reduce energy use by fossil fuels and replace it with something more environmentally sound. Santa Monica, which dubbed itself the "Sustainable City," formulated a policy in 1993 to slash citywide energy consumption 16 percent by the end of the decade. In a project funded by the California Energy Commission, the DOE, and Edison Technology Solutions, the Pacific Park on the Santa Monica Pier became home to the world's first solar-powered Ferris wheel in August 1998. The Ferris wheel was converted into a 50-kilowatt photovoltaic system, and the conversion was expected to save the park $7,000 a year in energy costs.

CURRENT CONDITIONS

One of the most significant barriers to PV systems over the last two decades was their high cost. But by 2000, the industry had succeeded in largely mitigating this difficulty, reducing the cost from over $50 per watt in the early 1980s to under $5 per watt, and most analysts expected this amount to come down

---

About... **THE FORCE BEHIND THE PV PHENOMENON**

Photovoltaic (PV) systems cannot operate without the Sun—the basis of the solar system and the source of heat, light, and energy for Earth. About 93 million miles from Earth, the Sun is 864,000 miles in diameter and has a mass about 330,000 times that of Earth. Scientists predict that the Sun will live approximately 10 billion years (it is currently about 4.5 billion years old). It is predicted that the Sun will remain stable and continue to burn hydrogen for about the same amount of time. At the end of its life, the Sun will dilate and its surface temperature of 5,800 degrees Kelvin will be cut in half. The Sun will then become about 50 times larger and about 300 times brighter, becoming what scientists call a "red giant."

Nuclear fusion at the core of the Sun is responsible for changing hydrogen into helium. The helium travels to the surface of the Sun and appears in the form of light. About one-third of this light is diffused by clouds or particles in the air when it enters Earth's atmosphere. Once this energy hits an object on Earth, it is absorbed and then redistributed through the object via conduction, convection, or radiation—all processes of transferring heat molecularly. Modern solar energy is a means of capturing this energy and redistributing it to heat and cool buildings, operate engines and pumps, heat water and swimming pools, and power appliances.

---

further as research efforts are coordinated and markets open up for a mass audience.

The efficiency of modern PV technology was noted by the accounting giant KPMG, which estimated that a large factory producing 5 million PV panels each year could power 250,000 households, thereby slashing energy costs by about 75 percent, according to *Earth Island Journal.* Such a factory could, according to KPMG, be built at a cost of about $660 million.

The Clinton administration took a role in the attempt to convert to efficient energy with the issuance of Executive Order 13123 along with the Million Solar Roofs Initiative, which aimed at adding solar-power systems to 1 million buildings throughout the United States by 2010. Shortly thereafter, a photovoltaic system was installed in the world's largest office building, the Pentagon, as part of the massive renovation of the structure. The system was expected to displace about 48,000 pounds of carbon dioxide per year. The Million Solar Roofs Initiative offers a 15 percent tax credit, with a $1,000 cap for solar thermal panels and a $2,000 cap for PV panels. The initiative had won over half a million commitments by the end of 1999. According to the Solar Energy Industries Association, the proposal for the million roofs will help deliver reliable PV-generated electricity to American consumers at a competitive price, lead to the construction of new plants in over 20 states, create 70,000 jobs in the PV industry, and increase the U.S. industry share from 40 to 60 percent.

By 2000 there were over 100,000 people using solar power and living "off the grid," or independent of utility companies in the United States. The cost for installing PV systems in an average home falls in the range of $6,000 to $10,000. Most systems in this range are capable of producing about 800 to 900 watts of power, enough to operate most of the basic electrical needs without the cost of monthly utility bills. By contrast, the start-up costs of powering new homes can be as high as $15,000.

While a range of PV cells were either commercially available or in production in the late 1990s, crystalline silicon cells accounted for the overwhelming bulk of PV shipments, at about 93 percent in 1998, though thin-film PV shipments were emerging rapidly, growing 76 percent that year. According to the Solar Energy Industries Association, total sales of photovoltaic solar systems reached an estimated $2.8 billion in 2000, up from about $2.2 billion the year before. Furthermore, electricity generation was the function of 45 percent of all PV systems, while communications and transportation also constituted strong end uses for the technology.

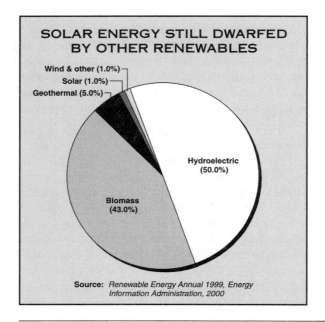

SOLAR ENERGY STILL DWARFED BY OTHER RENEWABLES

Wind & other (1.0%)
Solar (1.0%)
Geothermal (5.0%)

Hydroelectric (50.0%)

Biomass (43.0%)

Source: *Renewable Energy Annual 1999, Energy Information Administration, 2000*

The future dominance of renewable energy sources seemed secure, with solar energy expected to play a vital role. Even the major oil and gas companies committed large sums of money to develop new research and development outfits devoted to renewable energy. Royal Dutch/Shell Group, for instance, established Shell International Renewables in the late 1990s to study solar energy and biomass fuel, while British Petroleum (BP) established BP Solar, which opened a PV-system operation in California. Enron Corp. partnered with Amoco Corp. to form the world's second-largest producer of photovoltaic cells. The merger between Amoco and BP combined the leaders' solar operations to create BP Solarex, which by 2000 was one of the leading PV systems companies in the world.

INDUSTRY LEADERS

Siemens Solar, the photovoltaic division of the German global electronics giant Siemens AG, was a leading manufacturer of PV modules. The company produced about one-fifth of the total installed base of PV power worldwide. Founded in 1977, Siemens Solar emerged as the PV industry leader in 1990 through its purchase of California-based ARCO solar. The company maintained business partnerships with over 130 firms worldwide. Siemens Solar produced single crystalline PV modules with efficiencies of about 15 percent, and its SR 100 module was an industry-leading panel, generating 100 watts of electricity with a warranty of 25 years, the longest in the industry. Siemens Solar's products also included supplemental components such as sine wave inverters, charge controllers, and solar tiles. In the late 1990s Siemens collaborated with the World Bank to bring new photovoltaic systems to developing countries such as India, Indonesia, Sri Lanka, Zimbabwe, the People's Republic of China, and Kenya that aimed at providing electricity to rural areas.

BP Solarex was the world's largest solar electric company, combining BP Solar with Amoco's Solarex to produce over 30 megawatts (MW) of solar electric products for annual sales of more than $180 million. Solarex, founded in 1973, was a unit of Amoco-Enron Solar and the largest U.S.-owned manufacturer of photovoltaic products. The company participated in some groundbreaking projects, such as supplying about 40,000 square feet of the PV modules that made up the roof array located at the 1996 Olympics swimming facility in Atlanta, Georgia. The National Renewable Energy Lab in Golden, Colorado, which is part of the U.S. Department of Energy (DOE), contracted with Solarex in August 1997 to conduct further research on thin-film photovoltaics. At the time of the merger, BP already owned about 10 percent of global PV production capacity. The combined operations gave BP Amoco a nearly 20 percent share of the world market. The BP 590 module was one of the leading PV systems, carrying an 85-watt capacity and lasting 20 years. At a solar conversion rate of 27 percent, it was also the most efficient on the market at the end of 1999. The following year, the company went one up on itself with its Apollo brand, which generated efficiency of 10.9 percent, a thin-film record. BP Solarex expected revenues of over $200 million in 2000.

Boston-based Spire Corp., with 90 employees and $11.9 million in sales at the close of 1999, was a small but crucial player in the photovoltaic systems industry. Spire provided products and services to photovoltaics, optoelectronics, and biomedical markets worldwide, including the PV cell testers, tabbing and stringing assemblers, and other components. Their equipment was used by the PV industry worldwide for manufacturing solar modules; the company boasted that about 90 percent of PV systems on the market use Spire components.

AMERICA AND THE WORLD

The United States was a particularly influential market in the energy realm, in both economic and environmental terms, given that the nation's 105 million buildings consumed about 10 percent of the entire world's energy. Appropriately, then, much of the research performed on PV systems is concentrated in the United States, although some U.S. companies are involved in joint ventures with foreign manufacturers. For example, Energy Conversion Devices of Troy, Michigan, produces a metal roofing solar battery system that can replace a roof on an ordinary house. United Solar, a subsidiary of Energy Conversion Devices, makes the batteries in conjunction with Canon of Japan. The United States accounted for about 35 percent of the world's PV-system sales in 1998, followed by Japan, with 32 percent, and Europe, with 20 percent, primarily in Germany. Germany and Japan, meanwhile, account for 36 percent and 27 percent of U.S. photovoltaic exports, respectively, in 2000.

The European Union was firmly committed to the expansion of their solar-power base in the first decade of the 2000s. Like the United States, the European Union implemented an extensive subsidy program for

solar homes. In Germany, the world's largest and most technically advanced rooftop photovoltaic plant was installed by Siemens Solar on the hall rooftops of the New Munich Trade Fair Center. With a peak output of one MW, it will feed around 1 million kilowatt hours of solar power into the grid of the Trade Fair Center. In 1997 Germany's Ministry of Research and Technology announced it would provide financial support for two large solar manufacturing plants, and in Berlin, Germany, the city's construction industry made a commitment to install solar collectors in 75 percent of all new buildings.

German-owned Siemens also teamed up with the DOE's National Renewable Energy Lab in Golden, Colorado, to research film photovoltaics. In April 1998 Siemens Solar Industries and the Northwest Energy Efficiency Alliance, a consortium of Northwest electric utilities, state and local governments, public interest groups, and the private sector, signed an agreement to work together in cutting energy use and production time in the manufacture of silicon crystals for photovoltaic cells and computer chips.

The most efficient use of photovoltaic systems for residential energy, most analysts contend, will not arise from individual consumers sporadically buying panels for their own homes, but by integrating entire neighborhoods. One such ambitious undertaking was underway in the Netherlands, where the NV REMU power company was constructing a community of 500 homes with solar panels covering the roofs. The PV systems were expected to provide about 60 percent of the community's entire energy, with the rest pulled from the local power grid. Because the city of Amersfoot, where the community is being built, gets less sunshine than the world average, the PV cells were specially outfitted to respond to light reflected by clouds.

Australia continues to sit at the forefront of alternative and renewable energy applications. This is partly due to the geographic remoteness of areas in Australia where conventional electricity is not practicable. A joint venture between the University of South Wales and Pacific Power, known as Pacific Solar, was developing technology to set up the first manufacturing facility for PV products, with products on the market by 2002.

Developing nations have outpaced their industrialized counterparts in the growth rates for energy consumption for over 20 years, and in the short term, growing Asian markets such as China and India were likely to lead the world in the increase of energy consumption. The Indonesian, Pacific region, and Central and South American markets are also growing. More developing countries' predilections for PV systems have caused the solar-power market to grow an average of 15 percent per year between 1973 and 2000.

Ironically, 70 percent of the solar cells and solar-power systems manufactured in the United States are exported to Third World countries. Exports increased almost 40 percent in the mid-1990s. The export rate is expected to increase considerably, since about one-third of the world population lives without electricity. Although many of these countries initiated aggressive electrification programs, costs are too high to build large power plants or extend the electrical grid to thousands of the remote villages without power. Consequently, household solar-power systems may be an economically and environmentally sound alternative in these areas.

India is becoming a major world producer of PV modules, and the Indian government intends to install solar-powered telephones in every one of the country's 500,000 villages. In the Democratic Republic of the Congo (formerly Zaire), meanwhile, Hospital Bulape treats 50,000 patients every year and depends exclusively on solar power for everything from X-ray machinery to air conditioning systems. In Morocco, solar panels are sold in open markets next to carpets and produce.

Japan is the leading country for installations of PV panels, but the cost is about four times as high in U.S. dollars than traditional sourcing from utility companies. Japan, however, has a well-planned subsidy program for residential solar roofs, absorbing about half the cost. In early 1999 Japan cosponsored a two-day seminar on "Photovoltaic Technology in India and Japan," held in New Delhi, which covered 26 presentations and served as a nucleus for the exchange of information and technology. Japan and India remain second- and third-largest producers of PV cells, behind the United States.

There is a large-scale national program in place in Japan in which the Japanese government subsidizes homeowners for nearly half of the cost of a rooftop PV array. In fact, the Japanese government has increased its national budget for photovoltaics about 15 percent per year since 1992. In Tokyo there were about 1.5 million buildings with solar water heating, more than in the entire United States.

RESEARCH AND TECHNOLOGY

Thanks to extensive research, photovoltaic systems were no longer universally dependent on the Sun. New PV systems, of which the first commercial models were in development in 2000, utilized heat energy, or infrared radiation, instead of solar energy, thereby allowing them to operate more efficiently and durably during nighttime or overcast conditions. Thermophotovoltaics, as these systems are called, must use natural gas or some other fuel to generate heat, but the semiconductor conversion nonetheless generates significantly more efficiency than diesel generators, leading to cost and pollution savings.

The Finnish energy firm Fortum Corp. was a leading innovator of building-integrated photovoltaic (BIPV) systems, which are integrated into the building's architecture. BIPV systems were a central area of research for the nonresidential PV-applications market. The main centers of BIPV development were in Switzerland, Japan, Germany, and Finland, though the United States was beginning to catch up by 2000, as a number of architectural firms, such as Solar Design Associates of Massachusetts, devoted themselves to the new technology. BIPV systems are worked directly into the building's aesthetic and structural design, with excess energy fed into the central energy grid, which can also supply any necessary supplemental energy when the PV system fails to generate an amount sufficient to facilitate the building's normal functions. Fortum launched a pilot project in Zurich, Switzerland, for the headquarters of the Swiss retailer Migros, where the glass roof was integrated with PV cells.

Modern PV systems are being equipped with control inverters that can change normal solar energy into alternating current for use in households. Significantly, researchers are producing solar batteries that are in the 34 percent efficiency mark. That compares to earlier cells that were about 4 percent efficient. State-of-the-art, direct motorized tracking devices that aim the PV cells directly at the Sun at all times during the day are helping to improve systems by collecting more heat. Additionally, solar power and the PV industry are making inroads on traditional power-generating industries. Oil-fired power plants, for example, operate at only 35 percent efficiency.

One of the goals of PV system researchers is to improve the storage system currently in use. Another is to reduce the number of components in a system. The primary pieces of equipment in any solar system are the photovoltaic panels, which absorb and contain sunlight so that it begins conversion into useful power. Although they are made primarily of silicon, other materials have begun to be used, such as gallium arsenide, which is employed in the Russian space station Mir.

The number of panels needed in a given situation depends on the amount of energy required. For an average house, the number is determined by the kilowatts per hour actually used. Each panel generates about 50 watts of DC electricity for each hour of sunlight, and batteries are needed for the storage of the energy so that it can be used when needed. A power center must also be part of the system to regulate the flow of electricity going into the batteries so that they are not overcharged and to control the energy leaving the batteries. Inverters, which convert solar power into electricity, must also be obtained for a PV system. A generator is needed as a separate power source to serve as a backup if anything goes wrong and to replenish the system after a cloudy day.

Storage has long posed problems for solar energy researchers. Batteries are currently the most cost-effective method of storing power. They receive power from the inverters and store it until it is drawn upon. The number of batteries needed depends on the amount of power needed. The batteries provide adequate storage and require only modest attention. They must be replaced, however, about every 10 years at a cost of approximately $1,000 each. Researchers are seeking other, more inexpensive storage sources, such as thermal mass walls made of concrete, brick, adobe, or drywall; and superinsulated stress-skin panels to line walls. These panels are composed of a combination of oriented stranboard (which is similar to plywood) and chlorofluorocarbon-free Styrofoam.

Prabir Dutta, a professor of chemistry at Ohio State University, found a way to trap light energy and then store it chemically. Using a molecular cage, he managed to mimic photosynthesis. The charged light enters the cage and is then trapped in a zeolite cage, which prevents the charged molecule from returning to its donor molecule.

The National Aeronautics and Space Administration is also looking at ways to increase the amount of energy to be stored. The agency is experimenting with the use of a solar power satellite (SPS), which can deliver enormous amounts of energy to Earth. This can be accomplished by building huge photovoltaic structures (estimated to be as large as Manhattan) that are designed to deliver five to 10 gigawatts of electrical power. Just one of these monoliths would be sufficient to power Connecticut. The inventor of SPS, Dr. Peter Glaser, noted that they will be expensive to build, but cheap to operate and environmentally safe.

FURTHER READING

"BIPV Expanding the Solar Net." *European Power News,* November 1999.

Bull, Stanley R., and Lynn L. Billman. "Renewable Energy: Ready to Meet Its Promise?" *Washington Quarterly,* winter 2000.

Cook, Hugh. "Solar Goes Incognito." *Building Design & Construction,* October 1999.

Hellemans, Alexander. "Solar Homes for the Masses." *Science,* 30 July 1999.

Johnson, Jeff. "U.S. Photovoltaic Exports Jump." *Chemical & Engineering News,* 9 October 2000.

Kren, Lawrence. "The Future Looks Bright for Photovoltaics." *Machine Design,* 5 August 1999.

McVeigh, James, Dallas Burtraw, Joel Darmstadter, and Karen Palmer. "Renewables from Another Angle." *Electric Perspectives,* March/April 2000.

Morrison, David. "Industry Starts Building the Road to a Sun-Powered Future." *Electronic Design,* 20 March 2000.

"Most Efficient Thin Film PV." *Energy Conservation News,* July 2000.

Poole, Ian. "Phototransistor Basics." *Popular Electronics,* September 1999.

Poruban, Steven. "Major Frontrunners in Alternative Energy Investment." *Oil & Gas Journal,* 10 July 2000.

Schwartz, Joe. "Tapping the Sun." *Whole Earth,* winter 1999.

"Selling a Solar-Cell Future." *Christian Science Monitor,* 18 August 1999.

Shah, A., P. Torres, R. Tscharner, N. Wyrsch, and H. Keppner. "Photovoltaic Technology: The Case for Thin-Film Solar Cells." *Science,* 30 July 1999.

"Solar Power System Installed at Pentagon." *Air Conditioning Heating & Refrigeration News,* 6 December 1999.

"Solar Power Undimmed: Alternative Energy Gets a New Look as Fuel Prices Rise." *Denver Post,* 11 November 2000.

"Solarize Now!" *Earth Island Journal,* spring 2000.

U.S. Department of Energy. Energy Information Administration. "Renewable Energy Annual 1999." Available from http://www.eia.doe.gov/cneaf/solar.renewables/rea_data99/rea_sum.html.

U.S. Department of Energy. National Renewable Energy Laboratory. "World-Record Solar Cell a Step Closer to Cheap Solar Energy." 25 February 1999. Available from http://www.nrel.gov.

Wolcott, Barbara. "Sun Worship." *Mechanical Engineering,* June 1999.

PHYSICAL FITNESS PRODUCTS

INDUSTRY SNAPSHOT

In most exercise categories, the number of Americans working out grew considerably in the 1990s, leading to pumped up sales for producers of physical fitness products. The Sporting Goods Manufacturers Association (SGMA) reported that sales of sporting goods, including equipment, apparel, and athletic footwear, accelerated again in 1999, totaling $63.4 billion for growth of 4.4 percent. Sporting goods sales alone, meanwhile, failed to keep pace with the entire industry, growing 1.5 percent in 1999 to reach $17.81 billion, still significantly below the 1996 peak of $19.4 billion. Sales of exercise equipment, meanwhile, continued to rise at about 6 percent annually, and were expected to top $3.6 billion in 2000.

The SGMA and the Fitness Products Council reported that the number of Americans engaged in all sports, fitness, and outdoor activities increased 19 percent between 1987 and 1998, outpacing the population growth of 12 percent over this period, leaving 81.5 million Americans engaging in some form of physical fitness activity. Meanwhile, the ranks of health-club members swelled to 31 million in 1999, up from 17.4 million in 1987. Both men and women increasingly embraced the fitness craze, working out for a variety of reasons: to boost energy, tone muscles, improve self-image and self-confidence, and to add muscle bulk.

Perhaps the primary beneficiaries of all this activity, besides the increasingly fit segment of the population, has been the manufacturers and marketers of large exercise equipment such as treadmills, stair climbers, compact gyms, gliders, and elliptical exercisers. The SGMA reported that over 50 million households in the United States own exercise equipment, with 32.3 million households using the equipment frequently. Treadmill use, for instance, expanded a whopping 720 percent between the late 1980s and late 1990s. Meanwhile, both home-equipment sales and health clubs, situated in colleges, offices, and apartment buildings as well as in traditional commercial outlets, have enjoyed exploding popularity.

While overall Americans have been and are expected to continue increasing their physical activity to get fit, the purchase of higher-end exercise equipment is tied rather tightly to general U.S. economic health. On an individual level, research has long showed that fitness activity, especially activity requiring heavy equipment, is fairly commensurate with income level. Paradoxically, such activity generally diminishes with age, although the latter rule has grown far less pronounced in recent years. According to American Sports Data, Inc., the number of Americans aged 55 and older who were frequently engaged in fitness activity jumped 25 percent between 1987 and 1997 to reach 13 million, and by 2000, the use of physical fitness products, particularly free weights and treadmills, by this age group was soaring. And while advertisements for exercise equipment typically feature fit and toned young people, much of the growth in equipment sales was generated by older customers.

Fueled by the U.S. surgeon general's pronouncement that "physical activity is the key to good health for all Americans," individuals of all ages, but particularly the elderly, were investing both time and dollars in their own physical fitness. The American Council on Exercise (ACE), a nonprofit health and fitness organization, concluded that working out at work became popular as people tried to fit exercise into busy schedules. ACE found that state-of-the-art facilities were showing up in major corporations in the United States, including Gap, Oracle, Clif Bar, and 3Com. Manufacturers of exercise products have tried to meet the needs and desires of potential customers by developing products that are not only efficient and simple to use, but also enjoyable and reasonably affordable.

ORGANIZATION AND STRUCTURE

Fitness items are typically sold by the manufacturers, either directly to retailers, where price markup occurs before sale, or via distributors, who in turn sell to retailers. Often, high-end manufacturers give a retailer exclusive rights to sell their product in a certain region. Fitness products reach customers through a variety of outlets, the most notable being large sporting goods stores. Leading fitness specialty retailers in 2000 included Busy Body Fitness Warehouse; Omni Fitness; Gym Source; Exercise Equipment Center, Inc.; and Push Pedal Pull Group. Fitness products were also among the primary staples of late-night infomercials. Thirty-minute spots hawking Tae-Bo exercise videos, the Ab Rocker, and a host of other products were among the most successful infomercials in the late 1990s. Mail order and the Internet have also emerged as fresh marketing avenues for the promotion and sale of such products.

During the late 1990s, producers of fitness products witnessed significant changes within the industry, as mergers, acquisitions, and initial public offerings (IPOs) occurred with relative frequency. The largest notable acquisition in the area of sporting goods was that of Spalding Sports Worldwide by Kohlberg, Kravis, Roberts & Co. Estimated at over $1 billion, the deal was touted as the largest ever seen by the industry. Notable IPOs included those of Ridgeview Inc. and The North Face Inc. In 1998, Icon beat out two other bidders to acquire the well-known NordicTrack brand for $9.55 million when Nordic-Track filed for bankruptcy. Icon awarded sole distribution rights to NordicTrack, with the exception of about 20 NordicTrack stores acquired in the deal, to Sears, Roebuck & Co., Icon's best customer. Sears began to open NordicTrack specialty shops in stores across the country. Though NordicTrack's staple cross-country ski machines, one of the first major success stories in the exercise-equipment market, suffered from declining sales in the mid- and late 1990s, Icon greatly desired to capitalize on the astronomical brand-name recognition. NordicTrack now enjoys strong sales from treadmills and weight equipment in addi-

tion to its ski machines. Other notable acquisitions included Cybex's purchase of Tectrix, Precor's acquisition of Pacific Fitness, and Schwinn's takeover of Hebb Industries as well as GT Bikes.

BACKGROUND AND DEVELOPMENT

In the late 1980s the home-exercise segment of the wholesale fitness market stood at $750 million and was growing fast. Factors contributing to the emergence of the home-exercise phenomenon included convenience, proximity, the scarcity of available free time, and the added comfort and security of privacy—an issue of particular concern to those lacking confidence in either physical appearance or athletic ability. In 1988, *Forbes* magazine noted the comment of one expert who explained the reasoning behind people's preference for home exercise over health clubs: "When you couple a new behavior with a new environment, like a health spa, it represents a double threat to people, so they prefer to stay home." By the early 1990s, this concept became a mantra in the ads of at least one exercise equipment manufacturer. The Trotter Co. beckoned the market with its theme, "For those who consider exercise a matter of privacy."

In the late 1980s membership in health clubs began to level off after a period of sustained growth, and the major creators of exercise equipment realized the need to reorganize. Companies such as Nautilus Sports/Medical Industries and Universal Gym Equipment found themselves joined by such competitors as Precor, Inc. in the race to grab sales. Precor succeeded in creating its own niche by catering to consumers willing to pay for high-quality equipment that would stand up to years of use. Whereas in the early 1980s a treadmill, for example, could be purchased for as little as $200, by the decade's end, a sturdier and better designed product could be bought for about $1,000, a price not considered unreasonable.

Interestingly, Nautilus, designated the "grandfather" of the exercise equipment companies by industry insiders, chose not to push its products aggressively into the home-exercise market at that time. The firm, founded in 1970 by Arthur Jones, continued to focus on and provide its products primarily to health clubs and other commercial facilities. In 1998, however, the company's assets were acquired by Direct Focus, Inc., a direct-marketing firm.

Adding to the convenience of home-exercise equipment was the introduction of the exercise videotape. A $5.8-billion market by 1993, this segment of the industry faced significant challenges in initial distribution of its products in the early 1980s. Contributing to the difficulty of distribution was the lack of seriousness with which the industry viewed the coming aerobics boom. Industry pioneer Kathy Smith predicted that aerobics would be much more than a passing fad and that the industry would eventually realize this. A prophetic statement, since by 1992 Smith's combined 12 exercise videos sold more than 5 million copies. Names of other exercise gurus, particularly women, became common in American households by the 1990s. Models and actors, as well as professional trainers, cast their hats into the exercise-video ring by the late 1990s, sometimes with mixed results. Among the most successful entrepreneurs in this genre was Jane Fonda, who by 1989 made over 11 such tapes. While most exercise videos were initially geared toward aerobics and aerobic dancing, by the early 1990s stress management, stretching, body sculpting, and toning were highlighted topics as well.

In 1999 hundreds of videotapes were available, though not necessarily on the shelves of large sporting goods stores. Discount retailers such as Target carry some of the more popular ones, but the mail-order industry has the edge on exercise-video sales. Video sales were relatively dormant in the mid-1990s compared to the 1980s boom when Jane Fonda had seemingly everyone in aerobics workouts. By the end of the decade, however, exercise videos had been rejuvenated, largely on the strength of the Tae-Bo exercise series by Hollywood's Billy Blanks, which derived their sales primarily through its blockbuster infomercial.

CURRENT CONDITIONS

While sports participation has been declining for several years, physical fitness is on the rise. Describing the phases of exercise trends, the SGMA and the Fitness Products Council noted that while the 1970s were the running decade and in the 1980s everyone was in aerobics, the 1990s were dominated by the exercise machine. Equipment sales in this category grew 6 percent in 1999 to reach $3.57 billion, representing a slightly faster growth rate than the sporting goods industry as a whole. Sales of stationary equipment flattened in the late 1990s. Treadmills held steady at $1.6 billion in 1999, while stationary bicycles fell 3 percent to $380 million, and cross-country ski machines totaled $520 million. Elliptical trainers fell far short

of their inflated expectations in the late 1990s, a disappointment analysts attributed to an oversaturated market, customer confusion, and the wide range of prices, which ranged from $200 and $700. By 2001, the fitness-equipment retail market is expected to reach $4.9 billion.

For most of the 1990s, growth in the sporting goods industry was fueled by the fitness-products sector. About 49.6 million Americans use home-exercise equipment at least once a week, while an additional 4.9 million use such equipment less often. The most popular home-exercise equipment was free weights, used by about 42.8 million Americans, with treadmills following with 37.5 million and stationary bikes placing third at 31 million.

Other product trends in the late 1990s and early 2000s included sales of such items as: abdominal exercisers (also known as "ab trainers"); low-impact elliptical trainers, weight-resistance machines; recumbent bikes in which the user semi-reclines; and air walkers, flat-folding machines touted as providing "a complete workout" while inflicting no pounding impact on the body. While treadmills continue to reign as the best-selling equipment for home use, a resurgence in sales of exercise bikes began, in part due to the popularity of new group cardio classes, such as the group cycling class Spinning. Heart-rate monitors and body-fat measuring devices became popular and continued to sell into 2000 in conjunction with larger equipment.

The industry's customer-satisfaction component was expected to get a boost from the decision by Harris Black International, Ltd. and the American Council on Exercise (ACE) to issue customer surveys on home-exercise equipment. By randomly polling owners nationwide on issues such as affordability, ease of use, and physical fitness benefits, the surveys will result in awards to manufacturers in categories such as "best of price category" and "overall customer satisfaction," and will provide customers with a more comprehensive comparative view of the equipment market and manufacturers with greater detail on consumer wants and needs.

ACE reported that a primary objective for fitness-products manufacturers was enhancing the personalization of their products. Treadmills, elliptical exercisers, and other equipment increasingly feature personal adjustability as well as heart-rate monitors and programmable and adjustable training programs derived from health and strength data supplied by the user.

Recumbent bikes are often a feature in health clubs. (Kelly Quinn)

INDUSTRY LEADERS

ICON HEALTH & FITNESS, INC.

Icon, based in Logan, Utah, is the world's largest manufacturer and marketer of fitness equipment. Icon produces all types of major exercise equipment: elliptical motion trainers, cross-country ski machines, treadmills, stationary bikes, rowers, strength trainers, weight sets, and other equipment under brand names including Weider, Reebok, ProForm, Weslo, IMAGE, JumpKing, Healthrider, and NordicTrack. Icon's total sales fell to $710.2 million in 1999 from $749.3 the

year before, while employee ranks also fell from 4,800 to 4,300.

The company was formed as Weslo in 1977, and through a series of business deals built up its fitness operations, becoming Icon Health & Fitness in 1994. Icon's channels of distribution include direct sales (via the Internet and 800-numbers), Workout Warehouse (the company's catalog), department stores (Sears), mass merchandisers (Wal-Mart and Kmart), sporting goods stores (Sports Authority and Gart Sport Mart), specialty fitness retailers (Busy Body), catalog showrooms (Service Merchandise), and infomercials.

PRECOR, INC.

Founded in 1980, Precor was established by improving the design of a European rowing machine. A subsidiary of Premark International, Inc., Precor was absorbed by Illinois Tool Works, Inc. (ITW) in 1999 as part of the merger deal between ITW and Premark. Precor manufactures treadmills, elliptical fitness crosstrainers, and stair climbers, generating revenues of $100 million in 1999 while employing 900. In late 1998 Precor announced it had acquired Pacific Fitness Corp., manufacturer of high-end cardiovascular and flexibility equipment, greatly expanding its equipment operations.

CYBEX INTERNATIONAL, INC.

Cybex, of Medway, Massachusetts, employed 628 and posted sales of $123.8 million in 1999, a decline of 3 percent following a large increase in 1999, primarily as a result of its acquisition of stationary-bike and stair-climber manufacturer Tectrix. The firm manufacturers strength-training and cardiovascular equipment, focusing primarily on institutions such as health clubs, schools, and hotels. Cybex also reaches the consumer market through independent retailers. The company unveiled its new compact Cybex PG400 Personal Gym in 1998. Founded in 1973 as Trotter, Inc., the company grew steadily until it merged with Cybex International, Inc. in May 1997.

SCHWINN/GT CORP.

The well-known bicycle manufacturer, established in 1895 and headquartered in Boulder, Colorado, was also a leading manufacturer of physical fitness products. The firm achieved sales of $400 million in 1999, maintaining a payroll of 1,000 employees. In 2000 the company split into separate cycling and fitness divisions. Schwinn/GT Fitness produces stationary bikes, stair climbers, and treadmills geared toward home and institutional markets.

RESEARCH AND TECHNOLOGY

Fitness-products manufacturers and retailers were busily expanding their presence on the Internet, setting up online stores. Icon Fitness, for instance, maintains six companies carrying online stores. Even the equipment was taking on Web capabilities. The Web-based health and fitness concern Stayhealthy.com joined up with online insurance provider eHealthInsurance.com to market the CT1 Personal Calorie Tracker and BT1 Body Tracker, which monitor fitness

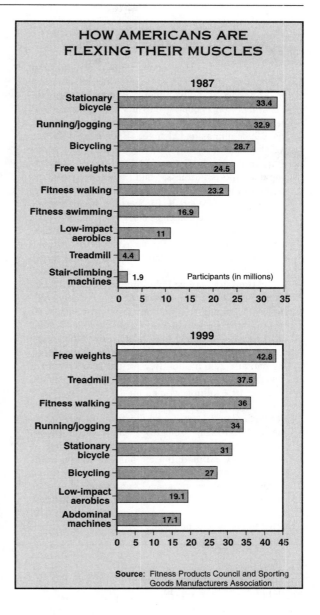

HOW AMERICANS ARE FLEXING THEIR MUSCLES

1987

Activity	Participants (in millions)
Stationary bicycle	33.4
Running/jogging	32.9
Bicycling	28.7
Free weights	24.5
Fitness walking	23.2
Fitness swimming	16.9
Low-impact aerobics	11
Treadmill	4.4
Stair-climbing machines	1.9

1999

Activity	Participants (in millions)
Free weights	42.8
Treadmill	37.5
Fitness walking	36
Running/jogging	34
Stationary bicycle	31
Bicycling	27
Low-impact aerobics	19.1
Abdominal machines	17.1

Source: Fitness Products Council and Sporting Goods Manufacturers Association

information such as caloric levels, blood pressure, body fat, weight, and muscle mass, displaying the data directly over the Internet. The devices are pocket-sized electronic boxes resembling pagers that link to a central processing station. A user need only access the Stayhealthy.com Web site to see their latest statistics.

Manufacturers also sought out ways to make their staple products less monotonous and more motivating. Icon's new NordicTrack EXP 100 treadmill was a multimedia exerciser, offering music and a computerized personal trainer to assist workouts. The program was built on software called iFit.com, which is run on the Internet, videos, or compact discs. Web sites, too, assumed the roles of personal trainers. Recognizing the increasing fitness consciousness but limited avail-

---

<table>
<tr><td>*Trends*</td><td>**PUMPING IRON**</td></tr>
</table>

Once upon a time, weightlifting was seen as primarily an activity for the self-obsessed or professional bodybuilders, although 98-pound weaklings were encouraged to hit the weights to avoid having sand kicked in their faces at the beach. By the late 1990s, things had changed. Exercising with free weights had emerged as the most popular fitness activity in the United States. Furthermore, of over 100 popular sports, fitness, and outdoor activities, weightlifting ranked fifth—after fishing, bowling, camping, and basketball. By the time strength training with resistance machines is factored in, more people were bulking up than were trying to catch fish, according to the Fitness Products Council.

The influential film industry was seen as partly responsible for the surge in female weightlifting. Linda Hamilton's ripped physique in the 1991 blockbuster *Terminator 2: Judgment Day* was widely credited with helping to spur female interest in weight workouts. While weight training has exploded among all groups, women have particularly flexed their muscles in this fitness sector. In 1987 only 30 percent of the nation's 22.6 million free-weight lifters were female; by 1999, that figure rose to about 45 percent, as some 19.4 million women hit the weights.

Gregg Hartley, executive director of the Fitness Products Council, attributed the surge in weightlifting to the growing "scientific" nature of the fitness industry that has focused consumers on the range of benefits, beyond mere muscle bulk, of weight training; the growing ranks of health-club members; an increased emphasis on shapely and toned physiques in the national media and entertainment industries; and the desire to boost energy levels to keep up with demanding work schedules.

able time among women, Joni Hyde, a Tae Kwon Do black belt and personal trainer, developed www.workoutsforwomen.com to offer personal-training consultation, fitness articles and assessments, and workout programs available over the Internet.

FURTHER READING

American Council on Exercise. "Nation's 'Workout Watchdog' Peers into the Future of Fitness." Washington: American Council on Exercise, 13 December 1999. Available from http://www.acefitness.org/newsreleases/121399.html.

Blumberg, Elizabeth. "Don't Kid Them." *Sportstyle,* April 1999.

Fetto, John. "Ready, Set, Go Nowhere!" *American Demographics,* November 1999.

"Icon Refinancing Is 'Critical' to Viability." *Sporting Goods Business,* 11 October 1999.

Newsome, Melba. "Which Exercise Videos Are Right for You?" *Investor's Business Daily,* 3 March 1999.

Reagan, Kellie. "Marketers Eluded by Ellipticals." *Response TV,* October 1998.

Sporting Goods Manufacturers Association. "America's Seniors Flex Their Muscles." North Palm Beach, FL: Sporting Goods Manufacturers Association, 30 July 1999. Available from http://www.sgma.com/press_room/1999_releases/m99-024.html.

———. "Fitness Equipment Drives Sporting Goods Growth." North Palm Beach, FL: Sporting Goods Manufacturers Association, 16 March 1999. Available from http://www.sgma.com/press_room/1999_releases/fitness99-001.html.

———. "Men Are Still Flexing Their Muscles." North Palm Beach, FL: Sporting Goods Manufacturers Association, 31 July 2000. Available from http://www.sgma.com/press_room/2000_releases/m2000-024.html.

———. "A Nation of Weightlifters?" North Palm Beach, FL: Sporting Goods Manufacturers Association, 16 June 1999. Available from http://www.sgma.com/press_room/1999_releases/fitness99-002.html.

———. "The Sports and Recreation Industry: Steady As She Goes." North Palm Beach, FL: Sporting Goods Manufacturers Association, 15 June 2000. Available from http://www.sgma.com/press_room/2000_releases/m2000-015.html.

———. "U.S. Sporting Goods Market Outlook for 2000." North Palm Beach, FL: Sporting Goods Manufacturers Association, 11 February 2000. Available from http://www.sgma.com/press_room/2000_releases/m2000-001.html.

———. "What's Driving Sporting Goods?" North Palm Beach, FL: Sporting Goods Manufacturers Association, 26 February 1999. Available from http://www.sgma.com/press_room/1999_releases/m99-008.html.

Stoneman, Bill. "Weighty Trends for Fitness Marketers." *American Demographics,* April 1999.

Troy, Mike. "Sporting Goods Category Batting Just above .500." *Discount Store News,* 12 July 1999.

Wellner, Alison. "The Ever-Shifting Fitness Market." *Response,* December 1999.

PREMIUM BOTTLED BEVERAGES

Dubbed "New Age" drinks, premium bottled beverages met the new millennium as a force to be reckoned with, drawing consumers' tastebuds away from soft drinks and alcoholic beverages. The 1999 Beverage Market Index reported that while soft drinks still captured 50 percent of the beverage market, premium bottled beverages were gaining ground. The developing, but still poorly defined, product category includes juice drinks, sports drinks, nutraceutical beverages, ready-to-drink (RTD) teas, and prepackaged iced coffee. The category excludes alcoholic beverages, soft drinks, and the increasingly popular bottled water.

The premium beverage market was worth about $8.6 billion by 1999, according to Beverage Marketing Corp. Information Resources of Chicago reported that 1999 category sales were up 14.8 percent over 1998. Juice-drink sales demonstrated a 13.8 percent dollar increase from October 1998 to October 1999 and RTD tea an 8.7 percent increase in the same period. Isotonic sports drinks posted a 4.3 percent increase.

The late 1990s were marked by especially strong growth in "nutraceutical" or "functional" drinks, which can consist of practically any type of premium beverage that contains ingredients touted as "enhancing" its "health benefits." Common nutraceutical ingredients include ginseng, kava kava, calcium, and vitamins C and A. The nutraceutical component of New Age beverages generated $350 million in wholesale industry sales in 1999 and Beverage Marketing predicted continued segment growth to $600 million by 2004. The research firm SPINS, however, pegged

2000 sales of the widely defined functional beverage sector at $1.17 billion. Of the 3,069 new beverages that debuted in 1999, 18.5 percent were described as "functional" or "good for you." This trend was expected to continue into the 2000s.

Producers of premium bottled beverages include companies of all sizes, from beverage industry giants Coca-Cola Co. and PepsiCo Inc. to specialty firms such as Snapple Beverages and even small regional manufacturers. Distribution varies according to a company's array of products and how each is manufactured. Coca-Cola and Pepsi dominate the distribution system in the United States by virtue of their size and market share.

Beverages are formulated and packaged using either a hot-fill or cold-fill processing method that is determined in part by the nature of the product in question. Hot fill, in which bottles are filled with hot liquid and immediately sealed, is the accepted method of bottling iced teas, for example. For cold-filled products, flavors are extracted from fruit or other ingredients while they are cold.

During the late 1990s, in response to the public's growing concern about *E. coli* and other food-borne diseases, manufacturers began paying extra attention to the bottling process in an effort to prevent contamination. Juice bottlers in particular have boosted quality control measures and turned to pasteurization, which kills potentially harmful bacteria, for added safety.

FRUIT JUICES AND JUICE DRINKS

Fruit juices and juice drinks (beverages containing less than 100 percent fruit juice) are the second-most popular type of beverage in the United States after carbonated soft drinks. They are typically available in single-serving portions that consumers might purchase in food-service establishments and convenience stores or from vending machines. Although juice consumption declined during the 1980s, it picked up again during the 1990s. Health-conscious consumers, clever marketing, expanded distribution, and a wider variety of flavors are credited with reversing the downward trend and boosting sales. In creating new flavors they hope will capture the public's fancy, juice makers experimented with juice blends as well as with single-fruit juice drinks. The American public's expanding awareness of nutrition boosted sales of some established products. For example, the health properties of purple grape juice, which contains the same antiartery clogging flavenoids as red wine, contributed to a 40-50 percent increase in sales of Welch's purple grape juice from 1995 to 1999.

READY-TO-DRINK TEA

Although ready-to-drink (RTD) tea had been on the market for several years when brands such as Snapple and AriZona arrived on the scene, it had not caught on with consumers. But Snapple and AriZona changed all that with single-serve, RTD beverages that actually tasted like brewed tea.

Snapple hit the national market in 1988. It enjoyed several good years during the early 1990s before sales fizzled in the middle of the decade, dropping 9 percent in 1995 and 8 percent in 1996. Purchased by Triarc Companies in 1997, Snapple recovered market share in 1998. AriZona Iced Tea was launched by Ferolito, Vultaggio & Sons in 1992 to compete with Snapple. Its unique packaging and competitive pricing helped draw consumers to the brand.

Lipton and Nestea, the traditional distributors of bottled iced tea, responded to their new competitors by forging alliances with Pepsi and Coca-Cola, the undisputed leaders in the soft drink industry. With the distribution and marketing might of Pepsi and Coke behind them, they remained the top-selling RTD teas. Lipton claimed about 38 percent market share in 1999 and Nestea 27 percent.

SPORTS DRINKS

Sports drinks experienced remarkable growth in the late 1990s. Quaker Oats' Gatorade, the granddaddy of the category, continued to maintain its overwhelming lead with nearly 80 percent of the domestic sports-drink market, despite increased competition in the form of new sports drinks from Pepsi, Coca-Cola, and other manufacturers. Gatorade constitutes a highly distinctive brand even beyond the beverage industry. Sales of Gatorade rose by 10 percent annually from 1994 to 2000, and alone generate about 40 percent of Quaker Oats' overall revenues. Quaker Oats also tailored the Gatorade line for a range of athletic abilities, from Frost (for less-energetic exercisers) to Fierce (for the more so). It also developed a flavored "workout water"—Propel Fitness Water—whose lighter taste and fewer calories were intended to draw female consumers.

Gatorade's chief competitors, Coca-Cola's POWERaDE and Pepsi's All Sport, together account for most of the remaining sports-drink market. Attempts by other companies to market sports drinks have often failed.

Sports drinks face another challenge in their efforts to snag a bigger share of the beverage market—criticism from health professionals. While doctors and others in the medical field agree that encouraging athletes to drink more fluids is laudable, they doubt the nutritional benefits of sports drinks. In fact, the high sugar content of such products as Gatorade translates into more calories, and its acidic nature (coupled with the high sugar content) helps promote tooth decay.

NUTRACEUTICAL DRINKS

Nutraceuticals or functional foods constituted the rising stars of the premium beverage industry. All nutraceutical foods, whether solid or liquid, contain ingredients that are reputed to increase the product's health-boosting potential beyond whatever inherent nutritional value it already possesses. Although some nutraceutical ingredients straddle the line between herbs, dietary supplements, and drugs, promoters of functional foods are prohibited by law from making any explicit claims that their products treat or prevent specific diseases or medical conditions. They may, however, provide general statements about the product's ability to enhance bodily structures and functioning. Manufacturers who ignore these guidelines run the risk of having the product classified as a drug instead of a food, and hence subjected to the stringent and costly clinical trials procedure required for U.S. Food and Drug Administration approval to market the product.

Manufacturers like nutraceutical drinks because they can charge premium prices for them. And the ultrabullish economy of the 1990s encouraged health-conscious, aging baby boomers to spend freely on items they perceived would help prolong their vitality and youth.

Orange juice was among the first beverages to earn nutraceutical status, with the addition of calcium to brands such as PepsiCo's Tropicana and Coca-Cola's Minute Maid. Snapple introduced a new nutraceutical drink line in the late 1990s—Elements. Each of the drinks is based on an elemental name, such as Sky. AriZona Beverages unveiled a new decaffeinated, tea-based Rx line of herb-infused health drinks, such as Rx Memory and Rx Stress, to address specific health concerns. But, cautioned Bart Vinza, AriZona's vice president of national accounts, "we make no claims at all for [their] health benefits." Quaker Oats entered a joint venture with the Consumer Health division of Switzerland's Novartis to create Altus Foods, a nutraceutical line under development for the North American market. Quaker also sought expansion into this sector on its own, bringing out a carbohydrate-laced fruit drink—Torq—to boost energy, which also contains B vitamins and antioxidants. Soy, heralded for its anticancer and antiheart-disease properties, popped up in South Beach Beverage's (SoBe) functional Soy Essentials, fruit-flavored elixirs supplemented with herbs.

CURRENT CONDITIONS

Americans keep getting thirstier. Total U.S. per capita beverage consumption increased by 2.7 gallons in 1998 alone. Sports-drink sales set records in 1999, according to the Beverage Marketing Corp. Total sales for 1999 were up 10 percent over those for 1998, with per capital U.S. consumption at 2.3 gallons.

Nutraceutical characteristics spilled into virtually every other premium beverage category, so that juice drinks, ready-to-drink (RTD) teas, and sports drinks all made room for new functional product mates. Manufacturers introduced functional beverages as extensions of existing product lines. For example, SoBe added Tsunami orange cream to its Lizard line and Lean Peach to its Lean teas. Tsunami contains taurine, guarana, zinc, and vitamins A, B-complex, C, and E. Minute Maid, an operating group of Coca-Cola, fortified its old standby line, Hi-C fruit drink, with calcium. Ocean Spray brought out Cranberry Juice Cocktail Plus, loaded with calcium and vitamins A, C, and E. These functional additions will enable Ocean Spray to charge 20-30 percent more than it does for its standard juices.

More On SPORTS DRINKS

Physical fitness fanatics gulp down over $1 billion worth of sports beverages every year. Gatorade, with 80 percent of the market, is among the 50 leading brand-name sellers in supermarkets. So what is the big attraction? According to David Whitford in *Fortune*, the sports beverage "looks like something Sam would serve with green eggs and ham." Where did it come from? Dr. Michael Cade of the University of Florida invented the beverage in the early 1960s to rehydrate the Florida Gators, the school football team. Cade's first recipes failed to pass the taste test and some players went so far as to heave the stuff after drinking it. It was Mrs. Mary Cade, the doctor's wife, who came up with an idea to introduce lemon juice in the formula. The lemon juice did the trick, and made the difference between drinkable and indigestible. Dr. Cade made the stuff in his lab until 1967 when he sold the rights to Stokely-Van Camp.

Are sports drinks particularly beneficial? Nutrition experts claimed that a quart of water can be just as beneficial except during an ultrastrenuous workout that lasts for 90 minutes or longer.

Among new nutraceutical launches, Snapple premiered a functional line, Zotics. Besides claiming nutraceutical properties, each Zotic drink is linked to an unusual fruit or botanical and to its country of origin. Thus, the yuzu fruit drink will bear a label tied to Japan; acerola berry to Barbados; pitaya to Brazil; mangosteen to Thailand; and ginseng green tea to Tibet. Hansen Natural Corp. came up with Energy and D Stress drinks, and Personal Health Development of Ventura, California, with Think! "interactive" sodas. Even omega-3 fatty acids wended their way into a new drink, Naked Superfood Tidal Wave Super Juice by California Day Fresh Foods. Among sports drinks, Hansen Natural Corp. introduced black-cherry flavored Hansen's Power, laced with B vitamins, glutamine, and the more controversial athletic supplement creatine.

Although nutraceutical beverages constituted the hottest new product segment at the turn of the 21st century, the American Dietetic Association reported that only about 20 percent of the Americans they polled were even familiar with the category. Moreover, the dosages of nutraceutical ingredients in many products are often too low to generate any appreciable impact on health. Still, this was the trendiest industry segment, a fact that many analysts thought could turn into a problem as companies flock to bring products of dubious quality to market under the "functional" banner, thus tarnishing the sector's image.

In 1999 RTD tea enjoyed a significant increase in sales, according to Beverage Marketing Corp.'s *1999 RTD Tea & Coffee Report.* Case sales equaled 515 million gallons, 8 percent above 1998, and wholesale sales reached $1.46 billion, 9 percent ahead of the previous year. Much of the renewed interest in the category resulted from increased consumer attention in nutrient-enhanced teas, such as those produced by SoBe and AriZona. Regular RTD teas posted a 4.7 percent increase in sales revenue for 1999, but those for nutraceutical tea climbed an impressive 172.8 percent.

Fruit drinks experienced the second-largest number of new product introductions in 1999 after teas, with an increase of 15.3 percent over 1998, according to Productscan Online.

Among exotic ingredients, guarana emerged from the Amazon basin as a new form of caffeine whose functional claims encompassed pumping up energy and libido while suppressing appetite and the urge to smoke. Although several industry heavy hitters attempted to introduce guarana-based drinks, without much success, the ingredient also appeared in the late 1990s as an offering from much smaller beverage companies. For example, Miami-based Hobarama Corp. unwrapped its Bawls Guarana in 1997; New York's Tribal Tonics also had a product containing guarana mixed with green tea and ginseng. PepsiCo tried an ill-fated launch in 1996 of guarana-based Josta, which failed to hook American teens; the product was abandoned. In an even bolder move, Coca-Cola brought guarana beverages to the Latin American market in the late 1990s. The initial reception from locals was less than enthusiastic, however.

Marketing, packaging, and distribution also changed. Part of increased consumer attention to the sector was due to a marketing shift from television commercials and national promotions to more localized ad and sampling efforts and a growing focus on tailoring new product development to various segments of the consumer population. Triarc learned this when it brought recently purchased Snapple out of a sales slump by generating a brand-new product platform—the dairy-based WhipperSnapple—rather than merely relying on extensions of the existing product lines to garner more sales. But it failed to pursue the same strategy with its other troubled brand, Mistic, which it acquired in 1995. In summer 1999, Triarc debuted two new major products, Mistic Italian Ice Smoothies and Sun Valley Squeeze, a cold-filled fruit drink in a "grabable" plastic bottle aimed at teen consumers. Bottling beverages in distinctive, wide-mouthed carafelike containers also proved successful for lifting sales of higher-priced, higher-juice content drinks.

Most premium beverage sales occur at convenience stores; only about 20 percent of all products are sold in supermarkets. Augmenting those sales was a priority with manufacturers, who found that offering their formulations in larger containers, in addition to single-serving bottles or cans, increased their appeal to supermarket shoppers.

Even a product with the overwhelming category domination of Gatorade sought to expand market presence by shifting distribution strategy to make it nearly as ubiquitous as water to thirsty, sweating athletes. In the mid-1990s, Quaker Oats identified nearly 100,000 likely sites that could extend the availability of Gatorade: country clubs, marinas, and stadiums, to name a few. The 40,000 new sales outlets on board by 1999 produced $100 million in additional sales that year, according to the company—or 25 percent of Gatorade's total sales. Gatorade also expanded its roster of star-athlete spokespeople beyond mainstay Michael Jordan, signing on Mia Hamm, Vince Carter, and Cal Ripken Jr. to broadcast the product's appeal.

By 2000, RTD iced-coffee drinks still failed to make much of an impact on consumers. Starbucks' Frappacino, produced in conjunction with PepsiCo, defined the sector with approximately 80 percent market share. The category overall demonstrated only 2 percent growth in 1999, with about $200 million in wholesale sales—roughly equal to 7 percent of those for RTD tea.

Entering the prepackaged beverage market in 1998 were various dairy-based "smoothie" drinks such as Triarc's WhipperSnapple and Hansen's Natural line. Tracking milk or other dairy drinks is done only on a limited basis by the beverage industry, however, since they are technically regarded as food items. To help make sure this category remains part of the milk industry rather than the beverage industry, the International Dairy Foods Association announced plans in 1997 to begin brokering the production and marketing of new products between dairies. The association also hoped to spur development and production of fruit and coffee drinks targeted at children and young people. SoBe's dairy based line was Lizard, and it planned two new product launches in the line per year.

INDUSTRY LEADERS

Quaker Oats Co. leads the premium bottled beverage industry as a result of Gatorade's success among sports drinks. Gatorade was the creation of Dr. Michael Cade, a researcher at the University of Florida who invented the greenish-yellow liquid to serve as a hydrating replacement for body fluids lost in athletic competition and during hot weather. Players for the Florida Gators football team who drank the concoction had fewer problems with dehydration and showed increased efficiency and greater endurance.

Dr. Cade sold the rights to Gatorade to Stokely-Van Camp in 1967. Quaker Oats bought Stokely in 1983 when Gatorade sales checked in at about $120 million. In 1999 the popular sports drink generated just over one-third of Quaker Oats' $4.725 billion in total sales. "Gatorade defines the category," declared Jesse Meyers, publisher of Beverage Digest, "There is not a beverage category in any country in the world that is so dominated by one producer." Gatorade claimed nearly 80 percent of the U.S. sports drink market in 2000. That year, Coca-Cola nearly agreed to acquire the firm, but broke off talks, only to have Pepsi move in and discuss takeover plans.

Coca-Cola Co. and PepsiCo Inc., best-known for soft drinks, maintain a prominent place in the alternative beverage field through their control of an assortment of familiar brands, including Coca-Cola's Minute Maid and Fruitopia fruit juices, Nestea iced tea, and POWERaDE sports drink. PepsiCo distributes Tropicana and Ocean Spray fruit juices, Lipton iced tea, and All Sport sports drink.

Ocean Spray Cranberries, Inc., is a cooperative of over 900 cranberry and citrus growers founded in 1930. It has been credited with reinventing the cranberry by coming up with new products and marketing strategies. Among the group's most successful endeavors are the "Crave the Wave" juice blends, estimated to account for about 80 percent of sales. Ocean Spray suffered a loss in sales' dollars in 1999 due to weak harvests and smaller rivals gaining market share. Ocean Spray has suffered from low prices and high harvests since 1981, but still controls 55 percent of the cranberry juice market. In addition, it produces Ruby Red grapefruit juice. Ocean Spray operates in 46 countries and had total sales of $1.48 billion in 1998.

Nantucket Nectars was founded by Tom First and Tom Scott, who met while attending Brown University. The pair started in business as provisioners in Nantucket Harbor and then opened a deli, where they began tinkering with concocting drinks. Their products include juice nectars, a "Super Nectars" line of functional drinks and herb-infused teas. Located in Cambridge, Massachusetts, Nantucket Nectars employed approximately 100 people and posted sales in the late 1990s of $45 million. In December 1997 it formed a partnership with rival Ocean Spray. Under

the terms of the agreement, Ocean Spray acquired a major stake in Nantucket Nectars, which continued operating as a free-standing company while taking advantage of the bigger firm's purchasing power and production expertise.

The standout among "alternative" premium beverages is South Beach Beverage (SoBe), a Norwalk, Connecticut-based company, whose primary production focus is herbally enhanced beverages. Though SoBe appeared on the scene only in 1995, they are the market leaders in their category. Sales increased 175 percent in 1999 to $166.4 million, from $67.3 million in 1998, demonstrating the fastest segment growth in the industry. Company founder Jerry Bello predicted sales would reach 225 million cases, or $275 million, in 2000. The company is credited with giving herbal drinks greater market visibility. In late 2000 the company, like Quaker Oats, was the subject of dramatic acquisition talks, first by Coca-Cola and then by Pepsi.

Among producers of RTD teas, Lipton (owned by PepsiCo) enjoys by far the largest market share. Yet two other brands, Snapple and AriZona, have attracted attention with quirky advertising, innovative packaging, and trendy flavors.

Snapple Beverage Corp. was established in 1986 in Brooklyn, New York. Founders Lenny Marsh, Hymie Golden, and Arnie Greenberg regarded their product as an alternative to sweet soft drinks. The national success it achieved during the early 1990s can be traced in part to a humorous series of television advertisements featuring Wendy, the "Snapple Lady." She was a bona fide marketing department employee of the company who read and answered customers' letters to Snapple on the air. Sales soared, reaching over $700 million by 1994, the year Quaker Oats bought the firm for $1.7 billion. But Quaker Oats soon sold Snapple to Triarc Companies after several years of declining sales that analysts blamed on distribution difficulties and a lack of promotion. A holding company with interests in several different industries, Triarc worked to turn the brand around, posting a 14 percent increase in case sales in the first quarter of 1999. Total sales for 1999 inched up 5 percent to reach $854 million. It also introduced a number of new products at the end of the 1990s, including WhipperSnapple smoothies, Snapple Farms juices, a line of herbal enhanced fruit drinks and teas called Elements, Mistic brand Italian Ice Smoothies, and Sun Valley Squeeze fruit-flavored drinks. In 2000 Triarc agreed to sell Snapple to Cardbury Schweppes.

Ferolito, Vultaggio & Sons, purveyors of the AriZona Iced Tea brand, started in business as beer distributors in Brooklyn, New York, during the 1970s. Their fleet eventually grew from one Volkswagen bus to 25 trucks. In 1986 they decided to try *making* beer rather than just delivering it. They experimented first with brewing malt liquors, then branched out to iced teas in 1992. Within two years, the AriZona brand was posting $300 million in sales. The company's innovative packaging, including larger-than-average portions and trendy "good-for-you" formulations featuring green teas and ginseng, helped build the AriZona brand. As of 1999, the AriZona brand of RTD teas accounted for $500 million in sales, ranking just behind Lipton and Snapple.

WORK FORCE

Increased regulations and more sophisticated equipment in bottling plants have created a need for better trained and more highly skilled employees in the beverage industry. Specialized courses of study such as the Beverage Technician certification program at Florida International University assure employers that their workers are properly educated.

Management-level employees are expected to have degrees in the sciences or engineering, with follow-up training and education from trade-specific groups such as the International Society of Beverage Technologists. For areas such as quality control, employment requirements might demand that candidates possess a degree in microbiology, biology, chemistry, or field science. Additional experience in statistical process control, blending, flavors, and sanitation is considered a plus.

AMERICA AND THE WORLD

U.S. companies dominate the worldwide beverage industry. Among the exceptions are two firms based in Mexico, PanAmerican Beverage, a Coca-Cola-affiliated distributor, and Pepsi-Gemex.

Soft drinks continued to invade developing nations, stealing beverage consumers away from more traditional beverages such as coffee and tea. In India, the world's largest consumer of tea, young people increasingly flocked to Western soft drinks, since they considered tea to be a "frumpy" drink of their elders. But tea producers and marketers looked to the nutraceutical properties of the drink to reinvigorate the flagging market. Tata Tea, whose acquisition of Tetley Tea made it the world's second-largest tea company, intended to introduce functional teas into the Indian market. And Hindustan Lever Ltd. was test-marketing its mass-brand tea A1 fortified with vitamins and minerals.

Beverage preferences vary widely from country to country. Americans tend to drink less fruit juice than Western Europeans, partly because of the popularity of soft drinks in the United States. The overall European market for flavors, which form key components of processed foods and premium beverages, was expected to increase to $1.65 billion from $1.27 billion in the period from 1997 to 2005, according to the Frost & Sullivan report, *The European Market for Flavours*. Functional foods won increased consumer attention in the late 1990s, with diary-based and vitamin-enhanced drinks especially popular in Germany, where the market segment grew by about 29 percent. In the Asian market, carbonated drinks are popular, but consumers also favor canned coffees and teas as well as mineral water. In Japan, for example, Georgia brand iced coffee, a Coca-Cola product, is a top-selling item.

RESEARCH AND TECHNOLOGY

Formulation and flavoring are ongoing preoccupations of premium beverage companies. With growing consumer demand for vitamins, minerals, and other health-related products, the challenge for flavoring companies trying to keep up with this trend is to provide beverage companies with nutritionally sound yet tasty products.

Many nutraceutical and flavoring ingredients in New Age beverages are difficult to work with because they have very strong flavors or odors, or because they add unaesthetic colorings to products. Food engineers both in the United States and abroad work to develop versions of these ingredients more amenable to combination in consumer beverages. In Europe, Zylepsis engaged in proprietary extraction work that permitted it to create black tea—a popular but hard-to-work-with flavor—as a white powder that is decaffeinated and becomes clear in beverage applications, thus eliminating the murky coloring it normally imparts to beverages. The U.S.-based Folexco/East Earth Herb focuses on creating blends of herbs and botanicals for use in beverages, scrutinizing the 25 most commonly used botanicals to identify pleasing combinations of what the company terms "collateral" flavors. These include echinacea extract combined with citrus, and the relaxation-inducing herb valerian, which "smells like dirty socks at high levels," according to company CEO Dave Wilson. The firm devised a microencapsulation technology that permits the ingredient to be time-released to avoid unpleasant odors while showcasing valerian's "berry notes." In search of ever-more exotic tastes, Givaudan Roure Flavours established a TasteTrek program to scout out new botanicals in the central African rainforest that would be extracted for further investigation in Givaudan's Swiss and American laboratories.

FURTHER READING

"Beverage Ownership Saga Has Yet to Play Out." *Atlanta Journal and Constitution,* 5 November 2000.

"The Beverage World Top 50." *Beverage World,* July 1999.

"Beverages." *Discount Merchandiser,* December 1999.

Buss, Dale. "Skepticism from Supermarkets over New Age Beverages." *Supermarket News,* 15 November 1999.

Cherkassky, Irene, and Greg Prince. "Functional's Juncture." *Beverage World,* 15 April 2000.

"Consumers' Taste for Alternative Drinks Grows." *Chain Drug Review,* 14 February 2000.

Dawson, Havis. "Snap! Crackle! Pop!" *Beverage World,* 15 July 1999.

Fanelli, Christa. "Live Deals: J.W. Childs Laps up Herbal Drink Co." *Buyouts,* 15 May 2000.

Gates, Kelly. "The Latest Buzz." *Brandmarketing,* December 1999.

Howell, Debbie. "Gatorade vs. the Beverage Giants—Going Head-to-Head in Sport Drinks." *Discount Store News,* 7 February 2000.

Khermouch, Gerry. "Mistical Quest." *Brandweek,* 26 July 1999.

MacArthur, Kate. "New Age Still the Rage in Beverages." *Advertising Age,* 15 May 2000.

Madley, Rebecca H. "The Nutraceutical Beverage Market." *Nutraceuticals World,* September 2000.

McKay, Betsy. "SoBe Hopes Edgy Ads Can Induce Masses to Try Its 'Lizard Fuel.'" *Wall Street Journal,* 28 April 2000.

"Millennial Trends." *Beverage World,* December 1999.

Murray, Barbara. "Drink to Your Health." *Supermarket News,* 21 February 2000.

"New Age Flavours." *Food Engineering International,* September 1999.

Phillips, Kent. "The Thriller in the Chiller." *Beverage World,* 15 November 1999.

"The Post-Mike Millennium." *Brandweek,* 3 January 2000.

Prince, Greg. "Beverage Market Index 1999." *Beverage World,* 15 May 1999.

————. "Gonna Fly Now." *Beverage World,* 15 December 1999.

————. "Greener Pastures." *Beverage World,* 15 March 2000.

Seraita, Steven, and Julie O'Donnell. "Don't Assume." *Beverage World,* 15 November 1999.

Staab, Deborah. "Tea Party." *Prepared Foods,* April 2000.

"State of the Industry Report." *Beverage Industry,* July 1999.

Thompson, Stephanie. "Seeking Momentum, Ocean Spray Readies Vitamin-Enhanced Cocktails." *Brandweek,* 12 July 1999.

"2000 Soft Drink Report: Wellness Fever Hits in 1999." *Beverage Industry,* March 2000.

Upbin, Bruce. "Breaking a Sweat." *Forbes,* 27 December 1999.

Vaishna, Roy. "The Cup That Needs Cheer." *Business Line,* 30 March 2000.

Whishart, George. "Tricky Iced Tea Targets." *Beverage World,* 15 January 2000.

Printers and Printer Accessories

As with many mainstream high-tech sectors, computer printer manufacturers have been faced with a competitive paradox: unit demand for their wares has been growing swiftly, but competition and technical advances have steadily eroded prices, and hence, per-unit dollar sales and profits. In fact, for common models of ink-jet and laser printers, manufacturers have found the repeat business of buying consumable supplies such as ink and toner cartridges more profitable than selling the machines needing those supplies. Manufacturers' margins on supplies have been estimated as high as 50 percent, compared to razor-thin margins on most popular printer models—some printer makers are believed to take a loss on some models in order to remain competitive.

Still, demand for most types of printers has been strong and is expected to remain healthy in the early 2000s. For Lyra Research, Inc., a market research firm specializing in imaging products, global printer shipments in 1999 rose 14 percent to nearly 75 million machines. By 2003, shipments were forecast to leap by one-third, approaching 100 million units. Industry revenues, on the other hand, were predicted to remain flat, at around $32 billion a year, over that period. The U.S. market accounted for about 30 percent of world purchases.

Fully two-thirds of printers shipped worldwide in 1999 were ink-jets, with sales driven by lower prices, better performance, and healthy new computer sales. Ink-jets have been wildly popular as personal printers almost since their debut, but more robust versions are now being bought for home offices and small work-group settings. Among the fastest-growing segments

within the ink-jet category in the early 2000s were multifunction models, which double as fax machines, scanners, or photocopiers, and network ink-jets, which allow office work-groups to share a single high-performance ink-jet printer. Lyra Research expected 2-3 million multifunction and network ink-jets to be flying off store shelves and warehouse pallets by 2002.

Other segments of the business have held their own as well. Color laser printers, luxury items in the mid-1990s, were growing more commonplace as prices came down and as the technology improved. And monochrome lasers, staples in most offices, continue to do moderate business, although their unit growth has been eclipsed by more versatile devices such as multifunction and color laser printers.

Current printers for ordinary home and office use rely on two technologies: ink-jet imaging and laser imaging. These two broad imaging technologies come in a wide array of specifications and capabilities, but together they have been so widely adopted that they have all but crowded out several competing imaging technologies—both in high-end and low-end applications—such as dye sublimation and dot-matrix.

RESOLUTION: COUNTING THE DOTS

A host of factors, such as print quality, speed, and printer capability, affect the cost of a printer. Measured horizontally and vertically, the number of dots per inch (dpi) determines the print quality or resolution. Most new printers in the early 2000s could produce at 600 by 600 dpi, a stark contrast to the mid-1990s when 300 dpi was the norm. Better printers today can readily print at 1,200 dpi and even 2,400 dpi—at or near professional-quality resolution, depending on what's being printed.

SPEED DEMONS AND DIVAS

Printer speed, measured in pages per minute (ppm), is most important to office workers and other high-volume users. Usually the technology to print faster costs more, although advances in this area, as is so often the case, have made speeds that were once considered appropriate for high-volume offices available at only moderate cost to home and small office users.

Manufacturers rate their printers with a target speed, say 12 ppm, but as many users and product reviewers find, printers often fall shy of this speed in real life. In general, laser printers work faster than ink-jets. In the early 2000s monochrome laser printers commonly came with rated speeds ranging between 8 ppm and 30 ppm, while color lasers often lagged at 4 ppm. Product tests, however, suggested the same printers in reality usually averaged half or even a quarter of their rated speeds. Typical ink-jet speed ratings were between 4 ppm and 10 ppm, but again, actual speeds tended to lag 50 percent or more.

DEMISE OF THE DOT-MATRIX

Dot-matrix printers at one time led the computer printer market, but are now relegated to such specialty commercial applications as printing multipart forms. The once industry-standard dot-matrix printer lost its appeal to the general market in the 1990s because the technology failed to keep up with competitive products. Dot-matrix technology employs some basic typewriter principles: the print head strikes a ribbon making contact with the paper to print characters. The noisy dot-matrix technology is cheap and easy to care for; however, the speed and print quality of dot-matrix printers lags far behind competing printer technologies, spurring its decline.

LASER PRINTERS UP CLOSE

Laser printers create images much as copy machines do, and rely on the same technology. As rollers advance paper through the printer, toner is dispensed to areas of the page that are to be shaded and heat is used to permanently bond it to the paper. This system creates a fast, reliable, and flexible printer with high-quality resolution. Laser printers require a new toner cartridge about every 2,000 to 8,000 pages.

INK-JETS EXAMINED

Ink-jet printers, on the other hand, work by funneling ink through small nozzles in the printer head where it makes contact with the paper. The ink-jet printer gradually evolved with its adoption of smaller and smaller nozzles since its inception, allowing it to produce enhanced quality print jobs. Technological advances also made the mid-1990s ink-jet printer a viable alternative to laser printers, not only for home use, but also for office use. In the mid-1990s, the industry-standard ink-jet printer included color and monochrome capabilities and contained two ink cartridges. The color cartridges included three to six base colors, where more base colors usually produce more realistic colors in images. Ink-jets may have a separate black cartridge for printing text documents; this tends to produce a better black than the alternative of mixing colors. Ink-jet printers need new ink cartridges about every 500 to 1,000 sheets of paper. In addition, most ink-jet printers require special coated paper to produce optimal output.

SPECIALTY PRINTERS

Besides these standard technologies, a number of specialty printers exist. These specialty models largely serve the image-arts sector. Wax thermal transfer printers produce high-quality transparencies, but they have limited capabilities for general and business-related printing needs. A related printer, the dye sublimation printer, creates some of the most compelling graphic images by injecting the ink in variously sized dots and allowing the colors to bleed together to yield more realistic images. Therefore, these printers offer a superb option for anyone needing to print photographs, advertisements, and otherwise graphically intense documents. A new line of ink-jet printers, phase-change ink-jet printers, also hit the market in the 1990s, providing a faster ink-jet solution for color printing. Averaging about four pages per minute, the phase-change printer works by melting ink sticks and spraying the molten form on to the paper where it becomes solid again. Higher-end ink-jets have stolen market share from technologies such as dye sublimation because they deliver similar quality.

TRADE ASSOCIATION BRINGS 'EM ALL TOGETHER

The North American Graphic Arts Suppliers Association (NAGASA) serves the industry by linking manufacturers, retailers, and users of computer printers designed for the graphics-arts market. NAGASA's members include printer industry behemoth Hewlett-Packard Co. The association strives to enhance its members' distribution channels, reducing their costs and improving their business. NAGASA also provides a noncommercial forum for discussing matters relevant to the graphics-arts and printing-related industries and encourages research to help advance printer technology.

CURRENT CONDITIONS

The trend toward low-cost ink-jets has dominated the industry, accounting for as much as 80 percent of U.S. printer shipments in 1999, according to a market study by Dataquest. The research firm reported that nearly 24 million printers were purchased by U.S. businesses and consumers in 1999, up 23 percent from the year before. Ink-jet growth outpaced that of the broader market, rising 30 percent in 1999.

CHEAP INK-JETS KEY

Low-cost ink-jet printers, which sell for as little as $50, have proven a battleground where up-and-coming manufacturers such as Lexmark International can challenge such traditional leaders as Hewlett-Packard (HP). Lexmark, which is credited with trailblazing sub-$100 printers in 1998, reportedly controlled upwards of 50 percent of that market in 1999. As computer prices dipped below $1,000, Lexmark realized that customers wanted to maintain the relative proportion of printer prices, and brought out their ultra-cheap modles to jump on this new market rather than try to compete against giants such as Hewlett-Packard in their specialty fields. HP, for its part, has fought back by launching the Apollo line of cheap, user-friendly personal printers. Printer makers see such devices being sold routinely through mass-merchandisers such as Wal-Mart Stores, Inc., where consumers might pick up a new printer and supplies much as they would a coffeemaker or filters.

For the time being, though, HP remains dominant both in laser and ink-jet printers. Dataquest estimated that in 1999 HP controlled 49 percent of the U.S. ink-jet market, trailed by Canon, Epson, and Lexmark, all of which were believed to have shares in the mid-teens.

In addition to those contenders, HP faces challenges in the ink-jet arena from Xerox Corp., which has been trying to elbow its way into the low-end printer business as part of a corporate turnaround strategy. In an alliance with Fuji and Sharp, Xerox unveiled in 2000 a new line of low-cost ink-jets that the company claimed would significantly outperform HP

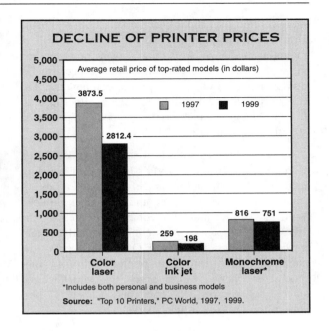

DECLINE OF PRINTER PRICES

Average retail price of top-rated models (in dollars)

■ 1997   ■ 1999

Color laser: 3873.5 (1997), 2812.4 (1999)
Color ink jet: 259 (1997), 198 (1999)
Monochrome laser*: 816 (1997), 751 (1999)

*Includes both personal and business models

Source: "Top 10 Printers," PC World, 1997, 1999.

models on both speed and ink conservation. In 1999 analysts reckoned Xerox had just 2 percent of the market, but the imaging giant appeared determined to wage an aggressive campaign to raise its profile in the business.

EMERGING CATEGORIES

Outside growth in the ink-jet market, printers that offer enhanced capabilities and performance have been driving nearly all the growth in the rest of the printer market. This is to the detriment of ordinary monochrome laser printers, which have been treading water in terms of unit sales. The monochrome market was still handily controlled by HP, which boasted as much as 72 percent of the market in the key 11-20 ppm monochrome laser market; Lexmark was a distant second in this category with 17 percent of the market. Important categories of enhanced devices include multifunction printers, color laser printers, and high-speed (30-50 ppm) monochrome lasers.

INDUSTRY LEADERS

Hewlett-Packard Co. (HP) continues to lead the printer industry with its popular laser and ink-jet models. Deriving 80 percent of its revenues from computer systems and peripherals sales, HP is a computer industry powerhouse. The company has a major presence in most segments of the computer printer business and in 2000 had commanding leads in the monochrome laser and ink-jet markets, both within the United States and in many parts of the world. It faces mounting challenges from other players, however, and in some cases is at a cost disadvantage because HP doesn't make all of its own printer components. The company had $42.4 billion in sales in its 1999, although imaging and printing goods represented slightly less than half, at $18.9 billion.

Epson America Inc., a division of Seiko Epson Corp., is another of the world's largest printer manufacturers. The Japanese company provides a host of state-of-the-art laser, ink-jet, and dot-matrix printers. With the stiff demand for computer printers in the 1990s, the company's sales climbed steadily, reaching $8.8 billion in fiscal 1999. Over 50 percent of the company's sales derive from printers and other computer components, which Epson has manufactured since 1982, and by 2000 commanded about 17 percent of the low-end printer market.

Lexmark International, a spin-off from IBM, increased its hold on the computer printer market in the 1990s. With three-quarters of its sales from computer printers and related wares, Lexmark excels in offering quality printers at competitive prices. Since Lexmark manufactures all of its printer components, the company can sell its products at a lower price than other printer markers. Lexmark produces all of the standard technologies: laser, ink-jet, and dot-matrix printers. Besides its printers, Lexmark manufacturers toner cartridges, ink-jet cartridges, coated paper, and connection cables. In 1999 Lexmark's sales were up 14 percent, to $3.5 billion, and its net earnings surged 31 percent.

Xerox Corp. had been scarcely visible in the printer business until the late 1990s, when it began aggressively rolling out low-end models to build market presence. Some of its printers were actually made by Lexmark. Xerox has also been increasingly involved in the color printer segment through its 1999 acquisition of Tektronix, a maker of higher-end printers. In 2000 Xerox teamed up with Fuji and Sharp to develop low-end ink-jet printers.

Other important computer printer manufacturers include Canon Inc.; Brother International Corp.; Panasonic, a division of Matsushita, a leading Japanese electronics manufacturer; and Okidata Inc., a U.S.-based subsidiary of Oki Electric Industry Co., Ltd. of Japan.

RESEARCH AND TECHNOLOGY

In 1996 Oberg Industries Inc. began using a new stamping technique for producing complex metal

---

Trends

NO DARKROOM, NO COMPUTER

Photography enthusiasts who are eager to try one of the new digital cameras, but who dislike the notion of working with a computer, have an alternate option. Early in 1999 Sony introduced the FVP-1 Mavica Photo Printer. The Mavica, a new concept in printing, creates 3-7/8 by 5-1/2-inch photographic images from 3.5-inch floppy disk. The process is as simple as it sounds—pop a floppy disk into a compatible camera; take one or more pictures. Pop out the floppy disk; place it into the printer and print the image. The Mavica hardware includes a self-contained floppy disk drive. An s-video outlet on the printer supports optional direct connection to a television or video camera via cable. The printer cannot and will not connect to a desktop computer.

The printer employs dye sublimation transfer technology to create images of 1.41 million pixels, an excellent level of detail, depending on the resolution at which the picture was taken. An easy-to-install ink ribbon cartridge fuels the printing mechanism. For brave-hearts who would save, edit, or otherwise enhance the images before or after printing, a Windows-based software bundle comes with the printer hardware. Sony's FVP-1 Mavica Photo Printer sells for a street price of well under $500. It weighs seven pounds and prints a photo in less than three minutes. Mavica is designed for compatibility with the Mavica FD81 camera.

---

components of computer printers, according to Richard J. Babyak in *Appliance Manufacturer*. Oberg expects the new stamping process to drastically cut costs of production and improve the overall design of the components. This process costs less because creating parts through stamping is cheaper than creating them through metal injection molding or pulverized metal fabrication—the competing methods. Printer manufacturers have used these parts as base yokes and armature in laser and dot-matrix printers.

Furthermore, Hewlett-Packard led a campaign in 1997 to make computer peripheral connections to local area networks, wide area networks, and to the Internet entirely seamless and independent of hardware and operating systems. HP's JetSend allows users to transmit text and images to peripherals without needing to know the configurations of the hardware—whether it's running a Mac or Windows operating system. This technology promises to help integrate the Internet and mobile communications technology with computer peripherals. JetSend lets a user send data via the Internet to a remote printer (or any remote peripheral), according to Scott Berinato in *PC Week*.

Lexmark was among the companies in 1998 to develop new technologies intending to produce higher quality ink-jet prints. Photorealistic output was a top priority, and new print heads and inks were launched. Epson built in new utilities to help with cleaning and aligning print heads, as well as nozzles. Network color laser printers also were improved, and prices continued to fall as quality rose.

FURTHER READING

Babyak, Richard J. "Cutting the Cost of Complexity." *Appliance Manufacturer,* June 1996.

Berinato, Scott. "HP to Launch 'Appliance Bid.'" *PC Week,* 21 July 1997.

Dominianni, Cheryl. "Printers: Low Prices and Superior Color Bring Photo-Quality Printing to the Desktop." *Windows Magazine,* 15 June 1998.

Flynn, Laurie. "Market for Home Color Printers Is Booming." *New York Times,* 20 May 1996.

Fusaro, Roberta. "Users Doubt Copier/E-mail Combo." *Computerworld,* 21 September 1998.

Gomes, Lee. "Computer-Printer Price Drop Isn't Starving Makers." *Wall Street Journal,* 16 August 1996.

"Hard Copy." *Fortune,* 1 December 1999.

Himowitz, Mike. "The Printer Market is True Blue." *The Baltimore Sun,* 4 September 2000.

Klein, Alec. "As Cheap Printers Take Off, H-P Is Forced to Play Catch-Up." *Wall Street Journal,* 21 April 1999.

————. "Lexmark Launches Six Printers in Bid to Grab Share from H-P." *Wall Street Journal,* 21 September 1999.

————. "Xerox to Offer Low-End Inkjet Printer in Bid to Take on Rival Hewlett-Packard." *Wall Street Journal,* 10 March 2000.

Lyra Research, Inc. "As the Century Closes, Vendors Mull over Industry's Future." *Hard Copy Observer,* January 2000. Available from http://www.lyra.com.

Manes, Stephen. "Banner Days for Ink-Jet Printers." *New York Times,* 30 April 1996.

Matzer, Marla. "Showing a Softer Side of Hardware." *Brandweek,* 7 October 1996.

Narisetti, Raju. "Pounded by Printers, Xerox Goes Digital." *Wall Street Journal,* 12 May 1998.

Perenson, Melissa J. "Convertible Printers." *PC Magazine,* 25 June 1996.

Peterson, Marilyn. "Network Printing Takes Off." *Managing Office Technology,* July/August 1988.

Roberts, John. "Lexmark's Road to Success." *Computer Reseller News,* 28 August 2000.

Roberts, John, and Al Senia. "Company Product Spending." *Computer Reseller News,* 29 June 1998.

Robinson, Phillip. "Laser Printers Still Beating Ink-Jet? Battleground Is Cost Per Page, 'Duty Cycle.'" *San Diego Union-Tribune,* 12 May 1998.

Shore, Joel. "Hard-Copy Spectrum." *Planet IT,* 5 July 1999.

Ward, Joe. "With So Many Printers, Which Do You Buy?" *USA Today,* 11 March 1998.

PROFESSIONAL EMPLOYER ORGANIZATIONS

Despite some icy patches on the road through its development years, employee leasing has emerged as one of the fastest-growing industries in the United States in the late 1990s and into the 2000s, growing at a 30 percent pace annually. The industry's 2,000 firms held responsibility for over $18 billion in wages and benefits for employees in 2000, while industry revenues topped $26 billion. The National Association of Professional Employer Organizations (NAPEO) forecast annual industry growth of 30 to 40 percent through the 2000s.

Professional employer organizations (PEOs), as firms engaged in employee leasing are known, assume the responsibility for a company's employees, placing them all on the PEO's payroll and handling all human resource and legal matters, and then leasing the employees back to the company for a marked-up fee. The larger PEOs, maintaining payrolls of several hundred thousand workers, achieve an economy of scale sufficient enough to offer more comprehensive benefits packages that smaller companies may not be able or willing to provide. Thus, PEOs can afford smaller firms with the ability to provide their employees, vicariously, with Fortune 500 level insurance benefits and other human resources benefits. Since smaller companies are often ill-staffed or insufficiently knowledgeable to manage modern regulatory compliance, legalities, safety and dispute resolutions, and other issues, PEOs can give these firms a leg up, freeing managers and executives to focus on business strategies.

Still, if all that sounds too good to be true, that's because it is. Several legal issues were still being ironed out in the late 1990s as to who was responsible for certain aspects of employment and the regulations that accompany them. While these issues sometimes proved contentious, causing a rift between PEOs and the client pool, the emerging industry was for the most part quite eager to work with regulators and companies to ensure the smoothest overall transition to the employee-leasing practice.

ORGANIZATION AND STRUCTURE

Employee-leasing firms are as varied in size and type as the client companies they represent. The biggest market for PEOs is among firms employing between five and 100 workers. Typically, a PEO will charge a fee to the company equal to between 3 and 6 percent of the client's payroll, plus between 9 and 20 percent of the firm's gross wages for benefits and the PEO's margin. In most cases, the company signs into a coemployment agreement with the PEO whereby the company becomes what is known as a "workside employer."

Employees still take their directions from the company's executives, who maintain control over all company policy and guidelines. Logistical employee concerns, however, such as paychecks, legal concerns, workers' compensation, and so on, are taken up with the PEO. From the employee's standpoint, then, the PEO functions much as a human resources department, although for the company itself, of course, the relationship is much different. Employees also receive the PEO's benefits package, which will generally include health and dental insurance, a 401(k) plan, assistance programs, credit-union membership, and possibly additional perks such as travel benefits or other discount packages.

One successful strategy lies in identifying and serving a particular industry niche. By targeting a particular type of client firm, a leasing company may specialize in terms of benefits offered, client size, payroll size, and risk ratios. PEOs may also assist in the training process for companies, producing training manuals and policy guidelines customized for the client. Often, a PEO will also provide on-site inspections to monitor for Occupational Safety and Health Administration (OSHA) compliance or other regulatory provisions.

Different client industries require different types of expertise from PEOs. Blue-collar manufacturing firms, for example, tend to employ people with lower average salaries but higher workers' compensation claims. White-collar employees in the computer software industry enjoy higher salaries and benefits, so a PEO needs to carve out a cost savings niche by relying on its economies of scale.

Key to the growing popularity of PEOs is the relief they offer in lifting administrative burdens from the shoulders of the client's managers. The U.S. Small Business Administration (SBA) puts the average cost of regulation, tax compliance, and paperwork for smaller companies (fewer than 500 employees) at about $5,000 per employee versus $3,400 for bigger firms. The SBA further estimated that between 7 and 25 percent of the small business owner's time is spent on employee-related paperwork.

A small business owner may be an expert at his or her product or service but a neophyte when it comes to processing workers' compensation claims, providing health insurance, or managing paperwork flow. A good PEO will take over this entire realm of activity, allowing the business owner to devote him- or herself solely to growing the business. While larger corporations have sufficient in-house expertise to handle such matters, smaller firms, especially those with 100 or fewer workers, usually lack such expertise. Few if any small manufacturers, for example, can devote a full-time manager solely to the task of monitoring and improving workplace safety. For these and other small firms, a good PEO can be extremely beneficial.

Small firms typically pay more for insurance and workers' compensation because their risk rating can be thrown off by a single unfortunate case. But in a leased environment, a PEO can merge a client's staff into very large pools of employees with a better overall risk rating. A single workers' compensation claim therefore won't have the same catastrophic effect on what the company pays.

This type of hand holding can take several forms. Many PEO clients are small manufacturers whose workers may suffer from a high number of repetitive strain injuries. PEO safety managers will analyze the patterns of work and attempt to devise ergonomic solutions to avoid such problems. Often, the solution may require a job rotation program or a change in the process or equipment involved. The key is to discover the root cause of injuries, then work with management and employees to eliminate those causes.

Many PEOs save their clients money by being very aggressive about return-to-work programs. When an employee is injured, the treating physician often places restrictions on when that employee may return to work. PEOs have been known to work directly with physicians to help them understand exactly what is required of specific employees. In such a case, a videotape of particular workplace procedures involved may serve this purpose. PEOs may also design a temporary "bridge" job that will allow the injured employee to return to lighter duty until fully recovered. Measures such as this have helped PEOs get employees back on the job sooner. This pays benefits in better morale, increased productivity, and lower workers' compensation costs.

The National Association of Professional Employment Organizations (NAPEO) based in Alexandria, Virginia, is the primary organization serving the industry. The organization has more than 350 member companies, 15 chapters representing 45 states, and 700 offices around the country. Its Institute for Accreditation of Professional Employment Organization (IAPEO) sets industry accreditation standards. To further shore up the industry's reputation, NAPEO launched its Seal of Assurance for Professional Employer Organizations (SAFPEO) program in early 2000. The SAFPEO is awarded to participating PEOs to acknowledge that they meet the industry's financial and ethical standards.

BACKGROUND AND DEVELOPMENT

Analysts offer varied and often fanciful explanations for the historical roots of employee leasing. Some point to the mercenary soldiers employed by Britain during the American Revolution. Others trace the industry's origins to Alan Pinkerton, founder of the Pinkerton National Detective Agency in 1852, who leased security guards to the railroads to prevent theft and to recover stolen property. Since the 1940s, another pool of leased employees has been

America's truck drivers. The Driver Employer Council of America reported that 30 percent of all private carriers use leased drivers, including many of the nation's largest firms.

In the 1970s, the employee-leasing industry developed a negative reputation as an arrangement used only to dodge certain tax and other obligations. For example, during this period many professional partnerships—such as those owned by physicians and dentists—viewed leasing only as a way to exclude clerical and other hourly help from the retirement plans of the more highly paid managers. The Internal Revenue Service (IRS) fought this arrangement in the tax courts and in 1982 the Tax Equity and Fiscal Responsibility Act (TEFRA) was enacted to ban the practice outright. TEFRA held that leased employees could be excluded from the client company's own pension plan only if the client contributed a substantial amount of money (equal to 7.5 percent of the employee's pay) to a fully vested pension plan. This could have ended the controversy, but further legislative revisions and tax-court rulings muddied the situation until the Tax Reform Act of 1986 ended once and for all the pension tax-related advantages of leasing employees. The Tax Reform Act was a boon for PEOs because it forced the leasing industry to come up with a more rational reason for its existence. From that time on, the best PEOs began to promote themselves as providing more and more of the client's total personnel needs.

The leasing industry still suffers its share of legal difficulties, however. In August 1989, embezzlement by managers sent CAP Staffing of North Carolina into bankruptcy, leaving leased employees with some $2.2 million in unpaid health claims. A few years later, Persona Management Corp., with nearly 100 client companies representing some 8,000 workers in Rhode Island and Massachusetts, was found by the IRS to have understated clients' payroll wages in 1992 and 1993 by $60 million, and to owe taxes of $13 million. To make matters worse, several larger companies were caught leasing out some of their lower-paid workers so as to escalate pension benefits for the higher-paid employees, thus making the benefits package appear more attractive to potential clients.

These incidents, even while tarnishing the industry's reputation, have provided an unexpected impetus to its growth. Many client companies that had a bad experience with an unscrupulous PEO found that the benefits of a leased arrangement so clearly outweighed the problems that they immediately sought to sign on with another, more reputable PEO. This churning of the client base continues, with the industry in a state of flux. Numerous clients try one or more PEOs for a year or so before settling with one that meets their needs. With so many PEOs vying for attention, client companies were forced to exercise due diligence before signing on with one of them. Since January 1996, the IAPEO has enforced its standards towards these ends. The process is costly, with annual accreditation fees ranging from $5,000 to $15,000.

CURRENT CONDITIONS

Thanks largely to mergers and acquisitions, the number of PEOs nationwide shrunk from 2,500 to about 2,000 between 1997 and 2000. But this trend belies the industry's longer-term growth; in 1985 there were fewer than 100 PEOs employing a total of about 10,000 workers. Florida, California, and Texas have the highest concentrations of PEO firms, with penetration in some regions reaching 30-40 percent. PEOs leased about 3 million workers to clients in the late 1990s, amounting to about $18 billion in payroll, according to the NAPEO. Through the late 1990s and early 2000s, moreover, sales and employee-retention pressures associated with a strong economy further spurred more and more small businesses to contract with PEOs.

And the reasons for doing so seem to be mounting in these days of mergers and consolidation. According to the SBA, small companies spend up to 80 percent more per employee than their larger counterparts on regulatory compliance. According to OSHA, meanwhile, workplace injuries cost an average of $15,745 if reported more than 30 days after the occurrence, whereas if reported within 10 days an injury will cost the company an average of $10,172, thus giving companies more incentive to place responsibility for such claims and filing in the hands of a knowledgeable team with the ability to process the information quickly.

Larger businesses are finding PEOs increasingly attractive as well. Since many firms operate across state boundaries, handing over control of their payroll to a PEO can alleviate the burden of trying to coordinate various state and local health-care networks. And as venture capitalists went wild in the late 1990s, many seeking quick, smooth growth found it easier to simply contract out their workers to a PEO. Finally, the increasing complexity of benefits administration and regulatory compliance poses the same difficulties to large firms as to small ones. Thus, as employee leasing develops and recovers its reputation from its rocky beginnings, larger firms will likely see less reason to avoid contracting out increasingly complex human resources operations.

At the same time, PEOs are often averse to entering into contracts that will give them a great deal of headaches. Administaff, Inc. president and CEO Paul Sarvadi, for instance, noted that his company generally tries to avoid companies with contentious work environments, high employee turnover, or high risk of employee injury. The reasons are fairly obvious; if the company is subject to one or more of these difficulties, the contract is likely to generate a relatively high level of work for the firm, thus cutting into profits. Throughout the employee-leasing industry, for related reasons, clientele tends to be more white collar than blue collar in orientation.

Moreover, some states, such as Colorado, require persons employed by PEOs to sign an agreement acknowledging themselves as such. Such an arrangement can make companies a bit skittish about signing on with a PEO, which would then claim the right to hire and fire workers, resulting in a loss of control some companies find too costly for the benefits a PEO can offer. PEO advocates counter, however, that making such moves without consulting with an employer would be ill advised for any PEO that hopes to keep getting business.

Generating new business through client referrals is a popular growth strategy among PEOs. Staff Leasing, Inc.'s Staffleads incentive program offers new clients travel and cash bonuses of up to $1,000 for each referral. Texas-based Administaff has a client relationship with American Express (AE) under which AE refers its smaller businesses to Administaff. In Memphis, the National Bank of Commerce's small business unit has agreed to refer some of its customers to Staff Line, Inc., a Memphis-based employee-leasing company.

The arrival of PEOs certainly confounded the regulatory climate, a development that had yet to be ironed out completely. The industry was still rife with legal wrangling in the late 1990s, as the dust settled on issues related to the responsibility for regulatory compliance. For instance, the Occupational Safety and Health Review Commission issued a ruling in 1999 whereby the responsibility for OSHA compliance rests with the person or entity who maintains control over the workplace. The ruling stemmed from a dispute originating with an OSHA inspection of an Ohio ceramics manufacturer that resulted in violation citations for both the ceramics firm and its PEO, TEAM America Corp. TEAM America fought the ci-

tation on the grounds that it could not be held responsible for such on-site violations. In this case, the review commission held that, although the PEO provided employment services and even agreed to run inspections for the company, TEAM's involvement in the on-site compliance was "indirect or theoretical," and thus was outside the purview of the OSHA citation. Rather, the commission ruled that the ceramics firm was in control of the work environment and thus responsible for compliance.

Meanwhile, state legislation tends to be aimed at past abuses and sometimes takes a distinctly antileasing tack. Moreover, attempts by the Clinton administration to broaden the availability of benefits to all workers might rob the leasing firms of their key advantage—the one-stop shopping approach they offer to clients in the often bewildering world of benefits. The threat from new state and federal regulatory change, however, appears to be rather slight. Leasing by now is well established and provides benefits that are so obvious it is unlikely that any concerted effort will be made to ban the practice. NAPEO reported that a number of state and federal lawmakers as well as the SBA have shown support for the industry and the services it offers to businesses. In addition, officials of state and federal regulatory agencies have met with NAPEO representatives and spoken at industry events.

Another issue comes in the form of competition from national firms such as Kelly Services, Inc., the temporary-help agency that in 1994 entered the leasing industry by purchasing the California-based PEO Your Staff. Given the marketing muscle of big players such as Kelly, many smaller PEOs will feel the pressure. A mitigating factor might be cultural; since the vast majority of PEO clients are small firms themselves, they may prefer to do business with a smaller leasing firm that can offer more personal service, rather than with a nationwide giant.

INDUSTRY LEADERS

Staff Leasing, Inc., based in Bradenton, Florida, is the largest PEO in the United States. After considering several buyout options in early 2000, the firm opted to remain independent. Staff Leasing maintains 47 sales offices, located in Alabama, Arizona, Colorado, Florida, Georgia, Minnesota, North Carolina, Tennessee, and Texas, and derives 25 percent of its clientele from the construction industry, including masons, roofers, and framers. The company prides itself on its Internet integration; about 19 percent of its employees had their payroll hours delivered over the Internet in 1999. It serves approximately 10,700 clients with about 134,350 employees, offering payroll and benefits administration, risk management, unemployment services, and human resource consulting. The company caters to small- and medium-size businesses with between 10 and 100 employees, and was increasingly shifting its focus to clients with higher wages. Staff Leasing had sales of $2.7 billion in 1999, up 13.7 percent from the year before.

The second-largest industry player was Administaff, Inc., based in Kingwood, Texas. Administaff operates 30 offices in 16 major markets in the United States and plans to add about 60 more offices in the coming years. The company focuses on small and medium companies seeking payroll management, medical and workers' compensation insurance programs, employee records management, employer liability management, government compliance, and employee recruiting and selection. Its client list includes 2,300 companies and 38,000 employees. American Express owns 17 percent of the company and has a marketing agreement with it. In 1999 Administaff reported sales of $2.3 billion, compared with $1.6 billion in 1998. The company also employed over 50,000 workers by January 2000, an increase of 22 percent from 1998, and *Fortune* magazine even named it to its list of America's most admired companies.

Employee Solutions, Inc. is another leading company in the industry. Like many other PEOs, Employee Solutions targets small and medium companies for its employee-leasing services. The company handles the administrative end of business (payroll, benefits, government regulations, tax services, etc.) for its 2,000 clients. Employee Solutions leases about 35,000 workers in 47 states, largely to clients in the transportation and service industries. The firm's revenues dipped slightly in 1999 to $939.8 million from $969.9 million in 1998, largely as a result of investment in the company pipeline and restructuring. However, the company's auditors issued a warning about its viability in 2000, causing Employee Solutions to be delisted from NASDAQ.

EPIX Holdings Corp. was the nation's largest privately held PEO with 50,000 employees placed with over 2,400 clients in 46 states. The company specializes in insurance, taxes, employee benefits programs, regulatory compliance, and payroll processing for mid-sized businesses. EPIX's sales jumped 36 percent in 1999 to reach $1 billion.

WORK FORCE

NAPEO estimates that about 10 million Americans were coemployed in a PEO arrangement at the end of 2000. The typical PEO client employs 16 workers with an average salary of $19,659, according to a 1997 survey. These small businesses run the gamut from accountants to zookeepers and include every profession in between, from doctors and retailers to mechanics and funeral home directors. As a rule, those who work for such companies do not have access to the menu of benefits available to employees of larger organizations. And, as reported by Rodney Ho in the *Wall Street Journal,* a survey by Dun & Bradstreet found that the number of small businesses offering employee benefits was decreasing.

PEO surveys indicated that employee satisfaction runs high because leased employees often enjoy a greater level of benefits than what was available to them prior to the leasing arrangement. According NAPEO, all member companies offered health plans by 2000, compared to 45 percent of small firms nationally offering health insurance. Dental care was offered by 97 percent of NAPEO members, 80 percent offered vision coverage, nearly 90 percent short- and long-term disability insurance, and 92 percent offered life insurance. More than 80 percent offered a 401(k) retirement savings plan.

As the leasing industry grows, the need to find experienced and capable managers becomes increasingly important. While it is possible to hire good people from related industries (such as risk managers from the insurance profession), there will no doubt be shortages as the leasing industry expands. Given the skyrocketing growth rates of the industry, this means it is likely that some PEO firms will contract with clients but be unable to deliver the required services. This is expected to result in a shakeout and consolidation of the industry over the next decade.

RESEARCH AND TECHNOLOGY

Industry consolidation yielded an unexpected benefit in the late 1990s. PEOprofits.com is a firm made up of employee-leasing industry veterans who came together to pool their expertise following the acquisitions of a number of PEOs in order to provide other PEOs with customized software and Internet solutions. In late 1999, PEOprofits.com teamed up with Ultimate Software, a provider of human resource and payroll e-business solutions, to offer Web-based payroll applications to PEO firms attempting to streamline their processing activities. This was the first such product specifically tailored to the employee-leasing industry, whose players typically had to adapt general accounting and payroll software packages to their operations.

FURTHER READING

Applegate, Jane. "Employee-Leasing Groups Help Smaller Companies." *Columbus Dispatch,* 3 May 1999.

Barnaba, Constance. "Want to Get the Best Employees? Ask a PEO." *HRFocus,* September 1999.

"Bringing in the Safety." *Workers' Compensation Monitor,* May 1999.

Brotherton, Phaedra. "HR Efficiency Without the Hassles." *Black Enterprise,* September 2000.

Buchanan Ingersoll Law Firm. "Employee Leasing Firm Not Liable for OSHA Violations." *Pennsylvania Employment Letter,* June 1999.

Flannery, William. "PEOs Change the Face of Human Resources." *St. Louis Post-Dispatch,* 24 August 1999.

France, Larry. "PEO: Professional Employer Organization —Or Potential Earnings Opportunities?" *Rough Notes,* November 2000.

Hirschman, Carolyn. "For PEOs, Business Is Booming." *HRMagazine,* February 2000.

Ho, Rodney. "Fewer Small Businesses Are Offering Health Care and Retirement Benefits." *Wall Street Journal,* 24 June 1998.

"PEO Cuts Clients' Work Comp Costs." *Managing Risk,* May 1999.

"PEO Industry Adopts Standard of Confidence." *Business Wire,* 3 February 1999.

"PEOprofits.com Selects Ultimate Software's E-business Model for Managing Employee and Client Company Needs." *PR Newswire,* 12 October 1999.

"Research Eyes Increased Use of Leased Workers." *Texas Worker's Comp Advisor,* 15 June 2000.

Schwab, Robert. "Employees Are a Lot of Work." *Denver Post,* 21 November 1999.

Shutan, Bruce. "Supplemental Benefits Admin: Professional Employer Organizations (PEOs) Take the Wide Angle on Growth by Expanding Their Services and Marketing Ambitions." *Employee Benefit News,* 1 February 2000.

Uhland, Vicky. "Outsourcing Human Resources." *Denver Rocky Mountain News,* 28 November 1999.

PROFESSIONAL EXECUTIVE RECRUITING

Tight U.S. job markets have been a boon to executive recruiters as companies have been willing to spend greater sums to lure in new talent. In 2000 revenues at top recruiting firms rose an average of 20 percent, netting the roughly 4,000 executive search firms an estimated $8.3 billion, and growth in 2001 was expected to match or exceed that rate. In addition to all the large, established companies that have relied on such services for years, the recent crop of well-funded Internet start-ups has created insatiable demand for veteran executives who can to steer "dot-coms" to riches.

Indeed, searches for e-commerce executives in 1999 accounted for as much as 25 percent of some recruiters' business, whereas that specialty didn't even exist a year or two earlier. In many cases the volume of demand caught recruiters off guard and the special requirements of Internet firms challenged recruiters to be more flexible. Recruiters who haven't been able to adapt—or do so quickly enough—risk losing ground to more agile competitors who can fill technology companies' needs.

ORGANIZATION AND STRUCTURE

Executive recruiters, often called headhunters, seek and place management personnel domestically and internationally in a wide variety of positions and industries. Companies retain the services of an executive recruiter to access a global network of candidates far beyond the scope of an in-house human resources department and to locate a suitable candidate quickly and efficiently.

Executive search firms are nonlicensed organizations that primarily place senior executives who earn a minimum of $50,000 per year. Top-level firms may restrict themselves to jobs paying $100,000 and above per year. Realistically, the differences between firms are disappearing as the industry sorts itself out and companies diversify.

When industry and business are operating at high levels, executive search services are in great demand. As downturns occur, businesses hire fewer managers, which cuts into the industry's employment levels and profits. Consequently, executive search firms are expanding their specialties to include such areas as business intelligence, outplacement, consulting, finance, benchmarking, employee testing, and temporary services. These additional services, combined with the expansion of the global market, provide an expanding opportunity for executive research firms.

The process of executive recruiting is multifaceted. A detailed job description, in writing, must be prepared by the search firm and client company at the onset. The recruiter then conducts an extensive search, contacts prospective candidates, and performs reference checks. Client interviews are arranged with the top two or three prospects from the pool of candidates. The most-promising candidate is selected.

TYPES OF HEADHUNTERS

The industry is divided into generalists and specialists. Some firms, such as Phyllis Solomon Executive Search Inc., based in Englewood Cliffs, New Jersey, concentrate on specific industries and clearly defined levels of management. Solomon focuses on middle- to upper-management personnel in the health-care field. Smaller firms such as Solomon also tend to seek relatively localized niches within the industry. Larger companies such as Korn/Ferry International tend to be more diverse and serve a wider array of clients in widespread geographical areas. They, too, constantly seek new clients in diverse businesses to serve. For example, A.T. Kearney Executive Search, which has been in business for more than 50 years, announced in 1997 that it was establishing an office in Santa Monica, California, to service the entertainment industry. It is vital to the success of executive search firms that they constantly establish niches and respond rapidly to changes in the business world.

Executive recruiting is becoming increasingly specialized. Contemporary recruiters use state-of-the-art technology to ensure the personnel recruited suitably fit the intended positions. They use tools such as computer software and paper-based tests to analyze items such as executives' skills and personality traits, then compare them to the requirements of the positions to be filled. Recruiters cannot trust luck, subjectivity, or hunches to select candidates. Clients can pay executive recruiting firms as much as one-third of a candidate's first year's salary as compensation, which means neither side can afford mistakes in matching the right candidate to a specific job. Recruiters can earn as much as $750,000, and repeat business, for the most high-profile job searches.

A SMALL MATTER OF MONEY

Firms generally work on one of two fee bases: contingent or retained. Contingency means that the client pays no money until a person is placed. Firms that work on a contingency basis usually recruit junior or mid-level executives, and are paid only if the search is successful for the client. Contingency fees can be as much as half of the target position's annual salary.

Under the retained structure, the client typically pays one-third of the fee up-front, another third halfway through the search, and the final third upon placement of a candidate. This fee can be as much as 33 percent of the position's annual compensation. The fee structure varies with the client's needs and the candidate's availability. In some cases, clients need people immediately—and temporarily. In others, they can afford long lead times to replace outgoing personnel or for the assumption of newly created positions.

Industry experts estimate that one office needs to sustain between $1 million and $3 million in business per year. Income is based to a great extent on location, however. For instance, fees for executive re-

cruiters' services may vary greatly between major geographic locations such as New York and Miami.

WANTED: CONNECTIONS AND FLEXIBILITY

Money is only part of the picture. Executive recruiters also need access to candidates with diverse backgrounds and skills. Because U.S. companies increasingly form joint ventures with companies in other parts of the world, there is a need for executives who not only speak foreign languages, but understand foreign cultures as well. The search for executives who can do both is best conducted by specialists in the field.

Often recruitment firms are called upon to place executives on a temporary basis. Many businesses today operate in a project mode in which they assign specialists to teams designed to complete a specific task. Once the task is completed, project members are reassigned or let go. Clients may need executives to fill in for short periods for key personnel. At other times, individuals may want to work only for a set period. These new practices have opened doors for recruitment firms to place executives on a temporary basis, which affects how they work. Placing temporary staff members generally means shorter time frames in identifying, testing, and placing executives. Clients seeking temporary personnel typically need them immediately. Consequently, recruiters sometimes must identify promising candidates quickly.

BACKGROUND AND DEVELOPMENT

The emergence of the U.S. executive recruitment industry can be traced back to the 1940s as businesses, growing after World War II, had a dearth of acceptable in-house candidates for promotions. For the most part, in the industry's first decades, the different types of recruiters were interchangeable. There was no sharp division of labor between personnel recruiters and executive search specialists.

In the early 1990s, a high-profile executive search helped reshape the industry. In early 1992, IBM Corp. launched a major search for a new chief executive. The corporation hired two top recruiters, Gerry Roche and Tom Neff, both of whom were acknowledged leaders in the field. (Both men have been included consistently in the top 250 executive recruiters in the United States.) This was an unusual move because Roche and Neff worked for different companies, Heidrick & Struggles International, Inc. and SpencerStuart, respectively. IBM also side-stepped a practice common in the executive recruiting industry known as "client blocks," in which major executive search firms do not approach individuals placed in jobs by competitors. Moreover, IBM was not shy about letting the world know how its search for a CEO was going. In fact, in a break with tradition, the corporation made public the names of executives who were ostensibly among the finalists for the position. The resulting publicity worked to the benefit of the executive search industry. For the first time, business experts and members of the public came face-to-face with an industry that had toiled in relative obscurity for most of its existence.

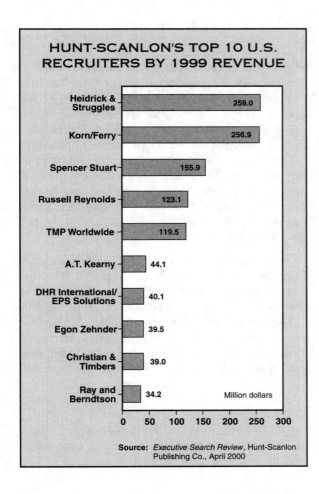

HUNT-SCANLON'S TOP 10 U.S. RECRUITERS BY 1999 REVENUE

Firm	Revenue
Heidrick & Struggles	259.0
Korn/Ferry	256.9
Spencer Stuart	155.9
Russell Reynolds	123.1
TMP Worldwide	119.5
A.T. Kearny	44.1
DHR International/EPS Solutions	40.1
Egon Zehnder	39.5
Christian & Timbers	39.0
Ray and Berndtson	34.2

Million dollars

Source: *Executive Search Review*, Hunt-Scanlon Publishing Co., April 2000

The notoriety helped fuel growth in the executive recruitment industry as executives from companies of all sizes became acquainted with the notion of professional recruiting firms. At the same time other changes in business practices spurred greater demand for these services. The global market proved to have an impact on American businesses, and recruiters found themselves involved in worldwide searches for executives to fill slots in multinational corporations.

There was also a revolution in the American workplace. Corporations began downsizing thousands of people to become "leaner and meaner." Those laid off included many high-ranking executives. Executive recruiters picked up some of the slack by matching laid-off professionals with new positions.

Ironically, the executive search industry experienced its own downsizing. Between 1992 and 1995, almost one-fifth of the country's retainer-type executive firms went out of business. Many of those remaining had to cut back staffing. In effect, they eliminated less productive recruiters.

ETHICAL WORRIES

An important issue in the late 1990s was recruiter ethics. In July 1997, John R. Walter resigned as president of AT&T Corp., after just seven months on the job. Although many laid sole responsibility at the feet of AT&T's board, some experts voiced concerns about the entire executive search system. As Judith Dobrzynski reported in the *New York Times,* the recruiters involved may not have heeded signs that the search was flawed, although many recruiters feel that the only way to ensure that this does not happen in the future is to fundamentally change the way recruiters are paid.

The Association of Executive Search Consultants (AESC), the leading trade group for retained search firms, maintains a code of ethics that members are supposed to follow, but critics say ethical guidelines are often set aside in the heat of a hunt. The AESC represents 160 member firms worldwide with a total of more than 700 offices and 3,000 consultants.

Kennedy Information, the publishers of *Executive Recruiter News,* an independent newsletter for the profession, says that clients must have a clear understanding of the search firm's replacement policy before booking a search. Search firms working on a contingency basis will usually guarantee a candidate for 60 days, while a search firm working on retainer will guarantee the candidate for a year or more. Should an executive leave before the duration of the time period, the firm should replace the candidate at a reduced or free rate.

CURRENT CONDITIONS

Executive recruiters saw brisk growth in the late 1990s thanks to a booming U.S. economy, exceptionally low unemployment, and a spate of start-ups seeking first-rate leadership. For example, the AESC reported that mid-1999 figures showed searches for e-commerce executives skyrocketed 1,407 percent from just a year earlier. Demand for top brass was also up sharply for telecommunications and general management positions. In the third quarter alone member firms conducted some 3,500 searches.

In spite of the industry's overall strength, a few of its target markets were markedly weak in 1999. Most prominently, based on AESC data for the third quarter, demand for executives in the computer hardware business and for those in corporate MIS roles was down significantly. Between third quarter 1998 and third quarter 1999, for instance, searches for computer and electronic equipment manufacturing management were off a surprising 37 percent. A different study by Korn/Ferry International produced conflicting results, though, showing a net gain for similar positions.

Overall, in 1999 revenues were up an average of 20 percent at large recruiting firms. According to analysis by Hunt-Scanlon Corp., which monitors the industry, the top 10 U.S. firms' combined revenues surpassed $1 billion for the first time. Only a year earlier, it took the combined revenues of the top 25 to reach $1 billion. As a whole, industry sales were expected to top $8.3 billion for 2000, continuing a growth rate of around 20 percent. Online recruiting, meanwhile, was predicted by Hunt-Scanlon to reach $8 billion in 2005, up from just $250 million in 1999.

The entry of so many small start-up firms into the executive recruiting market has made some recruiters alter their fees and other practices to accommodate firms with limited cash on hand but weighty demands. Some recruiters have entertained receiving stock options, for one thing, instead of the full fee in cash. High-tech start-ups also typically expect faster turnarounds and offer more ambiguous, fluid job descriptions to be filled.

INDUSTRY LEADERS

DUKING IT OUT AT THE TOP

In the late 1990s the industry's two biggest firms, Korn/Ferry International and Heidrick & Struggles, were quite self-consciously contending neck-and-neck for the industry's top spot. Korn/Ferry had peacefully resided in the number-one spot for decades, but aggressive competition from Heidrick & Struggles left Korn/Ferry playing catch-up by 1999, according to figures compiled by Hunt-Scanlon. In 2000 the press releases of both firms were each claiming the top seat.

KORN/FERRY STILL STRONG

Korn/Ferry International has been in the executive search industry since 1969. The company operates as one firm worldwide with more than 70 offices in 40 countries. Korn/Ferry recruits executive personnel for Fortune 500 companies in areas such as marketing, management, and finance. By the late 1990s, the company had about 4,100 clients each year and had completed over 75,000 searches in its history. Korn/Ferry brought in revenues of $500.7 million in 2000, including $200.2 million from U.S. clients and $106.6 million from Europe. Korn/Ferry maintained a sharp lead in the online executive recruiting business, with its Futurestep service raking in $22 million in 1999.

HEIDRICK & STRUGGLES IN HIGH GEAR

Heidrick & Struggles International, Inc. has been in the executive recruiting business since 1953. They operate 70 offices around the world. Organized into practice groups that specialize in areas such as information management, mining, and aerospace, the search firm recruits chief executives, boards of directors, and senior-level managers for Fortune 500 companies, not-for-profit organizations, and start-up ventures. In 1999 the company posted worldwide revenues of $435.8 million, with $259 million within the United States.

Contributing to its growth, in 1998 Heidrick & Struggles acquired rival Fenwick Partners. The firm was attempting to consolidate its lead in 2000 with the purchase of Chicago-based Lynch Miller Moore O'Hara, which specialized in recruiting for smaller, fast-growing firms. Heidrick & Struggles' online service, LeadersOnline, trails Futurestep by a huge margin, with only $2.6 million in revenues during 1999.

OTHER FIRMS NOT COMPLAINING

TMP Worldwide Inc., a provider of phone-book and help-wanted advertising, is a fairly new entrant into the business with its 1999 acquisition of LAI Worldwide, then the United States' fifth-largest executive recruiter, with $84 million in revenue. TMP also backs the popular job-hunting Web site Monster.com, giving it a hand in nearly all levels of the employee recruitment business. TMP went on a further acquisition spree in 1999 and 2000, snatching up specialty recruitment and consulting firms in several countries in an apparent bid to contend with the industry's top firms for global market share. The company's executive recruiting revenues totaled $295.7 million in 1999.

Another example of a growing company is Raymond Karsan Associates, based in Wayne, Pennsylvania. The worldwide firm has 450 employees in 24 offices. In 1998, for the fourth consecutive year, Raymond Karsan Associates was named one of the fastest-growing privately held companies by *Inc.* magazine. "Our company's growth has been fueled by corporate America's realization that human talent is their most important asset," said CEO Rudy Karsan. "We are proud to be included in this prestigious *Inc.* 500 ranking which salutes our sales growth of approximately $3.6 million to $36 million during the past five years."

WORK FORCE

The executive search industry doesn't employ large numbers of people, but its rapid growth has meant plenty of opportunities for people with the right skills. Many are sole proprietorships or small businesses. For example, the Curtiss Group employs 12 people and brings in about $1.5 million per year. Companies such as Curtiss employ recruiters, data processing and testing specialists, experts, and support people such as administrative assistants. Another example is the Compass Group, of Birmingham, Michigan, which employs only 22 people. The company, named one of the industry's top 50 firms by *Executive Recruiter News,* earns between $2 million and $5 million per year. Most of its employees are retired executives from Ford Motor Co. Only five of them are full-time employees.

Even industry leaders Korn/Ferry, which in 2000 had 1,837 total employees worldwide, and Heidrick & Struggles, with 1,621 the same year, don't have the large work forces one might expect from companies generating sales in excess of $450 million a year.

The majority of the recruiters are well-educated people with advanced degrees. Many recruiters have MBAs because a business background helps recruiters understand their clients' needs. One of the hallmarks of successful executive recruiters is in-depth knowledge of the fields they specialize in. Another is time in the industry. The average age of the top 250 executive recruiters is 55. They each average nearly 23 years in the business. Women and minorities make up a small but growing share of the industry's personnel. There are 28 women among the current top 250 recruiters, but only a handful of minorities.

AMERICA AND THE WORLD

The United States is by far the largest market in the world for executive search services. In the late 1990s it accounted for as much as two-thirds of the industry's estimated $7.5 billion in global revenues. Other regions, though, are growing at much faster rates, according to a large international study conducted by Korn/Ferry. Latin American revenues, for example, rose around 30 percent in 1999, while Asia/Pacific revenues grew some 24 percent. Europe, by contrast, was the slowest market, up just 8 percent in 1999.

Most of the top executive search firms in the United States have established offices throughout the world. For example, A. T. Kearney Executive Search currently has a multinational network of recruiting professionals with expertise in all principal industry and functional sectors. In fact, Kearney operates more than 60 offices in 30 countries. The Curtiss Group, based in Boca Raton, Florida, operates offices in Holland, Brazil, and Tokyo. This trend will continue as the global market expands and multinational corporations continue to grow. As they do, American executive search firms are likely to have a deep impact on international searches. By the same token, non-U.S. firms such as Switzerland's Egon Zehnder International have moved aggressively to capture a bigger piece of the booming U.S. market.

RESEARCH AND TECHNOLOGY

Computers have revolutionized the world of executive recruiting. Firms compile and reference large databases containing the names of people who can fill particular jobs with particular companies. Many executive search firms operate proprietary computerized information systems and employ in-house specialists to implement, maintain, and enhance them. For example, Compass Group maintains a database of more than 21,000 profiles and resumes of top candidates.

In recent years, executive search specialists began using software to help clients identify personality traits, simulate a day at the office, present models on how to conduct interviews properly, and a host of other tasks designed to facilitate the placement and hiring process. Software packages can range from $600 to $3,000 or more. State-of-the-art software and hardware have enhanced recruiters' abilities to place the right people in the right positions.

The Internet poses both challenge and opportunity for the industry. In June 1998, Korn/Ferry International and the *Wall Street Journal* announced the launch of Futurestep, an Internet service set up to recruit mid-level executives. Potential candidates log on to the system, answer informational questions, and respond to an assessment profile in lieu of submitting a resume. The information is then screened electronically and candidates who match current client requirements are called for a videoconference interview and must undergo a standard reference check. By 1999 the service was bringing in $22 million a year.

Although some online recruiters are thought to be resume wholesalers, because they solicit resumes via Web sites, many executive recruiters are expected to forge alliances with Internet content developers by the turn of the century.

FURTHER READING

Abelson, Reed. "Headhunters Turn a Few On Wall Street." *New York Times,* 16 July 2000.

Association of Executive Search Consultants. *AESC Online.* New York, 1999. Available from http://www.aesc.org.

Austin, Larry. "Recruitment Field Is Ripe for Harvesting Networks." *Houston Business Journal,* 3 December 1999.

Bennett, Julie. "Answering the Call: Not All Recruiters Are Created Equal, So Ask Questions." *Chicago Tribune,* 1 February 1998.

Burgess, Scott. "Boca Raton, Fla., Executive Search Firm Prides Itself on Luring Client." *Boca Raton News,* 11 March 1997.

Bushnell, Davis. "Suitors Line Up for Executives Recruiters: Roll Out the Limos in Headhunting for a Big Payoff." *Boston Globe,* 1 March 1998.

Curan, Catherine. "Recruiters Learn to Connect Dot-Coms." *Crain's New York Business,* 15 November 1999.

Dobrzynski, Judith H. "An Ethical Role for Recruiters." *New York Times,* 29 July 1997.

Drake, Samantha. "HR Firm Is after One-Stop Shopping." *Philadelphia Business Journal,* 11 April 1997.

Executive Recruiter News. Fitzwilliam, NH: Kennedy Information LLC, monthly. Available from http://www.kennedyinfo.com.

Flynn, Julia. "Egon Zehnder Plans U.S. Expansion as Executive Searches Go Global." *Wall Street Journal,* 4 January 2000.

Goodman, Cindy Krischer. "Giant Search Firms Make Miami Their Latin American Hub." *Miami Herald,* 9 June 1997.

Hayes, Cassandra. "1999 Executive Recruiter Directory." *Black Enterprise,* February 1999.

"Heidrick & Struggles." Chicago: Heidrick & Struggles, 1999. Available from http://www.heidrick.com.

"Invasion of the Body Snatchers." *Business Week,* 11 October 1999.

"Korn/Ferry International." Los Angeles: Korn/Ferry, 1999. Available from http://www.kornferry.com.

Kunde, Diana. "Execs Finding Short-Term Opportunities." *Dallas Morning News,* 26 January 1997.

Lee, Chris. "The Hunt for Skilled Workers." *Training,* 1 December 1997.

Logue, Charles H. *Outplace Yourself: Secrets of an Executive Outplacement Counselor.* Holbrook, MA: Bob Adams, Inc., 1993.

Lublin, Joann S. "Yellow Pages Giant TMP to Acquire Executive-Search Firm LAI Worldwide." *Wall Street Journal,* 12 March 1999.

Powell, Barbara. "Looking For Help." *San Diego Union-Tribune,* 26 June 2000.

"Raymond Karsan Associates." Princeton, NJ: Raymond Karsan Associates, 1999. Available from http://www.raymondkarsan.com.

Richtel, Matt. "A New Executive-Recruiting Service on the Web." *New York Times,* 8 June 1998.

Schellhardt, Timothy D. "Downsizing Thinned Ranks; 'Up-and-Coming' Go Fast." *Wall Street Journal,* 26 June 1997.

Sibbald, John. *The New Career Makers.* New York: Harper-Collins, 1995.

Sileo, Olia. "Matchmaker, Matchmaker." *New Jersey Record,* 9 April 1997.

Taylor, Robert. "Search for Executives in U.S. Continues to Grow Rapidly." *Financial Times,* 15 September 1999.

PUSH TECHNOLOGY

Wouldn't it be great to have an always-on Internet service that automatically sends real-time news and information to your desktop based on your interests? The answer is yes and no, judging from recent events.

Push technology is a software and networking paradigm in which content is selectively disseminated to users without them having to actively search for it. The technology is implemented as a software package or an online service, and the applications include so-called Webcasting or Netcasting (broadcasting content over the Internet) to defined audiences, as well as more sophisticated corporate systems that automate sending timely and targeted information to the appropriate people.

The phrase "push technology" entered the technophile lexicon in the mid-1990s, when a fledgling Internet service called PointCast, Inc. began beaming news stories and other information tidbits to users' computer screens via the firm's proprietary, Internet-enabled application. Both the company and the concept were considered exceptionally promising, but PointCast, for its part, failed to live up to expectations and ceased operation in 2000. The jury is still out on push technology in general, but some observers still find cause for optimism.

In all likelihood, a variety of factors caused Point-Cast to falter. Chief among them was simply that its software was bulky and intrusive, sapping resources from the personal computers (PCs) that ran it and wreaking havoc on corporate computer networks when many employees received a "push" of information all at once. By some accounts the information

PointCast offered wasn't unique or targeted enough to justify the burden of running its program. Some companies specifically banned the software from being run on their computers.

Other push technology firms, though, have continued to push the envelope, so to speak. More recent implementations of push technology offer what their proponents sometimes label as "polite" push features. Taking a cue from PointCast's dismal fate, developers of polite push technology have incorporated such features as messaging priorities, time-phased distribution, and thinner, nimbler programs.

Pull technology, or actively searching out and "pulling" information from a Web site, remains the most commonly used technique for retrieving information from the Internet, and search engines such as Infoseek, Yahoo!, HotBot, and Excite help users locate the desired site. The process can be extremely time-consuming and tedious, and users often become frustrated when unable to find exactly what they want.

According to Peter Weinstein in *Technology and Learning,* push technology can best be explained in terms of "who initiates and manages the transfer of content." Most people use push technology every day, if they use the Internet at all, when they send and receive e-mail. E-mail uses a very simple form of push technology. In other words, when you write an e-mail message, you then "push" it out over the Internet to the intended recipient.

PointCast, based in California, was the first company to see potential in delivering actual Web content to individuals instead of the other way around. The roots of the technology can be traced back to 1992, when Christopher and Gregg Hassett developed a product called *Journalist,* designed to deliver a customized electronic newspaper to CompuServe and Prodigy customers. Although *Journalist* flopped, the Hassett brothers went on to develop a new way of delivering customized news, soon to become PointCast.

PointCast began sending news and advertising directly to computers in 1996. Shortly thereafter, several other Silicon Valley firms, including Marimba, Inc. and BackWeb Technologies, Ltd., entered the market, each offering technologies to distribute and update software. Marimba was able to deliver Web content to all types of systems, mainly because its application, Castanet, was written in Java.

In order to receive pushed information, users download and install proprietary software. A push server can then send select information through broadcast "channels." The server manages distribution and maintenance of all available channels, although individual clients receive only those channels they have specified. Using the push software, users can configure it so that they can receive what they need, when they need it.

A "Netcast" or "Webcast" is a simple form of push technology. A server broadcasts the program over the Internet and individual computer users can tune in to the channel, just like tuning in to a television or radio program. The next step up from a Webcast is a push news and information service, which is delivered to subscribers through an application running on their local computer. PointCast used this technology.

PointCast, however, soon ran into trouble as its hefty software and massive broadcasts began to clog companies' computer networks and disrupt subscribers' computing tasks. Since most of its content was considered frivolous, PointCast easily drew the ire of information technology managers and the service's popularity began to ebb. After reportedly being valued (speculatively, of course) at several hundred million dollars in its first years, PointCast was finally bought out in 1999 by Launchpad Technologies, Inc. for a mere $7 million. The merged firm then changed its name to EntryPoint, offering a less invasive push information service, and the PointCast software and service were retired in early 2000.

CURRENT CONDITIONS

Although PointCast has faded from the scene, push technology is successfully embodied in a number of software products and services. The surviving companies have taken to heart the criticisms of PointCast. In essence, they compete with one another for using the least amount of network resources and providing the right amount of flexibility. Thus, applications such as BackWeb are intended to fit seamlessly into a company's existing systems and processes, rather than rolling in with a one-size-fits-all product that disregards users' work styles. For example, information distributed through BackWeb can be retrieved through an interface in the popular Microsoft Outlook e-mail package. That way, users can obtain information from the BackWeb system using a familiar tool that's regularly used for other purposes. BackWeb was also refining its Polite system to take advantage of the growing need for streamlined information geared toward business-to business e-commerce, and in 2000 struck a deal with the Dutch application service provider EC-Gate to develop B2B portals.

Software mechanisms for minimizing the network impact of push technology are growing ever more sophisticated. With leading packages such as BackWeb and Marimba's Castanet, network administrators can specify a maximum amount of system resources available to push activities. When the limit is reached, the software will wait until the bottleneck clears before attempting to introduce new traffic. Under different settings, these types of programs can also be configured to detect idle time or idle connections within the network before proceeding with distributing content. Other bandwidth-conserving measures include file compression and, in case of a file transfer interruption, file transfers that can be restarted where they left off rather than starting the whole thing over again.

Beyond using push technology for broadcasting messages and user-oriented content—and increasingly, for advertising—companies have begun to deploy push solutions for such tasks as software upgrades and system maintenance. Compaq Computer, for example, uses BackWeb behind the scenes to deliver and install periodic software patches and enhancements as a service to users of its desktop computers. Some have touted this method as a model for the future of software upgrades generally. Another emerging application is using push technology for targeted customer e-mailings, as part of customer relationship management software.

INDUSTRY LEADERS

BackWeb Technologies

BackWeb Technologies, Ltd. is a major push technology vendor based in San Jose, California, and Ramat Gan, Israel. BackWeb also has offices in Chicago, New York, Canada, the United Kingdom, and several other countries. BackWeb provides business customers with Internet communications systems and applications for managing critical business operations such as customer service, competitive analysis, and sales. The company is led by Eli Barkat, a former Israeli army paratrooper and founder of several other software ventures. BackWeb also has partnerships with many leading technology companies including Microsoft, Hewlett-Packard, Sun Microsystems, and others. It aspires to be at the center of an emerging multivendor standard for push applications, particularly those involving electronic commerce.

Among BackWeb's key products are an Internet communications software system called BackWeb Foundation, and a customer relations/sales package called BackWeb Sales Accelerator. BackWeb Foundation gathers important data in any format and delivers it to desktops throughout an organization. Sensitive to the bandwidth complaints that helped to drive original push technologies out of favor, BackWeb contains an array of features for conserving and managing network use.

BackWeb Sales Accelerator delivers key information such as new promotions, pricing, product announcements, and so on to organizations' sales forces. Additional system modules scan the Internet for market updates and industry news while other modules enhance organizations' internal messaging capabilities and provide access to industry-specific subscription services. Both products are designed to fit seamlessly into customers' existing management systems. BackWeb has licensed its software to more than 200 corporations. In 1999 it had annual sales of $23 million, but it has yet to turn a profit.

Marimba

Marimba, Inc., founded by four members of Sun Microsystems' original Java team, is based nearby in Mountain View, California. Kim Polese, one of Marimba's founders, is CEO. Marimba originally focused on content delivery, but by the late 1990s had turned its attention to developing applications enabling corporations to distribute and update software remotely via the Internet, corporate intranets, and extranets. Marimba's suite of Castanet products use client-server technology to update and maintain off-

the-shelf or custom applications. Castanet includes powerful security features such as authentication and encryption, among others. Organizations can add new modules to the Castanet system as needs expand. In addition to Castanet, the company also sells a line of software called Timbale for terminal server applications. In 1999 the company completed a public offering, but posted a net loss on its $31 million in annual sales. Marimba markets products worldwide.

Diffusion

Diffusion, Inc., is also based in Mountain View, California. Dr. Richard Schwartz founded Diffusion in 1995 and James Gagnard is president and CEO. Diffusion specializes in the customer relationship management market and has found a niche for itself in the financial services industry. Products such as Diffusion's Customer Relationship Management 3.0 software can automatically coordinate and manage key functions such as informing customers when account balances drop too low or when a fund transfer has taken place.

EntryPoint

The successor organization to industry pioneer PointCast, EntryPoint Inc. was formed in 1999 following the acquisition of PointCast by Launchpad Technologies, Inc. of San Diego. The merged company was renamed EntryPoint. The firm discontinued using the PointCast name and service in early 2000, opting instead to build up its new brand identity. The EntryPoint service is based on a premise similar to that of PointCast—online news and information delivered through a special program running on the subscriber's PC—but the company hoped the implementation this time would prove more appealing. The EntryPoint application is noteworthy for its relatively small size and modest interface toolbar that rests on the user's screen. Also unlike PointCast, EntryPoint has more of a shopping bent, which ties in well with the former Launchpad's eWallet electronic-cash product. In early 2000 EntryPoint, claiming some 2 million subscribers by then, secured a new round of private financing from a collection of prominent venture-capital groups.

AMERICA AND THE WORLD

American companies have yet to make a big impact in the international market, particularly Europe, mostly due to slow and unreliable telephone lines, which sometimes ceased to function when receiving heavy volumes of information all at once. Because of this, one of the most successful companies is a Canadian company, Lanacom, Inc. Led by CEO Tony Davis, Lanacom's Headliner (launched in December 1996) "reads" Internet news sites, and then delivers that information to registered users. The content is delivered to the desktop via a ticker-tape bar that runs on the top or bottom, or vertically along the side of the screen. Information can also be delivered in the form of a screen saver or can be downloaded directly to the user's hard drive.

Of the leaders in the American market, BackWeb has had the most success getting established in Europe.

FURTHER READING

Afzali, Cyrus. "PointCast Founder Preparing to Take Control of Push Pioneer." *InternetNew.com,* 3 April 1999. Available from http://www.internetnews.com.

Bertolucci, Jeff. "Browsers Get Pushy." *PC Computing,* 1 October 1997, 149.

Caruso, Denise. "My Life as a Mailbox/Garbage Can, or How I Came to Hate Push Technology." *New York Times,* 24 March 1997.

Chandrasekaran, Rajiv. "The Big Push? New Technology Could Change Way Web Is Used." *Washington Post,* 11 May 1997.

Cleary, Sharon. "The PointCast Network May Die, but Spirit Lives on in EntryPoint." *Wall Street Journal,* 24 March 2000.

Cortese, Amy. "A Way out of the Web Maze." *Business Week,* 24 February 1997.

"Diffusion." Mountain View, CA: Diffusion, Inc., 1999. Available from http://www.diffusion.com.

Duvall, Mel. "Push Pioneer Turns to CRM Market." *Interactive Week Online,* 20 January 1999. Available from http://www.zdnet.com/intweek/stories/news.

Eads, Stefani. "Can BackWeb Soar Where PointCast Stumbled?" *Business Week Online,* 30 April 1999. Available from http://www.businessweek.com.

Flynn, Laurie J. "Compressed Data: 'Push Technology' Returns in a Form That Is More Polite." *New York Times,* 13 March 2000.

Foremski, Tom. "Push Technologies." *Financial Times,* 12 March 1997, 6.

Gold, Howard R., and Kathy Yakal. "PointCast, Others Send News and Data Direct to the Desktop." *Barron's,* 12 May 1997, 58.

Gold, Steve. "BackWeb Looks to Market for Internet Push Standards." *Newsbytes,* 12 November 1999.

Lang, Amanda. "Push Came to Shove." *Financial Post Weekly,* 21 February 1998, IT3.

Moody, Glyn. "Pushing Technology off the Net." *Computer Weekly,* 14 May 1998, 66.

Nelson, Matthew G. "BackWeb Reinvents Push Technology." *Informationweek,* 31 July 2000.

"Push, Take 2." *Forbes,* 19 April 1999.

Rupley, Sebastian. "Pushing E-mail." *PC Magazine,* 18 April 2000.

Sliwa, Carol. "'Push' Thrives at Some Firms." *Computerworld,* 21 June 1999.

Strom, David. "The Best of Push." *Web Review,* 18 April 1997. Available from http://webreview.com/97/04/18/feature/index.html.

———. "Push Publishing Technologies," 13 May 1998. Available from http://www.strom.com/imc/t4a.html.

"Web Sight: Pushed, Push Pushes Back." *Telephony,* 6 September 1999.

Weinstein, Peter. "Pushing and Pulling on the Web." *Technology and Learning,* 1 January 1998, 24.

Whiting, Rick. "Push Technology Matures—And Makes a Comeback." *Informationweek,* 10 July 2000.

"Who's Pushing in Europe." *Wall Street Journal Europe,* 2 June 1997.

Wilder, Clinton, and Justin Hibbard. "Pushing outside the Enterprise: Companies Begin to Tap Push Technology's Potential as a Sales and Marketing Tool." *Information Week,* 4 August 1997, 20.

Wong, Wylie. "VARs Push Technology to Corporations: Developers' Solutions Target Specific Niches and Applications." *Computer Reseller News,* 9 February 1998, 99.

RETAIL AUTO LEASING

Consumers leased cars and trucks in droves during the 1990s thanks to favorable financing terms and aggressive marketing by manufacturers and finance companies. From less than a tenth of all new retail sales in 1990, reported CNW Marketing/Research, the number of consumer leases shot up in the early and mid-1990s to reach a third of all sales. By the 2000, narly 5 million new auto leases were originated in the United States each year, and total leases in effect were valued at more than $100 billion.

Despite the business's hare-footed growth, however, in the latter part of the decade the auto-leasing industry strained to reach a sustainable balance between rampant growth of lease signings and profitability. By most accounts, zealous lessors in the mid-1990s overestimated the residual values of the vehicles they leased. This practice created more favorable terms for customers—and helped spur the leasing boom—but also left lessors financially vulnerable a few years later when off-lease cars were returned and couldn't be resold at the lofty prices concocted for the lease. Softening in the used-car market, hence that for off-lease cars, aggravated the problem by keeping prices lower than even the more realistic forecasts. By the end of the 1990s, the majority of leases where the vehicle was returned to the lessor yielded a net loss for the lessor, all because residual values were lower than anticipated.

Auto lessors, as a consequence, approached the market more cautiously in the early 2000s, in hopes of trading quantity for quality. The growth of new leases slowed, even falling a bit in 1999 as a percentage of vehicle sales, and in some cases the terms were less favorable than in years past. Ironically, the strong U.S. economy may have also contributed to the slowdown, as one industry analyst explained, because consumers were more likely to buy than they were in a sluggish economy.

ORGANIZATION AND STRUCTURE

Ford Motor Co., General Motors Corp., and Chrysler Corp. (now DaimlerChrysler AG) introduced retail leasing in the late 1960s. Before that only large corporations that could afford to lease large fleets of vehicles had that opportunity. The automakers controlled retail leasing through their system of dealerships and captive financing arms—General Motors Acceptance Corp. (GMAC) and Ford Motor Credit Co. (FMCC), for example. They set up leasing desks at designated dealerships and one salesperson was designated as the lease specialist. The dealership was and still is the pass-through agent, and does not usually own the vehicle at any point in the transaction—the automaker owns the vehicle until it is sold to the leasing company. In the early days of leasing, the captive finance firms such as GMAC and FMCC had to supply the lease. Banks and credit unions later took over some of the lease contracts.

Affiliates of automakers still hold a disproportionate share of the market, though, and that's unlikely to change anytime soon. In the mid-1990s captive finance companies held 66 percent of the leasing market while banks had 29 percent, and independent finance companies and credit unions have the remaining market. Although banks and independent finance firms gained share during the boom, approaching 40 percent in 1998, losses in the wake of the residual-value shortfalls thinned out some of the independents, ceding market share back to the captive lessors.

NICHE MARKETS

Some lessors cater increasingly to niche markets. For instance, *Success* magazine pointed out that PMH Caramanning, Inc., a full-service marketing company located in Farmington Hills, Michigan, has targeted companies that lease or purchase fewer than 30 vehicles with their new unit, Business Vehicle Services in cooperation with General Motors. According to PMH president Peter McAteer, "These businesses don't usually qualify for corporate rates. They have to buy retail. But we train individuals at a participating auto dealerships to act as fleet managers for each company they deal with."

Auto-buying services have expanded into the lease market as well. Harried consumers can hire a lease-hunting professional to find the best lease for a fee of between $300 and $500. Car Bargains, AutoAdvisor, and CarSource are three such businesses mentioned in *Money* that will track down the desired vehicle and close the deal. Professional lease hunters usually do better than amateurs. Internet lessors are working the World Wide Web and an astute hunter can now find a good deal anywhere in the world. Two sites to find information on are Edmund's Web site (www.edmunds.com) and Microsoft Corp.'s CarPoint (www.carpoint.msn.com). Both offer prices, reviews, and an up-to-date listing of rebates. A shopper can click on IntelliChoice (www.intelichoice.com) to check manufacturers' leases and Carwizard (www.carwizard.com) to check the latest residual factors. Lastly, a new market niche is developing, the used-car lease fueled by high returns of expensive vehicles and the advent of the auto "superstore."

TYPES OF LEASES

Leasing companies use two types of leases. Most leases are closed-end where the lessee is not responsible for any end-of-lease payment. The other type of lease is open-end. The lessee or consumer takes the risk regarding the market value at the end of the lease. If the vehicle is worth more than the residual value or amount for which the vehicle can be purchased, the lessee must pay the difference if he chooses to purchase it. If the vehicle is worth less, the lessee may negotiate a rebate. In both types of leases the vehicle may be returned or purchased. The closed-end lease with a manufacturer subsidy or a subvented lease is the most popular of the two leases.

GOVERNMENT REGULATIONS AFFECT LEASING INDUSTRY

The federal Consumer Leasing Act of 1976 (CLA) was enacted for consumer use as an alternative to installment sales, reported *Business Lawyer*. As leasing became more prevalent in the early 1970s, the federal government realized that the consumer was confused as to what he was actually buying, a situation that was used by a few unscrupulous leasing companies. CLA requires that a leasing company make certain disclosures in writing. The lessor or owner of the vehicle may be the automaker's captive finance arm or a bank or finance company to which the automaker sells the lease and the vehicle. The name of the lessor can be found on the back of the contract. The lessor must give a brief description of the leased property. He must disclose the total amount of the initial payment required, including the acquisition fee or what the dealer pays the leasing company, usually $200-$500, to handle the lease for the vehicle. Marking up these fees increases profits. It may also include the adjusted capitalized cost, which is the capitalized cost minus the capitalized cost reduction. This can also be negotiated. The cap or capitalized cost is the purchase price and includes fees, taxes, warranty charges, insurance, and interest costs, and must be included in this disclosure. The capitalized cost reduction is also called the down payment on the lease and can be negotiated.

The lessor must disclose penalties for late payments or delinquencies. This includes early termination liability or the amount the lessee must pay to terminate the lease early. It can range from 30 to 100 percent of the remaining amount of the lease. The lessor must explain the warranty and who is responsible for the upkeep of the vehicle. Excess wear and tear is the amount the lessee pays for damage to the car at the end of the lease. It is not negotiable. The lessee should probably have it fixed himself. The lessee needs to know if the leasing company has a flexibility on moving clause. Some local and regional leasing companies do not allow the lessee to take the car when moving to another state. Some states also require the lease taxes to be paid again even if they have been paid to another state.

At the end of the lease the lessee has certain rights under CLA. The customer may have the option to purchase the vehicle. This is called the purchase option. At the end of the lease, the vehicle can be purchased for a "fixed" dollar amount or "fair market value." The fixed dollar amount is determined at the beginning of the lease, while the fair market value is determined at the end of the lease. The fixed purchase option is usually the better way to go. Both options can be negotiated if the lessor is willing to talk. The lessee must be given the residual value at the beginning of the lease. The purchase fee, usually $250, must also be disclosed. The purchase fee or the amount paid for the right to buy the vehicle can be negotiated.

If the lessee does not purchase the vehicle, he must pay the disposal or disposition fee, which covers the cost of moving, cleaning, and disposing of the car. This is charged by the leasing company and is waived if the vehicle is purchased; it can, however, be negotiated. Penalties for default or early termination must be reasonable.

Regulation M, revised federal rules that went into effect in October 1997, requires a standardized leasing form and simple language that tells the lessee exactly what the terms are. These terms include monthly depreciation, monthly rent charge, and the monthly payment. Monthly depreciation is the adjusted capital cost minus the residual value, divided by the number of months of the lease. The monthly rent charge also called the money factor is extremely important. It is the lease rate, or the cost of interest, on money borrowed. It is found by subtracting the monthly depreciation from the monthly payment. The monthly payment is the average monthly depreciation and average monthly rent charge, as well as federal, state, and local sales taxes.

State governments began to realize that some abuses existed in the leasing industry. At least 10 states have studied the leasing industry and enacted or amended consumer protection statutes covering automobile leasing. *Business Lawyer* reported that state government appears to be focusing on three issues: the punitive nature of default charges, gap insurance, and wear-and-tear damage. Illinois, Maryland, New Hampshire, New York, and Wisconsin have statutes that restrict the charge for early termination to a reasonable amount. States are beginning to require lessors to disclose whether they are providing gap insurance or informing the lessees that they must provide their own. Gap insurance protects lessees from paying the difference between the lease payoff and the vehicle's insured value if it is stolen or totaled. The dealer cost is about $200 and this insurance is vital to lessees.

Federal law authorizes lessors to determine the standards for abnormal damage to the vehicle. State laws in Connecticut, Illinois, Maryland, New Hampshire, New Jersey, New York, and Wisconsin are stepping in to help determine what is "normal" and what is "excessive" wear and tear. With the popularity of leasing, more states are expected to develop compre-

hensive state consumer leasing statutes. This trend was apparent at the National Conference of Commissioners on Uniform State Laws where a committee to draft a Uniform Consumer Leases Act was formed. More protection for both the lessee and the lessor is expected to be enacted.

Another aspect that state governments are looking into is the mileage allowance. The lessee is allowed to drive a certain number of miles, usually between 10,000 and 15,000 miles for each year of the lease. If the total mileage is exceeded, the lessee must pay a fee, usually 12-15 cents per mile. Some leasing companies give cash or credit for vehicles returned with less than the allowed mileage.

CURRENT CONDITIONS

Auto lessors closed out the 1990s on a mixed note, with lease volume failing to keep pace with the otherwise brisk market for new cars. U.S. car and truck sales swelled to record levels in 2000, at about 17.3 million vehicles, amid broadly based economic growth and low unemployment. Still, overall lease volume was up about 7 percent in 1999, with leases accounting for over a quarter of all retail sales, though that proportion was down from a 1997-98 high of more than 33 percent.

What made for a buoyant new-car market in the late 1990s, however, took steam out of demand for used cars. With used-car prices stagnant, lessors were saddled with an influx of off-lease cars that were worth significantly less than projected at lease signing. When consumers chose to purchase their leased vehicles, leasing firms made out all right because the buyers were locked into the higher residual price regardless of used-car market conditions. More often, though, consumers returned off-lease vehicles to the lessors, who had to sell the cars at a loss. Indeed, such losses had been mounting since the mid-1990s for some firms. GMAC, for one, lost in 1997 a stunning $500 million, most of that due to resale shortfalls from its leases. The next year, Banc One, which had some $10 billion worth of auto leases on its books, took a special charge of over $100 million for the same reason. Ford Motor Credit and other banks likewise had adverse results.

Banks were especially hard hit by lackluster auto leasing in the late 1990s and early 2000s. U.S. banks financed some $78 billion in auto leases in 1999. That year, 56 percent of vehicles were returned upon the expiration of the lease, up from 39 percent in 1998. Meanwhile, new cars weren't getting any more expensive; in September 2000, the average new vehicle price, according to Comerica, was only $207 more than in 1997. Analysts estimated that banks could wind up losing up to $11 billion from their auto leasing operations in 2000. Bank of America reported losses of $75 million each quarter directly attributable to auto leases.

Such harsh medicine has begun to reduce some banks' presence in the leasing business. First Union Corp., for instance, backed out of the leasing game altogether. Many others are simply assessing residual values more cautiously, preferring to err on the side of turning away business because their lease payments will be higher than to face millions of dollars in losses. For their part, though, automakers may continue to quote rosy residual values, resulting in more lenient leasing terms, and incur losses along the way. The logic has been that leasing is such a stimulus to new-car volume that the vertically integrated automakers can afford to take losses at the leasing stage because the benefits elsewhere in the supply chain outweigh the costs. In effect, carmakers have subsidized their leases and have a vested interest in doing so, whereas most banks and independent finance companies accrue no benefits from doling out unprofitable leases.

WEAR AND TEAR MADE LESS TAXING

Financial unease hasn't completely stymied innovation and customer promotions in the business. Responding to perennial complaints about expected and inconsistent end-of-lease charges for wear and tear, Chase Manhattan and others in 1999 started offering leases where the customer pays a small surcharge up front, as little as $100, and then isn't held responsible for any damage assessed at less than $1,500 at the lease's maturity. According to a CNW Marketing/Research estimate, about 7 percent of leasing customers choose not to lease again because of bad experiences with wear-and-tear fees. Since the average wear-and-tear fee industry-wide was over $1,600 in the late 1990s, this sort of program certainly wouldn't absolve all customers from paying damage fees, but would greatly reduce the number who must. DaimlerChrysler, at first critical of Chase Manhattan's policy, was considering in 2000 introducing a scaled-back version of a damage-waiver program and taking steps to improve customer communications at the end of the lease to minimize customers' dissatisfaction.

USED-CAR LEASING ON THE RISE

Another trend has been used-car leasing. According to GE Capital Auto Financial Services, a leasing firm, only 2 percent of used-car shoppers purchase a lease. Sandra Derickson, GE Capital Auto Financial Services' president, predicted in *Money,* "We think used-car leasing will be one of the fastest-growing parts of the industry." One in 10 luxury cars such as Mercedes-Benz and BMW are sold through used-car leases. With all the expensive Explorer and Expedition sport-utility vehicles (SUVs) coming back from new-car leases, Ford is offering used-car leases to people who would like an SUV but can't afford either the new or residual prices. A vehicle that is two or three years old has already taken its major depreciation and its value will decline much more slowly in the next three to four years. For example, a new Ford Explorer XLT will lose 42 percent of its value in the first two years, and only 45 percent more in the next four years, according to the *Automotive Leasing Guide,* a standard pricing reference for the industry.

E-LEASING

Some believe the Internet may help boost leasing rates in the future. So far a variety of companies have harnessed the Web for promoting sales of off-lease vehicles. Leasing companies have found that an Internet infrastructure and auction scheme tends to be less costly than shipping cars to ordinary real-life car auctions. For initiating new car sales, the Web may also be more amenable to leases because, aside from the vagaries of wear-and-tear charges, customers don't have to worry about disposing of their trade-in vehicle or getting the best price for it. Some observers have also argued that customers will be more willing to enter a leasing contract with an online merchant than a full-fledged financing agreement.

INDUSTRY LEADERS

The captive finance companies of the auto manufacturers dominate industry volume. They include Chrysler Financial Co. (a unit of DaimlerChrysler), Ford Motor Credit Co., General Motors Acceptance Corp., Nissan Motor Acceptance Corp., and Toyota Motor Credit Corp. These firms have been around for decades, and in most cases were the pioneers of auto leasing. They all offer traditional vehicle-purchase financing in addition to leases.

A range of large U.S. banks and independent finance companies also controls a sizable share of the auto-leasing market. These include such national and intraregional banks as Chase Manhattan, Bank of America, and Banc One, as well as deep-pocketed finance specialists such as GE Capital Auto Financial Services. These firms sometimes have special agreements with individual manufacturers, especially smaller ones, to handle leasing of their models.

Smaller independent auto lessors include Wheels Inc., Automotive Rentals Inc., Executive Car Leasing Co., Leasing Associates Inc., Always Rent a Car Co., Langhome Leasing and Messenger Service, Franklin Equity Leasing Co., Selex Systems Inc., A-Drive Corp., Jake Sweeney Auto Leasing Inc., and PHD Penske Leasing.

AMERICA AND THE WORLD

According to Daniel Howes in the *Detroit News,* the company that wins the race to be a world company will be the one that learns to use emerging technology to manage changing markets, customer preferences, and a diverse work force. Jacques Nasser, Ford Motor Co.'s president and chief executive, issued a challenge to Ford to become a "world-class consumer products company." He wanted to create a worldwide company that would offer a variety of services including sales, rental, leasing, and financing. General Motors chairman John F. Smith Jr. agreed. "The global auto companies of the future. . .are going to be more focused on the total life cycle of the vehicle and how their company participates in that there's no end to it." He also said, "As I look out, I don't see it being just a hardware game. I'm talking about info-tainment coming into the vehicle controlled by the manufacturer in such a way that we bill for the service." Apparently, Smith would lease "info-tainment" whether the customer bought or leased the vehicle.

DOWNSIDE TO THE WORLD MARKET

Nissan Motor Acceptance Co., the finance arm of Nissan, Japan's number-two automaker, held third place in the number of leases outstanding in the United States in 1999. Bob Thomas, president of Nissan Motor Corp., U.S.A., prophetically said in 1992, "Two years down the road you're going to be looking at those vehicles again. They will probably compete with your new vehicles. You've got half of your asset still remaining. You haven't depreciated it out. This is the risk side of it." Because it overestimated the value of its residuals, Nissan lost $2 billion in 1998 on returned leased vehicles. The economic crisis in Asia in the late

1990s made matters worse. Honda Motor Co. and Toyota also had serious losses, but not as deep as Nissan's. A lease company entering the world market must not only know the expected residual value in the home country, but must also keep a close eye on world economies as well.

NEW TECHNOLOGY

Not to be outdone by Ford and General Motors, DaimlerChrysler Financial Corp. moved to electronic training in the leasing business. Use of an intranet to train its leasing staff was expected to eliminate the need for thick manuals. LearnLinc I-Net is an electronic classroom tool made by Interactive Learning International Corp., of Troy, New York. More accurate leasing at a lower training cost and at a speedier pace are impressive results of the new technology. According to Don McCloud, manager of training and personnel development at DaimlerChrysler, in the *Detroit News,* "Leasing has become an increasingly large part of our business over the last six or seven years. And with state and federal leasing rules changing all the time, we can now be confident that the right information is getting to the right people" at each of DaimlerChrysler's offices worldwide. Others were adopting similar information networks to support their leasing operations.

FURTHER READING

Adelson, Andrea. "Owning and Leasing: Leases without Wear-and-Tear Fees." *New York Times,* 11 June 1999.

"Auto Leasing." *Consumer Trends,* International Credit Association, 1998.

Bivins, Larry. "Auto Lease Campaign Spells out Agreements." *Detroit News,* 10 December 1997.

Edgerton, Jerry. "Leasing in the Lap of Luxury." *Money,* October 1998.

———. "Secondhand News: Automakers Are Increasingly Pushing Used-Car Leases. Here's When One Makes Sense." *Money,* 1 April 1999.

Gelb, Joseph W., and Peter N. Cubita. "An Overview of State Automobile Leasing Legislation. (1997 Annual Survey of Consumer Financial Services Law.)" *Business Lawyer,* May 1997.

Harris, Donna. "Net Could Spark Boom in Leasing." *Automotive News,* 31 January 2000.

Harris, Sheryl. "Car Lease Math Goes Public, New Rules Should Take the Surprise out of Popular Transaction." *Detroit Free Press,* 9 March 1998.

Hearn, Albert D. "Auto Lease Guide." 1999. Available from http://www.leaseguide.com.

Henry, Ed. "Don't Buy a New Car—Lease It." *Kiplinger's Personal Finance Magazine,* December 1998.

Henry, Jim. "Banks Back Off." *Automotive News,* 27 March 2000.

———. "Leasing Snags a Quarter of Retail Market." *Automotive News,* 27 March 2000.

———. "Residual Losses Force GE to Quit Daimler-Chrysler Leasing." *Automotive News,* 24 August 1998.

———. "Value Subtracted: Average Residual Losses Are up to $1,400 a Leased Vehicle." *Automotive News,* 23 March 1998.

Howes, Daniel. "Strategy: To Win, Companies Must Change Quickly, Management Speed Will Determine Worldwide Success." *Detroit News,* 21 December 1998.

Keller, Maryann. "Leasing May Bite the Auto Industry." *Automotive Industries,* December 1999.

Mandaro, Laura. "Auto Lease Biz Pushes Banks Into Write-downs." *American Banker,* 24 October 2000.

McClelland, Paul. "Get Up To Speed On Auto Leasing." *Credit Union Executive Journal,* September/October 2000.

McReynolds, Rebecca. "The Scales Keep Tipping." *US Banker,* March 1999.

Nol, Michael. "Auto Leases Rolling Up Huge Losses For Banks." *Chicago Sun-Times,* 3 December 2000.

Phillips, David. "Car Sales on Record Pace." *Detroit News,* 8 April 1999.

Sakurai, Joji. "Nissan Struggles in Sea of Debt: Automaker Misread Consumer Trends to Fall on Hard Times." *Detroit News,* 16 February 1999.

"Summary of Consumer Credit Laws." *Credit and Financial Issues: Responsive Business Approaches to Consumer Needs.* Washington: U.S. Department of Commerce, May 1995.

Suttell, Scott. "Fed Steps in to Clear up Confusion in Auto Leasing." *Crain's Cleveland Business,* 27 October 1997.

Thornton, Emily, Joann Muller, Jeff Green, and Heather Timmons. "Losing at the Leasing Game." *Business Week,* 16 October 2000.

Welsh, Jonathan. "Chase Waives Some Charges on Auto Leases to Lure Buyers." *Wall Street Journal,* 1 June 1999.

Wilkinson, Stephanie. "Intranet Training Tool Gets a Road Test." *PC Week,* 2 February 1998.

RISK MANAGEMENT SERVICES

Any bid to secure or add to wealth entails some risk, which means that simply being in business is a risk in itself, consisting of a nearly unlimited number of specific risks depending on the particular business's structure and the climate in which it operates. Put simply, risk managers utilize their knowledge of market conditions and a company's situation to try to minimize the amount of damage that could result from risk exposure. This usually involves appropriating exposure and insurance coverage in such a way as to prevent or control losses in as efficient a manner as possible.

By 2000, the economy was producing new exposures so fast it was difficult for risk managers to keep up, particularly in the realms of developing technology, electronic commerce, and intellectual property rights, among others. For risk managers themselves, traditionalism was an ill-advised stance, as risk management was expected to alter rapidly in the early 21st century.

An estimated 20 percent of the commercial marketplace utilized full-time risk managers in the late 1990s. The relaxed regulatory climate in many industries also placed greater emphasis on risk assessment, which was increasingly a favored alternative to industry-wide regulatory standards and enforcement. Companies faced with such new-found responsibilities increasingly sought out professionals to sort out their exposures and position them for solid gains.

With so many risk categories, ranging from financial exposures to workers' compensation to environmental regulations to an uncountable host of others, companies find it necessary to either hire managers or contract with companies who specialize in risk. The intricacies of business are simply becoming too much for a nonspecialist to efficiently and effectively deal with.

ORGANIZATION AND STRUCTURE

The risk manager is an insurance broker who advises clients on insurance and risk; an independent consultant on risk working for a fee; or a salaried employee who manages risk for the employer. The profession's largest trade group, The Risk and Insurance Management Society, Inc. (RIMS), classified risk management service providers as anyone who protects an organization's financial and physical assets; buys insurance/risk transfer products for an organization; manages an employee benefit program; administers a self-funded property/casualty and/or employee benefits insurance program; or buys risk control services from independent suppliers.

Risk managers and risk management services first identify what the organization potentially may lose. In a disaster such as a chemical spill or fire, the company can lose physical property, such as buildings, vehicles, and equipment. They can lose income, since they are unable to do business while things are rebuilt or replaced. Companies can also lose personnel to a disaster. Employees would not necessarily need to die or be severely injured for the company to suffer losses. Whenever employees miss work and draw benefits, the employer pays for it. Another potential risk is liability. If the company produces something that accidentally harms its customers, the company could be liable for damages.

Risk control is intended to stop losses before they occur. One risk control technique is exposure avoidance, which means abandoning or not engaging in an activity that could bring a loss; for instance, a company might stop manufacturing children's pajamas with asbestos fibers. Loss prevention reduces the chance loss could occur, while loss reduction involves efforts to lessen the severity of a loss, such as disaster planning. Another technique is the segregation of loss exposure—spreading one's valuable assets to avoid being wiped out by one bad move. Examples of segregation are splitting up the company's inventory in different warehouses or sending its delivery trucks along different routes so if an accident occurs in one location, the company will not lose everything. Another form of risk control is contractual transfer, which shifts some legal and financial loss to another party. This is done by leasing or subcontracting risky activities, such as toxic chemical transport, to another firm that then shares the liability for a mishap.

Risk financing means paying for the losses that *did* occur, and this is done by either transfer or retention. Companies transfer losses by sharing responsibility for risks with other parties, such as contractors, or by taking out insurance policies with commercial insurance providers. Insurance generally covers property risks, liability risks, and transportation risks. Transfers completed without commercial insurance carriers often involved paying into a mutual insurance arrangement or "pool" maintained by other organizations sharing similar risks. In contrast, companies retain losses by paying for their own losses themselves by establishing special funds or by taking out loans.

The simplest form of retention is current expensing of losses, which means paying for the loss like any other current expense. Another method involves using an unfunded loss reserve, such as noting the loss as a potential liability to be paid later. Another financing method is a funded loss reserve, which means drawing from a company fund set aside for that reason. The company might also borrow the money to pay for the loss. The most complex retention method involves the use of a captive insurer, a private insurance carrier owned by the company and used to insure itself and its international subsidiaries. Many U.S. Fortune 1000 companies own captive insurance companies, and set them up offshore in locations such as Bermuda.

BACKGROUND AND DEVELOPMENT

Risk management is a relatively new industry, though the practice of risk management is as old as business itself. The industry really developed in the 1980s and 1990s amidst surging economic booms. Insurance

brokers in particular poured into risk management consulting as companies took advantage of strong markets to purchase less insurance, seek alternate financing sources such as captives, and lean towards longer-term agreements with insurers, leaving brokers with less commission and thus hungry for new business.

Particularly among the economy's largest firms, executives are leaning toward the retention of greater amounts of risk in order to save on traditional insurance, a trend that carries with it a greater responsibility for and awareness of risk exposure and how to manage it. One of the most popular methods of funding alternative financing was through some form of self-insurance.

The cost of risk steadily declined through much of the economic expansion of the 1990s, partly as a result of improved "loss control." The trend, however, reversed in 1998 and 1999, when greater retained losses and flat premiums pushed the cost up to $5.71 per $1,000 of revenue, equal to the 1996 level, from their low point of $5.25 in 1997.

As risk managers analyzed potential new problems, the insurance industry responded with even more products. As more companies did business on the Internet, some mistakenly assumed their existing general liability policies covered losses accrued from electronic transactions. As the information superhighway expanded, more risk managers also had to plan for telecommuters. And as more of the work force sat at computers, 55 percent of risk managers reported higher ergonomic repetitive motion claims, although 73 percent said their companies had programs to reduce the problem.

Leading up to the year-2000 date change and the unknown potential consequences of the Y2K computer bug, President Bill Clinton signed into law a bill, for which RIMS lobbied heavily, to protect U.S. businesses from severe legal costs by limiting lawsuits related to the computer date change. While the more apocalyptic fears proved unfounded as the crucial date passed, the legislation freed up a good deal of risk managers' activities, which could have been devoted almost exclusively to Y2K risk management through late 1999 (and well into 2000, if things had indeed fallen apart).

CURRENT CONDITIONS

Risk management was on the cusp of rapid maturity in 2000. One of the most prominent trends was enterprise management, which entailed the consolidation of all forms of a company's risk, including operational, financial, employment, hazard, and strategic, under one portfolio. Enterprise risk management was born of companies' evolving view of risk from separate exposures to a collective risk the company must face holistically. To date, enterprise risk management is more of a novelty, though the practice is expanding rapidly, led particularly by the financial services industries.

A massive shift toward enterprise risk management will, however, alter the game for risk managers, who will be expected to consider a wider range of risk exposures than just the traditional specialty exposures, such as financial or operational, that they are used to. While greater specialization will not disappear, firms could be a bit reluctant to pack their enterprise risk staffs with a bevy of traditionalist specialists if market pressures favor streamlined risk management geared toward a more generalist approach.

As global trade provisions heat up, so does the issue of intellectual property rights and the means of securing their protection. Aon Corp. in early 2000 introduced a new risk transfer service affording companies over $100 million in blanket protection for the enforcement of intellectual property such as trademarks, patents, and copyrights. Such intangible assets are assuming greater primacy in the global economy with the development of technology and the accelerating pace of patent grants; licensing revenues from patents are expected to reach $500 billion in 2005, compared with $100 billion in 1998. More dramatically, intellectual property losses exploded from an estimated $5 million in 1982 to $3.8 billion in 1998. The range of patents is also expanding, now including everything from software designs to production methods rather than simply new, physical inventions. Aon's new offering is a recognition that the risk management industry must catch up to this booming market sector with greater protection offerings. It allows coverage across all forms of intellectual property for use in legal defense, damage payments, or enforcement and damage reclamation if the company believes its own intellectual property rights have been violated.

The boundaries between previously demarcated professions such as loss adjusters and risk managers were also rapidly dissolving. Loss adjusters have witnessed their activities' expansion from simply sorting out losses following a claim to preventing the claim from occurring in the first place. In this case, firms are increasingly realizing the efficiency potential of more holistic risk management. Insurance companies hoping to maintain a strong footing are thus forced to diversify their services to include the expedient allocation and coverage of various exposures.

The rising costs of workers' compensation premiums constituted one of the primary concerns of risk managers in the late 1990s and early 2000s. An average of 1,500 employee complaints are filed every day in the United States. The expected hike in costs was to follow from pending rules to be issued by the Occupational Safety and Health Administration extending benefits stemming from ergonomic injuries. To reduce costs, many companies were taking more risk, delving into insurance schemes rewarding claims reduction.

The financial services industries provide some of risk management's best customers. Domestic and international banking systems and enterprises, facing massive deregulation and increased credit issuing, fell under greater scrutiny as regulatory bodies, such as the U.S. Federal Reserve and the Basel Committee for Banking Supervision of the Bank for International Settlements, noted the need for enhanced supervision and standardization of credit risk practices lest the more fluid and globalized financial markets suffer instability as a result of poorly managed risk exposures. Spurring the regulatory bodies into action regarding credit risk management were the disastrous effects of the Asian financial crisis of the late 1990s. As speculative bubbles grew in Southeast Asia, many companies protected their credit in the local economies, thereby increasing their risk exposure to the troubled economy

The Risk and Insurance Management Society (RIMS) expects more small and mid-sized companies to add risk managers to their staffs or to include risk management as part of the responsibility of these companies' chief financial officers or treasurers. Because of the trend towards risk management services among companies of all sizes, more insurance brokers are charging fees for their services, instead of receiving commissions for selling insurance products.

In the late 1990s risk managers faced not only the escalation of natural disasters, but also the increased stringency of environmental regulations. By addressing environmental issues such as pollution, waste management, and environmental liability, risk managers have the potential to aid companies in increasing their profitability and competitiveness. The development of pollution credits that can be traded on the market opened a new sector for risk management as companies attempted to rethink their waste management strategies.

The Internet posed a number of new risks as well. In 2000 risk managers realized the hazards that lurk on the information superhighway when the "Love Bug" computer virus was transported to millions of computers and cost companies in excess of $15

About... **ECONOMY, COMPANY, AND COMMUNITY: THREE LEVELS OF RISK MANAGEMENT**

Risk management has benefits on three levels: economy, company, and community. An economy's risk is the wasted resources, both natural and manmade, destroyed by or used to fight accidental losses. For example, resources are wasted by fires when buildings are destroyed. An effective risk management program for an economy minimizes the resources consumed and improves the allocation of resources.

Certain companies or organizations also face risks for potential and actual losses. An effective company risk management program will enable the organization to distinguish between good risks and unnecessary ones. This allows the company to become more prosperous—with-

out interfering with normal activities—while reducing the cost of risk.

A community's risk combines a company's and an economy's risks. Successful risk management on this level focuses on effects of actual or potential losses on a particular community.

While carrying out the duty of protecting the economy, companies, and the community, risk management services must work together to examine the interests of all levels, since all three have similar risks and similar resources allocated to establishing and maintaining risk management programs.

---

billion worldwide. Assurex International, a leading industry player, reported that one-fifth of Fortune 500 companies were victims of computer hackers in the late 1990s. And three-fourths of all respondents to the survey conducted by the Computer Security Institute and the U.S. Federal Bureau of Investigation (FBI) reported serious security breaches in their computer systems in 1999. With e-commerce becoming an ever-more integrated component of firms' operations, risk managers will need to shore up efforts to prevent any disruption of business due to new computer-based disasters.

During the 1990s insurance carriers marketed products covering all calamities. Several carriers offered kidnapping and extortion policies, especially designed to cover a company's top executives and their families when traveling or living abroad; some of these policies paid $25-$50 million for hostage negotiations. Aon Corp. offers insurance against hostile takeovers for smaller companies, and the policy covered up to $5 million in legal expenses to thwart an unwanted buyer. American International Group Inc. also offered political risk insurance for companies doing business abroad in case their overseas locations were nationalized or confiscated by an unexpected new government.

With the pace of mega mergers and acquisitions accelerating in almost all major industries, risk managers were increasingly brought in as consultants to develop solutions to problems and obstacles that cropped up during the consolidation process. For example, risk managers on the buying end must examine a target company's insurance policies, expenditures, loss experience, and other agreements and policies that could affect the management of its risk,

and then find solutions to any hurdles found in managing the prospective company's risks. Because of the brisk merger activity, risk managers can arrange insurance coverage so that it removes harmful liabilities from the balance sheets of companies to be acquired.

INDUSTRY LEADERS

One of the leading insurance brokerages offering risk management consulting is Marsh, Inc., a subsidiary of Marsh & McLennan Companies. The Marsh subsidiary garnered sales of $4.5 billion in 1999 for an increase of 32.4 percent from the previous year, and employed 8,900. The firm was rapidly diversifying its risk coverage and consultation services. They offer consultation on medical and legal cost containment, claims management, loss control, and employee benefits. Marsh generates over half of its revenues outside the United States, mainly in Asia, Europe, and South America. The company was aggressively pushing into the mid-sized client field.

Aon Corp. was the second-largest provider of risk management services, with 39,000 employees spread out over its brokerage and consulting operations. Aon acquired the brokerage Alexander & Alexander Services, another risk management consultant, in 1996, and the combined firm provides risk management to companies worldwide through a subsidiary, Aon Risk Services, Inc. Like Marsh, Aon spent the rest of the 1990s in a consolidation frenzy, teaming with Zurich U.S. to establish RiskAttack, a risk management enterprise geared specifically toward mid-sized technology firms. The company spent much of 1999 reorganizing to integrate its many acquisitions, but still managed to boost sales to $7.1 billion for all its operations in 1999 from $6.4 billion the year before.

Another diversified insurance firm providing risk management support is American International Group, Inc. (AIG). AIG raked in $35.9 billion in revenues in 1999, up from $30.7 billion in 1998, and employed 55,000. The company offers risk consulting services through a division called AIG Risk Management, Inc. In keeping with its name, AIG generated more than half of its revenue outside of the United States. Industry drama was enhanced by the fact that AIG chief executive officer Maurice Greenberg's son, Jeff, was president over at Marsh.

A good deal of networking paid off for U.S.-based Assurex International in 1999 when it partnered with Europe's Synergy groups to create the world's largest private insurance brokerage group, specializing in risk management services and global insurance. Providing an umbrella organization for some of the largest independent brokerages around the world, the Assurex/Synergy alliance helps firms assess and manage global risks by drawing on the knowledge of its local partners in the context of the alliance's international specialization. Assurex International employs 12,000 insurance and risk professionals and generate sales of about $1.3 billion.

WORK FORCE

The Risk and Insurance Management Society reported that 7,700 of their individual members handled some or all risk management tasks for their employers or clients in 2000. According to a survey of risk managers reported by Logic Associates, companies with sales of $200 million or less most often employ a full-time risk management staff of two. Annual salaries for risk managers at smaller companies were around $65,000. Companies with sales of $2 to $4 billion typically have risk management departments with professional workers who report to the chief financial officer. Companies with $4 to $7 billion in annual sales usually have risk management departments with four professional workers, while those with sales over $7 billion have staffs of five or more. Risk managers' salaries at sizable companies can be as high as $400,000, but for most industries, salaries at larger firms average around $180,000. Moreover, about 90 percent of risk managers at the largest companies enjoyed stock options, compared with only 38 percent at companies with sales less than $200 million.

AMERICA AND THE WORLD

U.S. risk managers often base a company's captive insurance office in another state or country because of the tax advantage. The top U.S. states for captive insurance companies are Colorado, Illinois, Vermont, and Hawaii. Common offshore captive domiciles include Panama, Barbados, and Grand Cayman. The world leader for captive insurance companies is Bermuda with over 1,150 firms. Bermuda's liberal corporate tax laws also attract many global specialty insurance and reinsurance firms.

As for competing in the world market, risk management increasingly required knowledge of not only international finance and legal issues, but also cultural and political variations as well, which, if improperly accounted for, can result in disastrous losses for a company.

RESEARCH AND TECHNOLOGY

Good risk managers should recognize their own risks as well as those of their clients. In that spirit, risk management institutions were trying to minimize their chances of losing or mishandling information crucial to their operations. A particularly popular remedy was the connected network backup (CNB) system from Connected Corp., which manages and protects electronic information assets. In the event of a computer or network malfunction, the CNB system is designed to retrieve lost information from its automatically created backup copy. With the rapidly expanding percentage of the work force engaged in telecommuting, and with more information stored electronically, such network protections are becoming an increasingly central part of a company's operating costs.

Along with the rise of e-commerce has come the inevitable rise of e-commerce fraud, another new risk source companies have grown anxious about. Since firms are less able to avoid the Internet as a marketing source if they hope to remain competitive, the high fraud rate, estimated at between 4 and an alarming 25 percent of all online transactions, is nonetheless unable to keep them from the cyber marketplace. CyberSource Corp., a leading provider of online risk management services, developed its CyberSource Internet Fraud Screen to reduce the risk from this hazard. The program was designed to quickly calculate risk assessments and allow online merchants to convert orders to sales while minimizing customer service overhead.

FURTHER READING

Bradford, Michael. "Job Market Tight for Risk Managers." *Business Insurance,* 28 August 2000.

Bradford, Michael, and Dave Lenckus. "Future Brings Challenges to Risk Manager." *Business Insurance,* 20 December 1999.

"Connected Corporation Signs Deal with Kemper Insurance to Manage and Protect Critical Corporate Data." *Business Wire,* 22 February 2000.

Deloitte & Touche. "Financial Risk Management Survey 1999." Deloitte & Touche. Available from http://www .deloitte.co.uk/sector/financial/bankingsecurities/riskman survey.html.

Dowding, Tony. "Commercial Risk Management; Broad Appeal." *Post Magazine,* 29 July 1999.

"Employers Seek Solutions to Reduce Anticipated Rise in Workers' Compensation Insurance Costs." *Business Wire,* 15 December 1999.

Kahn, Sharon. "Risks of the Internet." *Treasury & Risk Managment,* July 2000.

Katz, David M. "Risk Managers Not Doomed." *National Underwriter, Property & Casualty/Risk & Benefits Management Edition,* 19 April 1999.

Kroll, Karen M. "Covering Non-traditional Risks." *Industry Week,* 1 February 1999, 63.

McCrary, Ernest S. "Calling All Risks." *Global Finance,* April 2000.

Pillsbury, Dennis. "RIMS Looks at Harder Market, Effects of Internet." *Rough Notes,* July 2000.

"Risk and Insurance Management Society, Inc." Available from http://www.rims.org.

"Risk Management Supplement; Loss Adjusters Adjusting for Fewer Claims." *Post Magazine,* 16 September 1999.

Roberts, Sally, and Sarah Goddard. "Assurex Broadens Network: Little Overlap with New Partner Synergy." *Business Insurance,* 26 July 1999.

Robotics and Industrial Automation

INDUSTRY SNAPSHOT

Although it's been around for decades, the cyclical U.S. robotics industry grew vibrantly in the late 1990s and was expected to continue its upward trend in the early 2000s. In a banner year, the industry reveled in a sharp 39 percent jump in unit shipments in 1999 and a dramatic 60 percent spike in new orders.

Falling prices kept revenue from rising as quickly, growing just 17 percent in 1999, but industry analysts cited lower prices as one factor igniting new demand. Much of the recent growth can also be attributed to strength in the automotive business, which is the United States' biggest market for robotics and automation technology. Other sectors such as food processing also showed marked increases in demand for robots. Industry insiders say, moreover, that 90 percent of the potential U.S. market for first-time robotics purchases still remains untapped.

While the vast majority of robots so far are used in manufacturing, service robots are expected to be more commercially viable in the early 2000s. These devices won't resemble the intelligent android bots featured in movies and science fiction, but they will likely be harnessed in commercial settings for everyday drudgeries such as vacuuming and mowing lawns.

ORGANIZATION AND STRUCTURE

INDUSTRY MAKEUP

The robotics and industrial automation industry is made up of companies that produce robots and other industrial automation machines (including accessories such as "grippers," or "hands"); those that supply the software that controls them; and others, called system integrators, that bring the pieces together for a specific application for a specific customer. The 1998 *Robotics Industry Directory,* published by the Robotic Industries Association, listed more than 125 suppliers of robots and related automation products. The association's members included more than 175 manufacturers, distributors, system integrators, accessory suppliers, research groups, and consultant firms.

A small number of large corporations, most headquartered outside the United States, manufacture most of the world's robots and industrial automation systems. The larger number of mid-size and small companies, however, focusing on the needs of a specific industry or application, has expanded the frontiers of robotics. Typically, the automation supplier and the customer work closely together to develop a system to meet the specific requirements of the application and site.

ROBOTICS MARKET

The industry's customers are primarily manufacturing companies, with the automotive industry being the largest segment. Each year, however, more and more manufacturers in other industries such as food processing, electronics, and consumer goods invest in robotics and other automation systems. Semiconductor manufacturers are another important market segment. These companies use robots for such applications as welding, assembling parts, and transporting materials in the manufacturing process. In general, robots appeal to industry in two situations: first, when they can perform a task faster and more accurately than humans (in some cases, tasks impossible or un-

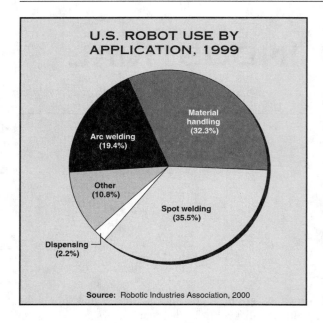

U.S. ROBOT USE BY APPLICATION, 1999

- Material handling (32.3%)
- Arc welding (19.4%)
- Other (10.8%)
- Spot welding (35.5%)
- Dispensing (2.2%)

Source: Robotic Industries Association, 2000

safe for humans), and secondly, when they are more cost-effective. Other fields, such as medicine, have also begun taking advantage of robots.

BACKGROUND AND DEVELOPMENT

In the 1890s, Nikola Tesla built the first radio-controlled vehicles in response to his vision of smart mechanisms that could emulate human movements. These were known as "automatons" until 1921, when a Czech novelist and playwright, Karel Capek, featured robots in his play, *R.U.R.,* short for "Rossum's Universal Robots." The term "robot" comes from the Czech word *robota,* which translates loosely into "serf," or compulsory labor. The word caught people's fancy, but robots did not exist in any great number outside the human imagination. It was not until the 1940s that true robots became reality. They were closely tied to the invention of computers.

Serious robot research began in the late 1950s when George Devol and Joe Engelberger developed the first industrial modern robots, known as Unimates. Devol earned the first patents for parts transfer machines. Engelberger formed Unimation, Inc., the first company to market robots, and consequently he has been called the father of robotics.

In the late 1960s, researchers at the Stanford Research Institute produced the first robot prototype, an experimental robot called Shakey. This machine processed information via a small computer and was capable of arranging blocks into stacks through the use of a television camera, which it used as a visual sensor. By itself, Shakey was not especially useful. It did, however, encourage other researchers to pursue useful functions for robots.

General Motors Corp. (GM) teamed up with the Massachusetts Institute of Technology (MIT) in the mid-1970s to develop robots. Using GM funds, MIT researcher Victor Scheinman refined a motor-driven arm he had invented. His work led to the production of a programmable universal manipulator for assembly, which marked the beginning of the so-called robot age. Because success in developing industrial robots did not come easily, there were failures galore in the early stages of experimentation.

In the early 1980s robotics was expected to be the "next industrial revolution." Zymark Corp. produced the first robots manufactured specifically for use in a laboratory in 1982. A few years later, Perkin-Elmer Corp. introduced the MasterLab, and Fisher Scientific Co. offered the MAXX 5, but neither was successful and both projects were dropped. In 1985 U.S.-based companies reported orders for a record 6,200 robots. Large corporations such as General Electric Co. (GE), IBM Corp., and Westinghouse got into the robotics business, along with many smaller companies.

In the mid-1980s, however, the boom turned to bust when the huge market that had been predicted failed to materialize. The big-name companies shut down robot operations, and many smaller companies merged or went out of business. The automobile industry accounted for more than 70 percent of robot orders, and cutbacks in capital investment there had devastating consequences. New orders for robots fell to just 3,700 in 1987.

Between 1987 and 1992 robot manufacturers improved the reliability and performance of their products, which would help to establish themselves in industries other than automotive. In 1991 Zymark introduced the XP robot, which featured programmable speeds and operated three times faster than other units in existence. That same year Hewlett-Packard Co. developed its Optimized Robot for Chemical Analysis, which used a special methods development language to operate. These machines revolutionized the laboratory robot industry and set the stage for important advances in the field. Robots were also developed for assembly, material handling, and many other applications.

After the severe slump in the mid- to late 1980s, the robotics industry made an impressive comeback. By the mid-1990s, the industry enjoyed a series of record-breaking sales years, with annual revenue in-

A technician assembling an industrial robot. (*Photo Researchers Inc./Rosenfeld Images Ltd./Science Photo Library*)

creases of as much as 25 percent. Although both the automotive and nonautomotive segments performed well, actual unit shipments still fluctuated in these years. Nevertheless, from 1992 to 1997 the industry posted gains in new orders of 131 percent.

Thus far there have been three generations of robots, each of which shows an increasing ability to accomplish more difficult tasks. Though some boast complex features, many amount to little more than electronic arms. In some cases each ensuing generation of robots is simply a more state-of-the-art arm. For instance, there are robotic arms today equipped

with tools to assist surgeons in performing delicate operations—a far cry from the primitive first generation of robots.

Industrial robots (such as information and painting robots and robots for education and automation in injection mold and welding lines) comprised the first generation of robots. Some were used in semiconductor and disk assembly, wafer inspection, and wafer disk carriers. The second generation gave birth to cleaning robots, security robots, and intelligent and assembly robots. As technology advanced, a third generation appeared. This group included more advanced service robots. This time, they did more than clean: they were personal robots. There were also medical/welfare robots used for rehabilitation and support for the elderly. In addition, this generation introduced cellular, navigation, biped, multi-arm and finger, and harvesting robots. Some featured artificial intelligence. There were also space robots, micro-robots for bionics, robots to work in hazardous environments, and maintenance robots.

Robots are dependent to a great extent on developments in computers. Like computers, their intelligence control systems are based on microprocessors. These systems provide continuous two-way communication between the robot's microprocessor and the arms. Whether the robots are classified as "playback" or "sequence" types, they rely on their microprocessors for directions.

Playback robots are capable of memorizing and repeating movements programmed by human operators. Sequence robots are less expensive than playback robots since manufacturers build their programs directly into the machines. Often, these robots move from point to point or from one assembly station to another. In either case, they work at a lower cost than humans, which accounts for their growing popularity. Comparisons between humans and robots on a typical production line suggest that robots far outperform humans at less cost overall. Moreover, they can function in places that pose hazards to humans. These advantages account for the surge in the number of industrial robots currently in place and the increasing number predicted to be installed in the near future.

Robots are classified as either industrial or nonindustrial. Industrial robots are used primarily on assembly lines. Robots with grippers perform tasks such as loading and unloading presses and other machines. A second type can use its grippers to manipulate tools and spray paint, weld, grind, drill, or rivet. Nonindustrial robots perform an entirely different range of services. For example, police departments use robots to detect bombs. This practice reduces the dangers that human officers might face in locating and defusing explosives. A Japanese university has developed a robot that simulates a human jawbone. The robot emulates human chewing motions, which the researchers hope will help them develop new dental treatments. A California-based manufacturer has invented a robot that performs hip replacements in dogs. Other companies have created robots that can patrol buildings as security guards; lift briefcases, open doors, and pour drinks for wheelchair-bound people; and clean washrooms. Of course, the National Aeronautics and Space Administration used robots to traverse the Moon and Mars.

CURRENT CONDITIONS

Despite a sluggish market in 1998, when both unit sales and revenues dipped, the Robotic Industries Association reported that the industry roared back in 1999 with record-setting orders, shipments, and revenues. Led by sharp upticks in orders for spot-welding and assembly robots, total new orders in 1999 soared 60 percent, reaching 17,591 units valued at $1.4 billion. Shipments that year also surged 39 percent to 15,063 devices worth $1.2 billion. At those levels, orders, shipments, and revenues were essentially double what they were in 1994.

Although they tend to cut into manufacturers' profits, tumbling prices have made robotic equipment accessible to a wider base of customers. In 1999 the average value of each machine shipped slid to about $80,000, down from $90,000 or more earlier in the decade. Worldwide, prices fell an estimated 40 percent from 1990 to 1999. A separate estimate placed the average net cost of installing a robot, including programming and other services, at $150,000. As newer robots based on personal computer (PC) technology continue to hit the market, average prices were expected to continue their downward course in the early 2000s.

The total installed base of robots in the United States was around 105,000 as of 2000. That number was up almost 14 percent from a year earlier and more than double the number operating back in 1990. By 2002, the U.S. robot count was expected to rise another 20 percent to 120,000 in use.

INDUSTRY LEADERS

The largest manufacturers of robots and industrial automation machines are multinational corporations such as ABB Ltd. of Zurich, Switzerland, FANUC Ltd. and Yaskawa Electric Corp., both of Japan, Thyssen AG of Germany, and Elsag Bailey Process Automation N.V. of the Netherlands. FANUC, Yaskawa, and Thyssen have U.S. subsidiaries. Rockwell International is the largest U.S.-based manufacturer of automation products, but not robots per se.

ABB

ABB Ltd. is considered the world's top producer of robotics equipment. A sprawling $30 billion engineering and industrial concern, ABB has sizable robotics operations in the United States through its ABB Flexible Automation Inc. subsidiary and other holdings. In 1999 the parent company's total revenues from robotics and automation were estimated at $8.65 billion. Its sales in 1999 were up some 26 percent as the company benefited from strong world demand and its acquisition of Netherlands-based Elsag Bailey, a large automation machinery maker in its own right.

FANUC

FANUC Robotics North America, Inc., of Rochester Hills, Michigan, is a subsidiary of Japan-based FANUC Ltd., generally regarded as the world's second-largest robot manufacturer. Originally called GMFANUC Robotics Corp., the firm was founded in 1982 as a joint venture between General Motors and FANUC Ltd. It became a wholly owned subsidiary of FANUC in 1992. While created in part to supply the auto industry, FANUC Robotics North America has diversified to serve most U.S. industries requiring robotics technology. The parent company has two other U.S. subsidiaries: FANUC America Corp. and GE FANUC Automation, a joint venture with General Electric. Approximately 45 percent of FANUC's unconsolidated revenues came from robotics as of 2000.

GIDDINGS & LEWIS

Giddings & Lewis, Inc., with headquarters in Wisconsin, is a subsidiary of Thyssen AG. It manufactures industrial automation equipment in Canada, Germany, and the United Kingdom, as well as in the United States. The company, bought out by Thyssen in 1997, primarily serves customers in heavy industries such as automotive, defense, and aerospace. Giddings & Lewis employs about 3,100 people.

ROCKWELL INTERNATIONAL

Rockwell International Corp., once a big defense contractor, is the largest U.S.-based industrial automation company. Between 1984 and 1998 it made more than 50 acquisitions and divested itself of 30 operations, getting out of the airframe, automotive components, and semiconductor businesses. Rockwell reported 2000 sales of $7.1 billion and net profits of $636 million. Automation accounted for more than 60 percent of sales. The company employed 41,200 worldwide.

MOTOMAN

Motoman, Inc., a subsidiary of Yaskawa Electric Manufacturing Co. of Japan, was founded in 1989, and by its tenth anniversary had more than 10,000 robot installations. The West Carrollton, Ohio, company has shipped more than 55,000 robots in total and is the third-largest robot maker in North America. Between 1989 and 1999 it experienced compound average growth of over 30 percent. In 2000 it employed about 500 people.

ADEPT TECHNOLOGY

Though it suffered setbacks in 1999, Adept Technology has installed over 15,000 robots worldwide and remains one of the United States' largest industrial robot producers. The San Jose, California-based manufacturer makes selective compliance assembly robot arms, or highly flexible multijointed robotic arms, for materials handling, assembly, and packaging. Other products include palletizing robots, robotic vision devices, and software.

In its fiscal year ended June 2000, Adept's sales grew 21 percent, to $99.2 million, from fiscal 1999. Slack demand in its high-tech markets of computer disk drives, telecommunications, and semiconductors was to blame. In July 1999 the company acquired BYE/Oasis Engineering, a microelectronics manufacturer, to help it branch into new lines of business.

PRI AUTOMATION

PRI Automation, Inc., of Billerica, Massachusetts, is the leading U.S. supplier of automation systems for computer-chip manufacturers, with 90 percent of the market. Its hardware and software automate the movement of silicon wafers between different steps of the manufacturing process, reducing the risk of error and contamination. Intel Corp. accounts for 21 percent of its sales. Other major customers include Advanced Micro Devices, Samsung, and Motorola. After fast sales growth in the early and mid-1990s, the company faced a sharp slowdown in the late 1990s because of weak demand in the semiconductor business. In its 1999 sales plunged to $136 million, down from $178.2 million the year before. That sales deficit slapped the company with a stinging 28 percent net loss on the year.

BROOKS AUTOMATION

Another major supplier to the chip industry is Brooks Automation, Inc. Its equipment uses vacuum technology to move, align, and hold the silicon wafers in the manufacturing process. The company supplies about 90 percent of the vacuum robots used in the semiconductor industry. While it managed to escape the bloodletting other suppliers to the chip business suffered, Brooks' sales in fiscal 1999 edged up just 4 percent to $104 million, while the company employed 850 workers. Three-fourths of its sales derive from

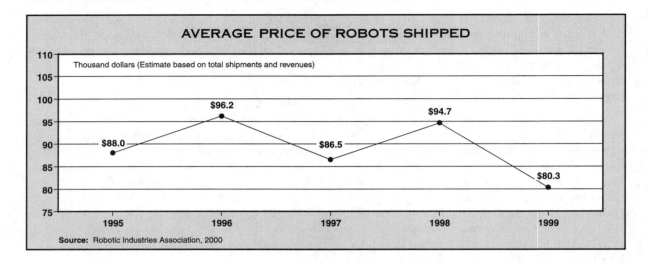

AVERAGE PRICE OF ROBOTS SHIPPED

Thousand dollars (Estimate based on total shipments and revenues)

$88.0 $96.2 $86.5 $94.7 $80.3

1995   1996   1997   1998   1999

Source: Robotic Industries Association, 2000

tool automation, while the rest comes from its factory automation products.

OTHER LEADERS

Other important U.S. robotics companies include Cognex Corp., the world's leading manufacturer of hardware and software systems that function as robot eyes with more than 100,000 vision systems shipped ($152 million in 1999 sales); Gerber Scientific, Inc., which makes automated manufacturing systems for the apparel, optical, sign making, and printing industries; Integrated Surgical Systems, Inc., with 1999 sales of $6.2 million; and Computer Motion, Inc., with 1999 sales of $18.1 million. Integrated Surgical Systems and Computer Motion both manufacture robotic systems for use in surgery.

WORK FORCE

Automation and robotics have a mixed effect on employment. Proponents argue that the increasing use of robots will add jobs. After all, there must be humans to design, build, and repair them. Opponents suggest otherwise. They say that more robots performing tasks heretofore carried out by humans will eliminate jobs. Early evidence does side with the proponents. The industry has generated more jobs in manufacturing, sales, and computer maintenance than it has eliminated. Although there are no hard figures at this point to substantiate either claim, it must be remembered that the robotics industry is in its infancy. Also, since it is allied closely with the computer industry, there may be a spillover effect between the two.

The industrial automation and robotics industry is also linked with other industries in a symbiotic manner. For example, there is a close relationship with the computer-aided design and computer-aided manufacturing, bionics, and laser industries. Jobs and career paths abound in all these industries. There is a growing need for robotics specialists in almost every industry, including electronics, shipbuilding, construction, automobile manufacturing, aerospace, computers, and medical technology. Job titles include robot programmer, robotics engineer, robotics repairperson, robotics designer, mechanical engineer, robot sales representative, robotics assembly supervisor, and robotics software writer, to name a few. Yet, with new jobs come increased demands for new skills. This is where the escalating use of industrial robots has an impact on the labor force.

Workers need new skills to cope with the new robots. There has been a reduction in the number of semiskilled workers as a result of industrial automation. The labor force needed in an automated plant requires skilled workers such as maintenance engineers, electricians, toolmakers, and computer programmers. Without such people, industry and robots cannot function. Thus, the increase in industrial automation and robots has created a demand for more training, without which neither industry nor robots can survive.

AMERICA AND THE WORLD

Worldwide in 1998 there were an estimated 720,300 industrial robots in operation, according to annual figures compiled by the United Nations Economic Commission for Europe (UNEC) and the International Federation of Robotics (IFR). By 2002, the total count was expected to rise 11 percent to just below 800,000 devices.

The value of all robots shipped in 1998, the most recent year for which statistics were available, was estimated at $4.2 billion, off 13 percent from 1997. The global market was weakened in the late 1990s by economic softness in Asia, particularly in Japan and South Korea, the region's biggest markets for robotics.

JAPAN

Japan led the world in robot technology with 57 percent of the world's installations in 1998, amounting to about 277 robots for every 10,000 manufacturing workers. That country has also been at the forefront of new research and product development. Japan's lead in robot use is expected to narrow, however, according to analysis by UNEC and IFR, which forecast Japan's share to dwindle to 46 percent by 2002. In addition to economic weakness at home, which stifled robot sales, Japan had long operated a disproportionate share of the world's robots, as much as two-thirds, so it was little surprise that other countries have begun to boost their shares. It wasn't until 1996 that the rest of the world's robot use ever exceeded Japan's.

UNITED STATES

The United States is the second-leading country in terms of robot deployment, with 11 percent of the world's robots in 1998. Its share was predicted to reach 15 percent in 2002. The U.S. industry has staged a comeback after setbacks in the 1980s and 1990s. In the early 1980s, the American robot industry grew quickly due in part to large investments by the automotive industry. The promising start to the fledgling industry, however, faltered when the integration of robots into production lines lagged and the economic viability of industrial automation and robots faded. As a result, there was a noticeable shakeout in the robot industry. Most of the American manufacturers went out of business, consolidated with others, or were sold to Japanese and European competitors. For a while, only one U.S. company, Adept, produced industrial robot arms.

GERMANY

Germany operates the third-largest number of industrial robots, with 10 percent of global installations as of 1998. The German share was expected to approach 13 percent by 2002, nearing 104,000 robots in operation.

RESEARCH AND TECHNOLOGY

Researchers work constantly to upgrade the quality and efficiency of robots. They concentrate primarily on true robots for industrial use. A true robot operates independently and automatically from a self-contained program built into it. There is also a class of robots called telecherics, which are human-operated machines. These machines can possess many features of a true robot, but they are always under human direction by cable or radio links. They serve such purposes as handling radioactive or explosive materials and sample specimens on the ocean floor. In all cases, though, operators behind the scenes must manipulate them. They are not as numerous as true robots.

True robots are generally stationary industrial robots located in factories. Early models handled assignments such as welding or painting that posed hazards to humans. These robots tend to be cumbersome. Researchers have developed a new generation of light-duty and inspection robots that address different problems. Modern true robots carry out monotonous, repetitive tasks with a high degree of precision. Some share work with human workers. Ironically, contemporary robots look nothing like the "creatures" portrayed in early movies, literature, and plays. Researchers have developed a new breed of robots with manipulators (the arms that define the machines' capabilities); controllers (the components that store information, instructions, and programs used to direct the manipulators' movements); and power supplies that drive the manipulators, which are smaller and more efficient than their forerunners. They have also improved on robots' degrees of freedom, geometrical configurations, and envelopes.

DEGREES OF FREEDOM

A robot's applications and flexibility are determined by its number of degrees of freedom (the number of movements it can perform). Many industrial-type robots are limited by sequence nature; that is, they are restricted to a low number of movements. The degrees of freedom are related closely to the robot's geometrical configuration.

GEOMETRICAL CONFIGURATION

Industrial robots feature four principal geometrical configurations: articulated, revolute, or jointed-arm; spherical (also called polar coordinate); rectangular (or Cartesian); and cylindrical. They can also be vertically jointed, horizontally mounted, and/or gantry or overhead mounted.

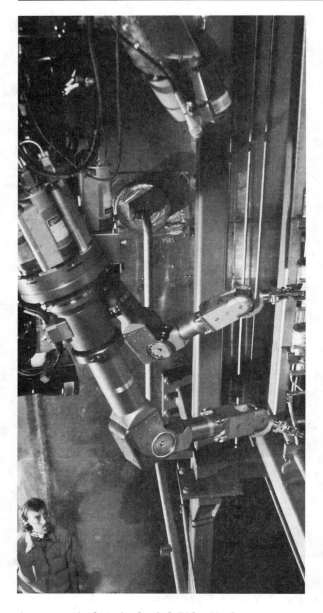

A servomanipulator in the Oak Ridge Nuclear Laboratories. (Photo Researchers Inc./Hank Morgan)

ENVELOPE

A robot's envelope is the three-dimensional contour formed by the motion of the end effector (a device used to produce a desired change in an object in response to input, such as a gripper) or wrist moved completely through the outer limits of motion.

As computers become more powerful, researchers make more changes to robots' degrees of freedom, geometrical configurations, and envelopes. That, in turn, means robots will become more flexible and capable of more advanced functions. In only one-quar-

ter of a century, researchers have made remarkable strides in robotics technology. Thus, the development of and need for advanced robots will continue to grow—as will the industrial automation industry.

THE FUTURE

By most indications, the robotics industry can look forward to a bright yet bumpy future. The automotive industry continues to be the dominant market, and electronics, aerospace, food and beverage, and appliance manufacturing have shown signs of strong growth. But robotics manufacturers will likely continue to face moody upswings and downswings brought about by business cycles in its target markets and by technological advances—and shortcomings—in its products.

Major technological factors on the horizon that bode well for the industry are the development of PC-based control systems, stimulated by the simultaneous development of low-cost PC-based vision systems. Vision systems, along with improved sensor technology, increase the possibilities for robot applications in currently labor-intensive processes. A survey of robotics professionals in *Robotics World* magazine reported that the shift away from proprietary control systems toward an open architecture would also be an important part of the future. Demographic and social trends also point toward greater adoption of robots, as aging populations, workplace safety concerns, and shorter workweeks will create demand for technological solutions.

FURTHER READING

International Federation of Robotics. "Robot Statistics." Geneva, Switzerland, 2000. Available from http://www.ifr.org.

Jefferson, Greg. "Robotics Entering New Era." *Indianapolis Business Journal,* 4 January 1999.

"Leading the Charge to a Productive 21st Century." *Robotics World,* fall 1998.

"1998 Industry Survey: Cautious Optimism the Industry Watchword." *Robotics World,* 1998/1999.

Robotic Industries Association. *Robotics Online.* Ann Arbor, MI, 2000. Available from http://www.roboticsonline.com.

"Robotics." Menlo Park, CA: SRI Consulting, 1998. Available from http://future.sri.com/TM/aboutROBO.html.

"The Robotics Market: Assessment and Forecast." *Robotics World,* 1998/1999.

"Will Robots Take Charge of the Factory." *Automation,* September 2000.

Williams, Frances. "Carmakers behind Rising Demand for Factory Robots." *Financial Times,* 5 October 1999.

"World Trade: More and More Robots Populate World's Factories." *Financial Times,* 14 October 1998.

Zheng, Y. F., ed. *Recent Trends in Mobile Robots.* Singapore: World Scientific, 1993.

SATELLITES

The global satellite market expanded into the stratosphere in the mid- and late 1990s. Global satellite revenues reached $41 billion in 1999, according to Merrill Lynch & Co., Inc., and, after some of the industry's kinks, quite evident at the turn of the century, worked themselves out, sales were expected to rocket to over $200 billion by 2009.

Throughout the 1990s, the industry restructured itself to capitalize on emerging consumer technologies incorporating satellite signals, and broadened from its weather-, space-, and military-centered operations of previous years, although those applications remained a cornerstone of satellite usage. Commercial launchings tripled during the 1990s following the rush of new satellite systems and technologies, including direct-to-home television broadcasting, satellite-based Internet service, telecommunications satellites, and the booming commercialization of existing technologies, such as global positioning systems. As a result of all this new activity, the entire industry's pace has accelerated rapidly. Whereas in the mid-1990s it took over two and a half years for a satellite to be built and launched, by 2000 the entire process generally required less than 18 months. Moreover, satellite manufacturers have taken broad steps to bring costs down so as to facilitate a more active consumer-based market, creating small satellites that cost less than $20 million, compared with the $100 million of yesteryear.

Still, the industry hit some rather sizable speed bumps in 1999 and 2000, including the sudden failure of two promising young companies, injecting a bit of sobriety into the otherwise rambunctious industry. Legislative difficulties also cut into the U.S. export market and ruffled the feathers of many industry executives. A growing contingent of other countries such as France, Russia, Japan, and the United Kingdom also make influential contributions and are capable of heavy competition with the United States. Still, the United States commanded about 65 percent of the global satellite system market in 2000.

ORGANIZATION AND STRUCTURE

Satellites serve as active repeaters of transmitted signals and, therefore, as an alternative method of sending information both short and long distances. Instead of wire, short-wave radio, cables, or fiber optics, communications satellites can send signals without interference across long distances and geographic boundaries. In addition, satellites are economical because their cost of operation does not depend on distance. Satellites, moreover, can relay signals from one terrestrial transmitter to a number of receivers within the coverage vicinity; they can also transmit broadband signals and hence can send large quantities of data. With enough satellites in the proper configuration, they could cover any point on the globe. In practice, however, the International Telecommunications Union (ITU) and the U.S. Federal Communications Commission (FCC)—regulatory bodies that oversee the development and operation of telecommunications technology—often restrict the coverage of satellites to a much more limited area.

Communications satellites function by taking the signal from an Earth-based transmitter antenna and relaying it to a receiver antenna elsewhere on Earth. That is, satellites contain equipment that receives signals, amplifies them, and sends them to Earth receiver stations. Hence, these features make satellites ideal for the one-to-many point transmissions of radio, television, data, and video.

Satellites can transmit and receive broadband microwave signals at a variety of different frequencies, which are allocated for specific uses. The Ku-band (extending from 10.7 to 18 gigahertz) and the Ka-band (18 to 31 gigahertz) frequencies were expected to replace C-band (3.7 to 7.25) frequencies for Earth stations with immobile antennas or fixed satellite services in the mid-1990s. While the popularity of Ku-band transponders, or receivers, was beginning to overtake that of its predecessors, the C-band transponders, by the late 1990s, companies, organizations, and individuals have a significant investment in C-band technology, especially in Earth station C-band equipment. Moreover, the typical backyard satellite dish receives C-band frequencies and there are an estimated 3 million U.S. households with such receivers. In order to placate both sides, companies have developed and launched satellites with both C-band and Ku-band capabilities.

Space satellites are propelled into orbit by spacecraft or rocket boosters. Satellite services rely on different kinds of orbits depending on the kinds of tasks they perform and on the size of the satellites. The most frequently used orbits include: low Earth orbits (LEOs), medium Earth orbits (MEOs), and geostationary orbits (GEOs). Many satellite projects under way in the late 1990s and early 2000s called for low Earth orbiting satellites. MEOs cover altitudes of about 6,000 miles from Earth and work best for larger satellites. Many of the communications satellites in the late 1990s, however, used GEOs, where they orbit at an altitude of 22,300 miles. From this point, the satellites' rotation mirrors Earth's, causing the satellites to maintain a constant position relative to Earth. This orbit, however, can hold only about 150 satellites and was almost full by the end of the 1990s.

The FCC and the ITU regulate satellite-related communications industries. The FCC focuses on issues concerning U.S. domestic use of satellites, while the ITU handles aspects of communications satellites with international ramifications. The FCC opened up the skies for U.S. satellites by rescinding the regulatory distinction between domestic and international satellites in a policy called Domestic International Satellite Consolidation in 1996. This policy allows satellite service providers access to international markets. The move, however, did not make the U.S. market more accessible to international satellite companies. On the other hand, the ITU allocates the use of various frequencies to different user groups and controls satellites in GEOs. The ITU makes its decisions concerning satellites use and radio frequencies at its World Administrative Radio Conferences.

BACKGROUND AND DEVELOPMENT

Russia launched the first successful satellite, the *Sputnik,* on 4 October 1957, taking the lead in space exploration. This event inspired the United States to redouble its efforts to catch up with and surpass Russia as the Cold War continued to brew. A few months later, on 1 February 1958, the United States launched its first satellite, becoming the second nation in space. On 3 November 1960, the National Aeronautics and Space Administration (NASA) launched its first satellite, *Explorer 8,* beginning the first of many NASA space expeditions.

Satellites first entered the commercial arena in the 1960s, providing alternative channels of data transmission for international telephone and telegraph services. That is, satellites competed with undersea cables for use in telephone and telegraph services. In the 1970s, companies started to deploy satellites within the United States for commercial purposes. These satellites not only transferred telephone signals for businesses, they also relayed network data. Companies relied on satellites for point-to-point and point-to-multipoint transmissions, between, say, an office and a production plant.

In addition, television networks began implementing satellites to send and receive transcontinental relays of broadcast signals in the 1970s. Satellites ultimately had a revolutionary effect on television broadcasting; with satellites, networks could cull the best resources from all the stations in the network. Stations could transmit or receive signals from other network stations via satellites. Later, television stations acquired portable Earth stations, allowing them to travel from event to event, to broadcast live from events, and to rove around town looking for events to broadcast.

CURRENT CONDITIONS

The opening of new markets was the most recognizable shift in the satellite industry through the mid- and late 1990s, and by 2000 the industry was poised to facilitate a range of services for the high-tech and perpetually connected economy. Telecommunications firms, Internet service providers, and direct broadcast satellite television companies poured money into satellite firms to capitalize on a market with seemingly endless opportunities.

TELECOMMUNICATIONS

The inundation of demand for cellular phones, voice message services, fax machines, and wireless communications devices fueled a massive surge in sales of low Earth orbit satellites. This market sector, however, seemingly hit a brick wall in late 1999, when Iridium World Communications Ltd. wound up in bankruptcy court. Iridium, an international point-to-point telecommunications network using 66 satellites in low orbit, was one of the most ambitious players in the satellite telecommunications sector, with a network designed to link its telecommunications satellites with mobile phones, solar-powered phone booths, fax machines, and pagers. Iridium's crash also resulted in suspended trading in public stock for satellite phone provider ICO Global. Thus, the telecommunications satellite boom that looked so unstoppable just a few years earlier was stuck in limbo by 2000, but most analysts held that it was foolish to consider the industry at a dead end.

Loral Space & Communications Ltd.'s Globalstar, for instance, pushed ahead with plans to offer a low-cost satellite-based phone service geared toward consumers who are not served by the cellular phone market, with an eye toward encroaching on that sector's business in the future. Hughes Electronics Corp.'s Spaceway, meanwhile, was building a telecommunications network with eight geostationary satellites to provide standard telephone, fax, data, video conferencing, and Internet services in North America by 2002. Orbcomm and Final Analysis were other companies engaged in the production of satellites capable of monitoring and transmitting information from space, tracking everything from mail items to household utility usage. And ICO Global was rescued from disaster by a proposed merger with Teledesic; the two companies planned to blend their data and voice satellite services for a commercial offering, expected about 2004.

BROADCAST SATELLITES

Broadcast satellites send audio, video, and data signals directly to subscribers. Dominated by Echostar and Hughes division DirecTV, direct broadcast satellite (DBS) television exploded in the late 1990s, as equipment and subscription costs diminished and service was significantly improved. Unlike the telecommunications sector, the broadcast satellite market met

with good news in 1999 and 2000. For instance, a federal ruling finally bore fruit to the industry's intensive lobbying campaign to allow DBS companies to sell signals in local markets, and the major companies lost no time in breaking into the nation's major cities to transmit local broadcasts.

The total number of DBS television subscribers was growing at an accelerating pace through 2000. From about 8.7 million subscribers at the end of 1998, the subscription base had catapulted to well over 11 million just over a year later, and an additional 4 million households signed up in 2000, according to the research firm Carmel Group. Broadcast television service was thus firmly established as one of the most successful commercial applications of satellite communications.

Digital audio radio satellites, the first of which were launched in late 2000, were slated to beam some 100 stations of commercial-free programming. Companies such as XM Satellite Radio Holdings Inc. and CD Radio threw their hats into the satellite-radio ring, seeking to compete with the heavily commercialized pop-music and talk format of conventional radio. These services were to offer a mix of music, talk, and news programming commercial-free over some 100 stations, commanding only a subscription fee of about $10 per month. They carry the additional advantage of being able to beam into areas of the country that have traditionally been underserved by commercial radio, which tends to gravitate toward the larger urban markets.

INTERNET SERVICE PROVIDERS

Satellites have also become a medium of Internet access, as researchers have sought faster ways of transmitting and downloading data. This segment of the industry could have a potential market of over $20 billion in 2005, according to Merrill Lynch. Analysts at Pioneer Consulting of Cambridge, Massachusetts predicted that broadband satellites would account for 30 percent of the Internet-access market by 2007, equal to 50 million users and generating revenues of $15 billion. Traditional telephone lines couldn't send large amounts of data quickly. Even upgraded to maximum capacity, about 56 bits per second in 2000, telephone lines couldn't compete with satellites, which can accommodate voice modems as well as send information at about 28 megabytes per second. QUALCOMM will use Globalstar's satellite system with added Transmission Control Protocol/Internet Protocol (TCP/IP) standard software, and the service was to offer wireless voice and data access. The common standards-based satellite technology, direct video broadcast, was modified to enable delivery of Internet services. Several other such projects were also in the works, including Lockheed Martin Corp.'s Astrolink and Loral Space's and Alcatel's CyberStar/Skybridge.

Some companies already offer wireless Internet access service. Metricom, Inc., for example, has had moderate success with its service even though it has only standard bandwidth of 33.6 kilobytes per second. Internet service providers (ISPs) use low-altitude satellites, which reduce transmission time and require less energy than higher altitude satellites. Satellites deliver data at a much greater rate than any other modem on the market—1,000 times faster than plain old telephone lines—and they also appeal to people in other countries in remote areas inaccessible by cable. Hughes Network Systems was the leading satellite ISP with its DirecPC service. Satellite ISPs, however, like satellite companies in general, must promote their services better in order to capture a greater share of the market.

GLOBAL POSITIONING SYSTEMS

Global positioning systems (GPSs) operate based on satellites and identify exact locations of users. The military first developed GPS, which runs on 24 U.S. Department of Defense satellites, for strategic and navigational purposes. Since then businesses have begun integrating the technology into a variety of products: cellular phones, dispatch hardware, and computers. The price of GPS equipment has also dropped, spurring an accelerated demand for it. Depending on the model, a GPS monitor can locate its whereabouts within 10 to 300 hundred feet of its actual position.

GPS has also experienced increased commercial popularity. The U.S. Department of Commerce predicted that this sector of the satellite industry alone might bring in as much as $8 billion worldwide in 2000 and $16 billion by 2003. The most common application for GPS was automobile navigation, with sales forecast to reach $1.6 billion by 2001. GPS is also used for aviation, marine, military, tracking, and surveying purposes. For example, shipping and transit services have implemented GPS to increase the efficiency of their services. With GPS in place, dispatchers always know where their vehicles are and assist them with directions, with finding alternate routes, and in emergencies. In addition, GPS was finding increasing favor in the agricultural industry, in which farmers and agribusiness managers used the systems to locate land for its particular characteristics and resources and plan the season's crop plantings accordingly.

OTHER APPLICATIONS

Consumer satellite communications helped facilitate the accelerating proliferation of distance-education programs for students enrolled in everything from elementary school to graduate courses to continuing education. Satellites render distance, geography, and infrastructure almost entirely irrelevant for education, with simultaneous reception of signals across an area of millions of square miles. In place of the limited point-to-point transmission of land-based communications, therefore, satellites facilitate ideal point-to-multipoint communication, which is more suitable for education and training courses.

Defense projects have also goaded the satellite industry on by using satellites for such varied purposes as tracking the weather and spying. Additionally, in 1998, NASA began efforts to award a $600-million-a-year contract to a team of companies that will control or monitor more than 100 existing and planned NASA spacecraft. Two teams, one headed by Lockheed Martin and the other by Boeing Co., hoped to change the way NASA scientists gather information from research spacecraft.

A small, albeit costly, segment of satellite production goes to space exploration projects. Recent missions, such as that by the *Galileo,* have photographed areas of celestial bodies that astronomers and other scientists wish to study but which are impracticable for human space missions. A series of NASA space-project failures in the late 1990s, however, gave pause to many researchers hoping to push ahead aggressively in this area.

CHALLENGES TO THE INDUSTRY

By 2000, the industry banded together to express its dissatisfaction with federal licensing policies. Since March 1999, the U.S. State Department has handled all licensing for the satellite industry, declaring that such equipment is classified as weaponry for export purposes. Previously, the task had been the responsibility of the U.S. Department of Commerce, which tended to be more permissive in its license grants. The switch came about after Congress feared Hughes and Loral might have given the Chinese missile defense system a boost when the companies investigated the failures of Chinese launchings of their satellites. Many industry executives complained that these stepped-up restrictions have severely damaged their international presence, slowing sales even to U.S. allies. For instance, in the wake of the authority switch, U.S. satellite exports fell 40 percent over the next year, according to the Aerospace Industry Association, while the U.S. share of the global market fell from 72 to 65 percent. Several European and Japanese satellite manufacturers, meanwhile, also strenuously objected to the U.S. government's action, arguing that it keeps them from acquiring necessary components from their U.S. counterparts, and that it effectively treats them as political enemies.

More than many industries, satellite companies are under particular pressure to begin generating returns on investments in fairly quick fashion. Satellites typically stay up in the air for a limited time, often falling out of orbit and necessitating replacement within seven years. Thus, in order to raise the cash necessary for new equipment, revenues must begin streaming in fairly quickly. The industry was also set back in 1999 by a series of failed launchings. In a little over a month in spring of that year, for instance, four satellites, including a U.S. military model, failed to reach their destination, either as a result of a botched launch or burning up in the atmosphere.

While satellite capabilities and demand increased and strengthened throughout the 1990s, the satellite industry also had to recognize a number of obstacles in its orbit. With all the space operations in the last few decades, the upper atmosphere was becoming inundated with cosmic debris. Thousands of rocket parts, shot satellites, and a host of other miscellaneous spacecraft components orbit around the galaxy, creating a perilous environment for new spacecraft. According to the *Economist,* 500 active satellites circulated throughout space, while some 2,000 inoperable ones, 1,400 used rocket boosters, and over 1,000 other pieces of debris polluted outer space in 1997.

INDUSTRY LEADERS

Boeing's purchase of industry leader Hughes Space and Communications Co. from General Motors Corp. for $3.75 billion catapulted Boeing to the forefront of the satellite manufacturing industry. Boeing's interest in Hughes dated back to 1997, and Boeing spent the late 1990s acquiring a variety of space-related enterprises to prepare for the move. For instance, Boeing purchased Rockwell International Corp.'s aerospace and defense operations in 1996, followed immediately by the purchase of McDonnell Douglas, which operated the Delta launch vehicle. Hughes thus exited from the satellite-manufacturing business to focus on its satellite services, which include DirecTV, PanAmSat, and Hughes Network Systems. Hughes was a market leader for decades, producing a third of all GEO satellites in the late 1990s. Hughes' satellite

manufacturing operations accounted for about 40 percent of its 1999 sales of $5.5 billion.

Lockheed Martin, based in Bethesda, Maryland, provides the Defense Department with space and satellite technology and plays a role in the commercial satellite market. Lockheed Martin designed spacecraft for Motorola's satellite network, equipment for the Hubble Space Telescope, satellites for weather monitoring, satellites for global positioning systems, technology for Iridium, and A2100 communications satellites. In 1999 Lockheed bought a 30 percent stake in Asia Cellular Service for $150 million and put up $400 million in a wireless satellite system known as Astrolink, a cooperative effort between Telecom Italia and the aerospace firm TRW Inc. That year, however, a series of launch failures set back its aggressive moves into the global commercial satellite business. The U.S. government accounted for 70 percent of sales. In 1999 the company recorded net income of $382 million on sales of $25.5 billion, while maintaining a payroll of 147,000 employees.

Loral Space & Communications Ltd., a high-technology company headquartered in New York and specializing in satellite manufacturing and satellite services, is the third-largest satellite producer. Loral owns a 42 percent share of Globalstar, a consortium developing a LEO satellite system for wireless communication, as well as a 51 percent interest in Space Systems/Loral, the company's dominant satellite manufacturer. The company also owns the communications service providers CyberStar, Skynet, and Orion Network Systems. Its development of new global satellite systems, including those of Globalstar, generated two straight years of net losses at the end of the 1990s, including a loss of $202 million in 1999 on revenues of $1.46 billion. About 77 percent of company sales derive from satellites. Loral employed 4,000 workers.

AMERICA AND THE WORLD

As the price of fiber-optic cable dropped, demand increased, taking a sizable chunk of the international telephone service business away from satellites. For example, in the late 1980s Intelsat, an organization of 143 member nations operating international communications satellites, handled about 50 percent of international phone calls, but in 1997 it handled only about 20 percent. As a result, organizations such as Intelsat that once thrived on international phone service, have turned to the direct-to-home television market in Asia,

More On STAR WARS

The satellite industry met with some high-stakes tension in early 2000 in the wake of concern by the U.S. government that China had acquired U.S. security and weapons-technology secrets. In particular, industry leader Lockheed Martin, a leading recipient of U.S. defense contracts, came under fire from several members of Congress and the State Department who claimed that Lockheed had engaged in some 30 export violations under the Arms Export Control Act when the company transferred satellite technology data to China.

The political nature of the controversy actually had its genesis back in 1996, when a Loral satellite was destroyed in an explosion of a Chinese rocket. During the ensuing investigation, Loral mistakenly sent some of its analysis to the Chinese team, after which Loral reported the incident to the State Department. From there, the political hubbub snowballed, particularly in the shadow of controversy over the Clinton administration's campaign-finance dealings related to China. Both Loral and Hughes were accused of sharing "sensitive" information, and President Bill Clinton came under fire from Congressional Republicans for being too soft on national security issues. Shortly beforehand, moreover, the Clinton administration had strongly promoted the transfer of licensing authority from the State Department to the Commerce Department following an aggressive lobbying campaign led by Hughes. By the time of the Lockheed allegations, the State Department was back in the licensing saddle.

The case against Lockheed, however, actually dated back further, although the suit came much later. The State Department's allegations stemmed from Lockheed's activities in 1994, when the company allegedly divulged results of a scientific evaluation of a Chinese-manufactured satellite motor with a client in Hong Kong without notifying the Department of Defense, in violation of export regulations. Denying any wrongdoing, Lockheed held that it received a license from the Commerce Department before the motor evaluation took place. Industry players criticized the government's aggressive stance, arguing that, even if violations did occur, the State Department charges failed to account for the fact that, since the incident occurred six years earlier, Lockheed's involvement was somewhat diluted; the scientists evaluating the motor worked for General Electric Co.'s satellite operation, which subsequently was bought by Martin Marietta Corp., which then merged with Lockheed. Lockheed's governmental detractors nonetheless insisted that China's ballistic-weapons capabilities were strengthened by the transaction.

As the industry became increasingly politicized in 1999 and 2000, the Aerospace Industries Association expressed concern that the industry would be hard-pressed to maintain its strong position in the global satellite export market. The transfer of regulatory and licensing responsibility for satellites between the Commerce and State Departments stood at the center of all parties' concerns, as the State Department was generally viewed as championing national security while the Commerce Department expressed the will of the free-trade advocates. The satellite industry thus found itself caught between proponents of two competing positions that usually went hand in hand in U.S. politics: national security and the free market.

which constituted one of the most rapidly expanding markets in the late 1990s.

The Asian satellite industry, however, suffered from severe oversupply in the wake of the late-1990s economic slowdown. The Association of South East Asian Nations had hoped to launch a regional satellite television network in 1999, but its plans were delayed when member nations were unable to agree which nation's satellite would be used for the broadcast. By 2000, however, it seemed that the Asian industry was poised to move out of its glut, and projects were being revived, spurred by both globalization and privatization efforts. Meanwhile, the Asia Cellular Satellite System, a partnership between Philippine Telecom, an Indonesian satellite operator, a Thai investment house, and Lockheed Martin launched its satellite in February 2000 to offer regional phone services.

France, Russia, the United Kingdom, and Japan have played instrumental roles in the progress of the satellite industry. Companies from these countries have contracts to collaborate on some of the largest satellite projects on the drawing boards. Boeing was collaborating with Ukrainian, Russian, and Norwegian companies to create a mobile launch system, the Odyssey. In addition, these countries have thriving satellite industries of their own. Russia, for example, developed the Proton spacecraft, which can carry up to seven satellites in just one mission. Also, France's Arianespace was among the world leaders for satellite launches. According to some analysts, the European and Japanese satellite industries have technological advantages over the U.S. industry in part because the governments in European countries and Japan have traditionally provided more support to satellite development.

RESEARCH AND TECHNOLOGY

In addition to the satellites, the launches that send them off into space are increasingly important. Currently planned satellites exceed the available number of launch pads. Companies, including Lockheed Martin, are developing reusable systems that should reduce the cost of a launch—currently running from $10 to $149 million—by one-tenth. In the late 1990s, NASA sponsored the production of the X-33 and X-34 programs, which promote the creation of reusable launch vehicles. The prototypes of Lockheed Martin's X-33 and Orbital Sciences' X-34 are forecasted to be completed in early 2001.

Satellite producers and operators constantly look for ways to reduce costs while maintaining the technological advantages of satellites in order to make their products financially accessible to mass markets. Sea Venture, a bevy of international companies led by Boeing Commercial Space, has been developing a mobile offshore launching platform, the Odyssey, for satellites. The Odyssey was to provide the advantages of launching satellites at the equator, where Earth's rotation is the fastest and the path to geostationary-transfer orbit, a stage of orbit prior to the final route to geostationary orbit, is the shortest. Therefore, launching satellites from equatorial points takes less energy than from other points.

FURTHER READING

Blake, Pat. "Stormy Skies." *Global Telephony,* November 2000.

Carroll, Kelly. "Beyond Iridium." *Telephony,* 4 September 2000.

———. "Satellite Industry Tries to Save Face." *Telephony,* 3 April 2000.

"Costs Soar as Satellites Fail to Reach Lofty Goals." *Toronto Star,* 6 May 1999.

Fernandez, Bob. "Satellite Services Caught on Launch Pad: Consumers Hold Key to Putting Profit into the Space Business." *San Diego Union-Tribune,* 5 December 1999.

Harris, Scott Blake. "A Precious Resource at Risk." *Toronto Star,* 3 April 2000.

Hirsh, Michael. "Left on the Launch Pad." *Newsweek,* 28 February 2000.

"ISPs Tune in to Satellite Broadcast." *Satellite Communications,* March 2000.

Loeb, Vernon. "Defense Advocates Applaud Action against Lockheed on Data Sharing." *Washington Post,* 7 April 2000.

———. "U.S. Satellite Firms Chafe at Tightened Export Controls." *Washington Post,* 12 May 1999.

"Lost in Space." *Economist,* 4 November 2000.

Mechem, Michael. "Asians Facing Era of Big Satellite Systems." *Aviation Week & Space Technology,* 14 February 2000.

Mooney, Elizabeth V. "Satellite Stumblers Expected to Come on Strong in 2000." *RCR Radio Communications Report,* 21 February 2000.

Noguchi, Yuki. "Competition in Low-Orbit Satellites Escalates." *Washington Post,* 1 September 1999.

Pollack, Andrew. "Export Rules Are Said to Be a Threat to Satellite Industry." *New York Times,* 1 August 1999.

Porter, Barry. "Regional TV Channel Beset by Bad News." *South China Morning Post,* 4 November 1999.

Rack, Michael, and Diana Cantu. "Under the Magnifying Glass: Distance Education and the Satellite Solution." *Satellite Communications,* March 2000.

Shiver, Jube, Jr. "Telecom Talk: Satellite Phone Services Still Have Lofty Hopes." *Los Angeles Times,* 9 September 1999.

Taverna, Michael A. "Industry Bullish on Broadband, But Impact on Satellites in Doubt." *Aviation Week & Space Technology,* 16 October 2000.

"To Boldly Dump: In Space, Nobody Ever Tidies Up." *Economist,* 29 March 1997, 87.

Williamson, Mark. "What's in a Name?" *Satellite Communications,* April 2000.

SECURITY PRODUCTS AND SERVICES

INDUSTRY SNAPSHOT

Security is a multibillion-dollar industry, consisting of a diverse group of corporations that supply personnel and products designed to protect public and private property and individuals from a variety of problems such as theft, arson, and personal attacks. Services include security guards, private investigators, and consultants. Products range from armored cars to X-ray scanning devices to bank vaults. In addition, an area of significant growth and importance for the security industry in the late 1990s and the early part of the new decade was securing intangibles, in particular intellectual property, computer-stored information or data, and computer networks. Throughout the world it is an especially important industry in view of real and assumed threats to national security, petroleum pipelines, nuclear power plants, and the global economy, among others. At the outset of the 21st century, factors driving the industry included heightened public concern about crime, decreased government spending on crime and crime prevention, corporate downsizing, and advances in security technology.

ORGANIZATION AND STRUCTURE

The security industry contains several distinct fields: civil and military service, public safety, private home and business security, data and information security, personal and consulting services, and a variety of guard services. The guard segment includes personnel such as bodyguards, border patrol officers, customs officials, private detectives, and park rangers. The industry contains many categories of services and products that are related by one common goal—the protection of individuals, groups, and property.

Numerous relatively small firms dominate the product manufacturing segment of the industry. Large firms such as Borg-Warner, through its Burns subsidiary, Pinkerton's, Inc., and Wackenhut Corp., dominate the guard segment of the industry, which provides executive protection, special events and strike coverage security, and patrol services, among others. Well-known companies, such as ADT and Brinks, lead the home and industrial security systems industry. To demonstrate the volatility of the industry, though, the acquisition of ADT by Tyco International indicated the ongoing competition for position in this rapidly growing field. Overall, the industry's revenues reached approximately $100 billion by 1999, up from $20 in 1980, according to *Los Angeles Business Journal*. The American Society for Industrial Security predicted that the industry's revenues will grow 8 percent through 2001 and by another 7 percent through 2004. Furthermore, Piper Jaffray Inc. reported that the Internet security segment would grow to almost $3 billion by the early 2000s.

BACKGROUND AND DEVELOPMENT

The concept of a "police department" is relatively new. King Louis XIV of France maintained a small group of 40 inspectors in the sixteenth century. Their primary job was to report on individuals' movements—not necessarily provide security for them. Beginning in 1633, the city of London hired watchmen to guard its streets at night. That practice carried over to the United States well into the 19th century. In 1829,

Sir Robert Peel (1788-1850) founded the first true police force in England by reorganizing the London metropolitan police force. The officers became known as "bobbies," in honor of Sir Robert.

The first organized U.S. police department came into existence in New York City in 1845. Boston became the next city to establish its own police force. Gradually, other cities followed suit. Private security, however, was still relatively unknown—until Allan Pinkerton (1819-1884) came along. Pinkerton is generally considered the father of private security. In 1850 he organized Pinkerton's National Detective Agency in Chicago. Eleven years later he recovered a large sum of money stolen from the Adams Express Co. and uncovered a plot to assassinate President Lincoln. Those coups enhanced his reputation and accelerated the development of the private security industry, which was helped by the Industrial Revolution.

As industry grew in the late 19th century in the United States, owners looked for ways to protect their property. This was especially true in the western sections of the United States as ranchers and manufacturers expanded throughout the territories. Not surprisingly, companies such as Pinkerton assumed much of the responsibility for protection of private goods and property. They took over the security for banks, department stores, museums, and other private buildings. That led to a spin-off industry of security system design (such as safes and vaults). Then, as home owners began to see the value of personal property security, companies such as ADT formed to provide it. Concomitantly, there was an outgrowth of the industry to provide security for government and privately owned facilities such as nuclear power facilities and oil pipelines. These demands created a need for better-trained protection personnel and more sophisticated security systems.

Starting in the late 1980s, technology made it possible for people to get away from traditional ways of buying products and banking. For example, people no longer needed to do their banking or shopping in person. They could do either of these by using automated teller machines (ATMs) or using computers, which added to the need for and development of security systems. Naturally, if people chose to do their banking at 2 A.M. through out-of-the-way ATMs, they ran a risk of becoming victims of criminals. That risk called for heightened security measures provided by banks. In addition, there grew a need for security systems for computerized transactions made by businesses, banks, financial institutions, and private citizens. The increasing use of computers to conduct business of all kinds had a dramatic impact on the security industry,

and companies emerged to fill the need. As a result, the commercial security services industry grew rapidly. That growth shows no signs of slowing down. In fact, the security industry is one of the fastest-growing—and most diverse—fields of employment in existence today.

The security industry expanded rapidly in the wake of highly publicized incidents such as the bombing of New York's World Trade Center in February 1993 and the bombing of the Oklahoma's Alfred Murrah Federal Building in April 1995. As a result of these incidents, the security firm Wackenhut, among others, grew by 20 percent and the government called for legislation mandating more stringent security measures. Furthermore, because of employee outrage at the stream of corporate downsizings in the 1980s and 1990s, more industries turned to security firms to protect their executives from employee retaliation. Between 1980 and 1996 the number of security companies rose from 70,000 to 160,000 and the number of security employees grew from 975,000 to 2 million.

CURRENT CONDITIONS

Overall, security products and services mushroomed into a $100 billion industry by the close of the 20th century, according to *Los Angeles Business Journal*. The security equipment sector of the industry is forecast to grow about 8 percent annually, reaching $4.25 billion in 2001, according to Frost & Sullivan, Inc. (an industry research group) and *Security Management*. Electronic article surveillance systems are forecast to drive much of the growth. In addition, *Security Management* reported that three trends in the late 1990s and early 2000s will also fuel this sector's expansion: increasing public concern about crime, federal and state budget cuts in public safety spending, and advances in security equipment. The Freedonia Group, Inc., however, cautioned that security expenditures are the first things to be cut in case of a recession and hence the growth of the industry is contingent on continued economic prosperity, which appeared uncertain by 2001.

The security equipment sector produces three kinds of equipment: perimeter security, interior security, and access control devices. Interior security and access control equipment together account for about 97 percent of the sector's revenues, according to *Security Management*. Sales of perimeter security equipment, which includes video motion detectors (VMDs), microwave sensors, and barrier sensors are predicted to double their mid-1990s levels and hit $39.1 million by 2001. VMDs are expected to spur most of the growth in the perimeter equipment market. In the mid-1990s, VMDs ran about $9,500, but prices continued to fall due to heightened competition in the industry. The access control portion of the industry remained the largest in the 1990s and *Security Management* predicted that it will continue to represent about 50 percent of the sector's sales through 2001, when access control equipment sales are slated to reach $2 billion. Falling access control prices, which cost about $921 in the mid-1990s, should spark the growth of these security products. Finally, the interior security equipment segment of the industry had sales of $675 million in the mid-1990s and is expected to have sales of $1.86 billion by 2001. Glass break sensors and closed-circuit television are forecast to lead the growth in interior security equipment.

Overall, U.S. companies spent an estimated $5.6 billion on computer security in 2000, a figure that was projected to reach $20 billion by 2004, according to Forrester Research. According to a study by the Computer Security Institute and the U.S. Federal Bureau of Investigation (F.B.I.), the 273 U.S. businesses surveyed had combined losses of $266 million in 1999 from Internet security breaches and some estimates indicate that total losses to computer crimes could be as high as $10 billion. Consequently, a growing area of increased need during the late 1990s and the early part of the new decade was in software security processors for banking, the Internet, and enterprise security application. These products use encryption technology embedded in hardware to help safeguard sensitive data that may be electronically communicated, for example, as in direct-deposit banking or credit-card purchases over the Internet.

Other computer security technologies include firewalls and authentication. Firewalls are combinations of hardware and software that control access between different networks, allowing only authorized users to gain access to a network's resources. Authentication also involves both software and hardware, requiring users to enter passwords or have requisite certificates, which are verified by a network before someone can gain access to its resources. By the early 2000s Piper Jaffray Inc. predicted that the Internet security sector will increase to nearly a $3 billion sector.

Theft of computer hardware is also of rising concern. The insurance company Safeware Inc., for instance, pegged the number of thefts of laptop computers at almost 319,000 in 1999, up from 303,000 the year before. Therefore, companies have developed and marketed products to prevent hardware theft. For in-

stance, Philadelphia Security Product's Flexguard Security System offers cable lock kits and pin lock kits to prevent desktop and laptop model computers from being stolen while connected to systems hardware.

Besides providing technology to secure the Internet, security companies also began to use the Internet to market their products and services. For example, SecureRite.com, a division of Clark Security Products (which is the nation's largest distributor of security products) announced an alliance in 1999 with over 500 independent locksmiths from across the country to offer online marketing of a wide array of home security products. Orders taken online are completed by the nearest affiliated locksmiths. The company hoped to attract more than 2,000 additional locksmiths as affiliate members by the year 2000. In 1999 Clark Security Products was a $100 million company with 12 warehouses nationwide.

Also in 1999, JAWS Technologies Inc. announced an alliance with Offsite Data Services Ltd. to offer companies both online and off-site backup and recovery software to ensure that client companies have uninterrupted and secure access to their information data. The president of Strategic Research, Michael Peterson, predicted to *Byte Magazine* in 1999 that "annual U.S. revenues for this type of online backup service will grow from a current $10 to $200 million over the next three years."

INDUSTRY LEADERS

Many companies in the security industry concentrate on specific niches. For example, Executive Protection Associates, Inc. (EPAI), based in Reno, Nevada, offers a broad range of security services including electronic debugging, background investigations, and antistalking operations.

In the field of personal security services, enterprises that dominated the market in late 1990s and the early part of the new decade included such notables as Flatfoot Investigation and Protection Agency (whose visibility was enhanced when it supplied bodyguard services during the 1996 Summer Olympics games) and the Anvil Group, which provides executive protection against terrorism, extortion, and kidnapping. Anvil also provides investigative services for alleged celebrity stalking. Other established protection service companies are Bodyguard Elite; Corporate Protection Professionals, Inc.; International Protection Services; and the National Bodyguard Network.

EPAI comprises several companies whose missions are to supply specific security-related products. County Communications, based in Silicon Valley, California, is a full-service radio communications engineering company specializing in communications scrambling systems and debugging for protective service and high-risk security applications. It is also a leading designer and manufacturer of surveillance equipment. Another of its companies, also based in Silicon Valley, is Layton and Associates, which provides licensed security and event staffing. Their personnel include Police Officer Standard Training trained security officers and event staff familiar with all aspects of security management and event security. A third arm is Executive Protection Associates, which is headquartered in Germany. The company provides full-service security throughout Europe. EPAI is but one of many corporations in the security field that offers diverse security on a worldwide basis.

One of the leading producers of security equipment is SafePak Corp., based in Portland, Oregon. SafePak develops and sells specialized deposit collection and ATM equipment to the banking industry, which is one of the biggest users of security services. The company developed a deposit retrieval system for night depositories and ATMs, which is considered the standard for the industry. SafePak's system dramatically reduces transportation and personnel costs involved in customer deposit collection and increases security for the deposits themselves. Moreover, it reduces dangers to bank customers, to the security personnel who are responsible for their safety, and the protection of banks' property and assets.

SafePak also produces other state-of-the-art equipment designed to protect banks' property. Much of it is in response to the trend away from direct-deposit banking, which resulted in an increase in the number of customers who do their banking transactions around the clock via ATMs. But as technology made it possible for people to bank 24-hours-a-day, it also increased the chances that they might become victims of enterprising criminals who also plied their trade around the clock. Thus grew the need for new security devices and guards to protect property and physical well-being.

Other SafePak products include special locks for cash cassettes on ATMs, and time-delay lock boxes for ATM keys. The company is always developing new products in response to increasing security needs—and to keep a step ahead of its competition, which is also cashing in on the escalating need for state-of-the-art technology systems.

Wackenhut Corp., founded by CEO and chairman George Wackenhut, ranked among the industry's largest security firms in the latter 1990s. During this period, Wackenhut won key contracts that included providing services to AT&T, the Kennedy Space Center, and Bank of America. By 1999, it had received two new lucrative accounts: first, as primary security provider for IBM Corp. at its world headquarters and 37 other locations in 14 states; and second, to provide fire and emergency services for Ciba Specialty Chemicals, commencing in May 1999 at Ciba's Alabama facility. In 2000, Wackenhut added the U.S. embassy in El Salvador to its list of clients, which includes 20 other embassies. That same year Wackenhut secured a five-year contract with the Federal Aviation Administration for the Atlantic City, New Jersey, International Airport. Based in Palm Beach Gardens, Florida, Wackenhut serves the commercial, industrial, and governmental security markets. Wackenhut also provides special security services such as airport security, executive security, and investigation. The company operates in 48 states and has a presence in 50 countries. Besides security services, Wackenhut's subsidiary Wackenhut Corrections also runs approximately 40 prisons throughout the country. Wackenhut's revenues rose 22 percent in 1999 to $2.15 billion, with a net income of $19.6 million. The company employed 76,000 workers in 1999.

The best-known company in the security business is Pinkerton's, Inc., which lists approximately half of the Fortune 500 companies as its clients. The company's chief focus is on integrated security systems (i.e., combining high-tech electronic access control and monitoring tools). It offers a variety of services, however, such as searches for missing persons; patent and trademark infringement investigations; security system consulting; design engineering; project management; security system sales, installation, and service; and guards. (Pinkerton's guard service generates 85 percent of the company's revenues.) The company operates about 220 offices located in Asia, Canada, Europe, Mexico, and the United States.

When Pinkerton bought northern California-based Omega Corp. and Cincinnati-based J. L. Torbec Co. in 1995, the company began expanding domestically and internationally. In 1996, acquisitions included Beltran's Security and Investigation Services; Colt Protective Services; Distribution Associates South; Security Services; and two Canadian security firms, Protection Canadlarme and VCS Securite, Inc. The trend continued in January 1997 when Pinkerton's acquired Security GmbH of Germany. Six months later, it acquired Steel S.A., a leading uniformed-officer security provider based in Santiago, Chile. The latter purchase was in keeping with Pinkerton's strategic expansion of its Latin American operations. In 1999, Pinkerton's itself was acquired. After the acquisition by Sweden-based Securitas AB, Pinkerton's became part of the largest security firm in the world, with $3.5 billion in revenues, 114,000 employees, and a presence in 32 countries.

Sensormatic Electronics Corp., based in Boca Raton, Florida, is another industry leader worth noting. The company is the world leader in electronic security. It is a fully integrated supplier of electronic security systems to retail, commercial, and industrial markets and manufactures integrated source tagging, i.e., antitheft labels, which are used by more than 1,000 companies in over 100 countries. The companies apply the labels during the packaging or manufacturing processes. Soft and hard goods retailers employ the company's electronic article surveillance, closed-circuit television, and exception monitoring systems to cut down on shoplifting and internal theft. Sensormatic contracted with British Petroleum, Saks Fifth Avenue, and Chevron Oil to provide security products for their facilities. Sensormatic's success is indicative of the growing need for security-related products and services worldwide. In 2000 the company booked sales of $1.1 billion and employed 5,500 workers, and planned to expand its workforce to keep pace with increased demand.

WORK FORCE

There are over 2.38 million people employed in the security services and equipment industry, including 1 million security guards (also called security technicians, patrollers, or bouncers), 132,000 production workers, 90,000 private investigators, and 16,500 armored car guards. There are also about 6,200 consultants and engineers in the field who design and implement security plans to protect personal property and goods. They generally work closely with company officials to develop comprehensive security programs to fit individual clients' needs. They also generate policies and procedures on the effective destruction of critical documents and the protection of data processing and other machinery. Once their systems are implemented, they remain responsible for overseeing their effectiveness and amending the plans as needed.

As one indication of the seriousness of the security industry in meeting society's needs, educational requirements for consultants have become quite rigid.

In the late 1990s and early 2000s, many companies preferred to hire security consultants with at least a college degree. Ideally, consultants should have a well-rounded education including courses in business management, communications, computers, sociology, and statistics. They should (but are not required to) have experience in police work, government, or other fields of crime prevention as well. The security industry needs a large variety of trained and experienced employees to develop and implement products and services required to combat sophisticated terrorists and criminals. *Security Management* however, reported that some companies have been forced to hire unskilled workers for security positions because of the shortage of skilled professionals. To compensate for the lack of experience, companies have turned to computer-aided training programs that provide simulated security problems for trainees to resolve.

The U.S. Bureau of Labor Statistics predicted that the security field will continue to grow well into the 21st century, creating numerous jobs for security guards, security managers, and other related personnel. In the late 1990s, the security service sector was the seventh-fastest-growing service industry in the country, according to the American Society for Industrial Security. Private security workers will be used increasingly to supplement or replace police officers in such activities as courtroom security, crowd control at airports, and at special events such as the Olympics, as state funding is reduced and companies continue to downsize. Meanwhile, others in the field will be employed by firms developing and selling security systems.

AMERICA AND THE WORLD

The world market for security services is projected to expand by 8 percent annually in the early 2000s, according to the American Society for Industrial Security. Developing economies are forecast to drive the growth of the industry during this period. The security industry in Western Europe had largely the same conditions as the United States during in the late 1990s and the early 2000s. As in the United States, information security is a top priority, followed by white-collar crime. The Western European market also has added opportunities because of corporate downsizing. Moreover, concern about violent crime in Western Europe led governments to install closed-circuit television (CCTV) systems in public areas, especially in city centers.

The Asian economic crisis of the late 1990s brought about political disquiet as well as greater opportunities for security providers. In Indonesia, for example, the economic slump caused the country, which previously was relatively free of violence, to suffer from more frequent civil disturbances, riots, and looting, according to *Security Management*. As a result, more companies in Indonesia sought to install new security systems or enhance their existing systems. Furthermore, Chinese government agencies have been purchasing CCTV equipment to monitor the population as well as traffic. In countries where labor is cheap, however, companies and organizations prefer hiring security guards to buying security equipment.

In Latin America, crimes such as abduction, hijacking, and armed robbery of production and warehouse facilities have led to the need for greater security measures, including both products and services. Mexico and Brazil in particular have increased their demand for security products and services, according to *Security Management*.

RESEARCH AND TECHNOLOGY

Research and technology are fueling the growth of the security industry. In every field of the industry, researchers are producing innovative, technologically advanced products that are revolutionizing the industry. Ademco Security Group, a division of the Pittway Corp., is one of the largest manufacturers on Long Island, New York, developing and implementing technologies that enhance security procedures and lower product costs. It markets over 1,500 security products, and worldwide helps protect 15 million businesses, offices, homes, government agencies, factories, etc. One form of its security technology is in its surface-mount devices that replaced its batch-processing system, in which circuit boards go through a series of steps in batches of hundreds or thousands. In the late 1990s, the company began using flexible manufacturing, whereby machines can complete a board of one design within two minutes and then make another of a completely different design.

Ademco is also active in wireless applications. Ten years ago, the company developed a wireless alarm system called AlarmNet. By reducing reliance on phone lines to send messages to monitoring companies, this product had immense implications in the home security area of the industry. If there is a problem with the phone systems, the warning systems are useless. So, Ademco created AlarmNet, which employs a cellular-like wireless radio frequency signal that sends multiple signals in case of trouble. Products and systems such as surface-mount devices and AlarmNet enhance the provision of security and assure growth for the entire industry.

Sensormatic Electronics Corp. is also aggressively pushing research and technology. For example, the company is integrating its Ultra*Max technology, which involves acousto-magnetic principles, with other label products. One result will be the incorporation of Ultra*Max right into bottle labels, which will reduce labeling costs and packaging steps for manufacturers and cut down on theft at the point of sales.

SafePak Corp. continually develops and markets products that improve security for bank tellers, armored car drivers, business managers, and other people involved in the transfer of funds. The company manufactures and sells specialized deposit collection equipment and ATM security equipment to the banking industry. Among the products it has developed are night deposit and ATM deposit retrieval systems, a cash bar system to lock in existing cash cassettes in ATMs, and optical deposit counters for night deposit safes. These eliminate the need for two bank employees to attend a night deposit safe, while also allowing armored guards to retrieve deposits in bulk from the safes without the presence of the bank employees. Similar security-related products are being developed constantly by firms in all niches of the industry.

At the Internet Security Conference held in San Jose, California, in April 1999, CyberSafe Corp. announced the release of a Centrax 2.2 upgrade to its newly acquired intrusion detection product suite. It is the only product to integrate host and network based intrusion detection, vulnerability assessment, and policy management under a single user-friendly interface. Host-based intrusion detection is directed at responding to internal compromises of a system (which account for 80 percent of unauthorized access), while network-based intrusion detection monitors external attack on the system's security integrity. CyberSafe Corp. was founded in 1991 and is privately held. Its products are designed to secure electronic business, such as its award-winning TrustBroker Security Suite, or Defensor and Centrax systems.

Companies such as IrisScan Inc. have also developed access control iris identification systems in the mid- to late 1990s. Such a system verifies a person's identity using images of the person's iris—the ring around the pupil. Iris scanning access control systems have been adopted by organizations and correctional institutions to ensure only authorized people gain access to sensitive and restricted resources. Iris scanning, unlike other methods such as photo identification and fingerprinting, cannot be circumvented easily. Photo identification requires a person to judge the resemblance of the photograph to the identification holder and fingerprints require a forensic expert to examine them. In contrast, an iris scan system is computerized and does not rely on human judgments.

FURTHER READING

Anderson, Teresa. "The Eyes Have It." *Security Management,* December 1999.

Booth, Jason. "Boom for Private Guards Despite Decline in Crime." *Los Angeles Business Journal,* 1 February 1999.

Bowman, Erik J. "Security Tools up for the Future." *Security Management,* January 1996, 30.

Brintliff, Russell L. *Crimeproofing Your Business: 301 Low-Cost, No-Cost Ways to Protect Your Office, Store, or Business.* New York: McGraw-Hill, 1994.

"Clairvest Group Inc. Acquires Second Largest Electronic Security Operations in Australasia." *Business Wire,* 17 March 1997.

"Employee Theft Soars." *Security,* 1 August 2000.

Fried, Edward R. *Oil Security: Retrospect and Prospect.* Washington: Brookings Institute, 1993.

Harowitz, Sherry L. "To Market, to Market." *Security Management,* May 1998.

"JAWS Technologies Signs Sales & Marketing Alliance with Offsite Data Services, Ltd." *Business Wire,* 22 April 1999.

Martin, William Flynn, et al. *Maintaining Energy Security in a Global Context.* New York: Trilateral Commission, 1996.

Prince, Paul. "Exodus Feels More Secure—New Hires Lead to New Security Offerings." *tele.com,* 13 November 2000.

"SecureRite.com Launches New Model for E-commerce Transactions." *Business Wire,* 21 April 1999.

"Sensormatic and Wallace Announce Production and Distribution Agreement." *Business Wire,* 11 February 1997.

"Study Predicts Huge E-commerce Gains." *PC Week,* 18 August 1997.

"Surveillance Sales Hard to Bear?" *Security Management,* December 1998.

"Welcome to the New World of Private Security." *Economist,* 19 April 1997, 21.

"World Business is Beset by Cybercrime." *Star Tribune,* (Minneapolis, MN), 11 December 2000.

SEMICONDUCTORS

The semiconductor business is far from new, but insatiable demand for computers, wireless communications equipment, and countless other electronic gadgets has made it a vibrant and dynamic industry. In addition to vigorous sales of personal computers (PCs), which are the largest market for semiconductors, growth in semiconductor manufacturing has been fueled by a multitude of consumer electronics such as digital audio players, digital cameras, communication devices, and information appliances.

Thoroughly internationalized, the semiconductor industry has delivered an occasionally spotty performance on the world stage, with years of solid growth punctuated by spells of overcapacity and price weakness. The low points are felt mostly by the industry's older, more established product lines such as dynamic random-access memory (DRAM) chips (the inexpensive chips used for main memory in PCs), a notoriously commoditized segment usually with low profit margins. Nonetheless, the worldwide industry is vast enough, at an estimated $204.8 billion in 2000, that even when revenues are off in such large segments as DRAM, there are any number of fast-moving emerging segments within the industry (recent examples being flash-memory and digital signal processors).

In the mid- to late 1990s the global industry suffered a pricing slump that dragged semiconductor revenues down more than 8 percent in 1998. To blame were excess production capacity and slack demand in some areas, notably east Asia because of financial turmoil. Sales in 1999 rebounded, however, jumping 15-18 percent by various tallies, as stronger-than-expected demand lifted production—along with prices.

Demand was so brisk that shortages occurred in some cases. Recovery in Asia, generally buoyant PC sales, and rampant growth of networking equipment and newer electronic devices such as cellular phones all contributed. What's more, analysts at the Semiconductor Industry Association predicted strong demand will keep industry sales heading decidedly upward through 2002.

Competition in the industry is vitally important. Although it's by no means a field that just any company can enter—cutting-edge digital-chip fabrication plants cost easily a billion dollars or more to build—competition can be credited with many of the ongoing innovations in the industry as well as the persistent downward creep of semiconductor prices over time. In one of the most visible face-offs, in 1999 and 2000 Advanced Micro Devices, Inc. (AMD) assaulted Intel Corp.'s stranglehold on the high-end PC microprocessor market by rolling out chips faster than Intel, including the first gigahertz-speed processor designed for a PC. AMD had formerly pursued a low-cost follower strategy, making chips that were cheaper than Intel's but usually the same speed or somewhat slower. Although Intel had comparable products close behind—and its sales still dwarfed AMD's—reinvigorated competition in the microprocessor arena had potential to chip away at Intel's huge lead and to spur further innovations and price cuts.

The semiconductor industry is divided according to the type of semiconductor produced. Each type has a separate function. All semiconductors, however, are broadly similar. They are all made from materials that conduct electricity, such as copper, iron, and aluminum, and from insulators, such as rubber, glass, and wood. Semiconductors are important because they can change the way an electric current behaves, or even change one form of energy (such as light) into another form (such as electricity).

Transistors, perhaps the most important form of semiconductors, are particularly important because they can control the flow of a very large electric current by means of a very small electric current at another point on their surface. They can act like switches in conducting electric current. For example, some transistors conduct electricity well over only a certain voltage—the amount of effort needed to move electricity in a current from one place to another. When the threshold voltage is reached, the transistor stops resisting the current and becomes a conductor of the current. This ability of transistors to act as both resistors and conductors of electricity allows them to serve as switches. Different settings of different switches allow information to be stored and communicated. This basic property of semiconductor material allowed scientists to develop the microprocessors and microcomputers that have so influenced the modern industrial world.

All semiconductor chips are manufactured using basically similar processes. They are most commonly made from a silicon matrix, composed of melted sand embedded with small crystals. Although other raw materials have been used to make semiconductors, including some plastics and ceramics, sand is most common; it is plentiful, inexpensive, and it works well. To make a semiconductor, a manufacturer melts sand into a column. Usually these columns are between six and eight inches in diameter, although recently they have expanded to 12 inches. The columns are cut into a series of thin wafers. Wafer manufacturing is usually separate from finished semiconductor manufacturing. Each wafer is then implanted or printed with a series of small circuits, which vary according to the function of the chip. The wafer is then cut into chips, which are sold to computer manufacturers, makers of electronic equipment, and hobbyists.

It is the imprinted circuits that make semiconductors function. They can be placed on the silicon matrix in a variety of ways. During the melting process, the manufacturer introduces impurities in the form of crystals of phosphorus, aluminum, boron, or gallium (called *dopants*), which change the semiconductor's ability to conduct electricity. This is commonly done by treating the wafer with chemicals. The first chemical makes it react like a piece of photo-

graphic paper. Next, a template called a photomask is placed over the wafer. The wafer is then treated with light-sensitive chemicals that cause tiny metal lines, some no thicker than 1/25 of a micron—finer than the finest human hair—to be deposited on its surface. Another way to imprint a circuit on a wafer is to flood the wafer with other dopants. The wafer is then heated to induce the dopant's atoms to line up in the desired pattern. Still another way is to shoot atoms of the dopant directly into the surface of the wafer. All these processes can be repeated on several different levels, so that a single microchip may contain several layers of semiconductors within its surface.

Manufacturers divide semiconductors into two large categories: analog and digital. Analog semiconductors pass electricity in continuous waves of fluctuating voltage. They can amplify or regulate voltages, coordinate signals between different systems, or convert data from analog or linear signals into digital signals and back again. Analog integrated circuits are used in amplifiers, electronic musical instruments, and electronic analog computers. Digital semiconductors process information as a series of extremely high-speed pulses, using the ability of transistors to function as on/off switches. Each pulse that passes through the circuit switches a transistor "on" or "off." Thus digital circuitry requires only two voltage levels ("on" voltage and "off" voltage) to communicate exact information quickly and accurately. High-speed microprocessors, such as Intel's Pentium processors, are capable of passing hundreds of millions of pulses per second that can then be translated into other types of information, through binary (two-digit) communication languages. Digital semiconductors are subdivided into three functional types: memory chips, microprocessors, and logic chips.

MEMORY CHIPS

Memory chips are made specifically to store information. Memory chips may be read-only memory (ROM) or random-access memory (RAM). Some semiconductors (volatile memory chips) lose the information they store when their power is interrupted, while others (nonvolatile memory chips) can retain data through a loss of power. These concepts translate into different classes of memory semiconductors.

Dynamic random-access memory (DRAM) chips are most common in PCs. They store information quickly and cheaply, and allow it to be accessed relatively rapidly. The counterpart to the DRAM chip is the static random-access memory (SRAM) semiconductor. SRAM performs the same functions as DRAM, but much faster. Unlike DRAM, SRAM does not require a constant electric current to operate—it can retain information with less current and operate much faster than DRAM. SRAM , however, is more complicated to manufacture and thus costs more than DRAM, so its use in computer systems is less common. Continually expanded processor power and function necessitates a corresponding upgrade in RAM modules. Extended data output random-access memory modules may be required for faster machines that process greater quantities of digitized data simultaneously.

The flash-memory chip is a nonvolatile semiconductor that can be erased and reprogrammed electrically. One example of a computer chip that uses flash memory is the binary input/output system (BIOS), a ROM chip that checks the hardware for system memory and the presence of installed devices such as disk drives. The BIOS directs the computer through the process of initial program load of the operating system. Flash-memory chips are found in communications equipment as well as in computing devices.

MICROPROCESSORS

Microprocessors are a specific type of chip used primarily in computers, but they are also important to the telecommunications, electronics, and automobile industries. They are sometimes called central processing units because they control and coordinate the processing of data from all other points of the computer. They consist of a series of specialized integrated circuits contained in a single chip. Microprocessors are what make computers such powerful tools. Microprocessors can pack thousands or even millions of transistors into a very small area—in some cases, less than the size of a human fingernail. The best-known of these microprocessors are the series manufactured by Intel, including the popular Pentium series.

LOGIC DEVICES

A third category of semiconductors is logic devices. They control the ways in which information is transmitted and interpreted within a single electronic system. While most other types of semiconductors can be used in different types of equipment without major changes, logic devices usually have to be designed to fit into a particular system. There are three main categories of logic devices: complex programmable logic devices, field programmable logic devices, and application-specific integrated circuits (ASICs). The two programmable logic devices are fairly standard across the industry. Their value lies in the fact that manufacturers can modify them to suit their particular needs by using electrical codes. The ASICs have to be designed and constructed for a particular function, and thus tend to be more expensive.

ENCRYPTION DEVICES

Early in 1999 industry leader Intel acknowledged plans to develop a new ASIC called an encryption chip, for a variety of applications including online banking and commerce transactions. Encryption technology originally emerged in the late 1990s as virtual private networks proliferated among business and industry. In order to achieve security over these networks, companies turned first to software packages but soon looked to hardware solutions for greater privacy. As a hardware component, the encryption chip would significantly expand the complexity of the array used to encrypt the data, far beyond the original U.S. Data Encryption Standard that permits a maximum of 56 computer digits. In addition to the expanded array, the dedicated encryption chip would support multiple passes of the data through the chip before the process would be complete for transmission. Encryption chip technology would be useful in a variety of security applications, including the protection of copyrighted electronic materials, such as videotaped releases, from unauthorized duplication.

BACKGROUND AND DEVELOPMENT

Semiconductors occur regularly in the natural environment. In 1874, Karl Ferdinand Braun used crystals of galena, an ore of lead, to make a simple semiconductor device to regulate electric current. Any atom that has more than three and fewer than six electrons in its outermost energy level can be a semiconductor. Inert gases such as helium and neon and rock-like materials such as mica have eight electrons in their outermost energy level and are very good insulators. Metals such as gold, silver, and copper are excellent conductors because they have only one electron in their outermost energy levels. The best semiconductors, such as silicon and germanium, have between three and six electrons. Even then, however, they have to be put through a manufacturing process in order to become commercially useful.

In the days before widespread development of semiconductors, scientists worked and experimented with other devices that could perform the same functions. Thomas Edison observed the principle behind the electron tube—the idea that an electric current would flow in only one direction through the device—as early as 1883. The electron tube was first developed in 1905 by Sir J. Ambrose Fleming, who used it to detect high-frequency radio waves. It works on the principle of heating or "cooking" electrons off a heated metal plate in order to affect current flow. Because this heating had to take place in a vacuum to prevent the plate from melting or oxidizing, these tubes were also called vacuum tubes. Electron tubes were common in early radio receivers and were common to nearly all telecommunications devices until the late 1950s and early 1960s. They are still seen in some microwave ovens, x-ray machines, and radar equipment.

Although the electron tube was indispensable in the development of the radio industry, it had its own problems. Electron tubes were bulky, inefficient, and fragile. In 1948, three scientists working at Bell Laboratories developed the first practical solid-state equivalent of the electron tube. Walter H. Brattain, John Bardeen, and William Shockley created the first transistors with the idea of replacing the tubes with something less fragile. The transistors were virtually unbreakable, gave off almost no heat, and were very small—in some cases no larger than the tip of a man's finger. In 1952 one of the original developers, Shockley, further refined the transistor, making it less fragile and more reliable.

In 1958 Jack Kilby created the first integrated circuit (IC), a complex electronic device that incorporated one or more semiconductors. Kilby's IC combined transistors with other electronic devices, such as resistors and capacitors, to create a solid-state electronic device. It represented a great advance over existing electronic devices because it was less fragile and more compact. The miniaturization potential of the IC made possible the development of the microcomputer in the 1960s.

The history of computing took another great leap forward in 1971 when Intel created the first microprocessor. The microprocessor made possible the coordination of great numbers of ICs into a single system. Only four years later, IBM Corp. introduced its first PC, and in 1976, Apple Computer Inc. introduced the first model in its popular Apple line. The PC had left the laboratory for the office, the classroom, and the home. Even more astounding were the strides made as embedded systems permeated the manufacturing environment. Embedded systems are complete one-chip computers that perform a comprehensive spectrum of maintenance functions for the electronic operation of a device or appliance. By the mid-1990s embedded systems were standard features on automobiles, security devices, household appliances, elevators, computer testing systems, and office machinery. The variety of potential applications for these systems will not be realized for years to come.

CURRENT CONDITIONS

The overall semiconductor market recovered in 1999 from a three-year lull. With global PC sales that

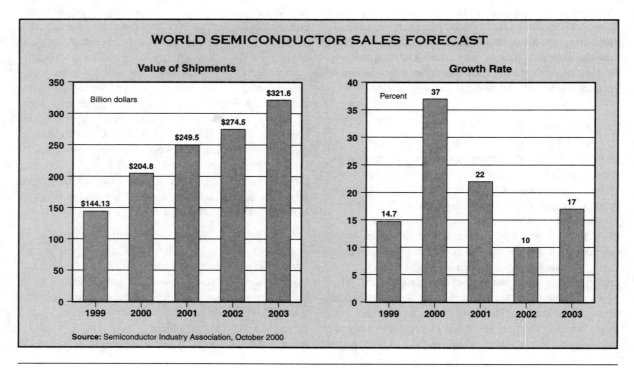

WORLD SEMICONDUCTOR SALES FORECAST

Value of Shipments (Billion dollars): 1999 $144.13; 2000 $204.8; 2001 $249.5; 2002 $274.5; 2003 $321.6

Growth Rate (Percent): 1999 14.7; 2000 37; 2001 22; 2002 10; 2003 17

Source: Semiconductor Industry Association, October 2000

year leaping more than 20 percent and sales of cell phones and network devices exploding, semiconductor revenues grew by a respectable 14.7 percent, based on estimates from the Semiconductor Industry Association, to $144 billion worldwide. About a third of those sales were from companies based in North and South America. Even stronger growth was expected through the early 2000s; the SIA and Dataquest separately forecast worldwide chip sales of over $300 billion by 2003, though most analysts expect a slight cooling off in 2001 following 37 percent growth in 2000, when the SIA estimated shipments of $204.8 billion.

Many segments of this diverse industry have been growing much faster. For instance, purchases of 32-bit microcontroller units, used in PCs and portable electronics, skyrocketed 86 percent in 1999. The larger flash-memory category also enjoyed fleet growth, rising 68 percent on the year. Even the massive yet battered DRAM category registered 40 percent sales growth, and was expected to reach $43.1 billion by 2002, according to SIA.

Surprising to many observers has been the buoyancy of analog chips. These speedy, often task-specific semiconductors have often been viewed as holdovers from a bygone era, as chips facing extinction. On the contrary, soaring demand for computers, multimedia devices, and other electronics has kept a steady flow of analog chips coming from top makers such as Texas Instruments Inc., Philips Electronics, and Motorola, Inc. as well as bevy of smaller specialized producers. Analog chips, in fact, tend to have a complementary relationship with their digital brethren, and hence the more digital chips needed, the more analog. Newer digital cell phones, for instance, have required more analog semiconductors than older models. Overall, as of 2000, analog chips represented nearly 15 percent of global semiconductor sales.

Aside from swift unit demand, the semiconductor recovery has been undergirded by stronger prices. Whereas ample supply, soft international markets, and price competition took their toll on prices in the mid-to late 1990s, by 1999 the industry found its products in relatively short supply and had to race to keep up with demand. Because of the inauspicious pricing climate, most manufacturers held the line on introducing new capacity, and few new fabrication plants were built. Indeed, in the latter part of 1998 the industry's capacity utilization dipped below 80 percent. As demand revived in 1999, however, utilization shot up toward 95 percent, where it was expected to stay in the early 2000s, since new facilities take over a year to build.

While the early 2000s were likely to be boom times for chip makers, industry veterans feared another slowdown was inevitable. The semiconductor business has been marked by pronounced business cycles in the past, as recently seen in the late 1990s, and some experts saw little reason to believe that won't continue. At least one analyst predicted that by late 2002 or early 2003 the industry as a whole would begin to face another downturn.

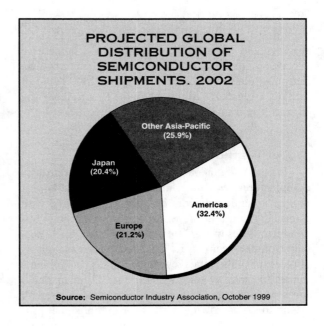

PROJECTED GLOBAL DISTRIBUTION OF SEMICONDUCTOR SHIPMENTS. 2002

Other Asia-Pacific (25.9%)

Japan (20.4%)

Europe (21.2%)

Americas (32.4%)

Source: Semiconductor Industry Association, October 1999

INDUSTRY LEADERS

INTEL

Maker of the first microprocessor, Intel Corp. is the leader in sales of semiconductors industry-wide. In 1971 Intel's founders created the 4004 series microprocessor, which had 2,300 transistors and a processing speed of 60,000 instructions per second. Intel's modern Pentium series processors regularly contain more than 5 million transistors and access them at a processing speed of 400 million instructions per second or better. The worldwide leader in sales of semiconductors, the company had semiconductor sales of $25.8 billion in 1999, marking a 13.3 percent gain for the year. Intel has become a household word in the United States because of the popularity of its Pentium microprocessors and its commercials advertising "Intel Inside."

Intel dominates the industry in the sale of microprocessors, with about 86 percent of the PC chip market. The firm worked with Hewlett-Packard to develop the powerful 64-bit Itanium microprocessor. Its major rivals are Advanced Micro Devices (AMD) and Cyrix, both of which produce microprocessors that rival Intel's Pentium series in performance. In the late 1990s the AMD K6 series microprocessors retailed at about 25 percent less than the equivalent Intel product, the Pentium II. The Cyrix equivalent of the Pentium II, the 6x86MX, sold at between 50 and 60 percent of Intel's price. Neither Cyrix nor AMD, however, has Intel's manufacturing capacity or its name recognition.

AMD has been making important strides, though, capturing a dominant share of the sub-$1,000 PC chip market and producing increasingly competitive processors that meet or beat Intel chips' performance. The most noteworthy example was the 2000 debut of AMD's 1 gigahertz Athlon chip, the first to break the gigahertz barrier in the general PC chip market.

TEXAS INSTRUMENTS

Texas Instruments Inc., a diversified electronics manufacturer, was the United States' second-largest maker of semiconductors in 1999, and was tied with Samsung Group for the world's fourth rank. Its semiconductor sales in 1999 totaled $7.1 billion, up 22 percent from the year before, and accounted for about 85 percent of TI's total revenues. Texas Instruments makes and sells an assortment of both digital and analog semiconductors, but perhaps its greatest strength lies in the fast-growing market for digital signal processing semiconductors. The company was increasingly focusing its semiconductor muscle on its digital light processor (DLP) technology for the creation of premium displays for personal computers, televisions, and movie theaters. Texas Instruments used these devices in electronic toys in the 1970s, but they have emerged as important components of high-speed modems and telephone technology.

MOTOROLA

The third-largest American producer of semiconductors is Motorola, Inc. In 2000 Motorola ranked sixth among the world's semiconductor producers, with worldwide sales of about $7.4 billion or nearly 22 percent of the company's overall sales. In 1999 Motorola sold off and shut down some of its semiconductor components operations to focus on its most profitable lines. As a result, Motorola's semiconductor sales actually dropped 9.4 percent that year, but rebounded nearly 20 percent the following year. The company's semiconductors are used in communication devices (including its own), networking equipment, transportation, and other applications.

LSI LOGIC

Much smaller and more specialized than such firms as Intel and Motorola, LSI Logic Corp. is nonetheless a sizable producer of application-specific integrated circuits for communications, networking, and storage systems. In 1999 the company produced $2.1 billion worth of semiconductors and related products, with sales rising 38 percent for the year.

RAMBUS

An innovator in more ways than one, Rambus Inc. is a small player whose business model differs greatly from most semiconductor firms. It designs high-performance semiconductor architectures, but lets other firms handle the physical production and marketing. Some of its most prominent designs allow processors to communicate much more rapidly with memory chips than mainstream technology allows. Rambus had only $43 million in sales during 1999, including $8.7 million in net income. Sony Corp. is one of Rambus' biggest customers, using the enhanced architecture in its game consoles. Other licensees include AMD, Intel, NEC, and Samsung.

AMERICA AND THE WORLD

Although U.S. companies have a major stake in the world's semiconductor business, they represent less than a third of global sales. The chief competitors of U.S. manufacturers are Japanese producers such as NEC Corp., Toshiba Corp., and Hitachi, Ltd. Two of the top-five manufacturers in 1999 were Japanese firms. NEC was ranked second only to Intel in semiconductor production with shipments valued at $9.2 billion. Toshiba was next, with $7.6 billion, and Hitachi ranked seventh in 1999 at $5.5 billion. Other top-10 semiconductor manufacturers are scattered across the world. Samsung in South Korea was tied for fourth place with Texas Instruments at $7.1 billion. Three European companies, Philips Electronics, STMicroelectronics, and Infineon Technologies, rounded out the top 10 in 1999.

Asia-Pacific countries outside Japan have amassed a striking presence in the industry. Indeed, Asian and Pacific Rim countries excluding Japan represent the second-largest semiconductor-producing region behind North America, with an estimated quarter share of world shipments in 2000. Production in the Asia-Pacific region has also been growing the fastest of any region.

RESEARCH AND TECHNOLOGY

Researchers continue to experiment with semiconductors in order to reduce price and increase performance. One simple way to reduce the cost of chips is to increase the size of the wafers they are made from. The industry standard until recently had been to use wafers cut from silicon columns that were only four inches in diameter. By 1997, wafer size had increased to between six and eight inches in diameter. Soon, industry analysts predict, manufacturers will move to a 12-inch or 300-millimeter size wafer. The increased wafer size will allow semiconductor makers to effectively double their chip capacity.

Currently, semiconductor manufacturers are experimenting with using new technology to bring their merchandise directly to consumers. They plan to place the entire series of circuits that make up the modern microcomputer on a single chip. This "system on a chip" technology could revolutionize computer manufacturing and electronic retailing. The creation of single chips that function like entire computer systems would allow the building of smaller, more powerful electronic devices and would speed the creation of new products. The first step in the development of systems on a chip is the integration of the function of memory chips and logic chips in a single semiconductor. LSI Logic, a company that specializes in the production of logic chips, already manufactures limited quantities of combined memory-logic chips. They have also begun development of specialized system chips for digital cameras and televisions.

Another technology that emerged in the late 1990s as commercially important is the digital signal processor (DSP). A DSP's only function is to change an analog signal into a digital one. It's capable, however, of handling these signals at speeds up to 10 times faster than the average microprocessor. DSPs have recently come down in price, and new technology allows them to be easily programmed. Although sales of DSPs amount to only a small portion of the semiconductor market, less than 3 percent in 1999, their sales have been growing at more than 20 percent a year. Some of the new applications in which DSPs could become important include voice-activated computers, videoconferencing, and downloading of digital television programs, movies, and games through consumers' television sets. Texas Instruments controls about 45 percent of the DSP manufacturing industry. The U.S. firm Lucent Technologies Inc. ranked 14th among the world's largest semiconductor manufacturers. Currently Lucent has an additional 29 percent of the DSP market, and the rest of the DSP industry is divided between several other firms, including Motorola.

Key to producing more powerful semiconductors is increasing the number of transistors that can fit on a single chip. The number of transistors on a single chip controls the chip's power. In 1971, when Intel produced its first microprocessor, its transistors measured 10 microns in size—much smaller than the original transistors first produced in 1948. In 1996, however, manufacturers regularly produced semiconductors containing transistors that measured a quarter of a micron or less in size.

Although semiconductor technology has advanced tremendously in the past 30 years, scientists are already predicting that there may be limits on how far semiconductor technology can progress. Even though his Moore's Law predicted the power of microchips could double every 18 months, Dr. Gordon Moore, one of the founders of Intel, has suggested more recently that such a progression may not last long. Moore foresees a limit to semiconductor power that may be reached in the next 10 years. In particular, he hinted that it may not be possible for line widths—the size of individual transistors on a single microchip—to be reduced to less than a 10th of a micron. That would limit how many transistors could be packed into a chip.

Researchers are trying to bypass this limit by placing semiconductors deeper inside a chip instead of in a small layer close to the surface, but this technology is not yet commercially viable. In April 1999 Lawrence Berkeley National Laboratory announced that researcher Othon Monteiro developed a method of applying copper inlay to the semiconductor wafer instead of the common aluminum alloys in general use. The copper reportedly supported accelerated speeds with better insulation, greater stability, and potentially smaller circuit runs.

FURTHER READING

Agres, Ted. "Roadmap Points to Crucial Semiconductor Needs." *R & D*, February 1998.

Arensman, Russ. "Analog Renaissance." *Electronic Business*, December 1999.

Carbone, James. "Supply Conditions Turn against Buyers." *Purchasing*, 13 January 2000.

"Chip Makers Predict Robust Growth through 2001." *Electronic Business*, December 1999.

Dick, Andrew Ronald. *Industrial Policy and Semiconductors: Missing the Target.* Washington: AEI Press, 1995.

Gawel, Richard. "Global Semiconductor Market Grows by Nearly 18% in 1999." *Electronic Design,* 7 February 2000.

Goldstein, Andrew, and William Aspray, eds. *Facets: New Perspectives on the History of Semiconductors.* New Brunswick, NJ: IEEE Center, 1997.

Howell, Thomas R., Brent L. Bartlett, and Warren Davis. *Creating Advantage: Semiconductors and Government Industrial Policy in the 1990s.* San Jose, CA: Semiconductor Industry Association/Dewey Ballantine, 1992.

"Industry Fishes for Chips as Sales Show Global Slump." *Electronics Times,* 11 December 2000.

Johnson, Grant. "Chip World Finally Firing on All Fronts." *Electronic News,* 3 January 2000.

Key, Angela. "Hello (Again), Mr. Chips." *Fortune,* 3 April 2000.

"MCUs Had Greatest Growth." *Purchasing,* 13 January 2000.

Merritt, Rick Boyd. "Sobering Realities." *Electronic Engineering Times,* 13 November 2000.

Murphy, Tom. "DRAM Advances Chip Growth." *Electronic News,* 10 January 2000.

Semiconductor Industry Association. "Industry Statistics and WSTS Subscribers." Available from http://www.semichips.org.

Souza, Crista. "Chip Forecast Sees Cooling Trend." *Electronic Buyers News,* 6 November 2000.

Willett, Hugh G. "Embedded Is Where It's At," *Electronic News,* 15 February 1999.

SMART CARDS

INDUSTRY SNAPSHOT

With everyone from Microsoft Corp. to American Express Co. to the Washington, D.C., subway system getting in on the action, in the early 2000s the U.S. smart-card business is beginning to wake from a decade of slumber. While the cards—credit-card-like devices containing integrated circuits for memory and processing power—have been the rage in Europe and Asia, introducing them in the United States had been slow and arduous. Since late 1999, however, American Express led the way in putting marketing muscle behind its new Blue smart card, and Visa, MasterCard, and others outside the financial industry were expected to follow suit in the early 2000s.

Smart cards are usually the same size as credit cards and are used for financial transactions, for security purposes, for long-distance phone accounts, to maintain medical and other records, and for a variety of related purposes. Perhaps their ultimate power lies in the ability of one card to support multiple applications. Students at certain universities, for instance, can use a single card to gain access to certain areas of campus restricted to outsiders, to access library records and grade information, and to check on their financial accounts, not only at the tuition office but even at the student cafeteria. While multiple-use cards offer myriad opportunities, they are difficult to implement outside contained environments such as university or office campuses. They require a shared infrastructure among all the supporting vendors and systems: the cafeteria, bookstore, and registrar all have to use compatible systems. But in coming years many of these problems are likely to dissolve as network integration and connectivity increase.

Some analysts believe that shifting to a smart-card economy would carry a cumulative price tag of $12 billion. Such costs would be borne mostly by industry unless companies find ways to make consumers willing to pay for the otherwise free plastic they tote in their wallets. Companies wishing to adopt smart cards must also contend with scant consumer awareness and, as a result, limited interest thus far.

Card Technology reported a total of 1.74 billion smart cards of all varieties in circulation in 2000, most of which were used for phone calls. The United States, however, accounted for only a tiny percentage of that total. In 1999 there were probably about 19 million in use in the U.S., according to Visa International, but most analysts expect Americans to be the largest contributors to industry growth in the early 2000s. The research firm Dataquest estimated worldwide smart card sales of $2.4 billion in 2000, a figure they expected to leap to $8.1 billion in 2004.

ORGANIZATION AND STRUCTURE

A smart card is a device that contains a microprocessor chip capable of storing large amounts of memory. Smart cards are different from magnetic-stripe cards in that the latter hold only a fraction of the information that smart cards do—and magnetic stripes are less secure.

Smart cards come in two varieties: "intelligent" cards, which can perform complex functions and have both a read and a write capacity; and memory cards, which store and gradually deduct value as it is used. A simple cash card or the telephone cards popular in

Europe and east Asia are specific examples of memory cards. Examples of intelligent cards are medical records cards that contain patients' vital statistics, prescription and allergy information, and medical histories. Some cards also include a digital image of the holder for identification.

Smart cards initially had three discrete functions—electronic purses, replacements for magnetic-stripe technology, and value-transfer cards—although newer cards support multiple applications, including applications well beyond these three. The electronic-purse function refers to systems designed to replace cash and coin with electronic credit. As a replacement for magnetic-stripe technology, smart cards were designed to replace credit and debit cards and provide superior security. Finally, as value-transfer cards, smart cards were designed to serve phone cards, copy cards, and so forth where users transfer cash value to the computer-chip cards.

There are also a variety of marketing applications for smart cards, including customer loyalty programs, in which the cardholder accrues points toward a gift from the issuer. An example is frequent-flyer miles earned toward a free plane ticket. Sometimes smart cards themselves become the commodity, as with card collecting—a booming side industry. Banks and other card-issuing institutions ultimately benefit from such unused cards. A $5 card issued by NYNEX during the 1992 Democratic National Convention in New York City, for example, was valued at $2,500 five years later.

Two principal industry-related organizations are the Smart Card Forum (SCF) and the Smart Card Industrial Association (SCIA). The former, established in 1993 by Citicorp, Bellcore, and the U.S. Treasury Financial Management Services Division, included in 1999 about 190 corporations and government agencies in Europe and the Americas. SCF promotes public policy initiatives in support of smart cards and works to develop both cooperation and competition among members of the industry.

SCIA was formed in 1989 and includes manufacturers, integrators, resellers, users, issuers, consultants, and nonprofit and educational institutions involved in some aspect of the smart-card industry. It sponsors CardTech/SecurTech, a conference for members of the advanced card and security technology industries; keeps members and the public informed about developments within the industry; publishes a newsletter, *Smart Link*; and educates the public about the developing smart-card industry. SCIA also provides links to principal financial card-issuing associations—Europay, MasterCard, and Visa—at its online

Web site. In an effort to become the premier trade association for the smart-card industry, the SCIA "relaunched" itself in early 1997 and has increased its efforts to educate businesses and the public about the industry's potential.

In order to kickstart sales in the laggard North American market, these two industry organizations joined together in 2000 to launch a $500,000 promotional effort in the United States and Canada over the following two years, primarily pitching the cards as a means for securing Internet transactions.

BACKGROUND AND DEVELOPMENT

A key element in the development of the smart card was the microchip, which was invented by Texas Instruments Inc. engineer Jack Kilby and Fairchild Semiconductor Corp. engineer Robert N. Noyce in 1959. Until that time, there was a direct relationship between a computer's size and its power. When, in 1971, Intel Corp. scientist Ted Hoff created a tiny silicon chip capable of holding as much memory as ENIAC, an early computer that weighed 18 tons, it was clear that the information industry was about to undergo monumental changes. Three years later, in 1974, Frenchman Roland Moreno conceived the idea of marrying chip technology with a credit-card-sized device, and the smart card was born. When, in 1980, Arlen R. Lessin, an American, learned about the smart card, which was then virtually unknown in North America, he said: "I knew the moment I saw the card demonstrated that it would revolutionize the way we conduct both our business and personal lives." Lessin obtained the rights from Moreno to market the card in the United States, and he founded the first U.S. company in the industry, SmartCard International, Inc.

Smart-card technology spawned a demand for computer chips capable of fitting inside a card and undergoing the same wear and tear as magnetic-stripe cards. In Europe, this technology was developing in the late 1970s and early 1980s as U.S. banks were just beginning to adopt the magnetic swipe card and as automated teller machines proliferated.

The United States' lag in smart-card use had its roots, ironically, in the high quality of U.S. telecommunications services. Running checks on credit cards via the phone lines was easy for U.S. merchants; hence, they felt little need for a card that would make it possible to instantly verify the customer's account information. In France, however, where phone services were not nearly as advanced as in the United

States, smart cards were an appealing alternative. By the mid-1990s, Moreno's home country alone had some 20 million banking smart cards and millions more phone cards in use.

Smart-card use in the United States was minimal until the nation's two leading credit-card companies, Visa and MasterCard, began to see them as a way to curtail credit-card fraud. In the mid-1990s, such fraud in the United States accounted for some $500 million a year in losses and $1.7 billion annually worldwide.

In 1995 three large financial institutions helped foster a major development that paved the way for wider use of smart cards. Europay, MasterCard, and Visa, all credit-card-licensing institutions, developed a set of technical standards—called the "EMV" specifications after their combined initials. These standards ensure that cards will be compatible with one another, preventing the proliferation of competing systems that could create costly failures analogous to Sony's ill-fated Betamax brand of videocassette technology.

Because of excitement over smart cards in the early 1990s, numerous companies flooded the market with smart-card technology as the number of competitors rose by 250 percent between 1992 and 1997, according to *Electronic Business*. Production equipment for smart cards jumped from $2 million to $1.36 billion during this period as companies prepared for a smart-card revolution. Despite the number of companies selling smart cards and smart-card equipment, consumer demand remained limited.

The Clinton administration took steps to increase the country's use of the new technology in the late 1990s. Under several government programs, federal employees have been carrying smart cards that serve as identification, credit cards, building access keys, and other functions. The federal government has partnered with a number of firms to develop and manage such technology, including a 1999 pilot program run by Citibank.

CURRENT CONDITIONS

Despite the languid pace of the 1990s, a few factors have motivated U.S. card issuers to continue moving toward broader adoption of smart cards. For one, some traditional credit-card companies such as Visa are worried that even if the cost of switching to smart cards is steep, they may have more to lose by not switching. In 1999 a study by Visa International warned that Visa issuers around the world could see competitors lure away up to $30 billion in transactions

if others are more nimble at rolling out feature-packed cards. In addition, Visa reported there were billions of dollars to be had in new business once card issuers bundled a compelling mix of services, including a potential influx of revenue from so-called micropurchases, daily expenses that amount to $20 or less, which are now usually paid with cash.

Predicting the rate of smart-card adoption in the United States remains a contentious matter. In the mid- and late 1990s a number of analysts prematurely foretold a massive roll-out of smart cards that would number in the hundreds of millions or even billions by 2000. Those proved inaccurate, but a more recent crop of forecasts still portends extraordinary growth for the industry.

For instance, Business Communications Co., of Norwalk, Connecticut, predicted in 1999 that the value of U.S. chip-card transactions would top $2 billion by 2003. Even at that level, U.S. transactions would amount to less than 14 percent of global volume, underscoring the slow pace of adoption. Experts also believe it will take at least until 2003 for sufficient infrastructure to be in place for widespread use of smart cards. The Freedonia Group, a Cleveland, Ohio, market research firm, projected that by 2003 the United States would have some 350 million cards in circulation, most of which would be single-function cards.

The Internet was a leading factor in the rosy forecasts for U.S. smart cards. Following a string of high-profile computer hackings in which hundreds of thousands of credit card numbers were stolen from online retailers, industry players planned to pitch smart cards as a method for ensuring safe online shopping. Since online merchants would never actually receive the credit card numbers, just an authorization code, customers could rest easy.

BLUE LOOKS GOOD ON AMEX

American Express pushed the smart-card envelope in September 1999 with the high-profile debut of its Blue card. Widely regarded as the first smart card in the United States aimed at a mass audience, Blue is a chip-driven credit card that uses digital certificates to authenticate users for online purchases. It also features a so-called wallet function that allows consumers to store information from multiple credit cards on it. The card relies on MultOS software and is expected to have additional applications developed for it over time. AmEx's goal was to have 2 million Blue cards in consumers' pockets by the end of 2000, a goal that was met comfortably and with strong expectations for the future.

WANTED: STANDARDS AND SECURITY

The smart-card movement in the United States has gained momentum thanks in part to greater agreement on standards—and more powerful standards enforcers. One of the contributors is Microsoft with the 1999 debut of its Windows for Smart Cards operating system. The software, an extension based on the company's dominant operating system for personal computers (PCs), provides a common environment for smart-card applications to run in. The Windows 2000 edition also included compatibility with some forms of smart-card technology. Microsoft's products compete with the previously issued JavaCard and MultOS systems. Microsoft likewise has backed other smart-card standards aimed at making them more universal.

Aside from getting its software onto smart cards and readers, Microsoft has lobbied fervently to make smart-card readers standard equipment with new PCs. The latter is a bid to bring electronic commerce (e-commerce) to a wider market because smart-card transactions, managed locally by a card reader attached to the PC, are believed more secure than customary Web-based security methods, which usually involve submitting encoded credit-card information over the Internet.

Although smart cards have gained a reputation for security—it's one of their biggest selling points where e-commerce is concerned—they are still vulnerable to a variety of security breaches. The techniques for hacking a smart card are different from those used on magnetic cards, and usually more sophisticated, but industry insiders have acknowledged they exist, and have taken some steps to shore up smart-card security further. Liabilities include the potential to infer a card's contents through reverse engineering (taking the card apart) or capturing signals a card emits while operating. Security critics have also noted possible problems with maintaining a user's anonymity when the person hasn't authorized identifying information to be released.

INDUSTRY LEADERS

Although many of the companies and institutions that use smart-card applications are well-known, such as Visa and MasterCard, those involved in manufacturing smart-card technology are far from household names: Schlumberger Ltd. and Gemplus S.A., for example.

Schlumberger, headquartered in New York, is an international company with annual sales of more than $8.7 billion in 1999 and with offices in approximately 100 countries. The company's Smart Cards & Terminals unit produces cards and readers for a wide range of purposes, including parking, transit, mobile phones, finance, and medical information. The diversified Schlumberger is primarily an oil services company.

Headquartered in France, Gemplus Card International was the world leader in smart cards and magnetic-stripe cards in the late 1990s. Created in 1988, the company employed about 6,000 people in 2000 and supplied products to more than 80 countries worldwide. It had total production capacity of 900 million plastic smart cards annually by the turn of the 21st century. In 1999 Gemplus brought in total sales of approximately $817 million, with smart-card revenue up 30 percent. Gemplus counts among its major clients IBM, Microsoft, Visa, and even the Vatican, which uses smart cards for access within Vatican City. Much of its growth has been driven by strong sales of cards for European wireless communications, which represented half of all Gemplus's sales in 1999.

Oberthur Card Systems, part of the French firm Groupe Francois-Charles Oberthur, has been a fast-rising leader in smart-card manufacturing. With its 1999 purchase of De La Rue plc of the United Kingdom, Oberthur became the world's top maker of microprocessor cards, with shipments of 22 million cards in 1999 The firm was more committed to the production of smart-card software than to the plastic, and purchased the U.K.-based SmartCards International in early 2000 for its card-management software operations. With U.S. operations based in Los Angeles, Oberthur ranked as the third-largest smart-card manufacturer overall.

Chip manufacturers are major component suppliers to the smart-card industry. Among chip manufacturers, the leader was Motorola, Inc., with 20 percent of the industry, followed by Texas Instruments and SGS-Thomson, with 15 percent each, and Siemens AG and Hitachi, Ltd., with 10 percent each. The remaining 30 percent of the chip market was held by all other companies involved, including Oki Semiconductor and Philips Semiconductor.

AMERICA AND THE WORLD

In the mid- to late 1990s, smart cards were one technological area in which the United States did not lead the world, although the Smart Card Industrial Association predicted that it would within a decade. During the 1990s, France was at the forefront in smart-card development, with the rest of Europe and the Pacific Rim close behind. In the mid- to late 1990s, Denmark had a stored-value cash system called Danmont, and Germany's national health-insurance program issued users smart cards. Japan, Singapore, and many of the emerging Eastern European nations were increasingly basing their monetary systems on smart cards.

Only about 2 percent of the world smart-card market was in the United States, with another 1 percent in Canada, compared to 70 percent in Western Europe, 11 percent in South America, 10 percent in Asia, and 6 percent in the rest of the world. The United States' share was expected to rise in the early 2000s as more cards were issued. On a transaction basis, U.S. purchases on smart cards were valued at only about 1 percent of global volume as of 1998, but that amount was expected to approach 14 percent by 2003, based on projections by Business Communications Co.

RESEARCH AND TECHNOLOGY

In the 1970s, Intel founder Gordon Moore postulated that computer-chip capacity and performance would double every 18 months, while prices would decrease at a similar rate. This concept, called "Moore's Law," applied mostly to microprocessor chip development. In the mid-1990s, because the smart-card industry was such a new one, the cards' capacity was not growing at the rate predicted—yet. But already in 1996, the industry was looking to rapidly grow as chip memory increased from 8 to 64 kilobytes and even 256 kilobytes. As memory expands, so does the likelihood that one day smart cards will constitute tiny PCs and even multimedia systems with voice and video capacities.

With the increase in memory capacity, the trend is toward multiple-application smart cards—that is, cards that can perform diverse functions. Other developments that were in progress in 1997 included smart-card systems that would allow secure access for users on the Internet or other networks. Hewlett-Packard Co., in conjunction with Informix and Gemplus, was an innovator in this technology, which it marketed as the ImagineCard. Overall, the Internet was expected to greatly expand the range of smart-card applications, and *America's Community Banker* reported in March 1997 that it would soon be possible for some bank customers to download cash online. In 1997 France launched a nationwide program that would ultimately replace cash with smart cards.

Smart-card hardware and peripherals were other areas that achieved significant growth in the 1990s. The high-tech smart cards of the mid-1990s required high-performance and yet user-friendly readers and other devices. Created mostly in Europe, such devices as modems with integrated smart-card readers allowed for secure e-commerce, home banking, and public online transactions.

Future versions of smart cards are likely to use their heightened processing power to perform tasks far beyond authorizing financial transactions and paying subway fares. Systems under development at Gemplus can automatically send and receive messages within a room, say, to track inventory or retrieve data from nearby computers. As such new applications develop, smart devices may no longer come as cards at all—they may be so-called smart objects whose form is dictated by the task they serve.

FURTHER READING

Allen, Catherine A., and William J. Barr, eds. *Smart Cards: Seizing Strategic Business Opportunities.* Chicago: Irwin Professional Publishing, 1997.

"BCC Predicts 22.7% Growth in Chip Card Transactions." *Report on Smart Cards,* 27 September 1999.

Bryant, Adam. "Plastic is Getting Smarter." *Newsweek,* 16 October 2000.

Coulton, Antoinette. "Examining Why Acceptance Lags in the U.S." *American Banker,* 29 April 1998, 5A.

Dvorak, John C. "Inside Track." *PC Magazine,* 6 April 1999, 89.

Egan, Jack. "The End of Cash and Carry." *U.S. News & World Report,* 27 October 1997, 61.

Fisher, Sara. "Local Firm Now the World's Largest Smart Card Maker." *Los Angeles Times,* 29 November 1999.

Fraone, Gina. "Smart-Card Vendors in for a Squeeze." *Electronic Business,* December 1998, 32.

Frook, John Evan. "Internet 'Smart Cards' on the Way." *Interactive Age,* 1 November 1996.

Kaplan, Jack M. *Smart Cards: The Global Information Passport.* Boston: International Thomson Computer, 1996.

Matlack, Carol. "The U.S. is Wising Up To Smart Cards." *Business Week,* 21 August 2000.

Mitchell, Richard. "The Smart Card's Chief Advocate." *Credit Card Management,* April 1997, 26.

"More Smart Cards: Access from the Inside Out." *Security,* April 1997, 24.

Mulqueen, John T. "V-One Secures New Clients." *Communications Week,* 4 November 1996, 87.

O'Sullivan, Orla. "From France, a Glimpse of Things to Come." *ABA Banking Journal,* March 1997, 57.

Roberts, Bill. "Internet Gives Smart Cards Whole New Life." *Computing Canada,* 3 March 1997, 14.

San Filippo, John. "ATMs: The Next Generation." *Credit Union Executive,* March/April 1997, 20.

"Smart Card Factoids." Smart Card Forum, 1998. Available from http://www.smartcrd.com.

"Smart Card Resource Center." Amerkore International, 1997. Available from http://www.smart-card.com.

Souccar, Miriam Kreinin. "Citi Committed to Chip Card as E-commerce Authenticator." *American Banker,* 6 December 1999.

———. "France's Oberthur Aiming for Top Rank." *American Banker,* 5 January 2000.

———. "Smart Cards Gather Momentum but U.S. Banks Still Lag." *American Banker,* 14 September 1999.

"Trade Groups Unite to Promote Smart Cards." *Card Fax,* 21 September 2000.

"Visa Smart Path Program Sets Global Milestones." *Report on Smart Cards,* 28 June 1999.

Young, Kung. "Cracking the Code." *Banker,* July 1999.

Zachary, G. Pascal. "Beyond Credit and Debit." *Wall Street Journal,* 20 September 1999.

SMOKING CESSATION PRODUCTS AND SERVICES

With heated criticism of tobacco companies and attacks on the smoking habit coming from a variety of sources, including the Oval Office and the halls of Congress, along with increased taxes for cigarette purchases, more and more smokers were trying to kick the habit in the early 2000s. Some studies estimated that as many as one-third of all smokers were interested in quitting.

According to the Centers for Disease Control and Prevention (CDC), tobacco smoking is responsible for over 20 percent of all preventable deaths in the United States, outpacing any other cause. The CDC added that smoking-related illnesses cost about $50 billion annually in health care in the mid-1990s. Smoking also is a major risk factor in six of the 14 leading causes of death among older people, and greatly aggravates other common conditions experienced by the elderly. According to the National Cancer Institute, smoking is the cause of 87 percent of all lung cancers, the most widespread form of cancer death, and also contributes substantially to cancers of the larynx, pharynx, oral cavity, esophagus, bladder, kidney, pancreas, and cervix.

Nicotine-replacement therapy involves the ingestion of small amounts of nicotine through various vehicles—including transdermal (through-the-skin) patches, nasal spray, chewing gum, inhalants, and tablets—during the process of quitting in order to mitigate some of the more aggravating side effects of nicotine withdrawal. Extensive research has concluded that smokers are far more likely to succeed at quitting with the aid of a nicotine replacement. Such products are usually classified as pharmaceuticals, and are sold both by prescription and over the counter. In addition, combining use of a nicotine replacement product with a behavior modification program increased the chance of success still more, up to double the cessation rate according to some studies.

Total smoking cessation product sales increased 7.5 percent in the year ended July 2000 to reach $643 million. Unit shipments, meanwhile, increased 6.7 percent to 17.3 million. Two products, Nicorette and NicoDerm CQ, both marketed by SmithKline Beecham PLC, accounted for about 95 percent of all sales. The largest sales categories were gum starter kits (such as Nicorette), with sales of $246.8 million for an increase of 15 percent; and patch starter kits (such as NicoDerm), which were down nearly 2 percent with sales totaling $234.6 million. The market for smoking cessation products and services was projected to reach $1.5 billion by 2007.

ORGANIZATION AND STRUCTURE

Much of the marketing efforts of smoking cessation companies, including the introduction of hopeful new products, are engineered to coincide with calendar events, such as New Year's Day or the Great American Smokeout, when customers generally try to turn over a new leaf and when building brand loyalty is at its greatest potential. Marketing of such products received a boost from the federal government in August 1999. While prescription drug advertising was already a $1.2 billion market, the U.S. Food and Drug Administration (FDA) issued a new ruling allowing direct marketing of pharmaceuticals on television and radio.

In an interesting financial reverse psychology, the Internal Revenue Service revoked its rule officially acknowledging nicotine as an addictive and hazardous drug in September 1999. As a result, taxpayers can deduct the cost of smoking cessation programs and prescription drugs from on their tax forms. Over-the-counter therapies, however, remain nondeductible.

The smoking cessation business is actually divided into two segments, the largest of which is a branch of the pharmaceutical industry. The second, and smaller, segment consists of counseling services, hypnotherapists, and self-help smoking cessation programs, such as SMOKENDERS.

The pharmaceuticals segment of the smoking cessation industry is made up mostly of large, diversified pharmaceutical companies, some of them international in scope. The smoking cessation products of these companies, in most cases, represent only a small percentage of their overall production and business. For example, SmithKline Beecham, the marketer of Nicorette chewing gum and NicoDerm CQ transdermal patches, produces mainly health and beauty aids.

Within the pharmaceutical-based smoking cessation aids, there is a division between those marketed over the counter, such as Nicorette chewing gum and some of the transdermal nicotine patches, and other, more potent products, such as Zyban, nicotine nasal spray, and the nicotine inhaler. The latter category of products was available only by prescription in the United States in 2000.

The services segment of the smoking cessation industry is often made up of groups formed by hospital and medical staff, volunteer organizations, addition counselors, and psychologists. Often these groups offer personalized quitting advice or 12-step programs. Behavioral or supportive therapy can be done in groups, by telephone contacts, through written materials, and even individual counseling.

BACKGROUND AND DEVELOPMENT

For as long as there have been smokers, there have been those among them who made a conscious decision to try to quit smoking. Not until the final decades of the 20th century did smokers finally get an arsenal of potent weapons that claimed to effectively treat nicotine withdrawal. Before that, people who chose to stop smoking had little choice but to grit their teeth and go cold turkey. Although there was undoubtedly some placebo effect from early over-the-counter products, the FDA announced in June 1993 that all such products were ineffective and would be withdrawn from the market after existing supplies ran out. Most of these products were sold as chewing gum or oral medication and carried such brand names as Cigarrest, Bantron, Tabmint, and Nikoban.

More than a decade before the FDA's withdrawal of some of these over-the-counter smoking deterrents from the market, the first nicotine-replacement product in the form of a chewing gum had made its debut. Called Nicorette and introduced originally by Marion Merrell Dow Inc., each piece of gum contained four milligrams of nicotine. Chewing an average of six to nine pieces daily, a smoker could gradually cut down on the number of cigarettes smoked without suffering sharp withdrawal pains.

During the 1980s, pharmaceutical companies introduced a new nicotine-replacement delivery system with the transdermal patch. The patches, in varying strengths depending on the magnitude of the smoker's habit, are applied directly to the skin and worn for 12 or more hours daily. Once the smoker has given up smoking and has gradually reduced the patch-delivered nicotine to its lowest level, he or she can stop using the patch and, ideally, stay off cigarettes.

Counseling services also were available for most of the second half of the 20th century, with most of the earliest ones relying heavily on hypnotherapy. Such services, many of them now affiliated with national and regional counseling services, continue to be available. In the 1960s, in the wake of the first urgent warning about the dangers of smoking, a number of stop-smoking programs, built around the concept of group therapy, started appearing. Such therapy, which typically worked with a group of smokers over a period of several weeks, claimed to be more successful than individual efforts in helping smokers quit.

The emergence of the fledgling smoking cessation industry was set against the backdrop of an increasingly health-conscious American landscape. Although health alarms about the use of tobacco products first sounded in the 1960s, it was not really until the last two decades of the century that smoking began to face strong social disapproval. This trend found its way into legislation that banned smoking in a wide range of public places. Additionally, smoking in the workplace was also becoming rare, with many places of business banning smoking altogether on their premises or limiting it to a few locations.

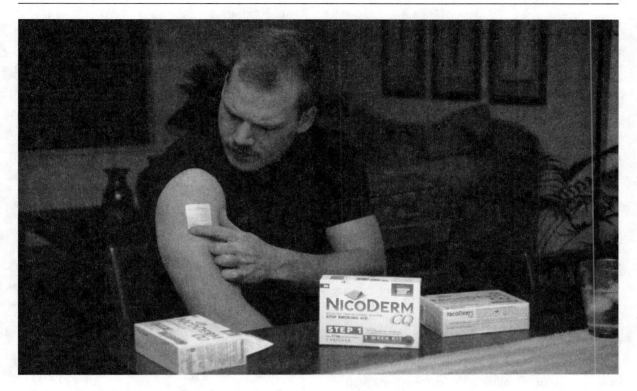

A man wearing a Nicoderm transdermal patch. *(Fieldmark Publications/Robert J. Huffman)*

PIONEERS IN THE FIELD

The breakthrough in drug therapies aimed at smoking cessation came in 1984 with Marion Merrell Dow's introduction of nicotine polacrilex gum—Nicorette. In 1992, another medium for nicotine replacement therapy was introduced—the transdermal patch. A number of companies, including Marion Merrell Dow and Parke-Davis, introduced the patches under such brand names as NicoDerm CQ, ProStep, Habitrol, and Nicotrol. The patches, available in a variety of strengths, were at first available only by prescription, as was Nicorette. Nicorette and NicoDerm CQ (also introduced by Marion Merrell Dow) were subsequently acquired by international pharmaceuticals giant SmithKline Beecham, based in the United Kingdom.

Among the pioneers in the nondrug programs aimed at stopping smoking, perhaps the best known and one of the earliest successes was SMOKENDERS. Founded by the wife of a dentist in Phillipsburg, New Jersey, the program attracted a wide following and was built around the concept of group therapy. Smokers interested in quitting would join the program and pay a fee to SMOKENDERS. Weekly sessions over six or seven weeks could even-

tually lead smokers to stop smoking. In its original form, the program did not use any pharmaceuticals; more recently, those enrolled in SMOKENDERS had the option of supplementing their behavior-modification techniques with pharmaceuticals. SMOKENDERS continues to attract a number of enrollees, and by 2000 included a program that an individual could follow outside of the group setting.

CURRENT CONDITIONS

The near monopoly on smoking cessation products enjoyed by the merging Glaxo Wellcome PLC and SmithKline Beecham was threatened at the turn of the century by the rush of generic products to market as patents expire. Market leaders were especially proprietary about their industry dominance. In fall 1999, SmithKline slapped California-based Watson Pharmaceuticals, Inc. with a lawsuit claiming that the user guide and audiocassette packaged with Watson's FDA-approved Polacrilex gum, a generic version of SmithKline's Nicorette, constituted a violation of SmithKline's copyright. SmithKline contended that the materials were too similar to those marketed with SmithKline's successful product. Watson protested that the materials were part of Nicorette's labeling. Under the Waxman-Hatch Act, generic products are required to use the innovator's labeling. Nonetheless, Watson was ordered by the Southern District of New York U.S. Circuit Court to cease distribution of the product and to recall previously shipped quantities.

Around the same time, Glaxo Wellcome sued Andrx Pharmaceuticals for patent infringement stemming from the latter's production of and FDA license request for its generic version of bupropion, the active ingredient in Zyban, Glaxo's innovative cessation tablet. Glaxo's patent of Zyban was set to expire in May 2000, and the lawsuit ensured that Andrx could not market its generic product for an additional 30 months unless the company could defeat Glaxo in court.

Despite growing product sales, some industry players decried retailers' frequent reluctance to more aggressively promote cessation products in their stores. Because of the relatively high cost of many of the products, retailers often keep them behind the counter or in a locked display case. Such restricted access, proponents claimed, discourages prospective quitters from inspecting and buying them. SmithKline Beecham held that its own studies revealed that retail sales of smoking cessation products could increase from 44 percent to 73 percent by placing the merchandise up front with other retail items, though retailers had theft and space concerns to contend with.

Meanwhile, the nation's medical students were deemed ill-prepared in smoking cessation treatments and techniques. A survey conducted by a consortium of university professors found that nicotine dependence was inadequately treated in U.S. medical schools, even though smoking is widely considered one of the most preventable and costly medical problem facing the nation. The survey reported that only 4.4 percent of all 126 U.S. medical schools included the smoking-related topics recommended by the National Cancer Institute and the Agency for Health Care Policy and Research in their curricula during the third or fourth year of study, and only 23.5 percent offered additional elective courses focused on smoking cessation. Moreover, nearly 70 percent of all schools did not require any training in smoking cessation techniques.

Like other industries, smoking cessation products and services were making room for themselves on the World Wide Web. SmithKline developed their Committed Quitters program, which tallies data on individuals' smoking habits and processes the information to produce individually tailored materials designed to help them quit. The 12-week program was offered free to purchasers of Nicorette, Nicorette Mint or Nico-Derm CQ, who can download a personalized program directly to their computer. Since studies have found that behavior-modification programs greatly enhance the likelihood of success when followed in conjunction with nicotine-replacement therapy, manufacturers increasingly sought out ways to develop programs and tailor them to individual customers, for which the Internet could prove a perfect vehicle.

A series of new cessation products hit stores in the late 1990s, offering smokers new methods by which to kick the habit. The Nicotinal nasal spray, released in 1996, contains nicotine that is absorbed through the user's nasal lining into the bloodstream. Like other nicotine-replacement therapies, the product was intended for use over relatively short durations—no more than six months. A little more than a year later, the FDA approved a Nicotrol nicotine inhaler, also available by prescription only. Users puff on a plastic mouthpiece containing a nicotine cartridge to receive approximately four milligrams of nicotine, about one-third of the nicotine in a regular cigarette.

The biggest leap forward in smoking cessation technology came in June 1997 when Glaxo Wellcome introduced Zyban into the prescription market. A tablet taken twice daily, Zyban offered a novel alternative to the gum, patch, and inhalant delivery systems. The drug, also marketed as an antidepressant called Wellbutrin SR, raises dopamine levels in the brain, thus reducing the smoker's craving. For smokers worried about an increase in weight, Zyban has the added appeal of helping to control appetite in the wake of smoking cessation, thus helping to alleviate the reluctance of potential quitters concerned about the weight gain often associated with smoking cessation.

For all nicotine-replacement products, users ran the risk of becoming addicted to the nicotine in the new medium. For these cessation products to be most effective, users must gradually reduce their intake of nicotine until they have completely weaned themselves off the substance.

Alternative therapies have proven successful as well. Psychotherapist and hypnotist Dr. Steven Rosenberg developed a 20-minute aversiotherapy antismoking session that has met with a remarkable success rate of 85 percent. In late 1999, Dr. Rosenberg offered the program for download on the Web for about $30.

Even with successful products, quitting smoking is no easy feat. A national poll conducted by the Hazelden Foundation in 1998 showed that it took smokers an average of 18.6 years before they finally quit. The poll also revealed that most smokers had tried to quit an average of 10.8 times before they finally succeeded. Current smokers revealed to Hazelden pollsters that they had already tried quitting an average of 3.4 times.

After years of speculation as to which smoking cessation products—including nicotine gum, patches, nasal sprays, inhalers, and prescription tablets—were the most effective, early comparative studies revealed little distinction. A British research team reported in the *Archives of Internal Medicine* in September 1999 that little difference occurred in levels of abstinence, cravings, or withdrawal symptoms across the different product types. Unlike in previous such studies, the research team required the subjects to purchase the products (at half price) in order to mimic market conditions. The findings revealed a 20 percent success rate without any significant correlation to product types, though compliance rates varied; smokers were most likely to abide by the recommended dosage with the patch, while those using gum or inhalers more frequently reduced their own dosage, presumably to save money.

INDUSTRY LEADERS

Perhaps the biggest news to hit the industry at the close of the 20th century was the merger between market leaders SmithKline Beecham PLC and Glaxo Wellcome PLC to create the runaway market leader in the smoking cessation products industry.

SmithKline reaped enormous rewards in 1999 from sales of Nicorette, which totaled $355.97 million, and NicoDerm CQ, with $224.48 million, accounting for 95 percent of the industry's product sales. In addition to its two flagship U.S. smoking cessation products, the U.K. firm marketed different smoking cessation patches in Europe and Australia. Overall, the company derived 43 percent of its sales from the United States and an equal percentage from Europe, while its Consumer Healthcare division accounted for 30 percent of total sales. With 53,300 employees, SmithKline Beecham posted net income of $3.1 billion in 1999 on sales of about $13.59 billion.

Glaxo Wellcome Inc., the U.S. subsidiary of U.K. pharmaceuticals giant Glaxo Wellcome PLC, marketed the prescription drug Zyban, the only oral pharmaceutical that reduced the craving for nicotine, although its sales disappointed in 1999, falling 26 percent to $114.32 million. Glaxo Wellcome PLC maintained a worldwide work force of about 60,000.

The parent company, along with Merck & Co. and Novartis AG, was one of the world's three largest manufacturers of prescription drugs. About 42 percent of Glaxo's business was in North America, 34 percent was in Europe, with the remaining 24 percent spread out over other regions. Sales increased 6 percent to $13.75 billion in 1999. The merger between Glaxo and SmithKline was expected to head off new competitors jumping into the market as patents expire.

The McNeil Consumer Products division of Johnson & Johnson markets three products in the arsenal of smoking cessation drug therapies. These are the Nicotrol transdermal patch, available over the counter, and the Nicotrol nasal spray and Nicotrol inhaler, both of which may be purchased only with a prescription. Johnson & Johnson, headquartered in New Brunswick, New Jersey, is the world's largest manufacturer of health-care products, as well as the most diversified. In addition to a wide range of consumer products such as Tylenol, Motrin, Band-Aid bandages, and Reach toothbrushes, the company produces and markets a wide range of medical equipment and pharmaceuticals through a number of its subsidiary operations. McNeil's flagship Nicotrol raked in sales of $16 million in 1999. The company employs more than 97,000 people worldwide, and achieved sales of $27.47 billion in 1999, representing an increase of 14.5 percent from the previous year. The consumer products division accounted for $6.86 billion, including $3.19 billion outside the United States.

Novartis AG, based in Basel, Switzerland, is the distributor of the Habitrol transdermal nicotine-replacement patch, which the company rolled out in 1999, and the Nicotinell flavored lozenge. Formed in 1996 by the $27 billion merger of Ciba-Geigy and Sandoz, Novartis' business focuses on three key areas: agribusiness, health care, and nutrition. The company's nutrition division produces Gerber baby foods and related products, while its agribusiness segment markets insecticides, herbicides, and fungicides to help protect farmers' crops. The health-care division produces about 60 percent of the company's total revenues, and its products include both prescription drugs and over-the-counter products. Employing about 82,000 worldwide, Novartis posted net income of $4.4 billion on revenue of $23.05 billion in 1999.

WORK FORCE

The international pharmaceutical industry, which manufactures and markets most smoking cessation products, employs hundreds of thousands of people around the world. The jobs available in the industry range from clerical to management positions in the pharmaceutical companies' offices. For those with an interest in chemical and medical research, this industry offers a broad range of opportunities, for it is through these companies' ongoing research that new products are brought to market.

Employment levels in the nondrug smoking cessation services field are relatively low. Most of these operations involve individual counselors or small teams, the majority of whom are trained professionals. There is a fairly limited number of support jobs available in these operations.

AMERICA AND THE WORLD

Although U.S. smokers may have felt more pressure to quit than smokers elsewhere in the world, there is a swelling tide of international opposition to the smoking habit. As in the United States, the pressure springs not only from health concerns but also from the fact that the smoking habit is becoming increasingly socially unacceptable. Many smoking cessation products are marketed internationally. Pharmacists, researchers, physicians, and other groups all contribute to promote the international No Smoking Day in March, with companies such as Pharmacia & Upjohn offering cash and other prize incentives to winners of regional competitions.

SmithKline Beecham invested close to $20 million in the United Kingdom to try to capture a majority of the U.K. smoking cessation market with the NiQuitin patch, and Glaxo's Zyban was released there in 2000. As a result of intensifying national campaigns against smoking in the United Kingdom, the smoking cessation market took off in 1999. Sales of nicotine replacement products jumped 28 percent, led by patches, such as NiQuitin CQ, which constituted 50 percent of the cessation market. The United Kingdom has about one-fourth as many smokers as the United States. Parliament launched its "Don't Stop Giving Up" campaign in December 1999, focusing primarily on advertising and support for cessation programs to reduce the national smoking rates and related diseases. Meanwhile, the Royal College of Practitioners placed nicotine on the same shelf as hard narcotics for its public health hazards. In early 2000, the U.K. Office for National Statistics reported that, despite such efforts, 28 percent of men and 26 percent of women were still habitual smokers, although this compared with 51 percent and 41 percent, respectively, in 1974.

Companies faced additional marketing difficulties in Europe, where, unlike in the United States, direct-to-consumer advertising of prescription drugs was prohibited. Thus, major firms were aggressively pushing their way into the Japanese market, which is home to the largest proportion of smokers in the industrialized world, with over 50 percent of men and 35 percent of women lighting up. In 1999 Novartis' Nicotinell TTS became the first transdermal patch to go on the market in Japan. SmithKline, meanwhile, was vocal in its plans to expand its presence in Japan.

RESEARCH AND TECHNOLOGY

Smoking cessation was not without its gender gaps. Researchers at London's Goldsmith College reported that women tend to respond better than men to nicotine-replacement therapy. A study at the University of California-Irvine further reported that smoking activity relates to varying mood swings between men and women, an insight likely to spur further tailoring of cessation products to more specialized markets. By asking 60 men and women to record their moods as they reached for a cigarette over a period of two days, the study revealed pronounced variations in moods associated with smoking urges. While general anger and anxiety were common to both sexes, men tended to light up when sad while women smoked when happy. Men were also more likely to smoke when suffering from fatigue, a feeling that produced no urge for women.

The effects of smoking varied as well. Smoking tended to aggravate anxiety among males and relieve it in females. Men, however, were more likely to calm their anger with a few puffs. In sum, researchers concluded that, contrary to conventional wisdom, men were as, if not more, likely than women to smoke to try to alter their mood. While the small scale of the study does not easily generalize across a market, manufacturers were likely to pay close attention to further studies in this area to get ahead on the development and marketing of products geared toward more focused consumer groups.

Meanwhile, though teenage smoking was targeted by a variety of groups as well as the Clinton administration, the teen quitting rate was markedly low, in part because most cessation programs are engineered and marketed for adults. A number of scientists and preventive medicine specialists decried the common perception of teenage smokers as unwilling to quit as inconsistent with the facts. Rather, they held, teenage smokers increasingly want to quit, but find little support on the market or in their communities. Research conducted by Dr. Richard Hurt of the Mayo Clinic's Nicotine Dependence Center revealed that teenagers attempting to quit met with little success with the patch; only 11 of 101 teens were able to kick the habit. Dr. Hurt surmised that this failure was in large part due to the absence of behavior-intervention components in the study, which would support the cessation process with information about how to deal with a craving.

A study of 17 teen cessation programs by Steve Sussman at the University of Southern California revealed an average success rate of only 6-7 percent, compared with the adult average of 50 percent with similar programs. Sussman likewise attributed the poor results to the failure of programs, which were based on adult models, to account for the specific needs and behavior of teens. Overall, researchers have found that teens have far more difficulty withstanding the headaches and anxiety associated with the cessation process, and thus programs need to be tailored to support them both physically and emotionally.

British American Tobacco, meanwhile, hoped to reduce the health hazards of smoking without decreasing sales of tobacco products; the company was testing its own "safe" cigarette using treated tobacco that has been stripped of the carcinogenic nitrosamines toxins. The product, however, met with almost universal dismissal from the medical profession.

FURTHER READING

Clark, Andrew. "Shares Slip on Poor Glaxo SmithKline Results." *Guardian* (London), 17 February 2000.

"Glaxo Brings Action against Andrx." *Financial Times* (London), 11 September 1999.

Medical Tribune News Service. "Men, Women Smoke to a Different Beat." *Arizona Republic,* 3 June 1999.

Needham, Christine B. "Medical Schools Draggin on Stop-Smoking Training." *Plain Dealer,* 1 November 1999.

O'Rourke, Kevin. "Free Shop Means to Quit." *Drug Store News,* 25 October 1999.

"Questions and Answers about the Benefits of Smoking Cessation." *CancerNet—National Cancer Institute,* 1 January 2000. Available from http://cancernet.nci.nih.gov/cgi-bin/srchcgi.exe?DBID=pdq&TYPE=search&SFMT=pdq_statement/1/0/0&ZUI=600811.

Scussa, Frank. "Down, but Not Out." *Med Ad News,* December 1999.

"Smoking Cessation Products." *MMR,* 18 September 2000.

"Smoking Out Sales." *Chemist & Druggist,* 9 September 2000.

"Stop Smoking: Little Difference in Results." *Gazette* (Montreal), 23 October 1999.

"Suit Yourself." *Chemist & Druggist,* 26 February 2000.

"Target Cancer." *Chemist & Druggist,* 5 June 1999.

"Teen Smoking: Cessation Programs Not Geared to Teens." *American Health Line,* 16 February 2000.

"Treatment Works. . .When You Choose to Stop Smoking." *APA Online,* 1999. Available from http://www.psych.org/public_info/nicotine.html.

White, Deborah. "Learning to Be a Quitter: Smoking Cessation Products Use a Variety of Methods." *Commercial Appeal* (Memphis, TN), 31 January 2000.

SPECIALTY COFFEE

Coffee is the world's second-most traded commodity, after oil. The premium variety is arabica coffee, which forms the basis of the U.S. specialty or gourmet coffee industry. The success of the industry is indicated by a number of trends in the overall coffee industry, but most significantly by the coffeehouse revival, the sale of whole-bean coffee, and the increase in coffee consumption.

According to the industry's trade group, the Specialty Coffee Association of America (SCAA), there were around 12,000 gourmet coffee outlets in the United States in 1999. That number stands in stark contrast to the 5,000 cafes in 1995, and in even starker contrast to the 250 cafes in 1979. In addition, whole-bean sales rose during the late 1990s as reflected by the 16 percent increase in whole-bean sales experienced by grocery, mass-merchant, and drug stores. Furthermore, overall coffee consumption has increased, fueled by the popularity of specialty coffee. In 1999, 76 percent of the country consumed coffee—at an average of 3.5 cups per day, according to *Restaurant Business*. The specialty coffee industry also generated over $1.5 billion in sales in the late 1990s. According to the SCAA, the industry grew quickly during the 1990s—about 25 percent per year. About 20 million Americans drink gourmet coffee beverages each day. The SCAA believed the gourmet category rejuvenated coffee sales as a whole, reversing a trend of declines from the 1960s that did not perk up again until the early 1990s.

As coffee prices rose during the 1990s, some analysts predicted that the specialty coffee business could only prosper. Since an ordinary cup of coffee was already considered expensive, specialty roasters and retailers believed consumers would spend slightly more for gourmet coffee. The array of products was never wider; retailers added more flavors to whole beans and variations to the basics of espresso and steamed milk. The more clever retailers added coffee shakes and iced-tea concoctions such as chai to their menus, to outdo competitors who offered mere iced lattes. Since most specialty retailers also retailed whole beans, their stores added home espresso machines, coffee grinders, and other brewing paraphernalia for add-on sales.

Many industry firms did all they could to increase market share: they ran catalog sales departments, added retail locations, and competed for new wholesale clients, such as restaurant chains and supermarkets. Several industry firms started sites on the World Wide Web during the 1990s to sell coffee beans over the Internet. Some roasters even created private label blends for their institutional customers. Starbucks Corp.'s Nordstrom Blend, for example, was created for the upscale department store chain. Courting corporate accounts became increasingly important because the top place for drinking coffee was the workplace in the late 1990s.

ORGANIZATION AND STRUCTURE

After growing in any of roughly 20 countries, coffee beans passed through many middlemen and brokers before coming to industry firms in the United States. Usually, the beans arrived green or unroasted, whereupon industry firms bought and roasted them in small batches. From there the beans reached consumers through several channels, including: supermarkets, gourmet delis, fancy food stores, houseware/gift stores, mail order, mass merchandisers, the Internet, specialty coffee stores, and coffee cafes. In nonproprietary retail stores, such as supermarkets, specialty coffee came prepackaged or in bulk, depending on the individual retailer's store format.

Industry firms often sold their beans through a combination of supermarkets, their own bean stores and/or cafes, mail order, and the Internet. There were 3,250 cafes, 2,125 coffee bars and kiosks, and 1,800 coffee carts selling coffee in the United States at one point in the late 1990s, according to the SCAA. The total number of specialty coffee retail outlets, however, climbed to 12,000 by 1999. The difference between a bean store and a cafe is that the former emphasizes selling beans (and assorted brewing gadgets) so consumers can make gourmet coffee at home, while a cafe prepares single drinks for customers to consume on the premises or to take out. Many industry firms such as Starbucks sell whole beans as well as individual drinks at their stores, and serve coffee drinks to consumers in two forms: the filtered, drip coffee familiar to most Americans, and European-style espresso, a more concentrated form of the brew, which is harder for consumers to make at home. Shots of espresso are "pulled" from espresso machines by cafe workers called *baristas,* a coffee bartender of sorts. Most espresso beverages have one or more shots combined with steamed or foamed milk to make such drinks as cappuccinos, caffe mochas, or cafe au laits.

The SCAA is a nonprofit trade organization with more than 2,500-member companies including roasters, retailers, exporters, and coffee brokers in the late 1990s. The group stated its purpose as being to "serve the specialty coffee industry through the development and dissemination of information that fosters coffee excellence within the trade." It is concerned with developing coffee quality standards, but also organizes trade shows and collects educational information for its members.

Although the coffee industry as a whole lacked standards for coffee brewing since 1975, the SCAA reinstituted such standards in the late 1990s. The SCAA's standards require that the coffee grounds to water ratio must fall between 3.25 and 4.25 ounces of ground coffee per every 64 ounces of water. Other standards cover water temperature and quality, brewing time, and coarseness or fineness of coffee grounds. As of late 1999, 30 restaurants had sought and received certification from the SCAA, having met the SCAA's standards.

According to an early 1990s study used by the SCAA, about 22 percent of Americans bought specialty coffee. The study noted above-average consumption in the Pacific, Middle Atlantic, and New England states. The study found gourmet coffee drinkers tended to be slightly more affluent than average and lived or worked in big cities. Gourmet coffee consumption also rose with the drinkers' educational level. Those who finished college bought 49 percent more gourmet coffee on average and those with some postgraduate education bought 71 percent more. They also found that households with kids and two working parents bought 28 percent more gourmet coffee. The SCAA described their typical customer as "an educated urban resident with the disposable income to spend on fine coffee."

BACKGROUND AND DEVELOPMENT

Until the 1960s, nearly all Americans bought their coffee at the supermarket. During the late 1960s, some entrepreneurs opened shops carrying hard-to-find gourmet food items, such as specialty coffees, aimed at affluent consumers. Some of these businesses even roasted their own coffee, to control the degree of roast and keep the coffee fresh. By 1969 the United States had about 50 specialty coffee stores. During the early 1970s, 100 gift/houseware stores and 1,200 specialty food stores carried gourmet coffee. In 1975 a killing frost in Brazil devastated the coffee crop, which raised coffee prices by 500 percent. Large roasters tried to calm consumer sticker shock by selling coffee in 13-ounce cans instead of the usual 16 ounce. Since consumers got less for their coffee dollar, some of them switched to the more flavorful gourmet blends following a quality versus quantity consumer trend.

Throughout the 1970s the industry experimented with roasting beans darker to make a smokier, more distinct coffee than the lighter supermarket roasts. Thus, many consumers came to associate dark roasted coffee with gourmet coffee and many specialty coffee companies developed proprietary house blends during the 1970s. Decaffeinated coffees became a popular seller during the 1980s, with 17 percent of the population drinking it by 1988. The demand for flavored coffees emerged in the mid-1980s, causing producers to add flavors such as cocoa, vanilla, or hazelnut in liquid or powder form to coffee beans. This required little capital investment and allowed specialty shops to sell flavored coffees at a higher price. Industry firms tried many different flavors, and several became big

A customer enjoying coffee at Starbucks. *(FieldMark Publications/Robert J. Huffman)*

hits, particularly by attracting new, younger coffee drinkers to the customer base.

Some coffee purists scoffed at flavored coffees, despite their apparent popularity. Starbucks, for example, refused to flavor its beans, but sold flavored syrup to add after brewing. Syrups provided retailers with more sales options than simply flavoring coffees. These could be used in Italian sodas, granitas, and other drink concoctions popular with the 18-to-35-year-old cafe patron. These drinks could also be sold at a premium. Standard flavors included vanilla, hazelnut, and raspberry; but companies such as Boyd Coffee expanded their lines to include wild huckleberry flavored syrups, and Stasero added praline, marshmallow, and a combination of passion fruit, orange, and guava. Marketing syrup-flavored drinks proved to fuel creativity from employee and customer alike. Signature drinks offered by some retailers included Lemon Meringue Pie Italian Soda; Nutty Buddy, a mocha spiked with three nut-flavored syrups; and Starburst, white chocolate and lemon syrups mixed in sparkling water.

Another trend included consumer requests for organic coffees. The industry in the 1990s, however, could not tell if consumers would pay more for the harder-to-find organics. Certainly more emphasis was placed by retailers on the beans' growing environ-ment. One growing environmental and economic concern within the industry was the plight of wintering songbirds. The shade trees sheltering coffee bushes of Central and South America have long been home to migratory birds. Ornithological surveys have found 150 or more bird species living in traditional coffee plantations. Strong demand for coffee and advice from the U.S. government caused growers to convert their land to so-called sun plantations. The U.S. Agency for International Development spent $81 million in efforts to get growers to change planting methods to increase volume. (Economic studies completed since dispute those assumptions.) The process of changing these once-fertile habitats from shade tree to sun plantation, started in 1978, has caused a decline in the migratory bird species population in these traditional locations.

Increased attention to the plight of the birds meant coffee drinkers began asking for shade-grown beans in an attempt to change the trend. Companies including Thanksgiving Coffee marketed specially labeled coffees to educate coffee lovers about the issue. According to a 1997 *Knight Ridder/Tribune News Service* article, most specialty coffee is actually shade grown. The SCAA said that most mass-market coffees are grown on sun plantations, where volume and price are a bigger factor.

Growth of the roaster/retailer segment shows how the industry evolved during the 1970s and 1980s. In 1979 there were about 50 coffee roaster/retailers in the United States; by 1989, there were 400. Growth of specialty coffee retail stores (no roasting on premises) was also dramatic: there were 250 of these stores in 1979 and 1,000 by 1989.

CURRENT CONDITIONS

The specialty coffee industry reaped sales of approximately $1.5 billion in the mid- to late 1990s, but the Specialty Coffee Association of America (SCAA) predicted that the industry's revenues would reach $3 billion by the early 2000s. The specialty coffee industry benefited in part from an overall surge in coffee consumption in the United States. By 1999, 76 percent of the population consumed coffee, including espresso and gourmet coffee potables as well as coffee consumed by occasional drinkers, according to *Restaurant Business*. This number represented the highest level of consumption in the last 40 years, surpassing the 1962 apex of coffee consumption when 64 percent of the population consumed coffee. Moreover, the number of cups consumed also rose in 1999, climbing to 3.5 cups a day, up from 3 cups earlier in the decade. As a final indicator of this growth, one-third of coffee drinkers used larger cups—8-ounce cups—in 1999, up 10 percent from 1998, according to *Restaurant Business*.

Led by specialty coffees, whole-bean sales by grocery, mass-merchant, and drug stores rose 16 percent in 1999, hitting $264.8 million, according to Information Resources Inc. These retailers reported that other coffee categories declined by 6.2 percent, as overall sales in grocery, mass-merchant, and drug stores dipped to $2 billion. While ground coffee sales dropped, however, whole-bean sales continued to sell well, more than tripling their 1989 level, according to the SCAA. Starbucks was a major catalyst in the growth of whole-bean sales, because the company began selling its whole beans in these stores in 1998. By 1999 Starbucks accounted for almost 10 percent of the whole-bean sales in these stores, with revenues of $23.8 million. The leader in this category was Eight O'Clock, whose sales fell about 10 percent due in part to Starbucks' presence. The SCAA expected whole-bean sales to continue increasing rapidly in 2000.

With strong demand for specialty coffee, more competitors entered the business during the late 1990s, with varied success. General Foods captured some market share from the smaller players with its line of Gevalia Coffees, sold only by mail order. Procter & Gamble, maker of Folgers, entered the specialty coffee fray in 1995 with its purchase of Millstone, which it distributes to about 7,000 stores. In 1999 Procter & Gamble even attempted to upgrade Folgers as a specialty coffee by selling whole coffee beans under the Folgers flag. In addition, another mass-market coffee producer, Chock full o' Nuts Corp., bought an industry firm called Quikava in 1994. Based in Boston, Quikava is a chain of drive-through espresso shops that offers franchising. Quikava kept expanding and Chock full o' Nuts set a precedent for other established retailers to enter the market with its streamlined business approach and its careful expansion plans. Sara Lee Corp. expanded its presence in the industry in 1999 by acquiring Chock full o' Nuts.

The influx of coffeehouses also has driven the specialty coffee industry, since many cafes and coffeehouses sell specialty coffee primarily or exclusively. The number of cafes jolted to 12,000 in 1999, up from just 5,000 in 1995. The SCAA, however, predicted that number will actually decline to about 10,000 within the early 2000s because the expansion outpaced demand.

As SCAA's forecast indicated, the cafe market may be maturing. Therefore, one industry trend of the late 1990s was the consolidation of specialty coffee companies (or the rumors of such consolidation), as smaller competitors scrambled to compete with the industry giant, Starbucks Corp. For example, the nation's number-two specialty coffee chain, Diedrich Coffee acquired Coffee People in 1999 for $23 million as well as Pannikin Coffee in 1997 for $2.8 million. In addition, Peabodys Coffee Inc. bought a number of smaller specialty coffeehouses, including Northern Lights Coffee in 1999 and Capitol Coffee and Arrosto Coffee Co. in 2000.

Some analysts said the industry trend toward consolidation indicated that the specialty coffee industry was maturing, and that mergers and acquisitions brought needed capital. Ted Lingle, head of the SCAA, said in a published story, "We see growth peaking in this industry around the year 2010, and between now and then you'll see a slow but steady increase in the number of mergers. After that, I don't think you'll see merger mania tapering off until after the year 2020."

"The definition of specialty coffee is changing," wrote Donald N. Schoenholt in a 1998 *Tea & Coffee Trade Journal* article. "The lines between specialty and commercial products are beginning to blur. The big companies' threat to the existence of regional brands increases. This is so even as specialty coffee's appeal continues to grow across the land. Our ranks have swelled, been thinned, and filled again with specialty coffee businesses that are in significant ways different kinds of businesses than those of the movement's founders. Many are extensions of much bigger companies whose primary products and services often have more to do with tobacco and soap than they do with any kind of coffee. None of this is bad by itself. But things have changed. . . . Today, 'specialty coffee' most often means a beverage of flavored coffee in a 12 oz. container to go. Enough said. Things change."

Schoenholt went on to say that aggressive business tactics by big companies served to "alienate some companies from their specialty coffee community roots." The roots of the industry, he wrote, were in a strong and viable independent group of businesses with the sole mission "to never let the blight of coffee sameness again creep over the land."

INDUSTRY LEADERS

Starbucks Corp., based in Seattle, Washington, led the industry in the late 1990s and looked poised to continue its dominance in the early 2000s. The company posted 1999 sales of $1.68 billion, up 28 percent, and had more than 2,800 retail locations spread throughout the world. Starbucks also distributes its specialty coffee to about 3,500 supermarkets. The company began in 1971 with one store in Seattle. Three entrepreneurs—Gordon Bowker, Jerry Baldwin, and Zev Siegl—founded the original business. They named it after a character who loved coffee from Herman Melville's classic novel *Moby Dick,* and they developed the now-familiar mermaid logo. Starbucks originally sold bulk tea and specialty coffee beans by the pound. They did not add a coffee bar to sell drinks until 1984. The coffee-bar idea came from Howard Schultz, who was the company's marketing director. Schultz quit the company in 1985 to start a chain of espresso cafes like those he'd seen in Milan, Italy. He called his cafes Il Giornale, and they served Starbucks coffee. In 1987 Schultz raised money from private investors and bought Starbucks from its founders for $3.8 million. The venture paid off for Schultz, whose personal fortune was $100 million in 1997, 75 percent of which came from Starbucks stock.

During the late 1980s, Starbucks built a larger roasting plant, started a mail-order catalog, and opened stores in British Columbia, Oregon, and the Chicago area. By 1992 the company grew to 165 stores and of-

fered stock on the Nasdaq stock exchange. Their specialty sales division landed prized institutional accounts throughout the 1990s including: Nordstrom's coffee bars, United Airlines, Barnes & Noble, ITT/Sheraton Hotels, Westin Hotels, and Star Markets. Starbucks also offered some of their catalog items on the Internet through America Online. In 1994 Starbucks had 425 U.S. stores and bought a smaller competitor, the Coffee Connection, Inc. In 1995 the company also bought a minority stake in Noah's New York Bagels, Inc., a coffee and bagel chain based in Golden, Colorado.

Starbucks began joint ventures from 1995 to 1997 to get its coffee into other products, including: Double Black Stout, a dark beer with a shot of espresso, developed with Redhook Ale Brewery; Frappucino, a bottled iced-coffee beverage, developed with PepsiCo Inc.; and a line of Starbucks coffee-flavored ice creams marketed with Dreyer's Grand Ice Cream, Inc., and sold in supermarkets. One of the company's few failures was a carbonated coffee beverage called Mazagran. Joint ventures extended to nonfood items as well, including the sale of music CDs in Starbucks stores, a concept developed with Capitol Records's Blue Note Jazz label. Furthermore, Starbucks also sells its beans via mail-order catalogs and the Internet.

Starbucks opened almost one new store per day in the late 1990s, including five on a single day in Toronto. During this period, Starbucks expanded to the Pacific Rim, opening stores in Hawaii, Japan, and Singapore. The expansion effort helped the company realize its goal of having 2,000 stores by the year 2000, which it handily exceeded by 800 cafes. Part of the company's expansion campaign also included the acquisition of Seattle Coffee Co. Seattle Coffee operates 68 cafes primarily in the United Kingdom, under the names Seattle's Best Coffee and Torrefazione Italia, as well as a roasting and packaging facility. Furthermore, Seattle Coffee products can be found in about 1,600 grocery stores nationwide. Starbucks bought the company in order to penetrate the European market. Despite critics calling them the "golden arches" of the specialty coffee industry, the company's cash registers kept ringing. Starbucks claimed to serve about 4 million customers per week, and hoped to maintain its good fortune through the opening of 1,000 more stores by 2003.

Starbucks' biggest competitor, publicly held Diedrich Coffee Inc. of Irvine, California, ranked second with 2000 sales of over $74.5 million, about 1,350 employees, more than 360 retail locations in operation, and plans to open as many as 1,500 retail outlets by the middle of the decade. Diedrich acquired another leading specialty coffee company, Coffee People, Inc., in 1999, propelling the company toward the top of the industry. Diedrich has stores and carts located in 38 states, plus wholesale and mail-order divisions, and roasts its own coffees from regional plants. Diedrich's coffee portfolio includes brands such as Diedrich Coffee, Gloria Jean's, and Coffee Plantation. The company also planned to open cafes in bank branches owned by Home Savings of America. Diedrich, founded in 1912, owns Central American plantations and is credited with designing and manufacturing "one of the world's most popular batch roasting machines."

Second Cup Ltd., a Toronto-based firm, slid out of the number-two spot in 1999 after liquidating its U.S. operations because of poor growth compared with its thriving Canadian business. With an empire of over 620 coffeehouses worldwide, the company reduced its number to 380. This divestiture included the sale of Coffee People of Portland, Oregon. Second Cup also provides coffee for use on Air Canada and VIA Rail Canada. The catering and restaurant concern Cara Operations owns Second Cup and reported sales of $572 million in 1999.

Caribou Coffee, started in 1992 with a mere $200,000, was the fourth-largest coffee retail chain in 1998. The privately owned company had 130 locations in Minnesota, Michigan, Ohio, Illinois, Georgia, and North Carolina in 1999 and also provides coffee to Delta Airlines. Planned expansion was to take Caribou Coffee throughout the Southeast and Midwestern United States. In the late 1990s, Caribou Coffee had estimated sales of $75 million. The company's strategy for the early 2000s was expansion in its core markets and exploring the possibility of a public offering. Another major player in the industry was Green Mountain Coffee, Inc. of Waterbury, Vermont, which posted 1999 sales of $64.9 million and had 388 employees. The firm sells gourmet coffee to 750,000 catalog patrons and has 5,000 institutional customers. Although Green Mountain once ran about 12 cafes, it decided to jettison them in the late 1990s to focus on its core wholesale business, for which it boasted over 6,000 customers.

One of Starbucks' founders, Jerry Baldwin, retained and runs privately held Peet's Coffee and Tea in the San Francisco Bay area (56 retail cafes in 2000). In the late 1990s, Peet's had estimated sales of over $50 million. Another Starbucks founder, Gordon Bowker, sat on the board of Peet's and Redhook Ale Brewery. In 1992 Starbucks expanded into northern California, thus competing with its own creators.

The independent cafe and retailer had long been an integral part of the growth of specialty coffee, however, they continued to face challenges from Starbucks in the late 1990s and the early 2000s. Independent retailers feeling stomped on by giant Starbucks didn't merely leave those business owners in their cups. In Boulder, Colorado, for example, in 1998, 10 local, independent cafes banded together to promote their stores. This effort included distributing coupons and to-go cups printed with a message promoting independent cafes—a message Solo Cup Co. refused to print because it provided cups for Starbucks.

AMERICA AND THE WORLD

Gourmet coffee comes from about 20 different countries. Free trade between the United States and producer countries is vital to the industry, since the domestic crop is so small. The only gourmet coffee grown on U.S. soil comes from the Kona area on the island of Hawaii. But Kona's crop was impractical for two reasons: price and authenticity. The coffee costs more than similar-tasting Latin American coffees, because American coffee pickers did not work for Third World wages. Since the beans are so expensive, scams occasionally surfaced. A case in point, in 1996 a Berkeley, California, wholesaler got caught diluting Kona beans with cheaper Latin American beans, after having fooled consumers, and some in the industry, for years.

Other specialty beans came from the Arab states and East Africa, including: Yemen, Ethiopia, Kenya, Tanzania, and Zimbabwe. The final group of coffees came from the Malay Archipelago, including such areas as Sumatra, Sulawesi, Java, and New Guinea. The most prominent coffee-growing region was Latin America. Brazil grew one-third of the world's coffee, but only a small portion of that was gourmet quality. The second-largest coffee-producing country was Colombia, which produced the most consistent coffee according to some analysts. Mexico, Ecuador, Peru, and Venezuela produced coffees most often used by specialty purveyors for blends, although better varieties from these countries were sometimes sold unblended. Some analysts believed Costa Rica grew the region's finest coffee, particularly the estate coffee, La Minita, from Tarrazu.

Conditions in Guatemala perhaps best represented the challenges facing industry firms doing business in the so-called Third World nations. The region produced a distinctive, sought-after coffee, but had a history of poverty, political turmoil, and human rights abuses. During 1994 and 1995, some human rights organizations picketed Starbucks, saying the company ignored the desperate conditions of Guatemalan coffee workers. Some analysts believed the company was singled out for attack because of its prominence and because the company was known for taking a stand on social issues. Starbucks countered that they did not own or control any of Guatemala's 33,000 coffee farms. The company also stated that they bought less than one-half of 1 percent of the world's coffee crop and lacked the leverage to solve entrenched social problems. In 1995, however, Starbucks wrote a "framework for a code of conduct," outlining what they expected from their suppliers: "We are dedicated to working with others to raise standards of health, education, workplace safety, and economic well-being in all communities where we do business."

Since 1997 Starbucks has collaborated in Guatemala with Appropriate Technology International on a program to improve efficiency and lessen environmental impact on some of Guatemala's small coffee farms. In 1996 Starbucks gave CARE (an international relief and development organization) a $250,000 donation, making it the charity's largest North American donor. Starbucks also merchandised "CARE packages" of coffees from countries where the charity operated (e.g., Kenya), donating some of the profit from those bean sales to CARE. In 2000 Starbucks increased its efforts to promote socially responsible coffee production and procurement and to appease activist groups. Starbucks agreed to sell Fair Trade Certified coffee, which is grown on small farms or cooperatives. This coffee will be bought for a minimum of $1.26 per pound and the proceeds will go directly to the farmers. In agreeing to these terms, Starbucks became the first large coffee company—specialty or run-of-the-mill—to adopt such a policy.

Despite the challenges presented with obtaining raw product abroad, there existed various international opportunities for specialty coffee purveyors outside the United States, particularly in the United Kingdom and Asia. Locations with the best opportunity for success included Singapore, Hong Kong, and Jakarta. Franchises in the United Kingdom included Seattle Coffee Co., Coffee Republic, Aroma and Costa Coffee with Nestlé announcing plans in April 1998 to open several Nescafé CoffeeHouse franchises, and Starbucks prepared to enter the market as well.

The primary challenge facing specialty coffee companies in the late 1990s continued to be how to expand while making their companies more competitive against the dominant Starbucks. The Specialty Coffee Association of America stated that the greatest opportunities for retailers had been between 1979 and 1983, but said ample room remained in the market. Orders were up 95.4 percent in 1998 in coffeehouses alone. "Specialty coffee is not a novelty anymore," remarked Michael Bregman, Second Cup Ltd., chairman and chief executive officer. "Most markets are fairly well served today, although there's lots of opportunity for growth. So, to go into a new market from scratch and expect them [consumers] to embrace a brand-new entrant into what's becoming a fairly competitive landscape requires a lot of capital, a lot of patience, and entails a lot of risk. We think that will continue to be the pattern."

FURTHER READING

Benson, Don. "Distinctive Coffee Blend Brings Success to Redlands, Calif., Business." *Knight Ridder/Tribune Business News,* 26 September 1999.

"The Cup Runneth: Retail and Specialty Products Are Helping Grow the Coffee and Tea Market." *Beverage Industry,* April 1997.

Dewar, Heather. "Decline in Shade Trees for Coffee Bushes May Be Linked to Decrease in Migratory Songbirds." *Knight Ridder/Tribune News Service,* 29 January 1997.

"Diedrich Coffee Co." Available from http://www.diedrich.com.

Earnest, Leslie. "Diedrich Coffee Struggles as Major Expansion Falters." *Los Angeles Times,* 2 December 2000.

Gillerlain, Sue. "State of the Industry Report 1998." *Specialty Coffee Retailer,* June 1998.

Gugino, Sam. "A Man Who Knows His Beans: If It Were up to John Martinez, Everyone Would Be Drinking Estate Coffee." *Cigar Aficionado,* August 1997.

Kramer, Louise. "Starbucks, P&G, Seattle Coffee in Grocery Scuffle." *Advertising Age,* 16 February 1998.

Kugiya, Hugo. "Seattle's Coffee King: Starbucks Boss Howard Schultz." *Seattle Times,* 15 December 1996.

McDonald, Barbara. "Specialty Coffee Prices May Heat up in Hurricane's Wake." *Supermarket News,* 18 January 1999.

Riell, Howard. "Harnessing Java's Jolt." *Supermarket Business,* March 1997.

Robert, Nancy. "Summertime Syrup Drinks." *Specialty Coffee Retailer,* June 1998.

Scarpa, James. "Gourmet Coffee Perks Up." *Restaurant Business,* 15 September 1999.

Schoenholt, Donald N. "The Times They Are a Changing." *Tea & Coffee Trade Journal,* April 1998.

Schulaka, Carly. "Boulder, Colo., Independent Coffee Shops Team up to Battle Corporate Chains." *Knight Ridder/Tribune Business News,* 15 June 1998.

Sheridan, Margaret. "Grinding It Out." *Restaurants & Institutions,* 15 May 1999.

"Specialty Coffee Association of America." Available from http://www.scaa.org.

"Thanksgiving Coffee Co." Available from http://www.thanksgivingcoffee.com.

"Whole Bean Coffee." *Discount Store News,* 20 March 2000.

Williams, Norman. "California Merger a Sign That Specialty Coffee Industry Is Maturing." *Knight Ridder/Tribune Business News,* 28 March 1997.

———. "Sacramento, Calif., Chain to Join with Wholesale Giant." *Knight Ridder/Tribune Business News,* 27 March 1997.

SPECIALTY TOURISM

From cycling to safaris, anthropological digs to spiritual retreats, the face of tourism changed dramatically during the late 1990s. Most often called specialty tourism, this rapidly emerging segment had begun to revolutionize the leisure travel industry as a whole. Once geared toward only high-end customers who were able to pay large sums of money for extravagant and individualized tours, by 2000 the industry had branched out, drawing in hundreds of thousands of "average" travelers annually, all interested in new and challenging ways to spend their leisure time.

In general, the bulk of specialty tours are targeted at specific groups—such as families, women, singles, or gays/lesbians—or specific activities, such as cycling, hiking, kayaking, or gambling. This targeted approach has led to a great deal of diversity in the field, with more than 80,000 companies offering services worldwide. Overall, the travel industry worldwide generated nearly $700 billion annually throughout the 1990s, and was expected to generate 100 million new jobs globally by 2010, according to the World Travel and Tourism Tax Policy Center. The specialty tourism segment of this market is expected to be increasingly significant, as much as 25 to 40 percent—more than $200 billion—by some estimates. Since the industry is so diverse, it is difficult to gauge the accuracy of these estimates, or give it an exact value. The trends, however, are obvious: specialty tourism will continue to grow and develop, and even emerge as a dominant force in the leisure travel industry well into the 21st century.

ORGANIZATION AND STRUCTURE

In general, the specialty travel industry has benefited from some emerging social, technological, and economic trends. Most importantly, travel has become easier, faster, and more important to our lifestyle. The cost of air and surface travel has been going down. There are more roads, air routes, airplanes, and surface vehicles to transport travelers to destinations previously very difficult to reach. Information for travelers is more abundant and more available. There are more businesses offering specialty services. The expanding network of local providers of lodging, guides, transport, equipment, and otherwise facilitating exploration of areas without a formal tourist infrastructure is growing rapidly. A prosperous economy has afforded more people the high incomes and security to expend discretionary income for the exotic experiences that specialty travel provides. And finally, specialty travel responds to the public's increased interest in healthy, active, educational activities.

There is no single organization or publication that speaks for the specialty travel industry, though several private entities attempt to provide unifying promotional services based on common needs for insurance, working with political or environmental policies, or for commercial promotion. Some operators are members of such traditional travel associations as the American Society of Travel Agents. The Adventure Travel Society of Boulder, Colorado, a private organization, has attempted to provide a forum for discussing adventure travel trends and problems. Each year they hold a World Congress for adventure travel at a different venue around the world. The organization, however, has no position on travel policy, nor does it include any democratic participation of members in establishing guidelines or directions. Generally, organizers of specialty travel may work with airlines or other transportation companies and derive a portion of their earnings from ticket commissions. In the 1990s, however, airlines dramatically reduced commissions to agents and some operators left the matter of reaching remote trip destinations in the hands of the traveler.

The lack of a unifying body for this segment of the travel industry also leads to marketing confusion. Often, adventure-travel land operators sell services through conventional travel agents, adventure agents, or directly to the consumer. This sometimes creates a dysfunctional marketing problem as diligent consumers may collect information from three or more different sources describing the price and features of a single adventure experience with varying criteria. Most specialty travel companies have Internet sites, which further complicate the problem of identifying and distinguishing services as unique. No conventions or common agreements have emerged to establish order in the marketing channels. Generally, consumers pay a fixed retail price, which may include commission for booking agents and remarketers at 10 to 35 percent, depending on booking volume and marketing commitment.

The retail costs of specialty travel vary greatly with destination, group size, duration, and types of service included. According to the Travelon Web site, which holds a database of several thousand trips, the cost of a guided, full-service, 8- to 12-day trip in Asia, Africa, or Latin America ranged from $900 to $2,500. Exploration cruising in the Amazon, Galápagos, or Antarctica generally cost between $200 and $400 per person per day. Himalayan trekking, African overland camping safaris, and other large group participation trips appealing to budget-minded travelers are usually priced under $100 per day, but may tally more than $200 per day. Cost was often a function of government fees. In Bhutan, for example, all local service providers were required by the Bhutan Tourism Ministry to charge overseas operators standard rates averaging more than $200 per person per day. The greatest costs of most African safaris are the fees for park entry, camping, and vehicle entry. Cost of tips to guides on all trips is usually additional. Consumers of specialty travel tend to enjoy above-average wealth, but trips must still be priced competitively. Specialty travel groups from different companies often meet at campsites, favored hotels, trailheads, key locations, or remote airports, and participants compare notes on price, quality, leadership, and experience. Every company understands the paramount importance of customer loyalty derived from having the best trip at the best price.

Though lacking any formal, collective organization, specialty tourism is categorized according to certain functional characteristics or business types. Tourism promotion offices are often associated with national, state, or regional government agencies and they usually promote all types of tourism. Inbound or receptive operators help groups of visitors or individual tourists and coordinate various portions of the overall itinerary, including lodging, transfers, activity reservations, guides, and meals. These inbound operators rely on local specialized service providers. These may be trekking, rafting, or diving operators; lodge owners; ski resorts; tour bus owners; or the owners and managers of any number of services. Most agents and operators who organize and conduct these trips are not members of organizations such as the American Society of Travel Agents or the U.S. Tour Operators Association, who serve to set standards and track development of the broader leisure tourism industry.

Specialty travel also relies on outbound operators, particularly in the case of foreign travel. Outbound operators design itineraries, print brochures, select inbound operators, specify services, negotiate prices, and promote services offered by their businesses as unique products for a national or international market. Often travelers who purchase vacation packages from outbound operators are not aware of this distinction. Outbound operators may rely on travel agents or independent trip organizers to fill trips. Each of the agents employed to reach the public may also specialize in some aspect of specialty travel, or more generally in leisure travel. Many travel agents have developed an interest or expertise in locating and evaluating special interest trips and the industry as a whole. Operators may try to fill trips through direct booking of clients and with the help of their own public relations agents. Increasingly, this purely promotional end of the specialty travel industry has proliferated to include the Internet, e-mail, video, magazines, database marketing, travel shows, and product or service cross-marketing schemes to reach prospective specialty travelers. All of these participate in the specialty travel industry, but none define it individually. Operators of specialty travel trips distinguish events less by the common standards than by the uniqueness of itineraries, leaders, style, qualifications, and value of services.

One of the best ways to assess the size and diversity of the industry is to attend one of the many adventure travel shows scheduled annually in large cities, including Chicago, Atlanta, Cincinnati, San Francisco, Baltimore, and New York. These shows bring participants, providers, tourist bureaus, guides, media publicists, adventure-travel site operators, airlines, hotel and lodge owners, and others with interest in adventure travel together. One can also gain a good sense for the diversity of this segment of the industry from the travel advertising sections of magazines such as *Outside, Sierra, Backpacker, Escape,* or *Men's Journal.*

ADVENTURE TOURISM

Adventure tourism is a broad term covering several smaller segments of specialty travel, all related to active pursuit of extreme sports, remote destinations, and unusual experiences. Increasing numbers of people are pursuing actively, physically, and intellectually challenging recreational experiences both close to home and in the most remote regions of the earth. In response to the demand for special travel information and services, thousands of small businesses around the world have emerged in the past 50 years.

Included are the more narrowly defined categories of adventure travel such as ecotourism, exploration cruising, trekking, mountaineering, rafting, kayaking, nature tourism, cultural tourism, scuba diving, dog sledding, and a panoply of other recreational outdoor sports. Many organized tours include a combination of these and other activities. All of these activities require a greater amount of exertion, higher degree of risk, and greater emphasis on the natural and cultural encounters of participants than conventional travel. Conversely, adventure tourism avoids or minimizes emphasis on luxury accommodations, nightlife, dining, relaxation, shopping, museums, or entertainment. More and more conventional tour and cruise operators, however, are expanding or redefining itineraries to include more active adventure activities as they detect market demand for authentic natural, cultural, and physical exploration on more spontaneous itineraries.

ECOTOURISM

Another large segment of the specialty travel industry is ecotourism. While not completely distinct from adventure tourism, ecotourism focuses on the experience of nature and culture while also paying attention to the economic and environmental impacts of travel itself. The adventure component of ecotourism may be more intellectual than physical. Some ecotourism operators seek the highest accommodation standards possible and avoid placing clients in circumstances demanding excessive physical exertion or use of primitive accommodations. Others presume clients are fit and flexible and that they anticipate the physical and intellectual challenges that accompany reaching pristine locations and/or cultures.

Ecotourism operators share a concern for enfranchising local communities in the economic process and benefits of tourism. Companies such as JOURNEYS International and International Expeditions also have nonprofit organizations or service divisions that help train local people in tourism-related fields and support schools, clinics, or local community projects. They view this as a way to help create a political and social environment for environmental preservation. Ecotourism is a process of learning, training, and improving the travel experience for participants and local hosts. It is also a way to move toward goals of sustainable activity and generate local community benefits without harming the local cultures or environments.

The recognized authority on ecotourism is the Ecotourism Society. This organization has memberships in various classes ranging from travelers to operators to researchers, all concerned with improving the standards and effects of ecotourism. They publish many pamphlets and brochures of interest to anyone trying to get started in the ecotourism business.

NATURE TOURISM

People more frequently formulate vacations around the primary objective of seeing and enjoying nature. Similar to ecotourism, nature tourism seeks nature for its own sake with less focus on human culture and less explicit concern for conservation or preservation. Bird watching, scuba diving, botany exploration, African wildlife safaris, sport fishing, whale watching, and other trips seek out nature and provide interpretation and education. Such trips may or may not support active conservation of the places they visit.

SPIRITUAL TOURISM

Increasing numbers of people join similarly educated or religiously oriented travelers to further spiritual understanding. Organized pilgrimages to holy places in the Middle East have taken place for decades, but in recent years more tours have promoted New Age spiritual orientations to visit ancient sites not usually associated with modern organized religion, such as the Mayan ruins of Central America or Stonehenge in Great Britain. Other trips adopt an agenda of self-realization similar to the vision quest of some Native American religions, without its doctrinal components. Many Americans explore Buddhism or other Eastern beliefs by joining tours to important religious sites in Asia, from the monasteries of Tibet and Nepal, to the ashrams of Hindu India to Islamic monuments of Pakistan or central Asia, to sacred sites of Native Americans in the United States.

SPORT TOURISM

Many people seek active vacations focusing on specific fitness activities. Bike trips, kayaking, golf, horseback riding, trekking, climbing, orienteering (competitive compass navigation), and even marathons increasingly draw people from all around the world to organized tours or events that may take place in exotic locations. Rafting, ballooning, sailing, and walking trips may require less physical exertion, but still demand a level of physical involvement, knowledge, and disciplined focus beyond the requirements of conventional leisure vacations. These types of vacations are typically organized by an individual or a company with knowledge of the sport and access to the specialized equipment required to perform the activity. They market expertise, access to optimal environments, the quality of their equipment and guides, and their ability to effectively coordinate necessary travel arrangements. The Discovery Channel's promotion of Eco-challenges, in which teams from around world compete to navigate a difficult course over difficult and varied terrain, has popularized a variety of sport tourism skills.

AFFINITY GROUP TRAVEL

Demographic factors offer another way to focus specialty travel events. Participants may all be members of an organization, occupation, ethnic group, or marital status. Operators organize trips for singles, families, grandparents and grandchildren, gays/lesbians, farmers, doctors, wine and food lovers, educators, students, or seniors. This kind of trip provides an experience tailored to specific common expectations and preferences of the group. Sometimes groups have an occupational focus that defines the primary goals of the trip. Health professionals, for example, may choose to take a trip such as the Himalayan Health Expedition, on which they have a full program of contact with local clinics, local healers, and shamans. A local doctor stimulates continuous dialogue with local people about health issues. Some operators offer an extensive variety of trips specifically geared to physicians.

Groups of people embarking on specialized trips appreciate knowing fellow participants will have the same personal and lifestyle views. Gay and lesbian tours are quite common, often with adventure or eco-tourist themes. Participants feel more comfort in knowing personal qualities such as sexual orientation or marital status will not create problems or confusion for other participants on the trip, allowing for more focus on the actual themes of the experience.

BACKGROUND AND DEVELOPMENT

The industry known as "specialty travel" was largely developed due to the increasing accessibility of once unknown, unattainable, or presumed hostile environments. Demystifying the dangers of wilderness, natural terrain, foreign travel, and wildlife created a psychological acceptance of the citizen as explorer and the traveler as student. Popular books, magazines, and movies about remote and wild places or attractive exotic locations also helped establish widespread desire to experience these places. Television programming on cable channels such as the Discovery Channel, the Travel Channel, the Learning Channel, and Animal Planet constantly remind viewers of the world they can explore. Additionally, specially designed clothing, luggage, medicines, and the spread of the English language have all facilitated adventure travel. Vastly expanded international air service has made it easier and quicker to reach exotic locations. And Peace Corps volunteers and other returned international workers bring back information on remote places and services for travelers. Increasingly, local residents of attractive adventure destinations were acquiring specialized activity knowledge, a hospitality infrastructure, and familiarity with international languages to allow them to act as guides and hosts for foreign visitors.

Prior to the 1970s, when the first special interest travel companies developed, travel excursions to remote areas were truly an adventure, undertaken without the benefit of guide books, organized services, or knowledgeable local interpretation. Simply reaching foreign lands was an all-consuming activity and contracting area diseases was expected. In the 1970s and 1980s, pioneering companies such as Mountain Travel, EarthWatch, JOURNEYS, and American Wilderness Experience established consistent activity and information-based itineraries that took the logistic hassles out of exotic travel and made it safer and healthier. Still, many people viewed specialty travel as more demanding or more uncertain than it really was and early growth was slow. Gradually, popular perception came to match reality, and this has spurred growth for all types of specialty travel.

In the 1990s, political and nonprofit environmental and wildlife preservation organizations began an almost religious support of ecotourism. Previously, conservation organizations viewed tourism as a destructive force in natural habitats. Research, however, demonstrated the economic rationale for some tourist activity helping natural and cultural preservation. Organizations such as the World Wildlife Fund, Conservation International, Sierra Club, and Nature Conservancy sponsor trips for members. They derive significant funding from adventure advertising in publications, and these groups actively support and facilitate development of accommodations in and adjacent to natural preserves where they conduct research.

This alliance between adventure travelers, local residents, and environmentalists serves as significant rationale in development planning for new facilities. The Sierra Club has always offered many trips that easily qualify as "adventure travel" or "ecotravel." More recently, organizations such as the World Wildlife Fund, Nature Conservancy, and Conservation International have offered more comfortable, less-physically demanding ecotravel. Some of these organizations are investing in large, luxurious expensive lodges adjacent to the natural areas they seek to preserve. The traveler who desires pristine nature and culture experiences (and will pay well for it) provides tangible, measurable, and direct measure of nature preservation benefits. This has become more convincing to policy makers than hypothetical and elusive rationales of preserving genetic diversity, protecting natural capital, balancing global gas emissions, or even reducing flooding from disturbed watersheds. Increasingly, adventure travel companies are closely aligned with efforts to preserve natural and cultural environments.

The growth of specialty travel as a broad industry in the last 20 years also reflects globalization of the underlying activities. In a world economy people are more interested in seeing the rest of the world, not just their own community, in the context of their own experience and interests. The concepts of "world records," "wonders of the world," and "world-class experience" have drawn people to take up hobbies and pastimes that extend that sense of personal interest worldwide. Specialty travel providers must understand not only tourism concepts, but also the underlying interests of the travelers.

Another important element in the development of an expanding specialty travel industry over the past two decades has included equipment innovation. It is now possible to travel lighter, more comfortably, and

more safely to previously hostile or inaccessible places. Safer climbing equipment, scuba gear, rafts, and other gear have taken much of the previous risk out of more adventurous travel. Lighter, stronger fabrics, better medicines, improved maps, field guides, and custom luggage have all become added incentives to prospective travelers seeking to turn fantasies into actual exploration.

PIONEERS IN THE FIELD

The merger of two of the oldest adventure travel companies formed Mountain Travel-Sobek (MTS) in 1991. MTS offers relatively high-priced group travel to all continents and is often considered a pioneer in both designing itineraries and promotional techniques. They currently offer more than 100 trips around the world. The company has changed ownership several times since its founding in 1967 and it is currently based in California.

JOURNEYS International, founded in 1978 by a former Peace Corps volunteer and his wife, specializes in active natural and cultural explorations of more than 60 worldwide destinations. Many of JOURNEYS trips support local conservation and cultural preservation projects. Local experts in each destination lead the group's programs. JOURNEYS is particularly known for Himalayan trekking, active African safaris, and small group adventure cruises.

American Wilderness Experience (AWE) is one of the oldest U.S. adventure travel companies. AWE describes its mission as promoting adventure travel, with dedication to program quality, customer service, and a commitment to support wilderness preservation, recycling, and ecologically sensitive tours. All AWE programs take place in North America.

CURRENT CONDITIONS

Economic prosperity in the United States, retirement security, the financial success of baby boomers, and the information revolution all served to expand the specialty tourism industry in the late 1990s. About 98 million U.S. adults took an adventure vacation in the second half of the decade, according to the Travel Industry Association of America's National Travel Survey. The Internet and the World Wide Web have made information about travel more accessible to anyone with a computer. They have also enabled travelers to contact local operators in remote places directly, resulting in reduced use of U.S.-based travel organizers and agents. According to *Travel Weekly,* since the mid-1990s airline ticket revenues have declined drastically as airlines reduce commissions and complete their own sales. While some adventure travel promoters suggest that this is a reason to expect travel agents will sell more adventure travel (a high-price product with at least a 10 percent commission to agents), fewer and fewer consumers are using travel agents to make their arrangements.

Yet, ironically, the same forces that expanded the industry have constrained the growth of new and established companies. The full employment economy has reduced the frequency and duration of American vacations, especially among the educated and high-income demographic groups. This has limited the growth of international trips and more lengthy expeditionary travel. The average length of American vacations was decreasing. As baby boomers aged, they were more able to afford the relatively high price of organized adventure travel. The debilitating effects of aging, however, have constrained participation in more active and physically demanding activities such as trekking, skiing, mountaineering, and scuba diving.

Other difficulties have also arisen. Highly publicized stories of criminal or terrorist actions against tourists in Egypt, Uganda, Turkey, and Colombia have created a generalized fear of foreign trips in travelers who might otherwise leave the United States. The risk of AIDS, cholera, virulent tuberculosis, and malaria in developing countries may seem like imposing obstacles to would-be travelers. There is a trend toward higher visa fees, higher tourism taxes, and increased park visitor fees in many foreign destinations. This was pushing the cost of international travel above the rate of inflation, or the rate that travel prices increase in North America.

These trends of shorter vacations and perceived instability favor U.S.-based operators of domestic adventure experiences such as cycling, rafting, whale watching, canoeing, and skiing. Participation in these activities within the United States insulates customers from political risk and provides a complete adventure experience in a relatively short period. Similarly, Canada, Europe, Australia, and New Zealand tend to be viewed as safe, stable, healthy destinations, and these will probably witness a higher rate by Americans visiting for specialty travel tours than less-developed areas of the world.

The Internet posed a dilemma for specialty tourism operators. If they create a Web site accessible to the public, they very visibly compete with other agents selling the same trip. This is particularly true if the site accepts direct bookings through the Web site or if they publish a toll-free telephone number for reservations. No tourism operators feel confident that a Web site will substitute for the traditional color brochure or catalog, yet virtually every operator feels a need for a credible Web presence. As a largely information-based industry, many operators feel Internet promotion will be increasingly important in the next decade and will provide an essential, if not yet fully defined promotional tool.

NEW BUSINESS START-UPS

Because reputation and references are so important for acquiring customers, new operators should expect four to six lean years while getting started. Many who lack substantial start-up capital must keep a part-time job until the business becomes established. Still, many newly established adventure travel companies do not survive into a second or third year. Due to the relatively high risk involved with travel to less-developed countries, insurance to cover professional liability and accidents is very expensive, especially for new operators without a proven safety record. This, combined with the well-known litigious character of the American consumer, has ended the existence of many start-up specialty travel businesses.

Another frequent cause of business failure is related to limited business opportunity. Specialty operators, for example, often have problems if they can offer certain tours only during certain seasons, and if the market they serve is too narrowly focused. Often, the specialty travel market is dispersed and hard to reach through traditional marketing avenues. Many excellent, well-planned, and fairly priced trips do not depart because the promoters failed to recruit enough participants in time to meet deposit or air reservation deadlines. When a specialty trip is sold to a broader market to achieve minimum enrollments, trip organizers and operators are often faced with participants with varied expectations and purposes. Still, according to the World Tourism Organization, as cited by the Ecotourism Society, 595 million travelers in 1997 spent an estimated $425 billion, and this expenditure was expected to grow by about 6.7 percent per year over the next two decades. The *Green Travel Newsletter* quoted the International Travel and Adventure Exposition organizers as estimating that adventure travel is a $200 billion industry, of which only 37 percent of tours are booked through travel agents.

INDUSTRY LEADERS

The specialty travel industry is diverse and rather specialized, consisting of thousands of companies that each provide unique, and often individualized services. It is therefore difficult to identify truly dominant companies in the field. There are, however, leading firms within different categories.

One of the first specialty travel companies, Earth-Watch is a unique nonprofit organization that helps sponsor and fund scientific research through expedition fees, paid by travelers who are then allowed to join the expedition in a limited capacity. EarthWatch works with scientists who make support arrangements for volunteer assistants, and as a nonprofit organization, some of the trips' costs are tax deductible.

International Expeditions, based in Helena, Alabama, specializes in quality guided nature explorations with particular focus on tropical rain forests and the African savannahs. They emphasize strong academic leadership and invest in training for many local guides in travel destinations.

Wilderness Travels was founded in the late 1970s, and offers quality group nature and cultural trips throughout the world. They have strong programs in the Galápagos, Peru, Turkey, and the Himalayas. Generally catering to the higher income market, these trips offer the best available standards of accommodation and dining in remote locations.

With more than 150 different bicycling, walking, hiking and multisport vacations in more than 85 destinations around the world, Backroads has become a leading specialty travel provider. In 2000 alone, Backroads offered more than 1,500 scheduled departures.

Abercrombie and Kent (A&K) of Oakbrook, Illinois, is an upscale company that bridges the conventional leisure travel market and specialty travel fields. Well known for cruises, safaris, and escorted trips to exotic locations, A&K is one of the most successful operators in the industry, marketing its programs worldwide through travel agents. A&K has 27 offices worldwide and their tours travel to 100 countries across the globe.

Victor Emanuel Nature Tours (VENT) specializes in birding tours. One of the oldest birding companies, VENT offers trips featuring expert birders and uses the best available accommodations for its relatively high-priced programs. They are also designing a program for birding cruises. In 1999 they offered nearly 140 tours.

WORK FORCE

By 2000, there were more than 83,000 adventure tour operators worldwide, according to the Adventure Travel Society. The Specialty Travel Index, which includes only the larger companies selling to the U.S. travel industry, listed 600, most of which were based in North America. The typical specialty travel operator was a small business employing the owner and two to five other people, none of whom were certified travel agents. There were no formal academic credentials required, though local licenses are required for some guides.

Most employees and owners of specialty travel companies do not spend time leading trips. While a single owner-operator-guide may be a basic model for operation, most people find that the challenge of running a profitable specialty travel business has more to do with understanding business, advertising, computers, communication, personnel management, and legal compliance than navigating difficult terrain. Most growing companies promoting international specialty travel require a competent staff of writers, salespeople, reservation agents, bookkeepers, and computer technicians to remain profitable. Many companies contract with guides as freelancers for individual trips or for a season of trips. Professional credentials, licenses, or training may be required.

While leading or guiding trips may be the most fun and hold the most glamour, guide pay and benefits are usually quite low, and the work can be physically and psychologically exhausting. Guide burnout is common, and extended guiding can be hard on personal relationships. Also, the work is often seasonal. Still, more people are seeking guide positions than are available for many types of trips. Most companies hiring guides require demonstrated leadership and communication skills, authoritative knowledge of the skills or contents of the activity, and some previous experience in the field. International specialty travel operators often hire local guides in destination countries, and company employees accompanying groups during international travel is relatively uncommon.

Specialty travel, especially adventure travel, is often a risky business. Owners of adventure companies are constantly concerned about safety, liability, and accurate record keeping. Errors in bookings, planning, reservations, or judgment can have extreme financial, legal, or medical consequences. At the same time, travel is traditionally a low-paying industry. According to the *Occupational Outlook Handbook,* "median annual earnings of travel agents on straight salary with less than one year experience were $16,400; from one to three years, $20,400; from three to five years, $22,300." The publication noted the problem this creates in competing for good people who can earn more in other industries.

In order to promote and sell the services a specialty tourist business offers, staff must have first-hand knowledge of the tours' activities and destinations. Being a specialized business requires more first-hand knowledge than generalized tour operators need. High quality, detailed written materials, reading lists, check lists, and predeparture booklets must be constantly rewritten and revised to emphasize the capacity of the operator to provide a safe and satisfying trip.

Owners hiring staff into public or client contact positions must be cautious in educating the staff to represent the company's policies and products accurately. Satisfaction with the personal treatment a company affords the traveler is a major factor in the participant taking future trips or recommending the company to friends.

AMERICA AND THE WORLD

In a 2000 study, the World Travel and Tourism Council estimated that tourism provided more than 12 percent of the jobs in the European Union, and accounted for more than 13 percent of the region's gross domestic product. While exact figures aren't available for the specialty tourism segment of the industry, it has been estimated that in the late 1990s, 25-40 percent of the European leisure travel industry consisted of so-called specialty and/or adventure tourism. This figure is not surprising, given that many industrialized countries in Europe have government support for vacations. In general, the average European vacation is more than three weeks in duration, as opposed to the average American vacation, which typically ranges from one week to 10 days.

The challenge of permits, visas, acquiring local transport, and foreign languages and culture often compound the adventure for travelers outside of the United States and provide further incentive for the traveler to seek the help of a specialized operator to assist with these requirements. Responsible adventure travel operators provide extensive safety, medical, cultural, environmental, and ecological information to foreign-bound travelers to minimize problems, as many areas attractive to adventure travelers have no

established local tourism industry. Accommodations, meals, standards of sanitation, legal and security services, and transportation fall far short of what would be reasonable minimum expectations in the United States.

Many international specialty travel operators pay special attention to the Travel Advisories and Warnings issued by the U.S. Department of State in planning or canceling trips to troubled areas. In addition, the advice and standards established by the Centers for Disease Control and Prevention in Atlanta often forms a basis for the health and immunization suggestions given by operators to clients traveling overseas. Both of these organizations have Web sites and e-mail lists to which operators may subscribe for current information.

For Americans traveling overseas the most popular adventure destinations include the Himalayas for trekking, east and southern Africa for safaris, southern Europe for bicycling and sailing trips, Costa Rica and Belize for tropical nature tours, Peru for hiking and pre-Columbian culture experience, and the Galápagos Islands of Ecuador and Antarctica for exploration cruises. Europe, perennially popular with conventional group tourists, also has a thriving specialty travel industry focusing on walking, bicycling, traditional cultural experiences, and dining and natural environment exploration.

In Latin America, emerging destinations include Panama, where visitors combine tours of the Panama Canal with rain-forest exploration. In Bolivia, the native cultures of the Andes, Amazon rain forest, and Inca ruins are attracting increasing numbers of visitors. The unique ecosystems and reverse seasons of Argentina and Chile and the spectacular scenery of Patagonia hold increasing interest for North American visitors.

Outer space is the new frontier for future adventure travel. Several companies suggested that they are prepared to book commercial spacecraft as soon as it becomes possible. More terrestrial limits for future specialty trips include circumpolar exploration cruises and icebreaker expeditions to the North Pole. In Asia, companies are offering hiking trips to remote parts of Tibet and Yunnan, China, climbing in Kyrgystan, dinosaur digs in Mongolia, and sea kayaking in the Far East. In Africa, adventurous travelers now travel in Mozambique, Ethiopia, Mali, Burkina Faso, Chad, and the Ivory Coast. Kilimanjaro climbs are extremely popular; Niger, Sudan, Somalia, the Congo, Rwanda, Algeria, and Libya, however, are still beyond the interest of even the most adventurous traveler.

FURTHER READING

"Adventure Travel Society." Englewood, CO: Adventure Travel Society, 2000. Available from http://www.adventuretravel.com.

"Backroads Fact Sheet." Berkeley, CA: Backroads, 2000. Available from http://www.backroads.com/media/factsmedia.html.

Ecotourism Society. "Ecotourism Explorer." North Bennington, VT: Ecotourism Society, 2000. Available from http://www.ecotourism.org.

"Explorers Index." *EXPLORE Magazine,* 1999. Available from http://www.hillside-visual.com/explore/explorers/weblinks.html.

Green Travel Newsletter. Auburn, MA: Green Travel Network, 1999. Available from http://www.greentravel.com.

Jacobs, Judy. "Evolution of Operators." *Travel Counselor Special Report,* February 1999.

Karwacki, Judy. "Indigenous Ecotourism: Overcoming Challenges." *Ecotourism Society Newsletter,* January/March 1999.

Lindberg, Kreg, et al. *Ecotourism: A Guide for Planners and Managers.* North Bennington, VT: Ecotourism Society, 1993.

McLaren, Deborah. *Rethinking Tourism and Ecotravel.* West Hartford, CT: Kumarian Press, 1998.

"Queen of the Mountain: Operators Are Developing More Women-Only Itineraries." *Travel Weekly,* 10 October 1996.

"Specialty Travel Index." San Anselmo, CA: Specialty Travel Index, 2000. Available from http://www.specialtytravel.com.

U.S. Bureau of Labor Statistics. *2000-2001 Occupational Outlook Handbook.* Available from http://www.bls.gov/oco/ocos173.htm.

STORAGE NETWORKING

INDUSTRY SNAPSHOT

Where corporate computer networks sprawl and data storage and retrieval grow ever more unwieldy, the storage networking industry promises to restore some semblance of efficiency and reliability. Storage networking is the business of selling hardware, software, and services to organizations with complex mass-storage needs.

The gist of storage networking is that specialized storage systems and software can do a better job at mundane file serving, backups, and other storage-related tasks in network environments than ordinary multipurpose network servers can. To wit, technologies such as storage area networks (SANs) and network-attached storage devices are added to existing Unix, NetWare, and Windows NT networks in order to take some of the burden off application servers and other network resources, improving speed, accessibility, reliability, and even cost-efficiency along the way.

With storage needs at data-laden companies now being tallied in terabytes, or trillions of bytes, the market for sophisticated storage systems, sometimes called enterprise storage, is flourishing. And while these systems were originally aimed mostly at Fortune 1000 companies, storage-networking vendors are beginning to target medium-sized organizations as well. According to one estimate, the market for such storage products and services in the late 1990s and early 2000s was doubling each year. The SAN market alone, according to analysts at Strategic Research Corp., is expected to surge tenfold between 1998 and 2003, topping $27 billion by the end of the period.

ORGANIZATION AND STRUCTURE

Networks have always contained storage resources, but not all of these qualify as storage network devices. Storage networking describes a fairly narrow set of technologies centered around dedicated yet versatile storage appliances that are based on open standards, high performance, and nearly universal connectivity with different kinds of network operating systems and hardware. Although storage networks had many precursors, especially in the mainframe arena, the current notion of storage networking came about largely in the late 1990s.

The set of technologies includes hardware, software, and services. More specifically, storage networks usually come in one of two hardware configurations: network-attached storage and SANs. These configurations consist of one or more—usually more—hardware devices that are attached to an existing computer network to provide greater storage capacity, greater manageability, and better performance. Storage networking also involves software for managing storage. Finally, services include consulting about storage needs, implementing and customizing a storage network, and in the extreme, hosting and managing a storage network for a client. Each aspect of storage networking is described below.

NETWORK-ATTACHED STORAGE

Network-attached storage (NAS) is a simple but powerful concept: let a speedy, focused appliance deal with storing and retrieving files so network servers can stick to the business of running applications and more advanced operations.

NAS devices, often called appliances or specialized servers, are the entry-level gear in storage networking. Priced anywhere from $1,000 to $80,000 or more, NAS servers are often used to enhance network performance on a work-group or department level; a single NAS server usually isn't enough to fix a big corporate network's storage woes. NAS systems can involve simply one such device hooked up to a local area network, or any number of NAS devices strung together.

Either way, NAS systems are optimized for saving and retrieving user files and communicating with other machines. They run on simplified, nimble operating systems that don't get bogged down in running databases, delivering e-mail, or hosting the boss's solitaire tournaments.

Inside the box, NAS servers typically contain a microprocessor, a generous helping of RAM, an array of hard disk drives (although some use optical or tape drives), and a variety of external ports for connecting the NAS to the network. Most NAS hardware can be readily upgraded, say, to add more storage capacity or additional network adapters. Top-notch systems use high-speed connection architecture, such as Fibre Channel or Ultra SCSI, to keep the whole system running at peak speed. Higher-end NAS devices also include one or more mechanisms (software or hardware or both) for fault tolerance and error handling, meaning the system can recover quickly and successfully from a problem without losing data or going out of service for long stretches—or better yet, never go down in the first place.

NAS servers are also designed for easy connectivity with existing network resources. The software is meant to be easily administered—often through Web- or Java-based utilities—and individual computers and servers can access the NAS much as they would any other shared resource on the network.

STORAGE AREA NETWORKS

Storage area networks (SANs) fill many of the same broad functions as NAS, but do so on a much grander scale and are decidedly more complex. In fact, they can contain any number of separate interworking devices, so there's no precise definition of what constitutes a SAN.

Five things are needed to achieve the kind of reliability, interconnectivity, and speed associated with an effective SAN: (1) a pool of logically (although not necessarily physically) centralized storage devices, be they disk arrays, tape drives, or otherwise; (2) at least two network servers to access the storage pool; (3) at least one hub or switch to mediate traffic between the servers and the storage devices; (4) a high-speed connection, usually via a Fibre Channel fiber-optic interface, between the hub and each of the servers and storage devices; and (5) software to manage it all. These are just the minimum requirements, and the way they're all put together has a huge impact on a SAN's performance and reliability.

Like NAS, a SAN frees up general network servers for more application processing, making networks run faster. By centralizing storage—a throwback to mainframe precepts—SANs also make network administration more efficient, and in many cases, have a lower total cost of ownership than conventional server-centric storage.

Whereas NAS servers are nearly plug-and-play devices, SANs often require a great deal of planning, consulting, and even integration work to implement. Indeed, heavy-duty SANs at big companies can easily cost several million dollars to set up. Clearly SANs are aimed at high-volume storage needs, whether for legions of general office workers or a smaller number of storage-intensive users such as graphic artists and medical image technicians. SANs likewise differ in that the file system isn't contained on the storage device, but on the server accessing the storage. SANs also have an extraordinary capacity to grow as needs change, known as scalability in the business, by adding more devices to the storage pool.

SOFTWARE

Software is mainly an issue for SANs, since NAS servers generally come with their own administration software. Most analysts believe software is key to realizing SANs' potential, although some also warn that management software for SANs is still underdeveloped.

SAN management software is the core of centralized storage administration. In addition to helping all the devices in the SAN function properly, these software utilities enable network administrators to configure SANs, allocate space effectively, and monitor storage resources.

SERVICES

The service side of the industry is again mostly aimed at SAN implementation and maintenance. Some SAN vendors, in fact, routinely sell service contracts along with the hardware. SAN services usually begin with consulting, which involves sizing up the client's current resources and present and future needs. The service vendor then formulates a network design that best uses resources and meets the client's needs.

Once a customer signs off on the plan, the work of implementing it begins. Implementation includes customizing old and new hardware so it all works with the SAN (for example, adding the appropriate network adapters), physically installing the new equipment and fiber-optic connections, and configuring software to run and administer the SAN. Most, if not all, of these tasks could be done by a customer's own information technology (IT) department; because SANs and the fiber optics that support them are relatively new technologies, however, service vendors may have expertise that internal staff lack.

Finally, service vendors perform ongoing maintenance and support of storage networks. This includes training, on-site repairs and troubleshooting, remote systems monitoring and problem detection, and phone-based technical support. Such services may be offered as part of the hardware sale, or may be purchased separately.

BACKGROUND AND DEVELOPMENT

Although storage networking has roots in mainframe technology and other areas of network computing, the current concept came about in the late 1990s due to four developments:

- Large computer networks running Unix, NetWare, and Windows NT were hobbled by costly, overtaxed all-purpose servers and spiraling storage needs.

- Storage device makers shifted away from proprietary technology and toward open standards that allowed different vendors' machines to work together.

- Standards groups and storage vendors agreed on new specifications for high-speed fiber-optic data transfer, namely Fibre Channel, that could support the speed and flexibility needed to ease the burdens on networks.

- Storage vendors focused increasingly on high performance over mere functionality.

Centralized storage was a common feature of mainframes since their inception. As businesses adopted distributed personal computer networking in the 1980s and 1990s, however, storage became increasingly fragmented and inefficient, parceled across different servers and sometimes different operating systems in what has come to be known as "islands of storage." Storage management was often done on a server-by-server basis, making it time consuming and occasionally technically challenging. When existing servers were maxed out, network managers added more storage capacity to individual servers or simply tacked on more servers, further fragmenting the organization's storage resources into an expansive archipelago.

Previous attempts at mass-storage networking met with mixed results. NAS-like file servers were used in Unix environments as early as the 1980s, but they had several deficiencies. They weren't particularly fast, were hard to manage, and tended to work only with specific kinds of systems. By the mid-1990s more options and flexibility had come along, but performance and interoperability—the ability to work with all kinds of machines and software—were still limited.

FIBER-OPTIC INTERFACE KEY

Emerging fiber-optic networking standards hastened the development of high-performance storage networking. Work on the Fibre Channel fiber-optic computer interface standard began in 1988 under the auspices of the American National Standards Institute and later under a collaboration between IBM Corp., Hewlett-Packard Co., and Sun Microsystems, Inc. called the Fibre Channel Systems Initiative. A few Fibre Channel standards were crafted for various purposes; the most popular for storage devices was the Fibre Channel Arbitrated Loop (FC-AL).

By 1994 a blueprint was in place for what Fibre Channel could offer—and the offerings were considerable. The technology boasted up to 1-gigabit-per-second data transfer rates (although 100 megabits was the standard in first-generation interfaces), long-distance connectivity up to 10 kilometers, and the ability to connect over a hundred devices in a single segment. By contrast, the aging, bulky small computer system interface (SCSI) at the time supported speeds only up to 20 megabits per second (40 Mbps more recently), a distance range of about 25 meters, and the ability to connect just 15 devices.

Importantly, Fibre Channel could also act both as a standard network communication interface and as a data channel for direct communication between a processor and a peripheral device. This was key to separating storage devices from processing on a network, paving the way for SANs and NAS servers. Fibre Channel also supported other communication protocols, including SCSI and the popular Internet

STORAGE SERVICE PROVIDERS: LETTING SOMEONE ELSE HANDLE STORAGE

With storage area network (SAN) technology being so complex and expensive, it's little wonder that a market for outsourcing storage needs exists. Storage service providers (SSPs) tap into this demand by providing general storage and SAN-like services, mostly to large companies and e-commerce start-ups. In addition to removing the administrative burdens of operating a large storage pool, SSPs can provide high-performance storage and tremendous flexibility to small Internet start-ups that can't afford to purchase the hardware on their own. According to one estimate, paying for high-end storage outsourcing services could save a company up to 35 percent over owning and maintaining its own storage network.

SSPs own the storage hardware and software and lease it out to companies, often charging a monthly fee based on the amount of storage needed. The cost could be as low as a few cents per megabyte, but most services expect clients to rent many gigabytes at a time. A few, though, such as Driveway Corp., offer smaller amounts of space for free, and then charge only after the customer reaches a certain level.

Outsourced storage prices also vary with the level of service and performance the customer requires. SSPs charge more for high availability guarantees, which can approach 99.999 percent from some vendors, and for management services such as backups, data recovery, and performance and needs monitoring. Customers can use SSPs for either primary storage, the active storage needed for day-to-day operations, or secondary storage, which is a backup system.

Customers can access the SSP in a couple of ways. High-end customers can get wired via fiber optics directly to the SSP's hardware. In theory, this service would be as fast as if the hardware were sitting right on the client's premises. Lower-cost services, on the other hand, use a simpler albeit slower Internet connection. Some SSPs have teamed up with Internet service providers and application service providers to reach customers and offer a package of services.

A bevy of contenders has sprung up to claim a stake in the SSP field. They include @Backup, Centripetal Inc., Driveway Corp., StorageNetworks, Inc., and USinternetworking, Inc.

Protocol, which made it highly compatible with existing technologies.

By 1996 enough manufacturers supported Fibre Channel and had begun to introduce devices to make it a commercially viable technology. Though it had helped create the Fibre Channel standards, IBM continued to tout a maverick interface called serial storage architecture (SSA). Despite IBM's clout, SSA was roundly seen as inferior to Fibre Channel—and even to SCSI—so few other manufacturers supported it. Still, IBM's competing interface contributed to uncertainty about Fibre Channel's future. Finally, in 1996 IBM entered a new collaboration with disk-drive giant Seagate Technology, Inc. and system-board manufacturer Adaptec, Inc. to meld SSA and FC-AL into a new interface called Fibre Channel Enhanced Loop, or simply Fibre Channel Loop. While the features of the new interface had yet to be determined, IBM's action was interpreted as its long-awaited endorsement of Fibre Channel and helped build confidence about Fibre Channel both in the industry and in the marketplace.

STORAGE NETWORKING COMES OF AGE

For the next couple years, storage vendors launched increasingly robust products using the emerging standards and began ramping up marketing as well. Meanwhile, the furious growth of the Internet and e-commerce had begun to multiply companies' storage problems. Web sites collected gigabyte-upon-gigabyte of traffic logs and potential customer data, all needing to be stored and analyzed. By some calculations, large companies' storage needs were doubling annually.

By 1998 a recognizable storage networking industry was in place. Leading companies that year formed the Storage Networking Industry Association, a Mountain View, California, trade group dedicated to promoting the technology and continuing collaboration on standards.

CURRENT CONDITIONS

The two dominant storage networking paradigms, NAS and SANs, have attracted an enthusiastic—and lucrative—following thus far. Estimates vary widely; market researcher Strategic Research Corp. predicted that the SAN side of the business, including hardware, software, and services, would be worth $14.8 billion in 2000, up fourfold from 1998. The number could surpass $27 billion in 2003, the firm said. Systems-management products for SANs were expected to leap from $500 million in 2000 to $3.3 billion by 2004. International Data Corp., meanwhile, forecast SAN market growth of 66 percent to reach $10.8 billion by 2003, which would account for nearly one-fourth of the external storage market. Nonetheless, a survey by Enterprise Management Associates of Boulder, Colorado, found that 80 percent of information technology professionals were hesitant about jumping on board with SANs due to a perceived lack of technology maturity, high costs, and a shortage of staff resources and expertise, according to *Washington Technology.*

Some analysts believe that NAS devices will reach a broader market faster because they are much cheaper and easier to install. Their relatively low price also may means the market is smaller, though. Peripheral Concepts, another research firm, estimated the NAS market at $2.2 billion as of 1999. Conservative forecasts pin the NAS sector at $7.2 billion in 2004. Using different numbers, Dataquest Inc. forecast the NAS market to reach $10.5 billion by 2002.

INDUSTRY LEADERS

Several of the industry's largest players are large, integrated computer manufacturers such as Compaq Computer Corp.; Hewlett-Packard; Hitachi, Ltd.; IBM; and Sun Microsystems. These companies often sell storage products as part of large new computer systems, such as mainframes or midrange servers, or as add-ons for customers who already own systems by the manufacturer. Among this group, in the late 1990s Compaq held the leading presence in the storage market, followed by IBM.

EMC

A diverse mix of smaller, more focused companies also produce storage networking products and services. One of the biggest of the independent manufacturers is EMC Corp., of Hopkinton, Massachusetts. Building SAN equipment was a natural extension for EMC, which had long made storage hardware for SAN-like configurations for mainframe systems. EMC sells its high-end equipment directly as well as through resellers and larger computer system manufacturers. In 1999 EMC's total revenues exceeded $6.7 billion, up an impressive 24 percent from a year earlier. Storage hardware accounted for 85 percent of EMC's revenues. Sales of two of its leading storage-networking products, Connectrix (for SANs) and Cel-

erra (for NAS), surged more than 40 percent. The company also markets storage software and services. To further solidify its place in the midrange market, in 1999 EMC acquired Data General Corp., maker of the CLARiiON line of storage products. The following year, the company purchased SOFTWORKS, a maker of data storage software.

NETWORK APPLIANCE

Network Appliance Corp., based in Sunnyvale, California, is another producer of higher-end storage-networking devices. In its fiscal 2000, Network Appliance, or NetApp, as it's known, posted a nearly 100 percent gain in revenue, a trend it maintained through the late 1990s, reaching $579.3 million for the period. At that time, storage solutions for e-commerce activities made up a third of NetApp's sales. Most of NetApp's products are NAS servers.

GADZOOX NETWORKS

Further down the food chain, Gadzoox Networks, Inc. of San Jose, California, is a leading supplier of Fibre Channel hubs, routers, and switches for SANs. For its 2000 fiscal year, Gadzoox pulled in almost $47.9 million, up over 97 percent from the year before, although it still wasn't turning a profit. In 1999 the small publicly traded company had an extensive indirect sales channel of 120 partners in 23 countries. Gadzoox's purchase of SmartSAN Systems, Inc. in 2000 gave it coverage in the SAN router market.

VERITAS SOFTWARE

In the SAN software arena, Veritas Software Corp. of Mountain View, California, is considered the largest vendor of storage management software. In 1998 the company took over Seagate's storage software business in a deal that gave Seagate a controlling stake in Veritas, though two years later Veritas purchased its shares back from Seagate. In 1999 Veritas reported $700 million in revenue, up more than 70 percent on the year.

RESEARCH AND TECHNOLOGY

Even though the industry has embraced Fibre Channel as its connectivity medium, particularly for SANs, rancorous debate continues about whether it's cost-effective to deploy the pricey fiber optics. Fibre Channel's main opponent is Ethernet, the predominant network interface for local area networks. Ethernet has undergone various upgrades over time, most recently in the late 1990s when the Gigabit Ethernet standard was unveiled. At this rate, some analysts said, Ethernet delivers performance comparable to Fibre Channel—and using cheaper technology that IT workers are more familiar with. In addition, future Ethernet specifications could potentially allow data transmissions of up to 10 gigabits per second (Gbps), whereas the current Fibre Channel road map goes only to two Gbps.

Separately, yet another connectivity standards initiative was close to being completed, this one with implications far beyond storage interfaces. In 1999 two rival camps developing standards for a new industry-wide high-bandwidth input/output medium agreed on a technical framework called the InfiniBand Architecture. The Next Generation Input/Output group had been backed by Intel Corp., while the Future Input/Output group had Compaq, Hewlett-Packard, and IBM on its side. The 1999 truce ended a couple years of standoffs and signaled potentially sweeping changes for all forms of computer input/output connections. The new medium, which could support copper and fiber-optic cables, was expected to reach speeds up to six Gbps, with room for growth in the future.

The InfiniBand Trade Association, the official trade group promulgating the standard, optimistically predicted that InfiniBand devices would begin hitting the market en masse in late 2001, but widespread adoption will likely take much longer. International Data Corp. expected about 100,000 servers would be supporting Infiniband by the end of 2001, with 800,000 servers signing on a year later. If InfiniBand catches on as intended, it could replace Fibre Channel altogether.

FURTHER READING

Adhikari, Richard. "Keeping Your Storage SANity." *Planet IT,* 13 November 1998. Available from http://www.planetit.com.

Bucholtz, Chris. "The Shifting Winds of Technology—How Much of Tomorrow's Cool Technology is Just Hot Air?" *VARBusiness,* 18 December 2000.

Chen, Elaine. "FC-AL Becomes a Show Stopper." *Electronic News,* 25 November 1996.

Edwards, Morris. "Mr. SAN Man, Send Me a Dream." *Communications News,* March 1999.

———. "Storage Needs Piling Up." *Communications News,* April 1998.

Fetters, Dave. "All that NAS." *Network Computing,* 12 July 1999.

———. "Siren Call of Online Commerce Makes SANs Appealing." *Planet IT,* 31 May 1999. Available from http://www.planetit.com.

Garvey, Martin J. "More Storage, Less Money." *Information Week,* 19 April 1999.

———. "Storage Nets: What Works?" *Information Week,* 6 November 2000.

Larsen DeCarlo, Amy. "SANs Appeal—Vendors Bulk Up SAN Switches to Meet Providers' Expanding Storage Needs." *tele.com,* 13 November 2000.

Lineback, J. Robert. "Fast Fibre Channel Could Redefine Local Area Network, I/O Worlds." *Electronic Business Buyer,* October 1994.

Matthews, Guy. "Infrastructure: It's Worth Watching This Unpredictable Storage Space." *Network News,* 13 December 2000.

Ohlson, Kathleen. "Network Storage Standards on Tap." *Computerworld,* 31 January 2000.

Sullivan, Kristina B. "SAN and Deliver." *PC Week,* 4 October 1999.

Surkan, Michael. "Just Say No to Fibre Channel SANs." *PC Week,* 15 February 1999.

Toigo, Jon. "Storage Area Networks." *Washington Technology,* 11 September 2000.

Vickers, Lauri. "Network Storage: Duking it Out over Data." *Electronic News,* 28 February 2000.

Walker, Christy. "Storage-Area Networks." *Computerworld,* 9 August 1999.

Webster, John. "Storage Meets Networking." *CIO,* 15 April 1999.

Wilkinson, Stephanie. "Install a Storage Area Network to Solve Info Glut." *Datamation,* September 1999.

SUPERDRUGS

INDUSTRY SNAPSHOT

Until recently, the mention of plague conjured up sinister images of the Black Death rampaging through the filth-ridden village streets of medieval Europe. By the 1970s, experts announced with satisfaction that epidemics such as smallpox and tuberculosis were on the way out due to the wonder drugs, such as penicillin and tetracycline, that had been administered for several decades. Such celebratory statements were premature, however. The discovery of acquired immunodeficiency syndrome (AIDS) in the early 1980s revealed all too clearly that pandemic infectious diseases had hardly been eradicated. Centuries-old killers such as tuberculosis (TB) and malaria also continued to kill many people, especially in the developing world. The World Health Organization (WHO) forecast in 1999 that 1 billion people would become infected with TB between 2000 and 2020. Even in the United States, 10-15 million people are estimated to be infected with latent TB; at least 17,000 active cases were reported in 1999, according to the Centers for Disease Control and Prevention. TB was spreading in other developed nations as well, increasing by 50 percent in one year in Germany, Denmark, and New Zealand, according to a WHO report released in March 2000.

Between 1976 and 2000, more than 30 dangerous new infectious agents appeared. The U.S. death rate from infectious diseases increased 58 percent between 1980 and 1992 alone. Resistance to established antibiotics is also rising, evident especially in increased illness and mortality from nosocomial infections (those spread in hospitals and clinical settings) that fail to respond to treatment even with vancomycin, usually the drug of last resort.

About one-third of the world's 50 million deaths each year result from infectious disease, yet only 2 percent of all biomedical research focuses on the diseases that target the developing world. Ironically, many features of modern living—burgeoning population and urbanization, increased air travel, centralized food processing and distribution, human penetration of previously remote habitats, even the overzealous administration of antimicrobial drugs themselves—have spawned the very climate required for infectious diseases to spread rapidly across borders and to mutate into stronger strains no longer susceptible to the drugs that once led to their demise.

The turn of the millennium refocused attention on the threat of infectious diseases and the need for a steady stream of new antimicrobial agents to attack them. Initiatives announced by the U.S. government and WHO, a large philanthropic donation from the Bill and Melinda Gates Foundation, and growing collaborations between old-line major pharmaceutical companies and younger biotech firms opened pathways for the development of new superdrugs.

ORGANIZATION AND STRUCTURE

While part of the long-established pharmaceutical industry, "superdrug" development is emerging in its own right. Although tremendous demand exists for these products, few have gone to market. Most smaller companies have not yet turned a profit, existing on venture capital, government grants, and research and development (R&D).

The industry can be divided into two broad sectors. One consists of traditional pharmaceutical companies—large multinationals that have been manufacturing antibiotics since the 1950s. They possess "libraries" of hundreds of thousands of chemical compounds. Most of these compounds have been developed and tested, but not used in commercial pharmaceuticals or prototypes. They consist of chemical variants of commercial pharmaceutical ingredients or compounds that exhibit interesting or useful characteristics previously unexploited in medicines. Such compounds can be derived from animal or botanical sources, or, increasingly, may be designed at the molecular level to possess particular pharmaceutical properties. New technologies in drug design have increased tremendously the pace at which compounds are being added to these libraries. (Also see the essay in this book entitled Molecular Design.)

Traditionally, in new drug trials compounds are tested on a pathological organism or condition on a mass-production scale until one compound exhibits a promising or desired result. It is then refined into a medication for human use. When bacteria that are resistant to a particular antibiotic emerge, the traditional response was to find another agent that would defuse the resistance and "piggyback" it onto the antibiotic, enabling it to function again. Since nearly all bacteria develop resistance to such combinations, drug research is moving away from simple modification toward such techniques as gene technology and automated drug screening to develop novel agents that bacteria have never encountered. Smaller, high-tech start-up companies, which began appearing in the 1980s and 1990s, use techniques such as genetic engineering to locate weak points in a pathogen's DNA. The techniques are usually based on the companies' own proprietary technologies, which they develop themselves or license from a university.

Smaller companies frequently form research partnerships with pharmaceutical firms. The small firms bring unique technology to the partnership, and the larger companies bring their chemical library and company infrastructure. Pharmaceutical products resulting from such research are licensed exclusively to the larger partner, with the smaller receiving a licensing fee and royalty payments.

REGULATION

Superdrugs must acquire U.S. Food and Drug Administration (FDA) approval, sanctioning their safety and effectiveness for human use, before being sold in the United States. They thus undergo preclinical tests followed by three clinical trials on healthy and ill human subjects. The entire process can last 15 years; the FDA, however, has sought to reduce the length of time

for final approval. A user fee program, refined under the Food and Drug Modernization Act of 1997, allows the FDA to hire more reviewers to speed up approvals. In 1998, 30 drugs received approval in an average of 11.7 months, compared with a 30-month average per drug before user fees.

Two fast-track programs help facilitate patient access to experimental drugs. "Expedited development and review" applies to drugs designed for patients with life-threatening diseases. The "accelerated approval program" is intended for new drugs that provide to patients therapeutic benefits that existing treatments lack. This program is generally limited to drugs for patients who are unresponsive to or intolerant of other available therapies.

In late 1999, the American Association of Pharmaceutical Scientists formed the Product Quality Research Institute, a collaboration of government, industry, and academia to evaluate the processes by which drug effectiveness and safety are ascertained. The collaboration means to help speed the clinical trials of promising new drugs without sacrificing safety or thoroughness.

BACKGROUND AND DEVELOPMENT

Attempts at vaccination aren't new. Centuries ago, the Chinese vaccinated against smallpox by blowing material from pox scabs through a blowpipe into the noses of uninfected people. In Turkey, smallpox "parties" were held at which guests were given small doses of smallpox through their skin. This procedure was noticed by the wife of the British ambassador to Turkey, who introduced the method to England in 1721 during an outbreak of the disease. Some West Africans also used this method. When the 1721 outbreak was transferred to Boston, a slave from the Ivory Coast demonstrated the method to his master, the famous preacher Cotton Mather. Benjamin Franklin broadcast the technique in his newspaper. Edward Jenner, a British doctor, refined the technique in 1798, adapting its use to the less lethal cowpox. Taking inoculation material from lesions on the hand of a dairymaid, Jenner called his prophylactic measure vaccination, from the Latin word for cow (vacca).

Louis Pasteur (1822-1895) established the science of bacteriology. He also discovered fermentation and pasteurization, and demonstrated the benefits of vaccinating sheep against anthrax by using a heat-attenuated strain of the disease. Robert Koch (1843-1910) discovered how to sterilize with dry heat and first isolated the agents of tuberculosis, anthrax, and cholera.

By accident, Alexander Fleming discovered penicillin in 1928 when he observed that *Penicillium notatum* inhibited growth of *Staphylococcus aureus.* By the 1950s, penicillin was recognized as a miracle drug. It was soon joined by other antibiotics, including the cephalosporins, tetracycline, streptomycin, erythromycin, and sulfa drugs.

By the 1970s most doctors believed that infectious diseases would soon be wiped out. Pharmaceutical manufacturers curtailed their R&D efforts, confident that existing remedies were adequate and fearful that the market was already saturated. This optimism proved premature, however, and by the 1990s the medical community recognized that many illnesses believed to have been conquered were reappearing.

Ironically, success contributed directly to the rise of resistant strains. The longer bacteria are exposed to a drug, the faster that resistant strains are able to become dominant. Furthermore, bacteria can exchange genetic material via little packets of DNA called plasmids, and thus pass resistance to as-yet nonresistant strains.

Doctors and patients both contribute to the problem. Doctors may prescribe antibiotics when they are not indicated, for example as treatment for the common cold, an illness caused by viruses, which do not respond to antibiotics. Patients often stop taking antibiotics as soon as they start feeling better instead of continuing the full regimen prescribed. This gives resistant bacteria an opportunity to survive, multiply, and become dominant.

Pharmaceutical companies responded to drug resistance by fighting the problem one-on-one: if a bacterium developed an enzyme to digest an antibiotic, researchers combined two drugs, the original antibiotic and another to short-circuit the enzyme. But bacteria can develop resistance more quickly than scientists can react. This is particularly true in regard to patients with compromised immune systems.

The drug of last resort during the late 1990s was vancomycin. More than 95 percent of hospital-acquired *S. aureus* infections are resistant to penicillin or ampicillin. Vancomycin is the only effective drug for these cases. In 1989 hospitals began reporting rapid increases in vancomycin resistance in enterococci (VRE) and realized that increased VRE can lead to cross-resistance in *S. aureus.* Public health officials fear that we could be rapidly approaching a window of vulnerability in which the existing antibiotics are

no longer effective and not enough new ones have yet been developed to take their place.

CURRENT CONDITIONS

A 1999 Pew Research Poll ascertained that 56 percent of Americans surveyed felt that the 21st century would witness an epidemic even more terrible than AIDS. Certainly, the numbers might give one pause. Despite substantial gains in treatment options, new cases of HIV/AIDS have appeared at a frightening rate in sub-Saharan Africa and the former Soviet Union, with a majority of those infected being women. Hepatitis C, generally acquired through blood transfusions or drug injections, has infected 3.9 million Americans. First identified only in 1988, the onset of illness sometimes appears years after the original infection, and a widespread outbreak is feared between 2000 and 2020. Even new diseases with limited outbreaks, such as ebola in the former Zaire during 1995, involve gruesome diseases that still lack both preventions and cures.

Increasing globalization seems poised to spawn a new heyday for infectious disease. With more air travel each year, many microbes will find a free ride to geographic areas far removed from their home turf. The sweeping internationalization of trade provides a means of transport as well. In 1991 a Chinese vessel emptied cholera-laced bilge water into a Chilean harbor, infecting local fish; a few weeks later, cholera appeared in Latin America, where it had been unknown for a century. Within a year the disease had spread to 11 adjacent countries. Population displacements from urbanization, deforestation, and warfare have exacerbated this dilemma. By the end of the 1990s, roughly 1 percent of the world's people were refugees of war, with infectious disease a common companion in refugee camps.

North America constitutes the world's largest pharmaceuticals market; in 1999, overall sales increased 18 percent to $138.8 billion. Although developing nations bear the brunt of infectious diseases, the aging U.S. population and the spread of drug-resistant strains of staphylococcus, pneumonia, and *E. coli* indicates a need for new antimicrobial drugs. This should spur new-drug research in this area, as well as in the more popular areas of cancer and heart disease.

According to the latest WHO report on global infectious disease, about 3,000 deaths occur daily due to malaria and 1.5 million deaths occur annually due to TB. HIV/AIDS has infected nearly 38 million people. According to the Jordan Report 2000, a century after Koch discovered cholera, there is still no highly effective vaccine for it. TB also lacks an effective vaccine and malarial treatments are inadequate as well.

Continuing and emerging global killers received intensified scrutiny in Washington at the turn of the 21st century. The U.S. 2001 budget encompassed a large increase in National Institutes of Health funds for malaria, TB, and HIV/AIDS vaccines. The Bill and Melinda Gates Foundation donated $750 million for vaccine purchases as part of the Global Alliance for Vaccines and Immunization. Public-private partnerships also were endorsed, such as the International AIDS Vaccine Initiative, with over $10 million dedicated to triple the number of possible AIDS vaccines being readied for clinical trials.

Industry leaders Merck & Co., American Home Products Corp., the merging Glaxo Wellcome and SmithKline Beecham, and Aventis Pharma AG pledged to donate millions of doses of vaccines in cooperation with the president's Millennium Vaccine Initiative. The Millennium Vaccine Initiative earmarked $50 million of the fiscal-year 2001 budget for purchase of vaccines for global immunizations and included a tax credit on vaccine sales to spur industry research and production.

The FDA approved 40 new medicines in 1999, but only one-fifth targeted infectious disease. In fall, the FDA granted approval to Aventis's Synercid, one of a group called streptogramins, to treat infections resulting from resistant *Enterococcus* and *Staphylococcus aureus*. Other approvals were granted for Glaxo's Agenerase, a protease inhibitor, to be used in treating HIV; Avelox, from Bayer, and Tequin, a new quinolone from Bristol-Myers Squibb, for respiratory infections; Nabi-HB from Nabi for hepatitis B, and Wellferon from Glaxo for hepatitis C. Two drugs for influenza A and B, Hoffmann-La Roche's Tamiflu and Glaxo's Relenza, were also approved.

In spring 1999, the FDA labeled Pharmacia's Zyvox a fast-track medicine. Zyvox (linezolid) is a member of the oxazolidinones, the first entirely new group of antibiotics developed in 35 years. The drug works by attacking bacteria very early in their protein-production cycle, shortcutting their ability to reproduce.

U.S. patents for drugs generating $43 billion will expire or lose exclusivity under FDA rules between 2000 and 2004, opening the road to production of cheaper generic versions. Though drug prices rose about 4.4 percent in 1999, according to IMS Health, generics will probably lower prices overall. OrbiMed

Advisors estimated that 30 of the 500 biotech companies they tracked would show a profit in 2000, as compared with only 16 in 1999.

Overall pharmaceutical R&D investment has doubled about every five years since 1970, according to International Trade Data System's 2000 industry profile. Future investment seems headed in the direction of pharmacogenomics, to identify the sequences of disease-causing microbes for both antibiotic/antiviral and vaccine development. (See the essay in this book entitled Pharmacogenomics.)

INDUSTRY LEADERS

Historically, the pharmaceutical industry was highly fragmented, with the top 10 manufacturers accounting for only 30 percent of drug sales. Expiring patents, however, precipitated a rash of mergers starting in the late 1990s that may radically alter the industry's terrain. Britain's Glaxo Wellcome and SmithKline Beecham agreed to become Glaxo SmithKline, the world's largest pharmaceutical company with annual sales of $25 billion and an R&D budget of about $3.6 billion. Monsanto Co. and Pharmacia & Upjohn, Inc. merged to become Pharmacia Corp. The merger created a firm valued at $52 billion that employed 29,900 and posted 1999 sales of $9.15 billion. Its annual R&D budget was about $2 billion. The company spun off its bioengineered-crops division, perceived as a liability in the wake of anti-genetic-modification protests heard throughout much of the world.

The merging Pfizer Inc. and Warner-Lambert announced they would increase R&D funding to $4.7 billion in 2000. The life-sciences divisions of France's Rhone-Poulenc SA joined with Germany's Hoechst AG, resulting in Aventis Co., with 101,000 employees worldwide and an R&D budget of $2.8 billion. Astra and Zeneca also merged.

Other prominent players include Bristol-Myers Squibb Co., with 1999 sales of $20.2 billion and 54,500 employees. It funded the only comprehensive global study of bacterial resistance, based at the University of Iowa. Merck, the biggest U.S. drug manufacturer, posted 1999 sales of $32.71 billion and had 62,300 employees.

Among biotech firms, Cubist Pharmaceuticals identified as drug targets 20 enzymes bacteria use to bind amino acids into protein. Cubist, with 75 employees, has collaborative agreements with Bristol-Myers Squibb, Merck, Novartis, and Pfizer to develop

About   A GERM PANIC ATTACK?

In 1998, 146 biological terrorist threats were received in the United States; though all turned out to be false alarms, their number highlights the new focus that media and government placed on the potential threats of biological warfare and bioterrorism in the new millennium.

Renewed warnings of the threat of potential bioterrorist attacks came in the wake of the 1995 Aum Shinrikyo release of Sarin gas in the Tokyo subway, and with the increase in so-called rogue states that possess chemical and biological warfare capability. Among possible biological weapons are botulism, smallpox, anthrax, and the viruses that cause hemorrhagic fevers. Bio-weapon attacks would mimic naturally occurring outbreaks and would therefore be hard to detect. In late 1999, the National Environmental Health Association announced its collaboration with the Agency for Toxic Substances and Disease Registry to launch a project to educate the public on how to respond to biological terrorism.

"The U.S. is currently unprepared for an attack," according to David Siegrist of the Potomac Institute for Policy Studies. The time lag that would follow a release of an infectious agent would facilitate its spread. Since symptoms would appear gradually, there would be no coordinated reporting system for diagnoses, and most physicians have no first-hand experience with diseases such as plague and anthrax.

The Clinton administration instituted an antibioterrorism initiative in 1999, on which the U.S. Department of Health and Human Services spent $158 million. The total was increased to $230 million for 2000. The plan encompassed increased education to familiarize doctors with the biological agents most likely to pose a threat. It also funded mass stockpiling of antibiotics and vaccines needed to combat diseases such as smallpox and anthrax.

While vaccines against smallpox and anthrax exist, nothing currently works against aerosolized plague. But quantities of proven pharmaceuticals are insufficient for widespread dissemination. According to Dr. Philip K. Russell, an infectious disease specialist who spoke at the National Symposium on Medical and Public Health Response to Bioterrorism in February 1999, only 7 million doses of smallpox vaccines were currently housed. Furthermore, production facilities for the vaccine were dismantled in 1980 because experts believed that the disease had been beaten. Thus, the military supply was far too small for general civilian use. The only feasible remedy would be a postattack treatment program, which the Centers for Disease Control and Prevention estimated could cost $26.2 billion per 100,000 people exposed to anthrax, for example.

Scientists have also identified a virtually indestructible bacterium, *Deinococcus radiodurans* ("terrible berry that survives radiation"). It can withstand a blast of gamma rays equivalent to thousands of lethal human doses. When "dead" *radiodurans* spores (which had been exposed to ultraviolet light for 100 years) in Antarctica were placed in a nutrient bath, their DNA reassembled itself and multiplied. If the genes could be added to anthrax, they might produce an anthrax virtually impossible to kill.

---

anti-infective drugs in its target-based Synthetase Program. In 1999 Cubist's revenues jumped 237 percent to reach $5.4 million, though its still registered a net loss of $17.1 million.

Sangamo BioSciences, Inc. has collaborative agreements with numerous companies to use its Universal Gene Tools in their internal research and validation programs. Sangamo concentrates on R&D of transcription factors, proteins that turn genes on and off to regulate gene expression by recognizing specific DNA sequences. The company registered a net loss of $3.8 on revenues of $2.2 in 1999.

Genome Therapeutics researches the genetic basis of disease. The company's superdrug research centers on its pathogen program. Its two most important technologies are whole-genome pathogen sequencing, which involves decoding and representing the genetic structure of a pathogen, and bioinformatics, which is the application of computers, software, and databases to the analysis of genomic research in order to compare sequences and identify a gene's function. Genome Therapeutics posted revenues of $24 million in 1999, an increase of 25 percent from the year before, and took a net loss of $6.3 million.

IntraBiotics of Sunnyvale, California, makes antimicrobials based on naturally occurring substances called host defense peptides, which are produced by the immune system to protect the host from infection with such immune-system-compromising viruses as the vancomycin-resistant enterococci (VRE) bacteria. IntraBiotics has several drugs under development, including Protegrins, which kill bacteria and fungi before attaching to their lipid membranes, a mechanism unique to this product. Ramoplanin, a naturally produced antibiotic for use against enterococci, was entering Phase III clinical trials.

RESEARCH AND TECHNOLOGY

The development, approval, and release of any new drug requires substantial amounts of cash and time. The Boston Consulting Group estimated that a company typically spends $500 million to debut a patentable new drug. The Tufts Center for the Study of Drug Development reported that, on average, an experimental drug is under development for 15 years. Only five of every 5,000 compounds proceed to human testing. Of those, only one ultimately earns approval for sale.

Perhaps the best way to conquer viruses is by preventing infection with vaccines. The old-fashioned way of making a vaccine is to grow a virus, kill or weaken it, then administer it to a host. The vaccine prods the immune system into making protective antibodies. But the approach can be too slow or costly to counter a sudden epidemic. Chiron Corp., in collaboration with the Institute for Genomic Research in Maryland, discovered a way to generate a meningitis vaccine based on the genetic structure for the bacterium that causes the disease. Chiron's computer-based genomics approach took only 18 months to complete and located 85 potential vaccine targets; in comparison, nearly 40 years of conventional research identified only about 20 potential vaccine targets.

Several tests were underway to add edible vaccines to genetically modified crops. Cornell University announced that it had embedded an anti-hepatitis-B vaccine into genetically modified potatoes, for example. Mice produced measles antibodies when fed edible vaccines in tobacco and lettuce in a project at Alfred Hospital in Sydney, Australia. Researchers are exploring applications for edible animal vaccines as well. ProdiGene of College Station, Texas, ran trials of genetically modified corn laced with a vaccine that fights the gastroenteritis virus in swine. This is a promising development, since the European Union banned in June 1999 the use of antibiotics in animal feed out of concern that the practice contributes to the development of drug-resistant microbes in both animals and humans.

Federal funding for antimicrobial resistance research rose from $7.8 million in 1992 to an estimated $13.8 million in 1998—a 75 percent increase. The Pharmaceutical Research and Manufacturing Association estimated that 15 percent of the pharmaceutical industry's outlay for R&D—an estimated $24 billion in 1999—is devoted to new anti-infectives.

Other simpler and relatively cheaper strategies cut down the expense and time to develop new drugs. New approaches cripple or inactivate bacteria instead of killing them so that resistance is less likely to develop. These "search-and-destroy" gene sequences resemble an enzyme found in all cells and so have the potential to be used in any kind of genetic material.

Quorex Pharmaceuticals Inc. discovered that many bacteria begin infection only after they have communicated with each other, such that a critical mass, or "quorum," of bacteria is present in the host. This communication takes place along a signaling pathway, which, if interrupted, could disable the pathogen's ability to cause infection. Quorex locates compounds that inhibit the pathway.

Paradoxically, future success in this industry will entail scaling back sales and controlling the distribution of antibiotics. Physicians and public health officials agree that bacteria will find a way to adapt to new drugs. The Centers for Disease Control and Prevention recommended that doctors prescribe antibiotics only when clearly necessary, and issued more stringent guidelines for the use of all antibiotics.

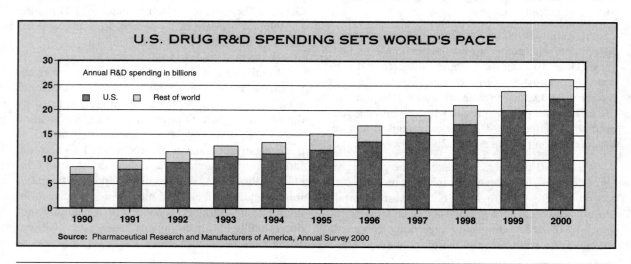

U.S. DRUG R&D SPENDING SETS WORLD'S PACE

Annual R&D spending in billions

■ U.S. □ Rest of world

Source: Pharmaceutical Research and Manufacturers of America, Annual Survey 2000

FURTHER READING

Abelson, Philip. "Biological Warfare." *Science,* 26 November 1999.

Alger, Alexandra. "War against the Microbes." *Forbes,* 14 June 1999.

"AMBI Receives Patent for Drug Candidate to Treat Serious Antibiotic-Resistant Bacterial Infections." *Business Wire,* 24 February 2000.

"Antibiotics: 'Miracle Drugs' to Fight 'Superbugs.'" *American Health Line,* 2 November 1999.

"Aventis Pharmaceuticals Submits U.S. Drug Application for First in New Family of Ketolide Antibiotics." *PR Newswire,* 6 March 2000.

Barrett, Amy. "Industry Outlook 2000: Life Sciences, Drugs." *Business Week Online,* 10 January 2000. Available from http://www.businessweek.com.

Benjamin, Georges. "Chemical and Biological Terrorism: Planning for the Worst." *Physician Executive,* January/February 2000.

Brooks, George. "Counterattacking Superbugs." *Equities,* March/April 1999.

Capell, Kerry. "AstraZeneca: A Drug Megamerger That's Working." *Business Week Online,* 15 November 1999. Available from http://www.businessweek.com.

Centers for Disease Control and Prevention. *Preventing Emerging Infectious Diseases: A Strategy for the 21st Century.* Atlanta: CDC, October 1998.

Chidley, Joe. "A Swatter for Superbugs." *Canadian Business,* 10 September 1999.

"The Clinton-Gore Administration: New Partnerships to Develop and Deliver Vaccines to Developing Countries." 2 March 2000. Available from http://www.niaid.nih.gov/publications/jordan/whitehouse.htm.

"Competition Accelerates Pharmaceutical Research." *Drug Discovery/Technology News,* January 2000.

Cook, Anne. "Livestock Antibiotics Linked to Drug Resistance in Humans." *News-Gazette* (Champaign-Urbana, IL), 16 January 2000.

Dimmitt, Barbara Sande. "Racing against Disease." *American Medical News,* 27 September 1999.

"Discovery of Antimicrobial Agents." *New England Journal of Medicine,* 6 January 2000.

"Drug Resistance: Antibiotic Shortage Raises Concern." *American Health Line,* 2 February 2000.

Farmer, Paul. "TB Superbugs: The Coming Plague on All Our Houses." *Natural History,* April 1999.

Goldberg, Ray A. "Transforming Life, Transforming Business: The Life-Science Revolution." *Harvard Business Review,* March/April 2000.

Hall, Carl. "Meningitis Bacteria's DNA Used in Designing Vaccine; Chiron Scientists Report Progress in Research." *San Francisco Chronicle,* 10 March 2000.

Henderson, C. W. "Report: Emerging Infectious Diseases of Wild Animals Are Threat to Biodiversity, Human Health." *World Disease Weekly,* 13 February 2000.

Hsu, Karen. "Firms Urge Incentives on Research." *Boston Globe,* 29 March 2000.

International Trade Data System. *Profile: The Pharmaceutical Industry.* March 2000. Available from http://www.itds.treas.gov/ITTA/pharmindustry.html.

Kaufman, Marc. "FDA Panel Clears New Antibiotic; Medication Controls Hospital Infections." *Washington Post,* 25 March 2000.

Key, Sandra W., and Michelle Marble. "Drug Shown Effective against Vancomycin-Resistant Bacteria." *World Disease Weekly Plus,* 29 March-5 April 1999.

———. "Legislation Introduced to Fight Infectious Disease on World TB Day." *World Disease Weekly Plus,* 19 April 1999.

———. "Researchers Advance Way to Stimulate Human Immune System." *Cancer Weekly Plus,* 16 August 1999.

Kmietowicz, Zosia. "Superbugs Are Beating at the Gates." *New Scientist,* 17 July 1999.

Ko, Albert, et al. "Urban Epidemic of Severe Leptospirosis in Brazil." *Lancet,* 4 September 1999.

Lueck, Sarah. "Panel Recommends Approval by FDA of First in a New Class of Antibiotics." *Wall Street Journal,* 27 March 2000.

"The Market for Community-Acquired Pneumonia Therapies Will Be Significantly Influenced by Increasing Levels of Antibiotic Resistance, States a Decision Resources Study." *PR Newswire,* 14 February 2000.

Martens, Pim, and Lisbeth Hall. "Malaria on the Move: Human Population Movement and Malaria Transmission." *Emerging Infectious Disease,* March/April 2000.

McConnell, Harvey. "Antibiotics and Superbugs." *Futurist,* February 1999.

Mulvaney, Kiernan. "The Scourge of Mankind." *E Magazine: The Environmental Magazine,* March/April 1999.

Noon, Daniel J., and Salynn Boyles. "AIDS Pandemic Seen Worsening Next Century." *AIDS Weekly Plus,* 11 October 1999.

O'Neil, John. "A Tough Battle with Drug-Resistant TB." *New York Times,* 21 March 2000.

Pilling, David. "Life Sciences and Pharmaceuticals: Brain versus Brawn in the Battle for Sales." *Financial Times,* 6 April 2000.

Preston, Richard. "What New Things Are Going to Kill Me?" *Time*, 8 November 1999.

"ProdiGene Is First to Demonstrate Vaccination with Edible Vaccines." *PR Newswire*, 15 February 2000.

"Quorex Funding Accelerates Novel Antibiotic Discovery Targeting Drug Resistant Bacteria." *Business Wire*, 13 March 2000.

"Responding to Chemical and Biological Terrorism." *Journal of Environmental Health*, November 1999.

Rovner, Julie. "Pharmaceutical Companies Pledge Vaccines for Developing Countries." *Lancet*, 11 March 2000.

"Rx Industry: Merger Mania for Major Players." *American Health Line*, 10 December 1999.

St. Pierre, Nicole. "Using Chicken Feed in the War on Superbugs." *Business Week*, 14 February 2000.

Schuchat, Anne. "Microbes without Borders: Infectious Disease, Public Health, and the Journal." *American Journal of Public Health*, February 2000.

Sikora, Martin. "M & A Roundup—More Megadeals Loom in the Drug Industry: After the Pfizer/Warner-Lambert Merger, Pressure Is on Holdouts to Combine." *Mergers and Acquisitions Journal*, 1 April 2000.

"Speeding up the FDA." *Drug Discovery/Technology News*, December 1999.

Stapleton, Stephanie. "New Superbug Renews Antibiotic Worries." *American Medical News*, 13 September 1999. Available from http://www.ama-assn.org/sci-pubs/amnews.

Stefanova, Kristina. "Maryland-Based Biotech Firm Targets Resistant Bacteria." *Washington Times*, 13 January 2000.

Sternberg, Steve, and Anita Manning. "Diseases Tighten Grip: Worldwide Health Grants Fight Rising Tide around the Globe." *USA Today*, 24 March 2000.

Stolberg, Sheryl. "Drug Agency Approves Antibiotic." *New York Times*, 22 September 1999.

Taggart, Stewart. "Food Gets Fed with Meds." *Wired News*, 26 January 2000.

Tomes, Nancy. "The Making of a Germ Panic, Then and Now." *American Journal of Public Health*, February 2000.

Uehling, Mark D. "Superbugs." *Popular Science*, May 1999.

U.S. Food and Drug Administration. *New and Generic Drug Approvals, 1998-2000.* 4 April 2000. Available from http://www.fda.gov/cder/approval/index.html.

Webster, Sarah. "New Drug Beefs up Arsenal: Zyvox Arrives in Nick of Time in Battle against Resistant Bacteria." *Detroit News*, 18 October 1999.

"World Health and Disease Is Now a Local Issue: The Effect of Globalisation on Healthcare Is Likely to Engage Politicians More Than They Expect." *Financial Times* (London), 3 January 2000.

SYSTEMS INTEGRATION

Company scrambles to develop electronic commerce (e-commerce) capabilities and better manage diverse information systems have given new steam to the decades-old business of systems integration (SI). Two growth trends, e-commerce deployment and enterprise application integration, are responsible for a large infusion of revenue that the industry has enjoyed since 1996, while activities such as corporate mergers and new technology adoption have contributed as well.

From 1996 to 1998 alone, according to government statistics, U.S. systems integrators' revenues vaulted 50 percent, approaching $32 billion, including consulting and related work. This torrid rate wasn't expected to continue industry-wide, but fast-moving segments such as e-commerce were predicted to yield strong double-digit percentage growth into the early 2000s. Based on the industry's compound annual growth rate from 1992 to 1998, revenue in 2000 was estimated at about $40 billion. International Data Corp. forecast worldwide systems integration revenues to reach $84 billion by 2003.

Vigorous demand for SI and related services has changed the competitive dynamics among integrators. In some cases, smaller firms are gaining an edge in the market for rapid e-commerce integration, where they are seen as more flexible, more responsive, possibly more knowledgeable, and better able to meet tight deadlines. Meanwhile, large integrators such as Electronic Data Systems Corp. (EDS) and IBM Global Services bring tremendous resources and bargaining power to the table, and are able to win larger, more complex contracts through their name recognition and stable brand image—even though they may subcontract the actual work to smaller, less-well-known operatives. The industry has also seen a swarm of mergers and acquisitions as companies seek the right mix of competencies and market access to best meet new demand.

ORGANIZATION AND STRUCTURE

Systems integration involves fitting together hardware and software to solve a business problem or create a competitive advantage. Often this occurs as part of deploying a new software application that was sold and installed by the integrator, who may also be called a reseller, but SI work can be performed at any point in a system's life cycle and by any service vendor that is retained to make two or more different systems interact as needed. Integration may also be performed by in-house staff instead of hiring an outside service.

One of the fastest-growing service areas within the information systems industry, systems integration was driven by fast-paced change in both business and technological environments during the 1980s and the 1990s. Drawing from traditional systems development approaches, systems integration nevertheless differs from this traditional systems model in a number of ways. The general assumption of most traditional systems development is that most—if not all—of the scope of the problem being attacked is within "design control" of the project. Traditional development assumes that the various parts of a system can be engineered to fit together and concentrates more on the development of applications and databases, giving little concern to interfacing those applications and databases. Systems integrators attack these development problems from the opposite direction, concentrating on building interfaces to make all system components work together.

Although it is separated from custom programming and other kinds of information technology (IT) services for statistical and analytical purposes, systems integration is in reality often done by firms that also perform such related services as custom application development, hardware and software installation, network management, system maintenance, and the like.

The systems integration (SI) process usually contains five steps: planning, design, development, implementation, and operation. SI brings about interaction between the hardware platform, software applications, and the operating system, and creates a base for all subsequent system-related uses and modifications.

Since systems integration can involve custom programming, Alan R. Earls explained in *Computerworld,* the initial stage of the integration process is one of the most crucial: clients must clearly specify exactly what capabilities they would like their systems to have and what the goals and requirements are. Systems integrators must also proceed carefully at this stage, ensuring that they fully comprehend client needs in order to deliver the expected service.

Furthermore, systems integrators and clients must take pains to draft thorough contracts that specify the tasks to be performed, as well as the deadlines for those tasks. Earls urged companies to conduct a rigorous selection process to make sure they choose systems integrators with skills and fees amenable to their needs. The screening process should involve lawyers, technicians, and contract specialists so that all aspects of the SI contractor are examined prior to selecting a SI firm and signing a contract with the integrator.

Earls noted that companies should consider the location of the systems integrators as well. If both parties cannot solve a problem via the phone, then an on-site visit is warranted, which could cause significant delays if the systems integrator has to travel a long distance. In fact, on-site service and special attention make up some of the most important features systems integrators can offer, according to a *Computerworld* survey, which small, nearby SI firms may excel at providing.

Depending on client needs and project specifications, systems integrators may use prepackaged software exclusively. They may also need to design custom applications or outsource this task to a custom

software developer. In addition, many systems integrators cater to specific markets, such as information system and manufacturing system markets, and they specialize in certain kinds of technology and computer system-related skills. Therefore, companies and organizations seeking SI services select firms based on the firms' focal markets and aptitudes. SI firms usually have a team of systems integrators work on contracts, so a given firm may have specialists in various aspects of system integration and employ specialists in various computer environments such as Windows and Unix.

BACKGROUND AND DEVELOPMENT

With the proliferation of computers into homes and businesses during the 1980s and 1990s, the demand for diverse computer applications increased. In the beginning of the computer boom, custom software constituted the most prevalent kind of applications for businesses. Companies would contract software developers to create applications to suit individual needs. Computer programmers would design everything from workplace automation software to customer information databases. Custom development, however, had two significant drawbacks: cost and lack of standardization. Other than financial powerhouses, most companies couldn't afford custom software development except in financially prosperous times. Furthermore, without industry standards, custom software clients could have trouble upgrading software and ensuring that all divisions had the same operating systems and compatible software, which sometimes hindered interaction between various branches of a company.

By decree of the U.S. Justice Department in 1969, IBM Corp. had to start selling its software separately from its computer hardware, ending IBM's stronghold on the prepackaged software industry and opening the doors for vigorous competition. Consequently, a plethora of software developers sprouted in the wake of the Justice Department's decision. Prepackaged software offered an economical solution to the needs not only of small and medium businesses with tight budgets, but also to home-computer users who used computers largely for uniform tasks such as word processing. Since software development required little capital investment, programmers could tinker away at novel and improved applications with very little financial risk. As a result, the prepackaged software industry blossomed in the 1980s and bore substantial fruit in the 1990s, producing high-quality products at much lower costs than custom-made counterparts.

Therefore, the custom software industry began to slow down as the prepackaged software industry soared ahead. Nonetheless, because of their unique tasks, many businesses and organizations still required custom applications to increase the efficiency and functionality of company software. This need continued to feed the custom software industry.

Another need, however, emerged as well: systems integration. Integrators were required to build and link diverse systems for various organizational functions, often to interface large, legacy systems on mainframes with more recent desktop computing environments. For example, a company might wish to access and manipulate data stored in a mainframe database from a Windows NT network. Such a project might involve creating intermediate programming—perhaps installing a middleware package—that allowed the Windows application to communicate with the mainframe application. Systems integration was beneficial anywhere companies needed to make unlike applications and platforms work together. This was especially true of massive proprietary applications, which were commonly used in government and large companies.

Cuts in federal spending in the early and mid-1990s reduced some opportunities for integrators serving the federal government, which was at one point the largest market for SI services. Still, as the number of federal employees decreased with government spending reductions, many systems integrators benefited as government agencies outsourced more projects. Thus, federal spending trends in the 1990s benefited the industry more than they hurt it. Streamlining of federal contract rules also changed the way federal contracts were obtained and under what terms, with a trend toward shorter, more task-specific contracts that rewarded high performance and penalized shoddy work.

CURRENT CONDITIONS

Demand for systems integration (SI) services escalated markedly in the mid-1990s and remains strong. As of 1998, U.S. Census Bureau figures pegged industry revenue at almost $32 billion a year, up some 20 percent from a year earlier. That amount included consulting and other work that isn't considered part of systems integration. Based on growth patterns in the 1990s, the industry stood to gain between 10 and 20 percent a year into the early 2000s, bringing sales somewhere around $40 billion as of 2000.

International Data Corp. (IDC), a market research firm, calculated U.S. industry revenue somewhat

---

About... SYSTEMS INTEGRATION INDUSTRY ORGANIZATIONS

Two organizations serve the systems integration industry: the Independent Computer Consultants Association (ICCA) and the National Association of Computer Consultant Businesses (NACCB). Founded in 1976, the ICCA reported having over 1,500 members and 24 chapters in 1999. The St. Louis-based association consists of entrepreneurs who are technical specialists in all aspects of computer hardware and software including systems integration. Before becoming members, computer consultants must pledge to uphold the organization's code of ethics. In addition, the nonprofit ICCA keeps members apprised of legislative activity that could affect small businesses and entrepreneurs, and it offers certification examinations.

The NACCB, meanwhile, lobbies for policies that will strengthen computer consultants' opportunities. The Washington-based association also uses the Internet to let computer consultants post their resumes to attract clients and requires its members to adhere to a code of ethics. The 300 businesses around the country that make up the NACCB work with contract computer consultants, including those who provide systems integration services. The member businesses are those that need temporary technical computer support.

---

lower, at $22.5 billion in 1998, but agreed that SI is growing strongly—both in the United States and around the world. IDC estimated that the global market for SI in 1998 was worth $50 billion and growing at 13 percent a year.

The need for e-commerce and Web integration is one of the factors driving the growth in demand. As companies flock to the Web to reach customers, they often require the Web interface to work with existing systems such as product catalog databases, order-entry databases, and customer databases. Integrators are needed to bridge the Web system with those sorts of systems, and demand for some specialties within Web integration was expected to double in the early 2000s. Not surprisingly, getting in on integration for e-commerce systems has been a high priority at SI firms large and small; EDS, the second-largest integrator, was banking on e-commerce as part of its new growth strategy unveiled in 1999.

Another important niche for integrators recently has been a shift toward large, interoperable corporate applications such as enterprise resource planning packages. Companies installed these powerful high-end applications to unify their data systems across different functional areas of the business, such as finance, human resources, and manufacturing, while still providing for the unique requirements of each area. Many also have industry-specific components intended for, say, telecommunications providers or financial services. These enterprise packages often require moderate customization for a particular client and often must be integrated to work with older systems. This kind of integration can extend not only to all of a company's major systems, but it may also include linkage between supplier or customer systems to further streamline the supply chain.

INDUSTRY LEADERS

IBM GLOBAL SERVICES

The reigning giant in the computer services business is IBM Global Services. This IBM division provides exhaustive IT services from consulting and design through implementation and management. It is commonly acknowledged as the world's largest systems integrator, although the company doesn't report its SI revenues separately from the rest of its diverse services. The Global Services unit generated $32.2 billion in revenue in 1999, gaining 11 percent from the year before.

ELECTRONIC DATA SYSTEMS

Electronic Data Systems Corp. (EDS) is generally considered the United States' second-biggest integrator. It, too, provides a full line of IT outsourcing services in addition to its SI business. In 1999 its systems and technology services operations posted revenues of $14.8 billion, up 14 percent from the year before. Including consulting and data center management services, EDS that year had total corporate revenues of $18.5 billion. Founded by Ross Perot, who now heads rival Perot Systems, the company was acquired by General Motors Corp. (GM) in 1984. Although it was spun off by GM in 1996, GM still supplies about a fifth of EDS's annual sales, down from 25 percent a few years earlier. Headquartered in Plano, Texas, EDS has an alliance with MCI World-Com, under which the two swap assets, employees, and services.

ANDERSEN CONSULTING

Another major company specializing in systems integration has been Andersen Consulting, newly re-named Accenture as of late 2000. Based in Chicago, Andersen (Accenture) is one of several large management consulting firms (others include Deloitte, Ernst & Young, KPMG, and PricewaterhouseCoopers) that are heavily involved in providing IT services. The company works closely with major computer and software suppliers. Andersen's 1999 sales from all operations totaled $8.9 billion, up 7 percent from the previous year.

AMERICAN MANAGEMENT SYSTEMS

Based in Fairfax, Virginia, American Management Systems Inc. (AMS) designs and integrates technological solutions for a wide variety of businesses worldwide. Although its largest individual customer is the U.S. government, the company's biggest market is the telecommunications industry, whose companies account for about 30 percent of AMS sales. The company is also a major provider of systems integration services to the banking and finance industries. AMS posted net income of $56.9 million on revenue of $1.24 billion in 1999. Net income was up 10 percent from 1998 levels, while sales improved 17 percent from the previous year.

PEROT SYSTEMS

Based in Dallas, Perot Systems Corp. provides IT consulting and services, including application development, systems management, and integration. The company went public in 1999, and more than 90 percent of its employees are shareholders under an employee stock ownership program. In 1999 the company reported net income of $75.5 million on revenue of $1.2 billion. Perot Systems employs more than 7,000 people worldwide.

UNISYS

Unisys Corp. ranks as one of the highest in terms of technical aptitude and customer service. Unisys offers systems integration services to both its corporate and government clients. Unisys' forte is building information architecture systems to allow clients to efficiently manage, store, and analyze data. When constructing a system, the company considers not only the data but also the customers, industry trends, business strategies, and competition in order to make the information system optimally functional. Unisys provides services throughout the world. The company also has strategic alliances with Microsoft, Hewlett-Packard, Sun Microsystems, PeopleSoft, Oracle, and Tandem. In 1999 Unisys posted net income of $511 million on revenue of $7.5 billion. Net income was up sharply from the previous year, by 36 percent, while revenue growth was subdued, at just 4 percent. The company's service operations, which include systems integration, accounted for $5.3 billion in revenue in 1999.

HEWLETT-PACKARD

Besides being a major provider of computer systems, servers, and peripherals, Hewlett-Packard Co. (HP) is a leading provider of systems integration services. In fiscal 1999 the company's IT services brought in $5.9 billion, up from $5.4 billion the year before. Services represented only a small part of HP's total revenues of $42 billion. Like other old-line hardware makers, HP's large services unit originated from its hardware support activities. The company now provides a full range of computer services.

COMPAQ

Compaq Computer Corp. is another key computer and Internet software and component producer that provides systems integration services as well. Its service arm is largely the result of its 1998 purchase of high-end hardware and services vendor Digital Equipment Corp. Flagging profits and strategic malaise forced out Compaq's longtime CEO Eckhard Pfeiffer in 1999, but the company managed to post a modest profit on the year. Total corporate revenues exceeded $38.5 billion that year, up 24 percent from 1998. Services contributed a minority of Compaq's revenue, with $6.6 billion in 1999, but that amount was up by nearly three-quarters from 1998 because of other acquisitions and aggressive marketing of services, which tend to carry higher profit margins than some areas of the hardware business.

COMPUTER SCIENCES

Founded in 1959, Computer Sciences Corp. (CSC) is a federal contractor that has increasingly courted the business market. Tech services to federal agencies accounted for as much as 70 percent of CSC's revenue back in the mid-1980s, but by 1999 the proportion was down to just 23 percent. In 1998 CSC was the target of a hostile takeover bid by software vendor Computer Associates International, which had been aggressively branching into services. No deal was ever reached, however. As of 2000, CSC had revenues of $9.37 billion, up 22 percent from 1999, and net income of $403 million, up 18 percent. Systems integration accounted for 24 percent of total revenues.

AMERICA AND THE WORLD

As the world economy becomes increasingly dependent on computer technology, the demand for systems integration services has witnessed rapid growth on the international scene. International Data Corp. (IDC) projected that the global market for SI would nearly double between 1998 and 2003, reaching $84 billion by the end of the period. Other research firms use broader definitions of systems integration (SI) services, and by their reckoning, the world's SI market was worth more than $200 billion in the early 2000s.

IDC estimated that, as of 1998, the United States represented 45 percent of the global SI market. Western Europe trailed at 28 percent, while Asia and the Pacific Rim accounted for less than 4 percent of the market. Nonetheless, Asia and other regions outside Europe and the United States were the fastest-growing markets, expanding around 20 percent a year compared to 13 percent for the world on average.

In June 1998 Digital Equipment Corp., now a part of Compaq Computer Corp., agreed to establish a new joint venture company with Beijing Founder Electronics Corp., the leading systems integrator in China. The new company, which will be called Beijing Founder Di Cheng Information Technology Co. Ltd., will become China's largest provider of network and systems integration services. China's booming information technology market is projected to experience a 35 percent compound annual growth by the year 2000. The Chinese market for systems integration was estimated at about $237 million in 2000, up from $71 million in 1996.

In early 1999, Siemens Computer Systems announced the formation of a strategic partnership with BSG, one of the leading systems integrators in the United Kingdom. Under the agreement, Siemens will combine its comprehensive portfolio of information and communications services with BSG's expertise in developing innovative information technology applications.

RESEARCH AND TECHNOLOGY

Integrating the Internet into other applications constitutes a major area of research and development in the industry. Among other applications, the Internet has stimulated research into the development of integrated systems for Internet service providers (ISPs). As demand for Internet access escalated in the mid-1990s, a spate of telephone companies rushed to begin offering such service. SI firms such as Technology Applications Inc. worked on developing systems to allow ISPs the efficiency of integrated Internet servers for network interface, online security, communications access, networking management, implementation, Web development, administration, and maintenance.

FURTHER READING

Alexander, Steve. "More than Just Hardware." *Computerworld,* 26 February 1996.

———. "Top-Down." *Computerworld,* 26 February 1996.

Caton, Michael. "The Great Systems Integrator Search." *PC Week,* 21 June 1999.

Earls, Alan R. "Who to Choose?" *Computerworld,* 26 February 1996. Available from http://www.computerworld .com.

Elgin, Ben. "Be Sure to Watch Your Back." *Sm@rt Reseller,* 27 September 1999.

Girishankar, Saroja. "Integrators Turn Their Attention to E-commerce." *Information Week,* 21 May 1999.

King, Julia. "Goliaths Losing Ground in Systems Integrator Market." *Computerworld,* 26 February 1996.

———. "IS Firm Looks beyond Tech Skills." *Computerworld,* 21 April 1997.

Klinger, Linda. "Fed Downsizing Sends Work to Systems Integrators." *Washington Business Journal,* 22 January 1999.

Madden, John. "Changing of the Guard." *PC Week,* 17 May 1999.

———. "CSC, EDS Jump into Web Hosting." *PC Week Online,* 2 March 2000. Available from http://www .pcweek.com.

Mullich, Joe. "Trends: Will the Real Network Integrator Please Stand Up." *InternetWeek,* 13 July 1998.

Schaff, William. "Scient's Signs Are Still Good." *Information Week,* 23 October 2000.

Uimonen, Terho. "IDC Bullish on Asia Systems Integration Arena." *ComputerWorld Today,* 22 October 1998.

Violino, Bob, and Bruce Caldwell. "Analyzing the Integrators." *Information Week,* 16 November 1998.

Vowler, Julia. "Contemplate a Mammoth Investment." *Computer Weekly,* 30 September 1999.

TELEMEDICINE

Perhaps it's not surprising that medicine would follow the two major trends of the information age: high-speed communications and easy, immediate access to a wealth of information. In line with both of these trends is the emerging telemedicine industry. While often broadly defined simply as the transfer of electronic medical data from one location to another, telemedicine really encompasses a broad range of emerging technologies—including telecommunications tools, information systems, and imaging technologies. Telemedicine is primarily intended to supplement the practice of conventional medicine and facilitate the exchange of information needed for diagnosis and treatment of illnesses.

The U.S. market for telemedicine was estimated at over $700 million by the end of the 1990s. Overall growth was projected at 35 percent annually from 1998 to 2002, with a 42 percent increase in public sector investments and 89 percent growth in sites. By 2005, prison telemedicine sites are expected to grow by 280 percent, and military investment is expected to double. The market for overall health-care-related information, however, is projected to grow by only 3 percent per year. If the predictions ring true, the telemedicine industry may serve to spark a health-care revolution in the 21st century.

ORGANIZATION AND STRUCTURE

Telemedicine typically involves interactive, *real-time* transactions (such as videoconferencing) that may require dedicated networks or even satellite links or *store-and-forward* systems that allow data, images, or patient information to be transmitted from a personal computer (PC) and inspected at the receiver's and sender's convenience. Transmission media include phone lines, coaxial or integrated services digital network lines, satellites, and other peripherals. Although complex dedicated networks provide the infrastructure for many institutional applications, telemedicine is rapidly evolving to encompass software and products for affordable desktop systems that can integrate voice, video, and data.

Applications range in complexity from the relatively simple transfer of digitized images or data via phone lines or the Internet to consultations and videoconferencing, to the monitoring of patients at home, or the direction of surgery or diagnostic procedures from a distance. Most applications have evolved from government-funded pilot programs, and a substantial proportion of telemedicine's advances were initially developed to meet the needs of military medicine and to improve health care in remote areas. Still in its infancy, telemedicine is available primarily to large institutions such as medical centers and prisons. In 1998 more than 700 companies supplied products and services for remote consultations, home health, teleradiology, telepathology, patient monitoring, distance education, and research.

The most popular application of telemedicine is the transmission of images in radiology, pathology, and dermatology, which do not require the patient's real-time involvement and can circumvent numerous legal problems created by cooperative diagnosis and treatment across state lines. The transmission of still images is also a well-established practice that Medicare and some other third parties will reimburse. Telemedicine in prisons, where the cost of patient transportation is exorbitant, has been highly successful. Interactive conferences for remote consults and distance education for practicing physicians and medical students are also becoming more widespread. At the end of the 1990s most managed care organizations were still examining the cost savings of telemedicine for home health care and many other applications.

HOME HEALTH

With the number of U.S. senior citizens growing at a nearly exponential rate, home health spending continues to increase at a steady pace. According to government estimates, home health spending exceeded $20 billion in 1999. Telemedical home health applications can range from phone-based call centers to integrated home telemonitoring systems that track the progress of chronically ill or recovering patients. In numerous pilot projects, at-home monitoring has been shown to reduce doctor and emergency visits and enable fewer home health nurses to see more patients more frequently in a shorter time. TeVital, a leading supplier of home-based monitoring equipment, estimated that per-cost home health visits can be reduced by one-third to one-half through the use of sensing and video systems. Although home health telemedicine promises enormous potential savings, only a handful of mostly university-based programs existed in the United States in 1999.

At least one special pilot program may promote more widespread use. American TeleCare, Inc.'s $1.5 million project—launched in early 1999—installed systems in 100 homes, thereby linking them with staff at Veteran's Hospital in Tampa, Florida. Connected via ordinary phone lines, the systems transmitted heart and lung sounds and vital signs in real-time between patient and hospital care staff. The initiative was expected to demonstrate improvements in accessibility of care and lower care costs, with fewer emergency room visits and inpatient days. While the final results were not yet recorded, as of 2000, physician, patient, and nurse responses were very positive.

RURAL HEALTH

According to the Health Resource and Services Administration, telemedicine was used to deliver patient care—primarily radiology services—in approximately one-third of all rural hospitals in the United States by the mid-1990s; 40 percent of those programs were nonexistent in 1994. The most common applications were for diagnostic consults, data transmissions, and chronic disease management. Many rural

hospitals are limited by the high cost of telecommunication technology, but federal attempts to offset those fees with a subsidy program were partly dismantled in 1998 by service providers' attempts to levy additional taxes. In January 1999, physicians in underserved rural areas became eligible for Medicare reimbursement for telemedicine services, with payment shared among practitioners. Although federal Medicaid law does not recognize telemedicine as a distinct service, services administered via telemedicine applications may be reimbursed at the state's option, according to a U.S. Department of Health and Human Services' Health Care Financing Administration Web page. As of 2000, at least 14 states reimbursed for services provided via telemedicine applications for reasons including improved access to specialists and reduction of transportation costs.

BACKGROUND AND DEVELOPMENT

Although interest in telemedicine was revived by the technological advances of the late 1990s, the use of communications technology to improve information sharing and to connect patients with doctors located elsewhere is not new. One of the first applications in the United States was a closed-circuit television system devised for a Nebraska state psychiatric institute in the 1950s. The National Aeronautics and Space Administration (NASA) began using telemetric devices to monitor the condition of astronauts in space in the 1960s and later to deliver health care to the Papago Indians of Arizona in the 1970s. Other early projects included a telemedicine station at Boston's Logan Airport to deliver emergency care to travelers, and an experimental network that used satellite-based video to provide health care in isolated regions of Alaska.

International prototypes of low-cost telemedicine to link rural populations with health-care providers included the Memorial University of Newfoundland's satellite-based audio and teleconferencing network that connected institutions throughout the province and was later linked to Kenya and five Caribbean nations. Using a government satellite, an Australian pilot project was begun in 1984 to provide health care to a remote group of islanders. In 1989 NASA established a satellite consultation network that used voice, video, and fax to aid earthquake victims in Soviet Armenia and was later extended to help burn victims after a railroad accident in Russia.

The U.S. government has actively supported a broad variety of mostly university-based demonstration projects for several decades, but many of its activities have never been systematically evaluated. Thirty-five organizations in nine government agencies spent more than $646 million on telemedicine projects between 1994 and 1996, but in 1997 the General Accounting Office found the projects to be poorly coordinated, and a U.S. Department of Commerce report questioned their cost-effectiveness.

After the National Information Infrastructure identified telemedicine as a key focus of information technology, joint agency ventures were reorganized to fulfill the requirements of the Telecommunications Reform Act of 1996, which mandated better reporting and evaluation of all federal telemedicine initiatives. Medicare was mandated to begin paying for some telemedicine consultations in 1999. Telecommunications carriers were required to provide service to rural health-care providers at rates comparable to those of urban areas in that state, with the support subsidy programs.

Yet the distribution of funds, capped annually at $400 million, was slow. An Office for the Advancement of Telehealth update stated that in mid-1999, 105 applications were waiting Federal Communications Commission (FCC) approval, and more than 200 additional applications were near completion for FCC submission. The FCC subsequently assigned the Universal Service Administrative Co. (USAC) to audit applications and administer the program. USAC recommendations outlined in a March 1999 report were intended to simplify the process and allow growth in health networks.

In 1996 the National Library of Medicine (NLM) and the Health Care Financing Administration, which administers Medicare, began a new series of demonstration projects to evaluate the use and cost-effectiveness of telemedicine in a wide variety of clinical settings. The NLM announced two additional projects in September 1997, and in 1998 awarded 24 contracts to various organizations to develop novel medical projects demonstrating Internet applications. These projects, including free Medline access on the Internet, with links to U.S. and international journals, continued to receive funding from the fiscal year 1999 presidential budget of $171.3 million for the NLM.

Additional funding to rural areas has been made available since 1993 through the U.S. Department of Agriculture. The 1999 Distance Learning and Telemedicine Loan and Grant Program had $150 million available for loans and $12.5 million for grants.

An army doctor working in a field/medical communication center. (Photo Researchers, Inc./Art Stein)

As of 2000, the program had funded nearly 300 projects—totaling more than $68 million—and improving health care in nearly 750 hospitals and rural health-care clinics.

CURRENT CONDITIONS

Many visionary projections about the future of telemedicine have not been realized, and early grant-funded projects suffered from lack of focus. In addition, market projections are difficult because products and services are often part of larger investments in telecommunications technologies and health-care delivery systems. Nevertheless, most industry projections were quite optimistic. The C. Everett Koop Institute estimated that as insurers recognize the savings provided by electronic links to patients and as technologies improve, telemedicine would become a $20 billion market consisting of software and hardware, biomedical equipment, and a standardized telecommunications infrastructure.

An ATSP survey further found that telemedicine programs for prison populations accounted for 20 percent of the reported activity. Remote care services were most commonly used for specialist consultation and second opinions; increasingly, however, telemedicine is being used for chronic illness management, emergency care, follow-up care, interpretation of diagnostic exams and home health care.

According to Feedback Research Services, in 1999 the U.S. market for telepathology, teleradiology, and videoconferencing systems was worth about $100 million. Telemedicine-related videoconferencing systems in Europe, North America, and the Pacific Rim accounted for $250 million, and worldwide sales of products and services approached $520 million in 1997. Annual worldwide growth is estimated at 15 percent, and Europe and the Pacific Rim may account for telemedicine expenditures of $1.4 billion by the year 2001.

Frost & Sullivan, an industry research group, estimated sales of picture archiving and communications systems and teleradiology systems in the United States—which accounts for 81 percent of the market—and Europe at $368.8 million in 1998. The estimated growth rate was projected at 28 percent, which would yield a total annual market of $1.6 billion by the year 2004.

A Healthcare Information and Systems Society survey of senior health-care executives also supported these projections: more than one-third of the organizations surveyed used telemedicine, 10 percent planned on using it within the next 21 months, and 28 percent were investigating its use in the future. In addition, 93 percent of telemedicine program managers surveyed by *Telemedicine and Telehealth Networks* planned to expand by 2003.

In December 2000 President Clinton signed legislation with strong bipartisan support that will greatly expand Medicare reimbursement for telemedicine services. The bill greatly expanded the range of telemedical services covered by Medicare. The bill will go into effect 1 October 2001. Reimbursement issues were seen as among the chief obstacles to telemedicine in the late 1990s. Feedback Research Services reported that U.S. telemedicine programs were reimbursed less than $10 million in 1999. because of the vagueness inherent in federal Medicaid law, states have the flexibility to reimburse the costs unique to telemedicine applications, such as technical support or line charges. As service caps become more universal and evidence of telemedicine's cost-effectiveness accumulates, managed care organizations may begin reimbursing telemedicine more widely, or even requiring its use when direct patient-physician interaction is not essential.

OBSTACLES

Although the cost of typical applications is quickly falling, telemedicine is not a common feature of the average medical practice. The most significant obstacles to its widespread use are licensure constraints, malpractice concerns, lack of reimbursement, technical compatibility problems, and physician resistance.

Technology. Many interactive applications require high-bandwidth carriers and are dependent on switched public network—expensive media not yet balanced by the overall cost savings of many telemedicine applications. Although networking solutions for expensive real-time teleconferencing and high-level data exchange will continue to be critical, lack of integration and standards have discouraged many institutions from investing heavily in transitional or quickly obsolescent technology.

Liability. Electronically administered medical care that transcends a single jurisdiction poses significant new licensing, credentialing, and malpractice problems. Except for military physicians, who are licensed in one state but may practice anywhere, physicians who wish to practice telemedicine across state lines must be licensed wherever they provide care. Although reciprocal licensing schemes have been proposed by the Federation of State Medical Boards, they have thus far been rejected by the American Medical Association and other influential physicians' groups. Malpractice claims have also already been made for misdiagnoses by consulting physicians based on inadequate image transmission. Several states have devised limited special-purpose licenses, but reciprocity among states is not expected until some time in 2001.

Physician Resistance. In addition to malpractice concerns, logistical and political barriers also exist among individual practitioners who perceive increasingly centralized and cooperative medical care as a threat to their livelihood. Many physicians also express resistance to expensive technologies that cannot be easily integrated into an existing medical practice. Because patient records still exist substantially in paper form, data from electronic transactions must often be manually added to a medical record, adding another level of administrative labor. Rural physicians, among others, express reservations about giving up existing referral structures in favor of monopolistic networks mandated by large health-care centers, and urban specialists accustomed to authority over their local resources express misgivings about relinquishing control over the quality of information available to them from distant sources. Many physicians cite inconvenience in existing telemedical consultation procedures and inconclusive evidence that telemedicine is in fact a better way to practice medicine.

Some observers believe that telemedicine will become one facet of a larger movement toward integrated health information systems that can streamline medical record-keeping and administration, which now account for up to 40 percent of the cost of medical care in the United States. Large-scale coordination of administrative and clinical data may dictate the use of multimedia electronic patient records and a level of information sharing and networking compatibility that raises serious questions about the security and confidentiality of patient data.

INDUSTRY LEADERS

Service providers and device manufacturers are quickly stepping in as telemedicine moves from a grant-funded series of pilot projects to a mature industry incorporated into mainstream health care. Telecommunications providers such as BellSouth and AT&T are participating in pilot projects to provide networks capable of integrating voice, video, data, and advanced imaging.

Ethernet local area networks and automated teller machine (ATM) networks are also being considered as backbones for multiservice networks, but experts believe significant compatibility and reliability problems still remain. Cisco Systems, a network provider, has expressed intentions to capture half of the healthcare network market and faces aggressive competition from 3Com and Bay Networks.

American TeleCare Inc. is prominent in the home health-care market. Its Personal Telemedicine System works with a PC over phone lines to send and receive physiologic data. Images can be stored and filed with patient information and notes. In March 2000, American TeleCare announced that it would be providing telemedicine equipment and services for a federally funded home telemedicine project for diabetes patients. The project is worth $28 million, the largest telemedicine grant ever funded by the U.S. government. The company formed a diabetes telemedicine partnership, called the Informatics for Diabetes Education and Telemedicine (IDEATel), with Gentiva Health Services in late 2000.

PictureTel, another videoconferencing provider, offers high-end graphics and group conferencing and participates in several U.S. Department of Defense pilot projects. In early 1999, Intel Corp. acquired 10 per-

A physician in a control room watches a simulated surgical procedure on monitors. (Photo Researchers, Inc./Jerome Yeats/Science Photo Library)

cent of PictureTel's equity, at a cost of more than $30 million. The company produces videoconferencing units with a range of technology requirements, including integrated services digital network (ISDN), T1/E1, or ATM backbones. Applications include everything from operating room and emergency care to consultations via local Internet connections. Despite the boost from Intel's acquisition, the company faced growing doubts about its future, with continuing net losses.

Vtel, the dominant video systems provider, produces videoconferencing and multimedia systems designed specifically for medical use that allow bedside input from endoscopes and other devices. The company claimed to have 1,500 systems installed worldwide. The Austin, Texas, company is second behind PictureTel, with customers such as Microsoft and the Drew Medical Center. Telemedicine products and accessories, including receivers, digital cameras, software kits and viewing stations, are highly adaptable from ISDN to ATM configurations, and Windows, Sun, or Macintosh platforms. Product distributors include Ameritech and Sprint long-distance carriers. Revenues for 2000 were $134.3 million, down from the 1999 total of $151.6 million. In late 1999, Vtel announced their new Galaxy line, and in January 2000 announced the formation of OnScreen24, a new business unit focused on high-impact visual communications. Projections for future revenues were optimistic as a result.

MedVision, Inc., a software company, produces a utility for viewing MRI, X ray, and other image and text data on any standard PC. The independent private company located in Minneapolis, Minnesota, develops software for medical practice management. Its customer base includes the Department of Defense, the University of Arizona, Canada's TechKnowledge, and the United Kingdom's United Medical Enterprises.

AMERICA AND THE WORLD

Developing nations have actively promoted telemedicine as a way of obtaining specialty care for their citizens in outlying areas, and international telemedicine consultations in turn circumvent some of the legal problems of providing interstate care domestically. International patients are linked through many consortia in Canada, Europe, and the United States, including WorldCare Ltd., a partnership between Duke University Medical Center, Massachusetts General Hospital, Johns Hopkins School of Medicine, and the Cleveland Clinic Foundation. In Malaysia, telemedicine is a cornerstone of the government's ambitious Multimedia Super Corridor, although investment was scaled back in 1998 in response to the region's economic difficulties. India participates in several consulting networks for obtaining second opinions and transmitting pathology and other data. In 1998 the first African telemedicine network was established in Mozambique.

World Care Technologies, Inc., a Cambridge, Massachusetts, company, provides telemedicine and medical management services accessible through the Internet. In 1999 the company formed a strategic alliance with Data General Corp., a leading information systems provider, and MarkCare Medical Systems, Inc., a medical imaging systems distributor. The alliance combines telemedicine and personal archiving and communication systems to interconnect healthcare providers. Initial installation sites included hospitals and clinics in Spain, Portugal, and Romania.

Canada has a long history of providing networked medical services to its remote provinces. The European Union has long advocated the use of information technology to reduce inequalities in European health care, and the European Commission has launched feasibility studies for its planned Global Emergency

Telemedicine System. Australia has been particularly aggressive in establishing telemedicine sites, and as a result, telemedical revenue grew from $36 million in 1997 to nearly $60 million in 1999, with projected sales at $4 billion by the 2005. In Great Britain, archaic record-keeping systems, bureaucratic opposition, and concern that short-term commercial interests would prevail over long-term goals have led to a few telemedicine trials but no large-scale applications.

RESEARCH AND TECHNOLOGY

Military medicine is an ideal laboratory for telemedicine technologies because of its freedom from reimbursement and licensure issues, and because its very purpose is to provide timely specialty care to remote locations. Portable medical communications systems and sensors for on-site assessment of key vital signs are being developed for possible future use on isolated job sites or in health-care settings. New electronic formats for medical information are also being developed, along with a personal information carrier intended to bridge the gap between treatment and access to a complete medical record. The importance of teleradiology was affirmed in 1998 during the U.S. mission to Bosnia-Herzegovina, where all radiological exams were conducted from neighboring countries. Numerous projects in teledentistry, teledermatology, telepsychiatry, and telepathology are in progress, including experimental uses of artificial intelligence to aid medical decision making under battlefield conditions and high-resolution diagnostic imaging provided by forward medical units to distant treatment centers.

Telemedicine is also being used outside clinical settings. Virgin Airlines and Princess Cruise Line both offer telemedicine services to travelers. A Florida homeless shelter has used telemedicine, especially to treat common ailments in homeless children. As the cost of technology falls and private companies gain a better understanding of the unique needs of health-care information systems, experts believe such commercial applications for routine health monitoring or emergency care will likely become more commonplace.

FURTHER READING

"American TeleCare, Inc." Available from http://www.americantelecare.com.

"ATA Applauds Presidential Signing of Major Telemedicine Legislation." *Business Wire*, 27 December 2000.

"ATSP '98 Telemedicine Report Chronicles Industry Growth, Diversification." *BW Healthwire*, 7 April 1999.

Bergeron, Bryan P. "Telepresence and the Practice of Medicine." *Post Graduate Medicine*, April 1998.

Bentivoglio, John. "Unleash the Internet: Outdated Laws and Regulations are Holding Back Advances in e-Health Ventures." *Modern Healthcare*, 6 November 2000.

Burns, Patrick. "Changing Times and the Business Case for 'Telestuff.'" *Health Management Technology*, July 1997.

"Data General, MarkCare Join Forces with WorldCare, Firms to Offer Integrated PACS/Telemedicine Systems." *PACS and Networking News*, February 1999.

"Data General, MarkCare Medical Systems and WorldCare Technologies Announce a Strategic Alliance to Provide Integrated Clinical Information Management Solutions to the Healthcare Industry." Westboro, MA: Data General Corp., 12 January 1999. Available from http://www.dg.com/news/html/01_12_99.html.

Davis, Stephania H. "What's Holding up the Telemedicine Explosion?" *Telephony*, 1 June 1998.

Dudman, Jane. "Health and Efficiency (Telemedicine in the United Kingdom)." *Computer Weekly*, 31 July 1997.

Evans, Jim. "Telemedicine: A Picture Is Worth. . . ." *Health Management Technology*, January 1998.

"Federal Telemedicine." Available from http://www.cbloch.com/about.html.

"HCFA Model for Telehealth out of Step with Current Practice." *Medical Outcomes and Guidelines Alert*, 18 June 1998.

Janah, Monua. "Health Care by Cisco." *Informationweek*, 23 February 1998.

"Killer Apps: The Telemedicine Breakthrough." *America's Network*, 15 January 1998.

Kim, Howard. "No Telemedicine 'Rush.'" *American Medical News*, 4 May 1998.

Larkin, Marilynn. "Telemedicine Finds Its Place in the Real World." *Lancet*, 30 August 1997.

"Latest Analysis Suggests a $4.2 Million Reimbursement Level for 1997 Telemedicine Services." *BW Healthwire*, 25 March 1999.

Linkous, Jonathan D. "Telemedicine Information & Resources: Predicting the Market for Telemedicine." Available from http://www.atmeda.org/resources/marketreports.html.

Magenau, Jeff L. "Digital Diagnosis: Liability Concerns and State Licensing Issues Are Inhibiting the Progress of Telemedicine." *Communications and the Law*, December 1997.

Meredith, Helen. "Exporting Skills Good Medicine for Health Care." *Australian Financial Review*, 17 July 1998.

Nairn, Geoffrey. "Internet Set for Key Role in Healthcare." *Financial Times*, 1 April 1998.

National Library of Medicine. "Fact Sheet: Telemedicine Related Programs." 11 December 1999. Available from http://www.nlm.nih.gov/pubs/factsheets/telemedicine.html.

"New Rules: Medicare to Pay for Interactive Consults Only." *Modern Healthcare*, 29 June 1998.

"NLM National Telemedicine Initiative." Bethesda, MD: National Library of Medicine, 5 April 1999. Available from http://www.nlm.nih.gov/research/telemedinit.html.

"Obstacles to Telemedicine's Growth." *Medical Economics*, 24 November 1997.

"PictureTel: Industries and Applications." 16 April 1999. Available from http://www.pictureTel.com.

"The Present Offers a Small Glimpse of Telemedicine's Future." *BBI Newsletter*, 1 May 1998.

Reid, Jim. "A Telemedicine Primer: Understanding the Issues." Available from http://www.atsp.org/telemedicine/primer.asp.

"Revolutionizing Science in a Digital World." *PR Newswire*, 4 December 2000.

Robinson, Kevin. "Telemedicine: Technology Arrives, but Barriers Remain." *Biophotonics International*, July/August 1998.

Rosenberg, Robert. "Telemedicine: An Expensive Prescription?" *Business Communications Review*, May 1997.

"Rural Providers Take $300 Million Hit as FCC Bows to Political Pressure." *Modern Healthcare*, 29 June 1998.

Sani, Rozana. "Ministry Cuts back on Telemedicine." *New Straits Times*, 25 May 1998.

Sherter, Alain L. "Using Telemedicine to Bring Care to Homeless." *Health Data Management*, March 1998.

Smith, Robert C., ed. "Telemedicine." *Medical and Healthcare Marketplace Guide 1997-1998*. Philadelphia: Dorland's Biomedical, 1998.

Snyder, Karyn. "Telemedicine: The New Frontier." *Drug Topics*, 4 August 1997.

Sorelle, Ruth. "Vision for the Future: Health Care Options Grow with Rural Telemedicine." *Houston Chronicle*, 7 July 1998.

———. "Vision for the Future: Medicine On-Screen." *Houston Chronicle*, 5 July 1998.

———. "Vision for the Future: Telemedicine May Be Just What the Doc Ordered in Space." *Houston Chronicle*, 6 July 1998.

———. "Vision for the Future: Telemedicine a Virtual Reality of the Future." *Houston Chronicle*, 8 July 1998.

Tieman, Jeff. "Monitoring a Good Opportunity: Telemedicine Grows as Method to Reach Poorly Served Regions." *Modern Healthcare,* 16 October 2000.

"Universal Fund Program: Options for the Future." Rockville, MD: Office for the Advancement of Telehealth, February 1999. Available from http://telehealth.hrsa.gov/univtxt.htm.

"Universal Service Administrative Company Report to the FCC: Evaluation of Rural Health Care Program." Washington: Federal Communications Commission, 29 March 1999. Available from http://www.fcc.gov.

U.S. Department of Health and Human Services. Health Care Financing Administration. "Medicaid and Telemedicine." 31 March 1999. Available from http://www.hcfa.gov/medicaid/telelist.html.

"Vtel: The Company." Available from http://www.vtel.com.

"World Care Technologies." 17 April 1999. Available from http://www.worldcaretech.com.

TELEPHONE SERVICES AND ACCESSORIES

INDUSTRY SNAPSHOT

As the telephone became a necessity and as telephone penetration peaked, telephone companies began expanding their services and telephone equipment manufacturers began developing new accessories to make telephone use more convenient and to give users greater options. The wide array of telephone accessories and services was developed mainly by research and development teams at some of the country's better-known telecommunications companies. An explosion of mergers and acquisitions during the late 1990s and early 2000s made this a corporate landscape subject to sharp changes from day to day. For the most part, telephone users avail themselves of these services through local service providers, although the product or technology may have been developed by another telecommunications company. Among the more popular telephone services and accessories are call block, call forwarding, caller ID, call waiting, call waiting ID, repeat dial, return call, signal ring, 900-call block, the cordless digital spread spectrum telephone, and conference calling.

The upsurge in U.S. telecommunications industry megamergers was traced by many to the Telecommunications Reform Act of 1996. Intended to deregulate the industry and stimulate competition, the statute instead appeared to set off a massive wave of corporate mergers. Of the original seven Baby Bells, three remained by 2001: Verizon (the product of the merger of Bell Atlantic and GTE), SBC Communications (which absorbed Baby Bell sibling Pacific Telesis), and BellSouth.

ORGANIZATION AND STRUCTURE

In the United States, the face of the telecommunications industry was forever altered in 1984 when the Justice Department's antitrust ruling broke the giant American Telephone & Telegraph (AT&T) into seven regional companies, one of which was Bell Atlantic. It should be noted, however, that Bell Atlantic's acquisition in the late 1990s of Baby Bell sibling NYNEX for $25.7 billion doubled its size and made it the number-two U.S. telecommunications service company after its former parent. Its merger with GTE Corp. in 2000 doubled the company's size again.

Mergers and acquisitions continued to change the structure of the U.S. telecommunications industry throughout the second half of the 1990s. As of mid-2000, the principal basic telephone service providers in the United States were SBC Communications, BellSouth, Qwest, WorldCom, Sprint, and Verizon. In addition, there were numerous small independent telephone companies located throughout the United States. These and other companies such as AT&T, Lucent Technologies, and Nortel also develop and market some of the highly successful new add-on services and devices.

Almost all of these companies, independents included, offer customers a broad range of add-on services and accessories, including caller ID, call block, and call forwarding. In addition to these services, American consumers have a number of other products to choose from, such as the PowerDialer from Technology Arts of Massachusetts. PowerDialer was designed to automatically redial busy numbers as quickly as the local telephone company could process the calls, as fast as 25 times in a minute. The product, which retailed for $249 in the late 1990s, is marketed directly by Technology Arts and is not available through local telephone companies.

The future promises an even broader range of services for telephone consumers with the spread of fiber-optic wiring, which will allow faster and better data transmission over telephone lines. A number of major telephone service providers also acquired an interest in television cable companies in preparation for the day when they would begin to offer television connections over telephone lines—and that day is not far off. Furthermore, the Internet and wireless telecommunications systems will most likely play a significant role in the development of the industry.

BACKGROUND AND DEVELOPMENT

Upheaval in the U.S. telecommunications industry in the mid-1980s, resulting from the Justice Department's antitrust ruling, left telephone companies in a brand-new competitive arena. Home and business telephone users, who had previously rented equipment from the local telephone company, could now purchase their own equipment and pay local providers for hooking up to their networks. Although most telephone companies offer a range of telephones for sale, consumers usually find they can get a better deal at the local discount chain or an electronics store.

Most telephone companies soon realized there was a virtual gold mine in marketing add-on products. Suddenly, services that previously had been available only to sophisticated business users were being sold to home service consumers. These included call-forwarding ability and the ability to dial back the number of the last caller (even if the phone was not answered). Some such services were even offered on a per-use basis. For example, telephone customers unable to get to a ringing phone in time could punch the star key and two numbers, typically six and nine, to activate this service, for which they would then be charged 75 cents or $1. Those who chose to have access to this service at all times paid a monthly fee for unlimited use.

Among the most popular services marketed by local telephone service providers are call block, which allows telephone customers to block all calls from certain telephone numbers, and call forwarding, which routes all calls to another telephone number or to voice mail when the phone is busy or not answered. Also

particularly popular is caller ID, the use of which requires a small box with a window to display a telephone number. This feature allows customers to determine the number (and sometimes the name of the caller) from which a call is coming.

The technology for cordless telephony has improved significantly since such equipment was first marketed. Reception on early cordless telephones left a great deal to be desired, and many purchasers of such early equipment soon abandoned it and returned to corded phones. In the late 1990s, digital spread spectrum technology vastly improved the reception and transmission quality of cordless telephones.

CURRENT CONDITIONS

The telephone accessories and services industry is a segment of the $250 billion telecommunications industry. Entering the new century, the worldwide telecommunications industry offered a vast selection of premium telephone accessories and services. Furthermore, such established services as call waiting and caller ID had gained strong levels of penetration by this point. In addition, these accessories and services adapted to the prominence wireless and Internet telecommunications technology as well as to changing user needs. Available from local telephone service providers, and in some cases from independent retailers, telephone accessories ran the gamut from caller ID boxes to a range of telephone instruments, both corded and cordless.

By the 21st century, the different models of telephones available to consumers became increasingly expansive. In contrast, about 20 years ago, choices would have been largely limited to console, wall, or princess telephones in black, white, or pink. With Ma Bell's control on telephones loosened by deregulation, a typical discount store routinely stocks a selection of about 50 cordless phones, 30 phones with cords, and at least a dozen cellular phones. That does not include the telephone/answering machine combinations, of which one might find at least half a dozen. Better yet, the increased competition in this marketplace has sent prices plummeting. By 2000, a 25-channel cordless telephone could be found at most discount retailers for less than $100, about half what it would have cost only a year earlier.

Furthermore, cordless telephones even outsold corded phones in the late 1990s. Jim Barry, a spokesman for the Consumer Electronics Manufacturers Association, predicted that the gap between cordless and corded phone sales was likely to grow larger over time. "What you're getting with a cordless phone is convenience," Barry said. "And the technology of cordless telephones is getting better." Cordless telephones also proved to be a very popular gift idea. For example, Ameritech, owned by local service behemoth SBC Communications, reported that about 45 percent of all its cordless telephones are sold in November, just in time for Christmas gift giving.

There are a number of reasons for the sharp increase in popularity of the cordless telephone, not the least of which is significantly improved reception. The first cordless phones on the market allowed a user to walk from one room of the house to another without dragging a telephone cord along with them, but they were subject to considerable interference, had a limited range, and lacked security. The first cordless phones transmitted sound from the handset to the telephone's base using an analog signal. Neighboring cordless phone users often found snippets of other conversations breaking into their own. Even transmissions from household baby monitors sometimes interfered with cordless phone calls. Modern cordless models broadcast over frequencies that are less crowded, offering much clearer signals. Even better, some new cordless phones use digital signals, reducing the chances that conversations would be intercepted. Sounds are converted into computer code, and then transmitted between the base and the handset.

In addition to increased dependability, cordless telephones today are available in a number of different models. Early cordless phones, operating on frequencies between 43 and 49 MHz, were highly susceptible to interference from computers, fluorescent lights, and other such devices. Transmissions at such low frequencies generally were not able to penetrate walls or other such obstructions. Most of these early cordless phones, few of which are still available in stores, operated over 10 channels. If interference was encountered on one channel, the phone would switch automatically to the next.

Improved reception is available on 25-channel analog cordless phones, which manage to avoid interference by using more channels. Some of the 25-channel phones come with built-in caller ID. If longer range and still clearer reception is required, 900-MHz analog phones are a good choice, according to CEMA's Jim Barry. He said that some such telephones operate dependably at three-quarters of a mile from the base. He pointed out, however, that since the signal is uncoded, users run the risk of having their conversations intercepted. That danger can be avoided if users opt for a 900-MHz digital phone, which convert sounds

into code for transmission from the handset to the base. To ensure even better reception, some 900-MHz phones use digital spread spectrum technology. If interference is encountered on one channel, the phone searches for a clear channel as far away as possible from the one that is blocked. This technology increases the clarity of reception and range. Finally, the superior cordless phone of the late 1990s and early 2000s was the 2.4-GHz model, available from Panasonic, Siemens, and Bang and Olufsen Telecom. These phones have twice the range of the 900-MHz models and offer increased clarity. In addition, telephone equipment makers included other features such as multiline capabilities and security features.

Although the performance of cordless telephones sharply improved, for many users the tried and true corded telephone was first choice because of its dependability and security. Other attractive features of corded phones are the lower price and the knowledge that they will still function in a power outage, something that cannot be said of cordless phones. The phone line itself supplies all the power needed to operate a corded telephone. For those who must use the telephone while typing or using their hands, however, a headset phone may make sense.

Of the add-on telephone services and accessories, the three most popular features are call waiting, caller ID, and voice mail, in that order. Call waiting achieved significant penetration by the late 1990s. Pacific Bell, for example, reported that 50 percent of its customers subscribed to its call-waiting service. Part of the appeal stems from the simplicity of obtaining and using this service, because call-waiting service is compatible with any telephone. When a user with this service is on the telephone and someone else calls, an audible signal can be heard on the line. The user may click the receiver button or push "flash" to answer the new call. No special equipment is needed for this service, although customers must pay a monthly fee to the local service provider. Moreover, by 2000 telephone companies merged two popular add-on services—call waiting and caller ID—apprising users of their callers so that they could decide whether or not to take incoming calls while already on the phone. This service requires a caller ID box, caller ID service, call-waiting service, and the new caller ID/call-waiting service, which cost $3 per month from Pacific Bell.

In addition, by the beginning of the new century, new call-waiting technology finally hit the market, enabling users to use call-waiting services while online. Companies such as Callwave, Pagoo, Prodigy, and MSN were among the first to offer programs for call-waiting service while using the Internet. Use of these programs cost $5 a month during this period. In addition, Actiontec developed a call-waiting modem that informs users of incoming calls and gives them the option of staying online or taking calls.

The average household trades approximately 115 messages a week, according to a household messaging study by Pitney Bowes. In addition, the average household also receives a plethora of telemarketing calls each week. Because of the influx of calls received, caller ID subscriptions quadrupled between 1995 and 1999, according to *American Demographics. American Demographics* also reported that about 40 percent of people between the ages of 16 and 74 in households with incomes of $25,000 or below use caller ID service. Unlike call waiting, caller ID service requires special equipment, specifically a liquid crystal display (LCD) screen to display information about incoming calls. Some newer models of phones, both corded and cordless, have a caller ID screen built in, or consumers who decide to opt for this service can purchase a small caller ID box with such a screen. Customers pay a monthly fee for caller ID service and also a rental fee if they use a caller ID box supplied by the telephone company. In the late 1990s, telephone companies started offering this service via the Internet, for managing calls while online. For example, Bell Atlantic (now Verizon) launched Internet Call Manager for $5.95 a month, which notifies users of incoming calls while they surf the Web. Voice-mail systems are covered in a separate essay in this book.

Increasingly popular in the late 1990s and early 2000s were two-line phones that allowed customers to use a line hooked up to a computer modem as a second voice line when the computer was not in use. Other telephone accessories or features available on the market included storage for telephone numbers called frequently, speakers for hands-free telephone use, and an answering machine for those who prefer that to voice mail.

INDUSTRY LEADERS

A leading player in the market for telephone services and accessories is Verizon, formerly Bell Atlantic, the largest of the surviving Baby Bells. Bell Atlantic's acquisition of Baby Bell sibling NYNEX doubled the company's size. Further expansion followed with the purchase of GTE Corp. to create Verizon. Based in New York City, Verizon is the second-largest telecommunications services company after AT&T and the largest local telephone service provider, edging ahead of SBC Communications with

its GTE acquisition. Verizon provides local telephone service to some 63 million homes and businesses in a 31-state area stretching from Maine to Virginia, and includes the District of Columbia. The company also boasts some 4 million long-distance customers. Verizon also operates, in conjunction with Vodafone, the leading wireless telephone service, Verizon Wireless. In 1999 Bell Atlantic posted net income of $4.2 billion on revenue of $33.1 billion, while GTE brought in net income of about $4 billion in 1999 on revenue of $25.3 billion.

Based in San Antonio, SBC Communications Inc. is the leading provider of local telephone service, after key acquisitions in the late 1990s, including Ameritech. With almost 61 million local-access lines in the states of Arkansas, California, Connecticut, Kansas, Missouri, Nevada, Oklahoma, and Texas, the company is the umbrella organization for such familiar subsidiaries as Southern New England Telecommunications, Southwestern Bell, and Pacific Bell. SBC is also active on the international front, holding interests in telecommunications companies in 10 countries outside the United States. Besides local service, SBC also is a major player in the wireless market, in which it combined with BellSouth to form Cingular Wireless, which boasted 19 million subscribersSBC is also a player in the long-distance, cable, and Internet access markets. The company reported revenues of $49.4 billion in 1999, with $8.1 billion in profit.

Lucent Technologies Inc., the former equipment manufacturing arm of AT&T, is today the largest U.S. manufacturer of telecommunications hardware and software. Based in Murray Hill, New Jersey, the company's products range from integrated circuits to sophisticated business communications systems. Lucent is also home to Bell Laboratories, AT&T's former research and development division. In fiscal year 1999, Lucent reported net income of $4.7 billion on revenue of $38.3 billion.

With 80 million customers, AT&T is the clear leader in the telecommunications industry. The company provides long-distance telephone, Internet, cable, wireless, and even local telephone services, though by 2001 it was preparing to split these operations into separate companies. At the turn of the century, AT&T, parent of the Baby Bells, was busily exploring ways to get back into the local telephone business that it lost when the company was broken up in 1984. In an effort to advance this strategy, AT&T acquired TeleCommuncations Inc. The purchase gave AT&T access to about 18 million homes through cable hookups. AT&T also acquired MediaOne, becoming the nation's largest cable provider. The company hoped to upgrade one-way cable lines into two-way connections, allowing AT&T to offer telephone, cable television, and high-speed Internet access over these connections. The company reported net income in 1999 of $3.4 billion and revenue of $62.3 billion.

Headquartered in Atlanta, BellSouth Corp. is the third largest provider of local telephone service, with 24 million subscribers in nine southeastern states. It is looking to Latin America for new business opportunities to offset some of the losses expected in local U.S. markets due to increased competition under deregulation. BellSouth posted 1999 net income of $3.45 billion on revenue of $25.2 billion. Net earnings showed a decrease of 2 percent over 1998, while revenue rose 9 percent over the previous year.

WorldCom Inc. (formerly called MCI World-Com), based in Clinton, Mississippi, is the second-leading player in the long-distance telephone market as well as a marketer of some telephone services and accessories. Formed by the 1998 merger of MCI Communications and WorldCom, the company has operations in more than 65 countries. In 2000 WorldCom announced another merger—this time with Sprint, but the deal was struck down by the U.S. Department of Justice. In 1999 it reported earnings of over $4 billion on revenue of $37.1 billion.

Headquartered in Brampton, Ontario, Nortel Networks, formerly Northern Telecom Ltd., is the second-largest manufacturer of telephone equipment in North America. Its products range from elaborate business communications systems to personal telephone equipment. About 60 percent of the company's revenue is generated by sales in the United States. In 1999 Northern Telecom reported a net loss of $537 million on revenue of $22.2 billion.

Sprint Corp., like most players in the U.S. telecommunications market, has irons in a number of fires. Already the number-three long-distance provider in the United States, the company also provides local phone and Internet services. The company's local service division boasted more than 8 million customers in 18 states as of late 2000. In 2000 its acquisition by WorldCom was denied by regulators. In 1999 the company's totaled $1.5 billion on revenue of $17.01 billion.

Based in Denver, Colorado, Qwest Communications International leapt to the top of the telephone services market with its purchase of Baby Bell U S West, which doubled the company's size, in 2000. The fourth-largest long-distance phone company in the United States, Qwest's acquisition of U S West also gave it 25 million local phone service subscribers, and

it was hoped that the move would discard U S West's reputation for poor service that earned it the nickname "U S Worst." In 1999 Qwest raked in sales of $3.9 billion and registered net income of $458 million, while U S West posted net income of $1.3 billion on revenue of $13.1 billion.

WORK FORCE

It is virtually impossible to isolate the segments of the telecommunications industry responsible for some of the specialized services and accessories covered here. The industry as a whole is a major employer in the United States as well as in most other Western countries with a sophisticated communications infrastructure. The world's growing dependence on communications technology is likely to ensure that this sector remains a major employer for the foreseeable future. It is possible, however, that some of the rationalizations in the industry brought by mergers and acquisitions may from time to time bring job reductions at some of the companies that are major players in this field.

According to employment records from the late 1990s, major employers in the telecommunications industry included Verizon, with a payroll of 145,000; SBC Communications Inc., which employed close to 204,530; and AT&T Corp., with about 148,000. BellSouth Corp. employed more than 96,200 as of 2000, while Sprint Corp. employed nearly 77,600 and WorldCom Inc. reported a payroll of 77,000 that same year. Canadian-based Nortel Networks employed 76,700, according to 2000 statistics.

Employment opportunities within the telecommunications industry run the gamut from entry-level clerical positions, to researchers and engineers, to high-paying management positions at the head of some of the industry's major players. For young people interested in participating in the technological revolution that continues to sweep this country and the world, the telecommunications industry is at the heart of this revolution, sponsoring much of the research that moved technological know-how forward during the late 20th century.

AMERICA AND THE WORLD

Demand for more powerful telephone services and accessories is not limited to the United States. Virtually all of the technology that has made possible most of these tools has either been exported to or developed independently in most of the countries of the industrialized world. And the advances are not limited to the industrialized world alone. Telephone customers in some of the developing countries are also getting an opportunity to avail themselves of these telephone products. Moreover, U.S. telephone service providers are major players in the international market and equipment manufacturers such Lucent have sought contracts and partnerships around the world. Likewise, telecommunications companies from other countries, including Siemens, Alcatel, and Ericsson, have established a presence in the United States through acquisitions and partnerships.

RESEARCH AND TECHNOLOGY

Just when it seems technological advancement has reached its limits, a company steps forward to announce a new groundbreaking product or a forward-looking variation to an existing product. Built on the popular caller ID technology, a new product called privacy manager was introduced in parts of Chicago and Detroit in the fall of 1998 by Ameritech. Caller ID was designed to help users screen out unwanted calls, particularly calls from telemarketers and other sales personnel. Cagey telemarketing firms, however, managed to dodge this barrier by using legal means to block both their identities and telephone numbers. Privacy manager uses caller ID technology to identify incoming calls from phone numbers that are either "unknown" or "unavailable." Such calls are intercepted by a recorded message that asks the caller to identify himself or herself. If the party placing the call chooses to disclose his or her identity, the call rings through to the privacy manager customer, who then hears a brief recording identifying the caller. The customer then has three options: accept the call, decline the call without explanation, or decline the call and have privacy manager ask that the caller not call again. In introducing the product, Diane Primo, Ameritech's president of product management, said: "The message is loud and clear. Our customers simply want control over telemarketing."

Moreover, because of the price wars among long-distance telephone service providers, Uniden America Corp. developed a phone called the Long Distance Manager to help users obtain the lowest long-distance rates. This telephone includes cordless 900-MHz technology coupled with capabilities designed to search a database of over 50 long-distance providers to select the lowest rate—all before the user finishes dialing a number. The database is updated every two weeks and the telephone cost between $50 and $80 in 1999.

One of the technologies that futurists have talked about endlessly for the last several decades has been the so-called picture phone, which allows both parties to a conversation to see each other. Although such telephones are available, thus far the technology is still rather shaky, the pictures not so clear, and the cost prohibitive for most telephone customers. This is one long-promised technological innovation that is almost certain to materialize in the early years of the 21st century. Another innovation offered by a number of electronics companies is the screen phone, which allows users to display caller ID information, surf the Web, or check e-mail. Sort of a marriage between a telephone and a computer, Cidco's iPhone was designed to appeal to customers who want to be able to check e-mail without booting up the personal computer. The iPhone retails for about $500.

A number of telecommunications companies are expected to aggressively pursue the cable television market in the next few years. Already the technology exists to offer cable television over existing telephone lines. Ongoing work to install fiber-optic telephone lines throughout the country will certainly step up action on this front in the near-term future. Qwest, which already offers 120 digital channels of television entertainment and information over telephone lines in the Phoenix area, is moving to offer the same sort of service in metropolitan Denver.

FURTHER READING

Carroll, Kelly. "Caller ID Takes to the Internet." *Telephony,* 29 November 1999.

Cummings, James. "Hold the Phone! Options Are Ringing off the Hook." *Atlanta Journal and Constitution,* 3 December 1998.

Day, Rebecca. "Phone Home: Phones of the Future That Do It All. Now. . . ." *Popular Mechanics,* 1 May 1998, 92.

Day, Sharri. "Pacific Bell to Offer a Merged Call Waiting— Caller ID Feature." *Knight Ridder/Tribune Business News,* 21 June 1999.

"Dialtone: PowerDialer—High-Tech Gadget Helps You Break Those AOL Busies." *Work-Group Computing Report,* 24 February 1997.

"Huaxu, Motorola Form Smart Card Joint Venture; Agreement Promises Bright Future for Smart Card Industry in China." *Business Wire,* 22 January 1998.

Irvine, Martha. "Phone Company Offers Service to Filter out Sales Calls." *AP Online,* 23 September 1998.

Lach, Jennifer. "Indicators: All Circuits Are Busy." *American Demographics,* December 1999.

———. "Who's Calling, Please?" *American Demographics,* October 1999.

Lewis, Jeff. "Uniden Phone Finds Lowest Long-Distance Rate." *HFN,* 4 January 1999.

Mason, Charles. "Cox Says Early Foray's Bearing Fruit." *America's Network,* 1 June 1998, 58.

Mathoda, Ranjit. "All Hell Breaks Loose in the Telephone Industry." *B.C. Intell. Prop. & Tech. F.,* 1998.

Meyers, Anne. "Family Tech: Smart Ways to Make Home Life Easier: Technology Keeps Ringing in New Customer Phone Services." *Atlanta Journal and Constitution,* 14 February 1999.

"NCTI Introduces Clearspeech-Phone Filter at Winter CES-Digitally Cancels Noise for Telephones." *Business Wire,* 7 January 1999.

Patalon, William III. "Watch These Babies Grow." *Kiplinger's Personal Finance Magazine,* December 2000.

Phillips, Sharon. "Ameritech EVP & CFO—Interview." *Wall Street Corporate Reporter,* 5 August 1998.

"Telecommunications." *Business Week,* 10 January 2000.

TELEPHONY

Telephony was finding ever more ways to connect people more quickly and clearly at the turn of the century. Bound primarily to the mammoth telecommunications industry, telephony was carried along for the whirlwind ride that industry experienced in the late 1990s, with mergers, acquisitions, and start-ups combining with an avalanche of technological innovation to produce a tempestuous market. Involving data transmission over wired and wireless networks, telephony faced a number of new challenges and opportunities in 2000. Telephony was evolving at an astonishing rate, with a number of new types of carrier services slated to go on the market in the first decade of the 2000s. In the meantime, the industry was awash with talk of convergence, or the integration existing forms of telephony into a seamless whole.

There are myriad ways for data and voice signals to get from one place to another, most of which were picking up steam at the outset of the 21st century. Long-distance phone calls generated revenues of $40 billion in the United States in the late 1990s. Internet Protocol (IP) telephony services were expected to reach $5 billion by 2002, according to Datamonitor. Other analysts estimated that 35 percent of all phone calls would be made using Internet-based public phone networks by 2002, potentially creating a $60 billion market. Fax transmissions, meanwhile, generate revenues of about $30 billion each year in the United States. The Strategis Group expected cable modem subscribers to total 18 million worldwide by 2003, generating a market of $6 billion. Voice Information Associates, Inc. released a study in 1999 in which it

was projected that speech recognition and telephony applications would total $1.17 billion by 2003.

In addition to telecommunications firms, the computers and electronics industries figure prominently in the development of telephony, providing switches, networking equipment, and computer-telephone integration technology used in faxes, voice mail, call centers, voice recognition, video-conferencing and interactive voice response systems.

ORGANIZATION AND STRUCTURE

The industry consists of three main businesses: provision of services to consumers, corporations, and individuals; installing infrastructure—from production of hardware to deployment of software; and managing or providing business services for these business activities within the industry and to consumers such as Yellow Pages publishing and custom database maintenance.

Voice is encoded and decoded through the telephone itself into electrical signals. These are transmitted over a network of copper or fiber-optic cable, radio, or satellite transceivers, and switches between one or more other telephones or networks. The majority of telephone services are designed for speech transmission, but with the advent of computerization and digitization, networks transmit other data as well. These include facsimile documents, audio and video, and big packets of secure data. Consumers want plain old telephone service, cellular telephone service, and Internet connections; corporations need sophisticated telephony networks for broadband transmission of voice, data, and even video. And what's more, they all want to transmit data at the fastest possible speed.

With over 600 million telephones throughout the world, it is small wonder that the telecommunications industry is as lucrative and as competitive as it is. Moreover, consumers, especially in industrialized countries (and most especially in the United States), increasingly owned several phones apiece, with telephones in several rooms throughout the house, cell phones, car phones, and so on. By the end of the 20th century, analog lines were being replaced or augmented with digital technology. And with the relaxation of the regulatory climate, competition was heating up to provide these customers with the fastest, most comprehensive service.

Telephony products cut a wide market swath. These include consumer products such as calling cards and actual handsets to sophisticated frame relay and network switching products, or software and servers for high-end corporate users or service providers. Among the companies making telephony hardware and software available in the late 1990s were high-profile companies such as AT&T, Siemens Rolm Communications, Lucent Technologies, Northern Telecom, Pacific Bell, and Internet telephony players IDT and VocalTec Communications. Also active in this area were Mitel, NTT, Teleport Communications Group, NetFrame Systems, Rhetorex, PairGain Technologies, Cubix, and Madge Networks.

GOVERNMENTAL AGENCIES

The telecommunications industry is regulated by the Federal Communications Commission (FCC). This independent agency, created in 1934, regulates interstate and international communications that originate in the United States and are transmitted via radio, TV, wire, cable, and satellite. As new technologies developed, for example, this agency has undertaken the task of allocation of the electromagnetic spectrum for transmission of television and wireless communications signals. The FCC traditionally has attempted to maintain a balance between the stronger market players while ensuring markets remain open to competition.

At the state level, public utilities commissions add another layer of regulation. These bodies, which do the bidding of state lawmakers, originally granted local franchises to local service providers and regulated utilities, namely gas and power companies. The National Association of Regulatory Utility Commissioners is an umbrella group designed to make sure there are uniform regulations for public utilities. Other levels of government responsible for various regulations, primarily for oversight of such things as franchise granting and infrastructure construction, exist at the county and municipal levels.

STANDARDS BODIES AND TRADE ASSOCIATIONS

The predominant standards body for the telephony industry is the United Nations's International Telecommunication Union, based in Geneva. This body assists governments and the private sector alike by providing a forum for determining technical methods by which data is sent. A good example is the ratification of the V.90 standard for 56K modems. The American National Standards Institute approves and publishes U.S. telecommunications standards. An array of other bodies, such as the Institute of Electrical and Electronics Engineers, promulgate standards as well. The U.S. Telephone Association, Telecommunications Industry Association, Multimedia Telecommunications Association, and National Exchange Carrier Association are among the various industry trade organizations formed to protect the interests of member companies within the industry.

IMPACT OF REGULATION

Regulation of the U.S. telecommunications market has primarily been shaped in the courts by antitrust actions brought against AT&T. In a 1949 case, the U.S. Department of Justice claimed that the Bell Operating Companies practiced illegal exclusion by purchasing goods from Western Electric, which was a part of the Bell system. The case, settled in 1956, resulted in AT&T holding on to Western Electric with the condition that they not enter the computer market. The second major antitrust suit, *United States vs. AT&T,* was initiated in 1974. The allegations included that AT&T monopolized the long-distance market and again asserted its relationship with Western Electric was illegal. The government sought divestiture of AT&T-owned manufacturing and long-distance businesses. The company broke up in 1982 after years of legal wrangling and formed seven regional Bell operating companies. The Baby Bells remained regulated monopolies, each with an exclusive franchise in its region. AT&T later spun off NCR and Lucent Technologies.

TELECOMMUNICATIONS REFORM ACT OF 1996

Although the breakup of AT&T was the watershed legal event causing telephony to evolve and thrive, perhaps the most notable factor pushing its convergence with the computer industry was the Telecommunications Reform Act of 1996. Congress, through this legislation, removed barriers to competition throughout the telecommunications industry and effectively paved the way for the industry to seek cross-industry alliances such as with computing. Telecommunications reform was spearheaded by the guidance of Reed Hundt, chairman of the FCC, who shepherded the act through Congress during his tenure, before stepping down in November 1997.

President Bill Clinton hailed the act as a revolutionary piece of legislation ushering in a new era of technology to reshape how we work and communicate with each other. Ostensibly, the act was intended to unleash the industry from the chains, such as outdated laws and regulations, that were determined to be holding it back, and to realize the virtues of the free market that were intended to push innovation, opportunities, and job creation.

Despite these promises, industry leaders chafed at regulatory challenges. Richard D. McCormick, chairman and chief operating officer of U S West Inc., was among them. In a 1996 address he told the U.S. Telephone Association that the FCC's new rules, far from creating a happy equilibrium and fairness, effectively gave the largest players free rein to steamroll smaller competitors, and insisted that the rules regarding industry interconnection were "not competition—they're confiscation."

While McCormick's view may seem hyperbolic to some observers, it was clear that the Telecommunications Reform Act had a somewhat more nuanced effect on the industry than President Clinton had predicted. The legislation resulted in corporate mergers and legal battles rather than better and more competitive consumer communications services. Rather than creating new networks from the ground up, companies are buying and selling customers to gain revenue, and buying companies to gain market position.

The resultant effect of the Telecommunications Reform Act of 1996 on telephony and other related communications businesses may take years to surface or to comprehend their impacts. And analysts were widely predicting future turmoil for the FCC and state regulators as they battled for regulatory turf. Effectively, these critics noted, the federal government had wrested away from states the right to determine telecommunications provisions and ownership patterns within their domains. Smaller local service providers, of course, were also none too pleased with the way the act was playing out.

Confusing issues further are taxes levied on telecommunications services. These include federal, state, and local charges for programs such as Universal Access, 911 service, and subsidies for school and hospital telephone service. Universal Access is a federal program designed to give rural residents and people in low-income brackets basic telephone service. What constitutes "basic" has been widely debated. The state of California, for example, in 1998 included a .41 percent charge to consumers be used to discount school, library, and hospital bills. On one bill for one phone line in San Francisco, as many as 11 agencies may tax phone use.

New entrants to the telephony market are perceived by telecommunications companies to have an unfair competitive advantage. Primarily, the grousing has been directed at Internet service providers (ISPs) who are unregulated and are not subject to the numerous taxes telecommunications firms have to pay. The regulation of IP telephony was becoming an increasingly heated political topic in the late 1990s. Regulatory constrictions on ISPs were being made on a select basis, solely on the complaints of telephone companies. With old technologies merging and new ones cropping up all the time, and with older ways of doing business seemingly antiquating by the day, some players and analysts even argued that telephony should be relieved of all regulatory oversight altogether, arguing that the FCC had outlived its usefulness.

BACKGROUND AND DEVELOPMENT

The history of telephony is entwined with the development and advances in electronics, telephone, and computer for communication. "The telephone utterly revolutionized human communication," stated Isaac Asimov. Hyperbole? Hardly. It was telegraph and telephone that propelled the desire for increasingly faster and more instant means of communications. Alexander Graham Bell is credited with inventing the telephone, initially to send voice via telegraph. Bell patented the device in 1876. Thomas Edison was the first to improve upon the invention.

Switching technologies have driven telephony development and deployment throughout the United States as it progressed from mechanical to analog to digital switching. The network and telephony devices are useless unless switching works properly to connect calls, whether for voice or data. In the early days, an operator manually plugged and removed circuits from a switchboard to initiate and terminate calls. The first technology leap was initiated in 1889 by Alom B. Strowger, an irate undertaker whose business was being diverted to a competitor by a less-than ethical operator. The Strowger system eliminated the need for a human to connect calls by utilizing mechanical devices to make a connection. This technology was standard throughout the United States for a period of about 50 years.

Beginning in about the 1940s, a series of analog switches were developed to replace huge and cumbersome devices. The new devices included cross-bar switches, the electronic switching system, and stored program control switches. Electronic switching systems were the first marriage of telephony and silicon. Computer technology was used within these systems to make operations efficient and thus reduce costs.

Regulation of the U.S. telecommunications market was shaped by antitrust actions brought against AT&T in 1949, 1956, and 1974. The company was finally broken up in 1982 after years of legal wrangling, forming seven regional Bell operating companies in 1984.

The 1970s, along with litigation against industry monolith AT&T, brought digital switching to the fore. These were faster, smaller, and more cost-efficient devices. A digital switch could accommodate between 1,000 and 10,000 subscribers on a network. These devices eventually automated and centralized maintenance. The late 1970s and 1980s were the age of fiber; the 1990s belonged to wireless, specifically digital wireless.

The telephone network was formed on twisted pair copper wires, but in the 1990s various means became available to transmit large bundles of data economically without wires. This shift actually had its beginning in the 1980s, when Bell was broken up and MCI started out to build its microwave network. After the government determined that the long-distance market for radio-based telephony was in fact competitive and, simultaneously, that the landline network amounted to a monopoly, new networks were immediately set up for wireless communication.

At that time other emergent technologies included cellular systems and low-power cellular or "personal communications services" networks. Also, the cost to companies for these various technologies was vastly different and the economics of scale constantly widening. In 1993 the cost associated with creating infrastructure for cellular networks was estimated as $1,000 per subscriber, while traditional copper-wired landlines cost about $1,500, with the costs increasing. Transmission equipment developed in the 1990s,

called Synchronous Option Network (SONET), were fiber-optic transport systems that increasingly provided the backbone for automated teller machines and broadband switching systems over which both voice and data can be carried. A steady, industry-wide transition toward an all-optical network was progressing in the late 1990s; at that time, however, the technology was not deemed cost-effective to make these types of networks commercially available. According to *Telephony*, companies such as international carriers with large investments in fiber optics were poised to be the first to employ these networks. Throughout this era, the industry became increasingly reliant upon computers for all aspects of telephony operations.

CURRENT CONDITIONS

The foremost buzzword throughout the telephony industry at the turn of the century was "convergence." Through convergence, the new-generation telephony company may eventually offer local, paging, long-distance, cellular, and Internet phone services all priced right and specially packaged. For the consumer, these convergent technologies may one day mean one number, one phone, and one bill.

Indicative of the accelerating convergence movement, computer telephony integration (CTI) was aided by enhanced technology for voice recognition for use with messaging products and for automatic call distribution. In coming years, moreover, hardware prices for CTI were likely to fall significantly, thereby relieving some of the pressure on companies to develop a production standard. CTI was generally a higher-margin system because it was geared mainly toward businesses. This technology was not expected to generate quite the level of excitement among major telecommunications firms, especially those focusing their operations on the individual consumer, since CTI is highly technical, even by modern telephony standards, and was thus expected to remain rarified, according to *Computer Reseller News*.

Demand for remote connectivity was greatly enhanced by the Internet, and the integration of wireless communications and Internet access was a very important priority among the major telecommunications and electronics firms. About one-third of the U.S. work force, amounting to 43 million individuals, were mobile—spending at least 20 percent of their working hours away from their workplace—in 1999, according to the Boston research firm the Yankee Group. And as business shifts increasingly to online networks, this culminates in a market just waiting to explode. Some analysts, however, worried that the demand for perpetual connectivity, particularly in wireless technology, was outpacing the ability of companies to meet expectations. Nonetheless, virtually every company recognized that wireless Internet access was a crucial component of its convergence scheme, and the race was on to streamline the process in order to bring the data transmission up to par with standard, personal computer-based connections. The Yankee Group predicted that the total number of mobile-data users would fall somewhere between 12 and 21.2 million by 2002, depending on how the technology develops amid the rapidly shifting telecommunications industry.

Cable telephony was another market area poised for dramatic growth in coming years. The Strategis Group predicted 20-fold global market expansion by 2003, with the United States expected to account for over one-third of the total 18 million subscribers, followed by China, Germany, Canada, Japan, India, and the United Kingdom.

Mergers and increased competitiveness caused companies to vie for customers in every sector, down to the heavy-use home user. The new generation telecommunications company wants to run the entire gamut of telephony services specially packaged for consumers. The furious drive toward convergence and the corresponding industry consolidation created some seemingly odd bedfellows. Cable-modem possibilities to connect to the elusive "final mile" meant matches were attempted with companies such as TCI, Cox, and Comcast to bring telephony services to consumers. There were many technology obstacles to overcome, but the possibilities were still being explored. And companies in other market niches, such as utilities, attempted to get a piece of telephony for their investors by investing in hybrid companies.

INDUSTRY LEADERS

Deregulation made telephony less a free market and more a free-for-all with merger mania making musical chairs of service market segments between 1996 and into 2000, with the ultimate economic and regulatory results remaining to be seen. The triumvirate of AT&T, WorldCom, and Sprint controlled over 80 percent of the long-distance market, a share that was expected to continue to be chipped away in coming years. There is truly no stagnation in this vibrant and ever-changing industry. Throughout the late 1990s, existing companies continued to spin off and merge

as well as consolidate services and refine their business focus to maximize profitability.

LONG-DISTANCE PROVIDERS

AT&T Corp. remained the United States' leading long-distance telephone carrier in 2000. The company, which had over 80 million customers and 148,000 employees in 2000, posted $62.4 billion in sales in 1999. With the advent of deregulation, increasing competition, and restructuring, AT&T broadened its focus to include wireless phone service, Internet access, and international and local telephone services. Meanwhile, the company has been gobbling up cable companies, including TCI and MediaOne, in an effort to compete with Time Warner for the position of leading cable operator. AT&T struck a deal with British Telecommunications in 1999 to provide worldwide wireless service through the Advance alliance.

WorldCom was founded in 1983 as discount long-distance carrier LDDS. The company grew through a series of acquisitions of some 40 competitors. In 1998 the company capped off a massive acquisition spree with a grand finale, merging with industry leader MCI. WorldCom employed 77,000 workers in 2000, but that year its acquisition of fellow big-three long-distance carrier Sprint, which would have propelled the company into even tighter competition with AT&T, was shot down by regulators. WorldCom's fiber-optic network was aimed at a global scale, and was already connected to several of the world's major cities through intercontinental cables. WorldCom's sales jumped to $37.1 billion in 1999 on the heals of the MCI merger, from $17 billion the year before.

Sprint Corp. was the third-largest long-distance service provider and the second-largest Baby Bell local provider. The company, which owns one of the largest fiber-optic networks, created neighborhood telephone stores with Radio Shack. In 1999 Sprint developed its Sprint Integrated On-Demand Network, which combined voice, video, and digital data transmissions through a single phone connection. After a competitive courting process, Sprint agreed to wed WorldCom in 2000, but the U.S. Justice Department struck the deal down. Sprint raked in revenues of $17 billion in 1999.

Qwest Communications International Inc., once an obscure telecommunications provider, grew to become the fourth-largest long-distance service provider in the United States by the end of the 1990s. Primarily operating in the western United States, the company was constructing an 18,800 mile fiber-optic network for more than 150 cities in the United States and Mexico. Qwest installs networks for companies such as Frontier, WorldCom, and Verizon alongside its own network, and sells network capacity to various parties. In addition to its long-distance operations, Qwest was a leading local phone service provider following its purchase of U S West, and also offered Internet access and multimedia services through its vast network. Qwest achieved sales of $3.9 billion in 1999.

LOCAL SERVICE PROVIDERS

Verizon, the product of the purchase by Bell Atlantic of GTE Corp., was number one in local phone service in 2000. Bell Atlantic Corp. was among the local service providing companies that emerged from the AT&T breakup. This Baby Bell purchased NYNEX—another Baby Bell—in 1997 to lift it to the top of the local service industry, and its purchase of GTE solidified its lead over SBC Communications. Verizon provided local phone service to 63 million customers in 31 states and the District of Columbia. In 1999 Bell Atlantic brought in revenues of $33.2 billion, while GTE achieved sales of $25.3 billion.

SBC Communications was the second-leading local phone service provider in 2000, maintaining industry staples Ameritech, Cellular One, Nevada Bell, Pacific Bell, SNET, and Southwestern Bell under its wing, with a payroll of 204,530 employees. SBC provides local service in 13 states, with plans to expand into a local-exchange carrier in 30 markets. The company also boasted 19 million wireless customers through its partnership with BellSouth called Cingular Wireless. Its other services included Internet access, paging, and directory publishing. SBC further struck up an alliance with Prodigy to offer nationwide Internet access. In 1999 the firm's revenues reached $49.5 billion, up from $28.8 billion the year before.

WIRELESS SERVICES

Vodafone AirTouch PLC was a wireless leader in 2000, formed by the 1999 acquisition by the United Kingdom's Vodafone Group of AirTouch Communications. Since that alliance, the company has continued its acquisition spree, purchasing Germany's Mannesman for $180 billion. Vodafone AirTouch claimed some 39.1 million customers in 24 countries, and employed 12,640 workers. In the United States, the company teamed up with Verizon to create Verizon Wireless, the leading wireless service in the nation with 26 million customers, plus an additional 4 million paging subscribers. In 1999 Vodafone AirTouch boosted revenues to $5.4 billion from $4.1 billion in 1998.

Nextel Communications of Reston, Virginia, was another leading wireless-phone service provider, with 5.1 million customers in the United States and an additional 500,000 foreign subscribers. Nextel pitches its services primarily toward businesses, yielding high returns but fewer customers overall. The company claimed the title of largest independent mobile phone operator in the United States, with 15,000 employees and revenues of $3.3 billion in 1999.

AMERICA AND THE WORLD

Traditionally, telephone services in nations other than the United States have traditionally been state-run; by 2000, however, many state monopolies had been privatized. Changing this industry internationally was the creation of a 1997 World Trade Organization agreement in which representatives from about 70 nations said they would open their national markets to international competition. Nations ratifying this process represented 90 percent of world telecommunications revenues. As a result, joint ventures between companies have created a crazy quilt of alliances and services for Internet service provision, infrastructure construction, and similar activities. These include Concert, which couples British Telecommunications and AT&T with assistance from Telefonica de Espana; and Global One, which combines Sprint and France Telecom.

British Telecommunications PLC (BT) was once the United Kingdom's government-run telephone company. The company offers a wide range of service, including international service—despite the fact that by the end of the 1990s the firm generated nearly all its revenues in the United Kingdom, where it boasted 28 million access lines. In addition to phone services, BT provides Internet access and corporate leased lines for data transmission. The company's subsidiary BT Cellnet was second only to Vodafone Air-Touch in U.K. cellular-phone service. With mounting competition at home, BT was increasingly looking outside the U.K. borders for new growth opportunities; it invested heavily in the United States, Asia, and Latin America. The company posted $27.3 billion in sales in 1999.

Deutsche Telekom AG, Europe's largest telecommunications provider, had 1999 sales of $35.8 billion, down significantly from 1998's $41.9 billion. Two-thirds owned by the German government, the company maintained over 48 million access lines in its domestic market, and claimed 22 million subscribers to its T-Mobil network. Like BT, Deutsche Telekom was pouring resources into other European, Asian, and North American markets, although it sold its stake in Global One, a joint venture with Sprint, to its European partner, France Telecom. France Telecom, for its part, maintained 34 million access lines and the remained the largest player in the French market it once monopolized.

Telecommunications operators were finally overcoming their wariness with Japan's long-frustrating market, which totaled about $90 billion by 1999. Major carriers such as WorldCom and Global Crossing set up joint ventures to take advantage of expected growth and an opening market by setting up their own infrastructure services, while AT&T and British Telecommunications partnered to purchase a 30 percent share of the long-distance giant Japan Telecom, offering their collective long-distance services to the Japanese outfit. The Chinese market, meanwhile, was also opening in a hurry, particularly as China moved to join the World Trade Organization. The market also carried a great deal of potential; there were some 87 million fixed-line telephone customers in China in 1998, and the Ministry of Information Industry planned to boost that number to 112 million by the end of 2000.

RESEARCH AND TECHNOLOGY

Technology advances have outpaced expectations. The changes have been amazingly rapid, from digital switching to fiber optics and beyond. Computers play an increasingly important role in telephony through development and deployment of technologies such as voice over networks. The past 20 years in this industry surpassed all expectations, but it is predicted that coming years will herald more developments in telephony than were brought about in the previous 50-year span.

Computing, photonics, satellites, and other technologies have become increasingly sophisticated, thus altering the foundation on which communications transmissions are made. Some telephony companies remain content to attempt to maximize their copper-wired infrastructure as long as possible without sacrificing service quality; significant capital investments, after all, have been made. Additional investments would be absorbed through service rate hikes.

The telephone network was designed based on conjecture that each call was three minutes in duration with no more than nine minutes's worth of calls made during peak-use hours. By the middle of the 1990s, however, the snowballing use of the Internet resulted in phone lines routinely tied up for well over 15 minutes at a time. Because Internet service providers and subscriber-based online services have arranged for users to incur no charges for local calls,

Web surfers can stay on indefinitely with no cost to them and there is no revenue for those local providers. The problem is further compounded by technology. While telephone companies had about $30 billion invested in the older circuit-switching infrastructure alone, packet switching technology is a digital, more efficient technology that will go a long way toward solving network traffic problems.

Examples of the latter technologies include asymmetric digital subscriber line (ADSL) and integrated services digital network. According to the ADSL Forum, by 1999 there were over 100,000 ADSL systems installed throughout the world. ADSL itself has grown more efficient as well, requiring only a few silicon chips, half as much as was necessary in 1998. According to Cahners In-Stat Group, the total number of digital subscriber lines worldwide was expected to grow about 125 percent annually between 1999 and 2000, much faster than the growth rate of cable modem subscribers, which was predicted at about 55 percent annually.

As a result, more and more companies were beginning to eye the mass purchase of ADSL technology as a viable option, particularly because it provides companies with a way to meet heightened consumer demand for high-speed access without ripping out their old copper-wire networks. Several North American phone companies purchased enough ADSL equipment from the French firm Alcatel in 1999 to provide high-speed Internet access to 80,000 households.

For equipment manufacturers, changes in the dynamics of the telephony market coupled with technological advances have made executives shift focus. Nortel, as an example, had more than 110-million digital switching lines internationally in the late 1990s in addition to SONET and microwave transmission products. Prior to deregulation, Tellabs Inc., for example, primarily made digital cross-connects for switching telephone traffic over large networks based on circuit switching. In the late 1990s, this was being replaced by packet switching, an industry segment dominated by companies such as Cisco Systems. Digital technologies are needed to enable voice traffic to be carried with data via Internet Protocol (IP) networks. As Bruce Upbin pointed out in a May 1998 *Forbes* article, "telephone technology is changing so fast that a hot product today could be obsolete in just a few years."

That's why companies such as Tellabs are investing in new technologies. It bought into photonics in 1997 with a $6 million purchase of the IBM wave division multiplexing technology. This technology allows light waves to be split to create more network bandwidth. In 1998, Lucent's Bell Laboratories was working with optical switching and Advance Intelligent Networking technology, wherein service "intelligence" placed in databases rather than switches was being deployed. Links with cable operators to provide wireless services were being explored by telephony companies.

Voice and data transmission networks are moving in the coming decade from traditional networks to specialized high-bandwidth networks such as IP networks. New generation telephony networks were in the design stage to carry data and voice traffic by using IP networking. Web phones that integrate mobile-phone capabilities with e-mail and, eventually, Web-based data, access were being developed. Such devices were primarily based on the Wireless Application Protocol, a language adapted from standard HTTP specifically for wireless services. The creation of these types of networks and devices would eliminate outdated copper-line transmission and enable businesses and individuals to simply mix and match an array of services from traditional telephone conversations to conducting teleconferences.

By 1996 data traffic outpaced voice traffic on backbone networks, thereby providing a crucial reason for technological convergence in the telephony industry. Nortel anticipated Internet users to number 300 million internationally by 2003. The forecasts for 2020 put U.S. Internet use at 80 percent of the total population. Indeed the early adapters seem to be large corporations most able to invest capital in these types of cutting-edge systems. Boeing and Ford Motor Co. were among those companies that deployed IP networks for their international, internal communication needs. Small business and consumer adoption of these technologies traditionally lags behind early adopters, with widespread use occurring as prices fall.

FURTHER READING

Adelson, Josh. "Internet Fax: What Can It Do for You?" *VoicePlus,* June 1999.

Brown, Patricia. "Blown Away." *tele.com,* 7 February 2000.

Cane, Alan. "Widening the Wire." *Financial Times,* 4 August 1999.

Carden, Philip. "Meet the New-Age Carriers." *Network Computing,* 12 July 1999.

Clancy, Heather. "Summit Updates CT Hopes, Hurdles." *Computer Reseller News,* 14 February 2000.

"DSL Will Vault to Broadband Leadership." *CED Buyer's Guide Supplement,* 15 November 2000.

"Digital Mobile Telephony Market Sees Strong Growth." *Computer Dealer News,* 29 October 1999.

Forman, Preston P. "CTI Industry Targets Small Businesses." *Computer Reseller News,* 16 August 1999.

Golden, Michael, William Rundquist, Arno Penzias, and Kelly Carroll. "New Media." *Telephony,* 10 May 1999.

Logan, Gail A. "Cable Gets Its Chance." *Telephony,* 13 December 1999.

Mason, Charles. "Tethered No More?" *America's Network,* 1 June 1999.

Nakamoto, Michiyo. "Telecoms Groups Feel Lure of Japan." *Financial Times,* 25 June 1999.

Neighly, Patrick. "Cable Telephony Market Grows to One in Three U.S. Households." *America's Network,* 1 December 1999.

"Publications and Reports." *Communications News,* October 1999.

Quinton, Brian. "Asleep at the Switch." *Telephony,* 13 September 1999.

Smith, Alan. "It's Not Just Television Anymore: Stroking the Revenue Stream Involves a Whole Lot More Than Pay TV These Days." *Multichannel News International Supplement,* May 1999.

Upbin, Bruce. "Survival Technique: Paranoia." *Forbes,* 18 May 1998.

"VOIP Seen as Global Weapon." *Business Communications Review,* May 1999.

Wang, John. "Signs of Opening in Telecom." *China Business Review,* May 1999.

TISSUE ENGINEERING

Though biomedically enhanced humans used to populate only 1970s television action shows and futuristic Hollywood offerings, the engineered production of human tissue was a reality by 2000—and the probability of engineering entire human organs, such as hearts and livers, loomed on the horizon. In the short term, tissue engineering—the process of converting isolated cells into complete tissues and, eventually, whole organs—will result in replacements for artificial joints, such nonliving processed tissues as heart valves, and tissues taken from a patient's own body or that of a donor.

Tissue engineering is a fledgling, highly interdisciplinary field that straddles the disciplines of materials science and biology, but draws on immunology, chemistry, and bioengineering as well. The aim of tissue engineering is to restore or replace human tissues or organs by introducing compatible, engineered live-cell tissue that becomes integrated into the recipient's body.

Producing engineered tissues is a bit like growing houseplants. The specialist starts with a trellislike scaffold (or matrix) made of collagen or biodegradable polymer, shapes it as necessary to facilitate development of the future tissue, seeds it with live cells, then nourishes the scaffold with growth factors to stimulate cell reproduction. The multiplying cells fill out the scaffold and grow into three-dimensional tissue. After being implanted in the body, intended tissue functions are re-created. Blood vessels attach themselves to the new tissue, the scaffold dissolves, and the tissue blends into the landscape. The procedure often uses stem cells, premature cells that were first identified in 1992. Implanting stem cells in appropriate places encourages them to grow into the intended type of cell, bone, tendon, or cartilage. Tissue-engineered systems can be either "open," and thus meant to be completely integrated into the recipient's body, or "closed" (encapsulated) to defend against rejection by the recipient's immune system. Controlled-release of growth factors may aid in the formation of blood vessels to nourish the newly introduced tissue matrix or to spur tissue-cell reproduction.

By 1998 the total capital of companies engaged in this emerging industry was valued at more than $3.5 billion, with an annual industry growth rate of 22.5 percent. Over 2,500 U.S. scientists and researchers were involved in industry-related research and development (R&D). The National Institute of Standards and Technology estimated that tissue-engineered remedies could find applications for treating disorders that account for half the nation's health-care costs. But tissue engineering also touches on sensitive legal, political, and ethical questions that have yet to be addressed by governments and the courts.

ORGANIZATION AND STRUCTURE

By 2000 approximately 40 companies were involved in tissue-engineering research. Most were small, private start-ups engaged in R&D in a nascent field where there's a high risk of failure. Despite the few products approved for the market, tissue engineering has yet to create a product that generates an appreciable amount of revenue. Because of the extensive interdisciplinary work the field requires, many firms collaborate with universities, larger phar-

Scanning electron micrograph (SEM) of cartilage growing on synthetic fibers. (Photo Researchers Inc./David Mooney/Science Photo Library)

maceutical companies, or each other in conducting their R&D.

Specialized programs in tissue engineering are slowly emerging, often as collaborations between two institutions whose departmental strengths complement each other. For example, in the late 1990s the Georgia Institute of Technology (GT) established a joint biomedical engineering department with Emory University's medical school. GT provided the engineering expertise and Emory, the medical. The department would be housed on both campuses and faculty appointments split between them as well.

Funding for tissue-engineering R&D comes from private foundations such as the Pugh Foundation, the Red Cross, the Howard Hughes Foundation, and the Whittaker Foundation, and from governmental sources such as the National Science Foundation and the National Institutes of Health (NIH). In 1997 the NIH established a Bioengineering Consortium devoted to this emerging science.

BACKGROUND AND DEVELOPMENT

By the dawn of the 21st century, the field of tissue engineering had existed less than three decades. Groundwork was laid as early as 1933, when the European researcher Bisceglie inserted mouse tumor cells, which he had enclosed in a polymer membrane, into a pig's abdominal cavity. The pig's immune system failed to kill the cells.

Though the Kennedy administration backed some tissue-engineering initiatives, the field really got its start in Boston at the Massachusetts Institute of Technology in the late 1970s. It resulted from the work of three research endeavors. Professor Howard Green pioneered research on skin (epithelial sheets and keratinocyte grafts). Professor Ioannis Yannas studied the creation of collagen scaffolds for skin repair. In conjunction with Dr. John Burke, a burn doctor at Boston's Shriners Hospital, Yannas developed an implant that could be used to guide the reformation of skin tissue. The technique became known as the Burke-Yannas Method. The third project, conducted by Robert Langer and Eugene Bell, involved the application of synthetic polymers in cell lattices. By the 1980s, scientists were trying to grow skin replacements with cells embedded in collagen gels—those attempts led to the tissue-engineered skin products on the market today. In the same decade the term "tissue engineering" was coined. In 1983 Langer and Dr. Joseph Vacanti developed a polymer scaffold for supporting tissue generation.

For its first 20 years, the focus of tissue engineering remained the development of skin products for burn wounds using autologous cells—those taken from the burn victim. The resultant tissue, which grafted well and was cosmetically acceptable, far surpassed the cadaver or pig skin previously used for the purpose. The material was also adapted for chronic wounds, such as leg and foot ulcers.

Many research milestones were reached only in the 1990s, several backed by funding from Geron Corp. In August 1997, Nobel Prize recipient Thomas Cech of the University of Colorado-Boulder and his team isolated the human gene responsible for telomerase reverse transcriptase (rTRT), which knits together the fraying edges, or telomeres, of aging cells. Later the same year, Jerry Shay and Woodring Wright of the University of Texas' Southwest Medical Center actually introduced the rTRT gene into cells and demonstrated the process in action. This discovery will benefit research aimed at extending the life span of new organs that may one day be engineered from a patient's own cells, which may be prematurely aged.

In 1998 both James Thompson of the University of Wisconsin and John Gearhart of Johns Hopkins University independently isolated human stem cells, whose existence had previously only been surmised. Stem cells form an ideal raw material for tissue-engineering research. By the end of the 1990s, scientists had also determined that adults, as well as embryos, possess stem cells that may carry on repair work on the body throughout life. This even proved to be true of adult neural stem cells, overturning the long-held belief that damage to the central nervous system (spinal cord and brain) was irreparable. The successful cloning of Dolly, the famous sheep, and the completed mapping of the human genome are breakthroughs with important implications for future field research as well.

CURRENT CONDITIONS

Since it's a nascent industry, virtually no tissue-engineering end products have been approved by the U.S. Food and Drug Administration (FDA) for the U.S. market. The first such material widely available was engineered skin tissue, which is grown commercially in "factories" engaged in continuous production for ready product availability to hospitals and research facilities. The replacement skins have a long shelf life and are fairly durable. TransCyte, a skin product from Advanced Tissue Sciences (ATS), uses donated human (allogeneic) dermal cells; they are cultivated on a polyglycolic-acid mesh. Rather than grafting onto a wound, the tissue covers it over and emits wound-healing signals to the patient's body, thus speeding recovery. The FDA approved TransCyte for burns, but the company was conducting trials for its applicability to venous and foot ulcers.

ATS also announced in March 2000 the first scientific demonstration that engineered tissue could stimulate the formation of new blood vessels (angiogenesis), essential for regenerating damaged heart tissue. In conjunction with members of the University of Arizona, ATS researchers tissue-engineered an epicardial patch that induced angiogenesis within two weeks. The patch was a living, human-based product that secreted growth factors and proteins.

Organogenesis produces Apligraf, a two-layered product that mimics the structure of human dermal and epidermal tissue, it's composed of a collagen matrix containing dermal cells (fibroblasts) overlaid with cultured epidermal cells (keratinocytes). In 1998 the product received approval for use with venous leg ulcers and in 2000 it was under review for diabetic foot ulcers. Nearly 2.6 million patients in the United States each year have dermal wounds that fail to heal properly, frequently due to complications from diabetes and circulation disorders, which often lead to amputation.

According to Datamonitor, the global market for replacement skin was valued at $106.2 million in 2000. But the firm projected a 126 percent increase to $240.3 million within five years. Reaping the economic rewards of that market, however, might prove difficult for the industry, since the products currently on the market are expensive and often receive limited reimbursement from insurance.

Collagen, which forms the basis for many scaffolds used in tissue-engineering research, is manufactured by Fibrogen. It was the first company to bring human-cell based collagen to market, rather than those derived from cow hides and tendons, which can cause inflammation in many recipients.

Ongoing research that may lead to fruitful commercial applications in the short term centers on the matrices and cells used in tissue engineering. Most matrices are composed either of synthetics, such as lactic-glycolic acid or polyacrylonitrile-polyvinyl, or natural materials, such as collagen and alginate. Bovine collagen was commonly used, raising alarms about possible contamination with mad-cow disease and its human counterpart, Creutzfeldt-Jakob disease. While synthetics permit more control over matrix ductility, strength, and permeability, natural materials offer better cell adhesiveness. Research in this sector thus seeks to uncover matrix-formulations that combine the best qualities of both. Research in the 1990s produced matrices capable of being shaped to support the growth of blood vessel and intestinal tubes, ear- and finger-shaped cartilage and bone, and heart-valve leaflets. Cartilage from the patient's own body has been used to treat juvenile urinary reflux and urinary stress incontinence in adults.

Cell studies for tissue engineering usually examine specific cell types. Autologous cartilage transplants are in clinical use for rebuilding damaged knees. For engineered skin tissue, dermal cells from neonates is used. Researchers are seeking to identify single sources from which a variety of cells could be drawn. The answer may lie in human stem cells. These undifferentiated cells, which appear at the period of earliest formation of the human embryo, later develop into all the various cell types found in the human body—bone, blood, nerve, cartilage, liver, and so on. Stem-cell research raised a public furor in the United States in the 1990s, because the cells are derived from aborted fetuses. Though initial results showed promise, further research was needed to solve technical problems of working with stem cells, such as methods to guarantee that stem-cell batches were contaminated with dermal cells, to prevent stem cells from sticking together during culturing, and to augment the production of mass quantities of stem cells that are needed for large-scale tissue generation.

Researchers have unveiled some significant advances in engineering structures composed of simpler tissues such as cartilage. Harvard surgery professor Dr. Joseph Vacanti grew an ear from a cartilage-cell seeded matrix embedded into a mouse's back. An American and Japanese research team, headed by Dr. William Landis of Northeastern Ohio University's College of Medicine and Dr. Noritoka Isogia of Kenki University in Osaka, successfully grew an articulated, humanlike finger joint on a mouse's back by wrapping bovine cells around a polymer scaffold. Within 20 weeks, blood vessels had formed in the joint. Initial future applications include the production of skeletal parts as replacements for toes and fingers. Liver-like tissues, bladders, and kidneys have also been engineered in animal studies.

Vacanti demonstrated the feasibility of constructing an entire circulatory system, artery to vein, for whole grown tissues, though his work did not appear successful for large vital organs. The more common way of inducing angiogenesis in organs is to graft the developing tissue onto the body of a live animal, so that the host's vascular network branches out to supply the tissue extension as well. ATS announced in March 2000 that its scientists, in conjunction with the University of Arizona, had stimulated angiogenesis in a damaged heart using its bioengineered tissue Dermagraft as a patch that secreted growth factors and proteins directly into the organ, prompting the development of new blood vessels.

In May 2000 researchers at Washington University restored damaged nerve tissue in mice using stem cells to regrow myelin, the tissue that covers nerve fibers. They cultured the stem cells with growth factors to become the key cells that form the nervous system; when injected into the mice, those cells prompted remyelation to occur.

Progress has even been made toward tackling the toughest challenge that confronts tissue engineers—engineering entire complex organs such as livers and hearts, One of the most encouraging developments to date occurred when Harvard Medical School's Dr. John Mayer and his colleagues announced that they had engineered entire heart valves from the blood ves-

---

| *More On* | POLICING THE HUMAN "SPARE PARTS" INDUSTRY |

Many of the same regulatory and bioethical issues that arise with cloning, human reproductive technologies, and genetic engineering impinge on the field of tissue engineering.

Increasingly, biomedical-technology law will have to settle questions regarding the ownership of the cell materials used to grow tissues, and of the resultant organs. As the field advances, issues of privacy and product liability will become ever more important. Eventually, governments around the world will have to articulate and enforce guidelines regarding the legalization of the reproduction, and possible engineered improvement, of human organs and other bodily structures. Although current U.S. federal law prohibits the sale of human organs that are harvested, no regulations govern organs that are grown, rather than harvested.

Despite the advantages of using stem cells to generate engineered tissues, the United States long prohibited the federal funding of any projects involving stem cells, because they must be obtained from embryos or aborted fetuses. The National Institutes of Health introduced suggested guidelines in 1999 to permit some such research, which finally passed review in August 2000. The industry was overjoyed to hear, in August 2000, that the U.S. government, through the NIH, would provide funding for research into human embryonic stem cells, despite the very vocal opposition of antiabortion groups and several members of Congress. To appease such opposition, the NIH ruled that stem cells can only be obtained from frozen embryos that were left over and would be discarded from fertility clinics. Scientists cannot solicit embryos specifically for their research.

Some questions concerning liability might be clarified when the FDA determines whether to classify and regulate engineered tissue as a biologic or medical device. Standard product liability laws would probably not come into play if the latter classification is adopted. In general, courts and legislative bodies have hesitated to recognize any transferable property interests in body parts. Statutes covering donation forbid the sale of human organs, for example, and blood donation is classified as a service.

---

sel cells of donor sheep. When implanted into those sheep, the valves functioned for up to five months.

INDUSTRY LEADERS

Advanced Tissue Sciences (ATS) of La Jolla, California, is among the more prominent of these firms. Its makes the skin replacement TransCyte, approved in the United States for use on burn victims, and Dermagraft, approved for use on diabetic foot ulcers in Canada and the United Kingdom. ATS posted sales of $42.8 million in 1999, a one-year increase of 108.8 percent, but it still represented a net loss of $21.3 million. ATS was pursuing several research ventures with the British firm Smith & Nephew.

Fibrogen, located in South San Francisco, is a private R&D firm specializing in the production of recombinant collagen and gelatin biomaterials for skin scarring, wound repair, and tissue regeneration. Founded in 1993, Fibrogen reported 1999 sales of under $1 million. It has developed the only known method for recombinantly producing human and animal collagen in a synthetic. Of the 20 types of collagen, it had nine by 1999. Now only two types are available for research. Matched collagen scaffolds might be able to function both as tissue regrowth matrix and active growth agent. Fibrogen maintains over 20 agreements with pharmaceutical companies and medical device manufacturers for the development of collagen.

Organogenesis, Inc. of Canton, Massachusetts, employs 205 and reported 1999 sales of $1.8 million, a decrease of 77.2 percent from 1998. The company's primary commercial product is Apligraf, a tissue-engineered skin replacement used for treating venous leg ulcers for which Novartis has global marketing rights. Organogenesis' research agenda focuses on Vitrix, a living-cell soft-tissue replacement for wound repair, a bioartificial liver, and vascular grafts.

Genzyme BioSurgery, of Cambridge, Massachusetts, is a separately traded division of Genzyme. Its main product is Carticel, used to heal knee cartilage. Its 1999 sales of $635.4 million represented a one-year increase of 11.6 percent, and resulted in net income of $142.1 million. Its Epicel Service grows skin grafts of patient skin; it can culture a body's worth of tissue from a postage-sized sample in four weeks. The company received FDA approval to grow autologous cartilage tissue, then implant it in human knees.

Other companies in the tissue-engineering flock include Osiris Therapeutics, Inc. of Baltimore, a privately held company pursuing the regeneration of bone, muscle, cartilage, and tendons using a patient's own stem cells. It maintained research collaborations with the University of Genoa, the University of Cincinnati, and

Collagenesis, among others. Ortec International, Inc., a New York-based start-up, received FDA approval for its Composite Cultured Skin (CCS), a wound-dressing derived from a bovine collagen matrix seeded with skin cells, to treat epidermolysis bullosa, a skin disorder that creates severe blistering and sloughing. Ortec, which posted 1999 sales of under $500,000, was exploring additional applications for CCS, including burns, skin ulcers, and reconstructive surgery.

WORK FORCE

The industry demands well-educated and highly trained individuals with the talent to combine skills from several disciplines. Although a bachelor's degree will often suffice for workers in technical support, most research positions require postgraduate education—with advanced degrees in the life sciences, medicine, and engineering quite common. Many tissue-engineering specialists possess postgraduate degrees in more than one field. Since it is a nascent industry, many of those who conduct tissue-engineering research are professors at major research universities. Given the potentially explosive ethical questions that tissue engineering raises, workers also must familiarize themselves with governmental regulations that affect developments in the field. Tissue-engineering scientists must be able to collaborate with others as part of an R&D team, since virtually all industry breakthroughs have resulted from the combined efforts of several specialists whose work foci complement each other.

For management positions in the industry, knowledge of the life sciences, medicine, or engineering is still essential. A combination of master's degrees is most desirable—one in the sciences and the other a master of business administration.

AMERICA AND THE WORLD

Research partnerships frequently cross international borders with scientists from leading universities throughout the world lending their expertise to ongoing research. The ethical challenges posed by stem-cell-based research and growing human organs must be shared as well, since all governments will need to determine how they will grapple with new developments that are rapidly approaching. Canada introduced a Human Reproductive and Genetic Technologies bill that would permit embryos to be grown from eggs har-

vested from aborted fetuses for research, citing the need for fetal tissue to aid work that targeted treatments for Parkinson's and Alzheimer's, among other diseases. In the United Kingdom, the establishment of the new Building Up Biomaterials initiative in the Department of Trade and Industry aimed to increase the United Kingdom's presence in the industry.

The Pittsburgh Tissue Engineering Initiative is a nonprofit, virtual global network of independent researchers dedicated to advances in tissue engineering. In 2000 Motorola, Inc. invested in Pittsburgh's Tissue Informatics proposal to build a global virtual tissue bank—a database of blueprints of all human tissues—that could function as road maps for researchers around the world.

The projected eventual availability of "farmed" human "spare parts," no doubt to be available on the world market, also raises the problems of organ and cell trafficking and the danger of the spread of disease through infected tissues. Global quality standards will be needed to assure safety and to adjudicate ethical and legal quandaries that will arise as tissue engineering moves from a fledgling, primarily research-oriented discipline to a full-blown commercial enterprise.

RESEARCH AND TECHNOLOGY

Private industry, universities, and federal agencies all contribute to ongoing research in the field. Much current research centers on deciphering how cells interact, and matching cells up with the right scaffold material to achieve desired results.

The National Institute of Standards and Technology's Advanced Technology Program sponsored 26 active or completed projects. Among the studies funded were those exploring xenogenic transplantation of pig cartilage for knee repair; three-dimensional fibrous scaffold for tissue engineering; and living heart-valve replacements of cryopreserved animal tissue and human cells.

Fertile ground for future work includes developing basic technologies for enabling viable cells to be mass-produced for commercial applications; storage facilities to prolong cell and tissue viability; technology for the manufacture of biocompatible materials; and the manufacture of products that will inhibit adverse reactions by the host-recipient.

Products undergoing FDA clinical trials include the development of a bioartificial liver, neuron transplants derived from pig cells to treat Parkinson's dis-

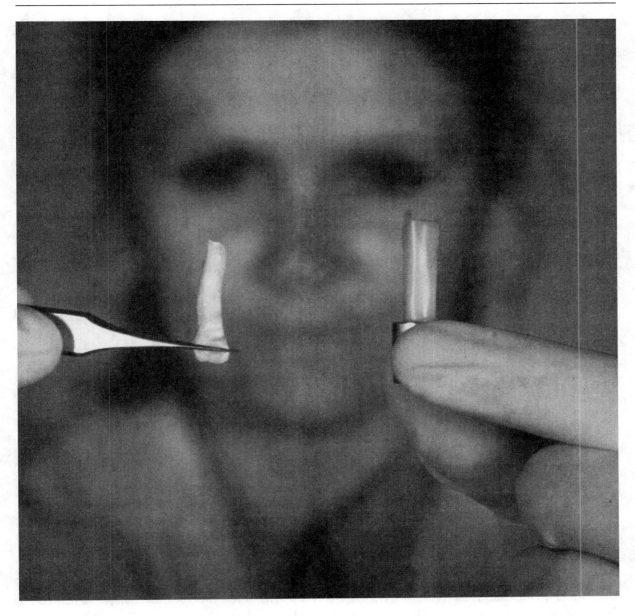

A lab technician holding a piece of human tendon and a smart-bandage. *(Photo Researchers Inc./Simon Fraser/Science Photo Library)*

ease, and additional applications for living skin replacements. A team at the Carolinas Medical Center is investigating the generation of soft-tissue masses for use in breast reconstruction for mastectomy patients.

Many mysteries of human biochemistry need to be solved for the field to advance. For example, the correct combination of growth factors must be identified for successful stimulation of each variety of engineered tissue or organ, and the exact mechanism that triggers blood-vessel development in tissues must be unraveled.

The production of entire, complex replacement organs, complete with their own networks of blood vessels, remains the daunting goal of tissue engineering. And despite growing public and market awareness of the industry, the goal still hovers in the distant future. In May 2000 a team of 44 scientists, coordinated by the University of Washington and Advanced Tissue Sciences, embarked on a 10-year project, funded by the National Institutes of Health, to grow an entire human heart using human stem cells. The project's interim goal was the development of an implantable, contractile cardial patch that could aid the functioning of weakened hearts in patients who were awaiting the availability of a human heart for transplant.

Ultimately, tissue engineering may be superfluous. Some scientists speculate that one day they will be able to inject a person's own stem cells back into his or her body. If all went well, the cells would migrate automatically to the destination where they were needed, and differentiate and grow to regenerate aging or failing body parts.

FURTHER READING

"Biomaterials." *Medical Device Technology,* April 2000.

"Datamonitor: Patient and Practitioner Awareness Key to Future Success of Skin Tissue." *PR Newswire,* 22 May 2000.

"Everything You Ever Wanted to Know About Stem Cells." *New Scientist,* 19 August 2000.

"FDA Advisory Panel Recommends Apligraf as Approvable for Use in the Treatment of Diabetic Foot Ulcers." *PR Newswire,* 8 May 2000.

"FDA Approves 'Donor Site' Pivotal Study of Ortec's Novel Tissue." *PR Newswire,* 7 June 1999.

Ferber, Dan. "Growing Human Corneas in the Lab." *Science,* 10 December 1999.

Friedrich, M. J. "Tissue Engineering in the Genitourinary System." *Journal of the American Medical Association,* 17 May 2000.

"Genetic Engineering News Reports Bioengineering Spurs Regenerative Medicine." *Business Wire,* 11 May 2000.

"Government Grant Received to Expand Tissue-Engineered Heart Valve Research." *Transplant Weekly,* 1 November 1999.

Gura, Trisha. "Custom-Made for You." *New Scientist,* 29 May 1999.

Hall, Alan. "Sculpting Life's Building Blocks." *Business Week,* 18 December 2000. Available from: http://www.businessweek.com.

Hedges, Stephen. "Tissue Imports Pose Hazards." *Chicago Tribune,* 22 May 2000.

"Japan Drafts Biotech Guidelines." *Nikkei Weekly,* 10 April 2000.

Leutwyler, Kristin. "Dolly's Legacy." *Scientific American,* 21 June 1999.

"The Magician of Body Plumbing." *Times Higher Education Supplement,* 3 September 1999.

Martinek, Vladimir, and Freddie H. Fu. "Gene Therapy and Tissue Engineering in Sports Medicine." *Physician & Sportsmedicine,* February 2000.

May, Mike. "Mother Nature's Menders." *Scientific American,* June 2000.

Milne, David. "Manmade Tissue No Longer Stuff of Science-Fiction: Production of Human-Like Finger Joint May Lead to Growing Arms, Legs." *Medical Post,* 7 September 1999.

Mooney, David, and Antonios Mikos. "Growing New Organs." *Scientific American,* special issue, September 1999.

Moran, Mark. "Tissue Engineering." *American Medical News,* 21 February 2000.

National Institutes of Health. "Stem Cells: A Primer." Available from http://www.nih.gov/news/stemcell/primer.htm.

Niklason, L. E. "Replacement Arteries Made to Order." *Science,* 19 November 1999.

Patrick, Charles W., Jr., et al., eds. *Frontiers in Tissue Engineering.* New York: Pergamon Press, 1998.

Recer, Paul. "Promise Seen for Spinal Injuries." *Associated Press,* 22 May 2000.

Restegar, Sohi. "Life Force." *Mechanical Engineering,* March 2000.

Rundle, Rhonda. "Biotech Firms Turn to Cosmetic-Surgery Market." *Wall Street Journal,* 12 May 1999.

Sobel, Rachel K. "Miracle Cells? Maybe." *U.S. News & World Report,* 4 September 2000.

"Tissue Banking: Motorola Invests in World's First Virtual Tissue Bank." *Breast Cancer Weekly,* 17 April 2000.

"Ultimate Materials Goal: A New Body?" *Professional Engineering,* 8 March 2000.

"UW Partners with Advanced Tissue Sciences and Others in $10 Million Grant to 'Grow' Human Heart Tissue."

Vacanti, Joseph, and Robert Langer. "Tissue Engineering: The Design and Fabrication of Living Replacement Devices for Surgical Reconstruction and Transplantation." *Lancet,* 31 July 1999.

Waldmeir, Patti. "U.S. Lawmakers 'Are Slow to Respond to New Ethics Issues.'" *Financial Times* (London), 10 August 1999.

Watt, Fiona M., et al. "Out of Eden: Stem Cells and Their Niches." *Science,* 25 February 2000.

Weiss, Samuel. "Pathways for Neural Stem Cell Biology and Repair." *Nature Biotechnology,* September 1999.

Wickware, Potter. "Exploring the Territory in Tissue Engineering." *Nature,* 27 January 2000.

Zorpette, Glenn, and Carol Ezell. "Your Bionic Future." *Scientific American,* special issue, September 1999.

Zuckerman, Mortimer. "Fountain of Youth." *U.S. News & World Report,* 22 November 1999.

USED COMPUTER EQUIPMENT RESELLING

Often overlooked in the computer hardware business, the used equipment trade is fragmented but vibrant. With an estimated 31.6 million personal computers (PCs) falling obsolete in 2000, there is ample supply of old hardware to be upgraded and refurbished. And that figure doesn't include recent models that are coming out of leases or being sold used for other reasons. Although estimates are scarce, one source placed the value of used PC sales in the United States at more than $6 billion as of 1998. Separately, a forecast by International Data Corp. expected annual unit trade to vault from 5.5 million machines in 1997 to 10 million by 2002, gaining about 14 percent a year over that period. Some observers believe, however, that continually falling prices in the new PC market will undercut the growth of used machine sales in the long run.

Companies dealing in used computers range from the Dells and IBMs of the world to small-time local dealers with perhaps just a few million dollars in sales. The big computer manufacturers often need to dispose of surplus stock after business computer leases end or after models are used for testing and demonstrations. Independent resellers, on the other hand, usually make a point of obtaining used equipment and parts, often performing some form of repair, upgrade, or refurbishment, to be resold for a profit.

An important trend in used computer sales has been the popularity of Internet auction sites, especially ones targeted at computer buyers and sellers. In addition to third-party and independent reseller sites, some of the notable entrants to the field have been auction sites from Dell and CompUSA, which may be seen as endorsements by larger companies that there's money to be made in used sales.

ORGANIZATION AND STRUCTURE

Sellers of used computer equipment are generally either retail stores or dealers. Although there are a few chains in the industry, notably Computer Renaissance, most retailers of used computers are small business owners. The *Wall Street Journal* offered an example of how one such store, Compuplan, does business. When a woman in Cedar Hill, Texas, wanted a computer to perform routine household operations such as keeping her finances, she went to Compuplan and purchased a used IBM 486 computer for $699. Her computer originally belonged to American Airlines, who used it for the airline's reservations system. Thus it did not have a great deal of consumer-oriented amenities, such as software. So Compuplan, which bought the unit from American for $250, invested another $300 in upgrading it. It then added $150 to the price (27 percent of the original investment) and sold the computer to the customer.

Retailers sell equipment of greatest interest to the consumer market: software, PCs, peripherals, and the occasional network card or memory chip for the do-it-yourself computer enthusiast. Dealers, on the other hand, sell all those things and more—including large systems for networking an entire company—but they do so in larger quantities. Typically, if consumers were to call a dealer and ask to buy or sell just one PC, the dealer would refer them to a retailer. Hence the difference between retailers and dealers is to some extent in what they sell, but more significantly in how they sell it. Dealers generally operate in an ordinary office, with a large storage and testing area in back, and do little of their business face-to-face; rather, they are highly dependent on telephone communications. Generally they buy from, and sell to, other businesses, including other dealers. They make their money primarily because of the information they possess: they know that on one side, Company X needs a certain item and is willing to pay $1,000 for it, and that on the other, Dealer Y has the item priced at $750. The dealer in the middle, because he is able to link up the two companies, makes the $250 profit.

One of the leading trade organizations for used computer sellers is the Information Technology Resellers Association (ITRA). It was formed in 1998 by the merger of the Computer Dealers and Lessors Association (CDLA) and the Digital Dealers Association. Founded in 1981, the CDLA itself brought together the Computer Lessors Association, which existed since 1967, and the Computer Dealers Association, formed in 1972. As its name implies, ITRA's constituency includes businesses that resell computer equipment. Besides sellers and lessors, the ITRA includes maintenance companies, refurbishment/reconfiguration firms, transportation companies, financial institutions, original equipment manufacturer finance companies, software distributors, and industry consultants. Among its principal services to the industry, and to the public, is ITRA's Code of Ethics, which its more than 300 members have signed. Since 1974, a

standing committee has arbitrated hundreds of cases regarding ethics violations.

More central to the life of the used computer business than industry associations ,however, are arenas and forums where dealers can exchange information about available equipment. Retailers, and to a certain extent wholesale dealers, watch for news of liquidations and auctions, including those run by local governments or federal institutions. Salespeople and equipment brokers often communicate with each other over the telephone in a complex network of interactions that spans the globe. A dealer in the Midwest, for instance, may learn that a buyer in San Francisco needs 300 personal computers. So she calls her contact in Denmark, who then gets in touch with a supplier in Australia. The Australian supplier puts in a call to a dealer in Los Angeles, who has the equipment and sends it. And thus the 300 PCs may travel around the world, back up the chain, in order simply to travel from Los Angeles to San Francisco. Outsiders might ask why the L.A. dealer was not put directly in touch with the San Francisco end user, but to equipment dealers, the answer is obvious: without the profit that accrues to a dealer as middleman, his business would be unable to continue to exist and the next time someone comes looking for equipment, he may be unable to locate it because there is no one to track it down.

Although voice interaction over the telephone remains a key element in arranging the movement of goods within the used computer industry, brokers also rely on weekly publications announcing equipment for sale, and are dependent on information-age technology to keep up-to-date on equipment offerings. A company with a large quantity of token rings to sell, for instance, might set up a fax broadcast to dealers and end users all over the United States or the world. The Internet is an emerging means of exchange as well. Numerous companies have their own Web sites, and there are sites as well for entities such as Daley Marketing Corp. (DMC), which sells primarily to dealers. Founded in 1980 as an IBM computer broker/lessor, DMC is in the business of providing timely, accurate, and detailed industry information through regular publication of its *DMC Computer Price List, DMC Broker and End-User Market Value Report,* and other items.

The market for used computer equipment is composed of three distinct segments: refurbished, used, and liquidated equipment. Refurbished equipment runs the gamut as far as quality is concerned, but all refurbished systems are previously owned computers that have been reconditioned. Many refurbished com-

More On **USED COMPUTER INDUSTRY ASSOCIATIONS**

Several organizations from different areas of the computer industry are of great interest to the used computer business. Among the most important are:

- Business Products Industry Association (www.bpia.org)
- Business Technology Association (www.btanet.org)
- Computing Technology Industry Association (www.comptia.org)
- Information Technology Association of America (www.itaa.org)
- Information Technology Resellers Association (www.itra.org)

All these groups represent some configuration of businesspeople, including storefront resellers, wholesale dealers, value-added resellers, and lessors.

puter systems are sold with warranties. Used equipment, on the other hand, may or may not be reconditioned. Finally, liquidated computers generally represent last year's models that were never sold. According to Christine Arrington, an analyst for International Data Corp., the used computer market "has been evolving from a dumping ground for unwanted and under-powered systems to an acceptable source of low-cost hardware to fit a variety of budget and power ranges." She predicted increasing competition between the new and used computer markets but said they will probably remain highly interdependent.

Late in the 1990s, cost-conscious school systems around the United States increasingly began to turn to refurbished personal computers to meet their needs in the classroom. The appearance on the used market of more and more used Pentium-based PCs has helped fuel this demand. Refurbished PCs are attractive to the folks running U.S. public schools for a number of reasons, not the least of which is the savings that can be realized. Many school systems operating under tight budgets are forced to cut corners on such basic supplies as paper and pencils, so an opportunity to save money on high-end purchases such as computers and peripheral equipment is appealing. By going the used computer route, school boards can double or triple the number of computers they can put into the classroom. Of the growing school market, Brian Kushner, chief executive officer of ReCompute, an Austin, Texas-based company that markets refurbished PCs, said: "To get three to four times the computational resource for the same dollar—that's an enormous leverage. Schools don't need—and often don't want—powerful systems targeted at multimedia, engineering, and software compilation applications."

BACKGROUND AND DEVELOPMENT

In 1993 an article on used computers in the Stockholm-based periodical *Tomorrow* approached the subject from a characteristically "green" northern European angle: concern over the environmental impact of nonrecyclable computer equipment. According to the article, the German Ministry of the Environment reported that western Germany alone generated some 800,000 metric tons of "electronic waste." This included batteries, cables, and other small items, but the bulk of it was in larger information and office systems. The situation pointed out the fact that computer equipment became obsolete at a quick rate, such that many companies considered it easier to dump such equipment into a landfill than to set about reselling it.

Trends   REUSE, RECYCLE, RESELL

A fast-growing business related to the used computer trade is hardware recycling. The National Safety Council estimated that of the 31.6 million or so PCs that were expected to become obsolete in 2000, just 11 percent would be recycled. A number of firms and nonprofit organizations have made raising that percentage a high priority, considering that some believe 99 percent of computer components are recyclable.

There are a few compelling reasons to recycle computer equipment rather than pitching it into a landfill. For one, some computer components contain toxic substances and harmful heavy metals that can't be buried or burned without risk of polluting the ground or air or both. Used equipment isn't useless, either; often computers can be upgraded or adapted to meet more advanced needs, or they can fit the needs of a less demanding user.

Comprenew Corp. of Belmont, Michigan, is one company that has gotten heavily into the recycling business. It takes in donations of nearly all kinds of electronic equipment for recycling, although it imposes a fee on computer monitors, which present special recycling problems because of their lead content. Comprenew has also partnered with nonprofits such as Goodwill Industries to take used computer equipment off their hands while providing Goodwill with revenue from the parts it can resell.

Resellers and recyclers sometimes have an uneasy coexistence, however, because their goals are different. Resellers seek to maximize the economic value of used equipment, usually by choosing to sell only the parts and equipment that will bring in the most revenue. Recyclers, however, are interested in salvaging as much hardware as possible, regardless of its monetary value. This tension has provoked some recyclers to accuse resellers of only making the recycling problem worse.

The infrastructure for such reselling, in the form of a healthy computer resale industry, was clearly only then developing—or at least, people's awareness of it was still in its early stages.

There was a time when IBM literally dumped old PCs, PC/XTs, and PC/AT models offshore to create an artificial reef, but that day is long gone. In 1997 *Computerworld* magazine reported that the industry giant had begun selling refurbished equipment on the World Wide Web. In fact, it was a 1956 U.S. Justice Department consent decree, restraining IBM's actions in the used equipment market and other areas, which laid the groundwork for the existence of the used computer industry. Of course, it would be many years before computers themselves became widely available to ordinary consumers, but the explosion in PC use during the 1980s paved the way for the growth of used computer sales.

Yet there was a period of lag, just as the used car business only came into its own approximately a decade after the advent of widespread sales of Fords and other models. For most of the 1980s and early 1990s, used equipment computer sales were primarily among dealers; only later did the industry see the appearance of numerous storefront retail operations. A study by the Gartner Group for the Computer Leasing and Remarketing Association at the end of 1993 found that volume had not grown for three years starting in 1991, a fact analysts attributed to caution on the part of consumers, as well as to the economic recession. In 1993, however, the volume of used computer leasing and sales was $19.4 billion, and by 1994 the figure had grown to $21.4 billion. Of that, approximately 30 percent, or $6.42 billion, was in used computer sales.

Aside from the growth in the economy and the differing methodology used to obtain the observations (for example, the first was a survey, the second a straight dollar accounting), the change can be attributed to rapid developments in computer technology during the middle and latter part of the 1990s. In quick succession, IBM upgraded the processing speed of its personal computers such that whereas a 286 was acceptable in 1990, by 1997 the technology had gone through three generations, to a 386, then a 486, and finally a Pentium processor. At the same time, the speed of Pentiums had also accelerated. Other changes were afoot as well: for instance, widespread access to the Internet dictated a need for faster and faster modems, and old 9,600- and 14,400-baud models were being cast off in favor of 28,800 or 56,000 models. The business world saw a revolution in local area networks, which required their own extensive range of equipment in order to be established. In upgrading their computers and systems, individuals and businesses had to go somewhere to sell off the old and, in many cases, to purchase the new or almost new.

By 1995 IBM was back in court challenging the 39-year-old Justice Department decree, but it faced strong opposition. One opponent, the very same judge who had presided over the original case—now 84 years old and still sitting on the bench—was removed from the case by a federal appeals court on the grounds that he could not be impartial. Another foe, Computer Leasing & Remarketing Association attorney Kevin Arguit, would not be so easily moved, though. According to the terms of the disputed de-

cree, IBM was prevented from immediately reselling returned equipment; instead, it had to wait 60 days and then offer it first to used equipment vendors at certain prices. These prices, which the company's representatives said were unreasonably high, further delayed sales of IBM's equipment. If the decree was lifted, Arguit responded, IBM would dominate the market. The dispute raged on.

CURRENT CONDITIONS

With so much of the computer industry's attention fixed on the newest, fastest machines, it's little wonder that the used computer business has remained somewhat obscure. In the words of David Bernstein, head of the refurbishing vendor Access Direct Inc., the used business may be seen as the "ugly twin sister" of new computer sales.

But obscurity, and even ugliness, hasn't stopped used box sellers from prospering. In the late 1990s refurbishers and resellers reported steady demand, even as new PC prices tumbled amid price wars. The market has also been ripe for used peripherals and components, which tend to wear out faster than computers themselves. In 1998 industry sales of used and refurbished PC equipment approached $6 billion, and that amount didn't include the smaller market for used high-end equipment such as mainframes.

Buyers of used computer equipment are a diverse bunch. Some are bona fide bargain hunters and cheapskates, but a good portion of them are technically savvy customers who know exactly what they want. This is particularly true with companies that are running large, older computer systems and wish to replace or add on with like machines. Many also purchase used computers, which may be less than a year old, because the technology is stable and proven. Of course, prices are more reasonable as well, enabling budget-conscious buyers to get more power for less money. To use Computer Renaissance president Taylor Bond's analogy, most used computer buyers "would prefer a used Ferrari to a brand-new Yugo."

There is some debate among analysts and industry veterans about what impact the ongoing erosion of new computer prices has on the remarketing segment. The standard logic is that given a choice between similarly priced, comparable machines, most buyers would opt for a new machine over an old. This prompts analysts such as Gabriel Griffith of International Data Corp. to predict a slowdown as new PC prices sink. Still, some in the business believe the relationship is

A used computer-equipment store. (FieldMark Publications/Robert J. Huffman)

more complex, and that low prices on new equipment can boost demand for used devices as well.

INDUSTRY LEADERS

The largest sellers of used computer equipment include many of the companies that make it and lease it new: in addition to IBM's resale wing, Dell Computer Corp., Compaq Computer Corp., AT&T Systems Leasing Corp., and GE Capital are important players. At another tier are high-volume dealers such as USA Computer in Long Island or Daktech in Fargo, North Dakota.

Formed in 1988, Computer Renaissance (CR) is a chain of 209 independent used computer franchises across the United States and Canada. The retail concept was franchised by Grow Biz International Inc. until Grow Biz sold it to Hollis Technologies LLC of Lakeland, Florida, in 1999 for $3 billion. Hollis was already a franchisee at several Florida outlets. The chain's revenue slipped 6.4 percent in 1999 because about a dozen franchises were closed and same-store sales were down. Sales that year totaled $145 million, down from $155 million in 1998. Most of CR's retail outlets show more computers than the superstores,

displaying an average of 30 systems per store. Shoppers are encouraged to tinker with the equipment before making a decision to purchase. All stores take trade-ins.

ReCompute International, based in Austin, Texas, refurbishes personal computers purchased from large companies that are upgrading their equipment, and from PC manufacturers that are liquidating unsold units to make room for new models. Brian Kushner, ReCompute's CEO, said, "We're the undertakers of the PC industry." For many computer users, individual as well as corporate, the older technology in some of the used computers marketed by ReCompute and others in the industry is more than sufficient for their needs. "The vast majority of buyers out there are paying for way more computer than they need," according to Dale Yates, a systems administrator for McLane Co., based in Temple, Texas. Yates and others responsible for corporate computer buying decisions are finding that there's no need to supply someone whose responsibilities are largely confined to word processing, for example, with a computer designed to perform far more sophisticated functions.

Other companies in this industry include Second Source, with six stores in Delaware and Pennsylvania; Computer Exchange, which matches buyers and sellers for a 10 percent commission; Boston Computer Exchange, a phone-based buying and selling dealership that reported $32 million in sales in 1996; Rumarson Technologies Inc., a refurbisher with about $25 million in 1998 sales; and U.S. Micro Corp., also a refurbisher with $20 to $25 million in sales. The Internet has several used computer selling sites, running from manufacturers that sell refurbished models to auctions.

WORK FORCE

Generally, a used computer operation, whether a wholesale dealer or a retail store, must employ at least one class of worker: salespeople. Salespeople, whether they work behind a counter or over the phone, may receive a salary, but usually commissions are used as an incentive for high performance. Because they generate the company's profit, salespeople are usually the most highly paid, and can often earn in the high five-digit figures, or even over $100,000 a year.

Also important are technical personnel, whose job is to evaluate equipment for problems, and then fix those problems as they arise. Tech workers may earn $20 an hour or more. In addition, used computer businesses, depending on their size, may employ shipping and receiving personnel, inventory workers, and administrative assistants.

AMERICA AND THE WORLD

The used computer business continues to grow internationally, where buyers in emerging countries are thrilled to purchase slightly used American equipment at a discount. Trading goes on between America and the economic powerhouses of Western Europe and the Pacific Rim, but a future area of growth is likely to be "second-tier countries," such as developing nations in Eastern Europe, the Middle East and Central Asia, East Asia (including China), and parts of Latin America and Africa.

One international market that was booming in the waning days of the 20th century was Brazil, where the supply of used computers in early 1999 was estimated at about 6.8 million. Many of these systems had been acquired from larger companies at cut-rate prices, according to Loja dos Micros, a São Paulo-based seller of used systems. Another player in the Brazilian market is Celty Informatica, also based in São Paulo. Both companies predict that as the devaluation of the

Brazilian currency increases the prices of new computers, the demand for used equipment will grow even stronger.

FURTHER READING

"Brazil: Growing Market for Used Computers." *South American Business Information,* 26 January 1999.

"Computer Dealer & Lessors Association." Available from http://www.cdla.org.

"Computer Industry Failing to Recycle Outdated Models." *Japan Times Weekly International Edition,* 27 May-2 June 1996, 14.

"Computers a Stupid Investment? (ReCompute Sells Used Equipment)." *Electronic News,* 20 July 1998, 40.

Dallabrida, Dale. "Savings Can Be Big on Used Computers." *Gannett News Service,* 18 February 1998.

"Dell Takes Outlet Store to Internet." *Newsbytes,* 28 February 2000.

Dennis, Raoul. "Second Time Around." *Black Enterprise,* August 1996, 26.

Doan, Amy. "Born-Again PCs." *Forbes,* 5 April 1999.

Eisenberg, Anne. "Used-PC Bargains Add Appeal to Life in the Slow Lane." *New York Times,* 4 March 1999.

Flynn, Laurie J. "Just Drive a Used PC off the Lot and Save." *New York Times,* 23 February 1997.

Gair, Cristina. "Secondhand PC Sales Going Strong." *Home Office Computing,* January 2000.

Gallaga, Omar L. "Dell Launches Auction Site for Used Computers." *Austin-American Statesman,* 20 July 1999.

Harrington, Mark. "Top Ten Retail Innovators: No. 4-Computer Renaissance." *Computer Retail Week,* 16 November 1998, 36.

Hepp, Rick. "Toxic Components Make Old Computers Dangerous, Raise Question of Recycling." *Chicago Tribune,* 28 February 2000.

Karl, Lisa Musolf. "Used, Not Obsolete." *Baltimore Business Journal,* 26 January 1998.

Kerstetter, Jim, and Peter Burrows. "Who May Prosper Despite the Fall." *Business Week,* 18 December 2000.

Mackenzie, Ian. "Lower Pentium PCs Set to Invade Used Computer Market." *Computer Dealer News,* 22 June 1998, 30.

Rigdon, Joan E. "FTC Inquires of PC Rivals on Used Parts." *Wall Street Journal,* 17 July 1995.

Rosa, Jerry. "Like Magic, Old PCs Reappear." *Computer Reseller News,* 15 February 1999.

Schwabach, Bob. "Refurbished Computers Cheaper, Plenty Powerful." *Star Tribune,* (Minneapolis, Minnesota), 3 August 2000.

"Secondhand Blues." *Computerworld,* 31 March 1997, 45.

"Secondhand Computers Hold Appeal." *Minneapolis Star Tribune,* 8 March 1999.

Templin, Neal. "Computers: Corporate Castoffs Fuel Market for Used PCs." *Wall Street Journal,* 10 June 1996.

———. "Computers: Midnight at the Oasis of Microprocessors." *Wall Street Journal,* 29 November 1995.

Vijayan, Jaikumar. "Suits over Used PCs End." *Computerworld,* 4 March 1996, 32.

Wasserman, Todd. "News: Refurb Chains Rethink Inventories —Retailers Alter Their New-to-Used Product Ratios to Help Sustain Margins." *Computer Retail Week,* 28 September 1998, 8.

Whelan, Carolyn. "Refurbished Systems Shift to Schools." *Electronic News,* 20 July 1998, 6.

VENTURE CAPITAL FIRMS

INDUSTRY SNAPSHOT

One of the more glamorous sectors of finance in the late 1990s and early 2000s, venture capital basked in its most glorious era, drawing new players and new money at a fantastic pace while generating record returns. About 100 new venture capital firms cropped up in 1999, bringing the U.S. total to over 600. However, the downturn in the technology markets in 2000 served as a painful reminder to venture capitalists that there was no such thing as a sure thing, and many players were ushered out of the game as quickly as they had entered. Still, with technology continuing to move the world economy, analysts predicted a central role for venture capitalists in financing tomorrow's innovative companies.

Venture capital is the equity invested in rapidly growing companies that investors believe hold excellent potential for future earnings. Venture capital firms thus fund enterprising upstart companies trying to get off the ground. Concentrated particularly heavily in high-tech industries, venture capital is generally pooled by institutions or deep-pocketed individuals in the hopes of generating huge profits over the long term. Traditionally, wealthy investors approached venture capital endeavors like buying lottery tickets. While these ventures do not always pan out, a few solid winners can usually make up for a string of disappointments, and venture capital firms typically have enough money in reserve to withstand a few stagnant underachievers. Thus, venture capital firms are often exactly the financial break young, struggling entrepreneurs need to get their companies on their feet.

Once the exclusive perch of the extremely wealthy, the venture capital industry drifted ever closer to the mainstream in the late 1990s, largely a direct result of the Internet explosion. Major corporations and financial institutions increasingly forged their own venture capital wings or subsidiaries. Meanwhile, the major venture capital firms have helped well-established organizations develop Internet-based companies. While still quite prohibitive owing to the lack of liquidity and long-term orientation, venture capital was drawing more average investors into the fold.

By 2000, venture capital was all the rage, drawing everyday investors in much the same manner as mutual funds did through the 1990s. With a strong U.S. economic climate, ecstatic news stories about the New Economy, and the explosion of Internet dot-com start-ups, the venture capital industry was at its most robust in early 2000, with few signs of a letup, save for analysts' prescient concerns over the long-term stability of the Internet business model. And with a soaring stock market inviting all sorts of get-rich-quick seekers, investors fell over each other to throw money at the next great dot-com idea. The tidal wave of money finally crashed in on investors in the latter half of 2000 as technology stocks declined. While hardly wiping out the VC industry, these events nonetheless injected some humility, forcing many to recall that fundamentals still matter in a dot-com world.

On the other hand, the tremendous success of venture capitalists shifted the industry dynamic 180 degrees. Gone are the days when eager opportunists would crawl hat-in-hand to venture capitalists seeking money. Nowadays, venture capital firms are scrambling to differentiate themselves amidst all the competition and the robust marketplace.

ORGANIZATION AND STRUCTURE

The venture capital industry is served by the National Venture Capital Association (NVCA), which represents over 350 venture capital and private equity firms. Established in 1973, the NVCA examines the intersection of the venture capital industry and the overall U.S. economy and facilitates the practice of funneling private equity to new business development. Two major research firms, VentureOne and Venture Economics, also supply information and analysis about the venture capital industry.

Most venture capital firms are private partnerships managed by small professional staffs. Venture capital firms derive their capital from pension funds, endowments, foundations, sympathetic nonfinancial corporations, banks, insurance companies, government, foreign investors, rich uncles, and a variety of other sources. Through the 1980s and up to the mid-1990s, pension funds provided about half of all money for venture capital (VC) funds. That proportion was a primary casualty of the massive VC boom of the late 1990s, however, as individual investments jumped to 19 percent of the total VC pool. Foundations provided an additional 18 percent and nonfinancial corporations kicked in 13 percent.

Far from the deep-pocketed individual investors of yesteryear, modern venture capital firms seek investment commitments from individuals, corporations, funds, and so on, and pool their money on the understanding that the money is committed for the long haul. This illiquidity generally places venturing beyond the scope of the average investor.

The majority of venture capital firms are independent of other financial institutions, though a growing number are subsidiaries of commercial and investment banks, a trend likely to accelerate following the passage of the Financial Services Modernization Act of 1999. Other firms are affiliated with nonfinancial corporations seeking to diversify their assets.

According to the NVCA, venture capitalists typically devote themselves to financing emerging companies that promise fast and lucrative growth; purchase equity securities; help companies develop new products and bring them to market; engage in high-risk, high-reward financing; and maintain a long-term orientation. Although in recent years venture capital deals have grown larger, VC firms usually sprinkle a little money here and there among a great number of businesses, and then actively work with the companies' management teams over the long term to help bring the business plan to fruition and generate strong returns on their investments. The firm then pools all its company investments into a single fund, thereby limiting the company-by-company risk.

Investment portfolios also vary widely. Some venture capital firms are generalists, investing across industries and company types. Others specialize in certain industries or even industry segments, geographic regions, or companies of certain types, such as those in the late stages of development. High-tech industry constitutes the overwhelming bulk of venture investment, but VC firms are spread far and wide, according to the NVCA, helping companies in industries from business services to construction, and in firms with special characteristics, such as those that constitute socially responsible investment.

There are several different stages of company development for which a venture capital firm may provide financing. The formative stage involves getting the initial idea off the ground, from a solid plan on paper to an actual firm with a structure and a basis of operation. Formative stage companies pull in the largest share of venture financing, about 42 percent of the total. Investment at this stage is known as seed financing, the most common type of funding people think of when they consider venture capital. A company receiving seed financing generally has yet to become fully operational, and probably has a product in development. Early-stage investment takes place when a company is well into its life cycle, perhaps looking to complete a current project or achieve new breakthroughs. Generally, early financing is directed at companies with a test or pilot product. Expansion financing fuels the renewed growth or widened reach of a product already on the market. The expansion

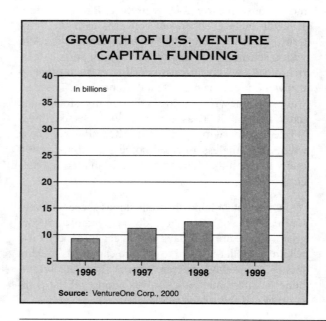

GROWTH OF U.S. VENTURE CAPITAL FUNDING

In billions

Source: VentureOne Corp., 2000

stage calls for funding to push a well-grounded company to the next level of viability. Such companies commanded about 32 percent of venture dollars in 1999.

Eventually, of course, a venture capital firm wants to realize a profit from its financial and management investment, and will try to cash out. Once a venture-backed company gets on its feet, the most common financing step is to announce an initial public offering (IPO), the proceeds of which may be used to cash out the venture capital firm. This is not always the case, however; some venture capital firms opt to stay in the game following the IPO, occasionally even forging a presence in the public company's management. Still, such guidance is not the main thrust of venture capitalists, who seek their fortune primarily in moving companies out of the gestation process. Venture capital firms may also throw money behind a proposed merger and acquisition to facilitate the smooth consolidation of promising firms.

Another pillar of the venture capital industry is the VC angel, who generally provides early financing to especially risky companies—those that are very young or that have poor financial histories. VC angels prepare a company for an IPO by providing the juice necessary to develop a new product or complete a key acquisition that will make the company viable for the public market. A VC angel will usually take a management position for as long as its money is invested. Angels are usually individual investors, a reemerging sector of the industry, willing to devote both finances and management expertise to a struggling start-up.

BACKGROUND AND DEVELOPMENT

While the practice of finding individuals or organizations wealthier than you to finance your better mousetrap probably dates back, in its various forms, to the earliest days of commerce, the modern venture capital industry emerged slowly from a tiny investment pool in the 1960s, with venture capital gradually evolving into a significant asset class. Prior to the 1960s, the venture capital industry was basically a number of tremendously wealthy individuals looking to make their mark funding innovative new companies. Particularly since World War II, the venture capital industry constituted the financial fuel for high-tech industry, and has, according to VentureOne, financed entire new industries, such as biotechnology and overnight shipping, almost singlehandedly, bringing

---

Profile

THE CIA INFILTRATES VC

Venture capitalists fund the innovative companies of tomorrow, helping to bring to market the products that will change the average consumer's life for the better. But that's not all they do.

With the announcement that the U.S. Central Intelligence Agency (CIA) would establish its own venture capital firm, In-Q-Tel, everybody's favorite conspiracy-theory target launched its very own high-tech investment scheme. The name wraps the word "intelligence" around "Q," the name of the purveyor of James Bond's high-tech gadgetry. In addition to its cute pop-culture nostalgia, the name signifies a certain reality. One of the firm's primary functions is to fund start-up tech companies developing products for use in the CIA's vast spy and analyst networks. Beyond that, the CIA simply wants the best high-tech gear that money can buy, including powerful search engines, language-translation software, and even the ability to roam around the Internet in secret. The agency thus intends to transform the methods by which it gathers intelligence.

In this case, the government acted as the VC angel. Congress funneled $61 million to the nonprofit firm to get it on its feet, though skeptics abound on Capitol Hill. Still, the program seemed to be generating some good business. In-Q-Tel's portfolio contained eight companies late in 2000, from small start-ups such as Graviton Inc. to such longtime government clients as Lockheed Martin Corp.

One of the CIA's first ventures fueled the growth of Silicon Valley software company PDH Inc., aimed at the development of technology capable of tracking and controlling the movement of digital information.

The federal government was keeping a curious eye on In-Q-Tel. Should the venture capital firm prove successful, other departments and agencies could follow suit, in effect altering the interaction of government and business. According to the *Wall Street Journal*, the U.S. Postal Service and the National Aeronautics and Space Administration were contemplating similar business models.

---

to life such current giants as Apple, Microsoft, Intel, Genentech, and Netscape.

Still, venture capitalists have had a bumpy road on their way to the mythic success of the late 1990s. One of the most notable busts occurred in the early 1990s, when the slate of much-hyped biotechnology companies failed to live up to inflated promises, proving a washout at the IPO stage.

The overall annual rates of return are subject to massive fluctuations, from as little as 0 percent in off years, such as 1984 and 1990, to 60 percent in good years such as 1980 and 1995, with the average usually hovering around 20 percent, although the late 1990s saw record returns of 85 percent.

CURRENT CONDITIONS

By the end of 1999 and into 2000, venture capital funds existed in a fairy tale world of tremendous profits and acquired a can't-lose reputation. While some of the euphoria surrounding venture capital, which emboldened herds of individual investors and corporations to participate in VC funds, was a bit overstated, the industry certainly had a glorious time. According to the National Venture Capital Association, venture capital funds investing in early-stage companies generated returns of 85 percent in 1999; the Standard & Poor's 500 (S&P 500) stock index, meanwhile, posted a 15 percent increase over the same period. Over a five-year period, the difference was less dramatic, but still clearly tilted in favor of venture capital, at 45 percent returns on early-stage ventures compared with 28 percent gains for the S&P 500.

Indeed, the venture capital industry closed out the 20th century with a bang, greatly accelerating investment to a total of $36.4 billion in 1999, easily the most lucrative venture year on record and outpacing the combined totals of the previous three years, according to VentureOne. The number of venture capital financings leaped 51 percent that year, while the total dollar amount behind those deals grew 155 percent. A total of about 4,000 companies received venture capital funding in 1999, up from about 2,900 the year before, while average funding rose from $5.2 million to $8.9 million.

The central development behind the massive late-1990s flow of dollars into start-up financings was the Internet; venture-backed Internet companies alone rode their way to viability on $25 billion in venture capital in 1999, four times the 1998 total. Thus, Internet start-ups accounted for a whopping 69 percent of all venture capital investment in 1999, compared with 43 percent the year before. The other booming industries propping up the venture capital industry in 1999 were telecommunications and networking segments, such as fiber optics, representing 21 percent of all VC investment at $7.6 billion.

Meanwhile, 248 venture-financed companies completed initial public offerings (IPOs) in 1999, according to VentureOne, bringing in $19.43 billion, doubling the record set in 1996 when the first wave

of Internet companies hit the public market en masse. The median valuation of these IPOs also took off as well in 1999, reaching $316.6 million from $169.6 million in 1998. Venture capital also financed a total of 256 merger-and-acquisition deals in 1999, nearly tripling the totals for 1997 and 1998, for a total of $39.18 billion.

In addition to traditional venture capital firms, major commercial banks increasingly assumed a venture capital demeanor, tripling their venture capital investment to over $4 billion between 1996 and 1999, with no sign of a letup. One of the most attractive aspects of venture capital for banks is the boosted returns relative to loan interest that has accompanied the massive start-up boom of the late 1990s. Amidst weakening bank stocks, the skyrocketing returns on venture investments have taken on greater importance as banks struggle to remain viable in their rapidly consolidating industry. For instance, Chase Manhattan Corp.'s subsidiary Chase Capital Partners sank nearly $2 billion into venture financing in 1999, and struck gold with such Internet start-ups as StarMedia Networks while maintaining a total of $7 billion to back some 500 companies. Chase Manhattan later purchased industry leader Hambrecht & Quist Private Equity. Wells Fargo & Co.'s Norwest Venture Capital put up $450 million to back new enterprises, especially in Silicon Valley.

The industry in the late 1990s and early 2000s also had a massive influx of average investors into venture capital, indicative of the can't-miss reputation the industry had acquired. While such investors still tend to be concentrated among the wealthier segments of the investing population, this trend has further relieved the superrich of their monopoly over venture capital. Not surprisingly, this demographic change has changed the face of the industry somewhat. While venture capital firms typically stay in for the long haul, not expecting any significant returns for about five to seven years, the late 1990s technology and Internet boom popularized the industry with a number of new players with a lot less patience.

With the sudden slump of the technology sector during the latter half of 2000, however, venture capital lost some, though by no means all, of its luster. Between April, when the NASDAQ first started to fall, and the end of the year, nearly 20 VC funds of over $1 billion closed. The general consensus among financial analysts held that such a trend was inevitable to counterbalance the overwhelming rush of dollars to back any and all high-tech, particularly dot-com, schemes, with little or no attention to sound fundamentals. Still, few predicted that venture capital was a passing fad. The wave of entrepreneurship and emergence of new, marketable technologies such as telecommunications and wireless equipment remained strong, and venture capital had proven enough of a money maker to keep it in the forefront of investors' minds for years to come.

The strong IPO market was in fact a major impetus to the rapid growth and diversification of the venture capital industry. Most analysts expected this trend to be long lasting, even in the face of a sour turn in the economy, as some predicted at the close of 2000. As a result, venture capital will assume more the look of a retail market, and VC firms will be forced to strive harder to showcase a unique and specialized strategy in order to survive the increasingly competitive marketplace.

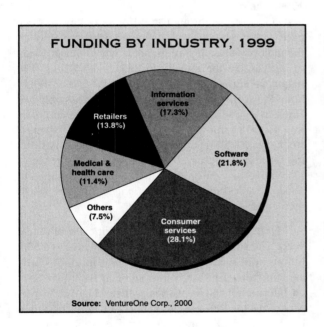

FUNDING BY INDUSTRY, 1999

Retailers (13.8%)
Information services (17.3%)
Software (21.8%)
Medical & health care (11.4%)
Others (7.5%)
Consumer services (28.1%)

Source: VentureOne Corp., 2000

INDUSTRY LEADERS

Based in San Francisco, Chase H&Q (formerly Hambrecht & Quist Private Equity) specialized in high-tech investment but also offered research and sales services, consulting, and merger-and-acquisition advisory services. A total of 25 of the company's venture-backed firms held IPOs between March 1999 and March 2000, and the value of those IPOs leaped 227 percent. Hambrecht & Quist, founded in 1968 on the personal savings of William Hambrecht and George Quist, went public itself in 1996. Although reeling from bad publicity generated by a federal price-fixing suit, the firm rebounded, forming a new company, WR Hambrecht, to take companies public via the Internet.

Hambrecht & Quist was purchased in the 1999 by Chase Manhattan, becoming a Chase subsidiary with 830 employees.

Kleiner Perkins Caufield & Byers (KPCB), based in Menlo Park, California, was a leading fuel provider to Silicon Valley. Since the company's inception in 1972, KPCB invested over $1 billion in more than 250 companies, featuring such blockbusters as Compaq, Genentech, Netscape, and Lotus. One of the firm's biggest dot-com success stories was its bankrolling of Amazon.com, Inc. KPCB's investment portfolio was divided into two sectors: Life Sciences, for health care, diagnostics, and drug discovery ventures; and Information Sciences, for software, communications, and semiconductors. The portfolio generated 18 IPOs between March 1999 and March 2000, and in the early 2000s was bulging with mobile computing firms.

Benchmark Capital held more than $1 billion in assets in 2000, the first venture capital firm to exceed that benchmark. The firm derived about one-third of its investment pool from individuals, including its own partners. The company's unique entrepreneur in residence ensured equal distribution of earnings among its partners. Also based in Menlo Park, California, Benchmark was another Silicon Valley giant, and was an early financial backer of the online auction company eBay Inc. Between March 1999 and March 2000, 15 of the firm's venture companies held IPOs. Benchmark generally dropped $3-$5 million in seed investments, but also delved in at later stages as well. Its investment was geared mainly toward high-tech industries such as the Internet, semiconductors, software, and telecommunications. The company counted among its investors Bill Gates and the Ford Foundation.

New Enterprise Associates of Baltimore, Maryland, held about $412 million in 121 companies in 2000. With individual investments ranging from $500,000 to $6 million, New Enterprise was devoted primarily to development-stage companies. Major winners in its portfolio history included 3Com Corp. and Vertex Pharmaceuticals Inc., highlighting its emphasis on high-tech, communications, and health care. More than 130 companies from New Enterprise's portfolio have gone public since the VC firm's founding in 1978, including 20 between March 1999 and March 2000, for a total return of about 420 percent.

Norwest Venture Capital of Minneapolis, Minnesota, split its operations into two divisions. Norwest Venture Partners fuels new companies in technology and health care as well as less glamorous industries such as retail stores and restaurants. Norwest Equity Partners funds consolidations, reorganizations, and management buyouts. The two divisions invested $247.5 million in 74 companies in 1999. Since 1961, over 300 countries have enjoyed financial backing from Norwest, with investments generally ranging from $1.5 to $30 million. The company was affiliated with the major banking firm Wells Fargo.

WORK FORCE

Professional venture capital fund managers, or general partners, are usually similar to mutual fund managers in that they assume control over the assets pooled by the investors and allocate them into a venture or into another fund, in most cases spreading out investments widely. Known as "gatekeepers," they enter into the firm as general partners, as opposed to the investors' limited partner status, and provide the resources and expertise the limited partners may lack. Venture capital firms recruit heavily from Wall Street investment banks and research departments. Compared with those positions, venture capital affords managers a great deal of independence, though the pay is a bit less.

AMERICA AND THE WORLD

While anxious market watchers have proclaimed continental Europe the next fertile venture capital soil for several years, it was only at the end of 1999 that the market began to show explosive growth, generating an avalanche of new venture funding in light of the booming market in the United States and the threat of encroachment on the European market by outside venture capitalists. U.S. venture capital firms, such as Benchmark Capital, Atlas Venture, and Chase H&Q, have been covetously eyeing the continental European market, and by 2000 began to move in aggressively, forcing the beginning of what was expected to be rapid consolidation among the European players.

European venture capital firms have traditionally been a great deal more conservative than their U.S. counterparts. Many European entrepreneurs grudgingly held that continental venture capital firms often demand an established management team and a proven clientele in addition to a strong business plan. Such cautiousness helped spur the influx of outside venture capital, and was forcing European firms to rethink their investment strategies.

Moreover, Forrester Research expected venture capital investment in Europe to double or triple dur-

ing the early 2000s as the Internet becomes more common throughout the continent. By the end of 1999, only 13 percent of European households were connected to the Internet, offering tremendous potential for market penetration and, simultaneously, venture capital influx. Nonetheless, by the end of 2000 there were warning signs of an early shakeout in the widening European VC industry, as one company after another reported difficulty. Analysts attributed this to more irrational exuberance surrounding the Internet, as dot-coms grew overwhelmingly fashionable overnight, leading to a financial backlash as risky investments failed to pan out.

In Japan, meanwhile, the Ministry of International Trade and Industry (MITI) took initial steps toward revitalizing the nation's venture capital industry in fall 1999. The number of new businesses in Japan was on a steady decline through the 1990s, failing to keep pace with the number of business closings; moreover, the majority of company founders were over 40 years of age, unlike the climate in the United States. The major venture capital firms in Japan were tightly bound to large stockbrokers, picking well-established firms to throw money into so as to put the company in a sound position when it breaks into the Japanese stock market. Some observers conclude that this structure is overly conservative, stifling the emergence of innovative new businesses. MITI therefore hoped to allocate more funds from the finance ministry for its own equity-investment boost.

Despite receiving its share of criticism in recent years, Canada's venture capital industry invested $2.7 billion in new cash in new companies in 1999, up 64 percent from the year before and centering primarily on Internet-related industries (which received 36 percent of the total) as well as on telecommunications and biotechnology. The industry, however, took some hits from the government and media for lacking the requisite patience and ingenuity to adequately finance growing industries. Despite gains in Canada's industry, Canada's average-deal growth in 1999 was way behind that of U.S. venture capital firms. The average Canadian deal grew by about $1.25 million, while the average U.S. investment growth doubled to $10 million in 1999.

FURTHER READING

Berenson, Alex. "Old Money Chasing the New: Seeing Windfalls, Big Banks Finance Start-Ups Again." *New York Times,* 24 December 1999.

Bruner, Richard. "Problems in Venture-Capital Land?" *ENEWS,* 11 December 2000.

Burton, Jonathan. "Putting Their Money Where the Future Is." *New York Times,* 29 March 2000.

"Consolidation Visits Venture Capital Sector." *Corporate Money,* 24 November 1999.

DeBellis, Matthew A., Georgie Raik-Allen, and Vanessa Richardson. "VCs in Europe." *RedHerring.com,* 15 March 2000. Available from http://www.redherring.com/vc/2000/0315/vc-fea-euro-home.html.

DeMont, Philip. "Capital Venture Industry Had Banner '99." *Ottawa Citizen,* 7 April 2000.

Dickson, Martin. "We Are All Venture Capitalists in the Brave New World." *Financial Times,* 11 March 2000.

"Dumbing Down." *Economist,* 30 October 1999.

Fulman, Ricki. "Performance Makes High Charges OK." *Pensions & Investments,* 20 March 2000.

Giussani, Bruno. "Give Me Shelter." *Industry Standard,* 18 December 2000.

Hahn, Avital Louria. "VCs Offer Analysts a Very Novel Bonus: Quality of Life." *Investment Dealers' Digest,* 22 November 1999.

King, Neil, Jr. "With a Nod to 007, the CIA Sets up Firm to Invest in High-Tech." *Wall Street Journal,* 3 April 2000.

Kroll, Luisa. "Mine's Bigger Than Yours." *Forbes,* 15 November 1999.

———. "Venture Vetting." *Forbes,* 10 January 2000.

Lipin, Steven. "Venture Capitalists 'R' Us: Now, Everyone Is Diving in, Seeing a No-Lose Situation." *Wall Street Journal,* 22 February 2000.

Nasr, Heidi. "Venture Cap Firms Lure Wall Street Talent." *Corporate Financing Week,* 11 October 1999.

"National Venture Capital Association." April 2000. Available from http://www.nvca.com.

PricewaterhouseCoopers. "The PricewaterhouseCoopers Money Tree Survey." March 2000. Available from http://www.pwcmoneytree.com.

Richardson, Vanessa. "The State of VC: Big." *RedHerring.com,* 11 February 2000. Available from http://www.redherring.com/vc/2000/0211/vc-stateofvc021100.html.

Saba, Jennifer. "Yes Dear, Money Does Grow on Trees." *MC: Technology Marketing Intelligence,* August 1999.

"A Squeeze in the Valley." *Economist,* 7 October 2000.

VentureOne. "1999 Venture-Backed IPOs Raise $19.4 Billion, Doubling Previous Record." Available from http://www.ventureone.com/news/press/Q499PRIPOMA.htm.

———. "Torrent of Venture Capital Financings in 1999 Outstrips '96, '97, '98 Totals Combined." Available from http://www.ventureone.com/news/press/Q499PRfinancings.htm.

———. "VentureOne: Information Partner to the Venture Capital Industry." April 2000. Available from http://www.ventureone.com.

VIDEO DISPLAYS

Advanced video-display technologies such as flat-panel screens and digital televisions have been around for general use since the mid-1990s, and with prices inching downward, they're gradually penetrating the mainstream of the $40 billion video-display market. As they gain favor, advanced displays are replacing, or at least supplementing, older display technologies, mainly bulky cathode-ray tube (CRT) computer monitors and TV sets. Smaller and increasingly high-quality displays are also showing up on a multitude of other electronic devices such as digital cameras and camcorders.

Different market conditions influence demand for the various types of advanced displays, but especially in the consumer market a common theme is pricing. Thus far, many advanced displays have commanded steep prices, often several thousand dollars per unit, and this has delayed wider rollout. Particularly for digital TV sets and digital computer monitors, competing standards have likewise been a nagging obstacle to mass marketing. Industry observers, however, held out hope that both pricing and standards would be more amenable to widespread adoption of newer video technologies in the early 2000s.

Market research on advanced displays has been decidedly upbeat for most types of devices. Flat-panel displays (FPDs) for notebook computers, for example, gained 26 percent in unit shipments during 1999, according to DisplaySearch, an industry consultancy. DisplaySearch predicted that the broader FPD market, which includes stand-alone displays for computers, TVs, home entertainment, and other uses, would swell by almost 25 percent a year through 2005. By that time, DisplaySearch estimated, the world market for FPDs would be valued at nearly $70 billion, up from just $18.5 billion in 1999. Indeed, by 2004, the firm envisioned FPDs outselling CRT displays, which hitherto have dominated the business. Research firm Stanford Resources, meanwhile, was more conservative in its predictions, estimating a rise from $19.9 billion in 2000 to $38.3 billion in 2006.

Other segments were expected to match or exceed that pace. Stanford Resources wagered that one of the newer categories, organic light-emitting displays, would grow from almost trivial sales as of 1999, at just $3 million, to reach a meaty $715 million by 2005.

DIGITAL TV

Digital TV consists of several formats and standards, the most celebrated being high-definition digital TV (HDTV). Besides the HDTV formats, it also includes a series of formats known collectively as standard-definition TV, which is more like conventional analog TV, but offers additional features, such as the ability to bundle multiple programs in one signal and potentially less distortion and interference.

HDTV marks a more dramatic departure from traditional TV. In contrast to analog TV with its 525 horizontal lines per frame, HDTV offers, depending on the format, either 720 or 1,080 horizontal lines, providing much clearer images and detail. HDTV can also provide wide-format viewing, much as movie theaters do, and fewer signal distortions. A standard analog television receives modulated radio waves that it reconstructs into a nearly square picture. An HDTV, on

---

Trends

FLAT PANEL NOT PORTABLE ENOUGH?
TRY A VIDEO HEADSET

The ever expanding portability of computing devices, gaming consoles, and most recently, digital video players creates a high-tech paradox: as display technology enables larger, crisper, more realistic graphics on reasonably portable screens, technology enthusiasts yearn for displays that are still larger, crisper, and more realistic. The problem is, at some point even lightweight displays will become unwieldy if their dimensions keep growing. How's an uncompromising videophile supposed to lug a 50-inch screen on the train to work? Some developers are banking that video headsets will be the answer.

Video headsets in some form or another have been around for years, used mostly for special applications and hard-core virtual-reality and gaming simulations. As display technology improves and as new portable video equipment such as digital video disc (DVD) players hits the market, though, manufacturers have begun to test selling upgraded versions of video headsets to a wider consumer audience.

Video headsets, also called head-mounted displays, rely on microdisplay technology and a bit of optical trickery to make users think they're seeing a much bigger image. Most employ a pair of tiny liquid crystal display (LCD) screens and magnifying optics to create a virtual image that appears larger to the eye than it is in real life, yet maintains very high resolution. In effect, a six-ounce headset can produce an experience comparable to a high-end 50-inch display, all completely portable and private for the user.

Some of the most promising applications for video headsets include personal movie viewing via portable DVD, portable Internet browsing and computing, and of course, gaming and simulations. Such manufacturers as Sony Corp. (which produces Glasstron), Olympus (Eye Trek), and Menlo Park, California, specialist i-O Display Systems (i-glasses) have unveiled consumer-oriented devices, some bundled with DVD players, priced anywhere from $400 to more than $2,000. Though these amounts are still steep for most consumers, firms such as i-O Display Systems have made noteworthy strides toward cracking the home and general-business markets. That company shipped more than 300,000 headsets in 1999, most under its i-glasses brand, and claimed leadership in the category. As with the rest of the advanced display market, as prices head downward, demand is expected to pick up.

---

the other hand, receives signals digitally as binary electronic signals, which the receiver then translates into a stream of images virtually free from broadcast distortion. Like analog signals, digital signals can be transmitted by broadcast, cable, or satellite. HDTV provides a 16/9 width-to-height ratio compared to the 4/3 ratio of conventional TV. HDTV also delivers digital sound, comparable in quality to an audio compact disc.

Digital TV hardware employs state-of-the-art computer technology to make it efficient and highly functional. Digital TV transmitters use computer technology to compress the signals for broadcast, allowing them to send two programs in one broadcast channel. Analog technology can deliver only one program per channel. Reciprocal technology must be present on the receiving end to interpret the digital signal.

Even though the Federal Communications Commission (FCC) has decreed that all commercial broadcasts must be offered digitally by 2002—and all analog broadcasts must cease by 2006—bickering over standards has made for an underwhelming debut by digital TV. Setting technical standards was complicated by the diverse range of business interests in the digital medium. In addition to television-set manufacturers, other industries vying to have their positions heard included broadcasting stations, broadcast-equipment makers, cable-system operators, computer-display manufacturers, and software developers. Often what was most beneficial to one of these industries was disadvantageous to others. For instance, computer hardware companies fought for a standard that would allow existing computer-display technology to work readily with digital TV, but most broadcasters and traditional TV manufacturers preferred technology closer to existing TVs.

Indeed, more than once standards were all but agreed upon, only to have one or more parties of the agreement break rank and lobby for changes. At companies' urging, the FCC has maintained a largely hands-off role, but regulators have been irked by the business's inability to resolve the disputes and get products on the market.

Some alternatives for receiving digital TV, however, don't involve buying a new display. Instead, some manufacturers have developed set-top conversion boxes that allow digital signals to be received by analog TVs. Such devices will be necessary as analog broadcasting is phased out, as the TV-set replacement rate is likely to lag behind the adoption of digital standards.

FLAT-PANEL DISPLAYS

Liquid crystal displays (LCDs) are the most common form of flat-panel display (FPD). LCDs work by having a layer of material that can regulate light and turn each picture element or pixel in an image on and off. LCD video displays comprise two primary kinds of laptop computer monitor technologies and constitute one of the costliest components of portable computers.

The most common technology used in higher-end FPDs are thin-film transistor screens, which provide the best image quality in terms of color saturation, response time, brightness, and color depth, according to Steve Preston in *EDN*. Lower-end notebook computers rely on super-twisted nematic (STN) screens, an older technology that delivers poorer-quality images. In particular, the pixels in STN screens take longer to turn on and off, thereby creating slower response times. STN displays are still widely used in some electronic gear, though, including handheld computers and wireless communications devices.

Manufacturers have integrated FPDs into an array of products such as watches, wide-screen wall TVs, and military, nautical, and aviation devices. Flat-panel technologies such as LCD displays make ideal components for these devices not only because of their size and weight, but also because they require substantially less power than cathode-ray tube displays.

BACKGROUND AND DEVELOPMENT

Video-display technology used in most desktop computers and TVs through the early 2000s has largely relied on one class of technology, the cathode-ray tube (CRT), to present images. CRTs function by projecting a beam of electrons from one end of the tube to the other, where the electrons cause a layer of chemical phosphors to glow, revealing different colors. Manufacturers have employed this long-standing technology ever since the first TVs were made—the analog TV technology of the mid-1990s paralleled that of the 1940s and 1950s.

Early televisions of the late 1920s supported 90-line resolution with monochrome pictures that flickered across the screen. The technology improved, however, almost on a yearly basis in that period. Between 1931 and 1939, resolution expanded from 120 lines to 441 lines. RCA released a 441-line video display in 1939 that sold for $600, or about half the cost of a new car.

The National Television Standards Committee (NTSC) established the TV broadcast format in 1941 that governed the industry until the FCC's 1996 decree that TV broadcasters convert to digital TV transmission by 2006. The NTSC's standard mandated that TV stations broadcast 525-line programs in the United States. With few alterations, this de facto standard remained for more than five decades, even though technology existed for higher-resolution broadcasting.

The modifications to the NTSC standard largely included making amendments for color broadcasting. Initially, the FCC adopted an ineffectual color-wheel method for color broadcasting in 1950. CBS developed the color-wheel technique, but it could produce only basic and inaccurate colors. The color wheel worked by creating the illusion of full color with a color wheel spinning inside the TV set, according to Joel Brinkley in the *New York Times*. In 1951, RCA introduced a different color system, which many companies and analysts extolled. Brinkley stated that RCA's electronic method created full-color images by shining three separate color images onto the screen. Consequently, the FCC repealed its original decision and made the RCA system the new standard.

In the 1970s and 1980s, companies such as Zenith Electronics Corp. and a number of Japanese companies led by the Japanese Broadcasting Corp. (NHK) started to research new television formats using digital technology. These digital TV projects led to the development of both digital standard-definition and digital high-definition television. The goals of this research were to create televisions with better resolution and to imbue TV pictures with a near three-dimensional quality and faster image scanning. Japan premiered its HDTV capabilities at the 1984 Los Angeles Olympics and began a 1,125-line resolution direct-broadcast service in 1989 called MUSE. Later, through a combined effort, NHK and Sony produced the regularly used HDTV system Hi-Vision, which promoted further development of HDTV technology.

Developers, however, couldn't integrate CRT displays into smaller electronic devices such as laptop computers, watches, calculators, and portable monitoring displays, because CRT displays require ample space for tubes. And the larger screens became, the more unwieldy they were with CRT technology because the size of the tube increases with that of the screen.

U.S. electronics corporations developed alternative or advanced video displays by the end of the 1970s working with LCD, plasma, and electroluminescent technologies. This research produced simple screens capable of presenting text and numbers as used in calculators and watches.

U.S. researchers, however, halted much of their research at this point, leaving the technology in an embryonic state, while Japanese companies continued to experiment with LCDs and developed active-matrix LCD displays for portable TVs in the 1980s. With this foundation in place, Japanese video-display manufacturers such as Sharp Corp. and NEC Corp. enhanced and refined existing FPD technology in the 1990s and conducted research on new flat-panel and advanced video-display technology.

CURRENT CONDITIONS

DIGITAL TV

Although squabbles over technical standards and high prices sidetracked sales of digital TV sets when they first came out in the late 1990s, manufacturers in 2000 steamed ahead with launching new products aimed at the mass market. Although early sets introduced in 1998 and 1999 carried rich prices of $6,000 or more, newer models were going for more affordable rates. The Consumer Electronics Association reported that by the end of 1999 more than 100,000 digital-ready TVs had been sold in the United States. Cahners In-Stat estimated that total at 431,000 units at the end of 2000.

The sales figures are somewhat misleading, though, because most of the sets sold to date weren't capable of receiving a digital signal on their own. Separately, consumers would have to obtain a digital receiver that actually allows them to harvest digital programming from the airwaves. While this division of technology may allow newer TVs to be more upgradable, somewhat like computers, it also reflects the extent to which the technical standards are still in flux.

The standards fracas rages on. In 1999 Sinclair Broadcasting, a leading operator of TV stations, caused a stir with an aggressive campaign to revamp the broad standards already being put into practice by some manufacturers. The broadcaster argued that the existing standard made TV reception difficult in some urban areas, and that it didn't allow enough flexibility for broadcasting digitally to mobile devices. Meanwhile, cable operators and set manufacturers reached an accord on some of their differences in early 2000, but still had a ways to go before reaching a comprehensive standard for delivering digital signals via cable.

FLAT-PANEL VIDEO DISPLAYS

The market for flat-panel displays (FPDs) has been thriving as robust sales of portable computers and communications devices have soared. In 1999 DisplaySearch estimated the global FPD market at $18.5 billion and predicted torrid 25 percent annual growth through 2005. Stanford Resources, meanwhile, estimated total sales of $19.9 billion in 2000, but predicted more modest growth to about $38.3 billion by 2006. Flat panels used for portable computers account for a large chunk of worldwide sales, but the nascent market for stand-alone FPDs gained significant momentum in 1999, albeit stronger in Japan than in the United States. FPDs for consumer electronics made up another major class of applications, followed by commercial, business, industrial, and transportation applications. Of the various flat-panel technologies, liquid crystal displays (LCDs) accounted for the majority of all FPDs sold, but newer forms of LCDs and other technologies such as organic light-emitting diodes will probably displace some sales of older-style LCDs. According to Stanford Resources, 3.7 million LCD monitors were shipped in 1999, while 2000 shipments were estimated at about 6.8 million. That still compared with some 105 million CRT monitors, but LCDs were expected to pass CRTs by the middle of the decade.

The large-format flat panels geared toward home entertainment have drawn public attention thanks to visible marketing campaigns by companies such as Philips Electronics N.V. Prices, however, remain in lofty territory—often above $10,000—and some media outlets have reported consumer dissatisfaction with the units, which usually hang on the wall. Some people complain that flat-panel TVs are hard to accommodate in homes and are unaesthetic; more to the heart of the problem, some believe the picture quality isn't particularly good. Sales of flat-panel TVs underwhelmed manufacturers in the late 1990s.

Some experts believe displays based on digital light processing (DLP) could steal market share from the more established LCD and plasma flat panels. DLP, which has been used since the mid-1990s in commercial projection systems, offers high resolution and a relatively compact design. Championed by Texas Instruments, makers of the chips that run the systems, DLP could be in a position to compete with other formats on price, as well, in the early 2000s.

Japanese and South Korean companies continue to lead FPD manufacturing. Other Asian countries such as Taiwan are also key players in the global flat-panel industry. In contrast to the United States, Japan invested billions of dollars in its flat-panel industry, which allowed the Japanese industry to prosper quickly as demand for FPDs in laptop computers burgeoned. As the decade progressed, this investment pushed the Japanese market to the forefront in both flat-panel production and sales.

INDUSTRY LEADERS

South Korea's Samsung Electronics is one of the industry's dominant players on the global level, ranking number one in 1999 thin-film transistor–liquid crystal display (TFT-LCD) screen production and supplying numerous other devices and components to the display market. According to figures compiled by International Data Corp. Japan, Samsung shipped 4.2 million TFT-LCDs, which are mainly used as notebook computer displays, and controlled almost 19 percent of that market worldwide. The same year it was likewise one of the world's top-five producers of stand-alone LCD computer monitors, a category it led within Europe. In digital TVs, Samsung also led the U.S. market in 1999 with roughly a 10 percent share. In 2000 the company announced a joint venture with NEC Corp. to develop electroluminescent (organic-EL) displays.

Philips Electronics N.V. of the Netherlands is another major force in the world display industry. Philips has long been a maker of TV sets and myriad other consumer electronics, and it has amassed an imposing presence in the advanced display business. Philips markets electronic displays under its own and the Magnavox brands, and in 1999 it formed a display joint venture with LG Electronics of South Korea, also a top producer of displays and parent to U.S. TV maker Zenith Electronics Corp. Ranking as the world's second-largest manufacturer of TFT-LCDs in 1999, the Korean joint venture was named LG Philips LCD and shipped 3.7 million TFT-LCDs that year.

NEC Corp. of Japan is a powerhouse in the market for advanced computer displays, with a dominant share of the stand-alone LCD market and sizable shares in other categories. Besides its video displays, NEC is a leading computer producer and a prominent manufacturer of semiconductors. In 2000 NEC employed 155,000 people and posted total revenues of $48.4 billion, most from activities outside the display industry. NEC splits ownership with Samsung on the new Samsung NEC Mobile Display Co. Ltd., a company formed to develop new organic-EL displays.

Sony Corp., an international electronics leader, competes in several segments of the advanced display business, including computer monitors, digital TVs, and specialty niches such as video headsets. It's also a top manufacturer of gaming consoles and DVD players. In 1999 the company recorded $39 billion in electronics sales, but only a small portion of that came from displays. Sony maintains a development partnership with Candescent Technologies to bring out next-generation FED technology for flat-panel displays.

Sharp Corp. was one of the first Japanese companies to follow up on initial U.S. research on FPDs in the 1970s. When U.S. companies such as Westinghouse and RCA halted their flat-panel experimentation, Sharp began exploring the technology. The company held nearly one-third of the LCD market at the end of the 1990s and made displays for products such as airplane instrumentation, calculators, and computer screens. Sharp had in 2000 a staff of 49,750 and gross sales of $17.6 billion.

Toshiba Corp. was the world's second-largest FPD producer in the 1990s. It also led the world market in portable personal computer manufacturing. Collaborating with IBM Corp., Toshiba manufactured advanced video displays for the computer and the consumer electronics industries. Toshiba also produced a diverse selection of electronics and energy products. Toshiba employed 198,000 in 2000, when it reported $54.5 billion in total sales.

In addition to the industry giants, there are quite a few prosperous companies in this industry segment, many of which are involved with the U.S. Display Consortium (USDC). The USDC, created in 1993 as a government-industry response to the Flat Panel Display Initiative, has as its mission to ensure that this segment of the high-definition display industry remains "on the leading edge." The group has been instrumental in creating and growing industry manufacturing infrastructures, and has funded more than 35 projects related to materials and components manufacturing since 1993. Those projects have been awarded to companies throughout the United States. In June 1998, the USDC was awarded an additional $10 million by the Defense Advanced Research Projects Agency for continuing research for the U.S. FPD industry. Among its more than 100 members, the USDC counts FPD manufacturers, developers, users, and equipment manufacturers and suppliers. These include companies such as Candescent Technologies Corp., Compaq Computer, Planar-Standish, Texas Instruments, Three-Five Systems, and Universal Display Corp.

Candescent Technologies Corporation attracted significant attention during the mid-1990s when it embarked on intensive research to perfect field emission display (FED) technology for flat display graphics applications. Candescent, once known as Silicon Video, is not alone in the quest for a high-voltage FED phosphor to mimic the function of cathode-ray tube (CRT) operation at the pixel level, although many in the industry look to Candescent to accomplish the painstaking project. Indeed, Japanese manufacturer Sony purchased an option for the production rights to the Candescent technology. Candescent persists in the development effort where dozens of other organizations have failed, not the least of which was Motorola, Inc. The technology, called ThinCRT, will facilitate FPD technology in the graphics display arena where active matrix liquid crystal display technology fails because of limitations in viewing angles, clarity, and power consumption. Despite ongoing technical advancements in Asia, Candescent continues as one of a dwindling number of U.S.-based industries involved in that field, although PixTech Inc. announced its intention in the first quarter of 1999 to undertake a similar research project.

Three-Five Systems, Inc., is a fast-growing Tempe, Arizona-based manufacturer of LCDs and light emitting diodes for a wide range of devices from pagers to military controls. About 90 percent of its annual sales come from original equipment manufacturers in the United States and Europe. Its largest customer has been Motorola, which accounts for about 86 percent of total sales. In 1999 the company posted sales of $147 million, up more than 50 percent from the year before, and by 2000 it had over 2,100 employees.

Planar Systems, Inc., with $123 million in 1999 sales, was North America's largest independent maker of industrial displays. Their electroluminescent displays, CRTs, and active- and passive-matrix LCDs were made for customers such as AlliedSignal and Siemens for products including industrial controls, aircraft instrumentation, and point-of-sale systems. The company purchased Standish Industries, a maker of lower-end liquid crystal displays, but in 1999 Planar announced the discontinuation of its FPD products because they were too expensive to manufacture in consideration of the limited demand. The Planar Systems rollback left PixTech in a bind as intermediary supplier of the Planar products. PixTech rebounded and agreed to purchase Micron Technology Inc., and announced an intention to begin research and development work toward perfecting FED technology for larger, brighter, slimmer screens.

RESEARCH AND TECHNOLOGY

The existing commercial CRT technology of the 1990s posed problems for developing large-screen TVs and monitors: weight and depth substantially increase with the size of the screen. Hence, larger desktop computer monitors are difficult to make so that they can actually fit on a desk. Sensitive to this problem, manufacturers started to examine placing electron guns at the side of the screen, reducing the tube depth and thereby making CRT video displays smaller and lighter, according to Alfred Poor in *PC Magazine*. Thin-film transistor–liquid crystal display (TFT-LCD) screens slowly began emerging in the marketplace. NEC Electronics Inc., in late May 1998, introduced flat-panel color monitors designed for desktop computing. These TFT-LCD monitors, with 18.1- and 15.4-inch displays, were estimated to cost between $2,100 and $4,000. *Publish* estimated that "flat-panel displays will still cost three times as much as comparable CRTs in 2001."

NEC and Sharp developed laboratory prototypes of LCD-based computer monitors that provided computer users with larger screens without increasing the weight and depth of the monitors. The cost of producing large-screen LCD displays was much greater than producing smaller ones—those under 20 inches diagonally. Consequently, Poor believed that LCD monitors would not compete in the large-screen market until their prices dropped. In addition, researchers continue to hone CRT displays for HDTV sets. HDTV specifications call for resolutions of 1,920 lines by 1,080 pixels.

While some companies expanded their LCD technologies, many U.S. and Japanese companies turned to competing flat-panel technologies in an effort to carve their niche in that market. Backed by the Advanced Research Projects Agency, U.S. producers experimented with electroluminescent and plasma displays, which they hoped would ultimately provide better resolution and more competitive prices than the standard LCD technology. Research on large flat-panel displays focused on color plasma technology, which producers believed would appeal to the market for 40- to 60-inch corporate and public wall-hanging displays. IBM prototyped its high-end Roentgen monitor late in 1998, with a 2,560 x 2,048 flat-panel display resolution. Companies also plan to integrate plasma flat-panel technology into emerging HDTV sets, but plasma HDTVs bore a hefty price of about $15,000 in 1997, making them financially accessible only to the corporate market. Furthermore, plasma displays could provide only a contrast ratio of 120:1, while CRT displays could deliver a ratio of 300:1, giving CRT technology an advantage in terms of image quality. Nonetheless, with adequate sales and expanded production, the prices of large-screen plasma displays could drop by 30 percent, according to Alfred Poor in *PC Magazine.*

The U.S. Display Consortium announced in May 1998 that it would begin exploring new markets for flat-panel displays, particularly field emission displays, projection display systems, and organic light emitting diodes. Markets for that technology include corporate presentations, education and training, and entertainment, as well as miniature liquid crystal displays. In a 1998 press release, the consortium stated that several areas that could benefit from these sorts of products, but have not yet been exploited, included areas such as home appliances, transportation, and medical instrumentation.

FURTHER READING

Ascierto, Jerry. "Candescent Delays Plant, Replaces CEO." *Electronic News,* March 1999.

———. "FCC Gives DTV Ultimatum." *Electronic News,* 17 January 2000.

Brinkley, Joel. "TV Goes Digital: Warts and Wrinkles Can't Hide." *New York Times,* 3 March 1997.

———. "Who Will Build Your Next Television? 2 Industries Fight for $150 Billion Prize." *New York Times,* 28 March 1997.

Brodesser, Claude, Michael Freeman, and Richard Katz. "The Resolution Will Not Be Televised." *Mediaweek,* 14 April 1997.

Brown, Peter. "LCD Shortage Looms." *Electronic News,* 30 March 1998.

Chinnock, Chris. "The Microdisplay Industry Is Beginning to Consolidate." *Electronic Design,* 4 October 1999.

———. "Walkman, Discman, DVDman?" *Electronic Design,* 8 March 1999.

Colman, David. "Flat-Panel TVs Sure Look Cool, but They Pose Design Dilemmas." *Wall Street Journal,* 27 August 1999.

"Demand Stays Healthy." *Electronics Times,* 6 November 2000.

DisplaySearch. *Press Room.* Austin, TX, 2000. Available from http://www.displaysearch.com.

"Flat-Panel Standard." *Computerworld,* 19 May 1997.

"The Good, the Bad, and the Flat." *Publish,* March 1998.

Hazlett, Thomas W. "Industrial Policy for Couch Potatoes." *Wall Street Journal,* 7 August 1996.

"HDTV Pushes Displays to Perform." *Design News,* 3 April 2000.

Karr, Albert R. "FCC Is Expected to Move Forward on HDTV Proposal." *Wall Street Journal,* 9 May 1996.

Krantz, Michael. "A Tube for Tomorrow." *Time,* 14 April 1997.

Lieberman, David. "Flat-Panel Displays Gain Favor On the Desktop." *Electronic Engineering Times,* 22 December 2000.

Nickerson, Steve. "Video." *U.S. Consumer Electronics Industry Today.* Arlington, VA: Consumer Electronics Association, 1999. Available from http://www.ce.org.

Poor, Alfred. "Future Display Technology." *PC Magazine,* 25 March 1997.

Preston, Steve. "Designing Graphics Systems for Notebook Computers." *EDN,* 16 April 1997.

Ramstad, Evan. "Digital-TV Panel Shows Willingness to Alter Industry Technical Standard." *Wall Street Journal,* 30 March 2000.

———. "TV Makers to Roll Out Digital-TV Sets Even as Standard Change Is Considered." *Wall Street Journal,* 10 April 2000.

"Television Timeline." *New York Times,* 2 December 1996.

"What Are Microdisplays?" *Microdisplay Report.* Norwalk, CT, 2000. Available from http://www.mdreport.com.

VIRTUAL REALITY

Although virtual reality is commonly associated with science fiction and video games, it is a bona fide technology formed from a meld of computer hardware and software. While virtual reality, or VR as it is referred to in the industry, grew slowly throughout a good portion of the 1990s, the technology seemed to be gaining wider acceptance by industry at the end of the decade. Spurred by lower prices and greater capabilities, industries and professions began adopting VR technology for a variety of applications including training and design. Virtual reality is, as its name suggests, a simulated version of reality wherein users feel they are "really" walking on a beach, flying a fighter jet, performing heart bypass surgery, or whatever else the VR software is programmed to do. According to CyberEdge Information Services, Inc., the VR market stood at $17.7 billion in 1999 and was estimated at about $23 billion in 2000.

Jaron Lanier, founder of VPL Research Inc., was the first to coin the term "virtual reality." Other related terms include "artificial reality," coined by Myron Krueger in the 1970s; William Gibson's "cyberspace," which debuted in 1984; and such terms as "virtual worlds" and "virtual environments," which first were used in the 1990s. The term "virtual reality" is today used in a wide variety of ways, often leading to some confusion. As originally coined by Lanier, the term was meant to describe total immersion in a three-dimensional (3-D) computer-generated world.

Although its entertainment potential is fairly obvious and was the first area to be exploited by the fledgling VR industry, virtual reality has some more practical educational applications that were being ex-plored seriously as the millennium neared its end. VR is expected (by its proponents) to reshape the relationship between information technology and people, offering a variety of new and novel ways to communicate information and visualize processes. Virtual reality allows the creation of a 3-D virtual environment that can be rooted in reality or abstract. Among the former could be such real systems as buildings, landscapes, human anatomy, crime scenes, automobile accidents, and spacecraft. Representations of abstract systems might include magnetic fields, mathematical systems, molecular models, and population densities.

BACKGROUND AND DEVELOPMENT

Computers have changed greatly since their inception. Early computers, in fact, lacked many of the elements users in the 1990s took for granted, such as memory and monitors. In the 1950s, computer scientists connected a typing board to a computer, and the notion of a monitor emerged soon afterwards, followed in the early 1960s by a movable pointer, which was quickly nicknamed a "mouse" because of the tail-like wire attached to it. Later came the idea of a graphical user interface (GUI), which allowed users to talk to or "interface" with the computer; an example of a GUI is an icon that users click to access a particular function. The icon is the side of the interface that the user sees, whereas the computer responds to a set of commands activated when the user clicks on the icon.

The basic concept underlying VR has been around for decades, although it began to take its present shape only in recent years. Simulators such as those used to train truck drivers and airline pilots were obvious forerunners of current virtual reality technology. It took the emergence of the computer and its ability to generate complex images and simulate interactive environments to truly energize the VR concept and spark the birth of a new industry.

Many people helped lay the groundwork for VR. In 1950 Douglas Engelbart envisioned a world of small computers that people would use for communication—an utterly foreign concept at a time when computers were mammoth structures that might fill up an entire house and yet be capable of little more than simple addition and subtraction. In 1960 J. C. R. Licklider predicted that the human mind and the computer would work in close harmony, in his essay "Man-Computer Symbiosis." This, too, seemed doubtful in an age when programmers could communicate with the computer only through punched-hole tape.

History

ALDOUS HUXLEY (1894-1963): THE FATHER OF VIRTUAL REALITY?

While the immediate roots of virtual reality go back only to the early 1980s, some of the fundamental technologies actually came into being along with the computer in the 1940s. Some, however, might see an even earlier root as far back as the 1930s, when Aldous Huxley's futuristic novel *Brave New World* depicted cinemagoers of the future accessing a full sensory experience through a contraption called a "feelie."

By the 1960s the notions that would later come to fruition as virtual reality were rapidly taking shape. In 1962 Morton Heilig built the Sensorama cubicle, which gave the user the illusion of driving a motorcycle. In 1965 Ivan Sutherland, "the father of computer graphics," had already imagined computer users being immersed in a separate reality created by graphics. In addition, Myron Krueger, a significant VR pioneer who in 1970 became the first to use the term "artificial reality," built the first of his many "responsive environments" in 1969. Called GLOWFLOW, it involved a platform surrounded by a screen. Viewers stood on the platform, and as they walked around, the shifting of their bodies' weight caused various pictures to appear on the screen.

From these early days the development of virtual reality was the product of a bizarre amalgam of players: computer scientists, many of whom worked in uni-

versity research labs; unconventional visionaries; and military and civilian personnel from the U.S. Department of Defense and the National Aeronautics and Space Administration (NASA). The government was an important contributor to VR research. After the Soviets launched the first space satellite, *Sputnik,* in 1957, the U.S. government reacted by launching vast new programs in military and flight engineering and science. Out of this came the Defense Advanced Research Projects Agency, which developed the beginnings of the Internet—then called the Arpanet—and invested in what would become virtual reality.

Futhermore, the military provided funding for J. C. R. Licklider, helping him to explore his ideas of "man-computer symbiosis." With its vast budget, the Defense Department facilitated the first use of a virtual reality system in the 1970s. NASA, on the other hand, had less money to spend, but its scientists were also interested in the possibilities for VR use in flight training and other aspects of space flight. Because of its limited budget, NASA was a key element in helping to develop relatively less expensive VR technology. NASA also explored the idea of telepresence, which would make it possible for someone to "do" something in one place while sitting in another. Following this concept, in July 1997 NASA programmers on Earth were able to operate a vehicle that rolled over the surface of Mars and collected soil and rock samples.

PIONEERS IN THE FIELD

Jaron Lanier was a leader in the early development and commercialization of virtual reality technology and products. Lanier is called the pioneer of virtual reality and is recognized for coining the term. Virtual reality was the name he gave to the goggles, gloves, and software that allow people to interact with each other in worlds generated by 3-D graphics. Lanier also developed software that made VR commercially viable.

Born in 1961, Lanier grew up in New Mexico, dropped out of high school, and set out to be a musician rather than a computer genius. Lanier was already developing the technology that would alter the future of humankind by the time he was in his twenties. Working with Atari in the early 1980s, he earned enough royalties from his Moondust video game to quit and start his own company. Legend has it that when *Scientific American* called to discuss a new programming language he had developed, the 22-year-old

Lanier was embarrassed to tell them his company had no name, so he made up the name VPL Research Inc. on the spot.

Lanier founded VPL Research in 1984 and headed the company until 1992. During that time, the company made many of the early advances that would later enable such interactive, networked 3-D games as Doom and Quake. "VPL's groundbreaking efforts and research have become an important influence on many virtual reality and 3-D graphics products that succeeded the company," according to Sun Microsystems, Inc., the company that later acquired VPL.

When Lanier left VPL in 1992 because of differences with Thomson-CFS, the French technology conglomerate that helped finance him, he gave up his patents. During the next four years, Greenleaf Medical financed VPL Systems. Greenleaf fought a four-year battle in bankruptcy court to keep Thomson from gaining exclusive control of the VPL patents. In February 1998, Sun Microsystems announced it had acquired VPL for an estimated $4 million. The deal settled debts and released approximately 35 patent applications, 12 of them already granted. The acquisition was looked on favorably by Wall Street and many in the VR industry.

Lanier has continued his involvement in the VR field as lead scientist for the National Tele-Immersion Initiative, a coalition of research universities working to create the next generation of virtual reality applications on the Internet.

CURRENT CONDITIONS

At the beginning of the 21st century, the virtual reality continued to search for a niche beyond entertainment and training. Nevertheless, the virtual reality market continued to expand, as a number of industries began adopting virtual reality technology as it became more powerful and less expensive. According to CyberEdge Information Services, Inc. the worldwide virtual reality market reached and estimated $23 billion in 2000, up nearly 30 percent from 1999. Despite this growth, market expansion remained slow throughout much of the 1990s. One of the factors that contributed to its relatively slow growth was the legal battle involving VPL Research. The legal battle involved custody of the patent rights to much of the technology that defines virtual reality. Since there was such uncertainty in the industry over the patents, interest in starting new companies waned during the four-year court battle (1993 to 1997).

That situation changed in 1998. By acquiring VPL, Sun Microsystems obtained the rights to the patent portfolio and technical assets of the company, which extend to networked 3-D graphics, human-based body input, and 3-D window systems. The acquisition provided stability in the volatile industry as a whole. According to Stuart Davidson, a partner in Labrador Ventures, a California high-tech venture capital firm, "this will help virtual reality get out of the cottage-industry stage. At the very least, by establishing hardware and software standards for the technology, Sun Microsystems should end costly duplication of effort among companies developing virtual reality."

In the late 1990s, virtual reality applications started establishing a presence in wide-ranging segments of American life. The primary areas of virtual reality penetration, however, were the entertainment, design and engineering, medicine, education and training, sales, and military industries.

Entertainment was an early area of VR application, and it remains significant in the early 2000s. For instance, one restaurant chain offers patrons the opportunity to experience virtual reality-based games, while another restaurant, Mars 2112, enables customers the chance to experience what landing on Mars would be like. In addition, the Evans and Sutherland Computer Corp. developed a system in late 1996 that inserts the viewer into a virtual setting on live television, and research at Carnegie Mellon University involved a VR application that would make it possible for someone watching a sport on television to view the action from anywhere on the field of play. Moreover, Disney opened DisneyQuest, a new family entertainment experience at Downtown Disney in Orlando. DisneyQuest features futuristic games and rides that use motion-based simulators and virtual reality environments. Disney partnered with Silicon Graphics, a leader in the VR field, for this project. DisneyQuest's Explore Zone is the entertainment world that features VR. Universal Studios also offers virtual reality rides at its theme parks, including the Amazing Adventures of Spider Man ride. Finally, a controversial area of VR entertainment in the late 1990s was virtual sex or "cybersex."

In the area of design and engineering, software for 3-D modeling assists designers in creating prototypes. Although virtual reality technology struggled to find marketable applications, some progress was made in the early 2000s as manufacturers teamed up with virtual reality developers to create virtual prototypes for the manufacturing industry. By replacing physical prototypes, manufacturers hoped to achieve greater cost efficiency and quicker transitions from model to market for new parts and products. The automotive, aerospace, and military industries expressed particular interest in the development of this technology. Because of prohibitive costs, industries have hesitated in using VR for prototype development. As VR costs dropped and VR systems became more powerful, however, VR technology gradually became a more viable technique for development. VR prototype development involves engineers using large visualization centers, such as Silicon Graphics' Reality Center, to see the minute and realistic details of their designs. The result of this research has been software such as Engineering Animation Inc.'s VisConcept, which enables engineers to create and project virtual prototypes. VR gives architects the ability to design and "build" whole structures and allows their prospective clients to "walk through" them. Many software companies also offer programs for the general public that allow users to create residential floor plans the way professionals create them. Industrial engineers also create virtual factories with employees, robots, machines, and products to explore better ways to make the factories function.

Medical advances in VR technology include the National Institutes of Health's development of "virtual bronchoscopy," a virtual and noninvasive imaging of the bronchial tree within the human respiratory system. Other advances make it increasingly possible to study human anatomy, without actually cutting open a cadaver, and to improve surgical techniques through virtual operations. Coined "cybersurgery," VR is a crucial tool in neurosurgery where a 3-D picture of the brain helps surgeons pinpoint the location of a brain tumor with extreme accuracy. In addition, developers have combined VR technology with robotics to advance cardiac surgery. The result is a VR system operated by a surgeon who controls a robot that performs the actual surgery. This technology makes cardiac surgery less invasive and speeds up recovery time. Furthermore, hospitals have implemented virtual reality technology to help relieve patient stress prior to serious operations, offering them tranquil escapes from the operating room environment.

While VR advocates once proclaimed that VR would revolutionize training for many different professions, VR training remained limited to a small but growing number of professionals, most notably pilots, doctors, and military personnel. Educational applications of VR range from knowledge of purely theoretical or historical interest to highly practical applications. Rome Reborn, an ambitious project being developed at the University of California-Los Ange-

les, would walk users through versions of Rome from 850 B.C. to A.D. 450. Virtual reality also is used to help people from a wide variety of occupations—doctors, factory workers, fighter pilots—improve their work by simulating their activities. In the late 1990s and early 2000s, the educational and training applications of VR continued to increase with the drop in VR technology prices and the improvement of performance.

Examples of VR applications in sales and marketing include uses in real estate such as Home Debut, which provides virtual tours of homes for sale. *Forbes* looked at VR technology enlisted by the marketing firm Coopers & Lybrand in an effort to predict the buying habits of 50,000 music consumers. Also, the journal *I/S Analyzer Case Studies* predicted that an increasing number of businesses would use VR technology because VR authoring software was now compatible with most programming platforms, and the cost of head-mounted displays and other equipment was dropping.

The military was one of VR's first advocates. In the late 1990s and early 2000s, virtual reality was being used more frequently to simulate combat, and experiments were exploring ways it could be used in actual combat. Called Simnet, VR was used to train soldiers on real-to-life tank and helicopter training simulations for the U.S. Army. One promising area is that of telepresence, which allows remote command functions to orchestrate activities in a distant location. Furthermore, the Department of Defense is a major investor in VR technology. In 1999 the U.S. Army reached a $45 million agreement with the University of Southern California to develop more realistic training simulators for the military.

Still very much in its infancy, VR technology in the late 1990s was being used extensively in the engineering, pharmaceutical, and entertainment fields. As noted, its value as a teaching tool in medicine, particularly surgery, has been recognized, and expansion of its use in this area can be expected. Almost any field in which it is helpful to construct a model that can be manipulated in real time can benefit from virtual reality technology. The images in VR simulations will become increasingly more realistic as computers grow ever more powerful. ScienceNet speculated that within 50 years, virtual environments that are essentially indistinguishable from real life will be readily created by computers.

Yet with the growing acceptance of VR in the marketplace came criticism. Some researchers found that people immersed in VR suffer side effects termed "cybersickness." The major problem with VR environments, according to these researchers, is the difficulty of adapting to the real world after a virtual experience. These adaptation problems include poor hand-eye coordination and poor eyesight. Other symptoms found were disorientation, nausea, and eyestrain. Furthermore, VR environments that require users to travel through a virtual landscape as a passive observer with little or no control of their movement seem to cause the most severe forms of cybersickness.

INDUSTRY LEADERS

SILICON GRAPHICS INC.

Silicon Graphics is one of the significant players in the VR field. Silicon Graphics computers were the dominant platform for virtual reality in the late 1990s and into the early 2000s. The company is a leading supplier of visual computing and high-performance systems. Its products include a broad range of computers, from desktop workstations to servers and high-end supercomputers. With corporate offices in Mountain View, California, and offices in 60 sites throughout the world, Silicon Graphics manufactures and markets its systems to the communications, energy, entertainment, government, manufacturing, and science industries.

In 1994 Silicon Graphics launched its Reality Center, a visualization facility for group virtual reality, which is used by hundreds of government and business employees. For example, in 2000 Silicon Graphics used its Reality Center in conjunction with software developer Engineering Animation Inc. to help General Motors Corp. develop virtual reality prototypes to replace physical ones. Furthermore, Silicon Graphics provided VR technology to the new DisneyQuest entertainment complex in Orlando. Its core virtual reality products include Onyx2 and Infinite-Reality, which offer computer graphics and high performance for the virtual reality experience. Silicon Graphics also developed the Onyx2 InfiniteReality System—a virtual reality supercomputer—which is currently used by the National Center for Supercomputing Applications, a unit of the University of Illinois. This supercomputer allows researchers to process high-resolution visualizations of their applications as they run them.

In fiscal 2000, which ended 30 June 2000, Silicon Graphics posted a net loss of $829 million on sales of $2.3 billion. That year, the company employed more than 6,700 people worldwide.

SUN MICROSYSTEMS, INC.

A chief competitor of Silicon Graphics is Sun Microsystems. Although not a high-profile player in the virtual reality field, the company's 1998 acquisition of VPL Research aimed to change that. The company was expected to establish hardware and software standards for the industry with this acquisition. In addition, Sun's operating systems are designed to be compatible with some of the leading VR authoring tools, including XvsLink and OrthoVista.

Sun has been a leading manufacturer of graphics workstations used for mechanical computer-aided design (MCAD). Founded in 1982, Sun is a leading provider of hardware, software, and services for the Internet. With more than $15 billion in annual revenues, Sun can be found in more than 150 countries around the world.

In the area of virtual reality, Sun has developed the Java 3-D View Model (a virtual reality viewing model), virtual holographic workstations, and virtual portals (three-screen immersive projections displays). Sun Microsystems' Java 3-D API is an application-programming interface used for writing 3-D graphics applications or Web-based 3-D applets. It provides an abstract, interactive imaging model for behavior and control of 3-D objects. The specification for this language is actually a result of collaboration between Sun Microsystems, Silicon Graphics, Intel Corp., and Apple Computer. Java 3-D is designed for use in virtual reality systems, 3-D games, computer-aided design applications, MCAD systems, and the design of Web pages and 3-D logos.

Headquartered in Palo Alto, California, Sun employed nearly 39,000 people worldwide in 1999. The company, led by Scott G. McNealy, chairman and chief executive officer, reported net earnings of $1.85 million for fiscal 2000, which ended 30 June 2000. Fiscal 2000 sales, totaling $15.7 billion, were up over 30 percent over the previous year.

AUTODESK

Autodesk is the fourth-largest personal computer (PC) software company worldwide. Its software products are focused on design solutions, visualization, and computer-aided automation software. Its Autocad, Autodesk, and Picture This software are used by architects, designers, engineers, animators, scientists, filmmakers, and educators to more easily conceptualize their ideas. Based in San Rafael, California, Autodesk posted net earnings of $9.8 million on sales of $820.2 million in fiscal 2000. Other significant players include Polhemus Inc. and Virtual Reality Inc.

OTHER LEADERS

Government and university entities also play a role in VR, the most prominent of the former being the Department of Defense and NASA. Among the latter are the University of Illinois, home of the National Center for Supercomputing Applications; the University of Washington; and the University of North Carolina-Chapel Hill.

WORK FORCE

Until virtual reality becomes widely used, jobs in this area will remain limited to design and production roles, though even these positions are limited. For example, in its heyday, VPL employed only about 35 individuals. The advantage for those interested in entering the field, however, is the fact that its territory is largely unmapped, and VR in the early 2000s is still to some extent a world open to visionaries.

AMERICA AND THE WORLD

Some industry analysts in the late 1990s expressed concern that America would fall behind other countries. This theme is familiar to those who observed the auto industry or various fields of electronics—Americans may have made the original innovations, but the Japanese were often more successful in developing and marketing the products. By the late 1990s, it appeared that Japan might well take the forefront in VR technology as well. Advantages enjoyed by the Japanese include the fact that Japanese industry in general—and high-tech industry in particular—operate according to national objectives, thus offering a modified form of the central planning espoused by command economies while enjoying the advantages of a free economy. The number of Japanese patent applications in the 1990s was double the number of those in the United States. Germany, France, and the United Kingdom also promise to be major players in the world of VR. As a result of Japanese efforts, the country boasts of an array of virtual reality applications including entertainment, medicine, and training, which have reached strong levels of consumer acceptance.

In the fall of 1998, Hong Kong Polytechnic University announced the installation of a $1.7 million virtual reality laboratory. The facility will substantially enhance the university's health education capabilities. Susie Lum, senior executive manager for nursing, said the facility "lowers risks associated with training on human patients and establishes standards and optimization of specific procedures."

To help prepare police officers in Australia's New South Wales to deal more effectively with such complex emergencies as hostage situations and major disasters, a VR training device called Minerva was introduced in early 1999. The video-based equipment simulates real-life crises and helps trainees to make split-second decisions. New South Wales Police Minister Paul Whelan, in introducing the VR trainer, likened its technology to simulators used in training race-car drivers and airline pilots.

RESEARCH AND TECHNOLOGY

In the late 1990s, VR technology seemed to be advancing only in the research labs and not in the marketplace. Despite the energetic experimentation and innovation in the VR industry, investors willing to throw a large chunk of money at the field for product development have been few and far between. The only area where marketability is progressing is in high-end industrial applications such as the creation of prototypes of commercial jets and cars.

Much of the discussion about VR technology focused on Virtual Reality Modeling Language (VRML) 2.0. VRML is a standard language for describing interactive 3-D objects and worlds on the Internet. Like Hypertext Markup Language (HTML), the modeling language typically used on the World Wide Web, VRML is a Web-authoring software, but it also gives users the ability to create sophisticated 3-D environments. It adds interaction, graphics, and extra dimensions to online communication.

A VRML Consortium was formed as the official mouthpiece for VRML evolution to provide a forum for creating and promoting standards for VRML and 3-D content on the Web. The consortium approved VRML 97 as the ISO standard in December 1997. In 1998 the nonprofit group was comprised of 65 organizations and, in March of that year, began work on formalizing its organizational structure by forming an executive committee and task groups to work on marketing and specification issues. Although many of the larger technology companies including Apple Computer, Cosmo Software (a Silicon Graphics company), Microsoft, Oracle, and Sony had joined the consortium, other major players, including Sun Microsystems and Intel, did not lend their support to VRML.

Indeed, by the end of 2000 even the VRML Consortium itself decided to distance itself from the specification, and it signaled its plans to shift to the next generation of 3-D modeling languages for the Web by changing its name to the Web 3-D (W3D) Consortium. As of late 2000, the consortium claimed 40 members, including Sun and Microsoft, and was working to bring out the extensible 3-D (X3D) language. X3D was based on extensible markup language (XML), the metalanguage endorsed by the World Wide Web Consortium (W3C) for structuring and labeling data and designing of specific markup languages. (Also see the essay in this book entitled XML.)

Central to the development of new VR technology is the controversy surrounding immersion technology versus wearable display gear. The primary piece of equipment for the VR experience is the head-mounted display (HMD)—a helmet hooked up to the computer that includes tiny monitors (television screens) to cover each eye. The screens each show slightly different views that, when viewed simultaneously, produce the illusion of looking at 3-D objects. Also inside the HMD is a tracking device that follows the user's head movements and changes the on-screen images accordingly, in order to maintain the sensation that one is operating within a fully spatial, rather than two-dimensional, realm. The HMD also includes speakers to further enhance the experience. Virtual reality users often avail themselves of tactile devices, most commonly a sensor glove, which is connected to the computer, just like the HMD. The glove senses movements of the user's hand and helps him or her to "move" within the virtual world seen through the screens on the headset. The headgear and the glove create an illusion of depth and the ability to manipulate objects. With prolonged use, these devices have proven to be awkward and uncomfortable. Head-mounted viewers such as Nintendo's Virtual Boy were expensive and ultimately unsuccessful. The most realistic computer-generated 3-D world, however, is currently displayed using these wearable displays.

Many scientists have come to embrace the idea of immersing a user in a 3-D environment on a computer screen without the use of wearable displays. Researchers are currently experimenting with these immersion VR environments. The National Center for Supercomputing Applications's computer animated virtual environment, at the University of Illinois-Chicago, is one such example. These environments completely surround the user, in effect transporting him or her to a different world through VR. The Laboratory for Integrated Medical Interface Technology at the University of Washington is another immersive environment. Other new immersive interface technologies are the Vision Dome from Alternate Realities Corp., Immersadesk from Pyramid Systems, and the Immersive Workbench from Fakespace.

Researchers in the late 1990s were looking at ways to improve the limitations of 3-D computer imaging on a two-dimensional display. Viewing 3-D scenes is still somewhat disorienting and has an unnatural feel. Objects in 3-D scenes are very difficult to grasp without jiggling them with a control device. Also, seeing virtual objects from different points of view currently requires the use of several screens.

Volumetric imaging was one development being researched in the late 1990s by Parvis Soltan at the Naval Command, Control, and Ocean Surveillance Center in San Diego. Soltan's research used volumetric imaging devices, which place points of light in all three dimensions using a panel that is twisted into a helix. The image is projected onto the helix, which is spinning very fast to make it virtually invisible, and it can be viewed from the top as well as the sides. Soltan's device looked crude and was very loud, but the images it created were surprisingly good. Two private companies have already started marketing the technology.

Another technology in development in the late 1990s was the solid-state crystal ball. Elizabeth Downing researched a whole new way to create 3-D images—by creating these images inside a solid piece of glass. The technology involves intersecting lasers in a fluoride-glass cube which contains elements that fluoresce when struck by these lasers. The energy created by the two intersecting beams release visible photons, thus creating the image. Applications for the crystal-ball technology include medicine, air-traffic control, design engineering and, eventually, 3-D television.

Virtual reality is being used in a hospital-based project in Atlanta to help rid veterans of the Vietnam War of some of the lingering psychological effects of that experience. Where traditional psychological therapy has largely failed to ease the posttraumatic stress that has plagued these veterans for decades, virtual reality seems to be having a positive effect. This was but one of more than a hundred VR applications outlined at an international conference, called Medicine Meets Virtual Reality, held in San Francisco in early 1999. Medicine has embraced both full virtual reality, and partial or augmented reality, in which the real and virtual worlds are blended together. Some of the problems that medicine has been addressing with VR technology include agoraphobia, anorexia, and impotence. Boston's Artificial Reality Corp. (ARC) has created a virtual environment for the training of physicians that allows trainees to experience both the smell and the feel of the patient and the operating room. Of this simulation, Peter Larson of ARC said, "When they go into the virtual world, they carry a backpack that contains a reservoir of smells. The computer follows their eye movements and when they look at something, the computer gives them the smell to go with it."

Moreover, researchers endeavored in the early 2000s to add or improve tactile effect offered by VR environments. While visual simulation requires 15-20 frames per second to create the sensation of movement, the sensation of touch requires stimulation of the skin hundreds of times per second. Although rudimentary forms of touch virtual reality exist in video games, which pulse and vibrate when players encounter certain situations, researchers of companies, universities, and the military are trying to develop applications for defense and industry, which have more realistic tactile effects.

FURTHER READING

"AlterVue Systems Releases First Practical Virtual Reality Application for Widespread Business Use." *Business Wire,* 12 May 1998.

Brown, Ed. "The Virtual Career of a Virtual Reality Pioneer." *Fortune,* 2 March 1998.

CyberEdge Information Services Inc. "Virtual Reality Market Measured." 1999. Available from http://www.cyberedge.com.

Ditlea, Steve. "False Starts Aside, Virtual Reality Finds New Roles." *New York Times,* 23 March 1998.

Dobson, Roger. "Science: Virtual Sanity." *Independent on Sunday,* 17 January 1999.

Dunn, Ashley. "Virtual Reality through a Crystal Ball." *New York Times,* 19 March 1997.

Dvorak, Paul. "Engineering Puts Virtual Reality to Work." *Machine Design,* 20 February 1997.

Fister, Sarah. "Virtual Reality: High Flier or Dead Duck?" *Training,* August 1999.

Gage, Deborah. "Virtual Reality: Net to Take on New Dimensions." *Computer Reseller News,* 24 February 1997.

Hayward, Tom. *Adventures in Virtual Reality.* Carmel, IN: Que, 1993.

Hempel, Carlene. "As Costs Drop, More Professions Find Use for Virtual Reality." *World Reporter,* 8 November 1999.

"How Businesses Are Cutting Costs through Virtual Reality: 30 Seconds." *I/S Analyzer Case Studies,* March 1997.

Koselka, Rita. "Playing the Game of Life." *Forbes,* 7 April 1997.

Larijani, L. Casey. *The Virtual Reality Primer.* New York: McGraw-Hill, 1994.

Larner, Monica. "For the Appian Way, Hit Command-A." *Business Week,* 14 April 1997.

"NSW: Virtual Reality to Give Police Edge in Crisis Management." *AAP General News,* 12 February 1999.

Rheingold, Howard. *Virtual Reality.* New York: Touchstone, 1991.

Silicon Graphics. "Cosmo Software Ships Cosmo PageFX, a New Web Authoring Tool for Designers." 1998. Available from http://www.sgi.com.

Sorid, Daniel. "Giving Computers a Sense of Touch." *New York Times,* 23 March 2000.

Stanney, Kay M., and Robert S. Kennedy. "The Psychometrics of Cybersickness." *Communications of the ACM,* August 1997.

"Times Books to Publish *The Visionary Position.*" *M2 PressWIRE,* 16 March 1999.

Valendorpe, Linda. "Breathe Easier with New Bronchoscopy." *R&D,* February 1997.

"Virtual Reality Market Study Continues; First Longitudinal Study Will Document Billion Dollar Market." *Business Wire,* 9 September 1998.

Von Schweber, Linda, and Eric Von Schweber. "Teams of Workers Will Visually Explore Virtual Prototypes Together and Interactively Conduct Simulations through VR Techniques." *PC Magazine,* 9 June 1998.

Waurzyniak, Patrick. "Virtual Models Gain Favor." *Manufacturing Engineering,* 1 April 2000.

VOICE RECOGNITION SYSTEMS AND SOFTWARE

By 2000, voice recognition systems were beginning to come into their own, taking hold in a number of industries that for years had looked upon the technology with a just-around-the-corner gaze. By improving on error rates in the translation of natural-voice input, voice recognition (VR) technology has finally become efficient enough to enjoy widespread application, and was poised to explode throughout a variety of industries in the early 2000s. According to the research firm PC Data, VR systems sold about 550,000 units in 1999, up from only 200,000 in 1997.

The uses for voice recognition systems and software were many and expanding quickly. One of the most prominent and established applications for VR technology was in the enhancement of office productivity. Several technologies were on the market allowing for quick and accurate voice dictation and for voice-based computer controls. Industrial applications afforded companies streamlined inventory management and order processing.

VR systems were also an element of the biometrics industry, generating high-level security systems through voice-based identification and verification. Banks and similar institutions were busily installing VR systems into their customer call centers, cutting down the account verification process. The convergence of wireless and other remote technologies with Internet applications also pushed the development of VR software for verification with electronic commerce.

The Internet, in fact, played an enormous role in speeding the growth of the VR systems and software industry. More and more people began to place a premium on perpetual connectivity in the late 1990s. The rapidly changing work environment and fast-paced economy drove many to require Internet connections at all hours of the day and without restrictions as to location. As a result, VR technology sped to market to allow commuters and others to check stock quotes, news, and e-mail, and even perform routine business tasks via voice commands while en route between locations. Typical of the technology's drive toward more efficient office productivity, voice recognition systems were even cropping up in automobiles in the early 2000s in an attempt to capitalize on perhaps the last untapped market for office connectivity.

BACKGROUND AND DEVELOPMENT

Judith Markowitz in *Using Speech Recognition* traced the development of speech recognition devices back to Alexander Graham Bell in the 1870s, though the result of his research was the telephone. Several decades later, a Hungarian scientist, Tihamer Nemes, sought a patent for a speech transcription apparatus that relied on the soundtracks of movies. Nemes wanted the device to recognize and transcribe speech sequences. The patent office, however, rejected the proposal. VR technology did not advance as quickly as Bell and Nemes had hoped. About 90 years after the initial endeavor to create a speech transcriber, AT&T Bell Laboratories finally developed a device that could recognize speech, especially digits, when uttered by a human voice. Matching a vocal stimulus with recorded patterns, the device required a lot of tuning before it could recognize someone's speech, yet it

AN EQUATION FOR EQUALITY

Advanced mathematics, as most high school and college students can tell you, is difficult enough without having to struggle just to deal with the extensive notation. Unfortunately, until recently, advanced mathematics was particularly prohibitive to many disabled students, for whom Braille or speech could not easily translate into complex mathematical symbols on paper.

To mitigate the plight of such students, Henry Gray, professor of statistics and mathematics at Southern Methodist University in Dallas, developed a system whereby voice commands can be translated into mathematical symbols, thus affording disabled students easier access to advanced mathematics education.

Incorporating systems from a variety of vendors, including the Dragon Dictate voice recognition system from Dragon Systems, Dr. Gray's MathTalk for the Visually Impaired allows for the mathematical information to be printed in Nemeth Braille, the standard notation for the blind. A teacher or assistant simply dictates the problem into the computer to generate a Braille printout for the student to work with. Moreover, MathTalk for the Visually Impaired can translate the completed Braille assignment sheets or take dictation from the student to generate a text copy to hand in to the teacher.

Students using MathTalk Scientific Notebook can actually dictate entire math assignments into the computer. This system was specifically designed for students with disabilities such that they are unable to perform on a keyboard. MathTalk Scientific Notebook can handle up to 3,000 mathematical commands as well as correcting words such as "erase."

Youngsters also benefit from Gray's software. The ArithmeticTalk system was designed specifically for elementary school students and includes recognition suitable for addition, subtraction, multiplication, and division problems.

---

was said to have almost 99 percent accuracy once successfully tuned.

Research in the mid-1960s taught developers a lesson: voice recognition technology depended on perceiving subtle and complex oral input—abilities researchers could not reasonably hope to imbue their devices with, according to Markowitz. Consequently, researchers limited their focus to a series of lesser goals that one day might lead to a more comprehensive and powerful voice recognition system. They devoted their study to developing devices that could recognize a single person's voice, known as speaker-dependent technology. The devices used oral stimuli punctuated by small pauses to allow the machine to process the input, and had small vocabularies of about 50 words. Speaker-dependent technology requires a training period—the speaker records sample pronunciations so that the device can create an archive of speech patterns and note a speaker's idiosyncratic inflections and cadences. Speakers must pause after each word with discrete devices. Hence, continuous speech is not possible with such technology and using a discrete-word device demands patience.

The rudiments of continuous speech recognition did not come until the 1970s. This technology did not become functional until the 1980s and remained under refinement in the 1990s. Threshold Technologies, Inc. created the first commercial VR product in the early 1970s, according to Markowitz. Threshold's VIP 100 had a small vocabulary and used a discrete-word, speaker-dependent format, but Markowitz reported that it proved moderately successful nonetheless.

Goaded by these successes, the Advanced Research Projects Agency (ARPA) started to experiment with voice recognition technology. ARPA pushed for large vocabulary, continuous speech-processing devices and helped launch the industry's collaboration with artificial intelligence research, according to Markowitz. ARPA also took a comprehensive approach to voice recognition technology, exploring the influence of word meaning, word structure, sentence structure, and contextual and social factors. By 1976, ARPA created systems that had vocabularies over 1,000 words, could process some continuous speech, could recognize the speech of several language users, had an artificial syntax, and recognized better than 90 percent of their input, according to Markowitz. ARPA contracted Carnegie Mellon University (CMU), Bolt Beranek and Newman, and the Massachusetts Institute of Technology to build these systems.

Markowitz reported that CMU developed one of the most successful early VR systems, Harpy, which could recognize over 1,000 words with an error rate of about 5 percent. CMU also implemented hidden Markov modeling (HMM) technology in its DRAGON device, which generated or predicted letter sequences based on language immersion. HMM became a staple part of most of the major VR applications that followed. By 1985, 1,000-word systems were still considered large, especially for commercial products, though Speech Systems, Inc. developed a product with an extremely large vocabulary for its time in 1986, the PE100. The PE100 could recognize as many as 20,000 words in continuous speech, and the system was not speaker-dependent. In the late 1980s, Dragon Systems raised the ante by creating a

30,000-word device, though it required discrete speech. Continuous speech VR technology became much more viable in the 1980s, and so did technology that could tolerate some background noise. The 1980s also brought the advent of portable VR devices, according to Markowitz. The machines of the early 1980s sold for as much as several thousand dollars and had only small vocabularies, whereas those of the late 1980s sold for a few hundred dollars replete with vocabularies over 1,000 words.

As personal computer (PC) prices fell in the mid-1990s, companies began to develop computer-based VR applications. In 1994 Philips Dictation Systems led the foray with software containing a large vocabulary that could process continuous speech. VR also began to expand its commercial potential at this point: companies integrated VR technology in videocassette recorder remote controls, air traffic control devices, and general computer software.

CURRENT CONDITIONS

Current voice recognition (VR) dictation programs have come a long way from the haphazard dictation of years past. Indeed, VR was becoming a standard software option. Industry revenue was expected to reach about $8 billion by 2001, compared with only $500 million in 1997. Long-term projections were even more optimistic, particularly where the Internet was concerned. The need for global connectivity to the Web, as well as for multilingualism, was expected to be a boon the VR industry in the early 2000s. Cahner's InStat Group forecast total sales of network-based speech products to reach $12 billion by 2005, with $1.6 billion coming from voice-based Web portals alone.

Major software developers provide simple VR technology in many of their applications, including the Microsoft and Apple operating systems. The leading voice recognition products of 2000 united two components that were found only separately in the previous 5-10 years: large vocabularies and continuous recognition. Top-of-the-line speech-to-text software, for example, wielded 60,000-word vocabularies and could process continuous speech. While the most recent developments still don't quite allow for natural (that is, lazy), everyday speech, clearly annunciated speech can turn results of 98 percent accuracy through the top VR systems, which can usually keep up with relatively fast speaking paces. Typically, the programs require a few "training" sessions so as to become accustomed to the user's voice, vocabulary, and syntax.

BUSINESS

Not only has standard dictation software benefited from the advances in VR technologies, businesses have turned to voice recognition applications to perform many tasks including providing automated telephone service, selling and trading stocks and bonds, and providing general information. Banks, brokerages, credit corporations, telephone services, online databases, and other businesses chose VR technology because, in addition to improved accuracy, it made fewer mistakes in general than did human counterparts, about 30 percent fewer on average.

In the late 1990s, more businesses turned to voice recognition systems to handle customer telephone calls. For example, stock-brokerage firm Charles Schwab & Co. used a VR system by Nuance Communications to handle 45,000 calls a day for stock quotes, and voice-automated stock trading became a reality on the Internet at a site called E*TRADE. UPS also implemented a VR system by Nuance for its 125,000 daily callers, which tells them when their packages will be delivered or where they were left. UPS said that the VR system cost only $1.75 per call, whereas employing a customer assistant would cost $4 per call.

VR systems, in some cases, were even helping contribute to the long-fabled paperless work environment. Especially in industrial warehouses, the technology was eliminating the necessity for large stacks of order forms and inventory items. Workers could track items and orders while keeping their hands free, simply reading bar-code numbers into portable microphone headsets. The central computer system then organized the product information as necessary. Speech recognition has also been used in factories to control machinery, enter data, inspect parts, and take inventory, thereby opening up a wealth of employment opportunities previously closed to those with disabilities.

Lernout & Hauspie Speech Products, N.V., meanwhile, developed its own simultaneous translation system to translate from one language into another in a natural voice. With a voice-to-text system receiving the words and text-to-voice software sending them back out with a text-to-text translator in between, Lernout & Hauspie's system produced a translation with a delay of about only one second.

BANKING AND SECURITY

Banks rapidly embraced VR technology beginning in the late 1990s. High-level systems for banks and other security-dependent institutions usually can identify a voice after only a few spoken words. In such institutions, customers could be relieved of the requirements of normal security checks, including passwords, mothers' maiden names, and so on. In place of such processes, the customers' voices would simply be checked against a stored "voice bank" for verification.

Banking systems also benefit by shortening the duration of phone calls into the remote access system, which then frees up the lines for other calls and, thus, other business. According to some analysts, VR technology can reduce the cost per call to banks by 32 cents, translating into hundreds of thousands of dollars in savings over the course of a year. Guardian Life and the U.S. pension division of the Canadian-based Manulife Financial Corp. added VR technology to their 401(k) call centers. The Gartner Group, Inc. technology research firm noted that such call centers were primed for incorporation of such technology since customers frequently call to access basic account information quickly.

Fidelity Investments, known officially as FMR Corp., uses Nuance Communications technology for its Fidelity Automated Service Telephone system, relieving customers of the burden of remembering long account numbers and ticker symbols when checking account information and stock quotes and performing transactions. The system was designed to handle 750,000 to 1 million calls daily.

TELEPHONE-BASED INTERNET CAPABILITY

The desire for perpetual Internet connectivity was a central driving force behind new developments in voice recognition technology. A number of companies were developing systems whereby a central computer could recognize a customer's voice to deliver e-mail and Web-based information over telephones. For businesspeople in constant travel away from a computer, new technologies were underway that provide the ability to compose new e-mail messages over the telephone using VR applications and then send them as text.

Silicon Valley VR firm Nuance built an invisible Web browser, called Voyager, to allow for voice-activated Web browsing directly over telephones. Most telephone-based Web browsers were activated by pushing telephone buttons and could display only a few lines at a time on a tiny screen. With the Voyager browser, users can navigate bookmarked Web sites purely by voice commands. Moreover, sending or receiving personalized information could be verified by voice recognition. Nuance was in negotiation with a number of Web site developers to make Web pages compatible with the Voyager system.

The BeVocal service, meanwhile, used voice recognition software in conjunction with a central cellular phone service to allow subscribers to call and get real-time information, including directions and e-mail, from an almost conversational computer. Voice-operated direction systems typically make use of global positioning satellites that map out selected areas, picking up on the signal from the driver's system to figure out the best route to the desired location.

AUTOMOBILES

In the late 1990s, researchers applied voice recognition technology to the automobile in an effort to transform the car into a mobile office, replete with e-mail and Internet access that could be activated and operated via voice commands. VR-based applications as designed for cars can control computers, radios, cell phones, televisions, and other gadgets.

By 2000, the drive to incorporate Internet capabilities into automobiles was generating furious competition in the auto industry, leading to strategic alliances between automakers and VR firms to develop voice user interfaces as the standard connectivity protocol. Nuance formed an alliance with General Motors Corp. (GM) to develop VR systems for GM cars, and Lernout & Hauspie did likewise with Ford Motor Co.

Clarion Corp.'s Auto PC was on the market in 2000, and several auto manufacturers offered the system as an option on new vehicles. Clarion and Microsoft Corp. collaborated to develop Auto PC with speech-to-text software from Lernout & Hauspie. The system was packaged to fit into the slot in which car stereos were installed in the factory, and could be used in most automobiles. Auto PC receives its signals through specialized FM radio signals. The technology responded to voice commands and read e-mail and Web information aloud to the driver, and could even provide directions to a favorite restaurant or the post office while the driver was en route.

Unfortunately, however, the Auto PC system, which acted essentially as a hands-free, automobile-based PC, was not without the occasional crashes associated with desktop models, in which case the radio system and whatever else the system was wired to was rendered inoperative. Fortunately, Clarion thought ahead for such possibilities, and did not manufacture the system to control the car's brakes or transmission.

Many 2001 GM models will include OnStar's Virtual Advisor system to enable Web and e-mail access through cellular phones and voice recognition systems. Unlike Auto PC, however, Virtual Advisor is wired to few of the automobile's actual systems, usually only the radio or other accessories.

Connectivity was not the only application for VR systems in automobiles. Visteon Automotive Systems developed a voice-activated computer system that was installed in the Jaguar S-Type to control the car's normal accessory functions, such as the heating and air-conditioning systems and radio controls, in addition to voice-activated telephone dialing. While the Auto PC is fairly easily transferable between vehicles, however, Visteon's is more or less hardwired into the car's system, and cannot be easily removed.

INTERNET "SPEAK"

New VR-based special access applications for the disabled, introduced in 1998, include several speech-activated Web browsers and a talking Web browser from IBM Corp. Conversational Computing Corp., known as Conversa, launched Converse Web, an inexpensive (under $70) voice-activated Web browser that allows any user with a multimedia computer to traverse the expanse of the Internet via oral commands, without using a mouse or keyboard. Motorola, Inc. took the concept one step further with its innovative Voice Markup Language (VoxML), a voice-activated language for voice-based browsers and Web pages. Motorola indicated its intent to submit VoxML to the World Wide Web Consortium for use as a standardized language. VoxML holds the potential for Web-based telephone conversations, whereby users would converse with the Internet over standard telephone lines.

MEDICAL TRANSCRIPTION

Early in 1999 voice recognition vendor Applied Voice Recognition Inc. (AVRI) reinvented itself as e-DOCS and announced its intention to specialize in voice recognition for medical transcription applications. In the process AVRI acquired at least six medical transcription companies between April 1998 and the same month in 1999. AVRI indicated that the acquisitions provided services for as many as 5,000 physicians. The new focus put AVRI in competition with MedQuist Inc., which employs human transcription personnel. AVRI further indicated its intent to retain its original name, while doing business as e-DOCS.net and trading on the Nasdaq stock exchange under the new symbol, e-DOCS.

The new e-DOCS transcription service ran on AVRI's Voice Commander 99 software, provided services to physicians via the Internet, and offered 24-hour online turnaround for transcribed documents. Physicians earned discounts as high as 20 per-

cent for realizing the highest accuracy rate of 95 to 100 percent. The discount incentives were an effort to encourage optimization of the technology, which required that dictators speak very clearly. AVRI offered to physicians contracts that included handheld dictation equipment along with the basic computer and printer. The Voice Commander software, conceived in 1994, was patented in 1997. By April 2000, e-DOCS.net provided Internet-based medical transcription services to about 6,000 physicians in the United States.

INDUSTRY LEADERS

Lernout & Hauspie Speech Products, N.V., based in Belgium, catapulted to the top of the industry with a series of mergers, acquisitions, and partnerships. In collaboration with Olympus, Lernout & Hauspie developed the Voice Xpress Mobile Professional System, a small, handheld device that can accept about 70 minutes of dictation and then transcribe it when connected to a PC's serial port. The company maintained alliances with Ford Motor Co. to build VR systems for integration into the latter's new models and with Delphi Automotive Systems to add voice recognition to handheld computers that link cars to the Internet. The firm also struck a joint-venture deal with Visteon to develop speech recognition software tailored to the automobile market. The company was on an acquisition frenzy in the late 1990s, acquiring four companies including industry pioneer Kurzweil Applied Intelligence, Inc. in 1997, in which it obtained Kurzweil's VoicePad, VoicePlus, and VoicePro products. Microsoft subsequently purchased a minority share of Lernout & Hauspie in 1998 in order to expedite the company's development of VR Web browsers and other related technologies. Microsoft maintained a 7 percent share of the firm in 2000. The two companies will cooperate and share their technology and Lernout & Hauspie will supply VR technology for Microsoft's Windows operating system. The company acquired Dictaphone, a producer of medical and telecommunications dictation equipment, in 2000. But perhaps the biggest news occurred later that year when L&H bought rival industry leader Dragon Systems for $460 million. Lernout & Hauspie's sales in 1999 climbed 63 percent to reach $344.2 million, while the firm employed 1,700 workers. However, L&H was in financial trouble at the end of 2000, having filed for bankruptcy and facing investigation for misreported revenues. Some analysts expected a breakup of the company.

Dragon Systems, Inc. of Newton, Massachusetts, had a total of nine voice recognition (VR) products on the market in 2000. Founded in 1982, Dragon focused predominantly on speech-related technology. A key innovator, in 1984 Dragon's VR technology became the first to be integrated in a portable computer. The Advanced Research Projects Agency also commissioned Dragon to develop speaker-independent, continuous speech recognition applications in the mid-1980s. In 1990, medical application developers used Dragon's technology for a speech recognition information management system. By 1994, Dragon had increased its flagship DragonDictate's vocabulary to 60,000 words, the industry's largest at that time. In 1997, Dragon introduced current industry leader NaturallySpeaking, combining a large vocabulary with continuous speech recognition capabilities as the world's first general-purpose large vocabulary continuous speech recognition application. The company withdrew an offer to go public in 1999, and was purchased the following year by Lernout & Hauspie. The firm, with 320 employees, maintained subsidiaries in France, Germany, and the United Kingdom.

Fonix Corp. attempted to redefine VR technology by developing new approaches to voice recognition. Fonix was dissatisfied with the direction voice recognition software was heading and sought alternative technology and models to replace some of the industry standards of the mid-1990s. Incorporated in 1985, Fonix strives to develop speaker independent, real-time, natural-language software that can house large vocabularies and recognize speech with greater than 97 percent accuracy. The firm maintained licensing agreements with Infineon Technologies, Lucent Technologies, Nortel Networks Corp., and General Magic, Inc. Salt Lake City-based Fonix conducts research and creates VR technologies, which it then licenses to other companies. Fonix's revenues from license fees and product sales totaled $440,000 in 1999, up 86 percent from the year before. The company employed 130 workers in 2000.

IBM Corp., the world's largest computer firm, continued to have a strong presence in the industry in the late 1990s. IBM's core voice recognition product during this period was ViaVoice, in its executive, office, and home versions. ViaVoice, a continuous speech program, features a 64,000-word base vocabulary, a 260,000-word backup dictionary, voice correction, and recognition of a wide range of voice frequencies. The Via Voice Millennium model integrates automatically with the leading Web browsers, facilitating e-mail and chat-room dictation. IBM also makes Simply Speaking and Simply Speaking Gold, VR

word-processing applications. In 1999, IBM garnered $87.5 billion in sales, though only a small percentage of that was devoted to voice recognition technology, and maintained a payroll of 300,000 employees.

The AT&T spinoff, Lucent Technologies, carrying on the vision of Alexander Graham Bell, extensively developed voice recognition technology. Specific to VR technology, Lucent created security systems, voice processing technology, networking systems, and telephones. One of its key products was Conversant, an automated speech recognition application with a 2,000-word vocabulary that allows clients 24-hour access to their accounts. Lucent also developed speech recognition technology for faxes and computer networking, and has developed Speech Application Platform, a programming platform for creating speech-based applications. Based in Murray Hill, New Jersey, Lucent employed over 140,000 people in 2000, and posted over $38.3 billion in 1999 sales.

RESEARCH AND TECHNOLOGY

In addition to battling traditional obstacles such as creating large vocabularies and implementing contextual information, the Speech Recognition Application Programming Interface Committee—which includes IBM, Dragon, Lernout & Hauspie, and Philips Dictation Systems—also aimed at the development of a programming interface in order to standardize VR software. This programming interface will enable independent software developers to integrate VR technology into their applications.

The identification market also sought convergence between computer-based encryption systems and voice recognition systems. Currently, the Internet employs a public key infrastructure operating system encouraging public key cryptography. As the Internet incorporates voice-controlled activity, however, encryption must be available for VR technology if the development is not to hamper electronic commerce.

For security purposes in general, voice recognition encompasses the standard set by the Speaker Verification Application Programming Interface, which included the U.S. Department of Defense, the Internal Revenue Service, and the Immigration and Naturalization Service, among other organizations.

Realizing that many customers will not commit to VR technology with anything less than 100 percent accuracy, major players strived to iron out the nagging, persistent bugs in most VR systems. Even the top-of-the-line models rang up the errors in trial runs, despite vast improvements in the late 1990s. Consequently, researchers looked to artificial intelligence for answers; in particular, to neural networks that simulate the performance of the human brain and are capable of learning from exposure to language. VR researchers hope that neural nets can supplement or replace reliance on statistical models of speech-sound frequency. This technology should reduce the effects of age, pitch, volume, and dialect in speech recognition.

FURTHER READING

Austen, Ian. "Need Restaurant Information? Phone a Web Server and Ask." *New York Times,* 13 April 2000.

————. "A Way to Use the Voice Instead of the Fingers." *New York Times,* 9 September 1999.

Beckman, David, and David Hirsch. "Live and Ready for Prime Time: Digital Recorders and Voice Recognition Software Team up to Get Good Ratings." *ABA Journal,* December 1999.

"Call Centers: New Voice Recognition Software Speeds Customer Service Calls at Manulife." *Future Banker,* 1 November 1999.

Clark, Lindsay. "Faster Voice Recognition." *Computer Weekly,* 30 September 1999.

Greenman, Catherine. "New Help for Disabled Math Students." *New York Times,* 30 March 2000.

Guernsey, Lisa. "Talking to the Web on Your Telephone." *New York Times,* 7 October 1999.

Hallenborg, John C. "The Identification Standards Movement." *ID World,* November 1999.

Innes, John. "Bank Security Takes Speech into Account." *Scotsman,* 25 January 2000.

Markowitz, Judith. *Using Speech Recognition.* Upper Saddle River, NJ: Prentice Hall PTR, 1996.

Marriott, Michel. "The Wind in Your Hair, Your E-Mail on the Dash." *New York Times,* 9 September 1999.

Meyer, Dan. "Voice Recognition Moves to Forefront of Enhanced-Services Offerings." *RCR Wireless News,* 6 November 2000.

Murray, Charles J. "Two Auto Giants Forge Partnerships to Develop Voice Technology—Kick the Tires? Nah. Hear It Talk." *Electronic Engineering Times,* 24 April 2000.

Paczkowski, John. "Mobile Computing Finds Its Voice." *Redherring.com,* 3 November 1999. Available from http://www.redherring.com/insider/1999/1103/news-mobile.html.

Quan, Margaret. "Speech Recognition Takes Network Turn." *Electronic Engineering Times,* 13 November 2000.

Sechler, Bob. "Small-Stock Focus: Applied Voice Recognition Transforms Itself to Catch Web Wave, but Technology Isn't Perfect." *Wall Street Journal,* 5 April 1999.

Sherter, Alain. "Speech Recognition Speaks Volumes." *Bank Technology News,* August 1999.

Small, Stefanie. "Talk Your Day Away: Voice-Recognition Systems Are Gaining Popularity in Warehouses." *Warehousing Management,* 31 May 1999.

Taub, Eric A. "The Blind Leading the Sighted." *New York Times,* 28 October 1999.

Water and Air Filtration and Purification Systems

INDUSTRY SNAPSHOT

Increased consumer awareness and concern about environmental quality helped the residential water and air purification industries flourish during the late 1990s with good prospects for the new decade. Both industries are highly fragmented and comprised of a large number of small companies manufacturing and distributing across various product lines. Nevertheless, a handful of companies, including divisions of industrial conglomerates, tended to dominate each industry.

Both industries are growing rapidly. In the late 1990s, the water quality products industry was valued at $25 billion worldwide, including all forms of treatment, filtration, and purification. The U.S. home water purification market was valued at over $1.38 billion in 1999 and is expected to continue to expand. Sales of portable units targeted for use outside the home were estimated to be about $15 million, but growth in that niche was shrinking. By 2000, the U.S. water filter market was estimated at nearly $2.5 billion. The air quality products industry was also on an upward trend. Sales of air purifiers, including the fast-selling portable air cleaners, grew by more than 10 percent a year in the mid- to late 1990s.

By 2000, both industries faced similar challenges. Each segment of the industry sold products that could be used either at a particular location in a home or throughout the whole house. Encouraging consumers to upgrade inexpensive entry-level purchases to high-end, large-scale, or whole-house purification systems was the next challenge for these industries. Furthermore, each segment began introducing more sophisticated filtration devices around 2000, each capable of removing more harmful substances than its predeces-

sor. Through various educational marketing techniques, the industry hoped to make consumers aware of the benefits and advantages of these new products. Additionally, consumer awareness of both air and water quality issues, especially in the home, continues to rise, due in large part to new regulations requiring the disclosure of such information and the consumer's ability to have his or her own home tested for air and water purity.

ORGANIZATION AND STRUCTURE

Both the water and air purification industries are comprised of companies that produce finished units, component manufacturers, and assemblers of finished units. Products are sold to industrial and commercial users as well as to residential homeowners. Although the largest industry leaders maintain their own networks of dealers and distributors, the large majority of firms sell products directly to retail outlets for resale.

WATER QUALITY PRODUCTS INDUSTRY

Products sold by water industry participants include softeners, reverse osmosis units, ultraviolet units, distillation units, ozonators, carbon and noncarbon filters, filtration carafes, faucet-mounted models, countertop models, and personal filtration units. Components manufactured for those products include mineral tanks, valves, controllers, membranes, faucets, and filters. Retail operations in the industry generally have a high percentage of revenues—sometimes as high as 70 percent—derived from recurring sales of consumables such as servicing equipment, replacement parts, and filters.

Retailers and manufacturers in the water treatment industry are represented by the Water Quality Association (WQA). The WQA is a not-for-profit international trade organization founded in 1950. The agency counted 2,200 members, all corporate manufacturers and retailers. A 1999 consumer survey commissioned by the WQA reported that the purchaser of water quality products and components is usually a dealership or original equipment manufacturer. As in many industries, assemblers and component manufacturers who make finished units sell more units to dealerships than to original equipment manufacturers.

The water quality products industry is not regulated by a government agency. Typically, however, units are labeled for retail sale with indications of how fine a filtration or purification system has been installed. The National Sanitation Foundation International Standard 42 indicates a filter equipped for handling aesthetic problems such as taste, smell, and appearance, while Standard 53 indicates a filter equipped for handling basic health problems such as lead and organic compounds. Such filters normally indicate the specific contaminants they can handle. The most-resistant filters—labeled as being certified "absolute one micron"—are those that can filter parasites.

The U.S. Environmental Protection Agency (EPA) did not regulate the manufacture or distribution of water filter units in the late 1990s. EPA policies and guidelines, however, as well as statutes such as the Safe Drinking Water Act of 1974 have had a great impact on the industry. The act contained water quality guidelines that many communities in the country failed to meet; the 1996 reauthorization of the act made certain provisions more rigorous. Thus, while communities fail to meet federal water standards and the public grows more skeptical of the water it drinks, the water quality products industry benefits.

The Safe Drinking Water Act Amendment of 1996 was signed into law in August of that year. Congress overwhelmingly approved the bill, which authorized billions of dollars to improve deteriorating water systems. The funds represent a sharp increase in spending for water systems, both municipal and rural. The law also included a "right to know" provision that requires water authorities to disclose what chemicals and bacteria are in drinking water and requires public notice of any dangerous contaminants within 24 hours of discovery. The bill also imposes a duty on the EPA to develop and apply more rigorous standards to fight cryptosporidium and other common drinking water contaminants posing significant health risks. Beginning in 1999, water utility companies were required to report what elements were found in their water. This information would allow consumers to make better choices when purchasing home water filtration products, and the responsibility placed on the EPA reflects a shift in federal policy away from identifying new pollutants toward controlling the most dangerous ones. The impact of the act is difficult to predict; its passage, however, reflects a growing discontent among Americans about the quality of water. That discontent makes itself felt in the booming sales figures for companies in the industry.

AIR QUALITY PRODUCTS INDUSTRY

The air quality products industry manufactures and markets air filters and purifiers for both whole-house applications and portable use. Within those two applications, there are three general types of air cleaners on the market: mechanical filters, electronic air cleaners, and ion generators.

Mechanical filters, which may be installed in whole-house or portable devices, are of two major types. The first type, known as flat or panel filters, normally consists of a dense medium, such as coarse glass fibers, animal hair, or synthetic fibers, which are then coated with a viscous substance such as oil to act as an adhesive for particulate material. Flat filters may also be made of "electret" media, which is comprised of a charged plastic film or fiber to which particles in the air are attracted. Although flat filters may collect large particles well, they remove only a small percentage of respirable-size particles.

The second type of mechanical filter is the pleated or extended surface filter. Due to its greater surface area, this type of filter generally attains greater efficiency for capture of respirable-size particles than do flat filters. This allows an increase in packing density without a significant drop in air flow rate.

In electronic air cleaners, an electrical field traps charged particles. Electronic air cleaners are usually electrostatic precipitators or charged-media filters. In electrostatic precipitators, particles are collected on a series of flat plates. In charged-media filter devices, the particles are collected on fibers in a filter. In most electrostatic precipitators, and some charged-media filters, the particles are ionized, or charged, before the collection process, resulting in a higher collection efficiency.

Like electronic air cleaners, ion generators use static charges to remove particles from indoor air. They act by charging the particles in a room, so they are attracted to walls, floors, or any surface. In some cases, these devices, which come in portable units only, contain a collector to attract the charged particles back to the unit. Both electronic air cleaners and ion generators can produce ozone. Some systems on the market are hybrid devices containing two or more of the particle removal devices.

The residential air quality products industry was also not regulated by a government agency in the late 1990s, nor has the government published any guidelines or standards for use in determining how well an air cleaner works in removing pollutants from indoor air. Standards for rating particle removal by air cleaners, both whole-house and portable, however, are published by two private trade associations. The Association of Home Appliance Manufacturers developed an American National Standards Institute-approved standard for portable air cleaners. Whole-house systems can be analyzed by Standard 52-761 of the American Society of Heating, Refrigerating & Air Conditioning Engineers, a trade group. Both standards estimate the effectiveness of an air-cleaning device in removing particles from indoor air.

One difficulty facing consumers is that air filtration standards focus only on particle removal. No standards exist to assess the comparative ability of air filters and purifiers to remove gaseous pollutants or radon—contaminants of increasing concern in the late 1990s and in the new century. The removal of gaseous materials from indoor air can be accomplished only in those units containing adsorbent or reactive materials.

Like the water quality products industry, the manufacture and sale of air quality products was on the upswing in the late 1990s. Both industries benefited from highly publicized findings of contaminants in homes and communities. The air quality industry, however, began its sharp increase in the early 1990s, meaning fewer companies were in that market than were in the water quality market.

Another major difference between the two industries lies in the perceived utility of the products themselves. While questions were raised as to whether the water quality of the vast majority of Americans is poor enough to require residential purification, testing typically showed that the products performed as advertised, reducing or eliminating the presence of various contaminants. As of the early 2000s, that question of effectiveness had not been answered for many air quality products. For example, by the end of the 20th century, the EPA had not taken a position on the value of home air cleaners, despite its recognition of the ill effects of air pollution on human health. Further, while standards exist for the quality of indoor air, standards for the products themselves are often difficult to compare across product lines.

BACKGROUND AND DEVELOPMENT

The water and air filtration and purification industries manufacture and sell systems and supplies that counter the effects of pollution and naturally occurring contaminants. Those effects range from the unhealthy and deadly to the aesthetic. Both industries have targeted the commercial and industrial markets for years—markets that are scrutinized by the EPA and the general public. More recent concerns about the safety of drinking water and the purity of indoor residential air drove an upswing in the retail market for those products. Both industries grew from being dominated by a few large manufacturers focusing on industrial and commercial applications to highly fragmented industries comprised of dozens of manufacturers, retailers, and distributors. Most were small businesses, all of whom vied for what appeared to be America's almost limitless appetite for contaminant-free living.

PUBLIC CONCERNS ABOUT WATER QUALITY

According to a trade group, the market for residential drinking water treatment nearly doubled from 1990 to 1995. By the end of the decade, the water purification industry was confronted with a public concerned about water quality and prepared to spend money to eliminate contaminants. The 1999 consumer survey commissioned by the Water Quality Association (WQA) revealed that the American public was increasingly suspicious of the tap water entering homes. Survey responses showed that three-quarters of consumers had some concern about their household water supply, and one in five consumers was dissatisfied with the quality of their water supply; one in three consumers felt that the water was not as safe as it should be. Despite these concerns, only one in four consumers reported ever having the water tested for contamination.

Consumer knowledge about water quality issues did not appear to be widespread. Forty-seven percent of respondents said that they wished they knew more about their household water supply; 23 percent, however, said that they did not know how to obtain information. The survey results point to continued solid growth for the water quality industry. Among all respondents, adults between the ages of 18 and 44 were the most likely to believe household water was unsafe.

Those consumers are also the least likely to know where to turn for information about their water. Increased reporting of water quality calamities in the 1990s, joined with the growing ubiquity of water purification devices in retail outlets, certainly had a great effect upon this consumer group.

The American consumer market appeared to be a sizable and growing market in the late 1990s, not just a fad. The WQA survey showed that due to increasing health concerns, about two-thirds of consumers were using some sort of water treatment method (either bottled water or a filtration device), compared to 53 percent in 1997. Thirty-eight percent of these consumers used a household water treatment device, compared to 32 percent in 1997 and 27 percent in 1995. Sales of "entry-level" devices, such as pour-through water carafes with filters, grew more quickly than any other type of water treatment device. The boom in entry-level devices demonstrated that the industry's marketing target has been met.

The growth of entry-level sales also has repercussions in the location of retail purchases. While 29 percent of Americans making water quality purchases in 1997 still purchased home water treatment devices from local water treatment dealers, department and discount stores grew in popularity as the site of purchase. Up from 7 percent in 1995, sales of water quality products at those stores tripled to 21 percent. As the industry offered more inexpensive products that required little expertise to install or maintain, accessibility through general retail outlets became possible.

Growing Evidence of Water Quality Failings

Growing distrust of the water supply may have been unfounded or overstated for the large majority of Americans in the 1990s. Most Americans receive water from a public water system where it has already been tested and treated under regulations derived from the Safe Drinking Water Act of 1974. Only those who get water from other sources, such as private wells or small water systems serving a relatively small number of customers, could not be as certain of the quality of their water. Still, well-publicized breakdowns of even the largest water systems cast uncertainty into the consumers' collective consciousness. For example, in the mid-1990s more than a dozen communities in the Midwest were informed that their tap water had heightened concentrations of a weed killer. More than 100 people were killed by the waterborne contaminant *cryptosporidia* in Milwaukee in 1993. Further, in 1996, Washington, D.C., residents were given a "boil

order" to combat unsafe bacteria levels. In addition, sporadic reports of nitrate—the cause of blue baby syndrome—and radon in drinking water also spurred the public's concern.

Adding to Americans' suspicions were widely publicized findings and studies. In the summer of 1997, for example, the U.S. Geological Survey asked U.S. and Canadian residents to aid in the scientific investigation of deformed frogs, toads, and salamanders. Citizens were encouraged to report sightings of abnormal and malformed amphibians they saw while outdoors. Whether the deformities arose from waterborne contaminants, and whether those contaminants could affect human health, had not been determined; it was known, however, that amphibians are highly sensitive to alterations in the aquatic environment.

The Centers for Disease Control and Prevention in Atlanta estimated that 1 million people annually develop illnesses due to U.S. drinking water and that nearly 1,000 people die as a result. The EPA also found water supplies falling below federal guidelines. A profile from the 1994 National Water Quality Inventory Report to Congress claimed that about 40 percent of surveyed rivers, lakes, and estuaries were not clean enough for basic uses such as fishing or swimming.

One study performed in 1995 by the National Resource Defense Council (NRDC) found that the tap water entering 80 million American homes contained significant levels of cancer-causing chemicals. The study found unsafe levels of arsenic, radon, and trihalomethanes.

A 1996 study by the Environmental Working Group (EWG) and the NRDC, using data compiled by the EPA, found that one in six Americans got water from a utility that had recent pollution problems. To compile the report, EWG and NRDC analyzed more than 16 million records submitted by public water suppliers to the EPA and state water agencies. A major finding of the report was that "more than 45 million Americans in thousands of communities were served drinking water during 1994-1995 that was polluted with fecal matter, parasites, disease-causing microbes, radiation, pesticides, toxic chemicals, and lead [when related to] standards established under the federal Safe Drinking Water Act." The report also claimed that, during 1994 and 1995, more than 18,500 public water supplies reported at least one violation of a federal drinking water standard. Although the report received harsh criticism from water utilities and industry groups such as the American Water Works Association, it was widely publicized—and studied by Congress since it debated amendments to the Safe Drinking Water Act.

NATIONWIDE RESPONSES TO WATER QUALITY CONCERNS

American concerns about water quality were reflected in the actions of elected representatives. In October 1996, President Bill Clinton announced an environmental initiative that allocated $45 million over four years for the U.S. Geological Survey (USGS) to extend water quality testing to 75 cities, which increased the examining of 35 river basins and groundwater systems. The initiative also made data collected on the major rivers, water-supply watersheds, and drinking water wells available to the public on the Internet. Through the USGS Water Resources Data Web site, consumers can get real-time water data from 3,000 stations throughout the United States, daily stream-flow reports from the National Water Information System, and records from the Water Quality Monitoring Network.

In addition, the amendment to the Safe Drinking Water Act of 1974, the Safe Drinking Water Act Amendment of 1996, created a revolving loan fund that will aid states in rebuilding and maintaining deteriorating water systems. That federal effort provided funds where the American public could see it in the form of a proposed budget giving every state at least $7 million. Up to $9.6 billion was authorized for payment to the states through 2003. Since fiscal 1994, President Clinton proposed $3 billion for that purpose each year in his budget requests.

DETERIORATING AIR QUALITY

While the market for residential air-cleaning products was already substantial and continued to grow in the late 1990s, fewer than 10 companies manufactured and marketed such products. With indoor air quality on the decline, however, that number was expected to increase, due in no small part to the well-publicized findings of agencies and scientists nationwide.

At the end of the 20th century, scientific experiments detected a reliable connection between human health problems and dirty air. Epidemiologists estimated that the annual U.S. death toll from air pollution is 50,000—resulting from heart disease, asthma, bronchitis, stroke, and similar conditions. Faced with these figures, in 1977 the EPA proposed strengthening air pollution standards. The most comprehensive air pollution legislation is the Clean Air Act Amendment of 1970. Despite this law, approximately 121 million Americans live in areas where the air falls below health standards and 46 million live in areas where pollutants such as carbon monoxide, ozone, lead, nitrogen dioxide, and sulfur dioxide exceed maximum levels set by the EPA.

According to the EPA, the average American spends roughly 90 percent of his or her time indoors, where the air is more polluted than the outdoor air in even the largest and most industrialized cities. Furthermore, the American Lung Association found that 87 percent of Americans are unaware that air pollution may be worse indoors than outdoors. In the 1990s, the EPA called indoor air pollution one of the country's top-five environmental issues. The EPA estimated that more than 50 percent of homes and offices suffered from highly polluted indoor air and the American Lung Association discovered that 40 percent of homeowners did not change their air filters for their air conditioners and heaters as recommended. The agency estimated that such pollution costs Americans tens of billions of dollars a year in direct medical expenses and lost productivity. An estimated one in five Americans suffered allergy-related illness at some point during their lives, with indoor allergens responsible for a substantial number of those cases. Because of this, in 1993 the Institute of Medicine of the National Academy of Sciences urged a comprehensive effort to clean up the air in America's homes, schools, and businesses.

More findings in the 1990s made indoor air quality appear grim and in need of immediate relief. Along with AIDS and tuberculosis, asthma is one of the three chronic diseases with an increasing mortality rate. The National Institutes of Health called allergic disease one of America's most common and expensive health problems. Asthma and allergies alone cause over 130 million lost school days and 13.5 million lost work days each year. Further, indoor allergens are blamed for much of the acute asthma in adults under the age of 50, according to the National Academy of Science.

Amid such well-publicized breakdowns in air quality, the residential air products industry is expected to thrive. To do so, however, it must overcome certain concerns about its products as well as a less tangibly fouled medium than the one being repaired by the water quality industry.

Air purifier sales climbed 11 percent in 1996 to $340 million, marking five years of consecutive sales growth, according to *HFN*. Retail sales accounted for the majority of the revenues at $275 million, while alternative distribution channels accounted for $65 million. Overall, the industry sold about 3.2 million units. Nonetheless, the industry's growth remained behind some projections that predicted revenues would expand by 30 to 40 percent in 1996. Still, some analysts believed air purifiers were among the most profitable small appliances since they have a 40 percent profit margin, according to *HFN*.

WATER PRODUCTS SALES GROWTH

From the late 1990s to 2000, the water filtration products industry experienced robust growth, which was expected to continue well into the new decade. The public's concerns about water quality and aesthetics were widely held and widely publicized during this period, and its willingness to purchase items claiming to rectify the problems at the spigot and throughout the house was on the rise. Greater consumer consciousness about water quality and mandatory Consumer Confidence Reports fueled and are expected to continue to fuel the industry's growth.

According to the Water Quality Association (WQA), 60 percent of adults believe the quality of drinking water has an impact on their health and about 50 percent are concerned about contaminants in their drinking water. Moreover, beginning in late 1999, the EPA required municipalities to send detailed reports on the drinking water they provide to their customers for compliance with the 1996 amendment to the Safe Drinking Water Act of 1974. Municipalities must submit these reports annually and water purification makers and manufacturers and retailers expect they will lead to greater consumer awareness and purifier sales. Makers and retailers used the Internet as an educational tool not only to demonstrate their purification wares and describe their features, but also to apprise consumers of water quality and contamination issues, according to *HFN*.

All types of water quality devices saw sales increases in that period; not surprisingly, more inexpensive entry-level products saw the greatest sales boom. Just as telling, consumers across all income brackets were more willing to purchase water quality equipment for the home. Water filter penetration increased from 27 percent in 1995 to 32 percent in 1997, to 38 percent in 1999, according to the National Consumer Water Quality Survey. Even with this growth, the industry still has plenty of room for expansion because of the increased consumer consciousness and the efforts of retailers to encourage current users of water purification devices to upgrade to faucet-mount, countertop, and under-sink models. In addition, some retailers tied water purification devices in with high-end and gourmet kitchenwares, emphasizing fashionable and costlier models, according to *HFN*. Consequently, the outlook for water filtration devices remains bright, and the WQA reported that about 10 percent of the U.S. population without water filters planned to purchase some kind of filtration device.

Predictions for growth in the water treatment industry were optimistic in the late 1990s. Revenue for residential water treatment products and systems, excluding bottled water sales, was valued at $1.01 billion in 1990. By the mid-1990s, that figure was $1.38 billion and was estimated at almost $2.5 billion by the year 2000.

Another significant development in the industry is the growing availability of products for retail sale outside of locations normally associated with water treatment. As entry-level products are created and increased competition drives some prices down, more product niches will be marketed through department stores and other chain outlets. Some of these products enable individuals to test their own water to see if it contains contaminants. Such a test is recommended to be performed up to four times per year depending on the source of water and the health needs of the individual.

In 2000, the cost of water purification units varied greatly by method. The most inexpensive alternative, the carafe models, were priced from about $17 to $30. The pour-through model was the fastest-growing and best-selling water filtration device in the late 1990s and early 2000s. The cost for filters ran from 50 cents to about $12. Faucet-mounted models, easily installed by the homeowner, cost from $15 to $55; replacement filters cost about $10 to $15. Countertop models, attached to the faucet, cost anywhere from $40 to $300; filters for these ran as high as $95. The faucet model grew quickly in the late 1990s, accounting for 20 percent of all water filters sold. Culligan Water Technologies, Inc. announced plans to reintroduce its dual-filtration faucet-mounted models, which ranged in price from about $25 to $40. These units guarantee that the levels of bacteria leaving the unit will not exceed the level of bacteria in the tap water as it enters the filter. Bacteria have actually been shown to multiply in household water systems, but this filter prevents that from occurring. These filters were introduced to limited markets in 1997, but improved marketing strategies have Culligan officials optimistic that the filters will be big sellers. Under-sink models, using two or three filter cartridges in a series and plumbed into the cold-water line, cost $45-$500; filters ran from $11 to $100. Under-sink reverse osmosis models were very effective against a wide range of contaminants. They cost anywhere from $150 to over $1,000, and filters ran as high as $165.

In addition, new portable filtration bottles were introduced into the market in the late 1990s, targeted to campers and sailors. These units contain a filter, secured inside the top of the bottle, which improves taste and cuts down on odor and removes virtually all chlorine (99.8 percent), microscopic pathogens that cause gastrointestinal illness, detergents, pesticides, industrial and agricultural wastes, and heavy metals. The 30-ounce bottles will filter 200 gallons, or more than 1,000 refills. These units ran from $15 to $40 and filters cost between $10 and $20.

CONSUMER ACCEPTANCE OF AIR QUALITY PRODUCTS

Growth in the industry in the late 1990s was primarily in the portable market. Variety among portable machines, however, grew greatly at that time as consumers demanded larger and more powerful units. Thus, the general trend in the market at that time was toward larger, console-sized models. Because installation of a whole-house unit requires great expense and retrofitting of air-flow sources, consumers appeared to want to solve air quality problems room-by-room with the largest units available, which usually operated in bedrooms and other highly trafficked areas. Most users, about 75 percent of those surveyed, indicated they purchased air purifiers because of allergies.

In the late 1990s, one indicator of the public's growing disenchantment with its indoor air could be seen in a battle of standards over the air in commercial establishments. Commercial indoor air quality is set by local code, often adopted from guidelines set out by the American Society of Heating, Refrigerating & Air Conditioning Engineers (ASHRAE). In 1997 ASHRAE proposed a new industry standard for ventilation. Its proposal carried great weight because its existing standard had become the most widely used and cited document for indoor air quality. The proposals by ASHRAE were far more rigorous and far-ranging than those in place. Of course, those standards, if adopted, will have no effect on residential air quality or products sold to consumers. The significant strengthening of the guidelines, however, gave an indication of the changes occurring on air issues; Americans find indoor air quality unacceptable and are prepared to pay greatly to improve their commercial and residential environments.

A major issue facing some manufacturers of air quality products in the late 1990s was the creation of ozone, a lung irritant, in certain products, either as a deliberate step to aid in air cleaning or as a by-product of the purification. In the late 1990s, the EPA was studying whether some products produced new pollutants or dispersed old ones. At least two manufacturers of portable units advertised that their products produced ozone to aid in removal of harmful gases; the EPA had not yet determined the possible health effects. Consumer confusion on the issue was high. For example, some marketing materials for products noted, without further explanation, that ozone is simply super-pure oxygen that occurs naturally on the planet. Certain advertising materials even compared the inhalation of ozone from a residential air purifier to the invigoration one feels after drinking water downstream from a waterfall.

Another technological concern for the industry was with studies showing that some electronic air cleaners themselves produce fine particulate material, or that filters and other devices remove particles from the environment and then re-emit gases and odors from the collected particles. In addition, some materials used in the manufacturing of air cleaners may themselves emit chemicals into indoor air; for example, formaldehyde may be emitted if particle board is used in the air-cleaner housing. Another technological hurdle facing the air quality products industry at the turn of the century was many units' inability to remove certain odors, primarily cigarette odor, from indoor environments. While most models are able to remove the particles from smoke, most are unable to remove the gaseous elements of cigarette residue. Some units are designed to scent the air, leading homeowners to believe the odor has been eradicated. Ion generators also generated concern; studies showed a correlation between them and a heightened deposit of particles in the human lung.

Two new air quality products on the horizon may prove to further increase sales in the market. In late 1998, Clean Air Systems installed filtration modules designed to eliminate cigarette smoke at Richmond International Airport. These filter modules operate by filtering out smoke, particles, and gases while returning clean air to the immediate environment. These filters are twice as efficient as previous filtration devices in absorbing 13 different chemical compounds found in cigarette smoke. Also in 1998, Environmental Elements Corp. was contracted by the EPA to develop a sterilizing filter capable of filtering more than 99 percent of microorganisms, including those that cause tuberculosis and Legionnaires' disease. This filter would enhance the collection and destruction of such microorganisms that along with inorganic particles contribute heavily to indoor air pollution. These new units will use electrically created plasma, which effectively destroys microorganisms without using chemicals or heat. Medical facilities, especially hospitals, would greatly benefit from such technology.

INDUSTRY LEADERS

WATER QUALITY INDUSTRY

In 2000, one company, Culligan Water Technologies, Inc., led the water purification and filtration industry and was followed at a long distance by other establishments that carved out portions of the market in particular product niches. Culligan, of Northbrook, Illinois, is a subsidiary of United States Filter Corp., which is owned by France-based Vivendi. Culligan manufactures water purification and treatment products for household, commercial, and industrial use. The company's products and services range from filters for tap water and household water softeners to advanced equipment and services for commercial and industrial applications. Culligan provides services in over 90 countries worldwide through a network of 1,400 sales and service centers.

Supporting its distribution network, Culligan maintains manufacturing facilities in the United States, Italy, Spain, and Canada. In addition, Culligan sells bottled water in the five-gallon bottled water market under names such as Elga, Everpure, and Bruner. In 1997 the company entered the consumer market selling filtration products directly to retailers. Culligan has been active in the water purification and treatment industry since 1936, and its brands are among the most recognized. Since the early 1980s, Culligan's residential water treatment systems have been installed in more than 3 million households in the United States, representing the largest installed base in the country, according to the company. In 1988 Culligan became the first company to be certified by the independent National Sanitation Foundation under its standard for residential reverse osmosis drinking water systems.

In 1997 Culligan created its new Consumer Market Division, which, through partnerships with other companies, sought quick access to niches of the retail market. The first products introduced by the division were faucet-mounted filters, which are sold through department stores. The division expanded its product line by aiming at the do-it-yourself market, selling under-counter systems, refrigerator water/ice maker filter systems, and a sediment and rust reduction whole-house filtration system. The division also announced the introduction of a designer, glass-pitcher filtration system and two monitored faucet-mount systems. In 1997 Culligan entered into a marketing partnership with Health-O-Meter Products, Inc., the parent of Mr. Coffee, for plastic pour-through pitchers, with a major appliance manufacturer to provide a refrigerator water/ice maker filtration system, and a long-term agreement with Moen Inc. to develop Moen products incorporating Culligan water filtration assemblies.

Through its Everpure subsidiary, Culligan also markets point-of-use filtration systems for homes and recreational vehicles such as Winnebago, Fleetwood, and Airstream. In 1997 Culligan Water Technologies merged with Ametek Inc. of Paoli, Pennsylvania, a global manufacturer of electrical and electromechanical products and a producer of parts for the residential water treatment market. In 1999 Culligan began selling and servicing Bruner water conditioning systems, in a move to position itself for increased emphasis on the commercial market, especially the food service, lodging, and grocery industries.

Kinetico Inc. of Newbury, Ohio, was a leader in the production of under-counter reverse osmosis models, as well as carbon filters, entering the new decade with sales of roughly $50 million. The privately held company employs 200 people and makes a line of products including a countertop filter model. Kinetico evolved from the Tangent Co., a small consulting design firm, eventually becoming a global organization of independent dealers, international distributors, and manufacturer representatives in more than 60 countries. The company uses a ceramic filter media developed by 3M Co., which Kinetico claims has proven very effective in the removal of microorganisms and contaminants such as methyl tertiary butyl ether (MTBE) from water. Because of the success of the ceramic filter, Kinetico now uses it in many of its applications, including residential, commercial, and industrial products.

Another leader in the 1990s was Teledyne Technologies Inc., the aftermath of the divestiture of Teledyne by Allegheny Ludlum. With approximate sales of $803.4 million in 1999, the company markets various products including a carafe model, a faucet-mounted model, and an under-sink model, as well as air purifiers in addition to its steel, industrial, and aerospace products. Teledyne Technologies employed 5,800 people in 1999.

With more than 70 years of experience, privately held EcoWater Systems Inc. claimed to be the oldest and largest manufacturer of residential water treatment equipment in the world. The firm, headquartered in Woodbury, Minnesota, is a composite of three former companies. One of these, the Lindsay Co., obtained the first patent for water conditioning in 1925. Lindsay pioneered several industry firsts, such as automatic controls, high-capacity resin, console units, iron-free systems, and rustproof fiberglass tanks. Lindsay became a member of the Marmon Group of companies in 1981 and, in 1983, purchased two other firms, after which the company was renamed EcoWater Systems in 1988. EcoWater is registered to the ISO 9001 Standard for Quality Systems and distributes its products through more than 1,400 independent water treatment dealers in the United States, Canada, Europe, Asia, and Africa. EcoWater Systems had sales estimated between $100 and $150 million in the late 1990s.

Brita, manufactured by the Clorox Corp. of Oakland, California, was a leader in the countertop carafe market with about a 55 percent market share during the late 1990s. The Brita unit is the most visibly successful of the carafe units and established an early lead in the brand-recognition battle. *HFN* reported that Brita controlled 60 percent of the water filter market by the late 1990s.

Aqua Care Systems, Inc., of Coral Springs, Florida, designs, manufactures, and markets filtration and water purification systems under its subsidiaries KISS, Di-Tech Systems, and Midwest Water Technologies. Sales in 1999 topped $23.4 million, a one-year sales growth of 11.7 percent.

The booming water purification market also served to lure large companies more known their for expertise in other areas. Entering the water treatment market in the late 1990s were appliance giant General Electric Co. (GE) and Honeywell International Inc., maker of thermostats and control products. GE officials expected water softening and water filtration products to become a $500 million business within five years. The company's new line included water filtration and water softening products, which the company called "SmartWater." According to the GE, these systems allow homeowners to adjust the softness of the water throughout the home. Benefits, GE said, include prolonged life of water-using appliances and plumbing, cleaner dishes and clothing, and increased water-heater efficiency. Honeywell signaled its entrance into the water-purification market in 1997 with its purchase of Filtercold Inc., a small Arizona-based maker of water-purification systems with between $5 and $10 million in annual sales. Honeywell primarily manufactures whole-house systems designed to remove sediment such as sand and clay. Another industrial behemoth also jumped into the fray as Procter and Gamble acquired Recovery Engineering— maker of Pur water purifiers—for $300 million in 1999. Recovery Engineering had sales of $77 million in the late 1990s.

AIR QUALITY INDUSTRY

Honeywell International Inc. was the leader in the air quality products industry in the late 1990s. Its Home and Building Control division is the division that manufactures and markets air quality systems. Sales for the division in 1999 were approximately $4 billion. The company expanded its product line in 1996 with its acquisition of the Duracraft Corp. of Southborough, Massachusetts, a company with annual sales of about $180 million. The following year, Honeywell's Home and Building Control division also bought Phoenix Controls Corp., which specializes in precision airflow systems. Total sales for Honeywell International Inc. topped $23.7 billion for 1999, placing Honeywell at number 65 in the Fortune 500. The company employed 120,000 people in 1999.

Other leaders in the industry include the Carrier Corp. of Farmington, Connecticut, a subsidiary of United Technologies Corp., and the Research Products Corp. of Madison, Wisconsin. Research Products employed 300 in the late 1990s with annual sales of over $50 million.

AMERICA AND THE WORLD

WATER PRODUCTS SALES GROW ABROAD

The water purification industry has an international scope, in no small part due to the questionable quality of water worldwide. Sales of water purification products to the international community have grown, and companies predicted that foreign exports will continue to increase. In 1997 the Water Quality Association (WQA) reported that approximately 44 percent of its members had a sales office outside the United States. Fifty-six percent indicated that they would acquire new or add to existing facilities outside the United States in the late 1990s. Even relatively small companies (those with revenues of less than $2 million annually) indicated that they will open a sales office offshore. Furthermore, the WQA and its affiliates have been working with the European Committee for Normalization in an effort to harmonize regulations between European countries and the United States to promote global trade.

AIR QUALITY PRODUCTS OVERSEAS

The air purification industry is expected to make large strides overseas as a new century begins. As America toiled to adhere to ever-increasing federal regulations on air pollution, nations around the world struggle with far worse pollution. Companies that focus on commercial applications of air filtration and purification equipment are expected to do even better business overseas. Those firms concentrating on the residential market are expected to do well also, especially in nations with a burgeoning middle class.

RESEARCH AND TECHNOLOGY

WATER QUALITY INDUSTRY

In the late 1990s, research developments in the water purification industry ranged from the simple to the highly complex. All capitalized on America's fear of the water it drinks. On a local level, research that aided drinking water came from watershed management, which helped to keep water clean before becoming polluted. One example was in New York's purification of its water supply by microorganisms as the water percolated through the soil of the Catskills. Any municipality doubting the economic value of prevention rather than cure could look to New York's example: The city planned to spend $660 million to preserve that watershed; the alternative, a water treatment plant, would have cost $4 billion to build. On a national level, watershed management and source water protection was made a part of national policy in the Safe Drinking Water Act Amendment of 1996. The amendment created a revolving fund that would aid states in keeping water supplies in good condition.

More high-technology research came from scientists with the Ernest Orlando Lawrence Berkeley National Laboratory. Dr. Ashok Gadgil's UV Waterworks is a simple device that uses ultraviolet (UV) light to safely and cheaply disinfect water of the viruses and bacteria that causes cholera, typhoid, dysentery, and other deadly diarrheal diseases. The strength of UV Waterworks lies in its differences from other ultraviolet-based water purifiers. The new system does not require pressurized water-delivery systems and electrical outlets to work. It uses gravity for water flow, allowing it to be used with any source of water; in addition, it only needs electricity for the UV light, which means it can be powered by a solar cell or a car battery. This ease of use offers a remarkably practical means of providing communities in developing nations with readily accessible supplies of safe drinking water.

In the UV system, passing water through the light inactivates the DNA of pathogens and purifies the water. The cost is estimated at about two cents per ton. It disinfects water at the rate of four gallons per minute, similar to the flow from a bathtub spout. In the late 1990s, a pilot project was being conducted in India; another was proposed for South Africa. Licensing of the technology is expected to be obtained by EEG Inc. of Chicago; the company will have world-wide rights to the product except in India, where Urminus Industries Ltd. of Bombay holds the rights.

Another research development led to the addition of iodine to water to disinfect as well as purify. One Florida company, Pure H2O Bio-Technologies, noted that the addition of iodine leads to a higher "kill" rate for bacterial pathogens, which can cause a number of diseases such as cholera and cryptosporidiosis. Similar to chlorine in its ability to destroy microorganisms, iodine cannot react with organic compounds to produce any carcinogens. The heightened effectiveness against pathogens can be of some value to the average water drinker, but it can be a matter of life and death for those with impaired immune systems, such as AIDS or cancer patients.

Moreover, with the strong penetration of pitcher water filters, manufacturers began to develop and launch new products with greater filtration capabilities and features in the late 1990s and into the new decade. Manufacturers created the new breed of water filters—removing more harmful microorganisms such as cryptosporidium, giardia, and cysts—to be portable and to monitor filter life electronically. Other developers created a nanoporous filter to remove from water carcinogens normally missed by carbon filters. These "nano sponge" filters are reusable and prevent organic contaminants from breeding after they are trapped. Further, researchers developed a countertop water filtration system using ozone, as used by municipalities and water bottlers for water purification. Since ozone is a very reactive form of oxygen, it can eliminate harmful organisms and substances, thereby enhancing the quality and taste of water.

AIR QUALITY INDUSTRY

By 2000, interest was renewed in UV light technology for the control of bioaerosols, a general name for microbial contaminants including fungi, bacteria, and viruses. These contaminants (and by-products) cause a wide range of adverse health effects, ranging from mild effects such as headaches and fatigue to serious illnesses such as asthma and Legionnaires' disease. Because exposure to UV radiation can adversely affect health, the technology formerly was not widely accepted. In addition, cold temperatures and high air velocity can harm UV lamps. Research in the late 1990s suggested that the high intensity of UV lamps can be maintained in hostile environments. Thus, the technology can be used in mechanical ventilation systems, especially in whole-building cleaning. The new century brought new designs to air purifiers. Instead of the standard box filter, one designer created a unit called the Daisy, which featured seven flowerlike appendages that emit the purified air. In addition, in 2000 Sharper Image released its personal air purifier, the Ionic Breeze Personal Air Purifier, which is worn around the neck. Selling for $60, the unit directs purified air toward the nose and mouth. Sharper Image's products include two innovations. One, they generate air electronically without fans and hence are silent. Two, they do not use filters, but electrostatic grids, which can be cleaned and reused.

FURTHER READING

"Air Filtration Modules Let Smokers 'Indulge.'" *Air Conditioning, Heating, & Refrigeration News,* 3 August 1998.

Blackwood, Francy. "Exporting Clean Air Imports Millions in Revenues." *San Francisco Business Times,* 17 March 1997.

Censky, Peter. "Thirst for Clean Water Boosts Water-Filter Products." *Appliance,* January 1999.

"Consumer Use of Household Water Treatment at an All-Time High as Americans Remain Concerned about Quality." Lisle, IL: Water Quality Association, 16 March 1999.

Eckhouse, Kim. "Culligan Expands Dual-Filtration Faucet-Mount Systems." *HFN,* 16 November 1998.

———. "Next Level in Water Filtration." *HFN,* 19 January 1998.

"EcoWater Profile." Woodbury, MN: EcoWater Systems Inc., 2000. Available from http://www.ecowater.com.

Ghahremani, Yasmin. "Troubled Waters in U.S. Homes." *CNN News,* 28 October 1995. Available from http://cnn.com/EARTH/9510/tap_water/index.html.

"Global Decline in Water Quality a Serious Problem, Say Researchers." *U.S. Water News Online,* July 1996. Available from http://www.uswaternews.com/archives/arcquality/6declwatq.html.

Hamilton, Martha M. "Liquid Assets, Pure and Simple; Bottled, Filtered or Treated, Water Products Tap a Big Market." *Washington Post,* 14 September 1996.

Hanania, Joseph. "Liquid Asset; The Right Filtration System Could Turn Your Hard Water into Pure Pleasure." *Los Angeles Times,* 13 May 1997.

Kerrigan, Karen. "Cleaning Up Indoor Air Carries Big Price Tag." *Washington Business Journal,* 11 November 1996.

Kinetico Inc. "About Kinetico Incorporated." Newbury, OH: Kinetico Quality Water Systems, 1999. Available from http://www.kinetico.com.

"Kinetico Reduces MTBE With Drinking Water Product Line." *PR Newswire,* 15 May 2000.

Lieber, Ed. "Sharper Image Unveils Personal Air Purifier." *HFN,* 20 March 2000.

Liu, Rea-Tiing. "Cleaning the Air." Trade Press Publishing Corp., 1997. Available from http://www.facilitiesnet.com/NS/NS3m7bb.html.

McLean, Bethany. "An Urge to Merge." *Fortune,* 13 January 1997.

McLoughlin, Bill. "Walking on Air." *HFN,* 24 November 1997.

Patton, Carol. "Ametek Moves to Sharpen Its Edge." *Philadelphia Business Journal,* 19 May 1997.

Pinches, Kate. "Water-Filter Pitchers Offer Low-Cost Convenience." *Home Improvement Market,* January 1998.

"President Clinton to Increase Water Quality Monitoring." *U.S. Water News Online,* October 1996. Available from http://www.uswaternews.com/archives/arcquality/6waterqual.html.

Remich, Norman C., Jr. "The 'Wow' Factor." *Appliance Manufacturer,* February 2000.

Romano, Jay. "Straining the Quality of Water." *New York Times,* 10 November 1996.

Sellers, Pamela. "Air's Still Rising." *HFN,* 17 March 1997.

Stevens, William K. "How Much Is Nature Worth? For You, $33 Trillion." *New York Times,* 20 May 1997.

"USGS—Water Resources Data." Reston, VA: U.S. Geological Survey, 1999. Available from http://h2o.er.usgs.gov/data.html.

"Water Filtration Pouring in Sales." *HFN,* 13 April 1998.

Water Quality Association. *1997 National Consumer Water Quality Survey.* Lisle, IL: Water Quality Association, 1999.

———. *Statistical and Market Data: Point-of-Use/Point-of-Entry Water Quality Improvement Industry.* Lisle, IL: Water Quality Association, 1996.

Yarris, Lynn. "Berkeley Lab Scientists Win Two Discover Awards." Berkeley, CA: Ernest Orlando Lawrence Berkeley National Laboratory, 3 June 1996. Available from http://www.lbl.gov/Science-Articles/Archive/Discover-awards.html.

Zaczkiewicz, Arthur. "Department Stores Bring Filtration Upscale." *HFN,* 22 November 1999.

———. "The Discovery Ozone." *HFN,* 13 September 1999.

———. "Get Ready for the Deluge." *HFN,* 16 August 1999.

WEB DEVELOPERS

Web development has come a long way since the World Wide Web was first brought to the public en masse in the mid-1990s. From long, bland pages featuring visually drab text and clumsily placed graphics, or wild eye-candy pages using every trick in the book with little attention to the finer virtues of subtlety, the Web has developed into a sophisticated portal to an endless supply of information and, especially in the late 1990s, commerce. From 10-year-old tech savvies designing intricate sites devoted to their cats to the world's largest multinational corporations, Web pages were an increasingly important source of public identification. By 2000, the World Wide Web had redefined everything from commercial transactions to communication to the daily vernacular. Behind it all are the developers who make the Web work.

By far, the factor most responsible for the rapid evolution of Web site development was the onslaught of electronic commerce (e-commerce). Businesses seeking to hawk products over the Web have spurred the technology and the developers into overdrive in attempts to tailor Web sites and their capabilities to the companies' marketing and distribution needs. With each new generation of server products mitigating low-end headaches such as object management and database connectivity, the role of Web developers was rapidly shifting to the creation of sites that distinguish the company and its product. The net result is a more differentiated Web environment.

International Data Corp. estimated that the market for Internet professional services, which include Web development, could grow from $7.8 billion in 1998 to $78.5 billion by 2003. The research firm ITEu-ropa.com coined the phrase "interactive architects" to describe the emerging companies dominating the race to provide companies with new online outfits to facilitate e-commerce. These companies included marchFIRST, Inc., Agency.com Ltd., and Razorfish, Inc., who more or less made their mark designing "brochure" sites for large corporations. Building on these early relationships, the interactive architects gradually shifted their focus to e-commerce as companies increasingly embraced the medium as a marketing vehicle.

ORGANIZATION AND STRUCTURE

Generally, the goal of a Web site is to combine optimal functionality with a unique and stimulating visual display. To achieve this, clients must clearly inform developers of what purposes their Web sites will serve and what features and information they should include. In return, developers must indicate what they can accomplish given their tools and the current state of technology so that clients do not expect more than developers can reasonably deliver.

Once the site is developed, the developer may take on the role of a Web site custodian, often called a Webmaster, depending on the contract and on the content of the Web site. If a company or organization wishes to keep its site up to date, then such a service is indispensable, whether performed by the developer, a third-party maintenance service, or the client itself.

Ownership of the Web site or its parts also depends on the contract between the developer and client. Some developers retain rights to Web pages and their graphics, but many clients prefer to own the copyright themselves. Ownership can be ambiguous if not negotiated in advance since most sites include content and ideas provided by the client, but encoded and implanted by the developer. Hardware to support the site is usually a separate matter, often provided by third-party vendors. Very little legislation existed in 2000 to guide clients and Web developers in these matters, so both parties eagerly awaited laws that will help avoid litigation stemming from ownership disputes.

Besides commissioning a Web site or purchasing it outright, organizations have two other options: renting a site or paying an initial fee and sharing the revenues the site generates. Renting is an economical method of getting on the Internet for companies with limited budgets, or companies looking to test the efficacy of a Web site. Retailers planning to use Web sites for online commerce could benefit from paying a development fee, which may start at about $20,000, and then paying a percentage of their revenues to the developers. The latter option offers clients shared risk if the site fails to draw many sales.

While one developer can design simple Web sites consisting of a few pages, generally a whole team of Web developers must undertake the design of more complex sites such as online stores or magazines. When working on larger projects, developers usually divide up the labor by allocating specific tasks to specific developers: one developer composes graphics, another codes the functional aspects, and yet another prepares the encoded text. Furthermore, a project manager often coordinates and oversees the entire production of Web sites.

Web pages are written using Hypertext Markup Language (HTML) codes for the basic layout of the site. HTML codes indicate how the information should appear in a browser: centered, boldfaced, colored, and so forth. Each style feature is separately coded. For graphics, developers can place digital photographs and images on pages with HTML codes referencing the external graphics files. Dynamic Internet graphics can be developed through programming languages such as Sun Microsystems, Inc.'s Java or Microsoft Corp.'s ActiveX. These languages allow the creation of active image applications—or applets—that rotate or change their form. Advanced Web authoring tools aid Web site development by allowing developers to use other programming languages such as Visual Basic or C++, or by automating parts of the design process such as writing complex strings of commonly used HTML codes. For instance, a development tool might allow the designer to create a document using standard word-processing techniques, which it converts to HTML. By 2000, Web server vendors were busily developing new customization tools to aid in the construction of networks. While this was intended to ease the developers' workload, this often resulted in having to learn the vendors' specific customization tools in the place of the more widely employed languages. Developers often decried these programs as stifling creativity and their companies' autonomy by tying them to the vendors' tools.

The Internet Engineering Task Force (IETF) functions as an organization of vendors, designers, operators, and researchers concerned with the progress of Internet operation and development. Founded in 1986, the IETF consists of a series of work groups responsible for various aspects of Internet operation and architecture. In 1996, the World Wide Web Consortium (W3C), an international group of Internet researchers—with the backing of both Netscape Communications Corp. and Microsoft Corp., the bitterly embattled manufacturers of browser technology—started to assume responsibility for developing HTML and Web authoring standards. Founded in 1994, the W3C strives to develop the Internet as an accessible and freely available worldwide medium, not dependent on proprietary features or specifications. The consortium is headed by the Massachusetts Institute of Technology's Laboratory for Computer Science and the National Institute for Research in Computer Science and Control, a public French research institute. In 2000, Tim Berners-Lee, the original author of HTML, served as the director of the W3C.

As Web development companies expanded their operations into providing online solutions to marketing needs and infrastructures, they increasingly squared off against major consulting firms. Since large consultancies generally contract, however, with major technology firms such as IBM Corp. for such work, development companies are often able to outprice them. This development portends the likelihood of a new competition between such firms for skilled personnel and, according to some observers, will eventually lead to a wave of merger activity.

BACKGROUND AND DEVELOPMENT

If the Internet and the World Wide Web had to be traced back to one man, it would inevitably fall on the shoulders of Ted Nelson. Although many different people have developed and designed the Web and the Internet as it is today, they would all agree their ideas were based in some way on Nelson's vision.

Nelson is credited as the inventor of hypertext, a term he coined in 1965, which is the basis for HTML, the language for designing Web pages. In 1960 Nelson began to envision computer networks as the repository of all human documentation, with notions of hyperlinked text and media, an almost unheard of concept at the time.

Prior to the advent of graphic Internet capabilities associated with the World Wide Web, however, the Internet offered little to the average person or even to companies. Scholars, businesses, and the U.S. military made up the primary users of Internet at this time. Use centered on exchange of information: posting text-only documents on browsable directory trees called gophers, and sending messages.

In 1990 Tim Berners-Lee created both HTML and the Hypertext Transfer Protocol (HTTP) that enables the global transfer of Web information, effectively developing the World Wide Web as it is known today. Three years later, the graphical Web browser revolutionized the medium and helped launch the Internet into mainstream society in the United States and across the globe. The National Center for Supercomputing Applications at the University of Illinois Urbana-Champaign developed the first browser, Mosaic, and licensed it to Spyglass, Inc., which in turn licensed it to other companies.

In 1995, as Web site development began to flourish as an industry, Kyle Shannon, cofounder of the Web design firm Agency.com Ltd., started the World Wide Web Artists Consortium to serve the needs and interests of Web site developers. The organization's focal points included advertising, digital imaging and graphics, e-commerce, Internet law, and database integration.

As more consumers subscribed to Internet service providers such as America Online, Microsoft Network, and Netcom, businesses and organizations began to use the Internet for more than internal company and organization communication. They found that they could promote, and in some cases deliver, their products and services via the World Wide Web. Unless they had a technically savvy staff, however, they could not expect to create a very exciting, functional, and informative Web site. Therefore, companies and organizations outsourced this task to competent agencies or individuals familiar with Web page creation. In addition, many software companies such as Microsoft and Novell developed HTML editing applications to allow users to create their own Web pages with templates and coding tools. Older programs required some familiarity with HTML and enabled

HTML novices to create only fairly generic pages based on templates or automated code generators known as "wizards." While newer programs made Web authoring easier, most still lacked capabilities for automated creation of original logos, graphics, and images that are common elements to Web pages. Hence, while Web developers may have started out by creating a basic, no-nonsense Web site, they evolved alongside the technology and came to provide more advanced services and greater expertise in Web site design that commercial software cannot provide.

CURRENT CONDITIONS

For several years, Web developers were torn between two competing browser standards: those of Netscape and those of Microsoft. Since each company's browser read similar coding in different ways as a result of the implementation of proprietary software technology, designers were forced to consider a variety of options to make their pages as accessible as possible for their intended audiences; either settling on a particular browser as the standard, creating duplicate pages while directing users to one or the other on the site's home page, or attempting to compromise in the coding so as to produce as little friction as possible between the competing browsers and their users. Both Netscape and Microsoft would submit their standards to the W3C so as to release news to the effect that their browsers were on the way to standardization. The net result was to keep Web developers focused on the lowest common denominator to ensure the greatest degree of backwards compatibility.

By 2000, the battle continued, but its rough edges were somewhat smoothed over when both companies retooled their rendering engines, the components that actually interpret the coding, to be compatible with emerging W3C standards. The development portends a less maddening future for Web developers, and could free up some of the more high-end technological and design developments for wider implementation.

High-end rich media capabilities afford Web developers the ability to create highly complex, visually stimulating, and interactive Web graphics and features, but by 2000, professional developers tended to use rich media only sparingly, for several reasons. Perhaps most crucially, developers recognize that a relatively small proportion of the browsing population actually has the bandwidth capable of effectively reading or even downloading such complex displays; despite the surging growth in e-commerce and Internet connectivity, only about 20 percent of the wired population was expected to use high-speed digital subscriber line (DSL) or cable modems by 2003, by the most optimistic projections, although this complication was significantly less pronounced for developers working on Web sites geared toward business-to-business activity. Moreover, current technology renders the delivery of rich media exceptionally complex, often requiring separate server infrastructure to set up. Nonetheless, with increasingly integrated standards, rich media was expected to gain an increasing foothold on the Web. By 2000, rich media was finding extensive application in e-commerce sites devoted to the online sale and distribution of music and video.

In 1999 and early 2000, a series of high-profile hackings into major commerce sites alarmed observers of the emerging electronic marketplace and focused developers' attention on heightening security measures. The Computer Emergency Response Team (CERT) Coordination Center at Carnegie Mellon University released a joint statement in February 2000 pertaining to the proliferation of software scripts hackers can post to Web sites unbeknownst to site operators. The scripts allow outsiders to access the systems to sabotage the infrastructure or intercept crucial information such as passwords or consumer profiles, including credit-card numbers. To protect their sites, CERT advised developers to recode dynamically produced sites to filter content during download and to dynamically code and filter incoming data from order forms and other messages. More broadly, IBM chief Louis Gerstner issued his own incentive to the e-commerce community to drastically step up security measures, noting simply that if companies didn't take such measures, government would, a development to which businesses would likely be ill-disposed.

Analysts were also advising increased care in the construction of Web sites, since, according to Forrester Research, a site fix can cost between $8,500 and $17,000, while a complete overhaul can run as high as $1.56 million. In the late 1990s, the average Web site cost about $267,000, while some ran over $3.4 million. To avoid such steep payments, observers noted, developers would do well to conduct a series of usability tests. Usability describes the access and information-retrieval capabilities a user experiences when visiting a site. Developers were charged with maintaining constant cognizance of variations in users' technological capabilities.

Meanwhile, activists for the disabled increasingly pressured Congress to enact legislation to push Web site operators toward greater accessibility for those with disabilities, particularly the blind. Under Title III of the Americans with Disabilities Act, public ac-commodations are required to be handicap-accessible. Leading the activists was the W3C, which held that the Web can use computers to transmit information in a variety of ways, including streaming audio, that accommodate the needs of the disabled. The legal applicability to the Internet of the Title III provisions, which are generally geared toward physical structures such as schools, remained unclear in early 2000, though some Internet industry proponents were calling for government-funded research to find the most effective way to implement such accessibility.

The Web development industry experienced a spate of consolidations in the late 1990s as a number of developers attempted to establish themselves as industry leaders. While there were about 40,000 Web developers overall, Forrester Research reported that only about 10 to 20 developers court major corporate accounts. In order to pique the curiosity of big companies, Web developers have merged to demonstrate that they are large and diverse enough to handle such accounts. For example, Web developers such as Agency.com and Razorfish made a plethora of acquisitions in the late 1990s, while USWeb/CKS, in perhaps a premonition of things to come, merged with the consultancy firm Whittman-Hart, Inc. in early 2000.

INDUSTRY LEADERS

The USWeb/CKS merger with Whittman-Hart created the industry giant marchFIRST, Inc., signifying the date of the deal in 2000. The move was intended to integrate the creative Web capabilities of USWeb/CKS with Whittman-Hart's experience in working with firms for their development needs. USWeb went on an expansion spree in the late 1990s to become the industry's biggest player. Founded in 1995, USWeb averaged an acquisition a month during the late 1990s. The developer specialized in helping businesses market themselves via the Internet, by designing intranets, extranets, Web sites, and Internet commerce systems. The new company expects to generate half its revenue from companies raking in revenues of less than $1 billion, 30 percent from Global 1,000 clients, and 20 percent from Internet start-ups. The firm also expects to compete in the world of big-time consulting against such global giants as Andersen Consulting and McKinsey Consulting & Co. The company released pro forma combined income statements for fiscal years 1998 and 1999, showing 1999 revenues of $1.13 billion, up from $822.8 million the year before. The company operates in 14 countries worldwide and employs 3,900.

Based in New York, Agency.com has successfully courted such major corporate clients as Metropolitan Life Insurance Co., American Express Co., Nike, Reuters, and GTE. Kyle Shannon and Chan Suh founded the firm in 1995 with only $80 and two employees. In 1996, the advertising powerhouse, Omnicom Group, acquired Agency.com for its Communicade division, its interactive marketing arm. In the following years, with strong corporate backing, Agency.com acquired Online Magic, a Web design company based in the United Kingdom with clients such as the *Economist* and Simon & Schuster, as well as Interactive Solutions and Spiral Media. In 1998, Agency.com continued its expansion by merging with Interactive Solutions, followed by an acquisition of Omnicom's Eagle River Interactive the following year, dramatically increasing its size before going public in late 1999. Agency.com was particularly drawn to the emerging wireless e-commerce market, reorganizing to focus more heavily on the convergence of the Web and wireless telephones. The company was an early member of the association that developed the Wireless Access Protocol (WAP) mobile Internet access specification. With clients in the United States, Europe, and Asia, Agency.com employed 1,100 people, bringing in sales of $87.8 million in 1999, 40 percent of which was garnered from companies committed to retainer relationships with Agency.com.

Through acquisitions, Razorfish became one of the industry's leading companies in the late 1990s, designing sites as well as refitting them for e-commerce capability. After buying Sunbather, CHBI, Plastic, Spray, and Avalanche Systems, Razorfish added such clients as the *Financial Times* to its roster of Web design clients, which included the *Wall Street Journal,* Time Warner, Charles Schwab, and CBS. With these acquisitions, Razorfish took a key step towards providing coast-to-coast service in the United States as well as in the globalization of the industry. In 1999, the company went public in an effort to raise additional money for expansion. Razorfish continued its aggressive acquisition campaign in 1999, boosting revenues 103 percent to $170.18 million and its payroll to 1,350 employees.

WORK FORCE

Web site developers launch their careers from a host of backgrounds. Some started out as graphic designers, while others trained as computer programmers. Moreover, a significant contingent switched to Web site design from a multitude of unrelated fields.

Knowledge of graphic design and computer programming facilitate Web site development, though many designers pick these skills up from Web development literature or from college courses on HTML and Web site design. Furthermore, certain Web authoring tools cater to novice programmers and require no familiarity with HTML or Java. Due to the rapid development of Web sites, however, education is something of a constant.

According to the *New York Times,* Web developers typically earned about $30,000 a year for HTML authoring and $100,000 a year for advanced programming using CGI and Perl—programming languages for advanced site functions such as image maps, forms, and database queries. Long-term job market projections, however, remain uncertain because software producers such as Microsoft, Adobe, and Novell continue to refine programs to streamline and simplify Web authoring. While such developments could diminish the value of such skills as HTML authoring, developers will be forced to market themselves on their creative expertise as it relates to page and infrastructure design, and the extent to which they can tailor that expertise to specific needs.

RESEARCH AND TECHNOLOGY

With mobile phone subscriptions projected to reach 500 million worldwide by 2003, and with 75 percent of those phones Internet-enabled through WAP and the Short Messaging Service (SMS), Web developers were already beginning to reconceptualize their design methods to allow for greater compatibility with this wireless medium, which differs markedly from the personal computer. By 2000, most "smart phones" were strictly text-based and could display only a few lines at any one time. SMS transmissions can rarely receive more than 160 characters in a single message, and thus split longer transmissions into separate messages. Studies have found mobile-phone users to be especially irritable when it comes to complex and multistep data reception, and thus Web developers were under pressure to simplify their content for this medium. For the time being, mobile Web development necessitates yet another set of languages: Handheld Device Markup Language (HDML) and Wireless Markup Language (WML). The pace at which these languages would be made compatible with standard languages such as HTML and XML (Extensible Markup Language) for seamless cross-format integration was yet to be determined. While the mobile Web format was in the gestation period and

A web designer at work. (Fieldmark Publications/Robert J. Huffman)

will develop rapidly, the intensifying consumer demand for perpetual connectivity will force Web developers to speed such accessibility no matter what the state of the format. Developers, used to constantly upgrading their work, will simply transform that experience to the mobile Web forum.

Computer hardware and software firms, meanwhile, have been hard at work developing systems aimed at facilitating the nonspecialist by taking some of the arcane nature out of Web authoring. Apple's WebObjects includes tools designed to simplify the deployment of the various languages and multimedia formats for a number of common standards. Microsoft's technology builds on its Distributed interNet Architecture (DNA) to offer features including Linkexchange software to facilitate the exchange of banner advertisements, messaging systems, identification and payment technology, and software to aid in users' system upgrades.

Emerging programming and Web design tools of the late 1990s included Dynamic Hypertext Markup Language (DHTML). DHTML provides users with greater control than conventional HTML for positioning graphics, frames, and text on Web pages. This technology includes cascading style sheets, which give Web designers complete control over the placement of text, images, and audio files on Web sites. Microsoft created scriplets, which are reusable segments of DHTML code, to offer programmers some advantages over Java. Like Java applets, Web designers can use scriplets to develop dynamic Web pages, but scriplets also allow developers to save and reuse parts of the code, such as the coding for navigation bars.

HTML does not easily allow the manipulation of data, and is hardly adequate to intelligently process information for e-commerce, since the language ascribes no meaning or value to any information. XML, on the other hand, was quickly emerging as "the lingua franca of e-commerce," according to Kristin Weller of the leading XML firm WebMethods, because it can actually interpret the meaning of words and figures such as product names and prices. With the refining of XML and its positioning as the dominant new high-end standard, some were pronouncing the era of Java over. XML is another permutation of HTML, which is also akin to Standard Generalized Markup Language (SGML), a markup language used for defining structure and content descriptions of electronic documents. Consequently, with its text parsing, tree management, and formatting capabilities, XML creates electronically sorted and searchable Web pages.

The XML specification, owned by the W3C, was developed for hierarchical data organization, with software interpreting the codes to reproduce the desired structure. In early 2000, the W3C rolled out its new XHTML 1.0 specification, which combines XML with HTML, essentially offering a bridge from the traditional HTML world to the future dominated by XML. The W3C simply took their most recent HTML version, HTML 4.0, and steered it toward XML to produce the new XHTML standard. XHTML allows for the merging of a page's data with its layout, thus facilitating easier manipulation and redesign. The integration of mobile transmission capabilities will be made significantly smoother through adoption of XHTML since mobile devices can simply ignore the data that is irrelevant or incompatible with their format.

FURTHER READING

Costlow, Terry. "Web Sites Begin To Focus On Accessibility." *Electronic Engineering Times,* 13 November 2000.

DeMarzo, Robert C. "Are You Like Agency.com? Our Survey Says 'Yes.'" *VAR Business,* 13 December 1999.

Dunn, Ashley. "Online Exchanges Open Door Wider for Technology Firms." *Los Angeles Times,* 20 March 2000.

Gunther, Tom. "Success with XML." *EXE,* 1 April 1999.

Harrison, Ann. "CERT Warns of Malicious Code on Web Sites." *Network World,* 3 February 2000.

Hayden, David. "Hello, Half a Billion of Us Want the Net via Phone." *Internet World,* 15 November 1999.

Head, Alison J. "Web Redemption and the Promise of Usability." *Online Magazine,* November 1999.

Jastrow, David. "Agency.com Set for Explosion of Mobile Internet Devices—Gearing up for Wireless Future." *Computer Reseller News,* 13 March 2000.

———. "USWeb/CKS Wants to marchFIRST." *Computer Reseller News,* 27 March 2000.

Krebs, Brian. "Congress Considers Handicapped-Accessible Web Sites." *Newsbytes,* 9 February 2000.

Levitt, Jason. "The Rendering Wars Emerge." *InformationWeek,* 20 March 2000.

Liebmann, Lenny. "App Servers Branch Out—E-commerce Shifts Developers' Focus to Customization." *InformationWeek,* 4 October 1999.

"Microsoft Builds on DNA for Web Builders." *Computing,* 16 September 1999.

Middleton, James. "E-business: Putting Markup Language in the Future Tense." *Network News,* 9 February 2000.

"Netviews: How XHTML Will Revolutionize the Web." *Network News,* 23 February 2000.

Pence, William. "Despite Growing Pains, Rich Media Has Bright Future." *iMarketing News,* 19 November 1999.

Poydner, Richard. "New Kids on the Digital Block." *Financial Times,* 1 March 2000.

Ward, Eric. "Equal Access Still Rare on the Web." *BtoB,* 9 October 2000.

"Web Function and Design." *Folio Hot Magazine Jobs Supplement,* December 2000.

WEB PORTALS AND ONLINE COMMUNITIES

According to two Internet research companies, Nielsen NetRatings and Media Matrix, each of the World Wide Web's 10 most heavily trafficked sites in 2000 was a Web portal, some of which sat at the very hub of the much-heralded New Economy. Often considered synonymous with "search engines," Web portals are actually far broader, though most include search engines in their arsenals. Web portals fulfill several different functions, and in fact their range of services was expanding almost daily in the late 1990s and early 2000s. At their most basic, they act as a sort of gateway to the World Wide Web, providing a starting point through which users can choose the direction in which they wish to go with the aid of the portal's extensive categorization and search engines. In addition, they provide original content, such as news and business headlines, and other features such as chat rooms and customization options.

As the Web became increasingly central to the world of commerce (and vice versa), so Web portals assumed a more commercial presence, not only acting as a central medium for companies to advertise and reach customers, but often acting as online merchants themselves. Inside the giant Yahoo! Labyrinth, for instance, consumers could hop around the different stores accumulating merchandise as if in a mall, and pay for the entire lot in one fell swoop.

While Web portals were indeed all the rage by 2000, several obstacles still kept the industry grounded. For instance, it was a rare Web portal that was actually making a profit, despite their popularity. Moreover, most portals were expected to see diminishing activity compared with the industry giants in the early 2000s. Forrester Research predicted that the percentage of Internet traffic commanded by the top-nine Web portals would reach 20 percent by 2003 from 15 percent in 1998. Thus, smaller players would likely find themselves scrambling for merger and acquisition partners.

Online communities are often a part of Web portals or can be completely separate entities. Such communities provide space where those with common interests or characteristics—such as women, basketball lovers, musicians, or any other group—can virtually meet and exchange information and ideas through bulletin boards, chat rooms, and e-mail lists. Most major Web portals included at least some of these elements. Like Web portals, as well, online communities proved a popular method of putting businesses in touch with each other.

Web portals come in a variety of flavors. The most well-known variety was the enormous generalist site, featuring a search engine, links pointing in all directions of the Internet, and an array of content for the average Net surfer. Modern Web portals generally include, but are not limited to, search engines. Since search engines, however, simply allow users to go elsewhere, Web portals realized that to keep Web users around on their sites, thereby attracting more advertising revenue, they needed to add value by expanding options and services. Depending on its precise focus and target audience, a Web portal typically augments its basic search engine and site categorization with additional services such as e-mail, chat rooms, virtual shopping centers, and directories.

By early 2000, most Web portals had begun to open online malls in a full embrace of electronic commerce (e-commerce), while streamlining their existing shopping services by adding ease-of-use features. For example, Excite@Home's Excite Shopping Service was designed to provide users with the ability to seek out a range of products, compare prices, and keep abreast of product availability, while America Online, Inc.'s ShopAOL offered electronic wallets, in which customers could store credit-card numbers and Web sites and easily toggle between product categories with a click of the mouse.

Along with the flourishing of e-commerce, a new breed of Web portals have cropped up, known as vertical portals, which focus not on general subject areas for any and all audiences but on specific users looking for specific sites or categories. Mostly, vertical portals are concentrated in the business-to-business (B2B) e-commerce sector, putting suppliers in touch with buyers and creating communities within industries. B2B portals enable companies to instantaneously compare prices and availability across a range of suppliers, and facilitate faster ordering and delivery. Vertical portals have also been constructed outside the B2B realm, catering to customers looking for certain kinds of products. Fashionmall.com, for instance, was a vertical portal designed to assist customers seeking out name-brand clothing.

Indeed, portals were beginning to emerge as the standard model by which businesses and information were organized. Companies began rearranging their manufacturing, advertising, and finance operations into a portal framework around the turn of the century, making applications simple to access and navigate. Business portals arrange corporate software and applications to perform their functions in the most efficient manner and facilitate the easy access of internal and external information. Software and Web giants, such as America Online and Netscape, have helped build customized Web portals for corporations such as FedEx and Lucent to allow their employees quick access to company software and information from Netscape's NetCenter Web site. This practice stands to revolutionize the business computing process, replacing the standard personal computer desktop applications with Web-based portals.

BACKGROUND AND DEVELOPMENT

Most of the major Web portals started out as simple search engines. As a result of the perpetual battle to draw more users, these search engines, including Yahoo!, Infoseek, Lycos, HotBot, Excite, and others, enhanced their home pages with expanded features and information. They began to streamline their Web site indexes to offer news headlines, sports scores, wire services, technology-based links, travel pages, and an almost endless supply of other features that added value to their sites, and invited users to stick around, drawing advertisers in their wake. By 1997, the leading Web portals, such as Yahoo!, recognized that many users felt simply overwhelmed with information and options when they hopped on the Web, and thus the portals began offering services, such as My Yahoo!, that allowed users to customize their options.

Rather quickly, Web portals became among the most famed of the dot-com companies, and greatly facilitated the onslaught of e-commerce, as companies eyeing their success at attracting Web surfers fell over themselves to establish marketing deals with the portal firms, which commanded handsome fees for the service.

For the most part, up until mid-1998, dot-com companies knew their places; while the e-tailers engaged in the commerce, the Web portals provided a site on which the merchants could hawk their goods. By 1999, things had begun to change, and Web portals began to aggressively promote new shopping sites and other e-commerce services directly on their own sites, while still maintaining their marketing contracts with e-merchants. Excite, for instance, launched its Express Order site at which customers could make purchases from any of the company's affiliated vendors, while Lycos, Inc. initiated an online store where customers could use a single interface to shop from more than 200 retailers.

CURRENT CONDITIONS

In the early 2000s, one of the most striking facts about Web portals, and indeed, much of the dot-com juggernaut in general, was that extremely few of them were yet operating in the black. Investors had hardly soured on Web portals, however. Indeed, Web portals were the second-best performing dot-com stock sector in 1999. For their part, the major Web portals were busily consolidating the dot-com industry in the late 1990s, buying up search engines, databases, and forming alliances with established portals, Internet service providers, and e-tailers. For instance, Infoseek, one of the leading early Web portals, teamed up with the Walt Disney Co. to create the giant GO.com, while Excite was purchased by Internet service provider @Home to create Excite@Home. Jupiter Communications, Inc., meanwhile, estimated that e-commerce emerging from Web portals would account for 20 percent of all online purchases by 2002, amounting to $8.7 billion, compared with about $2.4 billion in 1998.

Business-to-business (B2B) portals came into their own in 1999, providing companies with an extremely efficient way in which to procure equipment, supplies, and services, although the trend created a panic among manufacturing companies who feared the practice would undermine their operations and lead to diminished margins. Forrester Research expected that such portals would account for just over half of the $2.7 trillion in B2B e-commerce by 2004. While manufacturers scrambled for strategies to meet the rapidly shifting market conditions created by B2B portals, some have jumped on board in full force, even creating portals of their own. DuPont helped prepare the launch of Yet2.com as an electronic marketplace for technology purchasing, and teamed up with the Redwood City, California-based ImproveNet Inc. to create a construction-material portal and with Spec-Chem.com Inc. of Houston to build a site for chemicals.

Portals also tended to enjoy a surprising degree of loyalty. As customers became acclimated to one particular gateway's services and search methods, they often felt reluctant to deal with others. On the flip side of that loyalty was the "one-chance" mentality of users when it came to system crashes. Outside of the largest sites, users were quite often unforgiving of sites that delivered error messages and crashes. Thus, Web portals hoping to attract a lot of traffic were bound to extensively stress-test their systems to be sure they could handle the flood of site hits they hoped to generate.

Ironically, the borderless world of the Internet also helped local communities and businesses in some cases stave off competition from the encroachment of national chains and e-commerce giants. Local businesses have banded together to establish local portals as virtual neighborhoods in order to direct those in the community to the commerce, entertainment, and other Web sites and physical locations that will keep money and interest circulating inside the community. Ideally, local Web portals not only could keep small businesses alive in the New Economy and amidst the merger mania of the Old Economy, but could even help promote an active community life, providing links to local governments and organizations in addition to businesses, as well as keeping citizens on top of the local Little League standings or the results of the high school basketball team's game.

Local content was indeed one of the great prizes of the dot-com companies in 2000, and local portals generally found that they rarely had to pull teeth to persuade local businesses to sign up, usually for a monthly fee that could range from about $30 to $400, depending on the level of service provided by the portal. Local newspapers, with mountains of local content, also got into the act and helped propel the local portal craze by simply uploading their extensive files to the Web. The *Boston Globe,* for instance, created Boston.com in 1995 to link to other media in the Boston area, much to the skepticism of their brethren in the newspaper business. Soon, the site had developed into a full-blown portal, and was so successful that most other media were following suit by the turn of the century.

Like most portals, of course, it was a rare local portal that was making money in 2000, though they held great potential for expanded advertising revenues. Some were beginning to take on a localized version of the expansion of services offered by the major Web portals.

Media outlets, in general, quickly upgraded their Web sites to the portal model. The New York Times Co., Knight Ridder, and Dow Jones & Co. all announced plans to develop their sites into portals in 1999. It was hoped that, in this way, traffic on their sites would boom and advertisers would come calling, providing the ad revenue that lay at the heart of most newspaper companies' business.

Just as new Web portals were popping up continuously in the early 2000s, each with more and more specific audiences and functions, so online communities were created to bring together groupings of almost every conceivable variety. iVillage.com brought women together, Cancer.Home provided a place for cancer sufferers and their loved ones to exchange thoughts and feelings, and TheKnot.com helped engaged couples come together to share jitters and compare honeymoon and child plans. The Gay.com Network, formed by the merger of three online communities devoted to gay and lesbian Netizens, was one of the largest online communities.

Companies such as Participate.com specialized in helping businesses build online communities for business-to-business and business-to-customer applications. Online communities were attractive to businesses for fairly obvious reasons, aside from simply getting potential customers under their domain. For instance, companies could try to build brand loyalty by offering customers a place to come and share tips and opinions on the latest products, in effect building name recognition and word-of-mouth advertising.

More On

PORTALS AS RESEARCH AIDS

Though you might not know it from the euphoric press reports on the New Economy, Web portals actually served functions other than the facilitation of e-commerce. In fact, some portals were designed specifically to help researchers take advantage of the fabled information superhighway that received so much attention as the World Wide Web first achieved widespread popularity in the mid-1990s. Universities and corporations spent a good deal of time and money creating portals to act as virtual libraries for their research purposes, tailoring the categories, search engines, and databases to meet their specific needs. Enterprise information portals (EIPs) organize information along company, product, or topic lines for the purpose of integrating a company's or research outfit's internal and external resources.

One of the first uses of EIPs was by U S West Research & Information Group in 1996. The company's corporate intranet helped them provide customized research services to their clients, who requested information through a central Web page. Over time, these Web pages were customized to the clients' accumulated research practices, displaying current research status and past searches and even providing space for file storage and sharing.

Since then, the systems have found favor on college campuses, both for the entire university and for specific departments' high-level research. For instance, the University of Virginia's Health Sciences Library, the main electronic research facility for all the university's medical programs, implemented personalized portals to integrate research across all areas related to medical practices, including legal and business matters. Researchers were thus relieved of the time-consuming and often-frustrating chores of riffling through journal stacks and between different media.

Businesses, unsurprisingly, were beginning to adopt these customized Web portals in droves by 2000 in order to facilitate everything from market research, product development, advertising campaigns, and corporate structuring.

INDUSTRY LEADERS

With some 55 million visitors each month, Yahoo! Inc. boasted the most popular site on the Web. Unlike many of its chief competitors, however, Yahoo! did not moonlight as an Internet service provider, though the company planned to begin offering Internet access through a partnership with Kmart Corp. The company also branched out its services to include online auctions and retailing as well as e-mail and pag-

ing services. Yahoo! acquired GeoCities, which acted as a series of online neighborhoods for users to establish individual home pages. Based in Santa Clara, California, Yahoo! employed 2,000 workers in 2000, and finished off 1999 with revenues of $588.6 million, an increase of 189 percent over the year before, adding the distinction of being one of the few dot-com enterprises that was in the black, generating net income of $61.1 million. The company's heavy traffic attracted about 5,200 advertisers, Yahoo!'s main source of income, though other fees were extracted from its online auctions, e-commerce, and sponsorship agreements. The site's search engine organized some 1.2 million Web pages.

America Online, Inc. (AOL), the world's leading Internet service provider with 21 million subscribers, also maintained a leading Web portal, with a wide range of content that was greatly expanded and upgraded through its 2000 merger with media giant Time Warner. Based in Dulles, Virginia, the company employed 12,100. Established in 1991, AOL was one of the oldest dot-coms. AOL earned a net income of $1.2 billion in 2000 on revenues of $6.89 billion. Seventy percent of the company's revenues derived from the Internet service provider (ISP) subscription services, while the remainder was spread out over advertising, e-commerce, merchandising, and other sources.

Formed by the merger between the ISP @Home and the longtime Web portal leader Excite in 1999, Excite@Home's content was geared toward business and travel, which was augmented by its Work.com site, the product of a joint venture between the company and Dow Jones. In addition to chat rooms and search engines, the company also offered free e-mail, fax, and voice-mail services. Excite@Home launched a new Web site in early 2000 designed especially for its broadband customers, featuring high-end content such as streaming audio and video clips. The company was also working on a number of acquisitions to broaden its services and boost traffic. Based in Redwood City, California, Excite@Home employed 570 workers. The company's revenues reached $337 million in 1999, although it suffered a net loss of $1.46 billion.

Walt Disney Internet Group of North Hollywood, California, was the Internet arm of the media giant, maintaining the Web sites for ESPN and ABC as well as Disney Online. With 320 employees, the company's portal brought about 23 million visitors a month. Formerly called GO.com, which is still the name of the firm's Web portal, the company also ran Web sites for sporting associations such as the National Basketball Association, the National Football League, and

NASCAR. GO.com was the fruit of the merger between portal giant Infoseek and Disney's Buena Vista Internet Group, and the portal's forte, fittingly, was entertainment content. In 2000, the network's sales jumped 600 percent to reach $368.5 million, but operated in the red, with a net loss of $1 billion.

The software giant Microsoft Corp. counted the MSN.com portal, the third-most-visited site on the Web after Yahoo! and AOL, as part of its empire. Microsoft rolled out the Microsoft Network (MSN) in 1995, finally embracing the Internet, and MSN.com emerged as a force in the Web portal industry by 1998. MSN.com featured gift certificates, buyer's guides, and an e-wallet known as a "Passport" to store credit-card information and facilitate e-commerce, especially through its MSN marketplace. Microsoft was also hard at work building ways to link its software to the MSN portal. Microsoft's total sales reached $22.9 billion in 2000.

Lycos maintained the fourth-most-heavily trafficked site on the Web in 2000. The company enjoyed an exceptionally strong presence in Europe through its partnership with German media behemoth Bertelsmann AG, and also operated in Latin America and Asia. The Waltham, Massachusetts-based company's family included a series of popular Web sites such as HotBot, Wired News, Tripod, and Angelfire. The portal drew some 33 million visitors each month. About 70 percent of the company's revenue came from advertising, though it also maintained commercial partnerships with AT&T Corp. and Barnes & Noble. In 1999, Lycos planned a merger with USA Networks, Inc., but the deal fell though. Lycos also moonlighted as a venture capital firm, forming Lycos Ventures and LycosLabs to fund new dot-com start-ups. Started as a search engine in 1994, the Lycos company was founded a year later and went public in 1996. Lycos suffered a net loss of $52 million in 1999 on sales of $135.5 million, and employed 785 workers.

VerticalNet, Inc. was a leader in the business-to-business portal sector, with over 55 Web sites spread across disparate industries. The company also ran online communities related to chemical companies, food processing, and municipal water and waste treatment. Based in Horsham, Pennsylvania, VerticalNet maintained a payroll of nearly 700 employees in 2000. Founded in 1995, the company bought its way into prominence through scores of Web site acquisitions over the years before going public in 1999. The portal was home to a number of industry-specific sites, including career centers, buyer's guides, and news resources. The company also engaged in its own e-com-

merce and even held online auctions. VerticalNet expanded into Europe through a partnership with British Telecommunications and Internet Capital Group; together, the three companies ran VerticalNet Europe. The bulk of the firm's revenue derived from advertising. The company generated a net loss of $53.5 million on revenues of $20.8 million in 1999.

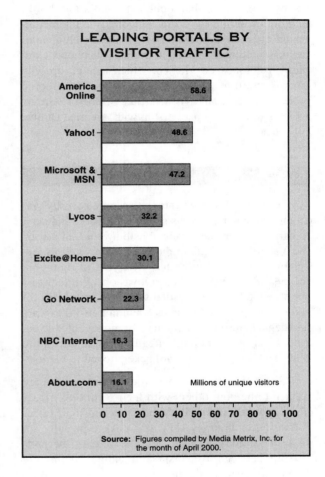

LEADING PORTALS BY VISITOR TRAFFIC

Portal	Millions of unique visitors
America Online	58.6
Yahoo!	48.6
Microsoft & MSN	47.2
Lycos	32.2
Excite@Home	30.1
Go Network	22.3
NBC Internet	16.3
About.com	16.1

Source: Figures compiled by Media Metrix, Inc. for the month of April 2000.

AMERICA AND THE WORLD

Most of the major Web portals maintained some sort of presence in the European market, often through joint ventures with foreign subsidiaries. Other markets, however, were seemingly not quite ready for the rush of portals experienced in the United States. In 1999, a flood of established and start-up portals saturated the Latin American market in hopes of getting a leg up in the rapidly expanding Internet market. The rush, however, got a bit ahead of itself, creating a glut of portals and other Internet services that outpaced the market's ability to sustain them, and several Latin American portals, such as StarMedia Network, saw their value decimated by the market. Analysts estimated that the market had room for only about four major portals of the StarMedia variety and was fairly similar for smaller, specialized portals as well.

Still, the Latin American market held great potential. International Data Corp. expected about 30 million Latin Americans to be plugged into the Internet by 2003, more than doubling 2000's total of 14 million. In addition to Terra Networks, the Internet division of Spain's Telefonica, StarMedia's chief competitors included Mexico's leading telephone company, Telefonos de Mexico, which teamed up with Microsoft Corp. to launch a Latin American portal called T1MSN; and Venezuela's Cisneros Group, which maintained a partnership with America Online.

RESEARCH AND TECHNOLOGY

As it was for most Internet sectors, security was among the chief concerns of the Web portal industry. In early 2000, hackers were able to invade and disrupt the Yahoo! site, sending the industry, as well as legislators, into a frenzy of activity trying to figure out the best way to ward off such invasions. While the issue was likely to be wrestled with on Capitol Hill for some time, portal companies could not afford to wait, and began pouring vast amounts of money into the development of technology safeguards in an attempt to plug the security holes that hackers loved to exploit.

Some Web portals even took an interactive approach to helping others with their technology troubles. In April 2000, AltaVista launched its own information technology (IT) help desk especially for IT professionals. The project was born of the partnership between AltaVista and online community Experts Exchange, a collection of IT eggheads. With common troubles categorized by topics such as Java and C++, AltaVista invited users to submit their queries, which were then answered by one of the Experts Exchange crew.

FURTHER READING

Blankenhorn, Dana. "Community Focus." *Advertising Age's Business Marketing,* June 1999.

Carlson, David. "Media Giants Create Web Gateways." *American Journalism Review,* September 1999.

"Click Here to Shop." *Fortune,* winter 2000.

Cohan, Peter. "Internet Sector Watch: Use Last Year's Lessons to Invest in 2000." *Boston Business Journal,* 25 February 2000.

Evarts, Eric C. "Web Shopping That Keeps Dollars Local." *Christian Science Monitor,* 24 April 2000.

Green, Heather, and Linda Himelstein. "Portals Are Mortal after All." *Business Week,* 21 June 1999.

Guenther, Kim. "Customized Data Delivery through Web Portals." *Online,* November/December 1999.

Hall, Mark. "IT Interest in Web Portals Tempered by Security Issues." *Computerworld,* 13 December 1999.

Jacso, Peter. "Rise of the Personalized Web Portals." *Information Today,* July/August 1999.

Kirkpatrick, David. "The Portal of the Future? Your Boss Will Run It." *Fortune,* 2 August 1999.

Malkin, Elisabeth. "Red Flags on the Latin Web." *Business Week,* 17 April 2000.

Notess, Greg R. "On the Net in 2000." *Online,* January 2000.

"Portals Moving Aggressively into E-commerce." *Electronic Advertising & Marketplace Report,* 9 March 1999.

Starr-Miller, Elizabeth. "Portal to the World." *Telephony,* 23 October 2000.

Swisher, Kara. "Behind the Portal." *Wall Street Journal,* 17 April 2000.

Tiazkun, Scott. "Corporate Portals Emerge as Desktop Alternative." *Computer Reseller News,* 26 July 1999.

Vijayan, Jaikumar. "B-to-B Portals Worry Industry." *Computerworld,* 21 February 2000.

WIRELESS COMMUNICATIONS AND WAP

INDUSTRY SNAPSHOT

Known by related monikers such as mobile, cellular, and personal communications services, wireless communications services are a huge and fast-growing business in the United States, and indeed, around the world. Consumers and businesses alike have been electronically tethering themselves in droves with wireless technology because of its convenience and increasing affordability. In 2000 alone, according to industry statistics, wireless carriers signed up about 23 million new subscribers in the United States, for a total of more than 109 million wireless subscribers by year's end. Industry revenue has grown in kind, reaching $45.1 billion that year, up from $37.2 billion in 1999. What's more, the U.S. wireless industry is widely regarded as underdeveloped compared to those of Japan and Western Europe, signaling ample opportunities for continued expansion.

Digital and broadband services are two wireless segments experiencing sharp growth in the early 2000s. Digital wireless services, which include personal communications services (PCS), have been available in the United States since the mid-1990s, but as of 2000 they still accounted for less than half of all wireless subscriptions in the country. Digital represents the so-called second generation of wireless communications, with the first being various analog systems that have been around for decades. Digital encoding enables greater volumes of information to be sent and received by wireless devices, and is capable of delivering higher sound quality and other features found wanting in analog service. Premium digital services offer users such conveniences as text messaging and caller ID.

Meanwhile, broadband wireless, a high-throughput communications link for tasks such as e-mailing and Internet browsing, heralds the third generation—one characterized by unified voice and data communications over digital networks. Using standards such as the nascent Wireless Application Protocol (WAP), broadband services have the potential to deliver applications and data to wireless phones that double as handheld organizers or computers. Much of the content delivered over broadband services, which began widespread rollout only in 2000, is Internet based. With competing interpretations, however, of the WAP standard running rampant among different companies—perhaps belying the existence of a true standard—wholesale adoption of broadband is likely to take longer than some optimistic industry forecasters envisaged.

Indeed, despite the industry's size and prominence, it's one still characterized by a bewildering set of incongruent technologies; there's no single wireless standard or type of wireless service within the United States, much less the world. Major technical distinctions include whether a service uses analog or digital signals, what kind of signal-separation scheme it employs to let multiple users share the same airwaves, and even what radio frequencies it uses. All these differences mean that portable phones and other wireless communications devices will work with some systems, but not others, and in some locations, but not all. This standards melange has resulted from technological change, proprietary competitive strategies of certain companies, and a failure to adopt wider standards before industry players invested heavily in one technology or another. Resolutions have been proposed that could improve cross-system compatibility.

Some industry insiders, however, dismiss the impact of competing standards as negligible, citing that pricing and features—rather than cross-system compatibility—are what drive new subscriptions.

ORGANIZATION AND STRUCTURE

The Federal Communications Commission (FCC) "sells air" by charging companies a fee to gain rights to a certain frequency. Beginning in 1994, for instance, the FCC auctioned off airspace for the new PCS technology and, in 1998 and 1999, it added licenses for local multipoint distribution service. Such purchasers may, in turn, sell air to other parties for a profit. The FCC also regulates and sets guidelines for various aspects of the telecommunications industry, such as cellular telephone service.

The six wireless divisions identified by the FCC—which are by no means equal in size and scope—are commercial mobile radio services, public mobile services, personal communications services, domestic public fixed radio services, private land mobile radio services, private operational-fixed microwave services, and personal radio services. Of these, only the first three are normally considered part of the commercial wireless industry.

COMMERCIAL MOBILE RADIO SERVICE

Commercial mobile radio service includes the cellular telephone industry. Cellular telephone systems use low-power radio-telephone transceivers. The cellular infrastructure in use in the United States at the end of the 1990s was largely analog, meaning that continuous electrical signals send and receive information. This differs from digital communications systems, which use digital signals to send and receive messages. Digital systems create virtually exact replicas of signals because they are fed through computers that assign binary codes—zeroes and ones—to each unit of information; analog systems create only very good copies of signals.

Geographic areas serviced by a cellular carrier are divided into small regions, sometimes only one mile across, called cells. Because of cooperation within the industry, it is possible for the cellular service customers to be "handed off" from one service provider's antenna to another as the user passes from cell to cell.

The advantage of using a cellular system is frequency reuse. Because the FCC grants a limited number of channels, or frequencies, to the cellular telephone service industry, it would be impossible to

have only one, or even a few, transceivers in each service area. Multiple cells allow the same frequency to be used by many callers in the same service area. Furthermore, each cell can be subdivided into sectors, usually three, using directional antennas. As a result, a single service area can have thousands of callers communicating on several hundred designated channels.

PUBLIC MOBILE SERVICES

Public mobile services includes pagers, air-to-ground service (such as aircraft-to-control tower communications), offshore service (for sailing vessels), and rural radio-telephone service.

PERSONAL COMMUNICATIONS SERVICE

Personal communications service (PCS) is a departure from "traditional" wireless telecommunications that require high power and relatively large cells to accommodate phones moving rapidly through space in motor vehicles. PCS systems are digital and are maintained by a network of small transmitter-receiver antennas installed throughout a community—such as on buildings. The antennas are connected to a master telephone switch that is connected to a main telephone network. PCS systems use comparatively low-powered phones that operate at a higher radio frequency. As a result, the systems use smaller cells that allow a greater concentration of users. The net result of PCS differences is a cellular network with as much as 20 times the capacity of a standard cellular service area. This increased capacity allows PCS to spread costs over a potentially larger subscriber base. In addition, PCS phones weigh less and are cheaper to manufacture than their cellular counterparts.

TELECOMMUNICATIONS REFORM ACT OF 1996

The Telecommunications Reform Act, signed into law 8 February 1996, swept away 62 years of regulation of the telecommunications industry. The legislation was intended to promote competition across the industry, thus resulting in the development of new technology, the creation of new business and new jobs, and ultimately lower prices. Local telephone companies, long-distance providers, wireless companies, and cable television operators were, in theory, free to offer any and all telecommunications services. Since all the major landline entities were already cellular providers, this did not have any immediate effect on the wireless industry, but the long-range goal of the major industry players was to provide "one-stop shopping" for consumer or business telecommunications

---

About... WIRELESS ACRONYM SOUP
HAS SOME STEWING

Accompanying the diverse range of technologies now used in the wireless industry has been, predictably, an abundance of technical terms and acronyms. Here's a summary of some of the most common:

- AMPS, or advanced mobile phone service, which dates to the early 1980s, is the most widely used analog wireless standard in the United States. The technology is nearly synonymous with first-generation cellular telephony. Today it's regarded as low tech, but as of 2000 there were still more U.S. subscribers to AMPS cellular services than to any digital format.

- CDMA, short for code division multiple access, is a complicated digital-signal-encoding scheme that lets multiple users share the same frequency. Developed by Qualcomm Inc. in the mid-1990s, CDMA is regarded as technically superior to time-sharing schemes such as TDMA and its international derivative, GSM, but its complexity and incompatibility with the more widely used systems have drawn the ire of some users and industry participants.

- GSM, or global system for mobile communications, is a time-sharing digital wireless standard used mostly outside the United States. In fact, as of 2000, more people used GSM than any other standard, a trend that was expected to continue. For various reasons, however, most U.S. wireless carriers have resisted of-

fering GSM services, rendering many U.S.-based cell phones useless abroad.

- LMDS, which stands for local multipoint distribution service, is a standard for broadband wireless access. The technology has the ability to send and receive high-speed data and even video, and can be used for business or personal Internet access instead of one of the wire-based methods.

- PCS, or personal communications service, is an FCC-designated class of digital wireless services that operate in a certain frequency range and share other characteristics. For most users, though, PCS isn't distinct from other second-generation digital wireless offerings.

- TDMA, or time division multiple access, is another standard for digital multiplexing, or enabling multiple users to share airspace. In essence, each user's signals are assigned to a series of tiny time slots that don't overlap with other users'. Some regard TDMA as inferior to CDMA, although several large U.S. carriers still back TDMA.

- WAP, the Wireless Application Protocol, is a communications and software standard for transmitting and displaying data over wireless networks, especially Internet content and functions. WAP can be used over any of the digital wireless formats (CDMA, TDMA, GSM) but requires special handling on both the sending and receiving ends.

---

needs. Mergers, acquisitions, and various kinds of joint ventures, already common in the wireless segment, drastically reshaped the broader telecommunications industry as companies tried to position themselves for future growth.

BACKGROUND AND DEVELOPMENT

The Detroit Police Department used one of the first mobile radio systems on 7 April 1928. The spectrum for radio transmission was broadened seven years later to include FM, or frequency modulation, signals. FM transmission technology paved the way for the mobile radio systems that were widely used during World War II. After the war, American Telephone and Telegraph (AT&T)—which at that time held a virtual monopoly over phone service in America—introduced the Improved Mobile Telephone Service, which made possible extremely limited cellular communication systems. The service was so restrictive that even by

1970, the Bell system in the city of New York could simultaneously sustain a total of only 12 mobile phone conversations.

Around 1980, under the guidance of AT&T, the first practical framework for mobile service in the United States, advanced mobile phone service (AMPS), was born. The FCC allocated space for AMPS in Washington, D.C., as a test market, but it was not until 1983, in the Chicago and Baltimore markets, that companies provided relatively inexpensive, efficient consumer cellular service in the United States.

In the mid-1980s cellular service grew rapidly in the industrialized world with the implementation of different networking systems in North America, parts of Europe, and Japan. The first generation of technology quickly ran its course, expanding to the furthest reaches of the airspace spectrum allocated for it; this was particularly true in Europe, where in the mid- to late 1980s the second generation of mobile communications technology was born.

The first PCS licenses, for the 51 major trading areas in the United States, were auctioned off between December 1994 and March 1995. A total of 18 bidders won 99 licenses, generating $7.7 billion for the U.S. Treasury. Sprint Spectrum, an alliance of Sprint Corp. and several cable TV concerns, spent $2.1 billion for 29 licenses. AT&T Wireless took 21 licenses for $1.69 billion, and PrimeCo, a venture of AirTouch Communications, Bell Atlantic, NYNEX Corp., and U S West Inc. spent $1.11 billion for 11 licenses.

The number of licenses purchased for each market put tremendous competitive pressure on everyone. Financial pressure was also great because of the cost of building the networks, along with the cost of the licenses. After purchasing these licenses, many PCS providers faced financial difficulty. Moreover, many communities opposed the construction of the many transmitting towers necessary for the low-power networks. The FCC, however, along with most industry observers, expected the investment to pay off bountifully within 10 years.

In the late 1990s, PCS carriers began adopting new networks that included both wire and wireless technology. Known as the "hybrid approach," the blend of wire and wireless technology allows carriers to bypass the traditional stationary wireless local loop technology, according to *Telephony*. U S West and BellSouth were among the first companies to choose the hybrid approach for their services. Europe has already widely developed this kind of integrated network.

CURRENT CONDITIONS

EARLY SIGNS OF MATURITY

Amid torrid growth since the mid-1990s, the wireless services industry has begun to show early signs of maturation. For one, mergers and acquisitions have concentrated ever greater market share in the hands of a few multinational players such as Verizon Wireless—a melding of AirTouch, Vodafone, GTE, and Bell Atlantic Corp.'s wireless interests. Regional Bells SBC Communications Inc. and BellSouth Corp. also announced in 2000 a merger of their wireless units, forming Cingular Wireless. The top-three U.S. carriers—Verizon, Cingular Wireless, and AT&T Wireless—controlled more than half the domestic wireless market by the end of 2000.

For the years 1999 and 2000, average wireless prices appeared to finally reach a plateau after a decade of annual declines, as major carriers began to focus more on solidifying financial returns over luring in new customers with unsustainably low prices and promotions. Meanwhile, approximately one-third of existing customers changed carriers during 2000, a phenomenon known as customer churn and a reflection of both more lenient subscriber contracts and greater customer willingness to shop around.

SUBSTANTIAL GROWTH STILL IN THE OFFING

This isn't to say growth is ebbing in the wireless market. Far from it, some industry forecasters expected the number of U.S. subscribers to double within

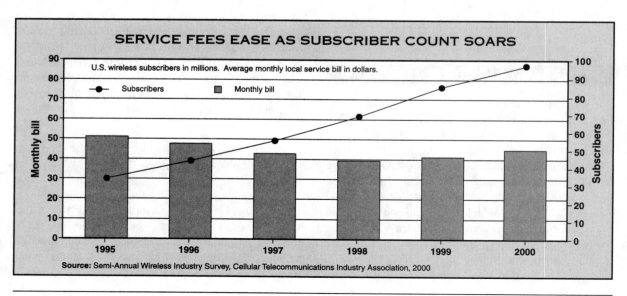

SERVICE FEES EASE AS SUBSCRIBER COUNT SOARS

U.S. wireless subscribers in millions. Average monthly local service bill in dollars.

Source: Semi-Annual Wireless Industry Survey, Cellular Telecommunications Industry Association, 2000

the first five years of the 2000s. The Strategis Group, a telecommunications market research firm, predicted the wireless penetration rate would soar from about 28 percent of the population in 1999 to 56 percent by 2004. By number of subscribers, that translates into a swell from about 97 million in mid-2000 to potentially more than 160 million, based on population growth estimates from the U.S. Census Bureau. In a separate estimate, the Cellular Telecommunications Industry Association reckoned there were more than 109 million U.S. subscribers at year-end 2000.

Not only are wireless carriers continuing to add new customers at a furious pace, but they're also benefiting from higher usage rates per customer. Research from International Data Corp., a leading technology research outfit, suggested that the average number of minutes used by consumers rose from 155 a month in 1999 to 247 in 2000, an increase of almost 60 percent.

Among other factors driving growth are new services such as wireless data and Internet access (see below), prepaid wireless service, and so-called dispatch services. Of these, prepaid was by far the largest in 1999, with an estimated 16 million subscribers, and was expected to remain one of the larger market niches into the early 2000s. Prepaid services appeal to rate-sensitive customers who may have occasional need for a wireless phone but prefer not to pay a monthly subscription fee. The Strategis Group estimated that prepaid users numbered nearly 16 million in 2000.

Dispatch services, one of the newest service segments, are expected to experience some of the fastest growth. With various services aimed at either businesses or consumers, wireless dispatch offers intercom-like communications among coworkers, family members, or friends who are in frequent contact. The services may be accessed using specialized devices or conventional cell phones with special features. Rates for contacting members of the family or workgroup would tend to be lower than those for using ordinary cell phones for the task. The number of dispatch users in the United States was estimated to top 1 million for the first time in 2000, but to skyrocket to more than 20 million by 2004, according to a report by the Strategis Group.

WAP AND BROADBAND TAKE DATA WIRELESS

Perhaps the wireless technology causing the most stir lately has been broadband data access via wireless device. The data arena opens the possibility of accessing Web pages, sending and receiving e-mail and two-way text paging, and the potential to transmit data

and application files without plugging into a conventional wired computer network. Moreover, fixed wireless broadband services such as local multipoint distribution service (LMDS) and multichannel multipoint distribution service can also support simultaneous voice and data transfer and, ultimately, advanced features such as video, although such capabilities are still at least a few years from widespread availability. In the meantime, LMDS and similar services will compete with such wired technologies as digital subscriber line (DSL) and cable for the high-speed data market.

One technology that many carriers, device makers, and content providers are banking on is Wireless Application Protocol (WAP). This communications standard was developed by a group of leading wireless hardware and service companies, and is intended to provide a universal foundation on which wireless applications can be built. Using a programming scheme called Wireless Markup Language, newer mobile phones and other devices can run wireless-oriented applications and transmit data over a common architecture that can be used in any number of digital wireless systems (CDMA, TDMA, GSM).

WAP requires specially outfitted devices that didn't begin commercial shipment until 2000. Still, with the backing of all the major wireless carriers and phone manufacturers, rollout was expected to be swift, especially in Europe, where cell-phone penetration rates are already vastly greater than in the United States. Indeed, International Data Corp. predicted that by 2001 all new digital cell phones would come equipped for WAP. Similar prognostications hold that within just a few years more people could be accessing the Internet via mobile WAP devices than with conventional personal computers. The Yankee Group reported that, by the end of 2000, about 1.8 million Americans had signed on to wireless data service. At the end of the third quarter, according to Yankee Group, market share was broken down as follows: Sprint PCS led the way with 320,000 subscribers; Verizon followed with 300,000; AT&T Wireless had 270,000 subscribers; Nextel reported 200,000; and Cingular Wireless was just entering the wireless-data field. Strategis Group expected the total number of subscribers to approach 13 million by 2004.

Another complication in WAP's deployment is the problem that most of the early WAP devices, many of which hit the market a year later than anticipated, aren't capable of the full range of WAP functions and activities. Within a few years, more sophisticated and powerful devices are expected that will render early models obsolete or severely limited by comparison. In short, while WAP technology represents the third gen-

THE PERILS OF UBIQUITOUS PHONES

It's often the case that technological advances bring with them unanticipated and even unsavory social and personal consequences, and wireless phones are no exception. While some decry the use of cell phones in any public space as a nuisance, at their worst cell phones can be out-and-out lethal when they preoccupy drivers on the road.

The tally of injuries and fatalities resulting from motor vehicle accidents where the driver was on the phone has been rising precipitously. The victims are often pedestrians or occupants of other vehicles. Indeed, statistics published in the *New England Journal of Medicine* suggested that drivers using cell phones are four times more likely than average to be involved in an accident, a rate comparable to that of drunk drivers. And separate figures indicated that the overwhelming majority of wireless phone owners are apt to use the devices at some point while they're driving.

Survivors of cell-phone-related accidents and other activists have been lobbying for laws to curtail the use of phones while driving. Over the objections of industry trade groups such as the Cellular Telecommunications Industry Association (CTIA), which favors driver education programs, many states and municipalities have begun to consider legislation that would restrict or outright ban using cell phones at the wheel. All told, 34 states had considered such a law by 2000, but no legislation had been passed. A few cities have limited wireless phone use to hands-free models, and in many places more radical steps are being considered.

Opponents of regulation argue that driver negligence is already dealt with under existing laws, and that cell-phone use is no more distracting than having a conversation with another person in the car, flipping radio stations, or doing other things while driving. The CTIA advocated responsible use of wireless phones and highlighted the safety benefits of having a cell phone in the car, including, ironically, the ability to call the police if someone spots a reckless driver on the road.

eration in mobile telephony, the first devices won't be close to being that generation's finest.

INDUSTRY LEADERS

VERIZON DOMINATES THE HORIZON

Mergers and acquisitions in the late 1990s and early 2000s have made some of the biggest wireless

carriers even bigger. By far the largest as of 2000 was a brand-new concern known as Verizon Wireless. Verizon Wireless is a joint venture of Vodafone AirTouch Plc (itself a merger of U.K. and U.S. wireless giants) and Bell Atlantic Corp, which absorbed GTE and its wireless unit in 2000. Verizon Wireless boasted more than 26 million subscribers just from the pooled interests. Once the merger was completed, Bell Atlantic and GTE took the Verizon name, which is a blend of the Latin *veritas* (truth) and "horizon."

The various pieces of Verizon Wireless had sales of about $7.7 billion in 1999. Separately, Vodafone AirTouch also has substantial presence in Europe, particularly in the wake of its 2000 acquisition of Mannesmann AG, Germany's biggest wireless operator.

SBC AND BELLSOUTH TIE THE KNOT, YIELDING CINGULAR WIRELESS

Another wireless merger on a grand scale was that of BellSouth Corp. and SBC Communications Inc., two regional Bells that had assembled sizable wireless services primarily in their local wireline coverage areas. The companies announced their plans in spring 2000 and concluded the transaction later that year, calling the firm Cingular Wireless. SBC was already the third-largest wireless carrier in its own right. The new firm had about 19 million wireless customers in 38 states, putting it second behind Verizon. The BellSouth and SBC wireless units posted about $10 billion in sales during 1999.

AT&T GOES IT ALONE

Once the dominant U.S. wireless carrier, AT&T Wireless Group's luster has perhaps been dimmed slightly in the shadow of the big mergers. In 2000 the company had a much ballyhooed initial public offering (IPO) of its tracking stock, at more than $10 billion the largest IPO in U.S. history, but AT&T Wireless has been criticized for being a weak and lumbering competitor in the fast-paced wireless business. The wireless unit, which is still part of AT&T despite having its own stock, traces its roots to AT&T's 1994 purchase of McCaw Cellular Communications, which paired the large, innovative McCaw with AT&T's home-grown cellular business. By the end of 2000, AT&T Wireless had more than 13 million subscribers worldwide. For its fiscal 1999, the company reported $7.6 billion in revenue.

SPRINT PCS TRAILS, BUT HAS POWERFUL BACKING

Sprint PCS, one of the leading carriers relying on CDMA technology, has lagged behind competitors such as AT&T and Verizon, but it has a strong retail presence and one of the most modern networks in the United States. The company was founded as a joint venture between long-distance carrier Sprint Corp. and three large cable system operators. Though Sprint PCS's subscribers numbered only 7.4 million in 2000, the attempted megamerger that year between MCI WorldCom (which became known as WorldCom in mid-2000) and Sprint Corp. was intended to revitalize Sprint PCS's business. The deal, however, was struck down by the U.S. Justice Department. Sprint PCS took in $3.2 billion in 1999.

NEXTEL, NEXTLINK ASCEND IN THE BUSINESS MARKET

A "different kind of wireless company," Nextel Communications, Inc. began as a specialized mobile radio company providing services for taxi drivers, truckers, and other work groups. In 1991 it began to develop a digital network with an infusion of capital from cellular phone service magnate Craig McCaw. With 6.2 million subscribers (primarily businesses) by 2000, it posted revenues in 1999 of $3.3 billion.

A separate McCaw venture with ties to Nextel is NEXTLINK Communications, Inc. A diversified independent telecommunications carrier, NEXTLINK has an early advantage in the fledgling fixed-wireless broadband arena through its dominant share of local multipoint distribution service licenses throughout the United States. NEXTLINK has begun to offer wireless Internet and voice services to businesses, focusing on the small business market.

AMERICA AND THE WORLD

In 2000, statistics collected by the GSM Association held that there were somewhat over 500 million wireless subscribers throughout the world, an amount approaching one out of every 12 people. About 55 percent of those subscribers, or 285 million, used the GSM digital standard, which is prevalent in Europe and Asia but uncommon in the United States. Separate estimates foresee the global subscriber count more than doubling by 2003, topping the 1 billion mark.

The United States trails a number of countries, notably those of northern Europe, in the rate and scope of wireless service deployment. The use of cell phones in Scandinavian countries is so prevalent—at more than 60 percent of the population by some estimates—that some observers speak of 100 percent penetration rates in the foreseeable future. In addition to wider adoption abroad, wireless services in Europe and parts of Asia also tend to be more technologically advanced than those of the United States. Wireless data services, for instance, were expected to be deployed faster in parts of Europe than in the United States.

As wealthy consumer and business markets such as those of Japan, Western Europe, and the United States approach saturation, multinational carriers are shifting their sights to other regions. Recognizing that half of the world's population lives more than 200 miles from the nearest telephone, many companies were striving to devise a blanket service that could deliver inexpensive wireless telephone service to every person on the globe. Even if a company

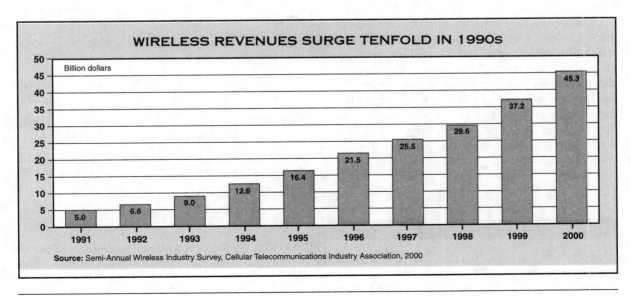

WIRELESS REVENUES SURGE TENFOLD IN 1990s

Billion dollars

Year	Revenue
1991	5.0
1992	6.6
1993	9.0
1994	12.6
1995	16.4
1996	21.5
1997	25.5
1998	29.6
1999	37.2
2000	45.3

Source: Semi-Annual Wireless Industry Survey, Cellular Telecommunications Industry Association, 2000

could capture just 1-2 percent of the global marketplace, it would enjoy a subscriber base of 50 to 100 million people.

While the United States has more than 64 main telephone lines and about 30 wireless phones for every 100 people, saturation rates in countries such as China are closer to seven main lines and two cell phones per hundred inhabitants. Although its saturation rate is low by comparison, China's prodigious population makes it one of the world's largest wireless markets in terms of number of subscribers. The 1.2 billion-person nation was expected to become the world's second-largest wireless market by subscriber count in the first years of the 2000s.

Penetration is even lower in places such as India and Indonesia, which have only two to three main lines and less than one wireless phone for every hundred people. Given such low penetration rates, wireless is seen by many as a cost-effective way to leapfrog wireline phones in such populous countries, offering greater access to telecommunications services without as great an investment as wiring entire countries practically from scratch.

RESEARCH AND TECHNOLOGY

AMPS, the first-generation analog system for U.S. cellular telecommunications, is rapidly being replaced by second-generation digital systems, such as GSM, CDMA, and TDMA. Even before the transition to digital has concluded, however, the third generation—often abbreviated as "3G" in the trade literature—is on the brink of being commercialized. 3G technology is characterized by integration with computer networks, especially the Internet, and broadening the scope of wireless communications into data, interactive applications, and ultimately, video. Although some devices with 3G features began reaching the market in 2000, they failed to incorporate all of the features hardware and software developers have been testing. As a result, analysts predicted considerable evolution during the early 2000s on both the hardware and service sides, labeling some of the transition devices "2.5G."

FURTHER READING

Bayne, Kim M. "Wireless Devices: The New Marketing Frontier." *e-Business Advisor,* December 2000.

Blake, Pat. "Fixed or Mobile? How about Both?" *Telephony,* 1 June 1998.

Cellular Telecommunications Industry Association. *CTIA's Wireless Industry Indices, 1985-1999.* Washington: Cellular Telecommunications Industry Association, 2000. Available from http://www.ctia.org.

Clark, Christopher. "Analyze This." *Wireless Review,* 1 October 1999.

Deardorff, Julie. "Victims Lead Drive to Ban Drivers from Using Cell Phones." *Chicago Tribune,* 24 March 2000.

Gilder, George, and Richard Vigilante. "AT&T's Wireless Debacle." *Wall Street Journal,* 1 May 2000.

Glanz, William. "Merger Mania Strikes World of Wireless Telecom, Spurs Debate over Industry." *Knight Ridder/ Tribune Business News,* 10 April 2000.

Goldman, Chris. "Wireless Data Still Looking for Momentum in U.S." *Wireless Review,* 31 December 2000.

"GSM/PCS Will Reach Half a Billion Users Worldwide in 2001." *Newsbytes,* 27 April 2000.

Jones, Stephen S. "Redefining Wireless." *Wireless Review,* 15 March 1999.

Luna, Lynette. "Promises, Promises." *Telephony,* 4 December 2000.

Mason, Charles. "Satellites: The New Direct-to-Consumer Tool." *America's Network,* 15 September 1998.

———. "Taking the Desktop to the Blacktop." *America's Network,* 1 March 1999.

Meyers, Jason. "Cellular Revisited." *Telephony,* 3 March 1997.

———. "Network Buildup." *Telephony,* 7 April 1997.

———. "Struggle for Survival: PCS Entrepreneurs Tread Dangerous Waters," 9 June 1997.

Nash, J. Madeleine. "Not in My Front Yard." *Time,* 4 November 1996.

O'Shea, Dan. "After the Discovery." *Telephony,* 31 March 1997.

Pappalardo, Denise. "NEXTLINK Bets the Farm on Wireless." *Network World,* 25 January 1999.

Pringle, David. "WAP Standard Runs into Trouble with Incompatible Technologies." *Wall Street Journal,* 9 May 2000.

"The Static in That AT&T Wireless IPO." *Business Week,* 1 May 2000.

Van, John. "Cellular Phone Users Switch Firms in Search of Better Service, Lower Prices." *Chicago Tribune,* 7 May 2000.

"Warning: Sharp Growth Ahead." *Communications News,* May 1998.

"Web Masters Will Have to Think of Wireless Users' Needs First." *EDP Weekly's IT Monitor,* 17 April 2000.

Wireless Application Protocol Forum Ltd. "Who We Are." Reading, U.K.: Wireless Application Protocol Forum, 2000. Available from http://www.wapforum.org.

XML

In the beginning, Web pages appeared in drab text, with clumsily placed graphics and sections separated by browser-length horizontal lines. Sophisticated design it was not. As the Web developed rapidly through the mid- and late 1990s, hotshot design specialists were quick to scoff at pages still incorporating such simple, first-generation design techniques. Meanwhile, by the close of the 20th century aesthetics were the least of the concerns of major electronic commerce (e-commerce) interests. What they wanted was a system to share data across a variety of platforms quickly and efficiently. The Hypertext Markup Language (HTML), the prevalent format for distributing information over the World Wide Web, was increasingly viewed as primitive and too inflexible to handle the dynamic information necessitated by increased e-commerce and technological capabilities.

Fortunately for the design snobs and the business folk, there appeared to be a single answer to these problems. Extensible Markup Language (XML) was poised to assume its position as the new lifeblood of the World Wide Web.

Markup languages, such as HTML and XML, define a document's attributes by inserting "tags" around select bits of information. HTML uses a limited number of relatively inflexible tags that determine only the document's form. XML, however, is nearly infinite in the number of possible tags, and XML tags can influence the document's content as well as its form. XML empowers users to develop and define languages of their own that suit their specific needs while remaining compatible with others' XML creations. Therein lies the beauty, and usefulness, of XML in the Web environment of the future.

Although it's called a language, XML technically bears a fancier description: a metalanguage. That is, it doesn't constitute the language in and of itself; rather, it acts as a grammar for the language, defining the language's rules and processes. It is for this reason that XML doesn't actually replace HTML, but rather works alongside it. Since most companies have, over the years, built Internet portals and e-marketplaces using a variety of frameworks instead of a single network in an effort to simply get the information or product into public view, one of XML's primary uses will be to integrate all this information.

XML furthermore allows for the seamless transfer between presentation media. That is, using the same set of criteria, XML can define content so as to appear in a particular way on a World Wide Web browser, for instance, and in a different way when printed on a hard copy.

Both XML and HTML are derived from an older format called Standard Generalized Markup Language (SGML), which was in use before the Web existed. HTML is a small subset of SGML using only about 70 tags, mainly to indicate how a document should be displayed or to link it to other documents. XML's tags, on the other hand, are not primarily presentation-oriented, and the metalanguage itself exists independently of any database file format. Rather, XML provides a way to define and use new tags that describe

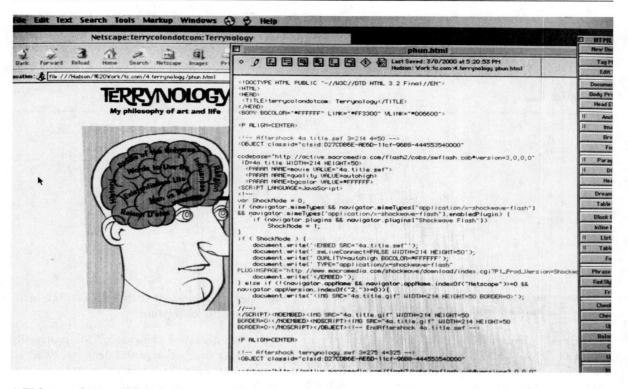

A Web-page showing HTML coding. *(FieldMark Publications/Robert J. Huffman)*

various elements of a document. Any elements that are opened and closed properly (using start and end tags) are considered "well formed" and are acceptable. There can be an unlimited number of tags, including "nested" hierarchies (although not overlapping tags that do not nest properly). So, for example, a student's transcript might have tags indicating the student's name, student ID, and courses. Along with the transcript would come a document type definition (DTD), a convention inherited from SGML, that describes how the document is organized. The document could be displayed in a Web browser or used with any other software capable of parsing it. A parser mediates between the document and the medium, such as a Web browser, both to ensure that the document is well formed and to present the information in the form tailored to that medium. Thus, the parser, rather than the application, actually reads the XML document. Parsers themselves are rendered in the XML format, usually conforming to the World Wide Web Consortium (W3C) XML standard. (The W3C is one of the major standards organizations for the Internet.) The generic nature of XML lends itself to marking up database records and other structured information.

Since XML tags generally pertain to how information is organized, rather than how it is to be displayed, the same document may be presented in any number of ways. Different application software packages or scripts might produce HTML for a Web display, a Braille version, or a file formatted for printing, all from the same XML document.

XML is intended to complement HTML, not compete with it. But older HTML-based tools and applications are not compatible with the new technology. HTML conforms to a single DTD, so it does not provide this description with every document. Rather, HTML tools are built to this single specification. XML documents use tags that are not part of HTML's fixed set; at the same time, XML is actually stricter about syntax rules, such as tags being properly closed. Newer software is being developed to take advantage of XML's capabilities. Web browsers are now able to support XML, and HTML specifications allow mixing of the two formats in a single document. E-commerce, data interchange, and information discovery are becoming important applications of XML.

The DTDs (which describe the tags) used in XML documents can be provided in a number of ways. They can either be part of the document itself or reside in a separate file. Developers working with SGML have been generating application-specific DTDs for years, and many of these are available for public use. An XML convention called the "namespace" allows a document to reference a universal resource locator (URL) address where a set of agreed-upon tag names has been published. Namespaces can be created by organizations, industries, hobbyist groups, companies, or other entities interested in making a set of tags available for the type of data they work with. Using namespaces, information can be exchanged with all the capabilities inherent in XML and without generating confusion by inadvertent use of the same name in different ways.

All Web standards, including HTML and XML, are overseen by the World Wide Web Consortium (W3C). The W3C was founded in 1994 and is chaired by Tim Berners-Lee, who first conceived the World Wide Web and invented HTML. The W3C has more than 180 members, most of whom are commercial software developers. Standards discussions can be contentious because each company wants to gain a market advantage by distinguishing itself, even as it recognizes a need to maintain the interoperability that drives the Web. Often a company will develop a technology, propose it to the W3C as a standard, and then market it by announcing that it is soon to be W3C-endorsed. In practice, inclusion in the popular Netscape or Microsoft Internet Explorer browsers have been at least as critical as W3C endorsement for advancing a technology.

For XML, agreeing on tag sets is an important area for cooperation between software vendors and other XML users. By mid-1998, there were efforts to establish an overall tag clearinghouse to head off naming conflicts. "Webcasting" or "push technology" applications, in which an "active channel" of information is sent directly to a user over the Web rather than having the user traverse links, were early adopters of XML. DataChannel, Inc. of Bellevue, Washington, a software company involved in Webcasting, formed the XML Active Content Technologies Council in March 1998. Within a few months there were proposals that the council, consisting of software developers and users, should perhaps be chaired by a more neutral organization such as the Organization for the Advancement of Structured Information Standards (OASIS), a nonprofit SGML/XML interest and advocacy group in Madison, Alabama. Other vendors questioned the necessity of such a move. (Also see the essay in this book entitled Push Technology.)

BACKGROUND AND DEVELOPMENT

HTML was one of the most important developments in the history of information technologies. By facilitating the explosion of the World Wide Web, it changed the way modern societies distribute information and do business; a few short years, however, is a long time on the Internet. As the Web is expected to provide ever-increasing functionality, and users struggle to find relevant information in a vast global network, HTML was beginning to show its age. Broken links—links that do not lead to an existing Web page—abound, limited document formatting makes some types of applications difficult, and search engines are getting bogged down in the sheer volume of documents on the Internet. Many technologies are being developed to address one or more of these problems.

XML was created to improve methods of organizing and finding data. Since tags can be tailored to a particular type of information, it can be navigated more efficiently. If entire industries or other groups agree on a set of tags, then search tools can be built to provide more relevant results when applied to the group's data stores. More data validation can be done by the browser, and all forms of publishing, including Internet, paper, and CD-ROM, can be done from the same XML document.

Development of XML began in September 1996. The W3C formed an XML Working Group, chaired by Jon Bosak of Sun Microsystems, and this group issued several draft specifications for review and comment. In December 1997, Version 1.0 of the XML specification, written by Tim Bray, was issued as a W3C recommendation at a meeting of the SGML/XML Conference in Washington, D.C. In February 1998, the W3C ratified XML as a standard. Software developers quickly perceived the potential of this technology. Tools were built to generate XML, and Internet software began to incorporate XML support. At a Seattle XML conference in March 1998, one month after adoption of the standard by the W3C, dozens of vendors announced new products. In the first year of XML's official existence, hundreds of SGML software packages were updated to support it.

The Extensible Style Language (XSL) describes how an XML document is formatted. XSL is a way to specify style sheets for XML documents, following the model of the cascading style sheets used with HTML. Software vendors Microsoft, ArborText, and Inso submitted a proposal for XSL to the W3C in August 1997, and the W3C created an XSL Working Group. XSL Version 1.0 was approved by the W3C in the summer of 1999. XSL was expected to complement and make up for the limitations of XML. As long as not all browsers support XML, developers may remain reluctant to shift to the new standard. In such cases, XSL can reformat the XML coding into an acceptable HTML format, which works with all browsers.

CURRENT CONDITIONS

Analysts were in near-universal agreement that XML was en route to becoming the lingua franca of the Web in particular and of data integration in general. By eliminating the need for and the utility of proprietary formats, XML was seen as a major boon to the quickly emerging business-to-business e-commerce industry.

The logical next step for e-commerce was the convergence of different markets, allowing quick, easy interchange between, say, auto companies and financing agencies or between various components of business-to-business transactions, including insurance and manufacturing. XML was lauded as the tool by which separate markets would be brought together. Companies that spent the mid- and late 1990s developing their own formats will simply use XML to bring their systems into alignment with those of the companies and customers with whom they do business.

Online financial data exchange was furthermore slowly becoming as globally integrated as the Web itself. The Extensible Business Reporting Language (XBRL) incorporates financial-reporting standards into the XML framework so as to seamlessly integrate the particular measurements and currencies across different countries' financial systems, ideally creating a universal e-commerce market. Since, despite efforts toward a worldwide system, accounting standards still differ even among the English-speaking nations, not to mention the rest of the world, the XML dynamic definition process can facilitate smooth financial information flow across borders. An ancillary benefit for companies adopting the XBRL standard is a simplified integration of new financial information upon merging with or acquiring other companies. The XBRL Project Committee was endorsed by over 30 companies and organizations, including Microsoft and the American Institute of Certified Public Accountants, in April 2000.

The Voice Extensible Markup Language (VXML) took advantage of the latest voice recognition technologies, readying e-commerce and other Web-based information for transmission via telephone. The VoiceXML Forum completed version 1.0 of the VoiceXML standard in early 2000. The forum, which counts among its 79 members IBM, Motorola,

Lucent, and AT&T submitted the specification to the W3C later that year for official ratification. VXML was expected to open new avenues of commercial convenience and communication by allowing consumers to comparison shop with a single telephone call to the Internet. Travelers could simply dial up the Internet on the telephone, and within minutes book a flight reservation, hotel room, and dinner at a favorite restaurant. One could even call in for interactive directions to the restaurant while en route.

The Resource Description Framework (RDF) lets applications exchange information about data within a document, such as whether the data's position within the document is important, ratings for child protection, security and privacy, and intellectual property rights. The RDF consolidates several earlier efforts in the same area, such as Netscape's Meta Content Framework and Microsoft's XML-Data. Netscape has included the use of RDF in the 5.0 version of Navigator to store bookmarks, history information, and mail preferences.

Open Financial Exchange is a framework for data exchange among financial institutions and with their customers. By moving to XML, banks can allow their customers the ability to download account statements, pay bills electronically, and basically manage their finances online. Originally based on SGML, the format required some modifications, such as end tags, to be compatible with XML. It integrates formats used by Microsoft, Intuit (which provides the popular financial software package Quicken), and electronic-banking vendor CheckFree.

A method for syndicating data for multiple uses on the Web is the Information and Content Exchange protocol. It allows one company to provide content to another through a content syndicated relationship. Business rules for the content and access rights to data can be enforced by using this protocol.

Specialized XML tags are also being developed in such fields as chemistry, astronomy, and genealogy. Chemical Markup Language, for example, provides a way of describing the structure of a molecule with advanced XML tags for the atoms, the bonds, and the isotopic constitution. A Mathematics Markup Language allows proper display and manipulation of mathematical symbols and equations for the first time since the inception of the Web.

XML, like any new technology working across such a wide range, was not without its bugs. Several XML parsers remained a little too strict and sensitive, often rejecting valid XML documents. Moreover, de-

Not surprisingly, wherever new Web-based technologies push ahead, e-commerce interests are right there, making sure the ball rolls in the direction that will most facilitate the easy transaction of goods, services, and money over the Internet.

In that spirit, some of the major regulatory bodies in the XML business and in the world combined to develop a single e-business standard encompassing existing and emerging XML standards. Sponsored by the United Nations Centre for Trade Facilitation and Electronic Business, as well as the Organization for the Advancement of Structured Information Standards (OASIS), representatives from business, government, and technology research met in early 2000 to continue work on the Electronic Business XML Initiative (ebXML).

Aimed particularly at facilitating easier e-market entry for businesses in developing nations, the ebXML initiative involved experts and officials from a wide range of industries and technical areas, including Internet technologies, business processes, e-commerce server intercommunications, XML, and a host of others.

Since such a wide variety of applications are currently used for e-commerce, from e-mail to Web forms to File Transfer Protocol, the ebXML team saw a chance to drastically boost levels of e-commerce by making each compatible with all the others. In addition, the team hoped to establish a single system to handle Internet credit-card purchases and confirmation and related encryption software and standards. The ebXML standard will enable clients to request e-commerce over any application protocol, using XML headers.

Final specifications were slated for summer 2001, after which evolving XML e-commerce applications and standards will likely take advantage of this new framework in which to develop.

spite efforts at cooperation and standardization, for the time being XML was likely to produce similar results as JavaScript before it. That is, different platforms will respond to documents differently, possibly rejecting them outright. Most observers expect such speed bumps to be ironed out within a few years, however, and XML will likely succeed as the document-transfer standard.

INDUSTRY LEADERS

Microsoft has been instrumental in the development of XML technology and tools. Its XML-ready tool for building Web sites, BizTalk, was released in summer 2000. BizTalk was tailored toward the generation and exchange of e-commerce information and documents, including purchase orders and invoices, via XML tags. Internet Explorer 4.0 uses XML to schedule active channel information delivery and can process and display XML documents. Internet Explorer 5.0 supports XML 1.0, XSL, XML Document Object Model (DOM), and XML Namespaces. Frontpage2000 also uses XML to support DOM, providing Web developers with the ability to specify documents by category. The company also marketed its MSXML tool, which parses an XML document into a hierarchical tree and provides Java programming language methods for manipulating the resulting structure. MSXML was integrated into Internet Explorer 5.0.

Late in 2000 the company released a specification for the XML Analysis protocol for the analysis of data between clients and development platforms.

Oracle Corp. was rapidly building XML into its offerings, developing publishing tools for storage and retrieval of XML data from the Oracle8i database. The company's XML parser went through several rapid upgrades by 2000. In late 1999, Oracle released a free version of its Oracle XML Developers Kit, previously used only to access the database XML features. The system runs on Java, C++, and Oracle's own database scripting language. By 2000, Oracle had XML-enabled the entire Oracle Internet Platform and released the Oracle XML Schema Processor for Java.

IBM has also been at the forefront of XML's development, creating over 20 XML technologies by 2000. Their proposal for XML Schema offers a way to overcome the limitations of document type definitions (DTDs) by allowing data-typing so that information, such as a date or integer, can be tagged and identified. IBM, Motorola, Lucent, and AT&T have formed the Voice Extensible Markup Language Forum to develop further XML-based methods to access Web content by telephone. IBM has submitted Speech Markup Language, and Motorola has developed VoxML, an XML-based method for creating voice activated Web sites and automated call centers for conducting business, in what Motorola has called "v-commerce." IBM's XML4J XML parser runs on a variety of different configurations. Together with

Lotus, IBM wrote the Simple Object Access Protocol specification for simple e-business XML exchange.

XML is well suited for use with object-oriented databases (OODBs) due to its linking ability and hierarchical architecture. Poet Software Corp. has bundled a Content Management Suite with its OODB, allowing storage, manipulation, and navigation of XML and SGML, as well as HTML, text, graphics, audio, and video formats. Poet's product supports content-based queries using XML tags. Object Design Inc.'s eXcelon serves XML files to a browser and makes them available for return visits to the site by storing them in the server's cache memory. Object Design later released its own eXcelon Stylus visual development tool.

Other leading XML development tools included Bluestone Software's Visual-XML, Extensibility's XML Authority, Icon Information-Systems' XML Spy, SoftQuad's XMetaL, and Vervet Logic's XML Pro.

RESEARCH AND TECHNOLOGY

Like XML, dynamic HTML (DHTML) is an effort to improve on HTML, this time by allowing changing information to be presented to the user with fewer, slow full-document downloads, resulting in greater control for the designer. The DHTML specification allows scripts to access structured data such as XML under program control. DHTML was first released in Internet Explorer 4.0. The 5.0 version increased the use of DHTML by making all the elements of a Web page, such as graphics, text, buttons, and forms, dynamic. In addition, layout preferences are retained by the browser for return visits to the page. DHTML, however, is taking hold more slowly than XML because of difficulties in reconciling different approaches by Netscape and Microsoft.

Another new markup language pushing HTML past its own boundaries was XHTML. In order to facilitate backwards compatibility during XML's early years on the market, the W3C issued a new XHTML 1.0 specification in early 2000. This standard basically acts as a bridge between HTML and XML, and was in fact built by steering the most recent HTML version, HTML 4.0, toward XML. Tim Berners-Lee commented that XHTML "connects the present Web to the future Web," according to *Network News,* that future being marked by XML. The system allows for seamless interoperability between those authors working with HTML and users with only HTML capability. The boosted flexibility afforded by XHTML

aims to facilitate the convergence of Web-capable wireless devices, which will process only that data relevant to the medium, thus widening accessibility over HTML, which in turn was likely to spur increased e-commerce.

Another proposed improvement to the workings of the Web is Extensible Link Language. This would support simple links between documents such as those currently used but also make possible names that are not dependent on the physical location of the data, bidirectional links, rings of links, and "transclusion," where linked documents appear to be part of the original document.

Several software vendors are developing ways to use XML as a "middleware" technology, tying together disparate resources over the Web. DataChannel's WebBroker software enables integration between Microsoft's Component Object Model, the competing Common Object Request Broker Architecture, and databases using Structured Query Language. WebMethods introduced B2B ("business-to-business"), allowing firms to exchange data from Microsoft Excel spreadsheets and applications built with Java, JavaScript, C, C++, Visual Basic, and ActiveX. Version 2.0 offers increased Open Database Connectivity and Java Database Connectivity support, as well as server-side XML data caching. If implemented at both ends, XML could allow users who are sent an e-mail with an attached spreadsheet to read it even if their own spreadsheet application comes from a different vendor.

XML can make related data stores appear as a single "virtual database" (VDB). This allows searching for information in a structured way, delivering better results than keyword searches over the entire Web. Yahoo, a leading provider of hierarchically organized directory information on the Web, is planning to use VDB technology to provide online comparison shopping. VDBs are also starting to be used in job recruitment applications.

The health-care industry may be an important future user of XML technology. Sequoia Software Corp. has received a grant from the National Institute of Standards and Technology to work on an XML-based Master Patient Index prototype. A URL for each patient would lead to an XML document with that patient's medical history and other information. In May 1998, Sequoia and Azron, Inc. announced the addition of an XML generator to Azron's Electronic Medical Record handheld device, used to gather patient information. A standard way to access medical records from any location should greatly facilitate telemedicine and coordination of specialist care. A health-care industry working group is developing Kona Architecture, an XML tag-naming convention using the same vocabulary as existing medical information transfer protocols. (Also see the essay in this book entitled Telemedicine.)

FURTHER READING

Abualsamid, Ahmad. "A Metalanguage for the Ages." *Network Computing,* 3 April 2000.

Booker, Ellis. "Vendors Debut XML Development Tools." *Internet Week,* 11 November 1999. Available from http://www.internetwk.com/story/INW19991111S0007.

Demers, Marie Eve. "Embracing XML: No Need to Wait For a Standard, Analysts Say." *ENEWS,* 28 August 2000.

Drummond, Rik. "XML: The Only Chance for a Worldwide Standard." *e-Business Advisor,* April 2000.

Gabel, David. "Making the Connection—XML Is the Standard That Brings E-markets Together." *VARBusiness,* 17 April 2000.

Hickman, Sam, and Philippe De Smedt. "ebXML is Emerging as a Reliable Standard." *Electronic Buyers' News,* 9 October 2000.

Luh, James C. "The ABCs of XML." *Internet World,* 1 March 2000.

Nelson, Matthew G. "XML Eases Integration on Marketplace Platforms." *InformationWeek,* 10 April 2000.

———. "XML to Speed Financial Data Online." *InformationWeek,* 17 April 2000.

"NetViews: How XHTML Will Revolutionize the Web." *Network News,* 23 February 2000.

Paul, Lauren Gibbons. "XML Standards Are Too Much of a Good Thing." *PC Week Online,* 12 April 1999. Available from http://www.zdnet.com/pcweek.

Perkins, Jon. "Getting Started with XML." *EXE,* 1 March 2000.

Radding, Alan. "XML: The Language of Integration." *Information Week,* 1 November 1999. Available from http://www.informationweek.com/759/xml.htm.

Ricadela, Aaron. "Microsoft Previews BizTalk Server 2000." *InformationWeek,* 17 April 2000.

Rist, Oliver. "XML Comes of Age." *Internet Week,* 16 August 1999. Available from http://www.techweb.com/se/directlink.cgi?INW19990816S0045.

Rupley, Sebastian. "XML Starts to Live Up to Its Hype." *PC Magazine,* 7 April 1999.

"VoiceXML Standard Opens Door to Web Browsing by Voice." *Network News,* 29 March 2000.

Walsh, Jeff. "IBM, W3C Advance XML Standards." *InfoWorld,* 22 February 1999.

Waltner, Charles. "Questions Still Surround XML Specification Standards." *InformationWeek,* 3 April 2000.

INDUSTRY INDEX

The Industry Index lists four-digit U.S. Standard Industrial Classification (SIC) codes, in numerical order, with the classification description following each code. The reference is followed by the page-number range(s) of relevant essays covered in this book.

SIC TO NAICS CONVERSION GUIDE

The following listing cross-references four-digit 1987 Standard Industrial Classification (SIC) codes with six-digit 1997 North American Industry Classification System (NAICS) codes pertinent to the topics covered within this book. Because the systems differ in specificity, some SIC categories correspond to more than one NAICS category.

AGRICULTURE, FORESTRY & FISHING

0742 Veterinary Services for Animal Specialties *see* NAICS 541940: Veterinary Services

0752 Animal Specialty Services, Except Veterinary; NAICS 115210: Support Activities for Animal Production; NAICS 812910: Pet Care (except Veterinary) Services

CONSTRUCTION INDUSTRIES

1731 Electrical Work *see* NAICS 561621: Security Systems Services (except Locksmiths); NAICS 235310: Electrical Contractors

FOOD & KINDRED PRODUCTS

2032 Canned Specialties *see* NAICS 311422: Specialty Canning; NAICS 311999: All Other Miscellaneous Food Manufacturing

2047 Dog and Cat Food *see* NAICS 311111: Dog and Cat Food Manufacturing

2048 Prepared Feed and Feed Ingredients for Animals and Fowls, Except Dogs and Cats *see* NAICS 311611: Animal (except Poultry) Slaughtering; NAICS 311119: Other Animal Food Manufacturing

2086 Bottled and Canned Soft Drinks and Carbonated Waters *see* NAICS 312111: Soft Drink Manufacturing; NAICS 312112: Bottled Water Manufacturing

2095 Roasted Coffee *see* NAICS 311920: Coffee and Tea Manufacturing; NAICS 311942: Spice and Extract Manufacturing

2099 Food Preparations, NEC *see* NAICS 311423: Dried and Dehydrated Food Manufacturing; NAICS 111998: All Other Miscellaneous Crop Farming; NAICS 311340: Non-Chocolate Confectionery Manufacturing; NAICS 311911: Roasted Nuts and Peanut Butter Manufacturing; NAICS 311991: Perishable Prepared Food Manufacturing; NAICS 311830: Tortilla Manufacturing; NAICS 311920: Coffee and Tea Manufacturing; NAICS 311941: Mayonnaise, Dressing, and Other Prepared Sauce Manufacturing; NAICS 311942: Spice and Extract Manufacturing; NAICS 311999: All Other Miscellaneous Food Manufacturing

TOBACCO PRODUCTS

2111 Cigarettes *see* NAICS 312221: Cigarette Manufacturing

TEXTILE MILL PRODUCTS

2296 Tire Cord and Fabrics *see* NAICS 314992: Tire Cord and Tire Fabric Mills

APPAREL & OTHER FINISHED PRODUCTS MADE FROM FABRICS & SIMILAR MATERIALS

2399 Fabricated Textile Products, NEC *see* NAICS 336360: Motor Vehicle Fabric Accessories and Seat Manufacturing; NAICS 315999: Other Apparel Accessories and Other Apparel Manufacturing; NAICS 314999: All Other Miscellaneous Textile Product Mills

PAPER & ALLIED PRODUCTS

2679 Converted Paper and Paperboard Products, NEC *see* NAICS 322215: Non-Folding Sanitary Food Container Manufacturing; NAICS 322222: Coated and Laminated Paper Manufacturing; NAICS 322231: Die-Cut Paper and Paperboard Office Supplies Manufacturing; NAICS 322298: All Other Converted Paper Product Manufacturing

PRINTING, PUBLISHING, & ALLIED INDUSTRIES

2741 Miscellaneous Publishing *see* NAICS 511140: Database and Directory Publishers; NAICS 512230: Music Publishers; NAICS 511199: All Other Publishers

CHEMICALS & ALLIED PRODUCTS

2833 Medicinal Chemicals and Botanical Products *see* NAICS 325411: Medicinal and Botanical Manufacturing

2834 Pharmaceutical Preparations *see* NAICS 325412: Pharmaceutical Preparation Manufacturing

2835 In Vitro and In Vivo Diagnostic Substances *see* NAICS 325412: Pharmaceutical Preparation Manufacturing; NAICS 325413: In-Vitro Diagnostic Substance Manufacturing

2836 Biological Products, Except Diagnostic Substances *see* NAICS 325414: Biological Product (except Diagnostic) Manufacturing

2841 Soaps and Other Detergents, Except Specialty Cleaners *see* NAICS 325611: Soap and Other Detergent Manufacturing

2842 Specialty Cleaning, Polishing, and Sanitary Preparations *see* NAICS 325612: Polish and Other Sanitation Good Manufacturing

2844 Perfumes, Cosmetics, and Other Toilet Preparations *see* NAICS 325620: Toilet Preparation Manufacturing; NAICS 325611: Soap and Other Detergent Manufacturing

2861 Gum and Wood Chemicals *see* NAICS 325191: Gum and Wood Chemical Manufacturing

RUBBER & MISCELLANEOUS PLASTICS PRODUCTS

3069 Fabricated Rubber Products, NEC *see* NAICS 313320: Fabric Coating Mills; NAICS 326192: Resilient Floor Covering Manufacturing; NAICS 326299: All Other Rubber Product Manufacturing

PRIMARY METALS INDUSTRIES

3357 Drawing and Insulating of Nonferrous Wire *see* NAICS 331319: Other Aluminum Rolling and Drawing; NAICS 331422: Copper Wire Drawing; NAICS 331491: Nonferrous Metal (except Copper and Aluminum) Rolling, Drawing, and Extruding; NAICS 335921: Fiber Optic Cable Manufacturing; NAICS 335929: Other Communication and Energy Wire Manufacturing

INDUSTRIAL & COMMERCIAL MACHINERY & COMPUTER EQUIPMENT

3535 Conveyors and Conveying Equipment *see* NAICS 333922: Conveyor and Conveying Equipment Manufacturing

3541 Machine Tools, Metal Cutting Type *see* NAICS 333512: Machine Tool (Metal Cutting Types) Manufacturing

3542 Machine Tools, Metal Forming Type *see* NAICS 333513: Machine Tool (Metal Forming Types) Manufacturing

3559 Special Industry Machinery, NEC *see* NAICS 333220: Rubber and Plastics Industry Machinery Manufacturing; NAICS 333319: Other Commercial and Service Industry Machinery Manufacturing; NAICS 333295: Semiconductor Manufacturing Machinery; NAICS 333298: All Other Industrial Machinery Manufacturing

3564 Industrial and Commercial Fans and Blowers and Air Purification Equipment *see* NAICS 333411: Air Purification Equipment Manufacturing; NAICS 333412: Industrial and Commercial Fan and Blower Manufacturing

3569 General Industrial Machinery and Equipment, NEC *see* NAICS 333999: All Other General Purpose Machinery Manufacturing

3571 Electronic Computers *see* NAICS 334111: Electronic Computer Manufacturing

3572 Computer Storage Devices *see* NAICS 334112: Computer Storage Device Manufacturing

3575 Computer Terminals *see* NAICS 334113: Computer Terminal Manufacturing

3577 Computer Peripheral Equipment, NEC *see* NAICS 334119: Other Computer Peripheral Equipment Manufacturing

3589 Service Industry Machinery, NEC *see* NAICS 333319: Other Commercial and Service Industry Machinery Manufacturing

3599 Industrial and Commercial Machinery and Equipment, NEC *see* NAICS 336399: All Other Motor Vehicle Part Manufacturing; NAICS 332999: All Other Miscellaneous Fabricated Metal Product Manufacturing; NAICS 333319: Other Commercial and Service Industry Machinery Manufacturing; NAICS 332710: Machine Shops; NAICS 333999: All Other General Purpose Machinery Manufacturing

ELECTRONIC & OTHER ELECTRICAL EQUIPMENT & COMPONENTS, EXCEPT COMPUTER EQUIPMENT

3629 Electrical Industrial Apparatus, NEC *see* NAICS 335999: All Other Miscellaneous Electrical Equipment and Component Manufacturing

3652 Phonograph Records and Prerecorded Audio Tapes and Disks *see* NAICS 334612: Prerecorded Compact Disc (Except Software), Tape and Record Reproducing; NAICS 512220: Integrated Record Production/Distribution

3661 Telephone and Telegraph Apparatus *see* NAICS 334210: Telephone Apparatus Manufacturing; NAICS 334416: Electronic Coil, Transformer, and Other Inductor Manufacturing; NAICS 334418: Printed Circuit/Electronics Assembly Manufacturing

3663 Radio and Television Broadcasting and Communication Equipment *see* NAICS 334220: Radio and Television Broadcasting and Wireless Communications Equipment Manufacturing

3674 Semiconductors and Related Devices *see* NAICS 334413: Semiconductor and Related Device Manufacturing

3679 Electronic Components, NEC *see* NAICS 334220: Radio and Television Broadcasting and Wireless Communications Equipment Manufacturing; NAICS 334418: Printed Circuit/Electronics Assembly Manufacturing; NAICS 336322: Other Motor Vehicle Electrical and Electronic Equipment Manufacturing; NAICS 334419: Other Electronic Component Manufacturing

3699 Electrical Machinery, Equipment, and Supplies, NEC *see* NAICS 333319: Other Commercial and Service Industry Machinery Manufacturing; NAICS 333618: Other Engine Equipment Manufacturing; NAICS 334119: Other Computer Peripheral Equipment Manufacturing; NAICS 335129: Other Lighting Equipment Manufacturing; NAICS 335999: All Other Miscellaneous Electrical Equipment and Component Manufacturing

TRANSPORTATION EQUIPMENT

3714 Motor Vehicle Parts and Accessories *see* NAICS 336211: Motor Vehicle Body Manufacturing; NAICS 336312: Gasoline Engine and Engine Parts Manufacturing; NAICS 336322: Other Motor Vehicle Electrical and Electronic Equipment Manufacturing; NAICS 336330: Motor Vehicle Steering and Suspension Components (except Spring) Manufacturing; NAICS 336340: Motor Vehicle Brake System Manufacturing; NAICS 336350: Motor Vehicle Transmission and Power Train Part Manufacturing; NAICS 336399: All Other Motor Vehicle Parts Manufacturing

3761   Guided Missiles and Space Vehicles *see* NAICS 336414: Guided Missile and Space Vehicle Manufacturing

MEASURING, ANALYZING, & CONTROLLING INSTRUMENTS

3812   Search, Detection, Navigation, Guidance, Aeronautical, and Nautical Systems and Instruments *see* NAICS 334511: Search, Detection, Navigation, Guidance, Aeronautical, and Nautical System and Instrument Manufacturing

3822   Automatic Controls for Regulating Residential and Commercial Environments and Appliances *see* NAICS 334512: Automatic Environmental Control Manufacturing for Regulating Residential, Commercial, and Appliance Use

3825   Instruments for Measuring and Testing of Electricity and Electrical Signals *see* NAICS 334416: Electronic Coil, Transformer, and Other Inductor Manufacturing; NAICS 334515: Instrument Manufacturing for Measuring and Testing Electricity and Electrical Signals

3827   Optical Instruments and Lenses *see* NAICS 333314: Optical Instrument and Lens Manufacturing

3829   Measuring and Controlling Devices, NEC *see* NAICS 339112: Surgical and Medical Instrument Manufacturing; NAICS 334519: Other Measuring and Controlling Device Manufacturing

3841   Surgical and Medical Instruments and Apparatus *see* NAICS 339112: Surgical and Medical Instrument Manufacturing

3845   Electromedical and Electrotherapeutic Apparatus *see* NAICS 334517: Irradiation Apparatus Manufacturing; NAICS 334510: Electromedical and Electrotherapeutic Apparatus Manufacturing

3851   Ophthalmic Goods *see* NAICS 339115: Ophthalmic Goods Manufacturing

3861   Photographic Equipment and Supplies *see* NAICS 333315: Photographic and Photocopying Equipment Manufacturing; NAICS 325992: Photographic Film, Paper, Plate and Chemical Manufacturing

MISCELLANEOUS MANUFACTURING INDUSTRIES

3944   Games, Toys, and Children's Vehicles, Except Dolls and Bicycles *see* NAICS 336991: Motorcycle, Bicycle, and Parts Manufacturing; NAICS 339932: Game, Toy, and Children's Vehicle Manufacturing

3949   Sporting and Athletic Goods, NEC *see* NAICS 339920: Sporting and Athletic Good Manufacturing

TRANSPORTATION, COMMUNICATIONS, ELECTRIC, GAS, & SANITARY SERVICES

4512   Air Transportation, Scheduled *see* NAICS 481111:

Scheduled Passenger Air Transportation; NAICS 481112: Scheduled Freight Air Transportation

4812   Radiotelephone Communications *see* NAICS 513321: Paging; NAICS 513322: Cellular and Other Wireless Telecommunications; NAICS 513330: Telecommunications Resellers

4813   Telephone Communications, Except Radiotelephone *see* NAICS 513310: Wired Telecommunications Carriers; NAICS 513330: Telecommunications Resellers

4841   Cable and Other Pay Television Services *see* NAICS 513210: Cable Networks; NAICS 513220: Cable and Other Program Distribution

4899   Communications Services, NEC *see* NAICS 513322: Cellular and Other Wireless Telecommunications; NAICS 513340: Satellite Telecommunications; NAICS 513390: Other Telecommunications

WHOLESALE TRADE

5043   Photographic Equipment and Supplies *see* NAICS 421410: Photographic Equipment and Supplies Wholesalers

5045   Computers and Computer Peripheral Equipment and Software *see* NAICS 421430: Computer and Computer Peripheral Equipment and Software Wholesalers; NAICS 443120: Computer and Software Stores

5065   Electronic Parts and Equipment, Not Elsewhere Classified *see* NAICS 421690: Other Electronic Parts and Equipment Wholesalers

5149   Groceries and Related Products, NEC *see* NAICS 422490: Other Grocery and Related Product Wholesalers

5199   Nondurable Goods, NEC *see* NAICS 541890: Other Services Related to Advertising; NAICS 422990: Other Miscellaneous Nondurable Goods Wholesalers

RETAIL TRADE

5411   Grocery Stores *see* NAICS 447110: Gasoline Stations with Convenience Stores; NAICS 445110: Supermarkets and Other Grocery (except Convenience) Stores; NAICS 452910: Warehouse Clubs and Superstores; NAICS 445120: Convenience Stores

5734   Computer and Computer Software Stores *see* NAICS 443120: Computer and Software Stores

5812   Eating and Drinking Places *see* NAICS 722110: Full-Service Restaurants; NAICS 722211: Limited-Service Restaurants; NAICS 722212: Cafeterias; NAICS 722213: Snack and Nonalcoholic Beverage Bars; NAICS 722310: Foodservice Contractors; NAICS 722320: Caterers; NAICS 711110: Theater Companies and Dinner Theaters

5941   Sporting Goods Stores and Bicycle Shops *see* NAICS 451110: Sporting Goods Stores

5945   Hobby, Toy, and Game Shops *see* NAICS 451120: Hobby, Toy and Game Stores

5961   Catalog and Mail-Order Houses *see* NAICS 454110: Electronic Shopping and Mail-Order Houses

5999   Miscellaneous Retail Stores, NEC *see* NAICS 446120: Cosmetics, Beauty Supplies, and Perfume Stores; NAICS 446199: All Other Health and Personal Care Stores; NAICS 453910: Pet and Pet Supplies Stores; NAICS 453920: Art Dealers; NAICS 443111: Household Appliance Stores; NAICS 443112: Radio, Television, and Other Electronics Stores; NAICS 448310:

Jewelry Stores; NAICS 453998: All Other Miscellaneous Store Retailers (except Tobacco Stores)

FINANCE, INSURANCE, & REAL ESTATE

6162   Mortgage Bankers and Loan Correspondents *see* NAICS 522292: Real Estate Credit; NAICS 522390: Other Activities Related to Credit Intermediation

6163   Loan Brokers *see* NAICS 522310: Mortgage and Other Loan Brokers

6211   Security Brokers, Dealers, and Flotation Companies *see* NAICS 523110: Investment Banking and Securities Dealing; NAICS 523120: Securities Brokerage; NAICS 523910: Miscellaneous Intermediation; NAICS 523999: Miscellaneous Financial Investment Activities

6221   Commodity Contracts Brokers and Dealers *see* NAICS 523130: Commodity Contracts Dealing; NAICS 523140: Commodity Brokerage

6231   Security and Commodity Exchanges *see* NAICS 523210: Securities and Commodity Exchanges

6282   Investment Advice *see* NAICS 523920: Portfolio Management; NAICS 523930: Investment Advice

6289   Services Allied With the Exchange of Securities or Commodities, NEC *see* NAICS 523991: Trust, Fiduciary, and Custody Activities; NAICS 523999: Miscellaneous Financial Investment Activities

6311   Life Insurance *see* NAICS 524113: Direct Life Insurance Carriers; NAICS 524130: Reinsurance Carriers

6321   Accident and Health Insurance *see* NAICS 524114: Direct Health and Medical Insurance Carriers; NAICS 525190: Other Insurance and Employee Benefit Funds; NAICS 524130: Reinsurance Carriers

6331   Fire, Marine, and Casualty Insurance *see* NAICS 524126: Direct Property and Casualty Insurance Carriers; NAICS 525190: Other Insurance and Employee Benefit Funds; NAICS 524130: Reinsurance Carriers

6411   Insurance Agents, Brokers, and Service *see* NAICS 524210: Insurance Agencies and Brokerages; NAICS 524291: Claims Adjusters; NAICS 524292: Third Party Administrators for Insurance and Pension Funds; NAICS 524298: All Other Insurance Related Activities

6513   Operators of Apartment Buildings *see* NAICS 531110: Lessors of Residential Buildings and Dwellings

SERVICE INDUSTRIES

7011   Hotels and Motels *see* NAICS 721110: Hotels (except Casino Hotels) and Motels; NAICS 721120: Casino Hotels; NAICS 721191: Bed and Breakfast Inns; NAICS 721199: All Other Traveler Accommodations

7041   Organization Hotels and Lodging Houses, on Membership Basis *see* NAICS 721110: Hotels (except Casino Hotels) and Motels; NAICS 721310: Rooming and Boarding Houses

7231   Beauty Shops *see* NAICS 812112: Beauty Salons; NAICS 812113: Nail Salons; NAICS 611511: Cosmetology and Barber Schools

7319   Advertising, NEC *see* NAICS 481219: Other Nonscheduled Air Transportation; NAICS 541830: Media Buying Agencies; NAICS 541850: Display Advertising; NAICS 541870: Advertising Material Distribution Services; NAICS 541890: Other Services Related to Advertising

7361   Employment Agencies *see* NAICS 541612: Human Resources and Executive Search Consulting Services; NAICS 561310: Employment Placement Agencies

7363   Help Supply Services *see* NAICS 561320: Temporary Help Services; NAICS 561330: Employee Leasing Services

7371   Computer Programming Services *see* NAICS 541511: Custom Computer Programming Services

7372   Prepackaged Software *see* NAICS 511210: Software Publishers; NAICS 334611: Software Reproducing

7373   Computer Integrated Systems Design *see* NAICS 541512: Computer Systems Design Services

7374   Computer Processing and Data Preparation and Processing Services *see* NAICS 514210: Data Processing Services

7375   Information Retrieval Services *see* NAICS 514191: On-Line Information Services

7376   Computer Facilities Management Services *see* NAICS 541513: Computer Facilities Management Services

7378   Computer Maintenance and Repair *see* NAICS 443120: Computer and Software Stores; NAICS 811212: Computer and Office Machine Repair and Maintenance

7379   Computer Related Services, NEC *see* NAICS 541512: Computer Systems Design Services; NAICS 541519: Other Computer Related Services

7381   Detective, Guard, and Armored Car Services *see* NAICS 561611: Investigation Services; NAICS 561612: Security Guards and Patrol Services; NAICS 561613: Armored Car Services

7382   Security Systems Services *see* NAICS 561621: Security Systems Services (except Locksmiths)

7515   Passenger Car Leasing *see* NAICS 532112: Passenger Cars Leasing

7812   Motion Picture and Video Tape Production *see* NAICS 512110: Motion Picture and Video Production

7819   Services Allied to Motion Picture Production *see* NAICS 512191: Teleproduction and Other Post-Production Services; NAICS 561310: Employment Placement Agencies; NAICS 532220: Formal Wear and Costumes Rental; NAICS 532490: Other Commercial and Industrial Machinery and Equipment Rental and Leasing; NAICS 541214: Payroll Services; NAICS 711510: Independent Artists, Writers, and Performers; NAICS 334612: Prerecorded Compact Disc (Except Software), Tape, and Record Manufacturing; NAICS 512199: Other Motion Picture and Video Industries

7822   Motion Picture and Video Tape Distribution *see* NAICS 421990: Other Miscellaneous Durable Goods Wholesalers; NAICS 512120: Motion Picture and Video Distribution

7829   Services Allied to Motion Picture Distribution *see* NAICS 512199: Other Motion Picture and Video Industries; NAICS 512120: Motion Picture and Video Distribution

7993   Coin Operated Amusement Devices *see* NAICS 713120: Amusement Arcades; NAICS 713290: Other Gambling Industries; NAICS 713990: All Other Amusement and Recreation Industries

7999   Amusement and Recreation Services, NEC *see* NAICS 561599: All Other Travel Arrangement and Reservation Services; NAICS 487990: Scenic and Sightseeing Transportation, Other; NAICS 711190: Other Performing Arts Companies; NAICS 711219: Other Spectator Sports; NAICS 713920: Skiing Facilities; NAICS 713940: Fitness and Recreational Sports Centers; NAICS 713210: Casinos (except Casino Hotels); NAICS 713290: Other Gambling Industries; NAICS 712190: Nature Parks and Other Similar Institutions; NAICS 611620: Sports and

Recreation Instruction; NAICS 532292: Recreational Goods Rental; NAICS 487110: Scenic and Sightseeing Transportation, Land; NAICS 487210: Scenic and Sightseeing Transportation, Water; NAICS 713990: All Other Amusement and Recreation Industries

8011   Offices and Clinics of Doctors of Medicine *see* NAICS 621493: Freestanding Ambulatory Surgical and Emergency Centers; NAICS 621491: HMO Medical Centers; NAICS 621112: Offices of Physicians; NAICS 621111: Offices of Physicians (except Mental Health Specialists)

8041   Offices and Clinics of Chiropractors *see* NAICS 621310: Offices of Chiropractors

8049   Offices and Clinics of Health Practitioners, NEC *see* NAICS 621330: Offices of Mental Health Practitioners (except Physicians); NAICS 621340: Offices of Physical, Occupational, and Speech Therapists and Audiologists; NAICS 621399: Offices of All Other Miscellaneous Health Practitioners

8059   Nursing and Personal Care Facilities, NEC *see* NAICS 623311: Continuing Care Retirement Communities; NAICS 623110: Nursing Care Facilities

8062   General Medical and Surgical Hospitals *see* NAICS 622110: General Medical and Surgical Hospitals

8071   Medical Laboratories *see* NAICS 621512: Diagnostic Imaging Centers; NAICS 621511: Medical Laboratories

8082   Home Health Care Services *see* NAICS 621610: Home Health Care Services

8099   Health and Allied Services, NEC *see* NAICS 621991: Blood and Organ Banks; NAICS 541430: Graphic Design Services; NAICS 541922: Commercial Photography; NAICS 621410: Family Planning Centers; NAICS 621999: All Other Miscellaneous Ambulatory Health Care Services

8211   Elementary and Secondary Schools *see* NAICS 611110: Elementary and Secondary Schools

8249   Vocational Schools, NEC *see* NAICS 611513: Apprenticeship Training; NAICS 611512: Flight Training; NAICS 611519: Other Technical and Trade Schools

8299   Schools and Educational Services, NEC *see* NAICS 611512: Flight Training; NAICS 611692: Automobile Driving Schools; NAICS 611710: Educational Support Services; NAICS 611691: Exam Preparation and Tutoring; NAICS 611610: Fine Arts Schools; NAICS 611630: Language Schools; NAICS 611430: Professional and Management Development Training Schools; NAICS 611699: All Other Miscellaneous Schools and Instruction

8322   Individual and Family Social Services *see* NAICS 624110: Child and Youth Services; NAICS 624210: Community Food Services; NAICS 624229: Other Community Housing Services; NAICS 624230: Emergency and Other Relief Services; NAICS 624120: Services for the Elderly and Persons with Disabilities; NAICS 624221: Temporary Shelter; NAICS 922150: Parole Offices and Probation Offices; NAICS 624190: Other Individual and Family Services

8361   Residential Care *see* NAICS 623312: Homes for the Elderly; NAICS 623220: Residential Mental Health and Substance Abuse Facilities; NAICS 623990: Other Residential Care Facilities

8731   Commercial Physical and Biological Research *see* NAICS 541710: Research and Development in the Physical Sciences and Engineering Sciences; NAICS 541720: Research and Development in the Life Sciences

8733   Noncommercial Research Organizations *see* NAICS 541710: Research and Development in the Physical Sciences and Engineering Sciences; NAICS 541720: Research and Development in the Life Sciences; NAICS 541730: Research and Development in the Social Sciences and Humanities

8742   Management Consulting Services *see* NAICS 541611: Administrative Management and General Management Consulting Services; NAICS 541612: Human Resources and Executive Search Consulting Services; NAICS 541613: Marketing Consulting Services; NAICS 541614: Process, Physical, Distribution, and Logistics Consulting

8743   Public Relations Services *see* NAICS 541820: Public Relations Services

8748   Business Consulting Services, NEC *see* NAICS 611710: Educational Support Services; NAICS 541618: Other Management Consulting Services; NAICS 541690: Other Scientific and Technical Consulting Services

8999   Services, NEC *see* NAICS 711510: Independent Artists, Writers, and Performers; NAICS 512210: Record Production; NAICS 541690: Other Scientific and Technical Consulting Services; NAICS 512230: Music Publishers; NAICS 541612: Human Resources and Executive Search Consulting Services; NAICS 514199: All Other Information Services; NAICS 541620: Environmental Consulting Services

PUBLIC ADMINISTRATION

9511   Air and Water Resource and Solid Waste Management *see* NAICS 924110: Air and Water Resource and Solid Waste Management

9512   Land, Mineral, Wildlife, and Forest Conservation *see* NAICS 924120: Land, Mineral, Wildlife, and Forest Conservation

NAICS TO SIC CONVERSION GUIDE

The following listing cross-references six-digit 1997 North American Industry Classification System (NAICS) codes with four-digit 1987 Standard Industrial Classification (SIC) codes that are pertinent to topics covered within this book. Because the systems differ in specificity, some NAICS categories correspond to more than one SIC category.

AGRICULTURE, FORESTRY, FISHING, & HUNTING

111998 All Other Miscellaneous Crop Farming *see* SIC 0139: Field Crops, Except Cash Grains, NEC; SIC 0191: General Farms, Primarily Crop; SIC 0831: Forest Nurseries and Gathering of Forest Products; SIC 0919: Miscellaneous Marine Products; SIC 2099: Food Preparations, NEC

115210 Support Activities for Animal Production *see* SIC 0751: Livestock Services, Except Veterinary; SIC 0752: Animal Specialty Services, Except Veterinary; SIC 7699: Repair Shops and Related Services, NEC

CONSTRUCTION

235310 Electrical Contractors *see* SIC 1731: Electrical Work

FOOD MANUFACTURING

311111 Dog and Cat Food Manufacturing *see* SIC 2047: Dog and Cat Food

311119 Other Animal Food Manufacturing *see* SIC 2048: Prepared Feed and Feed Ingredients for Animals and Fowls, Except Dogs and Cats

311340 Non-Chocolate Confectionery Manufacturing *see* SIC 2064: Candy and Other Confectionery Products; SIC 2067: Chewing Gum; SIC 2099: Food Preparations, NEC

311422 Specialty Canning *see* SIC 2032: Canned Specialties

311423 Dried and Dehydrated Food Manufacturing *see* SIC 2034: Dried and Dehydrated Fruits, Vegetables, and Soup Mixes; SIC 2099: Food Preparations, NEC

311611 Animal (except Poultry) Slaughtering *see* SIC 0751: Livestock Services, Except Veterinary; SIC 2011: Meat Packing Plants; SIC 2048: Prepared Feed and Feed Ingredients for Animals and Fowls, Except Dogs and Cats

311830 Tortilla Manufacturing *see* SIC 2099: Food Preparations, NEC

311911 Roasted Nuts and Peanut Butter Manufacturing *see* SIC 2068: Salted and Roasted Nuts and Seeds; SIC 2099: Food Preparations, NEC

311920 Coffee and Tea Manufacturing *see* SIC 2043: Cereal Breakfast Foods; SIC 2095: Roasted Coffee; SIC 2099: Food Preparations, NEC

311941 Mayonnaise, Dressing, and Other Prepared Sauce Manufacturing *see* SIC 2035: Pickled Fruits and Vegetables, Vegetables Sauces and Seasonings, and Salad Dressings; SIC 2099: Food Preparations, NEC

311942 Spice and Extract Manufacturing *see* SIC 2087: Flavoring Extracts and Flavoring Syrups NEC; SIC 2095: Roasted Coffee; SIC 2099: Food Preparations, NEC; SIC 2899: Chemicals and Chemical Preparations, NEC

311991 Perishable Prepared Food Manufacturing *see* SIC 2099: Food Preparations, NEC

311999 All Other Miscellaneous Food Manufacturing *see* SIC 2015: Poultry Slaughtering and Processing; SIC 2032: Canned Specialties; SIC 2087: Flavoring Extracts and Flavoring Syrups NEC; SIC 2099: Food Preparations, NEC

BEVERAGE & TOBACCO PRODUCT MANUFACTURING

312111 Soft Drink Manufacturing *see* SIC 2086: Bottled and Canned Soft Drinks and Carbonated Waters

312112 Bottled Water Manufacturing *see* SIC 2086: Bottled and Canned Soft Drinks and Carbonated Waters

312221 Cigarette Manufacturing *see* SIC 2111: Cigarettes

TEXTILE MILLS

313320 Fabric Coating Mills *see* SIC 2295: Coated Fabrics, Not Rubberized; SIC 3069: Fabricated Rubber Products, NEC

TEXTILE PRODUCT MILLS

314992 Tire Cord and Tire Fabric Mills *see* SIC 2296: Tire Cord and Fabrics

314999 All Other Miscellaneous Textile Product Mills *see* SIC 2299: Textile Goods, NEC; SIC 2395: Pleating, Decorative and Novelty Stitching, and Tucking for the Trade; SIC 2396: Automotive Trimmings, Apparel Findings, and Related Products; SIC 2399: Fabricated Textile Products, NEC

APPAREL MANUFACTURING

315999 Other Apparel Accessories and Other Apparel Manufacturing *see* SIC 2339: Women's, Misses' and Juniors' Outerwear, NEC; SIC 2385: Waterproof Outerwear; SIC 2387: Apparel Belts; SIC 2389: Apparel and Accessories, NEC; SIC 2396: Automotive Trimmings, Apparel Findings, and Related Products; SIC 2399: Fabricated Textile Products, NEC

PAPER MANUFACTURING

322215 Non-Folding Sanitary Food Container Manufacturing *see* SIC 2656: Sanitary Food Containers, Except Folding; SIC 2679: Converted Paper and Paperboard Products, NEC

322222 Coated and Laminated Paper Manufacturing *see* SIC 2672: Coated and Laminated Paper, NEC; SIC 2679: Converted Paper and Paperboard Products, NEC

322231 Die-Cut Paper and Paperboard Office Supplies Manufacturing *see* SIC 2675: Die-Cut Paper and Paperboard and Cardboard; SIC 2679: Converted Paper and Paperboard Products, NEC

322298 All Other Converted Paper Product Manufacturing *see* SIC 2675: Die-Cut Paper and Paperboard and Cardboard; SIC 2679: Converted Paper and Paperboard Products, NEC

CHEMICAL MANUFACTURING

325191 Gum and Wood Chemical Manufacturing *see* SIC 2861: Gum and Wood Chemicals

325411 Medicinal and Botanical Manufacturing *see* SIC 2833: Medicinal Chemicals and Botanical Products

325412 Pharmaceutical Preparation Manufacturing *see* SIC 2834: Pharmaceutical Preparations; SIC 2835: In Vitro and In Vivo Diagnostic Substances

325413 In-Vitro Diagnostic Substance Manufacturing *see* SIC 2835: In Vitro and In Vivo Diagnostic Substances

325414 Biological Product (except Diagnostic) Manufacturing *see* SIC 2836: Biological Products, Except Diagnostic Substances

325611 Soap and Other Detergent Manufacturing *see* SIC 2841: Soaps and Other Detergents, Except Specialty Cleaners; SIC 2844: Perfumes, Cosmetics, and Other Toilet Preparations

325612 Polish and Other Sanitation Good Manufacturing *see* SIC 2842: Specialty Cleaning, Polishing, and Sanitary Preparations

325620 Toilet Preparation Manufacturing *see* SIC 2844: Perfumes, Cosmetics, and Other Toilet Preparations

325992 Photographic Film, Paper, Plate and Chemical Manufacturing *see* SIC 3861: Photographic Equipment and Supplies

PLASTICS & RUBBER PRODUCTS MANUFACTURING

326192 Resilient Floor Covering Manufacturing *see* SIC 3069: Fabricated Rubber Products, NEC; SIC 3996: Linoleum, Asphalted-Felt-Base, and Other Hard Surface Floor Coverings, NEC

326299 All Other Rubber Product Manufacturing *see* SIC 3069: Fabricated Rubber Products, NEC

PRIMARY METAL MANUFACTURING

331319 Other Aluminum Rolling and Drawing, *see* SIC 3355: Aluminum Rolling and Drawing, NEC; SIC 3357: Drawing and Insulating of Nonferrous Wire

331422 Copper Wire Drawing *see* SIC 3357: Drawing and Insulating of Nonferrous Wire

331491 Nonferrous Metal (except Copper and Aluminum) Rolling. Drawing, and Extruding *see* SIC 3356: Rolling, Drawing, and Extruding of Nonferrous Metals, Except Copper and Aluminum; SIC 3357: Drawing and Insulating of Nonferrous Wire

FABRICATED METAL PRODUCT MANUFACTURING

332710 Machine Shops *see* SIC 3599: Industrial and Commercial Machinery and Equipment, NEC

332999 All Other Miscellaneous Fabricated Metal Product Manufacturing *see* SIC 3291: Abrasive Products; SIC 3432: Plumbing Fixture Fittings and Trim; SIC 3494: Valves and Pipe Fittings, NEC; SIC 3497: Metal Foil and Leaf; SIC 3499: Fabricated Metal Products, NEC; SIC 3537: Industrial Trucks, Tractors, Trailers, and Stackers; SIC 3599: Industrial and Commercial Machinery and Equipment, NEC; SIC 3999: Manufacturing Industries, NEC

MACHINERY MANUFACTURING

333220 Rubber and Plastics Industry Machinery Manufacturing *see* SIC 3559: Special Industry Machinery, NEC

333295 Semiconductor Manufacturing Machinery *see* SIC 3559: Special Industry Machinery, NEC

333298 All Other Industrial Machinery Manufacturing *see* SIC 3559: Special Industry Machinery, NEC; SIC 3639: Household Appliances, NEC

333314 Optical Instrument and Lens Manufacturing *see* SIC 3827: Optical Instruments and Lenses

333315 Photographic and Photocopying Equipment Manufacturing *see* SIC 3861: Photographic Equipment and Supplies

333319 Other Commercial and Service Industry Machinery Manufacturing *see* SIC 3559: Special Industry Machinery, NEC; SIC 3589: Service Industry Machinery, NEC; SIC 3599: Industrial and Commercial Machinery and Equipment, NEC; SIC 3699: Electrical Machinery, Equipment, and Supplies, NEC

333411 Air Purification Equipment Manufacturing *see* SIC 3564: Industrial and Commercial Fans and Blowers and Air Purification Equipment

333412 Industrial and Commercial Fan and Blower Manufacturing *see* SIC 3564: Industrial and Commercial Fans and Blowers and Air Purification Equipment

333512 Machine Tool (Metal Cutting Types) Manufacturing *see* SIC 3541: Machine Tools, Metal Cutting Type

333513 Machine Tool (Metal Forming Types) Manufacturing *see* SIC 3542: Machine Tools, Metal Forming Type

333618 Other Engine Equipment Manufacturing *see* SIC 3519: Internal Combustion Engines, NEC; SIC 3699: Electrical Machinery, Equipment, and Supplies, NEC

333922 Conveyor and Conveying Equipment Manufacturing *see* SIC 3523: Farm Machinery and Equipment; SIC 3535: Conveyors and Conveying Equipment

333999 All Other General Purpose Machinery Manufacturing *see* SIC 3569: General Industrial Machinery and Equipment, NEC; SIC 3599: Industrial and Commercial Machinery and Equipment, NEC

COMPUTER & ELECTRONIC PRODUCT MANUFACTURING

334111 Electronic Computer Manufacturing *see* SIC 3571: Electronic Computers

334112 Computer Storage Device Manufacturing *see* SIC 3572: Computer Storage Devices

334113 Computer Terminal Manufacturing *see* SIC 3575: Computer Terminals

334119 Other Computer Peripheral Equipment Manufacturing *see* SIC 3577: Computer Peripheral Equipment, NEC; SIC 3578: Calculating and Accounting Machines, Except Electronic Computers; SIC 3699: Electrical Machinery, Equipment, and Supplies, NEC

334210 Telephone Apparatus Manufacturing *see* SIC 3661: Telephone and Telegraph Apparatus

334220 Radio and Television Broadcasting and Wireless Communications Equipment Manufacturing *see* SIC 3663: Radio and Television Broadcasting and Communication Equipment; SIC 3679: Electronic Components, NEC

334413 Semiconductor and Related Device Manufacturing *see* SIC 3674: Semiconductors and Related Devices

334416 Electronic Coil, Transformer, and Other Inductor Manufacturing *see* SIC 3661: Telephone and Telegraph Apparatus; SIC 3677: Electronic Coils, Transformers, and Other Inductors; SIC 3825: Instruments for Measuring and Testing of Electricity and Electrical Signals

334418 Printed Circuit/Electronics Assembly Manufacturing *see* SIC 3661: Telephone and Telegraph Apparatus; SIC 3679: Electronic Components, NEC

334419 Other Electronic Component Manufacturing *see* SIC 3679: Electronic Components, NEC

334510 Electromedical and Electrotherapeutic Apparatus Manufacturing *see* SIC 3842: Orthopedic, Prosthetic, and Surgical Appliances and Supplies; SIC 3845: Electromedical and Electrotherapeutic Apparatus

334511 Search, Detection, Navigation, Guidance, Aeronautical, and Nautical System and Instrument Manufacturing *see* SIC 3812: Search, Detection, Navigation, Guidance, Aeronautical, and Nautical Systems and Instruments

334512 Automatic Environmental Control Manufacturing for Regulating Residential, Commercial, and Appliance Use *see* SIC 3822: Automatic Controls for Regulating Residential and Commercial Environments and Appliances

334515 Instrument Manufacturing for Measuring and Testing Electricity and Electrical Signals *see* SIC 3825: Instruments for Measuring and Testing of Electricity and Electrical Signals

334517 Irradiation Apparatus Manufacturing *see* SIC 3844: X-Ray Apparatus and Tubes and Related Irradiation Apparatus; SIC 3845: Electromedical and Electrotherapeutic Apparatus

334519 Other Measuring and Controlling Device Manufacturing *see* SIC 3829: Measuring and Controlling Devices, NEC

334611 Software Reproducing *see* SIC 7372: Prepackaged Software

334612 Prerecorded Compact Disc (Except Software), Tape and Record Reproducing *see* SIC 3652: Phonograph Records and Prerecorded Audio Tapes and Disks; SIC 7819: Services Allied to Motion Picture Production

ELECTRICAL EQUIPMENT, APPLIANCE, & COMPONENT MANUFACTURING

335129 Other Lighting Equipment Manufacturing *see* SIC 3648: Lighting Equipment, NEC; SIC 3699: Electrical Machinery, Equipment, and Supplies, NEC

335921 Fiber Optic Cable Manufacturing *see* SIC 3357: Drawing and Insulating of Nonferrous Wire

335929 Other Communication and Energy Wire Manufacturing *see* SIC 3357: Drawing and Insulating of Nonferrous Wire

335999 All Other Miscellaneous Electrical Equipment and Component Manufacturing *see* SIC 3629: Electrical Industrial Apparatus, NEC; SIC 3699: Electrical Machinery, Equipment, and Supplies, NEC

TRANSPORTATION EQUIPMENT MANUFACTURING

336211 Motor Vehicle Body Manufacturing *see* SIC 3711: Motor Vehicles and Passenger Car Bodies; SIC 3713: Truck and Bus Bodies; SIC 3714: Motor Vehicle Parts and Accessories

336312 Gasoline Engine and Engine Parts Manufacturing *see* SIC 3714: Motor Vehicle Parts and Accessories

336322 Other Motor Vehicle Electrical and Electronic Equipment Manufacturing *see* SIC 3679: Electronic Components, NEC; SIC 3694: Electrical Equipment for Internal Combustion Engines; SIC 3714: Motor Vehicle Parts and Accessories

336330 Motor Vehicle Steering and Suspension Components (except Spring) Manufacturing *see* SIC 3714: Motor Vehicle Parts and Accessories

336340 Motor Vehicle Brake System Manufacturing *see* SIC 3292: Asbestos Products; SIC 3714: Motor Vehicle Parts and Accessories

336350 Motor Vehicle Transmission and Power Train Part Manufacturing *see* SIC 3714: Motor Vehicle Parts and Accessories

336360 Motor Vehicle Fabric Accessories and Seat Manufacturing *see* SIC 2396: Automotive Trimmings, Apparel Findings, and Related Products; SIC 2399: Fabricated Textile Products, NEC; SIC 2531: Public Building and Related Furniture

336399 All Other Motor Vehicle Parts Manufacturing *see* SIC 3519: Internal Combustion Engines, NEC; SIC 3599: Industrial and Commercial Machinery and Equipment, NEC; SIC 3714: Motor Vehicle Parts and Accessories

336414 Guided Missile and Space Vehicle Manufacturing *see* SIC 3761: Guided Missiles and Space Vehicles

336991 Motorcycle, Bicycle, and Parts Manufacturing *see* SIC 3751: Motorcycles, Bicycles, and Parts; SIC 3944: Games, Toys, and Children's Vehicles, Except Dolls and Bicycles

MISCELLANEOUS MANUFACTURING

339112 Surgical and Medical Instrument Manufacturing *see* SIC 3829: Measuring and Controlling Devices, NEC; SIC 3841: Surgical and Medical Instruments and Apparatus

339115 Ophthalmic Goods Manufacturing *see* SIC 3851: Ophthalmic Goods; SIC 5995: Optical Goods Stores

339920 Sporting and Athletic Good Manufacturing *see* SIC 3949: Sporting and Athletic Goods, NEC

339932 Game, Toy, and Children's Vehicle Manufacturing *see* SIC 3944: Games, Toys, and Children's Vehicles, Except Dolls and Bicycles

WHOLESALE TRADE

421410 Photographic Equipment and Supplies Wholesalers *see* SIC 5043: Photographic Equipment and Supplies

421430 Computer and Computer Peripheral Equipment and Software Wholesalers *see* SIC 5045: Computers and Computer Peripheral Equipment and Software

421690 Other Electronic Parts and Equipment Wholesalers *see* SIC 5065: Electronic Parts and Equipment, Not Elsewhere Classified

421990 Other Miscellaneous Durable Goods Wholesalers *see* SIC 5099: Durable Goods, NEC; SIC 7822: Motion Picture and Video Tape Distribution

422490 Other Grocery and Related Product Wholesalers *see* SIC 5149: Groceries and Related Products, NEC

422990 Other Miscellaneous Nondurable Goods Wholesalers *see* SIC 5199: Nondurable Goods, NEC

RETAIL TRADE

443111 Household Appliance Stores *see* SIC 5999: Miscellaneous Retail Stores, NEC; SIC 7623: Refrigeration and Air-Conditioning Services and Repair Shops; SIC 7629: Electrical and Electronic Repair Shops, NEC

443112 Radio, Television, and Other Electronics Stores *see* SIC 5731: Radio, Television, and Consumer Electronics Stores; SIC 5999: Miscellaneous Retail Stores, NEC; SIC 7622: Radio and Television Repair Shops

443120 Computer and Software Stores *see* SIC 5045: Computers and Computer Peripheral Equipment and Software; SIC 5734: Computer and Computer Software Stores; SIC 7378: Computer Maintenance and Repair

445110 Supermarkets and Other Grocery (except Convenience) Stores *see* SIC 5411: Grocery Stores

445120 Convenience Stores *see* SIC 5411: Grocery Stores

446120 Cosmetics, Beauty Supplies, and Perfume Stores *see* SIC 5999: Miscellaneous Retail Stores, NEC

446199 All Other Health and Personal Care Stores *see* SIC 5047: Medical, Dental, and Hospital Equipment and Supplies; SIC 5999: Miscellaneous Retail Stores, NEC

447110 Gasoline Stations with Convenience Stores *see* SIC 5411: Grocery Stores; SIC 5541: Gasoline Service Stations

448310 Jewelry Stores *see* SIC 5944: Jewelry Stores; SIC 5999: Miscellaneous Retail Stores, NEC

451110 Sporting Goods Stores *see* SIC 5941: Sporting Goods Stores and Bicycle Shops; SIC 7699: Repair Shops and Related Services, NEC

451120 Hobby, Toy and Game Stores *see* SIC 5945: Hobby, Toy, and Game Shops

452910 Warehouse Clubs and Superstores *see* SIC 5399: Miscellaneous General Merchandise Stores; SIC 5411: Grocery Stores

453910 Pet and Pet Supplies Stores *see* SIC 5999: Miscellaneous Retail Stores, NEC

453920 Art Dealers *see* SIC 5999: Miscellaneous Retail Stores, NEC

453998 All Other Miscellaneous Store Retailers (except Tobacco Stores) *see* SIC 5261: Retail Nurseries, Lawn and Garden Supply Stores; SIC 5999: Miscellaneous Retail Stores, NEC

454110 Electronic Shopping and Mail-Order Houses *see* SIC 5961: Catalog and Mail-Order Houses

TRANSPORTATION & WAREHOUSING

481111 Scheduled Passenger Air Transportation *see* SIC 4512: Air Transportation, Scheduled

481112 Scheduled Freight Air Transportation *see* SIC 4512: Air Transportation, Scheduled

481219 Other Nonscheduled Air Transportation *see* SIC 0721: Crop Planting, Cultivating and Protecting; SIC 7319: Advertising, NEC; SIC 7335: Commercial Photography

487110 Scenic and Sightseeing Transportation, Land *see* SIC 4119: Local Passenger Transportation, NEC; SIC 4789: Transportation Services, NEC; SIC 7999: Amusement and Recreation Services, NEC

487210 Scenic and Sightseeing Transportation, Water *see* SIC 4489: Water Transportation of Passengers, NEC; SIC 7999: Amusement and Recreation Services, NEC

487990 Scenic and Sightseeing Transportation, Other *see* SIC 4522: Air Transportation, Nonscheduled; SIC 7999: Amusement and Recreation Services, NEC

INFORMATION

511140 Database and Directory Publishers *see* SIC 2741: Miscellaneous Publishing

511199 All Other Publishers *see* SIC 2741: Miscellaneous Publishing

511210 Software Publishers *see* SIC 7372: Prepackaged Software

512110 Motion Picture and Video Production *see* SIC 7812: Motion Picture and Video Tape Production

512120 Motion Picture and Video Distribution *see* SIC 7822: Motion Picture and Video Tape Distribution; SIC 7829: Services Allied to Motion Picture Distribution

512191 Teleproduction and Other Post-Production Services *see* SIC 7819: Services Allied to Motion Picture Production

512199 Other Motion Picture and Video Industries *see* SIC 7819: Services Allied to Motion Picture Production; SIC 7829: Services Allied to Motion Picture Distribution

512210 Record Production *see* SIC 8999: Services, NEC

512220 Integrated Record Production/Distribution *see* SIC 3652: Phonograph Records and Prerecorded Audio Tapes and Disks

512230 Music Publishers *see* SIC 2731: Books: Publishing, or Publishing and Printing; SIC 2741: Miscellaneous Publishing; SIC 8999: Services, NEC

513210 Cable Networks *see* SIC 4841: Cable and Other Pay Television Services

513220 Cable and Other Program Distribution *see* SIC 4841: Cable and Other Pay Television Services

513310 Wired Telecommunications Carriers *see* SIC 4813: Telephone Communications, Except Radiotelephone; SIC 4822: Telegraph and Other Message Communications

513321 Paging *see* SIC 4812: Radiotelephone Communications

513322 Cellular and Other Wireless Telecommunications *see* SIC 4812: Radiotelephone Communications; SIC 4899: Communications Services, NEC

513330 Telecommunications Resellers *see* SIC 4812: Radiotelephone Communications; SIC 4813: Telephone Communications, Except Radiotelephone

513340 Satellite Telecommunications *see* SIC 4899: Communications Services, NEC

513390 Other Telecommunications *see* SIC 4899: Communications Services, NEC

514191 On-Line Information Services *see* SIC 7375: Information Retrieval Services

514199 All Other Information Services *see* SIC 8999: Services, NEC

514210 Data Processing Services *see* SIC 7374: Computer Processing and Data Preparation and Processing Services

FINANCE & INSURANCE

522292 Real Estate Credit *see* SIC 6162: Mortgage Bankers and Loan Correspondents

522310 Mortgage and Other Loan Brokers *see* SIC 6163: Loan Brokers

522390 Other Activities Related to Credit Intermediation *see* SIC 6099: Functions Related to Deposit Banking, NEC; SIC 6162: Mortgage Bankers and Loan Correspondents

523110 Investment Banking and Securities Dealing *see* SIC 6211: Security Brokers, Dealers, and Flotation Companies

523120 Securities Brokerage *see* SIC 6211: Security Brokers, Dealers, and Flotation Companies

523130 Commodity Contracts Dealing *see* SIC 6099: Functions Related to Deposit Banking, NEC; SIC 6221: Commodity Contracts Brokers and Dealers; SIC 6799: Investors, NEC

523140 Commodity Brokerage *see* SIC 6221: Commodity Contracts Brokers and Dealers

523210 Securities and Commodity Exchanges *see* SIC 6231: Security and Commodity Exchanges

523910 Miscellaneous Intermediation *see* SIC 6211: Security Brokers, Dealers, and Flotation Companies; SIC 6799: Investors, NEC

523920 Portfolio Management *see* SIC 6282: Investment Advice; SIC 6371: Pension, Health, and Welfare Funds; SIC 6733: Trusts, Except Educational, Religious, and Charitable; SIC 6799: Investors, NEC

523930 Investment Advice *see* SIC 6282: Investment Advice

523991 Trust, Fiduciary and Custody Activities *see* SIC 6021: National Commercial Banks; SIC 6022: State Commercial Banks; SIC 6091: Nondeposit Trust Facilities; SIC 6099: Functions Related to Deposit Banking, NEC; SIC 6289: Services Allied With the Exchange of Securities or Commodities, NEC; SIC 6733: Trusts, Except Educational, Religious, and Charitable

523999 Miscellaneous Financial Investment Activities *see* SIC 6099: Functions Related to Deposit Banking, NEC; SIC 6211: Security Brokers, Dealers, and Flotation Companies; SIC 6289: Services Allied With the Exchange of Securities or Commodities, NEC; SIC 6792: Oil Royalty Traders; SIC 6799: Investors, NEC

524113 Direct Life Insurance Carriers *see* SIC 6311: Life Insurance

524114 Direct Health and Medical Insurance Carriers *see* SIC 6321: Accident and Health Insurance; SIC 6324: Hospital and Medical Service Plans

524126 Direct Property and Casualty Insurance Carriers *see* SIC 6331: Fire, Marine, and Casualty Insurance; SIC 6351: Surety Insurance

524130 Reinsurance Carriers *see* SIC 6311: Life Insurance; SIC 6321: Accident and Health Insurance; SIC 6324: Hospital and Medical Service Plans; SIC 6331: Fire, Marine, and Casualty Insurance; SIC 6351: Surety Insurance; SIC 6361: Title Insurance

524210 Insurance Agencies and Brokerages *see* SIC 6411: Insurance Agents, Brokers, and Service

524291 Claims Adjusters *see* SIC 6411: Insurance Agents, Brokers, and Service

524292 Third Party Administration for Insurance and Pension Funds *see* SIC 6371: Pension, Health, and Welfare Funds; SIC 6411: Insurance Agents, Brokers, and Service

524298 All Other Insurance Related Activities *see* SIC 6411: Insurance Agents, Brokers, and Service

525190 Other Insurance and Employee Benefit Funds *see* SIC 6321: Accident and Health Insurance; SIC 6324: Hospital and Medical Service Plans; SIC 6331: Fire, Marine, and Casualty Insurance; SIC 6733: Trusts, Except Educational, Religious, and Charitable

REAL ESTATE & RENTAL & LEASING

531110 Lessors of Residential Buildings and Dwellings *see* SIC 6513: Operators of Apartment Buildings; SIC 6514: Operators of Dwellings Other Than Apartment Buildings

532112 Passenger Cars Leasing *see* SIC 7515: Passenger Car Leasing

532220 Formal Wear and Costumes Rental *see* SIC 7299: Miscellaneous Personal Services, NEC; SIC 7819: Services Allied to Motion Picture Production

532292 Recreational Goods Rental *see* SIC 7999: Amusement and Recreation Services, NEC

532490 Other Commercial and Industrial Machinery and Equipment Rental and Leasing *see* SIC 7352: Medical Equipment Rental and Leasing; SIC 7359: Equipment Rental and Leasing, NEC; SIC 7819: Services Allied to Motion Picture Production; SIC 7922: Theatrical Producers (Except Motion Picture) and Miscellaneous Theatrical Services

PROFESSIONAL, SCIENTIFIC, & TECHNICAL SERVICES

541214 Payroll Services *see* SIC 7819: Services Allied to Motion Picture Production; SIC 8721: Accounting, Auditing, and Bookkeeping Services

541430 Graphic Design Services *see* SIC 7336: Commercial Art and Graphic Design; SIC 8099: Health and Allied Services, NEC

541511 Custom Computer Programming Services *see* SIC 7371: Computer Programming Services

541512 Computer Systems Design Services *see* SIC 7373: Computer Integrated Systems Design; SIC 7379: Computer Related Services, NEC

541513 Computer Facilities Management Services *see* SIC 7376: Computer Facilities Management Services

541519 Other Computer Related Services *see* SIC 7379: Computer Related Services, NEC

541611 Administrative Management and General Management Consulting Services *see* SIC 8742: Management Consulting Services

541612 Human Resources and Executive Search Consulting Services *see* SIC 7361: Employment Agencies; SIC 8742: Management Consulting Services; SIC 8999: Services, NEC

541613 Marketing Consulting Services *see* SIC 8742: Management Consulting Services

541614 Process, Physical, Distribution and Logistics Consulting *see* SIC 8742: Management Consulting Services

541618 Other Management Consulting Services *see* SIC 4731: Arrangement of Transportation of Freight and Cargo; SIC 8748: Business Consulting Services, NEC

541620 Environmental Consulting Services *see* SIC 8999: Services, NEC

541690 Other Scientific and Technical Consulting Services *see* SIC 0781: Landscape Counseling and Planning; SIC 8748: Business Consulting Services, NEC; SIC 8999: Services, NEC

541710 Research and Development in the Physical Sciences and Engineering Sciences *see* SIC 8731: Commercial Physical and Biological Research; SIC 8733: Noncommercial Research Organizations

541720 Research and Development in the Life Sciences *see* SIC 8731: Commercial Physical and Biological Research; SIC 8733: Noncommercial Research Organizations

541730 Research and Development in the Social Sciences and Humanities *see* SIC 8732: Commercial Economic, Sociological, and Educational Research; SIC 8733: Noncommercial Research Organizations

541820 Public Relations Services *see* SIC 8743: Public Relations Services

541830 Media Buying Agencies *see* SIC 7319: Advertising, NEC

541850 Display Advertising *see* SIC 7312: Outdoor Advertising Services; SIC 7319: Advertising, NEC

541870 Advertising Material Distribution Services *see* SIC 7319: Advertising, NEC

541890 Other Services Related to Advertising *see* SIC 5199: Nondurable Goods, NEC; SIC 7319: Advertising, NEC; SIC 7389: Business Services, NEC

541922 Commercial Photography *see* SIC 7335: Commercial Photography; SIC 8099: Health and Allied Services, NEC

541940 Veterinary Services *see* SIC 0741: Veterinary Service For Livestock; SIC 0742: Veterinary Services for Animal Specialties; SIC 8734: Testing Laboratories

ADMINISTRATIVE & SUPPORT, WASTE MANAGEMENT & REMEDIATION SERVICES

561310 Employment Placement Agencies *see* SIC 7361: Employment Agencies; SIC 7819: Services Allied to Motion Picture Production; SIC 7922: Theatrical Producers (Except Motion Picture) and Miscellaneous Theatrical Services

561320 Temporary Help Services *see* SIC 7363: Help Supply Services

561330 Employee Leasing Services *see* SIC 7363: Help Supply Services

561599 All Other Travel Arrangement and Reservation Services *see* SIC 4729: Arrangement of Passenger Transportation, NEC; SIC 7389: Business Services, NEC; SIC 7999: Amusement and Recreation Services, NEC; SIC 8699: Membership Organizations, NEC

561611 Investigation Services *see* SIC 7381: Detective, Guard, and Armored Car Services

561612 Security Guards and Patrol Services *see* SIC 7381: Detective, Guard, and Armored Car Services

561613 Armored Car Services *see* SIC 7381: Detective, Guard, and Armored Car Services

561621 Security Systems Services (except Locksmiths) *see* SIC 1731: Electrical Work; SIC 7382: Security Systems Services

EDUCATIONAL SERVICES

611110 Elementary and Secondary Schools *see* SIC 8211: Elementary and Secondary Schools

611430 Professional and Management Development Training Schools *see* SIC 8299: Schools and Educational Services, NEC

611511 Cosmetology and Barber Schools *see* SIC 7231: Beauty Shops; SIC 7241: Barber Shops

611512 Flight Training *see* SIC 8249: Vocational Schools, NEC; SIC 8299: Schools and Educational Services, NEC

611513 Apprenticeship Training *see* SIC 8249: Vocational Schools, NEC

611519 Other Technical and Trade Schools *see* SIC 8243: Data Processing Schools; SIC 8249: Vocational Schools, NEC

611610 Fine Arts Schools *see* SIC 7911: Dance Studios, Schools, and Halls; SIC 8299: Schools and Educational Services, NEC

611620 Sports and Recreation Instruction *see* SIC 7999: Amusement and Recreation Services, NEC

611630 Language Schools *see* SIC 8299: Schools and Educational Services, NEC

611691 Exam Preparation and Tutoring *see* SIC 8299: Schools and Educational Services, NEC

611692 Automobile Driving Schools *see* SIC 8299: Schools and Educational Services, NEC

611699 All Other Miscellaneous Schools and Instruction *see* SIC 8299: Schools and Educational Services, NEC

611710 Educational Support Services *see* SIC 8299: Schools and Educational Services, NEC; SIC 8748: Business Consulting Services, NEC

HEALTH CARE & SOCIAL ASSISTANCE

621111 Offices of Physicians (except Mental Health Specialists) *see* SIC 8011: Offices and Clinics of Doctors of Medicine; SIC 8031: Offices and Clinics of Doctors of Osteopathy

621112 Offices of Physicians, Mental Health Specialists *see* SIC 8011: Offices and Clinics of Doctors of Medicine; SIC 8031: Offices and Clinics of Doctors of Osteopathy

621310 Offices of Chiropractors *see* SIC 8041: Offices and Clinics of Chiropractors

621330 Offices of Mental Health Practitioners (except Physicians) *see* SIC 8049: Offices and Clinics of Health Practitioners, NEC

621340 Offices of Physical, Occupational, and Speech Therapists and Audiologists *see* SIC 8049: Offices and Clinics of Health Practitioners, NEC

621399 Offices of All Other Miscellaneous Health Practitioners *see* SIC 8049: Offices and Clinics of Health Practitioners, NEC

621410 Family Planning Centers *see* SIC 8093: Specialty Outpatient Facilities, NEC; SIC 8099: Health and Allied Services, NEC

621491 HMO Medical Centers *see* SIC 8011: Offices and Clinics of Doctors of Medicine

621493 Freestanding Ambulatory Surgical and Emergency Centers *see* SIC 8011: Offices and Clinics of Doctors of Medicine

621511 Medical Laboratories *see* SIC 8071: Medical Laboratories

621512 Diagnostic Imaging Centers *see* SIC 8071: Medical Laboratories

621610 Home Health Care Services *see* SIC 8082: Home Health Care Services

621991 Blood and Organ Banks *see* SIC 8099: Health and Allied Services, NEC

621999 All Other Miscellaneous Ambulatory Health Care Services *see* SIC 8099: Health and Allied Services, NEC

622110 General Medical and Surgical Hospitals *see* SIC 8062: General Medical and Surgical Hospitals; SIC 8069: Specialty Hospitals, Except Psychiatric

623110 Nursing Care Facilities *see* SIC 8051: Skilled Nursing Care Facilities; SIC 8052: Intermediate Care Facilities; SIC 8059: Nursing and Personal Care Facilities, NEC

623220 Residential Mental Health and Substance Abuse Facilities *see* SIC 8361: Residential Care

623311 Continuing Care Retirement Communities *see* SIC 8051: Skilled Nursing Care Facilities; SIC 8052: Intermediate Care Facilities; SIC 8059: Nursing and Personal Care Facilities, NEC

623312 Homes for the Elderly *see* SIC 8361: Residential Care

623990 Other Residential Care Facilities *see* SIC 8361: Residential Care

624110 Child and Youth Services *see* SIC 8322: Individual and Family Social Services; SIC 8641: Civic, Social, and Fraternal Associations

624120 Services for the Elderly and Persons with Disabilities *see* SIC 8322: Individual and Family Social Services

624190 Other Individual and Family Services *see* SIC 8322: Individual and Family Social Services

624210 Community Food Services *see* SIC 8322: Individual and Family Social Services

624221 Temporary Shelter *see* SIC 8322: Individual and Family Social Services

624229 Other Community Housing Services *see* SIC 8322: Individual and Family Social Services

624230 Emergency and Other Relief Services *see* SIC 8322: Individual and Family Social Services

ARTS, ENTERTAINMENT, & RECREATION

711110 Theater Companies and Dinner Theaters *see* SIC 5812: Eating and Drinking Places; SIC 7922: Theatrical Producers (Except Motion Picture) and Miscellaneous Theatrical Services

711190 Other Performing Arts Companies *see* SIC 7929: Bands, Orchestras, Actors, and Other Entertainers and Entertainment Groups; SIC 7999: Amusement and Recreation Services, NEC

711219 Other Spectator Sports *see* SIC 7941: Professional Sports Clubs and Promoters; SIC 7948: Racing, Including Track Operations; SIC 7999: Amusement and Recreation Services, NEC

711510 Independent Artists, Writers, and Performers *see* SIC 7819: Services Allied to Motion Picture Production; SIC 7929: Bands, Orchestras, Actors, and Other Entertainers and Entertainment Groups; SIC 8999: Services, NEC

712190 Nature Parks and Other Similar Institutions *see* SIC 7999: Amusement and Recreation Services, NEC; SIC 8422: Arboreta and Botanical or Zoological Gardens

713120 Amusement Arcades *see* SIC 7993: Coin Operated Amusement Devices

713210 Casinos (except Casino Hotels) *see* SIC 7999: Amusement and Recreation Services, NEC

713290 Other Gambling Industries *see* SIC 7993: Coin Operated Amusement Devices; SIC 7999: Amusement and Recreation Services, NEC

713920 Skiing Facilities *see* SIC 7999: Amusement and Recreation Services, NEC

713940 Fitness and Recreational Sports Centers *see* SIC 7991: Physical Fitness Facilities; SIC 7997: Membership Sports and Recreation Clubs; SIC 7999: Amusement and Recreation Services, NEC

713990 All Other Amusement and Recreation Industries *see* SIC 7911: Dance Studios, Schools, and Halls; SIC 7993: Coin Operated Amusement Devices; SIC 7997: Membership Sports and Recreation Clubs; SIC 7999: Amusement and Recreation Services, NEC

ACCOMODATION & FOODSERVICES

721110 Hotels (except Casino Hotels) and Motels *see* SIC 7011: Hotels and Motels; SIC 7041: Organization Hotels and Lodging Houses, on Membership Basis

721120 Casino Hotels *see* SIC 7011: Hotels and Motels

721191 Bed and Breakfast Inns *see* SIC 7011: Hotels and Motels

721199 All Other Traveler Accommodations *see* SIC 7011: Hotels and Motels

721310 Rooming and Boarding Houses *see* SIC 7021: Rooming and Boarding Houses; SIC 7041: Organization Hotels and Lodging Houses, on Membership Basis

722110 Full-Service Restaurants *see* SIC 5812: Eating and Drinking Places

722211 Limited-Service Restaurants *see* SIC 5499: Miscellaneous Food Stores; SIC 5812: Eating and Drinking Places

722212 Cafeterias *see* SIC 5812: Eating and Drinking Places

722213 Snack and Nonalcoholic Beverage Bars *see* SIC 5461: Retail Bakeries; SIC 5812: Eating and Drinking Places

722310 Foodservice Contractors *see* SIC 5812: Eating and Drinking Places

722320 Caterers *see* SIC 5812: Eating and Drinking Places

OTHER SERVICES

811212 Computer and Office Machine Repair and Maintenance *see* SIC 7378: Computer Maintenance and Repair; SIC 7629: Electrical and Electronic Repair Shops, NEC; SIC 7699: Repair Shops and Related Services, NEC

812112 Beauty Salons *see* SIC 7231: Beauty Shops

812113 Nail Salons *see* SIC 7231: Beauty Shops

812910 Pet Care (except Veterinary) Services *see* SIC 0752: Animal Specialty Services, Except Veterinary

PUBLIC ADMINISTRATION

922150 Parole Offices and Probation Offices *see* SIC 8322: Individual and Family Social Services

924110 Air and Water Resource and Solid Waste Management *see* SIC 9511: Air and Water Resource and Solid Waste Management

924120 Land, Mineral, Wildlife, and Forest Conservation *see* SIC 9512: Land, Mineral, Wildlife, and Forest Conservation

GENERAL INDEX

This index contains references to companies, associations, persons, government agencies, specific legislation, and terminology cited in the Encyclopedia of Emerging Industries. Citations are followed by the page number(s) in which the term is discussed.

A

ABB Ltd., 652–653

Abbot Laboratories
 AIDS drugs and, 12, 14
 in pharmacogenomics, 579
 in self testing products, 432

ABC. *See* American Broadcasting Company

Abdominal exercisers, 602, 603

Abe, Takeshi, 11

About.com, 832

Absolute Software (Company), 115–116

Abuzz Inc., 393

Academic achievement, charter schools and, 83, 84, 86

Accel Partners, 175

Accelerated Strategic Computing Initiative, 555

Accelerometers, 436, 437–438, 440–441, 540, 564

Accenture (Company), 379

Access Direct Inc., 770

Access to Medical Treatment Act, 29

Accidents, cellular telephones and, 838

Accounting firms, in IT consulting, 376, 378

Accuator/sensor systems, 440

Accuwave (Company), 324

ACNielsen Corporation, 430

ACORN. *See* Association of Community for Reform Now

Acquired immunodeficiency syndrome. *See* AIDS (Disease)

Acquisitions and mergers
 advice for, 228
 risk management for, 646
 venture capital for, 778, 779–780

Actiontec (Company), 746

Activase, 295

Active adult communities, 1

Active brake technology, 242

Active Tuned Mass Absorbers, 501

Actors, virtual, 98

ACTS Photonic Domain, 588

Acupuncture, 32–33, 306, 309, 489

Adaptec, Inc., 718

Adaptive Network Security Alliance, 111

Adaptive phased array, 449

ADC Telecommunications Inc., 261

Addiction, to gambling, 284

Ademco Security Group, 672

Adeno-associated virus, 298

Adept Technology, 653

Administaff, Inc., 624, 625

Administration. *See* Management

Administration on Aging, 1

Adobe Portable Document format, 218

Adobe Systems Inc.
 in desktop publishing, 133, 134
 in digital imaging, 140
 in encryption software, 220

Adoption, 252

Adrenalin Dreams Adventures, 244

ADSL (Asymmetric digital subscriber line), 757

ADT (Company), 667

Adult communities, **1–6**

Adult day care centers, 507, 508, 509–511
 corporate, 508, 509–510
 short-term, 510
 specialty, 509, 510

Adult education
 alternative, **19–27**
 history of, 21–23
 statistics on, 23
 virtual reality for, 794, 796
 vocational, 19–27, 632

Advance Intelligent Networking technology, 758

Advanced Casino Systems Corporation, 286

Advanced Cell Technology (Company), 49

Advanced Communications Technologies and Services program, 588

Advanced Fingerprint Recognition System, 71

Advanced Micro Devices, Inc., 675, 680

Advanced mobile phone service (AMPS), 835, 840

Advanced Networks and Services (Company), 368

Advanced Photo System, 140

Advanced planning and scheduling software, 406

Advanced Research Projects Agency
 in Internet development, 367–368
 in micromachines, 437, 439
 in optical storage, 534
 in photonics, 587
 in sensing devices, 542

Ecotourism, 707, 709
Ecotourism Society, 707, 710
EcoWater Systems Inc., 814, 815
EDAP Technomed Group, 448–449
Edelman Public Relations Worldwide, 313–314
EDFA. *See* Erbium-doped fiber amplifiers
EDI (Electronic Data Interchange), 167. *See also* Electronic
  funds
Edison, Thomas, 677–678, 753
Edison Schools, Inc., 83, 85–87, 90, 91, 92
Edison Technology Solutions, 595
Edmund's Web, 638
EDS. *See* Electronic Data Systems Corporation
Education. *See also* Schools
  adult (*See* Adult education)
  distance (*See* Distance education)
  for entrepreneurship, **227–232**
  franchises for, **89–93**
  history of, 21–23
  statistics on, 19, 20, 23
  virtual reality for, 794, 796, 798
  vocational (*See* Vocational education)
Education Alternative's Inc., 83, 86
Education Industry Group, 85
Education management organizations
  charter schools and, 81, 83, 86
  franchises for, 89–93
  profitability of, 85, 87
Educational products, 90
Educational television, 20, 23, 86
Educators in Private Practice, 92
EduClick.com, 90
Eduventures Inc., 89, 90
Eduventures.com, 24, 230
Edwards, Anthony, 349
Edwards, Robert, 252
Efab (Electrochemical fabrication), 439
EG&G Inc., 441
Egghead.com, Inc., 176, 182
Eggs, donor, 250
Egon Zehnder International, 631
eGrocer.com, 195
eHealthInsurance.com, 605
Ehrlich, Paul, 469
Eigen-ID, 464
Eight O'Clock (Company), 700
Einstein, Albert, 396
e4L, Inc., 348, 352
El-Sum, Hussein, 319
Elbrus International, 557
Eldeib, Hesham, 324
Elder care services, 270, **507–511**
Eldercare Locator, 509
Elderly. *See also* Aging
  adult communities for, 1–6
  apartment houses for, 1, 508
  day care for, 507, 508, 509–511
  managed care and, 414
  personal care services for, 507–511
  political clout of, 5
Electric utilities. *See also* Power generation
  fuel cells for, 273, 275, 277–278, 279
  fusion for, 395
  geographical information systems for, 146
Electric vehicles, 41, 42

Electrochemical fabrication, 439
Electroluminescent video displays, 785, 788
Electromagnetic fields, health effects of, 450
Electron beams, in holography, 319
Electron microscopes, holographic, 320
Electronic air cleaners, 808, 813
Electronic Bill of Rights, 73
Electronic Business XML Initiative, 847
Electronic commerce. *See* E-commerce
Electronic communications networks, **209–213**
Electronic currency. *See* Electronic funds
Electronic data interchange. *See* EDI (Electronic Data
  Interchange)
Electronic Data Systems Corporation, 379, 731, 732
Electronic file transfer, desktop publishing and, 133
Electronic funds
  development of, 167
  e-wallets, 122, 125, 635, 684, 828, 831
  electronic purse cards, 122, 125, 684, 828
  XML for, 846, 847
Electronic Industries Association, 542
Electronic ink, 220
Electronic mail systems. *See* E-mail
Electronic Medical Record, 739, 848–849
Electronic publishing, **215–221**
  advertising and, 217, 219
  of books, 215, 216, 217–218, 219
  copyright law and, 217, 220
  desktop publishing and, 131–136
  development of, 216–217
  distribution of, 132
  e-zines, 133–134, 218
  of magazines, 215, 216, 217, 218, 219
  of newspapers, 215, 216–217, 218–219
  pay-per-view for, 216
  pornography and, 217
  standards for, 218, 219
  subscriptions for, 216, 218
Electronic purse cards, 122, 125, 684, 828
Electronic records, archiving, 362, 529
Electronic Retailing Association, 347, 349, 350, 352
Electronic shopping. *See* E-commerce
Electronic signatures. *See* Digital signatures
Electronicast, 263
ElectroniCast Corporation, 584
Electronics Industry Association, 539
Electrons, 584, 593
Electrosurgical generators, 457
Eli Lilly Company, 471
Elix, Douglas T., 106
Elliptical trainers, 603, 604, 605
Ellison, Lawrence J., 26
Elsag Bailey Process Automation N.V., 652, 653
eLuxury.com, 173
Embargoes, oil, 39
Embedded systems, in desktop publishing, 135
Embryo research, 255, 762, 764
Embryologists, 254–255
Embryology laboratories, 251
EMC Corporation, 719
Emergency medical services, 417, 738
Emerging-market funds, 482
Emissions (Pollution)
  alternative fuels and, 40, 41
  carbon dioxide, 43

Health Care Financing Administration
    on home health care, 327, 328, 329, 332
    on telemedicine, 736, 737
Health Care Property Investors, Inc., 6
Health Care REIT, Inc., 6
Health clubs
    in health spas, 306
    juice bars in, 383
Health effects
    of cellular telephones, 450
    of electromagnetic fields, 450
Health foods. *See* Natural foods
Health insurance, 413–414. *See also* Health maintenance
  organizations; Managed health-care services
Health Insurance Association of America, 507
Health Insurance Portability and Accountability Act, 416
Health Maintenance Organization Act, 415
Health maintenance organizations, 413–420
    fertility medicine and, 249–250
    non-profit, 419
    open-ended, 414
Health-Mark Diagnostics, L.L.C., 433
Health-O-Meter Products Inc., 814
Health occupations, 29, 419
Health Partners of Minneapolis, 414
Health Resource and Services Administration, on telemedicine,
  736
Health spas, **305–310**
    in adult communities, 3
    alternative medicine in, 306, 307, 309
    in Asia, 309
    cost of, 307, 308
    day, 305, 306, 307
    destination, 305–306, 307–308
    for dogs, 308
    in Europe, 309
    history of, 306–307
    oxygen therapy in, 550
Healthcare Information and Systems Society, 738
Healthcor Holdings, 331
Healthquest Travel Inc., 510
HealthShield Technologies, 55
Heanue, John, 319
Hearing impairment, infomercials for, 348–349
Heart diseases
    heart replacement for, 765–766
    nutritional supplements for, 518
    tissue engineering for, 762–763, 764
Heart rate monitors, 603
Heart surgery, minimally invasive, 457–458
Heart-valve replacement, 762–763
HeartBar, 497
Heartland Wireless Communications, 449
Heat therapy, 449
Heating, microwave applications for, 445
Hebb Industries, 602
Heidrick & Struggles International, Inc., 628, 629, 630, 631
Heilig, Morton, 792
Heinz Pet Products, 569, 570, 572
Helicopters, noise from, 501
Helios airplanes, 280
Hemophilia, gene therapy for, 298
Henderson, Charles, 449
Hendrix, Gary, 113
Henry's Marketplace, Inc., 490

Henson, Paul, 259
Hepatitis
    drugs for, 295, 724
    home diagnostic tests for, 429, 432
    vaccines for, 726
Hepburn Act, 404
Herbal medicine, 513. *See also* Alternative medicine;
  Herbs
    demand for, 490, 517
    in Europe, 489
    in health spas, 309
    history of, 516
    for pets, 498
    spending on, 33
    use of, 516, 517
Herbalife International, Inc., 517
Herbicides, resistance to, 292
Herbs. *See also* Herbal medicine
    in anti-aging products, 46, 47, 48, 50, 51
    in premium beverages, 609, 612–613
Herceptin, 295
Herdrich, Cynthia, 418
Heritage Foundation, on patient's rights, 417
Hershey, Alfred, 292
Hershey Foods, 425
Hertz, Heinrich Rudolph, 446
Hesselink, Lambertus, 319
Heterodyne Mach-Zehnder inferometry, 319
Hewlett-Packard Company
    in digital imaging, 140
    handheld systems, 301, 303
    on input/output standards, 720
    in IT consulting, 379
    in knowledge management, 394
    laser printers, 133
    in molecular design, 465
    network support from, 104, 106
    printers, 616–618
    in robotics development, 650
    in semiconductors, 679–680
    in smart cards, 687
    in supercomputers, 556, 557, 558
    in systems integration, 733
Heymann, David, 15
HHS. *See* Department of Health and Human Services
High definition television
    development of, 157, 785
    digital micromirror devices for, 440
    direct broadcast, 164
    fiber optics for, 259
    holography for, 322–323
    micromachined chips for, 438
    transmission of, 160
    video displays for, 783–784
High Sierra Agreement, 531
High-tech PR firms, **311–315**
High-voltage FED phosphor video displays, 788
Higher Education Act, 23
Highways, noise control and, 501
Hiking, 711, 712
Hill and Knowlton, 314
Hill's Pet Nutrition, 572
Himalayan trekking, 712
Hinduism, 486
Hispanic Chamber of Commerce, 228

Hostile takeovers. *See also* Acquisitions and mergers
  insurance coverage of, 646
Hot-air balloons, 243
Hot springs, in spas, 306
HotBot, 218
Hotels and motels
  online reservations for, 203, 205, 207
  spas in, 306, 307–308
HotWired, 218
Housewares, sales of, 410, 411
Housing. *See also* Adult communities
  apartments, 1, 508
  smart, 335, 337
Howard, John, 30
Howes, Daniel, 641
HPC processors, 558
H&R Block, 266, 269
HTML, 820, 821, 823–825
  development of, 845
  editors for, 133
  vs. XML, 361
  XML and, 843, 844, 846
HTTP (Hypertext Transfer Protocol), 821
Hubble Space Telescope, 541, 542, 663
Huberts, Don, 276
Hubs (Network), 337, 719
Hughes, Eugene, 516
Hughes, Howard, gambling and, 282–283
Hughes' Development Corporation, 516
Hughes Electronics Corporation, 661
Hughes Network Systems, 161, 662
Hughes Space and Communications Company, 663
Huizenga, J.C., 85, 92
Human Authentication Application Programming Interface, 72, 74
Human Genome Project
  genetic engineering and, 289, 290, 293
  molecular design and modeling for, 464, 468
  pharmacogenomics and, 576, 577
Human Genome Sciences, Inc., 292, 579
Human growth hormone. *See* Somatotropin
Human immune virus. *See* HIV virus
Human Reproductive and Genetic Technologies Bill, 764
Human resource information management systems, 358
Humana Inc., 419
Humegon, 253
Hummingbird (Company), 393
Hundt, Reed, 753
Hunt-Scanlon Corporation, 630
Hurd, Earl, 96
Hurt, Richard, 695
Huxley, Aldous, 792
Hybrid computers, 469
Hybrid funds, 482
Hybridization, 290, 292
Hyde, Joni, 606
Hydro-Quebec, 395
Hydroelectric power, 596
Hydrogen
  fuel cells, 274, 275, 276, 278, 279–280
  fuel pumps, 277
  sensors for, 43
  vehicle fuels, 37, 42–43
Hydrogen peroxide therapy, 547
Hydrotherapy, 306–307, 309

Hyperbaric Oxygen Clinic, 547
Hyperbaric oxygen therapy, **545–551**
Hyperion Solutions, 360
Hyperopia, laser surgery for, 523, 527
HyperPlex, 558
Hypertext, 216
Hypertext Markup Language (HTML), 820, 821, 823–825
  development of, 845
  XML and, 843, 844, 846
Hypertext Transfer Protocol (HTTP), 821
Hyperthermia, 449
Hypnotherapy, for smoking cessation, 690, 692
Hypoxico, Inc., 547

I

i-glasses, 784
I/O Software, 72
i2 Technologies, 169
Iams Company, 572–573
IBM Corporation
  antitrust law and, 61
  in biometric identification systems, 69
  in digital imaging, 140
  in excimer lasers, 524
  executive recruitment for, 628–629
  in handheld systems, 300
  history of, 678, 730
  in holography, 319, 321
  in home networks, 338
  in information management systems, 360
  on input/output standards, 720
  in Internet development, 368
  as ISP, 368–369
  in knowledge management products, 391
  Network Computing Framework, 357
  in quantum computers, 590
  security for, 670
  in serial storage architecture development, 718
  in storage networks, 719
  in supercomputers, 554, 556, 557
  in used computer equipment, 769, 770, 771
  in video display development, 788
  in voice recognition systems, 803, 804
  in XML development, 847–848
IBM Global Services
  in IT consulting, 379
  in knowledge management, 391, 393
  in network support services, 105–106
  in systems integration, 732
Ice cream, coffee, 701
ICE (Information and Content Exchange protocol), 846
Iceland
  financial transactions in, 127
  fuel cells in, 279
ICN Pharmaceuticals, Inc., 48
ICO Global, 661
Icon Health & Fitness, Inc., 602, 604, 605
ICOS Corporation, 470
ICS Learning Systems, 26
ICSI (Intracytoplasmic sperm injection), 249, 251, 252, 256
ICTransducers, 437
Idaho National Engineering and Environmental Laboratory, 238
IDC. *See* International Data Corporation
ID3D HandKey Biometric System, 68

Itsy Bitsy Entertainment, 425
ITT Educational Services, Inc., 26
IUCRC. *See* Industry-University Cooperative Research Center
IVF (in vitro fertilization), 249–250, 251, 252, 254, 255–256
iVillage.com, 829
iXL Enterprises, 379–380

J

J. Crew Group Inc., 410
J & D Resources, Inc., 106
Jackson National Life, 11
Jacobson, Joseph, 220
Jago, David, 499
Jails. *See* Correctional institutions
Jamba Juice Company, 383, 385, 386
Japan
 anti-aging products in, 51
 biometric identification in, 73
 desktop publishing in, 135
 DVD in, 156
 e-commerce in, 177
 holography in, 322
 infomercials in, 352
 Internet use in, 372
 knowledge management in, 393
 mail-order sales in, 411
 micromachines development in, 441–442
 new age movement in, 491
 nutraceuticals in, 499
 nutritional supplements in, 518
 online brokers in, 189–190
 optical storage in, 533
 oxygen therapy in, 551
 photonics in, 588
 premium beverages in, 612
 robotics in, 655
 satellite television in, 163
 satellites and, 663, 664
 semiconductors in, 680
 sensing devices in, 542
 smart cards in, 687
 smoking cessation products in, 694
 solar power in, 597, 598
 spas in, 309
 telephone services in, 757
 toys in, 344
 vehicle navigation systems in, 149
 venture capital in, 780
 virtual reality development in, 796
Japanese Broadcasting Corporation, 785
Japanese Technology Evaluation Center, 533
Java 3-D View Model, 795
Java (Computer language), 361–362, 795
JavaCard, 686
JAWS Technologies Inc., 669
J.B. Hunt Logistics, 405–406
J.C. Penney Company, Inc., 410
J.D. Powers and Associates, on credit cards, 124
JDS Uniphase Corporation, 261–262
Jefferson, Richard A., 296–297
Jefferson Charter School, 85
Jenner, Edward, 722
Jennings & Company, 312
Jet aircraft, noise control for, 501, 502, 504

Jet Propulsion Laboratory, in holography, 321
Jet Skis, 503
JetSend technology, 618
Jetset Tours, 207
Jewelry, online sales of, 173
Jimmy Dean Foods, 495
J.L. Torbec Company, 670
Job creation, 229
Job placement agencies. *See* Employment services
Job training. *See* Vocational education
Jobs, Steve, 99
Joffe, Stephen N., 524
Johns Hopkins University, on adult communities, 5
Johnson, Magic, 8, 9
Johnson, Megan A., 34
Johnson & Johnson
 anti-aging products, 50
 antibacterial products, 55
 home diagnostic tests, 431–432
 in minimally invasive technologies, 454, 457
 nutraceuticals, 497
 smoking cessation products, 693
Johnson Controls, Inc., 504
Joint Commission on Accreditation of Healthcare Organizations,
 on home health care, 328
Jonas, Wayne, 34
Jones, Arthur, 602
Jones Institute for Reproductive Medicine, 253
Jordan Report, on cholera, 724
Jordan Whitney, Inc., 350
Jornada, 303
Joseph, James, 48
Journalists, public relations firms and, 313
Journals. *See* Magazines
JOURNEYS International, 709
Joy, Bill, 440
JP Morgan, communications networks and, 211
Juice & Smoothie Bar Consulting, 386
Juice bars, **383–387**
Juice Gallery, 383, 386
Juice It, 386
Juice Kitchen Inc., 386
Juice Stop, 386
Juices
 drinks, 607, 608, 609, 610
 fruit (*See* Fruit juices)
 unpasteurized, 385, 607
 vegetable, **383–387**
Junglee Corporation, 172
Jupiter Communications, Inc.
 on e-commerce, 165, 169, 173, 193, 829
 on electronic publishing, 217
 on online music, 197, 198, 200
 on online travel reservations, 205
Jurassic Park, 99
Just Juice, 386
Juvenile Products Manufacturers Association, 339, 340
JVC. *See* Victor Company of Japan, LTD

K

K-B Toys, 339, 340
K Laser Technology Corporation, 322
Ka-band, 660
Kaiser Permanente, 419

Loans. *See also* Mortgages
  online, 180, 476, 478
  subprime, 476
Local area networks. *See also* Network computers; Network
 servers
  history of, 367
  microwave applications in, 448
  printers for, 618
  support services for, 103, 104
Local multipoint distribution service (LMDS), 448, 835, 837
Local telephone service, 743, 744, 746. *See also* Telephone
 services
  fiber optics for, 257, 259, 260–261
  ISPs and, 369–370
  wireless communications for, 449–450
Local television broadcasting, 160, 161, 162
Lockheed Martin Corporation
  in infrared cameras, 540
  merger of, 540
  in satellite development, 149, 662, 663, 664, 665
  in sensing devices, 541
Lodging Management Systems, 286
Logic circuits, photonic, 586
Logic devices, 677
Logicon, Inc., 541
Logistics outsourcing services, **403–406**
Logitech International SA, 139–130
Loja dos Micros, 772
Long Distance Manager, 748
Long-distance telephone service, 746–747, 748. *See also*
 Telephone services
  fiber optics for, 257, 259
  providers of, 755–756
  revenues from, 751
Long-term care
  community-based, 5
  insurance for, 329, 507, 510
Loral Space & Communications Ltd., 661, 662, 663, 664
Lord Corporation, 502
L'Oreal SA, 50
Lorenzini, Beth, 384
Los Alamos National Laboratory, in supercomputers, 554
Loss prevention, 644, 645. *See also* Risk management
 services
Lost Arrow Corporation, 245
Lotteries, 282
Lotus Corporation, 357, 361
  knowledge management products, 391, 393
Low fat food, 493, 495
Lowestfare.com Inc., 207
LSI Logic Corporation, 680, 681
Lucas, George, 98, 99, 423
Lucas NovaSensor, 441
Lucent NetCare Services, 105
Lucent Technologies Inc.
  in call center software, 79
  in fiber optic technology, 261, 262
  history of, 752
  in home networking, 338
  in laser technology, 398–399
  network support from, 105
  in noise control, 501
  in optical switching, 758
  in photonics, 585, 587
  in semiconductors, 681

  in telephone services, 746
  in voice recognition systems, 804
  voice recognition systems for, 804
Lueg, Paul, 502
Lufthansa Air Cargo, 207
Lum, Susie, 796
Lung cancer, 689
Luteins (Carotenoids), 514
Lutz, Frank, 281
Luxury automobiles, 640
Luxury goods, online sales of, 173
Lycopene, 514, 518
Lycos, Inc., 218, 828, 831, 832
Lynch, Miller, Moore, O'Hara, 630
Lyra Research, Inc., 615

M

Machat, Jeffrey, 526
Machinima, 98
MacLaine, Shirley, 486
Macy's by Mail, 410
Madge Networks Inc., 338
Magazines
  distribution of, 132
  e-zines, 133–134, 218
  electronic, 215, 216, 217, 218, 219
  new age, 490
  postdistribution printing of, 135
Magna Doodle, 343
Magnetic resonance imaging, holographic, 319
Mail-order and catalog shopping, **407–412**
  in Asia, 411
  in business-to-business sales, 408
  for coffee, 700
  for computers, 410
  credit cards and, 124
  in Europe, 411
  for fitness products, 603
  for housewares, 410, 411
  for infant and preschool products, 340
  Internet based (*See* E-commerce)
  for medical self-testing products, 430
  for music CDs, 201
  sales by, 407, 408
  sales tax on, 409–410
  satisfaction with, 409
Mail services, for mail-order sales, 408
Maiman, Theodore Harold, 319, 396
Mainframe computers, 358
Mainframe Entertainment Inc., 99–100
Malaria, 723, 724
Malaysia, telemedicine for, 740
Managed Care Consumer Protection Act, 416
Managed Care Information Center, 417, 419
Managed health-care services, **413–420**
  call centers for, 78
  government regulation of, 413, 416, 417
  history of, 415–416
  litigation and, 417, 418
  Medicaid and, 414
  Medicare and, 417
  satisfaction with, 415, 417
  standards for, 415

for home health care, 327, 329, 331
managed care and, 414
telemedicine and, 736
Medical education, virtual reality for, 798
Medical equipment
endoscopic technology (See Endoscopes)
for home health care, 328
lasers for (See Laser surgery)
micromachines for, 437, 440, 441
microwave applications for, 448–449
nanobots, 440
virtual reality for, 794, 796, 797–798
Medical records, electronic, 739, 848–849
Medical self-testing products, **429–434**
Medical transcription, voice recognition systems for, 803
Medicare
eligibility for, 414
fraud, 329, 416
for home health care, 327, 328, 329, 331, 332
managed care and, 417
nursing homes and, 4
reform of, 417
reimbursement reductions, 416
telemedicine and, 736, 738
Medicinal chemistry, molecular modeling for, 467–471
Medicinal plants. See Herbal medicine; Herbs
Medicine. See also Health care; specific types of therapy, e.g., Hydrotherapy
alternative (See Alternative medicine)
Ayurvedic, 306, 489
fertility (See Fertility medicine)
herbal (See Herbal medicine)
homeopathy, 33–34 (See also Homeopathic products)
military, 735, 740
telecommunications for (See Telemedicine)
web portals for, 830
Medicus Group, 550
Meditation, 30, 485, 486, 489–490, 491
Medline, 737
MedQuist Inc., 803
MedVision, Inc., 740
Megastores. See Superstores
Melatonex, 50
Melatonin, in anti-aging products, 50
Melissa (Computer virus), 111
Memory cards, 683–684
Memory chips, 676–677
MEMS. See Microelectromechanical systems (MEMS)
Mendel, Gregor, 290
Meningitis, vaccines for, 726
Menlo Logistics, 405
Menorrhagia, 449
Menotropins, 251, 253
Mental health services, 331, 415, 692
Merced IA-64, 556
Mercedes-Benz, in fuel cell development, 279
Mercer Management Consulting, on logistics services, 406
Merck & Company, Inc.
AIDS and, 9, 14
hair restoration products, 50
in molecular modeling, 470
in pharmacogenomics research, 579
in vaccine development, 724
Mercury, cleanup of, 233
Mergers. See Acquisitions and mergers

MERIT, 368
Merlin, Joseph, 242
Merrill Lynch & Co., Inc.
on corporate education, 23–24
on educational franchises, 89
electronic communications networks and, 211
online accounts, 188
on satellites, 659, 661
Mertrodin, 251
Messaging systems. See also E-mail
satellites for, 661
MET-Rx Nutrition, 517
Metabolife International, 518
Metadata, 356
Metal roofing, solar, 597
Meteorology. See Weather forecasting
Methanol
fuels, 37, 38, 40, 277, 278
photovoltaic generation of, 594
Methyl tertiary butyl ether
cleanup of, 236, 238
water pollution from, 40–41, 277
MetLife Mature Market Institute, 509–510
Metricom, Inc., 662
Metrodin, 253
Metromedia Company, 262
Metromedia Fiber Network Inc., 262
Metropolitan area networks, 104
Mexico
beverage industry in, 612
satellite television in, 163
Meyers, Jesse, 611
MGM, in DVD development, 154
MGM Grand, Inc., 285
MGM Mirage Inc., 285
Michelson Doppler Imager, 323
Mickey Mouse, 422, 423, 424
Microalgae, 517, 518
Microban Products Company, 56
Microbolometers, 539
Microcomputers. See Computers; Personal computers
Microcoolers, 441
Microcosm, 436
Microdisplays, 436
Microelectromechanical systems (MEMS), 435–443. See also Nanotechnology
integrated, 437
for photonic switches, 589
for sensor development, 542
for surgery, 457–458
Microhydrin, 48
Microkeratomes, 527
Micromachines, **435–443**. See also Nanotechnology
in Europe, 441–442
funding for, 436–437, 439
government regulation of, 437
in Japan, 441–442
for medical equipment, 437, 440, 441
for photonic switches, 589
research in, 436–437, 442–443
for sensor development, 436, 438, 441, 542
for surgery, 457–458
Micron Technology Inc., 788
Microorganisms. See also Bacteria; Viruses
filtration of, 813, 816–817

Microphones, noise control, 504

Microprocessors. *See also* Semiconductors
  automated manufacturing of, 653
  development of, 678
  DNA, 439, 442–443
  field-programmable gate array, 555
  Itanium, 680
  MEMS, 436, 440
  for parallel processing, 556–557
  Pentium, 116, 679–680, 769, 770
  photonic, 584, 586, 589
  role of, 677
  sensors for, 542
  for smart cards, 683, 686
  transistors for, 681

Microrelays, 436, 441

Microscopes
  detection cantilevers for, 441
  holographic electron, 320
  photonics for, 587

Microscopic plumbers, 438–439

Microsoft Corporation
  antitrust law and, 393
  in biometric identification systems, 72
  in digital imaging, 140
  in electronic publishing, 218, 219
  in handheld systems, 301–302
  holographic labels for, 318
  infomercials for, 349
  in knowledge management, 391–392, 393, 394
  in online travel services, 206
  in optical storage, 531–532
  public relations firms for, 314
  in satellite television, 160
  in smart card development, 686
  software rentals and, 63
  in voice recognition systems, 802, 803
  web portals and, 831, 832
  World Wide Web Consortium and, 820
  in XML development, 847, 848

Microsoft Network, 369, 371, 831

Microsoft Outlook, 392, 393

Microsoft Windows
  based terminals, 62–63, 105
  for smart cards, 686
  voice recognition systems for, 803
  Windows CE, 299, 301–302, 303

MicroSpe, 43

Microsurgery, 458

Microsystems technology. *See* Nanotechnology

Microsystems Technology Office, 437

MicroTouch Systems Inc., 55

Microwave Bypass Systems, Inc., 448

Microwave Medical Corporation, 449

Microwave ovens, 445, 446, 447, 448, 450–451

Microwave Science LLC, 451

Microwave technology, **445–452**
  antennas for, 447, 450
  health effects of, 450
  in holography, 319
  in imaging systems, 449
  in medical equipment, 448–449
  in wireless communication systems, 445–448, 449–450

MidasPlus program, 465

Midwest Water Technologies, 815

Military industry. *See* Defense industry

Military medicine, telemedicine for, 735, 740

Milk, bovine somatotropin in, 296

Milken, Michael, 26

Millenium Vaccine Initiative, 9

Millennium Pharmaceuticals Inc., 578–579

Miller, Arthur R., 23

Miller, Cynthia, 489

Miller, Elliot, 486

Miller, Richard, 157

Million Solar Roofs Initiatives, 595–596

Millstone, 700

Milton Bradley, 344

Mind/body medicine, 29–30

MindSpring Enterprises, 370

MindSurf, 91

Mineral supplements, 513–518. *See also* Nutritional
  supplements

Minicomputers, 358

Minidiscs, 532–533

Minimally invasive technologies, **453–459**

Minolta, in digital imaging, 140

Minority groups, entrepreneurship training for, 228

Minoxidil, 46, 50

Minute Maid, 609

Mirage Resorts, Inc., 283, 285

Miramax Film Corporation, 156, 200, 201

Miraval Life, 308

Miros, Inc., 68–69, 70, 115

Mirrors, in digital micromirror devices, 440

Missiles
  lasers for, 396–397, 398
  sensors for, 537, 539, 541

MIT. *See* Massachusetts Institute of Technology

Mitsubishi Electric, 149, 152

Mitsubishi Motors Corporation, 279

MMDS (Multipoint multichannel distribution service), 447, 837

MMS-X system, 469

Mobile communication systems. *See* Wireless communication
  systems

Mobile computers. *See* Portable computers

Mobile radio service, 834

Modeling, molecular, **467–472**

Modems
  cable, 751, 755, 822
  call waiting, 746
  DSL, 260
  smart card readers for, 687

Molecular biotechnology, 462, 467–468

Molecular design, **461–466,** 722

Molecular Design Institute, 464, 465–466

Molecular field analysis, comparative, 465

Molecular Interactive Display and Simulation (MidasPlus), 465

Molecular modeling, **467–472**

Molecular Simulations Inc., 465, 468, 470

Moloch-2, 469

Molten carbonate fuel cells, 278

Moly (Software), 469

Monea, Paul, 353

Money management. *See* Financial planning services

Money market funds, 482–483

Money Store, 477

Monsanto Company, 293, 295–296, 463

Monteiro, Othon, 681

Montgomery Ward, 408

Nicotinell TTS, 694
Nidek, Inc., 525
Nielsen NetRatings, 827
Night vision devices, sensors for, 537, 540, 541
NIH. *See* National Institutes of Health
Nike, 176, 340
Nikon, in digital imaging, 138, 140
Nimbus CD International, 322
NiQuitin CQ, 694
Nissan Motor Acceptance Corporation, 640, 641
N2K Music Boulevard, 201
Noah's New York Bagels, Inc., 701
Nobel Learning Communities, Inc., 85, 87, 91–92
Noise Cancellation Technologies, Inc., 503–504
Noise Control Act, 502
Noise control and technology, **501–505**
Noise Control Technologies (Company), 503
NoiseBuster, 504
Nokia, 128
Nonaka, Ikujiro, 390, 393
Nonmedical senior care and personal services, **507–511**
Nonotubes, carbon, 439
Nonprofit organizations
    in adult housing, 5
    in AIDS care, 8
    ecotourism and, 709
    in managed care, 419
Nonsurgical embryo selective thinning & transfer (NEST), 249
NordicTrack, 602, 605
Norsk, 279
Nortel Networks Corporation
    in laser research, 399
    in photonics, 585, 588
    in telephone service, 747, 751
    voice recognition systems for, 804
North American Bungee Association, 241
North American Graphic Arts Suppliers Association, 616–617
North American Products Corporation, 322
North Atlantic Microwave Organization, 447
North Face, Inc., 245, 602
Northeastern University, on logistics services, 406
Northern Lights Coffee, 700
Northrop Grumman Corporation, 540, 541
Northwest Airlines, 205
Northwest Research Associates, Inc., 323
Norvir, 12
Norwest Equity Partners fund, 779–780
Norwest Venture Capital, 778, 779–780
Notebook computers, 299. *See also* Portable computers
Novartis AG
    Chiron Corporation and, 465
    in genetic engineering, 294
    in molecular modeling, 470
    in nutraceuticals, 499
    in premium beverages, 609
    smoking cessation products, 693, 694
Novartis Pharmaceuticals Corporation, 577–578
NovaSensor, 437
Novasoft, 362
Noyce, Robert N., 684
NPD Group, 339, 569
NPD Intelect, 139, 303
NSF. *See* National Science Foundation
Nuance Communications Inc., 79, 801, 802
Nuclear fusion, 395, 595

Nuclear waste cleanup, 233, 237, 238, 295
Nucleic acids, molecular design for, 466
NUON Technology, 157
Nurse call centers, 78
Nursing homes
    in congregate housing complexes, 1
    construction of, 328
    vs. continuing care retirement communities, 5
    day care in, 508
    government involvement in, 2
    Medicare and, 4
Nursing informatics, 332
Nutraceuticals, 493, 496–497, 513
    in beverages, 516, 607, 608–609, 612–613
    definition of, 514
    government regulation of, 497, 608
    for pets, 498
    producers of, 498–499
NuTrim, 495
Nutrition Labeling and Education Act, 514
Nutritional counseling, 489
Nutritional supplements, **513–519**. *See also* Vitamins
    advertising for, 515
    anti-aging, 45–46, 47, 48–49
    in Asia, 517–518
    claims of, 490
    definition of, 514
    in Europe, 518
    government regulation of, 514–515
    hormones in, 45, 46
    in juice bar products, 383, 384
    in new age products, 485
    for pets, 498
    sales of, 513, 516, 517
Nutropin, 295
NuvoMedia, Inc., 219
NV REMU, 597
NVX Active Noise and Vibration Control System, 502
NYNEX Corporation, 743, 746, 836

O

Oak Industries, 588
Oak Ridge National Laboratories, in sensing devices, 542
O'Barclay, Rebecca, 390
Oberg Industries Inc., 618
Oberthur Card Systems, 686
Object Design Inc., 848
Obstetricians, in fertility medicine, 248
Occupational education. *See* Vocational education
Occupational safety, professional employer organizations and, 622, 623, 624
Occupational Safety and Health Administration
    on bungee jumping, 241
    on ergonomic injuries, 645
    professional employer organizations and, 622, 623, 624
Occupational Safety and Health Review Commission, 624
Occupational therapy, in home health care, 328
Ocean Group Plc, 405
Ocean Hyperbaric Center, 550
Ocean Spray Cranberries, Inc., 609, 611
Odor control, 813
Odyssey (Launch system), 664
Office for the Advancement of Telehealth, 737
Office Noise Abatement and Control Expansion Act, 502

Restaurants, juice bars in, 383
Restraints
    child (*See* Child safety seats)
    passenger (*See* Passenger restraint systems)
Retail auto leasing, **637–642**
Retail stores
    biometrics for, 70
    chains (*See* Chain stores)
    discount, 430, 568
    groceries (*See* Grocery stores)
    infomercials for, 348
    online (*See* E-commerce)
    pet (*See* Pet stores)
    for used computer equipment, 770
Retin-A, 50
Retinal detachment, oxygen therapy for, 549
Retinal scanners, 69, 71
Retinoic acids, 48
Retinol, 48
Retirement, 1, 4
Retirement communities, **1–6**
Retirement plans
    financial advisors for, 265, 270
    in mutual funds, 481, 483
Reuters Group PLC, 212, 218–219
ReversAge, 48
Rexall Sundown, 517
RHK, on photonics, 586
Rhone-Poulenc SA, 14, 724
Ribonucleic acid (RNA), 291
Ricardo.de, 182
Rice, genetically engineered, 498
Rice University, in parallel processing, 559
Richard Milburn High School Inc., 91
Ride, Inc., 245
Ridgeview Inc., 602
Rights, of patients, 415, 417
Ringmaster software, 99
Ripper, John, 350
Risk and Insurance Management Society, Inc., 643, 644, 645
Risk control, 643–644
Risk management services, **643–648**
Riso National Laboratory, 322
Rite Aid, 517
Ritrovir. *See* Zidovudine
Rituxin, 295
Riverboat casinos, 281, 282
R.K. Hammer Investment Bankers, 122
RNA, 291
Robertson Stephens, 187–188
Robotic arms, 651, 653
Robotics, **649–657**
    artificial intelligence for, 652
    in Asia, 655
    for automotive manufacturers, 649, 653
    in Europe, 655
    for hazardous environments, 652
    history of, 650–652
    industrial, 649, 651–652, 653, 654–655
    microscopic plumbers and, 438–439
    nanotechnology and, 435
    PC-based control of, 656
    personal, 652
    playback *vs.* sequence, 652
    sales of, 652, 654

    service, 649, 652
    software for, 649
    for surgery, 456, 458, 652, 654
    systems integration for, 649
    in toys, 341
    vacuum, 653
    vision systems for, 654, 656
    for welding, 650
Robotics Industries Association, 649
Roche, Gerry, 628
Roche Bioscience, 470
Roche Diagnostics, 431
Roche Holding AG, 295, 517, 518
Rochester Photonics Corporation, 261
Rock climbing, 241–242, 243, 244, 245, 246
Rockwell International Corporation, 653
Rockwell Science Center, 321
Roebuck, Alvah, 408
Rofes, Eric, 84
Rogaine, 46, 50
Rohm & Haas Company, 469
Roller skates, 242
Rollerblade, Inc., 242, 245
Rollins Logistics, 405
Rome Reborn, 794
Roof, photovoltaic, 597
Roosevelt, Teddy, 422
Rosemount, 437
Roundup-ready seeds, 295–296, 463
Routers, 337, 719
Rowing machines, 604
Royal Ahold NV, 192, 194
Royal BodyCare, 48
Royal Dutch/Shell Group, 276, 596
R.R. Donnelly & Sons, 148
rTRT (Telomerase reverse transcriptase), 761
Rumarson Technologies Inc., 772
Rural areas, telemedicine for, 735, 736, 737–738
Russell, Philip K., 725
Russell Reynolds (Company), 629
Russia
    fiber optics for, 262
    satellites and, 147, 149, 664
Ryan White Act, 8–9
Ryan White Foundation, 9
Ryder Integrated Logistics, 405
Ryder Systems Inc., 85

S

Saab automobiles, head restraints, 563
Sabre Business Travel Solutions, 205
Sachs Group, on emergency care, 417
Safaris, 706, 709, 711
Safe Drinking Water Act, 808, 810, 816
Safe Drinking Water Act Amendment, 808, 812, 816
SafePak Corporation, 670, 672
Safety-Kleen Corporation, 237
Safety of products. *See* Product safety
Safeway Stores, 193
Saffo, Paul, 537
Sailing tours, 712
Saint Peter's University Hospital, 458
Salad bars, 384
Salads, prepared, 495

Searle Company, 469
Sears, Richard, 408
Sears Roebuck & Company, 349, 408, 602
Seat belts, 561, 565. *See also* Passenger restraint systems
    effectiveness of, 562, 563, 564
    smart, 564
Seattle Coffee Company, 701
Sechrist Industries, Inc., 550
Second Cup Ltd., 702
Second Source, 771
Secure Digital Music Initiative, 201
SecureRite.com, 669
Securities. *See also* Mutual funds
    bonds, 480, 482
    communications networks for, **209–213**
    ownership of, 266
    sales representatives, 483
    stocks, 209–213, 266, 269
Securities and Exchange Commission
    on communications networks, 209, 211
    on environmental liability, 235
    on financial planners, 267–268
    on mutual funds, 480
    on online brokers, 186
    Order Handling Rules, 211
Securities Exchange Act, 480
Securities exchanges, communications networks for, 209–213
Securities Industry Association, 479, 482
Security Analysis Tool for Auditing Networks (SATAN), 116
Security Capital Group, 358
Security GmbH, 670
Security products and services, **667–673**. *See also* Identification; Verification
    access control devices in, 668–669
    for airports, 670
    in Asia, 672
    biometrics for (*See* Biometrics)
    for computers (*See* Computer security)
    detectors (*See* Detectors)
    in Europe, 671
    for executives, 669, 670
    history of, 667–668
    home, 336, 667, 668
    industrial, 667
    in Latin America, 672
    for perimeter security, 668–669
    personal, 669
    revenues in, 668
Seeds
    genetically engineered, 290, 293, 295–296
    Roundup-ready, 295–296, 463
Seibert, Michael, 43
Seiko Epson Corporation, 618
Self-employment. *See also* Small businesses
    assistance programs, 230
    consultants and, 377–378
    financial advisors for, 265
Self-help groups, for smoking cessation, 690, 691
Self-insurance, 644
Self-tests, medical, **429–434**
Semiconductor Industry Association, 679
Semiconductor Laser International Corporation, 399
Semiconductors, **675–682**
    analog *vs.* digital, 676

in Asia, 675, 680
    automated manufacturing of, 653
    development of, 677–678
    digital light processor, 680
    digital signal processor, 681
    in Europe, 680
    lasers for, 396, 397
    memory chips, 676–677
    micromachines for, 442
    photonic, 584, 589
    robotic manufacturing for, 649
    sales of, 675, 678–679, 680
    sensors for, 542
    for solar power, 594, 598
Seminars, new age, 485–486
Senior citizens. *See* Elderly
Senior housing communities. *See* Adult communities
Senior Lifestyle Corporation, 6
SeniorNet, 26
Sensar, Inc., 69
Senseon, 440
Sensor/accuator systems, 440
Sensorama cubicles, 792
Sensormatic Electronics Corporation, 671, 672
Sensors
    accuator systems and, 440
    for airbags, 436, 437, 438, 440–441, 564
    in Asia, 542
    barium-strontium-titanate, 540
    for carbon monoxide, 540
    complementary metal oxide, 540
    for detectors, 541
    development of, 538–539
    for digital cameras, 538, 540, 542
    for earthquakes, 441
    energy-type, 539
    focal point array, 539
    for geographic information systems, 144
    glass break, 669
    for guidance systems, 537, 539, 541
    hydrogen, 43
    infrared, **537–543**
    integrated focal plane, 541
    MEMS and, 542
    micromachine, 435, 436, 438, 441
    for microprocessors, 542
    for night vision devices, 537, 540, 541
    optical, **537–543**
    photon-type, 539
    for pollution monitoring, 537, 540
    position, 441
    pressure, 438, 441, 542
    for remote controls, 144, 537
    semiconductor, 542
    silicon, 437
    for smart materials, 538, 539
    subminiature, 542
    for tracking systems, 537–538
    uncooled focal plane array, 539–540, 542
    vision, 542
    for weather satellites, 537
Sequent, 554
Sequoia Software Corporation, 205, 361, 848
Serafini, Anthony, 290–291
Serial storage architecture (SSA), 718